Foreign Trade

of the United States

Including State and Metro Area Export Data

Second Edition, 2001

Foreign Trade

of the United States

Including State and Metro Area Export Data

Second Edition, 2001

Editors
Cornelia J. Strawser
Sohair M. Abu-Aish
Linz Audain

BERNAN

ISBN: 0-89059-249-7

ISSN: 1524-3931

Printed by Automated Graphic Systems, Inc., White Plains, MD, on acid-free paper that meets the American National Standards Institute Z39-48 standard.

2002 2001   4 3 2 1

BERNAN
4611-F Assembly Drive
Lanham, MD 20706
800-274-4447
email: info@bernan.com
www.bernan.com

CONTENTS

ABOUT THE EDITORS

Foreign Trade of the United States was originally developed, and the first edition edited, by Dr. Courtenay M. Slater, formerly Manager of Economic Publications at Bernan Press, who previously served as Chief Economist for the Department of Commerce and Senior Economist at the President's Council of Economic Advisers and the Joint Economic Committee of Congress.

Dr. Cornelia J. Strawser, Sohair M. Abu-Aish, and Dr. Linz Audain edited this edition of *Foreign Trade*. Dr. Strawser, a senior economic consultant to Bernan, guided development of this edition, wrote the introductory article, and expanded "Using This Book" and the "Notes and Definitions" sections. She has been co-cditor of the last three editions of Bernan's *Business Statistics of the United States*. She was formerly Senior Economist at the U.S. House of Representatives Budget Committee and also has served at the Senate Budget Committee, the Congressional Budget Office, and the Federal Reserve Board, specializing in analysis of macroeconomic policy, current economic developments, and issues of economic measurement.

Sohair M. Abu-Aish, a Bernan data analyst, brought this book into being, developing the expanded selection of data introduced in this edition, preparing all the data tables, and updating and reviewing the textual components of the book. Ms. Abu-Aish, an Associate Editor of the latest edition of Bernan's *Handbook of U.S. Labor Statistics,* holds an M.S. in Economics from Zagazig University, Egypt, worked for the U.S. Bureau of the Census, and taught economics at Cairo University and Zagazig University.

Dr. Audain is a project consultant to Bernan. He has taught economics and statistics at the undergraduate and graduate level at seven different colleges and universities. He is an economist and an attorney. He is also a physician at the George Washington University Medical Center. He has published widely on economic, legal, and medical issues in various journals.

PREFACE

International commerce always has been of vital importance to the United States. The Revolutionary War was fought, in part, to gain freedom from the restrictions imposed by Great Britain on trade to and from the colonies that were to become the United States. Yet never have U.S. international economic relations been more important than in today's increasingly integrated global economy. U.S. exports make a contribution to the economy of every state and every major metropolitan area. Imports bring consumers an astounding variety of goods and services and introduce price competition that helps restrain inflation, but they also impact employment and profitability in industries beset by foreign competition.

Until the first edition of *Foreign Trade of the United States,* published by Bernan Press in 1999, the available wealth of basic statistical information about U.S. foreign trade had not been brought together in a single printed source. The first edition provided ready access to data on U.S. imports and exports of both goods and services, followed by data on exports from each state and most major metropolitan areas. This second edition includes and updates through 1999 all of the tables presented in the first edition. It contains important new additions as well, presenting measures of prices and real volumes of trade as well as current-dollar values, and providing alternative classification systems that allow comparisons with a greater variety of other national and international data.

Data on U.S. foreign trade and finance come from several major government sources. Estimates of trade in services are prepared by the Bureau of Economic Analysis of the U.S. Department of Commerce (BEA). BEA also prepares the balance of payments tables, relying not only on data on direct foreign investment collected by BEA but also on data on portfolio investment from the Department of the Treasury and the Federal Reserve. Data on government transactions abroad are assembled by BEA from information supplied by many government agencies.

Data on trade in goods are prepared by the Bureau of the Census, based on tallies supplied by the U.S. Customs Service. The International Trade Administration of the U.S. Department of Commerce (ITA) uses the Bureau of the Census data to prepare tables on exports by state and metropolitan area as well as summary tables of national trade highlights.

This diversity of source agencies, coupled with limitations on agency publication budgets, helps explain the lack (until *Foreign Trade of the United States*) of a single comprehensive reference volume. In particular, ITA lacks the resources to publish its state and metro area export data in printed form, although the data are available on its web site. And ITA's former publication *Foreign Trade Highlights,* containing national data, is now available only as a set of tables on the web.

Bernan's *Foreign Trade of the United States: Second Edition, 2001* assembles the most important data from the various government sources into one convenient volume. Annual time series are provided in all cases, so that year-to-year changes can be observed. A section on "Using This Book," immediately following this Preface, explains the organization of the book in more detail; demonstrates how to read the tables, illustrated by samples of the tables and interpretive material; and gives some general notes on the data. An introductory article analyzes trends in foreign trade, especially during the 1990s. Each of the five Parts begins with a graph highlighting the trends depicted in that Part, and is then introduced by Notes and Definitions specific to that Part.

All statistical data are subject to error arising from sampling variability, reporting and classification errors, incomplete coverage, imputation, and other causes. The responsibility of the editor and publisher of this volume is limited to reasonable care in the reproduction and presentation of data obtained from established sources.

The editors are deeply grateful to Lorrent Smith who prepared all graphics and Kara Gottschlich who prepared the layout. Copy editing was done by Jacalyn Houston, and Susan Huestis, Shanon Venegas, Alex Venezia, and Michele Venezia assisted with tables production. Special thanks go to Tamera L. Wells-Lee and Dan Parham for directing all editorial and production aspects. Profound thanks are due to each of these individuals for professionalism and cooperative effort. Finally, we are grateful to those at the Bureau of the Census, BEA, ITA, and elsewhere in government, who not only have been generous with assistance in obtaining and understanding their data, but who, through efforts extending over many years, have developed the statistical information that enables data users to better understand U.S. participation in the world economy.

USING THIS BOOK

Foreign Trade of the United States contains statistical information about U.S. exports and imports and related topics. The main body of the book is divided into five sections. Sections A, B, and C provide information for the United States as a whole; Section D provides statistics on the exports of each state by country or region of destination and by industry; Section E provides similar information for large metropolitan areas. Each section is described briefly below, with examples of the information found in that section and suggestions about how to read and use that information. GENERAL NOTES ON THE DATA at the end of this introductory chapter will provide general information about sources and definitions used throughout the book, and the NOTES AND DEFINITIONS in front of each part provide additional, specific notes for each section. Refer to the notes to learn how terms are defined, where to go for additional information, what countries are included in the regional totals shown in some tables, and how to interpret any symbols and abbreviations used in the tables.

The data in this book are annual time series, that is, they provide data pertaining to each year within a specified time span. This type of information allows examination of individual year-to-year changes as well as trends over longer periods. In general, the data are the latest available as of early 2001.

SECTION A. HIGHLIGHTS OF U.S. INTERNATIONAL TRANSACTIONS (pages 1–18)

Section A is an overview of U.S. trade in both goods and services and of other U.S. international transactions. This summary section provides data for a longer historical period than is possible in the other sections of the book. Tables A-1 through A-4 cover the longest time period, showing the aggregate values, prices and quantities of exports and imports as components of U.S. gross domestic product (GDP) each year from 1946 through 1999. Table A-5 summarizes exports, imports, and the trade balance as measured in the U.S. international transactions (balance of payments) accounts, and Table A-6 presents the full balance of payments accounts, from 1960 through 1999. Table A-7 shows the exchange value of the dollar against aggregates of other foreign currencies and individual currencies during the past several years.

USING SECTION A: SOME EXAMPLES

Table A-1. U.S. Gross Domestic Product [GDP], Exports, Imports, and Net Exports, 1946–1999
Table A-2. Exports, Imports, and Net Exports as a Percent of U.S. Gross Domestic Product, 1946–1999

Table A-2 includes columns showing the values of exports and imports as percentages of GDP, thus documenting the growing importance of foreign trade in the U.S. economy. From 1950 through 1969, exports only rarely reached 5 percent of GDP; the same was true of imports. Since 1969, however, both exports and imports have been rising as a percentage of GDP. In 1996 and 1997, exports were over 11 percent of GDP, and by 1999 imports exceeded 13 percent.

Table A-2. Exports, Imports, and Net Exports as a Percent of U.S. Gross Domestic Product, 1946–1999

(Percent of total gross domestic product.)

Year	Exports			Imports			Net exports
	Total	Goods	Services	Total	Goods	Services	
1950	4.18	3.47	0.71	3.94	3.09	0.85	0.24
1951	5.01	4.18	0.82	4.30	3.30	1.00	0.71
1952	4.55	3.74	0.81	4.27	3.01	1.25	0.28
1953	4.00	3.26	0.74	4.21	2.90	1.32	-0.21
1954	4.12	3.38	0.73	4.04	2.73	1.34	0.08
1955	4.24	3.47	0.77	4.14	2.77	1.37	0.10
1956	4.84	4.02	0.82	4.32	2.92	1.39	0.53
1957	5.18	4.25	0.93	4.31	2.88	1.45	0.87
1958	4.36	3.51	0.85	4.27	2.78	1.52	0.09
1959	4.06	3.25	0.83	4.39	3.02	1.38	-0.34
1960	4.80	3.89	0.91	4.32	2.88	1.44	0.46
1961	4.76	3.83	0.93	4.16	2.77	1.39	0.62
1962	4.67	3.70	0.97	4.26	2.88	1.38	0.41
1963	4.75	3.77	0.99	4.22	2.86	1.36	0.53
1964	5.06	4.02	1.04	4.23	2.92	1.31	0.83
1965	4.92	3.86	1.06	4.37	3.08	1.29	0.54
1966	4.93	3.89	1.04	4.70	3.33	1.36	0.24
1967	4.96	3.86	1.10	4.78	3.33	1.46	0.17
1968	4.97	3.87	1.10	5.11	3.72	1.38	-0.14
1969	5.00	3.89	1.12	5.13	3.73	1.39	-0.12
1995	11.06	7.89	3.17	12.20	10.24	1.96	-1.14
1996	11.19	7.91	3.27	12.33	10.35	1.98	-1.14
1997	11.62	8.28	3.34	12.69	10.64	2.05	-1.07
1998	10.99	7.76	3.23	12.71	10.59	2.13	-1.72
1999	10.65	7.52	3.13	13.38	11.28	2.10	-2.73

Table A-3. Real U.S. Gross Domestic Product [GDP], Exports, Imports, and Net Exports, 1946–1999
Table A-4. Chain-Type Quantity and Price Indexes for Exports and Imports, 1946–1999

These tables, new in this edition of *Foreign Trade of the United States*, are also derived from the National Income and Product Accounts. The price indexes shown in Table A-4 measure the changes in average prices for imports and exports, and the quantity indexes and 1996-dollar estimates indicate the trends in "real" trade volumes, removing the effects of price change. In 1999, the quantity indexes show that the volume of U.S. goods exports was 15 times what it had been in 1946, while the volume of service exports was 22 times that in 1946. This is consistent with the generally observed trend toward services in the composition of U.S. production. The volume of service imports in 1999 was 18 times that in 1946, while the volume of goods imports was 31 times that in 1946—a dramatic illustration of the increasing extent to which production overseas has supplied U.S. markets with goods.

Table A-4. Chain-Type Quantity and Price Indexes for Exports and Imports, 1946–1999

(1996=100.)

| Year | Quantity indexes | | | | | | Price indexes | | | | | |
| | Exports | | | Imports | | | Exports | | | Imports | | |
	Total	Goods	Services	Total	Goods	Services	Total	Goods	Services	Total	Goods	Services
1946	7.61	8.20	5.05	5.10	4.63	7.09	21.17	23.19	17.89	14.21	13.54	17.39
1947	8.69	9.43	5.55	4.84	4.45	6.52	24.61	27.60	18.24	17.02	16.62	19.43
1948	6.84	7.30	4.85	5.65	5.09	8.04	25.91	29.38	17.98	18.50	18.36	20.11
1949	6.78	7.26	4.71	5.45	4.89	7.85	24.34	27.22	18.30	17.63	17.38	19.56
1995	92.45	91.97	93.65	92.05	91.43	95.40	101.29	102.65	97.99	101.83	102.51	98.31
1996	100.00	100.00	100.00	100.00	100.00	100.00	100.00	100.00	100.00	100.00	100.00	100.00
1997	112.27	114.51	106.98	113.67	114.20	110.94	98.47	97.29	101.42	96.44	95.88	99.41
1998	114.80	117.01	109.58	127.15	127.67	124.42	96.26	94.25	101.34	91.26	90.16	97.09
1999	118.17	121.63	110.14	140.72	143.64	126.54	95.86	92.96	103.30	91.80	90.31	99.89

Table A-5. U.S. International Trade in Goods and Services, 1960–1999

This table further illustrates the increasing importance of U.S. trade in services. The value of service exports has more than doubled in the last ten years, rising from $127 billion in 1989 to $272 billion in 1999, when service exports exceeded service imports by $81 billion. The positive trade balance in services contrasts with the negative balance in goods, suggesting that the U.S. has a comparative advantage in services trade.

Table A-5. U.S. International Trade in Goods and Services, 1960–1999

(Balance of payments basis, billions of dollars.)

| Year | Exports | | | Imports | | | Trade balance | | |
	Total	Goods	Services	Total	Goods	Services	Total	Goods	Services
1987	348.9	250.2	98.7	500.6	409.8	90.8	-151.7	-159.6	7.9
1988	431.1	320.2	110.9	545.7	447.2	98.5	-114.6	-127.0	12.4
1989	489.2	362.1	127.1	579.8	477.4	102.5	-90.6	-115.2	24.6
1997	936.9	679.7	257.2	1 042.9	876.4	166.5	-105.9	-196.7	90.7
1998	933.0	670.3	262.7	1 099.9	917.2	182.7	-166.9	-246.9	80.0
1999	956.2	684.4	271.9	1 221.2	1 029.9	191.3	-265.0	-345.6	80.6

Technical note: The export and import values in Table A-5 differ slightly from those in Table A-1. The numbers in Table A-5 are compiled to be consistent with the financial flows measured in the international transactions accounts, but the numbers in Table A-1 have been adjusted to place them on a basis consistent with the GDP estimates. The NOTES AND DEFINITIONS provide information about this adjustment.

Table A-6. U.S. International Transactions, 1960–1999

The data in this table often are called the "balance of payments." They go beyond the flows of goods and services to provide a full picture of all U.S. international transactions, also including earnings on foreign investments and capital flows to and from the United States. They are designed to account not only for product and income flows but also for the international capital flows required to finance them. Unlike the other tables in this book, this table uses a minus sign to identify transactions that transfer dollars from U.S. to foreign governments, businesses, or individuals. Imports are an example: dollars are transferred to foreigners in payment. U.S. foreign investments are another example: the assets acquired are purchased from foreign entities. Earnings on past foreign investments are funds flowing back to the United States, however, and thus are a plus item in the accounts.

The broadest measure of the U.S. balance of payments is the "balance on current account," summarizing the effects of goods, services, and income flows and unilateral transfers; this was a negative $331 billion in 1999. A negative payments balance must be balanced by an equivalent inflow on the capital and financial accounts. In 1999, foreign investment in the U.S. ("Other foreign assets in the U.S., net") amounted to $711 billion, far exceeding U.S. investment abroad, which was $442 billion. The sum of these and the other items in the capital and financial accounts-including a "statistical discrepancy" arising from problems in measurement-exactly offsets the balance on current account.

Table A-6. U.S. International Transactions, 1960–1999—*Continued*
(Millions of dollars.)

Credits and debits	1990	1991	1992	1993	1994	1995	1996	1997	1998	1999
CURRENT ACCOUNT										
Memoranda:										
Balance on goods	-109 030	-74 068	-96 106	-132 609	-166 192	-173 729	-191 270	-196 665	-246 854	-345 559
Balance on services	30 173	45 802	60 440	63 660	69 153	77 782	89 157	90 733	79 956	80 588
Balance on goods and services	-78 857	-28 266	-35 666	-68 949	-97 039	-95 947	-102 113	-105 932	-166 898	-264 971
Balance on income	28 550	24 130	22 954	23 904	16 694	20 547	18 876	6 186	-6 211	-18 483
Balance on goods, services, and income	-50 307	-4 136	-12 712	-45 045	-80 345	-75 400	-83 237	-99 746	-173 109	-283 454
Unilateral current transfers, net	-26 654	10 752	-35 013	-37 637	-38 260	-34 057	-40 081	-40 794	-44 029	-48 025
Balance on current account	-76 961	6 616	-47 724	-82 681	-118 605	-109 457	-123 318	-140 540	-217 138	-331 479
CAPITAL AND FINANCIAL ACCOUNT										
U.S.-Owned Assets Abroad, Net	-81 234	-64 388	-74 410	-200 552	-176 056	-352 376	-413 923	-488 940	-335 436	-430 187
U.S. private assets, net	-81 393	-73 075	-76 644	-198 822	-181 012	-341 650	-419 602	-487 998	-328 231	-441 685
Foreign-Owned Assets In The United States, Net	141 571	110 808	170 663	282 040	305 989	465 684	571 706	756 962	482 235	753 564
Other foreign assets in the U.S., net	107 661	93 420	130 186	210 287	266 406	355 804	444 982	738 086	502 362	710 700
Direct investment	48 494	23 171	19 823	51 362	46 121	57 776	86 502	106 032	186 316	275 533
U.S. Treasury securities	-2 534	18 826	37 131	24 381	34 274	99 548	154 996	146 433	48 581	-20 464
U.S. securities other than U.S. Treasury securities	1 592	35 144	30 043	80 092	56 971	96 367	130 240	197 892	218 075	331 523
Statistical Discrepancy	23 204	-48 557	-49 141	1 281	-10 859	-4 223	-35 158	-127 832	69 702	11 602

Table A-7. Exchange Rates, 1992–1999

Table A-7 illustrates how the foreign exchange value of the dollar has risen in the last few years. According to the "Broad" index in the top line, based on January 1997=100, the average value of the dollar against the currencies included in this broad group rose from 76.3 in 1992 to 116.9 in 1999. Taking the percent change from the first to the second of these numbers, the average value of the dollar rose 53 percent. However, this is in some ways an exaggeration of the rise in the purchasing power of the dollar and the deterioration in competitive price advantage that has taken place. Some of the countries included in these indexes have had rapid inflation over this period, which has been reflected in an offsetting deterioration in their exchange rates. In the "real" indexes shown in the table—a new feature in this edition of *Foreign Trade of the United States*—the dollar has increased in price-adjusted purchasing power relative to the countries in the "Broad" index from 86.7 to 98.5 percent of the January 1997 average, an increase of only 14 percent in the "real" average value of the dollar.

The value of the dollar against more than 170 individual countries' currencies is also shown. In all cases, it is shown as foreign currency units per U.S. dollar, so that a rise consistently represents a stronger dollar/weaker foreign currency. The user should note that certain currencies—the U.K. and Irish pounds, the Australian and New Zealand dollars, and the new euro—are by convention often quoted (in newspapers, for example) in dollars per foreign currency unit. For example, the table here shows the U.K. pound value of the U.S. dollar as averaging 0.62 pounds in 1999, whereas many sources will show the pound as being worth $1.6172 ($1/0.61835).

Table A-7. Exchange Rates, 1992–1999

(Annual averages, currency units per U.S. dollar.)

Country and currency unit	1992	1993	1994	1995	1996	1997	1998	1999
TRADE-WEIGHTED INDEXES [1]								
Nominal								
Broad (January 1997=100)	76.29	84.45	90.42	92.52	97.40	104.44	116.48	116.87
Major currencies (March 1973=100)	85.45	87.73	86.25	81.39	84.60	91.24	95.79	94.07
Other important trading partners (January 1997=100)	52.88	66.01	80.51	92.51	98.26	104.67	126.03	129.94
G-10 (March 1973=100)	86.64	93.17	91.32	84.25	87.34	96.38	98.85	. . .
Real (adjusted for price change)								
Broad (January 1997=100)	86.73	87.59	87.25	84.69	86.63	91.24	99.21	98.53
Other important trading partners (January 1997=100)	100.66	98.14	97.79	97.14	94.40	95.58	108.10	107.22

Table A-7. Exchange Rates, 1992–1999—*Continued*

(Annual averages, currency units per U.S. dollar.)

Country and currency unit	1992	1993	1994	1995	1996	1997	1998	1999
United Kingdom, Pound Sterling	0.57	0.67	0.65	0.63	0.64	0.61	0.60	0.62
Uruguay, Peso	3.03	3.94	5.04	6.35	7.97	9.44	10.47	11.34
Vanuatu, Vatu	113.39	121.58	116.41	112.11	111.72	115.87	127.52	129.08
Venzuela, Bolivar	68.38	90.83	148.50	176.84	417.33	488.64	547.56	605.72
Yemen, Republic Of, Rial	12.01	12.01	12.01	40.84	94.16	129.28	135.88	159.50

SECTION B. U.S. FOREIGN TRADE IN SERVICES (pages 21–74)

Section B contains detailed information on U.S. international transactions in services. For services, the terms "exports" and "imports" do not refer to physical shipments of merchandise from or to the United States. Instead they refer to services provided by U.S. governments, businesses, or individuals to residents of other countries and to similar services provided by foreigners to U.S. residents. Important types of international service transactions are travel, transportation services, royalties and license fees, educational services, and business and professional services. Table B-1 summarizes U.S. receipts from (exports of) and payments for (imports of) services by type of service. Table B-2—new in this edition of *Foreign Trade of the United States*—shows indexes of export and import prices for selected categories of services. Table B-3 shows total trade in services by country or region. Tables B-4 through B-13 provide additional detail on the different categories of trade in services.

All of the data in Section B refer to private services transactions. The U.S. government also makes international service transactions, primarily defense related. Totals for these government transactions can be found in Table A-6: U.S. International Transactions, 1960–1999.

USING SECTION B: SOME EXAMPLES

Table B-1. U.S. Private Service Transactions by Type, 1986–1999

As this table shows, U.S. exports of private services reached $255 billion in 1999. Of this total, $75 billion (29 percent) was travel expenditure by foreign visitors to the United States, and $36 billion (14 percent) was royalties and license fees, such as those for use of U.S. patents and copyrights. (It is important to note that "travel" expenditure does not include passenger fares between the United States and other countries, which are tabulated separately; see NOTES AND DEFINITIONS.) Over the 13 years shown in the table, U.S. earnings from each of the major service categories have risen, some quite rapidly. Earnings from business, professional, and technical services, for example, have quintupled.

Table B-1. U.S. Private Service Transactions by Type, 1986–1999
(Millions of dollars.)

Type of service	Exports						
	1986	1987	1988	1989	1990	1991	1992
TOTAL PRIVATE SERVICES	77 545	87 030	100 971	117 935	137 232	152 437	163 688
Travel	20 385	23 563	29 434	36 205	43 007	48 385	54 742
Overseas	15 650	18 044	22 313	26 938	30 807	34 518	40 864
Canada	2 701	3 309	4 150	5 340	7 093	8 500	8 182
Mexico	2 034	2 210	2 971	3 927	5 107	5 367	5 696
Royalties And License Fees	8 113	10 174	12 139	13 818	16 634	17 819	20 841
Affiliated	6 174	7 888	9 493	10 961	13 250	14 106	15 659
U.S. parents transactions	5 994	7 668	9 238	10 612	12 867	13 523	14 925
U.S. affiliates transactions	180	220	256	349	383	583	733
Other Private Services	28 027	29 263	31 111	36 729	40 251	47 748	49 956
Unaffiliated services	19 641	20 769	21 544	24 433	26 629	33 210	33 134
Telecommunications	1 827	2 111	2 196	2 519	2 735	3 291	2 885
Business, professional, and technical services	4 813	4 765	5 970	6 823	7 752	12 045	11 722

Table B-1. U.S. Private Service Transactions by Type, 1986–1999 —*Continued*
(Millions of dollars.)

Type of service	Exports—*Continued*						
	1993	1994	1995	1996	1997	1998	1999
TOTAL PRIVATE SERVICES	171 588	187 357	203 768	222 633	239 444	244 099	254 665
Travel	57 875	58 417	63 395	69 809	73 426	71 286	74 881
Overseas	45 298	47 299	54 331	59 963	63 041	61 262	64 099
Canada	7 458	6 252	6 207	6 842	6 945	6 206	6 670
Mexico	5 119	4 866	2 857	3 004	3 440	3 818	4 112
Royalties And License Fees	21 695	26 712	30 289	32 470	33 639	36 197	36 467
Affiliated	15 688	20 275	22 859	24 556	24 876	26 809	26 307
U.S. parents transactions	14 936	19 250	21 399	22 719	23 091	24 720	24 576
U.S. affiliates transactions	752	1 025	1 460	1 837	1 785	2 089	1 731
Other Private Services	53 532	61 477	65 094	73 858	84 505	90 914	96 508
Unaffiliated services	36 718	41 652	44 611	50 927	57 252	62 517	67 565
Telecommunications	2 785	2 865	3 228	3 301	3 918	5 538	4 460
Business, professional, and technical services	12 958	15 330	16 078	19 466	21 450	22 175	24 368

Table B-2. U.S. Export and Import Price Indexes for Selected Categories of Services, 1991–1999

This table identifies price trends in exports and imports for passenger fares and other transportation services. For air passenger fares, there appears to be some similarity between export and import trends in individual geographic markets, probably reflecting competitive pressures, but considerable diversity between geographic markets, which could reflect differing degrees of competitive pressure and/or differing trends in demand. From 1991 to 1999, U.S. export fares to Latin America and the Caribbean rose 29 percent, and import fares in the same region rose 30 percent. In the Pacific market, on the other hand, export fares rose a bare 2 percent and import fares 11 percent.

Table B-2. U.S. Export and Import Price Indexes for Selected Categories of Services, 1991–1999

(1995=100, unless otherwise indicated; annual data are averages of March, June, September, and December.)

Category	1991	1992	1993	1994	1995	1996	1997	1998	1999
EXPORTS									
Air Passenger Fares	88.3	90.7	92.5	94.8	100.0	100.0	96.2	95.7	103.1
Pacific	85.8	88.4	94.5	96.2	100.0	93.3	82.8	78.9	87.8
Asia	...	...	...	96.7	100.0	90.0	77.4	75.5	84.3
Japan	...	...	...	96.5	100.0	87.3	78.5	76.2	86.7
Latin American and Caribbean	88.6	93.6	95.0	99.1	100.0	100.9	105.7	110.7	114.6
Air Passenger Fares	93.3	95.7	94.3	94.9	100.0	101.2	107.4	108.5	111.4
Pacific	90.9	90.0	94.3	96.1	100.0	97.1	104.1	102.0	100.7
Asia (December 1996=100)	...	...	...	...	...	...	108.7	105.4	104.9
Latin American and Caribbean	85.5	95.2	96.4	98.1	100.0	103.3	105.6	107.9	110.9
Caribbean (December 1996=100)	...	...	...	...	...	...	100.7	101.3	101.1

Table B-3. U.S. Private Service Transactions by Region and Country, 1986–1999

This table identifies the regions and countries with whose residents U.S. international service transactions took place. Only limited country detail is available for 1986-1991, much greater detail for 1992 and later years. The country purchasing the most services from the United States throughout the years shown was Japan, and, in each year shown, the United States had a large surplus on its services trade with Japan: in 1999, for example, the United States exported $30 billion of services to Japan while purchasing only $16 billion of Japanese services. Demonstrating the overwhelming competitive advantage of the United States in services, this country has a surplus in 1999 with every country and region shown.

Table B-3. U.S. Private Service Transactions by Region and Country, 1986–1999 —Continued

(Millions of dollars.)

Country or region	Exports—Continued						
	1993	1994	1995	1996	1997	1998	1999
ALL COUNTRIES	171 588	187 357	203 768	222 633	239 444	244 099	254 665
Japan	26 794	28 952	33 240	33 535	34 249	29 887	30 498

Table B-3. U.S. Private Service Transactions by Region and Country, 1986–1999 —Continued

(Millions of dollars.)

Country or region	Imports—Continued						
	1993	1994	1995	1996	1997	1998	1999
ALL COUNTRIES	107 940	119 101	128 781	137 102	152 042	167 607	174 825
Japan	11 785	12 584	13 463	12 907	14 053	13 522	15 692

Tables B-12 and B-13. U.S. Business, Professional, and Technical Service Receipts and Payments, 1996–1999.

These tables show U.S. receipts (Table B-12) and payments (Table B-13) by type of business, professional, or technical service by region and country. For example, in 1999 the United States earned $4.1 billion by supplying construction, engineering, architectural, and mining services, but paid only $0.5 billion to purchase such services from abroad. Of the $4.1 billion in receipts, $0.4 billion (almost 11 percent) came from the Middle East. Under Middle East in Table B-12 the "(D)" shown for Saudi Arabia and for "Other" indicates that, because some services were supplied by only a few large firms, the source agency for these data has suppressed this information so that the data pertaining to an individual firm cannot be separately identified. Two data cells must be suppressed here so that the value for a suppressed cell cannot be obtained by subtracting the remaining numbers from the total.

Table B-12. U.S. Business, Professional, and Technical Service Receipts, Unaffiliated, 1996–1999—*Continued*

(Millions of dollars.)

Country or region	Legal services				Construction, engineering, architectural, and mining services				Industrial engineering			
	1996	1997	1998	1999	1996	1997	1998	1999	1996	1997	1998	1999
ALL COUNTRIES	1 943	2 223	2 419	2 560	3 553	3 503	3 548	4 071	870	1 186	1 316	1 492
Middle East	49	65	60	54	1 028	616	571	447	46	120	(D)	96
Israel	13	23	22	26	26	14	7	7	5	(D)	14	9
Saudi Arabia	12	11	10	5	(D)	205	351	283	39	(D)	39	58
Other	24	32	28	22	(D)	398	213	157	3	(D)	(D)	29

Table B-13. U.S. Business, Professional, and Technical Service Payments, Unaffiliated, 1996–1999—*Continued*

(Millions of dollars.)

Country or region	Legal services				Construction, engineering, architectural, and mining services				Industrial engineering			
	1996	1997	1998	1999	1996	1997	1998	1999	1996	1997	1998	1999
ALL COUNTRIES	615	539	637	844	465	463	544	530	197	211	205	141
Middle East	11	9	11	12	(D)	(D)	84	95	(D)	(*)	(*)	3
Israel	5	4	5	6	(*)	4	(D)	13	(*)	(*)	. . .	1
Saudi Arabia	3	1	2	2	2	2	(D)	(D)	3	(*)	. . .	(*)
Other	4	4	4	4	(D)	(D)	(D)	(D)	(D)	(*)	(*)	2

Technical note: These tables distinguish between "affiliated" and "unaffiliated" transactions. Affiliated transactions are those between a parent company in one country and its foreign affiliate. Unaffiliated transactions are those between independent entities. Much of the detail by type of service is available only for unaffiliated transactions. The NOTES AND DEFINITIONS provide information about the distinction between affiliated and unaffiliated.

SECTION C. U.S. FOREIGN TRADE IN GOODS (pages 75–130)

Section C contains U.S. national totals for dollar values and price indexes of exports and imports of goods. Tables C-1, C-2, C-5, C-8, and C-9 show values according to different classification systems for the types of goods traded. Table C-3, new in this edition of *Foreign Trade of the United States*, shows values of exports and imports with the effects of price change removed (constant dollar or "real" basis). Tables C-4, C-6, C-7, and C-12—also new in this edition—show price indexes for exports and imports, using different classification systems. Tables C-10 and C-11 show total exports and imports by region and country.

USING SECTION C: SOME EXAMPLES

Table C-1. U.S. Foreign Trade in Goods, 1970–1999

This table shows total exports and imports of goods and divides these totals into four major groups: manufactured goods, agricultural products, mineral fuels, and other goods. The importance of manufactures to total U.S. goods trade is apparent; manufactures were 88 percent of all goods exports and 86 percent of all goods imports in 1999. Agricultural exports are also important, and the United States maintains a substantial surplus in this category, about $12 billion in 1999. For mineral fuels (which includes crude oil), imports are far larger than exports. The dollar value of mineral fuel imports fell by 27 percent from 1997 to 1998, and rose by 32 percent from 1998 to 1999. These movements reflect the collapse of oil prices in 1998 and their recovery in 1999, not quantity fluctuations; in fact, the quantity of petroleum products imported rose somewhat in 1998 and was little changed in 1999.

Table C-1. U.S. Foreign Trade in Goods, 1970–1999

(Census basis, billions of dollars.)

Year	Exports					Imports				
	Total goods	Manufactured goods	Agricultural products	Mineral fuels	Other goods	Total goods	Manufactured goods	Agricultural products	Mineral fuels	Other goods
1995	584.7	486.7	56.0	10.5	31.6	743.4	629.7	29.3	59.1	25.4
1996	625.1	524.7	60.6	12.4	27.4	795.3	658.8	32.6	78.1	25.8
1997	689.2	592.5	57.1	13.0	26.7	870.7	728.9	35.2	78.3	28.3
1998	682.1	596.6	52.0	10.4	23.2	911.9	790.8	35.7	57.3	28.1
1999	695.8	614.5	48.4	10.0	22.9	1 024.6	882.0	36.7	75.8	30.1

Table C-2. U.S. Foreign Trade in Goods by Principal End-Use Category, 1978-1999

Table C-2 can be used to examine the current value of exports and imports using the End-Use Classification. These end-use categories correspond roughly to categories in the National Income and Product Accounts, which characterize goods as either consumer goods or investment goods. Thus, imports and exports of automotive goods, other consumer goods, and capital goods can be related to overall measures of final demand for consumer goods and capital goods respectively, and trade in industrial supplies and materials can be treated as derived demand (derived from the final demands for consumer and capital goods) and related to levels of industrial activity. Six major categories are shown, and a trade balance is given for each category. The United States currently has small surpluses on trade in foods and capital goods, while it has substantial deficits on autos and other consumer goods and industrial supplies and materials (which includes petroleum and petroleum products).

Table C-2. U.S. Foreign Trade in Goods by Principal End-Use Category, 1978–1999

(Census basis, billions of dollars.)

Year	Foods, feeds, and beverages			Industrial supplies and materials			Capital goods, except automotive		
	Exports	Imports	Balance	Exports	Imports	Balance	Exports	Imports	Balance
1998	46.4	41.2	5.2	148.3	200.1	-51.9	299.6	269.6	30.1
1999	45.5	43.6	2.0	147.0	222.0	-75.0	311.4	297.1	14.3

Year	Automotive vehicles, engines, and parts			Consumer goods, except automotive			Other goods		
	Exports	Imports	Balance	Exports	Imports	Balance	Exports	Imports	Balance
1998	73.2	149.1	-75.9	79.3	216.5	-137.3	35.4	35.4	0.1
1999	75.8	179.4	-103.6	80.8	239.5	-158.7	35.3	43.0	-7.7

Table C-3. U.S. Exports and Imports of Goods by Principal End-Use Category: Constant Dollar Basis, 1985–1999

Table C-3 gives figures for the same end-use categories with the effects of price change removed. Values are shown in billions of 1996 dollars for the years 1994-1999. Values on this basis have not been calculated for earlier years, but are available in 1992 dollars. The 1992 dollar values are shown for 1986 through 1994, providing an overlap year so that the user may "link" the two sets of values to provide continuous time series for real imports and exports. For example, total exports in 1992 dollars were $522.3 billion in 1994 and $227.2 billion in 1986, a ratio of 2.299 (522.3/227.2). In 1996 dollars, total exports were $761.5 billion in 1999 and $518.6 billion in 1994, a ratio of 1.468. The product of the two ratios, 3.376, gives a measure of real exports in 1999 relative to 1986; equivalently, a linked index for 1999, 1986=100, is 337.6 (3.376x100); equivalently, real exports increased 238 percent from 1986 to 1999 [(3.376-1)x100], or at a 9.8 percent per year compounded annual rate of increase.

Table C-3. U.S. Exports and Imports of Goods by Principal End-Use Category: Constant Dollar Basis, 1985–1999

(Census basis; billions of 1996 dollars, unless otherwise indicated.)

Year	Total	Foods, feeds, and beverages	Industrial supplies and materials	Capital goods, except automotive	Automotive vehicles, engines, and parts	Consumer goods, except automotive	Other goods
EXPORTS							
1985	. . .	. . .	. . .	. . .	. . .	. . .	. . .
1986 [1]	227.2	22.3	57.3	75.8	21.7	. . .	. . .
1994 [1]	522.3	40.4	114.2	225.8	56.5	59.0	26.4
1994	518.6	50.8	131.9	187.0	59.1	61.6	28.3
1999	761.5	58.6	160.7	350.5	74.7	80.5	36.6

1. Values on the 1996 dollar basis are only available for 1994 to date. To provide more historical data, values on a 1992 dollar basis are shown for the years 1986-1994.

Table C-4. U.S. Export and Import Price Indexes for Selected Categories of Goods, by Principal End-Use Classification, 1991–1999

Using the same classification system as Tables C-2 and C-3, this table—new in this edition—shows price indexes for the years 1991 through 1999. In the aggregate, both export and import prices rose from 1991 to 1996 but fell back by 1999 to near the 1991 level.

Table C-4. U.S. Export and Import Price Indexes for Selected Categories of Goods, by Principal End-Use Classification, 1991–1999

(1995=100, unless otherwise indicated; annual data are averages of the 12 months.)

Category	End-use codes	1991	1992	1993	1994	1995	1996	1997	1998	1999
EXPORTS										
ALL COMMODITIES		92.6	92.7	93.2	95.2	100.0	100.5	99.2	95.9	94.7
IMPORTS										
ALL COMMODITIES		93.7	94.3	94.0	95.7	100.0	101.0	98.5	92.6	93.4

Table C-5. U.S. Foreign Trade in Goods Using Standard International Trade Classification [SITC] Product Groups, 1993–1999

This table, new in this edition, shows current-dollar values of U.S. goods exports and imports using Standard International Trade Classification product groups. We can read from this table that exports of office machines and ADP (data processing) equipment rose from $31.3 billion in 1993 to $51.6 billion in 1997, but fell back to $48.6 billion in 1999. Imports of such equipment rose steadily, however, from $43.2 billion in 1993 to $84.4 billion in 1999. The SITC classification system, created by the United Nations to categorize items by their traditional product categories and stage of production, provides the flexibility of great detail—so that users can combine data according to their own needs—and is particularly useful for international comparisons.

Table C-5. U.S. Foreign Trade in Goods Using Standard International Trade Classification [SITC] Product Groups, 1993–1999

(Census basis, preliminary; millions of dollars.)

Product	SITC code	Exports						
		1993	1994	1995	1996	1997	1998	1999
General industrial machinery	74	20 126	22 563	25 048	27 370	31 440	30 999	30 729
Office machines and ADP equipment	75	31 348	35 396	41 947	45 751	51 641	47 759	48 604
Telecommunications equipment	76	14 237	17 129	20 332	21 414	26 056	25 978	27 709

Table C-5. U.S. Foreign Trade in Goods Using Standard International Trade Classification [SITC] Product Groups, 1993–1999—*Continued*

(Census basis, preliminary; millions of dollars.)

Product	SITC code	Imports						
		1993	1994	1995	1996	1997	1998	1999
General industrial machinery	74	17 084	21 337	24 113	25 286	26 307	28 802	31 447
Office machines and ADP equipment	75	43 182	52 118	62 824	66 499	75 001	76 846	84 443
Telecommunications equipment	76	27 302	32 456	34 384	34 167	36 685	42 462	50 959

Table C-6. U.S. Export Price Indexes for Selected Categories of Goods, by SITC, 1991–1999

Tables C-6 and C-7 also use the SITC classification system. The all-commodities total price indexes are the same as those in Table C-4. In Table C-6, we can see how export prices of computer equipment and office machines fell 44 percent over the period ([{71.6/128.5}-1]x100).

Table C-6. U.S. Export Price Indexes for Selected Categories of Goods, by Standard International Trade Classification [SITC], 1991–1999—*Continued*

(1995=100, unless otherwise indicated; annual data are averages of the 12 months, unless otherwise indicated.)

Category	SITC code	1991	1992	1993	1994	1995	1996	1997	1998	1999
Computer equipment and office machines	75	128.5	122.7	115.0	106.0	100.0	92.5	84.7	77.1	71.6
Computer equipment	752	[1]143.1	[1]137.1	[1]122.1	109.8	100.0	89.8	79.9	73.5	67.3
Parts and accessories for computer equipment and office machines	759	[1]116.0	[1]111.5	[1]106.3	102.4	100.0	94.7	89.2	79.7	75.0

Table C-8. U.S. Foreign Trade in Goods by Industry Using North American Industry Classification System [NAICS] Product Groups, 1997–1999

Tables C-8 and C-9 provide time series of goods exports and imports using product groups that correspond to the product definitions used to classify industries in the United States. Data on production, employment, and capital in use are generally collected on an industry basis; hence, imports and exports need to be characterized on a similar basis in order to be linked with such data. All industry time series data currently being published for the United States currently use the 1987 Standard Industrial Classification (SIC) system, corresponding to the product classification system presented here in Table C-9. However, the United States, Canada, and Mexico are currently phasing out the SIC and replacing it with the North American Industry Classification System (NAICS), corresponding to the data presented in Table C-8. See the NOTES AND DEFINITIONS at the beginning of Part C for further information on NAICS and on the relationship of NAICS or SIC product codes to industry data.

The data in Table C-8, new in this edition, are among the first time series to be published using a NAICS-based system. Up to now, mainly single-year data from the 1997 Censuses of Business have been published on this basis. NAICS groupings are more appropriate for today's technology. For example, whereas the SIC classifies the manufacture of computers in "Industrial and Commercial Machinery" but places electronic components in "Electronic and Other Electrical Equipment," NAICS has a separate grouping for "Computer and electronic products," which is the largest single category in U.S. foreign trade; it accounted for 23 percent of U.S. goods exports and 20 percent of imports in 1999, and in that category imports exceeded exports by $44 billion.

Table C-8. U.S. Foreign Trade in Goods by Industry Using North American Industry Classification System [NAICS] Product Groups, 1997–1999

(Census basis, preliminary; millions of dollars.)

Product	NAICS code	1997	1998	1999
EXPORTS				
ALL COMMODITIES, TOTAL		687 598	680 474	692 821
Computer and electronic products	334	152 896	147 475	161 543
Electrical equipment, appliances, and component	335	22 917	22 383	23 716
Transportation equipment	336	118 101	131 890	132 042
IMPORTS				
ALL COMMODITIES, TOTAL		870 213	913 885	1 024 766
Computer and electronic products	334	175 011	181 202	205 604
Electrical equipment, appliances, and component	335	27 370	30 256	34 811
Transportation equipment	336	149 265	164 426	193 592

Table C-9. U.S. Foreign Trade in Goods by Industry Using Standard Industrial Classification [SIC] Product Groups, 1991–1997

Table C-9, using SIC product codes, provides more detail and a longer historical perspective. It shows, for example, that the value of exports of computers and office equipment rose 78 percent from 1991 to 1997, while imports of the same products rose 165 percent.

Table C-9. U.S. Foreign Trade in Goods by Industry Using Standard Industrial Classification [SIC] Product Groups, 1991–1997—Continued

(Census basis, millions of dollars.)

Product	SIC code	Exports						
		1991	1992	1993	1994	1995	1996	1997
Computers and office equipment	357	28 298	29 858	30 297	34 363	40 711	44 766	50 475
Refrigeration and service industry machinery	358	3 427	3 900	4 214	4 513	5 180	5 581	6 194
Miscellaneous industrial and commercial machinery and equipment	359	2 205	2 321	2 700	2 965	3 772	3 861	4 762

Table C-9. U.S. Foreign Trade in Goods by Industry Using Standard Industrial Classification [SIC] Product Groups, 1991–1997—Continued

(Census basis, millions of dollars.)

Product	SIC code	Imports						
		1991	1992	1993	1994	1995	1996	1997
Computers and office equipment	357	26 962	32 759	39 232	47 612	57 916	62 934	71 325
Refrigeration and service industry machinery	358	1 776	1 917	2 042	2 446	2 677	2 954	2 893
Miscellaneous industrial and commercial machinery and equipment	359	1 453	1 517	1 700	1 990	2 498	2 469	2 670

Table C-10. U.S. Foreign Trade in Goods, Summary by Region, 1991–1999

Tables C-10 and C-11 show exports and imports of all goods, agricultural products, and manufactures for each region of the world and each country with which the United States conducts any significant amount of trade. Table C-10 provides a one-page summary of trade by major geographic region. Of a $696 billion total for goods exports in 1999, $254 billion (36 percent) went to North America, that is to Canada and Mexico; $191 billion went to Asian destinations; and $172 billion to Europe. The pattern is not the same in all years, however. From 1991 to 1993 and again in 1995 and 1996, Asia rather than North America was the most important destination region. The increase in North American trade following the North American Free Trade Agreement (NAFTA) and the strengthening of the value of the dollar in recent years have both had their effects on these changes.

Table C-10. U.S. Foreign Trade in Goods, Summary by Regions, 1991–1999

(Census basis, millions of dollars.)

Region	1991	1992	1993	1994	1995	1996	1997	1998	1999
ALL DESTINATIONS									
Exports: All goods	421 730	448 164	465 091	512 627	584 742	625 075	689 182	682 138	695 797
NORTH AMERICA									
Exports: All goods	118 427	131 186	142 025	165 282	173 518	191 002	223 155	235 376	253 509
EUROPE									
Exports: All goods	123 469	122 617	119 785	123 479	140 564	148 810	163 273	170 008	171 834
ASIA									
Exports: All goods	130 629	138 262	146 725	160 995	197 402	207 328	213 547	187 566	190 881

Table C-11. U.S. Foreign Trade in Goods by Country or Region, 1991–1999

Table C-11 provides information by country as well as region. Almost 200 countries or country groups are included. The countries are arranged by geographic region, beginning with the Western Hemisphere and continuing through Europe, Asia, Australia and Oceania, and Africa. Within regions, the countries are arranged alphabetically. Some special regional groupings are found at the end of this table. Lists of the countries in each group are found in the NOTES AND DEFINITIONS in front of part C.

Table C-11. U.S. Trade in Goods by Country or Region, 1991–1999—*Continued*

(Census basis, millions of dollars.)

Country or region	1991	1992	1993	1994	1995	1996	1997	1998	1999
ASEAN (10 Countries)									
Exports: All goods	20 802	23 995	28 316	32 122	39 956	43 631	48 271	39 368	39 941
Agriculture	1 294	1 532	1 543	1 943	3 005	3 221	2 949	2 067	2 263
Manufactures	18 629	21 459	25 537	28 711	35 137	38 933	44 266	36 483	36 578
APEC (20 Countries)									
Exports: All goods	242 619	265 195	284 007	324 838	369 171	396 288	434 153	417 809	439 351
Agriculture	23 112	26 309	26 782	30 117	36 301	39 579	36 807	33 563	32 270
Manufactures	18 629	21 459	25 537	28 711	35 137	38 933	44 266	36 483	36 578
Caribbean Basin Initiative Countries									
Exports: All goods	10 449	11 744	12 748	13 801	15 671	16 350	18 961	20 773	20 454
Agriculture	1 494	1 532	1 736	1 760	2 155	2 426	2 565	2 684	2 587
Manufactures	7 740	9 025	9 849	10 950	12 329	12 617	14 978	16 927	16 774

Table C-12. U.S. Import Price Indexes for Selected Categories of Goods, by Locality of Origin, 1991–1999

This table, new in this edition, depicts price trends for imports from different regions. From 1991 to 1999, prices rose moderately for most regions and categories. However, prices declined for manufactured goods from developing countries and declined even more sharply for goods from the "Asian newly industrialized countries," reflecting the Asian financial crisis and consequent depreciation of currencies in several of these countries.

Table C-12. U.S. Import Price Indexes for Selected Categories of Goods, by Locality of Origin, 1991–1999

(1995=100, unless otherwise indicated; annual data are averages of the 12 months, unless otherwise indicated.)

Category	1991 [1]	1992 [2]	1993	1994	1995	1996	1997	1998	1999
DEVELOPING COUNTRIES	96.1	96.9	95.2	95.8	100.0	102.9	102.0	92.9	93.8
Manufactured goods	97.2	97.7	96.7	97.3	100.0	100.3	99.3	94.2	91.6
Nonmanufactured goods	94.7	95.8	89.7	90.2	100.0	113.1	109.7	81.6	100.3
ASIAN NEWLY INDUSTRIALIZED COUNTRIES	99.6	100.7	100.2	99.5	100.0	98.5	94.9	87.2	83.4

Technical notes: All dollar value data in Section C are on a "census basis." That is, they have not been adjusted to a basis consistent with the concepts and definitions used in the balance-of-payments. Therefore the data differ somewhat from the corresponding data in Tables A-5 and A-6. The NOTES AND DEFINITIONS in front of parts A and C provide information about each of these concepts and definitions.

SECTION D. STATE EXPORTS OF GOODS (pages 131–362) and
SECTION E. METROPOLITAN AREA EXPORTS OF GOODS (pages 363–438)

Sections D and E are similar in their organization. The first table in each section provides totals by year for exports of goods from each state (Table D-1) or from each of more than 250 metropolitan areas (Table E-1). Subsequent tables provide detail by destination or by industry. Table E-2, Metropolitan Area Exports of Goods by Industry, 1994-1999, provides industry detail for the 43 large metropolitan areas for which such information is available.

Data by state or metropolitan area can be provided only for exports of goods. Neither exports of services nor imports of either goods or services can be systematically assigned to any particular geographic area within the United States.

The assignment of goods exports to a state or metropolitan area is based on the location of the exporter of record. Such assignment may or may not reflect the location where the goods were produced. And, even if the final products were produced in the state to which they were assigned, these products may use parts manufactured elsewhere. An airplane assembled in Washington State, for example, is likely to contain parts produced in other states, or even in other countries. Thus, while the data in Sections D and E provide a good general indication of the role of exports in a local economy, they should be interpreted as only rough approximations.

USING SECTIONS D AND E: SOME EXAMPLES

Table D-1. State Exports of Goods, 1987 and 1991–1999

In 1999, total U.S. exports of goods increased from 1998 by about 2 percent, after a slight dip in 1998 from 1997, and following several years of strong growth. The pattern varied by state, however. Exports from California were up almost 4 percent, reflecting, in part, growth in demand for industrial machinery and computers. In contrast, exports from Washington State were down almost 3 percent, reflecting, in part, the slow down in world demand for transportation equipment.

Table D-1. State Exports of Goods, 1987 and 1991–1999

(Billions of dollars.)

State	1987	1991	1992	1993	1994	1995	1996	1997	1998	1999
ALL STATES	244.4	420.0	447.5	464.9	512.4	583.0	622.8	687.6	680.5	692.8
Arkansas	0.4	0.8	1.1	1.1	1.5	1.8	2.0	2.2	1.9	1.8
California	32.9	59.0	66.7	68.1	78.2	92.0	98.6	103.8	98.8	102.9
Washington	10.3	27.3	28.7	27.4	25.1	22.0	25.5	31.7	38.0	36.8
West Virginia	0.7	0.9	0.9	0.8	0.9	1.1	1.2	1.3	1.2	0.9
Wisconsin	2.9	4.9	5.8	5.8	6.9	8.0	8.4	9.8	9.2	9.5

Table D-3. ALABAMA: State Exports of Goods by Destination and Industry, 1994–1999

This table shows Alabama's exports by industrial classification and by destination; the succeeding tables show the same for each state, arranged in alphabetical order. Ten individual country destinations are shown; these are the ten countries to which the United States as a whole sends the most exports. Several regional groupings also are shown.

Two paired charts at the beginning of each state's segment illustrate the industrial composition of that state's exports. The pie chart on the left shows how the state's goods exports are divided into manufactures, agricultural and livestock products, and other commodities. For Alabama, like most states, manufactures make up the bulk of goods exports (95 percent in this case). The right-hand bar chart shows total exports of manufactures and the five top manufacturing industry groups. In Alabama's case transportation equipment accounts for $1.3 billion of the total of $4.7 billion of manufactured exports. Industrial machinery and computers accounts for another $0.7 billion.

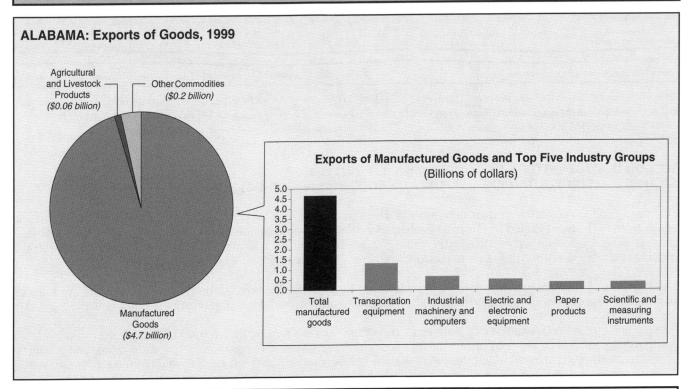

ALABAMA: Exports of Goods, 1999

Agricultural and Livestock Products ($0.06 billion)

Other Commodities ($0.2 billion)

Manufactured Goods ($4.7 billion)

Exports of Manufactured Goods and Top Five Industry Groups
(Billions of dollars)

Total manufactured goods — Transportation equipment — Industrial machinery and computers — Electric and electronic equipment — Paper products — Scientific and measuring instruments

Table D-3. ALABAMA: State Exports of Goods by Destination and Industry, 1994–1999

(Millions of dollars.)

Industry	All destinations						Canada					
	1994	1995	1996	1997	1998	1999	1994	1995	1996	1997	1998	1999
ALL GOODS	3 115.4	3 587.1	3 702.4	4 537.2	4 560.2	4 898.9	789.0	988.5	1 177.4	1 251.1	1 280.8	1 459.5
Manufactured Goods	2 796.6	3 167.0	3 359.9	4 207.7	4 262.3	4 665.6	745.6	939.9	1 118.6	1 199.4	1 235.7	1 416.9
Industrial machinery and computers	393.9	457.6	457.0	625.6	557.5	662.9	92.6	106.6	109.0	111.6	100.9	89.1
Electric and electronic equipment	487.9	610.0	819.6	1 140.0	538.2	517.3	211.7	239.9	358.2	210.5	181.1	186.6
Transportation equipment	591.6	418.8	400.5	357.8	1 034.2	1 313.8	101.7	207.1	250.2	232.6	267.4	335.6

Table E-3. Metropolitan Area Goods Exports by Destination, 1994–1999

This table shows the relative importance of each world region and each major country as an export market for each metropolitan area shown. Exports from Minneapolis-St. Paul, MN-WI, for example, are distributed fairly evenly across regions: in 1999, 31 percent went to Europe, 26 percent to Asia, another 26 percent to North America, and the remainder to the other world regions. In contrast, Brownsville-Harlingen-San Benito, TX, located on the Mexican border, sent 80 percent of its exports to Mexico. And San Jose, CA sent 54 percent to Asia.

The metropolitan areas in this table are arranged in alphabetical order and the export destinations listed alphabetically within major world region.

Table E-3. Metropolitan Area Exports of Goods by Destination, 1994–1999—*Continued*

(Millions of dollars.)

Destination	Minneapolis - St. Paul, MN - WI						Mobile, AL					
	1994	1995	1996	1997	1998	1999	1994	1995	1996	1997	1998	1999
ALL DESTINATIONS	8 863.5	11 071.8	12 384.0	12 006.7	11 652.4	12 401.3	395.3	415.8	459.9	498.7	426.1	570.8
North America	1 805.4	2 213.2	2 854.7	3 014.3	3 149.4	3 233.1	85.5	78.8	105.1	111.3	106.6	94.3
Canada	1 492.4	1 719.2	2 025.2	2 208.7	2 307.2	2 293.2	73.5	66.4	89.2	92.6	90.0	78.2
Mexico	313.1	494.0	829.5	805.6	842.2	940.0	11.9	12.4	15.9	18.6	16.7	16.1
Europe	3 479.4	4 101.6	4 293.2	4 111.3	3 878.5	3 860.2	186.3	177.8	167.3	146.3	105.1	137.6
Belgium	159.0	238.9	235.1	166.5	215.0	172.3	5.3	4.9	5.7	3.2	9.5	4.3
France	226.2	253.4	270.3	350.5	412.2	387.1	19.2	14.1	22.6	16.6	14.8	21.7
Asia	2 141.9	2 798.4	2 950.3	2 771.4	2 713.0	3 259.4	68.4	103.6	115.6	163.9	135.4	263.0
Japan	709.6	817.2	993.5	1 016.5	755.7	772.2	55.8	73.2	67.4	43.4	48.3	32.5
China	89.2	393.6	160.0	208.6	253.5	277.3	0.7	3.1	1.4	6.0	6.1	2.6

Table E-3. Metropolitan Area Exports of Goods by Destination, 1994–1999—*Continued*

(Millions of dollars.)

Destination	Bridgeport, CT						Brownsville - Harlingen - San Benito, TX					
	1994	1995	1996	1997	1998	1999	1994	1995	1996	1997	1998	1999
ALL DESTINATIONS	918.8	952.9	788.6	981.4	895.0	795.3	2 113.4	2 245.9	2 612.6	2 697.1	2 421.3	2 571.4
North America	188.3	170.4	194.5	237.3	212.8	181.9	2 060.9	2 178.1	2 560.9	2 634.0	2 301.2	2 448.6
Canada	115.2	133.9	148.3	170.9	161.9	151.4	133.9	453.1	372.9	467.8	361.8	397.7
Mexico	73.1	36.5	46.2	66.4	50.9	30.6	1 927.0	1 725.0	2 188.0	2 166.3	1 939.4	2 050.9

Table E-3. Metropolitan Area Exports of Goods by Destination, 1994–1999—*Continued*

(Millions of dollars.)

Destination	San Jose, CA						Santa Barbara - Santa Maria - Lompoc, CA					
	1994	1995	1996	1997	1998	1999	1994	1995	1996	1997	1998	1999
ALL DESTINATIONS	19 942.7	26 822.8	29 331.3	29 057.2	26 111.9	28 255.7	420.2	565.2	648.0	623.3	501.3	581.4
Asia	11 089.3	16 341.0	17 899.6	16 504.3	13 947.3	15 213.2	203.7	260.7	307.0	318.3	182.9	250.7
Japan	2 843.4	4 158.4	5 122.9	4 789.6	3 643.8	3 744.5	45.5	88.2	66.0	57.1	50.3	49.2
China	228.3	253.0	338.6	415.7	760.7	636.2	2.3	3.4	3.2	3.2	5.0	3.6

GENERAL NOTES ON THE DATA

TIME PERIOD COVERED

Starting dates vary depending on data availability. All tables continue through 1999.

DEFINITIONS

The following symbols are used for all of the tables in this volume.

... Data are not available, not applicable, or equal to zero for the item shown.
(D) Data are suppressed to protect confidentiality, that is, to avoid disclosure of data
      pertaining to an individual business.
(*) The value of this item is less than 500,000.

The following words or phrases are used throughout this volume, and apply to all tables.

f.a.s. Free Alongside Ship. The export value including the price of the merchandise, inland freight, insurance, and other costs in placing the goods alongside the carrier at the U.S. port of exportation.

f.o.b. Free on Board. The export value including the f.a.s. value and the cost of delivery to and placing on board a carrier at the port of exportation.

Values for *exports of goods* in the tables in this book are based on f.a.s. value.

Imports of goods are valued based on the U. S. Customs Service appraised value of merchandise. Typically, this is the price paid for merchandise for export to the United States. Import duties, freight, insurance, and other costs in bringing merchandise to the United States are excluded, as are customs duties.

Census Basis. The "census basis" goods data are compiled from the documents collected by the U.S. Customs Service and reflect the movement of goods between foreign countries and the 50 states, the District of Columbia, Puerto Rico, the U.S. Virgin Islands, and U.S. Foreign Trade Zones. They include government and non-government shipments of goods, and exclude shipments between the United States and its territories and possessions, transactions with U.S. military, diplomatic and consular installations abroad, U.S. goods returned to the United States by its armed forces, personal and household effects of travelers, and in-transit shipments. The general import values reflect the total arrival of merchandise from foreign countries that immediately enters consumption channels, warehouses, or Foreign Trade Zones.

Balance of Payments (BOP) Basis. Goods export values on a census basis are adjusted by the Bureau of Economic Analysis (BEA) to goods on a BOP basis to make the data consistent with the concepts and definitions used to prepare the international and national accounts. These adjustments are necessary to supplement coverage of the census basis data, to eliminate duplication of transactions recorded elsewhere in the international accounts, and to value transactions according to a standard definition.

The export adjustments include: (1) Deduction of U.S. military sales contracts, because the Census Bureau has included these contracts in the goods data, but BEA includes them in the service category "transfers under U.S. military sales contracts." BEA's source material for these contracts is more comprehensive, but has no distinction between goods and services. (2) Addition of private gift parcels mailed to foreigners by individuals through the U.S. Postal Service (Only commercial shipments are covered in census goods exports). (3) Addition to nonmonetary gold exports of gold that is purchased by foreign official agencies from private dealers in the United States and held at the Federal Reserve Bank of New York. The census data only include gold that leaves the customs territory. (4) Smaller adjustments including deductions for repairs of goods, exposed motion picture film, and military grant-aid, and additions for sales of fish in U.S. territorial waters, exports of electricity to Mexico, and vessels and oil rigs that change ownership for which no export document is filed.

The import adjustments include: (1) An addition for inland freight in Canada. Imports of goods from all countries are valued at the foreign port of export, including inland freight charges ("customs value"). In the case of Canada, this should be the cost of the goods at the U.S. border. However, the customs value for imports for certain Canadian goods is the point of origin in Canada. The BEA makes an addition for the inland freight charges of transporting these Canadian goods to the U.S. border to make the value comparable to the customs value as reported by all other countries (the same procedure is used for Mexico as an "other adjustment", but is much smaller). (2) Addition of nonmonetary gold imports is made for gold sold by foreign official agencies to private purchasers out of stock held at the Federal Reserve Bank of New York. The census data only includes gold that enters the customs territory. (3) Deduction of U.S. military sales contracts is made because the Census Bureau has included these contracts in the goods data, but BEA includes them in the service category "direct defense expenditures". BEA's source material is more comprehensive, but has no distinction between goods and services. (4) Smaller adjustments include deductions for repairs of goods, and exposed motion picture film, and additions for imported electricity from Mexico, conversion of vessels for commercial use, and repairs to U.S. vessels abroad.

National Income and Product Account (NIPA) basis. The BOP data on trade in goods and services require further adjustment in order to be fully consistent with the concepts and definitions used in the NIPA. The following adjustments are made to BOP basis trade data to reconcile it with NIPA concepts: (1) Beginning with 1967, BOP gold exports and imports are excluded from the NIPA; imports of gold in the NIPA is the excess of the value of gold in gross domestic purchases over the value of U.S. production of gold. (2) In the NIPA, transfers of goods and services under military grant programs, net, are excluded from exports and included in federal government consumption expenditures. Beginning with 1988, the BOP classify certain items as military grants that the NIPA do not. (3) In the NIPA, Puerto Rico, Northern Mariana Islands, and U.S. Territories are included in the rest of the world; in the BOP they are treated as part of the United States. Also, from 1946 to 1959 Alaska and Hawaii are included in the rest of the world. This ended in 1960 because they gained statehood in 1959. (4) Some transactions measured on a net basis in the BOP are measured on a gross basis in the NIPA accounts, resulting in higher import and export totals but no change on net exports (exports less imports).

SOURCES

Listed below are the agencies from which the data in this book were obtained.

Board of Governors of the Federal Reserve System
20th and Constitution Avenue, NW
Washington, DC 20551
Data Inquiries and Publication Sales:
Publications Services
Mail Stop 127
Board of Governors of the Federal Reserve System
Washington, DC 20551
(202) 452-3244
Monthly Publication: Federal Reserve Bulletin
Internet Address: http://www.federalreserve.gov

Bureau of Economic Analysis (BEA), U.S. Department of Commerce
Washington, DC 20233
Data Inquiries:
Public Information Office
(202) 606-9900
Monthly Publication: Survey of Current Business
Internet Address: http://www.bea.doc.gov

Bureau of the Census, U.S. Department of Commerce
Washington, DC 20233
Data Inquiries:
Foreign Trade Information: (301) 457-3041
Internet Address: http://www.census.gov

International Monetary Fund
Publication Sales:
Publication Services, Catalog Orders
700 19th Street, N.W.
Washington, D.C. 20431
Telephone: (202) 623-7430
Monthly Publication: International Financial Statistics
Internet Address: http://www.imf.org

Office of Trade and Economic Analysis (OTEA), International Trade Administration, U.S. Department of Commerce
Washington, D.C. 20230
Internet Address: http://www.ita.doc.gov/tradestats

Bureau of Labor Statistics, U.S. Department of Labor
Washington, D.C. 20212
Monthly publication: Monthly Labor Review
Internet address: http://stats.bls.gov

U.S. FOREIGN TRADE AT THE MILLENNIUM
by Cornelia J. Strawser

As the decade of the 1990s (and the 20th century and the millennium) drew to an end, the United States economy set a number of new records, not least in the area of foreign trade. This second edition of *Foreign Trade of the United States* documents foreign trade in goods and services in detail through 1999. Some of the major trends evident in those tables continued into 2000, according to preliminary data for that year, as shown in **Figure 1** and **Table 1**.

TABLE 1: MAJOR COMPONENTS OF U.S. INTERNATIONAL TRANSACTIONS, 1990, 1999 AND 2000
(BILLIONS OF DOLLARS)

	1990	1999	2000 (preliminary)
Current Account Balance, Total	-77.0	-331.5	-435.4
Balance on goods	-109.0	-345.6	-449.5
Balance on services	30.2	80.6	81.0
Balance on income	28.6	-18.5	-13.7
Unilateral transfers, net	-26.7	-48.0	-53.2
Selected Net Financial Flows:			
Selected U.S.-owned assets abroad [increase/financial outflow (-)]:			
Direct investment, private	-37.2	-150.9	-161.6
Foreign securities, private	-28.8	-128.6	-123.6
Selected foreign-owned assets in the United States [increase/financial inflow (+)]:			
Direct investment	48.5	275.5	316.5
U.S. Treasury securities	-2.5	-20.5	-52.2
Other U.S. securities	1.6	331.5	465.9

The "current account balance" is the broadest measure of balance in U.S. international transactions. **Table 1** shows that the U.S. current account deficit, which had been only $77 billion in 1990, widened from $331.5 billion in 1999 to $435 billion in 2000. Imports of goods exceeded exports of goods by $450 billion, an increase of $104 billion in the goods deficit from 1999. This increase was about the size of the total goods deficit in 1990. **Figure 1** shows the values of imports and exports (goods and services combined) as a percentage of gross domestic product, demonstrating that the widening of the trade gap reflected mainly a surge in the value of imports, more than offsetting a more moderate increase in the value of exports. Both the quantities and the prices of imports rose faster than those of exports.

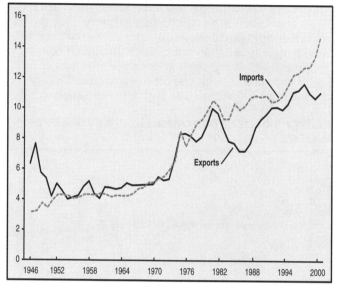

FIGURE 1: U.S. EXPORTS AND IMPORTS AS A PERCENTAGE OF GROSS DOMESTIC PRODUCT, 1946–2000

Yet the U.S. economy, in the aggregate, was in good health in 2000. Real gross domestic product grew 5.0 percent from 1999 to 2000, even faster than in the two preceding years. Growth rates slowed over the year, but in the fourth quarter, real GDP was nevertheless 3.4 percent above a year earlier. Unemployment, which had been 5.6 percent in 1990, averaged 4.0 percent of the civilian labor force during 2000 and also at yearend. This was the lowest rate since 1969 and one that many economists had thought could not be reached without setting off an acceleration in inflation. But inflation in the "core" Consumer Price Index (all items less food and energy) during 2000 (December 2000 from December 1999) was 2.6 percent, little changed from 1.9 percent during 1999.

In elementary economics textbooks, a surging U.S. trade deficit would be predicted to flood the rest of the world with unwanted dollars. Other countries, with plenty of dollars left over after paying for imports from the United States, would sell these dollars and drive down the price of the dollar relative to other currencies. As the dollar's value declined, imports to the United States would become more expensive to U.S. consumers and producers, while U.S. exports would become cheaper in the rest of the world; as a result, exports would tend to rise, imports to fall, and the trade deficit to be reduced by this equilibrating mechanism.

So far, however, nothing of the sort has happened to stem the rise in the trade deficit. As **Figure 2** shows, the dollar remained high relative to other major currencies (those of the other major industrial nations, whose currencies are freely traded in world markets) and also relative to our other important trading partners. (For the latter category, **Figure 2** shows an index corrected for relative changes in inflation rates, which provides a better measure for the longer-run price competitiveness of U.S. goods and services with respect to these countries; see the Notes and Definitions to Part A for explanation.)

FIGURE 2: INDEXES OF THE FOREIGN EXCHANGE VALUE OF THE U. S. DOLLAR, 1992–2000

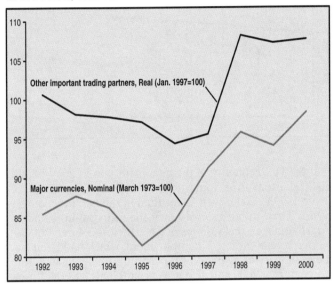

Why has the price of the dollar not declined in response to its increasing supply? The answer is that demand for the dollar has also increased. Foreigners do not use dollars just to buy U.S. goods and services; they need dollars for conducting other international business (including paying for petroleum, which is priced in dollars), as a store of value—providing assets that for inhabitants of many countries may be safer than holdings in their own currencies—and for investing in U.S. markets.

Investment in the United States continued to attract foreign money in 2000. **Table 1** shows recent trends for the major international financial flows that have enabled this country to finance its rising trade deficit without a decline in the dollar's value. Direct investment in the United States by foreigners rose by $41 billion in 2000, far greater than the $11 billion expansion in U.S. direct investment overseas. Foreigners bought $466 billion worth of U.S. nongovernment securities in 2000, an increase of $134 billion from 1999. U.S. stock markets were evidently as attractive to foreigners as to domestic investors. (As the U.S. federal government began to retire debt, foreigners sold Treasury securities, but as **Table 1** shows, these sales were small by comparison with the foreign direct investment and securities purchases.)

Yet, the stock market boom can hardly be the sole explanation for the continued strength of the dollar, since stock prices have been on a downtrend in recent months while as of late March 2001 the dollar is even stronger than it was in 2000. Weakness in the rest of the world—notably Japan's troubled economy—has accompanied the slowdown in U.S. economic indicators. Consequently, alternative major currencies, including the new euro, do not seem to have become more attractive.

In some developing countries, the dollar is used as a store of value or even as a circulating currency. This source of demand also strengthened in 1999, as can be seen in the "U.S. currency" holdings line in Table A-6, though by a smaller amount than the major inflows shown in **Table 1.**

Overall, the strength of the dollar and the absence of a strong growth engine overseas argue against any early growth in exports that could start to reverse the trend in the U.S. trade and current account deficits.

There was considerable apprehension about the state of the U.S. economy as this article was written. Many of the indicators that often presage recession, such as stock prices, had turned lower, and manufacturing output had been declining since September 2000. Payroll employment declined in March, and the unemployment rate edged up further to 4.3 percent.

At the end of the 20th century, the U.S. economy had demonstrated that strong economic growth, low unemployment, and a large and rising trade deficit could coexist—at least for a while. But as the 21st century begins, there is an unusual amount of uncertainty, at least about the immediate future of the U.S. economy.

Indeed, there is reason for concern about the health of the world economy. World financial problems began in Thailand in 1997 and spread during 1998. At first, these problems had effects on the United States that were both adverse and favorable. While U.S. exports weakened, the dollar strengthened and the United States was able to import goods to relieve any potential inflationary tendencies in domestic markets. By the same token, growing U.S. imports were a valued source of demand to other countries. But sustained slowing in U.S. incomes and production would remove some of this stimulus to other countries. The health of the economies of the United States and the rest of the world may depend on the ability of other countries to generate greater growth.

THE CHANGING COMPOSITION OF U.S. TRADE

Whatever the near-term prospects for the U.S. economy and its current account deficit, some important underlying factors are likely to continue. Exports of services and of advanced technology products have become increasingly important to U.S. trade, while the relative importance of agricultural exports has declined. Because the

U.S. is a heavy importer of crude petroleum and its products, changes in world prices for those goods can have dramatic effects on the value of imports and the trade balance.

Services have come to constitute an increasingly important share of total U.S. exports over the past half-century. Their growth was especially marked during the early and mid-1980s, when the services share of total trade rose from 19 percent in 1980 to more than 29 percent in 1987. Since 1987, with exports of both goods and services growing rapidly, the services share has remained in the vicinity of 29 percent.

FIGURE 3: U.S. TRADE IN PRIVATE SERVICES, 1999
(BILLIONS OF DOLLARS)

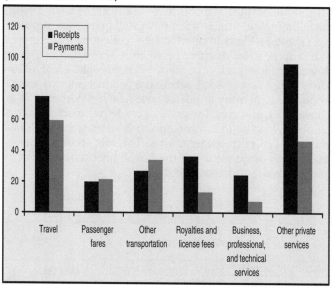

Figure 3 indicates the balances in 1999 between exports ("receipts") and imports ("payments") for the major categories of services. These categories are quite diverse.

- "Travel"—which does *not* include international passenger fares, but covers international travelers' expenditures for food, lodging, entertainment, retail shopping, local transportation, and such—reflects the rather low-tech tourist industry, and can be affected by major swings in exchange rates. The U.S. travel account is in surplus now, but was in deficit in 1986 through 1988; see Table B-1. In 1986 the value of the dollar relative to other major currencies was nearly 10 percent higher than in 2000, and it was even higher earlier in the 1980s. Travel by U.S. residents to Europe, Japan, and many other countries was therefore relatively cheap, while the United States was then more expensive for foreigners than it is now.

- Transportation (covered in "Passenger fares" and "other transportation") is a mature industry where international price competition is strong.

- The rest of the services category covers many activities in which the American advantages are not in relative prices but in popularity, creativity, and intellectual capital. The categories "royalties and license fees" and "other private services", in which the United States has large surpluses, include the activities of transnational entertainment and "brand-name" firms such as Coca-Cola, McDonalds, and Disney. U.S. surpluses in education and in a wide range of business and professional services are also substantial.

The rapid growth of service exports has earned the United States increasingly large surpluses on trade in services, reaching $81 billion in 1999 (See Table A-5) and remaining at that level in 2000. Exports more than doubled from 1989 to 1999, while imports rose 87 percent. (See Table B-1.) Some of the most impressive trade growth was in business, professional, and technical services, where both exports and imports more than quintupled. With exports starting from a larger base, net U.S. earnings on this category of service trade rose from $5 billion in 1989 to $17 billion in 1999. Another major earnings category for the United States was royalties and license fees, with a $23 billion surplus in 1999.

Total U.S. exports of *manufactured goods*, like those of services, more than doubled from 1989 to 1999, reaching $615 billion. (See Table C-1.) During the same period, however, U.S. imports more than doubled too, reaching $882 billion and increasing the U.S. trade deficit on manufactured goods from $92 billion in 1989 to $268 billion in 1999.

Advanced technology products dominate the U.S. manufacturing export picture. Four commodity groups—Electrical machinery, Motor vehicles, Transport equipment, and Office machines—accounted for more than 40 percent of U.S. manufactured exports in 1999. (See Table C-5). These are the groups that contain large concentrations of high-tech goods. A more precise measure of advanced technology products is shown in **Table 2.** The advanced technology values in this table are an aggregation of about 500 of the 22,000 commodity classification codes used in reporting U.S. goods trade. Only classifications dominated by leading-edge technology in a recognized high-technology field are included. In 1999 the United States exported $200.3 billion of these advanced technology products, and they have increased steadily in absolute value and as a share of U.S. goods exports.

TABLE 2: ADVANCED TECHNOLOGY PRODUCTS IN U.S. GOODS TRADE, 1995–2000

Year	Value of advanced technology products trade (Billions of dollars)			Percent of total goods	
	Exports	Imports	Balance	Exports	Imports
1995	138.5	124.8	13.7	23.7	16.8
1996	154.9	130.4	24.5	24.8	16.4
1997	179.5	147.3	32.2	26.0	16.9
1998	186.4	156.8	29.6	27.3	17.2
1999	200.3	181.2	19.1	28.8	17.7
2000 (preliminary)	227.1	222.1	5.0	29.1	18.3

However, imports of advanced technology products are also increasing in importance, and since 1997 they have been gaining on exports. By 2000, the positive U.S. balance in trade in these products was almost wiped out. The strong dollar may be a factor, increasing the price competitiveness of foreign high-tech producers.

Agricultural products have long been an area of strength in U.S. exports. With the more rapid growth of exports of manufactures, however, the agricultural share of total goods exports has diminished. Year-to-year fluctuations in foreign agricultural sales sometimes are large, reflect-

ing changes in weather, crop yields, world prices, and other highly variable factors. Comparing peak years, agricultural exports were 22 percent of total goods exports in 1974, 18 percent in 1983, 10 percent in 1995, and only 7 percent in 1999. In no year of the past quarter-century, however, has trade in agricultural products failed to produce a U.S. surplus in this category; the surplus reached $12 billion in 1999.

Oil. The mineral fuels category shown in Table C-1 includes petroleum and petroleum products. Here, imports greatly exceed exports, reflecting U.S. dependence on imported oil. This dependence has increased during the 1990s as domestic oil production declined. Quantities of energy-related petroleum products imported rose at an average rate of 4.8 percent per year from 1991 to 2000. The value of these imports held steady in the early 1990s as falling world prices offset increased quantities imported (**Table 3**). Costs jumped in 1996, reflecting a 20 percent jump in the price of crude petroleum. Then, by 1998, the lowest crude oil prices in many years brought a $20 billion drop in the cost of total petroleum product imports, even though the quantity imported rose nearly 8 percent. Since 1998, however, the price of crude has more than doubled, leading to a commensurate increase in the dollar value of U.S. petroleum imports. This rise accounts for $68 billion—one-third—of the $202.6 billion increase in the goods deficit from 1998 to 2000.

TABLE 3: IMPORTS OF PETROLEUM AND PETROLEUM PRODUCTS, 1991–2000

Year	Total energy-related petroleum products		Crude petroleum			
	Quantity (Millions of barrels)	Value (Billions of dollars)	Quantity (Millions of barrels)		Value (Billions of dollars)	Unit price (Dollars per barrel)
			Total	Average per day		
1991	2829.0	50.6	2146.1	5.9	37.5	17.46
1992	2947.6	50.5	2294.6	6.3	38.6	16.80
1993	3257.0	50.2	2534.4	7.0	38.5	15.13
1994	3416.0	49.5	2704.2	7.4	38.5	14.23
1995	3361.9	53.8	2767.3	7.6	43.7	15.81
1996	3622.4	70.2	2893.6	7.9	54.9	18.98
1997	3802.6	69.3	3069.4	8.4	54.2	17.67
1998	4088.0	49.1	3242.7	8.9	37.3	11.49
1999	4081.2	65.9	3228.1	8.8	50.9	15.80
2000	4299.7	116.9	3399.2	9.3	89.8	26.41

TRADE BY COUNTRY AND REGION

U.S. trade with individual countries and regions varies from year to year with fluctuations in economic conditions, shifts in exchange rates, and other factors. An underlying trend in the 1990s has been the increasing importance of trade within North America. For trade in goods, Canada has long been the most important U.S trading partner, and, since 1997, Mexico has been surpassing Japan as the second largest market for U.S. exports. (See Table C-11.) By 1999 these two North American countries accounted for 36 percent of U.S. goods exports and 30 percent of imports, up from 28 percent and 25 percent, respectively, in 1991. Although growth of trade among the North American countries was already well under way, the adoption of the North American Free Trade Agreement (NAFTA) in 1993 likely caused it to accelerate. As North American and other destinations have taken on increased importance, U.S. exports to Western Europe, while increasing in absolute value, have become a lesser share of the total, falling from 28 percent in 1991 to 24 percent in 1999. U.S. exports to Asian destinations rose from 31 percent of total goods exports in 1991 to almost 34 percent in 1995 but fell back to only 27 percent in 1999, as weak economies in many Asian countries reduced demand for U.S. goods.

The geographic pattern of trade in services differs from that of goods. Three countries—Canada, Japan, and the United Kingdom—account for nearly one-third of U.S. trade in services, and that proportion has varied little since 1986. (See Table B-3.) Japan is the strongest export market; the Japanese purchased $30.5 billion of U.S. services in 1999. The United Kingdom is the leading U.S. import source, selling U.S. residents $23.8 billion of services in 1999. With all three countries, passenger fares and other spending by travelers to the United States are the dominant sources of U.S. service export earnings. In 1999, the Japanese spent $9.7 billion for these services, the British $8.4 billion, and the Canadians $6.7 billion. U.S. residents spent $5.5 billion in 1999 to travel to Britain or on British passenger carriers and $6.1 billion for Canadian travel and transportation, but only $2.8 billion for travel and related services to Japan.

TRADE AND STATE AND LOCAL ECONOMIES

In a country as large and diverse as the United States, regions and localities may vary greatly in the volume of their exports, in the destinations to which they export, and in the types of products exported. Sections D and E of this book contain information on goods exports by state and metropolitan area. These data give an indication of the importance of exports to a particular area, but, for several reasons, they must be interpreted with caution. First, they pertain only to goods exports; comparable data about service exports are not available. Second, they identify the location (state or metropolitan area) of the seller of the export merchandise; often the merchandise is sold by the producer and the production occurs in the same state or metropolitan area as the sale, but this is not always the case. Third, even if the final product is produced in the state or metropolitan area to which it is assigned, the product likely contains materials and parts produced elsewhere. Hence, these data give a general impression of the importance of export production to a local economy, but not a precise measure.

FIGURE 4: MAJOR EXPORTING STATES, 1999
(STATE GOODS EXPORTS IN BILLIONS OF DOLLARS)

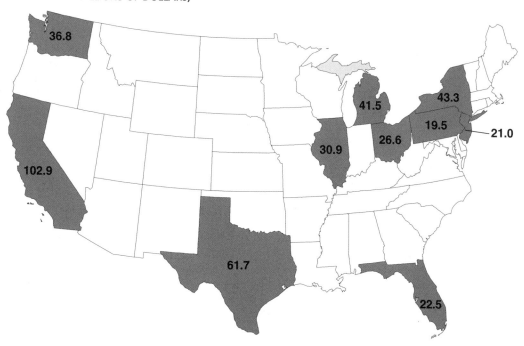

States. **Figure 4** locates the ten major exporting states. These ten states account for over one-half of all U.S. goods exports. California, Texas, and New York—the three states with the largest populations—each had even larger shares of exports. Together these states had 26 percent of the U.S. population in 1999 and 30 percent of exports. California is the biggest exporter to Asia, and to Europe as well. Texas, however, is the most important exporter to the Americas. (See graphs at the beginning of Part D.)

Florida, with the fourth largest population, has an export share which is large but below its population share, doubtless reflecting its large retired population and the relatively limited role of manufacturing in the Florida economy.

It is worth reiterating that these data cover only goods exports; they do not measure the overall participation of a state in the international economy. Hawaii's goods exports may be small, but its earnings from spending by foreign visitors are a vital factor in its economy. Florida has seen rapid growth of its goods exports in the past 10 years, but more important may be Florida's popularity as an international tourist destination and its role as a transportation hub for movement of people and goods to Latin America.

Metropolitan areas. The two metropolitan areas with the most goods exports in 1999 were Seattle-Bellevue-Everett, Washington, and San Jose, California, with about $32 billion and $28 billion of exports respectively. The first of these areas is a center of airplane manufacture; the second is the hub of Silicon Valley. Other metropolitan areas with exports in excess of $20 billion in 1999 were Detroit, Michigan; New York, New York; Los Angeles-Long Beach, California; and Chicago, Illinois. (See Table E-1.)

Although the totals are close, the export patterns of San Jose and New York are a study in contrasts. San Jose's exports have grown rapidly—almost 75 percent from 1993 to 1999; New York's 1999 exports were 13 percent less than those of 1993, and they had gone up and down in the intervening years. Of San Jose's manufactured exports in 1999, 96 percent were in the SIC categories of industrial machinery, electronic equipment, and instruments—the three categories that contain the bulk of high-tech manufacturing. New York's exports were more diversified, but 19 percent were primary metals (iron, steel, and nonferrous metals), an industry group marked by declining employment and no net output growth over the past two decades. And even New York's high-tech exports, which represent 15 percent of manufactured exports in 1999, have failed to experience the growth that San Jose has seen. (See Table E-2.) The two metropolitan areas also differ in the markets toward which their exports are directed. More than one-half of San Jose's exports went to Asian markets in 1999, including $3.7 billion to Japan and more than $2 billion each to South Korea and Taiwan. New York's exports are spread more broadly, with about 41 percent to Europe, 26 percent to Asia, and the remainder to other regions. (See Table E-3.)

Among other large metropolitan areas, San Diego, California, has experienced some of the most rapid export growth, with 1999 exports more than double those in 1993. Again, the picture is one of concentration in high-tech goods. Of $9 billion of total exports in 1999, more than 40 percent went to Mexico, while more than 1 billion to Asia and another $1 billion to Europe.

CONCLUDING CONSIDERATIONS

Foreign Trade of the United States: Second Edition presents a statistical depiction of U.S. foreign trade that is both broad and detailed. Inevitably, it does not answer all possible questions about the impact of trade on national, state, and local economies.

To take one example, large and growing trade deficits are clearly compatible with high levels of employment for the *aggregate* economy; but these data as collected cannot identify the impact of imports on employment in particular state and local economies. Detailed economic analysis holding other factors constant and tying imports to the domestic competing industries in the regional economies is required for such a study.

Secondly, many countries, including the United States, attempt to manage their international trade using tariffs, nontariff barriers such as import quotas, exchange rate manipulations, and regulations that attempt to discourage imports of goods and/or services. It is beyond the scope of this book to identify these policies. However, it should be noted that many economists believe that in a modern open economy, such policies can distort trade patterns in particular industries and with particular countries, but will have little effect on the overall trade deficit.

This argument takes as its starting point two accounting identities. One of these is the necessary identity between the current-account deficit and net financial inflows from abroad, discussed in the Introductory Notes to Part A of this book. This implies that a trade deficit must be financed by net foreign investment. If the foreigners don't invest enough to finance the trade deficit, the dollar will depreciate and reduce the trade deficit, as discussed earlier in this article. But if foreigners want to invest more funds in the United States than are supplied by the existing trade deficit, they will bid up the value of the dollar, which will increase the U.S. trade deficit.

The second is the necessary identity in the National Income and Product Accounts between net foreign investment and the gap between domestic private and government investment and saving. This implies that a domestic saving gap must be financed by foreigners; if they don't, domestic interest rates must rise, stifling investment and/or encouraging domestic saving.

Together, these identities are taken by many economists to mean that a deficit in the national saving-investment balance will require a corresponding deficit in international trade, and therefore should be regarded as the ultimate cause of the trade deficit.

This argument is an oversimplification, since most of the elements in the trade, saving, and investment accounts are outcomes of economic processes which themselves have many causes, rather than elements that can be considered to be independent "first causes." But it does provide some insight into past episodes of large trade deficits and financial inflows. For example, the trade deficits of the 1980s coincided with burgeoning Federal government deficits not financed by corresponding excesses of domestic saving over domestic investment. In the early 1990s, the Federal government deficits grew even larger, but domestic saving grew while domestic investment stagnated, so that those Federal deficits did not require much foreign financing. Then, trade deficits burgeoned in the late 1990s even as the Federal budget swung into surplus; these trade deficits are associated instead with surges in private business investment not financed by corresponding increases in domestic saving.

As this rather complicated analysis suggests, it is not possible to regard a large trade deficit as either unequivocally "good" or unequivocally "bad." Nor is it easy to devise policies that will affect its course—at least, not without attention to the broad fiscal and monetary policies that affect national spending and saving.

PART A. HIGHLIGHTS OF
U.S. INTERNATIONAL TRANSACTIONS

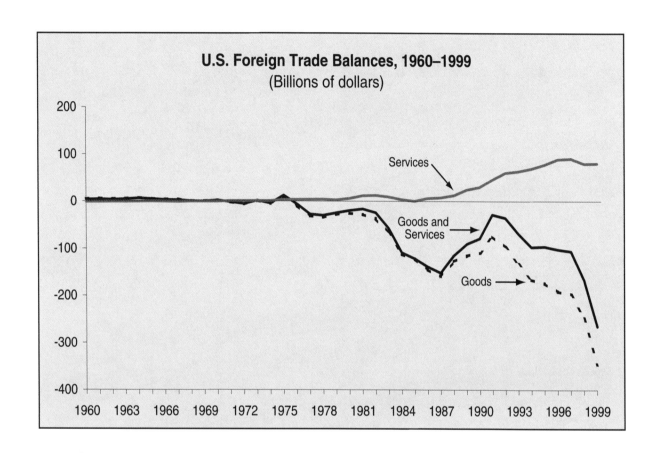

PART A. HIGHLIGHTS OF U.S. INTERNATIONAL TRANSACTIONS

NOTES AND DEFINITIONS

The data in tables A-1 through A-6 are from the U.S. economic accounts, a comprehensive and internally consistent set of accounts designed to provide a full picture of the U.S. economy, including its international economic transactions. These accounts are compiled and published by the U.S. Department of Commerce, Bureau of Economic Analysis. Table A-7 presents currency values compiled by the International Monetary Fund and the Board of Governors, Federal Reserve System.

Table A-1. U.S. Gross Domestic Product [GDP], Exports, Imports, and Net Exports, 1946–1999

Table A-2. Exports, Imports, and Net Exports as a Percent of U.S. Gross Domestic Product [GDP], 1946–1999

Table A-3. Real U.S. Gross Domestic Product [GDP], Exports, Imports, and Net Exports, 1946–1999

Table A-4. Chain-Type Quantity and Price Indexes for Exports and Imports, 1946–1999

Source: Bureau of Economic Analysis

DATA NOTES

The data in Tables A-1 through A-4 are from the National Income and Product Accounts (NIPAs), with percentages in Table A-2 calculated by the editors. These data show the relationship of exports and imports to U.S. gross domestic product (GDP). Exports are goods and services produced in the United States and are a component of total GDP. Imports are included in the other GDP components—personal consumption expenditures, private investment, and government consumption and gross investment—which are initially measured as total purchases without imports being separately identified. Therefore, imports must be subtracted from GDP purchases to avoid overestimating the total. Net exports (exports less imports) show the net contribution of foreign trade to GDP. BEA has adjusted the export and import numbers in this table from a balance of payments basis to a NIPA basis.

The measures of real exports and imports and quantity and price indexes are new in this edition of *Foreign Trade of the United States*. The aggregates presented in Table A-3 in billions of chained (1996) dollars do not necessarily add to totals because of the weighting procedure, and are therefore only presented at the broadest aggregate levels for years distant from 1996. However, the quantity indexes presented in Table A-4 provide more detailed chain-weighted measures of quantity trends over time with the effect of price change removed. The chain-type price indexes in Table A-4 summarize the average price trends for components of exports and imports.

DATA AVAILABILITY

Complete source data (from 1929 to 1999) are available from the BEA web site, or can be purchased on diskette. The latest comprehensive revision of these data is described in articles in the *Survey of Current Business* in August through December 1999 and April 2000.

New data normally are released toward the end of each month. The first estimates for each calendar quarter are released in the month after the quarter's end. Revisions for the most recent quarter are released in the second and third months after the quarter's end. In addition, "annual" revisions to the data for the last several years typically occur each July. "Comprehensive" revisions to the data for all time periods typically occur about once every five years. Revisions are published in the *Survey of Current Business*.

Table A-5. U.S. International Trade in Goods and Services, 1960–1999

Table A-6. U.S. International Transactions, 1960–1999

Source: Bureau of Economic Analysis

The U.S. international transactions accounts, or "balance of payments," provide a comprehensive view of economic transactions between the United States and foreign countries. The accounts include estimates of exports and imports of goods and of travel, transportation, and other services; earnings on assets abroad; foreign aid; and private and official capital flows, including direct investment. Data in the accounts have undergone extensive revision in the last few years to incorporate improved data sources and methodology.

The export and import data in Table A-5 are an integral part of the international transactions accounts and are reproduced in a separate table for easy reference. More detailed data on trade in private services are found in Section B of this book. More detailed data on trade in goods are found in Section C.

DEFINITIONS

Credits (+): In Table A-6, the following items are treated as credits [transactions that transfer dollars from foreign governments, businesses, or individuals to the United States] in the international transactions accounts: Exports of goods and services; income received on U.S. assets abroad and by U.S. employees abroad; unilateral transfers to the United States; capital account transactions receipts; and financial inflows—increases in foreign-owned assets (U.S. liabilities) or decreases in U.S.-owned assets (U.S. claims).

Debits (-): In Table A-6, the following items are treated as debits in the international transactions accounts, indicated by minus signs in the data cells [transactions that transfer dollars from the United States to foreign governments, businesses or individuals]: Imports of goods and services; income payments on foreign assets in the United States and to foreigners employed in the United States; unilateral transfers to foreigners; capital accounts transactions payments; and financial outflows—decreases in foreign-owned assets (U.S. liabilities) or increases in U.S.-owned assets (U.S. claims).

The balance rows represent the difference between the exports or receipts and the imports or payments. A negative amount indicates an excess of imports or payments over exports or receipts.

In concept, the balance on current account is necessarily offset exactly by the net capital and financial inflow or outflow; for example, a U.S. current account deficit results in more dollars held by foreigners, which must be reflected in additional claims on the United States held by foreigners, whether in the form of U.S. currency, securities, loans, or other forms of obligation. Because of different and incomplete data sources, however, the measured capital and financial accounts do not exactly offset the current account. The *statistical discrepancy* in the U.S. international accounts—the sum of all credits and debits, with the sign reversed—measures the amount by which measured net capital and financial flow would have to be augmented to offset the current account balance exactly.

DATA NOTES

Exports and imports of goods exclude exports of goods under U.S. military agency sales contracts identified in Census Bureau export documents and imports of goods under direct defense expenditures identified in import documents. They also reflect various other adjustments (for valuation, coverage, and timing) of Census Bureau statistics to a balance-of-payments basis.

Services include some goods, mainly military equipment (included in transfers under military agency sales contracts); major equipment, other materials, supplies, and petroleum products purchased abroad by U.S. military agencies (included in direct defense expenditures abroad); and fuels purchased by airline and steamship operators (included in other transportation).

Private remittances and other transfers includes taxes paid by U.S. private residents to foreign governments and taxes paid by private nonresidents to the U.S. government beginning in 1982.

Beginning with the data for 1982, *direct investment income* and the reinvested earnings component of *direct investment* capital are measured on a current-cost

(replacement-cost) basis after adjustment to reported depreciation, depletion, and expensed exploration and development costs. For prior years, depreciation is valued in terms of the historical cost of assets and reflects a mix of prices for the various years in which capital investments were made. See *Survey of Current Business*, June 1992, pages 72ff.

Repayments on U.S. credit and other long-term assets includes sales of foreign obligations to foreigners. The data for 1974 include extraordinary U.S. Government transactions with India, described in "Special U.S. Government Transactions," *Survey of Current Business*, June 1974, page 27.

Foreign official assets in the United States. U.S. Treasury securities consists of bills, certificates, marketable bonds and notes, and nonmarketable convertible and nonconvertible bonds and notes; other *U.S. Government securities* consists of U.S. Treasury and Export-Import Bank obligations, not included elsewhere, and of debt securities of U.S. government corporations and agencies; other *U.S. Government liabilities* includes, primarily, U.S. Government liabilities associated with military agency sales contracts and other transactions arranged with or through foreign official agencies; *other foreign official assets* consists of investments in U.S. corporate stocks and in debt securities of private corporations and state and local governments.

Estimates of *U.S. currency flows abroad* were introduced for the first time as part of the July 1997 revisions. Data for 1974 and subsequent years were affected (see *Survey of Current Business*, July 1997). Beginning with the 1998 revisions, currency flows are published separately from U.S. Treasury securities.

For 1978–83, *U.S. Treasury securities* includes foreign currency-denominated notes sold to private residents abroad.

Relation of balance on current account to net foreign investment. Conceptually, "net foreign investment" in the national income and product accounts (NIPAs) is equal to the balance on current account plus allocation of special drawing rights. However, the foreign transactions account in the NIPAs includes (a) adjustments to the international transactions accounts for the treatment of gold, (b) adjustments for the different geographical treatment of transactions with U.S. territories and Puerto Rico, and (c) services furnished without payment by financial pension plans except life insurance carriers and private noninsured pension plans. (Puerto Rico and the territories are not within the scope of the National Income and Product Accounts but are included with the United States in the international transactions accounts.) A reconciliation of the balance on goods and services from the international accounts and the NIPA net exports appears periodically in the "Reconciliation and

Other Special Tables" section of the *Survey of Current Business*. A reconciliation of the other foreign transactions in the two sets of accounts appears in Table 4.5 of the NIPAs.

DATA AVAILABILITY

Data on exports and imports of goods and services are published monthly in a joint Census-BEA press release (the FT900) available about six weeks after the close of the reference month. The data subsequently are published in the *Survey of Current Business*. The complete balance of payments data are available quarterly and monthly. Data first are reported in a BEA press release and subsequently published in the *Survey of Current Business*. Revisions to historical data are published annually. The most recent historical revisions appear in the July 2000 issue of the *Survey*. Complete historical data may be purchased on diskette from BEA. Historical data also are available on the BEA Internet site.

Table A-7. Exchange Rates, 1992–1999

Sources: *International Financial Statistics*, International Monetary Fund; and Board of Governors of the Federal Reserve System.

DATA NOTES

Trade-weighted indexes, compiled by the Federal Reserve Board, of the value of the dollar against groups of foreign currencies appear at the top of this table. The "Broad" index measures changes in the value of the dollar relative to the currencies of a broad group of U.S. trading partners. The "Major currencies" index is for a subset of currencies that circulate widely outside the country of issue, and so are particularly relevant to international financial flows. "Other major trading partners" measures the remaining currencies that do not circulate widely outside the country of issue.

These indexes are weighted based on trade flows. The weighting scheme can be summarized as the country's share of U.S. imports, the country's share of U.S. exports, and the country's share of exports that go to another country that is a large importer of U.S. goods.

The Broad Index (January 1997=100): Share of U.S. exports determines the selection of a country's currency

for the index. Basically, currencies were selected from countries that had a share of U.S. nonoil or nonagricultural exports of at least 0.5 percent. These countries are then divided up into the Major Currency and Other Important Trading Partners below. The selection of countries is updated annually when currency weights are adjusted.

Major Currency Index (March 1973=100): This index serves purposes similar to the older (and now discontinued) G-10 index: it is a gauge of financial pressure on the dollar and a measure of the competitiveness of U.S. goods and services in the major industrial countries. The index includes countries whose currencies are traded in deep and relatively liquid financial markets and for which information on short and long-term interest rates is readily available. A benefit of this country group is that it excludes economies that have been subject to high inflation. The large depreciation of those currencies would mask movement of the dollar's value against other currencies. As of October 1998, this index includes the currencies of the following countries: Canada, Euro area (Germany, France, Italy, Netherlands, Belgium and Luxembourg, Spain, Ireland, Austria, Finland, and Portugal), Japan, United Kingdom, Switzerland, Australia, and Sweden.

Other Important Trading Partners (OITP) Index (January 1997=100): This index captures the competitiveness of U.S. goods in key emerging markets in Latin America, Asia, the Middle East, and Eastern Europe. Because of the episodes of hyperinflation that some of the countries have experienced, the nominal version of this index is more useful for analysis of short-term exchange rate movements than for the study of longer-term competitiveness. The countries that make up this index include, as of October 1998, Mexico, China, Taiwan, South Korea, Singapore, Hong Kong, Malaysia, Brazil, Thailand, Indonesia, Philippines, Russia, India, Saudi Arabia, Israel, Argentina, Venezuela, Chile, and Colombia.

G-10 Index (March 1973=100): This measure is an index of the weighted average exchange value of the U.S. dollar against the currencies of other G-10 (industrialized) countries, which are Belgium, Canada, France, Germany, Italy, Japan, the Netherlands, Sweden, Switzerland, and the United Kingdom. This index was revised in August 1978. Unlike the previous three indexes, the weights on this index were fixed, and annual revisions were not necessary. These data are from the Federal Reserve and were published weekly in the H.10 release. The Federal Reserve ceased to calculate this index as of December 1998, as its function was better represented by the newer "Major Currencies" index.

The "real" indexes are adjusted for differential rates of inflation. Because of the occasional episodes of extreme inflation in some countries, the real indexes provide a better measure of the competitiveness of U.S. exports in such markets. To illustrate, a country whose currency has depreciated sharply versus the dollar has not become more competitive if the depreciation simply offsets a rapid rate of increase in that country's prices.

Foreign exchange rates include market, official, principal, and secondary rates as published by the IMF. The primary rates used were market and official rates. For the Democratic Republic of the Congo and Malawi, 1997 values are estimated using three quarters of data.
For the following countries or currencies, some values were estimated using partial year data, or end of year values were used when annual averages were unavailable: Azerbaijan, Belarus, Democratic Republic of Congo, Ethiopia, Guinea, Madagascar, Sao Tome and Principe, and Suriname.

DATA AVAILABILITY

The source for all of the national currency exchange rates is *International Financial Statistics*, International Monetary Fund. The data are reprinted by permission. Source for the trade weighted indexes is the Board of Governors of the Federal Reserve System. They may be found on the Federal Reserve Bank of St. Louis web site, (http://www.stls.frb.org/fred/data/exchange.html). Additional currency exchange rate information is available from the Federal Reserve web site (http://www.federalreserve.com), for daily, monthly, and annual data.

Table A-1. U.S. Gross Domestic Product [GDP], Exports, Imports, and Net Exports, 1946–1999

(Billions of dollars.)

Year	GDP	Exports			Imports			Net exports
		Total	Goods	Services	Total	Goods	Services	
1946	222.3	14.1	11.8	2.3	7.0	5.1	1.9	7.1
1947	244.4	18.7	16.1	2.6	7.9	6.0	2.0	10.8
1948	269.6	15.5	13.3	2.2	10.1	7.6	2.5	5.4
1949	267.7	14.4	12.2	2.2	9.2	6.9	2.4	5.2
1950	294.3	12.3	10.2	2.1	11.6	9.1	2.5	0.7
1951	339.5	17.0	14.2	2.8	14.6	11.2	3.4	2.4
1952	358.6	16.3	13.4	2.9	15.3	10.8	4.5	1.0
1953	379.9	15.2	12.4	2.8	16.0	11.0	5.0	-0.8
1954	381.1	15.7	12.9	2.8	15.4	10.4	5.1	0.3
1955	415.2	17.6	14.4	3.2	17.2	11.5	5.7	0.4
1956	438.0	21.2	17.6	3.6	18.9	12.8	6.1	2.3
1957	461.5	23.9	19.6	4.3	19.9	13.3	6.7	4.0
1958	467.9	20.4	16.4	4.0	20.0	13.0	7.1	0.4
1959	507.4	20.6	16.5	4.2	22.3	15.3	7.0	-1.7
1960	527.4	25.3	20.5	4.8	22.8	15.2	7.6	2.4
1961	545.7	26.0	20.9	5.1	22.7	15.1	7.6	3.4
1962	586.5	27.4	21.7	5.7	25.0	16.9	8.1	2.4
1963	618.7	29.4	23.3	6.1	26.1	17.7	8.4	3.3
1964	664.4	33.6	26.7	6.9	28.1	19.4	8.7	5.5
1965	720.1	35.4	27.8	7.6	31.5	22.2	9.3	3.9
1966	789.3	38.9	30.7	8.2	37.1	26.3	10.7	1.9
1967	834.1	41.4	32.2	9.2	39.9	27.8	12.2	1.4
1968	911.5	45.3	35.3	10.0	46.6	33.9	12.6	-1.3
1969	985.3	49.3	38.3	11.0	50.5	36.8	13.7	-1.2
1970	1 039.7	57.0	44.5	12.4	55.8	40.9	14.9	1.2
1971	1 128.6	59.3	45.6	13.8	62.3	46.6	15.8	-3.0
1972	1 240.4	66.2	51.8	14.4	74.2	56.9	17.3	-8.0
1973	1 385.5	91.8	73.9	17.8	91.2	71.8	19.3	0.6
1974	1 501.0	124.3	101.0	23.3	127.5	104.5	22.9	-3.1
1975	1 635.2	136.3	109.6	26.7	122.7	99.0	23.7	13.6
1976	1 823.9	148.9	117.8	31.1	151.1	124.6	26.5	-2.3
1977	2 031.4	158.8	123.7	35.1	182.4	152.6	29.8	-23.7
1978	2 295.9	186.1	145.4	40.7	212.3	177.4	34.8	-26.1
1979	2 566.4	228.7	184.0	44.7	252.7	212.8	39.9	-24.0
1980	2 795.6	278.9	225.8	53.2	293.8	248.6	45.3	-14.9
1981	3 131.3	302.8	239.1	63.7	317.8	267.8	49.9	-15.0
1982	3 259.2	282.6	215.0	67.6	303.2	250.5	52.6	-20.5
1983	3 534.9	277.0	207.3	69.7	328.6	272.7	56.0	-51.7
1984	3 932.7	303.1	225.6	77.5	405.1	336.3	68.8	-102.0
1985	4 213.0	303.0	222.2	80.8	417.2	343.3	73.9	-114.2
1986	4 452.9	320.3	226.0	94.3	452.2	370.0	82.2	-131.9
1987	4 742.5	365.6	257.5	108.1	507.9	414.8	93.1	-142.3
1988	5 108.3	446.9	325.8	121.1	553.2	452.1	101.1	-106.3
1989	5 489.1	509.0	371.7	137.3	589.7	484.5	105.2	-80.7
1990	5 803.2	557.2	398.5	158.6	628.6	508.0	120.6	-71.4
1991	5 986.2	601.6	426.4	175.2	622.3	500.7	121.6	-20.7
1992	6 318.9	636.8	448.7	188.1	664.6	544.9	119.8	-27.9
1993	6 642.3	658.0	459.7	198.3	718.5	592.8	125.7	-60.5
1994	7 054.3	725.1	509.6	215.5	812.1	676.7	135.4	-87.1
1995	7 400.5	818.6	583.8	234.7	902.8	757.6	145.2	-84.3
1996	7 813.2	874.2	618.4	255.8	963.1	808.3	154.8	-89.0
1997	8 318.4	966.4	688.9	277.5	1 055.8	885.1	170.7	-89.3
1998	8 790.2	966.0	682.0	284.0	1 117.5	930.5	187.0	-151.5
1999	9 299.2	990.2	699.2	291.0	1 244.2	1 048.6	195.6	-254.0

Table A-2. Exports, Imports, and Net Exports as a Percent of U.S. Gross Domestic Product, 1946–1999

(Percent of total gross domestic product.)

Year	Exports			Imports			Net exports
	Total	Goods	Services	Total	Goods	Services	
1946	6.34	5.31	1.03	3.15	2.29	0.85	3.19
1947	7.65	6.59	1.06	3.23	2.45	0.82	4.42
1948	5.75	4.93	0.82	3.75	2.82	0.93	2.00
1949	5.38	4.56	0.82	3.44	2.58	0.90	1.94
1950	4.18	3.47	0.71	3.94	3.09	0.85	0.24
1951	5.01	4.18	0.82	4.30	3.30	1.00	0.71
1952	4.55	3.74	0.81	4.27	3.01	1.25	0.28
1953	4.00	3.26	0.74	4.21	2.90	1.32	-0.21
1954	4.12	3.38	0.73	4.04	2.73	1.34	0.08
1955	4.24	3.47	0.77	4.14	2.77	1.37	0.10
1956	4.84	4.02	0.82	4.32	2.92	1.39	0.53
1957	5.18	4.25	0.93	4.31	2.88	1.45	0.87
1958	4.36	3.51	0.85	4.27	2.78	1.52	0.09
1959	4.06	3.25	0.83	4.39	3.02	1.38	-0.34
1960	4.80	3.89	0.91	4.32	2.88	1.44	0.46
1961	4.76	3.83	0.93	4.16	2.77	1.39	0.62
1962	4.67	3.70	0.97	4.26	2.88	1.38	0.41
1963	4.75	3.77	0.99	4.22	2.86	1.36	0.53
1964	5.06	4.02	1.04	4.23	2.92	1.31	0.83
1965	4.92	3.86	1.06	4.37	3.08	1.29	0.54
1966	4.93	3.89	1.04	4.70	3.33	1.36	0.24
1967	4.96	3.86	1.10	4.78	3.33	1.46	0.17
1968	4.97	3.87	1.10	5.11	3.72	1.38	-0.14
1969	5.00	3.89	1.12	5.13	3.73	1.39	-0.12
1970	5.48	4.28	1.19	5.37	3.93	1.43	0.12
1971	5.25	4.04	1.22	5.52	4.13	1.40	-0.27
1972	5.34	4.18	1.16	5.98	4.59	1.39	-0.64
1973	6.63	5.33	1.28	6.58	5.18	1.39	0.04
1974	8.28	6.73	1.55	8.49	6.96	1.53	-0.21
1975	8.34	6.70	1.63	7.50	6.05	1.45	0.83
1976	8.16	6.46	1.71	8.28	6.83	1.45	-0.13
1977	7.82	6.09	1.73	8.98	7.51	1.47	-1.17
1978	8.11	6.33	1.77	9.25	7.73	1.52	-1.14
1979	8.91	7.17	1.74	9.85	8.29	1.55	-0.94
1980	9.98	8.08	1.90	10.51	8.89	1.62	-0.53
1981	9.67	7.64	2.03	10.15	8.55	1.59	-0.48
1982	8.67	6.60	2.07	9.30	7.69	1.61	-0.63
1983	7.84	5.86	1.97	9.30	7.71	1.58	-1.46
1984	7.71	5.74	1.97	10.30	8.55	1.75	-2.59
1985	7.19	5.27	1.92	9.90	8.15	1.75	-2.71
1986	7.19	5.08	2.12	10.16	8.31	1.85	-2.96
1987	7.71	5.43	2.28	10.71	8.75	1.96	-3.00
1988	8.75	6.38	2.37	10.83	8.85	1.98	-2.08
1989	9.27	6.77	2.50	10.74	8.83	1.92	-1.47
1990	9.60	6.87	2.73	10.83	8.75	2.08	-1.23
1991	10.05	7.12	2.93	10.40	8.36	2.03	-0.35
1992	10.08	7.10	2.98	10.52	8.62	1.90	-0.44
1993	9.91	6.92	2.99	10.82	8.92	1.89	-0.91
1994	10.28	7.22	3.05	11.51	9.59	1.92	-1.23
1995	11.06	7.89	3.17	12.20	10.24	1.96	-1.14
1996	11.19	7.91	3.27	12.33	10.35	1.98	-1.14
1997	11.62	8.28	3.34	12.69	10.64	2.05	-1.07
1998	10.99	7.76	3.23	12.71	10.59	2.13	-1.72
1999	10.65	7.52	3.13	13.38	11.28	2.10	-2.73

Table A-3. Real U.S. Gross Domestic Product [GDP], Exports, Imports, and Net Exports, 1946–1999

(Billions of chained (1996) dollars.)

Year	GDP	Exports			Imports			Net exports
		Total	Goods	Services	Total	Goods	Services	
1946	1 505.5	66.5	. . .	. . .	49.1	. . .	. . .	. . .
1947	1 495.1	75.9	. . .	. . .	46.6	. . .	. . .	. . .
1948	1 560.0	59.8	. . .	. . .	54.4	. . .	. . .	. . .
1949	1 550.9	59.2	. . .	. . .	52.5	. . .	. . .	. . .
1950	1 686.6	51.8	. . .	. . .	62.0	. . .	. . .	. . .
1951	1 815.1	63.5	. . .	. . .	64.5	. . .	. . .	. . .
1952	1 887.3	60.6	. . .	. . .	70.1	. . .	. . .	. . .
1953	1 973.9	56.5	. . .	. . .	76.7	. . .	. . .	. . .
1954	1 960.5	59.3	. . .	. . .	72.9	. . .	. . .	. . .
1955	2 099.5	65.6	. . .	. . .	81.7	. . .	. . .	. . .
1956	2 141.1	76.5	. . .	. . .	88.4	. . .	. . .	. . .
1957	2 183.9	83.1	. . .	. . .	92.1	. . .	. . .	. . .
1958	2 162.8	71.8	. . .	. . .	96.4	. . .	. . .	. . .
1959	2 319.0	72.4	. . .	. . .	106.6	. . .	. . .	. . .
1960	2 376.7	87.5	. . .	. . .	108.0	. . .	. . .	. . .
1961	2 432.0	88.9	. . .	. . .	107.3	. . .	. . .	. . .
1962	2 578.9	93.7	. . .	. . .	119.5	. . .	. . .	. . .
1963	2 690.4	100.7	. . .	. . .	122.7	. . .	. . .	. . .
1964	2 846.5	114.2	. . .	. . .	129.2	. . .	. . .	. . .
1965	3 028.5	116.5	. . .	. . .	142.9	. . .	. . .	. . .
1966	3 227.5	124.3	. . .	. . .	164.2	. . .	. . .	. . .
1967	3 308.3	127.0	. . .	. . .	176.2	. . .	. . .	. . .
1968	3 466.1	136.3	. . .	. . .	202.4	. . .	. . .	. . .
1969	3 571.4	143.7	. . .	. . .	213.9	. . .	. . .	. . .
1970	3 578.0	159.3	. . .	. . .	223.1	. . .	. . .	. . .
1971	3 697.7	160.4	. . .	. . .	235.0	. . .	. . .	. . .
1972	3 898.4	173.5	. . .	. . .	261.3	. . .	. . .	. . .
1973	4 123.4	211.4	. . .	. . .	273.4	. . .	. . .	. . .
1974	4 099.0	231.6	. . .	. . .	267.2	. . .	. . .	. . .
1975	4 084.4	230.0	. . .	. . .	237.5	. . .	. . .	. . .
1976	4 311.7	243.6	. . .	. . .	284.0	. . .	. . .	. . .
1977	4 511.8	249.7	. . .	. . .	315.0	. . .	. . .	. . .
1978	4 760.6	275.9	. . .	. . .	342.3	. . .	. . .	. . .
1979	4 912.1	302.4	. . .	. . .	347.9	. . .	. . .	. . .
1980	4 900.9	334.8	. . .	. . .	324.8	. . .	. . .	. . .
1981	5 021.0	338.6	. . .	. . .	333.4	. . .	. . .	. . .
1982	4 919.3	314.6	. . .	. . .	329.2	. . .	. . .	. . .
1983	5 132.3	306.9	. . .	. . .	370.7	. . .	. . .	. . .
1984	5 505.2	332.6	. . .	. . .	461.0	. . .	. . .	. . .
1985	5 717.1	341.6	. . .	. . .	490.7	. . .	. . .	. . .
1986	5 912.4	366.8	. . .	. . .	531.9	. . .	. . .	. . .
1987	6 113.3	408.0	271.4	139.1	564.2	445.8	120.2	-156.2
1988	6 368.4	473.5	322.6	152.0	585.6	463.9	123.4	-112.1
1989	6 591.8	529.4	363.2	166.7	608.8	483.4	126.9	-79.4
1990	6 707.9	575.7	393.2	183.5	632.2	497.9	136.6	-56.5
1991	6 676.4	613.2	421.1	192.9	629.0	497.6	133.4	-15.8
1992	6 880.0	651.0	449.8	201.7	670.8	543.7	128.0	-19.8
1993	7 062.6	672.7	463.4	209.9	731.8	598.4	134.0	-59.1
1994	7 347.7	732.8	508.2	225.1	819.4	677.9	141.9	-86.5
1995	7 543.8	808.2	568.8	239.5	886.6	739.1	147.7	-78.4
1996	7 813.2	874.2	618.4	255.8	963.1	808.3	154.8	-89.0
1997	8 159.5	981.5	708.1	273.6	1 094.8	923.1	171.7	-113.3
1998	8 515.7	1 003.6	723.6	280.3	1 224.6	1 032.0	192.6	-221.0
1999	8 875.8	1 033.0	752.2	281.7	1 355.3	1 161.1	195.9	-322.4

Table A-4. Chain-Type Quantity and Price Indexes for Exports and Imports, 1946–1999

(1996=100.)

Year	Quantity indexes						Price indexes					
	Exports			Imports			Exports			Imports		
	Total	Goods	Services	Total	Goods	Services	Total	Goods	Services	Total	Goods	Services
1946	7.61	8.20	5.05	5.10	4.63	7.09	21.17	23.19	17.89	14.21	13.54	17.39
1947	8.69	9.43	5.55	4.84	4.45	6.52	24.61	27.60	18.24	17.02	16.62	19.43
1948	6.84	7.30	4.85	5.65	5.09	8.04	25.91	29.38	17.98	18.50	18.36	20.11
1949	6.78	7.26	4.71	5.45	4.89	7.85	24.34	27.22	18.30	17.63	17.38	19.56
1950	5.93	6.27	4.39	6.44	5.98	8.35	23.70	26.31	18.47	18.73	18.80	19.60
1951	7.27	7.64	5.57	6.69	5.86	10.62	26.78	30.16	19.40	22.63	23.60	20.75
1952	6.93	7.24	5.46	7.28	5.98	13.85	26.98	30.03	20.71	21.81	22.43	20.80
1953	6.47	6.75	5.12	7.97	6.32	16.36	26.90	29.73	21.36	20.88	21.47	19.90
1954	6.78	7.14	5.19	7.57	5.84	16.54	26.56	29.30	21.23	21.16	21.93	19.85
1955	7.50	7.89	5.77	8.49	6.52	18.67	26.81	29.58	21.42	21.05	21.87	19.63
1956	8.75	9.25	6.54	9.17	7.10	19.87	27.71	30.70	21.73	21.42	22.30	19.90
1957	9.51	9.98	7.35	9.56	7.31	21.24	28.76	31.70	23.09	21.66	22.50	20.23
1958	8.21	8.47	6.84	10.01	7.51	23.06	28.50	31.36	23.05	20.76	21.33	19.81
1959	8.28	8.41	7.35	11.07	8.82	22.61	28.53	31.66	22.30	20.95	21.48	20.05
1960	10.00	10.38	8.13	11.21	8.67	24.38	28.88	31.87	23.11	21.15	21.71	20.20
1961	10.17	10.43	8.67	11.14	8.66	23.96	29.29	32.48	22.98	21.15	21.50	20.58
1962	10.72	10.89	9.46	12.40	9.94	25.08	29.27	32.23	23.59	20.90	20.99	20.85
1963	11.52	11.75	10.06	12.74	10.34	25.06	29.22	32.12	23.71	21.30	21.18	21.71
1964	13.06	13.36	11.26	13.41	11.03	25.71	29.42	32.34	23.87	21.75	21.76	21.89
1965	13.33	13.43	12.15	14.84	12.59	26.47	30.38	33.46	24.46	22.06	21.86	22.66
1966	14.22	14.36	12.85	17.05	14.57	29.83	31.32	34.61	24.93	22.57	22.36	23.23
1967	14.53	14.43	13.97	18.29	15.34	33.47	32.56	36.06	25.68	22.66	22.39	23.45
1968	15.59	15.57	14.69	21.02	18.51	34.08	33.23	36.62	26.69	23.00	22.69	23.91
1969	16.44	16.39	15.59	22.21	19.52	36.22	34.29	37.75	27.62	23.60	23.33	24.40
1970	18.22	18.26	16.97	23.16	20.29	38.11	35.77	39.46	28.64	25.00	24.91	25.27
1971	18.35	18.18	17.77	24.40	21.99	37.03	36.98	40.51	30.31	26.53	26.19	27.55
1972	19.84	20.14	17.70	27.13	24.98	38.54	38.17	41.59	31.88	28.40	28.20	28.97
1973	24.19	24.77	20.85	28.39	26.74	37.24	43.40	48.27	33.47	33.34	33.23	33.51
1974	26.49	26.73	24.29	27.75	26.00	37.20	53.68	61.08	37.57	47.70	49.73	39.85
1975	26.32	26.11	25.91	24.66	22.72	35.59	59.24	67.89	40.22	51.67	53.90	43.08
1976	27.87	27.35	28.65	29.49	27.86	38.04	61.11	69.63	42.44	53.22	55.34	45.03
1977	28.57	27.71	30.67	32.70	31.25	39.94	63.58	72.16	44.77	57.92	60.42	48.23
1978	31.56	30.81	33.10	35.54	34.05	42.78	67.48	76.32	48.12	62.01	64.45	52.61
1979	34.59	34.45	33.64	36.13	34.64	43.37	75.63	86.40	51.91	72.62	76.00	59.42
1980	38.30	38.55	35.59	33.73	32.06	42.40	83.32	94.71	58.40	90.45	95.90	68.95
1981	38.74	38.14	39.32	34.61	32.72	44.85	89.41	101.38	63.32	95.32	101.25	71.94
1982	35.99	34.70	39.29	34.18	31.90	47.24	89.83	100.21	67.31	92.10	97.16	71.99
1983	35.11	33.70	38.86	38.49	36.24	51.06	90.24	99.48	70.12	88.65	93.10	70.81
1984	38.05	36.36	42.62	47.86	45.00	63.86	91.13	100.34	71.06	87.89	92.46	69.60
1985	39.08	37.58	43.01	50.95	47.80	68.71	88.70	95.62	73.43	85.02	88.84	69.51
1986	41.96	39.51	48.73	55.23	52.70	68.94	87.33	92.49	75.66	85.01	86.85	77.02
1987	46.67	43.89	54.38	58.58	55.15	77.64	89.62	94.89	77.70	90.02	93.04	77.48
1988	54.17	52.16	59.45	60.81	57.38	79.75	94.39	101.00	79.67	94.46	97.47	81.89
1989	60.56	58.74	65.18	63.21	59.80	81.98	96.15	102.33	82.37	96.87	100.23	82.94
1990	65.85	63.58	71.73	65.64	61.60	88.23	96.79	101.36	86.47	99.43	102.02	88.31
1991	70.15	68.09	75.40	65.31	61.56	86.18	98.10	101.26	90.85	98.93	100.62	91.15
1992	74.47	72.73	78.86	69.64	67.26	82.69	97.82	99.75	93.26	99.09	100.21	93.58
1993	76.95	74.93	82.07	75.98	74.03	86.60	97.82	99.21	94.47	98.18	99.06	93.78
1994	83.83	82.18	88.01	85.08	83.86	91.65	98.94	100.27	95.72	99.12	99.83	95.47
1995	92.45	91.97	93.65	92.05	91.43	95.40	101.29	102.65	97.99	101.83	102.51	98.31
1996	100.00	100.00	100.00	100.00	100.00	100.00	100.00	100.00	100.00	100.00	100.00	100.00
1997	112.27	114.51	106.98	113.67	114.20	110.94	98.47	97.29	101.42	96.44	95.88	99.41
1998	114.80	117.01	109.58	127.15	127.67	124.42	96.26	94.25	101.34	91.26	90.16	97.09
1999	118.17	121.63	110.14	140.72	143.64	126.54	95.86	92.96	103.30	91.80	90.31	99.89

Table A-5. U.S. International Trade in Goods and Services, 1960–1999

(Balance of payments basis, billions of dollars.)

Year	Exports			Imports			Trade balance		
	Total	Goods	Services	Total	Goods	Services	Total	Goods	Services
1960	25.9	19.7	6.3	22.4	14.8	7.7	3.5	4.9	-1.4
1961	26.4	20.1	6.3	22.2	14.5	7.7	4.2	5.6	-1.4
1962	27.7	20.8	6.9	24.4	16.3	8.1	3.4	4.5	-1.2
1963	29.6	22.3	7.3	25.4	17.0	8.4	4.2	5.2	-1.0
1964	33.3	25.5	7.8	27.3	18.7	8.6	6.0	6.8	-0.8
1965	35.3	26.5	8.8	30.6	21.5	9.1	4.7	5.0	-0.3
1966	38.9	29.3	9.6	36.0	25.5	10.5	2.9	3.8	-0.9
1967	41.3	30.7	10.7	38.7	26.9	11.9	2.6	3.8	-1.2
1968	45.5	33.6	11.9	45.3	33.0	12.3	0.3	0.6	-0.4
1969	49.2	36.4	12.8	49.1	35.8	13.3	0.1	0.6	-0.5
1970	56.6	42.5	14.2	54.4	39.9	14.5	2.3	2.6	-0.3
1971	59.7	43.3	16.4	61.0	45.6	15.4	-1.3	-2.3	1.0
1972	67.2	49.4	17.8	72.7	55.8	16.9	-5.4	-6.4	1.0
1973	91.2	71.4	19.8	89.3	70.5	18.8	1.9	0.9	1.0
1974	120.9	98.3	22.6	125.2	103.8	21.4	-4.3	-5.5	1.2
1975	132.6	107.1	25.5	120.2	98.2	22.0	12.4	8.9	3.5
1976	142.7	114.7	28.0	148.8	124.2	24.6	-6.1	-9.5	3.4
1977	152.3	120.8	31.5	179.5	151.9	27.6	-27.2	-31.1	3.8
1978	178.4	142.1	36.4	208.2	176.0	32.2	-29.8	-33.9	4.2
1979	224.1	184.4	39.7	248.7	212.0	36.7	-24.6	-27.6	3.0
1980	271.8	224.3	47.6	291.2	249.8	41.5	-19.4	-25.5	6.1
1981	294.4	237.0	57.4	310.6	265.1	45.5	-16.2	-28.0	11.9
1982	275.2	211.2	64.1	299.4	247.6	51.7	-24.2	-36.5	12.3
1983	266.1	201.8	64.3	323.9	268.9	55.0	-57.8	-67.1	9.3
1984	291.1	219.9	71.2	400.2	332.4	67.7	-109.1	-112.5	3.4
1985	289.1	215.9	73.2	411.0	338.1	72.9	-121.9	-122.2	0.3
1986	310.0	223.3	86.7	448.6	368.4	80.1	-138.5	-145.1	6.5
1987	348.9	250.2	98.7	500.6	409.8	90.8	-151.7	-159.6	7.9
1988	431.1	320.2	110.9	545.7	447.2	98.5	-114.6	-127.0	12.4
1989	489.2	362.1	127.1	579.8	477.4	102.5	-90.6	-115.2	24.6
1990	537.1	389.3	147.8	616.0	498.3	117.7	-78.9	-109.0	30.2
1991	581.2	416.9	164.3	609.4	491.0	118.5	-28.3	-74.1	45.8
1992	617.3	440.4	176.9	652.9	536.5	116.5	-35.7	-96.1	60.4
1993	642.8	456.8	185.9	711.7	589.4	122.3	-68.9	-132.6	63.7
1994	703.4	502.4	201.0	800.5	668.6	131.9	-97.0	-166.2	69.2
1995	795.1	575.8	219.2	891.0	749.6	141.4	-95.9	-173.7	77.8
1996	852.1	612.1	240.0	954.2	803.3	150.9	-102.1	-191.3	89.2
1997	936.9	679.7	257.2	1 042.9	876.4	166.5	-105.9	-196.7	90.7
1998	933.0	670.3	262.7	1 099.9	917.2	182.7	-166.9	-246.9	80.0
1999	956.2	684.4	271.9	1 221.2	1 029.9	191.3	-265.0	-345.6	80.6

Table A-6. U.S. International Transactions, 1960–1999

(Millions of dollars.)

Credits and debits	1960	1961	1962	1963	1964	1965	1966	1967	1968	1969
CURRENT ACCOUNT										
Exports Of Goods And Services And Income Receipts	30 556	31 402	33 340	35 776	40 165	42 722	46 454	49 353	54 911	60 132
Goods, balance of payments basis	19 650	20 108	20 781	22 272	25 501	26 461	29 310	30 666	33 626	36 414
Services	6 290	6 295	6 941	7 348	7 840	8 824	9 616	10 667	11 917	12 806
Transfers under U.S. military agency sales contracts	2 030	1 867	2 193	2 219	2 086	2 465	2 721	3 191	3 939	4 138
Travel	919	947	957	1 015	1 207	1 380	1 590	1 646	1 775	2 043
Passenger fares	175	183	191	205	241	271	317	371	411	450
Other transportation	1 607	1 620	1 764	1 898	2 076	2 175	2 333	2 426	2 548	2 652
Royalties and license fees [1]	837	906	1 056	1 162	1 314	1 534	1 516	1 747	1 867	2 019
Other private services [1]	570	607	585	613	651	714	814	951	1 024	1 160
U.S. Government miscellaneous services	153	164	195	236	265	285	326	336	353	343
Income receipts	4 616	4 999	5 618	6 157	6 824	7 437	7 528	8 021	9 367	10 913
Income receipts on U.S.-owned assets abroad	4 616	4 999	5 618	6 157	6 824	7 437	7 528	8 021	9 367	10 913
Direct investment receipts	3 621	3 823	4 241	4 636	5 106	5 506	5 260	5 603	6 591	7 649
Other private receipts	646	793	904	1 022	1 256	1 421	1 669	1 781	2 021	2 338
U.S. Government receipts	349	383	473	499	462	510	599	636	756	925
Compensation of employees	...	...	...	...	...	...	...	...	...	...
Imports Of Goods And Services And Income Payments	-23 670	-23 453	-25 676	-26 970	-29 102	-32 708	-38 468	-41 476	-48 671	-53 998
Goods, balance of payments basis	-14 758	-14 537	-16 260	-17 048	-18 700	-21 510	-25 493	-26 866	-32 991	-35 807
Services	-7 674	-7 671	-8 092	-8 362	-8 619	-9 111	-10 494	-11 863	-12 302	-13 322
Direct defense expenditures	-3 087	-2 998	-3 105	-2 961	-2 880	-2 952	-3 764	-4 378	-4 535	-4 856
Travel	-1 750	-1 785	-1 939	-2 114	-2 211	-2 438	-2 657	-3 207	-3 030	-3 373
Passenger fares	-513	-506	-567	-612	-642	-717	-753	-829	-885	-1 080
Other transportation	-1 402	-1 437	-1 558	-1 701	-1 817	-1 951	-2 161	-2 157	-2 367	-2 455
Royalties and license fees [1]	-74	-89	-100	-112	-127	-135	-140	-166	-186	-221
Other private services [1]	-593	-588	-528	-493	-527	-461	-506	-565	-668	-751
U.S. Government miscellaneous services	-254	-268	-296	-370	-415	-457	-513	-561	-631	-586
Income payments	-1 238	-1 245	-1 324	-1 560	-1 783	-2 088	-2 481	-2 747	-3 378	-4 869
Income payments on foreign-owned assets in the U.S.	-1 238	-1 245	-1 324	-1 560	-1 783	-2 088	-2 481	-2 747	-3 378	-4 869
Direct investment payments	-394	-432	-399	-459	-529	-657	-711	-821	-876	-848
Other private payments	-511	-535	-586	-701	-802	-942	-1 221	-1 328	-1 800	-3 244
U.S. Government payments	-332	-278	-339	-401	-453	-489	-549	-598	-702	-777
Compensation of employees	...	...	...	...	...	...	...	...	...	...
Unilateral Current Transfers, Net	-4 062	-4 127	-4 277	-4 392	-4 240	-4 583	-4 955	-5 294	-5 629	-5 735
U.S. Government grants	-3 367	-3 320	-3 453	-3 479	-3 227	-3 444	-3 802	-3 844	-4 256	-4 259
U.S. Government pensions and other transfers	-273	-373	-347	-339	-399	-463	-499	-571	-537	-537
Private remittances and other transfers	-423	-434	-477	-575	-614	-677	-655	-879	-836	-939
Memoranda:										
Balance on goods	4 892	5 571	4 521	5 224	6 801	4 951	3 817	3 800	635	607
Balance on services	-1 385	-1 376	-1 151	-1 014	-779	-287	-877	-1 196	-385	-516
Balance on goods and services	3 508	4 195	3 370	4 210	6 022	4 664	2 940	2 604	250	91
Balance on income	3 379	3 755	4 294	4 596	5 041	5 350	5 047	5 274	5 990	6 044
Balance on goods, services, and income	6 887	7 950	7 664	8 806	11 063	10 014	7 987	7 878	6 240	6 135
Unilateral current transfers, net	-4 062	-4 127	-4 277	-4 392	-4 240	-4 583	-4 955	-5 294	-5 629	-5 735
Balance on current account	2 824	3 822	3 387	4 414	6 823	5 431	3 031	2 583	611	399
CAPITAL AND FINANCIAL ACCOUNT										
Capital Account Transactions, Net	...	...	...	...	...	...	...	...	...	...
U.S.-Owned Assets Abroad, Net	-4 099	-5 538	-4 174	-7 270	-9 560	-5 716	-7 321	-9 757	-10 977	-11 585
U.S. official reserve assets, net	2 145	607	1 535	378	171	1 225	570	53	-870	-1 179
Gold	1 703	857	890	461	125	1 665	571	1 170	1 173	-967
Special drawing rights	...	...	...	...	...	...	...	...	...	...
Reserve position in the International Monetary Fund	442	-135	626	29	266	-94	537	-94	-870	-1 034
Foreign currencies	...	-115	19	-112	-220	-346	-538	-1 023	-1 173	822
U.S. Government assets, other than official reserve assets, net	-1 100	-910	-1 085	-1 662	-1 680	-1 605	-1 543	-2 423	-2 274	-2 200
U.S. credits and other long-term assets	-1 214	-1 928	-2 128	-2 204	-2 382	-2 463	-2 513	-3 638	-3 722	-3 489
Repayments on U.S. credits and other long-term assets	642	1 279	1 288	988	720	874	1 235	1 005	1 386	1 200
U.S. foreign currency holdings and short-term assets, net	-528	-261	-245	-447	-19	-16	-265	209	62	89
U.S. private assets, net	-5 144	-5 235	-4 623	-5 986	-8 050	-5 336	-6 347	-7 386	-7 833	-8 206
Direct investment	-2 940	-2 653	-2 851	-3 483	-3 760	-5 011	-5 418	-4 805	-5 295	-5 960
Foreign securities	-663	-762	-969	-1 105	-677	-759	-720	-1 308	-1 569	-1 549
U.S. claims on unaffiliated foreigners reported by U.S. nonbanking concerns	-394	-558	-354	157	-1 108	341	-442	-779	-1 203	-126
U.S. claims reported by U.S. banks, not included elsewhere	-1 148	-1 261	-450	-1 556	-2 505	93	233	-495	233	-570
Foreign-Owned Assets In The United States, Net	2 294	2 705	1 911	3 217	3 643	742	3 661	7 379	9 928	12 702
Foreign official assets in the U.S., net	1 473	765	1 270	1 986	1 660	134	-672	3 451	-774	-1 301
U.S. Government securities	655	233	1 409	816	432	-141	-1 527	2 261	-769	-2 343
U.S. Treasury securities	655	233	1 410	803	434	-134	-1 548	2 222	-798	-2 269
Other	...	...	-1	12	-2	-7	21	39	29	-74
Other U.S. Government liabilities	215	25	152	429	298	65	113	83	-15	251
U.S. liabilities reported by U.S. banks, not included elsewhere	603	508	-291	742	930	210	742	1 106	10	792
Other foreign official assets	...	...	...	...	...	...	...	...	...	...
Other foreign assets in the U.S., net	821	1 939	641	1 231	1 983	607	4 333	3 928	10 703	14 002
Direct investment	315	311	346	231	322	415	425	698	807	1 263
U.S. Treasury securities	-364	151	-66	-149	-146	-131	-356	-135	136	-68
U.S. securities other than U.S. Treasury securities	282	324	134	287	-85	-358	906	1 016	4 414	3 130
U.S. currency	...	...	...	...	...	...	...	...	...	...
U.S. liabilities to unaffiliated foreigners reported by U.S. nonbanking concerns	-90	226	-110	-37	75	178	476	584	1 475	792
U.S. liabilities reported by U.S. banks, not included elsewhere	678	928	336	898	1 818	503	2 882	1 765	3 871	8 886
Statistical Discrepancy	-1 019	-989	-1 124	-360	-907	-457	629	-205	438	-1 516

See footnotes at end of table.

Table A-6. U.S. International Transactions, 1960–1999—*Continued*

(Millions of dollars.)

Credits and debits	1970	1971	1972	1973	1974	1975	1976	1977	1978	1979
CURRENT ACCOUNT										
Exports Of Goods And Services And Income Receipts	68 387	72 384	81 986	113 050	148 484	157 936	172 090	184 655	220 516	287 965
Goods, balance of payments basis	42 469	43 319	49 381	71 410	98 306	107 088	114 745	120 816	142 075	184 439
Services	14 171	16 358	17 841	19 832	22 591	25 497	27 971	31 485	36 353	39 692
Transfers under U.S. military agency sales contracts	4 214	5 472	5 856	5 369	5 197	6 256	5 826	7 554	8 209	6 981
Travel	2 331	2 534	2 817	3 412	4 032	4 697	5 742	6 150	7 183	8 441
Passenger fares	544	615	699	975	1 104	1 039	1 229	1 366	1 603	2 156
Other transportation	3 125	3 299	3 579	4 465	5 697	5 840	6 747	7 090	8 136	9 971
Royalties and license fees [1]	2 331	2 545	2 770	3 225	3 821	4 300	4 353	4 920	5 885	6 184
Other private services [1]	1 294	1 546	1 764	1 985	2 321	2 920	3 584	3 848	4 717	5 439
U.S. Government miscellaneous services	332	347	357	401	419	446	489	557	620	520
Income receipts	11 748	12 707	14 765	21 808	27 587	25 351	29 375	32 354	42 088	63 834
Income receipts on U.S.-owned assets abroad	11 748	12 707	14 765	21 808	27 587	25 351	29 375	32 354	42 088	63 834
Direct investment receipts	8 169	9 160	10 949	16 542	19 157	16 595	18 999	19 673	25 458	38 183
Other private receipts	2 671	2 641	2 949	4 330	7 356	7 644	9 043	11 057	14 788	23 356
U.S. Government receipts	907	906	866	936	1 074	1 112	1 332	1 625	1 843	2 295
Compensation of employees	...	...	...	...	...	...	...	...	...	...
Imports Of Goods And Services And Income Payments	-59 901	-66 414	-79 237	-98 997	-137 274	-132 745	-162 109	-193 764	-229 870	-281 657
Goods, balance of payments basis	-39 866	-45 579	-55 797	-70 499	-103 811	-98 185	-124 228	-151 907	-176 002	-212 007
Services	-14 520	-15 400	-16 868	-18 843	-21 379	-21 996	-24 570	-27 640	-32 189	-36 689
Direct defense expenditures	-4 855	-4 819	-4 784	-4 629	-5 032	-4 795	-4 895	-5 823	-7 352	-8 294
Travel	-3 980	-4 373	-5 042	-5 526	-5 980	-6 417	-6 856	-7 451	-8 475	-9 413
Passenger fares	-1 215	-1 290	-1 596	-1 790	-2 095	-2 263	-2 568	-2 748	-2 896	-3 184
Other transportation	-2 843	-3 130	-3 520	-4 694	-5 942	-5 708	-6 852	-7 972	-9 124	-10 906
Royalties and license fees [1]	-224	-241	-294	-385	-346	-472	-482	-504	-671	-831
Other private services [1]	-827	-956	-1 043	-1 180	-1 262	-1 551	-2 006	-2 190	-2 573	-2 822
U.S. Government miscellaneous services	-576	-592	-589	-640	-722	-789	-911	-951	-1 099	-1 239
Income payments	-5 515	-5 435	-6 572	-9 655	-12 084	-12 564	-13 311	-14 217	-21 680	-32 961
Income payments on foreign-owned assets in the U.S.	-5 515	-5 435	-6 572	-9 655	-12 084	-12 564	-13 311	-14 217	-21 680	-32 961
Direct investment payments	-875	-1 164	-1 284	-1 610	-1 331	-2 234	-3 110	-2 834	-4 211	-6 357
Other private payments	-3 617	-2 428	-2 604	-4 209	-6 491	-5 788	-5 681	-5 841	-8 795	-15 481
U.S. Government payments	-1 024	-1 844	-2 684	-3 836	-4 262	-4 542	-4 520	-5 542	-8 674	-11 122
Compensation of employees	...	...	...	...	...	...	...	...	...	...
Unilateral Current Transfers, Net	-6 156	-7 402	-8 544	-6 913	-9 249	-7 075	-5 686	-5 226	-5 788	-6 593
U.S. Government grants	-4 449	-5 589	-6 665	-4 748	[2]-7 293	-5 101	-3 519	-2 990	-3 412	-4 015
U.S. Government pensions and other transfers	-611	-696	-770	-915	-939	-1 068	-1 250	-1 378	-1 532	-1 658
Private remittances and other transfers	-1 096	-1 117	-1 109	-1 250	-1 017	-906	-917	-859	-844	-920
Memoranda:										
Balance on goods	2 603	-2 260	-6 416	911	-5 505	8 903	-9 483	-31 091	-33 927	-27 568
Balance on services	-349	957	973	989	1 213	3 501	3 401	3 845	4 164	3 003
Balance on goods and services	2 254	-1 303	-5 443	1 900	-4 292	12 404	-6 082	-27 246	-29 763	-24 565
Balance on income	6 233	7 272	8 192	12 153	15 503	12 787	16 063	18 137	20 408	30 873
Balance on goods, services, and income	8 487	5 969	2 749	14 053	11 211	25 191	9 981	-9 109	-9 355	6 308
Unilateral current transfers, net	-6 156	-7 402	-8 544	-6 913	-9 249	-7 075	-5 686	-5 226	-5 788	-6 593
Balance on current account	2 331	-1 433	-5 795	7 140	1 962	18 116	4 295	-14 335	-15 143	-285
CAPITAL AND FINANCIAL ACCOUNT										
Capital Account Transactions, Net	...	...	...	...	...	...	...	...	...	...
U.S.-Owned Assets Abroad, Net	-8 470	-11 758	-13 787	-22 874	-34 745	-39 703	-51 269	-34 785	-61 130	-64 915
U.S. official reserve assets, net	3 348	3 066	706	158	-1 467	-849	-2 558	-375	732	6
Gold	787	866	547	...	...	...	...	-118	-65	-65
Special drawing rights	16	468	7	9	-172	-66	-78	-121	1 249	3
Reserve position in the International Monetary Fund	389	1 350	153	-33	-1 265	-466	-2 212	-294	4 231	-189
Foreign currencies	2 156	382	-1	182	-30	-317	-268	158	-4 683	257
U.S. Government assets, other than official reserve assets, net	-1 589	-1 884	-1 568	-2 644	366	-3 474	-4 214	-3 693	-4 660	-3 746
U.S. credits and other long-term assets	-3 293	-4 181	-3 819	-4 638	-5 001	-5 941	-6 943	-6 445	-7 470	-7 697
Repayments on U.S. credits and other long-term assets	1 721	2 115	2 086	2 596	[2]4 826	2 475	2 596	2 719	2 941	3 926
U.S. foreign currency holdings and short-term assets, net	-16	182	165	-602	[2]541	-9	133	33	-131	25
U.S. private assets, net	-10 229	-12 940	-12 925	-20 388	-33 643	-35 380	-44 498	-30 717	-57 202	-61 176
Direct investment	-7 590	-7 618	-7 747	-11 353	-9 052	-14 244	-11 949	-11 890	-16 056	-25 222
Foreign securities	-1 076	-1 113	-618	-671	-1 854	-6 247	-8 885	-5 460	-3 626	-4 726
U.S. claims on unaffiliated foreigners reported by U.S. nonbanking concerns	-596	-1 229	-1 054	-2 383	-3 221	-1 357	-2 296	-1 940	-3 853	-5 014
U.S. claims reported by U.S. banks, not included elsewhere	-967	-2 980	-3 506	-5 980	-19 516	-13 532	-21 368	-11 427	-33 667	-26 213
Foreign-Owned Assets In The United States, Net	6 359	22 970	21 461	18 388	35 341	17 170	38 018	53 219	67 036	40 852
Foreign official assets in the U.S., net	6 908	26 879	10 475	6 026	10 546	7 027	17 693	36 816	33 678	-13 665
U.S. Government securities	9 439	26 570	8 470	641	4 172	5 563	9 892	32 538	24 221	-21 972
U.S. Treasury securities	9 411	26 578	8 213	59	3 270	4 658	9 319	30 230	23 555	-22 435
Other	28	-8	257	582	902	905	573	2 308	666	463
Other U.S. Government liabilities	-456	-510	182	936	301	1 517	4 627	1 400	2 476	-40
U.S. liabilities reported by U.S. banks, not included elsewhere	-2 075	819	1 638	4 126	5 818	-2 158	969	773	5 551	7 213
Other foreign official assets	...	...	185	323	254	2 104	2 205	2 105	1 430	1 135
Other foreign assets in the U.S., net	-550	-3 909	10 986	12 362	24 796	10 143	20 326	16 403	33 358	54 516
Direct investment	1 464	367	949	2 800	4 760	2 603	4 347	3 728	7 897	11 877
U.S. Treasury securities	81	-24	-39	-216	697	2 590	2 783	534	2 178	4 060
U.S. securities other than U.S. Treasury securities	2 189	2 289	4 507	4 041	378	2 503	1 284	2 437	2 254	1 351
U.S. currency	...	...	...	...	1 100	1 500	1 500	1 900	3 000	3 000
U.S. liabilities to unaffiliated foreigners reported by U.S. nonbanking concerns	2 014	369	815	1 035	1 844	319	-578	1 086	1 889	1 621
U.S. liabilities reported by U.S. banks, not included elsewhere	-6 298	-6 911	4 754	4 702	16 017	628	10 990	6 719	16 141	32 607
Statistical Discrepancy	-219	-9 779	-1 879	-2 654	-2 558	4 417	8 955	-4 099	9 236	24 349

See footnotes at end of table.

Table A-6. U.S. International Transactions, 1960–1999—*Continued*

(Millions of dollars.)

Credits and debits	1980	1981	1982	1983	1984	1985	1986	1987	1988	1989
CURRENT ACCOUNT										
Exports Of Goods And Services And Income Receipts	344 440	380 928	366 983	356 106	399 913	387 612	407 098	457 053	567 862	650 494
Goods, balance of payments basis	224 250	237 044	211 157	201 799	219 926	215 915	223 344	250 208	320 230	362 120
Services	47 584	57 354	64 079	64 307	71 168	73 155	86 689	98 661	110 919	127 087
Transfers under U.S. military agency sales contracts	9 029	10 720	12 572	12 524	9 969	8 718	8 549	11 106	9 284	8 564
Travel	10 588	12 913	12 393	10 947	[3]17 177	17 762	20 385	23 563	29 434	36 205
Passenger fares	2 591	3 111	3 174	3 610	[3]4 067	4 411	5 582	7 003	8 976	10 657
Other transportation	11 618	12 560	12 317	12 590	13 809	14 674	[3]15 438	17 027	19 311	20 526
Royalties and license fees [1]	7 085	7 284	5 603	5 778	6 177	6 678	8 113	10 174	12 139	13 818
Other private services [1]	6 276	[3]10 250	17 444	18 192	19 255	20 035	[3]28 027	29 263	31 111	36 729
U.S. Government miscellaneous services	398	517	576	666	714	878	595	526	664	587
Income receipts	72 606	86 529	91 747	90 000	108 819	98 542	97 064	108 184	136 713	161 287
Income receipts on U.S.-owned assets abroad	72 606	86 529	91 747	90 000	108 819	98 542	96 156	107 190	135 718	160 270
Direct investment receipts	37 146	32 549	[3]29 469	31 750	35 325	35 410	36 938	46 288	58 445	61 981
Other private receipts	32 898	50 300	58 160	53 418	68 267	57 633	52 806	55 592	70 571	92 638
U.S. Government receipts	2 562	3 680	4 118	4 832	5 227	5 499	6 413	5 311	6 703	5 651
Compensation of employees	...	...	...	...	...	...	908	994	995	1 017
Imports Of Goods And Services And Income Payments	-333 774	-364 196	-355 975	-377 488	-473 923	-483 769	-530 142	-594 443	-663 741	-721 307
Goods, balance of payments basis	-249 750	-265 067	-247 642	-268 901	-332 418	-338 088	-368 425	-409 765	-447 189	-477 365
Services	-41 491	-45 503	-51 749	-54 973	-67 748	-72 862	-80 147	-90 787	-98 526	-102 479
Direct defense expenditures	-10 851	-11 564	-12 460	-13 087	-12 516	-13 108	-13 730	-14 950	-15 604	-15 313
Travel	-10 397	-11 479	-12 394	-13 149	[3]-22 913	-24 558	-25 913	-29 310	-32 114	-33 416
Passenger fares	-3 607	-4 487	-4 772	-6 003	[3]-5 735	-6 444	-6 505	-7 283	-7 729	-8 249
Other transportation	-11 790	-12 474	-11 710	-12 222	-14 843	-15 643	[3]-17 766	-19 010	-20 891	-22 172
Royalties and license fees [1]	-724	-650	-795	-943	-1 168	-1 170	-1 401	-1 857	-2 601	-2 528
Other private services [1]	-2 909	[3]-3 562	-8 159	-8 001	-9 040	-10 203	[3]-13 146	-16 485	-17 667	-18 930
U.S. Government miscellaneous services	-1 214	-1 287	-1 460	-1 568	-1 534	-1 735	-1 686	-1 893	-1 921	-1 871
Income payments	-42 532	-53 626	-56 583	-53 614	-73 756	-72 819	-81 571	-93 891	-118 026	-141 463
Income payments on foreign-owned assets in the U.S.	-42 532	-53 626	-56 583	-53 614	-73 756	-72 819	-78 893	-91 553	-116 179	-139 177
Direct investment payments	-8 635	-6 898	[3]-2 114	-4 120	-8 443	-6 945	-6 856	-7 676	-12 150	-7 045
Other private payments	-21 214	-29 415	-35 187	-30 501	-44 158	-42 745	-47 412	-57 659	-72 314	-93 768
U.S. Government payments	-12 684	-17 313	-19 282	-18 993	-21 155	-23 129	-24 625	-26 218	-31 715	-38 364
Compensation of employees	...	...	...	...	...	...	-2 678	-2 338	-1 847	-2 286
Unilateral Current Transfers, Net	-8 349	-11 702	-16 544	-17 310	-20 335	-21 998	-24 132	-23 265	-25 274	-26 169
U.S. Government grants	-5 486	-5 145	-6 087	-6 469	-8 696	-11 268	-11 883	-10 309	-10 537	-10 860
U.S. Government pensions and other transfers	-1 818	-2 041	-2 251	-2 207	-2 159	-2 138	-2 372	-2 409	-2 709	-2 775
Private remittances and other transfers	-1 044	[3]-4 516	[3]-8 207	-8 635	-9 479	-8 593	-9 877	-10 548	-12 028	-12 534
Memoranda:										
Balance on goods	-25 500	-28 023	-36 485	-67 102	-112 492	-122 173	-145 081	-159 557	-126 959	-115 245
Balance on services	6 093	11 852	12 329	9 335	3 419	294	6 543	7 874	12 393	24 607
Balance on goods and services	-19 407	-16 172	-24 156	-57 767	-109 073	-121 880	-138 538	-151 684	-114 566	-90 638
Balance on income	30 073	32 903	35 164	36 386	35 063	25 723	15 494	14 293	18 687	19 824
Balance on goods, services, and income	10 666	16 731	11 008	-21 381	-74 010	-96 157	-123 044	-137 391	-95 879	-70 814
Unilateral current transfers, net	-8 349	-11 702	-16 544	-17 310	-20 335	-21 998	-24 132	-23 265	-25 274	-26 169
Balance on current account	2 317	5 030	-5 536	-38 691	-94 344	-118 155	-147 177	-160 655	-121 153	-96 982
CAPITAL AND FINANCIAL ACCOUNT										
Capital Account Transactions, Net	...	...	199	209	235	315	301	365	493	336
U.S.-Owned Assets Abroad, Net	-85 815	-113 054	-127 882	-66 373	-40 376	-44 752	-111 723	-79 296	-106 573	-175 383
U.S. official reserve assets, net	-7 003	-4 082	-4 965	-1 196	-3 131	-3 858	312	9 149	-3 912	-25 293
Gold	...	(4)	...	...	...	...	...	...	...	...
Special drawing rights	1 136	-730	-1 371	-66	-979	-897	-246	-509	127	-535
Reserve position in the International Monetary Fund	-1 667	-2 491	-2 552	-4 434	-995	908	1 501	2 070	1 025	471
Foreign currencies	-6 472	-861	-1 041	3 304	-1 156	-3 869	-942	7 588	-5 064	-25 229
U.S. Government assets, other than official reserve assets, net	-5 162	-5 097	-6 131	-5 006	-5 489	-2 821	-2 022	1 006	2 967	1 233
U.S. credits and other long-term assets	-9 860	-9 674	-10 063	-9 967	-9 599	-7 657	-9 084	-6 506	-7 680	-5 608
Repayments on U.S. credits and other long-term assets	4 456	4 413	4 292	5 012	4 490	4 719	6 089	7 625	10 370	6 725
U.S. foreign currency holdings and short-term assets, net	242	164	-360	-51	-379	117	973	-113	277	115
U.S. private assets, net	-73 651	-103 875	-116 786	-60 172	-31 757	-38 074	-110 014	-89 450	-105 628	-151 323
Direct investment	-19 222	-9 624	[3]-4 556	-12 528	-16 407	-18 927	-23 995	-35 034	-22 528	-43 447
Foreign securities	-3 568	-5 699	-7 983	-6 762	-4 756	-7 481	-4 271	-5 251	-7 980	-22 070
U.S. claims on unaffiliated foreigners reported by U.S. nonbanking concerns	-4 023	-4 377	6 823	-10 954	533	-10 342	-21 773	-7 046	-21 193	-27 646
U.S. claims reported by U.S. banks, not included elsewhere	-46 838	-84 175	-111 070	-29 928	-11 127	-1 323	-59 975	-42 119	-53 927	-58 160
Foreign-Owned Assets In The United States, Net	62 612	86 232	96 589	88 694	117 752	146 115	230 009	248 634	246 522	224 928
Foreign official assets in the U.S., net	15 497	4 960	3 593	5 845	3 140	-1 119	35 648	45 387	39 758	8 503
U.S. Government securities	11 895	6 322	5 085	6 496	4 703	-1 139	33 150	44 802	43 050	1 532
U.S. Treasury securities	9 708	5 019	5 779	6 972	4 690	-838	34 364	43 238	41 741	149
Other	2 187	1 303	-694	-476	13	-301	-1 214	1 564	1 309	1 383
Other U.S. Government liabilities	615	-338	605	602	739	844	2 195	-2 326	-467	160
U.S. liabilities reported by U.S. banks, not included elsewhere	-159	-3 670	-1 747	545	555	645	1 187	3 918	-319	4 976
Other foreign official assets	3 145	2 646	-350	-1 798	-2 857	-1 469	-884	-1 007	-2 506	1 835
Other foreign assets in the U.S., net	47 115	81 272	92 997	82 849	114 612	147 233	194 360	203 247	206 764	216 425
Direct investment	16 918	25 195	...	10 372	24 468	19 742	35 420	58 470	57 735	68 274
U.S. Treasury securities	2 645	2 927	7 027	8 689	23 001	20 433	3 809	-7 643	20 239	29 618
U.S. securities other than U.S. Treasury securities	5 457	6 905	6 085	8 164	12 568	50 962	70 969	42 120	26 353	38 767
U.S. currency	4 500	3 200	4 000	5 400	4 100	5 200	4 100	5 400	5 800	5 900
U.S. liabilities to unaffiliated foreigners reported by U.S. nonbanking concerns	6 852	917	-2 383	-118	16 626	9 851	3 325	18 363	32 893	22 086
U.S. liabilities reported by U.S. banks, not included elsewhere	10 743	42 128	65 633	50 342	33 849	41 045	76 737	86 537	63 744	51 780
Statistical Discrepancy	20 886	21 792	36 630	16 162	16 733	16 478	28 590	-9 048	-19 289	47 101

See footnotes at end of table.

Table A-6. U.S. International Transactions, 1960–1999—*Continued*

(Millions of dollars.)

Credits and debits	1990	1991	1992	1993	1994	1995	1996	1997	1998	1999
CURRENT ACCOUNT										
Exports Of Goods And Services And Income Receipts	708 881	730 387	749 324	776 933	868 867	1 006 576	1 075 874	1 194 283	1 191 422	1 232 407
Goods, balance of payments basis	389 307	416 913	440 352	456 832	502 398	575 845	612 057	679 702	670 324	684 358
Services	147 832	164 261	176 916	185 941	201 031	219 229	240 007	257 235	262 653	271 884
Transfers under U.S. military agency sales contracts	9 932	11 135	12 387	13 471	12 787	14 643	16 446	16 836	17 628	16 334
Travel	43 007	48 385	54 742	57 875	58 417	63 395	69 809	73 426	71 286	74 881
Passenger fares	15 298	15 854	16 618	16 528	16 997	18 909	20 422	20 868	20 098	19 776
Other transportation	22 042	22 631	21 531	21 958	23 754	26 081	26 074	27 006	25 604	27 033
Royalties and license fees [1]	16 634	17 819	20 841	21 695	26 712	30 289	32 470	33 639	36 197	36 467
Other private services [1]	40 251	47 748	[3]49 956	53 532	61 477	65 094	73 858	84 505	90 914	96 508
U.S. Government miscellaneous services	668	690	841	883	887	818	928	955	926	885
Income receipts	171 742	149 214	132 056	134 159	165 438	211 502	223 810	257 346	258 445	276 165
Income receipts on U.S.-owned assets abroad	170 570	147 924	130 631	132 725	163 895	209 741	222 054	255 544	256 511	273 957
Direct investment receipts	65 973	58 718	57 538	67 246	77 344	95 260	102 505	115 536	106 407	118 802
Other private receipts	94 072	81 186	65 977	60 353	82 423	109 768	114 958	136 449	146 503	151 958
U.S. Government receipts	10 525	8 019	7 115	5 126	4 128	4 713	4 591	3 559	3 601	3 197
Compensation of employees	1 172	1 290	1 425	1 434	1 543	1 761	1 756	1 802	1 934	2 208
Imports Of Goods And Services And Income Payments	-759 189	-734 524	-762 035	-821 977	-949 212	-1 081 976	-1 159 111	-1 294 029	-1 364 531	-1 515 861
Goods, balance of payments basis	-498 337	-490 981	-536 458	-589 441	-668 590	-749 574	-803 327	-876 367	-917 178	-1 029 917
Services	-117 659	-118 459	-116 476	-122 281	-131 878	-141 447	-150 850	-166 502	-182 697	-191 296
Direct defense expenditures	-17 531	-16 409	-13 835	-12 086	-10 217	-10 043	-11 061	-11 698	-12 241	-13 650
Travel	-37 349	-35 322	-38 552	-40 713	-43 782	-44 916	-48 078	-52 051	-56 509	-59 351
Passenger fares	-10 531	-10 012	-10 603	-11 410	-13 062	-14 663	-15 809	-18 138	-19 971	-21 405
Other transportation	-24 966	-24 975	-23 767	-24 524	-26 019	-27 034	-27 403	-28 959	-30 363	-34 137
Royalties and license fees [1]	-3 135	-4 035	-5 161	-5 032	-5 852	-6 919	-7 837	-9 614	-11 713	-13 275
Other private services [1]	-22 229	-25 590	[3]-22 296	-26 261	-30 386	-35 249	-37 975	-43 280	-49 051	-46 657
U.S. Government miscellaneous services	-1 919	-2 116	-2 263	-2 255	-2 560	-2 623	-2 687	-2 762	-2 849	-2 821
Income payments	-143 192	-125 084	-109 101	-110 255	-148 744	-190 955	-204 934	-251 160	-264 656	-294 648
Income payments on foreign-owned assets in the U.S.	-139 728	-121 058	-104 349	-105 123	-142 792	-184 692	-198 634	-244 494	-257 547	-287 059
Direct investment payments	-3 450	2 266	-2 189	-7 943	-22 150	-30 318	-33 093	-43 601	-38 679	-56 098
Other private payments	-95 508	-82 452	-63 079	-57 804	-76 450	-97 004	-97 901	-112 843	-127 749	-135 830
U.S. Government payments	-40 770	-40 872	-39 081	-39 376	-44 192	-57 370	-67 640	-88 050	-91 119	-95 131
Compensation of employees	-3 464	-4 026	-4 752	-5 132	-5 952	-6 263	-6 300	-6 666	-7 109	-7 589
Unilateral Current Transfers, Net	-26 654	10 752	-35 013	-37 637	-38 260	-34 057	-40 081	-40 794	-44 029	-48 025
U.S. Government grants	-10 359	29 193	-16 320	-17 036	-14 978	-11 190	-15 401	-12 472	-13 270	-13 774
U.S. Government pensions and other transfers	-3 224	-3 775	-4 043	-4 104	-4 556	-3 451	-4 466	-4 191	-4 305	-4 401
Private remittances and other transfers	-13 070	-14 665	-14 650	-16 497	-18 726	-19 416	-20 214	-24 131	-26 454	-29 850
Memoranda:										
Balance on goods	-109 030	-74 068	-96 106	-132 609	-166 192	-173 729	-191 270	-196 665	-246 854	-345 559
Balance on services	30 173	45 802	60 440	63 660	69 153	77 782	89 157	90 733	79 956	80 588
Balance on goods and services	-78 857	-28 266	-35 666	-68 949	-97 039	-95 947	-102 113	-105 932	-166 898	-264 971
Balance on income	28 550	24 130	22 954	23 904	16 694	20 547	18 876	6 186	-6 211	-18 483
Balance on goods, services, and income	-50 307	-4 136	-12 712	-45 045	-80 345	-75 400	-83 237	-99 746	-173 109	-283 454
Unilateral current transfers, net	-26 654	10 752	-35 013	-37 637	-38 260	-34 057	-40 081	-40 794	-44 029	-48 025
Balance on current account	-76 961	6 616	-47 724	-82 681	-118 605	-109 457	-123 318	-140 540	-217 138	-331 479
CAPITAL AND FINANCIAL ACCOUNT										
Capital Account Transactions, Net	-6 579	-4 479	612	-88	-469	372	693	350	637	-3 500
U.S.-Owned Assets Abroad, Net	-81 234	-64 388	-74 410	-200 552	-176 056	-352 376	-413 923	-488 940	-335 436	-430 187
U.S. official reserve assets, net	-2 158	5 763	3 901	-1 379	5 346	-9 742	6 668	-1 010	-6 783	8 747
Gold	. . .	. . .	. . .	. . .	. . .	. . .	. . .	. . .	. . .	. . .
Special drawing rights	-192	-177	2 316	-537	-441	-808	370	-350	-147	10
Reserve position in the International Monetary Fund	731	-367	-2 692	-44	494	-2 466	-1 280	-3 575	-5 119	5 484
Foreign currencies	-2 697	6 307	4 277	-797	5 293	-6 468	7 578	2 915	-1 517	3 253
U.S. Government assets, other than official reserve assets, net	2 317	2 924	-1 667	-351	-390	-984	-989	68	-422	2 751
U.S. credits and other long-term assets	-8 410	-12 879	-7 408	-6 311	-5 383	-4 859	-5 025	-5 417	-4 678	-6 175
Repayments on U.S. credits and other long-term assets	10 856	16 776	5 807	6 270	5 088	4 125	3 930	5 438	4 111	9 560
U.S. foreign currency holdings and short-term assets, net	-130	-974	-66	-310	-95	-250	106	47	145	-634
U.S. private assets, net	-81 393	-73 075	-76 644	-198 822	-181 012	-341 650	-419 602	-487 998	-328 231	-441 685
Direct investment	-37 183	-37 889	-48 266	-83 950	-80 167	-98 750	-91 885	-105 016	-146 052	-150 901
Foreign securities	-28 765	-45 673	-49 166	-146 253	-60 309	-122 506	-149 829	-118 976	-135 995	-128 594
U.S. claims on unaffiliated foreigners reported by U.S. nonbanking concerns	-27 824	11 097	-387	766	-36 336	-45 286	-86 333	-122 888	-10 612	-92 328
U.S. claims reported by U.S. banks, not included elsewhere	12 379	-610	21 175	30 615	-4 200	-75 108	-91 555	-141 118	-35 572	-69 862
Foreign-Owned Assets In The United States, Net	141 571	110 808	170 663	282 040	305 989	465 684	571 706	756 962	482 235	753 564
Foreign official assets in the U.S., net	33 910	17 389	40 477	71 753	39 583	109 880	126 724	18 876	-20 127	42 864
U.S. Government securities	30 243	16 147	22 403	53 014	36 827	72 712	120 679	-2 161	-3 589	32 527
U.S. Treasury securities	29 576	14 846	18 454	48 952	30 750	68 977	115 671	-6 690	-9 921	12 177
Other	667	1 301	3 949	4 062	6 077	3 735	5 008	4 529	6 332	20 350
Other U.S. Government liabilities	1 868	1 367	2 191	1 313	1 564	-105	-982	-1 041	-3 550	-3 255
U.S. liabilities reported by U.S. banks, not included elsewhere	3 385	-1 484	16 571	14 841	3 665	34 008	5 704	22 286	-9 501	12 692
Other foreign official assets	-1 586	1 359	-688	2 585	-2 473	3 265	1 323	-208	-3 487	900
Other foreign assets in the U.S., net	107 661	93 420	130 186	210 287	266 406	355 804	444 982	738 086	502 362	710 700
Direct investment	48 494	23 171	19 823	51 362	46 121	57 776	86 502	106 032	186 316	275 533
U.S. Treasury securities	-2 534	18 826	37 131	24 381	34 274	99 548	154 996	146 433	48 581	-20 464
U.S. securities other than U.S. Treasury securities	1 592	35 144	30 043	80 092	56 971	96 367	130 240	197 892	218 075	331 523
U.S. currency	18 800	15 400	13 400	18 900	23 400	12 300	17 362	24 782	16 622	22 407
U.S. liabilities to unaffiliated foreigners reported by U.S. nonbanking concerns	45 133	-3 115	13 573	10 489	1 302	59 637	39 404	113 921	-7 001	34 298
U.S. liabilities reported by U.S. banks, not included elsewhere	-3 824	3 994	16 216	25 063	104 338	30 176	16 478	149 026	39 769	67 403
Statistical Discrepancy	23 204	-48 557	-49 141	1 281	-10 859	-4 223	-35 158	-127 832	69 702	11 602

1. Beginning in 1982, this item is presented on a gross basis. The definition of exports is revised to exclude U.S. parents' payments to foreign affiliates and to include U.S. affiliates' receipts from foreign parents. The definition of imports is revised to include U.S. parents' payments to foreign affiliates and to exclude U.S. affiliates' receipts from foreign parents.
2. For 1974, includes extraordinary U.S. Government transactions with India.
3. Break in series.
4. Value less than $500,000 (+/-).

Table A-7. Exchange Rates, 1992–1999

(Annual averages, currency units per U.S. dollar.)

Country and currency unit	1992	1993	1994	1995	1996	1997	1998	1999
TRADE-WEIGHTED INDEXES [1]								
Nominal								
Broad (January 1997=100)	76.29	84.45	90.42	92.52	97.40	104.44	116.48	116.87
Major currencies (March 1973=100)	85.45	87.73	86.25	81.39	84.60	91.24	95.79	94.07
Other important trading partners (January 1997=100)	52.88	66.01	80.51	92.51	98.26	104.67	126.03	129.94
G-10 (March 1973=100)	86.64	93.17	91.32	84.25	87.34	96.38	98.85	. . .
Real (adjusted for price change)								
Broad (January 1997=100)	86.73	87.59	87.25	84.69	86.63	91.24	99.21	98.53
Other important trading partners (January 1997=100)	100.66	98.14	97.79	97.14	94.40	95.58	108.10	107.22
NATIONAL CURRENCIES								
Afghanistan, Islamic State Of, Afghani	50.60	50.60	425.10	833.33	2 333.33	3 000.00	3 000.00	3 000.00
Albania, Lek	75.03	102.06	94.62	92.70	104.50	148.93	150.63	137.69
Algeria, Algerian Dinar	21.84	23.35	35.06	47.66	54.75	57.71	58.74	66.57
Antigua and Barbuda, East Caribbean Dollar [4]	2.70	2.70	2.70	2.70	2.70	2.70	2.70	2.70
Argentina, Peso	0.99	1.00	1.00	1.00	1.00	1.00	1.00	1.00
Armenia, Dram	. . .	9.11	288.65	405.91	414.04	490.85	504.92	535.06
Aruba, Aruban Florin	1.79	1.79	1.79	1.79	1.79	1.79	1.79	1.79
Australia, Australian Dollar	1.36	1.47	1.37	1.35	1.28	1.35	1.59	1.55
Austria, Schilling [2]	10.99	11.63	11.42	10.08	10.59	12.20	12.38	12.92
Azerbaijan, Manat	54.20	99.98	1 570.22	4 413.54	4 301.26	3 985.37	3 869.00	4 042.00
Bahamas, The, Bahamian Dollar	1.23	1.00	1.00	1.00	1.00	1.00	1.00	1.00
Bahrain, Dinar	0.38	0.38	0.38	0.38	0.38	0.38	0.38	0.38
Bangladesh, Taka	38.95	39.57	40.21	40.28	41.79	43.89	46.91	49.09
Barbados, Barbados Dollar	2.00	2.00	2.00	2.00	2.00	2.00	2.00	2.00
Belarus, Rubel	. . .	. . .	. . .	. . .	13 984.00	25 964.10	46 070.00	276 000.00
Belgium, Belgium Franc [2]	32.15	34.60	33.46	29.48	30.96	35.77	36.30	37.86
Belize, Belize Dollar	2.00	2.00	2.00	2.00	2.00	2.00	2.00	2.00
Benin, CFA Franc [3]	264.69	0.03	555.21	499.15	511.55	583.67	589.95	615.70
Bhutan, Ngultrum	0.02	0.03	0.05	32.43	35.43	36.31	41.26	43.06
Bolivia, Boliviano	3.90	4.27	4.62	4.80	5.07	5.25	5.51	5.81
Botswana, Pula	2.11	2.42	2.68	2.77	3.32	3.65	4.23	4.62
Brazil, Real	. . .	0.03	0.64	0.92	1.01	1.08	1.16	1.81
Bulgaria, Lev	0.02	0.03	0.05	0.07	0.18	1.68	1.76	1.84
Burkina Faso, CFA Franc [3]	264.69	283.16	555.21	499.15	511.55	583.67	589.95	615.70
Burundi, Burundi Franc	208.30	242.78	252.66	249.76	302.75	352.35	447.77	563.56
Cambodia, Riel	1 266.60	2 689.00	2 545.25	2 450.83	2 624.08	2 946.25	3 744.42	3 807.83
Cameroon, CFA Franc [3]	264.69	283.16	555.21	499.15	511.55	583.67	589.95	615.70
Canada, Canadian Dollar	1.21	1.29	1.37	1.37	1.36	1.38	1.48	1.49
Cape Verde, Escudo	68.02	80.43	81.89	76.85	82.59	93.18	98.16	102.70
Central African Republic, CFA Franc [3]	264.69	283.16	555.21	499.15	511.55	583.67	589.95	615.70
Chad, CFA Franc [3]	264.69	283.16	555.21	499.15	511.55	583.67	589.95	615.70
Chile, Peso	362.59	404.17	420.18	396.77	412.27	419.30	460.29	508.78
China, People's Republic: Mainland, Yuan	5.52	5.76	8.62	8.35	8.31	8.29	8.28	8.28
China, People's Republic: Hong Kong, Hong Kong Dollar	7.74	7.74	7.73	7.74	7.73	7.74	7.75	7.76
Colombia, Peso	759.28	863.07	844.84	912.83	1 036.69	1 140.96	1 426.04	1 629.31
Comoros, Comorian Franc	264.69	283.16	416.40	374.36	383.66	437.75	442.46	461.78
Congo, Democratic Republic Of, New Zaire	0.22	2.51	1 194.12	7 024.43	44 339.00	125 181.00	. . .	. . .
Congo, Republic Of, CFA Franc [3]	264.69	283.16	555.21	499.15	511.55	583.67	589.95	615.70
Costa Rica, Colon	134.51	142.17	157.07	179.73	207.69	232.60	257.23	285.69
Cote D' Ivoire, CFA Franc [3]	264.69	283.16	555.21	499.15	511.55	583.67	589.95	615.70
Croatia, Kuna	. . .	3.58	6.00	5.23	5.43	6.10	6.36	7.11
Cyprus, Cyprus Pound	0.45	0.50	0.49	0.45	0.47	0.51	0.52	0.54
Czech Republic, Koruny	. . .	29.15	28.79	26.54	27.14	31.70	32.28	34.57
Denmark, Krone	6.04	6.48	6.36	5.60	5.80	6.60	6.70	6.98
Djibouti, Djibouti Franc	177.72	177.72	177.72	177.72	177.72	177.72	177.72	177.72
Dominica, East Caribbean Dollar [4]	2.70	2.70	2.70	2.70	2.70	2.70	2.70	2.70
Dominican Republic, Peso	12.77	12.68	13.16	13.60	13.77	14.27	15.27	16.03
Ecuador, Sucre	1 533.96	1 919.10	2 196.73	2 564.49	3 189.47	3 998.27	5 446.57	11 786.80
Egypt, Egyptian Pound	3.32	3.35	3.39	3.39	3.39	3.39	3.39	3.40
El Salvador, Colon	9.17	8.70	8.73	8.75	8.76	8.76	8.76	8.76

See footnotes at end of table.

Table A-7. Exchange Rates, 1992–1999—*Continued*

(Annual averages, currency units per U.S. dollar.)

Country and currency unit	1992	1993	1994	1995	1996	1997	1998	1999
Equatorial Guinea, CFA Franc [3]	264.69	283.16	555.21	499.15	511.55	583.67	589.95	615.70
Estonia, Kroon	...	13.22	12.99	11.46	12.03	13.88	14.07	14.68
Ethiopia, Birr	2.80	5.00	5.47	6.16	6.35	6.71	7.12	7.76
European Monetary Union, EURO [2]	...	...	...	...	...	...	...	0.94
Fiji, Fiji Dollar	1.50	1.54	1.46	1.41	1.40	1.44	1.99	1.97
Finland, Markka [2]	4.48	5.71	5.22	4.37	4.59	5.19	5.34	5.58
France, Franc [2]	5.29	5.66	5.55	4.99	5.12	5.84	5.90	6.16
Gabon, CFA Franc [3]	264.69	283.16	555.21	499.15	511.55	583.67	589.95	615.70
Gambia, The, Dalasi	8.89	9.13	9.58	9.55	9.79	10.20	10.64	11.31
Germany, Deutsche Mark [2]	1.56	1.65	1.62	1.43	1.50	1.73	1.76	1.84
Ghana, Cedi	437.09	649.06	956.71	1 200.43	1 637.23	2 050.17	2 314.15	2 647.32
Greece, Drachma	190.62	229.25	242.60	231.66	240.71	273.06	295.53	305.65
Grenada, East Caribbean Dollar [4]	2.70	2.70	2.70	2.70	2.70	2.70	2.70	2.70
Guatemala, Quetzal	5.17	5.64	5.75	5.81	6.05	6.07	6.39	7.39
Guinea, Franc	902.00	955.49	976.64	991.41	1 004.02	1 095.33	1 236.83	1 372.80
Guinea-Bissau, Franc	106.68	155.11	198.34	278.04	405.75	583.67	589.95	615.70
Guyana, Guyana Dollar	125.00	126.73	138.29	141.99	140.38	142.40	150.52	178.00
Haiti, Gourde	9.80	12.82	15.04	15.11	15.70	16.65	16.77	16.94
Honduras, Lempira	5.50	6.47	8.41	9.47	11.71	13.00	13.39	14.21
Hungary, Forint	78.99	91.93	105.16	125.68	152.65	186.79	214.40	237.15
Iceland, Krona	57.55	67.60	69.94	64.69	66.50	70.90	70.96	72.35
India, Rupee	25.92	30.49	31.37	32.43	35.43	36.31	41.26	43.06
Indonesia, Rupiah	2 029.92	2 087.10	2 160.75	2 248.61	2 342.30	2 909.38	10 013.60	7 855.15
Iran, Islamic Republic Of, Rial	65.55	1 267.77	1 748.75	1 747.93	1 750.76	1 752.92	1 751.86	1 752.93
Iraq, Dinar	0.31	0.31	0.31	0.31	0.31	0.31	0.31	0.31
Ireland, Irish Pound [2]	0.59	0.68	0.67	0.62	0.63	0.66	0.70	0.74
Israel, New Sheqel	2.46	2.83	3.01	3.01	3.19	3.45	3.80	4.14
Italy, Lira [2]	1 232.41	1 573.67	1 612.44	1 628.93	1 542.95	1 703.10	1 736.21	1 817.40
Jamaica, Jamaica Dollar	22.96	24.95	33.09	35.14	37.12	35.40	36.55	39.04
Japan, Yen	126.65	111.20	102.21	94.06	108.78	120.99	130.91	113.91
Jordan, Dinar	0.68	0.69	0.70	0.70	0.71	0.71	0.71	0.71
Kazakistan, Tenge	...	...	35.54	60.95	67.30	75.44	78.30	119.52
Kenya, Kenya Shilling	32.22	58.00	56.05	51.43	57.11	58.73	60.37	70.33
Korea, South, Won	780.65	802.67	803.45	771.27	804.45	951.29	1 401.44	1 188.82
Kuwait, Dinar	0.29	0.30	0.30	0.30	0.30	0.30	0.30	0.30
Kyrgyz Republic, Som	...	...	10.84	10.82	12.81	17.36	20.84	39.01
Lao People's Democratic Republic, Kip	716.08	716.25	717.67	804.69	921.02	1 259.98	3 298.33	7 102.03
Latvia, Lats	0.74	0.68	0.56	0.53	0.55	0.58	0.59	0.59
Lebanon, Lebanese Pound	1 712.79	1 741.36	1 680.07	1 621.41	1 571.44	1 539.45	1 516.13	1 507.84
Lesotho, Loti	2.85	3.27	3.55	3.63	4.30	4.61	5.53	6.11
Liberia, Liberian Dollars	1.00	1.00	1.00	1.00	1.00	1.00	1.00	1.00
Libya, Libyan Dinars	0.28	0.31	0.32	0.35	0.36	0.38	0.39	0.46
Lithuania, Litas	1.77	4.34	3.98	4.00	4.00	4.00	4.00	4.00
Luxembourg, Franc [2]	32.15	34.60	33.46	29.48	30.96	35.77	36.30	37.86
Macedonia, Denar	...	...	43.26	37.88	39.98	50.00	54.46	56.90
Madagascar, Malagasy Franc	1 863.97	1 913.78	3 067.34	4 265.63	4 061.25	5 090.89	5 441.40	6 249.80
Malawi, Kwacha	3.60	4.40	8.74	15.28	15.31	16.44	31.07	44.09
Malaysia, Ringgit	2.55	2.57	2.62	2.50	2.52	2.81	3.92	3.80
Maldives, Rufiyaa	10.57	10.96	11.59	11.77	11.77	11.77	11.77	11.77
Mali, CFA Franc [3]	264.69	283.16	555.21	499.15	511.55	583.67	589.95	615.70
Malta, Maltese Lira	0.32	0.38	0.38	0.35	0.36	0.39	0.39	0.40
Mauritania, Ouguiya	87.03	120.81	123.58	129.77	137.22	151.85	188.48	209.51
Mauritius, Rupee	15.56	17.65	17.96	17.39	17.95	21.06	23.99	25.19
Mexico, New Peso	3.09	3.12	3.38	6.42	7.60	7.92	9.14	9.56
Moldova, Leu	...	...	...	4.50	4.60	4.62	5.37	10.52
Mongolia, Togrog	42.56	...	412.72	448.61	548.40	789.99	840.83	1 021.87
Morocco, Dirham	8.54	9.30	9.20	8.54	8.72	9.53	9.60	9.80
Mozambique, Metical	2 516.50	3 874.24	6 038.59	9 024.33	11 293.70	11 543.60	11 874.60	12 775.10
Myanmar, Kyat	6.10	6.16	5.97	5.67	5.92	6.24	6.34	6.29
Namibia, Namibia Dollar	2.85	3.27	3.55	3.63	4.30	4.61	5.53	6.11

See footnotes at end of table.

Table A-7. Exchange Rates, 1992–1999—*Continued*

(Annual averages, currency units per U.S. dollar.)

Country and currency unit	1992	1993	1994	1995	1996	1997	1998	1999
Nepal, Rupee	42.72	48.61	49.40	51.89	56.69	58.01	65.98	68.25
Netherlands Antilles, Guilder	1.79	1.79	1.79	1.79	1.79	1.79	1.79	1.79
Netherlands, Guilder [2]	1.76	1.86	1.82	1.61	1.69	1.95	1.98	2.07
New Zealand, New Zealand Dollar	1.86	1.85	1.69	1.52	1.45	1.51	1.87	1.89
Nicaragua, Cordoba	5.00	5.62	6.72	7.55	8.44	9.45	10.58	11.81
Niger, CFA Fanc [3]	264.69	283.16	555.21	499.15	511.55	583.67	589.95	615.70
Nigeria, Naira	17.30	22.07	22.00	21.90	21.88	21.89	21.89	21.89
Norway, Krone	6.21	7.09	7.06	6.34	6.45	7.07	7.55	7.80
Oman, Rial Omani	0.38	0.38	0.38	0.38	0.38	0.38	0.38	0.38
Pakistan, Rupee	25.08	27.95	30.39	31.46	35.87	40.87	44.92	50.55
Panama, Balboa	1.00	1.00	1.00	1.00	1.00	1.00	1.00	1.00
Papua New Guinea, Kina	0.96	0.98	1.01	1.28	1.32	1.44	2.07	2.54
Paraguay, Guarani	1 500.26	1 744.35	1 904.80	1 963.00	2 056.80	2 177.90	2 726.50	3 119.10
Peru, New Sol	1.25	1.99	2.20	2.25	2.45	2.66	2.93	3.38
Philippines, Peso	25.51	27.12	26.42	25.71	26.22	29.47	40.89	39.09
Poland, Zloty	1.36	1.81	2.27	2.42	2.70	3.28	3.48	3.97
Portugal, Escudo [2]	135.00	160.80	165.99	151.11	154.24	175.31	180.10	188.18
Qatar, Riyal	3.64	3.64	3.64	3.64	3.64	3.64	3.64	3.64
Romania, Leu	307.95	760.05	1 655.09	2 033.28	3 084.22	7 167.94	8 875.58	15 332.80
Russia, Ruble	. . .	0.99	2.19	4.56	5.12	5.78	9.71	24.62
Rwanda, Rwanda Franc	133.35	144.31	. . .	262.20	306.82	301.53	312.31	333.94
Samoa, Tala	2.47	2.57	2.53	2.48	2.46	2.57	2.96	3.02
Sao Tome and Principe, Dobra	321.34	429.85	732.63	1 420.34	2 203.16	4 552.55	6 883.20	7 072.10
Saudi Arabia, Riyal	3.75	3.75	3.75	3.75	3.75	3.75	3.75	3.75
Senegal, CFA Franc [3]	264.69	283.16	555.21	499.15	511.55	583.67	589.95	615.70
Seychelles, Rupee	5.12	5.18	5.06	4.76	4.97	5.03	5.26	5.34
Sierra Leone, Leone	499.44	567.46	586.74	755.22	920.73	981.48	1 563.62	1 804.19
Singapore, Singapore Dollar	1.63	1.62	1.53	1.42	1.41	1.48	1.67	1.69
Slovak Republic, Koruna	. . .	30.77	32.04	29.71	30.65	33.62	35.23	41.36
Slovenia, Tolar	81.29	113.24	128.81	118.52	135.36	159.69	166.13	181.77
Solomon Islands, Solomon Island Dollar	2.93	3.19	3.29	3.41	3.57	3.72	4.82	4.84
South Africa, Rand	2.85	0.05	3.55	3.63	4.30	4.61	5.53	6.11
Spain, Peseta [2]	102.38	127.26	133.96	124.69	126.66	146.41	149.40	156.17
Sri Lanka, Rupee	43.83	48.32	49.42	51.25	55.27	58.99	64.59	70.40
St. Kitts and Nevis, East Caribbean Dollar [4]	2.70	2.70	2.70	2.70	2.70	2.70	2.70	2.70
St. Lucia, East Caribbean Dollar [4]	2.70	2.70	2.70	2.70	2.70	2.70	2.70	2.70
St. Vincent and the Grenadines, East Caribbean Dollar [4]	2.70	2.70	2.70	2.70	2.70	2.70	2.70	2.70
Sudan, Sudanese Pound	9.74	15.93	28.96	58.09	125.08	157.57	200.80	252.55
Suriname, Guilder	1.79	1.79	134.12	442.23	401.26	401.00	401.00	844.00
Swaziland, Lilangeni	2.85	3.27	3.55	3.63	4.30	4.61	5.53	6.11
Sweden, Krona	5.82	7.78	7.72	7.13	6.71	7.63	7.95	8.26
Switzerland, Swiss Franc	1.41	1.48	1.37	1.18	1.24	1.45	1.45	1.50
Syrian Arab Republic, Syrian Pound	11.23	11.23	11.23	11.23	11.23	11.23	11.23	11.23
Taiwan, Taiwan dollar	. . .	26.42	26.47	26.50	27.47	28.78	33.55	32.32
Tajikistan, Tajik Ruble	. . .	10.36	24.49	122.86	295.50	562.33	776.63	. . .
Tanzania, Tanzanian Shilling	297.71	405.27	509.63	574.76	579.98	612.12	664.67	774.76
Thailand, Baht	25.40	25.32	25.15	24.92	25.34	31.36	41.36	37.84
Togo, CFA Franc [3]	264.69	283.16	555.21	499.15	511.55	583.67	589.95	615.70
Tonga, Pa'anga	1.35	1.38	1.32	1.27	1.23	1.26	1.49	1.59
Trinidad and Tobago, TT Dollar	4.25	5.35	5.92	5.95	6.01	6.25	6.30	6.30
Tunisia, Dinar	0.88	1.00	1.01	0.95	0.97	1.11	1.14	1.18
Turkey, Lira	6 872.40	10 984.60	29 608.70	45 845.10	81 404.90	151 865.00	260 724.00	418 783.00
Uganda, Uganda Shilling	1 133.83	1 195.02	979.45	968.92	1 046.08	1 083.01	1 240.31	1 454.80
Ukraine, Hryvnia	. . .	0.05	0.33	1.47	1.83	1.86	2.45	4.13
United Arab Emirates, Dirham	3.67	3.67	3.67	3.67	3.67	3.67	3.67	3.67
United Kingdom, Pound Sterling	0.57	0.67	0.65	0.63	0.64	0.61	0.60	0.62
Uruguay, Peso	3.03	3.94	5.04	6.35	7.97	9.44	10.47	11.34
Vanuatu, Vatu	113.39	121.58	116.41	112.11	111.72	115.87	127.52	129.08
Venezuela, Bolivar	68.38	90.83	148.50	176.84	417.33	488.64	547.56	605.72
Yemen, Republic Of, Rial	12.01	12.01	12.01	40.84	94.16	129.28	135.88	159.50
Zambia, Kwacha	172.21	452.76	669.37	864.12	1 207.90	1 314.50	1 862.07	2 388.02
Zimbabwe, Zimbabwe Dollar	5.10	6.48	8.15	8.67	10.00	12.11	23.68	38.30

1. Value of the U.S. dollar relative to other currencies.
2. The Euro became the official currency of the 11 Euro area (EMU) nations on January 1, 1999. The 1999 values are computed values for the former national currencies.
3. CFA Franc is used in Benin, Burkina Faso, Cameroon, Central African Republic, Chad, Republic of the Congo, Cote D'Ivoir, Equitorial Guinea, Gabon, Mali, Niger, Senegal, and Togo.
4. The East Caribbean Dollar is used in Antigua and Barbuda, Dominica, Grenada, St. Kitts and Nevis, St. Lucia, and St. Vincent and the Grenadines.

PART B. U.S. FOREIGN TRADE IN SERVICES

U.S. Trade in Services, 1999
(Billions of dollars)

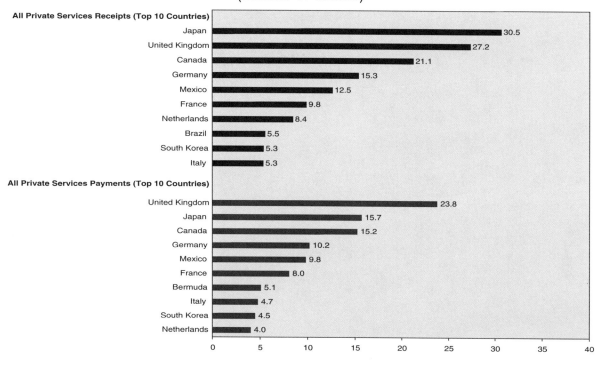

All Private Services Receipts (Top 10 Countries)

Japan	30.5
United Kingdom	27.2
Canada	21.1
Germany	15.3
Mexico	12.5
France	9.8
Netherlands	8.4
Brazil	5.5
South Korea	5.3
Italy	5.3

All Private Services Payments (Top 10 Countries)

United Kingdom	23.8
Japan	15.7
Canada	15.2
Germany	10.2
Mexico	9.8
France	8.0
Bermuda	5.1
Italy	4.7
South Korea	4.5
Netherlands	4.0

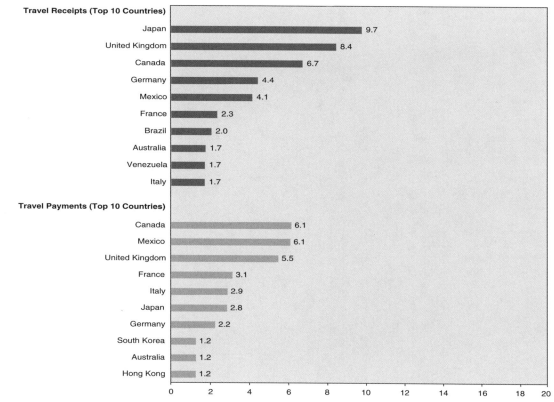

Travel Receipts (Top 10 Countries)

Japan	9.7
United Kingdom	8.4
Canada	6.7
Germany	4.4
Mexico	4.1
France	2.3
Brazil	2.0
Australia	1.7
Venezuela	1.7
Italy	1.7

Travel Payments (Top 10 Countries)

Canada	6.1
Mexico	6.1
United Kingdom	5.5
France	3.1
Italy	2.9
Japan	2.8
Germany	2.2
South Korea	1.2
Australia	1.2
Hong Kong	1.2

PART B. U.S. FOREIGN TRADE IN SERVICES

NOTES AND DEFINITIONS

For all tables except Table B-2, the source is the Bureau of Economic Analysis. Table B-2 is from the Bureau of Labor Statistics.

General notes for all tables:
(*) Less than $500,000
(D) Suppressed to avoid disclosure of data of individual companies.

DATA NOTES

Data in this section are for private service transactions.

The data cover what are referred to as "cross-border" transactions, that is, transactions between residents of the United States and residents of another country. (In this context, "residents" includes businesses as well as individuals.) The transactions may be between independent entities (unaffiliated) parties, or may represent trade within a multinational company (affiliated). In both cases, the transactions are included in the international transactions accounts of both countries, as an export for the seller's country and an import for the buyer's country.

Because the international transactions accounts are based on residency, transactions with foreigners by foreign affiliates of U.S. companies are transactions between two foreign entities, and are not considered U.S. international transactions. Transactions between U.S. residents and U.S. affiliates of foreign companies are domestic transactions within the United States, and do not enter into the international transactions accounts except to the extent that the profits from such transactions are transferred from the country of residency to the country of ownership. (For example, suppose that a U.S. resident purchases financial services from a local branch of a foreign-owned firm. The labor that supplies those services is located in the United States, and the establishment may be in part locally owned. Only the profits repatriated to the owning country are considered international transactions.)

Since 1989, a majority of U.S. purchases of services from foreign entities have been purchases from foreign affiliates in the United States, that is, transactions that are not included in these international trade data. Since 1996, sales of services to foreigners by foreign affiliates of U.S. firms have exceeded U.S. cross-border sales. Sales of services to foreigners by foreign affiliates of U.S.-owned firms have exceeded sales of services to U.S. persons by U.S. affiliates of foreign firms each year from 1987 through 1998, all the years for which data are currently available. (For more information, see "U.S. International Services: Cross-Border Trade in 1999 and Sales Through Affiliates in 1998," *Survey of Current Business*, October 2000.)

DEFINITIONS

Travel: This category covers purchases of goods and services by U.S. persons traveling abroad and by foreign persons traveling in the United States for business or personal reasons for less than 1 year. It does not include the passenger fares, which are reported separately. The types of goods and services most likely to be purchased are lodging, food, recreation and entertainment, local transportation, and gifts. U.S. travel transactions with both Canada and Mexico include border transactions, which often involve stays of less than 24 hours.

Passenger fares: This category covers fares paid by residents of one country to airline and vessel operators that reside in another country. Exports consist of fares received by U.S. operators for transporting foreign residents between the United States and a foreign country and between foreign countries. Imports consist of fares paid to foreign operators by U.S. residents for travel to and from the United States.

Other transportation: This category primarily covers transactions for freight and port services for the transportation of goods by ocean, air, and truck to and from the United States. Freight receipts of U.S. carriers are for transporting U.S. goods exports and for transporting goods between two foreign points; freight payments to foreign carriers are for transporting U.S. goods imports. Port services receipts are the value of the goods and services procured by foreign carriers in both U.S. sea and air ports; port services payments are the value of goods and services procured by U.S. carriers in foreign sea and airports.

Royalties and license fees: This category covers transactions with foreign residents that involve patented and unpatented techniques, processes, formulas, and other intangible property rights used in the production of goods; transactions involving copyrights, trademarks, franchises, broadcast rights, and other intangible rights; the rights to distribute, use, and reproduce computer software; and the rights to sell products under a particular trademark, brand name, or signature.

Other private services: This category consists of a variety of services: Education; financial services; insurance; telecommunications; business, professional, and technical services; and other affiliated and unaffiliated services.

Education receipts consist of expenditures for tuition and living expenses by foreign students enrolled in U.S. colleges and universities; payments consist of tuition and living expenses of U.S. students for study abroad.

Financial services covers a variety of services, including funds management, credit card services, explicit fees and commissions on transactions in securities, fees on credit-related activities, and other miscellaneous financial services; implicit fees paid and received on bond trading are also covered.

Insurance includes premiums earned and paid for primary insurance and for reinsurance; losses paid by U.S. insurers and losses recovered from foreign insurers are netted against the premiums. Primary insurance consists of life insurance, accident and health insurance, and property and casualty insurance. Each type of primary insurance may be reinsured; reinsurance is the ceding of a portion of a premium to another insurer, who then assumes a corresponding portion of the risk. Reinsurance is one way of providing coverage for events with so high a degree of risk or liability that a single insurer is unwilling or unable to underwrite insurance against their occurrence.

Telecommunications consists of settlements between U.S. and foreign communications companies for the transmission of messages between the United States and other countries; channel leasing; telex, telegram, and other jointly provided (basic) services; value-added services, such as electronic mail and video conferencing; and telecommunications support services.

Business, professional, and technical services covers a wide variety of services, including accounting, auditing, and bookkeeping services; advertising; agricultural services; computer and data processing services; construction, engineering, architectural, and mining services; data base and other information services; industrial engineering; installation, maintenance, and repair of equipment; legal services; mailing, reproduction, and commercial art; management of health care facilities; management, consulting, and public relations services; medical services; miscellaneous disbursements; operational leasing; personnel supply services; research, development, and testing services; sports and performing arts; training services; and other business, professional, and technical services. *Other business, professional, and technical services* consists of language translation services, security services, collection services, actuarial services, salvage services, satellite photography services, oil spill and toxic waste clean-up services, and merchanting (purchase and resale of goods to unaffiliated foreign persons) services.

DATA AVAILABILITY

The most recent data are published in the October 2000 *Survey of Current Business*. Data are also available on the BEA web site, or may be purchased on diskette.

Table B-2. U.S. Export and Import Price Indexes for Selected Categories of Services, 1991–1999

The Bureau of Labor Statistics calculates price indexes for selected categories of internationally traded services. The price measures are aggregated using 1995 U.S. trade values as weights.

Table B-3. U.S. Private Service Transactions by Region and Country, 1986–1999

DATA NOTES

The *European Union* comprises Belgium, Denmark, France, Germany, Greece, Ireland, Italy, Luxembourg, Netherlands, Portugal, Spain, United Kingdom, Austria, Finland, and Sweden. The last three countries joined the Union on January 1, 1995. The European Union totals prior to 1995 do not include these three countries. Note that the European Union is not the same as the euro currency area.

Eastern Europe comprises Albania, Armenia, Azerbaijan, Belarus, Bulgaria, Czech Republic, Estonia, Georgia, Hungary, Kazakhstan, Kyrgyzstan, Latvia, Lithuania, Moldova, Poland, Romania, Russia, Slovakia, Tajikistan, Turkmenistan, Ukraine, and Uzbekistan.

Table B-4: U.S. Travel, Passenger Fare, and Other Transportation Receipts, 1996–1999

Table B-5: U.S. Travel, Passenger Fare, and Other Transportation Payments, 1996–1999

DATA NOTES

Other port services receipts and payments for Canada are shown below, in millions of dollars:

OTHER PORT SERVICES RECEIPTS AND PAYMENTS, CANADA, 1996–1999

(Millions of dollars)

Year	Receipts	Payments
1996	160	82
1997	154	84
1998	160	86
1999	167	98

Table B-6. U.S. Royalty and License Fee Receipts, 1996–1999

Table B-7. U.S. Royalty and License Fee Payments, 1996–1999

DATA NOTES

Other unaffiliated receipts and payments are shown below for the rights to distribute, use, and reproduce computer software in billions of dollars:

OTHER UNAFFILIATED RECEIPTS AND PAYMENTS, 1996–1999

(Millions of dollars)

Year	Receipts	Payments
1996	...	...
1997	2.7	0.5
1998	3.1	0.5
1999	3.7	0.5

Table B-12. U.S. Business, Professional, and Technical Service Receipts, 1996–1999

Table B-13. U.S. Business, Professional, and Technical Service Payments, 1996–1999

DATA NOTES

Receipts for engineering, architectural, construction, and mining services are published net of merchandise exports, which are included in merchandise trade in the U.S. international transactions accounts, and net of outlays abroad for wages, services, materials, and other expenses. Gross receipts and the deductions taken to arrive at net receipts are shown below for 1996–1999.

Payments for engineering, architectural, construction, and mining services are not published net of merchandise imports and outlays for wages and other expenses. Data are not collected for merchandise imports and wages and other expenses, and no estimates are made because they are believed to be small.

Other receipts and payments consists of accounting, auditing, and bookkeeping services, agricultural services, mailing, reproduction, and commercial art, management of health care facilities, medical services, miscellaneous disbursements, operational leasing, personnel supply services, sports and performing arts, training services, and other business, professional, and technical services. *Other business, professional, and technical services* consists of language translation services, security services, collection services, actuarial services, salvage services, satellite photography services, oil spill and toxic waste clean-up services, and merchanting services.

ENGINEERING, ARCHITECTURAL, CONSTRUCTION, AND MINING SERVICE RECEIPTS, 1996–1999

(Millions of dollars)

Year	Gross operating revenue	Merchandise exports	Foreign expenses	Net receipts
1996	6521	1535	1433	3553
1997	7319	1958	1858	3503
1998	8654	1861	3244	3548
1999	8724	1330	3322	4071

Table B-1. U.S. Private Service Transactions by Type, 1986–1999

(Millions of dollars.)

Type of service	Exports						
	1986	1987	1988	1989	1990	1991	1992
TOTAL PRIVATE SERVICES	77 545	87 030	100 971	117 935	137 232	152 437	163 688
Travel	20 385	23 563	29 434	36 205	43 007	48 385	54 742
Overseas	15 650	18 044	22 313	26 938	30 807	34 518	40 864
Canada	2 701	3 309	4 150	5 340	7 093	8 500	8 182
Mexico	2 034	2 210	2 971	3 927	5 107	5 367	5 696
Passenger Fares	5 582	7 003	8 976	10 657	15 298	15 854	16 618
Other Transportation	15 438	17 027	19 311	20 526	22 042	22 631	21 531
Freight	4 864	5 452	6 491	7 209	8 379	8 651	8 441
Port services	10 574	11 575	12 820	13 318	13 662	13 979	13 088
Royalties And License Fees	8 113	10 174	12 139	13 818	16 634	17 819	20 841
Affiliated	6 174	7 888	9 493	10 961	13 250	14 106	15 659
U.S. parents transactions	5 994	7 668	9 238	10 612	12 867	13 523	14 925
U.S. affiliates transactions	180	220	256	349	383	583	733
Unaffiliated	1 939	2 286	2 646	2 857	3 384	3 712	5 183
Industrial processes	. . .	1 593	1 863	1 947	2 333	2 435	2 525
Other	. . .	694	782	910	1 052	1 277	2 657
Other Private Services	28 027	29 263	31 111	36 729	40 251	47 748	49 956
Affiliated services	8 385	8 494	9 568	12 295	13 622	14 538	16 823
U.S. parents transactions	5 577	5 658	6 808	9 117	9 532	9 975	10 479
U.S. affiliates transactions	2 808	2 836	2 760	3 179	4 090	4 563	6 344
Unaffiliated services	19 641	20 769	21 544	24 433	26 629	33 210	33 134
Education	3 495	3 821	4 142	4 575	5 126	5 679	6 186
Financial services	3 301	3 731	3 831	5 036	4 417	5 012	4 034
Insurance, net	1 385	1 573	847	103	230	491	682
Premiums	3 424	3 615	3 534	3 117	3 388	3 365	3 852
Losses	2 039	2 042	2 687	3 015	3 158	2 874	3 170
Telecommunications	1 827	2 111	2 196	2 519	2 735	3 291	2 885
Business, professional, and technical services	4 813	4 765	5 970	6 823	7 752	12 045	11 722
Accounting, auditing, and bookkeeping services	21	27	37	124	119	168	164
Advertising	94	109	145	145	130	274	315
Agricultural services	4	7	4	3	4	56	54
Computer and data processing services	985	649	1 198	978	1 031	1 738	776
Construction, engineering, architectural, and mining services	759	668	790	939	867	1 478	1 935
Data base and other information services	124	133	196	205	283	442	641
Industrial engineering	98	304	278	219	473	363	212
Installation, maintenance, and repair of equipment	1 033	1 087	1 276	1 717	2 031	2 574	2 744
Legal services	97	147	272	397	451	1 309	1 358
Mailing, reproduction, and commercial art	(D)	22	29	9	8	18	14
Management of health care facilities	1	. . .	(*)	. . .	. . .	22	22
Management, consulting, and public relations services	306	327	344	300	354	870	728
Medical services	490	516	541	588	630	672	708
Miscellaneous disbursements	. . .	. . .	. . .	. . .	. . .	89	97
Operational leasing	384	484	544	671	801	796	854
Personnel supply services	(D)	38	(D)	2	1	160	127
Research, development, and testing services	282	177	231	375	384	602	611
Sports and performing arts	32	11	(D)	43	47	71	43
Training services	73	60	54	109	138	345	320
Other business, professional, and technical services [1]	. . .	. . .	. . .	. . .	. . .	. . .	. . .
Other unaffiliated services [2]	4 821	4 769	4 558	5 378	6 369	6 693	7 625

See footnotes at end of table.

Table B-1. U.S. Private Service Transactions by Type, 1986–1999—Continued

(Millions of dollars.)

Type of service	Exports—Continued						
	1993	1994	1995	1996	1997	1998	1999
TOTAL PRIVATE SERVICES	171 588	187 357	203 768	222 633	239 444	244 099	254 665
Travel	57 875	58 417	63 395	69 809	73 426	71 286	74 881
Overseas	45 298	47 299	54 331	59 963	63 041	61 262	64 099
Canada	7 458	6 252	6 207	6 842	6 945	6 206	6 670
Mexico	5 119	4 866	2 857	3 004	3 440	3 818	4 112
Passenger Fares	16 528	16 997	18 909	20 422	20 868	20 098	19 776
Other Transportation	21 958	23 754	26 081	26 074	27 006	25 604	27 033
Freight	8 594	9 575	11 273	11 146	11 789	11 048	11 667
Port services	13 364	14 180	14 809	14 929	15 217	14 557	15 365
Royalties And License Fees	21 695	26 712	30 289	32 470	33 639	36 197	36 467
Affiliated	15 688	20 275	22 859	24 556	24 876	26 809	26 307
U.S. parents transactions	14 936	19 250	21 399	22 719	23 091	24 720	24 576
U.S. affiliates transactions	752	1 025	1 460	1 837	1 785	2 089	1 731
Unaffiliated	6 007	6 437	7 430	7 914	8 763	9 388	10 160
Industrial processes	2 820	3 026	3 513	3 566	3 544	3 573	3 551
Other	3 187	3 411	3 917	4 348	5 219	5 814	6 609
Other Private Services	53 532	61 477	65 094	73 858	84 505	90 914	96 508
Affiliated services	16 813	19 825	20 483	22 931	27 253	28 397	28 943
U.S. parents transactions	10 902	13 313	13 033	14 118	17 288	18 232	18 111
U.S. affiliates transactions	5 911	6 512	7 450	8 813	9 965	10 165	10 832
Unaffiliated services	36 718	41 652	44 611	50 927	57 252	62 517	67 565
Education	6 738	7 174	7 515	7 887	8 346	9 037	9 572
Financial services	4 999	5 763	7 029	8 229	10 243	11 273	13 925
Insurance, net	1 020	1 676	1 296	2 168	2 473	2 189	2 295
Premiums	3 981	4 921	5 491	5 929	6 118	7 265	8 259
Losses	2 961	3 245	4 195	3 761	3 645	5 076	5 964
Telecommunications	2 785	2 865	3 228	3 301	3 918	5 538	4 460
Business, professional, and technical services	12 958	15 330	16 078	19 466	21 450	22 175	24 368
Accounting, auditing, and bookkeeping services	164	132	181	222	316	353	440
Advertising	338	487	425	543	607	488	414
Agricultural services	47	30	30	19	23	22	25
Computer and data processing services	986	1 306	1 340	1 617	2 011	1 922	2 291
Construction, engineering, architectural, and mining services	2 407	2 474	2 550	3 553	3 503	3 548	4 071
Data base and other information services	694	1 026	1 078	1 158	1 479	1 524	1 741
Industrial engineering	268	575	726	870	1 186	1 316	1 492
Installation, maintenance, and repair of equipment	2 978	3 497	3 218	3 648	3 272	3 212	3 487
Legal services	1 442	1 617	1 667	1 943	2 223	2 419	2 560
Mailing, reproduction, and commercial art	12	10	4	33	17	15	23
Management of health care facilities	19	18	18	18	23	23	26
Management, consulting, and public relations services	826	1 134	1 489	1 460	1 632	1 841	1 910
Medical services	750	794	856	1 005	1 113	1 204	1 302
Miscellaneous disbursements	222	222	251	333	144	146	195
Operational leasing	834	925	978	1 482	2 012	2 366	2 606
Personnel supply services	113	85	95	99	92	106	102
Research, development, and testing services	464	522	638	681	893	833	767
Sports and performing arts	77	86	116	149	149	104	98
Training services	319	388	421	388	447	419	408
Other business, professional, and technical services [1]	. . .	. . .	. . .	246	308	313	408
Other unaffiliated services [2]	8 220	8 845	9 465	9 874	10 821	12 305	12 946

See footnotes at end of table.

Table B-1. U.S. Private Service Transactions by Type, 1986–1999—Continued

(Millions of dollars.)

Type of service	Imports						
	1986	1987	1988	1989	1990	1991	1992
TOTAL PRIVATE SERVICES	64 731	73 945	81 002	85 295	98 210	99 934	100 379
Travel	25 913	29 310	32 114	33 416	37 349	35 322	38 552
Overseas	20 311	23 313	25 260	25 746	28 929	26 506	29 838
Canada	3 034	2 939	3 232	3 394	3 541	3 705	3 554
Mexico	2 568	3 058	3 622	4 276	4 879	5 111	5 160
Passenger Fares	6 505	7 283	7 729	8 249	10 531	10 012	10 603
Other Transportation	17 766	19 010	20 891	22 172	24 966	24 975	23 767
Freight	12 512	12 618	13 792	13 997	15 046	14 554	13 571
Port services	5 254	6 392	7 099	8 176	9 920	10 421	10 197
Royalties And License Fees	1 401	1 857	2 601	2 528	3 135	4 035	5 161
Affiliated	916	1 309	1 426	1 704	2 206	2 955	3 396
U.S. parents transactions	118	168	141	71	239	166	189
U.S. affiliates transactions	799	1 142	1 285	1 632	1 967	2 789	3 207
Unaffiliated	484	547	1 175	824	929	1 080	1 766
Industrial processes	...	435	488	568	666	796	818
Other	...	112	689	256	265	283	948
Other Private Services	13 146	16 485	17 667	18 930	22 229	25 590	22 296
Affiliated services	3 915	5 356	6 043	7 911	9 117	9 732	9 640
U.S. parents transactions	2 391	3 050	3 461	4 783	5 334	5 260	5 355
U.S. affiliates transactions	1 524	2 307	2 582	3 128	3 784	4 472	4 285
Unaffiliated services	9 231	11 129	11 624	11 019	13 111	15 859	12 656
Education	433	452	539	586	658	698	767
Financial services	1 769	2 077	1 656	2 056	2 475	2 669	986
Insurance, net	2 200	3 241	2 628	823	1 910	2 467	1 324
Premiums	7 217	8 538	8 954	9 909	10 222	11 207	11 738
Losses	5 017	5 297	6 326	9 086	8 312	8 740	10 414
Telecommunications	3 253	3 736	4 576	5 172	5 583	6 608	6 052
Business, professional, and technical services	1 303	1 367	1 926	2 059	2 093	3 015	3 102
Accounting, auditing, and bookkeeping services	29	37	31	22	57	89	104
Advertising	77	128	188	228	243	301	450
Agricultural services	5	7	4	2	(*)	22	21
Computer and data processing services	32	74	107	46	44	116	71
Construction, engineering, architectural, and mining services	301	163	307	443	170	315	261
Data base and other information services	23	25	39	31	54	51	72
Industrial engineering	75	103	133	53	74	30	112
Installation, maintenance, and repair of equipment	467	496	616	704	714	538	191
Legal services	40	56	98	81	111	244	311
Mailing, reproduction, and commercial art	12	9	9	8	8	38	37
Management of health care facilities	(*)	...	2	(*)	(*)	13	13
Management, consulting, and public relations services	60	67	73	143	135	271	243
Medical services	...	...	...	...	...	...	...
Miscellaneous disbursements	...	...	...	...	...	342	395
Operational leasing	50	48	78	88	202	229	337
Personnel supply services	25	7	10	10	5	15	14
Research, development, and testing services	76	114	182	133	210	241	225
Sports and performing arts	21	25	40	54	48	84	145
Training services	7	9	10	13	17	77	101
Other business, professional, and technical services [1]	...	...	...	...	...	...	...
Other unaffiliated services [2]	272	255	298	323	392	402	425

See footnotes at end of table.

Table B-1. U.S. Private Service Transactions by Type, 1986–1999—*Continued*

(Millions of dollars.)

Type of service	Imports—Continued						
	1993	1994	1995	1996	1997	1998	1999
TOTAL PRIVATE SERVICES	107 940	119 101	128 781	137 102	152 042	167 607	174 825
Travel	40 713	43 782	44 916	48 078	52 051	56 509	59 351
Overseas	31 859	34 534	35 281	37 436	40 667	44 395	47 142
Canada	3 692	3 914	4 319	4 670	4 904	5 718	6 135
Mexico	5 162	5 334	5 316	5 972	6 480	6 396	6 074
Passenger Fares	11 410	13 062	14 663	15 809	18 138	19 971	21 405
Other Transportation	24 524	26 019	27 034	27 403	28 959	30 363	34 137
Freight	14 518	16 006	16 455	16 539	17 654	19 412	22 214
Port services	10 005	10 013	10 579	10 864	11 305	10 950	11 925
Royalties And License Fees	5 032	5 852	6 919	7 837	9 614	11 713	13 275
Affiliated	3 386	3 933	5 256	5 406	7 202	8 754	10 208
U.S. parents transactions	234	420	583	761	1 379	1 755	2 134
U.S. affiliates transactions	3 152	3 513	4 673	4 645	5 823	6 999	8 074
Unaffiliated	1 646	1 919	1 663	2 431	2 412	2 959	3 067
Industrial processes	1 054	1 034	948	1 319	1 417	1 536	1 883
Other	592	884	714	1 112	995	1 423	1 185
Other Private Services	26 261	30 386	35 249	37 975	43 280	49 051	46 657
Affiliated services	10 677	12 451	13 634	15 548	17 817	19 756	22 437
U.S. parents transactions	5 721	6 538	6 861	7 084	9 012	10 406	11 427
U.S. affiliates transactions	4 956	5 913	6 773	8 464	8 805	9 350	11 010
Unaffiliated services	15 585	17 935	21 615	22 427	25 463	29 295	24 220
Education	857	972	1 125	1 253	1 396	1 591	1 840
Financial services	1 371	1 654	2 472	2 907	3 347	3 561	3 574
Insurance, net	3 095	4 034	5 360	3 885	5 873	9 080	4 078
Premiums	12 093	14 075	15 284	14 522	15 211	20 290	21 242
Losses	8 998	10 041	9 925	10 637	9 338	11 210	17 164
Telecommunications	6 365	6 928	7 305	8 290	8 346	7 687	6 766
Business, professional, and technical services	3 504	3 869	4 822	5 547	6 047	6 869	7 430
Accounting, auditing, and bookkeeping services	103	130	170	218	279	318	531
Advertising	646	728	833	971	773	886	757
Agricultural services	18	14	17	11	9	8	9
Computer and data processing services	101	83	126	276	276	399	432
Construction, engineering, architectural, and mining services	319	280	345	465	463	544	530
Data base and other information services	110	141	160	146	128	151	198
Industrial engineering	142	100	160	197	211	205	141
Installation, maintenance, and repair of equipment	175	164	160	239	307	310	302
Legal services	321	383	469	615	539	637	844
Mailing, reproduction, and commercial art	33	17	22	42	30	30	32
Management of health care facilities	11	12	16	8	10	10	10
Management, consulting, and public relations services	287	321	465	497	687	888	867
Medical services	...	...	...	...	...	...	...
Miscellaneous disbursements	371	538	843	750	1 075	1 139	1 257
Operational leasing	356	401	407	325	189	174	162
Personnel supply services	13	3	4	28	18	18	20
Research, development, and testing services	239	294	364	379	564	667	782
Sports and performing arts	156	122	120	200	260	240	270
Training services	101	137	145	140	153	165	175
Other business, professional, and technical services [1]	...	...	...	40	75	79	111
Other unaffiliated services [2]	394	477	532	546	453	507	532

1. Other business, professional, and technical services consists of language translation services, security services, collection services, actuarial services, oil spill and toxic waste cleanup services, and merchanting services.
2. Exports include mainly film and tape rentals and expenditures of foreign governments and international organizations in the United States. Imports include mainly expenditures of U.S. residents temporarily working abroad and film and tape rentals.

Table B-2. U.S. Export and Import Price Indexes for Selected Categories of Services, 1991–1999

(1995=100, unless otherwise indicated; annual data are averages of March, June, September, and December.)

Category	1991	1992	1993	1994	1995	1996	1997	1998	1999
EXPORTS									
Air Freight (December 1996=100)	...	...	...	...	...	...	96.6	95.4	89.6
Air Passenger Fares	88.3	90.7	92.5	94.8	100.0	100.0	96.2	95.7	103.1
Atlantic	90.9	93.2	90.0	91.4	100.0	105.6	104.8	109.2	108.8
Europe	...	...	...	91.5	100.0	105.9	105.2	110.1	109.7
Pacific	85.8	88.4	94.5	96.2	100.0	93.3	82.8	78.9	87.8
Asia	...	...	...	96.7	100.0	90.0	77.4	75.5	84.3
Japan	...	...	...	96.5	100.0	87.3	78.5	76.2	86.7
Latin American and Caribbean	88.6	93.6	95.0	99.1	100.0	100.9	105.7	110.7	114.6
IMPORTS									
Air Freight	87.9	87.0	88.7	92.8	100.0	97.0	88.9	82.3	87.3
Atlantic	102.6	100.3	89.4	91.8	100.0	98.0	89.5	88.2	85.6
Pacific	79.0	78.8	86.6	92.1	100.0	97.1	89.6	77.9	89.6
Air Passenger Fares	93.3	95.7	94.3	94.9	100.0	101.2	107.4	108.5	111.4
Atlantic	96.3	97.8	93.8	93.7	100.0	101.6	111.0	108.4	114.1
Europe (December 1996=100)	...	...	...	...	...	...	113.6	110.0	116.3
United Kingdom (December 1996=100)	...	...	...	...	...	...	103.0	97.9	103.3
Pacific	90.9	90.0	94.3	96.1	100.0	97.1	104.1	102.0	100.7
Asia (December 1996=100)	...	...	...	...	...	...	108.7	105.4	104.9
Latin American and Caribbean	85.5	95.2	96.4	98.1	100.0	103.3	105.6	107.9	110.9
Caribbean (December 1996=100)	...	...	...	...	...	...	100.7	101.3	101.1
Crude Oil Tanker Freight	88.2	79.9	87.9	74.4	100.0	96.0	97.3	84.5	72.1
Gulf	90.9	76.6	80.9	67.2	100.0	91.5	89.8	76.1	61.3
Ocean Liner Freight	92.4	92.1	92.1	94.0	100.0	100.0	96.0	99.0	121.7
U.S. East Coast	89.5	86.8	90.5	92.6	100.0	102.0	99.0	98.8	106.1
From Atlantic	84.9	80.6	86.8	92.7	100.0	103.5	98.8	97.2	96.6
From Pacific	90.5	92.2	91.8	91.4	100.0	100.4	98.2	100.6	119.6
U.S. West Coast	94.9	97.2	93.8	95.3	100.0	98.1	93.1	98.6	133.0

Table B-3. U.S. Private Service Transactions by Region and Country, 1986–1999

(Millions of dollars.)

Country or region	Exports						
	1986	1987	1988	1989	1990	1991	1992
ALL COUNTRIES	77 545	87 030	100 971	117 935	137 232	152 437	163 688
Canada	8 465	9 371	10 703	13 323	15 684	17 750	17 380
Mexico	4 531	4 445	4 911	4 822	8 590	9 666	10 492
Europe	24 896	30 259	35 754	41 593	48 192	53 570	60 182
Belgium and Luxembourg	1 027	1 025	1 209	1 475	1 763	1 946	2 308
France	2 912	3 648	3 885	4 642	5 542	6 168	6 998
Germany [1]	4 001	5 196	5 881	6 134	7 364	8 825	10 867
Italy	1 852	2 143	2 452	2 676	3 279	3 680	4 496
Netherlands	1 938	2 106	2 456	2 579	3 269	3 576	3 747
Norway	...	...	...	...	...	...	1 118
Spain	...	...	...	...	...	...	2 443
Sweden	...	...	...	...	...	...	1 756
Switzerland	...	...	...	...	...	...	2 894
United Kingdom	6 502	8 389	10 105	12 448	12 989	14 091	15 726
Other	...	...	...	...	...	...	7 834
Latin America And Other Western Hemisphere [2]	14 206	14 398	15 669	17 842	21 957	24 842	26 722
South and Central America [2]	11 472	11 744	13 027	15 142	18 447	21 174	23 228
Argentina	...	...	...	...	...	...	1 797
Brazil	...	...	...	...	...	...	2 499
Chile	...	...	...	...	...	...	620
Venezuela	937	829	914	1 027	1 273	1 563	1 993
Other	...	...	...	...	...	...	5 832
Other Western Hemisphere	2 740	2 652	2 642	2 699	3 509	3 667	3 494
Bermuda	...	...	...	...	...	...	414
Other	...	...	...	...	...	...	3 077
Africa, Middle East, And Asia And Pacific	25 602	28 258	33 335	39 327	45 321	51 167	54 855
Africa	...	...	...	...	...	...	2 234
South Africa	...	...	...	...	...	...	465
Other	...	...	...	...	...	...	1 771
Middle East	...	...	...	...	...	...	3 965
Israel	...	...	...	...	...	...	896
Saudi Arabia	...	...	...	...	...	...	1 356
Other	...	...	...	...	...	...	1 713
Asia And Pacific	...	...	...	...	...	...	48 656
Australia	1 593	1 842	2 311	2 825	3 260	3 214	3 459
China	...	...	...	...	...	...	1 568
Hong Kong	...	...	...	...	...	...	2 259
India	...	...	...	...	...	...	1 094
Indonesia	...	...	...	...	...	...	775
Japan	10 273	12 376	14 827	18 363	21 159	23 981	25 554
Malaysia	...	...	...	...	...	...	601
New Zealand	...	...	...	...	...	...	761
Philippines	...	...	...	...	...	...	968
Singapore	...	...	...	...	...	...	2 155
South Korea	...	...	...	...	...	...	3 375
Taiwan	...	...	...	...	...	...	3 173
Thailand	...	...	...	...	...	...	750
Other	...	...	...	...	...	...	2 160
International Organizations And Unallocated	4 376	4 745	5 510	5 850	6 077	5 109	4 548
European Union	20 752	25 259	29 447	34 307	39 149	44 150	51 140
Eastern Europe	283	298	403	686	956	1 140	1 163

See footnotes at end of table.

Table B-3. U.S. Private Service Transactions by Region and Country, 1986–1999—*Continued*

(Millions of dollars.)

Country or region	Exports—*Continued*						
	1993	1994	1995	1996	1997	1998	1999
ALL COUNTRIES	171 588	187 357	203 768	222 633	239 444	244 099	254 665
Canada	16 971	17 216	17 927	19 492	20 505	19 156	21 134
Mexico	10 440	11 344	8 705	9 442	10 789	11 706	12 544
Europe	62 138	67 473	73 092	81 274	86 497	93 864	96 193
Belgium and Luxembourg	2 207	2 782	2 843	2 882	2 861	3 005	3 050
France	6 816	6 694	7 965	8 862	9 400	9 657	9 821
Germany [1]	11 346	11 573	12 692	13 370	14 018	14 912	15 326
Italy	4 080	4 264	4 533	4 858	4 992	5 499	5 300
Netherlands	4 109	5 476	6 119	7 012	7 271	7 705	8 396
Norway	1 241	1 157	1 210	1 401	1 391	1 378	1 341
Spain	2 246	2 678	2 991	3 098	3 432	3 506	3 812
Sweden	1 728	1 747	1 890	2 474	2 385	2 599	2 312
Switzerland	2 922	3 695	3 843	4 294	4 331	4 915	4 708
United Kingdom	17 163	17 848	18 625	20 204	23 829	26 559	27 224
Other	8 276	9 558	10 381	12 819	12 588	14 129	14 903
Latin America And Other Western Hemisphere [2]	29 126	32 740	32 872	35 736	42 511	47 094	49 795
South and Central America [2]	25 219	27 931	27 639	29 826	35 064	38 320	38 709
Argentina	2 147	2 482	2 403	2 759	3 347	3 581	3 569
Brazil	2 949	3 737	4 997	5 205	6 404	6 618	5 494
Chile	777	1 156	991	1 189	1 421	1 334	1 437
Venezuela	2 428	2 145	2 496	2 409	2 695	3 074	3 260
Other	6 480	7 070	8 049	8 820	10 410	12 007	12 404
Other Western Hemisphere	3 904	4 809	5 234	5 910	7 447	8 776	11 086
Bermuda	533	755	606	849	903	1 056	1 190
Other	3 371	4 056	4 628	5 062	6 544	7 719	9 894
Africa, Middle East, And Asia And Pacific	58 604	64 937	74 508	80 154	84 223	77 800	81 547
Africa	2 328	2 579	2 869	3 036	3 484	4 372	4 660
South Africa	494	625	801	843	1 004	1 056	1 238
Other	1 835	1 954	2 069	2 195	2 481	3 317	3 422
Middle East	4 147	5 052	5 796	6 681	6 844	7 201	7 350
Israel	1 106	1 484	1 637	1 899	1 918	2 050	2 167
Saudi Arabia	1 239	1 864	2 084	1 689	1 911	1 970	1 986
Other	1 802	1 702	2 074	3 095	3 013	3 181	3 196
Asia And Pacific	52 130	57 306	65 843	70 437	73 895	66 226	69 536
Australia	3 558	3 791	4 266	4 510	4 901	4 724	5 021
China	1 919	2 049	2 531	3 164	3 579	3 966	3 932
Hong Kong	2 365	2 804	2 998	3 338	3 633	3 488	3 287
India	1 138	1 226	1 320	1 496	1 593	1 892	2 099
Indonesia	893	874	1 157	1 415	1 770	1 459	1 506
Japan	26 794	28 952	33 240	33 535	34 249	29 887	30 498
Malaysia	680	892	1 032	1 278	1 257	1 044	1 120
New Zealand	794	835	996	1 177	1 252	1 130	1 183
Philippines	1 247	1 187	1 059	1 237	1 490	1 310	1 422
Singapore	2 414	2 646	3 148	3 854	4 103	3 844	4 150
South Korea	3 638	4 599	5 693	7 435	7 082	4 770	5 339
Taiwan	3 466	4 168	4 429	4 048	4 735	4 004	4 860
Thailand	1 016	1 020	1 188	1 216	1 243	1 159	1 112
Other	2 205	2 267	2 786	2 734	3 005	3 549	4 006
International Organizations And Unallocated	4 750	4 990	5 365	5 971	5 707	6 187	5 997
European Union	52 374	56 013	63 938	70 372	75 309	81 950	84 659
Eastern Europe	1 673	2 183	2 580	3 283	3 398	3 630	3 588

See footnotes at end of table.

Table B-3. U.S. Private Service Transactions by Region and Country, 1986–1999—*Continued*

(Millions of dollars.)

Country or region	Imports						
	1986	1987	1988	1989	1990	1991	1992
ALL COUNTRIES	64 731	73 945	81 002	85 295	98 210	99 934	100 379
Canada	6 311	6 854	8 350	8 640	9 130	9 716	8 688
Mexico	3 681	4 506	5 068	5 976	6 731	7 056	7 269
Europe	24 132	28 313	30 866	33 010	39 815	39 262	39 718
Belgium and Luxembourg	604	556	622	813	1 022	958	1 028
France	2 264	2 679	2 931	3 517	4 169	3 927	4 581
Germany [1]	3 982	5 198	5 540	6 048	6 819	6 438	6 376
Italy	2 258	2 509	2 870	2 863	3 469	3 299	3 177
Netherlands	1 032	1 305	1 317	1 609	1 935	2 157	2 479
Norway	...	...	...	...	...	...	1 034
Spain	...	...	...	...	...	...	1 271
Sweden	...	...	...	...	...	...	779
Switzerland	...	...	...	...	...	...	1 710
United Kingdom	7 542	8 918	9 411	9 795	11 564	12 111	10 538
Other	...	...	...	...	...	...	6 746
Latin America And Other Western Hemisphere [2]	13 010	14 964	15 648	16 840	18 643	19 602	20 127
South and Central America [2]	7 522	9 074	10 241	11 180	12 737	13 254	13 439
Argentina	...	...	...	...	...	...	449
Brazil	...	...	...	...	...	...	679
Chile	...	...	...	...	...	...	332
Venezuela	480	526	619	487	659	584	633
Other	...	...	...	...	...	...	4 077
Other Western Hemisphere	5 488	5 892	5 407	5 659	5 905	6 348	6 690
Bermuda	...	...	...	...	...	...	1 522
Other	...	...	...	...	...	...	5 167
Africa, Middle East, And Asia And Pacific	19 371	21 999	23 617	24 232	27 976	29 285	29 120
Africa	...	...	...	...	...	...	1 472
South Africa	...	...	...	...	...	...	199
Other	...	...	...	...	...	...	1 276
Middle East	...	...	...	...	...	...	2 053
Israel	...	...	...	...	...	...	1 016
Saudi Arabia	...	...	...	...	...	...	337
Other	...	...	...	...	...	...	698
Asia And Pacific	...	...	...	...	...	...	25 595
Australia	1 163	1 495	1 644	1 748	2 290	2 386	2 215
China	...	...	...	...	...	...	1 044
Hong Kong	...	...	...	...	...	...	1 420
India	...	...	...	...	...	...	636
Indonesia	...	...	...	...	...	...	440
Japan	6 662	7 527	8 396	8 927	10 529	11 772	10 607
Malaysia	...	...	...	...	...	...	265
New Zealand	...	...	...	...	...	...	525
Philippines	...	...	...	...	...	...	785
Singapore	...	...	...	...	...	...	684
South Korea	...	...	...	...	...	...	2 041
Taiwan	...	...	...	...	...	...	1 978
Thailand	...	...	...	...	...	...	389
Other	...	...	...	...	...	...	2 569
International Organizations And Unallocated	1 907	1 815	2 521	2 573	2 646	2 069	2 726
European Union	20 412	23 961	25 813	28 057	33 394	32 924	32 960
Eastern Europe	345	477	508	582	797	1 052	1 596

See footnotes at end of table.

Table B-3. U.S. Private Service Transactions by Region and Country, 1986–1999—*Continued*

(Millions of dollars.)

Country or region	Imports—*Continued*						
	1993	1994	1995	1996	1997	1998	1999
ALL COUNTRIES	107 940	119 101	128 781	137 102	152 042	167 607	174 825
Canada	9 223	10 132	11 160	12 451	13 544	15 128	15 222
Mexico	7 410	7 849	7 930	8 918	9 838	9 870	9 783
Europe	44 417	48 996	52 708	53 856	61 606	70 812	72 079
Belgium and Luxembourg	1 048	1 245	1 480	1 498	1 733	1 917	1 997
France	4 958	5 749	5 951	6 023	6 770	7 598	8 027
Germany [1]	6 806	7 280	7 586	7 705	7 963	9 810	10 179
Italy	3 142	3 433	3 743	3 492	3 672	4 145	4 743
Netherlands	2 211	2 613	3 191	3 157	3 455	4 462	3 992
Norway	1 414	1 184	1 162	1 281	1 287	805	813
Spain	1 081	1 140	1 109	1 304	1 457	1 882	2 174
Sweden	942	857	844	884	872	840	965
Switzerland	1 945	2 317	2 285	2 636	2 768	3 809	3 670
United Kingdom	13 634	14 692	16 063	16 186	21 355	23 206	23 750
Other	7 237	8 486	9 293	9 690	10 276	12 343	11 771
Latin America And Other Western Hemisphere [2]	20 588	22 783	24 252	26 954	29 840	32 367	32 346
South and Central America [2]	13 582	14 850	15 500	17 711	19 158	19 795	20 124
Argentina	464	572	572	779	864	938	922
Brazil	734	904	1 165	1 421	1 765	1 803	1 765
Chile	362	415	427	519	526	809	777
Venezuela	714	761	701	767	708	709	718
Other	3 899	4 352	4 708	5 308	5 457	5 666	6 162
Other Western Hemisphere	7 005	7 933	8 750	9 244	10 682	12 571	12 222
Bermuda	1 278	1 832	2 713	2 867	3 652	4 653	5 065
Other	5 727	6 100	6 036	6 377	7 029	7 917	7 156
Africa, Middle East, And Asia And Pacific	31 789	35 300	38 542	41 580	45 130	46 763	53 191
Africa	1 527	1 911	1 947	2 380	2 550	2 540	2 699
South Africa	228	294	398	543	725	855	866
Other	1 298	1 616	1 548	1 837	1 827	1 683	1 834
Middle East	2 172	2 240	2 663	3 152	3 225	3 660	4 030
Israel	1 068	1 192	1 171	1 369	1 505	1 427	1 652
Saudi Arabia	339	307	559	437	576	855	951
Other	764	740	936	1 346	1 143	1 377	1 428
Asia And Pacific	28 090	31 148	33 933	36 048	39 356	40 562	46 462
Australia	2 163	1 929	2 142	2 573	2 677	3 286	3 478
China	1 303	1 459	1 674	1 936	2 205	2 279	2 666
Hong Kong	1 336	1 881	1 901	2 920	3 042	3 249	3 809
India	687	760	851	1 093	1 223	1 532	1 516
Indonesia	428	438	443	550	548	305	338
Japan	11 785	12 584	13 463	12 907	14 053	13 522	15 692
Malaysia	299	355	451	456	532	377	375
New Zealand	538	567	601	661	697	897	1 121
Philippines	851	1 036	1 121	1 361	1 456	1 265	1 246
Singapore	938	1 155	1 232	1 817	2 094	1 852	2 181
South Korea	2 343	2 796	3 581	4 124	4 530	4 157	4 458
Taiwan	2 381	2 649	2 856	2 702	3 371	2 930	3 514
Thailand	377	475	677	802	758	794	920
Other	2 659	3 062	2 944	2 148	2 163	4 119	5 151
International Organizations And Unallocated	1 926	1 889	2 119	2 266	1 921	2 538	1 986
European Union	36 680	40 238	45 301	45 486	52 929	60 658	62 478
Eastern Europe	1 513	1 965	2 171	2 346	2 148	2 558	2 471

1. Prior to 1990, data are only for the Federal Republic of Germany. Beginning in 1990, data also include the former German Democratic Republic.
2. Includes Mexico.

Table B-4. U.S. Travel, Passenger Fare, and Other Transportation Receipts, 1996–1999

(Millions of dollars.)

Country or region	Travel				Passenger fares			
	1996	1997	1998	1999	1996	1997	1998	1999
ALL COUNTRIES	69 809	73 426	71 286	74 881	20 422	20 868	20 098	19 776
Canada	6 900	6 945	6 206	6 670	1 339	1 361	1 478	1 540
Mexico	3 004	3 438	3 818	4 112	761	859	958	952
Europe	23 171	23 314	24 112	25 581	6 867	6 822	7 024	7 093
Belgium and Luxembourg	557	514	487	562	294	294	262	232
France	2 327	2 496	2 348	2 330	954	932	993	1 002
Germany	4 403	4 146	4 155	4 398	1 714	1 370	1 341	1 287
Italy	1 691	1 647	1 907	1 691	461	613	651	517
Netherlands	1 141	972	922	1 216	222	188	217	352
Norway	336	405	428	439	1	. . .	1	82
Spain	831	964	961	1 043	366	339	386	310
Sweden	635	665	675	674	234	183	263	259
Switzerland	1 363	1 124	1 146	1 252	353	219	180	169
United Kingdom	6 450	7 102	7 600	8 398	1 805	2 199	2 258	2 535
Other	3 437	3 279	3 483	3 578	463	485	472	348
Latin America And Other Western Hemisphere [1]	14 984	18 123	19 498	19 799	4 098	4 713	5 600	5 455
South and Central America [1]	12 888	15 453	16 810	16 748	3 601	4 162	4 901	4 662
Argentina	1 224	1 536	1 519	1 457	485	634	627	655
Brazil	2 588	3 021	2 753	2 034	839	841	1 071	837
Chile	489	549	552	540	164	193	181	159
Venezuela	1 401	1 440	1 592	1 697	203	291	323	275
Other	4 182	5 469	6 576	6 908	1 149	1 344	1 741	1 784
Other Western Hemisphere	2 096	2 670	2 688	3 051	497	551	699	793
Bermuda	14	16	18	17	4	7	7	9
Other	2 082	2 654	2 670	3 034	493	544	692	784
Africa	766	1 054	1 183	1 317	77	65	31	42
South Africa	285	370	386	386	7	. . .	. . .	. . .
Other	481	684	797	931	70	65	31	42
Middle East	1 979	2 316	2 403	2 686	425	509	626	398
Israel	694	822	809	866	264	290	412	281
Saudi Arabia	454	558	542	583	454	11	19	3
Other	831	936	1 052	1 237	161	208	195	114
Asia And Pacific	22 009	21 674	17 884	18 828	7 616	7 398	5 339	5 248
Australia	1 709	1 839	1 562	1 735	540	621	548	520
China	807	1 101	1 140	777	100	142	151	170
Hong Kong	624	741	746	698	380	471	383	267
India	544	634	779	861	42	50	57	34
Indonesia	337	392	179	248	19	24	109	168
Japan	11 790	11 068	9 424	9 711	5 790	5 442	3 616	3 585
Malaysia	262	268	172	206	262	. . .	. . .	11
New Zealand	608	616	488	542	121	108	79	90
Philippines	476	585	469	579	82	84	92	103
Singapore	377	383	299	349	49	77	64	55
South Korea	2 345	2 056	991	1 251	308	132	44	20
Taiwan	1 370	1 287	1 035	1 189	84	114	80	95
Thailand	421	349	209	260	3	15	21	35
Other	339	355	391	422	98	118	95	95
International Organizations And Unallocated	. . .	. . .	. . .	. . .	. . .	. . .	. . .	. . .
European Union	20 004	20 273	20 963	22 369	6 391	6 431	6 646	6 700
Eastern Europe	1 213	1 249	1 257	1 184	104	144	159	78

See footnotes at end of table.

Table B-4. U.S. Travel, Passenger Fare, and Other Transportation Receipts, 1996–1999—*Continued*

(Millions of dollars.)

Country or region	Other transportation							
	Total				Freight			
					Total			
	1996	1997	1998	1999	1996	1997	1998	1999
ALL COUNTRIES	26 074	27 006	25 604	27 033	11 146	11 789	11 046	11 667
Canada	2 394	2 414	2 317	2 479	1 816	1 905	1 856	1 967
Mexico	549	567	549	690	186	239	205	321
Europe	8 138	8 224	8 827	8 429	2 842	3 003	3 037	3 118
Belgium and Luxembourg	326	355	423	400	270	304	307	299
France	417	580	893	845	241	266	290	300
Germany	860	964	1 153	1 037	368	411	394	396
Italy	338	349	411	379	109	126	126	126
Netherlands	883	766	1 046	1 015	395	386	420	452
Norway	503	360	228	193	20	21	28	21
Spain	195	182	231	245	90	98	139	134
Sweden	308	300	220	199	45	59	69	63
Switzerland	311	228	278	266	40	64	61	61
United Kingdom	1 359	1 726	1 742	1 719	599	688	747	794
Other	2 638	2 414	2 202	2 131	665	580	456	472
Latin America And Other Western Hemisphere [1]	3 178	3 657	3 282	3 368	1 746	2 041	1 896	1 864
South and Central America [1]	2 598	3 103	2 909	2 933	1 504	1 817	1 719	1 687
Argentina	152	202	191	151	84	113	106	77
Brazil	290	623	542	480	217	330	287	240
Chile	158	196	153	210	50	62	54	56
Venezuela	159	201	192	159	116	165	155	116
Other	1 290	1 314	1 282	1 243	851	908	912	877
Other Western Hemisphere	580	554	373	435	242	224	177	177
Bermuda	4	4	8	5	4	4	8	5
Other	576	550	365	430	238	220	169	172
Africa	450	389	491	418	215	190	208	190
South Africa	84	132	77	97	18	16	18	21
Other	366	257	414	321	197	174	190	169
Middle East	1 073	1 023	1 016	1 093	634	507	527	576
Israel	481	287	297	398	348	162	172	275
Saudi Arabia	88	125	124	131	49	87	86	85
Other	504	611	595	564	237	258	269	216
Asia And Pacific	10 312	10 750	9 103	10 691	3 875	4 129	3 506	3 941
Australia	304	307	282	360	154	168	163	199
China	597	565	510	627	132	209	200	211
Hong Kong	459	509	463	512	389	432	447	490
India	156	167	132	144	126	140	107	110
Indonesia	86	91	63	88	41	50	60	81
Japan	3 190	3 230	2 819	3 089	1 329	1 290	1 048	1 144
Malaysia	174	162	142	170	109	126	106	125
New Zealand	130	178	187	191	30	25	20	24
Philippines	227	253	179	225	93	136	103	129
Singapore	626	684	456	641	220	272	221	335
South Korea	2 339	2 040	1 231	1 477	374	340	206	294
Taiwan	1 115	1 491	985	1 244	283	268	259	300
Thailand	127	142	123	118	95	96	73	64
Other	782	931	1 531	1 805	500	577	493	435
International Organizations And Unallocated	529	549	568	555	16	14	16	11
European Union	6 092	6 487	7 406	7 092	2 386	2 571	2 722	2 782
Eastern Europe	475	434	270	344	302	291	166	215

See footnotes at end of table.

Table B-4. U.S. Travel, Passenger Fare, and Other Transportation Receipts, 1996–1999—*Continued*

(Millions of dollars.)

Country or region	Other transportation—*Continued*											
	Freight—*Continued*											
	Ocean				Air				Other			
	1996	1997	1998	1999	1996	1997	1998	1999	1996	1997	1998	1999
ALL COUNTRIES	4 703	4 575	3 783	3 930	3 956	4 608	4 758	5 046	2 485	2 610	2 505	2 691
Canada	32	54	59	52	59	69	71	76	1 725	1 782	1 726	1 839
Mexico	96	96	48	51	86	95	104	213	4	48	53	57
Europe	1 522	1 455	1 361	1 311	1 226	1 443	1 578	1 699	94	105	98	108
Belgium and Luxembourg	204	226	222	210	61	72	79	83	5	6	6	6
France	59	54	52	51	176	205	231	242	6	7	7	7
Germany	132	156	135	133	223	240	245	248	13	15	14	15
Italy	40	51	47	42	64	70	75	79	5	5	4	5
Netherlands	281	253	269	284	83	99	119	133	31	34	32	35
Norway	16	14	16	9	4	7	12	12	. . .	. . .	. . .	. . .
Spain	47	52	76	74	43	46	63	60	. . .	. . .	. . .	. . .
Sweden	18	23	22	25	27	36	47	38	. . .	. . .	. . .	. . .
Switzerland	. . .	18	. . .	. . .	40	46	61	61	. . .	. . .	. . .	. . .
United Kingdom	188	182	203	174	401	494	534	608	10	12	10	12
Other	537	426	319	309	104	128	112	135	24	26	25	28
Latin America And Other Western Hemisphere [1]	661	725	479	448	799	1 013	1 125	1 100	286	307	292	316
South and Central America [1]	499	591	408	381	754	960	1 055	1 030	251	269	256	276
Argentina	25	49	28	12	59	64	78	65	. . .	. . .	. . .	. . .
Brazil	63	111	45	18	154	219	242	222	. . .	. . .	. . .	. . .
Chile	28	35	17	22	22	27	37	34	. . .	. . .	. . .	. . .
Venezuela	48	64	33	25	61	93	113	82	7	8	9	9
Other	239	236	237	253	372	462	481	414	240	213	194	210
Other Western Hemisphere	162	134	71	67	45	53	70	70	35	38	36	40
Bermuda	. . .	. . .	. . .	. . .	4	4	8	5	. . .	. . .	. . .	. . .
Other	162	134	71	67	41	49	62	65	35	38	36	40
Africa	182	152	155	143	26	29	34	28	7	9	19	19
South Africa	8	4	5	8	3	3	5	5	7	9	8	8
Other	174	148	150	135	23	26	29	23	. . .	. . .	11	11
Middle East	565	430	449	473	69	77	78	103	. . .	. . .	. . .	. . .
Israel	318	162	142	224	30	. . .	30	51	. . .	. . .	. . .	. . .
Saudi Arabia	. . .	57	68	72	. . .	30	18	13	. . .	. . .	. . .	. . .
Other	198	211	239	177	39	47	30	39	. . .	. . .	. . .	. . .
Asia And Pacific	1 725	1 745	1 264	1 492	1 777	1 977	1 872	2 040	373	407	370	409
Australia	14	4	8	17	99	119	113	134	41	45	42	48
China	76	120	115	118	56	89	85	93	. . .	. . .	. . .	. . .
Hong Kong	139	157	154	170	250	275	293	320	. . .	. . .	. . .	. . .
India	119	128	92	91	7	12	15	19	. . .	. . .	. . .	. . .
Indonesia	33	35	53	73	8	15	7	8	. . .	. . .	. . .	. . .
Japan	522	470	319	355	720	725	640	693	87	95	89	96
Malaysia	23	25	24	41	86	101	82	84	. . .	. . .	. . .	. . .
New Zealand	9	. . .	. . .	. . .	8	11	7	8	13	14	13	16
Philippines	61	61	36	56	32	75	67	73	. . .	. . .	. . .	. . .
Singapore	39	57	54	98	181	215	167	237	. . .	. . .	. . .	. . .
South Korea	238	231	146	178	136	109	60	116	. . .	. . .	. . .	. . .
Taiwan	183	101	104	109	100	167	155	191	. . .	. . .	. . .	. . .
Thailand	52	36	19	19	43	60	54	45	. . .	. . .	. . .	. . .
Other	217	320	140	167	51	4	127	19	232	253	226	249
International Organizations And Unallocated	16	14	16	11	. . .	. . .	. . .	. . .	. . .	. . .	. . .	. . .
European Union	1 156	1 132	1 167	1 091	1 148	1 350	1 471	1 599	82	89	84	92
Eastern Europe	265	249	124	178	27	32	32	25	10	10	10	12

See footnotes at end of table.

Table B-4. U.S. Travel, Passenger Fare, and Other Transportation Receipts, 1996–1999—*Continued*

(Millions of dollars.)

Country or region	Other transportation—*Continued*											
	Port services											
	Total [2]				Ocean				Air			
	1996	1997	1998	1999	1996	1997	1998	1999	1996	1997	1998	1999
ALL COUNTRIES	14 929	15 217	14 558	15 366	7 799	7 659	7 145	7 807	6 971	7 404	7 253	7 392
Canada	578	509	461	512	60	68	38	63	358	287	263	282
Mexico	363	328	344	369	88	75	86	109	275	253	258	260
Europe	5 296	5 221	5 790	5 311	2 880	2 901	2 693	2 342	2 416	2 320	3 097	2 969
Belgium and Luxembourg	56	51	116	101	19	24	46	37	37	27	70	64
France	176	314	603	545	6	23	27	22	170	291	576	523
Germany	492	553	759	641	393	460	587	484	99	93	172	157
Italy	229	223	285	253	89	102	66	54	140	121	219	199
Netherlands	488	380	626	563	68	61	73	61	420	319	553	502
Norway	483	339	200	172	483	339	200	172	...	...	...	...
Spain	105	84	92	111	...	...	2	2	105	84	90	109
Sweden	263	241	151	136	167	135	62	53	96	106	89	83
Switzerland	271	164	217	205	45	...	52	45	226	164	165	160
United Kingdom	760	1 038	995	925	135	312	217	118	625	726	778	807
Other	1 973	1 834	1 746	1 659	1 475	1 445	1 361	1 294	498	389	385	365
Latin America And Other Western Hemisphere [1]	1 432	1 616	1 386	1 504	395	347	237	339	1 037	1 269	1 149	1 165
South and Central America [1]	1 094	1 286	1 190	1 246	275	233	171	219	819	1 053	1 019	1 027
Argentina	68	89	85	74	2	2	...	...	66	87	85	74
Brazil	73	293	255	240	16	10	10	13	57	283	245	227
Chile	108	134	99	154	68	50	27	35	40	84	72	119
Venezuela	43	36	37	43	26	20	20	26	17	16	17	17
Other	439	406	370	366	75	76	28	36	364	330	342	330
Other Western Hemisphere	338	330	196	258	120	114	66	120	218	216	130	138
Bermuda	...	...	...	...	...	...	...	...	...	...	...	...
Other	338	330	196	258	120	114	66	120	218	216	130	138
Africa	235	199	283	228	49	44	39	52	186	155	244	176
South Africa	66	116	59	76	3	6	7	21	63	110	52	55
Other	169	83	224	152	46	38	32	31	123	45	192	121
Middle East	439	516	489	517	147	157	131	174	292	359	358	343
Israel	133	125	125	123	...	...	...	...	133	125	125	123
Saudi Arabia	39	38	38	46	...	...	...	...	39	38	38	46
Other	267	353	326	348	147	157	131	174	120	196	195	174
Asia And Pacific	6 437	6 621	5 597	6 750	3 755	3 607	3 455	4 293	2 682	3 014	2 142	2 457
Australia	150	139	119	161	15	23	20	7	135	116	99	154
China	465	356	310	416	301	173	115	154	164	183	195	262
Hong Kong	70	77	16	22	69	75	16	21	1	2	...	1
India	30	27	25	34	11	5	3	3	19	22	22	31
Indonesia	45	41	3	7	...	3	...	...	45	38	3	7
Japan	1 861	1 940	1 771	1 945	1 175	1 113	1 093	1 180	686	827	678	765
Malaysia	65	36	36	45	28	3	7	9	37	33	29	36
New Zealand	100	153	167	167	...	...	...	...	100	153	167	167
Philippines	134	117	76	96	46	23	26	35	88	94	50	61
Singapore	406	412	235	306	258	264	91	121	148	148	144	185
South Korea	1 965	1 700	1 025	1 183	1 092	809	564	754	873	891	461	429
Taiwan	832	1 223	726	944	686	1 076	582	778	146	147	144	166
Thailand	32	46	50	54	1	4	2	3	31	42	48	51
Other	282	354	1 038	1 370	73	36	936	1 228	209	318	102	142
International Organizations And Unallocated	513	535	552	544	513	535	552	544	...	...	...	...
European Union	3 706	3 916	4 684	4 310	1 770	1 873	1 863	1 629	1 936	2 043	2 821	2 681
Eastern Europe	173	143	104	129	98	73	36	44	75	70	68	85

1. Includes Mexico.
2. Data may include value of Other port services, not shown separately. See "Notes and Definitions" for more information.

Table B-5. U.S. Travel, Passenger Fare, and Other Transportation Payments, 1996–1999

(Millions of dollars.)

Country or region	Travel				Passenger fares			
	1996	1997	1998	1999	1996	1997	1998	1999
ALL COUNTRIES	48 078	52 051	56 509	59 351	15 809	18 138	19 971	21 405
Canada	4 670	4 904	5 718	6 135	391	470	587	712
Mexico	5 972	6 480	6 396	6 074	650	777	809	960
Europe	15 932	17 866	20 481	21 411	7 766	9 081	10 554	11 053
Belgium and Luxembourg	268	236	385	369	149	221	297	266
France	2 427	2 751	2 997	3 118	524	611	723	805
Germany	2 013	1 984	2 063	2 230	939	1 225	1 454	1 685
Italy	1 843	2 109	2 446	2 865	515	441	389	488
Netherlands	495	670	756	799	688	865	910	800
Norway	140	235	222	190	26	36	38	39
Spain	671	832	1 138	1 223	155	136	172	289
Sweden	200	171	209	203	39	49	48	91
Switzerland	650	655	755	800	490	590	701	833
United Kingdom	3 788	4 703	5 142	5 457	2 756	3 212	3 896	3 818
Other	3 437	3 520	4 368	4 157	1 485	1 695	1 926	1 939
Latin America And Other Western Hemisphere [1]	14 141	15 375	15 725	16 403	2 438	2 781	2 894	3 039
South and Central America [1]	10 010	11 038	11 671	11 809	1 968	2 209	2 234	2 331
Argentina	352	443	563	465	134	143	124	140
Brazil	418	615	764	831	389	462	405	336
Chile	228	232	525	375	93	92	87	93
Venezuela	256	281	358	355	80	104	122	111
Other	2 784	2 987	3 065	3 709	622	631	687	691
Other Western Hemisphere	4 131	4 337	4 054	4 594	470	572	660	708
Bermuda	314	411	356	416	. . .	. . .	. . .	. . .
Other	3 817	3 926	3 698	4 178	470	572	660	708
Africa	1 300	1 269	1 185	1 201	286	435	484	490
South Africa	268	272	362	283	124	239	273	308
Other	1 032	997	823	918	162	196	211	182
Middle East	1 227	1 164	1 510	1 748	447	399	441	475
Israel	446	493	428	541	261	253	328	368
Saudi Arabia	208	270	472	629	71	75	77	73
Other	573	401	610	578	115	71	36	34
Asia And Pacific	10 808	11 473	11 890	12 453	4 481	4 972	5 011	5 636
Australia	1 068	997	1 201	1 243	507	546	587	642
China	733	918	924	1 050	107	149	139	161
Hong Kong	1 101	948	1 189	1 225	480	421	460	571
India	502	602	812	751	120	135	133	113
Indonesia	276	296	139	168	62	66	10	. . .
Japan	2 905	3 036	2 719	2 845	712	757	784	858
Malaysia	202	228	163	129	66	75	67	73
New Zealand	300	254	391	475	193	217	293	401
Philippines	754	736	658	604	235	268	160	224
Singapore	474	559	539	572	309	249	183	199
South Korea	945	1 207	1 175	1 244	763	1 083	1 141	1 180
Taiwan	622	780	797	859	633	678	656	720
Thailand	440	392	442	472	81	111	139	125
Other	486	520	741	816	213	217	259	369
International Organizations And Unallocated	. . .	. . .	. . .	. . .	. . .	. . .	. . .	. . .
European Union	13 155	15 118	17 261	18 325	6 839	7 956	9 135	9 577
Eastern Europe	1 223	946	1 326	1 274	250	317	452	370

See footnotes at end of table.

Table B-5. U.S. Travel, Passenger Fare, and Other Transportation Payments, 1996–1999—*Continued*

(Millions of dollars.)

Country or region	Other transportation							
	Total				Freight			
					Total			
	1996	1997	1998	1999	1996	1997	1998	1999
ALL COUNTRIES	27 403	28 959	30 363	34 137	16 539	17 654	19 412	22 214
Canada	2 790	3 037	2 910	3 224	2 249	2 415	2 285	2 510
Mexico	525	800	958	1 070	106	118	111	151
Europe	9 753	10 566	11 323	11 410	5 768	6 340	6 929	6 746
Belgium and Luxembourg	445	454	513	522	119	132	157	174
France	706	687	758	765	163	226	257	243
Germany	1 545	1 748	1 873	1 786	776	924	1 186	1 116
Italy	422	468	547	536	246	337	445	422
Netherlands	700	708	797	837	297	283	336	333
Norway	958	881	349	367	957	876	346	361
Spain	99	105	116	124	28	41	35	37
Sweden	344	253	171	192	335	244	161	184
Switzerland	114	138	224	294	105	111	205	269
United Kingdom	1 605	2 205	2 397	2 507	481	786	764	743
Other	2 815	2 919	3 578	3 480	2 261	2 380	3 037	2 864
Latin America And Other Western Hemisphere [1]	2 253	2 464	2 351	2 607	811	761	647	762
South and Central America [1]	1 569	1 747	1 822	2 096	517	479	471	600
Argentina	22	28	13	31	8	10	7	15
Brazil	93	121	86	111	44	58	40	49
Chile	116	117	89	154	105	105	75	112
Venezuela	235	182	82	105	51	51	33	46
Other	578	499	594	625	203	137	205	227
Other Western Hemisphere	684	717	529	511	294	282	176	162
Bermuda	...	...	...	...	...	...	...	...
Other	684	717	529	511	294	282	176	162
Africa	177	147	165	216	86	53	83	112
South Africa	18	29	36	64	10	22	29	54
Other	159	118	129	152	76	31	54	58
Middle East	493	599	503	634	273	347	335	477
Israel	251	283	187	203	75	80	77	77
Saudi Arabia	22	51	27	31	20	23	20	20
Other	220	265	289	400	178	244	238	380
Asia And Pacific	10 959	11 053	11 727	14 899	6 374	6 645	7 749	10 460
Australia	308	230	214	197	51	63	64	45
China	611	636	707	1 008	557	516	482	728
Hong Kong	585	587	604	789	141	165	217	318
India	98	65	56	69	44	22	23	26
Indonesia	63	22	35	56	38	14	9	8
Japan	4 207	4 182	4 219	4 986	2 032	2 045	2 425	2 937
Malaysia	34	24	45	43	28	20	35	35
New Zealand	76	80	75	72	17	23	22	22
Philippines	128	128	109	151	61	59	55	76
Singapore	713	811	572	778	542	654	442	634
South Korea	1 950	1 762	1 403	1 551	1 690	1 502	1 295	1 422
Taiwan	1 112	1 528	1 070	1 552	912	1 368	938	1 384
Thailand	116	52	58	152	8	25	28	102
Other	958	946	2 560	3 495	253	169	1 714	2 723
International Organizations And Unallocated	978	1 093	1 384	1 147	978	1 093	1 384	1 147
European Union	7 456	8 144	8 969	9 284	3 773	4 238	4 878	4 956
Eastern Europe	317	279	219	229	201	178	124	119

See footnotes at end of table.

Table B-5. U.S. Travel, Passenger Fare, and Other Transportation Payments, 1996–1999—*Continued*

(Millions of dollars.)

Country or region	Other transportation—*Continued*											
	Freight—*Continued*											
	Ocean				Air				Other			
	1996	1997	1998	1999	1996	1997	1998	1999	1996	1997	1998	1999
ALL COUNTRIES	11 258	11 904	13 652	15 726	3 201	3 543	3 624	4 137	2 080	2 207	2 136	2 351
Canada	112	131	97	101	60	80	56	62	2 077	2 204	2 132	2 347
Mexico	95	104	101	140	8	11	6	7	3	3	4	4
Europe	4 539	5 031	5 434	5 133	1 229	1 309	1 495	1 613	...	...	...	...
Belgium and Luxembourg	41	58	81	74	78	74	76	100	...	...	...	...
France	16	66	92	85	147	160	165	158	...	...	...	...
Germany	501	639	892	815	275	285	294	301	...	...	...	...
Italy	180	271	377	345	66	66	68	77	...	...	...	...
Netherlands	123	123	171	157	174	160	165	176	...	...	...	...
Norway	957	876	346	361	...	...	...	...	...	...	...	...
Spain	...	2	7	7	28	39	28	30	...	...	...	...
Sweden	299	204	124	138	36	40	37	46	...	...	...	...
Switzerland	...	...	97	102	105	111	108	167	...	...	...	...
United Kingdom	217	474	409	304	264	312	355	439	...	...	...	...
Other	2 205	2 318	2 838	2 745	56	62	199	119	...	...	...	...
Latin America And Other Western Hemisphere [1]	659	591	475	582	149	167	168	176	3	3	4	4
South and Central America [1]	374	317	307	429	140	159	160	167	3	3	4	4
Argentina	2	3	...	1	6	7	7	14	...	...	...	...
Brazil	22	11	18	25	22	47	22	24	...	...	...	...
Chile	73	56	42	59	32	49	33	53	...	...	...	...
Venezuela	50	51	33	46	1	...	...	...	...	...	...	...
Other	132	92	113	158	71	45	92	69	...	...	...	...
Other Western Hemisphere	285	274	168	153	9	8	8	9	...	...	...	...
Bermuda	...	...	...	...	...	...	...	...	...	...	...	...
Other	285	274	168	153	9	8	8	9	...	...	...	...
Africa	81	41	67	98	5	12	16	14	...	...	...	...
South Africa	5	14	21	45	5	8	8	9	...	...	...	...
Other	76	27	46	53	...	4	8	5	...	...	...	...
Middle East	178	228	238	352	95	119	97	125	...	...	...	...
Israel	...	...	...	...	75	80	77	77	...	...	...	...
Saudi Arabia	...	...	...	...	20	23	20	20	...	...	...	...
Other	178	228	238	352	...	16	...	28	...	...	...	...
Asia And Pacific	4 711	4 789	5 957	8 313	1 663	1 856	1 792	2 147	...	...	...	...
Australia	24	36	37	16	27	27	27	29	...	...	...	...
China	343	253	262	386	214	263	220	342	...	...	...	...
Hong Kong	139	162	215	316	2	3	2	2	...	...	...	...
India	35	14	13	19	9	8	10	7	...	...	...	...
Indonesia	34	8	5	7	4	6	4	1	...	...	...	...
Japan	1 482	1 467	1 927	2 362	550	578	498	575	...	...	...	...
Malaysia	7	7	14	21	21	13	21	14	...	...	...	...
New Zealand	...	...	...	...	17	23	22	22	...	...	...	...
Philippines	43	36	37	54	18	23	18	22	...	...	...	...
Singapore	426	519	323	475	116	135	119	159	...	...	...	...
South Korea	1 249	945	840	1 237	441	557	455	185	...	...	...	...
Taiwan	757	1 203	778	1 145	155	165	160	239	...	...	...	...
Thailand	2	8	7	10	6	17	21	92	...	...	...	...
Other	170	131	1 499	2 265	83	38	215	458	...	...	...	...
International Organizations And Unallocated	978	1 093	1 384	1 147	...	...	...	...	...	...	...	...
European Union	2 670	3 063	3 615	3 550	1 103	1 175	1 263	1 406	...	...	...	...
Eastern Europe	193	167	110	100	8	11	14	19	...	...	...	...

See footnotes at end of table.

Table B-5. U.S. Travel, Passenger Fare, and Other Transportation Payments, 1996–1999—*Continued*

(Millions of dollars.)

Country or region	Other transportation—*Continued*											
	Port services											
	Total [2]				Ocean				Air			
	1996	1997	1998	1999	1996	1997	1998	1999	1996	1997	1998	1999
ALL COUNTRIES	10 864	11 305	10 951	11 923	2 231	2 187	1 930	1 973	8 551	9 034	8 935	9 852
Canada	541	622	625	714	131	165	158	170	328	373	381	446
Mexico	419	682	847	919	82	123	71	50	337	559	776	869
Europe	3 985	4 226	4 394	4 664	691	660	648	601	3 294	3 566	3 746	4 063
Belgium and Luxembourg	326	322	356	348	98	111	118	90	228	211	238	258
France	543	461	501	522	44	46	43	37	499	415	458	485
Germany	769	824	687	670	102	107	102	96	667	717	585	574
Italy	176	131	102	114	21	25	13	12	155	106	89	102
Netherlands	403	425	461	504	142	118	130	131	261	307	331	373
Norway	1	5	3	6	1	5	3	6	...	...	...	...
Spain	71	64	81	87	13	20	27	25	58	44	54	62
Sweden	9	9	10	8	9	9	10	8	...	...	...	...
Switzerland	9	27	19	25	...	...	...	...	9	27	19	25
United Kingdom	1 124	1 419	1 633	1 764	118	111	111	84	1 006	1 308	1 522	1 680
Other	554	539	541	616	143	108	91	112	411	431	450	504
Latin America And Other Western Hemisphere [1]	1 442	1 703	1 704	1 845	493	566	337	285	949	1 137	1 367	1 560
South and Central America [1]	1 052	1 268	1 351	1 496	397	450	296	244	655	818	1 055	1 252
Argentina	14	18	6	16	14	18	6	2	...	...	...	14
Brazil	49	63	46	62	29	43	22	6	20	20	24	56
Chile	11	12	14	42	11	12	5	17	...	...	9	25
Venezuela	184	131	49	59	66	126	45	47	118	5	4	12
Other	375	362	389	398	195	128	147	122	180	234	242	276
Other Western Hemisphere	390	435	353	349	96	116	41	41	294	319	312	308
Bermuda	...	...	...	...	...	...	...	...	...	...	...	...
Other	390	435	353	349	96	116	41	41	294	319	312	308
Africa	91	94	82	104	79	75	71	91	12	19	11	13
South Africa	8	7	7	10	4	2	2	4	4	5	5	6
Other	83	87	75	94	75	73	69	87	8	14	6	7
Middle East	220	252	168	157	146	82	96	92	74	170	72	65
Israel	176	203	110	126	107	57	52	72	69	146	58	54
Saudi Arabia	2	28	7	11	...	12	1	8	2	16	6	3
Other	42	21	51	20	39	13	43	12	3	8	8	8
Asia And Pacific	4 585	4 408	3 978	4 439	691	639	620	734	3 894	3 769	3 358	3 705
Australia	257	167	150	152	9	1	5	3	248	166	145	149
China	54	120	225	280	50	5	62	127	4	115	163	153
Hong Kong	444	422	387	471	65	51	40	94	379	371	347	377
India	54	43	33	43	46	43	28	33	8	...	5	10
Indonesia	25	8	26	48	25	8	26	48	...	...	...	...
Japan	2 175	2 137	1 794	2 049	177	165	135	151	1 998	1 972	1 659	1 898
Malaysia	6	4	10	8	6	4	10	8	...	...	...	...
New Zealand	59	57	53	50	2	1	2	1	57	56	51	49
Philippines	67	69	54	75	13	8	10	25	54	61	44	50
Singapore	171	157	130	144	6	10	10	27	165	147	120	117
South Korea	260	260	108	129	116	114	65	90	144	146	43	39
Taiwan	200	160	132	168	81	50	42	31	119	110	90	137
Thailand	108	27	30	50	19	5	8	23	89	22	22	27
Other	705	777	846	772	76	174	177	73	629	603	669	699
International Organizations And Unallocated	...	...	...	...	...	...	...	...	...	...	...	...
European Union	3 683	3 906	4 091	4 328	585	574	580	506	3 098	3 332	3 511	3 822
Eastern Europe	116	101	95	110	75	58	51	75	41	43	44	35

1. Includes Mexico.
2. Data may include value of Other port services, not shown separately. See "Notes and Definitions" for more information.

Table B-6. U.S. Royalty and License Fee Receipts, 1996–1999

(Millions of dollars.)

Country or region	Total 1996	1997	1998	1999	Affiliated Total 1996	1997	1998	1999	By U.S. parents from their foreign affiliates 1996	1997	1998	1999
ALL COUNTRIES	32 470	33 639	36 197	36 467	24 556	24 876	26 809	26 307	22 719	23 091	24 720	24 576
Canada	1 526	1 597	1 651	1 696	1 279	1 287	1 330	1 339	1 229	1 249	1 290	1 300
Mexico	474	651	762	798	(D)	556	620	684	384	506	534	602
Europe	16 863	16 324	19 097	19 024	14 120	13 283	15 503	14 910	12 866	12 533	14 202	13 880
Belgium and Luxembourg	816	681	688	669	683	585	563	509	623	569	558	504
France	2 419	2 261	2 245	2 149	2 115	1 923	1 854	1 673	1 720	1 851	1 825	1 647
Germany	2 841	2 765	3 227	3 109	2 174	2 069	2 321	2 070	2 099	2 005	2 115	1 895
Italy	1 170	1 062	1 060	963	949	810	801	680	906	772	777	664
Netherlands	2 169	2 419	2 838	2 990	(D)	2 267	2 686	2 848	1 859	2 107	2 561	2 760
Norway	108	98	117	117	84	72	83	80	83	71	82	77
Spain	709	599	558	585	591	454	417	419	589	454	417	418
Sweden	546	402	489	436	(D)	(D)	(D)	210	244	215	245	205
Switzerland	632	682	912	859	510	561	764	715	471	467	589	604
United Kingdom	3 017	2 996	3 621	3 517	2 532	2 410	2 996	2 710	2 204	2 125	2 342	2 189
Other	2 435	2 358	3 342	3 630	(D)	(D)	(D)	2 995	2 067	1 898	2 691	2 918
Latin America And Other Western Hemisphere [1]	1 599	2 120	2 683	2 720	1 205	1 711	2 125	(D)	1 183	1 644	1 953	2 028
South and Central America [1]	1 454	1 757	2 079	1 991	1 100	1 370	1 578	(D)	1 080	1 306	1 408	1 377
Argentina	202	204	255	237	148	158	(D)	185	145	157	177	179
Brazil	426	493	584	514	311	359	(D)	(D)	311	355	394	302
Chile	46	48	60	55	22	27	34	31	20	26	29	29
Venezuela	110	131	141	143	(D)	97	101	108	82	96	99	105
Other	196	230	277	244	138	172	210	(D)	138	166	175	161
Other Western Hemisphere	145	362	604	729	105	341	547	(D)	102	338	544	651
Bermuda	83	78	(D)	82	(D)	78	79	58	(D)	78	79	58
Other	62	284	(D)	646	(D)	263	468	(D)	(D)	260	466	593
Africa	237	232	328	403	144	121	229	(D)	142	121	204	250
South Africa	164	160	188	268	102	97	(D)	(D)	102	97	99	156
Other	73	72	140	136	41	24	(D)	97	40	24	105	94
Middle East	117	169	154	204	32	39	32	38	28	35	28	34
Israel	57	67	76	104	19	18	18	25	19	18	18	25
Saudi Arabia	32	52	40	52	6	14	7	5	6	13	6	5
Other	28	50	38	48	7	8	7	7	4	3	3	3
Asia And Pacific	10 407	11 387	10 408	10 501	6 546	7 191	6 247	6 192	6 132	6 354	5 806	5 855
Australia	696	684	728	721	542	520	538	544	540	516	518	528
China	153	250	315	304	90	165	215	217	87	164	213	215
Hong Kong	338	343	261	218	260	(D)	181	149	256	256	176	143
India	66	76	62	61	19	20	17	24	19	20	17	23
Indonesia	80	86	45	50	32	37	18	23	31	36	18	23
Japan	5 940	6 700	5 977	6 054	3 584	4 086	3 563	3 528	3 220	3 363	3 237	3 300
Malaysia	127	118	119	92	72	81	53	53	71	77	50	53
New Zealand	80	97	79	74	57	73	54	48	57	73	54	48
Philippines	92	102	85	97	66	70	52	66	65	68	52	65
Singapore	1 457	1 379	1 174	1 143	1 374	1 301	1 106	1 062	(D)	1 282	1 092	1 057
South Korea	823	879	847	947	231	(D)	(D)	(D)	(D)	241	161	170
Taiwan	402	497	594	627	135	160	156	169	131	159	154	166
Thailand	134	160	107	93	83	96	64	60	83	96	60	55
Other	21	15	15	20	2	3	(D)	(D)	2	3	4	8
International Organizations And Unallocated	1 720	1 811	1 874	1 916	1 230	1 243	1 342	1 314	1 138	1 154	1 236	1 229
European Union	15 924	15 230	17 676	17 647	13 416	12 481	14 438	13 886	12 202	11 830	13 324	12 982
Eastern Europe	145	218	296	277	83	140	182	161	83	137	164	145

See footnote at end of table.

Table B-6. U.S. Royalty and License Fee Receipts, 1996–1999—*Continued*

(Millions of dollars.)

Country or region	Affiliated—*Continued* By U.S. affiliates from their foreign parents				Unaffiliated Total				Unaffiliated Industrial processes			
	1996	1997	1998	1999	1996	1997	1998	1999	1996	1997	1998	1999
ALL COUNTRIES	1 837	1 785	2 089	1 731	7 914	8 763	9 388	10 160	3 566	3 544	3 573	3 551
Canada	50	38	40	39	247	310	321	358	82	92	83	100
Mexico	(D)	51	86	82	(D)	94	142	114	26	32	40	26
Europe	1 254	750	1 301	1 029	2 743	3 040	3 594	4 115	1 042	979	1 194	1 365
Belgium and Luxembourg	59	16	6	5	134	96	124	160	90	57	72	103
France	395	72	29	26	304	337	391	476	123	92	143	196
Germany	74	64	206	175	668	696	906	1 040	219	184	248	332
Italy	43	38	24	17	221	252	259	282	66	77	53	84
Netherlands	(D)	160	125	89	(D)	152	152	142	80	71	59	42
Norway	(*)	1	1	3	24	27	34	37	3	4	3	1
Spain	1	(*)	...	1	118	145	141	166	28	29	28	23
Sweden	(D)	(D)	(D)	5	(D)	(D)	(D)	226	137	115	149	151
Switzerland	39	95	175	111	122	121	148	144	84	76	90	94
United Kingdom	328	285	654	522	485	586	625	806	129	147	157	163
Other	(D)	(D)	(D)	76	(D)	(D)	(D)	636	84	126	192	175
Latin America And Other Western Hemisphere [1]	22	67	173	(D)	394	409	557	(D)	82	81	112	87
South and Central America [1]	19	64	170	(D)	354	387	500	(D)	(D)	81	(D)	60
Argentina	3	2	(D)	6	54	46	(D)	53	4	5	7	8
Brazil	...	5	(D)	(D)	115	134	(D)	(D)	14	17	18	11
Chile	2	1	5	2	25	21	25	24	6	6	5	3
Venezuela	(D)	(*)	2	3	(D)	35	40	36	7	11	12	7
Other	1	6	35	(D)	58	58	67	(D)	(D)	11	(D)	5
Other Western Hemisphere	3	3	3	(D)	40	21	57	(D)	(D)	1	(D)	27
Bermuda	...	...	(*)	...	(D)	1	(D)	24	(D)	(*)	(D)	22
Other	3	3	3	(D)	(D)	21	(D)	(D)	(*)	(*)	1	5
Africa	1	...	25	(D)	93	111	99	(D)	28	15	17	20
South Africa	...	...	(D)	(D)	62	63	(D)	(D)	23	11	14	16
Other	1	...	(D)	3	31	48	(D)	38	5	4	3	3
Middle East	4	5	4	4	85	129	123	167	25	41	21	51
Israel	...	...	...	...	38	49	59	79	8	(D)	4	17
Saudi Arabia	(*)	(*)	(*)	(*)	26	39	34	47	11	17	11	21
Other	4	4	4	4	21	42	30	41	5	(D)	6	14
Asia And Pacific	414	837	441	338	3 861	4 196	4 161	4 309	2 299	2 299	2 136	1 921
Australia	2	4	20	16	154	165	190	178	36	32	33	30
China	3	1	1	1	63	85	100	87	43	52	47	29
Hong Kong	3	(D)	4	5	78	(D)	80	70	19	21	27	16
India	...	...	...	1	47	56	45	37	37	29	20	16
Indonesia	1	(*)	(*)	(*)	48	50	27	27	13	26	11	17
Japan	364	723	326	227	2 356	2 613	2 413	2 526	1 429	1 508	1 199	1 077
Malaysia	1	3	3	(*)	55	38	67	39	(D)	12	43	12
New Zealand	...	...	(*)	(*)	23	24	25	26	5	4	2	3
Philippines	2	1	...	1	26	33	33	31	2	7	7	6
Singapore	(D)	19	15	5	83	78	68	81	37	39	41	41
South Korea	(D)	(D)	(D)	(D)	593	(D)	(D)	(D)	478	389	489	489
Taiwan	4	1	2	3	267	337	438	458	130	144	194	168
Thailand	...	...	4	5	51	64	43	33	27	36	19	14
Other	...	...	(D)	(D)	19	12	(D)	(D)	(D)	1	2	3
International Organizations And Unallocated	92	89	10	86	490	568	532	602	8	36	10	7
European Union	1 214	652	1 114	903	2 508	2 749	3 238	3 761	937	885	1 082	1 243
Eastern Europe	...	3	18	17	62	79	114	115	11	7	14	22

See footnote at end of table.

Table B-6. U.S. Royalty and License Fee Receipts, 1996–1999—*Continued*

(Millions of dollars.)

Country or region	Books, records, and tapes				Broadcasting and recording of live events				Franchise fees			
	1996	1997	1998	1999	1996	1997	1998	1999	1996	1997	1998	1999
ALL COUNTRIES	323	316	324	403	315	202	242	248	419	475	506	569
Canada	15	17	19	22	12	23	(D)	14	36	29	41	35
Mexico	4	5	6	8	11	6	8	7	7	7	9	11
Europe	193	197	188	228	122	129	173	172	170	192	230	253
Belgium and Luxembourg	3	4	3	4	4	4	3	3	2	2	3	3
France	26	33	25	28	20	19	31	33	10	18	15	15
Germany	41	39	39	48	28	27	68	47	81	76	80	89
Italy	21	20	20	22	10	11	12	12	3	3	20	22
Netherlands	9	9	9	11	6	7	6	7	3	5	6	8
Norway	2	1	2	3	1	1	1	1	2	3	5	6
Spain	13	18	12	19	9	9	10	12	4	5	5	10
Sweden	5	5	6	5	5	4	4	4	4	4	6	7
Switzerland	5	5	6	7	3	3	4	3	2	2	2	1
United Kingdom	52	48	48	58	(D)	32	21	36	34	42	48	53
Other	16	16	19	24	(D)	12	12	13	23	31	40	39
Latin America And Other Western Hemisphere [1]	24	24	31	35	68	18	17	17	38	44	53	56
South and Central America [1]	23	23	29	32	60	16	16	16	26	31	36	38
Argentina	4	5	6	5	17	3	4	4	3	3	3	3
Brazil	11	11	12	13	19	6	4	4	2	3	4	2
Chile	1	1	1	1	5	(*)	(*)	(*)	2	3	3	3
Venezuela	1	1	1	3	2	(*)	(*)	(*)	1	1	2	3
Other	2	1	3	2	7	1	1	1	11	14	15	16
Other Western Hemisphere	1	1	2	2	8	1	(*)	1	12	14	16	18
Bermuda	. . .	. . .	. . .	. . .	(*)	(*)	. . .	. . .	(*)	(*)	(*)	(*)
Other	1	1	2	2	8	1	(*)	1	12	14	16	18
Africa	5	4	5	6	1	2	1	2	9	12	12	14
South Africa	4	3	4	5	1	2	1	2	3	(D)	6	6
Other	1	1	1	1	(*)	(*)	(*)	(*)	6	(D)	7	8
Middle East	7	9	6	9	(*)	1	1	1	24	34	38	43
Israel	4	4	4	5	(*)	1	1	1	8	8	9	9
Saudi Arabia	3	5	1	3	. . .	. . .	. . .	. . .	7	9	12	13
Other	(*)	1	1	1	(*)	. . .	. . .	. . .	9	17	18	21
Asia And Pacific	64	49	62	83	(D)	28	32	39	131	148	123	147
Australia	13	9	10	13	9	7	5	6	14	15	12	13
China	1	1	(*)	2	1	1	1	1	5	5	5	5
Hong Kong	2	2	3	5	4	6	1	1	10	11	11	13
India	1	(*)	1	1	(*)	(*)	1	1	1	4	4	4
Indonesia	4	2	1	(*)	3	(*)	1	1	5	10	3	5
Japan	30	26	36	49	30	10	12	16	41	28	31	35
Malaysia	(*)	1	1	1	(D)	(*)	1	1	8	14	9	10
New Zealand	1	(*)	1	1	2	(*)	6	6	3	4	3	4
Philippines	2	3	3	2	1	1	1	1	4	6	7	8
Singapore	3	1	1	2	1	(*)	(*)	(*)	8	5	4	5
South Korea	4	2	2	4	1	1	1	2	9	16	9	14
Taiwan	2	2	3	3	4	(*)	(*)	1	10	15	13	16
Thailand	1	1	(*)	(*)	1	1	3	3	10	11	8	9
Other	(*)	(*)	(*)	(*)	(D)	(*)	(*)	(*)	3	3	4	4
International Organizations And Unallocated	15	14	13	20	(D)	2	(D)	4	11	17	9	22
European Union	182	186	175	210	116	122	164	163	153	170	204	227
Eastern Europe	4	4	5	6	3	2	4	3	8	8	11	9

See footnote at end of table.

Table B-6. U.S. Royalty and License Fee Receipts, 1996–1999—*Continued*

(Millions of dollars.)

Country or region	Unaffiliated—*Continued*							
	Trademarks				Other			
	1996	1997	1998	1999	1996	1997	1998	1999
ALL COUNTRIES	964	1 105	1 111	1 176	2 326	3 121	3 631	4 214
Canada	35	48	49	51	67	100	(D)	136
Mexico	17	19	44	18	(D)	27	36	44
Europe	333	372	317	353	882	1 171	1 492	1 743
Belgium and Luxembourg	11	8	9	8	23	21	33	38
France	37	41	25	33	87	133	153	172
Germany	32	25	25	24	267	345	446	500
Italy	45	44	39	33	78	97	115	110
Netherlands	13	7	5	4	(D)	54	68	70
Norway	6	2	2	3	11	16	20	22
Spain	40	44	47	53	25	41	39	48
Sweden	7	8	5	5	(D)	(D)	(D)	53
Switzerland	8	5	7	6	21	29	40	32
United Kingdom	49	77	44	67	(D)	241	307	430
Other	85	110	110	117	(D)	(D)	(D)	268
Latin America And Other Western Hemisphere [1]	101	110	181	136	81	131	164	(D)
South and Central America [1]	98	108	177	129	(D)	129	(D)	(D)
Argentina	20	16	28	21	6	14	(D)	11
Brazil	30	38	53	46	38	59	(D)	(D)
Chile	9	8	11	11	2	4	5	6
Venezuela	7	10	14	10	(D)	12	10	12
Other	15	18	27	23	(D)	13	(D)	(D)
Other Western Hemisphere	3	2	4	7	(D)	3	(D)	(D)
Bermuda	(*)	...	1	1	(*)	(*)	(D)	1
Other	3	2	3	6	(D)	2	(D)	(D)
Africa	21	22	24	28	28	56	39	(D)
South Africa	11	9	(D)	(D)	18	(D)	38	40
Other	10	12	(D)	(D)	10	(D)	1	(D)
Middle East	13	10	13	11	16	36	44	52
Israel	7	5	8	8	11	(D)	33	41
Saudi Arabia	3	2	2	2	2	5	8	7
Other	3	2	3	2	3	(D)	3	4
Asia And Pacific	454	516	508	567	(D)	1 156	1 300	1 552
Australia	22	25	23	16	61	77	107	99
China	7	6	5	9	6	20	42	41
Hong Kong	31	27	19	17	13	(D)	19	19
India	3	11	2	1	5	11	17	14
Indonesia	15	5	9	1	8	5	2	1
Japan	309	374	401	476	517	668	735	874
Malaysia	3	2	2	1	(D)	10	11	14
New Zealand	5	4	4	3	8	12	10	9
Philippines	13	14	11	11	4	2	4	4
Singapore	4	5	2	2	30	27	19	31
South Korea	21	22	13	13	80	(D)	(D)	(D)
Taiwan	9	11	12	10	111	165	216	260
Thailand	8	4	3	3	4	13	10	4
Other	5	5	3	4	(D)	2	(D)	(D)
International Organizations And Unallocated	6	27	18	29	(D)	471	(D)	520
European Union	302	325	272	320	818	1 059	1 341	1 598
Eastern Europe	8	(D)	11	4	28	(D)	71	71

1. Includes Mexico.

Table B-7. U.S. Royalty and License Fee Payments, 1996–1999

(Millions of dollars.)

Country or region	Total				Affiliated							
					Total				By U.S. parents to their foreign affiliates			
	1996	1997	1998	1999	1996	1997	1998	1999	1996	1997	1998	1999
ALL COUNTRIES	7 837	9 614	11 713	13 275	5 406	7 202	8 754	10 208	761	1 379	1 755	2 134
Canada	225	321	427	608	128	187	296	407	22	30	25	110
Mexico	65	117	107	(D)	(D)	101	72	62	11	20	24	10
Europe	4 835	5 728	6 888	7 446	3 705	4 393	5 372	5 808	541	687	894	957
Belgium and Luxembourg	118	136	160	220	(D)	100	(D)	(D)	(D)	23	(D)	22
France	470	632	836	895	203	281	393	433	30	28	21	30
Germany	719	896	1 311	1 285	543	682	1 102	1 065	60	67	52	24
Italy	126	126	115	99	73	78	58	63	18	26	17	17
Netherlands	393	398	777	782	366	347	(D)	736	16	17	(D)	411 ·
Norway	12	16	11	26	4	2	4	15	1	1	1	1
Spain	16	20	17	44	13	12	9	(D)	11	10	7	12
Sweden	104	149	138	158	54	(D)	(D)	98	3	6	1	6
Switzerland	687	781	822	1 221	589	678	712	1 081	68	73	82	82
United Kingdom	1 915	2 114	2 058	1 748	1 589	1 796	1 682	1 269	165	259	130	118
Other	275	461	644	968	(D)	(D)	494	831	(D)	176	(D)	233
Latin America And Other Western Hemisphere [1]	201	(D)	860	1 054	123	(D)	(D)	(D)	26	(D)	(D)	(D)
South and Central America [1]	164	162	187	186	(D)	115	100	(D)	(D)	28	35	20
Argentina	38	9	(D)	11	(D)	7	9	8	4	1	2	1
Brazil	1	11	23	21	(*)	1	(*)	1	. . .	1	(*)	1
Chile	(*)	1	(*)	4	(*)	. . .	(*)	4	(*)	. . .	(*)	(*)
Venezuela	35	2	8	7	(D)	1	7	5	2	1	4	1
Other	24	24	(D)	(D)	(D)	5	12	(D)	(D)	4	5	8
Other Western Hemisphere	37	(D)	673	868	(D)	(D)	(D)	(D)	(D)	(D)	(D)	(D)
Bermuda	2	(D)	622	818	2	(D)	(D)	(D)	(*)	(D)	(D)	(D)
Other	35	52	50	49	(D)	27	(D)	(D)	(D)	23	21	(D)
Africa	6	18	4	5	1	5	3	(D)	1	5	3	2
South Africa	6	11	2	5	1	1	1	(D)	1	1	1	2
Other	(*)	7	2	1	(*)	4	2	1	(*)	4	2	(*)
Middle East	14	14	7	21	2	2	(*)	(D)	(*)	1	(*)	(D)
Israel	12	13	7	20	2	2	(*)	. . .	. . .	1	. . .	. . .
Saudi Arabia	(*)	1	(*)	(*)	(*)	(*)	(*)	(D)	(*)	(*)	(*)	(D)
Other	2	(*)	(*)	1	. . .	. . .	. . .	. . .	. . .	. . .	. . .	. . .
Asia And Pacific	1 641	(D)	2 629	3 507	1 153	(D)	(D)	(D)	129	(D)	(D)	(D)
Australia	35	90	41	70	18	(D)	24	27	11	9	1	4
China	(D)	(D)	(D)	108	(*)	1	(*)	5	(*)	1	(D)	4
Hong Kong	14	30	19	18	6	(D)	11	11	6	10	11	10
India	7	13	(D)	6	. . .	(*)	. . .	(*)	. . .	(*)	. . .	(*)
Indonesia	2	3	1	3	1	1	1	2	1	1	1	2
Japan	1 434	2 065	2 365	3 161	1 069	1 625	1 937	2 501	87	86	84	77
Malaysia	3	4	(*)	(*)	. . .	. . .	. . .	. . .	. . .	. . .	. . .	. . .
New Zealand	(D)	10	2	3	(*)	(*)	(*)	(*)	(*)	. . .	. . .	. . .
Philippines	3	2	3	9	(*)	(*)	(*)	8	(*)	(*)	(*)	8
Singapore	(D)	7	5	10	(D)	(D)	3	(D)	1	1	2	(D)
South Korea	47	(D)	36	85	(D)	(D)	(D)	(D)	10	(D)	(D)	17
Taiwan	16	22	14	23	14	16	3	7	11	15	1	1
Thailand	2	9	(*)	4	2	5	(*)	3	2	5	(*)	3
Other	(*)	(D)	(D)	9	. . .	1	(*)	(D)	. . .	1	(*)	. . .
International Organizations And Unallocated	916	489	897	634	294	299	363	425	42	57	72	89
European Union	4 071	4 832	5 967	6 113	3 106	3 702	4 647	4 706	467	602	803	869
Eastern Europe	12	18	12	12	6	6	8	5	5	5	7	4

See footnote at end of table.

Table B-7. U.S. Royalty and License Fee Payments, 1996–1999—*Continued*

(Millions of dollars.)

Country or region	Affiliated—Continued — By U.S. affiliates to their foreign parents				Unaffiliated — Total				Unaffiliated — Industrial processes			
	1996	1997	1998	1999	1996	1997	1998	1999	1996	1997	1998	1999
ALL COUNTRIES	4 645	5 823	6 999	8 074	2 431	2 412	2 959	3 067	1 319	1 417	1 536	1 883
Canada	106	157	271	297	97	134	131	201	66	89	90	152
Mexico	(D)	80	48	53	(D)	16	35	(D)	5	(D)	(D)	(D)
Europe	3 164	3 706	4 478	4 851	1 129	1 335	1 516	1 638	782	729	763	830
Belgium and Luxembourg	70	77	102	(D)	(D)	36	(D)	(D)	(D)	30	29	31
France	173	253	372	404	267	351	443	462	192	(D)	(D)	(D)
Germany	483	615	1 049	1 042	176	214	209	220	148	149	124	161
Italy	55	52	41	46	52	48	56	35	49	35	48	23
Netherlands	350	330	354	325	27	52	(D)	46	24	30	44	36
Norway	3	1	3	14	7	14	7	11	5	9	6	9
Spain	1	2	2	(D)	4	8	8	(D)	1	1	4	(D)
Sweden	51	(D)	(D)	92	50	(D)	(D)	60	49	61	55	54
Switzerland	520	605	629	999	98	103	110	140	72	86	82	105
United Kingdom	1 423	1 537	1 552	1 151	326	318	377	479	135	118	152	189
Other	34	(D)	(D)	597	(D)	(D)	150	138	(D)	(D)	(D)	112
Latin America And Other Western Hemisphere [1]	97	98	73	(D)	78	71	(D)	(D)	51	50	113	115
South and Central America [1]	92	87	65	(D)	(D)	47	87	(D)	(D)	28	(D)	80
Argentina	(D)	6	7	8	(D)	2	(D)	2	(D)	(*)	(*)	(*)
Brazil	(*)	(*)	...	...	1	9	22	20	(*)	4	(D)	18
Chile	...	...	(*)	4	(*)	1	(*)	(*)	...	...	...	...
Venezuela	(D)	...	2	4	(D)	1	1	3	1	(*)	(*)	(*)
Other	(*)	1	8	(D)	(D)	18	(D)	(D)	(D)	(D)	(D)	(D)
Other Western Hemisphere	5	11	8	(D)	(D)	24	(D)	(D)	(D)	22	(D)	35
Bermuda	1	7	(D)	2	(*)	...	(D)	(D)	...	...	(D)	(D)
Other	4	4	(D)	(D)	(D)	24	(D)	(D)	(D)	22	(D)	(D)
Africa	...	...	...	(D)	5	13	1	(D)	4	5	1	(*)
South Africa	...	...	...	(D)	5	11	(*)	(D)	4	5	(*)	(*)
Other	...	...	...	(*)	(*)	3	1	(*)	...	...	1	...
Middle East	2	1	(*)	...	12	12	7	(D)	12	9	5	15
Israel	2	1	(*)	...	10	11	6	20	10	9	5	15
Saudi Arabia	...	...	...	...	(*)	1	(*)	(D)	...	...	(*)	(*)
Other	...	...	...	...	2	(*)	(*)	1	2	...	(*)	...
Asia And Pacific	1 024	1 620	1 886	2 510	488	655	(D)	(D)	401	530	563	766
Australia	6	(D)	23	23	17	(D)	17	43	9	9	6	7
China	...	...	(D)	(*)	(D)	(D)	(D)	104	(D)	(D)	(D)	103
Hong Kong	...	(D)	...	1	8	(D)	8	7	2	2	7	2
India	...	...	...	...	7	13	(D)	6	(D)	(D)	5	5
Indonesia	...	...	...	(*)	1	1	(*)	1	(*)	(*)	(*)	1
Japan	982	1 540	1 853	2 425	366	440	428	659	308	360	385	610
Malaysia	...	...	...	...	3	4	(*)	(*)	3	3	(D)	(*)
New Zealand	(*)	(*)	(*)	(*)	(D)	2	10	3	1	(*)	(D)	(*)
Philippines	...	...	...	...	3	2	3	1	1	(*)	2	1
Singapore	(D)	(D)	1	1	2	(D)	2	(D)	(*)	2	2	(*)
South Korea	(D)	5	(D)	(D)	(D)	17	(D)	(D)	(D)	(D)	15	(D)
Taiwan	2	2	2	5	3	6	11	16	2	4	9	(D)
Thailand	...	...	...	...	(*)	4	(*)	(*)	...	3	(*)	(*)
Other	...	...	...	(D)	(*)	(D)	(D)	(D)	(*)	(D)	(D)	(D)
International Organizations And Unallocated	252	242	291	336	622	190	534	209	3	4	3	4
European Union	2 639	3 100	3 844	3 837	965	1 130	1 320	1 407	649	558	599	643
Eastern Europe	1	1	1	1	6	12	4	6	4	2	2	1

See footnote at end of table.

Table B-7. U.S. Royalty and License Fee Payments, 1996–1999—*Continued*

(Millions of dollars.)

Country or region	Unaffiliated—*Continued*											
	Books, records, and tapes				Broadcasting and recording of live events				Franchise fees			
	1996	1997	1998	1999	1996	1997	1998	1999	1996	1997	1998	1999
ALL COUNTRIES	146	151	163	214	523	60	436	102	6	4	4	7
Canada	20	17	17	27	3	9	9	8	...	...	(*)	...
Mexico	3	(D)	3	(D)	1	1	1	(D)	...	...	(*)	...
Europe	94	107	124	160	(D)	40	(D)	68	6	4	4	6
Belgium and Luxembourg	(*)	1	1	1	(*)	(*)	(*)	(*)	...	...	...	...
France	6	6	6	6	4	5	5	8	...	...	...	...
Germany	4	4	3	5	(*)	(*)	(*)	1	...	...	...	...
Italy	2	2	1	2	1	1	(*)	(*)	...	...	...	...
Netherlands	2	2	3	3	(*)	(*)	(*)	(*)	...	...	...	...
Norway	(*)	(*)	(*)	2	...	1	...	...	...	...	...	...
Spain	1	1	2	4	(*)	1	(*)	(*)	...	...	...	...
Sweden	1	1	2	4	(*)	(*)	(*)	(*)	...	...	...	...
Switzerland	3	2	2	6	(D)	8	(D)	(D)	...	...	...	...
United Kingdom	71	84	102	124	33	21	36	41	...	...	...	...
Other	3	3	3	3	(*)	2	(D)	(D)	6	4	4	6
Latin America And Other Western Hemisphere [1]	6	(D)	6	6	1	2	1	(D)	...	...	(*)	...
South and Central America [1]	4	(D)	5	(D)	1	1	1	(D)	...	...	(*)	...
Argentina	1	(*)	1	1	...	(*)	(*)	...	...	...	...	...
Brazil	(*)	(*)	(*)	(*)	(*)	(*)	(*)	(*)	...	...	(*)	...
Chile	...	...	...	...	...	(*)	...	...	...	...	(*)	...
Venezuela	(*)	(*)	1	1	(*)	(*)	(*)	(*)	...	...	(*)	...
Other	1	(*)	(*)	(*)	...	...	...	...	...	...	...	...
Other Western Hemisphere	1	(*)	1	(D)	...	1	...	...	...	...	...	...
Bermuda	...	...	...	...	...	...	...	...	...	...	...	...
Other	1	(*)	1	(D)	...	1	...	...	...	...	...	...
Africa	1	1	(*)	(*)	...	4	...	...	(*)	...	...	...
South Africa	1	(*)	(*)	(*)	...	1	...	...	(*)	...	...	...
Other	(*)	(*)	(*)	...	...	3	...	...	...	...	...	...
Middle East	(*)	(*)	(*)	(*)	...	...	...	...	...	...	(*)	(*)
Israel	(*)	(*)	(*)	(*)	...	...	...	...	...	...	...	(*)
Saudi Arabia	...	...	...	...	...	...	...	...	...	...	(*)	...
Other	...	...	...	...	...	...	...	...	...	...	...	...
Asia And Pacific	20	15	8	13	1	5	1	(D)	...	...	(*)	(*)
Australia	4	4	5	9	(*)	2	1	(D)	...	...	...	...
China	...	(*)	...	...	...	...	...	...	...	...	...	...
Hong Kong	1	1	(*)	2	...	...	...	(*)	...	...	...	...
India	...	...	...	...	...	1	...	...	...	...	(*)	...
Indonesia	(*)	...	...	...	...	...	...	...	...	...	...	...
Japan	(D)	1	1	1	(*)	1	(*)	(*)	...	...	...	...
Malaysia	...	...	...	...	...	...	...	...	...	...	...	...
New Zealand	(D)	8	1	1	...	...	...	...	...	...	...	...
Philippines	1	2	1	(*)	...	...	...	(*)	...	...	...	...
Singapore	(*)	...	(*)	(*)	...	(*)	...	...	...	...	...	...
South Korea	...	(*)	(*)	(*)	...	...	...	...	...	...	...	...
Taiwan	(*)	(*)	(*)	...	...	...	...	...	...	...	...	...
Thailand	...	...	...	...	...	(*)	...	...	...	...	...	...
Other	(*)	...	...	...	...	1	...	...	...	...	...	(*)
International Organizations And Unallocated	5	(D)	7	9	(D)	(*)	(D)	(*)	...	(*)	...	...
European Union	89	103	121	150	38	30	64	51	6	4	4	6
Eastern Europe	2	2	1	2	...	(*)	(*)	(*)	...	...	...	1

See footnote at end of table.

Table B-7. U.S. Royalty and License Fee Payments, 1996–1999—*Continued*

(Millions of dollars.)

Country or region	Unaffiliated—*Continued*							
	Trademarks				Other			
	1996	1997	1998	1999	1996	1997	1998	1999
ALL COUNTRIES	145	203	197	211	293	577	623	651
Canada	2	4	6	6	7	14	9	8
Mexico	(*)	(*)	1	(*)	(D)	4	(D)	(D)
Europe	(D)	93	(D)	105	126	362	452	469
Belgium and Luxembourg	1	2	2	3	(*)	3	(D)	(D)
France	3	5	3	5	(D)	(D)	(D)	(D)
Germany	10	(D)	5	7	14	(D)	76	47
Italy	1	4	4	6	(*)	6	3	4
Netherlands	(*)	(D)	12	2	1	(D)	(D)	4
Norway	(*)	(*)	(*)	(*)	2	3	1	(*)
Spain	(*)	1	1	1	(*)	5	1	1
Sweden	(*)	6	2	(*)	(*)	(D)	(D)	3
Switzerland	(D)	2	2	1	(*)	5	(D)	(D)
United Kingdom	42	51	48	67	44	43	40	57
Other	1	(*)	(D)	11	(D)	(D)	5	(D)
Latin America And Other Western Hemisphere [1]	(D)	1	2	2	(D)	(D)	(D)	(D)
South and Central America [1]	(D)	1	2	2	(D)	(D)	(D)	(D)
Argentina	(*)	...	(*)	(*)	(*)	1	(D)	2
Brazil	(*)	(*)	(*)	(*)	(*)	5	(D)	1
Chile	...	...	(*)	(*)	(*)	1	(*)	...
Venezuela	(D)	(*)	(*)	(*)	(*)	(*)	(*)	(*)
Other	1	1	1	1	(D)	(D)	(D)	(*)
Other Western Hemisphere	...	...	1	1	(*)	1	(D)	...
Bermuda	...	...	...	...	(*)	...	(D)	...
Other	...	...	1	1	(*)	1	...	...
Africa	...	...	(*)	(*)	(*)	3	(*)	(D)
South Africa	...	...	(*)	(*)	(*)	3	(*)	(D)
Other	...	...	(*)	(*)	(*)	...	...	...
Middle East	(*)	1	1	(*)	(*)	2	1	(D)
Israel	(*)	1	(*)	(*)	(*)	1	1	4
Saudi Arabia	(*)	(*)	(*)	(*)	(*)	1	(*)	(D)
Other	...	...	...	...	(*)	(*)	...	1
Asia And Pacific	15	26	26	32	52	79	(D)	32
Australia	1	2	1	1	2	(D)	4	(D)
China	...	(*)	(*)	(*)	(*)	1	(*)	(*)
Hong Kong	4	(*)	(*)	(*)	1	(D)	1	3
India	...	...	6	(*)	(D)	(D)	(D)	(*)
Indonesia	...	...	(*)	(*)	(*)	1	...	...
Japan	9	23	18	30	(D)	55	24	18
Malaysia	...	...	(*)	(*)	(*)	1	...	(*)
New Zealand	(*)	(*)	(*)	(*)	(*)	3	1	2
Philippines	...	(*)	(*)	(*)	1	1	(*)	(*)
Singapore	(*)	...	(*)	(*)	1	(D)	(*)	(D)
South Korea	(*)	(*)	(*)	(*)	(*)	(D)	(D)	(D)
Taiwan	(*)	...	(*)	(*)	1	2	1	(D)
Thailand	...	...	(*)	(*)	(*)	(*)	...	(*)
Other	...	...	(*)	(*)	(*)	...	...	...
International Organizations And Unallocated	(D)	78	(D)	66	(D)	(D)	111	130
European Union	58	90	84	100	124	345	449	458
Eastern Europe	...	(*)	(*)	2	(*)	8	1	1

1. Includes Mexico.

Table B-8. U.S. Other Private Service Receipts, 1996–1999

(Millions of dollars.)

Country or region	Total				Affiliated							
					Total				By U.S. parents from their foreign affiliates			
	1996	1997	1998	1999	1996	1997	1998	1999	1996	1997	1998	1999
ALL COUNTRIES	73 858	84 505	90 914	96 508	22 931	27 253	28 397	28 943	14 118	17 288	18 232	18 111
Canada	7 333	8 188	7 504	8 749	3 626	4 242	3 617	3 973	2 387	2 964	2 860	3 020
Mexico	4 654	5 274	5 619	5 992	351	432	477	581	292	372	398	481
Europe	26 235	31 813	34 804	36 066	11 752	13 922	15 224	14 805	7 348	9 129	9 470	8 901
Belgium and Luxembourg	889	1 017	1 145	1 187	(D)	391	428	454	330	362	371	373
France	2 745	3 131	3 178	3 495	1 426	1 447	1 534	1 499	814	870	888	826
Germany	3 552	4 773	5 036	5 495	1 735	2 414	2 683	2 743	580	1 173	1 345	1 337
Italy	1 198	1 321	1 470	1 750	441	445	477	417	298	337	354	314
Netherlands	2 597	2 926	2 682	2 823	1 801	2 077	1 768	1 796	1 408	1 789	1 345	1 313
Norway	453	528	604	510	209	231	276	265	79	79	96	112
Spain	997	1 348	1 370	1 629	(D)	(D)	529	600	173	297	348	406
Sweden	751	835	952	744	275	290	366	103	46	52	54	55
Switzerland	1 635	2 078	2 399	2 162	926	1 117	1 460	1 097	613	664	730	283
United Kingdom	7 573	9 806	11 338	11 055	3 317	4 172	4 664	4 302	2 274	2 892	3 263	2 993
Other	3 846	4 052	4 630	5 216	965	(D)	1 040	1 529	734	613	675	890
Latin America And Other Western Hemisphere [1]	11 877	13 898	16 031	18 453	1 398	1 582	1 787	2 066	898	1 064	1 233	1 458
South and Central America [1]	9 285	10 589	11 621	12 375	894	1 068	1 198	1 204	674	842	951	999
Argentina	696	771	989	1 069	(D)	79	85	114	72	64	72	108
Brazil	1 062	1 426	1 668	1 629	171	200	275	208	132	185	245	178
Chile	332	435	388	473	(D)	29	34	59	28	25	27	31
Venezuela	536	632	826	986	55	86	91	88	48	69	85	87
Other	2 003	2 053	2 131	2 225	208	243	236	154	101	127	125	113
Other Western Hemisphere	2 592	3 310	4 412	6 078	504	514	589	861	224	222	282	458
Bermuda	744	798	910	1 077	260	213	198	301	80	71	42	121
Other	1 849	2 512	3 501	5 000	244	301	391	560	144	151	239	337
Africa	1 506	1 744	2 339	2 480	117	171	223	208	92	132	194	170
South Africa	303	342	405	487	(D)	50	71	80	17	47	70	74
Other	1 205	1 403	1 935	1 992	(D)	121	153	128	75	85	124	95
Middle East	3 087	2 826	3 002	2 969	296	230	292	266	91	78	109	147
Israel	403	452	456	518	37	54	38	44	9	17	15	33
Saudi Arabia	1 115	1 165	1 245	1 217	(D)	(D)	(D)	101	19	10	7	6
Other	1 571	1 207	1 301	1 233	(D)	(D)	(D)	121	63	51	88	108
Asia And Pacific	20 093	22 686	23 492	24 268	5 665	7 027	7 192	7 544	3 227	3 843	4 304	4 335
Australia	1 261	1 450	1 604	1 685	388	440	491	530	359	403	438	466
China	1 507	1 521	1 850	2 054	(D)	171	227	209	84	117	151	143
Hong Kong	1 537	1 569	1 635	1 592	578	660	666	675	518	579	580	598
India	688	666	862	999	18	23	27	44	18	22	27	44
Indonesia	893	1 177	1 063	952	90	99	88	54	84	89	86	53
Japan	6 825	7 809	8 051	8 059	2 887	3 542	3 638	3 813	880	986	1 172	1 177
Malaysia	715	709	611	641	105	161	(D)	219	99	154	172	189
New Zealand	238	253	297	286	39	(D)	25	20	38	25	24	20
Philippines	360	466	485	418	46	76	77	78	39	68	74	75
Singapore	1 345	1 580	1 851	1 962	884	1 046	1 195	1 257	788	1 000	1 159	1 140
South Korea	1 620	1 975	1 657	1 644	242	(D)	(D)	155	105	143	130	141
Taiwan	1 077	1 346	1 310	1 705	154	191	237	385	114	156	167	194
Thailand	531	577	699	606	82	87	104	91	73	76	95	85
Other	1 494	1 586	1 517	1 664	(D)	23	31	14	26	23	29	13
International Organizations And Unallocated	3 722	3 347	3 745	3 526	76	79	63	81	76	79	63	81
European Union	21 961	26 888	29 259	30 851	10 452	12 448	13 349	13 296	6 493	8 263	8 514	8 375
Eastern Europe	1 346	1 353	1 648	1 705	65	76	89	86	59	70	73	77

See footnote at end of table.

Table B-8. U.S. Other Private Service Receipts, 1996–1999—*Continued*

(Millions of dollars.)

Country or region	Affiliated—*Continued* By U.S. affiliates from their foreign parents				Unaffiliated Total				Education			
	1996	1997	1998	1999	1996	1997	1998	1999	1996	1997	1998	1999
ALL COUNTRIES	8 813	9 965	10 165	10 832	50 927	57 252	62 517	67 565	7 887	8 346	9 037	9 572
Canada	1 239	1 278	757	953	3 707	3 946	3 886	4 777	425	439	445	472
Mexico	59	60	79	99	4 303	4 842	5 142	5 412	153	167	183	190
Europe	4 404	4 793	5 755	5 904	14 483	17 893	19 580	21 260	1 352	1 447	1 573	1 675
Belgium and Luxembourg	(D)	29	58	81	(D)	626	716	733	17	18	18	20
France	612	578	645	673	1 319	1 683	1 645	1 996	103	108	117	127
Germany	1 155	1 241	1 338	1 406	1 817	2 359	2 353	2 752	162	171	182	194
Italy	143	108	123	103	757	876	993	1 333	50	54	60	62
Netherlands	393	287	423	484	796	849	913	1 027	35	36	38	37
Norway	130	152	180	153	244	297	328	245	40	42	45	47
Spain	(D)	(D)	181	194	(D)	(D)	841	1 029	84	86	83	82
Sweden	229	238	312	48	476	545	586	641	70	76	85	91
Switzerland	313	453	730	813	709	961	939	1 065	30	34	36	37
United Kingdom	1 044	1 279	1 401	1 309	4 256	5 634	6 674	6 753	143	142	152	162
Other	230	(D)	365	639	2 881	(D)	3 590	3 687	619	678	756	816
Latin America And Other Western Hemisphere [1]	500	518	554	608	10 479	12 317	14 246	16 388	837	914	984	1 090
South and Central America [1]	220	226	247	205	8 391	9 521	10 423	11 171	643	702	777	859
Argentina	(D)	15	13	6	(D)	692	904	955	38	42	47	52
Brazil	39	15	30	30	891	1 226	1 393	1 421	97	115	134	159
Chile	(D)	4	7	28	(D)	406	354	414	18	18	22	27
Venezuela	7	16	7	1	481	547	734	898	79	85	91	101
Other	107	116	111	41	1 795	1 810	1 895	2 071	259	274	300	329
Other Western Hemisphere	280	292	307	403	2 088	2 796	3 823	5 217	194	212	207	231
Bermuda	180	142	156	180	484	585	712	776	11	11	10	10
Other	100	150	151	223	1 605	2 211	3 110	4 440	183	201	196	221
Africa	26	39	30	39	1 389	1 573	2 116	2 272	359	400	431	508
South Africa	(D)	3	1	6	(D)	292	334	407	35	36	37	39
Other	(D)	36	29	33	(D)	1 282	1 782	1 864	324	364	394	469
Middle East	205	153	183	120	2 791	2 596	2 710	2 703	363	359	369	412
Israel	28	37	23	11	366	398	418	474	45	45	50	60
Saudi Arabia	(D)	(D)	(D)	95	(D)	(D)	(D)	1 116	72	77	85	96
Other	(D)	(D)	(D)	13	(D)	(D)	(D)	1 112	245	237	235	257
Asia And Pacific	2 438	3 184	2 888	3 208	14 428	15 659	16 300	16 724	4 551	4 787	5 235	5 415
Australia	28	37	52	64	874	1 010	1 111	1 155	43	44	49	54
China	(D)	54	76	66	(D)	1 350	1 623	1 845	556	626	718	815
Hong Kong	60	80	86	77	959	909	969	917	169	161	148	140
India	(*)	(*)	(*)	1	670	643	835	955	446	451	517	599
Indonesia	6	10	2	2	803	1 078	975	898	180	183	203	194
Japan	2 007	2 556	2 466	2 637	3 939	4 266	4 413	4 245	785	834	868	880
Malaysia	5	8	(D)	30	610	548	(D)	422	197	214	223	185
New Zealand	1	(D)	1	1	199	(D)	272	266	15	15	18	19
Philippines	7	8	3	3	314	390	408	340	44	41	43	46
Singapore	96	45	37	117	461	534	656	705	58	55	59	64
South Korea	137	(D)	(D)	14	1 378	(D)	(D)	1 489	509	547	656	626
Taiwan	39	35	70	192	923	1 155	1 073	1 320	459	449	472	496
Thailand	8	11	9	6	449	490	595	515	171	199	231	200
Other	(D)	1	1	1	(D)	1 563	1 616	1 650	921	968	1 033	1 099
International Organizations And Unallocated	...	...	...	...	3 646	3 268	3 682	3 444	...	...	...	...
European Union	3 958	4 185	4 835	4 921	11 510	14 440	15 910	17 555	699	722	764	798
Eastern Europe	6	6	15	9	1 283	1 279	1 568	1 622	252	291	349	390

See footnote at end of table.

Table B-8. U.S. Other Private Service Receipts, 1996–1999—*Continued*

(Millions of dollars.)

Country or region	Financial services				Unaffiliated—*Continued* Insurance							
					Net				Premiums			
	1996	1997	1998	1999	1996	1997	1998	1999	1996	1997	1998	1999
ALL COUNTRIES	8 229	10 243	11 273	13 925	2 168	2 473	2 189	2 295	5 929	6 118	7 265	8 259
Canada	593	593	771	1 090	357	389	112	207	1 011	996	887	940
Mexico	249	282	325	365	43	47	47	75	98	114	132	152
Europe	3 563	4 309	4 703	5 510	683	1 003	752	199	2 727	2 553	2 791	2 639
Belgium and Luxembourg	166	158	174	186	65	53	28	17	138	98	100	100
France	303	409	396	492	31	131	37	101	204	220	293	348
Germany	270	271	310	438	129	214	120	-16	312	469	447	343
Italy	166	155	173	282	15	39	39	21	74	78	90	106
Netherlands	216	227	239	319	-14	-38	3	7	42	41	31	36
Norway	27	41	59	64	44	11	22	-31	65	49	48	44
Spain	102	148	132	234	9	16	6	-5	33	24	42	44
Sweden	89	100	86	159	20	10	3	-12	42	28	25	17
Switzerland	338	435	414	575	-41	-1	2	-4	86	55	53	68
United Kingdom	1 488	1 979	2 274	2 385	385	518	475	128	1 602	1 333	1 459	1 347
Other	398	386	446	376	40	50	17	-6	129	157	202	184
Latin America And Other Western Hemisphere [1]	2 022	2 890	3 244	4 373	416	600	897	1 626	1 033	1 391	2 451	3 443
South and Central America [1]	916	1 222	1 191	1 439	229	163	13	206	553	595	764	755
Argentina	160	233	220	268	43	4	89	114	122	115	219	245
Brazil	173	294	262	332	5	8	7	6	22	26	24	20
Chile	57	72	66	96	26	20	8	6	65	80	96	57
Venezuela	71	98	95	84	19	11	1	-6	26	29	28	28
Other	206	243	223	294	94	73	-139	11	220	232	264	252
Other Western Hemisphere	1 106	1 668	2 053	2 934	187	438	884	1 419	480	796	1 688	2 688
Bermuda	290	434	561	667	108	66	53	16	352	364	601	952
Other	816	1 234	1 492	2 267	79	372	831	1 403	128	432	1 086	1 736
Africa	101	128	230	281	5	7	1	-18	16	16	18	10
South Africa	26	27	39	45	1	4	3	2	7	8	10	4
Other	75	101	191	236	4	4	-1	-20	9	9	8	6
Middle East	249	261	339	437	17	13	15	-11	45	50	73	71
Israel	62	67	63	110	7	(*)	7	11	25	35	52	42
Saudi Arabia	62	61	73	81	1	2	4	-1	4	3	7	3
Other	125	133	203	246	10	10	5	-22	16	12	13	27
Asia And Pacific	1 688	2 053	1 973	2 229	441	394	304	249	911	894	847	956
Australia	157	201	212	220	36	32	36	1	111	117	124	159
China	39	70	52	78	(*)	-14	18	2	10	14	12	17
Hong Kong	264	281	202	253	25	12	17	19	53	37	37	35
India	31	35	32	51	3	(*)	-1	(*)	7	7	9	7
Indonesia	61	87	41	53	4	-2	-3	-6	16	15	9	5
Japan	480	532	628	583	319	287	182	231	520	484	453	552
Malaysia	42	31	30	56	2	3	(*)	3	14	13	8	8
New Zealand	21	14	20	19	7	9	8	8	15	13	14	12
Philippines	45	46	50	73	6	5	2	-7	15	15	13	14
Singapore	165	193	197	240	12	20	12	-2	25	30	26	32
South Korea	121	160	175	226	7	6	12	(*)	25	23	32	34
Taiwan	77	132	109	148	14	28	18	5	87	111	90	61
Thailand	45	43	34	52	5	8	5	(*)	12	14	15	17
Other	140	228	191	177	. . .	. . .	-3	-6	. . .	2	4	3
International Organizations And Unallocated	13	9	13	5	249	66	107	44	186	216	198	200
European Union	3 056	3 657	4 029	4 752	660	979	724	238	2 548	2 418	2 615	2 466
Eastern Europe	76	94	115	147	9	11	3	-4	21	25	60	43

See footnote at end of table.

Table B-8. U.S. Other Private Service Receipts, 1996–1999—*Continued*

(Millions of dollars.)

Country or region	Insurance—*Continued* Losses				Telecommunications				Business, professional, and technical services			
	1996	1997	1998	1999	1996	1997	1998	1999	1996	1997	1998	1999
ALL COUNTRIES	3 761	3 645	5 076	5 964	3 301	3 918	5 538	4 460	19 466	21 450	22 175	24 368
Canada	654	606	774	733	294	305	305	301	1 637	1 879	1 771	2 223
Mexico	55	67	85	77	350	445	463	380	648	796	850	947
Europe	2 044	1 550	2 039	2 440	915	1 206	2 016	1 461	6 005	7 420	7 629	8 858
Belgium and Luxembourg	73	45	73	83	32	91	138	114	182	234	294	325
France	172	89	256	248	84	90	96	99	617	750	723	835
Germany	183	255	327	359	77	81	95	83	737	921	975	1 129
Italy	60	39	51	86	46	45	50	42	289	329	397	577
Netherlands	56	79	28	29	32	59	63	61	447	500	471	506
Norway	21	37	26	75	40	89	76	21	62	89	100	118
Spain	24	8	36	50	34	37	32	27	220	237	189	278
Sweden	22	18	22	29	20	36	78	39	224	280	265	279
Switzerland	127	56	50	71	36	57	47	36	317	408	405	380
United Kingdom	1 217	815	984	1 219	287	356	1 032	720	1 614	2 210	2 144	2 629
Other	89	107	185	190	227	265	309	219	1 295	1 462	1 665	1 801
Latin America And Other Western Hemisphere [1]	617	791	1 555	1 817	854	1 012	1 274	1 009	2 916	3 147	3 784	4 018
South and Central America [1]	324	433	751	549	736	892	1 144	880	2 477	2 846	3 297	3 587
Argentina	79	111	130	131	30	36	57	49	279	299	411	384
Brazil	17	18	17	15	86	111	181	145	407	559	595	570
Chile	40	61	88	51	35	47	45	33	135	209	171	208
Venezuela	7	17	27	34	40	49	47	65	234	257	432	568
Other	126	159	403	241	194	204	350	207	774	726	838	910
Other Western Hemisphere	294	358	804	1 268	118	120	130	129	439	301	487	430
Bermuda	245	298	548	936	15	15	12	10	55	54	69	66
Other	49	60	256	332	103	106	118	119	384	247	417	364
Africa	11	9	17	28	109	143	447	478	752	825	940	935
South Africa	6	4	7	2	51	60	69	80	104	117	120	154
Other	5	5	10	26	58	83	378	397	649	707	819	781
Middle East	28	37	58	83	162	205	251	205	1 925	1 667	1 649	1 548
Israel	18	34	45	31	52	71	85	82	162	176	180	172
Saudi Arabia	3	1	4	3	30	40	54	31	741	849	876	878
Other	6	2	9	48	80	93	111	92	1 022	641	593	498
Asia And Pacific	470	501	543	707	963	1 040	1 245	1 006	5 929	6 383	6 239	6 574
Australia	75	85	88	158	68	89	98	108	434	473	472	534
China	10	28	-6	15	183	98	105	67	526	482	634	782
Hong Kong	28	25	19	16	67	100	248	96	403	310	316	372
India	4	7	10	6	52	58	58	81	128	90	218	212
Indonesia	12	17	12	11	23	43	43	37	508	739	674	605
Japan	201	197	271	322	213	223	352	236	1 892	2 113	1 904	1 907
Malaysia	12	9	8	5	14	22	19	12	341	244	118	129
New Zealand	8	4	6	4	13	16	30	15	102	120	140	151
Philippines	9	10	11	21	36	45	35	28	157	225	236	174
Singapore	12	10	15	34	36	47	55	57	173	193	306	317
South Korea	18	18	20	34	126	127	141	118	539	568	414	454
Taiwan	74	83	72	56	80	117	122	93	262	383	291	516
Thailand	7	6	10	17	21	23	29	24	183	196	275	212
Other	. . .	2	6	9	30	31	41	32	279	246	240	209
International Organizations And Unallocated	-62	150	91	155	4	6	(*)	(*)	302	129	162	213
European Union	1 888	1 438	1 891	2 228	691	887	1 672	1 262	4 672	5 915	6 115	7 308
Eastern Europe	12	13	57	48	101	125	183	88	729	633	749	785

See footnote at end of table.

Table B-8. U.S. Other Private Service Receipts, 1996–1999—*Continued*

(Millions of dollars.)

Country or region	Unaffiliated—*Continued* Other services				Addendum: film and tape rentals			
	1996	1997	1998	1999	1996	1997	1998	1999
ALL COUNTRIES	9 874	10 821	12 305	12 946	4 982	5 944	7 033	7 556
Canada	401	342	482	484	341	315	406	394
Mexico	2 860	3 105	3 275	3 454	65	83	117	139
Europe	1 964	2 506	2 904	3 558	3 234	3 938	4 316	4 950
Belgium and Luxembourg	(D)	70	64	72	81	72	67	72
France	180	193	276	343	426	431	573	588
Germany	443	700	670	924	524	755	717	1 001
Italy	190	255	272	349	232	295	330	399
Netherlands	81	65	99	97	865	977	841	871
Norway	31	25	26	26	27	21	22	21
Spain	(D)	(D)	399	412	292	427	473	495
Sweden	53	43	68	85	68	53	77	91
Switzerland	29	27	35	41	29	24	30	35
United Kingdom	338	430	597	728	487	655	906	1 013
Other	302	(D)	397	481	204	227	281	362
Latin America And Other Western Hemisphere [1]	3 434	3 752	4 063	4 274	325	409	587	600
South and Central America [1]	3 389	3 696	4 001	4 201	311	396	573	586
Argentina	(D)	78	80	88	38	48	48	55
Brazil	123	139	214	209	109	147	249	220
Chile	(D)	40	42	44	17	24	24	26
Venezuela	39	45	67	85	35	37	63	80
Other	269	289	323	320	47	57	73	65
Other Western Hemisphere	45	56	62	73	14	13	14	15
Bermuda	5	6	7	7	4	4	4	4
Other	41	51	55	66	10	9	10	11
Africa	63	71	68	88	59	54	62	85
South Africa	(D)	48	66	87	55	42	57	78
Other	(D)	23	2	1	4	12	5	6
Middle East	75	91	87	112	38	52	63	89
Israel	37	39	33	39	22	22	23	28
Saudi Arabia	(D)	(D)	(D)	32	7	5	8	26
Other	(D)	(D)	(D)	41	9	24	33	34
Asia And Pacific	856	1 002	1 304	1 251	960	1 149	1 516	1 313
Australia	134	171	245	240	240	284	361	346
China	(D)	88	96	101	7	9	11	16
Hong Kong	31	45	38	37	32	44	41	36
India	11	9	11	12	2	2	3	4
Indonesia	27	28	17	15	21	21	9	8
Japan	251	278	480	408	433	469	776	579
Malaysia	14	34	(D)	37	10	30	30	32
New Zealand	40	(D)	56	55	37	49	52	51
Philippines	26	28	43	26	19	20	33	17
Singapore	18	26	27	29	17	25	26	27
South Korea	76	(D)	(D)	64	88	118	80	83
Taiwan	31	46	62	62	33	60	77	84
Thailand	24	21	22	27	19	15	14	20
Other	(D)	89	114	139	2	2	3	7
International Organizations And Unallocated	3 081	3 058	3 398	3 180	25	27	83	126
European Union	1 732	2 278	2 603	3 199	3 088	3 797	4 120	4 703
Eastern Europe	116	126	169	215	60	72	101	143

1. Includes Mexico.

Table B-9. U.S. Other Private Service Payments, 1996–1999

(Millions of dollars.)

Country or region	Total				Affiliated							
					Total				By U.S. parents to their foreign affiliates			
	1996	1997	1998	1999	1996	1997	1998	1999	1996	1997	1998	1999
ALL COUNTRIES	37 975	43 280	49 051	46 657	15 548	17 817	19 756	22 437	7 084	9 012	10 406	11 427
Canada	4 375	4 812	5 486	4 543	2 494	2 721	3 080	2 458	536	790	730	748
Mexico	1 706	1 664	1 600	1 575	168	172	239	324	108	125	127	191
Europe	15 570	18 365	21 566	20 759	8 522	9 467	11 397	12 526	4 014	4 966	6 395	6 588
Belgium and Luxembourg	518	686	562	620	(D)	476	373	387	(D)	271	274	310
France	1 896	2 089	2 284	2 444	1 111	1 191	1 377	1 513	489	565	632	650
Germany	2 489	2 110	3 109	3 193	1 450	1 355	1 616	1 604	617	620	664	590
Italy	586	528	648	755	276	208	267	280	104	72	89	97
Netherlands	881	814	1 222	774	630	677	934	997	222	270	286	296
Norway	145	119	185	191	93	68	83	111	20	6	5	11
Spain	363	364	439	494	73	(D)	100	141	51	49	74	119
Sweden	197	250	274	321	168	179	175	218	28	26	25	44
Switzerland	695	604	1 307	520	652	521	724	600	122	175	187	220
United Kingdom	6 122	9 121	9 713	10 220	3 206	4 113	5 105	5 906	1 971	2 707	3 838	3 961
Other	1 678	1 681	1 827	1 227	(D)	(D)	643	769	(D)	207	321	289
Latin America And Other Western Hemisphere [1]	7 921	8 597	10 537	9 243	1 005	974	1 017	2 042	534	565	559	745
South and Central America [1]	3 999	4 002	3 881	3 702	446	404	490	614	251	330	346	386
Argentina	233	241	228	275	33	55	49	82	33	55	48	82
Brazil	520	556	525	466	136	123	148	102	77	111	133	75
Chile	82	84	108	151	3	2	8	57	1	1	2	2
Venezuela	(D)	139	139	140	(D)	18	15	19	9	11	12	14
Other	(D)	1 316	1 281	1 097	(D)	33	31	29	23	27	22	23
Other Western Hemisphere	3 922	4 595	6 655	5 541	559	570	528	1 428	282	234	213	359
Bermuda	2 551	2 832	3 675	3 831	273	288	257	937	159	100	88	231
Other	1 371	1 762	2 980	1 710	285	282	271	491	123	134	125	127
Africa	611	681	702	787	65	(D)	92	175	29	59	88	117
South Africa	127	174	182	207	(D)	(D)	85	102	24	57	85	96
Other	484	509	518	581	(D)	4	7	73	5	2	3	21
Middle East	971	1 049	1 199	1 152	170	(D)	271	320	156	204	257	303
Israel	399	463	477	520	148	194	246	286	138	(D)	237	277
Saudi Arabia	136	179	279	218	6	4	5	4	6	4	5	4
Other	436	406	442	415	16	(D)	19	30	12	(D)	15	23
Asia And Pacific	8 159	9 437	9 305	9 967	3 244	4 317	3 873	4 889	1 766	2 398	2 352	2 900
Australia	655	814	1 243	1 326	220	313	353	459	193	276	321	355
China	432	398	404	339	14	24	29	28	12	16	20	15
Hong Kong	740	1 056	977	1 206	413	590	572	873	295	523	500	727
India	366	408	521	577	12	(D)	(D)	60	6	10	18	16
Indonesia	147	161	120	111	29	23	14	4	26	22	11	4
Japan	3 649	4 013	3 435	3 842	2 169	2 653	2 159	2 651	1 002	1 101	1 000	1 251
Malaysia	151	201	102	130	63	118	(D)	53	49	77	27	46
New Zealand	81	136	136	170	27	(D)	44	43	25	36	41	41
Philippines	241	322	335	258	2	16	17	18	(*)	16	17	18
Singapore	307	468	553	622	158	305	378	426	90	218	292	269
South Korea	419	439	402	398	73	(D)	(D)	107	34	39	27	59
Taiwan	319	363	393	360	47	77	100	117	27	44	50	54
Thailand	163	194	155	167	14	20	25	46	3	16	22	42
Other	491	458	532	462	3	(D)	(D)	3	2	3	6	2
International Organizations And Unallocated	372	339	257	205	50	31	27	26	50	31	27	26
European Union	13 965	16 879	19 326	19 179	7 760	8 852	10 546	11 755	3 866	4 770	6 178	6 321
Eastern Europe	544	588	549	586	10	25	37	15	5	12	6	13

See footnote at end of table.

Table B-9. U.S. Other Private Service Payments, 1996–1999—*Continued*

(Millions of dollars.)

Country or region	Affiliated—*Continued* By U.S. affiliates to their foreign parents				Unaffiliated Total				Education			
	1996	1997	1998	1999	1996	1997	1998	1999	1996	1997	1998	1999
ALL COUNTRIES	8 464	8 805	9 350	11 010	22 427	25 463	29 295	24 220	1 253	1 396	1 591	1 840
Canada	1 958	1 931	2 350	1 710	1 881	2 092	2 406	2 085	10	12	15	18
Mexico	60	48	112	133	1 537	1 491	1 361	1 251	157	170	180	200
Europe	4 508	4 501	5 002	5 939	7 048	8 898	10 172	8 232	714	802	924	1 081
Belgium and Luxembourg	107	206	100	77	(D)	209	188	233	9	8	10	12
France	622	627	745	862	785	897	907	932	93	101	120	140
Germany	833	735	952	1 014	1 039	755	1 493	1 589	43	46	51	59
Italy	173	136	178	183	308	320	381	475	95	110	124	145
Netherlands	408	407	648	701	251	137	287	-223	8	11	13	16
Norway	74	61	78	101	52	51	102	80	. . .	. . .	2	2
Spain	22	(D)	26	23	290	(D)	339	353	103	114	134	159
Sweden	140	153	150	173	29	71	99	103	1	1	5	5
Switzerland	530	346	537	380	43	83	583	-80	3	3	9	9
United Kingdom	1 235	1 406	1 266	1 946	2 917	5 008	4 608	4 313	249	287	336	399
Other	365	(D)	322	480	(D)	(D)	1 184	458	109	120	120	134
Latin America And Other Western Hemisphere [1]	471	409	459	1 296	6 917	7 623	9 516	7 201	359	394	435	486
South and Central America [1]	194	74	144	227	3 554	3 598	3 391	3 088	310	340	374	417
Argentina	(*)	(*)	(*)	(*)	200	186	179	193	8	10	13	14
Brazil	58	12	15	28	384	433	377	364	10	11	13	15
Chile	2	1	6	55	79	82	100	94	15	18	24	27
Venezuela	(D)	7	3	5	(D)	121	124	121	5	4	6	7
Other	(D)	6	9	7	(D)	1 283	1 250	1 068	115	128	138	154
Other Western Hemisphere	276	336	315	1 069	3 363	4 025	6 127	4 113	49	54	61	69
Bermuda	114	188	169	705	2 278	2 544	3 418	2 894	. . .	1	1	1
Other	162	147	146	363	1 086	1 480	2 709	1 219	49	53	60	69
Africa	36	(D)	4	58	546	(D)	610	612	26	33	39	46
South Africa	(D)	(D)	. . .	6	(D)	(D)	97	105	7	4	6	8
Other	(D)	1	4	51	(D)	505	511	508	19	28	33	38
Middle East	14	(D)	14	17	801	(D)	928	832	22	23	27	31
Israel	10	(D)	10	10	251	269	231	234	21	22	26	30
Saudi Arabia	. . .	. . .	. . .	(*)	130	175	274	214	. . .	. . .	. . .	. . .
Other	4	4	5	7	420	(D)	423	385	1	. . .	1	1
Asia And Pacific	1 479	1 919	1 521	1 989	4 915	5 120	5 432	5 078	122	133	152	178
Australia	27	37	32	104	436	501	889	866	38	44	50	61
China	2	8	9	13	418	374	375	311	9	9	12	14
Hong Kong	119	67	72	145	327	466	405	333	3	2	1	1
India	5	(D)	(D)	44	354	(D)	(D)	517	3	3	4	4
Indonesia	3	1	3	1	118	138	106	107	1	1	1	1
Japan	1 166	1 552	1 160	1 400	1 481	1 360	1 275	1 190	24	25	28	32
Malaysia	14	41	(D)	6	88	83	(D)	77	. . .	. . .	. . .	. . .
New Zealand	2	(D)	3	2	54	(D)	92	127	. . .	5	7	9
Philippines	1	(*)	(*)	(*)	239	306	318	240	. . .	. . .	1	1
Singapore	69	88	86	157	149	163	175	196	1	1	1	1
South Korea	39	(D)	(D)	48	346	(D)	(D)	291	3	2	2	2
Taiwan	20	33	50	63	272	286	293	243	1	1	1	1
Thailand	11	4	3	4	149	174	130	121	1	1	1	1
Other	1	(D)	(D)	1	488	(D)	(D)	459	39	38	43	49
International Organizations And Unallocated	. . .	. . .	. . .	. . .	322	307	231	178	. . .	. . .	. . .	. . .
European Union	3 894	4 081	4 367	5 434	6 205	8 026	8 782	7 423	639	723	843	995
Eastern Europe	6	12	31	2	536	570	529	573	38	39	40	41

See footnote at end of table.

Table B-9. U.S. Other Private Service Payments, 1996–1999—*Continued*

(Millions of dollars.)

Country or region	Financial services				Insurance							
					Net				Premiums			
	1996	1997	1998	1999	1996	1997	1998	1999	1996	1997	1998	1999
ALL COUNTRIES	2 907	3 347	3 561	3 574	3 885	5 873	9 080	4 078	14 522	15 211	20 290	21 242
Canada	173	200	227	203	458	518	712	232	1 060	1 077	1 225	612
Mexico	125	82	42	63	-3	-4	3	3	2	2	5	7
Europe	1 651	2 029	2 169	2 217	553	1 835	2 607	81	6 547	6 925	7 954	9 534
Belgium and Luxembourg	52	47	34	56	30	35	33	41	72	80	128	137
France	126	128	158	129	158	319	220	274	477	561	538	712
Germany	181	103	139	151	253	162	846	880	1 298	1 311	1 615	2 338
Italy	43	24	59	39	-24	. . .	-14	15	60	70	100	124
Netherlands	71	51	70	62	-5	-109	6	-477	27	32	39	476
Norway	8	11	11	19	11	1	12	3	17	15	16	14
Spain	22	38	39	42	5	2	6	10	11	7	10	13
Sweden	26	29	39	46	-51	-9	-22	-38	54	72	61	74
Switzerland	114	135	114	113	-272	-247	237	-417	684	591	1 214	790
United Kingdom	901	1 354	1 353	1 386	461	1 755	1 256	621	3 332	3 694	3 753	4 289
Other	107	109	153	174	-12	-74	25	-829	515	492	480	566
Latin America And Other Western Hemisphere [1]	390	489	502	428	2 822	3 265	5 224	3 265	6 347	6 644	10 500	10 589
South and Central America [1]	273	271	198	224	41	-11	17	8	91	45	48	57
Argentina	26	34	16	28	1	-5	-3	-9	(D)	(D)	(D)	15
Brazil	63	75	46	61	35	-8	(*)	8	(D)	1	1	9
Chile	8	8	4	11	2	-1	2	1	2	1	1	1
Venezuela	5	10	13	10	6	-1	. . .	(*)	6	4	(*)	(*)
Other	46	62	77	51	(*)	9	16	6	19	(D)	(D)	24
Other Western Hemisphere	117	218	304	204	2 782	3 276	5 207	3 257	6 256	6 599	10 452	10 532
Bermuda	53	36	76	61	2 201	2 469	3 295	2 705	4 087	4 357	7 116	7 426
Other	64	182	228	143	581	806	1 913	552	2 169	2 242	3 337	3 106
Africa	18	37	51	59	3	5	3	1	5	8	5	3
South Africa	7	9	10	11	(*)	-1	-1	. . .	1	1	1	1
Other	11	28	41	48	3	6	3	1	4	6	4	2
Middle East	10	11	32	49	18	3	5	1	10	6	8	7
Israel	4	6	10	12	12	-1	-1	-2	2	1	(*)	1
Saudi Arabia	2	1	10	25	. . .	. . .	(*)	1	(*)	(*)	(*)	(*)
Other	4	4	12	12	6	4	6	2	9	5	7	7
Asia And Pacific	662	581	580	613	6	200	528	517	536	514	588	480
Australia	56	57	74	63	48	83	426	413	132	188	243	178
China	5	2	1	. . .	4	-14	-3	-2	1	1	-4	3
Hong Kong	70	98	65	88	-85	19	27	20	80	6	(D)	5
India	15	17	14	19	. . .	1	2	-2	3	3	4	2
Indonesia	17	19	10	15	3	3	1	1	3	3	1	1
Japan	268	180	189	210	15	93	62	89	278	272	292	270
Malaysia	39	28	17	15	(*)	-1	-1	. . .	(*)	(*)	(*)	(*)
New Zealand	9	3	1	. . .	7	10	8	-1	(D)	12	9	1
Philippines	11	40	29	34	1	-4	7	1	1	1	5	1
Singapore	32	39	48	84	3	-1	8	(*)	5	6	14	2
South Korea	19	28	20	33	6	4	-4	3	12	9	10	14
Taiwan	9	14	17	27	(*)	. . .	-2	-1	6	5	2	2
Thailand	16	12	16	10	2	3	-3	. . .	2	5	2	(*)
Other	96	44	79	15	3	2	. . .	-3	(D)	3	(D)	2
International Organizations And Unallocated	3	. . .	. . .	5	25	47	2	-18	16	38	10	18
European Union	1 457	1 839	1 983	2 007	810	2 078	2 357	498	5 846	6 317	6 722	8 728
Eastern Europe	14	14	29	34	(*)	3	. . .	-2	(*)	1	1	(*)

See footnote at end of table.

Table B-9. U.S. Other Private Service Payments, 1996–1999—*Continued*

(Millions of dollars.)

Country or region	Insurance—*Continued* Losses				Telecommunications				Business, professional, and technical services			
	1996	1997	1998	1999	1996	1997	1998	1999	1996	1997	1998	1999
ALL COUNTRIES	10 637	9 338	11 210	17 164	8 290	8 346	7 687	6 766	5 547	6 047	6 869	7 430
Canada	602	559	514	380	350	332	309	220	681	837	946	1 204
Mexico	5	7	2	4	1 162	1 104	1 016	827	89	136	113	151
Europe	5 994	5 090	5 347	9 452	1 374	1 370	1 171	1 315	2 594	2 708	3 143	3 369
Belgium and Luxembourg	42	45	95	97	40	35	29	29	60	81	75	84
France	319	242	317	438	102	111	100	86	273	220	290	286
Germany	1 045	1 149	769	1 458	119	123	115	107	424	295	320	377
Italy	84	71	114	109	105	102	87	113	81	75	114	148
Netherlands	33	141	33	953	50	57	42	37	113	117	140	127
Norway	7	14	3	11	10	23	14	13	22	15	63	44
Spain	6	5	4	4	72	64	54	58	81	69	99	81
Sweden	105	80	83	112	16	22	19	12	33	27	57	78
Switzerland	956	839	977	1 207	58	60	57	51	123	124	157	155
United Kingdom	2 870	1 939	2 496	3 669	270	276	250	334	996	1 274	1 378	1 506
Other	527	566	455	1 394	531	496	405	476	389	410	450	484
Latin America And Other Western Hemisphere [1]	3 525	3 378	5 276	7 324	2 978	2 984	2 781	2 301	322	480	540	703
South and Central America [1]	50	55	31	49	2 582	2 544	2 303	1 867	304	444	486	557
Argentina	(D)	(D)	(D)	24	133	103	99	84	31	43	53	73
Brazil	(D)	8	1	1	202	249	201	144	72	105	116	135
Chile	1	2	-1	(*)	40	36	55	37	13	21	15	18
Venezuela	(*)	6	(*)	...	91	92	80	74	21	16	23	28
Other	19	(D)	(D)	19	954	960	851	702	78	122	165	152
Other Western Hemisphere	3 474	3 323	5 245	7 275	395	440	478	433	18	36	54	146
Bermuda	1 887	1 887	3 821	4 721	18	19	17	11	6	19	29	116
Other	1 588	1 436	1 424	2 554	378	420	461	423	12	17	26	30
Africa	2	2	2	2	346	345	357	334	152	171	159	170
South Africa	(*)	2	1	1	52	254	60	57	20	21	21	28
Other	1	1	1	1	294	292	297	278	132	150	137	142
Middle East	-8	4	3	7	560	495	491	421	190	296	368	326
Israel	-10	2	1	3	169	140	111	93	45	102	85	101
Saudi Arabia	(*)	(*)	1	...	109	92	100	76	19	79	159	109
Other	3	1	1	4	282	263	280	252	127	114	124	117
Asia And Pacific	531	314	61	-37	2 439	2 593	2 386	2 015	1 608	1 556	1 711	1 655
Australia	85	105	-182	-235	84	138	121	112	195	170	209	201
China	-3	15	-1	5	356	324	295	238	44	53	70	61
Hong Kong	165	-13	(D)	-15	210	212	192	110	129	134	120	113
India	4	2	2	4	300	314	335	330	36	41	118	165
Indonesia	(*)	(*)	(*)	...	68	75	69	60	29	40	25	30
Japan	263	179	230	181	308	318	251	192	824	716	716	656
Malaysia	...	1	1	(*)	32	36	31	20	17	20	14	11
New Zealand	(D)	1	(*)	2	24	60	55	103	13	19	19	16
Philippines	(*)	5	-2	-1	184	210	187	146	42	59	73	58
Singapore	1	7	6	1	63	67	68	42	50	57	50	67
South Korea	6	5	14	12	238	222	192	145	80	79	106	108
Taiwan	6	5	3	3	188	200	184	132	74	71	93	84
Thailand	(*)	1	5	(*)	91	94	75	60	38	64	41	41
Other	(D)	1	(D)	4	294	323	330	325	37	32	57	46
International Organizations And Unallocated	-9	-10	7	36	244	228	191	160	(*)	(*)	2	3
European Union	5 036	4 240	4 365	8 229	927	938	822	891	2 233	2 302	2 643	2 877
Eastern Europe	(*)	-2	1	3	295	273	210	283	189	242	237	216

See footnote at end of table.

Table B-9. U.S. Other Private Service Payments, 1996–1999—Continued

(Millions of dollars.)

Country or region	Unaffiliated—Continued Other services				Addendum: film and tape rentals			
	1996	1997	1998	1999	1996	1997	1998	1999
ALL COUNTRIES	546	453	507	532	183	159	181	256
Canada	208	193	197	209	76	45	51	62
Mexico	7	4	7	6	(*)	(*)	1	1
Europe	162	157	158	171	72	85	64	106
Belgium and Luxembourg	(D)	4	5	4	1	2	2	11
France	33	17	21	18	19	7	6	12
Germany	20	25	22	14	2	(D)	1	4
Italy	8	8	10	15	(*)	2	(D)	16
Netherlands	14	11	16	13	5	4	5	8
Norway	...	...	...	1	...	...	...	...
Spain	6	(D)	7	6	...	(*)	1	3
Sweden	4	1	1	2	(*)	1	1	1
Switzerland	17	9	9	11	17	7	6	7
United Kingdom	41	63	35	66	26	52	24	39
Other	(D)	(D)	31	21	1	(D)	(D)	5
Latin America And Other Western Hemisphere [1]	46	11	34	18	6	5	26	8
South and Central America [1]	44	9	14	15	4	4	(D)	7
Argentina	1	1	2	3	1	1	2	3
Brazil	2	1	1	1	2	1	1	1
Chile	...	...	...	...	(*)	...	(*)	(*)
Venezuela	(D)	1	1	2	(*)	1	1	2
Other	(D)	2	3	3	(*)	(*)	(D)	(*)
Other Western Hemisphere	2	2	21	3	1	2	(D)	1
Bermuda	...	...	...	...	1	1	1	1
Other	2	2	21	3	(*)	1	(D)	(*)
Africa	1	(D)	1	2	...	(*)	(*)	(*)
South Africa	(D)	(D)	1	1	...	(*)	(*)	(*)
Other	(D)	1	...	1	...	...	...	...
Middle East	...	(D)	5	4	...	3	5	3
Israel	...	...	...	...	...	...	(*)	(*)
Saudi Arabia	...	3	5	3	...	3	5	3
Other	...	(D)	...	1	...	...	...	...
Asia And Pacific	78	56	76	100	25	19	34	75
Australia	16	9	8	17	3	6	4	14
China	...	...	1	1	...	...	1	1
Hong Kong	1	1	...	1	1	1	1	1
India	...	(D)	(D)	...	(*)	2	(*)	(*)
Indonesia	...	...	...	...	...	...	...	...
Japan	42	29	29	13	19	8	7	16
Malaysia	...	...	(D)	31	...	...	...	(D)
New Zealand	...	(D)	...	...	...	(*)	...	...
Philippines	...	...	21	...	(*)	(*)	(D)	...
Singapore	...	...	...	2	...	(*)	(*)	2
South Korea	...	(D)	(D)	...	2	(*)	(D)	1
Taiwan	...	...	...	...	...	...	...	...
Thailand	...	...	...	9	(*)	(*)	...	(D)
Other	19	(D)	(D)	26	...	1	...	...
International Organizations And Unallocated	50	32	35	29	5	1	1	1
European Union	140	146	133	154	55	79	44	98
Eastern Europe	1	(*)	15	2	...	...	...	2

1. Includes Mexico.

Table B-10. U.S. Insurance Receipts, 1996–1999

(Millions of dollars.)

Country or region	Total											
	Net				Premiums received				Losses paid			
	1996	1997	1998	1999	1996	1997	1998	1999	1996	1997	1998	1999
ALL COUNTRIES	2 168	2 473	2 189	2 295	5 929	6 118	7 265	8 259	3 761	3 645	5 076	5 964
Canada	357	389	112	207	1 011	996	887	940	654	606	774	733
Mexico	43	47	47	75	98	114	132	152	55	67	85	77
Europe	683	1 003	752	199	2 727	2 553	2 791	2 639	2 044	1 550	2 039	2 440
Belgium and Luxembourg	65	53	28	17	138	98	100	100	73	45	73	83
France	31	131	37	101	204	220	293	348	172	89	256	248
Germany	129	214	120	-16	312	469	447	343	183	255	327	359
Italy	15	39	39	21	74	78	90	106	60	39	51	86
Netherlands	-14	-38	3	7	42	41	31	36	56	79	28	29
Norway	44	11	22	-31	65	49	48	44	21	37	26	75
Spain	9	16	6	-5	33	24	42	44	24	8	36	50
Sweden	20	10	3	-12	42	28	25	17	22	18	22	29
Switzerland	-41	-1	2	-4	86	55	53	68	127	56	50	71
United Kingdom	385	518	475	128	1 602	1 333	1 459	1 347	1 217	815	984	1 219
Other	40	50	17	-6	129	157	202	184	89	107	185	190
Latin America And Other Western Hemisphere [1]	416	600	897	1 626	1 033	1 391	2 451	3 443	617	791	1 555	1 817
South and Central America [1]	229	163	13	206	553	595	764	755	324	433	751	549
Argentina	43	4	89	114	122	115	219	245	79	111	130	131
Brazil	5	8	7	6	22	26	24	20	17	18	17	15
Chile	26	20	8	6	65	80	96	57	40	61	88	51
Venezuela	19	11	1	-6	26	29	28	28	7	17	27	34
Other	94	73	-139	11	220	232	264	252	126	159	403	241
Other Western Hemisphere	187	438	884	1 419	480	796	1 688	2 688	294	358	804	1 268
Bermuda	108	66	53	16	352	364	601	952	245	298	548	936
Other	79	372	831	1 403	128	432	1 086	1 736	49	60	256	332
Africa	5	7	1	-18	16	16	18	10	11	9	17	28
South Africa	1	4	3	2	7	8	10	4	6	4	7	2
Other	4	4	-1	-20	9	9	8	626	5	5	10	1
Middle East	17	13	15	-11	45	50	73	71	28	37	58	83
Israel	7	(*)	7	11	25	35	52	42	18	34	45	31
Saudi Arabia	1	2	4	-1	4	3	7	3	3	1	4	3
Other	10	10	5	-22	16	12	13	27	6	2	9	48
Asia And Pacific	441	394	304	249	911	894	847	956	470	501	543	707
Australia	36	32	36	1	111	117	124	159	75	85	88	158
China	(*)	-14	18	2	10	14	12	17	10	28	-6	15
Hong Kong	25	12	17	19	53	37	37	35	28	25	19	16
India	3	(*)	-1	(*)	7	7	9	7	4	7	10	6
Indonesia	4	-2	-3	-6	16	15	9	5	12	17	12	11
Japan	319	287	182	231	520	484	453	552	201	197	271	322
Malaysia	2	3	(*)	3	14	13	8	8	12	9	8	5
New Zealand	7	9	8	8	15	13	14	12	8	4	6	4
Philippines	6	5	2	-7	15	15	13	14	9	10	11	21
Singapore	12	20	12	-2	25	30	26	32	12	10	15	34
South Korea	7	6	12	(*)	25	23	32	34	18	18	20	34
Taiwan	14	28	18	5	87	111	90	61	74	83	72	56
Thailand	5	8	5	(*)	12	14	15	17	7	6	10	17
Other	. . .	. . .	-3	-6	. . .	2	4	3	. . .	2	6	9
International Organizations And Unallocated	249	66	107	44	186	216	198	200	-62	150	91	155
European Union	660	979	724	238	2 548	2 418	2 615	2 466	1 888	1 438	1 891	2 228
Eastern Europe	9	11	3	-4	21	25	60	43	12	13	57	48

See footnote at end of table.

Table B-10. U.S. Insurance Receipts, 1996–1999—*Continued*

(Millions of dollars.)

Country or region	Primary insurance											
	Net				Premiums received				Losses paid			
	1996	1997	1998	1999	1996	1997	1998	1999	1996	1997	1998	1999
ALL COUNTRIES	710	444	406	1 685	967	865	939	2 078	257	421	533	393
Canada	115	83	35	21	286	186	141	86	170	103	106	65
Mexico	19	22	21	32	26	31	32	36	7	9	11	4
Europe	194	163	91	109	263	222	234	158	69	59	143	49
Belgium and Luxembourg	5	2	-3	1	8	5	5	2	3	3	8	1
France	12	7	2	3	20	12	21	5	8	5	19	2
Germany	16	11	2	5	25	17	21	7	9	6	19	2
Italy	6	3	-5	2	9	5	8	2	3	2	13	(*)
Netherlands	5	2	4	7	6	5	4	4	1	3	-1	-3
Norway	(D)	(D)	2	...	(D)	(D)	10	5	4	5	8	5
Spain	5	2	-5	2	8	4	(D)	2	3	2	(D)	...
Sweden	4	2	-3	1	8	4	3	1	4	2	6	...
Switzerland	4	2	-1	(D)	8	4	5	(D)	3	2	6	6
United Kingdom	113	115	98	64	133	137	138	95	19	23	40	30
Other	(D)	(D)	1	(D)	(D)	(D)	(D)	(D)	11	7	(D)	6
Latin America And Other Western Hemisphere [1]	118	130	128	1 515	175	191	302	1 569	57	60	174	54
South and Central America [1]	112	115	68	(D)	163	172	229	(D)	51	57	161	47
Argentina	38	33	69	96	51	45	90	100	12	12	21	4
Brazil	8	10	6	7	9	13	8	8	1	2	2	2
Chile	6	6	(D)	12	7	7	(D)	13	1	1	1	1
Venezuela	8	9	9	7	8	10	10	8	1	1	1	1
Other	33	36	(D)	(D)	62	67	(D)	(D)	29	32	124	36
Other Western Hemisphere	6	15	60	(D)	12	18	73	(D)	6	3	13	7
Bermuda	-1	4	(*)	4	2	4	8	4	3	1	8	1
Other	7	11	59	(D)	11	14	64	(D)	4	3	5	6
Africa	3	2	1	1	4	3	3	2	1	1	2	1
South Africa	1	1	(*)	(*)	1	1	(*)	(*)	(*)	(*)	(*)	(*)
Other	2	1	1	2	3	3	3	1	1	1	2	-21
Middle East	2	2	2	-1	4	2	2	2	1	(*)	(*)	3
Israel	1	(*)	(*)	-1	1	1	1	1	(*)	(*)	(*)	2
Saudi Arabia	1	1	(*)	...	1	1	1	(*)	1	...	(*)	(*)
Other	(*)	1	1	(*)	1	1	1	(*)	1	(*)	(*)	(*)
Asia And Pacific	50	26	58	58	80	82	115	142	30	56	57	85
Australia	7	-4	11	2	20	19	35	49	13	23	25	48
China	(*)	(*)	(*)	(*)	1	(*)	1	1	(*)	(*)	(*)	1
Hong Kong	8	1	8	6	13	(D)	14	14	5	(D)	6	8
India	(*)	...	(*)	(*)	1	1	(*)	(*)	(*)	1	(*)	(*)
Indonesia	1	1	1	(*)	2	1	1	1	(*)	(*)	(*)	1
Japan	9	7	16	30	11	11	24	32	2	5	8	2
Malaysia	(*)	1	1	1	1	1	1	1	(*)	(*)	...	...
New Zealand	1	1	(*)	(*)	1	1	1	1	(*)	(*)	(*)	(*)
Philippines	1	...	1	1	2	2	1	2	1	2	(*)	1
Singapore	11	8	6	8	(D)	(D)	(D)	(D)	(D)	(D)	(D)	(D)
South Korea	2	1	7	10	3	5	8	11	1	3	2	2
Taiwan	8	10	3	2	(D)	12	11	(D)	(D)	3	8	(D)
Thailand	1	1	3	-2	1	1	(D)	2	(*)	(*)	(D)	5
Other	(*)	(*)	(*)	(*)	1	(*)	(*)	(*)	(*)	...	(*)	(*)
International Organizations And Unallocated	229	38	91	-19	156	178	142	118	-72	140	51	137
European Union	171	147	88	88	232	198	217	125	61	51	129	37
Eastern Europe	1	(*)	1	(*)	2	1	1	1	1	1	...	(*)

See footnote at end of table.

Table B-10. U.S. Insurance Receipts, 1996–1999—*Continued*

(Millions of dollars.)

Country or region	Reinsurance											
	Net				Premiums received				Losses paid			
	1996	1997	1998	1999	1996	1997	1998	1999	1996	1997	1998	1999
ALL COUNTRIES	1 458	2 029	1 783	610	4 962	5 253	6 326	6 181	3 504	3 224	4 543	5 571
Canada	242	306	77	186	725	810	746	854	484	504	669	668
Mexico	23	25	27	43	72	82	100	116	48	58	74	73
Europe	489	840	661	90	2 464	2 331	2 557	2 481	1 975	1 491	1 896	2 391
Belgium and Luxembourg	61	51	30	17	130	94	95	99	69	43	65	82
France	19	125	35	98	184	209	272	344	165	84	237	246
Germany	113	203	118	-21	287	452	426	336	174	249	308	357
Italy	9	36	44	19	65	73	82	104	56	37	38	85
Netherlands	-19	-40	-1	-1	36	37	27	32	55	77	28	33
Norway	(D)	(D)	21	-31	(D)	(D)	39	39	17	32	18	70
Spain	4	13	10	-7	25	20	(D)	43	21	6	(D)	50
Sweden	15	8	6	-13	34	24	22	16	18	16	16	29
Switzerland	-46	-3	4	(D)	78	51	48	(D)	124	53	44	65
United Kingdom	272	403	377	64	1 470	1 196	1 321	1 253	1 198	793	944	1 189
Other	(D)	(D)	17	(D)	(D)	(D)	(D)	(D)	77	101	(D)	185
Latin America And Other Western Hemisphere [1]	298	470	769	110	858	1 201	2 150	1 874	560	731	1 381	1 763
South and Central America [1]	118	47	-55	(D)	390	423	535	(D)	273	376	590	502
Argentina	5	-29	20	18	71	70	130	145	66	99	109	127
Brazil	-2	-3	1	-1	13	13	16	12	15	16	15	13
Chile	19	14	(D)	-5	58	74	(D)	44	39	60	88	50
Venezuela	11	3	-8	-13	18	19	18	20	7	16	25	33
Other	61	37	(D)	(D)	158	164	(D)	(D)	98	127	279	206
Other Western Hemisphere	181	423	824	(D)	468	778	1 615	(D)	287	355	791	1 262
Bermuda	109	62	53	13	351	360	593	948	242	298	540	935
Other	72	361	771	(D)	117	418	1 022	(D)	45	57	251	326
Africa	2	5	(*)	-19	11	13	15	8	9	8	15	27
South Africa	(*)	3	3	2	6	7	10	4	5	4	7	2
Other	2	2	-2	4	6	6	6	25	4	4	8	1
Middle East	15	11	13	-11	41	48	70	70	26	37	57	80
Israel	6	...	6	12	24	34	51	41	18	34	45	29
Saudi Arabia	(*)	1	3	-1	3	3	7	2	2	2	4	3
Other	9	10	4	-22	15	11	12	26	6	2	9	48
Asia And Pacific	391	368	246	191	831	812	732	814	440	444	486	623
Australia	30	36	26	-1	92	98	89	110	62	62	63	110
China	...	-15	18	1	9	14	12	15	10	28	-6	14
Hong Kong	17	11	9	13	40	(D)	23	21	23	(D)	14	7
India	2	(*)	-1	...	6	6	9	6	4	6	10	6
Indonesia	2	-3	-4	-7	14	14	8	4	12	16	12	11
Japan	310	280	166	201	509	472	429	521	199	192	263	320
Malaysia	2	3	...	3	13	12	7	7	12	9	8	5
New Zealand	7	9	8	8	14	12	14	11	7	3	6	4
Philippines	6	5	1	-7	13	13	12	13	7	8	11	20
Singapore	2	11	6	-9	(D)	(D)	(D)	(D)	(D)	(D)	(D)	(D)
South Korea	4	5	5	-9	22	19	23	23	18	14	18	32
Taiwan	6	19	15	2	(D)	99	79	(D)	(D)	80	64	(D)
Thailand	4	7	2	3	11	13	(D)	15	7	6	(D)	12
Other	-1	-1	-3	-6	-1	1	3	3	-1	2	6	9
International Organizations And Unallocated	20	28	16	63	30	38	56	82	10	10	40	18
European Union	488	833	636	150	2 316	2 220	2 398	2 341	1 827	1 387	1 762	2 191
Eastern Europe	8	11	1	-5	19	23	59	43	11	12	57	47

1. Includes Mexico.

Table B-11. U.S. Insurance Payments, 1996–1999

(Millions of dollars.)

Country or region	Total											
	Net				Premiums paid				Losses recovered			
	1996	1997	1998	1999	1996	1997	1998	1999	1996	1997	1998	1999
ALL COUNTRIES	3 885	5 873	9 080	4 078	14 522	15 211	20 290	21 242	10 637	9 338	11 210	17 164
Canada	458	518	712	232	1 060	1 077	1 225	612	602	559	514	380
Mexico	-3	-4	3	3	2	2	5	7	5	7	2	4
Europe	553	1 835	2 607	81	6 547	6 925	7 954	9 534	5 994	5 090	5 347	9 452
Belgium and Luxembourg	30	35	33	41	72	80	128	137	42	45	95	97
France	158	319	220	274	477	561	538	712	319	242	317	438
Germany	253	162	846	880	1 298	1 311	1 615	2 338	1 045	1 149	769	1 458
Italy	-24	...	-14	15	60	70	100	124	84	71	114	109
Netherlands	-5	-109	6	(D)	27	32	39	(D)	33	141	33	(D)
Norway	11	1	12	3	17	15	16	14	7	14	3	11
Spain	5	2	6	10	11	7	10	13	6	5	4	4
Sweden	-51	-9	-22	-38	54	72	61	74	105	80	83	112
Switzerland	-272	-247	237	-417	684	591	1 214	790	956	839	977	1 207
United Kingdom	461	1 755	1 256	621	3 332	3 694	3 753	4 289	2 870	1 939	2 496	3 669
Other	-12	-74	25	(D)	515	492	480	(D)	527	566	455	(D)
Latin America And Other Western Hemisphere [1]	2 822	3 265	5 224	3 265	6 347	6 644	10 500	10 589	3 525	3 378	5 276	7 324
South and Central America [1]	41	-11	17	8	91	45	48	57	50	55	31	49
Argentina	1	-5	-3	-9	(D)	(D)	(D)	15	(D)	(D)	(D)	24
Brazil	35	-8	(*)	8	(D)	1	1	9	(D)	8	1	1
Chile	2	-1	2	1	2	1	1	1	1	2	-1	(*)
Venezuela	6	-1	...	(*)	6	4	(*)	(*)	(*)	6	(*)	...
Other	(*)	9	16	6	19	(D)	(D)	24	19	(D)	(D)	19
Other Western Hemisphere	2 782	3 276	5 207	3 257	6 256	6 599	10 452	10 532	3 474	3 323	5 245	7 275
Bermuda	2 201	2 469	3 295	2 705	4 087	4 357	7 116	7 426	1 887	1 887	3 821	4 721
Other	581	806	1 913	552	2 169	2 242	3 337	3 106	1 588	1 436	1 424	2 554
Africa	3	5	3	1	5	8	5	3	2	2	2	2
South Africa	(*)	-1	-1	...	1	1	1	1	(*)	2	1	1
Other	3	6	3	2	4	6	4	1	1	1	1	2
Middle East	18	3	5	1	10	6	8	7	-8	4	3	7
Israel	12	-1	-1	-2	2	1	(*)	1	-10	2	1	3
Saudi Arabia	...	...	...	1	(*)	(*)	(*)	(*)	(*)	(*)	1	...
Other	6	4	6	2	9	5	7	7	3	1	1	4
Asia And Pacific	6	200	528	517	536	514	588	480	531	314	61	-37
Australia	48	83	426	413	132	188	243	178	85	105	-182	-235
China	4	-14	-3	-2	1	1	-4	3	-3	15	-1	5
Hong Kong	-85	19	27	20	80	6	(D)	5	165	-13	(D)	-15
India	...	1	2	-2	3	3	4	2	4	2	2	4
Indonesia	3	3	1	1	3	3	1	1	(*)	(*)	(*)	...
Japan	15	93	62	89	278	272	292	270	263	179	230	181
Malaysia	(*)	-1	-1	...	(*)	(*)	(*)	(*)	...	1	1	(*)
New Zealand	7	10	8	-1	(D)	12	9	1	(D)	1	(*)	2
Philippines	1	-4	7	1	1	1	5	1	(*)	5	-2	-1
Singapore	3	-1	8	(*)	5	6	14	2	1	7	6	1
South Korea	6	4	-4	3	12	9	10	14	6	5	14	12
Taiwan	(*)	...	-2	-1	6	5	2	2	6	5	3	3
Thailand	2	3	-3	...	2	5	2	(*)	(*)	1	5	(*)
Other	3	2	...	-3	(D)	3	(D)	2	(D)	1	(D)	4
International Organizations And Unallocated	25	47	2	-18	16	38	10	18	-9	-10	7	36
European Union	810	2 078	2 357	498	5 846	6 317	6 722	8 728	5 036	4 240	4 365	8 229
Eastern Europe	(*)	3	...	-2	(*)	1	1	(*)	(*)	-2	1	3

See footnote at end of table.

Table B-11. U.S. Insurance Payments, 1996–1999—*Continued*

(Millions of dollars.)

Country or region	Primary insurance											
	Net				Premiums paid				Losses recovered			
	1996	1997	1998	1999	1996	1997	1998	1999	1996	1997	1998	1999
ALL COUNTRIES	1 310	1 558	1 117	1 451	1 528	1 644	1 295	1 580	217	86	178	129
Canada	60	108	115	37	(D)	108	115	38	(D)	(*)	(*)	1
Mexico	(*)	(*)	1	1	(*)	(*)	1	1	...	(*)	(*)	(*)
Europe	897	1 149	833	1 092	985	1 188	887	1 161	88	40	55	68
Belgium and Luxembourg	9	14	(D)	3	9	14	(D)	3	...	(*)	(*)	(*)
France	66	88	44	51	(D)	88	47	51	(D)	1	3	(*)
Germany	16	33	18	19	16	33	19	20	(*)	(*)	1	1
Italy	1	3	1	7	1	3	1	7	(*)	(*)	(*)	(*)
Netherlands	(*)	(*)	1	(*)	(*)	(*)	1	(*)	...	(*)	(*)	(*)
Norway	12	7	10	9	(D)	10	10	9	(D)	2	(*)	(*)
Spain	(*)	(*)	(*)	(*)	(*)	(*)	(*)	(*)	(*)	(*)	(*)	(*)
Sweden	1	1	1	1	2	1	1	1	1	(*)	(*)	(*)
Switzerland	16	28	20	10	16	34	21	16	(*)	6	1	6
United Kingdom	774	964	726	989	853	995	775	1 051	79	31	49	62
Other	3	10	(D)	3	3	10	(D)	3	(*)	(*)	(*)	(*)
Latin America And Other Western Hemisphere [1]	338	280	140	288	443	325	260	348	105	45	121	60
South and Central America [1]	(D)	25	19	24	(D)	26	19	24	...	(*)	(*)	(*)
Argentina	(*)	(*)	(*)	(*)	(*)	(*)	(*)	(*)	...	(*)	(*)	(*)
Brazil	(*)	(*)	(*)	(*)	(*)	(*)	(*)	(*)	...	(*)	(*)	(*)
Chile	2	1	1	1	2	1	1	1	...	(*)	(*)	(*)
Venezuela	5	(D)	(*)	(*)	5	(D)	(*)	(*)	...	(*)	(*)	(*)
Other	(D)	(D)	17	21	(D)	(D)	17	21	...	(*)	(*)	(*)
Other Western Hemisphere	(D)	255	121	265	(D)	300	241	325	105	45	120	60
Bermuda	307	242	123	261	412	287	(D)	311	105	45	(D)	50
Other	(D)	12	-2	3	(D)	13	(D)	14	(*)	1	(D)	11
Africa	4	2	1	2	4	2	1	2	...	(*)	(*)	(*)
South Africa	...	(*)	(*)	(*)	...	(*)	(*)	(*)	...	(*)	...	(*)
Other	4	2	1	2	4	2	1	(*)	...	(*)	(*)	-1
Middle East	8	2	5	5	8	2	5	5	(*)	(*)	(*)	(*)
Israel	2	(*)	(*)	(*)	2	(*)	(*)	(*)	...	(*)	...	(*)
Saudi Arabia	...	(*)	...	(*)	...	(*)	(*)	(*)	...	(*)	(*)	...
Other	6	2	5	5	6	2	5	5	(*)	(*)	(*)	...
Asia And Pacific	2	19	25	26	(D)	19	26	26	(D)	(*)	1	(*)
Australia	-8	9	13	8	(D)	9	14	8	(D)	(*)	(*)	(*)
China	...	(*)	(*)	2	...	(*)	(*)	2	...	(*)	(*)	...
Hong Kong	4	3	2	3	(D)	3	2	3	(D)	(*)	...	(*)
India	...	(*)	...	(*)	...	(*)	(*)	(*)	...	(*)	(*)	(*)
Indonesia	2	1	1	1	2	1	1	1	...	...	(*)	(*)
Japan	2	5	5	11	2	5	5	11	(*)	(*)	(*)	(*)
Malaysia	...	(*)	...	(*)	...	(*)	...	(*)	...	(*)	...	...
New Zealand	...	(*)	2	(*)	...	(*)	2	(*)	...	(*)	...	...
Philippines	(*)	(*)	(*)	(*)	(*)	(*)	(*)	(*)	...	(*)	...	(*)
Singapore	(*)	(*)	(*)	(*)	(*)	(*)	(*)	(*)	...	(*)	(*)	...
South Korea	(*)	(*)	(*)	(*)	(*)	(*)	(*)	(*)	...	(*)	(*)	...
Taiwan	(*)	(*)	(*)	(*)	(*)	(*)	(*)	(*)	...	(*)	(*)	...
Thailand	...	(*)	(*)	(*)	...	(*)	(*)	(*)	...	(*)	(*)	...
Other	2	(*)	1	(*)	(D)	(*)	1	(*)	(D)	(*)	(*)	(*)
International Organizations And Unallocated	2	(*)	...	...	3	(*)	...	...	1	...	...	...
European Union	869	1 112	802	1 073	956	1 144	855	1 135	87	32	54	63
Eastern Europe	(*)	(*)	(*)	(*)	(*)	(*)	(*)	(*)	...	(*)	(*)	(*)

See footnote at end of table.

Table B-11. U.S. Insurance Payments, 1996–1999—*Continued*

(Millions of dollars.)

Country or region	Reinsurance											
	Net				Premiums paid				Losses recovered			
	1996	1997	1998	1999	1996	1997	1998	1999	1996	1997	1998	1999
ALL COUNTRIES	2 575	4 315	7 963	2 627	12 994	13 567	18 995	19 662	10 420	9 252	11 032	17 035
Canada	398	411	597	194	(D)	969	1 110	574	(D)	559	513	380
Mexico	-3	-5	2	1	2	2	4	6	5	7	2	4
Europe	-344	687	1 775	-1 011	5 563	5 737	7 067	8 373	5 907	5 050	5 292	9 384
Belgium and Luxembourg	21	21	(D)	37	63	66	(D)	134	42	45	95	97
France	92	232	176	223	(D)	473	490	661	(D)	241	314	438
Germany	236	129	828	860	1 282	1 278	1 596	2 318	1 045	1 149	768	1 457
Italy	-25	-3	-15	8	59	68	99	117	84	71	114	109
Netherlands	-5	-110	6	(D)	27	31	38	(D)	33	141	32	(D)
Norway	-1	-6	3	-6	(D)	5	6	6	(D)	11	3	11
Spain	5	2	6	9	11	7	10	13	6	5	4	4
Sweden	-52	-10	-22	-39	52	70	61	73	104	80	83	112
Switzerland	-288	-276	217	-427	668	557	1 193	774	956	833	976	1 201
United Kingdom	-312	791	531	-369	2 479	2 699	2 978	3 239	2 792	1 908	2 447	3 607
Other	-15	-84	(D)	(D)	513	481	(D)	(D)	527	566	455	(D)
Latin America And Other Western Hemisphere [1]	2 484	2 985	5 084	2 977	5 904	6 318	10 240	10 240	3 420	3 333	5 155	7 263
South and Central America [1]	(D)	-36	-2	-16	(D)	19	29	33	50	55	31	49
Argentina	1	-5	-3	-9	(D)	(D)	(D)	15	(D)	(D)	(D)	24
Brazil	35	-8	...	8	(D)	(*)	(*)	9	(D)	8	(*)	1
Chile	-1	-2	...	1	(*)	(*)	(*)	(*)	1	2	-1	(*)
Venezuela	1	-6	...	(*)	1	(D)	(*)	(*)	(*)	(D)	(*)	...
Other	(D)	-10	-1	-16	(D)	(D)	(D)	3	(*)	(D)	(D)	19
Other Western Hemisphere	(D)	3 021	5 086	2 993	(D)	6 299	10 211	10 207	3 370	3 278	5 124	7 215
Bermuda	1 894	2 227	3 172	2 444	3 676	4 070	(D)	7 115	1 782	1 843	(D)	4 671
Other	(D)	794	1 914	549	(D)	2 229	(D)	3 092	1 588	1 435	(D)	2 543
Africa	-1	3	1	-1	1	6	4	1	2	2	2	2
South Africa	(*)	-1	-1	...	1	1	1	1	(*)	2	1	1
Other	-1	4	2	1	(*)	5	3	1	1	(*)	1	(*)
Middle East	10	1	(*)	-4	3	4	3	2	-8	44	3	7
Israel	10	-1	-1	-3	(*)	1	(*)	(*)	-10	2	1	3
Saudi Arabia	...	...	...	1	(*)	(*)	(*)	(*)	(*)	(*)	1	...
Other	...	2	1	-2	3	3	3	2	3	1	1	4
Asia And Pacific	4	181	503	490	(D)	495	562	453	(D)	314	59	-37
Australia	56	75	413	404	(D)	180	230	170	(D)	105	-183	-235
China	4	-14	-3	-4	1	1	-4	1	-3	15	-1	5
Hong Kong	-89	16	25	17	(D)	3	(D)	2	(D)	-13	(D)	-15
India	...	1	2	-2	3	3	4	2	4	2	2	4
Indonesia	1	2	...	(*)	1	2	(*)	(*)	(*)	(*)	(*)	...
Japan	13	89	57	77	275	267	287	258	263	179	230	181
Malaysia	(*)	-1	-1	...	(*)	(*)	(*)	(*)	...	1	1	(*)
New Zealand	7	10	6	-1	(D)	11	7	1	(D)	1	(*)	2
Philippines	1	-4	7	1	1	1	5	(*)	(*)	5	-2	-1
Singapore	3	-1	7	(*)	4	6	14	2	1	7	6	1
South Korea	5	3	-4	2	12	9	10	14	6	5	14	12
Taiwan	(*)	-1	-2	-1	6	4	1	2	6	5	3	3
Thailand	2	3	-3	...	2	5	2	(*)	(*)	1	5	(*)
Other	1	2	-1	-3	(D)	3	(D)	1	(D)	1	(D)	4
International Organizations And Unallocated	23	47	2	-18	13	38	10	18	-10	-10	7	36
European Union	-59	966	1 556	-574	4 890	5 174	5 867	7 592	4 949	4 208	4 311	8 167
Eastern Europe	(*)	3	...	-3	(*)	(*)	(*)	(*)	(*)	-2	1	3

1. Includes Mexico.

Table B-12. U.S. Business, Professional, and Technical Service Receipts, Unaffiliated, 1996–1999

(Millions of dollars.)

Country or region	Total				Advertising				Computer and data processing services			
	1996	1997	1998	1999	1996	1997	1998	1999	1996	1997	1998	1999
ALL COUNTRIES	19 466	21 450	22 175	24 368	543	607	488	414	1 617	2 011	1 922	2 291
Canada	1 637	1 879	1 771	2 223	101	114	82	90	202	227	231	244
Mexico	648	796	850	947	11	15	13	7	62	57	61	51
Europe	6 005	7 420	7 629	8 858	251	267	238	197	713	875	867	1 134
Belgium and Luxembourg	182	234	294	325	(D)	4	9	13	16	33	35	44
France	617	750	723	835	27	42	32	19	81	98	73	97
Germany	737	921	975	1 129	36	42	34	35	107	145	136	170
Italy	289	329	397	577	19	25	21	21	24	28	34	44
Netherlands	447	500	471	506	4	9	4	4	109	85	69	95
Norway	62	89	100	118	1	1	1	1	13	21	24	36
Spain	220	237	189	278	6	12	5	5	16	28	30	41
Sweden	224	280	265	279	(D)	(D)	(D)	30	36	39	29	26
Switzerland	317	408	405	380	13	17	21	16	50	45	28	31
United Kingdom	1 614	2 210	2 144	2 629	89	66	62	44	194	264	291	391
Other	1 295	1 462	1 665	1 801	8	(D)	(D)	10	66	88	119	159
Latin America And Other Western Hemisphere [1]	2 916	3 147	3 784	4 018	80	112	89	70	204	207	249	211
South and Central America [1]	2 477	2 846	3 297	3 587	38	68	55	41	195	195	231	190
Argentina	279	299	411	384	1	4	1	3	25	19	19	19
Brazil	407	559	595	570	3	9	(D)	6	66	74	96	47
Chile	135	209	171	208	(D)	(D)	2	1	8	4	8	8
Venezuela	234	257	432	568	1	1	(*)	(*)	15	18	17	33
Other	774	726	838	910	(D)	(D)	(D)	25	20	22	30	32
Other Western Hemisphere	439	301	487	430	41	44	34	28	9	13	18	21
Bermuda	55	54	69	66	(D)	(D)	(D)	10	2	2	7	8
Other	384	247	417	364	(D)	(D)	(D)	19	7	11	10	13
Africa	752	825	940	935	1	3	3	3	22	35	34	52
South Africa	104	117	120	154	(*)	1	(*)	(*)	12	23	17	30
Other	649	707	819	781	(*)	2	3	2	10	12	17	22
Middle East	1 925	1 667	1 649	1 548	5	6	10	5	38	53	65	91
Israel	162	176	180	172	3	4	3	2	9	12	17	28
Saudi Arabia	741	849	876	878	1	1	3	2	21	32	38	46
Other	1 022	641	593	498	1	1	3	1	7	9	10	17
Asia And Pacific	5 929	6 383	6 239	6 574	106	103	67	50	438	613	477	559
Australia	434	473	472	534	4	11	3	3	75	94	60	75
China	526	482	634	782	2	2	2	3	17	23	20	19
Hong Kong	403	310	316	372	33	11	15	7	22	24	20	39
India	128	90	218	212	1	1	2	1	9	12	15	16
Indonesia	508	739	674	605	2	1	(*)	(*)	9	10	8	15
Japan	1 892	2 113	1 904	1 907	40	51	30	22	195	290	200	209
Malaysia	341	244	118	129	(*)	1	1	1	11	16	15	22
New Zealand	102	120	140	151	1	1	(*)	(*)	7	8	10	15
Philippines	157	225	236	174	1	2	1	(*)	14	12	15	10
Singapore	173	193	306	317	6	5	4	6	9	23	26	28
South Korea	539	568	414	454	6	7	3	3	30	53	37	40
Taiwan	262	383	291	516	8	8	3	2	21	35	33	43
Thailand	183	196	275	212	2	2	1	1	17	10	15	21
Other	279	246	240	209	(*)	(*)	1	(*)	1	3	4	6
International Organizations And Unallocated	302	129	162	213	. . .	(*)	(*)	(*)	. . .	(*)	(*)	(*)
European Union	4 672	5 915	6 115	7 308	236	244	211	176	621	774	778	996
Eastern Europe	729	633	749	785	1	2	3	2	24	29	29	57

See footnote at end of table.

Table B-12. U.S. Business, Professional, and Technical Service Receipts, Unaffiliated, 1996–1999—*Continued*

(Millions of dollars.)

Country or region	Database and other information services				Research, development, and testing services				Management, consulting, and public relations services			
	1996	1997	1998	1999	1996	1997	1998	1999	1996	1997	1998	1999
ALL COUNTRIES	1 158	1 479	1 524	1 741	681	893	833	767	1 460	1 632	1 841	1 910
Canada	115	162	174	181	49	63	87	116	124	160	201	170
Mexico	32	54	57	70	9	9	9	13	49	53	47	40
Europe	564	703	718	774	216	361	395	305	553	623	657	838
Belgium and Luxembourg	17	25	28	22	9	22	23	10	12	9	10	20
France	74	79	75	76	24	28	40	33	21	51	56	93
Germany	71	99	86	93	38	68	95	82	54	80	113	141
Italy	70	95	99	112	7	27	28	14	18	17	11	20
Netherlands	25	30	29	34	12	14	13	14	17	27	29	40
Norway	5	6	8	9	2	2	3	7	1	3	3	4
Spain	16	21	23	27	5	8	5	5	3	6	4	10
Sweden	19	24	23	27	13	38	31	32	15	15	17	23
Switzerland	25	36	37	36	47	64	61	27	24	33	47	61
United Kingdom	172	175	204	209	43	46	52	43	135	173	166	179
Other	72	115	105	129	16	43	44	38	253	208	200	244
Latin America And Other Western Hemisphere [1]	86	149	169	225	24	30	30	47	177	231	260	219
South and Central America [1]	69	132	150	200	23	27	30	47	153	210	231	195
Argentina	7	15	21	21	(*)	2	5	9	8	8	8	7
Brazil	10	25	29	51	5	5	3	6	23	67	54	41
Chile	4	7	10	12	(*)	(*)	(*)	(*)	1	4	3	2
Venezuela	8	11	16	21	1	1	3	3	9	12	35	26
Other	8	20	17	26	8	10	9	16	62	67	84	79
Other Western Hemisphere	17	17	19	25	(*)	3	(*)	1	24	21	30	24
Bermuda	4	5	6	5	(*)	1	(*)	(*)	5	3	1	1
Other	13	12	13	20	(*)	2	(*)	(*)	19	18	29	23
Africa	39	45	51	60	14	19	20	17	146	135	146	142
South Africa	(D)	30	35	41	5	4	3	6	8	12	14	19
Other	(D)	15	16	19	9	14	18	11	139	123	132	123
Middle East	51	67	63	74	97	19	19	40	119	124	167	157
Israel	17	9	8	7	6	5	4	5	24	17	20	20
Saudi Arabia	(D)	22	25	29	88	11	12	33	63	64	88	78
Other	(D)	35	31	38	3	2	3	3	32	44	59	59
Asia And Pacific	303	353	348	426	280	398	276	235	340	354	407	379
Australia	74	76	82	112	27	30	25	19	41	49	78	42
China	5	6	10	12	4	5	7	4	10	10	10	10
Hong Kong	24	24	29	35	2	7	2	5	23	12	16	11
India	13	19	26	29	3	4	8	4	15	15	12	9
Indonesia	2	5	3	4	13	10	6	5	37	24	21	21
Japan	100	110	86	94	169	238	159	142	88	128	140	161
Malaysia	6	7	9	12	4	3	(*)	2	3	7	4	3
New Zealand	12	19	22	26	(*)	3	1	1	8	2	3	1
Philippines	3	5	4	5	3	3	5	2	21	26	25	20
Singapore	32	33	37	47	5	7	7	7	6	6	8	9
South Korea	13	19	10	16	23	36	19	8	10	11	12	15
Taiwan	6	11	11	12	19	33	19	21	12	3	4	6
Thailand	7	10	11	13	5	13	(D)	12	8	16	13	15
Other	4	7	7	9	3	6	(D)	4	58	47	62	57
International Organizations And Unallocated	. . .	(*)	1	(*)	1	4	5	7	2	5	2	5
European Union	519	615	631	681	163	277	321	263	288	393	427	555
Eastern Europe	7	32	33	37	4	17	9	7	224	165	149	180

See footnote at end of table.

Table B-12. U.S. Business, Professional, and Technical Service Receipts, Unaffiliated, 1996–1999—*Continued*

(Millions of dollars.)

Country or region	Legal services				Construction, engineering, architectural, and mining services				Industrial engineering			
	1996	1997	1998	1999	1996	1997	1998	1999	1996	1997	1998	1999
ALL COUNTRIES	1 943	2 223	2 419	2 560	3 553	3 503	3 548	4 071	870	1 186	1 316	1 492
Canada	123	162	156	184	98	99	15	144	(D)	87	111	194
Mexico	32	30	39	39	81	104	139	116	24	12	34	78
Europe	1 003	1 211	1 329	1 410	434	717	572	806	105	187	262	402
Belgium and Luxembourg	60	70	87	80	(D)	4	10	3	2	2	11	8
France	194	214	212	237	15	19	4	14	4	9	11	18
Germany	153	158	160	189	23	48	63	70	9	18	24	69
Italy	26	38	44	50	(D)	11	25	(D)	2	4	13	13
Netherlands	27	42	63	46	43	16	11	13	(D)	(D)	37	24
Norway	9	12	8	9	1	1	3	2	1	2	2	2
Spain	11	12	13	15	38	10	7	7	(D)	20	11	32
Sweden	25	23	32	31	3	2	7	2	10	8	12	15
Switzerland	36	46	71	59	7	(D)	10	11	(D)	(D)	(D)	12
United Kingdom	364	467	508	566	58	286	10	157	12	26	40	110
Other	98	130	130	128	203	(D)	421	(D)	13	34	(D)	98
Latin America And Other Western Hemisphere [1]	111	143	156	162	591	460	775	923	247	147	219	207
South and Central America [1]	75	104	104	109	410	430	618	800	245	139	213	196
Argentina	8	11	15	12	23	23	24	27	24	24	(D)	(D)
Brazil	14	17	18	23	61	49	31	57	7	11	22	20
Chile	4	10	9	8	51	68	54	74	(D)	(D)	4	5
Venezuela	7	14	10	10	99	100	245	377	21	19	(D)	4
Other	10	22	14	16	95	86	125	149	(D)	(D)	58	(D)
Other Western Hemisphere	36	39	52	53	181	31	158	123	3	8	6	11
Bermuda	19	18	27	26	(*)	(*)	3	2	(*)	(*)	(*)	(*)
Other	17	21	25	27	181	31	155	121	3	8	6	11
Africa	10	8	8	7	235	300	371	368	(D)	42	(D)	29
South Africa	8	4	5	4	10	9	7	8	(D)	(*)	(*)	(*)
Other	2	4	3	3	225	291	364	360	8	41	(D)	29
Middle East	49	65	60	54	1 028	616	571	447	46	120	(D)	96
Israel	13	23	22	26	26	14	7	7	5	(D)	14	9
Saudi Arabia	12	11	10	5	(D)	205	351	283	39	(D)	39	58
Other	24	32	28	22	(D)	398	213	157	3	(D)	(D)	29
Asia And Pacific	645	634	710	744	1 166	1 309	1 244	1 382	376	602	508	564
Australia	32	40	45	50	37	5	5	29	6	10	6	19
China	19	19	17	37	165	170	210	362	34	52	(D)	5
Hong Kong	78	77	76	89	3	19	12	11	1	1	1	3
India	3	2	11	3	30	2	93	98	25	10	10	5
Indonesia	8	9	8	7	248	602	535	469	(D)	9	13	10
Japan	415	372	403	390	178	106	41	78	104	219	237	191
Malaysia	2	2	2	2	183	60	10	26	(D)	(D)	13	7
New Zealand	3	4	4	4	. . .	0	1	(*)	(*)	1	5	2
Philippines	6	3	7	4	53	114	116	81	5	1	1	4
Singapore	8	13	18	18	14	12	73	75	13	9	18	7
South Korea	48	57	74	96	137	146	48	45	32	51	21	38
Taiwan	15	24	28	31	28	22	55	70	40	(D)	17	(D)
Thailand	4	5	3	6	49	43	38	35	11	(D)	(D)	(D)
Other	4	5	13	7	41	10	8	4	(D)	25	23	21
International Organizations And Unallocated	1	(*)	(*)	(*)	(*)	(*)	1	1	. . .	1	(D)	(*)
European Union	901	1 073	1 162	1 264	250	487	343	632	78	156	172	307
Eastern Europe	51	72	84	74	153	102	208	156	4	17	(D)	77

See footnote at end of table.

Table B-12. U.S. Business, Professional, and Technical Service Receipts, Unaffiliated, 1996–1999—*Continued*

(Millions of dollars.)

Country or region	Installation, maintenance, and repair of equipment				Other			
	1996	1997	1998	1999	1996	1997	1998	1999
ALL COUNTRIES	3 648	3 272	3 212	3 487	3 994	4 645	5 072	5 634
Canada	273	240	227	331	(D)	566	486	569
Mexico	158	219	207	246	191	243	244	286
Europe	965	937	901	986	1 200	1 539	1 689	2 006
Belgium and Luxembourg	25	34	25	23	(D)	31	57	103
France	83	96	94	98	95	115	125	150
Germany	112	123	130	135	135	139	134	144
Italy	34	45	79	59	(D)	39	43	(D)
Netherlands	122	110	92	93	(D)	(D)	121	144
Norway	12	11	15	11	18	30	34	37
Spain	62	54	21	53	(D)	67	69	84
Sweden	41	37	36	44	(D)	(D)	(D)	50
Switzerland	41	36	20	31	(D)	94	(D)	95
United Kingdom	226	243	259	296	322	465	552	634
Other	206	149	130	144	361	386	413	(D)
Latin America And Other Western Hemisphere [1]	417	412	461	507	978	1 256	1 374	1 447
South and Central America [1]	371	382	404	477	898	1 161	1 261	1 333
Argentina	71	17	57	66	112	176	(D)	(D)
Brazil	50	74	69	85	170	227	(D)	234
Chile	6	5	11	27	39	60	69	73
Venezuela	24	21	14	11	50	59	(D)	82
Other	62	45	45	42	337	396	(D)	(D)
Other Western Hemisphere	47	30	57	30	80	95	113	114
Bermuda	1	(*)	1	1	(D)	(D)	(D)	14
Other	46	30	56	29	(D)	(D)	(D)	100
Africa	130	65	45	31	(D)	173	(D)	226
South Africa	8	16	12	17	(D)	19	26	27
Other	122	50	34	14	(D)	155	(D)	198
Middle East	418	496	406	431	73	99	(D)	153
Israel	28	49	45	29	31	(D)	40	40
Saudi Arabia	354	379	293	329	(D)	(D)	16	15
Other	37	68	68	73	(D)	(D)	(D)	98
Asia And Pacific	1 435	1 116	1 162	1 194	841	900	1 041	1 042
Australia	75	88	86	91	63	69	84	93
China	140	66	95	97	130	130	(D)	232
Hong Kong	104	35	67	85	114	100	78	87
India	13	9	21	20	16	15	20	26
Indonesia	62	32	41	35	(D)	37	39	37
Japan	429	412	384	404	174	186	224	217
Malaysia	74	38	38	35	(D)	(D)	26	21
New Zealand	14	23	28	31	57	59	66	70
Philippines	27	30	37	29	24	30	25	20
Singapore	66	65	77	92	13	20	37	27
South Korea	186	135	130	123	54	52	59	72
Taiwan	82	71	86	113	31	(D)	36	(D)
Thailand	69	51	42	28	11	(D)	16	(D)
Other	93	61	29	10	(D)	81	(D)	91
International Organizations And Unallocated	9	6	8	8	289	112	(D)	192
European Union	755	801	810	906	859	1 094	1 259	1 529
Eastern Europe	114	32	26	11	148	165	(D)	183

1. Includes Mexico.

Table B-13. U.S. Business, Professional, and Technical Service Payments, Unaffiliated, 1996–1999

(Millions of dollars.)

Country or region	Total				Advertising				Computer and data processing services			
	1996	1997	1998	1999	1996	1997	1998	1999	1996	1997	1998	1999
ALL COUNTRIES	5 547	6 047	6 869	7 430	971	773	886	757	276	276	399	432
Canada	681	837	946	1 204	46	50	48	34	38	71	78	67
Mexico	89	136	113	151	22	8	14	19	2	3	3	1
Europe	2 594	2 708	3 143	3 369	417	303	372	263	155	104	153	162
Belgium and Luxembourg	60	81	75	84	13	14	10	9	3	7	2	3
France	273	220	290	286	54	32	51	27	(D)	7	7	3
Germany	424	295	320	377	99	63	59	40	(D)	14	27	44
Italy	81	75	114	148	23	16	20	16	1	1	3	2
Netherlands	113	117	140	127	6	5	8	5	6	6	1	(*)
Norway	22	15	63	44	2	2	3	2	9	(*)	(D)	(D)
Spain	81	69	99	81	37	26	34	19	2	9	3	1
Sweden	33	27	57	78	7	3	8	5	1	1	4	1
Switzerland	123	124	157	155	15	13	19	12	3	4	5	7
United Kingdom	996	1 274	1 378	1 506	136	106	137	113	45	47	68	87
Other	389	410	450	484	25	22	25	15	3	9	(D)	(D)
Latin America And Other Western Hemisphere [1]	322	480	540	703	56	44	71	85	5	9	14	10
South and Central America [1]	304	444	486	557	55	42	69	82	5	7	12	7
Argentina	31	43	53	73	6	2	9	9	(*)	(*)	2	2
Brazil	72	105	116	135	17	16	23	38	1	2	1	1
Chile	13	21	15	18	2	2	2	4	(*)	(*)	(*)	(*)
Venezuela	21	16	23	28	1	1	2	1	(*)	1	1	1
Other	78	122	165	152	7	13	19	11	(*)	1	4	1
Other Western Hemisphere	18	36	54	146	1	1	2	4	(*)	2	2	2
Bermuda	6	19	29	116	(*)	1	1	(*)	(*)	1	1	1
Other	12	17	26	30	1	1	1	3	(*)	1	1	1
Africa	152	171	159	170	6	6	8	5	(*)	1	2	1
South Africa	20	21	21	28	3	3	5	3	(*)	1	(*)	(*)
Other	132	150	137	142	2	2	4	2	(*)	(*)	1	1
Middle East	190	296	368	326	31	13	20	18	2	7	13	17
Israel	45	102	85	101	(D)	1	3	2	1	2	7	13
Saudi Arabia	19	79	159	109	(*)	2	5	4	1	4	5	3
Other	127	114	124	117	(D)	10	12	11	(*)	(*)	(*)	(*)
Asia And Pacific	1 608	1 556	1 711	1 655	416	358	366	352	76	84	139	176
Australia	195	170	209	201	25	21	24	15	11	11	7	5
China	44	53	70	61	4	5	4	4	1	2	2	2
Hong Kong	129	134	120	113	18	10	14	8	5	11	5	2
India	36	41	118	165	2	4	4	2	2	8	82	131
Indonesia	29	40	25	30	3	2	1	(*)	1	1	2	2
Japan	824	716	716	656	310	261	274	284	39	20	21	15
Malaysia	17	20	14	11	2	2	1	1	(*)	1	(*)	(*)
New Zealand	13	19	19	16	3	4	4	1	(*)	1	1	(*)
Philippines	42	59	73	58	2	2	3	1	5	9	9	11
Singapore	50	57	50	67	11	8	5	3	5	5	4	2
South Korea	80	79	106	108	21	18	13	14	2	4	1	1
Taiwan	74	71	93	84	11	14	14	16	4	9	3	4
Thailand	38	64	41	41	2	3	3	1	(*)	2	(*)	(*)
Other	37	32	57	46	3	3	2	2	(*)	(*)	1	1
International Organizations And Unallocated	(*)	(*)	2	3	...	(*)	(*)	...	...	...	(*)	...
European Union	2 233	2 302	2 643	2 877	393	280	343	244	142	96	135	143
Eastern Europe	189	242	237	216	3	4	4	1	(*)	4	1	(*)

See footnote at end of table.

Table B-13. U.S. Business, Professional, and Technical Service Payments, Unaffiliated, 1996–1999—*Continued*

(Millions of dollars.)

Country or region	Database and other information services				Research, development, and testing services				Management, consulting, and public relations services			
	1996	1997	1998	1999	1996	1997	1998	1999	1996	1997	1998	1999
ALL COUNTRIES	146	128	151	198	379	564	667	782	497	687	888	867
Canada	6	6	18	21	33	54	61	86	72	80	120	173
Mexico	(*)	(*)	(*)	(*)	3	4	6	3	6	20	14	28
Europe	107	84	95	133	246	320	453	510	203	249	324	381
Belgium and Luxembourg	(*)	(*)	1	1	5	5	10	14	5	9	9	13
France	8	(D)	11	(D)	11	21	17	25	20	13	17	38
Germany	4	3	11	13	33	35	45	56	25	20	23	45
Italy	(*)	(*)	(*)	1	2	10	6	13	6	3	3	4
Netherlands	20	11	14	15	9	20	27	24	6	8	19	12
Norway	(*)	(*)	(*)	(*)	3	4	22	5	1	1	1	2
Spain	4	7	1	(*)	3	3	5	7	4	3	9	7
Sweden	(*)	(*)	(*)	(*)	8	7	14	39	3	1	3	2
Switzerland	2	3	4	6	31	25	29	45	8	14	8	5
United Kingdom	64	42	46	48	68	103	205	197	94	147	183	196
Other	5	(D)	6	(D)	73	87	72	86	30	30	48	57
Latin America And Other Western Hemisphere [1]	1	3	1	1	32	32	31	33	40	89	83	83
South and Central America [1]	(*)	2	(*)	1	29	30	29	31	38	86	78	81
Argentina	(*)	(*)	(*)	(*)	2	3	4	4	4	3	3	3
Brazil	(*)	1	(*)	(*)	13	12	8	9	8	32	26	22
Chile	...	(*)	(*)	(*)	2	2	2	2	3	3	1	1
Venezuela	...	(*)	(*)	(*)	(*)	(*)	1	1	4	2	5	4
Other	...	(*)	(*)	(*)	9	9	8	12	13	26	29	24
Other Western Hemisphere	1	1	(*)	(*)	3	2	2	1	2	3	5	2
Bermuda	(*)	(*)	(*)	(*)	(*)	1	1	(*)	1	1	2	(*)
Other	1	1	(*)	(*)	3	1	1	1	1	2	3	2
Africa	(*)	4	(*)	(*)	25	26	(D)	28	35	34	(D)	(D)
South Africa	(*)	1	(*)	(*)	2	1	1	6	1	2	1	2
Other	(*)	3	(*)	(*)	22	25	(D)	22	34	32	(D)	(D)
Middle East	(*)	1	1	2	4	(D)	(D)	49	12	(D)	(D)	(D)
Israel	(*)	(*)	1	2	2	(D)	(D)	46	4	2	2	2
Saudi Arabia	(*)	(*)	...	(*)	2	(*)	1	2	3	(D)	(D)	(D)
Other	...	(*)	(*)	(*)	(*)	2	1	1	5	7	3	5
Asia And Pacific	31	30	36	42	39	(D)	64	76	135	(D)	209	126
Australia	1	1	2	2	7	9	13	15	17	22	33	20
China	3	2	3	4	2	2	3	3	1	6	13	8
Hong Kong	1	1	1	1	(*)	1	2	1	7	6	6	3
India	(*)	1	3	3	3	3	3	5	4	5	4	4
Indonesia	(*)	(*)	(*)	(*)	1	5	2	4	4	8	5	6
Japan	20	16	20	20	14	24	19	25	29	29	37	14
Malaysia	(*)	(*)	(*)	(*)	(*)	(*)	(*)	(*)	7	(D)	7	4
New Zealand	(*)	(*)	(*)	(*)	3	2	4	2	2	1	1	1
Philippines	4	2	3	5	1	3	3	3	14	28	(D)	22
Singapore	(*)	4	3	3	1	1	1	1	3	3	3	5
South Korea	1	1	(*)	2	2	4	6	8	(D)	13	10	5
Taiwan	1	(*)	(*)	(*)	1	4	3	2	4	2	(D)	12
Thailand	(*)	1	(*)	(*)	2	(D)	3	3	(D)	(D)	(D)	(D)
Other	(*)	1	(*)	(*)	2	(D)	3	4	9	4	5	(D)
International Organizations And Unallocated	...	...	(*)	...	...	(*)	(*)	(*)	(*)	(*)	(*)	(*)
European Union	105	78	89	125	156	226	351	405	169	210	277	329
Eastern Europe	(*)	3	1	1	55	61	48	46	22	20	26	32

See footnote at end of table.

Table B-13. U.S. Business, Professional, and Technical Service Payments, Unaffiliated, 1996–1999—*Continued*

(Millions of dollars.)

Country or region	Legal services				Construction, engineering, architectural, and mining services				Industrial engineering			
	1996	1997	1998	1999	1996	1997	1998	1999	1996	1997	1998	1999
ALL COUNTRIES	615	539	637	844	465	463	544	530	197	211	205	141
Canada	53	33	36	44	100	61	56	86	24	44	37	29
Mexico	12	14	15	19	4	9	3	4	1	1	2	2
Europe	309	275	343	413	166	220	264	201	46	49	81	68
Belgium and Luxembourg	7	7	11	15	4	(D)	1	(*)	1	1	(*)	(*)
France	24	19	29	29	13	3	44	(D)	(D)	4	2	2
Germany	64	45	58	60	(D)	10	8	6	(D)	19	11	2
Italy	11	8	9	16	1	1	11	4	3	2	(D)	(D)
Netherlands	9	7	10	9	21	34	(D)	9	(*)	(*)	1	(*)
Norway	4	4	5	6	1	(*)	4	11	(*)	(*)	1	1
Spain	11	9	9	11	(*)	(*)	(*)	(*)	2	(*)	(D)	16
Sweden	6	5	6	6	. . .	(*)	(*)	(*)	(*)	1	(D)	8
Switzerland	7	8	11	15	7	4	23	7	(*)	1	2	2
United Kingdom	130	128	149	176	22	81	60	80	19	14	8	18
Other	37	37	47	69	(D)	(D)	(D)	(D)	2	6	1	(D)
Latin America And Other Western Hemisphere [1]	49	61	74	176	12	33	17	39	3	2	5	16
South and Central America [1]	46	54	61	(D)	11	31	16	39	2	2	4	16
Argentina	6	7	8	9	(*)	(*)	(*)	7	(*)	(*)	(*)	1
Brazil	11	15	16	18	(*)	5	2	2	1	(*)	(*)	(D)
Chile	3	2	3	3	1	1	(*)	2	. . .	(*)	(*)	(*)
Venezuela	4	4	4	5	1	(*)	(*)	1	(*)	(*)	(*)	1
Other	9	12	16	18	5	(D)	3	(D)	(*)	1	1	(D)
Other Western Hemisphere	3	7	13	(D)	1	2	1	(*)	(*)	1	1	(*)
Bermuda	1	4	9	(D)	. . .	2	(*)	(*)	(*)	1	1	(*)
Other	1	2	4	4	1	(*)	(*)	(*)	. . .	(*)	(*)	(*)
Africa	5	6	8	10	31	24	26	27	(*)	3	2	3
South Africa	2	2	2	3	(*)	(*)	(*)	1	. . .	(*)	. . .	(*)
Other	3	3	6	7	31	24	25	27	(*)	3	2	3
Middle East	11	9	11	12	(D)	(D)	84	95	(D)	(*)	(*)	3
Israel	5	4	5	6	(*)	4	(D)	13	(*)	(*)	. . .	1
Saudi Arabia	3	1	2	2	2	2	(D)	(D)	3	(*)	. . .	(*)
Other	4	4	4	4	(D)	(D)	(D)	(D)	(D)	(*)	(*)	2
Asia And Pacific	188	155	164	189	(D)	(D)	98	78	(D)	113	80	22
Australia	21	21	23	22	28	5	15	21	2	1	(*)	(*)
China	7	8	10	13	3	1	1	(*)	2	1	1	1
Hong Kong	27	26	20	24	(*)	1	12	11	(*)	(*)	(*)	(*)
India	5	2	4	5	(*)	(*)	1	1	2	(D)	(D)	1
Indonesia	2	3	3	3	5	2	1	1	. . .	(*)	(*)	(*)
Japan	87	57	54	70	(D)	24	32	5	(D)	(D)	(D)	(D)
Malaysia	1	1	1	2	(*)	(*)	(*)	(*)	(*)	(*)	. . .	(*)
New Zealand	4	4	5	6	(*)	(*)	(*)	(*)	. . .	(*)	. . .	(*)
Philippines	2	2	2	4	8	3	3	4	. . .	(*)	(*)	(*)
Singapore	5	6	5	5	1	7	2	(D)	. . .	2	(D)	(D)
South Korea	16	14	17	18	(*)	1	(D)	(D)	1	4	(*)	1
Taiwan	9	8	9	9	1	2	6	1	(*)	(*)	(*)	(*)
Thailand	3	2	4	6	3	4	2	2	(*)	(*)	(*)	(*)
Other	1	2	7	4	9	(D)	(D)	2	. . .	(D)	(*)	(*)
International Organizations And Unallocated	. . .	(*)	(*)	1	(*)	(*)	. . .	2	. . .	. . .	. . .	. . .
European Union	277	242	301	357	132	148	155	133	46	45	77	63
Eastern Europe	16	17	18	27	(D)	(D)	(D)	(D)	(*)	3	1	1

See footnote at end of table.

Table B-13. U.S. Business, Professional, and Technical Service Payments, Unaffiliated, 1996–1999—*Continued*

(Millions of dollars.)

Country or region	Installation, maintenance, and repair of equipment				Other			
	1996	1997	1998	1999	1996	1997	1998	1999
ALL COUNTRIES	239	307	310	302	1 763	2 099	2 181	2 576
Canada	26	60	87	102	282	378	405	561
Mexico	2	3	5	7	37	75	51	67
Europe	158	173	111	138	786	931	947	1 100
Belgium and Luxembourg	1	2	2	(*)	20	(D)	30	30
France	3	7	6	3	64	(D)	106	109
Germany	10	11	10	26	99	76	68	86
Italy	9	2	1	29	26	30	(D)	(D)
Netherlands	3	3	4	4	33	23	(D)	47
Norway	(*)	3	8	3	2	2	(D)	(D)
Spain	3	(*)	7	1	15	12	(D)	18
Sweden	2	3	1	6	5	6	(D)	10
Switzerland	(*)	5	2	1	49	47	54	55
United Kingdom	(D)	133	63	43	(D)	473	458	548
Other	(D)	5	7	22	(D)	134	136	146
Latin America And Other Western Hemisphere [1]	5	7	41	10	120	200	204	250
South and Central America [1]	5	6	40	9	112	184	176	(D)
Argentina	1	(*)	3	(*)	11	(D)	16	(D)
Brazil	3	2	(D)	1	17	21	(D)	(D)
Chile	(*)	(*)	(*)	(*)	2	12	7	6
Venezuela	(*)	(*)	(*)	(*)	11	7	10	13
Other	(*)	1	(D)	(*)	34	(D)	(D)	(D)
Other Western Hemisphere	...	1	1	1	7	16	28	(D)
Bermuda	...	1	(*)	(*)	3	7	14	(D)
Other	...	(*)	1	1	4	8	14	17
Africa	1	1	1	1	50	65	68	(D)
South Africa	(*)	(*)	1	(*)	11	10	10	13
Other	1	1	(*)	1	39	55	58	(D)
Middle East	3	5	10	2	(D)	51	62	(D)
Israel	(*)	(*)	7	1	(D)	(D)	16	16
Saudi Arabia	1	2	2	(*)	3	(D)	(D)	10
Other	1	2	1	(*)	(D)	(D)	(D)	(D)
Asia And Pacific	46	61	59	48	(D)	473	494	545
Australia	(D)	4	5	3	(D)	74	86	97
China	3	2	2	2	19	25	32	25
Hong Kong	1	6	3	2	68	72	57	60
India	(*)	1	1	(*)	18	(D)	(D)	12
Indonesia	1	1	2	1	11	17	8	12
Japan	(D)	19	16	17	197	(D)	(D)	(D)
Malaysia	2	2	(*)	(*)	4	(D)	4	3
New Zealand	1	(*)	(*)	(*)	2	7	4	6
Philippines	1	1	(*)	(*)	6	8	(D)	9
Singapore	1	6	(D)	7	24	16	20	24
South Korea	1	3	(D)	8	(D)	18	24	(D)
Taiwan	4	(D)	9	6	40	(D)	(D)	32
Thailand	1	2	1	1	(D)	(D)	(D)	(D)
Other	...	(D)	(*)	(*)	13	15	(D)	(D)
International Organizations And Unallocated	...	(*)	...	...	...	(*)	1	...
European Union	152	164	100	117	660	812	814	959
Eastern Europe	1	1	1	1	(D)	(D)	(D)	(D)

1. Includes Mexico.

PART C. U.S. FOREIGN TRADE IN GOODS

U.S. Trade in Goods, 1999
(Billions of dollars)

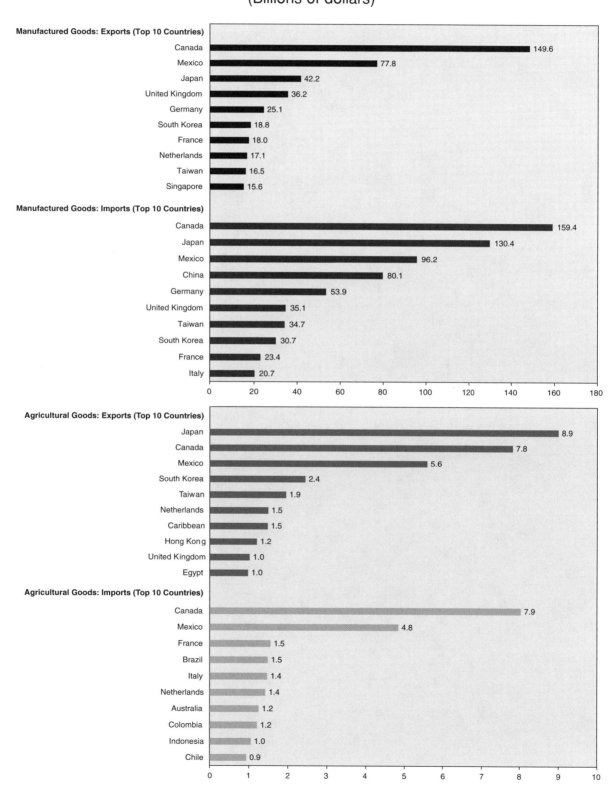

Manufactured Goods: Exports (Top 10 Countries)

Canada	149.6
Mexico	77.8
Japan	42.2
United Kingdom	36.2
Germany	25.1
South Korea	18.8
France	18.0
Netherlands	17.1
Taiwan	16.5
Singapore	15.6

Manufactured Goods: Imports (Top 10 Countries)

Canada	159.4
Japan	130.4
Mexico	96.2
China	80.1
Germany	53.9
United Kingdom	35.1
Taiwan	34.7
South Korea	30.7
France	23.4
Italy	20.7

Agricultural Goods: Exports (Top 10 Countries)

Japan	8.9
Canada	7.8
Mexico	5.6
South Korea	2.4
Taiwan	1.9
Netherlands	1.5
Caribbean	1.5
Hong Kong	1.2
United Kingdom	1.0
Egypt	1.0

Agricultural Goods: Imports (Top 10 Countries)

Canada	7.9
Mexico	4.8
France	1.5
Brazil	1.5
Italy	1.4
Netherlands	1.4
Australia	1.2
Colombia	1.2
Indonesia	1.0
Chile	0.9

PART C. U.S. FOREIGN TRADE IN GOODS

NOTES AND DEFINITIONS

Tables C-1 through C-3, C-5, and C-8 through C-11 are all based on current-dollar trade value data collected by the U.S. Bureau of the Census and compiled by the International Trade Administration, Office of Trade and Economic Analysis (OTEA). Tables C-4, C-6, C-7, and C-12 present price indexes compiled by the U.S. Department of Labor, Bureau of Labor Statistics.

All the values in this and subsequent chapters are reported on the "Census basis," which differs from both the NIPA values for goods exports and imports and the values reported in Table A-6 on the "balance of payments basis" (BOP). The differences among the three systems of valuation are described in the "General Notes on the Data" section of "Using This Book."

The export statistics are initially collected and compiled by the Bureau of the Census into the approximately 8,000 commodity classifications contained in *Schedule B, Statistical Classification of Domestic and Foreign Commodities Exported from the United States*. Schedule B is a U.S. Bureau of the Census publication and is based on the Harmonized Commodity Description and Coding System (Harmonized System).

The import statistics are initially collected and compiled in terms of the approximately 14,000 commodity classifications in the *Harmonized Tariff Schedule of the United States Annotated for Statistical Reporting Purposes*.

Related to the Harmonized System is the Standard International Trade Classification (SITC). This is an international statistical classification of the commodities in world trade, maintained by the United Nations. These uniform classifications facilitate the international comparison of trade-by-commodity data. The values in Table C-5 use the SITC, as do the price indexes in Tables C-6 and C-7.

The data in Table C-8 for 1997 through 1999 use the new North American Industry Classification System (NAICS); the data for earlier years in Table C-9 are based on Standard Industrial Classification (SIC) product codes. These data have been converted from the Harmonized System by the Bureau of the Census. Classification of goods exports into a NAICS or SIC product code does not necessarily imply that all the goods so classified are produced in the corresponding industry, nor that all the products produced by the SIC industry appear in the SIC product code. The SIC industry codes classify establishments by type of activity, and each producing establishment is coded based on its principal activity. However, one establishment sometimes may produce more than one type of product. Exports and imports are classified by product irrespective of whether the product was produced in an establishment primarily producing this product.

The new North American Industry Classification System (NAICS) is being adopted by all three NAFTA members, and in the United States, it is replacing the Standard Industrial Classification (SIC). The first data on a NAICS basis were released during 1999, and NAICS will be fully implemented around 2004 or later. Bernan Press, in cooperation with the National Technical Information Service, is the official publisher and distributor of the manual: *North American Industry Classification System, United States, 1997*, Executive Office of the President, Office of Management and Budget. Tables matching NAICS to SIC definitions are included, as is a complete index. The manual is available in hardcover, softcover or as a CD-ROM by calling Bernan (1-800-865-3457) or placing an order through the Bernan internet site, www.bernan.com.

Table C-1. U.S. Foreign Trade in Goods, 1970–1999

Source: Bureau of the Census; data compiled by Office of Trade and Economic Analysis (OTEA), International Trade Administration.

DATA NOTES

Census data concordances link the 1980–1992 trade figures into time series that are as consistent as possible. Data for 1970 to 1979 are not linked and are from published sources. Import values are based on transaction prices whenever possible ("free alongside ship" [f.a.s.] from 1974 to 1979, and customs basis thereafter), maintaining a consistent data series over time. Import data before 1974 do not exist on a transaction price basis. 1991 imports include revisions for passenger cars, trucks, petroleum, and petroleum products not included elsewhere. *Total goods* includes military grant aid and trade between the U.S. Virgin Islands and foreign countries. For all categories other than total goods, data for 1970 to 1980 exclude trade between the U.S. Virgin Islands and foreign countries.

Manufactured goods include commodity sections 5 through 9 under Schedules A and E for 1970 to 1982, and SITC (Standard International Trade Classification) revision 3 for 1983 to present. Manufactures include undocumented exports to Canada, nonmonetary gold (excluding gold ore, scrap, and base bullion), and special category shipments.

Agricultural products from 1983 forward utilize the latest Census definition that excludes manufactured goods that were previously classified as manufactured agricultural products.

Mineral fuels include commodity section 3 under SITC revision 1 for 1970 to 1976, SITC revision 2 for 1977 to 1982, and SITC revision 3 from 1983 forward. This category includes petroleum, petroleum products, and natural gas and related products.

DATA AVAILABILITY

This table, formerly published by OTEA in *Foreign Trade Highlights*, now may be found on the OTEA website, http://www.ita.doc.gov/tradestats.

Table C-2. U.S. Foreign Trade in Goods by Principal End-Use Category, 1978–1999

Table C-3. U.S. Foreign Trade in Goods by Principal End-Use Category: Constant Dollar Basis, 1985–1999

Source: Bureau of the Census; data compiled by Office of Trade and Economic Analysis (OTEA), International Trade Administration.

DATA NOTES

Data in this table are classified in accordance with the use for which the goods are intended.

Foods, feeds, and beverages include alcoholic beverages, animal feeds, bakery products, corn, dairy products, eggs, fish, shellfish, fruits, frozen juices, meat, poultry, nonagricultural foods, nuts, oilseeds, food oils, rice sorghum, barley, oats, soybeans, vegetables, wheat, and other foods.

Industrial supplies and materials include aluminum and alumina; chemical fertilizers; inorganic and organic chemicals; other chemicals; coal and other fuels; copper; cotton fiber cloth; raw cotton; crude oil; electric energy; finished metal shapes; finished textile supplies; fuel oil; natural gas; plate and sheet glass; hair, waste materials; hides and skins; industrial rubber products; iron and steel products; leather and furs; logs and lumber; manmade cloth; metallurgical grade coal; manufactured mineral supplies; natural gas liquids; newsprint; nonferrous metals; nonmetallic minerals; nonmonetary gold; nontextile floor tiles; nuclear fuel materials; petroleum products; plastic materials; precious metals; pulpwood and woodpulp; shingles, molding, and wallboard; steelmaking materials; primary synthetic rubber; audio and video tapes; unmanufactured tobacco; manufactured wood supplies and other industrial supplies.

Capital goods, except automotive include agricultural machinery and equipment; business machines and equipment; civilian aircraft; commercial vessels; computer accessories; computers; drilling and oilfield equipment; electric apparatus; engines for civilian aircraft; excavating machinery; food and tobacco machinery; generators, accessories; industrial engines; other industrial machines; laboratory testing instruments; marine engines and parts; materials handling equipment; measuring, testing, and control instruments; medicinal equipment; metalworking machine tools; nonfarm tractors and parts; parts for civilian aircraft; photographic and service industry machinery; pulp and paper machinery; railway transportation equipment; semiconductors; non-military spacecraft; specialized mining; telecommunications equipment; textile

sewing machines; vessels, except scrap; and wood, glass, and plastic.

Automotive vehicles, engines, and parts includes semis and heavy trucks, as well as automobiles and light trucks. Vehicles for both commercial and personal use are included.

Consumer goods include textile apparel and household goods; nontextile apparel and household goods; artwork, antiques, and stamps; books and printed matter; cookware, cutlery, and tools; furniture and household goods; gem diamonds; glassware and chinaware; household appliances; jewelry; musical instruments; numismatic coins; nursery stock; other household goods; pharmaceutical preparations; pleasure boats and motors; records, tapes, and disks; rugs; sports apparel and gear; stereo equipment; manufactured tobacco; toiletries and cosmetics; toys, games, and sporting goods; TV's and VCR's; and writing and art supplies.

DATA AVAILABILITY

Data available from the OTEA website. More detailed data are released each month in the joint Census-BEA release (FT900). Historical data for recent years are available from the Census Bureau web site, <http://www.census.gov>.

Table C-4. U.S. Export and Import Price Indexes for Selected Categories of Goods, by Principal End-Use Classification, 1991–1999

Table C-6. U.S. Export Price Indexes for Selected Categories of Goods, by Standard International Trade Classification (SITC), 1991–1999

Table C-7. U.S. Import Price Indexes for Selected Categories of Goods, by Standard International Trade Classification (SITC), 1991–1999

Table C-12. U.S. Import Price Indexes for Selected Categories of Goods, by Locality of Origin, 1991–1999

Source: U.S. Department of Labor, Bureau of Labor Statistics.

DATA NOTES

BLS produces monthly and quarterly export and import price indexes for nonmilitary goods, and selected services, traded between the United States and the rest of the world. The export price index provides a measure of price change for all products sold by U.S. residents to foreign buyers. The import price index provides a measure of price change for goods purchased from other countries by U.S. residents. Price data are collected primarily by mail questionnaire, usually directly from the exporter or importer. To the extent possible, the data refer to prices at the U.S. border for exports and at either the foreign or the U.S. border for imports. Survey respondents are asked to indicate all discounts, allowances, and rebates applicable. Weights are based on 1995 trade values. For the export price indexes, the preferred pricing is f.a.s. (free alongside ship) U.S. port of exportation. When firms report export prices f.o.b. (free on board), production point information is collected which enables the Bureau to calculate a shipment cost to the port of exportation. For imports, prices may be either the import price f.o.b. at the foreign port of exportation or the import price c.i.f. (costs, insurance and freight) at the U.S. port of importation, not including duty charges.

BLS does not publish annual price indexes. The annual data shown have been calculated by the editors of *Foreign Trade of the United States* using all available monthly data for the year. The months used are indicated in the headings and footnotes to each table.

DATA AVAILABILITY

Current data, along with descriptive information, are published in a monthly press release and in the *Monthly Labor Review*. Current and historical data are available on the Internet at http://stats.bls.gov/ipphome.

Table C-5. U.S. Foreign Trade in Goods Using Standard International Trade Classification [SITC] Product Groups, 1993–1999

DATA AVAILABILITY

Available at the OTEA web site, http://www.ita.doc.gov/tradestats.

Table C-8. U.S. Foreign Trade in Goods by Industry Using North American Industry Classification System [NAICS] Product Groups, 1997–1999

Table C-9. U.S. Foreign Trade in Goods by Industry Using Standard Industrial Classification [SIC] Product Groups, 1991–1997

Source: Bureau of the Census, U.S. Department of Commerce; data compiled by Office of Trade and Economic Analysis (OTEA), International Trade Administration, U.S. Department of Commerce.

DATA NOTES

Data are on a Census basis. Exports are on an f.a.s. value basis, imports are on a Customs Service value basis. The data are classified on the basis of NAICS and SIC product codes, respectively, as explained above.

DATA AVAILABILITY

These compilations may be found on the OTEA web site.

Table C-10. U.S. Foreign Trade in Goods, Summary by Region, 1991–1999

Table C-11. U.S. Foreign Trade in Goods by Country or Region, 1991–1999

Source: Bureau of the Census, U.S. Department of Commerce; data compiled by Office of Trade and Economic Analysis (OTEA), International Trade Administration, U.S. Department of Commerce.

DATA NOTES

Data are based on the Harmonized System of commodity classification and converted to other classification systems using recent Census data concordances to produce consistent time series. Therefore, the data in this table will differ from values in other published sources. Manufactured goods are as defined in SITC (revision 3) 5-9. Data in this table are not necessarily revised to reflect revisions in total U.S. exports and imports. (See the general notes for this section, above, for an explanation of these classification systems.)

Exports are on a Census basis, f.a.s. value. Imports are on a Census basis, customs value. When necessary, country and regional foreign trade data were adjusted to create data series that utilize the same country definitions over time.

COUNTRY AND REGION NOTES

Western Hemisphere includes the countries listed below as parts of North America, South America, Central America, and the Caribbean. In addition, Western Hemisphere totals include *Other Western Hemisphere* which includes Bermuda, Cuba, the Falkland Islands, French Guiana, French West Indies, Greenland, and St. Pierre and Miquelon.

North America includes Canada and Mexico.

South and Central America and Caribbean include all the countries listed below in the individual regions.

Caribbean countries include the Bahamas, Barbados, Belize, Cayman Islands, Dominican Republic, Guyana, Haiti, Jamaica, Leeward and Windward Islands (i.e., Antigua, British Virgin Islands, Dominica, Grenada, Montserrat, St. Christopher-Nevis and Anguilla, St. Lucia, and St. Vincent), Netherlands Antilles and Aruba, Suriname, Trinidad and Tobago, and Turks and Caicos Islands.

Central American countries consist of Costa Rica, El Salvador, Guatemala, Honduras, Nicaragua, and Panama.

South America includes Argentina, Bolivia, Brazil, Chile, Colombia, Ecuador, Paraguay, Peru, Uruguay, and Venezuela.

Europe consists of Western Europe and Eastern Europe.

Western Europe includes the European Union (EU) and non-EU Western Europe. *The European Union* includes Austria, Belgium/Luxembourg, Denmark, Finland, France, Germany (both East and West), Greece, Ireland, Italy, Netherlands, Portugal (including Azores and the Madeira Islands), Spain (including Spanish Africa and the Canary Islands), Sweden, and the United Kingdom.

Western Europe, except European Union include Cyprus, Gibraltar, Iceland, Malta, Norway, Switzerland, Turkey, Yugoslavia (former), and, after 1987, other non-EU Western Europe (Andorra, Faroe Islands, Liechtenstein, Monaco, San Marino, Svalbard and Jan Mayen Island, and Vatican City).

Yugoslavia (former) consists of Bosnia-Herzegovina, Croatia, Macedonia, Serbia and Montenegro, and Slovenia. In June 1992 the U.S. Bureau of the Census began to report trade figures for the new republics of the former Yugoslavia; therefore 1992 trade figures do not reflect the entire year for these republics. However, 1992 trade figures for Yugoslavia (former) do reflect the entire year.

Eastern Europe and Former Soviet Republics includes Albania, Bulgaria, Czech Republic and Slovakia (former Czechoslovakia), Hungary, Poland, Romania and the Former Soviet Republics.

Czechoslovakia ceased to exist effective January 1, 1993, and became two countries, the Czech Republic and Slovakia.

Former Soviet Republics consist of Armenia, Azerbaijan, Belarus, Estonia, Georgia, Kazakhstan, Kyrgyzstan, Latvia, Lithuania, Russia, Tajikistan, Turkmenistan, Ukraine and Uzbekistan. In January 1992 the U.S. Bureau of the Census began to report trade figures for Estonia, Latvia and Lithuania. In February 1992 the U.S. Bureau of the Census began to report trade figures for the republics of the former USSR; therefore, 1992 trade figures do not reflect the entire year for these republics. However, the 1992 total trade figure for the Former Soviet Republics does reflect the entire year.

Asia, including Middle East includes Afghanistan, Bangladesh, Bhutan, Brunei, Burma, Cambodia, China, Hong Kong, India, Indonesia, Japan, Laos, Macao, Malaysia, Maldive Islands, Mongolia, Nepal, North Korea, Pakistan, Philippines, Singapore, South Korea, Sri Lanka, Taiwan, Thailand, Vietnam and the Middle East

The Middle East includes Bahrain, Iran, Iraq, Israel (including the Gaza Strip and the West Bank), Jordan, Kuwait, Lebanon, the Neutral Zone, Oman, Qatar, Saudi Arabia, Syria, United Arab Emirates and the Yemen Arab Republic.

Australia and Oceania consists of: Australia, Australian island dependencies (i.e., Christmas Island, Cocos Island, Heard and McDonald Islands, and Norfolk Island), French Pacific Islands (i.e., French Polynesia, New Caledonia, and Wallis and Futuna), New Zealand, New Zealand island dependencies (i.e., Cook Islands, Niue, and Tokelau Islands), Papua New Guinea, Southern Pacific Islands (i.e., Kiribati, Pitcairn Island, Solomon Islands, Tuvalu, and Vanuatu), Former Trust Territory (i.e., Federated States of Micronesia, Marshall Islands, and Palau), Western Samoa, and Other Pacific Islands NEC (i.e., Fiji, Nauru, and Tonga).

Africa consists of all the countries on the continent. French Indian Ocean areas include Reunion and French Southern and Antarctic Lands. Western Africa NEC includes Cape Verde, Guinea-Bissau, and Sao Tome and Principe. Effective July 1, 1993, the Census Bureau began collecting data for Eritrea.

The ten *Association of Southeast Asian Nations [ASEAN]* members are Brunei, Burma, Cambodia, Indonesia, Laos, Malaysia, Philippines, Singapore, Thailand, and Vietnam. Cambodia was not a member in previous years.

The twenty-one *Asian Pacific Economic Cooperation [APEC]* countries are Australia, Brunei, Canada, Chile, China, Hong Kong, Indonesia, Japan, Malaysia, Mexico, New Zealand, Papua New Guinea, Peru, Philippines, Russia, Singapore, South Korea, Taiwan, Thailand, United States, and Vietnam.

Caribbean Basin Initiative countries consist of the Caribbean countries and the Central American countries.

DATA AVAILABILITY

Full data are available from the OTEA web site. Monthly data for a large number of countries are available from the Census web site, or in the FT900 report.

Table C-1. U.S. Foreign Trade in Goods, 1970–1999

(Census basis, billions of dollars.)

Year	Exports					Imports				
	Total goods	Manufac- tured goods	Agricul- tural products	Mineral fuels	Other goods	Total goods	Manufac- tured goods	Agricul- tural products	Mineral fuels	Other goods
1970	43.8	31.7	7.3	1.6	3.1	40.4	27.3	5.8	3.1	4.2
1971	44.7	32.9	7.8	1.5	2.5	46.2	32.1	5.8	3.7	4.6
1972	50.5	36.5	9.5	1.6	2.9	56.4	39.7	6.5	4.8	5.3
1973	72.5	48.5	17.9	1.7	4.5	70.5	47.1	8.5	8.2	6.7
1974	100.0	68.5	22.3	3.4	5.8	102.6	57.8	10.4	25.5	8.9
1975	109.3	76.9	22.1	4.5	5.9	98.5	54.0	9.5	26.5	8.6
1976	117.0	83.1	23.3	4.2	6.4	123.5	67.6	11.2	34.0	10.7
1977	123.2	88.9	24.2	4.2	5.9	151.0	80.5	13.6	47.2	9.8
1978	145.9	103.6	29.8	3.9	8.6	174.8	104.3	15.0	42.0	13.4
1979	186.5	132.7	35.2	5.7	12.9	209.5	117.1	16.9	59.9	15.5
1980	225.7	160.7	41.8	8.2	15.1	245.3	133.0	17.4	78.9	15.9
1981	238.7	171.7	43.8	10.3	12.8	261.0	149.8	17.2	81.2	12.8
1982	216.4	155.3	37.0	12.8	11.3	244.0	151.7	15.7	65.3	11.3
1983 [1]	411.2	297.2	72.6	19.6	21.9	516.0	342.1	32.5	115.6	25.9
1984	224.0	164.1	37.9	9.7	12.3	330.7	230.9	19.3	60.8	19.6
1985	218.8	168.0	29.3	10.3	11.2	336.5	257.5	19.5	53.7	5.9
1986	227.2	179.8	26.3	8.4	12.6	365.4	296.7	20.9	37.2	10.7
1987	254.1	199.9	28.7	8.0	17.5	406.2	324.4	20.3	44.1	17.4
1988	322.4	255.6	37.1	8.5	21.2	441.0	361.4	20.7	41.0	17.8
1989	363.8	287.0	41.6	9.9	25.3	473.2	379.4	21.1	52.6	20.0
1990	393.6	315.4	39.6	12.4	26.3	495.3	388.8	22.3	64.7	19.5
1991	421.7	345.1	39.4	12.3	24.9	488.5	392.4	22.1	54.1	19.8
1992	448.2	368.5	43.1	11.3	25.2	532.7	434.3	23.4	55.3	19.7
1993	465.1	388.7	42.8	9.9	23.7	580.7	479.9	23.6	55.9	21.2
1994	512.6	431.1	45.9	9.0	26.7	663.3	557.3	26.0	56.4	23.6
1995	584.7	486.7	56.0	10.5	31.6	743.4	629.7	29.3	59.1	25.4
1996	625.1	524.7	60.6	12.4	27.4	795.3	658.8	32.6	78.1	25.8
1997	689.2	592.5	57.1	13.0	26.7	870.7	728.9	35.2	78.3	28.3
1998	682.1	596.6	52.0	10.4	23.2	911.9	790.8	35.7	57.3	28.1
1999	695.8	614.5	48.4	10.0	22.9	1 024.6	882.0	36.7	75.8	30.1

1. Data for 1983 are on the old basis (Non Harmonized System) of commodity classification.

Table C-2. U.S. Foreign Trade in Goods by Principal End-Use Category, 1978–1999

(Census basis, billions of dollars.)

Year	Foods, feeds, and beverages			Industrial supplies and materials			Capital goods, except automotive		
	Exports	Imports	Balance	Exports	Imports	Balance	Exports	Imports	Balance
1978	25.6	15.8	9.7	39.0	79.2	-40.1	46.9	19.7	27.2
1979	30.3	18.0	12.3	57.3	102.6	-45.3	58.8	24.9	33.9
1980	36.0	18.5	17.5	70.6	124.7	-54.1	74.8	31.1	43.7
1981	38.6	18.5	20.1	67.7	130.7	-63.0	82.5	37.0	45.5
1982	32.0	17.5	14.5	62.1	107.7	-45.6	75.1	38.4	36.7
1983	30.7	18.5	12.2	57.4	105.3	-47.8	70.6	39.4	31.2
1984	31.3	21.5	9.8	62.6	121.6	-59.1	76.4	58.0	18.5
1985	24.1	22.3	1.8	59.2	114.1	-54.9	78.9	62.4	16.4
1986	22.5	24.5	-2.0	62.0	102.9	-40.9	81.8	72.6	9.2
1987	24.3	26.8	-2.6	66.7	117.3	-50.6	86.2	87.0	-0.8
1988	32.3	24.8	7.5	85.1	118.3	-33.2	109.2	101.4	7.8
1989	37.2	25.1	12.1	99.3	132.3	-33.0	138.8	113.3	25.5
1990	35.1	26.6	8.4	104.4	143.2	-38.8	152.7	116.4	36.3
1991	35.7	26.5	9.2	109.7	131.6	-21.9	166.7	120.7	45.9
1992	40.3	27.6	12.7	109.1	138.6	-29.5	175.9	134.3	41.7
1993	40.6	27.9	12.8	111.8	145.6	-33.8	181.7	152.4	29.3
1994	42.0	31.0	11.0	121.4	162.1	-40.7	205.0	184.4	20.7
1995	50.5	33.2	17.3	146.2	181.8	-35.6	233.0	221.4	11.6
1996	55.5	35.7	19.8	147.7	204.5	-56.8	252.9	229.1	23.8
1997	51.5	39.7	11.8	158.2	213.8	-55.5	294.5	253.3	41.3
1998	46.4	41.2	5.2	148.3	200.1	-51.9	299.6	269.6	30.1
1999	45.5	43.6	2.0	147.0	222.0	-75.0	311.4	297.1	14.3

Year	Automotive vehicles, engines, and parts			Consumer goods, except automotive			Other goods		
	Exports	Imports	Balance	Exports	Imports	Balance	Exports	Imports	Balance
1978	14.6	25.9	-11.3	11.1	29.6	-18.5	8.6	3.1	5.5
1979	16.6	26.9	-10.3	13.4	31.3	-17.9	9.9	3.4	6.5
1980	16.0	28.2	-12.1	17.2	34.3	-17.2	11.1	4.6	6.5
1981	18.3	30.7	-12.5	17.1	38.4	-21.2	14.4	5.7	8.8
1982	16.0	34.3	-18.3	15.7	39.6	-24.0	15.6	6.5	9.1
1983	15.4	42.1	-26.7	16.2	46.3	-30.1	15.3	6.5	8.8
1984	18.6	55.1	-36.5	16.4	61.4	-45.0	17.9	8.1	9.8
1985	20.6	66.6	-46.0	15.8	69.9	-54.1	20.7	10.0	10.7
1986	19.9	78.5	-58.6	17.8	80.3	-62.5	23.6	11.2	12.3
1987	24.6	87.5	-62.8	17.7	93.6	-76.0	34.6	12.2	22.4
1988	29.3	87.7	-58.4	23.1	95.9	-72.8	43.4	12.8	30.6
1989	34.8	86.1	-51.3	36.4	102.9	-66.4	17.2	13.6	3.6
1990	37.4	87.3	-49.9	43.3	105.7	-62.4	20.7	16.1	4.6
1991	40.0	85.7	-45.6	45.9	108.0	-62.1	23.7	15.9	7.7
1992	47.0	91.8	-44.8	51.4	122.7	-71.2	24.4	17.7	6.7
1993	52.4	102.4	-50.0	54.7	134.0	-79.4	23.9	18.4	5.5
1994	57.8	118.3	-60.5	60.0	146.3	-86.3	26.5	21.3	5.2
1995	61.8	123.8	-62.0	64.4	159.9	-95.5	28.7	23.4	5.3
1996	65.0	128.9	-63.9	70.1	171.0	-100.9	33.8	26.1	7.7
1997	74.0	139.8	-65.8	77.4	193.8	-116.4	33.5	29.3	4.2
1998	73.2	149.1	-75.9	79.3	216.5	-137.3	35.4	35.4	0.1
1999	75.8	179.4	-103.6	80.8	239.5	-158.7	35.3	43.0	-7.7

NOTE: Categories may not sum to totals due to rounding and revisions.

Table C-3. U.S. Exports and Imports of Goods by Principal End-Use Category: Constant Dollar Basis, 1985–1999

(Census basis; billions of 1996 dollars, unless otherwise indicated.)

Year	Total	Foods, feeds, and beverages	Industrial supplies and materials	Capital goods, except automotive	Automotive vehicles, engines, and parts	Consumer goods, except automotive	Other goods
EXPORTS							
1985	. . .	. . .	. . .	. . .	. . .	. . .	. . .
1986 [1]	227.2	22.3	57.3	75.8	21.7	. . .	. . .
1987 [1]	254.1	24.3	66.7	86.2	24.6	. . .	. . .
1988 [1]	322.4	32.3	85.1	109.2	29.3	. . .	. . .
1989 [1]	363.8	37.2	99.3	138.8	34.8	. . .	. . .
1990 [1]	393.6	35.1	104.4	152.7	37.4	39.2	18.7
1991 [1]	421.7	35.7	109.7	166.7	40.0	40.4	21.1
1992 [1]	448.2	40.3	109.1	175.9	47.0	43.6	21.7
1993 [1]	471.2	40.2	111.1	190.0	51.9	54.0	23.9
1994 [1]	522.3	40.4	114.2	225.8	56.5	59.0	26.4
1994	518.6	50.8	131.9	187.0	59.1	61.6	28.3
1995	569.9	57.8	138.6	216.6	62.7	65.4	29.0
1996	625.0	55.7	147.2	253.3	65.1	69.9	33.8
1997	711.9	55.8	160.1	312.0	73.4	77.0	33.6
1998	730.0	56.1	159.9	326.2	72.4	79.0	36.5
1999	761.5	58.6	160.7	350.5	74.7	80.5	36.6
IMPORTS							
1985	. . .	. . .	. . .	. . .	. . .	. . .	. . .
1986 [1]	365.4	24.4	101.3	71.8	78.2	79.4	. . .
1987 [1]	406.2	24.8	111.0	84.5	85.0	88.7	. . .
1988 [1]	441.0	24.8	118.3	101.4	87.7	95.9	. . .
1989 [1]	473.2	25.1	132.3	113.3	86.1	102.9	. . .
1990 [1]	495.3	26.6	146.2	116.4	87.3	105.7	14.5
1991 [1]	488.5	26.5	131.6	120.7	85.7	108.0	14.2
1992 [1]	532.7	27.6	138.6	134.3	91.8	122.7	15.5
1993 [1]	591.5	28.0	151.3	160.2	100.7	132.9	18.4
1994 [1]	675.1	29.5	168.8	199.6	112.1	144.2	20.8
1994	676.0	31.8	188.1	161.7	122.4	149.3	22.7
1995	730.1	32.4	193.0	194.8	125.0	161.0	23.9
1996	794.4	35.6	203.7	229.0	129.0	171.0	26.0
1997	914.2	38.9	219.6	290.8	139.4	195.9	29.6
1998	1 021.5	41.6	241.4	331.7	148.5	221.8	36.4
1999	1 148.5	45.3	246.8	387.3	177.2	247.5	44.5

1. Values on the 1996 dollar basis are only available for 1994 to date. To provide more historical data, values on a 1992 dollar basis are shown for the years 1986-1994.

Table C-4. U.S. Export and Import Price Indexes for Selected Categories of Goods, by Principal End-Use Classification, 1991–1999

(1995=100, unless otherwise indicated; annual data are averages of the 12 months.)

Category	End-use codes	1991	1992	1993	1994	1995	1996	1997	1998	1999
EXPORTS										
ALL COMMODITIES		92.6	92.7	93.2	95.2	100.0	100.5	99.2	95.9	94.7
Foods, feeds, and beverages	0	87.5	87.5	88.5	91.8	100.0	113.7	102.5	92.5	88.1
Industrial supplies and materials	1	84.6	82.5	83.5	89.0	100.0	95.5	95.1	89.7	88.5
Capital goods	2	98.4	99.8	99.7	99.2	100.0	100.7	99.9	97.8	96.5
Automotive vehicles, parts and engines	3	94.9	96.7	97.8	98.8	100.0	101.1	102.1	102.4	103.3
Consumer goods, excluding automotive	4	94.4	96.8	98.4	98.7	100.0	101.3	102.2	102.1	102.0
Agricultural Commodities	AG	86.9	86.1	87.7	91.9	100.0	111.4	101.3	91.4	85.0
Nonagricultural Commodities	EXAG	93.1	93.4	93.9	95.6	100.0	99.2	98.9	96.4	95.8
IMPORTS										
ALL COMMODITIES		93.7	94.3	94.0	95.7	100.0	101.0	98.5	92.6	93.4
Foods, feeds, and beverages	0	86.5	86.2	86.1	95.1	100.0	98.1	99.3	96.2	93.5
Industrial supplies and materials	1	96.0	93.4	90.3	90.5	100.0	105.2	102.4	88.1	95.2
Capital goods	2	95.5	97.2	97.5	98.4	100.0	97.6	91.7	85.7	82.7
Automotive vehicles, parts and engines	3	90.5	92.1	93.7	97.0	100.0	100.6	100.9	101.1	101.7
Consumer goods, excluding automotive	4	93.8	96.6	97.6	98.4	100.0	100.4	99.5	98.3	97.7
All Imports Excluding Petroleum	EXPET	92.0	93.3	93.8	96.2	100.0	99.2	97.1	93.7	92.4

Table C-5. U.S. Foreign Trade in Goods Using Standard International Trade Classification [SITC] Product Groups, 1993–1999

(Census basis, preliminary; millions of dollars.)

Product	SITC code	Exports						
		1993	1994	1995	1996	1997	1998	1999
ALL COMMODITIES, TOTAL	0-9	464 858	512 416	583 031	622 827	687 598	680 474	692 821
Manufactures	5-9	388 538	430 844	484 967	522 658	591 233	595 222	611 780
Non-Manufactures	0-4	76 322	81 572	98 060	100 167	96 363	85 256	81 038
Live animals	00	522	591	544	535	694	683	658
Meat and meat preparations	01	4 373	5 208	6 478	7 005	6 943	6 431	6 372
Dairy products and birds' eggs	02	788	732	796	713	836	808	747
Fish (except marine mammal)	03	3 099	3 153	3 298	3 059	2 739	2 272	2 858
Cereals and cereal preparation	04	11 826	11 281	16 054	18 152	12 648	11 491	11 652
Vegetables and fruit	05	6 562	7 295	7 697	7 947	8 105	7 942	7 779
Sugars, sugar preparations	06	463	538	597	630	679	668	638
Coffee, tea, cocoa	07	756	944	891	918	1 045	1 047	1 012
Feeding stuff for animals	08	3 583	3 458	3 798	4 387	4 867	4 305	3 635
Miscellaneous edible	09	1 833	2 218	2 018	2 443	2 720	2 671	2 886
Beverages	11	1 013	1 275	1 418	1 361	1 475	1 524	1 566
Tobacco and tobacco	12	5 584	6 741	6 668	6 664	6 587	6 309	5 198
Hides, skins and furskins	21	1 310	1 551	1 777	1 711	1 687	1 279	1 156
Oil seeds and oleaginous	22	4 980	4 725	5 921	7 855	7 984	5 441	5 037
Crude rubber	23	937	1 082	1 262	1 364	1 305	1 173	1 186
Cork and wood	24	5 799	5 581	5 666	5 543	5 179	4 133	4 299
Pulp and waste paper	25	3 006	3 839	6 279	4 079	3 899	3 485	3 616
Textile fibers	26	2 684	3 989	5 403	4 403	4 279	3 942	2 232
Crude fertilizers	27	1 409	1 553	1 577	1 581	1 697	1 676	1 614
Metalliferous ores	28	3 343	3 773	5 595	4 382	4 740	3 627	3 558
Crude animal and vegetable materials	29	1 169	1 201	1 325	1 366	1 433	1 504	1 479
Coal, coke and briquettes	32	3 201	2 964	3 714	3 853	3 567	3 192	2 261
Petroleum, petroleum products	33	5 957	5 432	5 946	7 546	8 137	6 138	6 760
Gas, natural and manufactured	34	597	548	747	757	794	555	699
Electric current	35	61	30	47	69	124	185	206
Animal oils and fats	41	503	606	835	613	571	686	516
Fixed vegetable fats and oils	42	836	1 120	1 525	1 032	1 402	1 830	1 184
Animal and vegetable fats and oils processed and waste	43	128	144	184	199	227	259	234
Organic chemicals	51	11 238	13 064	16 395	15 012	16 766	15 181	15 754
Inorganic chemicals	52	3 887	4 153	4 581	4 749	5 429	4 842	4 701
Dyeing, tanning and coloring materials	53	2 033	2 353	2 621	2 771	3 351	3 528	3 687
Medicinal and pharmaceutical products	54	5 842	6 184	6 554	7 330	8 231	9 661	11 247
Essential oils	55	3 142	3 644	3 943	4 438	5 020	4 888	5 013
Fertilizers	56	1 823	2 706	3 226	3 076	3 074	3 282	3 117
Plastics in primary form	57	7 407	8 721	10 756	10 988	12 166	11 560	11 771
Plastics in nonprimary form	58	3 419	3 864	4 337	4 693	5 412	5 315	5 364
Chemical materials	59	7 077	7 763	9 288	9 873	11 378	11 014	11 333
Leather, leather manufactures	61	910	850	836	862	1 006	1 026	1 042
Rubber manufactures	62	2 726	3 096	3 554	3 850	4 705	4 902	4 901
Cork and wood manufactures	63	1 528	1 609	1 718	1 786	2 055	1 801	1 857
Paper, paperboard	64	6 527	7 522	9 675	9 992	10 439	10 082	10 100
Textile yarn, fabrics	65	6 025	6 592	7 372	8 008	9 187	9 205	9 504
Nonmetallic mineral	66	5 266	5 975	6 708	7 217	8 056	7 968	8 744
Iron and steel	67	3 602	3 903	5 803	5 251	6 197	6 026	5 450
Nonferrous metals	68	4 703	5 382	7 514	7 174	7 767	7 575	6 910
Manufactures of metals	69	7 874	9 066	10 282	11 623	12 865	13 221	13 650
Power generating machinery	71	19 676	20 870	22 430	23 169	28 135	29 963	32 380
Machinery specialized	72	18 338	20 669	24 286	26 628	30 375	28 688	26 120
Metalworking machinery	73	3 405	4 112	4 865	5 503	6 051	5 717	5 718
General industrial machinery	74	20 126	22 563	25 048	27 370	31 440	30 999	30 729
Office machines and ADP equipment	75	31 348	35 396	41 947	45 751	51 641	47 759	48 604
Telecommunications equipment	76	14 237	17 129	20 332	21 414	26 056	25 978	27 709
Electrical machinery, apparatus and appliances	77	43 178	52 921	65 638	70 286	78 302	76 872	88 655
Motor vehicles	78	41 178	46 305	49 222	51 703	57 429	56 469	56 640
Transport equipment	79	33 394	32 377	27 720	34 356	43 212	55 724	52 742
Prefabricated buildings; sanitary, plumbing, etc.	81	1 120	1 281	1 323	1 402	1 583	1 462	1 377
Furniture and bedding	82	2 855	3 275	3 306	3 530	4 219	4 675	4 701
Travel goods, handbags	83	223	263	286	339	369	343	384
Articles of apparel and clothing	84	4 952	5 616	6 651	7 511	8 672	8 793	8 269
Footwear	85	703	758	791	879	920	851	839
Professional scientific instruments	87	15 844	17 207	19 372	21 441	25 042	25 386	26 905
Photographic apparatus, equipment and optical goods	88	4 398	4 681	5 200	5 916	6 501	6 381	6 950
Miscellaneous manufactured articles	89	24 282	26 539	28 515	30 694	31 781	31 798	32 206
Special transactions	93	4 433	4 975	4 695	5 132	5 685	5 287	5 500
Coin including gold	95	101	79	66	43	65	40	37
Coin (other than gold)	96	4	4	8	16	12	6	5
Gold, nonmonetary	97	9 063	5 677	5 098	6 671	5 694	5 407	5 225
Estimate of low valued import transaction	98	...	...	...	...	...	...	...
Low value shipments	99	10 651	11 700	13 005	14 211	14 945	15 547	15 940

See NOTE at end of table.

Table C-5. U.S. Foreign Trade in Goods Using Standard International Trade Classification [SITC] Product Groups, 1993–1999—*Continued*

(Census basis, preliminary; millions of dollars.)

Product	SITC code	Imports						
		1993	1994	1995	1996	1997	1998	1999
ALL COMMODITIES, TOTAL	0-9	580 469	663 830	743 505	791 315	870 213	913 885	1 024 766
Manufactures	5-9	480 017	557 870	629 630	659 864	728 573	792 418	882 729
Non-Manufactures	0-4	100 452	105 957	113 877	131 449	141 640	121 463	142 038
Live animals	00	1 539	1 392	1 727	1 595	1 654	1 718	1 642
Meat and meat preparations	01	2 797	2 636	2 322	2 317	2 656	2 847	3 258
Dairy products and birds' eggs	02	544	583	620	717	711	904	1 018
Fish (except marine mammal)	03	5 820	6 593	6 741	6 657	7 687	8 105	8 902
Cereals and cereal preparation	04	1 390	1 834	1 808	2 075	2 404	2 350	2 480
Vegetables and fruit	05	5 666	6 074	6 581	7 514	7 744	8 372	9 261
Sugars, sugar preparations	06	1 194	1 224	1 379	1 860	1 881	1 687	1 626
Coffee, tea, cocoa	07	3 014	3 976	4 856	4 715	5 963	5 782	5 136
Feeding stuff for animals	08	481	520	510	682	711	658	599
Miscellaneous edible	09	539	620	687	778	845	991	1 171
Beverages	11	3 961	4 307	4 567	5 271	5 963	6 493	7 405
Tobacco and tobacco	12	1 551	861	739	1 332	1 626	1 263	1 210
Hides, skins and furskins	21	179	205	200	207	207	172	149
Oil seeds and oleaginous	22	169	287	267	357	407	376	326
Crude rubber	23	1 361	1 539	2 264	2 070	1 873	1 675	1 451
Cork and wood	24	5 632	6 683	6 153	7 532	8 185	7 625	8 925
Pulp and waste paper	25	1 887	2 315	3 827	2 648	2 639	2 443	2 597
Textile fibers	26	726	803	886	1 056	787	737	744
Crude fertilizers	27	938	1 027	1 174	1 176	1 340	1 298	1 270
Metalliferous ores	28	3 026	3 252	4 000	4 048	4 156	4 101	3 657
Crude animal and vegetable materials	29	1 456	1 611	1 992	2 205	2 436	2 675	2 601
Coal, coke and briquettes	32	513	646	703	606	654	726	665
Petroleum, petroleum products	33	49 685	49 325	52 569	65 242	69 249	49 370	65 887
Gas, natural and manufactured	34	4 722	5 481	5 079	6 278	7 297	6 511	7 316
Electric current	35	662	960	856	902	978	1 039	1 334
Animal oils and fats	41	38	37	38	43	56	47	47
Fixed vegetable fats and oils	42	871	1 057	1 171	1 416	1 375	1 324	1 219
Animal and vegetable fats and oils processed and waste	43	91	109	161	150	156	174	142
Organic chemicals	51	9 316	10 799	13 325	14 820	16 852	18 300	21 860
Inorganic chemicals	52	3 285	4 104	4 655	4 954	5 137	5 118	5 173
Dyeing, tanning and coloring materials	53	1 700	1 868	2 080	2 165	2 482	2 470	2 632
Medicinal and pharmaceutical products	54	4 133	4 680	5 544	7 076	8 737	10 885	13 542
Essential oils	55	1 809	1 995	2 309	2 443	2 677	2 893	3 151
Fertilizers	56	1 135	1 296	1 392	1 400	1 378	1 568	1 500
Plastics in primary form	57	2 724	3 512	4 331	4 449	4 946	5 084	5 442
Plastics in nonprimary form	58	2 123	2 422	2 821	2 994	3 298	3 480	3 835
Chemical materials	59	2 941	3 238	3 921	4 568	4 819	4 822	5 072
Leather, leather manufactures	61	943	1 095	1 212	1 193	1 239	1 236	1 185
Rubber manufactures	62	4 138	4 783	5 149	5 177	5 654	6 463	7 156
Cork and wood manufactures	63	2 956	3 471	3 798	4 172	4 815	5 799	7 254
Paper, paperboard	64	8 639	9 065	12 472	11 637	11 703	12 796	13 407
Textile yarn, fabrics	65	8 438	9 208	9 985	10 248	11 949	12 890	13 575
Nonmetallic mineral	66	11 558	13 313	14 363	15 650	17 827	19 519	22 450
Iron and steel	67	10 112	14 218	14 211	15 263	16 082	19 190	15 132
Nonferrous metals	68	8 826	11 565	14 524	13 619	15 200	16 145	17 208
Manufactures of metals	69	10 559	12 084	13 729	14 690	16 505	18 029	19 627
Power generating machinery	71	17 163	19 561	20 486	22 499	24 504	28 132	31 533
Machinery specialized	72	13 546	16 755	18 990	18 509	21 192	22 970	21 632
Metalworking machinery	73	3 675	4 614	5 925	6 789	7 319	7 928	6 787
General industrial machinery	74	17 084	21 337	24 113	25 286	26 307	28 802	31 447
Office machines and ADP equipment	75	43 182	52 118	62 824	66 499	75 001	76 846	84 443
Telecommunications equipment	76	27 302	32 456	34 384	34 167	36 685	42 462	50 959
Electrical machinery, apparatus and appliances	77	46 752	57 672	75 169	75 525	80 317	79 366	88 592
Motor vehicles	78	83 332	95 128	100 254	103 664	112 767	121 310	146 202
Transport equipment	79	7 939	8 601	8 336	9 844	11 856	16 118	18 277
Prefabricated buildings; sanitary, plumbing, etc.	81	1 764	2 024	2 282	2 579	2 945	3 391	4 327
Furniture and bedding	82	6 249	7 567	8 339	9 431	11 143	13 338	16 178
Travel goods, handbags	83	2 654	3 080	3 411	3 581	3 842	3 944	4 148
Articles of apparel and clothing	84	33 787	36 744	39 526	41 559	48 407	53 743	56 413
Footwear	85	11 176	11 716	12 106	12 749	14 018	13 879	14 068
Professional scientific instruments	87	8 452	9 964	11 572	12 385	13 947	15 505	17 641
Photographic apparatus, equipment and optical goods	88	8 619	9 213	10 164	10 508	11 173	11 700	12 585
Miscellaneous manufactured articles	89	31 783	33 602	36 467	38 844	43 547	47 470	51 313
Special transactions	93	13 714	16 312	18 024	20 532	23 016	26 419	31 783
Coin including gold	95	239	182	122	192	279	291	367
Coin (other than gold)	96	5	8	5	14	12	20	11
Gold, nonmonetary	97	2 015	1 932	2 153	2 737	3 028	3 571	3 034
Estimate of low valued import transaction	98	4 250	4 568	5 157	5 453	5 968	8 526	11 788
Low value shipments	99	...	...	...	...	...	...	...

NOTE: Data are unrevised and will not agree exactly with other revised tables of U.S. Foreign Trade in Goods.

Table C-6. U.S. Export Price Indexes for Selected Categories of Goods, by Standard International Trade Classification [SITC], 1991–1999

(1995=100, unless otherwise indicated; annual data are averages of the 12 months, unless otherwise indicated.)

Category	SITC code	1991	1992	1993	1994	1995	1996	1997	1998	1999
ALL COMMODITIES		92.6	92.7	93.2	95.2	100.0	100.5	99.2	95.9	94.7
Food And Live Animals	0	[1]85.6	[2]86.4	86.9	90.2	100.0	113.5	99.9	90.7	87.8
Meat and meat preparations	01	[2]88.0	90.9	94.0	93.5	100.0	99.2	95.6	93.8	94.1
Meat of bovine animals, fresh, chilled or frozen	011	[1]87.7	[1]91.2	[1]92.3	[1]88.8	100.0	91.2	90.0	86.1	94.3
Meat, not of bovine animals, and edible offal, fresh, chilled, or frozen	012	. . .	. . .	[1]94.5	[1]98.2	100.0	104.9	97.8	97.7	91.7
Fish, crustaceans, aquatic invertebrates and preparations thereof	03	[1]79.7	[1]82.1	[1]78.1	86.4	100.0	91.5	91.9	89.2	104.6
Fish, fresh (live or dead), chilled or frozen (December 1996=100)	034	. . .	. . .	. . .	. . .	. . .	. . .	100.1	97.2	116.3
Cereals and cereal preparations	04	[1]81.1	[2]83.8	82.7	86.7	100.0	126.6	97.0	82.0	73.9
Wheat (including spelt) and meslin, unmilled	041	[1]63.7	[1]80.3	[1]73.1	77.9	100.0	118.0	94.2	76.4	69.8
Maize (not including sweet corn) unmilled	044	[1]88.9	[3]167.2	253.6	89.1	100.0	136.7	95.4	79.1	69.9
Vegetables, fruit and nuts, fresh or dried	05	[1]92.8	[2]84.2	89.2	91.7	100.0	104.3	99.6	97.4	96.7
Vegetables, fresh, chill, frozen, and preserved; roots	054	[1]97.4	[3]86.3	92.1	101.5	100.0	101.3	99.0	104.5	97.3
Fruit and nuts (not including oil nuts), fresh or dried	057	[1]91.9	[1]78.4	[1]87.5	86.6	100.0	105.6	99.3	94.1	93.8
Feeding stuff for animals (not including unmilled cereals)	08	[1]99.1	[1]98.6	[1]99.9	100.2	100.0	121.9	121.0	95.3	89.8
Miscellaneous edible products and preparations	09	[1]100.5	[1]100.8	[1]99.6	[1]98.9	[1]100.0	[1]103.1	103.9	105.5	107.1
Other food and live animals (December 1996=100)	0R	. . .	. . .	. . .	. . .	. . .	. . .	103.3	97.4	90.5
Beverages And Tobacco	1	[1]92.6	[1]96.0	[1]98.4	98.6	100.0	100.5	100.7	100.1	101.4
Tobacco and tobacco manufactures	12	[1]92.6	[1]96.0	[1]98.4	[1]98.5	[1]100.0	[1]100.5	100.6	99.9	101.5
Tobacco, manufactured (including tobacco substitutes)	122	. . .	. . .	[1]98.1	[1]97.8	[1]100.0	[1]100.3	99.9	98.8	100.7
Crude Materials, Inedible, Except Fuels	2	[1]75.0	[2]74.1	78.2	86.3	100.0	90.8	91.5	80.8	76.0
Hides, skins and furskins, raw	21	[1]79.4	[2]83.4	81.7	98.3	100.0	100.7	105.9	84.1	83.3
Oil seeds and oleaginous fruits	22	[1]98.5	[2]92.6	102.4	103.1	100.0	123.7	124.7	101.5	81.0
Cork and wood	24	[1]64.0	[2]76.2	97.1	98.3	100.0	96.5	92.5	83.0	82.6
Wood in the rough or roughly squared	247	[1]57.5	[1]69.6	[1]99.8	97.0	100.0	97.6	85.4	69.6	70.7
Wood, simply worked and railway sleepers of wood	248	[1]74.7	[1]83.8	[1]100.2	104.2	100.0	96.9	101.5	95.2	95.0
Pulp and waste paper	25	[1]54.5	[2]52.8	44.7	62.2	100.0	60.7	64.4	62.6	69.2
Textile fibers and their waste	26	[1]79.4	[2]65.8	66.1	80.6	100.0	89.2	83.3	76.2	67.0
Cotton textile fibers	263	[1]78.6	[1]61.7	[1]61.6	77.5	100.0	87.9	80.8	73.1	61.6
Crude fertilizers and crude minerals	27	[1]101.8	[2]99.8	97.1	97.6	100.0	97.8	97.6	96.6	93.5
Metalliferous ores and metal scrap	28	[1]74.1	[2]69.7	70.2	81.1	100.0	87.9	90.2	74.9	72.2
Ferrous waste and scrap	282	[1]76.8	[1]71.0	[1]83.7	[1]90.7	100.0	91.8	90.7	71.9	64.0
Nonferrous base metal waste and scrap	288	[1]74.3	[1]72.2	[1]62.6	[1]84.8	100.0	82.9	85.4	68.5	67.5
Other crude materials, inedible, except fuels (December 1996=100)	2R	. . .	. . .	. . .	. . .	. . .	. . .	101.0	97.0	90.5
Mineral Fuels, Lubricants And Related Materials	3	[1]100.0	[2]95.6	94.8	95.4	100.0	110.8	112.0	100.3	107.3
Coal, coke and briquettes	32	[1]102.2	[2]100.1	97.3	96.8	100.0	102.3	102.0	100.0	98.3
Petroleum, petroleum products and related materials	33	[1]97.8	[2]92.7	92.4	94.3	100.0	117.7	121.0	102.0	114.1
Petroleum oils and oils from bituminous minerals (other than crude)	334	[1]95.6	[1]93.7	[1]92.7	95.0	100.0	116.4	119.4	102.8	123.5
Residual petroleum products, n.e.s. and related materials	335	[1]101.1	[1]75.3	[1]85.8	92.4	100.0	122.2	123.7	99.0	89.6
Animal And Vegetable Oils, Fats And Waxes	4	[1]79.4	[2]80.5	84.3	95.3	100.0	94.3	97.1	103.2	82.0
Chemicals And Related Products, n.e.s.	5	[1]87.5	[2]84.9	84.0	88.6	100.0	96.7	96.0	92.6	91.7
Organic chemicals	51	[1]80.8	[1]78.5	[1]76.9	82.1	100.0	87.6	84.7	77.1	77.0
Hydrocarbons, n.e.s. and their derivatives	511	[1]68.5	[1]68.3	[1]69.8	84.0	100.0	89.5	93.4	75.5	80.7
Alcohols, phenols, phenol-alcohols and their derivatives	512	[1]80.0	[1]74.1	[1]72.4	76.5	100.0	88.1	81.8	79.3	75.6
Carboxylic compounds and derivatives	513	. . .	. . .	. . .	. . .	[1]100.0	[1]75.6	68.8	63.6	62.3
Nitrogen-function compounds	514	[1]79.0	[1]76.2	[1]74.0	[1]79.8	100.0	89.6	88.6	79.0	77.2
Organo-inorganic and heterocylics, nucleic acids and their salts	515	. . .	. . .	. . .	[1]93.6	100.0	99.2	89.2	86.3	86.1
Organic chemicals, n.e.s.	516	. . .	. . .	[1]84.1	[1]87.1	[1]100.0	[1]84.1	89.2	88.4	86.8
Inorganic chemicals	52	. . .	. . .	[1]82.6	[1]83.9	100.0	102.4	99.3	103.3	100.8
Inorganic chemical elements, oxides and halogen salts	522	[1]84.0	[1]76.4	[1]56.7	[1]62.6	[1]100.0	[1]102.5	91.4	104.1	99.1
Dyeing, tanning and coloring materials	53	. . .	. . .	. . .	98.6	100.0	101.1	102.2	100.8	101.0
Pigments, paints, varnishes and related materials	533	. . .	. . .	[1]95.6	98.8	100.0	100.4	101.1	99.3	99.1
Medicinal and pharmaceutical products	54	[1]93.3	[1]95.7	[1]98.6	99.5	100.0	101.7	101.2	101.5	100.2
Medicinal and pharmaceutical products, other than medicaments	541	. . .	. . .	[1]98.7	99.6	100.0	102.6	102.6	104.5	102.3
Medicaments (including veterinary medicaments)	542	[1]94.4	[1]95.5	[1]98.2	99.2	100.0	99.6	98.1	95.6	95.9
Essential oils; polishing and cleansing preparations	55	[1]91.2	[2]92.7	93.8	97.4	100.0	100.9	102.6	101.7	102.0
Perfumery, cosmetics, or toilet preparations, excluding soaps (December 1997=100)	553	. . .	. . .	. . .	. . .	. . .	. . .	. . .	100.5	101.9
Fertilizers (December 1996=100)	56	. . .	. . .	. . .	. . .	. . .	. . .	95.8	95.2	87.5
Plastics in primary forms	57	. . .	. . .	75.4	84.7	100.0	94.1	95.4	89.1	89.2
Polymers of ethylene, in primary forms	571	. . .	. . .	[1]63.0	74.4	100.0	91.0	94.9	84.2	85.9
Polyacetals, other polyethers and epoxide resins, in primary forms	574	. . .	. . .	[1]90.5	91.2	100.0	104.1	103.2	99.0	95.8
Plastics, n.e.s., in primary forms	575	. . .	. . .	[1]76.1	85.3	100.0	96.2	96.4	92.3	92.0
Plastics in nonprimary forms	58	. . .	. . .	90.3	92.6	100.0	99.3	98.8	98.1	97.0
Plates, sheets, film, foil and strips of plastic	582	. . .	. . .	[1]91.7	93.1	100.0	100.7	100.4	101.0	100.2
Chemical materials and products, n.e.s.	59	[1]89.8	[2]89.3	91.7	94.6	100.0	102.2	103.5	100.9	99.6
Prepared additives and lubricatory preparation materials	597	. . .	. . .	[1]91.9	94.1	100.0	101.4	101.8	96.4	94.9
Miscellaneous chemical products, n.e.s.	598	[1]92.3	[1]92.0	[1]93.5	96.3	100.0	102.8	103.0	101.0	100.0

See footnotes and NOTE at end of table.

Table C-6. U.S. Export Price Indexes for Selected Categories of Goods, by Standard International Trade Classification [SITC], 1991–1999—*Continued*

(1995=100, unless otherwise indicated; annual data are averages of the 12 months, unless otherwise indicated.)

Category	SITC code	1991	1992	1993	1994	1995	1996	1997	1998	1999
Manufactured Goods Classified Chiefly By Material	6	[1]87.1	[2]87.6	88.1	91.8	100.0	97.8	98.1	97.6	97.2
Rubber manufactures, n.e.s.	62	[1]90.2	[2]91.0	93.1	94.0	100.0	102.7	102.6	102.9	106.8
Tires and inner tubes of rubber	625	[1]89.9	[1]91.9	[1]93.6	[1]93.0	100.0	102.5	101.0	101.0	107.7
Cork and wood manufactures other than furniture	63	. . .	. . .	[1]97.3	[1]102.6	100.0	91.5	91.3	91.6	95.0
Paper, paperboard, and articles of paper pulp, paper or paperboard	64	[1]80.9	[2]79.8	76.8	81.0	100.0	88.9	84.1	83.1	84.0
Paper and paperboard	641	[1]75.1	[1]74.1	[1]70.6	76.5	100.0	86.6	80.2	79.4	80.7
Paper, paperboard, cut to size, and articles thereof	642	. . .	. . .	[1]97.3	96.2	100.0	96.7	95.6	94.4	94.4
Textile yarn, fabrics, and made-up articles, n.e.s.	65	[1]93.3	[1]95.3	[1]95.9	[1]95.8	[1]100.0	[1]103.1	103.0	102.3	99.1
Special yarns, special textile fabrics and related products	657	[1]90.2	[1]91.7	[1]91.9	[1]91.0	[1]100.0	[1]106.1	107.7	107.2	104.6
Nonmetallic mineral manufactures, n.e.s.	66	[1]92.8	[2]94.5	96.5	98.1	100.0	102.4	104.9	107.0	106.3
Glass	664	. . .	. . .	[1]93.2	[1]96.7	[1]100.0	[1]99.0	98.1	98.8	98.3
Iron and steel	67	. . .	. . .	. . .	[1]94.0	[1]100.0	[1]101.9	103.1	100.0	95.2
Iron and steel tubes, pipes, and fittings for tubes and pipes (December 1996=100)	679	. . .	. . .	. . .	. . .	. . .	. . .	101.5	102.9	94.0
Nonferrous metals	68	[1]78.1	[2]76.3	73.1	83.8	100.0	91.2	92.2	88.3	86.8
Copper	682	. . .	. . .	[1]72.6	83.8	100.0	85.7	79.4	62.7	60.3
Aluminum	684	[1]75.3	[1]73.0	[1]69.1	81.8	100.0	87.1	90.9	87.6	83.2
Manufactures of metals, n.e.s.	69	[1]90.7	[1]91.9	[1]93.4	95.2	100.0	101.7	104.0	105.9	107.8
Tools for use in hand or in machines	695	[1]87.1	[1]89.8	[1]92.3	[1]95.5	[1]100.0	[1]102.2	102.8	102.7	104.6
Manufactures of base metal, n.e.s.	699	[1]87.5	[1]88.8	[1]90.5	[1]93.2	100.0	99.6	101.6	102.4	103.0
Machinery And Transport Equipment	7	[1]98.4	[2]99.8	99.7	99.3	100.0	100.6	100.4	98.8	97.6
Power generating machinery and equipment	71	[1]90.9	[2]94.7	96.2	98.0	100.0	103.8	105.9	107.1	109.9
Internal combustion piston engines and parts thereof, n.e.s.	713	. . .	. . .	. . .	99.9	100.0	102.2	104.1	105.0	107.6
Gas turbine engines and reaction engines; parts thereof n.e.s.	714	. . .	. . .	. . .	. . .	100.0	105.4	108.4	110.3	115.2
Rotating electric plant and parts thereof, n.e.s.	716	[1]91.3	[1]93.9	[1]95.2	96.1	100.0	102.0	102.5	102.9	102.6
Machinery specialized for particular industries	72	[1]91.5	[2]94.0	95.9	97.2	100.0	102.7	104.2	105.2	105.8
Agricultural machinery (excluding tractors) and parts thereof	721	[1]92.4	[1]94.8	[1]97.3	98.6	100.0	102.0	103.0	103.1	103.9
Civil engineering and contractors' plant, equipment and parts, n.e.s.	723	[1]91.6	[1]91.3	[1]93.5	96.6	100.0	101.5	102.7	105.8	107.1
Machinery and equipment specialized for particular industries, and parts	728	[1]90.8	[1]95.4	[1]97.4	96.9	100.0	104.4	106.3	106.2	106.0
Metalworking machinery	73	[1]94.8	[1]97.3	[1]99.0	98.6	100.0	101.9	104.4	108.1	109.0
Machine tools for removing metal or other material (December 1996=100)	731	. . .	. . .	. . .	. . .	. . .	. . .	99.8	101.6	101.7
General industrial machinery, equipment, and parts, n.e.s.	74	[1]92.9	[2]95.4	97.0	98.5	100.0	102.4	104.8	106.2	107.4
Heating and cooling equipment and parts thereof, n.e.s.	741	[1]94.9	[1]95.5	[1]98.1	99.4	100.0	101.5	102.6	102.5	102.5
Pumps for liquids; liquid elevators; and parts thereof	742	[1]90.6	[1]93.2	[1]95.9	97.4	100.0	102.2	106.1	110.9	113.5
Pumps, compressors, fans, centrifuges, and filtering apparatus	743	[1]90.5	[1]93.6	[1]95.5	97.1	100.0	104.2	108.3	109.3	110.2
Mechanical handling equipment, and parts thereof, n.e.s.	744	. . .	. . .	. . .	[1]100.3	[1]100.0	101.6	102.4	103.9	105.3
Nonelectrical machinery, tools and mechanical apparatus, and parts	745	[1]93.4	[1]96.2	[1]96.7	98.4	100.0	101.3	102.2	102.1	103.2
Taps, cocks, valves and similar appliances for pipes, boiler shells	747	[1]92.9	[3]95.7	[1]96.9	97.4	100.0	103.1	102.3	103.4	105.3
Computer equipment and office machines	75	[1]128.5	[2]122.7	115.0	106.0	100.0	92.5	84.7	77.1	71.6
Computer equipment	752	[1]143.1	[1]137.1	[1]122.1	109.8	100.0	89.8	79.9	73.5	67.3
Parts and accessories for computer equipment and office machines	759	[1]116.0	[1]111.5	[1]106.3	102.4	100.0	94.7	89.2	79.7	75.0
Telecommunications and sound recording and reproducing apparatus and equipment	76	[1]100.3	[2]102.0	101.9	100.8	100.0	100.5	99.7	98.2	97.0
Telecommunications equipment and parts, n.e.s.	764	[1]99.7	[1]101.5	[1]102.3	100.7	100.0	100.6	99.7	98.1	97.2
Electrical machinery and equipment	77	[1]98.4	[2]100.6	99.9	99.5	100.0	98.8	96.1	92.0	88.4
Electric power machinery (except rotating power machinery) and parts	771	. . .	. . .	[1]101.6	100.0	100.0	100.0	98.7	97.2	98.6
Electrical circuitry equipment	772	[1]95.9	[1]96.9	[1]97.1	98.2	100.0	101.0	102.8	103.7	99.7
Equipment for distributing electricity, n.e.s. (December 1996=100)	773	. . .	. . .	. . .	. . .	. . .	. . .	100.2	97.4	96.2
Electro-diagnostic apparatus for medical use	774	[1]103.0	[1]105.8	[1]103.3	101.0	100.0	99.6	99.8	99.1	100.6
Household type electrical and nonelectrical equipment, n.e.s.	775	[1]93.3	[1]95.4	[1]96.7	96.9	100.0	99.3	99.2	97.0	93.4
Electronic valves and tubes, diodes, transistors and integrated circuits	776	[1]102.1	[1]105.2	[1]102.5	100.6	100.0	97.2	91.0	84.3	79.2
Electrical machinery and apparatus, n.e.s.	778	[1]93.0	[1]95.1	[1]96.7	98.8	100.0	100.5	101.5	100.4	98.9
Road vehicles	78	[1]94.9	[2]96.5	97.3	98.5	100.0	101.0	101.8	102.0	102.5
Motor vehicles (excep public transport) designed to transport people	781	[1]94.2	[1]95.7	[1]96.4	97.9	100.0	101.6	102.3	102.9	103.9
Motor vehicles for the transport of goods and multi-purpose motor vehicles	782	. . .	. . .	. . .	98.8	100.0	101.0	102.5	104.2	106.0
Parts and accessories for tractors, motor cars and other motor vehicles	784	[1]96.1	[1]97.2	[1]98.4	98.9	100.0	100.7	101.2	100.6	100.3
Miscellaneous Manufactured Articles	8	[1]96.6	[1]98.4	[1]98.9	99.2	100.0	100.8	101.7	101.0	101.1
Furniture and parts thereof	82	[1]103.1	[1]103.8	[1]100.2	[1]100.2	100.0	101.8	103.3	104.2	104.9
Articles of apparel and clothing accessories	84	. . .	. . .	. . .	[1]99.7	[1]100.0	[1]100.4	102.1	103.1	100.5
Apparel, of textile fabrics, knitted or crocheted, n.e.s. (December 1996=100)	845	. . .	. . .	. . .	. . .	. . .	. . .	99.1	99.8	94.3
Professional, scientific and controlling instruments and apparatus, n.e.s.	87	[1]93.1	[2]95.4	96.8	98.6	100.0	101.6	103.4	103.8	105.3
Instruments and appliances; for medical, surgical, dental, and veterinary use	872	[1]93.7	[1]98.4	[1]98.8	98.6	100.0	101.5	102.3	101.7	101.2
Measuring, checking, analysing and controlling instruments, n.e.s.	874	[1]93.1	[1]95.3	[1]97.0	98.8	100.0	101.4	103.3	103.9	106.2
Photographic apparatus, equipment and supplies and optical goods, n.e.s.	88	[1]95.9	[1]96.2	[1]97.7	[1]99.5	[1]100.0	[1]98.9	98.5	94.0	95.4
Photographic and cinematographic supplies	882	[1]96.4	[1]97.6	[1]99.2	[1]99.7	100.0	97.1	96.0	85.6	88.4
Miscellaneous manufactured articles, n.e.s.	89	[1]100.2	[1]101.8	[1]100.9	99.6	100.0	100.6	100.4	98.7	98.2
Printed matter	892	[1]93.5	[1]96.0	[1]97.2	98.1	100.0	103.8	106.3	108.9	110.8
Articles, n.e.s. of plastics	893	[1]99.3	[1]100.3	[1]99.0	97.3	100.0	100.7	98.9	97.3	96.6
Baby carriages, toys, games and sporting goods	894	[1]99.8	[1]101.0	[1]99.4	[1]98.4	100.0	100.1	100.7	100.7	100.5
Musical instruments, LDs, tapes, and other sound recordings	898	[1]116.4	[1]112.3	[1]109.0	103.9	100.0	98.1	95.5	90.4	89.3
Miscellaneous manufactured articles, n.e.s. (December 1996=100)	899	. . .	. . .	. . .	. . .	. . .	. . .	100.8	98.9	98.3
Other miscellaneous manufactured articles (December 1996=100)	8R	. . .	. . .	. . .	. . .	. . .	. . .	101.0	102.3	102.1
Gold, nonmonetary (excluding gold ores and concentrates)	971	. . .	. . .	[1]93.6	100.4	100.0	100.6	87.7	76.3	72.6

1. Average of March, June, September, and December.
2. Average of March, June, September, October, November, and December.
3. Average of March, June, July, August, September, October, November, and December.

NOTE: n.e.s. = not elsewhere specified.

Table C-7. U.S. Import Price Indexes for Selected Categories of Goods, by Standard International Trade Classification [SITC], 1991–1999

(1995=100, unless otherwise indicated; annual data are averages of the 12 months, unless otherwise indicated.)

Category	SITC code	1991	1992	1993	1994	1995	1996	1997	1998	1999
ALL COMMODITIES		93.7	94.3	94.0	95.7	100.0	101.0	98.5	92.6	93.4
Food And Live Animals	0	[1]87.9	[2]86.2	86.6	95.9	100.0	95.8	100.1	97.0	93.3
Meat and meat preparations	01	[1]118.3	[2]110.2	112.3	107.8	100.0	95.9	102.4	98.3	95.5
Fish, crustaceans, aquatic invertebrates and preparations thereof	03	[1]86.6	[2]87.2	88.0	98.0	100.0	96.3	103.2	105.3	104.5
Fish, fresh (live or dead), chilled or frozen	034	[1]95.4	[1]96.1	[1]94.2	96.3	100.0	98.5	102.5	111.1	117.6
Crustaceans, aquatic invert. fresh, chilled, frozen, dried, or salted	036	[1]80.0	[1]79.5	[1]81.9	97.4	100.0	92.6	103.0	102.2	99.7
Vegetables, fruit and nuts, fresh or dried	05	[1]91.3	[2]93.8	91.3	88.6	100.0	103.8	103.2	103.9	103.2
Fruit and nuts (not including oil nuts), fresh or dried	057	[1]92.7	[1]87.9	[1]89.8	93.4	100.0	101.4	102.3	99.0	104.9
Coffee, tea, cocoa, spices and manufactures thereof	07	[1]58.1	[2]50.9	55.4	93.7	100.0	81.6	96.2	83.4	67.9
Coffee and coffee substitutes	071	[1]46.1	[1]38.3	[1]44.7	93.3	100.0	74.7	93.7	71.3	52.0
Other food and live animals (December 1996=100)	0R	...	...	...	...	...	...	99.8	94.7	92.8
Beverages And Tobacco	1	[1]96.0	[2]147.9	97.6	98.2	100.0	103.8	107.4	109.5	110.9
Beverages	11	[1]95.8	[2]98.2	97.8	98.2	100.0	101.8	104.0	106.2	107.7
Crude Materials, Inedible, Except Fuels	2	[1]75.8	[2]116.9	80.1	87.0	100.0	96.0	97.2	87.9	89.5
Cork and wood	24	[1]72.7	[2]83.1	103.7	111.8	100.0	112.1	121.1	106.7	118.5
Pulp and waste paper	25	[1]67.9	[2]66.9	56.4	65.0	100.0	72.3	66.7	62.7	61.3
Metalliferous ores and metal scrap	28	[1]88.6	[2]86.2	82.2	85.3	100.0	99.1	103.8	96.9	93.2
Crude animal and vegetable materials, n.e.s. (December 1996=100)	29	...	...	...	...	...	...	108.4	110.6	108.4
Other crude materials, inedible, except fuels (December 1996=100)	2R	...	...	...	...	...	...	96.9	90.0	90.3
Mineral Fuels, Lubricants And Related Materials	3	[1]108.3	[2]107.3	97.3	91.9	100.0	118.4	111.9	78.5	102.7
Petroleum, petroleum products and related materials	33	[1]107.8	[2]106.9	96.3	90.7	100.0	118.8	110.0	74.3	100.6
Petroleum oils and oils from bituminous minerals, crude	333	[1]109.9	[2]109.8	96.3	90.0	100.0	119.5	110.2	72.1	101.5
Petroleum oils and oils from bituminous minerals (other than crude)	334	[1]107.3	[1]101.9	[1]94.7	92.6	100.0	117.6	111.7	85.6	98.8
Gas, natural and manufactured	34	[1]116.4	[2]114.0	113.6	110.9	100.0	117.4	133.2	112.6	124.0
Natural gas, whether or not liquefied	343	[1]127.2	[1]123.0	[1]131.3	[1]123.7	[1]100.0	[1]126.0	138.0	119.5	131.1
Chemicals And Related Products, n.e.s.	5	[1]90.5	[2]91.8	91.5	93.1	100.0	99.5	96.6	92.8	91.1
Organic chemicals	51	[1]97.0	[1]94.8	[1]92.6	95.5	100.0	98.9	97.0	91.7	91.3
Organo-inorganic and heterocylics, nucleic acids and their salts	515	...	98.8	[1]98.1	97.8	100.0	104.9	100.1	93.7	94.3
Inorganic chemicals	52	[1]90.2	[2]88.2	89.5	90.5	100.0	101.4	100.0	94.9	87.5
Inorganic chemical elements, oxides and halogen salts	522	[1]87.9	[1]84.3	[1]81.1	85.1	100.0	102.1	98.7	88.9	79.3
Dyeing, tanning and coloring materials	53	...	92.7	92.8	94.6	100.0	102.1	96.7	95.3	91.9
Medicinal and pharmaceutical products	54	[1]81.1	[2]87.1	90.5	94.0	100.0	100.3	96.3	95.4	96.8
Medicinal and pharmaceutical products, other than medicaments	541	...	88.9	[1]93.5	[1]95.8	100.0	100.6	97.3	96.7	95.5
Medicaments (including veterinary medicaments)	542	...	84.8	[1]88.6	[1]91.9	100.0	99.8	94.7	93.6	97.2
Essential oils; polishing and cleansing preparations	55	[1]83.9	[2]87.7	89.7	89.9	100.0	102.2	97.8	94.8	92.6
Plastics in primary forms	57	...	...	91.7	93.2	100.0	98.2	91.9	92.9	93.2
Plastics in nonprimary forms	58	...	...	87.1	88.0	100.0	87.6	86.1	77.9	75.9
Plates, sheets, film, foil and strips of plastic	582	...	...	[1]90.0	91.1	100.0	97.7	91.5	87.1	84.6
Chemical materials and products, n.e.s.	59	[1]89.5	[2]99.5	97.8	95.9	100.0	107.1	103.8	100.8	98.3
Miscellaneous chemical products, n.e.s. (December 1996=100)	598	...	...	...	...	...	...	99.9	95.6	87.7
Manufactured Goods Classified Chiefly By Material	6	[1]88.7	[2]88.7	88.2	90.8	100.0	98.3	96.3	93.7	92.4
Rubber manufactures, n.e.s.	62	[1]96.0	[2]98.1	98.9	97.4	100.0	99.8	96.7	94.7	94.6
Tires and inner tubes of rubber	625	[1]98.8	[1]101.3	[1]102.3	99.2	100.0	101.3	99.3	97.8	97.1
Cork and wood manufactures other than furniture	63	[1]82.8	[1]90.0	[1]100.3	[1]101.0	[1]100.0	[1]99.8	99.5	94.7	101.7
Veneers, plywood, particle board, and other wood, worked, n.e.s.	634	[1]73.8	[1]81.5	[1]100.5	[1]104.5	[1]100.0	[1]98.6	93.9	85.1	98.4
Paper, paperboard, and articles of paper pulp, paper or paper board	64	[1]80.1	[2]75.7	75.9	77.3	100.0	98.4	87.1	87.4	85.0
Paper and paperboard (December 1996=100)	641	...	...	...	...	...	...	101.2	101.3	98.4
Textile yarn, fabrics, made-up articles, n.e.s., and related products	65	[1]91.9	[1]94.4	[1]94.2	95.7	100.0	100.5	100.2	97.3	95.0
Made-up articles, wholly or chiefly of textile materials, n.e.s.	658	[1]90.7	[1]91.4	[1]91.1	94.6	100.0	100.1	97.7	93.8	93.5
Nonmetallic mineral manufactures, n.e.s.	66	[1]92.9	[2]94.9	96.6	97.6	100.0	101.8	102.7	100.6	101.0
Pearls, precious and semiprecious stones, unworked or worked	667	[1]95.1	[3]96.3	97.5	98.8	100.0	100.4	100.9	99.0	99.5
Iron and steel	67	[1]90.9	[1]89.1	[1]89.7	91.8	100.0	97.8	96.3	92.2	86.3
Pig iron, sponge iron, iron or steel granules, powders, and ferroalloys	671	[1]94.5	[1]87.5	[1]81.3	84.1	100.0	99.5	91.4	82.6	79.5
Iron, nonalloy steel flat-rolled products not clad, plated, coated	673	...	...	[1]84.8	[1]92.2	100.0	95.0	97.1	92.1	87.2
Iron and steel bars, rods, angles, shapes, sections, and sheet piling	676	[1]90.7	[1]88.6	[1]90.9	[1]90.3	[1]100.0	[1]96.7	95.0	94.2	91.3
Iron and steel tubes, pipes, and fittings for tubes and pipes (December 1996=100)	679	...	...	...	...	...	...	98.2	95.3	89.8
Nonferrous metals	68	[1]84.0	[2]81.9	73.2	83.6	100.0	90.4	92.4	88.7	88.9
Silver, platinum and other platinum group metals	681	[1]212.0	[1]191.7	[1]394.8	100.7	100.0	94.3	101.1	130.1	147.8
Copper (December 1997=100)	682	...	...	...	...	...	...	...	96.1	93.2
Aluminum	684	[1]74.8	[1]70.8	[1]67.6	79.8	100.0	87.8	91.4	84.8	81.2
Manufactures of metals, n.e.s.	69	[1]92.1	[2]94.3	94.3	95.3	100.0	101.1	98.9	96.8	96.1
Nails, screws, nuts, bolts, rivets, of iron, steel, copper or aluminum	694	[1]86.1	[1]88.1	[1]90.1	91.9	100.0	96.7	93.4	88.6	85.3
Tools for use in hand or in machines	695	[1]96.1	[1]98.1	[1]97.6	[1]98.5	[1]100.0	[1]103.7	103.1	103.6	101.2
Household equipment of base metal, n.e.s.	697	[1]94.1	[1]93.9	[1]94.2	[1]96.4	[1]100.0	[1]103.7	102.9	101.3	100.0
Manufactures of base metal, n.e.s.	699	[1]91.3	[1]94.9	[1]95.7	[1]96.3	100.0	101.7	100.7	98.4	98.4

See footnotes and NOTE at end of table.

Table C-7. U.S. Import Price Indexes for Selected Categories of Goods, by Standard International Trade Classification [SITC], 1991–1999—*Continued*

(1995=100, unless otherwise indicated; annual data are averages of the 12 months, unless otherwise indicated.)

Category	SITC code	1991	1992	1993	1994	1995	1996	1997	1998	1999
Machinery And Transport Equipment	7	[1]93.6	[2]95.3	96.0	97.9	100.0	98.9	95.5	91.9	90.3
Power generating machinery and equipment (December 1996=100)	71	. . .	. . .	. . .	. . .	. . .	. . .	99.3	98.2	98.6
Gas turbine and reaction engines; parts thereof, n.e.s. (December 1997=100)	714	. . .	. . .	. . .	. . .	. . .	. . .	. . .	100.2	100.1
Rotating electric plant and parts thereof, n.e.s.	716	[1]88.2	[1]89.7	[1]91.7	94.5	100.0	99.2	96.6	93.7	92.5
Machinery specialized for particular industries	72	[1]89.5	[2]93.2	92.4	95.1	100.0	101.4	99.3	97.8	97.9
Civil engineering and contractors' plant, equipment and parts, n.e.s.	723	[1]85.0	[1]86.8	[1]90.9	95.2	100.0	101.1	102.1	102.5	104.9
Textile and leather machinery, and parts thereof, n.e.s.	724	[1]90.8	[1]94.4	[1]93.7	94.8	100.0	100.3	98.3	96.5	95.5
Printing and bookbinding machinery, and parts thereof (December 1996=100)	726	. . .	. . .	. . .	. . .	. . .	. . .	95.9	94.6	93.3
Machinery and equipment specialized for particular industries, and parts	728	[1]87.6	[1]90.4	[1]90.2	93.8	100.0	100.3	97.2	95.2	94.3
Metalworking machinery	73	[1]85.3	[1]87.5	[1]89.7	92.8	100.0	101.5	98.4	97.2	95.5
Machine tools for removing metal or other material	731	. . .	. . .	[1]87.5	[1]92.5	100.0	101.5	99.1	98.5	98.0
General industrial machinery, equipment, and machine parts, n.e.s.	74	[1]89.2	[2]92.0	92.0	94.7	100.0	100.9	98.2	97.0	97.7
Heating and cooling equipment and parts thereof, n.e.s. (December 1996=100)	741	. . .	. . .	. . .	. . .	. . .	. . .	99.7	98.8	98.5
Pumps for liquids; liquid elevators; and parts thereof	742	[1]88.7	[1]91.4	[1]93.1	95.4	100.0	104.8	101.7	101.5	100.2
Pumps, compressors, fans, centrifuges, and filtering apparatus	743	[1]93.3	[1]95.3	[1]96.2	97.4	100.0	101.2	99.4	97.4	97.4
Mechanical handling equipment, and parts thereof, n.e.s. (December 1996=100)	744	. . .	. . .	. . .	. . .	. . .	. . .	94.9	94.1	93.4
Nonelectrical machinery, tools and mechanical apparatus, and parts	745	[1]85.6	[1]88.3	[1]87.3	90.5	100.0	100.8	96.7	93.8	99.5
Taps, cocks, valves and similar appliances for pipes, boiler shells	747	[1]87.8	[1]90.9	[1]92.4	96.0	100.0	101.5	97.3	96.3	96.5
Parts for mechanical power transmission	748	. . .	. . .	[1]90.2	93.9	100.0	103.6	101.3	100.2	103.6
Computer equipment and office machines	75	[1]116.1	[2]114.3	109.5	103.6	100.0	92.3	80.9	70.4	63.1
Office machines	751	[1]87.5	[1]91.0	[1]94.7	96.8	100.0	98.1	90.7	88.9	87.7
Computer equipment	752	[1]136.7	[1]131.2	[1]120.1	108.6	100.0	93.0	80.5	66.4	55.0
Parts and accessories for computer equipment and office machines	759	[1]105.0	[1]102.0	[1]99.9	99.6	100.0	89.2	78.3	71.6	69.3
Telecommunications and sound recording and reproducing apparatus and equipment	76	[1]99.6	[2]99.2	99.9	99.4	100.0	97.3	93.2	89.7	87.3
Television receivers, including monitors, projectors and receivers	761	[1]98.5	[1]99.7	[1]100.7	100.6	100.0	98.9	92.0	86.8	81.9
Radio-broadcast receivers	762	[1]100.3	[1]100.2	[1]100.3	99.9	100.0	98.3	96.6	93.4	90.9
Sound recorders or reproducers; television image and sound recorders	763	[1]99.6	[1]98.3	[1]99.8	99.5	100.0	96.4	91.3	87.9	85.7
Telecommunications equipment and parts, n.e.s.	764	[1]99.2	[1]98.9	[1]99.7	99.0	100.0	97.0	93.1	89.7	87.8
Electrical machinery and equipment	77	[1]94.3	[2]95.3	97.2	98.8	100.0	95.6	89.4	84.6	82.9
Electric power machinery (except rotating power mach) and parts thereof	771	[1]89.7	[1]92.0	[1]93.8	94.5	100.0	101.2	101.3	100.5	97.7
Electrical circuitry equipment	772	[1]92.2	[1]94.3	[1]94.9	96.5	100.0	99.1	97.8	95.9	92.9
Equipment for distributing electricity, n.e.s. (December 1999=100)	773	. . .	. . .	. . .	. . .	. . .	. . .	. . .	. . .	. . .
Electro-diagnostic apparatus for medical use (December 1996=100)	774	. . .	. . .	. . .	. . .	. . .	. . .	98.2	96.4	95.5
Household type electrical and nonelectrical equipment, n.e.s.	775	[1]99.9	[1]100.8	[1]100.2	99.9	100.0	100.9	100.0	99.5	96.8
Electronic valves and tubes, diodes, transistors and integrated circuits	776	[1]94.8	[1]94.6	[1]100.5	102.4	100.0	88.9	76.8	69.5	68.2
Electrical machinery and apparatus, n.e.s.	778	[1]92.1	[1]93.4	[1]94.2	96.0	100.0	99.9	97.9	94.7	93.7
Road vehicles	78	[1]89.5	[2]91.4	93.1	97.0	100.0	100.7	101.0	101.2	102.2
Motor vehicles designed to transport people (except public transportation)	781	[1]89.4	[3]91.0	[1]93.5	97.0	100.0	100.8	101.7	102.1	103.3
Motor vehicles for the transport of goods and multi-purpose motor vehicles	782	. . .	. . .	. . .	96.3	100.0	100.9	100.8	100.7	102.1
Road vehicles, n.e.s. (December 1998=100)	783	. . .	. . .	. . .	. . .	. . .	. . .	. . .	. . .	101.2
Parts and accessories for tractors, motor cars and other motor vehicles	784	[1]92.2	[1]92.5	[1]94.1	97.1	100.0	100.1	98.2	97.4	97.8
Motorcycles and cycles, motorized and not motorized (December 1996=100)	785	. . .	. . .	. . .	. . .	. . .	. . .	99.0	95.8	96.9
Miscellaneous Manufactured Articles	8	[1]94.5	[1]97.1	[1]97.7	98.3	100.0	100.7	100.1	98.7	98.0
Prefabricated buildings; plumbing, heat and lighting fixtures, n.e.s.	81	[1]95.2	[1]98.4	[1]98.5	[1]97.1	100.0	100.9	96.4	95.5	92.8
Lighting fixtures and fittings, n.e.s. (December 1996=100)	813	. . .	. . .	. . .	. . .	. . .	. . .	97.2	97.1	95.8
Furniture and parts thereof	82	[1]96.4	[1]98.4	[1]97.8	98.2	100.0	101.0	102.8	101.4	99.0
Travel goods, handbags and similar containers	83	[1]92.5	[1]96.5	[1]96.7	96.8	100.0	101.1	101.1	100.5	101.5
Articles of apparel and clothing accessories	84	[1]96.5	[1]98.6	[1]99.0	99.0	100.0	101.2	102.4	102.7	101.9
Mens or boys clothing, coats, underwear, and suits, of woven textiles	841	. . .	. . .	[1]97.3	98.3	100.0	100.7	103.5	104.4	103.2
Women or girls woven trousers, underwear, coats, dresses, skirts, and suits	842	. . .	. . .	. . .	98.9	100.0	101.4	102.5	102.9	101.8
Men's or boys' coats, jackets, suits, trousers, shirts, etc. (December 1996=100)	843	. . .	. . .	. . .	. . .	. . .	. . .	99.9	96.3	92.1
Women's or girl's outer and undergarments, knitted or crocheted	844	. . .	. . .	[1]101.3	[1]99.7	100.0	101.6	100.1	99.7	100.0
Apparel, of textile fabrics, knitted or crocheted, n.e.s.	845	. . .	. . .	[1]98.2	[1]99.3	100.0	101.4	102.5	101.6	104.9
Headgear and non-textile apparel and clothing accessories	848	. . .	. . .	[1]95.5	[1]97.0	[1]100.0	101.9	104.3	102.1	98.7
Footwear	85	[1]99.6	[2]102.0	98.9	98.6	100.0	101.0	101.1	100.9	100.9
Professional, scientific and controlling instruments and apparatus, n.e.s.	87	[1]89.1	[1]91.6	[1]94.0	97.0	100.0	100.1	97.2	95.0	94.6
Instruments and appliances; for medical, surgical, dental, and veterinary use	872	. . .	. . .	. . .	[1]96.1	100.0	99.7	95.0	91.7	92.1
Measuring, checking, analysing and controlling instruments/apparatus, n.e.s.	874	[1]89.9	[1]92.1	[1]94.6	[1]97.6	100.0	100.5	98.4	96.9	96.1
Photographic apparatus, equipment and supplies and optical goods, n.e.s.	88	[1]89.4	[2]92.3	93.9	96.4	100.0	98.1	94.5	91.2	91.7
Photographic apparatus and equipment, n.e.s.	881	[1]87.4	[1]89.6	[1]93.2	[1]96.3	100.0	96.3	89.9	84.6	85.8
Photographic and cinematographic supplies	882	[1]96.7	[1]95.6	[1]97.5	[1]97.8	100.0	99.4	98.8	95.9	96.2
Optical goods, n.e.s.	884	[1]89.6	[1]92.4	[1]95.3	[1]97.4	100.0	96.9	94.9	90.4	91.4
Watches and clocks	885	[1]86.2	[1]90.0	[1]90.8	94.5	100.0	99.7	94.7	93.8	93.6
Miscellaneous manufactured articles, n.e.s.	89	[1]93.2	[1]97.0	[1]97.9	98.5	100.0	100.8	99.2	96.2	95.1
Printed matter	892	. . .	. . .	. . .	[1]96.7	100.0	100.2	100.8	99.1	99.3
Articles of plastics, n.e.s.	893	[1]91.3	[1]94.8	[1]93.5	94.7	100.0	102.6	102.2	97.5	96.1
Baby carriages, toys, games and sporting goods	894	[1]91.9	[1]100.8	[1]101.2	100.7	100.0	101.5	100.3	97.6	96.1
Jewelry and other articles of precious materials, n.e.s.	897	[1]96.4	[1]94.5	[1]94.8	98.4	100.0	101.0	99.7	98.8	98.9
Musical instruments, LDs, tapes, other sound recordings	898	[1]102.7	[1]101.9	[1]102.1	[1]99.3	[1]100.0	97.8	91.7	84.0	81.0
Miscellaneous manufactured articles, n.e.s.	899	[1]91.6	[1]94.3	[1]96.5	96.3	100.0	99.9	99.6	98.5	99.5
Gold, nonmonetary (excluding gold ores and concentrates)	971	. . .	. . .	[1]96.1	101.3	100.0	100.4	87.6	77.0	73.2

1. Average of March, June, September, and December.
2. Average of March, June, September, October, November, and December.
3. Average of March, June, July, August, September, October, November, and December.

NOTE: n.e.s. = not elsewhere specified.

Table C-8. U.S. Foreign Trade in Goods by Industry Using North American Industry Classification System [NAICS] Product Groups, 1997–1999

(Census basis, preliminary; millions of dollars.)

Product	NAICS code	1997	1998	1999
EXPORTS				
ALL COMMODITIES, TOTAL		687 598	680 474	692 821
Agricultural products	111	29 216	25 034	22 733
Livestock and livestock products	112	1 150	1 121	1 039
Forestry products, nesoi	113	2 023	1 550	1 568
Fish, fresh, chilled, or frozen and other marine products	114	2 564	2 127	2 601
Oil and gas	211	1 674	1 257	1 460
Minerals and ores	212	6 052	5 411	4 451
Food manufacturing	311	26 314	25 163	24 113
Beverages and tobacco products	312	6 739	6 528	5 536
Textiles and fabrics	313	5 587	5 672	6 055
Textile mill products	314	2 197	2 218	2 211
Apparel and accessories	315	8 551	8 708	8 194
Leather and allied products	316	2 623	2 693	2 570
Wood products	321	5 523	4 651	4 859
Paper	322	14 593	13 820	14 131
Printing, publishing and similar products	323	4 864	4 955	4 866
Petroleum and coal products	324	7 201	5 388	6 007
Chemicals	325	69 124	67 531	69 870
Plastics and rubber products	326	14 036	14 522	15 197
Nonmetallic mineral products	327	6 420	6 211	6 527
Primary metal manufacturing	331	20 855	20 130	18 667
Fabricated metal products, nesoi	332	19 191	19 985	20 136
Machinery, except electrical	333	82 874	79 445	76 388
Computer and electronic products	334	152 896	147 475	161 543
Electrical equipment, appliances, and component	335	22 917	22 383	23 716
Transportation equipment	336	118 101	131 890	132 042
Furniture and fixtures	337	2 497	2 613	2 563
Miscellaneous manufactured commodities	339	20 228	20 478	21 970
Waste and scrap	910	4 474	3 570	3 623
Public administration	920	2 710	3 330	2 848
U.S. goods returned to Canada (exports only)	980	2 378	1 933	1 703
Special classification provisions, nesoi	990	22 023	22 682	23 635
IMPORTS				
ALL COMMODITIES, TOTAL		870 213	913 885	1 024 766
Agricultural products	111	12 404	12 364	12 237
Livestock and livestock products	112	2 478	2 675	2 682
Forestry products, nesoi	113	1 675	1 512	1 242
Fish, fresh, chilled, or frozen and other marine products	114	6 539	6 608	7 124
Oil and gas	211	63 450	45 362	59 475
Minerals and ores	212	2 851	2 891	2 566
Food manufacturing	311	16 713	17 364	18 425
Beverages and tobacco products	312	6 478	6 995	7 877
Textiles and fabrics	313	6 403	6 533	6 481
Textile mill products	314	4 794	5 615	6 362
Apparel and accessories	315	47 201	52 376	55 141
Leather and allied products	316	19 408	19 554	20 025
Wood products	321	12 910	13 288	16 003
Paper	322	14 675	15 610	16 435
Printing, publishing and similar products	323	3 214	3 475	3 789
Petroleum and coal products	324	13 019	10 490	13 713
Chemicals	325	49 620	53 722	60 963
Plastics and rubber products	326	12 885	14 226	15 984
Nonmetallic mineral products	327	10 472	11 512	13 224
Primary metal manufacturing	331	35 948	40 622	36 930
Fabricated metal products, nesoi	332	20 914	22 797	24 487
Machinery, except electrical	333	65 662	70 981	72 186
Computer and electronic products	334	175 011	181 202	205 604
Electrical equipment, appliances, and component	335	27 370	30 256	34 811
Transportation equipment	336	149 265	164 426	193 592
Furniture and fixtures	337	8 985	10 797	13 173
Miscellaneous manufactured commodities	339	43 016	47 144	50 961
Waste and scrap	910	1 907	1 756	1 710
Public administration	920	3 958	4 593	5 424
U.S. goods returned and reimported items (imports only)	980	21 801	25 363	30 888
Special classification provisions, nesoi	990	9 186	11 777	15 252

NOTE: Data are unrevised and will not agree exactly with other revised tables of U.S. Foreign Trade in Goods. nesoi = not elsewhere specified or identified.

Table C-9. U.S. Foreign Trade in Goods by Industry Using Standard Industrial Classification [SIC] Product Groups, 1991–1997

(Census basis, millions of dollars.)

Product	SIC code	Exports						
		1991	1992	1993	1994	1995	1996	1997
ALL COMMODITIES, TOTAL	0	421 854	447 471	464 858	512 416	583 031	622 827	687 598
Agricultural Products, Total	01	21 704	23 206	22 222	22 915	30 161	33 134	28 290
Cash grains and other crops	011	13 799	15 296	14 991	13 988	19 909	23 966	18 564
Field crops, except cash grains	013	4 548	4 383	3 519	4 744	5 968	4 971	5 204
Vegetables and melons	016	862	906	1 007	1 073	1 111	1 040	1 132
Fruits and tree nuts	017	2 134	2 245	2 313	2 704	2 742	2 719	2 865
Horticultural specialties	018	361	375	393	406	430	438	526
Livestock And Livestock Products, Total	02	1 000	928	847	980	962	998	1 150
Livestock, except dairy and poultry	021	265	268	207	289	175	194	312
Dairy farms	024	50	43	39	47	31	36	34
Poultry and eggs	025	204	207	214	225	227	226	238
Animal specialties	027	480	410	387	420	530	542	566
Forestry Products, total	08	286	306	293	285	297	292	301
Standing timber	081	63	66	77	62	58	66	72
Forestry products	083	223	240	215	223	239	226	229
Commercial Fishing, Total	09	2 822	3 068	2 703	2 787	2 952	2 716	2 453
Metallic Ores And Concentrates, Total	10	1 126	1 258	852	1 023	1 586	1 169	1 282
Iron ore	101	156	187	168	162	184	232	236
Copper ore	102	382	445	342	393	486	287	211
Lead and zinc ores	103	364	441	191	188	265	305	414
Gold and silver ores	104	4	5	3	16	9	10	22
Ferroalloy ores, except vanadium	106	148	136	102	218	580	264	327
Miscellaneous metal ores	109	71	45	45	46	61	71	71
Coal And Lignite, Total	12	4 628	4 242	3 092	2 859	3 574	3 697	3 408
Bituminous coal and lignite	122	4 593	4 210	3 062	2 826	3 523	3 646	3 362
Anthracite mining	123	35	31	30	33	50	51	45
Oil And Gas Extraction, Total	13	693	741	591	586	734	1 214	1 674
Crude petroleum and natural gas	131	105	262	138	159	126	583	1 013
Natural gas liquids	132	588	479	453	426	607	632	661
Nonmetallic Minerals, Except Fuels, Total	14	1 148	1 159	1 116	1 208	1 303	1 322	1 402
Dimension stone (includes granite, marble, etc.)	141	70	57	48	60	58	63	74
Crushed and broken limestone	142	32	46	58	53	69	66	63
Sand and gravel	144	95	98	97	106	113	117	130
Clay, ceramic, and refractory minerals	145	571	634	635	706	757	770	808
Chemical and fertilizer minerals	147	154	92	73	71	88	87	102
Nonmetallic minerals, except fuels	149	227	232	204	211	218	220	226
Food And Kindred Products, Total	20	17 726	20 059	20 847	23 459	26 401	27 568	29 109
Meat products and meat packing products	201	5 262	5 842	5 880	6 936	8 435	8 878	8 811
Dairy products	202	571	851	965	883	894	850	1 066
Canned, frozen, and preserved fruits and vegetables	203	2 019	2 272	2 339	2 603	2 885	3 015	3 202
Grain mill products	204	3 233	3 476	3 710	3 951	4 093	4 289	4 351
Bakery products	205	224	295	340	368	362	378	411
Sugar and confectionery products	206	1 452	1 532	1 700	1 868	1 919	2 160	2 015
Fats and oils	207	2 455	2 877	2 681	2 951	3 799	3 681	4 693
Beverages and flavorings	208	1 261	1 460	1 558	1 890	2 104	2 161	2 338
Miscellaneous food preparations and kindred products	209	1 249	1 454	1 674	2 008	1 910	2 155	2 222
Tobacco Products, Total	21	4 581	4 518	4 262	5 424	5 264	5 268	5 005
Cigarettes	211	4 239	4 200	3 934	5 011	4 812	4 765	4 456
Cigars	212	7	9	6	7	8	12	18
Chewing and smoking tobacco, and snuff	213	266	245	268	337	346	401	461
Manufactured tobacco, including processed tobacco	214	70	64	53	68	98	90	70
Textile Mill Products, Total	22	4 215	4 583	4 809	5 270	5 830	6 315	7 225
Cotton broad woven fabrics	221	552	591	641	725	834	906	965
Silk and manmade fiber broad woven fabrics	222	816	922	1 007	1 076	1 127	1 235	1 330
Wool broad woven fabrics	223	66	104	88	90	118	122	140
Narrow woven fabrics	224	246	256	292	350	409	431	546
Knit fabrics and hosiery	225	441	519	585	625	759	829	1 038
Carpets and rugs	227	724	734	727	695	673	737	823
Yarns and thread	228	280	248	219	299	398	452	519
Miscellaneous textile goods	229	1 089	1 208	1 249	1 410	1 512	1 604	1 865

Table C-9. U.S. Foreign Trade in Goods by Industry Using Standard Industrial Classification [SIC] Product Groups, 1991–1997—*Continued*

(Census basis, millions of dollars.)

Product	SIC code	Imports						
		1991	1992	1993	1994	1995	1996	1997
ALL COMMODITIES, TOTAL	0	488 873	532 017	580 469	663 830	743 505	791 315	870 213
Agricultural Products, Total	01	7 323	7 262	7 427	8 745	9 818	11 096	12 284
Cash grains and other crops	011	402	538	599	890	770	896	1 122
Field crops, except cash grains	013	1 344	1 281	1 310	1 209	1 081	1 955	1 779
Vegetables and melons	016	984	849	1 122	1 227	1 486	1 729	1 763
Fruits and tree nuts	017	3 944	3 878	3 617	4 584	5 490	5 396	6 428
Horticultural specialties	018	649	716	779	835	991	1 119	1 192
Livestock And Livestock Products, Total	02	1 645	2 032	2 159	2 046	2 441	2 374	2 483
Livestock, except dairy and poultry	021	1 178	1 408	1 521	1 348	1 690	1 505	1 564
Dairy farms	024	10	28	26	16	23	25	16
Poultry and eggs	025	28	35	42	40	36	39	37
Animal specialties	027	428	561	571	643	693	806	865
Forestry Products, total	08	847	956	1 068	1 208	1 932	1 809	1 625
Standing timber	081	30	31	29	30	34	36	40
Forestry products	083	817	925	1 039	1 179	1 898	1 773	1 585
Commercial Fishing, Total	09	4 587	4 570	4 797	5 515	5 615	5 525	6 479
Metallic Ores And Concentrates, Total	10	1 500	1 435	1 243	1 379	1 535	1 597	1 523
Iron ore	101	437	396	415	510	486	556	551
Copper ore	102	67	107	42	126	137	76	67
Lead and zinc ores	103	204	248	116	90	102	162	118
Gold and silver ores	104	45	49	31	54	87	74	42
Ferroalloy ores, except vanadium	106	136	114	110	109	206	186	190
Miscellaneous metal ores	109	611	520	529	490	518	542	556
Coal And Lignite, Total	12	112	127	218	229	248	238	257
Bituminous coal and lignite	122	112	122	210	218	247	235	255
Anthracite mining	123	0	5	8	11	1	3	2
Oil And Gas Extraction, Total	13	42 181	42 902	44 291	45 041	48 961	58 325	63 450
Crude petroleum and natural gas	131	39 487	40 949	41 685	42 381	46 046	54 500	59 501
Natural gas liquids	132	2 694	1 954	2 606	2 661	2 915	3 825	3 949
Nonmetallic Minerals, Except Fuels, Total	14	828	747	769	842	915	915	1 090
Dimension stone (includes granite, marble, etc.)	141	25	21	21	18	21	24	24
Crushed and broken limestone	142	32	43	52	61	71	72	95
Sand and gravel	144	9	9	8	8	7	9	11
Clay, ceramic, and refractory minerals	145	22	23	25	28	34	38	43
Chemical and fertilizer minerals	147	430	324	244	318	349	367	442
Nonmetallic minerals, except fuels	149	310	328	418	408	432	405	476
Food And Kindred Products, Total	20	15 741	16 944	16 599	17 799	18 713	21 295	23 006
Meat products and meat packing products	201	3 182	3 020	3 092	2 971	2 692	2 684	3 036
Dairy products	202	701	807	785	860	1 058	1 218	1 158
Canned, frozen, and preserved fruits and vegetables	203	2 286	2 616	2 339	2 515	2 610	3 052	3 180
Grain mill products	204	567	653	706	863	893	1 101	1 196
Bakery products	205	376	419	468	540	599	658	706
Sugar and confectionery products	206	2 144	2 228	2 098	2 132	2 377	2 896	3 129
Fats and oils	207	942	1 182	1 193	1 388	1 524	1 874	1 883
Beverages and flavorings	208	3 639	4 096	4 025	4 387	4 625	5 338	6 015
Miscellaneous food preparations and kindred products	209	1 905	1 922	1 893	2 142	2 334	2 474	2 701
Tobacco Products, Total	21	221	360	607	163	184	280	497
Cigarettes	211	130	265	496	72	64	69	75
Cigars	212	45	45	52	64	94	188	403
Chewing and smoking tobacco, and snuff	213	46	50	59	27	25	19	14
Manufactured tobacco, including processed tobacco	214	0	0	0	0	1	3	5
Textile Mill Products, Total	22	5 447	5 943	6 258	6 618	7 037	7 233	8 437
Cotton broad woven fabrics	221	1 282	1 493	1 554	1 499	1 634	1 535	1 712
Silk and manmade fiber broad woven fabrics	222	1 440	1 531	1 589	1 630	1 586	1 622	1 799
Wool broad woven fabrics	223	246	240	232	243	258	267	297
Narrow woven fabrics	224	179	193	226	265	291	307	346
Knit fabrics and hosiery	225	516	414	536	644	715	944	1 370
Carpets and rugs	227	586	705	662	743	845	824	932
Yarns and thread	228	298	363	381	437	458	478	583
Miscellaneous textile goods	229	901	1 003	1 078	1 157	1 251	1 256	1 397

Table C-9. U.S. Foreign Trade in Goods by Industry Using Standard Industrial Classification [SIC] Product Groups, 1991–1997—Continued

(Census basis, millions of dollars.)

Product	SIC code	Exports						
		1991	1992	1993	1994	1995	1996	1997
Apparel And Related Products, Total	23	3 866	4 806	5 603	6 350	7 428	8 400	9 654
Suits and coats, mens and boys	231	165	203	244	302	280	279	267
Shirts, nightwear, underwear, mens and boys	232	1 229	1 635	2 009	2 243	2 536	2 895	3 383
Ladies outerwear (blouses, dresses, etc.)	233	387	556	632	635	766	788	905
Womens, girls, and infants undergarments	234	363	416	479	533	676	675	845
Headwear	235	44	57	72	69	68	71	65
Outerwear of textile materials	236	472	639	718	936	1 293	1 766	2 038
Fur goods	237	71	77	61	66	78	78	96
Miscellaneous apparel and accessories	238	273	280	330	389	466	439	454
Miscellaneous fabricated textile products	239	812	903	1 015	1 149	1 239	1 382	1 577
Lumber And Wood Products, Total	24	6 627	6 877	7 420	7 317	7 506	7 486	7 398
Logs, pulpwood, and timber	241	2 718	2 762	3 087	2 920	3 032	2 853	2 373
Sawmill and planing mill products	242	2 289	2 427	2 564	2 523	2 496	2 504	2 598
Millwork, plywood, veneer, and structural wood products	243	872	1 023	1 083	1 102	1 165	1 242	1 431
Wood containers	244	63	62	65	66	65	74	98
Wood buildings and mobile homes	245	202	77	60	88	91	112	119
Miscellaneous wood products	249	483	525	560	618	656	702	779
Furniture And Fixtures, Total	25	2 205	2 625	2 901	3 173	3 140	3 307	3 918
Household furniture	251	82	86	90	103	106	118	139
Office furniture	252	5	6	6	6	9	8	7
Partitions, shelving, lockers, and office and store fixtures	254	104	132	142	195	147	160	193
Miscellaneous furniture and fixtures	259	2 014	2 402	2 663	2 869	2 878	3 021	3 579
Paper And Allied Products, total	26	9 361	10 123	9 533	11 123	15 119	14 205	14 703
Pulp mill products	261	2 945	3 259	2 501	2 998	4 765	3 397	3 281
Paper mill products	262	4 107	4 299	4 212	4 841	6 478	6 416	6 615
Paperboard	263	0	0	0	0	1	1	2
Paperboard containers and boxes	265	597	697	786	918	1 152	1 288	1 405
Converted paper and paperboard products, except boxes	267	1 711	1 868	2 034	2 366	2 724	3 104	3 401
Printing, Publishing, And Allied Industries, Total	27	3 765	3 970	4 192	4 193	4 570	4 632	4 905
Newspapers	271	38	30	27	35	31	28	34
Periodicals, unbound	272	705	732	738	791	828	822	868
Books and pamphlets	273	1 542	1 689	1 739	1 785	1 846	1 864	1 958
Miscellaneous publishing	274	62	79	84	73	95	90	92
Commercial printed matter	275	1 209	1 205	1 363	1 226	1 384	1 396	1 482
Manifold business forms	276	14	13	13	17	16	15	15
Greeting cards	277	50	58	60	84	149	161	182
Blankbooks and looseleaf binders	278	90	103	110	119	142	174	195
Printing blocks, cylinders, and plates	279	55	60	58	64	78	83	79
Chemicals And Allied Products, Total	28	42 159	42 829	43 493	49 735	58 813	59 590	66 397
Industrial inorganic chemicals	281	5 578	5 873	5 517	6 048	7 106	7 300	8 310
Plastic materials and synthetic resins	282	10 016	9 532	9 600	11 180	13 811	14 248	15 468
Drugs	283	5 843	6 912	7 370	7 737	8 212	9 168	10 695
Soap, detergents, cleaners, perfumes, and cosmetics	284	2 301	2 604	2 952	3 462	3 816	4 250	4 894
Paints, varnishes, and allied products	285	688	758	818	943	1 021	1 108	1 332
Industrial organic chemicals	286	10 375	10 344	10 702	12 729	16 063	14 608	15 978
Agricultural chemicals	287	4 685	4 147	3 654	4 704	5 489	5 376	5 743
Miscellaneous chemicals	289	2 673	2 660	2 881	2 933	3 296	3 532	3 978
Petroleum Refining And Related Products, total	29	7 166	6 434	6 239	5 578	6 081	7 305	7 518
Petroleum Refinery Products	291	6 552	5 827	5 715	5 025	5 398	6 442	6 619
Asphalt paving and roofing materials	295	71	88	93	102	94	96	123
Miscellaneous petroleum and coal products	299	543	519	431	450	589	767	776
Rubber And Miscellaneous Plastics Products, Total	30	7 096	7 947	8 722	10 174	11 306	12 397	14 549
Tires and inner tubes	301	1 282	1 418	1 473	1 630	1 901	2 004	2 466
Rubber and plastics footwear	302	145	143	144	152	159	132	133
Rubber and plastics hose and belting	305	919	977	1 080	1 257	1 447	1 730	2 054
Miscellaneous fabricated rubber products	306	730	750	809	955	1 026	1 115	1 325
Miscellaneous plastics products	308	4 020	4 659	5 215	6 180	6 773	7 416	8 572
Leather And Leather Products, Total	31	1 453	1 573	1 664	1 681	1 715	1 890	2 091
Tanned and finished leather	311	702	732	795	720	709	733	845
Shoe and boot cut stock and findings	313	124	139	152	158	182	273	315
Footwear, except rubber	314	371	399	393	433	425	447	446
Leather gloves	315	14	13	16	15	15	12	8
Luggage	316	119	146	150	180	191	250	276
Handbags and other personal leather goods	317	58	69	77	84	97	92	94
Miscellaneous leather goods	319	64	75	81	91	95	82	107

Table C-9. U.S. Foreign Trade in Goods by Industry Using Standard Industrial Classification [SIC] Product Groups, 1991–1997—*Continued*

(Census basis, millions of dollars.)

Product	SIC code	Imports						
		1991	1992	1993	1994	1995	1996	1997
Apparel And Related Products, Total	23	27 598	32 924	35 632	38 699	41 307	43 158	50 315
Suits and coats, mens and boys	231	679	793	826	955	1 044	1 135	1 319
Shirts, nightwear, underwear, mens and boys	232	7 602	9 405	10 393	11 548	13 323	14 124	16 822
Ladies outerwear (blouses, dresses, etc.)	233	6 348	7 327	7 834	8 100	8 600	9 132	10 015
Womens, girls, and infants undergarments	234	1 269	1 536	1 787	2 071	2 443	2 492	2 887
Headwear	235	407	576	663	679	693	739	704
Outerwear of textile materials	236	6 609	8 073	8 229	8 961	8 925	9 220	11 288
Fur goods	237	173	142	176	190	151	193	184
Miscellaneous apparel and accessories	238	2 140	2 468	2 582	2 737	2 561	2 500	2 902
Miscellaneous fabricated textile products	239	2 370	2 605	3 142	3 458	3 567	3 623	4 193
Lumber And Wood Products, Total	24	5 311	6 766	8 919	10 547	10 400	12 205	13 553
Logs, pulpwood, and timber	241	199	219	265	273	293	291	323
Sawmill and planing mill products	242	2 855	3 723	5 279	6 277	5 745	7 066	7 597
Millwork, plywood, veneer, and structural wood products	243	984	1 251	1 531	1 738	1 789	2 109	2 528
Wood containers	244	44	50	49	55	72	91	145
Wood buildings and mobile homes	245	9	10	10	22	24	42	44
Miscellaneous wood products	249	1 222	1 514	1 785	2 182	2 477	2 605	2 916
Furniture And Fixtures, Total	25	5 069	5 567	6 265	7 525	8 307	9 325	11 013
Household furniture	251	375	465	495	579	672	769	986
Office furniture	252	13	13	12	9	13	12	16
Partitions, shelving, lockers, and office and store fixtures	254	96	118	131	166	194	216	265
Miscellaneous furniture and fixtures	259	4 586	4 971	5 626	6 771	7 429	8 330	9 745
Paper And Allied Products, total	26	10 517	10 467	10 897	11 782	16 771	14 798	14 852
Pulp mill products	261	2 142	2 104	1 868	2 285	3 745	2 601	2 572
Paper mill products	262	6 926	6 737	7 224	7 370	10 235	9 158	9 059
Paperboard	263	1	1	1	1	1	1	0
Paperboard containers and boxes	265	177	233	254	342	466	488	497
Converted paper and paperboard products, except boxes	267	1 272	1 392	1 550	1 784	2 324	2 551	2 723
Printing, Publishing, And Allied Industries, Total	27	1 892	2 058	2 217	2 424	2 904	2 999	3 211
Newspapers	271	48	53	52	9	9	9	9
Periodicals, unbound	272	121	134	194	209	222	217	204
Books and pamphlets	273	870	951	965	1 018	1 188	1 242	1 298
Miscellaneous publishing	274	52	45	50	51	64	61	69
Commercial printed matter	275	504	543	604	704	883	882	975
Manifold business forms	276	1	2	3	3	14	17	10
Greeting cards	277	46	54	59	103	109	121	136
Blankbooks and looseleaf binders	278	240	269	288	321	409	444	502
Printing blocks, cylinders, and plates	279	10	6	4	5	6	6	8
Chemicals And Allied Products, Total	28	23 491	26 474	27 917	32 190	38 194	42 254	47 468
Industrial inorganic chemicals	281	4 743	4 671	4 546	5 232	6 153	6 573	6 769
Plastic materials and synthetic resins	282	3 036	3 507	4 207	5 218	6 172	6 260	6 948
Drugs	283	4 882	6 016	6 322	6 935	8 555	11 221	14 110
Soap, detergents, cleaners, perfumes, and cosmetics	284	1 221	1 491	1 636	1 855	2 147	2 294	2 495
Paints, varnishes, and allied products	285	141	184	197	261	343	393	440
Industrial organic chemicals	286	6 758	7 499	7 629	9 085	10 630	11 064	12 112
Agricultural chemicals	287	1 689	1 891	2 086	2 250	2 603	2 744	2 702
Miscellaneous chemicals	289	1 021	1 216	1 293	1 354	1 589	1 705	1 892
Petroleum Refining And Related Products, total	29	11 510	10 990	10 355	10 018	9 022	13 548	13 464
Petroleum Refinery Products	291	11 362	10 831	10 191	9 789	8 816	13 312	13 205
Asphalt paving and roofing materials	295	84	88	103	123	124	138	132
Miscellaneous petroleum and coal products	299	65	71	61	107	82	98	127
Rubber And Miscellaneous Plastics Products, Total	30	10 360	11 870	13 225	14 566	16 181	17 097	18 513
Tires and inner tubes	301	2 275	2 470	2 685	2 985	3 095	3 030	3 370
Rubber and plastics footwear	302	2 381	2 693	3 101	3 006	3 240	3 442	3 728
Rubber and plastics hose and belting	305	952	1 109	1 217	1 480	1 663	1 819	1 990
Miscellaneous fabricated rubber products	306	885	1 127	1 343	1 576	1 829	2 015	2 065
Miscellaneous plastics products	308	3 867	4 470	4 879	5 520	6 354	6 790	7 360
Leather And Leather Products, Total	31	10 352	10 911	11 818	13 056	13 708	14 285	15 562
Tanned and finished leather	311	582	644	751	869	954	921	1 004
Shoe and boot cut stock and findings	313	327	367	424	467	409	423	457
Footwear, except rubber	314	6 748	6 994	7 556	8 133	8 357	8 771	9 710
Leather gloves	315	171	193	216	259	290	294	309
Luggage	316	1 137	1 285	1 423	1 711	1 983	2 054	2 336
Handbags and other personal leather goods	317	1 247	1 270	1 281	1 421	1 485	1 583	1 548
Miscellaneous leather goods	319	140	158	168	195	229	239	198

Table C-9. U.S. Foreign Trade in Goods by Industry Using Standard Industrial Classification [SIC] Product Groups, 1991–1997—*Continued*

(Census basis, millions of dollars.)

Product	SIC code	Exports						
		1991	1992	1993	1994	1995	1996	1997
Stone, Clay, Glass And Concrete Products, Total	32	3 464	3 751	3 978	4 393	4 921	5 229	5 988
Flat glass	321	500	502	588	632	697	806	825
Glass and glassware, pressed or blown	322	801	843	841	936	1 120	1 199	1 423
Glass products, made of purchased glass	323	374	424	484	537	555	595	818
Cement, hydralulic	324	47	51	49	47	56	60	61
Structural clay products	325	132	124	136	131	163	174	205
Pottery and related products	326	368	409	486	549	630	579	722
Concrete, gypsum, and plaster products	327	131	158	130	133	143	175	224
Cut stone and stone products	328	43	36	36	37	32	31	31
Abrasive, asbestos, and miscellaneous nonmetallic mineral products	329	1 068	1 203	1 227	1 392	1 525	1 612	1 679
Primary Metal Products, Total	33	15 004	14 558	18 981	16 812	20 812	21 902	23 526
Steel works, blast furnaces, and rolling and finishing mill products	331	4 061	3 391	3 204	3 477	5 264	4 696	5 536
Iron and steel foundry products	332	301	365	310	314	410	478	484
Smelted and refined nonferrous metals	333	5 794	5 757	10 267	6 895	7 405	8 675	8 184
Secondary smelting and refining of nonferrous metals	334	10	9	12	18	20	20	26
Rolled, drawn and extruded nonferrous metals	335	4 615	4 834	4 960	5 854	7 336	7 697	8 889
Nonferrous foundries (castings)	336	64	38	45	52	78	87	95
Miscellaneous primary metal products	339	160	164	183	202	298	249	312
Fabricated Metal Products, Except Machinery, Total	34	11 905	13 065	13 867	13 770	15 562	17 103	18 487
Metal cans and shipping containers	341	261	350	346	346	412	354	372
Cutlery, handtools, and general hardware	342	1 665	1 883	2 077	2 383	2 480	2 676	2 931
Heating equipment except electric and warm air, and plumbing fixtures	343	333	390	335	362	355	362	456
Fabricated structural metal products	344	1 358	1 506	1 745	1 844	2 114	2 368	2 934
Bolts, nuts, screws, rivets and washers	345	645	702	739	939	1 089	1 410	1 381
Metal forgings and stampings	346	1 464	1 734	1 882	609	523	531	581
Ordnance and accessories, except vehicles and guided missiles	348	2 422	2 558	2 391	2 229	2 687	2 649	2 428
Miscellaneous fabricated metal products	349	3 758	3 941	4 351	5 058	5 903	6 754	7 404
Industrial And Commercial Machinery And Computer Equipment, Total	35	70 387	74 004	77 828	88 528	103 239	111 983	127 707
Engines and turbines	351	5 148	5 782	6 700	8 133	9 303	8 852	10 650
Farm and garden machinery and equipment	352	2 763	2 862	3 243	3 496	4 005	4 653	5 517
Construction, mining, and materials handling machinery	353	10 811	10 831	10 712	11 931	13 352	14 979	17 381
Metalworking machinery and parts	354	3 915	4 444	4 857	5 682	5 885	6 546	7 597
Special industry machinery, except metalworking machinery	355	5 228	5 211	5 864	6 901	9 369	10 193	10 534
General industrial machinery and equipment	356	8 591	8 795	9 241	10 543	11 662	12 550	14 597
Computers and office equipment	357	28 298	29 858	30 297	34 363	40 711	44 766	50 475
Refrigeration and service industry machinery	358	3 427	3 900	4 214	4 513	5 180	5 581	6 194
Miscellaneous industrial and commercial machinery and equipment	359	2 205	2 321	2 700	2 965	3 772	3 861	4 762
Electronic And Other Electrical Equipment Except Computers, Total	36	47 802	52 938	60 831	73 949	90 377	94 880	108 276
Electric transmission and distribution equipment	361	670	747	798	855	996	1 139	1 378
Electrical industrial apparatus	362	3 393	3 840	4 065	4 421	5 169	5 323	6 105
Household appliances	363	2 384	2 603	2 835	2 975	3 053	3 257	3 514
Electric lighting and wiring equipment	364	2 848	3 224	3 594	4 166	4 710	5 061	5 553
Household audio and video equipment and audio recordings	365	4 745	5 512	6 224	7 214	7 627	7 108	8 376
Communications equipment	366	6 235	7 476	9 179	11 275	13 814	14 520	17 719
Electronic components and accessories	367	21 006	22 510	26 364	34 357	45 514	47 976	54 289
Miscellaneous electrical machinery, equipment, and supplies	369	6 521	7 026	7 771	8 687	9 495	10 497	11 343
Transportation Equipment, Total	37	77 765	84 652	82 492	88 159	85 752	96 568	112 259
Motor vehicles and motor vehicle equipment	371	32 410	37 473	41 286	47 128	49 524	52 138	58 342
Aircraft and parts	372	41 842	42 891	37 623	36 331	31 134	38 797	48 635
Ship and boat building and repairing	373	1 113	1 407	929	1 173	1 196	1 015	1 319
Railroad equipment	374	468	494	462	605	766	732	1 097
Motorcycles, bicycles, and parts	375	709	749	783	762	905	955	1 012
Guided missiles, space vehicles, and parts	376	27	36	24	26	56	134	16
Miscellaneous transportation equipment	379	1 195	1 601	1 386	2 135	2 172	2 797	1 838
Scientific And Professional Instruments; Photographic And Optical Goods, Total	38	23 573	24 888	26 135	28 162	31 392	34 804	39 397
Search, detection, navigation and guidance systems	381	2 242	2 151	2 139	2 048	1 948	2 054	2 535
Analytical, optical, measuring, and controlling instruments	382	9 536	10 041	10 886	11 999	13 613	14 936	17 527
Surgical, medical, and dental instruments and supplies	384	7 009	7 860	8 331	9 166	10 281	11 669	12 777
Opthalmic goods	385	455	474	506	556	646	786	842
Photographic equipment and supplies	386	4 062	4 089	3 973	4 075	4 573	5 026	5 342
Watches, clocks, clockwork operated devices and parts	387	269	274	299	318	331	332	373

Table C-9. U.S. Foreign Trade in Goods by Industry Using Standard Industrial Classification [SIC] Product Groups, 1991–1997—*Continued*

(Census basis, millions of dollars.)

Product	SIC code	Imports						
		1991	1992	1993	1994	1995	1996	1997
Stone, Clay, Glass And Concrete Products, Total	32	5 549	5 935	6 454	7 620	8 553	9 132	10 220
Flat glass	321	283	278	342	416	399	463	495
Glass and glassware, pressed or blown	322	1 126	1 259	1 344	1 606	1 831	1 998	2 204
Glass products, made of purchased glass	323	352	376	412	526	613	692	698
Cement, hydralulic	324	335	251	284	444	542	596	753
Structural clay products	325	422	484	540	583	639	709	817
Pottery and related products	326	1 527	1 747	1 815	2 021	2 211	2 124	2 315
Concrete, gypsum, and plaster products	327	97	114	134	227	337	418	560
Cut stone and stone products	328	475	404	399	444	498	560	680
Abrasive, asbestos, and miscellaneous nonmetallic mineral products	329	932	1 022	1 184	1 353	1 483	1 571	1 698
Primary Metal Products, Total	33	21 291	21 610	22 940	30 266	33 790	34 705	37 924
Steel works, blast furnaces, and rolling and finishing mill products	331	9 312	9 457	10 218	14 403	14 379	15 296	16 085
Iron and steel foundry products	332	215	200	218	301	411	397	403
Smelted and refined nonferrous metals	333	7 520	7 256	7 703	9 785	11 704	11 794	12 772
Secondary smelting and refining of nonferrous metals	334	623	820	703	764	895	873	1 184
Rolled, drawn and extruded nonferrous metals	335	3 388	3 633	3 835	4 730	6 044	5 981	6 987
Nonferrous foundries (castings)	336	39	43	38	47	65	45	59
Miscellaneous primary metal products	339	193	200	226	236	292	318	434
Fabricated Metal Products, Except Machinery, Total	34	11 231	12 297	13 400	15 012	16 615	17 889	19 602
Metal cans and shipping containers	341	147	185	186	210	229	301	287
Cutlery, handtools, and general hardware	342	2 388	2 684	2 963	3 456	3 765	4 165	4 661
Heating equipment except electric and warm air, and plumbing fixtures	343	328	379	427	497	518	593	683
Fabricated structural metal products	344	640	566	644	792	1 036	1 386	1 369
Bolts, nuts, screws, rivets and washers	345	1 121	1 247	1 407	1 693	1 935	1 879	1 939
Metal forgings and stampings	346	1 076	1 159	1 159	737	772	747	643
Ordnance and accessories, except vehicles and guided missiles	348	501	568	682	762	649	608	578
Miscellaneous fabricated metal products	349	5 029	5 507	5 933	6 864	7 711	8 211	9 441
Industrial And Commercial Machinery And Computer Equipment, Total	35	56 098	63 116	73 928	90 294	107 219	113 601	126 310
Engines and turbines	351	2 306	2 362	2 726	3 202	3 701	3 523	3 639
Farm and garden machinery and equipment	352	2 034	2 162	2 316	3 097	3 268	3 224	3 679
Construction, mining, and materials handling machinery	353	3 924	4 342	5 428	6 842	7 586	7 676	9 107
Metalworking machinery and parts	354	5 590	5 036	6 045	7 753	9 429	9 961	10 941
Special industry machinery, except metalworking machinery	355	5 326	5 716	6 513	7 585	8 900	8 717	9 681
General industrial machinery and equipment	356	6 728	7 305	7 925	9 766	11 243	12 144	12 375
Computers and office equipment	357	26 962	32 759	39 232	47 612	57 916	62 934	71 325
Refrigeration and service industry machinery	358	1 776	1 917	2 042	2 446	2 677	2 954	2 893
Miscellaneous industrial and commercial machinery and equipment	359	1 453	1 517	1 700	1 990	2 498	2 469	2 670
Electronic And Other Electrical Equipment Except Computers, Total	36	61 992	69 917	79 161	96 678	116 198	115 277	122 571
Electric transmission and distribution equipment	361	695	807	936	990	1 231	1 276	1 493
Electrical industrial apparatus	362	3 316	3 777	4 334	5 367	6 145	6 476	7 268
Household appliances	363	3 693	4 292	4 571	5 005	5 416	5 717	6 128
Electric lighting and wiring equipment	364	3 895	4 459	5 184	5 892	6 287	6 481	7 070
Household audio and video equipment and audio recordings	365	12 633	14 680	15 200	18 037	18 746	17 533	18 475
Communications equipment	366	9 321	9 896	10 982	13 372	14 300	15 396	16 538
Electronic components and accessories	367	21 886	24 514	29 520	37 926	53 320	51 057	53 250
Miscellaneous electrical machinery, equipment, and supplies	369	6 552	7 492	8 435	10 090	10 753	11 342	12 349
Transportation Equipment, Total	37	88 205	92 990	101 072	115 377	120 877	127 707	140 615
Motor vehicles and motor vehicle equipment	371	73 419	77 407	85 990	99 784	105 519	109 846	118 597
Aircraft and parts	372	12 422	12 930	11 532	11 728	10 958	13 138	17 256
Ship and boat building and repairing	373	212	270	920	750	765	974	824
Railroad equipment	374	532	595	587	969	1 088	1 128	1 158
Motorcycles, bicycles, and parts	375	1 370	1 574	1 759	1 801	2 179	2 046	2 117
Guided missiles, space vehicles, and parts	376	1	0	0	0	1	134	179
Miscellaneous transportation equipment	379	249	212	283	346	367	439	484
Scientific And Professional Instruments; Photographic And Optical Goods, Total	38	19 183	20 990	22 698	25 065	28 127	29 353	31 995
Search, detection, navigation and guidance systems	381	876	915	803	763	868	932	1 166
Analytical, optical, measuring, and controlling instruments	382	4 904	5 460	6 125	7 524	8 814	9 387	10 368
Surgical, medical, and dental instruments and supplies	384	4 181	4 618	4 923	4 946	5 564	5 975	6 610
Opthalmic goods	385	1 010	1 130	1 146	1 216	1 413	1 522	1 605
Photographic equipment and supplies	386	6 018	6 653	7 277	8 099	8 837	8 862	9 537
Watches, clocks, clockwork operated devices and parts	387	2 195	2 214	2 424	2 518	2 631	2 675	2 708

Table C-9. U.S. Foreign Trade in Goods by Industry Using Standard Industrial Classification [SIC] Product Groups, 1991–1997—*Continued*

(Census basis, millions of dollars.)

Product	SIC code	Exports						
		1991	1992	1993	1994	1995	1996	1997
Miscellaneous Manufactured Goods, Total	39	6 626	7 257	7 642	8 622	9 620	10 338	11 107
Jewelry, silverware, and plated ware	391	2 527	2 505	2 677	3 074	3 488	3 864	4 163
Musical instruments	393	309	346	369	401	425	447	446
Dolls, toys, games, and sporting and athletic goods	394	1 930	2 276	2 487	2 894	3 350	3 502	3 695
Pens, pencils, and other artists materials	395	550	586	587	641	696	766	889
Costume jewelry, novelties, buttons, and miscellaneous notions	396	249	274	289	304	294	309	381
Miscellaneous manufactured products	399	1 061	1 270	1 233	1 308	1 367	1 451	1 532
Manufactured Commodities Not Identified By Kind	3X	11 588	11 769	11 800	13 023	14 182	15 408	16 328
Scrap And Waste	91	4 050	3 311	3 452	4 300	6 251	4 684	4 414
Used Or Second-Hand Merchandise	92	2 965	2 582	2 653	2 470	2 218	2 286	2 725
U.S. Goods Exported And Returned	98	1 090	1 222	1 418	1 592	1 661	2 032	2 378
Special Classification Provisions	99	2 007	2 222	2 382	2 515	2 301	2 707	2 573

Table C-9. U.S. Foreign Trade in Goods by Industry Using Standard Industrial Classification [SIC] Product Groups, 1991–1997—*Continued*

(Census basis, millions of dollars.)

Product	SIC code	Imports						
		1991	1992	1993	1994	1995	1996	1997
Miscellaneous Manufactured Goods, Total	39	19 759	22 714	25 272	26 910	28 765	31 164	35 648
Jewelry, silverware, and plated ware	391	7 536	8 007	9 387	10 357	10 765	11 607	13 025
Musical instruments	393	611	685	737	789	923	899	961
Dolls, toys, games, and sporting and athletic goods	394	7 841	9 622	10 446	10 570	11 440	13 013	15 598
Pens, pencils, and other artists materials	395	739	803	897	1 005	1 077	1 076	1 168
Costume jewelry, novelties, buttons, and miscellaneous notions	396	814	925	926	987	918	878	851
Miscellaneous manufactured products	399	2 217	2 671	2 878	3 202	3 642	3 690	4 043
Manufactured Commodities Not Identified By Kind	3X	. . .	. . .	. . .	. . .	. . .	. . .	. . .
Scrap And Waste	91	1 135	1 040	1 105	1 431	1 926	1 761	1 903
Used Or Second-Hand Merchandise	92	2 053	2 182	2 861	2 690	2 880	3 050	3 952
U.S. Goods Exported And Returned	98	11 040	12 281	13 067	15 720	17 223	19 594	21 801
Special Classification Provisions	99	4 806	5 641	5 827	6 374	7 141	7 727	8 589

Table C-10. U.S. Foreign Trade in Goods, Summary by Region, 1991–1999

(Census basis, millions of dollars.)

Region	1991	1992	1993	1994	1995	1996	1997	1998	1999
ALL DESTINATIONS									
Exports: All goods	421 730	448 164	465 091	512 627	584 742	625 075	689 182	682 138	695 797
Agriculture	39 468	43 134	42 949	46 300	56 364	60 562	57 092	52 005	48 230
Manufactures	345 428	368 165	388 537	430 845	484 971	522 660	591 233	595 218	611 781
Imports: All goods	488 453	532 665	580 659	663 256	743 445	795 289	870 671	911 896	1 024 618
Agriculture	22 184	23 447	23 664	25 949	29 260	32 568	35 148	35 741	36 731
Manufactures	393 820	434 256	480 016	557 871	629 632	659 867	728 574	792 422	882 729
Balance: All goods	-66 723	-84 501	-115 568	-150 629	-158 703	-170 214	-181 489	-229 758	-328 821
NORTH AMERICA									
Exports: All goods	118 427	131 186	142 025	165 282	173 518	191 002	223 155	235 376	253 509
Agriculture	8 076	9 166	9 387	10 673	9 936	12 230	12 666	13 848	13 309
Manufactures	104 300	114 972	125 941	147 279	153 951	168 730	198 709	209 615	227 402
Imports: All goods	122 194	133 841	151 134	177 900	206 470	230 190	253 172	267 885	308 432
Agriculture	5 805	6 416	7 273	8 071	9 329	10 443	11 390	12 290	12 671
Manufactures	92 685	102 225	115 858	140 139	164 366	181 409	201 318	223 365	255 639
Balance: All goods	-3 767	-2 655	-9 109	-12 618	-32 952	-39 188	-30 017	-32 509	-54 923
SOUTH AND CENTRAL AMERICA, AND THE CARIBBEAN									
Exports: All goods	29 659	34 785	36 170	41 127	49 095	51 870	62 088	62 651	54 512
Agriculture	2 605	2 797	3 141	3 474	4 350	4 901	5 090	5 094	4 341
Manufactures	24 356	29 381	30 578	35 127	41 706	43 713	53 608	54 906	48 034
Imports: All goods	31 306	33 518	34 433	38 443	42 429	49 505	53 657	50 247	58 430
Agriculture	5 475	5 668	5 310	6 015	6 373	7 243	8 110	7 396	7 468
Manufactures	12 478	14 329	15 398	18 583	19 984	21 077	23 938	26 194	29 964
Balance: All goods	-1 647	1 267	1 737	2 684	6 666	2 365	8 431	12 404	-3 918
EUROPE									
Exports: All goods	123 469	122 617	119 785	123 479	140 564	148 810	163 273	170 008	171 834
Agriculture	10 203	10 525	9 660	8 774	10 767	11 912	11 446	9 961	7 187
Manufactures	102 223	101 770	102 337	105 710	118 591	126 467	141 712	151 682	156 146
Imports: All goods	104 062	112 707	119 082	136 562	152 376	164 587	181 440	202 874	224 790
Agriculture	5 127	5 168	5 088	5 574	6 233	7 077	7 398	7 763	8 400
Manufactures	92 665	100 138	106 055	121 421	137 558	147 152	164 164	186 631	204 835
Balance: All goods	19 407	9 910	703	-13 083	-11 812	-15 777	-18 167	-32 866	-52 956
ASIA									
Exports: All goods	130 629	138 262	146 725	160 995	197 402	207 328	213 547	187 566	190 881
Agriculture	16 104	17 393	17 576	20 121	27 360	27 641	24 694	20 113	19 582
Manufactures	98 462	104 949	113 551	125 095	151 612	162 859	166 544	156 544	159 130
Imports: All goods	210 207	233 130	256 424	291 318	321 647	326 611	354 997	367 661	408 542
Agriculture	3 212	3 710	3 647	4 065	5 103	5 392	5 635	5 376	5 171
Manufactures	191 633	213 227	238 203	272 402	302 014	304 103	332 063	347 915	383 727
Balance: All goods	-79 578	-94 868	-109 699	-130 323	-124 245	-119 283	-141 450	-180 095	-217 661
AUSTRALIA AND OCEANIA									
Exports: All goods	9 797	10 682	9 938	11 687	12 794	14 087	14 450	14 216	14 163
Agriculture	379	378	455	522	485	463	525	511	460
Manufactures	8 960	9 904	9 074	10 812	11 920	13 170	13 474	13 343	13 310
Imports: All goods	5 337	5 097	4 752	4 914	5 085	5 601	6 465	7 373	7 381
Agriculture	1 902	1 895	1 724	1 559	1 528	1 511	1 718	1 981	2 160
Manufactures	2 032	1 939	1 848	2 322	2 410	2 771	3 257	4 006	3 884
Balance: All goods	4 460	5 585	5 186	6 773	7 709	8 486	7 985	6 843	6 782
AFRICA									
Exports: All goods	8 820	9 907	9 428	9 219	9 904	10 615	11 390	11 167	9 880
Agriculture	1 858	2 500	2 381	2 413	2 829	2 712	2 255	2 069	2 090
Manufactures	6 464	6 869	6 411	6 330	6 431	7 133	8 443	8 435	7 228
Imports: All goods	14 002	14 346	14 798	14 091	15 481	18 744	19 925	15 825	16 990
Agriculture	661	589	621	665	694	903	897	933	859
Manufactures	2 315	2 386	2 632	2 986	3 281	3 338	3 797	4 292	4 647
Balance: All goods	-5 182	-4 439	-5 370	-4 872	-5 577	-8 129	-8 535	-4 658	-7 110

Table C-11. U.S. Foreign Trade in Goods by Country or Region, 1991–1999

(Census basis, millions of dollars.)

Country or region	1991	1992	1993	1994	1995	1996	1997	1998	1999
ALL DESTINATIONS									
Exports: All goods	421 730	448 164	465 091	512 627	584 742	625 075	689 182	682 138	695 797
Agriculture	39 468	43 134	42 949	46 300	56 364	60 562	57 092	52 005	48 230
Manufactures	345 428	368 165	388 537	430 845	484 971	522 660	591 233	595 218	611 781
Imports: All goods	488 453	532 665	580 659	663 256	743 445	795 289	870 671	911 896	1 024 618
Agriculture	22 184	23 447	23 664	25 949	29 260	32 568	35 148	35 741	36 731
Manufactures	393 820	434 256	480 016	557 871	629 632	659 867	728 574	792 422	882 729
Balance: All goods	-66 723	-84 501	-115 568	-150 629	-158 703	-170 214	-181 488	-229 758	-328 821
WESTERN HEMISPHERE									
Exports: All goods	148 592	166 395	178 870	206 994	223 470	243 567	286 183	298 780	308 668
Agriculture	10 757	12 037	12 600	14 220	14 360	17 208	17 832	19 016	17 719
Manufactures	129 061	144 675	157 098	182 897	196 417	213 030	253 139	265 138	275 968
Imports: All goods	153 521	167 385	185 603	216 371	248 930	279 721	306 878	318 163	366 914
Agriculture	11 281	12 086	12 584	14 086	15 703	17 686	19 500	19 686	20 140
Manufactures	105 174	116 566	131 278	158 740	184 368	202 503	225 293	249 578	285 636
Balance: All goods	-4 929	-911	-6 733	-9 376	-25 460	-36 153	-20 695	-19 383	-58 247
NORTH AMERICA									
Exports: All goods	118 427	131 186	142 025	165 282	173 518	191 002	223 155	235 376	253 509
Agriculture	8 076	9 166	9 387	10 673	9 936	12 230	12 666	13 848	13 309
Manufactures	104 300	114 972	125 941	147 279	153 951	168 730	198 709	209 615	227 402
Imports: All goods	122 194	133 841	151 134	177 900	206 470	230 190	253 172	267 885	308 432
Agriculture	5 805	6 416	7 273	8 071	9 329	10 443	11 390	12 290	12 671
Manufactures	92 685	102 225	115 858	140 139	164 366	181 409	201 318	223 365	255 639
Balance: All goods	-3 767	-2 655	-9 108	-12 618	-32 952	-39 188	-30 016	-32 509	-54 923
Canada									
Exports: All goods	85 150	90 594	100 444	114 439	127 226	134 210	151 767	156 603	166 600
Agriculture	5 129	5 453	5 864	6 201	6 479	6 863	7 544	7 755	7 754
Manufactures	75 900	80 421	89 979	103 177	113 649	119 952	135 823	139 834	149 585
Imports: All goods	91 064	98 630	111 216	128 406	144 370	155 893	167 234	173 256	198 711
Agriculture	3 291	4 032	4 566	5 210	5 549	6 730	7 373	7 713	7 905
Manufactures	69 685	75 127	84 476	99 782	113 837	120 444	129 523	140 048	159 441
Balance: All goods	-5 914	-8 036	-10 772	-13 967	-17 144	-21 682	-15 467	-16 653	-32 111
Mexico									
Exports: All goods	33 277	40 592	41 581	50 844	46 292	56 792	71 388	78 773	86 909
Agriculture	2 947	3 714	3 523	4 472	3 456	5 367	5 123	6 094	5 555
Manufactures	28 400	34 551	35 962	44 103	40 302	48 778	62 885	69 781	77 817
Imports: All goods	31 130	35 211	39 917	49 494	62 101	74 297	85 938	94 629	109 721
Agriculture	2 514	2 385	2 707	2 860	3 780	3 713	4 018	4 578	4 766
Manufactures	23 000	27 098	31 382	40 357	50 528	60 965	71 795	83 317	96 198
Balance: All goods	2 148	5 381	1 664	1 350	-15 809	-17 506	-14 549	-15 857	-22 812
SOUTH AND CENTRAL AMERICA, AND CARIBBEAN									
Exports: All goods	29 659	34 785	36 170	41 127	49 095	51 870	62 088	62 651	54 512
Agriculture	2 605	2 797	3 141	3 474	4 350	4 901	5 090	5 094	4 341
Manufactures	24 356	29 381	30 578	35 127	41 706	43 713	53 608	54 906	48 034
Imports: All goods	31 306	33 518	34 433	38 443	42 429	49 505	53 657	50 247	58 430
Agriculture	5 475	5 668	5 310	6 015	6 373	7 243	8 110	7 396	7 468
Manufactures	12 478	14 329	15 398	18 583	19 984	21 077	23 938	26 194	29 964
Balance: All goods	-1 647	1 267	1 737	2 684	6 666	2 365	8 431	12 404	-3 918
CARIBBEAN									
Exports: All goods	6 184	6 341	6 784	7 173	8 259	8 608	9 962	10 618	10 257
Agriculture	961	950	1 010	996	1 275	1 402	1 496	1 445	1 475
Manufactures	4 502	4 763	5 085	5 533	6 331	6 474	7 703	8 549	8 104
Imports: All goods	5 252	5 720	5 910	6 471	6 721	7 676	8 188	7 820	8 340
Agriculture	368	338	347	416	387	495	587	478	347
Manufactures	2 946	3 321	3 665	4 209	4 681	4 744	5 289	5 459	5 613
Balance: All goods	932	621	874	702	1 538	932	1 774	2 797	1 917

See footnotes and NOTE at end of table.

Table C-11. U.S. Foreign Trade in Goods by Country or Region, 1991–1999—*Continued*

(Census basis, millions of dollars.)

Country or region	1991	1992	1993	1994	1995	1996	1997	1998	1999
Bahamas									
Exports: All goods	721	712	704	685	661	726	810	816	842
Agriculture	111	112	137	120	118	135	114	108	116
Manufactures	468	483	440	445	444	481	610	620	651
Imports: All goods	469	605	328	203	157	165	155	142	195
Agriculture	3	5	3	3	2	2	3	2	3
Manufactures	348	404	202	79	78	87	83	76	87
Balance: All goods	252	107	376	482	505	561	655	673	647
Barbados									
Exports: All goods	166	128	145	161	186	223	281	281	305
Agriculture	34	25	29	31	38	52	49	42	45
Manufactures	118	90	104	120	133	155	205	223	237
Imports: All goods	31	31	34	35	38	41	42	35	59
Agriculture	2	1	. . .	. . .	. . .	1	1	1	1
Manufactures	27	28	30	30	33	36	36	30	53
Balance: All goods	135	97	111	127	148	181	239	247	246
Belize									
Exports: All goods	114	117	136	115	100	107	115	120	136
Agriculture	19	21	19	19	15	16	16	17	16
Manufactures	89	91	107	90	80	86	89	100	116
Imports: All goods	45	59	54	51	52	68	77	66	81
Agriculture	18	30	20	20	17	31	35	20	23
Manufactures	21	22	26	21	21	22	21	24	24
Balance: All goods	69	58	82	64	48	39	38	54	55
Cayman Islands									
Exports: All goods	117	282	164	202	180	208	270	422	369
Agriculture	10	8	9	14	16	17	32	40	32
Manufactures	97	245	154	179	155	179	219	368	319
Imports: All goods	18	10	35	53	18	17	20	18	9
Agriculture	. . .	. . .	. . .	. . .	. . .	. . .	. . .	. . .	. . .
Manufactures	1	3	24	44	10	8	12	15	6
Balance: All goods	99	272	130	150	162	191	251	404	359
Dominican Republic									
Exports: All goods	1 743	2 100	2 350	2 799	3 015	3 191	3 924	3 944	4 100
Agriculture	243	250	286	279	368	412	533	499	556
Manufactures	1 408	1 754	1 965	2 391	2 509	2 637	3 221	3 338	3 386
Imports: All goods	2 008	2 373	2 672	3 091	3 399	3 575	4 327	4 441	4 287
Agriculture	286	240	244	309	298	369	451	371	240
Manufactures	1 699	2 099	2 394	2 740	3 035	3 087	3 633	3 829	3 847
Balance: All goods	-265	-273	-322	-292	-384	-384	-403	-497	-186
Guyana									
Exports: All goods	86	118	122	110	141	137	143	146	145
Agriculture	11	17	18	20	26	29	28	22	22
Manufactures	73	98	101	87	113	105	111	117	118
Imports: All goods	83	101	91	98	107	110	113	137	121
Agriculture	1	13	6	9	3	10	11	8	7
Manufactures	10	10	12	29	47	39	36	34	29
Balance: All goods	3	17	32	12	34	27	30	9	25
Haiti									
Exports: All goods	395	209	228	205	550	475	499	549	614
Agriculture	115	137	107	105	224	188	198	210	214
Manufactures	258	75	110	98	289	248	275	312	370
Imports: All goods	284	107	154	59	130	144	188	272	301
Agriculture	11	. . .	6	3	9	6	10	9	9
Manufactures	270	106	148	55	117	135	173	256	287
Balance: All goods	111	102	74	146	420	331	311	277	313

See footnotes and NOTE at end of table.

Table C-11. U.S. Foreign Trade in Goods by Country or Region, 1991–1999—*Continued*

(Census basis, millions of dollars.)

Country or region	1991	1992	1993	1994	1995	1996	1997	1998	1999
Jamaica									
Exports: All goods	961	938	1 116	1 066	1 420	1 491	1 417	1 304	1 293
Agriculture	136	118	134	128	167	204	198	190	185
Manufactures	695	697	838	807	1 095	1 105	1 032	983	939
Imports: All goods	576	599	720	747	847	838	738	755	678
Agriculture	32	31	43	45	36	48	47	49	49
Manufactures	304	335	471	525	622	589	541	496	476
Balance: All goods	385	340	396	319	573	653	678	549	615
Leeward And Windward Islands									
Exports: All goods	378	342	368	344	342	356	444	701	525
Agriculture	78	63	66	63	65	79	76	73	64
Manufactures	260	244	256	244	279	273	312	587	419
Imports: All goods	67	79	104	89	71	61	108	89	135
Agriculture	4	5	13	5	4	2	8	2	3
Manufactures	55	70	89	80	84	78	81	79	118
Balance: All goods	311	264	263	255	270	295	336	612	390
Netherlands Antilles And Aruba									
Exports: All goods	861	766	785	795	751	764	714	1 102	905
Agriculture	95	95	98	100	105	111	109	109	101
Manufactures	533	486	463	525	475	491	475	855	681
Imports: All goods	748	856	854	887	711	1 243	1 190	778	1 059
Agriculture	. . .	. . .	. . .	7	2	2	2	2	1
Manufactures	27	65	48	78	71	128	150	147	154
Balance: All goods	114	-90	-69	-92	41	-479	-476	324	-155
Suriname									
Exports: All goods	134	142	114	122	190	223	183	187	144
Agriculture	12	17	13	14	21	25	23	22	16
Manufactures	117	118	102	106	165	191	153	159	124
Imports: All goods	52	46	58	43	100	97	92	106	123
Agriculture	. . .	. . .	. . .	. . .	. . .	. . .	1	. . .	. . .
Manufactures	1	2	5	10	43	14	7	7	16
Balance: All goods	83	96	56	79	90	126	92	81	21
Trinidad And Tobago									
Exports: All goods	468	448	529	541	689	666	1 106	983	785
Agriculture	94	82	91	98	108	132	116	109	101
Manufactures	352	350	426	417	565	486	950	830	661
Imports: All goods	866	848	803	1 113	1 086	1 313	1 134	977	1 287
Agriculture	10	12	13	13	15	22	19	14	12
Manufactures	183	175	216	518	521	518	515	466	514
Balance: All goods	-398	-400	-274	-573	-397	-648	-28	6	-501
Turks And Caicos Islands									
Exports: All goods	40	38	22	29	34	44	59	64	95
Agriculture	3	4	3	3	4	4	5	5	7
Manufactures	34	33	17	25	29	37	51	56	83
Imports: All goods	4	6	4	4	5	5	5	5	6
Agriculture	. . .	. . .	. . .	. . .	. . .	. . .	. . .	. . .	. . .
Manufactures	. . .	. . .	. . .	1	. . .	2	1	1	3
Balance: All goods	36	32	18	25	29	38	53	59	89
CENTRAL AMERICA									
Exports: All goods	4 265	5 403	5 964	6 628	7 412	7 742	8 999	10 155	10 197
Agriculture	534	583	725	764	880	1 024	1 069	1 239	1 112
Manufactures	3 237	4 262	4 763	5 417	5 999	6 143	7 275	8 378	8 669
Imports: All goods	3 241	3 981	4 546	5 126	6 169	7 120	8 788	9 564	11 411
Agriculture	1 387	1 516	1 566	1 571	1 816	1 915	2 184	2 044	1 917
Manufactures	1 560	2 164	2 646	3 152	3 895	4 743	5 929	6 942	8 871
Balance: All goods	1 023	1 422	1 419	1 502	1 243	622	210	591	-1 214

See footnotes and NOTE at end of table.

Table C-11. U.S. Foreign Trade in Goods by Country or Region, 1991–1999—*Continued*

(Census basis, millions of dollars.)

Country or region	1991	1992	1993	1994	1995	1996	1997	1998	1999
Costa Rica									
Exports: All goods	1 034	1 357	1 542	1 870	1 736	1 816	2 024	2 297	2 381
Agriculture	84	102	147	161	162	217	188	198	179
Manufactures	881	1 167	1 330	1 633	1 513	1 540	1 778	2 015	2 130
Imports: All goods	1 154	1 412	1 541	1 647	1 843	1 974	2 323	2 745	3 968
Agriculture	475	535	552	550	637	682	747	773	829
Manufactures	639	839	951	1 049	1 161	1 229	1 494	1 908	3 059
Balance: All goods	-120	-55	1	223	-107	-158	-299	-449	-1 587
El Salvador									
Exports: All goods	534	742	873	931	1 111	1 075	1 400	1 514	1 519
Agriculture	106	116	143	130	173	192	230	244	200
Manufactures	374	575	685	754	870	821	1 088	1 223	1 281
Imports: All goods	303	384	488	609	812	975	1 346	1 438	1 605
Agriculture	130	134	134	92	88	101	154	131	101
Manufactures	157	233	332	493	694	931	1 158	1 271	1 474
Balance: All goods	231	358	385	322	298	99	54	76	-86
Guatemala									
Exports: All goods	945	1 205	1 312	1 352	1 647	1 566	1 730	1 938	1 812
Agriculture	119	124	195	211	239	272	260	308	271
Manufactures	655	902	975	1 029	1 283	1 172	1 330	1 514	1 446
Imports: All goods	899	1 081	1 194	1 283	1 527	1 679	1 990	2 072	2 265
Agriculture	472	503	510	548	648	660	778	686	694
Manufactures	389	535	632	682	812	914	1 091	1 302	1 446
Balance: All goods	46	124	118	70	120	-112	-261	-134	-453
Honduras									
Exports: All goods	625	811	899	1 012	1 279	1 643	2 019	2 318	2 370
Agriculture	88	76	88	85	113	132	162	185	192
Manufactures	481	635	718	886	1 101	1 398	1 717	2 052	2 098
Imports: All goods	557	782	914	1 098	1 441	1 795	2 322	2 544	2 713
Agriculture	213	251	231	238	279	277	296	301	134
Manufactures	242	423	574	733	1 033	1 366	1 842	2 077	2 410
Balance: All goods	68	28	-15	-86	-162	-153	-303	-227	-344
Nicaragua									
Exports: All goods	150	185	150	186	250	262	290	337	374
Agriculture	43	52	44	52	69	65	67	75	83
Manufactures	99	129	99	126	170	186	210	249	280
Imports: All goods	60	69	128	167	239	350	439	453	495
Agriculture	40	44	74	77	71	80	95	93	74
Manufactures	2	6	24	43	95	192	230	276	325
Balance: All goods	90	116	22	19	11	-88	-150	-116	-122
Panama									
Exports: All goods	978	1 103	1 187	1 277	1 390	1 381	1 536	1 753	1 742
Agriculture	95	113	108	127	124	148	162	228	188
Manufactures	748	854	956	989	1 061	1 026	1 152	1 325	1 434
Imports: All goods	269	254	280	322	307	346	367	312	365
Agriculture	58	50	65	65	93	115	115	59	85
Manufactures	131	128	133	152	99	110	114	109	157
Balance: All goods	709	850	908	955	1 082	1 034	1 169	1 441	1 378
SOUTH AMERICA									
Exports: All goods	19 210	23 041	23 422	27 326	33 424	35 520	43 127	41 878	34 058
Agriculture	1 110	1 264	1 406	1 714	2 195	2 475	2 525	2 410	1 754
Manufactures	16 617	20 356	20 730	24 177	29 376	31 096	38 630	37 979	31 261
Imports: All goods	22 813	23 817	23 977	26 846	29 539	34 709	36 681	32 863	38 679
Agriculture	3 720	3 814	3 397	4 028	4 170	4 833	5 339	5 204	
Manufactures	7 972	8 844	9 087	11 222	11 408	11 590	12 720	13 793	15 480
Balance: All goods	-3 602	-776	-556	480	3 885	811	6 446	9 015	-4 621

See footnotes and NOTE at end of table.

Table C-11. U.S. Foreign Trade in Goods by Country or Region, 1991–1999—*Continued*

(Census basis, millions of dollars.)

Country or region	1991	1992	1993	1994	1995	1996	1997	1998	1999
Argentina									
Exports: All goods	2 045	3 223	3 776	4 462	4 189	4 517	5 810	5 886	4 950
Agriculture	43	89	81	109	122	157	344	188	135
Manufactures	1 900	3 009	3 559	4 188	3 893	4 213	5 305	5 570	4 719
Imports: All goods	1 287	1 256	1 206	1 725	1 761	2 279	2 228	2 231	2 598
Agriculture	568	487	392	417	475	730	686	621	676
Manufactures	531	481	602	986	841	652	848	985	1 054
Balance: All goods	758	1 967	2 570	2 736	2 428	2 238	3 582	3 655	2 352
Bolivia									
Exports: All goods	192	222	218	185	214	270	295	417	298
Agriculture	35	41	27	31	28	40	31	22	19
Manufactures	151	176	180	150	179	223	259	378	289
Imports: All goods	208	162	191	260	262	275	223	224	224
Agriculture	20	10	9	20	10	14	20	17	15
Manufactures	153	134	157	191	190	200	149	156	163
Balance: All goods	-17	60	27	-75	-49	-6	72	193	75
Brazil									
Exports: All goods	6 148	5 751	6 058	8 102	11 439	12 718	15 915	15 142	13 203
Agriculture	251	146	190	474	462	561	514	455	195
Manufactures	5 178	4 968	5 294	7 057	10 230	11 279	14 594	14 049	12 550
Imports: All goods	6 717	7 609	7 479	8 683	8 833	8 773	9 626	10 102	11 314
Agriculture	1 250	1 378	1 203	1 298	1 183	1 349	1 502	1 278	1 452
Manufactures	4 746	5 475	5 394	6 451	6 618	6 522	7 178	7 697	8 572
Balance: All goods	-569	-1 858	-1 421	-581	2 607	3 944	6 289	5 040	1 889
Chile									
Exports: All goods	1 839	2 466	2 599	2 774	3 615	4 140	4 368	3 979	3 078
Agriculture	69	91	107	98	164	128	123	132	150
Manufactures	1 673	2 260	2 384	2 544	3 244	3 766	4 006	3 740	2 829
Imports: All goods	1 302	1 388	1 462	1 821	1 931	2 262	2 293	2 453	2 953
Agriculture	444	497	457	534	545	753	747	784	912
Manufactures	629	634	653	819	790	885	875	845	1 205
Balance: All goods	537	1 078	1 137	953	1 684	1 877	2 075	1 527	125
Colombia									
Exports: All goods	1 952	3 286	3 235	4 064	4 624	4 714	5 197	4 816	3 560
Agriculture	119	216	218	302	456	609	523	557	427
Manufactures	1 732	2 970	2 923	3 671	4 040	3 907	4 471	4 138	3 014
Imports: All goods	2 736	2 837	3 032	3 171	3 791	4 424	4 737	4 656	6 259
Agriculture	784	881	811	1 021	1 134	1 121	1 426	1 293	1 184
Manufactures	647	798	860	908	1 055	1 064	1 077	1 212	1 527
Balance: All goods	-784	449	203	893	833	291	460	160	-2 699
Ecuador									
Exports: All goods	948	999	1 100	1 195	1 538	1 259	1 526	1 683	910
Agriculture	101	57	90	71	160	156	187	177	105
Manufactures	826	885	962	1 085	1 279	1 046	1 224	1 369	746
Imports: All goods	1 327	1 344	1 399	1 726	1 940	1 958	2 055	1 752	1 821
Agriculture	470	394	355	517	550	539	549	519	569
Manufactures	40	49	82	104	89	112	121	128	157
Balance: All goods	-380	-345	-299	-532	-402	-700	-529	-69	-911
Paraguay									
Exports: All goods	374	415	521	788	992	898	913	786	515
Agriculture	10	13	17	21	24	33	31	10	10
Manufactures	307	348	444	719	915	821	833	721	479
Imports: All goods	43	35	50	80	55	42	41	34	48
Agriculture	8	5	10	6	14	9	12	12	14
Manufactures	35	30	39	72	40	32	28	18	28
Balance: All goods	331	380	471	708	937	855	873	752	467

See footnotes and NOTE at end of table.

Table C-11. U.S. Foreign Trade in Goods by Country or Region, 1991–1999—*Continued*

(Census basis, millions of dollars.)

Country or region	1991	1992	1993	1994	1995	1996	1997	1998	1999
Peru									
Exports: All goods	840	1 005	1 072	1 408	1 775	1 774	1 953	2 063	1 697
Agriculture	160	170	189	205	297	307	192	355	294
Manufactures	629	737	804	1 079	1 417	1 409	1 725	1 646	1 356
Imports: All goods	776	738	754	841	1 035	1 261	1 772	1 976	1 928
Agriculture	105	81	61	116	187	154	273	228	221
Manufactures	482	457	421	488	514	702	1 019	1 376	1 384
Balance: All goods	64	266	318	566	741	513	181	87	-232
Uruguay									
Exports: All goods	216	231	253	311	396	483	548	591	495
Agriculture	7	4	6	10	11	16	14	11	11
Manufactures	202	220	238	285	372	440	509	563	464
Imports: All goods	237	266	266	168	167	261	229	256	199
Agriculture	37	37	29	27	28	62	60	54	62
Manufactures	178	208	215	113	108	177	145	176	110
Balance: All goods	-21	-35	-12	143	229	222	319	335	296
Venezuela									
Exports: All goods	4 656	5 444	4 590	4 039	4 640	4 749	6 602	6 516	5 354
Agriculture	315	437	479	393	472	467	566	503	408
Manufactures	4 019	4 783	3 942	3 400	3 808	3 991	5 806	5 806	4 814
Imports: All goods	8 179	8 181	8 140	8 371	9 764	13 173	13 477	9 181	11 335
Agriculture	36	44	70	72	43	102	64	68	100
Manufactures	531	579	665	1 090	1 163	1 244	1 280	1 200	1 280
Balance: All goods	-3 522	-2 737	-3 550	-4 332	-5 124	-8 424	-6 876	-2 666	-5 981
OTHER WESTERN HEMISPHERE									
Bermuda									
Exports: All goods	232	242	265	300	299	282	338	400	344
Agriculture	65	62	61	62	64	68	65	66	60
Manufactures	150	165	185	222	220	192	241	289	246
Imports: All goods	8	7	15	9	10	12	30	12	25
Agriculture	...	...	...	...	...	...	...	1	1
Manufactures	7	6	13	8	9	10	29	10	24
Balance: All goods	224	236	250	291	288	270	308	389	319
Cuba									
Exports: All goods	1	1	2	5	6	6	10	4	5
Agriculture	...	...	...	...	...	...	...	...	...
Manufactures	1	1	3	4	6	5	9	3	5
Imports: All goods	...	...	...	...	...	...	...	...	1
Agriculture	...	...	...	...	...	...	...	...	...
Manufactures	...	...	...	...	...	...	...	...	1
Balance: All goods	1	1	2	5	6	6	10	4	4
French Guiana									
Exports: All goods	150	82	323	196	442	301	494	247	194
Agriculture	1	1	1	1	1	1	1	1	1
Manufactures	148	78	322	194	441	300	492	245	191
Imports: All goods	1	3	3	3	5	5	2	3	4
Agriculture	...	...	...	...	...	...	...	...	...
Manufactures	1	3	3	3	5	5	2	3	4
Balance: All goods	149	79	320	192	436	296	491	243	190
French West Indies									
Exports: All goods	119	93	81	82	108	101	92	90	98
Agriculture	11	11	9	9	9	8	8	6	8
Manufactures	101	74	66	65	91	84	74	72	85
Imports: All goods	2	2	6	5	3	2	6	3	4
Agriculture	...	...	1	...	...	...	...	...	...
Manufactures	2	1	5	5	3	2	5	3	3
Balance: All goods	117	91	75	77	104	99	86	87	95

See footnotes and NOTE at end of table.

Table C-11. U.S. Foreign Trade in Goods by Country or Region, 1991–1999—*Continued*

(Census basis, millions of dollars.)

Country or region	1991	1992	1993	1994	1995	1996	1997	1998	1999
EUROPE									
Exports: All goods	123 469	122 617	119 785	123 479	140 564	148 810	163 273	170 008	171 834
Agriculture	10 203	10 525	9 660	8 774	10 767	11 912	11 446	9 961	7 187
Manufactures	102 223	101 770	102 337	105 710	118 591	126 467	141 712	151 682	156 146
Imports: All goods	104 062	112 707	119 082	136 562	152 376	164 587	181 440	202 874	224 790
Agriculture	5 127	5 168	5 088	5 574	6 233	7 077	7 398	7 763	8 400
Manufactures	92 665	100 138	106 055	121 421	137 558	147 152	164 164	186 631	204 835
Balance: All goods	19 407	9 911	702	-13 084	-11 812	-15 778	-18 167	-32 865	-52 957
WESTERN EUROPE									
Exports: All goods	118 682	117 100	113 681	118 177	134 863	141 543	155 384	162 571	165 952
Agriculture	7 614	8 068	7 604	7 576	9 223	9 816	9 759	8 621	6 172
Manufactures	100 341	99 186	98 572	102 011	114 823	122 086	136 386	146 191	151 747
Imports: All goods	102 262	110 727	115 557	130 730	145 356	157 601	172 957	191 971	212 969
Agriculture	4 904	4 970	4 876	5 384	6 033	6 744	7 209	7 544	8 183
Manufactures	91 359	98 610	103 209	116 266	131 202	141 175	156 672	176 762	194 857
Balance: All goods	16 420	6 374	-1 876	-12 553	-10 493	-16 058	-17 573	-29 400	-47 018
EUROPEAN UNION (EU-15)									
Exports: All goods	108 417	107 844	101 501	107 777	123 671	127 711	140 774	149 034	151 814
Agriculture	7 003	7 339	6 881	6 872	8 272	8 723	8 570	7 603	6 166
Manufactures	91 668	91 446	87 768	92 894	105 387	110 025	123 656	134 254	138 917
Imports: All goods	93 030	101 201	105 493	119 467	131 871	142 947	157 528	176 380	195 227
Agriculture	4 266	4 474	4 402	4 881	5 481	6 107	6 565	6 950	7 605
Manufactures	83 777	90 885	95 067	107 202	120 380	129 993	144 498	163 534	180 479
Balance: All goods	15 387	6 643	-3 993	-11 690	-8 200	-15 236	-16 755	-27 346	-43 412
Austria									
Exports: All goods	1 056	1 256	1 326	1 372	2 017	2 010	2 075	2 143	2 588
Agriculture	35	35	30	41	22	28	26	22	14
Manufactures	995	1 196	1 267	1 300	1 964	1 945	2 012	2 450	2 535
Imports: All goods	1 264	1 307	1 411	1 750	1 963	2 200	2 368	2 561	2 909
Agriculture	66	49	51	61	27	36	39	31	27
Manufactures	1 184	1 232	1 308	1 645	1 903	2 138	2 277	2 464	2 794
Balance: All goods	-208	-50	-85	-378	54	-191	-294	-418	-321
Belgium And Luxembourg									
Exports: All goods	10 789	10 047	9 439	11 168	12 840	12 774	14 132	14 524	13 365
Agriculture	452	449	452	470	602	675	612	591	493
Manufactures	7 991	7 451	7 210	8 055	9 590	9 784	11 421	12 053	11 634
Imports: All goods	4 117	4 703	5 402	6 642	6 288	6 980	8 151	8 813	9 510
Agriculture	97	111	113	128	136	137	162	175	158
Manufactures	3 832	4 285	5 122	6 220	5 947	6 573	7 649	8 293	8 943
Balance: All goods	9 971	5 344	4 037	4 526	6 552	5 795	5 982	5 711	3 855
Denmark									
Exports: All goods	1 574	1 473	1 092	1 215	1 518	1 731	1 757	1 874	1 726
Agriculture	117	126	144	141	173	188	226	191	147
Manufactures	1 256	1 175	904	1 027	1 251	1 468	1 484	1 633	1 532
Imports: All goods	1 661	1 667	1 664	2 122	1 945	2 142	2 138	2 395	2 819
Agriculture	443	356	390	430	430	416	417	411	425
Manufactures	1 126	1 223	1 234	1 637	1 551	1 733	1 752	1 969	2 403
Balance: All goods	-87	-194	-572	-907	-427	-411	-381	-521	-1 093
Finland									
Exports: All goods	952	785	848	1 068	1 250	2 439	1 741	1 915	1 669
Agriculture	46	47	44	72	74	126	125	72	75
Manufactures	777	621	677	821	968	2 128	1 484	1 730	1 490
Imports: All goods	1 085	1 185	1 608	1 801	2 270	2 389	2 392	2 596	2 908
Agriculture	77	50	68	83	48	55	65	69	65
Manufactures	991	1 108	1 474	1 645	2 118	2 100	2 190	2 421	2 664
Balance: All goods	-133	-400	-761	-732	-1 020	50	-650	-681	-1 239

See footnotes and NOTE at end of table.

Table C-11. U.S. Foreign Trade in Goods by Country or Region, 1991–1999—*Continued*

(Census basis, millions of dollars.)

Country or region	1991	1992	1993	1994	1995	1996	1997	1998	1999
France									
Exports: All goods	15 345	14 593	13 267	13 619	14 245	14 456	15 965	17 729	18 877
Agriculture	566	588	568	431	522	490	535	471	343
Manufactures	13 685	13 109	12 099	12 639	12 983	13 199	14 769	16 648	17 965
Imports: All goods	13 333	14 797	15 279	16 699	17 209	18 646	20 636	24 016	25 709
Agriculture	637	735	692	765	881	958	1 131	1 237	1 518
Manufactures	11 950	13 272	13 875	15 125	15 611	16 861	18 683	21 875	23 404
Balance: All goods	2 012	-205	-2 013	-3 080	-2 964	-4 190	-4 672	-6 287	-6 831
Germany									
Exports: All goods	21 302	21 249	18 932	19 229	22 394	23 495	24 458	26 657	26 800
Agriculture	1 052	1 121	1 057	1 052	1 208	1 439	1 294	1 206	897
Manufactures	19 442	19 217	17 193	17 417	20 166	21 177	22 201	24 544	25 081
Imports: All goods	26 137	28 820	28 562	31 744	36 844	38 945	43 122	49 842	55 228
Agriculture	537	560	524	532	659	712	728	762	739
Manufactures	25 489	27 954	27 734	30 909	35 915	37 901	41 995	48 688	53 895
Balance: All goods	-4 834	-7 572	-9 630	-12 515	-14 450	-15 450	-18 663	-23 185	-28 428
Greece									
Exports: All goods	1 039	901	880	829	1 519	825	949	1 355	996
Agriculture	110	111	104	113	129	139	148	118	89
Manufactures	841	728	729	665	1 330	618	750	1 193	861
Imports: All goods	429	370	348	455	397	506	453	467	563
Agriculture	154	152	132	133	104	159	135	124	203
Manufactures	192	159	193	231	268	276	296	319	331
Balance: All goods	609	531	533	374	1 121	319	496	889	432
Ireland									
Exports: All goods	2 681	2 862	2 728	3 419	4 109	3 669	4 642	5 647	6 384
Agriculture	188	192	190	196	235	211	227	268	195
Manufactures	2 398	2 568	2 468	3 136	3 796	3 377	4 334	5 268	6 089
Imports: All goods	1 948	2 262	2 519	2 894	4 079	4 804	5 867	8 401	10 994
Agriculture	59	77	83	94	97	140	142	219	207
Manufactures	1 736	2 015	2 252	2 607	3 816	4 463	5 505	7 955	10 572
Balance: All goods	733	600	209	525	30	-1 135	-1 224	-2 754	-4 611
Italy									
Exports: All goods	8 570	8 721	6 464	7 183	8 862	8 797	8 995	8 991	10 091
Agriculture	673	669	597	541	695	787	750	676	490
Manufactures	6 375	6 705	4 972	5 607	6 752	6 820	7 108	7 375	8 690
Imports: All goods	11 764	12 314	13 216	14 802	16 348	18 325	19 408	20 959	22 357
Agriculture	752	852	777	898	1 067	1 303	1 370	1 369	1 437
Manufactures	10 458	10 839	11 973	13 460	15 212	16 680	17 730	19 374	20 731
Balance: All goods	-3 194	-3 593	-6 752	-7 620	-7 487	-9 528	-10 413	-11 968	-12 266
Netherlands									
Exports: All goods	13 511	13 752	12 839	13 582	16 558	16 663	19 827	18 978	19 437
Agriculture	1 676	1 833	1 658	1 675	2 033	2 015	1 891	1 496	1 487
Manufactures	10 331	10 602	10 256	11 066	13 145	13 415	16 763	16 562	17 097
Imports: All goods	4 811	5 300	5 443	6 007	6 405	6 583	7 293	7 599	8 475
Agriculture	710	752	849	943	1 096	1 149	1 230	1 315	1 390
Manufactures	3 775	4 230	4 447	4 749	5 066	5 238	5 665	5 927	6 731
Balance: All goods	8 699	8 451	7 395	7 575	10 153	10 079	12 534	11 378	10 962
Portugal									
Exports: All goods	792	1 025	727	1 054	898	961	954	888	1 092
Agriculture	228	238	216	231	269	290	249	156	139
Manufactures	449	675	425	757	527	561	606	648	843
Imports: All goods	695	664	785	899	1 057	1 017	1 138	1 265	1 356
Agriculture	44	41	43	43	47	62	70	65	72
Manufactures	552	557	665	747	841	835	907	1 056	1 138
Balance: All goods	96	361	-59	156	-158	-56	-184	-377	-264

See footnotes and NOTE at end of table.

Table C-11. U.S. Foreign Trade in Goods by Country or Region, 1991–1999—*Continued*

(Census basis, millions of dollars.)

Country or region	1991	1992	1993	1994	1995	1996	1997	1998	1999
Spain									
Exports: All goods	5 474	5 537	4 168	4 622	5 526	5 500	5 539	5 454	6 133
Agriculture	928	916	775	850	1 168	1 060	1 137	1 036	678
Manufactures	3 795	3 866	2 827	3 119	3 637	3 737	3 700	3 775	4 868
Imports: All goods	2 848	3 002	2 992	3 555	3 880	4 280	4 606	4 780	5 059
Agriculture	373	426	353	411	458	507	546	602	716
Manufactures	2 081	2 254	2 281	2 812	3 186	3 451	3 753	3 887	4 078
Balance: All goods	2 626	2 535	1 176	1 067	1 647	1 220	933	673	1 074
Sweden									
Exports: All goods	3 287	2 845	2 354	2 518	3 080	3 431	3 314	3 822	4 251
Agriculture	138	145	152	160	124	128	125	126	99
Manufactures	3 006	2 533	2 074	2 208	2 772	3 137	3 025	3 539	3 995
Imports: All goods	4 524	4 716	4 534	5 041	6 256	7 153	7 299	7 848	8 103
Agriculture	108	91	88	87	81	75	105	106	88
Manufactures	4 234	4 426	4 281	4 752	5 971	6 880	6 890	7 450	7 653
Balance: All goods	-1 238	-1 871	-2 180	-2 522	-3 177	-3 722	-3 985	-4 026	-3 852
United Kingdom									
Exports: All goods	22 046	22 800	26 438	26 900	28 857	30 963	36 425	39 058	38 407
Agriculture	794	868	895	899	1 019	1 148	1 223	1 174	1 020
Manufactures	20 327	21 000	24 665	25 078	26 506	28 658	33 997	36 836	36 237
Imports: All goods	18 413	20 093	21 730	25 058	26 930	28 979	32 659	34 838	39 237
Agriculture	209	224	238	273	349	399	427	466	559
Manufactures	16 175	17 331	18 228	20 662	22 975	24 862	29 207	31 857	35 141
Balance: All goods	3 633	2 707	4 708	1 842	1 927	1 984	3 766	4 220	-830
WESTERN EUROPE, EXCEPT EUROPEAN UNION									
Exports: All goods	10 265	9 256	12 180	10 401	11 192	13 833	14 611	13 536	14 138
Agriculture	612	729	724	704	952	1 093	1 188	1 018	815
Manufactures	8 673	7 740	10 804	9 116	9 437	12 061	12 730	11 937	12 830
Imports: All goods	9 232	9 526	10 063	11 264	13 486	14 654	15 429	15 591	17 742
Agriculture	638	496	474	503	552	637	644	594	578
Manufactures	7 582	7 725	8 142	9 065	10 821	11 182	12 174	13 229	14 378
Balance: All goods	1 033	-270	2 117	-863	-2 294	-822	-818	-2 054	-3 605
Cyprus									
Exports: All goods	119	166	138	209	258	257	245	162	192
Agriculture	31	42	43	31	44	37	37	11	21
Manufactures	63	72	59	58	67	73	75	74	86
Imports: All goods	12	11	16	18	13	17	16	32	31
Agriculture	1	1	1	1	1	1	1	2	2
Manufactures	10	9	12	15	10	15	13	28	27
Balance: All goods	107	155	122	191	245	240	228	130	160
Iceland									
Exports: All goods	156	119	147	112	171	257	179	237	298
Agriculture	10	11	11	12	15	18	16	20	30
Manufactures	132	96	127	86	137	218	149	204	246
Imports: All goods	209	165	233	249	233	236	231	268	304
Agriculture	1	2	. . .	1	2	3	1	2	1
Manufactures	21	17	24	28	44	45	37	66	55
Balance: All goods	-53	-45	-86	-137	-62	21	-52	-31	-6
Malta And Gozo									
Exports: All goods	57	58	172	88	107	125	121	267	190
Agriculture	11	11	4	6	10	20	8	7	11
Manufactures	41	45	166	79	93	103	109	254	172
Imports: All goods	65	91	104	96	132	209	224	340	325
Agriculture	. . .	. . .			. . .		. . .		. . .
Manufactures	63	89	96	96	132	208	222	334	323
Balance: All goods	-8	-33	68	-8	-26	-84	-103	-73	-135

See footnotes and NOTE at end of table.

Table C-11. U.S. Foreign Trade in Goods by Country or Region, 1991–1999—*Continued*

(Census basis, millions of dollars.)

Country or region	1991	1992	1993	1994	1995	1996	1997	1998	1999
Norway									
Exports: All goods	1 489	1 279	1 212	1 267	1 293	1 559	1 721	1 709	1 439
Agriculture	98	93	88	124	110	128	81	74	65
Manufactures	1 309	1 142	1 095	1 109	1 124	1 362	1 576	1 572	1 294
Imports: All goods	1 624	1 969	1 958	2 353	3 087	3 993	3 752	2 872	4 043
Agriculture	29	35	28	25	27	26	29	33	39
Manufactures	929	879	865	961	1 241	1 436	1 451	1 430	1 578
Balance: All goods	-135	-690	-745	-1 086	-1 794	-2 434	-2 031	-1 162	-2 603
Switzerland									
Exports: All goods	5 557	4 540	6 806	5 624	6 227	8 373	8 307	7 247	8 371
Agriculture	204	157	147	165	179	180	204	172	165
Manufactures	5 317	4 346	6 615	5 406	6 019	8 155	8 062	6 999	8 153
Imports: All goods	5 576	5 645	5 973	6 373	7 594	7 793	8 405	8 690	9 539
Agriculture	86	99	92	108	137	132	147	127	130
Manufactures	5 427	5 525	5 845	6 219	7 411	7 636	8 195	8 509	9 406
Balance: All goods	-19	-1 105	834	-749	-1 366	581	-98	-1 443	-1 167
Turkey									
Exports: All goods	2 467	2 735	3 429	2 752	2 768	2 847	3 540	3 506	3 217
Agriculture	214	378	379	268	516	615	742	666	488
Manufactures	1 539	1 777	2 552	2 152	1 730	1 850	2 381	2 532	2 514
Imports: All goods	1 006	1 110	1 198	1 575	1 798	1 778	2 121	2 543	2 629
Agriculture	420	300	294	326	343	419	422	397	357
Manufactures	529	750	784	1 203	1 401	1 286	1 635	2 060	2 191
Balance: All goods	1 462	1 625	2 231	1 178	970	1 068	1 419	963	588
Yugoslavia (former) [1]									
Exports: All goods	371	310	234	297	301	356	437	349	380
Agriculture	42	36	50	98	74	82	95	63	30
Manufactures	242	230	165	193	220	265	330	264	323
Imports: All goods	674	463	454	467	475	504	525	555	542
Agriculture	101	54	57	42	41	54	43	32	46
Manufactures	570	406	395	421	433	449	481	521	493
Balance: All goods	-303	-153	-220	-170	-174	-148	-88	-206	-162
Bosnia-Herzegovina									
Exports: All goods	...	5	25	39	28	59	103	40	44
Agriculture	...	...	8	36	22	30	31	23	7
Manufactures	...	5	7	3	7	28	70	17	31
Imports: All goods	...	10	7	4	3	10	8	7	15
Agriculture	...	1	...	1	...	...	...	...	...
Manufactures	...	9	7	3	3	10	8	7	14
Balance: All goods	...	-4	18	35	25	49	94	33	29
Croatia									
Exports: All goods	...	91	103	147	140	106	139	97	108
Agriculture	...	9	15	48	33	18	27	18	3
Manufactures	...	68	84	96	102	84	107	76	102
Imports: All goods	...	43	106	115	94	71	83	73	110
Agriculture	...	7	17	16	15	13	10	7	8
Manufactures	...	35	88	95	78	57	71	64	101
Balance: All goods	...	48	-3	32	46	35	56	24	-3
Macedonia									
Exports: All goods	...	4	11	14	21	14	34	15	56
Agriculture	...	...	3	3	6	3	8	3	10
Manufactures	...	4	8	11	15	11	25	11	45
Imports: All goods	...	47	111	82	89	125	147	175	137
Agriculture	...	11	34	19	17	26	23	18	32
Manufactures	...	35	77	63	72	99	124	157	104
Balance: All goods	...	-42	-100	-68	-68	-111	-113	-161	-80

See footnotes and NOTE at end of table.

Table C-11. U.S. Foreign Trade in Goods by Country or Region, 1991–1999—*Continued*

(Census basis, millions of dollars.)

Country or region	1991	1992	1993	1994	1995	1996	1997	1998	1999
Serbia And Montenegro									
Exports: All goods	. . .	6	2	1	2	46	49	74	59
Agriculture	. . .	1	. . .	. . .	. . .	13	1	. . .	. . .
Manufactures	. . .	4	1	1	2	32	47	59	46
Imports: All goods	. . .	39	. . .	. . .	. . .	8	10	13	5
Agriculture	. . .	4	. . .	. . .	. . .	2	1	1	1
Manufactures	. . .	36	. . .	. . .	. . .	6	9	12	4
Balance: All goods	. . .	-33	2	1	2	38	39	62	54
Slovenia									
Exports: All goods	. . .	38	92	96	110	131	113	123	114
Agriculture	. . .	7	24	11	13	17	28	19	10
Manufactures	. . .	28	65	83	95	110	82	100	98
Imports: All goods	. . .	101	229	266	289	289	277	287	276
Agriculture	. . .	3	6	6	9	14	9	6	5
Manufactures	. . .	95	224	259	279	276	268	280	270
Balance: All goods	. . .	-63	-137	-169	-180	-158	-164	-164	-162
EASTERN EUROPE AND FORMER SOVIET REPUBLICS									
Exports: All goods	4 787	5 517	6 104	5 301	5 701	7 267	7 889	7 438	5 882
Agriculture	2 588	2 456	2 056	1 197	1 544	2 096	1 688	1 340	1 015
Manufactures	1 882	2 584	3 765	3 699	3 768	4 381	5 326	5 491	4 399
Imports: All goods	1 800	1 980	3 526	5 832	7 020	6 986	8 483	10 903	11 821
Agriculture	223	197	212	190	200	333	189	218	217
Manufactures	1 306	1 528	2 846	5 154	6 356	5 977	7 492	9 868	9 978
Balance: All goods	2 987	3 537	2 578	-531	-1 319	280	-594	-3 465	-5 939
Albania									
Exports: All goods	18	36	34	16	14	12	3	15	25
Agriculture	9	25	29	14	7	8	2	10	6
Manufactures	2	9	5	2	7	4	1	5	18
Imports: All goods	3	5	8	6	9	10	12	12	9
Agriculture	3	4	4	2	4	4	7	8	3
Manufactures	. . .	1	3	4	6	7	4	4	6
Balance: All goods	15	31	27	10	4	2	-9	3	16
Bulgaria									
Exports: All goods	142	85	115	110	132	138	110	112	103
Agriculture	35	6	26	6	10	30	6	9	9
Manufactures	51	41	48	52	63	46	45	60	67
Imports: All goods	56	79	159	216	188	127	171	219	199
Agriculture	36	36	54	16	35	19	18	31	43
Manufactures	20	43	104	184	148	107	154	182	154
Balance: All goods	86	6	-44	-106	-57	11	-62	-107	-96
Czechoslovakia (former) [2]									
Exports: All goods	123	413	301	340	424	475	672	680	737
Agriculture	21	20	16	16	20	14	17	11	9
Manufactures	97	383	280	317	376	437	623	613	683
Imports: All goods	145	241	342	447	493	607	775	839	923
Agriculture	17	19	18	18	21	13	13	16	16
Manufactures	127	222	321	425	472	591	762	822	907
Balance: All goods	-22	171	-41	-107	-69	-132	-104	-159	-186
Czech Republic									
Exports: All goods	. . .	. . .	267	297	363	412	590	569	610
Agriculture	. . .	. . .	15	16	18	13	16	9	7
Manufactures	. . .	. . .	247	275	317	376	543	504	557
Imports: All goods	. . .	. . .	277	316	363	482	610	673	754
Agriculture	. . .	. . .	14	14	17	10	11	14	14
Manufactures	. . .	. . .	262	301	346	471	598	658	741
Balance: All goods	. . .	. . .	-10	-19	-1	-70	-20	-104	-144

See footnotes and NOTE at end of table.

Table C-11. U.S. Foreign Trade in Goods by Country or Region, 1991–1999—*Continued*

(Census basis, millions of dollars.)

Country or region	1991	1992	1993	1994	1995	1996	1997	1998	1999
Slovakia									
Exports: All goods	...	...	34	43	61	63	82	111	127
Agriculture	...	...	...	1	1	1	2	2	2
Manufactures	...	...	34	42	59	61	80	109	125
Imports: All goods	...	...	65	131	129	125	166	166	169
Agriculture	...	...	4	4	3	3	2	2	2
Manufactures	...	...	60	124	126	120	164	163	166
Balance: All goods	...	...	-31	-88	-69	-62	-84	-55	-42
Hungary									
Exports: All goods	256	295	435	309	295	331	486	483	504
Agriculture	13	12	11	11	14	9	25	18	20
Manufactures	241	277	421	296	280	320	458	458	479
Imports: All goods	367	347	401	470	54/	676	1 079	1 567	1 893
Agriculture	92	61	55	56	54	66	56	50	32
Manufactures	273	287	343	411	491	608	1 021	1 516	1 858
Balance: All goods	-111	-52	34	-161	-252	-345	-594	-1 084	-1 389
Poland									
Exports: All goods	459	641	912	625	776	968	1 170	882	826
Agriculture	36	83	178	87	112	218	111	114	62
Manufactures	399	528	719	522	643	711	1 002	711	704
Imports: All goods	357	375	454	651	664	628	696	784	816
Agriculture	67	63	65	67	58	61	63	76	78
Manufactures	271	301	378	553	599	559	614	683	697
Balance: All goods	102	266	458	-26	112	340	474	98	10
Romania									
Exports: All goods	209	248	324	340	253	266	258	337	176
Agriculture	74	95	102	67	49	46	15	25	13
Manufactures	66	96	172	208	114	131	124	249	146
Imports: All goods	69	87	69	195	222	249	400	393	442
Agriculture	2	2	4	4	1	1	1	1	2
Manufactures	66	54	64	153	220	206	329	374	389
Balance: All goods	140	161	254	145	31	17	-142	-57	-266
FORMER SOVIET REPUBLICS [3]									
Exports: All goods	3 579	3 799	3 984	3 562	3 807	5 078	5 191	4 930	3 511
Agriculture	2 400	2 216	1 694	996	1 333	1 771	1 512	1 154	896
Manufactures	1 026	1 250	2 119	2 302	2 285	2 733	3 072	3 395	2 303
Imports: All goods	802	845	2 094	3 848	4 895	4 690	5 350	7 089	7 539
Agriculture	6	12	11	27	27	169	31	36	43
Manufactures	548	621	1 633	3 425	4 421	3 899	4 608	6 287	5 966
Balance: All goods	2 777	2 954	1 890	-286	-1 088	388	-159	-2 159	-4 028
Armenia									
Exports: All goods	...	25	78	74	70	57	62	51	51
Agriculture	...	20	49	50	42	42	22	23	10
Manufactures	...	5	29	24	29	16	39	24	38
Imports: All goods	...	1	1	1	16	2	6	17	15
Agriculture	...	...	...	...	...	...	1	...	...
Manufactures	...	1	1	1	1	1	5	16	14
Balance: All goods	...	23	77	73	54	56	56	35	36
Azerbaijan									
Exports: All goods	...	...	37	27	36	54	62	123	55
Agriculture	...	...	...	14	12	6	6	9	10
Manufactures	...	...	37	13	23	48	48	48	30
Imports: All goods	...	...	...	...	1	5	6	5	26
Agriculture	...	...	...	...	...	1	1	1	2
Manufactures	...	...	...	...	1	3	4	4	6
Balance: All goods	...	...	36	27	35	50	57	118	29

See footnotes and NOTE at end of table.

Table C-11. U.S. Foreign Trade in Goods by Country or Region, 1991–1999—*Continued*

(Census basis, millions of dollars.)

Country or region	1991	1992	1993	1994	1995	1996	1997	1998	1999
Belarus									
Exports: All goods	...	25	92	46	48	53	41	30	26
Agriculture	...	16	70	21	15	11	1	...	...
Manufactures	...	9	22	25	33	37	34	26	24
Imports: All goods	...	25	34	54	45	52	66	105	94
Agriculture	...	...	...	...	...	...	...	...	...
Manufactures	...	25	33	53	44	51	65	102	86
Balance: All goods	...	...	58	-7	3	1	-25	-75	-68
Estonia									
Exports: All goods	...	59	54	33	139	84	47	87	163
Agriculture	...	32	30	8	74	27	25	52	126
Manufactures	...	26	23	23	59	54	21	34	34
Imports: All goods	...	12	20	29	62	55	77	125	237
Agriculture	...	1	...	...	...	...	...	...	1
Manufactures	...	8	10	25	56	49	56	62	48
Balance: All goods	...	46	34	4	77	29	-29	-38	-74
Georgia									
Exports: All goods	...	16	48	78	95	83	141	137	84
Agriculture	...	14	32	59	55	48	30	62	32
Manufactures	...	2	16	20	40	35	110	74	38
Imports: All goods	...	7	21	1	11	8	7	14	18
Agriculture	...	...	...	...	...	...	...	2	3
Manufactures	...	...	...	1	10	7	6	12	15
Balance: All goods	...	9	27	77	85	75	134	122	65
Kazakhstan									
Exports: All goods	...	15	68	130	81	138	346	103	180
Agriculture	...	9	2	3	1	1	...	12	2
Manufactures	...	5	63	127	77	128	253	88	176
Imports: All goods	...	21	41	62	123	121	129	169	229
Agriculture	...	...	1	...	...	...	...	...	...
Manufactures	...	21	37	58	122	112	114	163	222
Balance: All goods	...	-6	27	68	-42	17	217	-66	-50
Kyrgyzstan									
Exports: All goods	...	2	18	6	25	47	28	21	23
Agriculture	...	0	16	3	14	17	11	9	6
Manufactures	...	2	3	3	11	30	16	11	15
Imports: All goods	...	1	2	8	8	5	2	...	1
Agriculture	...	...	...	...	...	...	...	...	...
Manufactures	...	1	2	4	7	5	2	...	...
Balance: All goods	...	1	16	-2	16	42	26	20	22
Latvia									
Exports: All goods	...	55	90	101	89	167	218	187	218
Agriculture	...	26	12	5	10	91	119	111	146
Manufactures	...	23	71	87	78	71	98	73	68
Imports: All goods	...	11	22	41	82	103	145	115	229
Agriculture	...	...	...	...	...	...	...	1	1
Manufactures	...	8	15	49	60	18	46	74	91
Balance: All goods	...	44	67	60	8	64	73	72	-11
Lithuania									
Exports: All goods	...	44	57	41	52	63	87	62	66
Agriculture	...	25	18	19	12	15	15	2	2
Manufactures	...	17	38	22	39	48	64	59	61
Imports: All goods	...	5	16	15	26	34	80	81	97
Agriculture	...	1	1	6	7	11	10	17	23
Manufactures	...	4	5	10	19	23	33	51	48
Balance: All goods	...	39	41	26	26	29	8	-19	-31

See footnotes and NOTE at end of table.

Table C-11. U.S. Foreign Trade in Goods by Country or Region, 1991–1999—*Continued*

(Census basis, millions of dollars.)

Country or region	1991	1992	1993	1994	1995	1996	1997	1998	1999
Moldova									
Exports: All goods	. . .	9	31	23	10	22	20	21	11
Agriculture	. . .	8	28	20	5	12	4	6	3
Manufactures	. . .	1	3	4	5	9	16	14	7
Imports: All goods	. . .	. . .	. . .	3	25	30	54	109	87
Agriculture	. . .	. . .	. . .	1	1	4	3	4	2
Manufactures	. . .	. . .	. . .	2	24	26	48	108	87
Balance: All goods	. . .	9	31	20	-15	-8	-34	-89	-77
Russia									
Exports: All goods	. . .	2 112	2 970	2 578	2 823	3 346	3 365	3 553	2 060
Agriculture	. . .	1 108	1 221	637	1 032	1 352	1 234	841	517
Manufactures	. . .	745	1 593	1 691	1 620	1 550	1 744	2 501	1 291
Imports: All goods	. . .	481	1 743	3 245	4 030	3 577	4 319	5 747	5 921
Agriculture	. . .	5	7	11	8	12	10	7	5
Manufactures	. . .	361	1 356	2 847	3 631	3 057	3 814	5 139	4 825
Balance: All goods	. . .	1 631	1 227	-667	-1 207	-231	-954	-2 195	-3 861
Tajikistan									
Exports: All goods	. . .	9	12	15	18	17	19	12	14
Agriculture	. . .	8	10	10	14	12	16	10	9
Manufactures	. . .	1	2	5	4	5	3	2	3
Imports: All goods	. . .	2	18	60	41	33	9	33	23
Agriculture	. . .	. . .	. . .	2	6	3	. . .	. . .	. . .
Manufactures	. . .	1	18	58	35	29	8	32	23
Balance: All goods	. . .	7	-6	-44	-23	-16	10	-21	-9
Turkmenistan									
Exports: All goods	. . .	35	46	137	34	201	118	28	18
Agriculture	. . .	. . .	15	22	11	12	. . .	. . .	3
Manufactures	. . .	35	30	115	24	188	117	28	15
Imports: All goods	. . .	1	2	2	1	1	2	3	9
Agriculture	. . .	. . .	1	1	1	. . .	2	. . .	1
Manufactures	. . .	1	1	1	. . .	. . .	. . .	2	8
Balance: All goods	. . .	34	44	136	33	200	116	25	10
Ukraine									
Exports: All goods	. . .	307	310	180	223	395	403	368	205
Agriculture	. . .	164	137	62	38	44	29	16	23
Manufactures	. . .	119	171	116	181	244	278	269	169
Imports: All goods	. . .	89	165	323	406	507	410	531	529
Agriculture	. . .	. . .	. . .	6	3	2	1	1	1
Manufactures	. . .	45	146	315	394	492	369	490	472
Balance: All goods	. . .	218	145	-143	-182	-112	-7	-164	-324
Uzbekistan									
Exports: All goods	. . .	51	73	90	63	352	234	147	339
Agriculture	. . .	49	55	62	. . .	81	. . .	. . .	6
Manufactures	. . .	2	17	26	63	269	232	145	331
Imports: All goods	. . .	1	7	3	19	159	39	34	26
Agriculture	. . .	. . .	. . .	. . .	. . .	134	2	2	4
Manufactures	. . .	1	7	3	16	24	37	32	21
Balance: All goods	. . .	50	66	87	45	193	195	113	313
ASIA, INCLUDING MIDDLE EAST									
Exports: All goods	130 629	138 262	146 725	160 995	197 402	207 328	213 547	187 566	190 881
Agriculture	16 104	17 393	17 576	20 121	27 360	27 641	24 694	20 113	19 582
Manufactures	98 462	104 949	113 551	125 095	151 612	162 859	174 465	156 544	159 130
Imports: All goods	210 207	233 130	256 424	291 318	321 647	326 611	354 997	367 661	408 542
Agriculture	3 212	3 710	3 647	4 065	5 103	5 392	5 635	5 376	5 171
Manufactures	191 633	213 227	238 203	272 402	302 014	304 103	332 063	347 915	383 727
Balance: All goods	-79 578	-94 868	-109 698	-130 321	-124 245	-119 282	-141 450	-180 095	-217 661

See footnotes and NOTE at end of table.

Table C-11. U.S. Foreign Trade in Goods by Country or Region, 1991–1999—*Continued*

(Census basis, millions of dollars.)

Country or region	1991	1992	1993	1994	1995	1996	1997	1998	1999
Afghanistan									
Exports: All goods	3	4	9	5	4	17	12	7	18
Agriculture	...	...	7	...	...	8	2	...	5
Manufactures	1	3	2	4	3	8	7	5	13
Imports: All goods	4	2	3	6	5	16	10	17	9
Agriculture	3	1	2	5	5	5	7	3	6
Manufactures	1	1	1	1	1	1	3	5	4
Balance: All goods	-2	2	7	-1	-1	1	2	-10	9
Bangladesh									
Exports: All goods	179	188	254	232	325	210	259	318	274
Agriculture	94	118	56	159	217	88	120	159	123
Manufactures	84	61	175	61	95	110	133	149	140
Imports: All goods	524	831	886	1 080	1 257	1 343	1 679	1 846	1 918
Agriculture	7	4	2	1	2	1	1	2	2
Manufactures	479	759	804	979	1 188	1 231	1 544	1 751	1 801
Balance: All goods	-345	-643	-632	-848	-932	-1 133	-1 420	-1 528	-1 644
Brunei									
Exports: All goods	162	453	473	376	190	375	178	123	67
Agriculture	...	2	2	4	1	1	2	1	1
Manufactures	159	448	473	367	187	371	175	122	65
Imports: All goods	26	30	30	46	38	48	56	211	389
Agriculture	...	...	...	...	...	...	...	...	...
Manufactures	13	30	27	46	38	49	56	124	128
Balance: All goods	136	424	442	330	152	326	122	-88	-322
Burma									
Exports: All goods	23	4	12	11	16	32	20	32	9
Agriculture	1	...	...	1	1	2	1	...	1
Manufactures	23	4	12	10	15	30	19	31	8
Imports: All goods	27	39	46	67	81	108	115	164	232
Agriculture	2	1	3	6	6	9	6	6	6
Manufactures	15	30	37	51	69	89	98	149	213
Balance: All goods	-4	-34	-34	-56	-65	-76	-95	-132	-224
Cambodia									
Exports: All goods	...	16	16	8	27	22	19	11	20
Agriculture	...	...	...	1	4	1	2	1	2
Manufactures	...	16	15	7	21	18	15	8	13
Imports: All goods	...	...	1	1	5	4	103	365	593
Agriculture	...	...	...	...	4	1	1	...	1
Manufactures	...	...	1	1	1	3	102	364	590
Balance: All goods	...	16	15	6	22	17	-84	-354	-573
China									
Exports: All goods	6 278	7 418	8 763	9 282	11 754	11 993	12 862	14 241	13 111
Agriculture	724	545	370	1 082	2 634	2 080	1 592	1 330	839
Manufactures	5 000	6 251	7 725	7 655	8 330	9 131	10 357	12 234	11 406
Imports: All goods	18 969	25 728	31 540	38 787	45 543	51 513	62 558	71 169	81 788
Agriculture	311	357	420	412	463	568	654	711	734
Manufactures	17 705	24 354	30 486	37 623	44 154	49 928	60 708	69 484	80 139
Balance: All goods	-12 691	-18 309	-22 777	-29 505	-33 790	-39 520	-49 695	-56 927	-68 677
Hong Kong									
Exports: All goods	8 137	9 077	9 874	11 441	14 231	13 966	15 117	12 925	12 652
Agriculture	769	863	874	1 225	1 480	1 471	1 689	1 483	1 200
Manufactures	6 734	7 585	8 530	9 706	12 011	11 781	12 817	10 981	11 093
Imports: All goods	9 279	9 793	9 554	9 696	10 291	9 865	10 288	10 538	10 528
Agriculture	103	114	102	108	90	92	83	72	71
Manufactures	9 148	9 650	9 423	9 557	10 170	9 742	10 172	10 433	10 426
Balance: All goods	-1 141	-716	319	1 745	3 940	4 102	4 829	2 387	2 124

See footnotes and NOTE at end of table.

Table C-11. U.S. Foreign Trade in Goods by Country or Region, 1991–1999—*Continued*

(Census basis, millions of dollars.)

Country or region	1991	1992	1993	1994	1995	1996	1997	1998	1999
India									
Exports: All goods	1 999	1 917	2 778	2 294	3 296	3 328	3 608	3 564	3 688
Agriculture	103	145	204	120	195	112	153	200	156
Manufactures	1 480	1 457	2 354	1 948	2 727	2 928	3 243	3 171	3 353
Imports: All goods	3 192	3 780	4 554	5 310	5 726	6 170	7 322	8 237	9 071
Agriculture	253	273	328	423	425	484	571	600	771
Manufactures	2 659	3 251	4 021	4 606	5 058	5 395	6 475	7 280	8 021
Balance: All goods	-1 193	-1 863	-1 776	-3 016	-2 430	-2 841	-3 715	-4 673	-5 383
Indonesia									
Exports: All goods	1 891	2 779	2 770	2 809	3 360	3 977	4 522	2 299	2 038
Agriculture	298	342	342	480	811	847	770	452	536
Manufactures	1 364	2 159	2 169	2 045	2 251	2 856	3 461	1 672	1 199
Imports: All goods	3 241	4 529	5 435	6 547	7 435	8 250	9 188	9 341	9 525
Agriculture	680	829	810	1 003	1 411	1 529	1 531	1 305	1 026
Manufactures	1 891	2 942	3 838	4 508	5 146	5 831	6 813	7 144	7 501
Balance: All goods	-1 349	-1 750	-2 665	-3 738	-4 076	-4 273	-4 666	-7 042	-7 487
Japan									
Exports: All goods	48 125	47 813	47 891	53 488	64 343	67 607	65 549	57 831	57 466
Agriculture	7 718	8 413	8 752	9 346	11 015	11 620	10 485	9 084	8 917
Manufactures	31 386	30 260	30 266	35 309	43 598	46 969	47 621	42 824	42 205
Imports: All goods	91 511	97 414	107 246	119 156	123 479	115 187	121 663	121 845	130 864
Agriculture	200	198	207	230	272	255	267	269	316
Manufactures	91 757	96 483	106 563	118 377	122 786	114 503	120 461	121 102	130 409
Balance: All goods	-43 385	-49 601	-59 355	-65 668	-59 137	-47 580	-56 115	-64 014	-73 398
Macao									
Exports: All goods	10	20	27	21	30	30	65	41	42
Agriculture	1	1	1	1	1	0	1	1	2
Manufactures	10	18	27	20	29	29	65	39	39
Imports: All goods	581	721	668	791	895	858	1 021	1 109	1 124
Agriculture	3	1	. . .	. . .	. . .	. . .	. . .	1	1
Manufactures	575	715	663	786	892	855	1 019	1 106	1 122
Balance: All goods	-750	-702	-641	-770	-865	-828	-956	-1 068	-1 083
Malaysia									
Exports: All goods	3 900	4 363	6 064	6 969	8 816	8 546	10 780	8 957	9 060
Agriculture	153	165	195	229	534	610	477	278	309
Manufactures	3 673	4 166	5 732	6 625	8 161	7 747	10 210	8 586	8 681
Imports: All goods	6 101	8 294	10 563	13 982	17 455	17 829	18 027	19 000	21 424
Agriculture	307	359	311	336	395	370	394	353	354
Manufactures	5 611	7 766	10 125	13 482	16 912	17 265	17 302	18 332	20 713
Balance: All goods	-2 202	-3 931	-4 499	-7 013	-8 639	-9 283	-7 247	-10 043	-12 364
Mongolia									
Exports: All goods	12	2	17	6	14	4	34	20	10
Agriculture	4	. . .	14	3	. . .	. . .	2	5	2
Manufactures	9	2	2	3	14	4	32	15	8
Imports: All goods	1	7	34	27	23	31	42	42	61
Agriculture	1	2	5	2	. . .	2	2	. . .	. . .
Manufactures	. . .	4	28	22	22	26	35	40	60
Balance: All goods	11	-4	-17	-20	-9	-27	-8	-22	-51
Nepal									
Exports: All goods	6	5	6	7	10	9	27	16	21
Agriculture	1	. . .	. . .	. . .	. . .	1	. . .	1	1
Manufactures	5	4	5	7	9	8	26	15	20
Imports: All goods	55	73	91	117	96	117	114	139	178
Agriculture	2	2	4	2	2	8	3	2	1
Manufactures	47	71	87	115	94	109	110	138	177
Balance: All goods	-49	-68	-85	-109	-86	-108	-87	-124	-156

See footnotes and NOTE at end of table.

Table C-11. U.S. Foreign Trade in Goods by Country or Region, 1991–1999—*Continued*

(Census basis, millions of dollars.)

Country or region	1991	1992	1993	1994	1995	1996	1997	1998	1999
Pakistan									
Exports: All goods	950	881	811	718	941	1 271	1 240	720	497
Agriculture	150	267	186	245	453	352	441	194	89
Manufactures	662	545	542	452	448	890	771	515	314
Imports: All goods	662	866	897	1 012	1 197	1 266	1 442	1 692	1 741
Agriculture	23	27	16	21	17	32	20	23	22
Manufactures	611	817	856	955	1 155	1 203	1 401	1 653	1 695
Balance: All goods	288	15	-86	-293	-256	6	-202	-971	-1 244
Philippines									
Exports: All goods	2 265	2 759	3 529	3 886	5 295	6 142	7 417	6 737	7 222
Agriculture	368	510	476	564	752	877	851	701	770
Manufactures	1 795	2 100	2 872	3 134	4 286	5 001	6 447	5 943	6 343
Imports: All goods	3 471	4 355	4 894	5 719	7 007	8 161	10 445	11 947	12 353
Agriculture	418	553	436	434	565	593	627	601	477
Manufactures	2 929	3 672	4 345	5 168	6 309	7 436	9 638	11 160	11 719
Balance: All goods	-1 206	-1 596	-1 364	-1 833	-1 712	-2 019	-3 028	-5 211	-5 131
Singapore									
Exports: All goods	8 804	9 626	11 678	13 020	15 333	16 720	17 696	15 694	16 247
Agriculture	191	206	227	265	292	281	276	206	211
Manufactures	8 283	9 047	10 961	12 110	14 526	15 955	17 089	15 197	15 606
Imports: All goods	9 957	11 313	12 798	15 358	18 561	20 343	20 075	18 356	18 191
Agriculture	52	53	45	57	65	47	58	75	98
Manufactures	9 761	11 062	12 513	15 071	18 290	20 093	19 780	18 032	17 841
Balance: All goods	-1 153	-1 687	-1 120	-2 338	-3 227	-3 623	-2 378	-2 662	-1 944
South Korea									
Exports: All goods	15 505	14 639	14 782	18 025	25 380	26 621	25 046	16 486	22 958
Agriculture	2 091	2 213	1 912	2 311	3 736	3 828	2 833	2 208	2 436
Manufactures	11 131	10 240	10 723	13 641	18 980	20 413	19 959	13 202	18 825
Imports: All goods	17 018	16 682	17 118	19 629	24 184	22 655	23 173	23 942	31 179
Agriculture	54	58	63	67	69	84	79	81	92
Manufactures	16 747	16 325	16 730	19 226	23 717	22 275	22 710	23 423	30 650
Balance: All goods	-1 514	-2 043	-2 336	-1 604	1 196	3 966	1 873	-7 456	-8 220
Sri Lanka									
Exports: All goods	121	178	203	198	279	211	155	190	167
Agriculture	61	95	110	92	156	92	40	62	55
Manufactures	59	81	90	103	120	117	113	125	110
Imports: All goods	604	789	1 002	1 093	1 260	1 393	1 620	1 767	1 742
Agriculture	19	20	21	25	30	29	32	37	28
Manufactures	583	767	977	1 063	1 225	1 355	1 584	1 720	1 703
Balance: All goods	-483	-612	-798	-895	-981	-1 182	-1 465	-1 576	-1 575
Taiwan									
Exports: All goods	13 182	15 250	16 168	17 109	19 290	18 460	20 366	18 165	19 131
Agriculture	1 892	1 892	2 035	2 136	2 581	2 953	2 598	1 786	1 948
Manufactures	10 031	12 213	13 125	13 853	15 613	14 404	16 830	15 650	16 511
Imports: All goods	23 023	24 596	25 101	26 706	28 972	29 907	32 629	33 125	35 204
Agriculture	172	121	108	113	136	155	168	167	174
Manufactures	22 638	24 231	24 708	26 316	28 566	29 517	32 192	32 660	34 696
Balance: All goods	-9 841	-9 346	-8 934	-9 597	-9 682	-11 447	-12 263	-14 960	-16 073
Thailand									
Exports: All goods	3 753	3 989	3 766	4 865	6 665	7 198	7 349	5 239	4 985
Agriculture	283	306	301	382	586	569	530	407	402
Manufactures	3 328	3 514	3 289	4 259	5 466	6 379	6 619	4 674	4 412
Imports: All goods	6 122	7 529	8 542	10 306	11 348	11 336	12 602	13 436	14 330
Agriculture	521	653	670	701	891	875	844	728	671
Manufactures	4 636	5 927	6 809	8 199	9 194	9 318	10 545	11 259	12 021
Balance: All goods	-2 369	-3 540	-4 775	-5 441	-4 683	-4 139	-5 252	-8 198	-9 345

See footnotes and NOTE at end of table.

Table C-11. U.S. Foreign Trade in Goods by Country or Region, 1991–1999—*Continued*

(Census basis, millions of dollars.)

Country or region	1991	1992	1993	1994	1995	1996	1997	1998	1999
Vietnam									
Exports: All goods	3	4	7	173	253	616	287	274	292
Agriculture	. . .	. . .	. . .	17	24	33	40	21	31
Manufactures	4	4	7	149	223	573	228	247	250
Imports: All goods	. . .	. . .	. . .	51	199	332	389	554	608
Agriculture	. . .	. . .	. . .	38	152	132	158	188	158
Manufactures	. . .	. . .	. . .	5	28	72	136	163	210
Balance: All goods	3	4	7	122	54	285	-102	-280	-317
MIDDLE EAST									
Exports: All goods	15 315	16 873	16 821	16 045	17 537	19 967	20 928	23 661	20 885
Agriculture	1 204	1 307	1 512	1 458	1 882	1 815	1 785	1 529	1 541
Manufactures	13 241	14 767	14 446	13 618	14 496	17 132	18 221	21 128	18 500
Imports: All goods	15 813	15 726	15 387	15 812	16 567	19 852	20 403	18 766	25 422
Agriculture	79	85	92	78	103	122	126	150	162
Manufactures	3 803	4 335	5 129	6 226	6 980	7 781	9 146	10 342	11 821
Balance: All goods	-497	1 147	1 434	234	970	115	526	4 895	-4 537
Bahrain									
Exports: All goods	500	489	636	444	255	244	406	295	348
Agriculture	16	14	23	21	23	19	9	22	27
Manufactures	465	455	605	396	199	188	364	248	309
Imports: All goods	87	61	97	148	134	116	116	156	225
Agriculture	. . .	. . .	. . .	. . .	. . .	. . .	. . .	. . .	. . .
Manufactures	47	59	93	154	128	105	117	144	219
Balance: All goods	413	428	539	296	121	128	290	139	122
Iran									
Exports: All goods	527	747	616	329	277	. . .	1	. . .	48
Agriculture	13	51	115	86	136	. . .	. . .	. . .	48
Manufactures	478	680	488	233	136	. . .	1	. . .	. . .
Imports: All goods	231	1	. . .	1	. . .	. . .	. . .	. . .	2
Agriculture	. . .	. . .	. . .	. . .	. . .	. . .	. . .	. . .	. . .
Manufactures	4	1	. . .	1	. . .	. . .	. . .	. . .	2
Balance: All goods	297	474	616	328	277	. . .	1	. . .	46
Iraq									
Exports: All goods	. . .	. . .	4	1	. . .	3	82	106	10
Agriculture	. . .	. . .	3	. . .	. . .	3	82	96	9
Manufactures	. . .	. . .	1	. . .	. . .	. . .	. . .	10	. . .
Imports: All goods	6	. . .	. . .	. . .	. . .	. . .	312	1 183	4 226
Agriculture	. . .	. . .	. . .	. . .	. . .	. . .	. . .	. . .	. . .
Manufactures	. . .	. . .	. . .	. . .	. . .	. . .	. . .	. . .	. . .
Balance: All goods	-6	. . .	4	1	. . .	3	-230	-1 077	-4 217
Israel									
Exports: All goods	3 911	4 077	4 429	4 994	5 621	6 012	5 995	6 983	7 691
Agriculture	299	363	331	383	477	608	528	358	420
Manufactures	3 406	3 561	3 909	4 403	4 861	5 167	5 266	6 374	7 011
Imports: All goods	3 484	3 815	4 420	5 229	5 709	6 434	7 326	8 640	9 864
Agriculture	70	70	77	66	81	88	98	115	118
Manufactures	3 389	3 703	4 299	5 122	5 622	6 320	7 205	8 488	9 733
Balance: All goods	428	262	9	-232	-88	-422	-1 331	-1 657	-2 174
Jordan									
Exports: All goods	219	258	361	287	335	345	403	353	276
Agriculture	128	103	173	127	163	151	143	87	89
Manufactures	85	138	179	151	159	172	240	236	163
Imports: All goods	6	18	19	29	29	25	25	16	31
Agriculture	. . .	. . .	. . .	. . .	. . .	1	1	1	. . .
Manufactures	6	18	19	28	28	23	24	15	30
Balance: All goods	213	240	342	258	306	320	377	337	245

See footnotes and NOTE at end of table.

Table C-11. U.S. Foreign Trade in Goods by Country or Region, 1991–1999—*Continued*

(Census basis, millions of dollars.)

Country or region	1991	1992	1993	1994	1995	1996	1997	1998	1999
Kuwait									
Exports: All goods	1 228	1 337	999	1 176	1 437	1 984	1 390	1 524	864
Agriculture	15	31	43	51	66	42	46	50	56
Manufactures	1 190	1 256	921	1 071	1 302	1 888	1 298	1 377	795
Imports: All goods	36	281	1 818	1 458	1 335	1 651	1 816	1 266	1 439
Agriculture	. . .	. . .	. . .	. . .	. . .	. . .	. . .	. . .	. . .
Manufactures	1	10	51	32	51	28	17	29	36
Balance: All goods	1 192	1 055	-819	-282	102	332	-426	258	-575
Lebanon									
Exports: All goods	165	311	377	442	592	627	552	514	357
Agriculture	39	50	84	48	114	134	99	69	77
Manufactures	102	137	191	219	271	286	258	236	179
Imports: All goods	27	28	27	25	35	42	78	83	51
Agriculture	5	6	6	5	15	23	19	25	13
Manufactures	22	21	20	20	20	15	52	57	38
Balance: All goods	138	283	350	417	557	586	474	431	305
Oman									
Exports: All goods	202	257	251	219	222	217	341	303	188
Agriculture	11	11	10	12	14	14	12	18	18
Manufactures	184	223	215	199	195	193	317	262	156
Imports: All goods	115	186	277	458	295	414	242	217	220
Agriculture	. . .	. . .	. . .	. . .	. . .	. . .	. . .	. . .	. . .
Manufactures	48	86	84	113	138	129	161	189	209
Balance: All goods	87	72	-26	-239	-73	-198	98	86	-31
Qatar									
Exports: All goods	147	189	166	162	226	208	379	354	146
Agriculture	5	6	7	6	9	6	7	10	9
Manufactures	136	177	154	145	208	194	344	336	129
Imports: All goods	30	70	65	81	91	157	157	220	272
Agriculture	. . .	. . .	. . .	. . .	. . .	. . .	. . .	. . .	. . .
Manufactures	30	66	62	76	77	157	130	197	179
Balance: All goods	118	119	101	81	135	51	222	134	-127
Saudi Arabia									
Exports: All goods	6 557	7 167	6 661	6 013	6 155	7 311	8 438	10 520	7 912
Agriculture	500	459	446	458	519	551	619	503	447
Manufactures	5 689	6 457	5 932	5 279	5 288	6 468	7 555	9 753	7 161
Imports: All goods	10 900	10 371	7 708	7 688	8 377	10 467	9 365	6 241	8 254
Agriculture	. . .	1	1	. . .	1	1	1	. . .	1
Manufactures	122	160	235	374	493	538	534	572	651
Balance: All goods	-4 343	-3 205	-1 047	-1 675	-2 222	-3 156	-927	4 279	-342
Syria									
Exports: All goods	209	165	186	198	223	226	180	161	173
Agriculture	38	29	23	22	69	50	63	49	57
Manufactures	162	137	145	134	131	153	104	101	99
Imports: All goods	25	42	130	64	61	15	28	46	95
Agriculture	2	5	4	3	4	5	4	4	23
Manufactures	4	7	10	8	11	10	11	35	48
Balance: All goods	184	123	56	134	162	211	153	116	78
United Arab Emirates									
Exports: All goods	1 455	1 553	1 811	1 599	2 006	2 533	2 607	2 366	2 708
Agriculture	71	71	95	112	158	123	112	189	189
Manufactures	1 220	1 344	1 549	1 343	1 693	2 288	2 384	2 090	2 430
Imports: All goods	713	812	727	449	459	499	920	660	714
Agriculture	. . .	1	1	. . .	1	1	1	2	3
Manufactures	130	204	255	290	410	454	894	610	671
Balance: All goods	742	741	1 084	1 150	1 547	2 034	1 687	1 706	1 994

See footnotes and NOTE at end of table.

Table C-11. U.S. Foreign Trade in Goods by Country or Region, 1991–1999—*Continued*

(Census basis, millions of dollars.)

Country or region	1991	1992	1993	1994	1995	1996	1997	1998	1999
Yemen Arab Republic									
Exports: All goods	191	322	322	178	186	256	153	178	157
Agriculture	67	119	160	132	133	114	65	76	95
Manufactures	123	202	157	44	51	133	87	99	62
Imports: All goods	152	41	98	183	42	31	16	38	24
Agriculture	1	2	2	3	2	3	3	2	3
Manufactures	. . .	1	1	2	6	3	. . .	6	1
Balance: All goods	40	281	224	-5	144	225	137	140	133
AUSTRALIA AND OCEANIA									
Exports: All goods	9 797	10 682	9 938	11 687	12 794	14 087	14 450	14 216	14 163
Agriculture	379	378	455	522	485	463	525	511	460
Manufactures	8 960	9 904	9 074	10 812	11 920	13 170	13 474	13 343	13 310
Imports: All goods	5 337	5 097	4 752	4 914	5 085	5 601	6 465	7 373	7 381
Agriculture	1 902	1 895	1 724	1 559	1 528	1 511	1 718	1 981	2 160
Manufactures	2 032	1 939	1 848	2 322	2 410	2 771	3 257	4 006	3 884
Balance: All goods	4 460	5 585	5 186	6 773	7 709	8 485	7 986	6 843	6 782
Australia									
Exports: All goods	8 404	8 876	8 276	9 781	10 789	12 008	12 063	11 918	11 818
Agriculture	270	254	313	387	323	301	331	306	297
Manufactures	7 772	8 327	7 620	9 104	10 157	11 347	11 380	11 325	11 203
Imports: All goods	3 988	3 688	3 297	3 202	3 323	3 869	4 602	5 387	5 280
Agriculture	1 159	1 130	1 026	896	798	794	917	1 078	1 224
Manufactures	1 609	1 510	1 417	1 615	1 638	2 035	2 437	3 181	3 063
Balance: All goods	4 416	5 188	4 979	6 579	7 466	8 140	7 461	6 531	6 538
French Pacific Islands									
Exports: All goods	124	118	125	99	105	118	140	119	135
Agriculture	24	26	26	26	28	35	37	36	31
Manufactures	61	63	82	54	60	65	80	65	82
Imports: All goods	33	26	33	37	54	72	87	54	51
Agriculture	. . .	. . .	. . .	2	1	. . .	5	3	4
Manufactures	32	23	29	26	36	45	48	43	46
Balance: All goods	91	92	92	62	51	46	52	65	84
New Zealand									
Exports: All goods	1 007	1 307	1 249	1 508	1 691	1 729	1 962	1 887	1 923
Agriculture	50	60	77	73	96	88	112	120	100
Manufactures	914	1 185	1 129	1 399	1 543	1 573	1 782	1 718	1 781
Imports: All goods	1 209	1 218	1 208	1 421	1 452	1 463	1 579	1 645	1 748
Agriculture	708	720	654	623	690	676	755	837	863
Manufactures	338	329	315	569	554	604	658	636	652
Balance: All goods	-202	89	41	87	240	265	383	242	175
New Zealand Island Dependencies									
Exports: All goods	4	3	3	2	33	32	39	12	7
Agriculture	. . .	1	. . .	. . .	. . .	. . .	. . .	5	0
Manufactures	4	3	3	2	32	32	38	6	6
Imports: All goods	4	1	6	6	7	3	4	4	6
Agriculture	1	. . .	4	. . .	1	. . .	. . .	. . .	. . .
Manufactures	3	1	2	3	6	4	3	4	6
Balance: All goods	1	1	-3	-4	25	29	35	8	1
Papua New Guinea									
Exports: All goods	96	72	50	66	51	69	117	65	37
Agriculture	1	1	2	2	7	4	6	4	3
Manufactures	92	70	49	63	44	65	110	61	34
Imports: All goods	34	64	98	115	50	86	65	130	145
Agriculture	23	26	25	26	27	25	26	41	52
Manufactures	11	1	2	1	1	1	8	37	3
Balance: All goods	61	8	-47	-49	1	-16	52	-64	-107

See footnotes and NOTE at end of table.

Table C-11. U.S. Foreign Trade in Goods by Country or Region, 1991–1999—*Continued*

(Census basis, millions of dollars.)

Country or region	1991	1992	1993	1994	1995	1996	1997	1998	1999
Southern Pacific Islands									
Exports: All goods	33	90	34	26	9	12	6	46	16
Agriculture	1	2	...	...	...	...	1	1	...
Manufactures	32	88	34	25	6	12	5	45	16
Imports: All goods	3	7	9	5	6	3	4	9	4
Agriculture	1	...	...	...	...	1	...	4	2
Manufactures	1	1	3	1	1	2	1	2	1
Balance: All goods	30	84	26	20	3	8	1	37	12
Trust Territory (former)									
Exports: All goods	97	76	70	66	63	71	68	70	75
Agriculture	26	28	28	25	21	22	27	26	20
Manufactures	63	40	36	36	36	42	37	37	48
Imports: All goods	9	21	27	24	30	24	32	30	36
Agriculture	1	1	1	2	3	2	3	1	1
Manufactures	7	17	22	17	26	22	38	30	33
Balance: All goods	88	55	43	42	33	47	36	40	40
Western Samoa									
Exports: All goods	7	73	10	7	8	12	11	10	12
Agriculture	2	3	4	4	3	5	4	4	4
Manufactures	4	69	6	3	4	6	6	6	8
Imports: All goods	1	1	1	...	...	1	3	7	5
Agriculture	1	...	1	...	...	...	...	2	...
Manufactures	...	...	...	...	...	...	2	2	2
Balance: All goods	6	72	9	7	7	11	9	4	7
Other Pacific Islands									
Exports: All goods	23	65	117	124	40	34	41	87	134
Agriculture	4	4	4	6	6	7	7	8	5
Manufactures	16	56	113	117	32	25	33	77	127
Imports: All goods	49	72	73	103	84	79	88	107	105
Agriculture	8	17	12	9	9	13	12	14	14
Manufactures	32	55	58	89	68	58	60	72	76
Balance: All goods	-26	-7	44	21	-44	-45	-46	-21	29
AFRICA									
Exports: All goods	8 820	9 907	9 428	9 219	9 904	10 615	11 390	11 167	9 880
Agriculture	1 858	2 500	2 381	2 413	2 829	2 712	2 255	2 069	2 090
Manufactures	6 464	6 869	6 411	6 330	6 431	7 133	8 443	8 435	7 228
Imports: All goods	14 002	14 346	14 798	14 091	15 481	18 744	19 925	15 825	16 990
Agriculture	661	589	621	665	694	903	897	933	859
Manufactures	2 315	2 386	2 632	2 986	3 281	3 338	3 797	4 292	4 647
Balance: All goods	-5 182	-4 439	-5 370	-4 872	-5 577	-8 129	-8 535	-4 658	-7 110
Algeria									
Exports: All goods	727	688	938	1 192	774	635	692	651	459
Agriculture	427	368	479	586	410	294	316	257	221
Manufactures	256	258	372	580	339	321	361	372	220
Imports: All goods	2 103	1 586	1 583	1 527	1 750	2 126	2 440	1 638	1 824
Agriculture	...	...	...	...	...	...	1	2	1
Manufactures	3	1	7	4	6	30	30	7	62
Balance: All goods	-1 376	-898	-645	-335	-976	-1 491	-1 748	-987	-1 366
Angola									
Exports: All goods	186	158	174	197	260	268	281	355	252
Agriculture	16	11	8	37	33	28	28	28	23
Manufactures	169	134	158	155	220	231	242	320	226
Imports: All goods	1 775	2 303	2 092	2 061	2 232	2 902	2 779	2 241	2 418
Agriculture	...	...	...	...	...	...	...	...	...
Manufactures	11	11	8	12	10	9	6	4	11
Balance: All goods	-1 589	-2 145	-1 918	-1 864	-1 973	-2 633	-2 499	-1 886	-2 166

See footnotes and NOTE at end of table.

Table C-11. U.S. Foreign Trade in Goods by Country or Region, 1991–1999—*Continued*

(Census basis, millions of dollars.)

Country or region	1991	1992	1993	1994	1995	1996	1997	1998	1999
Benin									
Exports: All goods	26	27	22	26	34	27	52	44	31
Agriculture	9	13	6	8	10	2	5	6	2
Manufactures	6	6	6	7	17	13	29	22	16
Imports: All goods	23	10	16	10	10	14	8	4	18
Agriculture	...	...	...	1	1	1	1	2	15
Manufactures	...	...	1	2	1	5	1	1	...
Balance: All goods	3	18	7	16	24	14	44	40	14
Botswana									
Exports: All goods	31	47	25	23	36	29	43	36	33
Agriculture	...	2	...	1	4	1	3	1	1
Manufactures	31	45	24	22	32	27	40	35	32
Imports: All goods	13	12	8	14	21	27	25	20	17
Agriculture	...	...	1	...	...	...	...	...	...
Manufactures	13	12	7	13	21	27	25	20	17
Balance: All goods	18	34	17	9	15	2	19	16	17
Burkina Faso									
Exports: All goods	24	13	18	7	15	10	18	16	11
Agriculture	16	6	8	2	6	3	6	9	6
Manufactures	5	5	8	4	5	5	10	5	3
Imports: All goods	1	...	...	...	...	4	1	1	3
Agriculture	...	...	...	...	...	4	...	...	2
Manufactures	1	...	...	...	...	...	1	1	...
Balance: All goods	23	13	17	7	14	7	17	16	8
Burundi									
Exports: All goods	2	10	2	18	3	2	1	5	3
Agriculture	...	...	...	15	...	...	...	3	1
Manufactures	2	9	2	2	2	1	1	1	2
Imports: All goods	8	8	3	8	21	2	14	8	6
Agriculture	8	6	1	3	18	1	14	6	6
Manufactures	...	...	...	2	...	...	...	...	...
Balance: All goods	-6	1	...	10	-18	...	-13	-3	-4
Cameroon									
Exports: All goods	45	57	49	54	46	71	121	75	37
Agriculture	13	22	21	11	3	3	12	6	6
Manufactures	27	31	23	39	37	59	105	58	21
Imports: All goods	127	84	101	55	57	65	57	53	77
Agriculture	8	7	8	9	19	21	20	10	10
Manufactures	3	2	2	5	5	7	9	12	10
Balance: All goods	-81	-27	-53	-1	-12	7	64	22	-40
Central African Republic									
Exports: All goods	1	1	5	3	6	4	4	5	4
Agriculture	...	...	1	...	...	...	1	...	...
Manufactures	1	1	4	2	6	3	3	4	3
Imports: All goods	1	1	1	...	...	...	1	3	2
Agriculture	1	1	1	...	...	...	1	2	3
Manufactures	...	...	...	...	...	...	...	...	...
Balance: All goods	...	...	4	2	6	4	2	2	1
Chad									
Exports: All goods	14	5	8	8	11	3	3	4	3
Agriculture	5	...	1	1	1	2	2	...	1
Manufactures	8	5	7	7	10	1	1	3	1
Imports: All goods	...	...	...	1	3	7	3	8	7
Agriculture	...	...	...	1	...	...	...	1	...
Manufactures	...	...	...	...	...	2	...	...	...
Balance: All goods	14	5	8	6	8	-4	...	-4	-4

See footnotes and NOTE at end of table.

Table C-11. U.S. Foreign Trade in Goods by Country or Region, 1991–1999—*Continued*

(Census basis, millions of dollars.)

Country or region	1991	1992	1993	1994	1995	1996	1997	1998	1999
Congo									
Exports: All goods	43	59	27	38	55	63	75	92	47
Agriculture	2	6	. . .	6	6	7	5	8	9
Manufactures	41	53	27	31	48	55	65	77	34
Imports: All goods	410	511	500	403	207	315	472	315	415
Agriculture	. . .	3	3	. . .	. . .	3	7	1	4
Manufactures	6	3	4	15	19	24	18	12	22
Balance: All goods	-366	-452	-473	-365	-152	-252	-397	-223	-368
Democratic Republic Of The Congo									
Exports: All goods	62	33	35	40	77	73	38	34	21
Agriculture	15	8	10	10	31	24	14	10	3
Manufactures	40	19	18	22	34	39	18	22	17
Imports: All goods	294	250	238	180	267	259	282	172	229
Agriculture	3	5	2	1	5	3	2	2	2
Manufactures	117	123	97	70	121	116	125	95	121
Balance: All goods	-232	-218	-203	-140	-190	-185	-244	-138	-208
Djibouti									
Exports: All goods	10	11	13	7	8	8	7	20	26
Agriculture	2	2	2	2	3	2	2	5	13
Manufactures	4	4	4	3	2	2	2	10	12
Imports: All goods	. . .	. . .	. . .	. . .	. . .	. . .	. . .	1	. . .
Agriculture	. . .	. . .	. . .	. . .	. . .	. . .	. . .	. . .	. . .
Manufactures	. . .	. . .	. . .	. . .	. . .	. . .	. . .	. . .	. . .
Balance: All goods	10	11	13	7	8	8	7	20	26
Egypt									
Exports: All goods	2 720	3 088	2 768	2 855	2 985	3 153	3 835	3 059	3 001
Agriculture	701	763	646	850	1 309	1 255	964	903	979
Manufactures	1 901	2 201	2 011	1 882	1 523	1 723	2 710	1 987	1 859
Imports: All goods	206	434	613	549	606	681	658	660	618
Agriculture	10	11	10	15	15	25	13	21	26
Manufactures	153	198	240	325	415	411	545	585	533
Balance: All goods	2 515	2 654	2 155	2 306	2 379	2 473	3 178	2 398	2 383
Equatorial Guinea									
Exports: All goods	13	11	3	2	5	17	47	87	221
Agriculture	2	2	. . .	. . .	. . .	. . .	. . .	. . .	1
Manufactures	10	8	3	2	5	17	47	86	220
Imports: All goods	. . .	. . .	. . .	. . .	31	76	30	67	43
Agriculture	. . .	. . .	. . .	. . .	. . .	. . .	. . .	. . .	. . .
Manufactures	. . .	. . .	. . .	. . .	3	1	2	2	1
Balance: All goods	12	11	3	2	-26	-59	17	20	178
Ethiopia And Eritrea									
Exports: All goods	210	250	140	152	164	162	138	114	167
Agriculture	59	66	69	91	65	43	21	44	30
Manufactures	151	183	67	59	97	116	114	68	138
Imports: All goods	15	9	22	34	33	36	71	53	31
Agriculture	9	7	20	32	31	24	66	45	28
Manufactures	6	1	2	2	2	9	3	3	1
Balance: All goods	196	241	118	118	131	126	67	61	137
Gabon									
Exports: All goods	85	55	48	40	54	56	85	62	45
Agriculture	1	1	1	1	1	0	1	1	2
Manufactures	83	53	46	37	53	54	81	57	39
Imports: All goods	712	921	961	1 134	1 464	1 984	2 202	1 259	1 543
Agriculture	4	3	1	1	1	1	. . .	. . .	1
Manufactures	3	2	1	2	2	4	6	19	62
Balance: All goods	-627	-866	-913	-1 094	-1 410	-1 928	-2 118	-1 197	-1 498

See footnotes and NOTE at end of table.

Table C-11. U.S. Foreign Trade in Goods by Country or Region, 1991–1999—*Continued*

(Census basis, millions of dollars.)

Country or region	1991	1992	1993	1994	1995	1996	1997	1998	1999
Gambia									
Exports: All goods	11	10	10	4	6	9	10	9	10
Agriculture	2	2	2	1	2	2	2	2	2
Manufactures	6	6	5	2	3	5	6	4	5
Imports: All goods	2	1	2	2	2	2	3	2	. . .
Agriculture	. . .	. . .	6	. . .	. . .	. . .	. . .	. . .	. . .
Manufactures	2	1	2	2	2	2	3	2	. . .
Balance: All goods	9	9	8	2	4	7	7	7	9
Ghana									
Exports: All goods	141	124	215	125	167	296	315	225	233
Agriculture	15	26	43	36	45	64	51	46	51
Manufactures	85	77	160	79	104	206	233	161	156
Imports: All goods	152	96	216	199	196	171	155	143	209
Agriculture	67	30	48	13	55	32	13	26	43
Manufactures	59	38	133	153	129	114	118	88	133
Balance: All goods	-11	27	. . .	-74	-29	124	160	82	24
Guinea									
Exports: All goods	88	60	59	50	67	87	83	65	55
Agriculture	11	13	14	12	15	12	10	5	8
Manufactures	48	31	29	30	34	59	61	52	32
Imports: All goods	138	102	117	92	99	117	128	115	117
Agriculture	. . .	1	1	0	0	2	6	4	1
Manufactures	7	8	7	4	5	6	12	14	18
Balance: All goods	-50	-42	-58	-42	-32	-29	-45	-50	-62
Ivory Coast									
Exports: All goods	81	87	89	111	173	141	151	151	104
Agriculture	27	26	25	23	37	20	18	6	21
Manufactures	45	57	58	84	127	110	124	137	75
Imports: All goods	223	187	178	185	214	397	289	426	350
Agriculture	172	143	137	150	180	310	238	386	297
Manufactures	30	22	18	28	28	32	16	14	9
Balance: All goods	-141	-100	-90	-74	-41	-256	-138	-275	-246
Kenya									
Exports: All goods	91	124	131	170	114	105	225	199	189
Agriculture	8	48	29	58	34	10	31	60	28
Manufactures	81	75	84	108	76	89	188	133	153
Imports: All goods	69	73	92	109	101	107	114	99	106
Agriculture	42	37	42	51	46	55	56	48	35
Manufactures	22	28	41	56	54	46	57	49	70
Balance: All goods	22	51	39	61	13	-2	111	100	83
Lesotho									
Exports: All goods	3	3	7	3	2	3	2	1	1
Agriculture	2	2	2	3	1	2	1	1	. . .
Manufactures	2	1	1	1	. . .	1	1	. . .	1
Imports: All goods	27	53	56	63	62	65	87	100	111
Agriculture	. . .	. . .	. . .	. . .	. . .	. . .	. . .	. . .	. . .
Manufactures	27	53	56	63	62	65	86	100	111
Balance: All goods	-24	-50	-48	-60	-60	-63	-84	-99	-110
Liberia									
Exports: All goods	47	31	39	46	42	50	43	50	45
Agriculture	37	14	13	36	30	35	18	13	16
Manufactures	9	14	5	9	8	13	20	33	24
Imports: All goods	9	12	3	4	10	27	5	25	30
Agriculture	6	9	1	1	. . .	. . .	2	25	29
Manufactures	3	2	2	2	10	27	3	. . .	1
Balance: All goods	38	18	36	43	32	23	38	25	14

See footnotes and NOTE at end of table.

Table C-11. U.S. Foreign Trade in Goods by Country or Region, 1991–1999—*Continued*

(Census basis, millions of dollars.)

Country or region	1991	1992	1993	1994	1995	1996	1997	1998	1999
Madagascar									
Exports: All goods	14	6	11	48	10	12	12	15	106
Agriculture	8	2	4	2	3	2	5	6	2
Manufactures	7	4	7	46	7	10	7	9	104
Imports: All goods	47	53	43	57	57	46	63	71	80
Agriculture	42	48	36	47	39	26	40	42	28
Manufactures	2	2	4	7	14	15	19	26	50
Balance: All goods	-33	-47	-32	-9	-47	-34	-51	-57	26
Malawi									
Exports: All goods	55	14	26	19	18	13	18	15	7
Agriculture	9	2	6	4	8	...	...	...	...
Manufactures	46	12	10	15	10	10	15	14	7
Imports: All goods	72	60	58	57	41	73	83	60	73
Agriculture	66	49	51	53	38	71	82	60	71
Manufactures	6	9	8	4	3	2	...	...	2
Balance: All goods	-18	-46	-32	-38	-23	-59	-65	-46	-65
Mali									
Exports: All goods	18	11	33	19	23	18	26	25	30
Agriculture	9	2	...	1	...	...	3	2	1
Manufactures	6	4	29	17	19	16	18	18	27
Imports: All goods	2	1	1	6	4	5	4	3	9
Agriculture	...	...	...	...	...	1	...	...	3
Manufactures	1	1	1	4	5	4	4	3	6
Balance: All goods	17	10	31	13	20	14	22	22	21
Mauritania									
Exports: All goods	22	59	20	14	43	15	21	20	25
Agriculture	4	3	4	1	1	1	3	2	1
Manufactures	15	51	15	8	16	10	9	5	12
Imports: All goods	11	9	6	4	6	5	...	...	1
Agriculture	...	...	...	...	...	...	...	...	...
Manufactures	1	2	1	...	...	...	...	...	1
Balance: All goods	10	51	13	11	38	10	21	19	24
Mauritius									
Exports: All goods	15	22	18	24	25	25	31	23	39
Agriculture	...	...	1	...	...	...	...	1	...
Manufactures	14	21	17	22	24	25	31	22	38
Imports: All goods	132	136	198	217	230	217	238	272	259
Agriculture	16	2	14	11	8	14	16	13	6
Manufactures	113	134	182	207	219	193	208	252	251
Balance: All goods	-117	-113	-180	-193	-205	-192	-207	-248	-220
Morocco									
Exports: All goods	404	496	600	409	517	476	435	561	566
Agriculture	132	164	307	136	156	233	162	122	154
Manufactures	195	269	231	205	262	136	211	372	374
Imports: All goods	154	178	185	192	239	247	296	343	386
Agriculture	40	36	33	25	40	46	49	37	49
Manufactures	62	72	93	90	110	129	166	213	235
Balance: All goods	250	318	415	217	278	229	139	218	180
Mozambique									
Exports: All goods	101	150	59	39	49	23	46	46	35
Agriculture	22	70	25	19	28	10	26	29	18
Manufactures	77	79	11	18	17	10	13	14	13
Imports: All goods	23	19	9	15	28	27	31	26	10
Agriculture	21	19	7	14	24	25	28	23	8
Manufactures	1	1	2	1	1	1	2	1	1
Balance: All goods	78	130	50	24	22	-4	15	20	25

See footnotes and NOTE at end of table.

Table C-11. U.S. Foreign Trade in Goods by Country or Region, 1991–1999—*Continued*

(Census basis, millions of dollars.)

Country or region	1991	1992	1993	1994	1995	1996	1997	1998	1999
Namibia									
Exports: All goods	33	34	22	16	26	23	25	51	196
Agriculture	. . .	2	9	1	5	5	1	. . .	. . .
Manufactures	32	32	10	15	22	17	25	51	195
Imports: All goods	35	23	22	28	11	27	63	52	30
Agriculture	1	4	6	3	1	. . .	. . .	1	. . .
Manufactures	25	16	12	20	8	14	32	18	2
Balance: All goods	-3	11	-1	-11	15	-5	-38	-1	166
Niger									
Exports: All goods	10	13	16	12	40	27	25	18	19
Agriculture	4	3	2	1	2	1	2	2	. . .
Manufactures	5	8	12	5	28	7	8	7	10
Imports: All goods	5	3	3	2	2	1	30	2	12
Agriculture	. . .	. . .	. . .	. . .	. . .	. . .	. . .	. . .	. . .
Manufactures	3	3	3	2	1	1	41	1	5
Balance: All goods	5	10	13	10	38	27	-5	16	6
Nigeria									
Exports: All goods	831	1 001	895	509	603	818	813	817	628
Agriculture	36	71	140	68	117	177	115	150	172
Manufactures	787	911	713	436	460	617	653	636	424
Imports: All goods	5 168	5 103	5 301	4 430	4 930	5 978	6 349	4 194	4 385
Agriculture	37	30	46	43	38	34	24	13	8
Manufactures	10	7	26	18	20	13	8	13	14
Balance: All goods	-4 337	-4 101	-4 407	-3 921	-4 328	-5 160	-5 536	-3 377	-3 757
Rwanda									
Exports: All goods	2	3	9	35	38	37	35	22	48
Agriculture	. . .	. . .	5	30	32	33	27	10	18
Manufactures	2	1	1	4	6	3	7	12	30
Imports: All goods	7	5	4	2	2	9	4	4	4
Agriculture	6	2	1	. . .	1	7	3	2	2
Manufactures	1	. . .	. . .	. . .	. . .	. . .	. . .	. . .	. . .
Balance: All goods	-5	-2	5	33	37	29	31	18	44
Senegal									
Exports: All goods	76	80	70	42	68	56	52	59	63
Agriculture	24	24	37	12	12	7	7	16	4
Manufactures	37	40	23	18	40	33	31	31	46
Imports: All goods	10	10	8	11	5	6	7	5	9
Agriculture	3	1	. . .	. . .	. . .	. . .	. . .	. . .	. . .
Manufactures	6	5	4	7	5	5	6	4	8
Balance: All goods	66	70	63	31	63	50	45	54	54
Seychelles									
Exports: All goods	2	2	65	6	7	103	6	10	8
Agriculture	. . .	. . .	. . .	. . .	. . .	1	1	. . .	. . .
Manufactures	2	2	64	6	7	102	5	10	7
Imports: All goods	1	1	4	3	2	3	2	2	5
Agriculture	. . .	. . .	. . .	. . .	. . .	. . .	. . .	. . .	. . .
Manufactures	1	1	4	3	2	2	2	2	5
Balance: All goods	1	1	60	3	5	100	4	8	2
Sierra Leone									
Exports: All goods	25	28	22	24	18	28	16	24	13
Agriculture	7	14	6	10	10	15	9	16	5
Manufactures	15	11	10	11	5	9	4	6	7
Imports: All goods	48	61	47	51	29	22	18	12	10
Agriculture	. . .	1	. . .	. . .	2	. . .	. . .	. . .	. . .
Manufactures	13	23	21	28	21	20	18	12	9
Balance: All goods	-23	-33	-25	-27	-11	6	-3	11	3

See footnotes and NOTE at end of table.

Table C-11. U.S. Foreign Trade in Goods by Country or Region, 1991–1999—*Continued*

(Census basis, millions of dollars.)

Country or region	1991	1992	1993	1994	1995	1996	1997	1998	1999
Somalia									
Exports: All goods	7	21	46	30	8	4	3	3	3
Agriculture	4	20	11	16	6	3	1	2	2
Manufactures	4	1	20	14	2	1	1	1	1
Imports: All goods	3	2	...	...	...	...	...	1	...
Agriculture	...	...	...	...	...	...	...	...	...
Manufactures	...	...	...	...	...	...	...	...	...
Balance: All goods	5	18	46	30	8	4	2	2	3
South Africa									
Exports: All goods	2 113	2 434	2 188	2 172	2 751	3 112	2 997	3 628	2 586
Agriculture	80	465	238	141	258	288	211	176	169
Manufactures	1 958	1 864	1 856	1 895	2 342	2 597	2 598	3 255	2 276
Imports: All goods	1 728	1 727	1 845	2 031	2 208	2 323	2 510	3 049	3 194
Agriculture	5	48	57	67	78	107	101	109	104
Manufactures	1 475	1 422	1 490	1 646	1 763	1 789	1 985	2 476	2 636
Balance: All goods	385	707	344	142	543	789	487	579	-609
Sudan									
Exports: All goods	92	52	59	55	43	51	36	7	9
Agriculture	53	14	24	38	11	16	11	6	8
Manufactures	39	39	29	16	33	34	26	...	...
Imports: All goods	16	11	12	35	23	19	12	3	...
Agriculture	2	3	5	10	5	7	4	...	...
Manufactures	1	...	1	2	4	2	2	...	...
Balance: All goods	77	41	47	19	21	33	24	4	9
Swaziland									
Exports: All goods	5	4	3	5	3	2	5	8	9
Agriculture	...	...	...	2	2	...	1	2	1
Manufactures	4	3	2	4	1	2	4	7	8
Imports: All goods	28	23	21	38	32	30	44	25	38
Agriculture	18	7	6	17	9	8	23	3	8
Manufactures	8	14	13	19	17	19	20	20	28
Balance: All goods	-23	-20	-18	-32	-29	-28	-39	-17	-28
Tanzania									
Exports: All goods	34	34	33	49	66	50	65	67	68
Agriculture	4	5	4	16	13	5	13	8	17
Manufactures	23	20	21	26	47	34	42	51	44
Imports: All goods	15	11	11	15	22	19	27	32	35
Agriculture	10	6	6	4	7	4	5	6	9
Manufactures	5	4	5	10	13	12	17	20	17
Balance: All goods	20	23	21	34	44	31	38	35	33
Togo									
Exports: All goods	24	20	13	12	19	20	26	25	26
Agriculture	8	8	6	3	4	5	3	...	3
Manufactures	12	9	5	8	11	13	10	23	21
Imports: All goods	3	6	3	4	3	4	9	2	3
Agriculture	2	2	1	1	1	1	1	1	2
Manufactures	1	1	2	3	2	2	1	1	1
Balance: All goods	21	13	9	8	15	16	16	23	23
Tunisia									
Exports: All goods	172	232	232	327	215	189	252	196	280
Agriculture	73	92	121	106	89	90	118	81	71
Manufactures	84	122	102	213	114	84	119	104	201
Imports: All goods	25	48	41	54	70	76	63	62	75
Agriculture	6	5	4	4	5	...	3	4	5
Manufactures	16	24	25	38	59	34	47	47	60
Balance: All goods	146	184	192	273	145	113	189	134	206

See footnotes at end of table.

Table C-11. U.S. Foreign Trade in Goods by Country or Region, 1991–1999—*Continued*

(Census basis, millions of dollars.)

Country or region	1991	1992	1993	1994	1995	1996	1997	1998	1999
Uganda									
Exports: All goods	13	15	21	28	22	17	35	30	25
Agriculture	5	5	9	7	5	4	17	11	7
Manufactures	6	7	9	18	14	12	17	16	16
Imports: All goods	18	12	10	35	13	16	38	15	20
Agriculture	18	12	10	34	13	16	37	12	17
Manufactures	. . .	. . .	. . .	. . .	. . .	. . .	1	2	. . .
Balance: All goods	-5	3	11	-7	9	1	-3	15	5
Zambia									
Exports: All goods	23	68	42	33	49	46	29	22	20
Agriculture	. . .	44	11	2	3	. . .	. . .	1	1
Manufactures	22	21	23	26	43	43	26	19	19
Imports: All goods	42	70	41	64	33	64	56	47	38
Agriculture	1	. . .	1	1	. . .	. . .	. . .	1	2
Manufactures	41	70	40	63	32	64	55	46	35
Balance: All goods	-19	-2	2	-31	16	-18	-27	-26	-18
Zimbabwe									
Exports: All goods	53	144	84	93	122	91	82	93	61
Agriculture	1	88	25	3	9	1	. . .	4	9
Manufactures	52	55	58	89	112	89	79	88	50
Imports: All goods	90	106	110	102	98	133	140	127	133
Agriculture	30	39	47	46	11	49	40	21	31
Manufactures	57	66	61	51	80	77	94	103	98
Balance: All goods	-37	38	-25	-10	24	-42	-58	-34	-72
ASEAN (10 Countries)									
Exports: All goods	20 802	23 995	28 316	32 122	39 956	43 631	48 271	39 368	39 941
Agriculture	1 294	1 532	1 543	1 943	3 005	3 221	2 949	2 067	2 263
Manufactures	18 629	21 459	25 537	28 711	35 137	38 933	44 266	36 483	36 578
Imports: All goods	28 947	36 094	42 318	52 085	62 139	66 428	71 013	73 395	77 658
Agriculture	1 980	2 448	2 276	2 578	3 489	3 556	3 620	3 258	2 791
Manufactures	24 857	31 435	37 702	46 537	55 997	60 171	64 484	66 747	70 948
Balance: All goods	-8 145	-12 099	-14 001	-19 963	-22 183	-22 797	-22 742	-34 027	-37 718
APEC (20 Countries)									
Exports: All goods	242 619	265 195	284 007	324 838	369 171	396 288	434 153	417 809	439 351
Agriculture	23 112	26 309	26 782	30 117	36 301	39 579	36 807	33 563	32 270
Manufactures	18 629	21 459	25 537	28 711	35 137	38 933	44 266	36 483	36 578
Imports: All goods	318 221	351 680	392 518	454 525	512 802	538 133	588 893	618 685	692 791
Agriculture	11 061	12 169	12 677	13 777	16 092	17 557	18 981	19 817	20 121
Manufactures	24 857	31 435	37 702	46 537	55 997	60 171	64 484	66 747	70 948
Balance: All goods	-75 602	-86 485	-108 511	-129 687	-143 631	-141 845	-154 739	-200 876	-253 439
Caribbean Basin Initiative Countries									
Exports: All goods	10 449	11 744	12 748	13 801	15 671	16 350	18 961	20 773	20 454
Agriculture	1 494	1 532	1 736	1 760	2 155	2 426	2 565	2 684	2 587
Manufactures	7 740	9 025	9 849	10 950	12 329	12 617	14 978	16 927	16 774
Imports: All goods	8 493	9 701	10 456	11 597	12 890	14 796	16 976	17 384	19 751
Agriculture	1 755	1 855	1 913	1 986	2 204	2 410	2 771	2 521	2 265
Manufactures	4 507	5 485	6 311	7 361	8 576	9 486	11 218	12 402	14 484
Balance: All goods	1 956	2 043	2 292	2 204	2 781	1 554	1 985	3 389	703

1. Data for Yugoslavia (former) reflect all months of 1992. Data for the new republics reflect June-December of 1992.
2. Effective January 1, 1993 Czechoslovakia ceased to exist and became two countries, the Czech Republic and Slovakia.
3. Data for USSR (former), Estonia, Latvia, and Lithuania reflect all months of 1992. Data for the remaining new republics reflect February through December of 1992 only.

NOTE: Data reflect all revisions through June 20, 2000. Detail may not sum to aggregates due to rounding.

Table C-12. U.S. Import Price Indexes for Selected Categories of Goods, by Locality of Origin, 1991–1999

(1995=100, unless otherwise indicated; annual data are averages of the 12 months, unless otherwise indicated.)

Category	1991 [1]	1992 [2]	1993	1994	1995	1996	1997	1998	1999
DEVELOPED COUNTRIES	89.5	91.3	92.1	94.7	100.0	100.2	97.9	95.0	96.4
Manufactured goods	89.1	91.0	92.0	94.7	100.0	99.6	97.3	95.6	96.2
Nonmanufactured goods	95.6	97.3	95.0	95.6	100.0	113.3	110.5	88.9	105.0
DEVELOPING COUNTRIES	96.1	96.9	95.2	95.8	100.0	102.9	102.0	92.9	93.8
Manufactured goods	97.2	97.7	96.7	97.3	100.0	100.3	99.3	94.2	91.6
Nonmanufactured goods	94.7	95.8	89.7	90.2	100.0	113.1	109.7	81.6	100.3
CANADA	93.3	93.2	91.7	93.5	100.0	100.6	99.7	96.2	97.9
Manufactured goods	93.9	93.0	91.6	93.4	100.0	98.9	98.5	97.3	97.1
Nonmanufactured goods	93.7	95.9	93.4	93.9	100.0	116.1	112.6	91.9	107.6
EUROPEAN UNION	94.2	96.8	93.4	94.7	100.0	102.5	101.2	100.2	100.5
Manufactured goods	93.3	96.7	93.3	94.6	100.0	102.1	100.9	100.7	100.9
Nonmanufactured goods	102.1	103.0	99.2	99.1	100.0	115.8	113.8	85.0	96.1
LATIN AMERICA (December 1997=100)	...	...	...	...	...	...	...	94.0	97.6
Manufactured goods (December 1997=100)	...	...	...	...	...	...	...	97.3	96.6
Nonmanufactured goods (December 1997=100)	...	...	...	...	...	...	...	84.6	101.3
JAPAN	84.9	87.2	91.3	95.7	100.0	97.8	93.0	88.6	88.8
ASIAN NEWLY INDUSTRIALIZED COUNTRIES	99.6	100.7	100.2	99.5	100.0	98.5	94.9	87.2	83.4

1. Average of March, June, September, and December.
2. Average of March, June, September, October, November, and December.

PART D. STATE EXPORTS OF GOODS

Leading Exporting States, 1999
(Billions of dollars)

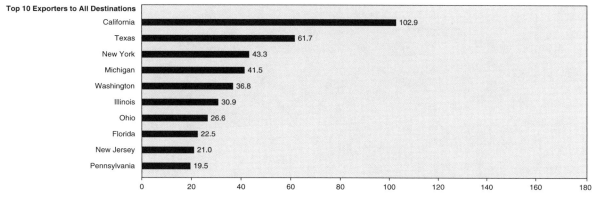

Top 10 Exporters to All Destinations

California	102.9
Texas	61.7
New York	43.3
Michigan	41.5
Washington	36.8
Illinois	30.9
Ohio	26.6
Florida	22.5
New Jersey	21.0
Pennsylvania	19.5

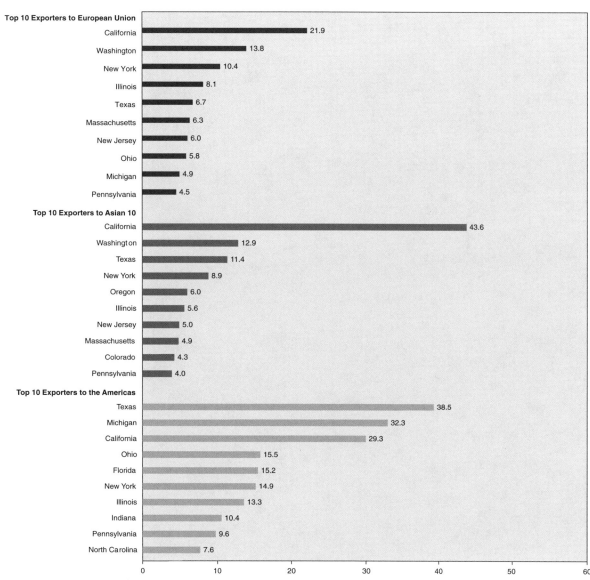

Top 10 Exporters to European Union

California	21.9
Washington	13.8
New York	10.4
Illinois	8.1
Texas	6.7
Massachusetts	6.3
New Jersey	6.0
Ohio	5.8
Michigan	4.9
Pennsylvania	4.5

Top 10 Exporters to Asian 10

California	43.6
Washington	12.9
Texas	11.4
New York	8.9
Oregon	6.0
Illinois	5.6
New Jersey	5.0
Massachusetts	4.9
Colorado	4.3
Pennsylvania	4.0

Top 10 Exporters to the Americas

Texas	38.5
Michigan	32.3
California	29.3
Ohio	15.5
Florida	15.2
New York	14.9
Illinois	13.3
Indiana	10.4
Pennsylvania	9.6
North Carolina	7.6

PART D. STATE EXPORTS OF GOODS

NOTES AND DEFINITIONS

State Exporter Location (EL) Data

Source: Bureau of the Census; compiled by Office of Trade and Economic Analysis (OTEA), International Trade Administration.

DATA NOTES

All of the state data shown have been compiled from the Census Bureau's Exporter Location (EL) series by the Office of Trade and Economic Analysis, International Trade Administration, U.S. Department of Commerce. All of the state data are based on f.a.s. (free alongside ship) value. All state data exclude timing adjustments and Canada adjustment. Timing adjustment is adjustment to a previous period's data because the data were not reported in a timely manner; the Canada adjustment is for inland freight that is sometimes included in Canadian exports. All figures are based on initial, unrevised data.

The EL series show export sales by exporters of record located in the state listed. Typically, the EL data reflect the point of sale, that is, the marketing origin of the exports. This is not necessarily the location where the goods are produced. *Thus, the EL series provide an approximation, rather than a precise record, of the production origin of U.S. exports.* The data are best viewed as a measure of international sales activity. They should be interpreted with caution as a measure of export-related production or jobs.

About three-fourths of manufacturing exports are generated by manufacturers who do their own exporting. For these shipments the production origin and the sales origin are generally, but not always, the same. For the remaining one-fourth of manufactured exports and most non-manufactured exports, the seller (the exporter of record) is not the producer. The production may or may not have occurred in the same state. In some cases, the exporter of record may be a headquarters or central office that may or may not engage in international marketing activity. Overall, Census Bureau research suggests that, for manufacturing establishments, the zip code location of the exporter of record is the same as the physical location of production for about 88 percent of the value of exports.

The data measure final sales of goods leaving the country. Even where the final product was produced in the same location as the sale, it may contain raw materials and intermediate products produced elsewhere.

There are significant differences between the EL series and the alternative Origin of Movement (OM) state export series, also prepared by the Bureau of the Census. Data from these two series cannot be compared to each other. The OM series measures the transportation origin of exports, which inflates the exports of states with major

shipping ports. Also, the OM series is only available for states, while the EL series can show both states and metropolitan areas.

The export figures shown in these tables for states and metropolitan areas can be used together. That is, it is possible to use the data for a metropolitan area to estimate its share of the state's export sales.

Commodity categories shown in state tables are based on the Standard Industrial Classification (SIC) product codes. (See the general notes for Section C for an explanation of SIC and other classifications.) Manufactured goods that cannot be classified by type, for example those with incomplete data, are labeled "unidentified manufactures".

DATA AVAILABILITY

All data are available on the OTEA web site.

Table D-1. State Exports of Goods, 1987 and 1991–1999

DATA NOTES

All figures reflect sales by exporters of record located in the jurisdictions shown. The location from which exports are sold is not always the same as where the goods were produced. The category "Unallocated" represents exports that, because of faulty reporting of the zip code of the exporter, cannot be allocated to any state.

Table D-2. State Exports of Goods by Destination, 1994–1999

Tables D-3 through D-55. State Exports of Goods by Destination and Industry, 1994–1999

DATA NOTES

Central and South America, and Caribbean includes the following country categories. *Central America* includes Costa Rica, El Salvador, Guatemala, Honduras, Nicaragua, and Panama. South America includes Argentina, Bolivia, Brazil, Chile, Colombia, Ecuador, Paraguay, Peru, Uruguay, and Venezuela. *The Caribbean* includes the Bahamas, Barbados, Belize, Cayman Islands, Dominican Republic, Guyana, Haiti, Jamaica, Leeward and Windward Islands [i.e., Antigua, British Virgin Islands, Dominica, Grenada, Montserrat, St. Christopher-Nevis and Anguilla, St. Lucia, and St. Vincent], Netherlands Antilles and Aruba, Suriname, Trinidad and Tobago, and Turks and Caicos Islands.

European Union includes Austria, Belgium, Luxembourg, Denmark, Finland, France, Germany, Greece, Ireland, Italy, Netherlands, Portugal, Spain, Sweden, and the United Kingdom.

131

The Asian 10 include China, Hong Kong, Indonesia, Japan, Malaysia, Philippines, Singapore, South Korea, Taiwan, and Thailand.

The Middle East includes Bahrain, Iran, Iraq, Israel (including the Gaza Strip and the West Bank), Jordan, Kuwait, Lebanon, the Neutral Zone, Oman, Qatar, Saudi Arabia, Syria, United Arab Emirates and the Yemen Arab Republic.

Africa consists of all the countries on the continent.

The *Former Soviet Republics* consist of Armenia, Azerbaijan, Belarus, Estonia, Georgia, Kazakhstan, Kyrgyzstan, Latvia, Lithuania, Moldova, Russia, Tajikistan, Turkmenistan, Ukraine and Uzbekistan.

Table D-1. State Exports of Goods, 1987 and 1991–1999

(Billions of dollars.)

State	1987	1991	1992	1993	1994	1995	1996	1997	1998	1999
ALL STATES	244.4	420.0	447.5	464.9	512.4	583.0	622.8	687.6	680.5	692.8
Alabama	1.5	2.4	2.7	2.5	3.1	3.6	3.7	4.5	4.6	4.9
Alaska	0.5	1.1	1.1	0.8	0.9	0.9	0.9	1.0	0.8	0.9
Arizona	2.5	4.5	5.0	5.8	7.0	8.4	9.9	13.6	10.8	10.1
Arkansas	0.4	0.8	1.1	1.1	1.5	1.8	2.0	2.2	1.9	1.8
California	32.9	59.0	66.7	68.1	78.2	92.0	98.6	103.8	98.8	102.9
Colorado	4.8	6.1	6.0	6.2	7.8	9.7	10.1	11.3	10.7	11.2
Connecticut	4.7	6.7	10.5	10.2	10.3	12.9	13.1	12.9	12.1	11.3
Delaware	2.7	3.5	3.7	3.5	3.8	4.4	4.6	5.1	5.0	4.9
District of Columbia	0.4	0.4	0.4	4.7	5.2	5.3	5.1	4.9	4.4	4.3
Florida	7.8	12.6	14.4	14.7	16.6	18.6	19.6	22.9	23.2	22.5
Georgia	2.4	5.2	6.0	6.1	7.1	8.6	8.6	9.8	11.2	11.1
Hawaii	0.2	0.2	0.1	0.2	0.2	0.3	0.3	0.3	0.2	0.2
Idaho	0.4	1.0	1.1	1.2	1.5	1.9	1.6	1.7	1.5	2.1
Illinois	10.2	16.4	19.0	20.3	24.5	30.5	32.2	34.2	33.8	30.9
Indiana	3.7	6.7	7.3	8.4	9.5	11.1	12.1	13.1	13.9	14.6
Iowa	1.1	1.4	1.5	2.0	2.3	2.6	2.7	3.1	3.4	3.0
Kansas	1.9	2.9	3.1	3.1	3.5	4.5	5.0	5.1	4.4	4.9
Kentucky	1.7	3.3	3.8	3.3	4.2	5.0	5.8	6.9	7.4	8.0
Louisiana	3.0	3.1	3.4	3.2	3.6	4.6	4.7	4.4	4.4	3.9
Maine	0.5	1.0	1.0	1.1	1.1	1.3	1.2	1.6	1.7	1.8
Maryland	1.5	2.7	2.7	2.7	2.8	3.4	3.5	3.9	4.0	4.1
Massachusetts	8.3	11.2	11.6	11.6	12.6	14.4	15.4	17.4	16.5	17.1
Michigan	19.5	18.8	22.0	25.3	36.8	37.1	38.1	37.9	39.3	41.5
Minnesota	5.6	7.9	9.0	10.0	10.0	12.4	13.9	13.8	13.5	14.4
Mississippi	0.4	0.8	0.8	0.8	1.1	1.4	1.2	1.4	1.4	1.5
Missouri	3.4	4.3	4.3	4.7	5.2	5.7	6.6	7.0	6.8	7.4
Montana	0.1	0.2	0.2	0.2	0.3	0.3	0.3	0.4	0.4	0.4
Nebraska	0.3	0.7	1.5	1.7	2.0	2.3	2.5	2.5	2.5	2.0
Nevada	0.3	0.4	0.4	0.5	0.5	0.7	0.7	0.8	0.8	1.1
New Hampshire	0.7	0.9	1.0	1.1	1.2	1.5	1.7	1.9	2.0	2.2
New Jersey	7.6	13.7	13.9	14.5	16.8	18.4	18.5	20.8	20.0	21.0
New Mexico	0.1	0.2	0.2	0.4	0.5	0.4	0.9	1.8	1.9	3.0
New York	29.6	37.5	36.8	40.7	37.3	44.1	45.0	48.9	45.6	43.3
North Carolina	3.5	6.2	7.4	8.0	9.0	10.6	11.6	13.1	12.9	13.6
North Dakota	0.2	0.3	0.3	0.3	0.4	0.5	0.6	0.6	0.7	0.6
Ohio	6.5	13.6	15.2	17.7	19.5	20.9	22.6	25.1	24.8	26.6
Oklahoma	1.0	2.4	2.6	2.3	2.2	2.5	2.5	2.7	2.6	2.4
Oregon	3.1	5.0	5.7	6.2	7.0	9.9	8.5	8.4	8.1	11.2
Pennsylvania	7.2	12.2	13.2	13.2	14.7	17.7	17.4	19.3	19.1	19.5
Rhode Island	0.4	0.7	0.7	0.9	1.0	1.0	1.0	1.1	1.1	1.1
South Carolina	1.0	2.0	2.7	3.2	3.5	4.5	4.9	5.7	5.9	6.5
South Dakota	. . .	0.2	0.2	0.2	0.3	0.3	0.4	0.4	0.4	1.1
Tennessee	3.0	5.0	5.7	6.2	7.5	9.5	9.3	9.9	9.9	9.3
Texas	18.0	31.9	33.9	35.6	40.5	45.2	48.3	56.3	59.0	61.7
Utah	0.7	1.7	2.2	2.0	2.2	2.3	2.8	3.3	3.1	2.8
Vermont	0.3	2.0	1.8	2.3	2.3	2.7	2.6	2.6	2.8	2.8
Virginia	3.1	8.8	8.5	8.1	9.9	10.4	10.9	11.5	11.5	10.7
Washington	10.3	27.3	28.7	27.4	25.1	22.0	25.5	31.7	38.0	36.8
West Virginia	0.7	0.9	0.9	0.8	0.9	1.1	1.2	1.3	1.2	0.9
Wisconsin	2.9	4.9	5.8	5.8	6.9	8.0	8.4	9.8	9.2	9.5
Wyoming	0.1	0.1	0.1	0.1	0.1	0.1	0.1	0.2	0.2	0.2
Puerto Rico	2.0	3.8	4.2	4.4	4.6	4.7	5.2	5.5	6.1	7.9
Virgin Islands	. . .	. . .	0.1	0.2	0.2	0.2	0.2	0.2	0.1	0.2
Unallocated	19.6	53.1	45.2	39.1	35.8	39.0	48.7	57.8	55.0	53.1

Table D-2. State Exports of Goods by Destination, 1994–1999

(Millions of dollars.)

Destination	U.S. total						Alabama					
	1994	1995	1996	1997	1998	1999	1994	1995	1996	1997	1998	1999
ALL DESTINATIONS	512 415.6	583 030.5	622 827.1	687 598.0	680 473.1	692 820.6	3 115.4	3 587.1	3 702.4	4 537.2	4 560.2	4 898.9
Canada	114 254.7	126 024.1	132 583.9	150 124.4	154 151.1	163 912.8	789.0	988.5	1 177.4	1 251.1	1 280.8	1 459.5
Mexico	50 840.3	46 311.5	56 760.8	71 378.3	79 010.1	87 044.0	222.6	193.1	324.9	813.7	380.4	456.4
Central and South America and Caribbean	77 944.2	93 130.2	98 269.4	117 819.0	118 995.2	103 500.0	374.0	308.3	304.4	407.7	500.8	415.4
Argentina	4 466.3	4 189.5	4 515.8	5 807.8	5 885.3	4 938.5	22.9	21.4	26.6	25.5	29.8	11.4
Brazil	8 118.4	11 443.6	12 699.2	15 912.3	15 157.0	13 249.0	21.6	53.0	51.1	77.5	65.5	60.4
Chile	2 775.9	3 613.1	4 131.5	4 375.1	3 985.2	3 079.0	13.9	10.3	9.8	15.1	8.1	5.9
Colombia	4 070.3	4 628.2	4 708.7	5 198.6	4 816.7	3 532.0	23.3	24.0	18.1	39.7	96.0	37.6
Dominican Republic	2 799.5	3 016.6	3 183.2	3 928.2	3 977.4	4 085.6	20.6	27.7	22.9	30.7	35.8	37.7
Venezuela	4 041.7	4 641.2	4 740.8	6 607.5	6 519.8	5 372.9	7.3	9.1	10.5	13.0	22.2	9.7
European Union	207 237.4	238 465.8	244 130.4	271 602.0	287 384.8	291 601.6	723.4	883.0	820.1	864.6	1 326.4	1 497.2
Belgium	10 944.2	12 459.2	12 519.9	13 430.8	13 918.1	12 384.9	52.7	62.1	78.4	74.4	71.2	46.3
France	13 622.3	14 240.5	14 427.8	15 981.6	17 728.0	18 838.5	108.1	96.4	71.7	79.9	127.2	110.5
Germany	19 236.9	22 376.4	23 473.9	24 466.9	26 641.9	26 788.9	112.5	119.2	100.0	124.2	452.5	421.4
Ireland	3 415.5	4 094.8	3 659.6	4 641.1	5 653.0	6 374.7	32.2	6.1	8.9	11.3	20.7	19.4
Italy	7 192.6	8 862.3	8 784.9	8 973.2	9 027.0	10 094.0	95.2	147.9	116.3	98.5	117.6	113.9
Luxembourg	228.4	374.4	242.0	711.8	606.1	983.5	0.2	0.3	1.6	9.0	1.2	3.3
Netherlands	13 590.8	16 558.5	16 614.5	19 821.6	19 003.8	19 412.1	87.3	127.3	165.5	151.1	178.2	165.8
Spain	4 624.8	5 529.4	5 486.1	5 543.8	5 464.6	6 131.6	69.0	48.4	46.4	41.5	55.0	58.0
United Kingdom	26 832.7	28 826.9	30 916.0	36 435.1	39 070.2	38 337.8	127.8	187.2	198.6	247.6	235.1	302.7
Switzerland	5 614.0	6 240.8	8 370.5	8 306.4	7 251.3	8 364.7	72.2	36.5	36.3	12.5	38.0	34.1
Former Soviet Republics	6 910.4	7 123.8	9 642.2	9 660.5	9 480.5	6 292.6	7.1	10.0	6.8	11.0	18.3	7.3
Asian 10	140 865.5	174 163.6	180 972.9	186 919.0	158 651.5	164 797.6	615.0	878.8	761.1	867.4	660.1	739.1
China	9 286.8	11 748.4	11 977.9	12 805.4	14 258.0	13 117.7	30.9	57.1	54.3	58.0	52.3	28.5
Hong Kong	11 445.3	14 220.4	13 955.8	15 114.8	12 923.5	12 647.1	31.7	52.9	42.3	51.3	32.3	32.5
Indonesia	2 811.0	3 356.0	3 965.0	4 531.7	2 290.9	1 938.9	8.3	11.3	11.5	24.2	8.7	7.2
Japan	53 480.8	64 297.9	67 535.5	65 672.6	57 887.9	57 483.5	342.2	491.6	382.5	322.8	331.7	268.1
Malaysia	6 964.8	8 818.4	8 521.3	10 827.8	8 952.9	9 079.0	8.5	8.9	17.3	20.9	9.6	12.6
Philippines	3 888.3	5 294.2	6 124.7	7 427.4	6 736.2	7 226.2	2.7	4.3	7.4	5.1	8.8	14.3
Singapore	13 021.6	15 318.2	16 685.5	17 727.4	15 673.5	16 246.4	26.3	62.4	57.4	62.5	40.1	28.4
South Korea	18 028.4	25 413.2	26 583.1	25 066.8	16 538.3	22 954.0	125.2	140.9	129.8	268.8	131.0	299.7
Taiwan	17 077.7	19 295.0	18 412.8	20 387.9	18 157.1	19 121.1	28.3	37.2	38.9	34.0	24.8	26.9
Thailand	4 861.0	6 401.9	7 211.4	7 357.2	5 233.4	4 983.5	10.9	12.3	19.5	19.9	20.8	20.9
India	2 296.3	3 295.7	3 318.1	3 615.6	3 544.7	3 707.4	5.2	15.4	20.3	10.1	13.2	12.9
Australia	9 780.7	10 788.5	11 991.7	12 040.8	11 929.3	11 810.7	124.1	60.6	56.8	71.0	66.1	95.7
Middle East	30 684.2	33 093.3	37 070.7	39 404.2	44 100.8	38 867.2	69.4	112.1	93.3	95.7	133.6	55.8
Israel	5 006.0	5 593.2	6 009.0	5 992.5	6 977.5	7 694.5	18.0	29.1	22.4	19.6	47.6	28.6
Saudi Arabia	6 010.5	6 085.0	7 295.3	8 450.8	10 524.9	7 901.7	21.0	24.8	21.6	28.5	23.2	14.0
Africa	8 332.7	10 288.7	11 627.2	11 695.5	12 563.2	10 526.8	16.4	24.0	29.6	44.6	40.8	51.9

Destination	Alaska						Arizona					
	1994	1995	1996	1997	1998	1999	1994	1995	1996	1997	1998	1999
ALL DESTINATIONS	887.7	891.5	850.4	969.0	758.5	950.0	6 970.6	8 402.8	9 937.8	13 556.7	10 753.0	10 123.0
Canada	120.6	195.7	181.2	305.4	229.4	279.7	644.2	839.0	970.2	1 072.2	1 058.6	1 159.1
Mexico	1.3	0.9	1.5	2.0	4.9	4.5	1 206.5	1 265.6	1 622.2	1 963.1	1 993.1	2 195.5
Central and South America and Caribbean	3.3	11.9	9.3	4.1	36.9	4.7	92.7	111.8	154.7	218.9	295.9	358.5
Argentina	0.2	5.0	0.6	0.7	0.2	0.9	13.5	10.9	12.6	19.7	23.2	15.8
Brazil	0.1	1.4	1.0	0.5	0.5	0.9	29.7	46.1	68.4	124.3	136.4	141.3
Chile	0.2	1.9	4.7	0.7	0.2	0.2	23.2	26.4	31.3	18.1	53.0	34.4
Colombia	0.9	0.3	0.7	0.2	1.7	0.3	3.9	7.0	3.3	5.5	3.6	3.1
Dominican Republic	0.2	0.1	. . .	0.2	0.1	0.5	1.4	0.5	1.8	1.3	0.7	3.6
Venezuela	0.2	0.8	1.2	0.6	2.7	0.2	4.9	3.3	7.0	6.4	9.2	14.2
European Union	121.2	113.0	134.5	237.6	174.7	197.2	1 879.5	2 443.8	2 448.6	3 686.4	2 542.4	2 064.4
Belgium	44.5	37.9	49.7	92.4	62.1	114.1	57.6	71.9	76.3	81.6	92.3	80.6
France	6.9	11.9	2.4	2.0	3.7	9.4	206.7	285.7	324.9	382.2	439.4	381.4
Germany	27.1	33.3	18.2	30.7	19.8	24.2	349.8	410.8	392.9	413.7	529.7	454.3
Ireland	0.1	0.1	0.1	. . .	0.4	1.1	90.1	132.3	105.0	96.7	136.9	76.9
Italy	0.6	2.8	7.6	7.0	11.7	3.5	58.4	88.7	79.8	94.0	79.1	67.2
Luxembourg	. . .	. . .	. . .	. . .	. . .	. . .	0.5	0.3	. . .	0.7	1.1	18.0
Netherlands	1.6	15.3	35.5	44.9	19.7	2.4	134.1	291.1	558.5	1 454.6	408.1	100.2
Spain	29.4	0.6	11.3	3.1	11.1	2.1	13.9	21.6	19.8	23.3	42.5	39.2
United Kingdom	9.4	6.6	7.3	55.4	44.5	37.4	906.0	1 085.1	827.2	1 061.5	720.2	752.5
Switzerland	16.3	8.5	0.8	0.8	0.8	0.8	24.2	30.9	32.7	108.5	135.3	111.3
Former Soviet Republics	56.9	20.9	18.7	9.4	11.4	5.2	7.9	8.9	7.3	166.1	90.5	7.8
Asian 10	558.0	521.6	492.3	392.6	293.6	425.7	2 859.9	3 437.2	4 451.6	5 975.8	4 129.7	3 810.9
China	28.9	20.5	38.3	11.6	5.4	4.0	63.5	92.5	121.2	123.7	243.0	167.7
Hong Kong	1.8	1.8	1.3	2.1	1.7	1.9	279.3	387.0	392.7	503.5	329.6	365.4
Indonesia	. . .	1.9	1.2	0.2	. . .	0.3	14.6	22.2	16.5	53.4	25.4	26.9
Japan	412.6	327.5	270.0	259.2	214.0	325.8	808.3	1 125.5	1 356.2	1 806.4	679.6	799.7
Malaysia	0.3	0.6	1.6	0.8	0.5	0.3	374.6	427.3	709.5	1 233.9	1 069.6	906.8
Philippines	0.2	4.1	0.2	0.1	0.1	0.2	94.4	101.8	140.3	310.8	407.8	258.0
Singapore	1.1	5.1	6.1	0.9	2.8	7.8	351.4	302.8	364.6	473.2	301.3	312.2
South Korea	75.6	93.7	127.6	97.4	60.6	72.5	206.2	230.2	287.8	296.9	352.9	334.6
Taiwan	34.5	61.4	40.7	18.4	7.7	12.5	604.3	648.2	895.4	1 062.8	624.5	490.3
Thailand	2.9	5.0	5.4	2.0	0.7	0.5	63.2	99.5	167.5	111.3	96.0	149.3
India	0.2	0.8	0.4	2.8	0.2	1.2	21.8	26.7	15.9	35.1	20.0	14.5
Australia	0.7	3.7	1.0	1.4	0.5	16.9	108.0	80.3	82.7	94.2	120.8	115.1
Middle East	3.2	3.1	2.0	7.9	2.5	1.7	53.9	62.5	72.0	85.2	102.2	122.5
Israel	. . .	0.5	0.8	1.3	1.1	0.6	29.4	33.6	45.7	38.6	49.1	72.2
Saudi Arabia	. . .	2.1	1.0	1.8	0.7	0.1	13.0	17.2	14.9	28.3	33.3	34.0
Africa	0.5	0.4	5.6	1.2	0.5	0.6	16.1	42.9	18.4	40.3	38.1	30.0

Table D-2. State Exports of Goods by Destination, 1994–1999—*Continued*

(Millions of dollars.)

Destination	Arkansas						California					
	1994	1995	1996	1997	1998	1999	1994	1995	1996	1997	1998	1999
ALL DESTINATIONS	1 470.9	1 794.4	1 997.2	2 211.6	1 934.1	1 828.9	78 190.4	92 038.4	98 634.0	103 802.5	98 809.0	102 863.8
Canada	521.1	574.1	614.9	820.4	687.5	751.3	8 054.5	9 537.7	10 577.1	11 492.4	12 644.1	13 245.9
Mexico	94.2	59.8	102.2	140.8	179.4	207.9	5 957.0	6 171.6	7 787.3	9 942.0	10 798.2	12 230.9
Central and South America and Caribbean	41.6	80.1	75.6	84.6	90.2	67.5	2 662.7	2 952.3	3 357.7	4 307.0	4 700.5	3 871.6
Argentina	4.9	12.1	9.4	9.6	10.9	4.4	399.9	340.8	390.3	616.3	672.2	464.4
Brazil	6.2	25.4	21.2	23.0	24.7	11.8	866.1	1 031.5	1 260.8	1 395.6	1 407.0	1 179.6
Chile	2.5	3.0	5.1	5.6	7.5	3.3	274.2	332.9	352.2	488.6	432.6	364.8
Colombia	2.7	7.3	5.3	4.2	4.4	2.9	172.2	170.3	193.1	228.8	267.6	217.4
Dominican Republic	1.1	1.2	0.8	4.6	4.7	5.7	113.6	98.8	116.3	161.7	180.1	187.6
Venezuela	1.1	1.7	2.5	5.1	4.9	1.9	140.3	146.9	187.3	264.6	284.9	222.7
European Union	185.8	258.3	268.6	302.9	321.1	274.6	17 147.1	18 897.0	18 687.0	19 709.4	21 428.1	21 887.4
Belgium	24.1	40.5	42.8	41.4	39.5	39.8	887.1	958.8	1 060.8	1 027.9	1 157.3	975.3
France	13.0	20.3	30.8	45.8	53.9	37.9	2 387.9	2 443.8	2 552.3	2 422.7	2 239.2	2 334.1
Germany	24.4	34.0	43.3	45.4	48.0	40.4	3 406.8	3 752.9	3 798.6	3 761.4	4 369.2	4 232.6
Ireland	7.6	5.8	6.5	8.6	8.2	4.2	637.3	702.1	647.8	735.2	946.2	1 153.2
Italy	4.8	19.9	20.7	27.7	25.2	17.5	1 302.1	1 377.5	1 079.5	1 140.6	1 205.1	1 419.4
Luxembourg	0.9	1.0	1.3	1.3	4.7	0.1	51.0	49.3	41.9	107.7	208.7	72.8
Netherlands	23.0	27.6	28.0	31.8	30.1	40.7	2 624.3	2 914.3	2 138.1	3 096.0	3 569.5	4 165.1
Spain	5.9	14.6	6.2	4.8	7.6	4.5	593.3	777.7	769.0	716.0	735.4	818.6
United Kingdom	64.4	76.2	74.5	84.8	88.5	72.1	3 835.4	4 507.1	4 779.0	5 109.8	5 361.8	5 195.5
Switzerland	16.0	21.9	25.0	14.0	17.9	19.5	787.0	812.2	881.0	1 205.5	1 061.0	874.7
Former Soviet Republics	140.0	283.5	401.4	300.3	189.0	49.9	280.4	328.8	380.7	426.8	479.2	491.9
Asian 10	361.1	381.8	391.0	417.2	317.6	357.3	37 949.6	47 427.4	51 192.1	49 784.3	40 385.4	43 550.1
China	5.6	13.7	30.2	21.4	10.3	14.8	1 507.6	1 349.3	1 933.0	2 274.3	2 472.2	2 678.6
Hong Kong	66.0	98.0	109.2	146.9	108.8	126.6	3 019.6	3 541.3	3 481.6	3 926.2	3 502.7	3 692.8
Indonesia	2.8	3.7	6.7	5.1	1.5	1.7	404.6	499.6	771.5	801.8	321.1	287.9
Japan	157.1	139.4	126.9	117.2	90.2	106.0	14 536.6	18 288.8	19 704.6	17 927.4	14 939.2	14 653.2
Malaysia	7.4	6.3	5.2	10.0	4.8	3.8	2 342.9	3 816.2	3 252.5	3 025.7	2 590.6	2 509.9
Philippines	24.6	16.7	17.1	25.9	26.3	30.1	1 213.1	1 616.0	1 800.8	1 739.2	1 404.7	1 632.8
Singapore	25.7	25.4	22.0	20.5	14.1	13.5	3 993.9	4 647.7	5 559.7	5 336.7	4 368.1	4 515.6
South Korea	33.8	37.2	41.4	33.1	24.4	32.1	4 557.5	6 406.6	7 398.8	6 494.2	4 005.1	5 890.7
Taiwan	32.4	32.8	24.2	30.3	34.1	25.4	4 923.9	5 503.5	5 396.5	6 184.8	5 577.9	6 528.7
Thailand	5.7	8.5	7.9	6.9	3.0	3.4	1 449.7	1 758.4	1 893.0	2 074.0	1 203.9	1 159.9
India	1.4	2.3	2.1	2.4	2.1	1.5	253.5	393.0	405.8	397.5	397.9	399.9
Australia	15.6	16.4	13.8	24.1	22.2	18.9	1 970.8	1 895.3	1 910.4	2 045.2	1 963.4	2 109.1
Middle East	45.4	37.7	35.3	44.0	37.4	29.1	1 083.0	1 292.3	1 372.2	1 827.2	2 481.6	2 044.2
Israel	2.9	1.8	1.9	3.5	3.5	2.3	385.2	499.8	587.3	609.9	592.8	823.9
Saudi Arabia	30.5	19.2	25.9	32.6	25.3	19.8	265.4	304.6	281.7	721.6	1 414.1	811.2
Africa	12.1	8.3	7.8	8.1	5.6	10.2	378.7	320.7	337.7	372.3	405.4	361.6

Destination	Colorado						Connecticut					
	1994	1995	1996	1997	1998	1999	1994	1995	1996	1997	1998	1999
ALL DESTINATIONS	7 802.1	9 688.8	10 064.9	11 329.2	10 733.3	11 171.2	10 272.0	12 942.1	13 052.5	12 897.1	12 139.7	11 335.1
Canada	524.2	602.8	609.7	671.6	729.3	920.7	1 481.1	1 660.2	1 603.9	1 847.7	1 872.8	1 973.5
Mexico	636.8	692.7	902.5	1 418.0	1 105.4	868.4	441.4	321.9	521.5	529.5	544.1	699.2
Central and South America and Caribbean	521.4	518.4	519.2	516.7	457.0	418.8	1 122.0	1 421.9	1 333.5	1 410.1	1 362.8	1 084.8
Argentina	100.3	70.7	60.5	73.4	73.2	66.2	105.9	94.1	84.3	108.4	111.0	67.0
Brazil	263.0	261.2	276.7	244.2	172.6	160.2	269.3	380.6	359.9	276.5	317.9	240.5
Chile	24.3	30.7	34.6	33.8	32.8	33.5	82.6	75.3	96.0	83.9	93.4	77.1
Colombia	27.2	30.4	31.0	35.0	33.9	30.9	92.1	147.5	145.2	124.7	119.5	54.4
Dominican Republic	3.8	6.4	2.7	2.7	3.7	3.3	67.4	84.5	94.7	152.4	156.4	172.6
Venezuela	22.7	27.9	33.3	34.7	51.3	39.1	97.8	111.6	95.9	84.6	86.9	59.6
European Union	3 263.6	3 741.7	3 674.0	3 693.1	3 905.4	3 999.1	2 584.7	3 413.6	3 416.0	3 636.7	3 708.2	3 253.8
Belgium	131.3	102.0	118.7	109.4	91.7	85.6	342.6	405.7	453.2	482.2	435.3	209.5
France	512.6	715.6	624.2	521.9	567.0	532.0	252.7	297.6	298.5	314.6	732.2	810.0
Germany	769.9	900.5	735.0	669.4	678.4	820.7	477.8	583.3	658.4	721.9	684.1	509.6
Ireland	51.8	108.2	84.2	191.4	315.3	410.0	127.0	178.2	122.0	107.0	157.2	156.0
Italy	364.7	380.2	557.0	694.2	586.6	538.4	224.0	242.5	242.1	199.6	150.9	165.7
Luxembourg	0.1	1.4	0.3	1.6	0.1	0.3	2.4	0.6	0.3	4.7	3.7	1.7
Netherlands	363.0	428.8	548.5	500.2	613.2	619.1	291.1	378.0	449.8	466.9	346.0	388.9
Spain	144.3	138.5	181.8	166.6	195.6	73.7	188.9	304.5	220.1	230.0	135.1	118.3
United Kingdom	780.3	811.4	671.6	689.3	714.5	757.2	500.4	604.1	693.7	813.0	773.7	649.2
Switzerland	50.1	71.9	84.8	82.5	119.9	145.4	142.2	142.6	204.4	139.5	172.7	143.7
Former Soviet Republics	29.8	29.3	52.0	162.4	66.9	15.3	65.7	39.2	52.8	33.9	30.1	12.8
Asian 10	2 299.4	3 400.4	3 574.9	4 098.4	3 746.0	4 296.0	3 077.2	4 034.5	4 004.2	3 740.2	3 242.1	2 798.9
China	22.8	29.4	52.2	74.3	166.6	177.8	261.9	475.8	416.5	291.2	301.6	134.5
Hong Kong	273.5	388.5	325.7	403.5	383.3	461.9	179.1	240.3	233.9	207.5	176.0	186.0
Indonesia	14.3	33.7	36.1	55.0	113.9	45.3	98.9	139.7	227.4	240.5	152.3	94.8
Japan	1 158.7	1 555.6	1 590.1	1 691.4	1 370.8	1 407.9	1 050.2	1 222.5	1 178.6	1 189.8	1 005.9	935.0
Malaysia	91.0	96.7	95.5	104.1	116.1	129.1	101.5	132.4	160.7	144.9	124.2	92.7
Philippines	32.5	33.2	53.5	112.7	90.0	174.7	49.1	93.4	104.9	74.6	59.3	50.4
Singapore	308.6	591.7	638.9	622.5	745.9	736.1	349.9	357.3	287.3	270.2	282.9	243.5
South Korea	174.8	250.4	342.2	609.0	365.1	570.2	577.5	763.3	879.2	812.9	581.4	628.3
Taiwan	130.4	205.7	197.2	214.2	217.7	357.2	333.6	429.2	331.2	364.4	418.8	308.9
Thailand	92.8	215.6	243.5	211.8	176.6	235.8	75.5	180.6	184.6	144.2	139.7	124.8
India	12.6	19.5	36.9	31.2	30.5	37.8	64.7	153.6	71.0	228.7	72.8	71.3
Australia	310.1	396.4	390.9	330.7	266.6	207.9	155.4	154.3	147.2	133.0	114.6	101.6
Middle East	52.5	73.6	73.0	53.1	82.7	57.5	184.0	281.6	297.7	260.6	229.5	281.2
Israel	19.7	38.7	35.4	24.5	35.1	33.7	80.9	94.6	123.6	87.9	87.9	133.6
Saudi Arabia	17.5	14.7	25.2	14.4	20.4	10.6	42.0	59.9	89.5	62.6	51.6	44.8
Africa	28.0	37.4	24.0	29.7	40.2	38.4	129.3	213.6	223.7	234.9	200.5	112.3

Table D-2. State Exports of Goods by Destination, 1994–1999—*Continued*

(Millions of dollars.)

Destination	Delaware						District of Columbia					
	1994	1995	1996	1997	1998	1999	1994	1995	1996	1997	1998	1999
ALL DESTINATIONS	3 758.1	4 396.8	4 584.5	5 103.9	4 968.6	4 856.8	5 150.7	5 323.5	5 084.8	4 881.0	4 392.4	4 344.5
Canada	692.5	717.5	739.7	788.3	937.9	989.5	120.9	81.8	102.1	142.1	157.8	113.5
Mexico	212.6	183.1	286.1	308.2	290.2	257.1	30.0	12.3	8.9	17.1	28.7	29.6
Central and South America and Caribbean	414.8	505.9	516.0	611.5	498.9	433.4	209.6	96.2	141.2	168.5	166.7	185.3
Argentina	59.9	83.8	102.8	119.8	91.2	75.6	14.5	4.3	3.3	12.1	10.1	11.5
Brazil	167.0	214.7	230.2	277.8	239.0	219.7	47.5	54.1	95.7	111.4	75.9	65.1
Chile	35.9	50.2	52.2	60.8	35.3	32.6	5.5	10.6	10.0	13.7	11.8	13.4
Colombia	43.3	48.4	50.9	53.0	41.1	36.2	115.1	1.7	10.1	1.8	5.2	2.6
Dominican Republic	4.6	6.8	1.4	2.4	2.6	3.6	1.0	3.1	2.7	1.5	1.2	2.7
Venezuela	25.1	34.8	24.1	32.2	28.1	19.3	3.5	0.5	2.0	1.5	23.7	2.6
European Union	1 154.7	1 465.6	1 455.8	1 536.6	1 704.4	1 588.1	937.8	1 288.2	929.3	1 177.8	1 148.6	1 302.3
Belgium	484.6	695.9	662.1	656.7	731.9	675.1	1.6	2.9	4.3	7.5	8.2	6.8
France	99.7	112.6	89.9	99.9	105.3	119.3	44.7	89.8	43.5	46.9	105.8	264.4
Germany	170.0	156.9	178.3	166.2	220.2	185.3	130.9	98.6	96.8	187.2	71.9	103.6
Ireland	9.4	28.2	30.9	31.7	35.7	44.4	1.5	2.5	1.7	2.0	3.5	3.5
Italy	25.0	44.8	36.1	39.9	44.2	42.5	34.9	55.7	35.3	36.2	27.3	26.2
Luxembourg	22.9	23.0	23.3	18.7	14.7	11.9	1.9	0.1	0.3	0.2	0.1	0.5
Netherlands	165.0	200.9	210.7	269.9	270.9	253.7	14.6	22.8	18.7	11.3	19.7	20.2
Spain	16.1	17.3	36.2	26.1	27.1	29.1	44.6	30.8	15.5	32.1	14.6	33.1
United Kingdom	140.4	160.1	166.5	195.6	229.2	198.2	513.6	390.5	546.3	500.1	579.5	575.0
Switzerland	7.1	10.5	11.5	15.7	30.6	26.1	39.7	75.4	404.4	214.4	43.1	41.1
Former Soviet Republics	14.9	14.0	22.2	24.5	8.5	8.3	99.9	82.2	56.8	57.7	81.9	93.4
Asian 10	1 004.5	1 173.7	1 263.7	1 514.1	1 198.6	1 274.6	1 037.1	1 144.6	873.0	1 194.8	920.5	1 128.7
China	54.2	64.2	68.4	73.6	69.0	102.9	4.8	4.0	6.0	9.0	9.5	8.1
Hong Kong	64.9	79.4	99.7	87.3	75.1	88.0	5.3	17.3	16.3	11.8	8.4	7.4
Indonesia	50.5	68.1	69.0	79.2	43.0	43.4	6.4	19.7	18.5	29.0	4.8	11.3
Japan	370.2	433.0	441.5	556.0	531.5	444.0	127.9	213.9	86.7	116.4	294.0	465.4
Malaysia	24.2	29.6	31.2	90.5	15.2	11.3	24.1	20.4	32.6	64.3	25.6	27.2
Philippines	9.2	9.1	9.2	11.2	8.4	10.3	27.2	57.2	39.2	19.3	8.3	8.6
Singapore	74.6	88.8	105.1	147.5	135.4	157.9	29.9	35.6	34.6	41.4	37.1	45.8
South Korea	155.9	172.5	208.0	190.2	114.8	174.4	39.9	19.2	34.8	37.1	17.0	19.4
Taiwan	149.0	170.4	167.9	205.1	166.5	200.5	676.2	649.7	491.3	602.8	447.9	515.9
Thailand	51.8	58.6	63.7	73.4	39.6	41.8	95.4	107.5	113.0	263.7	67.8	19.6
India	23.4	40.5	39.6	45.4	42.2	42.9	77.7	121.7	88.8	77.4	38.7	31.0
Australia	97.5	100.4	84.0	82.8	97.8	80.9	215.9	253.9	187.0	260.7	441.1	473.0
Middle East	41.5	55.1	46.6	55.3	55.0	51.1	1 467.1	1 615.2	1 633.1	885.4	646.3	357.7
Israel	14.2	21.0	19.4	24.1	28.9	26.4	47.3	3.8	6.1	5.5	15.9	9.9
Saudi Arabia	18.6	21.7	14.6	24.6	20.3	12.3	1 318.0	1 271.0	904.1	514.7	498.3	237.0
Africa	36.2	45.7	47.2	53.2	54.1	37.3	52.1	91.1	117.8	57.4	97.8	63.3

Destination	Florida						Georgia					
	1994	1995	1996	1997	1998	1999	1994	1995	1996	1997	1998	1999
ALL DESTINATIONS	16 559.2	18 564.4	19 618.2	22 888.6	23 172.6	22 544.2	7 108.1	8 626.8	8 618.0	9 810.0	11 212.1	11 060.6
Canada	1 504.8	1 608.2	1 631.6	1 928.4	2 057.7	2 094.9	1 646.3	1 820.7	1 896.9	1 999.7	2 115.9	2 221.4
Mexico	993.6	536.2	737.0	1 220.8	1 271.5	1 426.8	469.5	403.8	516.9	685.7	1 135.7	1 327.6
Central and South America and Caribbean	9 041.1	10 070.1	10 742.6	12 819.2	12 851.4	11 661.5	1 203.2	1 490.0	1 418.1	1 575.5	1 957.9	1 481.5
Argentina	865.3	695.9	794.6	889.5	907.7	734.7	198.3	152.0	130.2	152.9	196.2	119.2
Brazil	1 115.9	1 687.6	2 092.2	2 586.5	2 272.2	2 099.8	130.0	316.9	277.0	339.8	472.3	281.9
Chile	423.9	437.5	483.5	462.3	402.7	463.2	69.7	95.2	123.6	73.1	72.7	68.9
Colombia	1 072.6	1 202.7	1 185.0	1 321.5	1 105.2	847.3	82.9	96.3	97.8	122.0	167.4	117.7
Dominican Republic	684.4	724.5	768.2	989.2	943.4	1 034.3	124.7	112.2	102.5	130.8	140.2	120.8
Venezuela	786.0	887.0	903.0	1 339.4	1 532.1	1 174.6	61.8	75.3	58.9	78.5	115.8	74.2
European Union	2 033.6	2 612.9	2 909.9	2 772.9	2 886.1	3 184.2	1 578.2	2 010.8	1 818.5	2 351.4	3 048.7	2 898.6
Belgium	116.6	125.0	106.3	147.4	161.5	140.6	122.1	136.4	115.7	241.0	477.3	279.3
France	311.1	395.4	494.2	397.5	348.3	483.0	172.8	243.4	246.2	279.6	291.3	276.1
Germany	309.9	399.4	408.1	383.4	450.9	512.4	259.3	298.9	311.5	340.0	338.3	403.8
Ireland	50.0	77.5	67.1	88.4	100.6	133.8	24.3	32.0	33.0	92.5	64.8	54.1
Italy	138.6	191.8	317.2	207.6	201.6	238.2	130.3	211.1	137.3	226.8	166.4	185.3
Luxembourg	2.4	2.3	2.2	3.2	12.4	8.5	8.1	5.8	2.9	1.4	5.9	6.5
Netherlands	247.9	332.6	378.7	399.6	416.2	409.2	241.1	282.2	259.5	380.2	367.3	422.8
Spain	128.9	259.5	245.7	193.8	181.3	188.8	78.0	96.1	96.3	106.6	105.2	127.0
United Kingdom	489.9	560.1	601.3	687.1	742.7	821.7	385.8	459.8	426.6	489.3	1 005.7	916.8
Switzerland	75.8	104.2	105.3	94.4	123.8	127.8	61.7	55.4	55.6	57.5	87.8	42.8
Former Soviet Republics	36.3	59.8	40.5	68.9	37.5	32.1	122.0	130.5	293.0	160.0	128.1	79.8
Asian 10	1 862.9	2 288.8	2 082.8	2 474.2	2 192.3	2 471.5	1 287.8	1 874.8	1 732.9	1 976.8	1 690.3	1 795.7
China	533.4	565.9	358.6	640.1	494.7	502.5	105.6	136.1	136.5	186.9	148.5	173.3
Hong Kong	173.3	228.7	188.5	193.0	158.3	188.8	176.4	242.4	267.5	301.5	224.3	229.4
Indonesia	27.8	36.3	52.9	26.6	11.3	17.0	71.5	41.2	78.3	79.9	45.8	49.2
Japan	487.4	584.1	554.2	588.2	541.7	553.2	401.8	589.9	567.6	622.3	589.6	708.2
Malaysia	88.9	75.3	108.4	114.1	135.4	155.8	53.1	42.2	49.5	58.3	57.4	62.2
Philippines	36.9	26.8	52.7	67.4	44.1	56.5	29.8	36.6	52.5	48.2	47.6	56.0
Singapore	140.1	218.5	236.9	319.9	449.1	474.8	92.8	134.3	158.2	213.3	134.2	172.6
South Korea	179.2	357.8	351.6	341.3	216.6	266.4	174.1	429.1	236.5	253.5	233.4	132.0
Taiwan	153.4	155.3	122.2	131.2	96.9	167.0	138.9	138.8	120.9	136.4	149.5	163.4
Thailand	42.6	40.1	56.7	52.4	44.2	89.5	43.8	84.3	65.4	76.4	59.9	49.5
India	56.0	152.1	66.6	163.5	185.1	275.1	63.7	92.6	84.4	103.0	101.4	92.8
Australia	227.2	238.6	332.9	304.3	309.4	275.7	101.8	142.4	176.4	225.3	277.1	484.5
Middle East	275.9	304.1	334.2	404.3	424.2	391.0	262.1	245.9	238.6	255.6	286.6	311.1
Israel	96.7	120.8	153.5	112.8	185.3	168.3	26.8	41.7	36.0	51.1	88.8	118.4
Saudi Arabia	100.2	95.8	92.9	173.4	135.0	132.9	129.0	114.8	108.8	101.6	101.4	83.7
Africa	136.8	168.6	138.6	149.6	160.7	123.8	106.9	116.4	142.5	151.5	135.8	113.6

Table D-2. State Exports of Goods by Destination, 1994–1999—*Continued*

(Millions of dollars.)

Destination	Hawaii						Idaho					
	1994	1995	1996	1997	1998	1999	1994	1995	1996	1997	1998	1999
ALL DESTINATIONS	237.4	255.7	295.2	303.2	211.4	243.5	1 530.5	1 892.6	1 610.1	1 716.1	1 460.0	2 116.6
Canada	13.4	53.1	69.8	33.3	16.8	21.5	208.7	292.3	276.5	277.9	280.5	280.9
Mexico	6.0	0.3	0.7	1.0	1.9	0.8	33.7	29.1	37.4	44.2	56.2	64.4
Central and South America and Caribbean	0.7	0.8	1.2	1.1	2.0	1.6	18.7	24.3	18.7	27.0	24.7	43.0
Argentina	...	...	...	...	...	...	6.3	3.5	3.4	6.1	4.6	9.5
Brazil	...	0.1	0.1	0.2	0.1	0.4	2.9	2.5	2.2	2.3	1.9	4.9
Chile	...	...	...	0.1	0.1	0.6	0.8	1.2	3.9	3.7	4.2	2.9
Colombia	...	...	...	0.1	0.1	0.1	1.0	0.6	0.7	1.1	1.8	1.0
Dominican Republic	...	...	...	...	...	...	0.1	0.1	0.1	0.7	0.7	1.6
Venezuela	...	...	0.5	...	...	...	0.6	0.5	0.6	1.8	1.7	1.3
European Union	6.5	7.8	9.4	7.1	10.5	11.8	428.5	528.8	384.9	460.9	430.1	571.3
Belgium	...	...	0.1	0.1	0.1	0.3	12.2	5.8	3.2	2.1	9.7	40.2
France	1.6	1.9	1.5	1.3	1.1	1.5	49.2	66.7	26.2	17.4	20.6	41.4
Germany	2.3	2.4	2.5	1.4	3.7	3.1	82.4	83.0	92.0	132.2	89.6	82.5
Ireland	...	...	...	0.2	...	...	21.2	47.3	14.7	13.9	8.1	8.9
Italy	0.2	0.1	0.3	0.7	0.2	0.6	26.7	38.9	37.8	23.4	34.4	27.9
Luxembourg	...	...	...	...	...	...	...	...	0.1	...	...	...
Netherlands	0.8	1.1	1.5	0.4	0.9	1.0	16.0	57.1	71.5	73.1	42.4	17.3
Spain	0.2	0.1	0.1	0.1	0.2	0.1	5.6	6.6	6.0	7.6	9.3	10.4
United Kingdom	0.9	1.1	2.9	2.0	2.3	3.9	186.6	194.2	116.4	169.8	189.6	294.9
Switzerland	1.0	1.3	1.0	1.2	4.9	0.6	5.8	6.3	5.9	23.5	8.7	9.3
Former Soviet Republics	...	...	0.1	0.3	0.3	1.0	2.1	0.7	3.9	20.8	4.9	13.3
Asian 10	180.0	170.8	190.8	217.2	152.3	170.3	768.1	922.6	805.5	796.5	592.2	1 022.3
China	4.9	0.6	0.8	6.2	1.2	1.4	5.9	22.3	16.0	17.4	25.1	28.0
Hong Kong	13.2	5.4	4.5	8.1	6.2	4.5	29.6	41.3	35.8	72.5	36.2	78.7
Indonesia	0.5	0.4	0.6	3.9	0.5	0.8	6.8	5.3	23.8	10.8	3.8	2.1
Japan	120.1	126.7	161.2	173.0	126.9	136.7	352.8	348.0	309.4	317.1	233.5	229.7
Malaysia	0.2	0.7	0.6	0.3	0.1	0.2	17.8	40.7	41.7	51.9	58.1	201.7
Philippines	2.3	1.8	3.9	1.4	1.1	5.3	57.8	75.9	120.3	73.7	33.1	20.5
Singapore	2.1	5.6	5.1	11.9	6.6	7.6	149.5	208.6	154.8	120.2	99.0	248.9
South Korea	26.2	24.8	9.3	9.7	5.5	10.7	29.2	35.5	36.8	32.5	21.5	41.9
Taiwan	9.6	3.8	4.2	2.1	3.6	2.4	110.6	132.0	60.4	97.2	77.5	161.8
Thailand	0.9	1.0	0.6	0.6	0.6	0.8	8.0	13.1	6.7	3.1	4.3	8.9
India	...	...	...	0.1	...	...	0.7	2.0	1.1	0.6	2.6	5.2
Australia	14.0	5.4	5.1	3.3	3.3	6.0	17.8	18.9	11.0	20.1	16.7	18.5
Middle East	0.2	0.6	0.3	3.2	1.2	1.1	14.7	19.8	25.7	20.2	19.1	35.4
Israel	0.1	0.5	0.1	0.3	0.8	0.8	13.3	14.8	13.5	8.5	9.5	12.5
Saudi Arabia	0.1	...	0.1	0.3	0.2	0.1	0.5	1.5	5.8	3.9	3.2	2.7
Africa	0.6	0.1	0.1	0.2	0.6	0.5	4.5	7.1	3.0	4.3	5.5	8.5

Destination	Illinois						Indiana					
	1994	1995	1996	1997	1998	1999	1994	1995	1996	1997	1998	1999
ALL DESTINATIONS	24 534.2	30 478.2	32 224.9	34 225.0	33 838.1	30 856.5	9 534.0	11 052.0	12 119.0	13 097.3	13 949.1	14 583.9
Canada	5 763.1	6 452.6	6 767.3	8 044.2	7 942.8	7 885.6	4 593.6	4 594.8	4 630.3	5 060.3	5 671.6	6 391.4
Mexico	1 825.4	1 366.1	1 844.7	2 189.7	2 797.9	2 886.2	1 492.6	1 955.7	2 529.3	2 573.3	3 046.4	3 225.7
Central and South America and Caribbean	2 044.2	2 186.9	2 368.8	3 012.3	3 067.7	2 567.3	315.9	486.2	511.1	716.0	778.7	788.1
Argentina	265.3	259.2	293.5	459.1	390.4	322.0	45.2	59.5	65.4	133.1	68.0	74.3
Brazil	654.5	690.2	763.5	1 070.5	1 109.6	868.5	103.5	188.8	227.0	353.0	479.8	524.9
Chile	219.2	256.5	297.8	235.1	210.3	169.4	18.5	36.7	38.1	41.0	28.2	22.7
Colombia	195.1	195.4	196.9	239.0	237.6	184.0	27.2	63.8	50.2	55.7	64.5	32.5
Dominican Republic	76.8	94.5	101.5	106.2	116.6	136.5	11.0	5.6	6.1	7.3	7.5	10.0
Venezuela	182.5	157.9	181.4	335.5	310.1	251.7	39.5	33.9	36.6	28.5	25.6	17.0
European Union	5 970.4	7 419.0	8 062.6	8 713.5	8 715.4	8 112.0	1 555.7	1 901.8	2 149.5	2 377.7	2 405.5	2 285.8
Belgium	928.7	1 077.1	1 150.4	1 260.6	1 395.1	1 358.3	84.8	116.5	96.1	77.1	84.7	66.3
France	646.1	791.7	811.8	916.1	834.1	717.7	170.1	191.2	298.8	389.2	444.0	538.3
Germany	1 224.9	1 491.2	1 597.7	1 643.5	1 769.7	1 587.1	294.1	290.3	288.9	337.3	318.2	295.5
Ireland	84.0	120.6	136.6	275.9	386.5	324.9	46.7	54.9	71.9	109.7	147.0	93.9
Italy	334.6	501.2	539.3	524.3	481.4	510.4	103.8	116.8	147.2	132.1	144.1	160.6
Luxembourg	1.4	1.5	1.6	2.7	4.8	2.9	2.9	2.2	2.1	3.0	4.8	9.4
Netherlands	788.6	915.8	1 171.3	1 369.3	1 030.2	980.6	175.2	250.4	301.9	364.8	279.1	208.8
Spain	270.3	479.8	513.6	399.4	394.8	316.5	46.8	62.6	56.7	49.8	54.8	55.7
United Kingdom	1 276.0	1 572.1	1 641.8	1 830.8	1 826.2	1 689.8	495.7	627.5	644.0	704.8	713.1	673.6
Switzerland	105.7	119.6	134.4	119.2	130.8	133.1	28.3	35.8	46.6	42.5	52.7	54.3
Former Soviet Republics	207.8	129.2	185.3	281.6	339.2	273.8	8.2	10.5	9.7	10.9	15.9	9.3
Asian 10	5 894.1	8 803.2	8 626.1	7 714.3	6 721.0	5 647.8	1 182.1	1 528.6	1 691.4	1 757.0	1 439.0	1 333.5
China	1 001.6	1 219.9	1 040.4	1 005.0	900.9	761.1	40.6	81.4	154.6	132.1	90.4	94.1
Hong Kong	378.5	763.0	629.9	985.4	572.0	382.5	81.8	100.9	105.4	131.6	112.8	92.2
Indonesia	127.3	258.1	339.4	317.7	85.4	58.7	8.9	14.5	14.9	18.0	8.8	10.4
Japan	2 121.5	2 940.1	3 024.6	2 437.4	2 953.2	2 304.5	571.0	733.6	747.2	729.9	696.7	687.8
Malaysia	152.3	365.0	334.2	261.8	187.1	179.9	46.5	40.5	45.5	63.3	34.0	27.4
Philippines	139.7	335.8	297.7	324.9	149.8	129.1	29.9	66.4	33.7	50.3	38.9	27.1
Singapore	356.3	649.7	744.7	720.6	516.3	581.7	126.5	149.8	188.1	185.2	149.8	134.8
South Korea	698.1	1 266.2	1 301.0	892.6	626.8	690.0	158.7	183.0	199.3	227.1	132.9	132.9
Taiwan	637.8	592.1	512.2	496.1	516.9	443.1	79.0	116.1	140.9	134.4	129.2	101.7
Thailand	281.1	413.4	401.9	272.8	212.6	117.2	39.3	42.5	61.7	85.2	50.7	25.2
India	142.8	222.8	166.8	184.0	310.1	371.9	18.7	35.6	46.7	50.7	34.6	40.7
Australia	786.3	1 131.2	1 243.1	1 196.2	1 149.4	1 017.7	152.2	168.3	201.1	201.0	179.8	145.8
Middle East	695.4	903.9	942.2	969.8	1 011.2	821.1	82.0	120.3	128.6	105.4	99.7	112.0
Israel	220.9	371.0	436.1	372.4	427.8	419.2	22.6	31.1	35.6	33.0	30.3	33.9
Saudi Arabia	213.2	200.7	251.4	349.1	314.3	197.3	33.7	35.1	32.9	41.0	38.5	28.8
Africa	299.1	439.3	583.7	570.1	575.0	324.2	24.9	39.7	39.5	43.4	41.4	35.3

Table D-2. State Exports of Goods by Destination, 1994–1999—*Continued*

(Millions of dollars.)

Destination	Iowa						Kansas					
	1994	1995	1996	1997	1998	1999	1994	1995	1996	1997	1998	1999
ALL DESTINATIONS	2 331.4	2 577.8	2 695.1	3 116.7	3 411.7	2 985.2	3 498.3	4 461.5	4 971.3	5 133.2	4 402.8	4 856.3
Canada	1 152.8	1 220.5	1 277.2	1 569.1	1 742.2	1 439.2	571.2	687.0	696.0	834.4	878.9	847.5
Mexico	99.2	81.9	110.3	167.7	158.2	153.0	366.0	348.8	643.1	449.2	484.9	489.6
Central and South America and Caribbean	83.3	108.0	140.5	182.8	169.0	132.8	407.3	580.5	699.7	931.2	597.6	583.5
Argentina	14.1	17.8	24.9	37.6	29.9	22.4	33.3	45.5	39.2	97.3	30.2	17.7
Brazil	14.7	25.4	31.5	46.3	44.5	28.7	40.8	50.5	58.0	126.1	73.7	93.8
Chile	15.0	16.3	23.5	27.7	20.3	10.5	18.5	68.3	47.0	17.9	19.1	18.9
Colombia	5.9	7.9	14.0	16.7	14.4	10.2	78.6	106.7	147.3	167.7	128.4	134.2
Dominican Republic	1.9	2.5	2.8	3.4	3.3	4.6	42.4	57.3	79.5	67.8	51.7	46.9
Venezuela	6.1	8.0	7.9	11.3	13.6	14.5	71.4	104.7	120.7	216.0	141.7	106.9
European Union	430.0	483.4	507.3	524.9	718.6	641.5	488.4	483.8	636.9	744.6	693.1	914.4
Belgium	24.5	24.5	21.7	17.6	18.7	17.7	57.5	64.5	63.5	75.6	90.0	77.9
France	54.7	46.6	63.1	81.0	119.1	109.6	52.3	64.3	108.1	98.2	98.1	124.8
Germany	52.6	71.4	84.1	86.2	117.6	136.9	121.5	98.0	94.9	114.8	125.0	178.5
Ireland	12.2	10.4	10.3	9.3	16.6	15.6	2.6	12.9	11.5	13.7	20.9	24.1
Italy	56.6	64.9	73.7	59.0	96.4	58.1	42.4	35.2	44.7	38.3	37.3	47.6
Luxembourg	0.4	0.9	0.8	0.2	0.1	1.0	0.2	0.5	6.1	1.7	1.9	1.0
Netherlands	82.8	108.0	92.0	84.5	116.8	71.0	36.1	32.6	73.1	102.0	52.7	83.8
Spain	17.7	27.4	18.4	21.2	32.5	20.0	27.4	37.4	23.1	33.0	19.9	33.3
United Kingdom	85.0	87.9	93.2	114.1	150.3	156.2	92.7	90.5	129.6	173.4	189.3	273.4
Switzerland	5.1	14.7	6.2	7.4	9.6	13.9	27.4	38.4	34.6	49.6	29.8	48.7
Former Soviet Republics	40.1	12.8	22.5	13.6	29.9	7.4	8.4	12.3	5.7	12.4	18.1	5.9
Asian 10	394.7	486.5	465.6	464.2	401.2	402.2	1 125.3	1 827.4	1 761.2	1 501.7	1 219.5	1 485.1
China	18.4	27.3	22.6	25.1	31.9	30.9	45.7	49.6	30.7	62.6	39.2	25.3
Hong Kong	22.4	31.3	33.5	27.3	24.8	27.2	15.5	26.6	70.6	29.3	27.5	32.0
Indonesia	12.6	12.5	10.7	12.9	3.8	5.1	15.4	9.6	16.0	20.0	22.3	43.2
Japan	111.1	145.1	159.3	161.5	176.7	162.0	697.4	1 057.3	1 075.0	921.8	830.3	947.7
Malaysia	12.2	17.2	15.4	19.7	11.8	17.7	41.2	72.9	57.8	28.2	4.8	5.9
Philippines	9.1	16.2	16.4	15.1	11.8	10.8	6.3	15.7	18.3	35.7	22.9	9.5
Singapore	50.1	65.8	61.6	55.0	56.8	51.5	25.3	24.0	51.2	33.5	24.5	42.4
South Korea	83.0	87.3	82.8	90.8	46.9	54.2	107.7	341.5	239.3	179.1	127.3	186.5
Taiwan	56.9	61.3	41.3	35.1	26.4	28.7	159.5	216.3	171.6	153.3	85.9	182.3
Thailand	19.0	22.5	22.0	21.7	10.3	14.2	11.4	14.1	30.7	38.1	34.8	10.4
India	2.1	12.8	5.5	7.4	7.3	5.8	24.1	45.8	14.5	46.6	45.4	12.0
Australia	44.0	60.1	54.3	65.2	50.5	74.4	61.6	63.5	170.4	98.7	53.3	89.4
Middle East	32.4	28.4	35.5	36.6	42.4	34.6	72.3	96.2	57.5	117.5	101.4	100.1
Israel	10.5	10.4	12.8	9.5	15.7	10.9	8.5	7.5	24.6	9.1	12.6	13.5
Saudi Arabia	9.5	8.3	11.6	10.9	11.3	11.6	20.3	18.1	14.5	64.8	51.7	39.0
Africa	17.0	25.6	16.4	21.2	14.9	13.4	83.6	81.7	107.9	104.8	85.2	140.3

Destination	Kentucky						Louisiana					
	1994	1995	1996	1997	1998	1999	1994	1995	1996	1997	1998	1999
ALL DESTINATIONS	4 188.2	5 030.1	5 824.2	6 904.1	7 440.0	8 016.2	3 576.9	4 580.7	4 730.8	4 373.5	4 391.9	3 947.3
Canada	1 571.1	1 804.7	1 905.3	2 368.9	2 325.0	2 801.4	449.1	557.4	542.9	663.1	735.9	745.0
Mexico	232.1	188.0	280.1	345.1	450.7	566.6	108.9	79.8	145.5	132.6	196.1	246.2
Central and South America and Caribbean	156.5	304.0	446.6	573.0	849.1	819.3	391.8	537.4	517.6	597.1	799.9	463.6
Argentina	26.2	24.1	29.5	35.2	39.1	35.9	28.6	21.3	17.6	34.4	45.2	29.0
Brazil	15.8	39.7	46.6	69.2	83.8	76.6	30.8	54.5	56.1	70.2	60.2	59.0
Chile	12.4	17.4	23.3	24.1	21.0	17.5	12.9	17.3	41.1	41.6	20.9	10.8
Colombia	12.1	20.7	19.3	29.1	21.7	24.2	24.8	59.8	37.9	37.9	18.4	14.9
Dominican Republic	6.2	35.1	68.0	92.8	154.4	146.9	16.6	15.5	11.9	18.9	12.9	29.3
Venezuela	8.7	21.4	12.5	27.3	20.8	25.6	70.0	62.9	72.6	87.0	93.8	60.4
European Union	718.4	790.2	1 099.0	1 202.7	1 455.1	1 547.5	785.6	1 072.2	976.6	841.6	711.3	525.3
Belgium	123.0	58.4	56.2	51.2	121.8	131.0	206.8	241.0	237.1	187.6	124.7	96.3
France	166.8	151.6	258.9	366.5	359.4	338.9	82.4	110.9	60.2	65.1	44.1	28.2
Germany	136.6	228.6	229.6	232.7	327.1	351.6	70.4	63.6	122.1	90.1	71.3	67.4
Ireland	22.1	17.6	23.1	25.6	35.5	60.5	24.6	24.9	16.3	6.9	5.2	3.7
Italy	36.8	34.4	39.9	41.7	52.0	56.7	31.2	52.5	40.3	53.3	44.8	29.2
Luxembourg	. . .	0.1	0.1	. . .	. . .	0.1	. . .	0.5	0.3	0.2	. . .	0.9
Netherlands	56.7	60.3	114.3	132.6	121.2	117.2	155.8	288.6	226.8	180.0	141.8	102.3
Spain	33.9	35.9	51.3	53.3	48.1	62.9	86.8	111.6	126.0	105.6	125.5	72.3
United Kingdom	114.7	167.2	283.9	255.2	309.0	349.7	73.0	113.6	97.2	97.9	108.8	96.0
Switzerland	8.8	9.7	7.2	18.6	18.1	38.7	10.8	9.4	9.4	3.6	5.0	8.9
Former Soviet Republics	3.9	8.1	19.1	28.2	86.5	33.8	34.3	30.7	27.9	22.9	35.3	15.6
Asian 10	1 109.8	1 478.6	1 605.4	1 816.8	1 719.0	1 676.4	1 272.7	1 701.7	1 978.3	1 568.4	1 398.9	1 360.7
China	14.6	17.7	30.2	36.4	28.4	34.9	51.4	236.2	131.6	92.3	174.0	91.7
Hong Kong	64.6	64.1	66.6	41.8	37.3	39.8	21.0	31.0	26.4	27.7	27.1	19.8
Indonesia	4.7	11.1	9.4	14.3	6.5	4.8	213.5	92.3	68.6	39.7	18.9	24.3
Japan	752.3	1 041.8	1 143.0	1 385.0	1 436.1	1 372.2	800.5	879.8	1 111.3	974.2	792.9	746.1
Malaysia	12.3	20.4	23.2	43.1	29.6	25.2	9.7	42.1	92.4	55.9	13.1	21.7
Philippines	46.9	49.6	33.0	22.8	15.2	27.5	6.5	6.4	9.2	10.6	3.9	24.0
Singapore	90.3	88.6	96.0	91.6	57.6	35.9	47.9	37.8	51.8	45.6	48.8	43.9
South Korea	72.2	107.0	116.1	99.6	45.1	72.7	61.1	98.9	144.8	127.0	126.0	155.9
Taiwan	38.6	53.6	66.5	58.2	40.7	42.7	50.2	247.3	324.3	173.4	172.4	189.3
Thailand	13.2	24.7	21.5	24.1	22.6	20.7	10.9	30.0	17.8	21.9	21.9	44.0
India	3.8	9.8	12.1	22.1	19.6	26.5	10.0	25.0	21.8	20.0	13.6	12.8
Australia	78.1	90.8	117.9	140.0	131.6	150.5	55.4	57.9	69.5	72.8	43.5	50.8
Middle East	186.4	191.3	158.0	157.5	167.5	120.8	211.5	247.4	207.4	227.6	218.3	210.5
Israel	31.1	38.7	36.7	33.0	41.2	29.6	46.6	60.3	38.0	25.6	31.4	35.6
Saudi Arabia	48.7	40.0	29.0	40.1	31.6	25.8	73.6	91.1	115.7	138.2	114.6	111.0
Africa	16.4	18.7	17.3	22.4	26.5	24.0	96.9	78.7	109.7	97.0	81.9	96.3

Table D-2. State Exports of Goods by Destination, 1994–1999—*Continued*

(Millions of dollars.)

Destination	Maine						Maryland					
	1994	1995	1996	1997	1998	1999	1994	1995	1996	1997	1998	1999
ALL DESTINATIONS	1 138.9	1 318.2	1 248.8	1 590.2	1 664.3	1 785.2	2 848.5	3 439.0	3 509.9	3 861.0	4 013.7	4 068.3
Canada	406.2	469.8	489.0	557.4	528.3	639.7	621.4	551.9	553.3	653.2	690.4	847.6
Mexico	36.0	10.7	12.3	18.4	17.2	30.4	100.4	94.5	174.9	199.2	337.2	330.2
Central and South America and Caribbean	39.2	36.7	40.6	52.0	59.3	58.7	250.8	288.8	262.4	270.1	301.9	191.3
Argentina	1.5	1.3	1.2	7.6	4.4	2.1	42.4	43.3	33.7	36.3	39.3	30.2
Brazil	3.5	6.1	6.0	5.5	12.9	15.7	33.4	73.2	62.3	51.3	56.7	46.4
Chile	3.1	1.4	3.0	1.7	2.4	1.5	29.9	47.5	54.4	48.4	33.7	17.3
Colombia	2.3	1.0	1.3	2.8	5.1	3.1	23.0	24.3	25.1	35.5	63.6	15.8
Dominican Republic	15.6	11.3	13.1	13.3	14.1	22.4	35.8	4.2	7.5	8.0	9.2	5.0
Venezuela	2.0	3.0	1.8	5.7	6.1	3.6	25.8	9.2	7.7	9.9	14.1	13.2
European Union	204.5	228.3	208.0	220.8	212.1	196.6	886.9	1 167.7	1 076.3	1 077.5	1 200.0	1 274.5
Belgium	30.5	10.4	8.4	8.7	9.6	20.2	196.6	166.4	167.1	197.7	237.8	291.1
France	36.9	56.5	61.3	46.1	35.5	25.3	89.4	107.8	84.2	108.8	114.1	118.4
Germany	27.6	30.9	34.0	28.4	47.3	34.5	87.9	121.7	138.5	165.3	139.4	196.9
Ireland	0.9	1.2	2.4	7.7	5.1	9.7	14.0	16.5	15.8	11.0	14.1	18.4
Italy	15.1	13.5	18.1	12.6	16.0	14.9	58.4	64.8	71.6	76.6	92.7	72.3
Luxembourg	. . .	. . .	. . .	0.2	. . .	0.2	2.6	1.8	0.2	1.9	1.7	2.4
Netherlands	19.1	16.7	11.8	11.2	18.9	28.5	167.9	226.6	201.8	128.3	174.4	196.6
Spain	5.5	5.9	8.3	17.7	5.5	2.6	30.3	68.4	31.2	29.4	23.0	29.9
United Kingdom	43.8	62.4	44.5	59.1	52.1	47.3	189.9	329.9	308.6	286.7	313.5	274.1
Switzerland	1.8	3.6	3.4	5.2	5.6	3.3	11.2	14.8	12.3	9.0	38.8	68.6
Former Soviet Republics	2.8	1.5	1.7	0.9	1.1	0.7	34.1	60.1	130.7	157.9	66.9	31.7
Asian 10	364.7	489.8	400.5	668.6	783.6	794.2	448.6	608.8	663.8	766.2	675.6	698.7
China	3.0	7.8	6.2	17.2	12.9	13.3	39.6	68.1	99.6	84.9	75.3	127.9
Hong Kong	50.1	48.6	43.7	44.4	30.0	34.0	50.4	56.6	54.1	73.0	90.1	93.8
Indonesia	6.5	7.4	4.1	4.5	5.6	10.0	8.8	63.7	75.1	80.2	20.4	7.5
Japan	109.1	102.1	99.6	88.2	68.8	79.1	134.3	153.1	171.1	158.6	189.0	179.5
Malaysia	102.0	176.5	95.2	242.2	281.2	163.6	28.9	16.9	14.7	24.7	15.4	14.0
Philippines	1.2	3.2	3.5	5.4	10.5	15.1	25.4	38.8	23.7	40.4	61.0	30.3
Singapore	36.5	46.3	47.9	166.1	290.5	389.9	31.6	64.5	72.5	51.4	44.0	51.3
South Korea	18.2	49.2	69.2	65.6	42.7	44.4	48.1	60.8	74.6	95.4	67.0	88.7
Taiwan	28.9	37.5	19.6	21.3	27.5	28.7	67.2	66.0	57.4	64.7	67.0	74.3
Thailand	9.3	11.3	11.6	13.7	13.8	16.2	14.3	20.4	21.0	92.8	46.3	31.2
India	1.6	3.0	2.9	2.3	3.6	5.7	15.6	28.1	23.2	59.0	59.1	36.4
Australia	18.2	15.1	15.8	6.5	8.4	6.3	47.7	68.3	73.6	83.5	93.3	73.1
Middle East	47.9	40.4	50.8	18.3	10.7	21.5	180.2	251.2	139.7	186.7	219.4	215.1
Israel	22.2	26.6	39.7	9.6	7.3	14.4	34.4	35.4	27.6	23.4	33.0	20.5
Saudi Arabia	17.7	7.9	7.3	4.5	0.9	3.3	98.8	115.9	62.6	94.1	112.2	80.3
Africa	3.9	4.2	8.1	16.9	10.1	4.2	106.2	91.4	109.8	107.6	132.5	124.2

Destination	Massachusetts						Michigan					
	1994	1995	1996	1997	1998	1999	1994	1995	1996	1997	1998	1999
ALL DESTINATIONS	12 586.0	14 396.4	15 368.4	17 368.1	16 467.3	17 105.8	36 812.1	37 102.3	38 128.2	37 920.1	39 268.8	41 489.9
Canada	2 860.4	3 339.9	3 486.8	3 677.5	3 387.6	3 256.8	20 809.1	21 935.9	21 949.6	19 760.2	19 665.9	21 992.1
Mexico	535.1	316.7	388.8	467.6	564.5	715.5	7 088.5	5 002.8	4 686.8	6 458.0	7 888.1	9 294.9
Central and South America and Caribbean	464.7	542.7	582.9	677.4	651.3	630.7	752.5	1 028.8	1 209.6	1 613.8	1 684.9	1 013.5
Argentina	73.6	56.5	52.8	68.9	59.2	77.2	77.0	68.6	137.1	219.2	297.3	83.4
Brazil	134.6	181.6	219.6	264.1	219.9	242.8	299.7	471.4	491.8	550.5	598.6	416.9
Chile	44.6	50.2	43.9	50.2	48.2	41.3	81.9	148.3	152.2	167.3	120.7	59.1
Colombia	41.9	44.3	42.0	55.0	62.5	43.9	36.0	35.2	26.1	40.9	38.3	26.0
Dominican Republic	20.1	15.1	35.0	34.1	21.4	20.6	20.0	18.1	12.2	6.5	11.7	24.0
Venezuela	32.5	39.9	35.8	46.0	57.7	35.6	110.0	112.8	214.9	446.3	279.8	236.3
European Union	4 629.8	5 288.6	5 353.1	5 889.3	6 200.1	6 304.9	3 553.2	4 193.2	4 155.6	4 745.7	5 110.0	4 944.4
Belgium	245.2	326.6	492.1	417.7	316.7	302.6	541.4	608.8	581.4	1 081.1	951.6	787.5
France	542.0	528.2	562.8	626.7	673.5	761.1	392.3	345.9	283.7	297.6	314.4	274.5
Germany	851.8	1 040.5	1 098.8	1 019.4	1 163.8	1 057.9	893.6	1 054.5	999.4	1 057.0	1 047.9	900.9
Ireland	379.1	368.8	316.4	330.4	429.1	432.0	20.8	27.6	20.0	31.8	34.4	45.3
Italy	275.2	298.9	309.9	360.4	375.4	396.4	124.8	158.8	154.3	143.0	156.9	151.4
Luxembourg	5.1	12.0	5.4	2.8	3.4	2.4	10.7	13.2	35.1	23.2	19.8	29.3
Netherlands	710.1	763.4	692.3	928.9	903.9	1 013.3	155.3	175.6	205.8	238.7	217.0	233.9
Spain	108.6	150.8	154.2	137.1	152.5	138.0	150.5	156.7	140.3	138.7	168.8	163.4
United Kingdom	1 245.0	1 479.0	1 415.2	1 706.4	1 794.5	1 826.5	688.7	588.6	633.8	742.8	934.0	1 329.2
Switzerland	133.2	149.5	153.4	161.6	162.7	145.2	96.0	93.1	73.2	66.7	56.5	52.4
Former Soviet Republics	48.4	62.8	40.2	58.8	42.2	31.6	65.6	80.5	69.0	91.3	65.7	15.9
Asian 10	3 023.8	3 713.9	4 316.5	5 323.4	4 419.6	4 878.9	2 471.6	2 822.0	3 300.4	3 083.8	2 550.0	2 426.2
China	130.9	144.8	162.7	159.8	235.4	247.0	148.8	143.2	216.3	365.5	264.1	225.5
Hong Kong	378.0	464.4	432.4	536.6	424.6	408.6	149.7	179.7	192.6	216.4	213.4	190.1
Indonesia	35.3	47.6	74.1	85.6	43.5	31.5	28.2	29.4	36.4	37.2	23.7	28.8
Japan	1 155.1	1 396.4	1 680.5	1 969.0	1 859.3	1 793.0	1 223.4	1 451.8	1 789.5	1 444.3	1 394.3	1 120.9
Malaysia	78.2	154.8	131.9	205.6	169.6	278.1	38.4	54.5	69.8	77.2	36.2	88.2
Philippines	72.3	126.1	198.6	331.2	304.5	273.4	63.0	44.3	47.7	44.6	50.5	83.9
Singapore	329.0	352.4	409.0	544.8	430.4	583.9	84.0	119.0	110.5	117.5	105.4	132.0
South Korea	348.4	432.5	530.7	616.5	320.1	464.4	243.0	367.2	435.7	369.3	148.8	241.9
Taiwan	427.6	489.6	592.3	789.0	557.2	697.8	359.6	293.3	198.8	207.6	174.0	168.3
Thailand	69.1	105.3	104.2	85.4	74.9	101.1	133.4	139.7	203.0	204.2	139.6	146.7
India	55.8	60.6	54.7	61.6	67.9	63.2	22.8	56.9	60.2	58.0	44.7	40.1
Australia	282.9	316.6	326.6	314.8	285.2	300.0	329.7	405.5	567.4	543.9	547.0	482.6
Middle East	243.0	241.5	282.9	316.2	304.7	354.3	1 337.3	1 160.2	1 656.1	1 153.7	1 318.9	910.8
Israel	139.8	134.8	159.3	176.5	206.9	236.6	194.1	236.3	211.1	129.5	133.6	89.3
Saudi Arabia	56.4	52.3	61.6	69.4	44.2	57.0	675.5	477.6	793.1	618.0	666.0	481.7
Africa	79.1	98.4	102.6	97.9	96.2	99.1	44.3	53.5	62.1	54.2	81.1	51.8

Table D-2. State Exports of Goods by Destination, 1994–1999—*Continued*

(Millions of dollars.)

Destination	Minnesota						Mississippi					
	1994	1995	1996	1997	1998	1999	1994	1995	1996	1997	1998	1999
ALL DESTINATIONS	10 011.1	12 404.3	13 884.1	13 793.3	13 499.4	14 400.8	1 099.9	1 368.7	1 221.7	1 421.3	1 414.0	1 454.3
Canada	2 108.5	2 442.2	2 860.6	3 190.2	3 389.5	3 443.4	352.1	372.7	387.8	430.4	492.8	520.7
Mexico	329.8	505.7	846.3	822.8	870.4	974.1	65.7	87.9	91.3	127.4	242.4	293.0
Central and South America and Caribbean	450.7	686.6	762.1	780.8	787.0	687.1	208.5	245.1	254.0	232.5	242.6	272.9
Argentina	44.1	33.3	40.9	89.2	56.0	40.8	6.6	2.8	5.9	5.5	9.2	6.9
Brazil	88.8	81.2	143.3	118.3	139.5	85.5	3.0	6.9	7.7	12.5	22.3	34.5
Chile	29.4	69.2	54.5	54.9	55.6	86.4	12.3	11.9	6.6	8.4	6.7	2.0
Colombia	33.5	65.7	88.0	58.9	58.6	54.0	4.5	4.6	8.0	9.1	10.8	5.6
Dominican Republic	14.7	22.9	10.7	36.3	38.1	38.5	14.4	21.7	20.1	19.7	21.8	21.3
Venezuela	34.0	95.2	84.4	98.4	72.1	71.0	3.2	6.0	8.6	7.2	12.4	33.7
European Union	3 393.6	4 049.7	4 075.7	4 025.2	3 785.0	3 732.3	169.8	223.3	208.1	266.9	254.3	208.9
Belgium	163.7	245.7	239.7	173.4	218.9	174.6	6.5	10.0	19.3	47.0	28.8	25.0
France	236.7	265.4	280.2	362.9	420.8	400.6	17.7	24.0	17.5	12.0	12.7	6.5
Germany	473.8	514.1	658.7	593.4	577.8	550.2	20.2	20.2	17.3	17.4	26.1	29.4
Ireland	177.6	216.9	244.1	265.6	265.6	405.0	0.5	0.6	1.6	12.0	23.1	6.6
Italy	229.9	322.6	288.2	236.3	234.4	246.7	20.4	32.0	30.8	40.3	41.6	33.5
Luxembourg	1.2	1.8	0.8	0.7	0.7	0.4	0.2	...	0.1	0.1	0.1	0.1
Netherlands	968.5	1 072.8	989.1	846.2	758.5	641.2	22.1	32.8	26.3	26.1	22.2	27.8
Spain	376.8	451.1	323.5	432.9	367.8	309.2	4.6	3.3	6.2	5.0	7.9	5.7
United Kingdom	448.3	540.9	599.3	703.8	638.8	688.4	68.5	91.3	75.2	80.9	70.4	57.0
Switzerland	59.4	66.4	58.6	71.3	72.5	95.3	1.9	1.5	2.8	2.4	1.0	4.9
Former Soviet Republics	97.3	32.3	121.5	44.7	37.0	31.7	24.0	40.7	85.0	148.5	42.3	15.8
Asian 10	2 292.4	2 935.4	3 126.2	3 027.7	2 984.5	3 639.5	78.4	177.8	127.9	139.8	88.0	84.5
China	92.5	400.5	176.7	233.8	315.5	322.8	4.5	28.1	14.8	17.3	6.1	5.0
Hong Kong	185.0	273.7	259.8	255.4	365.4	339.6	14.7	28.7	15.8	15.2	11.1	18.9
Indonesia	71.3	68.5	94.5	146.5	51.5	125.8	0.4	6.1	3.1	2.6	0.6	0.9
Japan	761.6	863.6	1 047.8	1 089.8	822.3	894.7	17.9	26.5	39.0	49.2	44.3	24.3
Malaysia	208.6	148.3	114.1	82.5	121.8	124.3	1.5	1.2	0.4	0.9	1.5	1.4
Philippines	55.3	101.6	105.8	222.1	306.0	340.3	1.3	12.7	9.2	23.4	6.2	4.8
Singapore	190.0	230.2	259.2	245.4	317.7	295.8	12.1	10.6	12.1	9.2	8.4	8.3
South Korea	261.2	435.4	488.3	268.4	301.3	570.2	16.0	29.3	19.7	11.2	4.6	9.7
Taiwan	262.9	255.8	449.9	257.1	269.0	364.2	8.1	19.9	8.8	7.0	3.4	7.1
Thailand	204.1	157.9	129.9	226.8	114.0	261.8	2.0	14.6	5.0	3.6	2.1	4.0
India	17.2	40.7	33.6	31.3	30.2	29.9	0.7	0.6	4.0	5.4	1.1	2.9
Australia	160.5	176.5	189.7	203.3	199.4	197.3	7.8	14.3	13.6	14.2	12.9	19.5
Middle East	386.7	442.2	396.8	352.0	275.8	404.7	160.1	179.9	18.5	21.1	17.0	16.5
Israel	171.3	158.9	204.5	155.8	71.5	133.6	149.1	149.6	5.2	6.0	5.4	2.6
Saudi Arabia	65.5	78.4	64.3	67.5	50.9	64.0	5.8	9.5	7.0	7.6	5.4	7.9
Africa	113.4	163.4	164.0	138.8	118.9	131.6	9.6	5.3	7.4	8.3	4.8	3.6

Destination	Missouri						Montana					
	1994	1995	1996	1997	1998	1999	1994	1995	1996	1997	1998	1999
ALL DESTINATIONS	5 234.8	5 689.9	6 590.5	7 043.0	6 832.4	7 431.1	260.0	279.2	340.9	429.8	390.0	404.0
Canada	1 347.9	1 369.7	1 288.1	1 490.1	1 570.3	1 570.2	140.1	140.2	160.6	236.5	192.8	200.1
Mexico	773.4	699.0	1 089.0	1 042.4	1 189.6	1 272.5	5.1	8.1	46.2	20.6	59.5	76.6
Central and South America and Caribbean	498.6	660.2	788.2	797.1	733.7	875.3	4.3	5.7	3.8	3.5	7.4	6.4
Argentina	78.1	88.3	125.0	115.3	97.9	174.9	0.2	0.3	0.2	0.2	0.5	0.4
Brazil	103.1	170.7	194.7	199.7	148.8	188.5	0.3	1.7	1.3	1.4	1.2	1.3
Chile	19.5	30.5	39.8	39.8	29.1	24.2	0.1	0.1	0.1	0.2	0.4	0.7
Colombia	42.8	69.2	84.8	60.8	64.9	60.8	...	0.9	0.3	0.3	0.1	0.3
Dominican Republic	11.7	18.6	18.7	20.5	24.7	33.7	...	...	...	0.1	0.1	...
Venezuela	64.3	88.2	81.2	67.0	98.9	78.6	1.0	0.9	1.2	0.2	0.1	...
European Union	1 123.4	1 330.8	1 493.0	1 701.7	1 527.4	1 689.4	84.1	88.0	82.5	106.9	83.1	50.8
Belgium	291.8	373.4	376.5	386.8	221.6	399.1	53.1	47.3	43.6	73.5	34.5	1.4
France	77.6	91.6	72.1	81.2	119.9	90.9	3.4	3.8	8.0	9.6	6.0	4.8
Germany	117.3	156.5	171.6	202.7	217.8	216.9	7.0	16.5	13.0	8.0	21.9	21.4
Ireland	40.9	39.8	60.3	69.0	77.5	86.4	0.4	1.0	1.0	0.4	0.5	0.3
Italy	92.1	106.9	148.8	103.2	80.7	120.2	2.7	1.4	0.7	1.1	1.0	1.9
Luxembourg	0.4	0.5	1.2	1.2	1.2	1.2	...	...	...	...	...	...
Netherlands	122.7	117.3	137.7	129.7	78.6	108.1	1.7	5.7	3.6	2.4	4.7	4.1
Spain	72.9	127.3	149.9	237.0	95.5	103.9	0.1	0.5	0.3	0.5	1.0	0.8
United Kingdom	262.5	195.6	193.7	235.8	293.5	345.8	14.3	11.1	8.3	9.1	12.0	13.9
Switzerland	14.7	24.5	30.9	24.2	22.0	22.9	0.4	2.4	4.6	1.2	2.0	0.5
Former Soviet Republics	41.9	57.2	60.1	84.5	36.2	31.0	0.3	0.1	0.2	0.1	0.1	...
Asian 10	945.5	986.8	1 152.2	1 205.3	1 059.6	1 240.8	17.3	26.5	32.8	54.5	36.4	47.0
China	48.7	80.3	162.6	167.4	137.8	155.1	0.1	0.2	1.6	14.2	0.6	1.0
Hong Kong	75.5	112.5	102.3	81.7	102.1	71.5	0.6	1.3	1.5	1.6	0.9	1.4
Indonesia	23.4	39.2	64.3	79.4	49.2	42.3	...	0.1	0.1	0.2	0.1	...
Japan	259.4	282.0	275.5	307.6	367.8	317.7	10.9	16.8	20.5	23.1	19.4	28.5
Malaysia	51.6	49.5	54.1	58.1	45.8	86.3	0.1	0.2	0.6	0.6	0.6	0.5
Philippines	107.5	33.4	36.7	63.0	40.4	93.3	0.1	0.8	0.3	0.8	0.4	0.5
Singapore	81.5	103.9	104.2	102.1	108.7	137.6	0.4	0.9	1.9	4.0	6.1	3.9
South Korea	104.9	131.0	152.1	151.7	72.5	135.8	3.9	4.7	4.5	4.3	3.1	2.5
Taiwan	137.1	106.7	163.4	166.4	113.9	143.4	1.2	1.2	1.1	5.3	5.2	8.6
Thailand	55.9	48.2	37.0	27.9	21.3	57.9	0.1	0.4	0.5	0.4	...	0.2
India	22.1	19.2	26.4	25.5	37.2	35.0	0.1	0.1	0.1	0.1	...	...
Australia	111.2	123.9	162.2	165.5	164.6	159.0	2.9	2.0	2.7	2.4	2.2	3.0
Middle East	195.4	189.1	218.8	203.2	179.2	203.3	1.1	1.8	2.0	1.9	1.8	0.9
Israel	107.6	125.6	129.4	126.8	114.9	91.1	0.3	0.3	0.7	1.3	0.8	0.6
Saudi Arabia	35.3	32.2	32.8	34.4	26.1	40.4	0.7	1.1	1.2	0.4	0.5	0.2
Africa	22.7	67.4	75.0	67.9	72.6	89.7	0.2	1.0	0.9	0.2	2.5	14.7

Table D-2. State Exports of Goods by Destination, 1994–1999—*Continued*

(Millions of dollars.)

Destination	Nebraska 1994	1995	1996	1997	1998	1999	Nevada 1994	1995	1996	1997	1998	1999
ALL DESTINATIONS	1 957.9	2 255.3	2 452.8	2 493.7	2 471.6	1 991.4	458.5	711.1	691.6	807.1	764.9	1 083.4
Canada	327.1	352.3	418.7	529.0	523.9	502.3	148.9	211.8	265.6	272.1	300.7	549.4
Mexico	108.8	80.0	168.0	142.0	142.9	178.4	14.5	12.8	9.2	59.9	22.5	57.3
Central and South America and Caribbean	66.5	74.8	123.1	176.4	131.5	133.9	22.5	34.6	44.7	34.3	38.0	39.2
Argentina	3.3	3.0	14.8	15.3	14.3	8.7	1.0	5.3	4.6	4.6	4.1	6.6
Brazil	2.0	3.2	12.2	21.2	21.0	23.1	2.4	3.7	6.4	6.1	4.7	5.7
Chile	1.7	1.8	2.3	3.2	3.0	6.0	1.4	4.0	3.1	3.0	2.6	4.5
Colombia	0.6	0.8	1.8	3.4	3.8	2.7	1.5	2.2	1.5	3.1	3.0	1.9
Dominican Republic	0.1	2.9	4.4	11.5	9.1	5.3	. . .	0.3	1.1	0.2	0.1	0.3
Venezuela	45.2	49.7	76.4	110.8	68.9	38.0	0.4	0.8	1.4	2.4	4.5	3.7
European Union	221.8	213.1	237.8	285.7	407.7	343.8	97.3	103.6	114.2	181.5	174.9	190.8
Belgium	22.6	16.9	37.6	47.1	87.0	59.6	2.6	2.1	3.1	10.6	8.4	9.5
France	18.3	16.2	20.5	22.2	29.8	27.6	14.7	12.1	18.0	24.1	23.3	30.2
Germany	30.8	29.0	35.8	39.0	44.3	37.4	12.6	19.7	22.1	20.2	29.1	34.5
Ireland	10.2	11.0	8.2	13.3	24.0	20.9	2.1	2.3	2.0	3.2	5.6	4.8
Italy	27.5	23.6	29.6	23.6	36.2	32.6	4.0	12.7	5.8	8.7	16.6	12.7
Luxembourg	. . .	. . .	. . .	. . .	. . .	. . .	0.1	0.6	. . .	7.3	0.0	0.1
Netherlands	62.3	73.6	58.7	60.4	73.9	52.3	10.3	9.1	13.4	17.2	17.4	17.8
Spain	6.3	5.2	6.1	6.5	28.7	27.9	0.7	1.2	2.3	3.2	7.1	5.8
United Kingdom	30.5	27.9	30.2	40.7	58.7	51.2	45.2	28.1	32.6	64.5	49.1	53.0
Switzerland	1.9	1.7	2.8	11.6	6.2	6.3	4.3	13.8	5.8	5.7	8.4	10.6
Former Soviet Republics	1.3	2.0	12.9	2.4	3.2	1.3	4.4	4.8	4.5	3.2	5.0	2.0
Asian 10	1 137.3	1 426.7	1 366.0	1 206.4	1 115.4	619.3	109.7	269.3	176.6	197.0	135.0	153.1
China	4.1	8.6	16.4	9.8	33.4	14.8	10.9	7.5	9.1	4.6	9.8	8.5
Hong Kong	16.8	15.0	8.2	14.3	17.9	15.6	7.1	10.4	12.4	14.5	16.2	15.4
Indonesia	12.1	19.7	26.7	32.6	8.5	6.2	0.7	2.6	5.3	1.5	0.6	0.9
Japan	912.8	1 162.7	1 103.1	870.8	808.3	309.0	34.6	82.6	77.7	82.9	63.8	60.6
Malaysia	2.1	3.6	6.5	17.1	5.3	5.3	1.4	4.0	10.9	14.8	4.2	12.4
Philippines	1.3	2.1	7.4	9.2	48.0	70.0	29.1	131.4	12.3	33.3	2.0	3.5
Singapore	16.7	23.8	23.8	29.0	25.1	34.9	5.9	7.0	7.5	10.6	10.6	8.2
South Korea	146.1	160.8	134.3	184.7	111.4	106.1	11.0	13.3	24.7	21.8	10.9	28.3
Taiwan	10.8	13.2	16.8	24.9	34.3	30.2	7.6	8.5	13.6	10.6	14.9	13.1
Thailand	14.5	17.3	22.9	14.0	23.3	25.9	1.5	2.0	3.2	2.5	2.1	2.2
India	1.4	2.9	1.3	2.5	2.0	1.4	1.7	4.5	3.8	2.9	3.0	5.3
Australia	27.1	28.1	48.1	58.5	59.2	55.9	13.6	17.4	17.9	19.5	18.6	16.7
Middle East	31.5	28.1	21.1	18.1	15.4	51.2	9.2	14.1	11.2	7.8	18.2	18.8
Israel	12.5	13.2	14.3	7.3	6.8	0.0	6.2	4.8	4.3	2.5	4.6	13.6
Saudi Arabia	4.8	1.6	3.1	6.3	5.1	13.1	1.4	2.3	2.9	1.7	2.1	1.0
Africa	10.1	7.6	11.3	16.7	9.3	19.7	7.6	9.3	9.4	7.7	23.8	15.9

Destination	New Hampshire 1994	1995	1996	1997	1998	1999	New Jersey 1994	1995	1996	1997	1998	1999
ALL DESTINATIONS	1 247.9	1 478.6	1 744.9	1 931.0	1 986.5	2 159.1	16 760.8	18 368.6	18 458.4	20 815.4	20 032.9	21 007.6
Canada	422.4	494.4	642.4	672.2	643.4	726.3	2 943.7	3 167.2	3 379.1	3 836.8	3 872.7	3 902.1
Mexico	43.4	45.2	63.6	73.8	86.1	78.3	1 068.1	583.8	679.2	883.8	953.7	1 079.5
Central and South America and Caribbean	92.3	97.3	92.7	117.1	109.7	102.5	1 433.6	1 808.6	1 932.9	2 107.8	1 997.2	1 921.0
Argentina	6.6	4.8	3.5	5.8	6.7	6.6	177.9	139.1	148.4	202.4	187.2	177.8
Brazil	21.7	38.6	28.1	30.7	16.2	14.0	282.6	439.5	496.1	627.2	573.7	523.9
Chile	2.6	2.0	3.0	4.5	3.1	5.5	128.7	141.8	145.4	185.6	135.1	139.9
Colombia	2.8	4.1	3.0	3.4	4.7	4.9	118.6	159.0	140.0	139.3	121.4	131.3
Dominican Republic	48.2	34.2	31.8	39.9	46.5	41.7	124.2	194.1	144.9	182.0	157.3	139.3
Venezuela	3.1	3.0	7.8	7.1	3.1	5.1	123.9	156.5	167.8	167.4	155.6	153.4
European Union	349.8	459.5	500.3	580.1	652.6	695.2	4 350.9	4 792.2	4 499.6	5 269.0	5 700.7	6 011.2
Belgium	13.5	15.1	10.6	15.2	27.7	19.0	415.8	510.6	412.9	473.5	544.3	607.0
France	36.9	38.1	48.3	50.0	45.1	44.0	488.6	525.3	493.0	577.6	610.1	736.2
Germany	60.4	95.3	93.5	144.9	135.5	118.0	798.3	920.8	871.5	912.4	904.6	924.6
Ireland	43.7	88.3	119.0	94.5	137.1	158.8	265.6	306.0	233.9	435.9	353.1	287.0
Italy	19.8	22.3	24.3	26.8	28.4	30.6	295.5	351.0	280.9	350.1	465.5	468.5
Luxembourg	0.3	0.1	. . .	0.1	0.1	0.4	1.7	3.0	1.8	2.2	2.7	4.9
Netherlands	46.2	50.2	58.4	62.5	65.8	85.4	566.0	648.1	747.2	1 016.1	1 057.0	1 051.3
Spain	10.5	9.5	11.3	19.2	15.3	21.8	184.4	206.3	193.6	193.5	275.2	276.2
United Kingdom	95.7	104.7	102.7	132.5	147.0	168.6	999.0	955.7	854.9	901.1	1 026.1	1 146.8
Switzerland	7.7	9.5	9.4	11.6	10.7	9.8	263.3	321.9	252.8	310.7	390.2	339.7
Former Soviet Republics	4.5	3.5	15.3	13.0	4.9	6.3	151.7	151.1	149.1	171.7	137.3	100.0
Asian 10	242.8	289.3	344.9	360.2	374.4	417.7	4 410.9	5 154.1	4 862.1	5 264.4	4 205.9	4 954.0
China	10.6	15.0	9.0	18.0	18.4	23.9	283.1	606.8	405.0	348.9	668.5	558.2
Hong Kong	15.7	24.9	43.5	49.7	59.8	81.0	326.8	424.5	407.6	420.6	442.4	394.0
Indonesia	4.1	4.3	6.0	8.6	6.2	11.9	65.2	122.2	138.0	301.9	50.5	64.1
Japan	60.4	59.0	81.8	109.0	96.3	88.7	1 357.7	1 470.2	1 577.5	1 648.2	1 432.0	1 880.1
Malaysia	3.7	5.5	5.0	13.2	13.0	9.3	78.1	100.8	89.5	103.8	83.5	105.9
Philippines	5.6	5.4	7.1	5.6	5.0	7.6	146.8	139.3	165.2	150.8	101.0	106.4
Singapore	60.5	76.1	50.3	56.7	68.9	93.5	262.1	249.6	231.4	304.0	214.9	373.7
South Korea	40.7	52.5	48.3	31.7	14.7	28.0	1 260.9	1 359.6	1 279.5	1 356.7	693.2	861.1
Taiwan	34.8	36.0	57.4	49.5	79.8	56.3	517.6	519.0	440.3	484.7	443.6	467.0
Thailand	6.7	10.5	36.4	18.2	12.3	17.4	112.5	162.1	128.2	144.7	76.3	143.6
India	5.4	9.1	6.5	6.3	5.5	5.3	93.2	135.2	142.5	90.0	91.9	108.4
Australia	25.8	23.0	22.5	28.8	27.4	26.6	275.8	321.7	319.0	333.6	333.9	335.1
Middle East	15.9	17.3	23.1	27.8	33.4	43.7	1 001.0	1 081.0	1 094.9	1 299.4	1 485.4	1 455.9
Israel	10.4	10.7	18.5	18.1	21.6	27.5	660.4	708.7	745.9	863.5	986.2	927.7
Saudi Arabia	2.7	1.4	1.9	2.9	5.1	11.5	196.7	243.1	198.8	264.6	341.4	373.5
Africa	4.5	6.5	4.6	6.1	7.7	10.7	129.3	178.7	157.1	168.0	183.5	198.3

Table D-2. State Exports of Goods by Destination, 1994–1999—*Continued*

(Millions of dollars.)

Destination	New Mexico						New York					
	1994	1995	1996	1997	1998	1999	1994	1995	1996	1997	1998	1999
ALL DESTINATIONS	488.5	426.6	917.4	1 779.9	1 896.2	2 964.9	37 259.7	44 080.1	44 964.7	48 885.3	45 564.5	43 296.8
Canada	47.5	41.7	51.2	55.6	67.8	75.8	7 487.2	9 243.7	8 956.7	10 616.0	9 957.1	9 735.9
Mexico	93.9	77.1	100.0	86.6	86.6	114.0	1 323.9	994.0	1 303.1	1 804.9	1 936.0	2 031.1
Central and South America and Caribbean	7.2	10.7	8.9	13.8	29.0	53.4	3 054.5	3 401.8	3 536.8	4 088.6	4 046.1	3 111.3
Argentina	0.8	1.2	1.0	1.2	1.5	1.7	304.3	242.4	260.5	358.5	426.6	295.6
Brazil	2.2	1.3	2.1	1.5	1.2	3.2	803.0	970.6	964.1	1 171.2	1 158.3	983.0
Chile	0.3	0.5	1.0	0.8	6.6	1.1	239.5	219.9	247.0	245.5	174.0	112.6
Colombia	0.7	1.2	0.3	0.2	4.1	0.5	219.7	345.7	368.1	392.7	320.6	140.9
Dominican Republic	...	1.8	...	0.1	0.1	0.2	350.5	260.3	289.1	365.6	330.9	253.7
Venezuela	0.4	0.3	0.4	0.4	0.6	5.3	175.2	225.9	187.4	255.9	390.5	303.8
European Union	114.3	112.6	103.2	153.8	110.0	206.4	8 152.9	9 474.6	9 958.1	10 108.2	11 210.5	10 362.3
Belgium	2.2	5.0	6.5	24.0	11.0	3.5	875.0	1 011.5	909.5	923.6	1 004.0	1 038.7
France	12.1	20.8	27.6	32.3	30.5	41.5	826.0	929.9	1 057.9	1 270.4	1 345.3	1 299.4
Germany	32.9	26.1	19.1	18.8	13.4	47.2	1 212.8	1 577.1	1 503.8	1 684.7	1 768.7	1 801.8
Ireland	1.6	5.3	19.6	24.6	17.5	51.6	211.9	244.0	165.8	265.7	266.3	226.0
Italy	8.1	5.9	4.9	5.6	2.4	2.3	651.8	841.5	814.8	795.7	777.2	624.0
Luxembourg	0.7	0.8	0.5	0.9	0.6	0.3	7.7	21.7	37.4	42.0	32.2	37.2
Netherlands	4.4	16.3	4.9	21.3	6.3	24.4	846.6	1 090.9	906.5	874.9	1 019.1	1 054.8
Spain	1.2	1.1	2.0	1.6	1.3	2.5	287.1	383.2	362.9	376.9	393.1	342.7
United Kingdom	46.4	26.7	10.7	13.4	15.8	23.2	2 703.6	2 744.8	3 593.4	3 140.1	3 898.6	3 344.3
Switzerland	9.9	4.2	1.9	15.5	1.5	6.0	1 237.2	2 205.3	3 126.0	3 413.4	2 998.1	3 698.9
Former Soviet Republics	15.2	2.3	2.7	4.1	5.8	2.9	484.2	453.2	353.0	317.4	367.9	382.6
Asian 10	186.5	165.9	630.8	1 426.6	1 570.8	2 450.3	10 724.2	13 013.6	12 191.5	12 122.7	9 275.2	8 880.4
China	2.0	8.2	10.3	28.5	147.3	208.0	588.9	636.5	807.0	766.2	678.6	685.1
Hong Kong	19.5	14.1	10.1	13.6	7.6	12.9	1 498.1	1 631.9	1 461.2	1 646.6	1 163.2	1 179.8
Indonesia	0.1	0.6	0.5	8.7	3.6	0.8	209.4	332.0	198.0	211.3	96.6	123.2
Japan	44.2	21.2	45.7	60.1	26.1	30.9	4 634.8	5 463.9	5 422.1	5 369.3	4 536.0	4 224.3
Malaysia	1.4	4.1	79.8	271.0	152.6	338.1	272.1	287.3	351.3	413.8	182.6	210.7
Philippines	5.8	4.8	203.4	688.3	750.8	954.6	215.0	277.4	278.3	396.0	314.8	191.5
Singapore	2.8	8.1	5.4	2.6	1.8	7.8	613.1	628.0	563.1	609.1	423.3	459.2
South Korea	68.7	59.1	184.4	197.2	375.9	784.9	1 344.7	1 954.8	1 793.2	1 423.3	747.9	944.2
Taiwan	6.9	13.6	53.4	115.7	67.5	66.9	1 082.3	1 442.7	956.0	944.7	784.0	623.6
Thailand	35.3	32.2	37.9	40.8	37.6	45.5	265.7	359.2	361.4	342.5	348.4	238.9
India	0.4	0.3	0.6	1.8	0.4	0.4	406.8	525.2	498.5	543.5	387.6	472.3
Australia	3.1	3.3	5.0	10.9	5.3	14.8	503.1	625.7	711.0	744.6	652.7	577.6
Middle East	5.5	5.0	7.0	6.2	7.1	33.6	2 098.2	2 280.2	2 536.4	3 141.8	3 106.8	2 789.5
Israel	2.1	3.8	5.7	3.1	5.1	32.2	1 007.0	1 141.8	1 295.0	1 499.4	1 750.7	1 706.9
Saudi Arabia	0.5	0.6	0.4	2.3	0.9	0.4	648.9	642.3	805.2	1 075.8	873.7	635.1
Africa	0.9	0.5	1.5	1.6	4.2	2.2	482.2	647.4	656.0	696.9	555.8	448.1

Destination	North Carolina						North Dakota					
	1994	1995	1996	1997	1998	1999	1994	1995	1996	1997	1998	1999
ALL DESTINATIONS	8 968.8	10 567.4	11 586.6	13 102.1	12 919.9	13 571.4	388.9	488.6	576.2	623.1	657.4	634.6
Canada	2 782.8	3 168.5	3 520.4	3 748.2	3 719.3	4 006.8	250.6	315.3	378.8	427.6	386.8	345.3
Mexico	493.1	653.8	922.2	1 320.5	1 564.7	1 843.6	1.8	16.8	11.5	17.6	17.6	12.5
Central and South America and Caribbean	1 072.2	1 490.6	1 589.0	1 814.6	1 667.3	1 716.7	10.7	15.0	10.3	14.7	14.2	12.1
Argentina	84.2	79.1	98.4	121.2	91.0	82.4	3.0	3.4	2.5	5.0	6.3	3.1
Brazil	142.4	242.4	243.8	343.2	259.4	255.2	1.3	3.5	2.0	2.0	0.3	0.8
Chile	44.8	65.0	71.8	72.2	58.7	93.5	0.6	1.1	1.7	1.5	1.3	0.9
Colombia	90.6	105.6	94.1	89.1	103.3	83.3	2.4	2.0	1.3	2.1	0.5	0.4
Dominican Republic	63.6	104.7	119.0	144.1	115.2	165.1	0.4	1.7	...	0.4	0.4	0.3
Venezuela	32.2	48.1	52.7	59.3	72.3	45.5	0.4	0.6	...	0.2	1.2	0.3
European Union	1 994.4	2 300.0	2 533.0	2 870.7	2 877.7	2 935.0	98.1	106.1	127.7	110.7	188.1	216.8
Belgium	417.0	474.9	441.5	378.2	377.4	302.1	68.1	68.9	72.2	56.4	131.0	142.5
France	131.1	165.4	191.9	298.3	315.7	317.7	1.6	1.3	2.8	5.0	3.3	4.1
Germany	396.0	476.5	482.9	550.1	515.4	591.1	12.7	14.7	17.9	20.7	15.8	18.4
Ireland	75.2	72.2	82.3	79.9	100.9	84.5	0.3	0.2	0.1	0.3	1.0	0.3
Italy	101.9	132.6	145.5	146.7	154.3	178.4	1.0	0.9	1.1	2.0	3.1	21.4
Luxembourg	0.6	0.2	0.5	1.4	0.6	2.2	...	...	...	...	...	...
Netherlands	215.5	225.7	237.6	291.5	282.0	289.5	1.7	2.8	11.9	4.2	9.0	3.9
Spain	97.6	105.6	130.8	152.1	189.4	156.4	6.6	7.5	11.0	7.7	8.1	11.1
United Kingdom	391.4	446.8	552.8	716.5	708.6	762.4	4.2	7.2	8.7	12.6	13.7	12.6
Switzerland	79.2	90.8	73.6	143.8	117.5	97.1	0.6	0.3	0.1	0.3	0.4	0.3
Former Soviet Republics	8.6	27.5	43.0	42.4	36.9	58.8	1.0	1.6	3.2	1.6	1.3	1.0
Asian 10	1 652.3	1 904.2	1 984.5	2 175.2	1 951.9	1 984.9	22.2	20.4	26.8	30.1	27.6	21.2
China	135.5	175.1	185.7	230.4	215.6	210.0	0.7	1.7	1.9	3.6	4.4	4.4
Hong Kong	180.5	234.7	197.9	270.8	246.3	262.5	0.2	0.8	2.5	2.0	1.3	1.4
Indonesia	60.0	82.3	69.8	73.3	50.6	66.5	0.5	0.6	0.8	0.8	0.3	0.4
Japan	743.4	760.7	824.0	811.0	779.6	731.0	7.4	5.3	6.1	9.7	6.1	6.6
Malaysia	59.7	72.3	91.5	105.2	86.9	85.8	0.5	2.0	0.9	1.4	1.1	0.4
Philippines	38.5	52.4	67.5	79.7	61.4	61.9	0.9	1.1	2.4	0.8	0.3	0.4
Singapore	91.4	96.2	119.3	111.9	109.7	166.5	0.6	1.9	1.4	1.8	1.6	0.7
South Korea	132.2	183.2	201.9	202.8	151.4	200.0	1.1	2.9	7.5	4.5	1.0	2.2
Taiwan	120.7	126.8	115.1	166.1	168.5	122.1	10.2	2.9	2.4	4.4	3.5	4.2
Thailand	90.3	120.5	111.9	124.1	82.1	78.6	0.1	1.3	0.8	1.0	7.9	0.6
India	18.0	24.2	31.6	35.0	34.6	49.3	...	...	1.0	0.5	0.4	1.2
Australia	152.8	180.0	192.6	177.3	179.2	194.2	2.0	8.6	10.6	14.7	12.5	15.3
Middle East	306.0	287.6	232.1	224.4	213.1	209.3	0.5	1.1	0.8	1.0	5.2	3.1
Israel	58.7	60.8	67.6	63.4	59.7	77.6	0.2	0.5	0.6	0.7	0.5	0.9
Saudi Arabia	81.4	86.1	71.3	75.5	61.3	55.8	0.2	0.4	0.1	0.2	4.1	0.6
Africa	91.9	112.7	105.3	114.1	131.0	99.0	0.3	0.4	0.4	0.1	0.8	0.6

Table D-2. State Exports of Goods by Destination, 1994–1999—*Continued*

(Millions of dollars.)

Destination	Ohio						Oklahoma					
	1994	1995	1996	1997	1998	1999	1994	1995	1996	1997	1998	1999
ALL DESTINATIONS	19 478.2	20 926.5	22 555.2	25 106.5	24 814.8	26 561.7	2 172.0	2 467.3	2 537.6	2 721.6	2 623.2	2 405.3
Canada	8 501.4	8 881.3	9 580.4	10 471.6	10 669.1	11 963.4	497.1	492.4	570.9	669.9	656.1	663.7
Mexico	1 423.2	1 362.2	1 345.1	1 583.7	1 958.6	2 251.8	139.3	120.3	178.7	239.6	294.6	283.0
Central and South America and Caribbean	1 003.1	1 249.0	1 226.7	1 624.6	1 621.2	1 283.9	360.3	498.6	433.3	453.2	507.6	306.9
Argentina	123.8	122.5	158.5	160.8	149.2	126.6	57.7	55.4	78.7	55.3	92.2	55.1
Brazil	225.1	339.8	348.3	615.7	690.4	601.5	49.8	58.6	62.2	60.9	69.0	36.5
Chile	71.0	91.4	101.0	127.8	110.9	77.8	10.6	18.3	20.4	15.2	28.5	12.0
Colombia	119.8	131.7	126.7	131.7	121.6	72.7	44.3	81.3	44.9	34.0	39.5	19.6
Dominican Republic	34.7	41.1	54.9	68.2	75.9	54.4	0.5	0.9	8.0	1.1	1.7	3.1
Venezuela	126.6	150.2	116.1	159.7	173.2	114.8	89.7	147.2	92.2	171.7	115.1	52.4
European Union	4 369.4	4 472.4	4 725.6	5 380.7	5 732.9	5 833.9	477.2	540.1	500.1	535.7	450.0	444.4
Belgium	330.1	371.0	425.9	444.4	397.1	328.2	36.8	47.2	37.2	42.0	40.2	34.4
France	1 794.2	1 344.3	1 331.9	1 757.2	1 947.9	1 949.0	42.0	49.1	58.0	80.6	63.5	48.9
Germany	604.5	727.9	725.6	737.9	712.3	740.8	63.2	80.1	64.2	60.0	64.2	127.6
Ireland	107.6	126.7	101.8	146.1	176.4	171.2	2.9	5.0	2.5	5.1	9.3	14.5
Italy	212.7	275.7	279.8	287.3	331.8	280.0	52.3	65.0	76.8	56.1	47.7	16.1
Luxembourg	19.6	16.3	17.2	26.0	20.1	17.0	0.9	1.3	0.7	0.9	0.7	3.7
Netherlands	208.4	247.3	290.3	330.6	331.1	369.2	161.0	145.9	130.7	151.6	87.3	56.9
Spain	140.0	123.2	150.7	157.7	166.1	155.7	11.8	8.9	7.3	16.0	17.9	24.7
United Kingdom	730.7	942.2	1 089.5	1 173.5	1 290.0	1 512.7	86.1	109.9	98.1	100.7	100.6	95.7
Switzerland	134.2	142.0	139.1	102.6	118.4	160.5	4.2	13.5	9.9	9.7	8.7	7.9
Former Soviet Republics	13.4	58.1	29.7	35.5	51.9	21.9	28.0	36.1	47.8	20.9	48.0	39.9
Asian 10	2 723.4	3 326.4	3 927.3	4 233.4	3 229.0	3 726.3	399.3	458.9	473.7	446.4	300.1	271.0
China	197.3	211.4	269.5	477.4	359.0	404.0	60.3	80.7	53.9	50.3	38.2	30.4
Hong Kong	171.2	229.1	287.8	361.3	251.3	262.4	18.7	23.0	17.8	15.7	12.8	12.4
Indonesia	53.9	87.0	93.8	79.3	67.0	46.1	8.3	18.2	30.3	24.9	20.7	25.3
Japan	1 033.0	1 124.0	1 254.0	1 190.9	976.5	1 206.9	129.6	133.6	194.9	178.7	97.8	75.3
Malaysia	139.1	150.4	172.5	214.6	127.3	158.1	25.6	5.0	6.5	12.9	6.8	6.8
Philippines	34.4	70.3	91.3	102.4	82.9	68.4	22.0	16.8	11.6	14.0	4.3	3.8
Singapore	329.3	395.5	454.4	488.6	432.0	523.4	55.2	56.7	56.3	70.4	66.3	56.0
South Korea	374.2	538.0	773.0	804.9	445.6	662.2	45.8	66.8	66.0	45.3	11.3	28.6
Taiwan	294.7	379.3	384.6	368.9	379.5	301.5	20.1	27.7	16.4	15.6	29.5	20.7
Thailand	96.2	141.6	146.3	145.2	107.9	93.4	13.7	30.1	20.1	18.6	12.4	11.6
India	71.0	109.1	99.7	176.5	82.4	77.0	20.0	17.6	10.7	32.6	36.6	130.7
Australia	347.6	362.7	382.7	397.8	381.7	415.6	38.9	48.6	67.3	60.9	50.9	56.4
Middle East	316.3	346.1	374.1	415.9	362.5	289.5	61.3	76.9	96.6	90.7	99.5	63.7
Israel	93.7	112.6	135.6	148.2	106.4	103.2	4.9	12.5	7.5	5.9	8.2	5.0
Saudi Arabia	125.1	114.5	109.6	142.0	137.3	90.5	23.2	22.8	34.6	34.0	27.3	17.8
Africa	146.8	161.8	191.1	160.9	147.8	111.9	23.1	26.6	45.8	46.3	37.1	34.5

Destination	Oregon						Pennsylvania					
	1994	1995	1996	1997	1998	1999	1994	1995	1996	1997	1998	1999
ALL DESTINATIONS	6 987.4	9 902.1	8 481.3	8 358.6	8 143.5	11 164.3	14 698.6	17 680.2	17 445.6	19 298.4	19 138.8	19 527.7
Canada	1 020.9	1 097.5	890.2	1 081.7	1 328.6	1 675.2	4 066.5	4 671.8	4 773.7	5 615.7	5 856.9	5 927.2
Mexico	120.6	86.1	52.8	88.8	452.0	991.2	866.4	741.2	879.0	1 140.3	1 425.2	2 306.2
Central and South America and Caribbean	123.9	196.2	122.0	193.4	181.9	154.6	1 363.6	1 689.8	1 550.3	1 820.8	1 567.0	1 377.6
Argentina	13.2	11.4	10.5	12.1	9.8	9.0	201.8	161.8	127.0	154.0	156.0	120.9
Brazil	19.0	29.2	14.9	30.6	23.9	44.7	491.1	679.1	603.6	744.7	502.7	501.2
Chile	43.4	85.4	37.7	41.7	31.6	21.2	70.9	130.6	129.3	173.4	108.0	61.5
Colombia	11.2	11.5	9.1	10.5	10.0	10.6	119.2	128.9	116.8	103.6	99.9	100.8
Dominican Republic	0.6	1.6	6.9	6.1	3.3	2.5	50.8	70.5	97.2	115.2	114.7	94.0
Venezuela	3.5	3.4	4.1	41.8	30.2	7.4	138.4	150.9	118.5	131.5	151.0	95.1
European Union	1 164.3	1 725.3	952.9	1 061.8	1 077.2	1 726.1	3 277.5	4 365.0	4 373.1	4 487.9	4 698.5	4 513.7
Belgium	50.4	75.8	43.4	49.3	43.6	120.9	263.3	409.9	376.4	369.1	463.7	308.8
France	115.5	242.6	117.5	81.2	95.0	142.5	278.0	388.4	411.8	446.8	457.3	459.0
Germany	305.7	414.2	306.1	213.0	171.2	238.5	583.8	692.1	631.1	652.4	681.1	753.7
Ireland	76.7	225.3	119.3	145.8	146.9	83.7	107.6	120.1	97.4	108.6	96.1	99.6
Italy	91.8	96.7	56.8	68.4	73.4	109.3	281.1	338.4	343.3	336.2	335.3	369.0
Luxembourg	0.9	1.1	0.1	. . .	. . .	. . .	2.9	4.5	3.7	3.1	4.3	8.8
Netherlands	106.9	178.9	46.1	198.3	200.7	535.6	500.7	725.6	647.8	664.7	767.3	667.5
Spain	30.7	33.7	19.3	20.0	19.6	40.6	140.6	174.2	193.8	184.8	186.2	249.6
United Kingdom	304.9	352.4	161.6	191.0	225.5	325.1	812.3	1 146.9	1 369.9	1 436.3	1 405.5	1 270.1
Switzerland	17.9	24.8	20.4	28.6	16.5	26.0	88.2	82.3	97.2	86.9	78.6	112.0
Former Soviet Republics	45.5	36.7	11.9	26.0	34.4	31.9	48.6	78.2	134.7	101.4	73.6	29.4
Asian 10	3 654.0	5 675.0	5 419.7	5 147.9	4 544.2	6 033.1	3 676.7	4 416.3	4 030.3	4 429.7	3 818.0	3 976.1
China	33.7	75.2	96.2	107.0	129.5	216.4	255.8	314.8	242.5	245.2	296.6	315.5
Hong Kong	148.2	276.8	451.7	225.3	183.9	223.8	274.6	347.3	360.4	376.6	332.6	374.1
Indonesia	42.4	142.0	123.2	77.9	49.2	79.8	62.1	124.9	121.9	167.9	65.3	69.1
Japan	1 389.1	1 778.7	1 487.2	1 271.4	1 145.2	1 603.0	861.7	1 098.6	1 119.4	1 162.0	961.1	956.1
Malaysia	166.5	431.6	207.3	261.2	255.9	525.6	194.3	173.2	137.9	171.9	128.7	316.0
Philippines	283.2	302.3	371.2	520.3	481.5	509.6	89.6	136.0	154.3	142.6	87.2	117.4
Singapore	252.0	507.3	560.8	449.8	284.4	298.4	486.8	592.9	627.8	675.0	548.7	462.2
South Korea	550.9	936.5	905.5	1 037.8	1 353.5	1 910.6	641.1	694.9	593.3	593.8	459.9	415.0
Taiwan	688.4	1 057.7	1 047.0	1 063.4	593.8	585.9	565.3	727.6	428.1	521.3	591.3	645.4
Thailand	99.5	167.0	169.5	133.5	67.2	79.9	245.4	206.0	244.6	373.4	346.6	305.4
India	9.3	19.2	23.7	26.2	15.6	22.0	99.0	133.5	135.1	161.2	165.7	115.8
Australia	205.5	302.8	253.2	168.1	112.8	168.9	317.6	457.7	426.4	417.3	375.3	320.5
Middle East	86.2	144.1	203.9	131.9	85.4	89.1	402.4	510.7	479.1	415.1	423.0	344.9
Israel	26.5	27.8	48.0	38.6	21.5	45.4	113.2	137.6	155.8	128.2	141.4	128.4
Saudi Arabia	9.6	45.5	11.5	40.3	5.9	6.8	163.6	196.3	181.3	154.6	135.6	100.8
Africa	60.4	52.0	43.9	42.5	40.5	44.9	152.2	184.2	166.6	153.2	174.1	143.0

Table D-2. State Exports of Goods by Destination, 1994–1999—*Continued*

(Millions of dollars.)

Destination	Puerto Rico						Rhode Island					
	1994	1995	1996	1997	1998	1999	1994	1995	1996	1997	1998	1999
ALL DESTINATIONS	4 618.9	4 704.5	5 188.4	5 528.1	6 126.5	7 893.6	1 011.5	956.8	954.8	1 126.5	1 113.1	1 104.7
Canada	671.3	535.9	575.8	689.5	657.4	798.8	268.8	294.3	322.6	329.6	371.5	360.5
Mexico	137.0	205.5	226.9	216.8	160.2	164.2	27.6	15.4	23.2	77.3	68.1	80.9
Central and South America and Caribbean	852.6	950.1	981.7	1 097.1	1 089.8	1 156.9	53.1	42.7	28.7	64.8	47.1	41.0
Argentina	51.4	32.9	39.1	38.6	41.8	42.8	10.6	3.9	2.8	6.1	5.2	4.8
Brazil	106.2	115.3	116.7	129.8	110.2	109.7	8.4	9.3	6.7	32.3	15.7	10.8
Chile	8.4	6.2	8.8	5.3	4.6	5.2	10.2	7.4	3.8	3.7	2.8	2.0
Colombia	27.4	22.8	28.0	29.6	27.6	18.2	3.1	3.1	1.3	2.6	3.3	2.0
Dominican Republic	393.5	455.0	473.5	549.1	565.5	580.0	1.0	1.4	0.8	2.7	2.0	2.2
Venezuela	34.0	42.8	26.3	37.3	25.9	29.0	2.0	4.0	2.2	4.1	3.7	3.1
European Union	1 787.3	2 042.1	2 277.3	2 115.0	2 944.1	4 139.8	387.9	324.8	296.6	342.1	285.1	265.3
Belgium	202.3	194.6	214.6	185.8	182.9	260.5	40.7	25.3	24.3	39.4	27.7	29.1
France	209.9	309.9	309.8	318.2	407.2	590.0	19.2	18.3	16 4	18.3	17.7	19.6
Germany	652.5	781.6	935.6	532.8	667.7	1 233.8	25.2	30.2	38.6	41.2	29.3	30.5
Ireland	92.2	72.8	87.5	69.4	85.8	97.9	31.3	16.4	30.8	35.0	42.3	17.9
Italy	127.0	156.5	254.6	350.7	535.5	696.7	14.7	23.0	14.2	17.7	14.2	16.4
Luxembourg	0.1	. . .	5.7	. . .	. . .	. . .	1.5	1.5	3.1	2.6	0.7	1.9
Netherlands	164.9	206.8	235.5	415.6	686.1	629.9	48.4	29.1	24.7	20.8	16.9	22.7
Spain	38.4	37.8	42.4	32.1	36.5	69.3	17.4	13.5	12.8	25.3	18.0	12.0
United Kingdom	249.9	238.3	148.4	179.4	279.2	499.6	147.0	84.0	64.1	91.7	66.0	60.3
Switzerland	267.2	75.1	92.2	359.1	242.4	438.5	25.9	19.0	17.1	26.3	18.6	13.0
Former Soviet Republics	3.8	4.5	7.4	11.0	3.4	5.0	3.0	3.7	4.1	4.4	1.5	1.2
Asian 10	611.0	697.5	841.5	797.8	788.5	934.3	191.6	209.9	216.9	236.1	273.2	270.5
China	5.6	11.8	13.7	17.5	78.0	31.3	17.7	6.1	8.1	6.9	10.5	10.8
Hong Kong	17.5	22.9	19.1	28.5	21.8	31.5	33.7	30.3	34.9	34.5	41.8	40.9
Indonesia	14.2	8.2	11.5	17.7	3.6	3.7	0.8	0.6	1.5	1.0	0.7	1.5
Japan	397.3	400.5	413.1	448.7	428.0	547.8	46.7	65.8	61.8	89.4	114.9	83.1
Malaysia	23.1	16.9	41.1	34.4	27.1	30.7	18.2	23.3	28.5	24.9	26.9	30.3
Philippines	5.6	8.4	6.2	6.8	5.4	6.4	9.5	10.8	16.0	15.2	26.1	27.7
Singapore	71.4	140.9	244.8	149.8	125.2	147.6	22.1	23.9	19.7	18.4	16.9	24.8
South Korea	43.1	61.7	51.5	35.0	32.5	32.9	24.8	28.6	26.8	20.2	11.6	18.8
Taiwan	29.5	23.0	37.7	56.4	63.4	97.2	13.3	14.3	12.4	20.0	19.0	22.2
Thailand	3.8	3.1	2.8	3.0	3.6	5.1	4.9	6.2	7.2	5.5	4.8	10.5
India	10.5	10.0	5.2	11.5	9.1	16.1	4.9	4.6	2.5	2.1	1.9	4.1
Australia	181.3	96.0	86.2	92.2	86.3	74.0	11.0	13.2	14.7	9.7	16.9	9.4
Middle East	12.8	11.6	14.1	12.6	23.4	37.0	10.4	11.6	11.4	9.0	9.7	8.9
Israel	3.8	6.1	8.2	7.5	10.7	16.7	5.4	6.5	5.6	4.3	3.3	3.9
Saudi Arabia	2.3	0.4	1.4	3.5	8.0	3.2	1.9	2.0	1.9	0.9	3.5	2.8
Africa	15.5	12.0	11.0	13.3	17.2	20.5	3.9	3.2	3.0	3.4	3.2	33.4

Destination	South Carolina						South Dakota					
	1994	1995	1996	1997	1998	1999	1994	1995	1996	1997	1998	1999
ALL DESTINATIONS	3 510.1	4 497.9	4 924.9	5 673.8	5 856.9	6 476.5	263.9	348.6	397.3	435.3	373.5	1 143.4
Canada	1 252.7	1 538.5	1 478.2	1 620.7	1 710.8	1 989.7	130.8	142.1	164.1	167.3	165.9	178.9
Mexico	450.0	641.4	661.8	935.9	1 054.3	1 296.8	5.5	5.3	7.8	11.5	18.6	17.9
Central and South America and Caribbean	237.7	337.9	309.2	439.6	528.3	536.8	5.8	11.9	17.4	14.8	16.7	15.7
Argentina	13.7	21.3	23.3	38.1	40.3	19.5	0.3	0.2	0.2	0.5	0.8	1.1
Brazil	26.3	75.1	63.8	87.7	88.7	119.0	1.0	2.5	1.6	4.2	1.9	1.6
Chile	30.6	23.0	27.9	26.6	25.9	15.4	0.5	0.3	2.7	1.1	0.4	0.7
Colombia	20.9	20.6	18.6	26.9	31.9	17.8	0.4	1.0	0.6	0.8	0.4	0.1
Dominican Republic	23.1	31.4	32.9	50.2	73.2	71.4	0.1	0.1	0.2	0.2	0.1	6.4
Venezuela	6.3	15.3	19.8	41.4	13.5	13.8	0.4	0.5	0.6	1.7	5.1	0.9
European Union	786.2	926.8	1 452.0	1 592.9	1 618.4	1 569.4	69.5	111.2	105.8	121.7	92.6	114.7
Belgium	70.2	91.5	102.0	110.8	123.7	162.8	0.9	0.9	1.6	2.4	1.5	1.7
France	73.0	86.0	92.8	108.0	94.3	103.9	4.2	6.7	7.2	7.4	5.0	6.1
Germany	214.8	233.6	727.4	854.7	748.4	654.4	8.3	10.6	17.1	18.2	22.9	15.7
Ireland	42.7	34.7	25.3	23.6	18.8	14.2	17.3	24.1	11.8	21.6	20.5	26.8
Italy	51.9	77.4	89.9	99.1	118.8	110.5	1.1	2.7	2.2	3.1	3.4	19.4
Luxembourg	0.4	0.5	0.5	0.6	0.3	0.8	0.3	1.1	0.7	. . .	. . .	. . .
Netherlands	88.6	102.4	121.9	96.7	88.1	119.7	25.7	26.6	31.7	29.6	6.4	14.8
Spain	24.3	28.6	30.0	35.4	31.2	46.6	0.1	0.6	0.9	0.5	1.7	1.8
United Kingdom	177.3	225.5	210.0	212.9	337.1	295.6	8.7	35.5	29.6	35.7	27.4	25.5
Switzerland	15.4	17.1	17.8	23.4	29.8	95.1	1.0	1.1	0.6	0.9	0.6	0.9
Former Soviet Republics	1.9	1.3	4.8	4.3	5.2	2.6	0.4	1.3	0.4	0.2	0.3	0.7
Asian 10	585.5	760.5	712.9	773.0	647.9	721.0	38.2	58.4	81.9	104.5	66.5	798.3
China	29.0	54.0	55.9	45.9	35.3	58.3	0.4	0.6	0.3	3.8	2.6	9.7
Hong Kong	96.6	144.6	92.6	103.0	97.6	66.7	3.1	4.8	15.0	15.6	7.9	16.2
Indonesia	11.4	12.0	12.0	35.3	9.2	7.3	0.1	0.1	0.2	0.7	. . .	9.5
Japan	180.5	181.5	201.6	273.1	247.8	236.0	22.1	38.6	28.0	22.0	14.7	580.7
Malaysia	9.5	21.2	30.5	16.4	16.3	11.8	0.5	1.0	12.9	17.0	14.6	10.7
Philippines	5.4	11.0	13.5	9.3	8.9	9.9	0.5	0.4	1.2	0.7	0.4	0.8
Singapore	55.5	50.6	49.8	44.7	32.6	36.2	3.9	3.9	2.9	4.7	4.1	13.7
South Korea	112.4	115.2	66.9	67.5	44.9	164.3	2.6	1.0	3.2	4.7	0.7	125.9
Taiwan	71.0	154.1	165.8	160.3	135.6	113.3	4.2	6.2	14.0	32.0	9.4	25.8
Thailand	14.2	16.4	21.3	17.3	19.8	17.2	0.7	1.8	4.2	3.3	12.0	5.4
India	11.0	32.8	24.8	29.3	18.9	22.0	0.4	0.3	0.6	0.3	0.4	0.7
Australia	50.5	70.2	68.6	83.9	63.9	85.5	2.6	5.9	5.2	5.2	4.1	8.3
Middle East	54.0	85.9	99.3	71.6	76.0	69.8	4.6	5.1	3.7	2.9	4.2	1.8
Israel	11.5	24.6	22.4	20.4	22.1	13.8	0.8	1.7	2.8	1.1	3.4	0.7
Saudi Arabia	22.3	34.1	44.6	25.9	22.7	26.9	2.0	1.0	0.2	1.1	0.1	0.1
Africa	16.3	19.1	24.5	22.7	26.3	17.6	1.7	2.2	1.0	0.6	0.9	0.6

Table D-2. State Exports of Goods by Destination, 1994–1999—Continued

(Millions of dollars.)

Destination	Tennessee						Texas					
	1994	1995	1996	1997	1998	1999	1994	1995	1996	1997	1998	1999
ALL DESTINATIONS	7 506.2	9 460.5	9 328.3	9 916.9	9 872.5	9 342.7	40 489.0	45 192.6	48 252.1	56 292.9	59 029.3	61 705.6
Canada	1 976.2	2 101.0	2 199.9	2 389.4	2 589.1	2 919.3	4 830.4	6 142.0	6 616.4	8 117.6	8 505.9	9 295.9
Mexico	752.4	839.4	913.6	1 188.1	1 288.3	975.0	14 364.9	12 589.0	15 586.7	18 864.1	21 626.6	23 329.6
Central and South America and Caribbean	492.1	707.9	771.9	894.1	982.2	769.9	3 976.2	5 073.2	5 180.2	6 402.8	6 180.0	5 846.5
Argentina	53.7	59.8	71.3	75.0	101.0	114.5	366.3	529.1	475.7	504.9	508.3	600.9
Brazil	137.2	206.3	267.9	251.8	205.7	170.1	492.0	878.1	1 023.6	1 230.5	1 171.3	1 302.9
Chile	21.9	45.4	27.1	52.7	71.3	45.6	169.7	272.7	259.6	378.2	348.2	329.0
Colombia	44.4	53.9	48.1	88.3	77.8	59.6	530.5	620.3	696.7	782.3	585.4	549.1
Dominican Republic	49.1	70.7	61.8	72.8	80.6	62.0	122.4	108.1	120.5	156.9	124.3	133.9
Venezuela	31.1	29.3	30.7	34.4	50.4	51.6	1 027.0	1 136.4	1 175.8	1 375.5	1 290.8	1 279.6
European Union	1 708.0	1 898.8	1 869.1	2 132.4	2 314.2	2 290.6	4 957.7	5 803.7	5 419.8	6 162.9	7 118.6	6 723.6
Belgium	90.9	145.7	147.2	156.5	160.8	179.8	445.3	557.0	434.0	561.9	595.6	679.3
France	209.7	202.3	240.5	283.6	298.9	246.9	539.8	557.1	570.8	584.5	737.3	727.5
Germany	334.8	323.5	371.8	403.1	366.7	377.5	563.2	722.2	719.0	882.7	970.0	1 056.6
Ireland	26.3	41.3	40.4	34.8	60.8	51.8	148.3	153.8	136.8	143.1	270.5	437.0
Italy	134.2	162.2	133.5	133.3	163.0	186.2	245.7	331.3	265.6	297.9	355.4	385.7
Luxembourg	0.9	1.0	1.0	4.8	1.0	0.8	3.3	1.7	2.5	8.0	7.1	7.9
Netherlands	372.8	413.1	343.1	385.7	417.0	430.2	934.3	1 128.6	1 105.2	1 161.0	1 364.2	1 099.8
Spain	51.6	73.7	72.7	87.3	91.7	82.7	174.3	194.4	168.1	181.3	182.1	185.4
United Kingdom	378.4	422.9	395.5	531.7	619.9	604.5	1 674.6	1 915.5	1 717.1	1 979.3	2 236.7	1 672.9
Switzerland	14.7	16.3	23.2	25.4	25.5	28.5	112.3	127.3	104.0	106.2	132.0	130.1
Former Soviet Republics	16.1	14.8	25.0	125.3	52.9	15.0	227.8	256.6	347.6	326.6	286.1	395.4
Asian 10	1 949.4	2 984.1	2 693.9	2 247.4	1 744.3	1 561.2	8 159.0	10 826.5	9 981.2	11 006.0	9 707.5	11 408.0
China	384.0	1 100.6	872.5	433.2	154.7	113.0	482.4	715.0	605.4	651.8	583.4	810.3
Hong Kong	214.6	256.8	208.5	217.7	239.0	162.9	633.0	1 070.3	906.3	974.4	784.2	732.1
Indonesia	70.7	150.4	114.7	65.5	59.7	46.9	257.8	302.2	413.0	344.1	237.6	225.8
Japan	563.3	674.3	727.7	692.8	614.7	555.0	1 558.4	2 181.0	2 073.9	2 218.4	1 846.4	2 109.5
Malaysia	36.3	46.2	43.4	37.0	37.9	49.6	836.6	1 023.9	837.4	972.8	832.4	1 182.0
Philippines	48.7	80.8	73.0	65.6	61.2	68.7	490.7	598.3	754.1	882.1	935.9	1 129.1
Singapore	87.0	85.1	83.2	165.7	152.2	170.1	1 529.3	1 755.5	1 528.7	2 015.8	1 964.4	1 629.6
South Korea	230.4	284.4	320.6	279.2	187.6	157.0	923.6	1 474.0	1 354.2	1 352.6	1 084.4	1 841.4
Taiwan	249.4	213.1	176.6	226.2	200.7	202.9	1 200.4	1 371.4	1 179.0	1 348.3	1 211.8	1 539.8
Thailand	65.0	92.5	73.6	64.5	36.6	35.1	246.9	335.7	329.2	245.6	226.8	208.5
India	25.3	44.4	26.3	31.9	35.9	37.4	158.9	281.6	253.5	242.7	296.0	197.0
Australia	129.6	158.7	162.7	206.3	209.1	210.5	472.7	634.6	723.4	636.7	618.9	584.0
Middle East	117.2	171.0	146.6	185.7	166.5	119.0	1 194.2	1 334.9	1 705.8	1 882.8	2 004.4	1 645.9
Israel	28.4	29.7	34.7	40.2	34.8	37.2	120.7	227.5	262.6	271.5	221.7	223.7
Saudi Arabia	50.7	58.7	56.4	60.6	55.7	40.4	576.6	594.0	668.9	814.7	1 037.2	828.3
Africa	59.8	70.0	73.6	99.3	122.9	94.8	486.2	800.1	952.3	1 046.7	1 054.9	932.3

Destination	Utah						Vermont					
	1994	1995	1996	1997	1998	1999	1994	1995	1996	1997	1998	1999
ALL DESTINATIONS	2 233.1	2 313.4	2 768.5	3 293.3	3 099.4	2 789.3	2 304.3	2 683.6	2 610.8	2 592.1	2 757.7	2 826.7
Canada	342.9	413.1	443.3	514.5	505.2	563.2	2 064.5	2 509.9	2 377.6	2 310.3	2 486.3	2 477.4
Mexico	82.7	66.7	76.4	73.0	87.5	113.6	15.9	10.4	8.5	8.7	10.8	14.7
Central and South America and Caribbean	50.2	86.3	96.4	109.8	102.9	107.7	8.0	10.0	16.8	22.8	23.2	25.3
Argentina	3.3	3.4	3.6	6.4	5.5	8.3	0.6	0.9	0.9	1.0	0.7	0.8
Brazil	8.0	6.9	20.8	29.8	38.8	44.3	1.8	3.4	3.6	2.8	2.7	5.3
Chile	15.1	37.7	28.3	28.5	17.0	7.0	0.4	0.7	0.6	1.1	1.1	1.6
Colombia	5.0	10.6	5.3	10.6	6.3	6.9	0.9	0.9	1.1	3.6	5.1	0.9
Dominican Republic	2.6	7.4	11.2	3.3	3.1	3.5	0.2	0.1	1.3	0.1	0.2	0.5
Venezuela	3.3	4.2	8.3	9.3	6.9	9.7	1.0	1.4	0.7	1.0	0.9	1.1
European Union	522.5	619.2	895.1	1 257.1	1 132.4	1 122.2	123.7	73.9	96.6	136.6	139.1	168.0
Belgium	83.7	129.7	64.3	81.6	44.6	48.2	1.9	2.2	3.3	3.7	6.5	3.0
France	16.1	26.8	42.2	41.1	37.2	48.7	8.4	7.1	11.3	19.7	14.3	17.4
Germany	187.9	196.7	210.2	146.5	114.5	120.8	16.4	12.0	13.5	27.8	25.6	22.6
Ireland	20.8	24.5	21.6	43.4	50.7	65.1	30.4	3.3	1.5	2.5	4.9	5.0
Italy	13.0	17.7	26.3	48.6	26.1	42.6	5.2	5.9	7.6	9.3	11.7	13.6
Luxembourg	0.4	0.6	1.6	0.1	0.3	1.2	. . .	. . .	0.9	0.6	1.3	2.7
Netherlands	117.6	90.9	116.1	118.1	106.9	120.3	20.4	3.1	15.4	6.0	9.2	11.1
Spain	5.1	7.3	19.0	14.0	17.7	11.3	2.9	1.6	1.9	3.1	2.7	3.3
United Kingdom	60.8	108.8	365.9	735.1	697.7	626.5	29.5	29.7	32.8	49.1	47.6	69.3
Switzerland	78.7	4.5	6.0	17.7	8.1	14.3	4.2	4.4	4.3	5.8	8.9	8.6
Former Soviet Republics	3.4	12.0	5.3	7.4	11.0	6.2	3.5	0.4	0.4	0.4	0.2	0.2
Asian 10	1 086.8	1 021.0	1 116.0	1 204.5	857.7	718.8	65.8	54.3	78.7	80.3	63.8	95.1
China	13.8	16.4	28.1	11.7	17.8	24.9	4.9	3.4	5.2	2.9	1.8	7.3
Hong Kong	384.2	59.0	36.1	39.1	33.3	49.9	2.4	3.2	4.5	4.1	4.0	13.0
Indonesia	7.8	7.9	11.8	8.4	3.3	4.2	0.6	1.1	1.1	4.2	1.2	0.8
Japan	296.1	404.8	468.9	516.8	387.9	281.0	18.0	26.0	33.5	31.3	26.4	35.8
Malaysia	14.9	9.7	45.9	171.6	112.7	58.1	0.3	1.1	1.1	0.6	3.5	5.1
Philippines	32.6	65.7	52.1	97.0	111.2	83.0	1.2	0.9	1.9	1.4	1.3	0.9
Singapore	24.1	82.5	131.9	64.6	41.0	46.8	13.2	8.5	8.1	10.5	4.7	6.9
South Korea	89.6	159.4	140.7	107.1	46.3	92.5	5.4	5.7	9.3	17.6	13.2	5.8
Taiwan	172.6	144.9	138.8	112.8	54.1	54.7	17.0	3.4	12.1	6.3	7.0	19.0
Thailand	51.2	70.6	61.8	75.4	50.1	23.9	2.6	1.0	1.7	1.4	0.7	0.4
India	1.7	4.5	4.1	19.4	8.2	9.3	0.4	0.7	1.2	2.2	0.6	1.1
Australia	27.9	35.0	34.5	36.9	312.6	42.7	5.9	4.9	5.1	6.8	6.3	8.6
Middle East	12.8	20.0	49.6	24.3	26.1	31.4	6.1	5.0	12.3	8.8	7.2	13.3
Israel	6.1	12.6	9.7	14.6	10.7	16.1	1.5	1.0	1.6	4.5	2.2	1.9
Saudi Arabia	3.1	2.9	22.5	3.7	4.3	4.0	3.4	2.6	9.9	1.2	2.5	9.4
Africa	4.2	6.0	11.8	9.1	9.8	12.2	1.2	1.2	1.2	1.6	1.9	2.4

Table D-2. State Exports of Goods by Destination, 1994–1999—Continued

(Millions of dollars.)

Destination	Virgin Islands						Virginia					
	1994	1995	1996	1997	1998	1999	1994	1995	1996	1997	1998	1999
ALL DESTINATIONS	158.0	228.6	192.4	242.7	114.5	180.9	9 947.3	10 425.2	10 926.0	11 512.4	11 459.9	10 722.4
Canada	7.5	12.4	7.4	4.3	2.8	2.9	1 220.5	1 465.8	1 356.7	1 535.8	1 835.9	2 138.0
Mexico	3.8	5.6	11.7	3.9	0.7	1.9	365.8	320.8	342.1	430.2	547.2	644.6
Central and South America and Caribbean	71.6	134.6	123.7	114.8	73.7	92.2	619.5	694.4	750.1	903.6	833.0	608.6
Argentina	0.2	0.6	6.4	0.2	2.7	...	49.6	68.8	45.2	84.8	67.6	41.2
Brazil	6.8	23.3	8.4	1.3	0.4	1.8	171.2	256.4	273.4	407.3	347.2	228.1
Chile	0.4	...	0.2	...	...	...	29.6	47.8	76.4	58.5	73.3	48.9
Colombia	0.6	0.7	7.3	1.1	0.3	0.3	21.7	34.8	58.8	46.8	65.8	27.2
Dominican Republic	6.4	13.2	9.2	9.6	5.1	1.1	25.2	13.4	12.4	19.4	15.5	24.5
Venezuela	...	0.7	0.2	0.2	...	3.2	47.2	42.7	40.7	48.1	51.8	41.9
European Union	32.4	14.3	24.4	83.2	20.4	43.6	3 077.9	3 244.3	3 414.4	3 326.2	3 389.8	2 670.1
Belgium	0.1	...	...	0.3	2.3	2.1	1 406.8	1 379.6	1 303.3	1 164.5	1 048.6	439.1
France	0.3	0.1	0.1	1.8	0.1	0.7	153.8	154.0	194.7	210.5	249.0	204.6
Germany	0.3	0.6	0.1	5.8	1.8	0.3	480.4	531.0	672.5	670.7	620.4	679.0
Ireland	...	...	...	...	11.2	...	7.1	16.3	15.8	22.1	60.0	32.9
Italy	12.8	9.6	13.6	16.7	3.1	28.2	162.1	197.1	233.5	268.3	198.3	170.7
Luxembourg	...	...	...	...	...	...	14.4	14.7	22.5	31.3	31.6	37.8
Netherlands	16.4	2.5	8.4	57.5	0.7	10.9	185.2	262.0	202.6	211.0	331.4	285.7
Spain	0.3	0.1	0.1	...	0.2	0.1	178.9	141.1	192.6	184.3	238.9	190.6
United Kingdom	1.0	0.7	1.0	0.4	0.9	1.4	286.0	315.7	338.2	323.3	346.2	338.1
Switzerland	0.3	0.2	0.1	0.3	...	0.1	37.7	43.3	59.9	69.2	79.3	113.4
Former Soviet Republics	0.3	0.2	...	0.2	...	0.1	343.2	332.9	682.3	588.2	390.1	87.2
Asian 10	38.4	45.6	14.7	19.2	1.9	10.7	2 907.6	3 008.5	2 899.7	3 094.5	2 813.2	2 861.7
China	2.6	3.0	1.8	...	...	0.1	65.1	119.9	107.2	134.2	109.7	106.9
Hong Kong	0.2	0.9	...	0.1	0.3	...	153.7	176.3	198.4	262.3	202.7	168.8
Indonesia	0.3	...	...	...	0.2	...	28.2	31.2	35.2	48.4	16.8	22.7
Japan	1.9	16.1	6.4	0.1	1.1	0.8	1 401.9	1 256.2	1 385.5	1 434.2	1 458.0	1 476.2
Malaysia	0.7	...	...	0.4	...	...	33.6	59.5	60.8	64.0	49.6	85.6
Philippines	0.1	...	...	0.1	0.1	...	15.9	25.9	41.4	50.6	47.7	43.4
Singapore	8.5	0.8	0.1	0.1	...	3.9	96.3	126.3	107.7	133.4	118.7	159.1
South Korea	18.3	17.3	6.3	18.4	...	5.8	856.4	971.6	737.6	751.7	605.1	645.6
Taiwan	6.0	7.4	0.1	0.1	0.1	...	202.2	181.5	156.1	152.8	135.6	112.6
Thailand	...	...	...	...	...	...	54.5	60.3	69.7	62.9	69.3	40.8
India	...	4.1	0.1	2.3	...	...	29.7	21.4	34.1	30.5	27.8	29.8
Australia	0.3	0.2	...	...	0.7	0.4	95.5	113.4	113.5	101.5	116.9	176.6
Middle East	0.5	1.2	0.3	0.7	0.1	0.6	612.2	562.1	676.1	766.0	763.3	711.2
Israel	0.1	0.2	...	...	...	...	90.3	107.7	124.6	140.8	133.6	115.1
Saudi Arabia	...	0.9	0.1	...	...	0.2	321.7	234.9	251.5	276.5	285.5	364.8
Africa	0.9	2.9	7.6	0.3	0.5	0.5	214.0	151.3	137.1	95.8	82.2	107.0

Destination	Washington						West Virginia					
	1994	1995	1996	1997	1998	1999	1994	1995	1996	1997	1998	1999
ALL DESTINATIONS	25 062.3	22 032.0	25 498.0	31 745.6	37 960.4	36 825.9	940.6	1 097.9	1 217.9	1 298.8	1 178.2	897.1
Canada	1 856.4	2 288.6	2 437.4	2 457.5	2 360.0	2 507.7	334.6	334.2	377.5	478.5	503.4	373.0
Mexico	411.2	188.1	254.9	272.4	582.9	385.2	16.7	16.4	19.3	34.4	55.8	29.6
Central and South America and Caribbean	410.4	482.4	651.0	952.2	1 193.6	979.5	66.2	91.1	101.7	65.5	62.6	70.0
Argentina	36.5	97.5	44.3	60.4	119.5	263.8	4.1	2.5	4.8	2.7	2.5	3.5
Brazil	98.9	105.5	106.7	414.2	392.7	188.5	45.1	78.0	81.6	46.1	45.1	55.3
Chile	27.6	140.5	338.8	291.8	430.3	138.8	1.0	1.2	2.5	2.8	4.0	2.3
Colombia	94.7	33.2	32.0	48.3	28.6	22.7	5.7	2.7	3.7	3.6	3.1	2.0
Dominican Republic	1.8	1.5	2.4	3.1	6.8	8.5	0.9	0.4	2.0	3.4	0.9	0.4
Venezuela	13.8	16.4	26.4	44.1	43.6	125.2	1.5	0.9	1.4	1.2	1.6	0.9
European Union	5 114.5	4 469.0	4 869.4	8 889.1	10 281.5	13 815.8	291.5	412.9	419.6	403.3	305.9	259.0
Belgium	166.7	148.6	219.2	299.9	354.2	234.7	10.0	25.5	53.8	47.4	48.5	30.9
France	415.7	297.5	218.9	342.5	971.3	1 500.9	20.9	23.3	24.0	34.0	19.0	37.4
Germany	829.1	896.6	923.4	1 518.4	2 401.9	2 249.2	24.1	29.3	19.4	28.0	22.1	24.8
Ireland	45.1	57.0	39.7	52.9	86.9	427.8	0.5	1.6	2.0	4.8	2.0	1.8
Italy	282.6	431.4	432.0	285.5	156.2	813.0	63.3	104.5	102.3	50.1	39.4	29.0
Luxembourg	1.8	162.5	2.1	326.5	164.8	658.5	...	...	...	0.1	...	0.1
Netherlands	448.4	713.7	904.2	877.1	479.3	961.3	71.3	73.0	57.2	64.4	26.9	32.6
Spain	388.6	152.6	141.9	192.2	77.0	957.7	13.4	19.5	34.8	25.0	20.8	11.3
United Kingdom	2 297.4	1 272.3	1 688.5	4 488.1	4 455.9	4 431.9	57.7	100.6	100.0	127.2	116.4	76.8
Switzerland	59.2	24.0	61.7	68.0	105.6	118.0	1.0	0.3	1.7	2.1	1.4	1.9
Former Soviet Republics	442.0	274.8	555.1	272.8	989.8	483.6	0.6	1.3	0.6	0.2	0.6	0.3
Asian 10	14 039.7	13 043.6	13 920.2	14 870.6	16 362.0	12 860.7	200.1	193.4	231.1	218.3	188.9	124.2
China	1 887.1	1 088.4	1 463.9	1 805.7	3 172.2	2 070.7	22.1	20.5	12.6	9.0	16.8	10.1
Hong Kong	465.0	553.7	828.4	297.0	597.5	412.1	35.3	19.4	22.2	14.8	7.3	8.2
Indonesia	383.5	78.0	81.2	253.3	266.0	51.9	0.7	0.9	1.6	3.0	1.6	1.7
Japan	6 372.5	6 703.0	6 316.4	6 561.6	6 287.0	6 056.1	58.7	94.7	112.0	105.5	115.2	70.6
Malaysia	853.2	206.3	260.6	977.6	1 308.9	432.7	10.1	2.4	2.2	4.7	2.5	2.4
Philippines	57.8	191.3	237.8	109.1	77.2	98.3	0.9	1.2	1.4	2.1	1.3	1.4
Singapore	1 295.0	1 037.4	966.3	1 276.1	1 403.4	1 218.9	30.5	18.9	28.0	21.0	21.0	7.2
South Korea	1 408.3	1 851.6	2 023.9	1 889.2	965.3	1 398.8	16.7	21.2	24.5	29.8	11.6	14.0
Taiwan	993.8	933.0	893.6	797.0	1 541.6	550.9	15.2	10.1	17.1	13.2	7.5	6.1
Thailand	323.5	400.7	848.0	904.0	742.9	570.3	10.0	4.2	9.6	15.2	4.1	2.6
India	169.2	37.6	414.6	205.2	390.7	345.1	1.1	4.2	4.6	3.3	3.5	2.3
Australia	469.5	241.0	610.0	479.1	500.7	574.4	11.4	16.3	21.8	24.8	27.2	13.2
Middle East	768.4	288.0	643.9	1 683.4	2 918.5	2 507.7	5.0	11.7	17.2	25.5	14.4	10.7
Israel	343.6	211.6	54.8	101.6	33.9	520.7	1.3	7.1	12.1	3.9	5.6	4.5
Saudi Arabia	27.2	31.7	135.4	955.4	2 202.0	1 255.2	2.6	3.5	2.3	10.8	3.0	2.6
Africa	103.8	110.1	270.7	206.1	644.6	462.8	4.8	7.9	5.3	16.1	5.1	3.2

Table D-2. State Exports of Goods by Destination, 1994–1999—*Continued*

(Millions of dollars.)

Destination	Wisconsin						Wyoming					
	1994	1995	1996	1997	1998	1999	1994	1995	1996	1997	1998	1999
ALL DESTINATIONS	6 927.9	8 004.5	8 409.7	9 791.5	9 221.4	9 546.3	95.4	101.2	123.7	175.9	158.4	155.8
Canada	2 438.4	2 808.6	2 685.6	3 096.3	3 457.3	3 716.2	48.6	50.7	69.4	88.3	75.9	89.1
Mexico	411.9	311.0	350.5	427.3	512.1	596.1	4.1	4.1	3.5	4.9	5.9	12.6
Central and South America and Caribbean	464.1	577.6	664.0	785.1	736.3	604.1	3.5	4.2	4.2	11.7	8.9	6.4
Argentina	74.9	60.9	85.3	102.2	97.8	92.5	0.5	0.4	0.1	1.4	0.8	0.4
Brazil	109.1	176.6	187.2	243.9	228.1	148.8	0.4	0.2	0.7	2.4	1.6	0.7
Chile	70.5	94.3	139.6	129.3	103.9	79.0	0.2	0.3	0.4	0.3	0.7	0.3
Colombia	43.9	45.0	41.0	42.6	44.7	31.3	0.4	0.3	0.1	0.5	0.4	0.2
Dominican Republic	15.1	22.8	21.4	28.8	25.3	29.6	0.3	0.1	0.5	0.7	0.1	0.1
Venezuela	23.6	29.8	27.2	52.9	48.8	33.7	0.2	0.3	1.7	2.2	1.2	1.4
European Union	1 725.6	1 915.6	2 097.3	2 493.0	2 203.9	2 299.0	16.5	17.4	17.8	39.5	46.4	21.2
Belgium	124.8	147.3	178.5	205.3	163.9	161.5	0.1	0.2	3.1	9.8	7.4	0.7
France	317.4	358.2	319.4	454.0	327.7	412.5	1.2	1.5	0.6	1.3	1.9	0.9
Germany	325.0	387.1	441.4	462.2	445.6	382.5	4.0	2.7	1.9	1.7	3.4	0.5
Ireland	22.4	28.6	40.6	47.8	58.0	44.4	0.3	...	0.3	1.0	1.2	0.8
Italy	120.2	133.7	146.9	160.2	167.2	197.4	0.5	0.5	0.2	1.7	1.5	1.4
Luxembourg	1.0	1.2	1.9	1.7	2.7	1.7	...	...	...	...	...	...
Netherlands	179.4	238.9	254.8	238.9	261.2	268.3	0.5	1.1	0.9	15.0	18.2	3.6
Spain	48.2	60.9	78.2	75.4	80.0	71.3	0.6	2.9	3.6	0.9	1.1	1.2
United Kingdom	447.2	400.3	441.9	612.6	513.1	583.4	8.6	7.6	6.8	6.9	10.2	9.9
Switzerland	64.5	71.0	57.9	51.5	47.5	46.5	0.5	0.6	0.6	0.3	0.2	0.5
Former Soviet Republics	13.7	12.0	24.7	162.7	48.3	10.5	4.2	1.3	0.9	0.1	0.1	0.1
Asian 10	1 172.6	1 557.6	1 696.5	1 830.6	1 470.2	1 547.7	13.3	17.2	24.0	22.8	15.1	18.8
China	89.0	102.6	110.1	146.2	118.7	149.2	...	0.4	0.4	2.6	1.2	0.8
Hong Kong	158.7	184.1	186.6	186.9	171.8	170.5	1.4	1.2	0.5	2.4	1.3	2.3
Indonesia	11.1	26.6	42.6	92.0	22.6	11.2	...	1.0	0.3	0.4	0.8	1.0
Japan	463.9	581.6	677.9	693.7	639.6	680.6	6.9	9.6	18.4	11.1	3.6	4.7
Malaysia	24.5	47.0	62.4	69.8	34.1	36.2	0.4	0.4	0.1	0.2	0.5	0.7
Philippines	23.5	33.9	59.4	71.9	136.7	66.5	0.4	0.4	1.8	0.2	0.2	0.2
Singapore	112.8	124.5	137.3	149.3	87.5	123.8	1.0	1.1	0.6	1.3	1.8	1.7
South Korea	123.4	167.4	172.1	187.9	79.7	119.7	1.1	0.9	1.2	3.3	3.8	5.3
Taiwan	119.1	214.2	164.6	160.3	147.7	151.6	2.0	1.8	0.7	1.1	1.9	2.1
Thailand	46.6	75.6	83.6	72.8	31.8	38.3	0.1	0.5	0.1	0.2	0.1	0.1
India	20.6	41.2	37.6	34.9	37.3	46.6	0.1	0.1	0.2	0.5	0.5	1.1
Australia	258.1	239.1	290.0	380.6	267.5	267.1	1.8	1.4	1.3	2.1	1.8	1.2
Middle East	132.2	206.8	170.5	174.0	164.5	159.0	1.0	1.6	0.6	2.4	1.3	2.3
Israel	26.4	48.7	35.0	31.2	33.9	37.2	0.3	0.7	0.2	0.2	0.7	0.4
Saudi Arabia	56.5	75.7	67.2	73.0	70.9	57.8	0.2	...	0.2	0.7	0.2	1.1
Africa	66.3	78.1	113.2	106.3	72.3	58.5	1.1	0.3	0.3	0.5	0.4	0.5

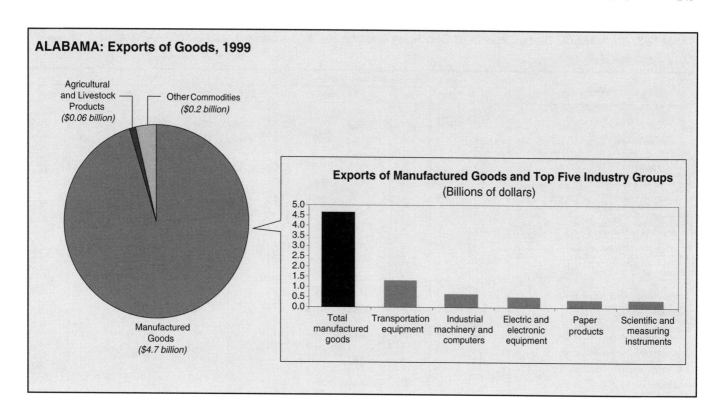

ALABAMA: Exports of Goods, 1999

Agricultural and Livestock Products ($0.06 billion)

Other Commodities ($0.2 billion)

Manufactured Goods ($4.7 billion)

Exports of Manufactured Goods and Top Five Industry Groups
(Billions of dollars)

Total manufactured goods / Transportation equipment / Industrial machinery and computers / Electric and electronic equipment / Paper products / Scientific and measuring instruments

Table D-3. ALABAMA: State Exports of Goods by Destination and Industry, 1994–1999

(Millions of dollars.)

Industry	All destinations						Canada					
	1994	1995	1996	1997	1998	1999	1994	1995	1996	1997	1998	1999
ALL GOODS	3 115.4	3 587.1	3 702.4	4 537.2	4 560.2	4 898.9	789.0	988.5	1 177.4	1 251.1	1 280.8	1 459.5
Manufactured Goods	2 796.6	3 167.0	3 359.9	4 207.7	4 262.3	4 665.6	745.6	939.9	1 118.6	1 199.4	1 235.7	1 416.9
Food products	32.4	49.6	40.9	52.1	41.9	49.4	26.6	41.3	31.0	37.8	27.7	36.9
Tobacco products	1.1	0.7	2.4	1.5	2.7	6.1	. . .	. . .	. . .	. . .	0.1	0.2
Textile mill products	66.0	83.9	86.0	122.4	135.5	156.5	35.9	34.6	25.1	32.2	32.8	48.7
Apparel	79.4	94.8	129.6	168.4	213.9	272.0	11.3	12.9	13.5	18.1	18.8	21.5
Lumber and wood products	129.9	143.1	140.2	143.6	137.0	153.5	6.9	5.4	7.3	20.9	12.5	15.1
Furniture and fixtures	32.2	25.6	21.9	27.5	26.7	64.9	22.0	21.0	15.3	20.5	21.4	57.0
Paper products	333.0	500.5	440.1	442.6	417.3	376.9	35.1	56.6	81.5	89.6	101.3	98.3
Printing and publishing	4.9	4.3	3.2	5.6	3.7	4.5	2.8	2.7	0.9	0.8	0.7	1.0
Chemical products	219.6	292.7	335.2	356.8	383.8	228.1	51.6	57.0	56.4	69.8	67.4	69.1
Refined petroleum products	0.8	1.5	9.4	3.1	2.9	6.6	0.2	0.2	8.1	1.4	1.1	5.6
Rubber and plastic products	61.3	56.6	64.8	82.5	93.6	84.9	31.4	24.1	24.3	42.5	40.6	40.6
Leather products	0.5	0.7	1.7	1.3	1.5	1.7	0.1	0.4	0.4	0.1	0.3	0.3
Stone, clay and glass products	42.3	49.5	46.2	47.8	56.5	59.2	9.6	10.2	12.1	13.4	12.0	11.8
Primary metals	140.5	187.9	146.5	199.0	194.9	167.5	40.0	50.0	48.0	82.8	62.4	54.8
Fabricated metal products	79.9	90.7	110.0	165.0	86.9	121.2	26.6	31.3	33.6	28.7	28.7	55.3
Industrial machinery and computers	393.9	457.6	457.0	625.6	557.5	662.9	92.6	106.6	109.0	111.6	100.9	89.1
Electric and electronic equipment	487.9	610.0	819.6	1 140.0	538.2	517.3	211.7	239.9	358.2	210.5	181.1	186.6
Transportation equipment	591.6	418.8	400.5	357.8	1 034.2	1 313.8	101.7	207.1	250.2	232.6	267.4	335.6
Scientific and measuring instruments	62.1	64.0	63.8	220.0	298.0	371.2	24.1	26.3	28.1	172.5	249.4	280.2
Miscellaneous manufactures	27.0	24.1	31.1	32.8	23.2	30.8	14.0	10.2	13.7	10.1	6.3	6.4
Unidentified manufactures	10.2	10.2	9.6	12.1	12.5	16.7	1.6	2.0	1.9	3.4	3.0	2.8
Agricultural And Livestock Products	69.2	125.4	64.8	69.5	81.9	59.7	21.3	25.8	30.7	22.3	18.1	13.8
Agricultural products	65.5	121.3	58.3	62.4	74.2	49.5	19.2	24.1	27.3	17.9	14.4	9.7
Livestock and livestock products	3.8	4.1	6.5	7.1	7.7	10.2	2.1	1.6	3.5	4.3	3.7	4.1
Other Commodities	249.5	294.7	277.8	259.9	216.0	173.5	22.1	22.9	28.1	29.4	27.0	28.8
Forestry products	0.3	0.6	0.4	0.3	0.5	0.5	0.1	0.2	0.1	0.1	. . .	. . .
Fish and other marine products	11.6	13.7	9.2	4.6	4.5	5.1	6.3	4.2	2.9	3.4	3.5	2.8
Metallic ores and concentrates	1.0	1.8	2.2	2.0	0.1	0.1	1.0	1.2	1.4	2.0	0.1	0.1
Bituminous coal and lignite	199.5	235.1	218.7	204.9	149.1	83.5	0.8	. . .	0.7	. . .	. . .	0.4
Crude petroleum and natural gas	. . .	. . .	2.6	. . .	. . .	0.1	. . .	. . .	2.6	. . .	. . .	. . .
Nonmetallic minerals	3.5	4.5	4.7	6.9	5.8	8.6	1.0	2.7	3.6	5.9	3.5	5.8
Scrap and waste	2.7	8.0	5.8	5.6	7.9	10.1	0.6	3.1	1.9	2.7	2.0	2.9
Used merchandise	6.4	7.6	7.7	7.4	7.6	8.4	1.2	1.1	1.1	1.6	0.7	1.5
Goods imported and returned unchanged	8.7	7.9	11.9	12.7	16.3	10.6	8.7	7.9	11.9	12.7	16.3	10.6
Special classification provisions	15.7	15.6	14.6	15.6	24.3	46.6	2.4	2.5	2.0	1.2	0.8	4.9

Table D-3. ALABAMA: State Exports of Goods by Destination and Industry, 1994–1999—*Continued*

(Millions of dollars.)

Industry	South and Central American and Caribbean						Mexico					
	1994	1995	1996	1997	1998	1999	1994	1995	1996	1997	1998	1999
ALL GOODS	374.0	308.3	304.4	407.7	500.8	415.4	222.6	193.1	324.9	813.7	380.4	456.4
Manufactured Goods	338.9	253.0	259.9	345.0	429.9	375.1	218.8	190.6	323.1	809.0	368.2	444.9
Food products	1.5	1.7	1.8	4.3	2.8	3.1	0.6	0.3	1.0	0.9	4.0	0.5
Tobacco products	0.1	0.1	1.1	0.2	0.3	3.7	...	...	0.1	0.2	0.2	0.1
Textile mill products	5.4	15.3	24.5	46.6	62.8	25.8	2.2	3.8	5.7	11.5	16.7	57.0
Apparel	42.7	42.5	56.1	92.9	120.4	157.3	12.2	26.1	43.7	42.0	66.4	83.1
Lumber and wood products	6.7	8.0	12.8	14.3	17.9	18.1	3.5	2.0	0.6	0.5	1.2	0.5
Furniture and fixtures	1.3	1.7	2.6	1.8	1.6	2.8	4.0	0.7	0.5	0.8	0.5	1.1
Paper products	7.2	14.1	20.6	20.0	19.8	17.4	11.2	11.3	8.1	10.2	6.3	11.6
Printing and publishing	0.3	0.1	0.2	0.1	0.2	0.1	0.4	0.4	0.6	2.9	1.2	0.8
Chemical products	9.3	19.8	22.4	28.1	35.4	21.5	13.8	12.4	15.2	19.8	21.2	20.2
Refined petroleum products	0.1	0.3	0.4	0.5	0.4	0.2	0.1	...	0.2	0.1	...	...
Rubber and plastic products	6.1	8.3	8.5	9.3	4.9	3.4	5.8	3.8	6.5	4.9	4.6	9.7
Leather products	0.1	...	0.3	...	...	0.6	...	...	...	...	0.5	...
Stone, clay and glass products	1.9	1.8	1.8	1.9	2.3	4.2	2.0	2.3	3.2	3.2	4.5	6.3
Primary metals	11.5	16.2	17.1	13.2	23.7	30.9	49.7	26.6	23.6	28.2	27.5	38.1
Fabricated metal products	10.4	15.2	14.3	16.8	8.1	9.6	2.8	5.8	7.3	15.7	17.1	22.3
Industrial machinery and computers	26.9	32.2	38.2	54.9	49.5	49.4	19.5	12.4	20.4	33.8	33.9	50.0
Electric and electronic equipment	11.6	21.7	10.1	13.5	10.1	10.3	82.7	75.6	176.8	618.1	146.4	115.7
Transportation equipment	192.1	48.2	23.7	18.5	64.0	8.9	1.6	1.3	2.7	4.5	3.3	6.2
Scientific and measuring instruments	1.7	2.4	1.2	6.0	1.7	4.1	5.9	3.8	2.3	3.6	5.5	7.3
Miscellaneous manufactures	1.4	2.8	1.8	1.5	2.4	1.7	0.3	0.2	4.1	7.7	5.2	12.2
Unidentified manufactures	0.8	0.7	0.4	0.4	1.3	2.1	0.6	1.8	0.3	0.4	2.0	2.2
Agricultural And Livestock Products	13.7	13.5	7.1	13.4	18.5	16.3	0.3	1.3	1.3	4.0	11.6	8.6
Agricultural products	12.9	12.6	6.0	11.8	15.9	13.4	0.2	0.9	0.9	3.3	10.6	5.6
Livestock and livestock products	0.8	0.9	1.2	1.7	2.6	2.9	0.1	0.5	0.4	0.7	1.1	3.0
Other Commodities	21.4	41.8	37.4	49.3	52.4	23.9	3.5	1.2	0.5	0.8	0.6	2.9
Forestry products	...	0.1	...	0.1	0.3	0.5	0.1	0.1	...	...	...	...
Fish and other marine products	...	...	...	...	...	0.6	...	...	...	...	...	0.1
Metallic ores and concentrates	...	...	...	...	...	...	...	...	...	...	...	0.1
Bituminous coal and lignite	19.8	39.8	35.5	46.9	38.8	16.5	2.1	...	...	...	...	...
Crude petroleum and natural gas	...	...	...	...	...	...	...	...	...	...	...	...
Nonmetallic minerals	1.2	0.8	0.3	0.5	1.6	1.8	0.9	0.5	0.1	0.2	0.1	0.2
Scrap and waste	0.1	0.2	0.1	0.3	0.3	0.4	0.4	0.5	0.3	0.3	0.2	0.1
Used merchandise	0.2	0.7	0.6	1.4	3.3	1.9	...	0.1	0.1	0.1	0.2	1.0
Goods imported and returned unchanged	...	...	...	...	...	...	...	...	...	...	...	...
Special classification provisions	0.2	0.1	0.7	0.1	8.1	2.4	...	...	...	0.1	0.1	1.4

Industry	European Union						United Kingdom					
	1994	1995	1996	1997	1998	1999	1994	1995	1996	1997	1998	1999
ALL GOODS	723.4	883.0	820.1	864.6	1 326.4	1 497.2	127.8	187.2	198.6	247.6	235.1	302.7
Manufactured Goods	632.1	749.9	697.1	748.3	1 231.3	1 425.6	109.9	169.2	179.9	221.5	224.1	293.3
Food products	1.4	1.0	2.5	2.9	2.5	2.5	0.3	0.4	1.1	1.1	1.2	1.3
Tobacco products	0.1	0.2	0.3	0.3	0.8	0.8	...	...	0.2	...	0.1	0.1
Textile mill products	10.5	11.5	13.0	13.2	11.6	13.6	4.3	4.0	5.3	6.5	2.8	2.0
Apparel	8.5	4.6	3.9	7.3	1.4	4.5	5.4	1.5	2.5	1.1	0.9	3.8
Lumber and wood products	71.8	73.7	74.2	65.2	64.2	86.1	8.9	8.2	6.8	8.1	13.4	31.2
Furniture and fixtures	1.1	0.6	1.2	2.5	1.5	2.7	...	...	0.1	0.6	0.2	0.4
Paper products	88.1	138.6	119.6	123.7	148.5	98.8	24.7	37.0	29.6	23.3	35.5	26.5
Printing and publishing	0.9	0.8	0.7	1.0	1.0	2.2	0.1	...	0.2	0.2	0.1	0.1
Chemical products	28.2	46.3	60.8	81.5	64.6	43.4	8.1	27.2	30.1	51.1	2.8	4.2
Refined petroleum products	0.1	0.3	0.3	0.4	0.8	0.2	...	...	0.1	0.1	...	...
Rubber and plastic products	10.6	12.1	16.4	18.1	31.8	15.7	1.0	1.4	6.7	5.1	3.2	2.5
Leather products	0.2	0.2	1.0	1.0	0.4	0.3	0.1	...	...	...	0.1	...
Stone, clay and glass products	17.7	23.6	17.7	15.1	24.8	22.1	1.2	2.1	3.0	1.8	2.5	3.3
Primary metals	12.8	22.1	9.6	17.3	22.9	20.8	3.0	3.1	2.0	2.5	5.1	7.0
Fabricated metal products	15.9	11.9	15.8	15.1	17.0	20.0	5.5	5.9	7.7	5.6	5.3	5.7
Industrial machinery and computers	142.4	167.4	157.9	175.4	194.0	187.6	16.1	36.1	36.3	59.1	69.1	68.6
Electric and electronic equipment	86.6	121.4	122.0	127.7	89.1	94.9	17.2	30.6	36.7	43.2	25.2	24.5
Transportation equipment	117.0	94.7	59.8	55.2	528.0	770.4	7.9	6.6	7.8	5.2	47.4	104.4
Scientific and measuring instruments	12.2	12.0	12.8	17.0	19.7	29.4	3.7	3.0	2.0	5.4	6.4	5.6
Miscellaneous manufactures	3.3	3.9	3.3	3.2	2.8	3.2	1.8	1.6	1.6	1.2	1.2	1.2
Unidentified manufactures	2.6	3.4	4.3	5.3	3.9	6.6	0.5	0.4	0.2	0.3	1.5	1.0
Agricultural And Livestock Products	4.3	12.1	5.8	7.1	11.3	2.8	3.3	3.3	1.8	2.0	0.1	0.1
Agricultural products	3.8	11.8	5.1	6.9	11.2	2.7	3.3	3.2	1.6	2.0	0.1	0.1
Livestock and livestock products	0.5	0.3	0.6	0.2	0.1	0.1	...	0.1	0.2	...	...	...
Other Commodities	87.0	121.0	117.2	109.3	83.9	68.8	14.6	14.6	16.8	24.1	10.9	9.3
Forestry products	0.1	0.1	0.1	0.1	0.1	...	...	0.1	0.1	...	...	...
Fish and other marine products	...	0.4	0.3	0.1	0.1	0.1	...	...	...	...	...	...
Metallic ores and concentrates	...	0.6	...	...	...	0.1	...	0.6	0.6	...	...	0.1
Bituminous coal and lignite	77.0	105.9	106.3	96.4	70.3	48.9	9.5	9.5	12.3	18.9	4.1	2.9
Crude petroleum and natural gas	...	...	...	...	...	...	...	...	...	...	...	...
Nonmetallic minerals	0.3	0.3	0.6	0.2	0.4	0.8	...	...	0.2	0.1	0.1	...
Scrap and waste	0.4	1.2	1.1	0.8	1.3	0.5	0.2	...	0.5	0.4	1.0	0.5
Used merchandise	3.6	3.6	3.4	2.0	2.5	2.9	1.4	0.8	0.7	0.4	1.1	1.5
Goods imported and returned unchanged	...	...	...	...	...	...	...	...	...	...	...	...
Special classification provisions	5.7	8.8	4.9	9.7	9.3	15.6	3.4	3.5	2.6	4.3	4.5	4.3

Table D-3. ALABAMA: State Exports of Goods by Destination and Industry, 1994–1999—*Continued*

(Millions of dollars.)

Industry	Germany						France					
	1994	1995	1996	1997	1998	1999	1994	1995	1996	1997	1998	1999
ALL GOODS	112.5	119.2	100.0	124.2	452.5	421.4	108.1	96.4	71.7	79.9	127.2	110.5
Manufactured Goods	110.8	115.2	97.8	120.2	448.6	414.5	106.5	92.7	70.6	76.8	126.0	106.1
Food products	0.1	0.2	0.4	0.6	0.5	0.1	0.1	0.2	...	0.1	0.2	0.4
Tobacco products	...	0.1	...	...	...	0.2	...	...	0.1	...	...	...
Textile mill products	0.4	1.2	1.6	0.7	0.9	0.5	0.3	0.4	1.0	0.5	0.2	1.1
Apparel	1.1	1.1	0.6	0.2	0.2	...	0.2	...	0.2	...	...	0.2
Lumber and wood products	7.8	8.0	6.9	6.3	4.6	6.0	2.2	1.7	2.5	2.4	1.1	0.8
Furniture and fixtures	...	0.2	0.1	0.4	0.2	0.6	...	...	0.1	0.7	0.3	0.2
Paper products	12.1	17.0	26.1	37.7	28.8	12.3	17.9	30.4	20.9	19.7	23.9	8.4
Printing and publishing	0.1	...	0.1	...	...	0.5	0.1	0.1	0.1	0.1	...	0.3
Chemical products	1.9	2.7	9.8	14.2	22.8	13.3	0.9	0.8	0.5	1.1	1.9	2.7
Refined petroleum products	...	0.2	0.2	...	0.6	...	...	...	...	0.1	...	...
Rubber and plastic products	1.8	2.8	1.2	3.2	6.3	2.0	2.7	2.4	3.2	4.5	7.9	3.1
Leather products	...	...	0.9	0.4	0.2	0.2	0.1	0.1	...	0.1	...	...
Stone, clay and glass products	8.4	10.4	6.1	4.6	10.7	8.3	2.1	1.8	2.3	3.4	3.3	3.5
Primary metals	6.1	7.2	3.8	8.2	11.7	8.0	2.0	3.4	1.1	3.7	3.1	3.0
Fabricated metal products	3.6	2.7	4.0	4.4	2.6	6.6	1.4	0.5	0.6	1.3	2.1	1.8
Industrial machinery and computers	32.8	21.4	12.6	10.5	10.5	15.0	19.8	20.6	7.9	9.4	23.4	20.8
Electric and electronic equipment	16.3	19.7	11.1	12.1	8.5	6.2	15.3	13.0	3.5	3.9	5.0	6.2
Transportation equipment	15.8	16.2	9.2	13.9	335.2	321.8	38.4	13.9	22.2	20.5	48.9	49.9
Scientific and measuring instruments	2.0	2.0	2.1	2.3	3.7	11.1	2.6	3.3	4.0	5.2	4.5	3.4
Miscellaneous manufactures	0.3	1.3	0.7	0.3	0.2	0.6	0.1	0.2	0.3	0.2	...	0.3
Unidentified manufactures	0.3	0.8	0.2	0.1	0.4	1.2	0.1	0.1	0.1	0.1	0.1	0.1
Agricultural And Livestock Products	0.1	0.6	0.4	1.3	0.8	1.7	0.2	0.1	0.1	0.1	0.1	...
Agricultural products	...	0.6	0.4	1.2	0.8	1.7	0.1	...	...	0.1	0.1	...
Livestock and livestock products	...	...	...	0.1	...	...	0.1	0.1	0.1	...	...	...
Other Commodities	1.6	3.4	1.9	2.8	3.1	5.2	1.4	3.5	1.0	3.0	1.1	4.3
Forestry products	...	...	...	...	...	...	...	...	...	...	...	...
Fish and other marine products	...	0.3	0.3	0.1	...	...	...	...	...	...	...	...
Metallic ores and concentrates	...	...	...	...	...	...	...	...	...	...	...	...
Bituminous coal and lignite	...	...	...	...	...	...	...	...	...	...	0.4	3.1
Crude petroleum and natural gas	...	...	...	...	...	...	...	...	...	...	...	...
Nonmetallic minerals	0.2	0.3	...	0.1	0.3	0.7	...	...	...	...	...	...
Scrap and waste	0.1	0.5	0.3	...	0.1	...	...	...	...	...	...	...
Used merchandise	1.2	2.0	1.2	1.3	1.0	0.6	0.3	0.4	0.6	0.1	0.1	0.1
Goods imported and returned unchanged	...	...	...	...	...	...	...	...	...	...	...	...
Special classification provisions	...	0.2	0.1	1.3	1.5	3.9	1.0	3.1	0.4	2.9	0.7	1.1

Industry	The Netherlands						Asian 10					
	1994	1995	1996	1997	1998	1999	1994	1995	1996	1997	1998	1999
ALL GOODS	87.3	127.3	165.5	151.1	178.2	165.8	615.0	878.8	761.1	867.4	660.1	739.1
Manufactured Goods	86.0	124.1	164.6	148.4	155.1	141.1	482.3	742.0	687.9	825.6	621.5	694.6
Food products	...	...	0.3	0.2	0.4	0.2	0.8	1.2	2.1	4.4	2.5	4.6
Tobacco products	...	...	...	...	0.1	...	...	...	0.1	0.1	0.3	0.5
Textile mill products	1.6	1.2	1.3	1.2	1.4	1.8	2.1	2.7	3.7	3.9	5.2	5.2
Apparel	0.4	0.4	0.1	0.1	...	0.1	3.4	7.8	11.0	6.3	4.6	4.1
Lumber and wood products	2.1	2.2	3.6	4.8	2.3	3.1	32.9	45.7	38.7	36.6	35.1	26.8
Furniture and fixtures	0.2	0.1	0.1	0.1	0.1	...	0.2	0.5	1.1	0.7	0.6	0.4
Paper products	1.3	1.9	4.5	8.0	15.1	11.8	181.1	262.9	178.9	190.8	134.7	146.4
Printing and publishing	0.1	0.1	...	0.1	0.1	...	0.4	0.2	0.2	0.5	0.1	0.3
Chemical products	4.6	3.4	0.7	0.6	14.4	2.5	69.0	109.0	137.4	135.8	161.8	56.4
Refined petroleum products	...	...	...	...	...	...	0.2	0.1	0.1	0.1	0.4	0.6
Rubber and plastic products	1.5	0.7	...	0.1	0.2	0.2	3.8	4.8	4.5	3.1	5.6	11.4
Leather products	...	...	...	0.4	...	...	...	0.1	0.1	...	0.2	0.4
Stone, clay and glass products	2.7	4.2	1.9	2.4	5.1	2.3	6.7	7.1	6.3	9.0	7.1	8.8
Primary metals	0.2	1.0	0.5	0.2	0.3	0.4	14.3	25.8	12.4	15.2	7.9	8.9
Fabricated metal products	1.2	0.5	1.0	0.4	1.4	0.5	13.4	17.3	27.7	76.7	5.1	6.3
Industrial machinery and computers	45.8	65.1	81.8	69.0	71.1	64.6	60.2	87.0	91.9	178.8	123.8	238.7
Electric and electronic equipment	22.2	34.8	58.6	54.1	35.3	42.7	64.1	112.8	120.7	132.9	87.8	97.2
Transportation equipment	0.7	7.4	9.5	5.9	7.2	9.0	16.5	42.2	33.0	10.5	18.7	30.6
Scientific and measuring instruments	0.9	0.5	0.5	0.4	0.2	1.6	7.9	10.2	10.7	12.5	14.9	40.2
Miscellaneous manufactures	0.2	0.3	0.1	0.3	0.2	0.3	3.8	3.2	5.1	6.5	4.1	5.1
Unidentified manufactures	0.1	0.2	0.1	0.2	0.1	0.1	1.6	1.4	2.3	1.2	1.1	1.7
Agricultural And Livestock Products	0.4	0.1	0.3	0.2	0.1	0.1	27.6	47.8	17.1	15.9	13.6	14.1
Agricultural products	0.1	0.1	0.1	0.1	0.1	0.1	27.5	47.3	16.5	15.8	13.4	14.0
Livestock and livestock products	0.3	...	0.2	0.1	...	...	0.2	0.5	0.6	0.1	0.2	0.1
Other Commodities	0.9	3.0	0.6	2.5	23.0	24.6	105.1	89.0	56.0	25.9	25.0	30.4
Forestry products	...	...	...	...	...	...	...	0.1	0.1	...	...	...
Fish and other marine products	...	...	...	...	...	...	5.3	9.1	5.9	1.1	0.9	1.5
Metallic ores and concentrates	...	...	...	...	...	...	...	...	0.2	...	...	...
Bituminous coal and lignite	...	2.7	...	2.3	22.9	23.7	94.9	77.5	45.2	20.4	17.0	11.2
Crude petroleum and natural gas	...	...	...	...	...	...	...	...	...	...	...	...
Nonmetallic minerals	...	...	0.3	...	...	...	0.1	0.1	0.1	0.1	0.2	0.1
Scrap and waste	...	0.1	...	...	...	...	0.1	0.1	0.4	0.1	2.7	4.6
Used merchandise	0.1	...	...	...	...	...	0.2	0.6	1.2	0.2	0.1	0.1
Goods imported and returned unchanged	...	...	...	...	...	...	...	...	...	...	...	...
Special classification provisions	0.8	0.2	0.2	0.1	0.1	0.9	4.4	1.5	2.8	3.9	4.0	13.0

Table D-3. ALABAMA: State Exports of Goods by Destination and Industry, 1994–1999—*Continued*

(Millions of dollars.)

Industry	Japan						South Korea					
	1994	1995	1996	1997	1998	1999	1994	1995	1996	1997	1998	1999
ALL GOODS	342.2	491.6	382.5	322.8	331.7	268.1	125.2	140.9	129.8	268.8	131.0	299.7
Manufactured Goods	234.5	393.1	323.2	297.6	308.6	251.1	119.1	133.7	126.6	265.4	126.0	293.4
Food products	0.5	. . .	0.5	0.8	1.1	1.8	0.3	1.0	1.3	3.0	0.7	1.6
Tobacco products	. . .	. . .	. . .	. . .	. . .	0.1	. . .	. . .	. . .	. . .	. . .	. . .
Textile mill products	0.2	0.3	0.7	0.4	1.5	0.4	0.2	0.4	0.4	0.2	. . .	0.7
Apparel	2.9	6.9	10.2	5.0	3.4	1.9	. . .	. . .	0.1	0.1	. . .	0.1
Lumber and wood products	29.9	40.2	34.4	33.4	32.8	24.1	0.4	0.4	0.3	0.1	. . .	0.2
Furniture and fixtures	0.1	0.3	0.4	0.3	0.3	0.2	. . .	0.1	. . .	. . .	. . .	0.1
Paper products	112.9	182.2	111.0	118.3	107.6	102.0	68.0	79.8	63.7	53.6	19.2	40.1
Printing and publishing	0.1	0.1	0.1	0.1	. . .	0.2	0.1	. . .	0.1	0.2	0.1	0.0
Chemical products	33.7	39.8	57.6	39.5	70.4	21.7	8.9	16.1	25.9	21.8	22.7	12.6
Refined petroleum products	. . .	. . .	. . .	. . .	. . .	. . .	. . .	. . .	. . .	0.1	0.3	0.4
Rubber and plastic products	0.1	0.1	1.1	0.4	1.7	7.2	2.7	3.7	2.5	1.0	0.5	0.5
Leather products	. . .	. . .	. . .	. . .	. . .	0.1	. . .	. . .	. . .	. . .	. . .	. . .
Stone, clay and glass products	3.4	3.0	1.4	2.3	1.5	3.3	0.2	0.2	0.6	0.7	0.4	0.8
Primary metals	0.6	5.4	0.5	2.9	0.6	1.8	0.4	1.2	1.6	2.1	0.1	0.8
Fabricated metal products	3.6	0.9	0.9	1.1	0.7	1.2	3.5	5.1	5.0	59.6	0.8	0.7
Industrial machinery and computers	20.0	24.3	27.7	25.5	25.5	15.0	11.8	12.5	11.3	103.6	69.9	197.5
Electric and electronic equipment	16.9	50.0	56.4	59.6	38.7	47.0	19.8	9.7	6.1	12.0	6.1	5.0
Transportation equipment	6.7	33.5	15.0	2.8	12.5	11.6	0.5	2.0	4.5	1.2	0.8	6.7
Scientific and measuring instruments	1.7	5.2	3.3	3.8	8.7	10.7	1.2	0.9	2.6	5.3	3.9	24.6
Miscellaneous manufactures	0.7	0.7	1.8	1.4	1.3	0.8	1.0	0.5	0.5	0.6	0.4	0.5
Unidentified manufactures	0.4	0.2	0.1	0.1	0.2	0.4	0.1	0.1	. . .	0.3	0.1	0.5
Agricultural And Livestock Products	7.2	11.3	6.9	3.5	5.4	3.0	6.1	6.7	3.0	3.4	2.3	1.5
Agricultural products	7.1	11.1	6.3	3.5	5.2	3.0	6.1	6.5	3.0	3.4	2.3	1.5
Livestock and livestock products	0.1	0.1	0.6	0.1	0.1	0.1	. . .	0.3	. . .	. . .	. . .	. . .
Other Commodities	100.6	87.3	52.4	21.7	17.7	13.9	. . .	0.5	0.2	. . .	2.6	4.8
Forestry products	. . .	. . .	. . .	. . .	. . .	. . .	. . .	. . .	. . .	. . .	. . .	. . .
Fish and other marine products	5.3	9.1	5.7	1.0	0.7	1.3	. . .	. . .	. . .	. . .	. . .	. . .
Metallic ores and concentrates	. . .	. . .	0.2	. . .	. . .	. . .	. . .	. . .	. . .	. . .	. . .	. . .
Bituminous coal and lignite	94.9	77.5	45.2	20.4	17.0	11.2	. . .	. . .	. . .	. . .	. . .	. . .
Crude petroleum and natural gas	. . .	. . .	. . .	. . .	. . .	. . .	. . .	. . .	. . .	. . .	. . .	. . .
Nonmetallic minerals	0.1	0.1	. . .	. . .	. . .	. . .	. . .	. . .	. . .	. . .	. . .	. . .
Scrap and waste	. . .	. . .	. . .	. . .	. . .	. . .	. . .	. . .	. . .	. . .	2.6	3.5
Used merchandise	0.2	0.5	1.0	0.1	. . .	. . .	. . .	. . .	0.1	. . .	. . .	. . .
Goods imported and returned unchanged	. . .	. . .	. . .	. . .	. . .	. . .	. . .	. . .	. . .	. . .	. . .	. . .
Special classification provisions	. . .	0.1	0.2	0.1	. . .	1.4	. . .	0.5	0.1	. . .	. . .	1.3

Industry	Taiwan						Singapore					
	1994	1995	1996	1997	1998	1999	1994	1995	1996	1997	1998	1999
ALL GOODS	28.3	37.2	38.9	34.0	24.8	26.9	26.3	62.4	57.4	62.5	40.1	28.4
Manufactured Goods	24.0	31.1	37.8	31.6	22.4	23.3	26.1	61.7	56.0	59.5	37.3	25.1
Food products	. . .	. . .	0.1	0.2	0.2	. . .	. . .	. . .	. . .	0.1	. . .	. . .
Tobacco products	. . .	. . .	. . .	. . .	0.1	0.1	. . .	. . .	. . .	. . .	0.1	. . .
Textile mill products	0.2	0.1	0.1	0.2	0.2	0.7	0.8	0.7	1.0	0.9	0.4	0.4
Apparel	0.3	0.6	0.3	0.8	0.1	0.1	0.1	0.2	0.1	0.1	. . .	0.2
Lumber and wood products	1.9	3.6	1.5	0.9	0.5	0.5	. . .	0.1	. . .	0.2	. . .	. . .
Furniture and fixtures	. . .	. . .	. . .	. . .	. . .	. . .	. . .	. . .	. . .	. . .	. . .	. . .
Paper products	. . .	0.2	. . .	0.9	0.6	0.9	. . .	. . .	. . .	0.1	0.1	. . .
Printing and publishing	0.2	0.1	. . .	. . .	. . .	. . .	. . .	. . .	. . .	. . .	. . .	. . .
Chemical products	5.0	8.0	9.5	8.7	6.3	5.0	9.2	21.9	20.8	29.0	18.8	6.2
Refined petroleum products	0.1	. . .	0.1	. . .	0.1	. . .	. . .	. . .	. . .	. . .	. . .	. . .
Rubber and plastic products	0.1	0.2	0.2	0.1	0.2	0.2	. . .	0.1	0.1	0.2	0.2	0.1
Leather products	. . .	. . .	0.1	. . .	. . .	. . .	. . .	. . .	. . .	. . .	. . .	0.4
Stone, clay and glass products	0.8	0.9	1.1	1.5	0.9	0.4	0.4	0.8	1.0	1.5	1.4	0.9
Primary metals	0.9	2.1	1.2	1.5	1.3	1.3	2.1	10.6	0.4	0.7	0.3	0.9
Fabricated metal products	1.1	2.1	3.5	2.5	0.2	0.6	1.3	3.1	2.8	2.4	0.8	1.1
Industrial machinery and computers	4.3	3.7	3.3	8.1	3.3	4.9	5.2	4.2	9.6	8.4	6.9	6.2
Electric and electronic equipment	6.2	7.4	7.8	3.9	5.1	4.7	5.0	16.0	15.2	12.9	6.1	6.2
Transportation equipment	1.5	0.6	8.0	0.4	2.4	3.0	0.8	3.1	3.4	1.7	1.0	1.3
Scientific and measuring instruments	0.7	1.1	0.7	1.5	0.4	0.4	0.6	0.2	0.3	0.5	0.6	0.2
Miscellaneous manufactures	0.4	0.2	0.3	0.3	0.5	0.3	0.3	0.3	1.0	0.8	0.6	0.7
Unidentified manufactures	0.2	0.1	. . .	0.1	0.1	0.2	0.3	0.2	. . .	0.1	0.1	. . .
Agricultural And Livestock Products	4.1	6.2	0.5	2.3	2.3	3.0	0.1	. . .	. . .	. . .	. . .	. . .
Agricultural products	4.1	6.2	0.5	2.3	2.3	3.0	0.1	. . .	. . .	. . .	. . .	. . .
Livestock and livestock products	. . .	. . .	. . .	. . .	. . .	. . .	. . .	. . .	. . .	. . .	. . .	. . .
Other Commodities	0.1	. . .	0.6	0.1	0.1	0.6	0.2	0.7	1.4	3.0	2.8	3.4
Forestry products	. . .	. . .	. . .	. . .	. . .	. . .	. . .	. . .	. . .	. . .	. . .	. . .
Fish and other marine products	. . .	. . .	. . .	. . .	. . .	. . .	. . .	. . .	. . .	. . .	. . .	. . .
Metallic ores and concentrates	. . .	. . .	. . .	. . .	. . .	. . .	. . .	. . .	. . .	. . .	. . .	. . .
Bituminous coal and lignite	. . .	. . .	. . .	. . .	. . .	. . .	. . .	. . .	. . .	. . .	. . .	. . .
Crude petroleum and natural gas	. . .	. . .	. . .	. . .	. . .	. . .	. . .	. . .	. . .	. . .	. . .	. . .
Nonmetallic minerals	. . .	. . .	. . .	0.1	0.1	. . .	. . .	. . .	. . .	. . .	. . .	. . .
Scrap and waste	0.1	. . .	. . .	. . .	. . .	. . .	. . .	. . .	. . .	. . .	. . .	. . .
Used merchandise	. . .	. . .	. . .	. . .	. . .	. . .	0.1	0.1	0.1	0.1	0.1	. . .
Goods imported and returned unchanged	. . .	. . .	. . .	. . .	. . .	. . .	. . .	. . .	. . .	. . .	. . .	. . .
Special classification provisions	. . .	. . .	0.6	. . .	0.1	0.6	0.1	0.6	1.3	3.0	2.7	3.3

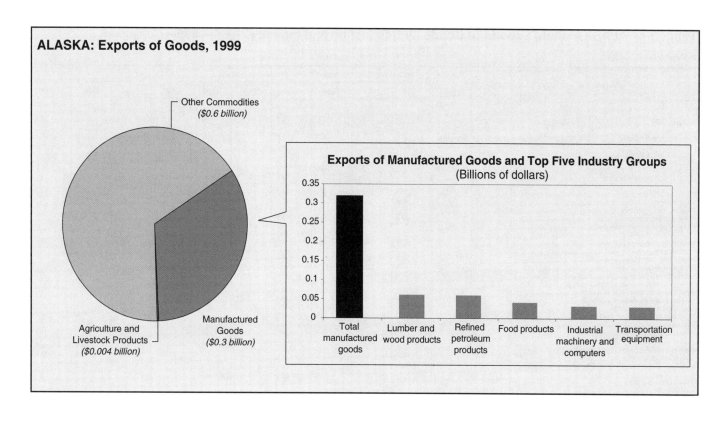

ALASKA: Exports of Goods, 1999

Other Commodities ($0.6 billion)

Agriculture and Livestock Products ($0.004 billion)

Manufactured Goods ($0.3 billion)

Exports of Manufactured Goods and Top Five Industry Groups
(Billions of dollars)

Total manufactured goods | Lumber and wood products | Refined petroleum products | Food products | Industrial machinery and computers | Transportation equipment

Table D-4. ALASKA: State Exports of Goods by Destination and Industry, 1994–1999

(Millions of dollars.)

Industry	All destinations						Canada					
	1994	1995	1996	1997	1998	1999	1994	1995	1996	1997	1998	1999
ALL GOODS	887.7	891.5	850.4	969.0	758.5	950.0	120.6	195.7	181.2	305.4	229.4	279.7
Manufactured Goods	486.2	406.3	345.2	332.3	222.6	318.7	67.5	85.4	102.6	118.7	105.8	129.7
Food products	22.5	34.8	44.0	31.8	26.2	41.6	7.5	10.7	30.6	23.0	20.8	26.3
Tobacco products	...	...	...	...	...	...						
Textile mill products	0.3	0.7	0.5	1.2	0.4	1.0	0.1	0.2	0.1	0.4	0.1	0.1
Apparel	0.4	0.7	0.8	1.2	0.5	0.6	0.1	0.1	...	0.2	0.1	0.1
Lumber and wood products	153.9	79.2	44.1	65.7	40.6	61.1	3.5	19.4	6.0	21.9	27.3	22.0
Furniture and fixtures	0.5	0.3	0.2	0.7	0.4	7.2	0.1	0.1	0.1	0.2	0.1	4.2
Paper products	84.0	108.6	79.3	31.0	5.6	6.9	0.8	2.0	2.3	2.2	4.8	6.2
Printing and publishing	1.2	1.2	0.5	0.6	0.7	0.9	0.9	1.0	0.3	0.4	0.1	0.5
Chemical products	20.1	16.2	12.3	11.1	9.0	15.5	0.8	3.3	3.4	5.8	3.2	2.8
Refined petroleum products	58.4	46.6	60.1	45.9	23.0	59.9	10.4	12.0	21.1	26.9	22.9	25.6
Rubber and plastic products	1.6	8.3	4.7	5.3	3.7	4.0	1.0	1.8	0.9	0.8	1.7	2.4
Leather products	0.2	0.2	...	0.2	0.2	0.2	0.1	0.1	...	...	...	0.1
Stone, clay and glass products	0.5	0.7	0.9	1.3	0.7	0.9	0.2	0.3	0.3	0.3	0.1	0.1
Primary metals	3.6	4.5	2.1	7.7	5.5	11.6	1.8	2.5	1.6	5.7	4.3	9.7
Fabricated metal products	19.5	7.1	3.2	5.1	1.8	7.6	17.9	1.0	0.4	1.3	0.9	1.1
Industrial machinery and computers	16.3	24.0	28.7	50.3	18.9	32.4	6.6	6.1	9.4	10.2	4.9	8.1
Electric and electronic equipment	9.4	14.9	19.9	27.7	12.3	13.3	1.1	3.1	11.7	2.9	2.9	1.7
Transportation equipment	76.3	43.4	29.5	26.8	64.0	31.1	5.1	17.7	8.6	8.9	9.4	9.3
Scientific and measuring instruments	13.1	9.7	11.5	15.9	7.3	20.4	6.7	2.5	4.9	6.3	1.5	8.8
Miscellaneous manufactures	1.5	2.3	1.4	1.0	0.6	1.3	0.8	0.7	0.1	0.4	0.1	0.1
Unidentified manufactures	2.7	3.0	1.6	1.9	1.2	1.3	2.1	0.9	0.9	0.8	0.6	0.6
Agricultural And Livestock Products	4.1	4.7	2.3	2.9	2.3	4.3	1.2	2.9	0.9	2.0	1.0	3.5
Agricultural products	3.2	4.1	1.9	2.2	1.4	3.1	0.4	2.2	0.6	1.3	0.1	2.3
Livestock and livestock products	0.9	0.6	0.4	0.8	0.9	1.2	0.7	0.6	0.3	0.8	0.8	1.2
Other Commodities	397.3	480.5	502.9	633.8	533.6	627.0	51.9	107.4	77.8	184.7	122.7	146.5
Forestry products	...	...	...	...	...	...	...	...	...	...	...	...
Fish and other marine products	121.6	94.9	101.0	68.8	59.3	99.1	17.2	26.2	34.4	24.9	25.0	34.0
Metallic ores and concentrates	97.8	194.8	215.5	362.5	306.2	356.3	21.4	66.7	30.8	126.5	83.0	98.2
Bituminous coal and lignite	22.9	29.5	26.7	42.8	10.5	15.0	...	...	...	17.4	0.0	0.0
Crude petroleum and natural gas	140.0	144.7	144.9	141.0	144.4	149.3	...	...	...	...	3.4	8.3
Nonmetallic minerals	0.1	0.9	0.4	0.1	...	0.2	...	...	0.2	...		
Scrap and waste	5.0	3.5	2.1	2.1	0.7	0.6	4.9	3.1	1.8	2.1	0.7	0.5
Used merchandise	2.5	1.4	1.9	1.5	0.3	1.4	1.1	0.6	0.4	1.1	0.2	0.8
Goods imported and returned unchanged	7.0	10.5	10.0	12.2	10.3	4.4	7.0	10.5	10.0	12.2	10.3	4.4
Special classification provisions	0.4	0.2	0.5	2.7	1.9	0.7	0.1	0.1	0.1	0.3	0.1	0.2

Table D-4. ALASKA: State Exports of Goods by Destination and Industry, 1994–1999—*Continued*

(Millions of dollars.)

Industry	South and Central American and Caribbean						Mexico					
	1994	1995	1996	1997	1998	1999	1994	1995	1996	1997	1998	1999
ALL GOODS	3.3	11.9	9.3	4.1	36.9	4.7	1.3	0.9	1.5	2.0	4.9	4.5
Manufactured Goods	3.1	11.9	9.1	4.1	36.8	4.6	1.3	0.9	1.5	1.9	0.9	4.4
Food products	0.1	0.2	...	...	...	0.5	0.1	...	...	...	...	0.1
Tobacco products	...	...	...	...	...	...	...	...	...	...	...	...
Textile mill products	0.1	...	...	...	...	...	...	...	0.2	...	0.1	0.7
Apparel	...	0.1	0.1	0.6	0.1	...	0.1	...	0.1	...	0.1	0.2
Lumber and wood products	...	...	...	...	...	0.1	...	...	...	...	...	...
Furniture and fixtures	...	0.1	...	...	0.1	0.2	...	...	...	...	...	...
Paper products	0.5	1.3	0.8	0.1	...	0.1	0.1	0.1	0.1	0.1	0.1	...
Printing and publishing	...	...	...	...	...	...	...	...	...	...	...	...
Chemical products	0.1	1.0	0.3	0.4	0.4	0.5	0.5	...	0.1	0.1	0.1	0.1
Refined petroleum products	...	...	...	...	...	...	...	...	...	...	...	...
Rubber and plastic products	...	0.5	0.4	0.3	0.2	0.5	...	...	...	0.2	...	0.2
Leather products	...	...	...	0.1	...	...	...	...	...	...	...	...
Stone, clay and glass products	...	0.1	0.1	...	...	...	0.1	...	...	...	...	...
Primary metals	...	0.5	0.1	...	...	...	0.1	0.1	...	...	...	...
Fabricated metal products	0.2	0.1	0.8	...	...	0.1	...	...	...	...	...	2.3
Industrial machinery and computers	0.7	1.6	4.7	1.3	0.4	0.4	0.1	0.3	0.5	0.3	0.1	0.3
Electric and electronic equipment	0.4	5.7	0.8	0.4	2.8	1.1	0.1	0.2	0.3	0.5	...	0.2
Transportation equipment	1.0	0.5	0.1	0.4	32.7	0.3	...	...	...	...	...	0.1
Scientific and measuring instruments	...	0.2	0.3	0.2	0.1	0.4	...	...	0.3	0.7	0.2	0.1
Miscellaneous manufactures	...	...	0.5	0.1	...	0.2	...	...	...	...	...	0.1
Unidentified manufactures	...	...	...	...	...	...	...	...	...	...	...	0.1
Agricultural And Livestock Products	0.1	...	0.1	...	...	...	...	0.1	...	...	0.1	0.1
Agricultural products	0.1	...	0.1	...	...	...	...	0.1	...	...	0.1	0.1
Livestock and livestock products	...	...	...	...	...	...	...	...	...	...	...	...
Other Commodities	...	...	0.1	...	...	0.1	...	...	...	...	4.0	...
Forestry products	...	...	...	...	...	...	...	...	...	...	...	...
Fish and other marine products	...	...	...	...	...	...	...	...	...	...	...	...
Metallic ores and concentrates	...	...	...	...	...	...	...	...	...	...	4.0	...
Bituminous coal and lignite	...	...	...	...	...	...	...	...	...	...	...	...
Crude petroleum and natural gas	...	...	...	...	...	...	...	...	...	...	...	...
Nonmetallic minerals	...	...	...	...	...	...	...	...	...	...	...	...
Scrap and waste	...	...	...	...	...	...	...	...	...	...	...	...
Used merchandise	...	...	...	...	...	...	...	...	...	...	...	...
Goods imported and returned unchanged	...	...	...	...	...	...	...	...	...	...	...	...
Special classification provisions	...	...	...	...	...	...	...	...	...	...	...	...

Industry	European Union						United Kingdom					
	1994	1995	1996	1997	1998	1999	1994	1995	1996	1997	1998	1999
ALL GOODS	121.2	113.0	134.5	237.6	174.7	197.2	9.4	6.6	7.3	55.4	44.5	37.4
Manufactured Goods	59.0	40.0	27.6	69.3	19.8	38.3	6.3	5.1	2.5	34.9	7.6	10.4
Food products	1.1	3.2	1.3	0.8	1.2	6.6	0.4	0.4	0.4	0.3	...	...
Tobacco products	...	...	...	...	...	...	...	...	...	...	...	...
Textile mill products	...	0.2	0.1	0.5	...	...	...	...	...	0.1	...	...
Apparel	...	...	0.1	0.1	...	0.1	...	...	...	...	...	0.1
Lumber and wood products	0.1	0.2	0.1	0.1	...	...	...	...	...	...	...	...
Furniture and fixtures	...	...	0.1	...	0.2	1.9	...	...	...	...	...	0.7
Paper products	14.0	15.2	11.0	3.5	0.1	0.1	...	...	...	...	...	...
Printing and publishing	...	...	...	...	0.1	0.1	...	...	...	...	...	0.1
Chemical products	1.0	1.3	2.4	1.5	0.4	6.0	0.8	0.3	0.2	0.5	0.2	0.8
Refined petroleum products	...	...	...	...	0.1	0.1	...	...	...	...	0.1	0.1
Rubber and plastic products	0.1	0.5	1.6	3.2	1.6	0.3	0.1	0.2	0.4	0.3	0.1	...
Leather products	...	...	...	0.1	0.2	0.1	...	...	...	...	...	...
Stone, clay and glass products	...	...	0.2	0.2	0.4	0.4	...	...	...	...	...	...
Primary metals	0.3	0.2	0.2	0.8	0.8	0.4	...	...	...	0.2	...	...
Fabricated metal products	0.7	3.9	1.1	3.2	0.3	1.0	0.4	2.4	...	3.0	...	0.1
Industrial machinery and computers	3.9	3.5	4.7	29.1	5.8	10.8	2.9	0.7	0.4	25.9	3.5	5.4
Electric and electronic equipment	1.8	0.8	1.3	17.6	2.5	2.8	1.1	0.2	0.1	1.8	0.1	0.1
Transportation equipment	35.2	9.2	1.9	2.7	4.2	5.4	0.5	0.2	0.8	1.6	2.3	2.0
Scientific and measuring instruments	0.5	1.5	1.4	5.6	1.8	2.0	...	0.5	0.1	1.3	1.1	1.1
Miscellaneous manufactures	0.1	0.1	0.1	0.1	...	0.1	0.1	0.1	...	...	...	...
Unidentified manufactures	...	0.1	...	0.3	0.1	0.1	...	...	...	...	...	...
Agricultural And Livestock Products	2.0	1.5	0.3	0.1	0.5	0.2	1.5	0.7	...	...	0.1	...
Agricultural products	1.9	1.5	0.3	0.1	0.5	0.2	1.5	0.7	...	...	0.1	...
Livestock and livestock products	...	...	...	...	...	...	...	...	...	...	...	...
Other Commodities	60.2	71.5	106.6	168.2	154.5	158.7	1.6	0.8	4.8	20.5	36.8	27.0
Forestry products	...	...	...	...	...	...	...	...	...	...	...	...
Fish and other marine products	5.2	5.0	4.8	3.6	3.8	7.0	0.6	0.6	0.4	0.5	0.5	0.1
Metallic ores and concentrates	53.9	66.2	101.7	164.4	150.5	151.5	...	0.1	4.4	19.8	36.3	26.8
Bituminous coal and lignite	...	...	...	...	...	...	...	...	...	...	...	...
Crude petroleum and natural gas	...	...	...	...	...	...	...	...	...	...	...	...
Nonmetallic minerals	...	...	...	...	...	0.1	...	...	...	...	...	...
Scrap and waste	...	0.2	...	...	...	...	...	0.1	...	...	...	...
Used merchandise	1.0	...	...	0.1	...	...	1.0	...	...	0.1	...	...
Goods imported and returned unchanged	...	...	...	...	...	...	...	...	...	...	...	...
Special classification provisions	0.1	...	...	0.1	0.2	0.1	...	...	...	0.1	...	...

Table D-4. ALASKA: State Exports of Goods by Destination and Industry, 1994–1999–*Continued*

(Millions of dollars.)

Industry	Germany 1994	1995	1996	1997	1998	1999	France 1994	1995	1996	1997	1998	1999
ALL GOODS	27.1	33.3	18.2	30.7	19.8	24.2	6.9	11.9	2.4	2.0	3.7	9.4
Manufactured Goods	14.0	18.7	13.2	5.2	4.6	8.5	4.5	9.0	1.1	1.5	2.6	8.5
Food products	0.1	0.2	0.4	0.1	0.1	0.3	...	...	...	0.2	0.6	5.7
Tobacco products	...	...	...	...	...	...	...	...	...	...	...	...
Textile mill products	...	0.2	...	...	...	...	...	...	...	...	...	...
Apparel	...	...	...	0.1	...	...	...	...	...	...	...	...
Lumber and wood products	...	0.1	...	...	...	...	...	...	...	...	...	...
Furniture and fixtures	...	...	0.1	...	...	0.5	...	...	...	...	0.1	0.4
Paper products	12.0	15.1	9.5	3.1	...	...	...	...	0.1	...	...	...
Printing and publishing	...	...	...	...	...	...	...	...	...	...	...	...
Chemical products	...	...	0.1	0.1	...	...	...	0.2	0.7	0.1	0.1	0.1
Refined petroleum products	...	...	...	...	...	...	...	...	...	...	...	...
Rubber and plastic products	0.1	0.1	0.1	...	...	0.2	...	...	...	0.1	...	0.1
Leather products	...	...	...	...	...	...	...	...	...	...	0.1	0.1
Stone, clay and glass products	...	...	0.2	0.1	0.4	0.4	...	...	...	...	...	...
Primary metals	...	...	...	...	0.1	0.2	...	0.2	...	0.2	0.6	0.2
Fabricated metal products	0.3	1.3	1.1	...	...	0.1	...	...	...	...	0.1	0.7
Industrial machinery and computers	0.1	0.1	0.1	0.3	0.8	2.2	0.1	0.5	...	0.2	0.3	1.1
Electric and electronic equipment	0.2	0.2	0.2	0.4	1.6	1.7	0.1	...	...	0.1	0.2	...
Transportation equipment	0.7	0.4	0.9	0.7	1.3	2.6	4.3	8.0	0.1	0.1	0.3	0.1
Scientific and measuring instruments	0.4	0.9	0.4	0.2	0.2	0.1	...	...	0.2	0.5	0.1	...
Miscellaneous manufactures	...	...	0.1	...	...	...	...	...	...	...	...	...
Unidentified manufactures	...	...	...	...	...	...	...	...	...	...	...	...
Agricultural And Livestock Products	0.1	...	...	...	0.4	...	0.2	0.2	...	...	...	...
Agricultural products	0.1	...	...	...	0.4	...	0.2	0.2	...	...	...	...
Livestock and livestock products	...	...	...	...	...	...	...	...	...	...	...	...
Other Commodities	13.1	14.6	4.9	25.5	14.9	15.7	2.1	2.8	1.3	0.5	1.1	0.9
Forestry products	...	...	...	...	...	...	...	...	...	...	...	...
Fish and other marine products	0.4	0.1	0.6	0.5	0.3	1.2	2.1	2.8	1.3	0.5	1.1	0.9
Metallic ores and concentrates	12.6	14.4	4.4	25.0	14.6	14.4	...	...	...	...	...	...
Bituminous coal and lignite	...	...	...	...	...	...	...	...	...	...	...	...
Crude petroleum and natural gas	...	...	...	...	...	...	...	...	...	...	...	...
Nonmetallic minerals	...	...	...	...	...	...	...	...	...	...	...	...
Scrap and waste	...	...	...	...	...	...	...	...	...	...	...	...
Used merchandise	...	...	...	...	...	...	...	...	...	...	...	...
Goods imported and returned unchanged	...	...	...	...	...	...	...	...	...	...	...	...
Special classification provisions	0.1	...	...	...	...	...	...	...	...	...	...	...

Industry	The Netherlands 1994	1995	1996	1997	1998	1999	Asian 10 1994	1995	1996	1997	1998	1999
ALL GOODS	1.6	15.3	35.5	44.9	19.7	2.4	558.0	521.6	492.3	392.6	293.6	425.7
Manufactured Goods	1.2	0.9	5.4	23.2	3.2	2.3	273.4	222.0	176.6	114.0	49.5	116.1
Food products	...	0.2	0.2	0.1	0.2	0.3	5.0	13.4	5.0	5.0	2.5	6.0
Tobacco products	...	...	...	...	...	...	...	...	...	...	...	...
Textile mill products	...	...	...	0.5	...	...	...	0.1	...	0.1	...	0.1
Apparel	...	...	...	...	...	...	0.1	0.5	0.4	0.2	0.1	0.1
Lumber and wood products	...	...	...	...	...	...	150.1	59.5	37.9	41.0	13.3	39.1
Furniture and fixtures	...	...	...	...	...	...	...	...	...	...	0.1	0.9
Paper products	...	...	...	0.2	0.1	...	65.7	83.9	63.6	25.0	0.5	0.4
Printing and publishing	...	...	...	...	...	...	0.1	...	...	0.1	0.1	...
Chemical products	...	0.3	...	...	...	0.1	1.6	1.5	5.2	2.3	4.7	5.9
Refined petroleum products	...	...	...	...	...	...	26.4	34.4	36.0	18.9	...	34.3
Rubber and plastic products	...	0.1	0.3	1.5	1.4	...	0.1	4.8	1.0	0.5	0.2	0.3
Leather products	...	...	...	...	...	...	...	...	...	...	...	...
Stone, clay and glass products	...	...	...	...	...	...	0.2	0.1	0.1	0.7	0.2	0.3
Primary metals	...	...	0.1	0.2	...	...	0.2	0.4	0.1	0.1	0.1	1.2
Fabricated metal products	...	...	0.1	...	...	...	0.2	0.6	0.4	0.4	0.4	0.8
Industrial machinery and computers	0.1	0.2	3.3	2.6	0.9	1.8	2.1	1.3	1.7	1.7	5.6	5.1
Electric and electronic equipment	0.4	...	0.9	15.2	0.4	0.1	1.1	1.4	3.5	2.2	2.7	4.1
Transportation equipment	0.6	0.1	...	0.2	0.1	...	17.6	14.5	17.5	12.8	15.5	12.5
Scientific and measuring instruments	...	...	0.5	2.4	0.1	...	2.1	4.1	3.5	2.4	2.9	4.4
Miscellaneous manufactures	...	...	0.1	...	...	...	0.5	1.2	0.4	0.4	0.4	0.5
Unidentified manufactures	...	...	...	0.2	...	...	0.2	0.2	0.2	0.1	0.2	0.2
Agricultural And Livestock Products	0.1	0.3	0.1	...	0.1	...	0.2	0.1	0.4	0.3	0.6	0.3
Agricultural products	0.1	0.3	0.1	...	0.1	...	0.1	0.1	0.4	0.3	0.5	0.3
Livestock and livestock products	...	...	...	...	...	...	...	...	0.1	...	...	...
Other Commodities	0.3	14.1	30.0	21.7	16.4	...	284.4	299.5	315.3	278.4	243.5	309.3
Forestry products	...	...	...	...	...	...	...	...	...	...	...	...
Fish and other marine products	0.3	0.1	0.3	...	0.3	...	98.8	63.2	60.9	38.8	29.4	56.7
Metallic ores and concentrates	...	14.1	29.7	21.7	16.2	...	22.5	61.2	82.3	71.1	61.0	95.9
Bituminous coal and lignite	...	...	...	...	...	...	22.9	29.5	26.7	25.3	10.5	15.0
Crude petroleum and natural gas	...	...	...	...	...	...	140.0	144.7	144.9	141.0	140.9	141.0
Nonmetallic minerals	...	...	...	...	...	...	0.1	0.9	...	...	...	0.1
Scrap and waste	...	...	...	...	...	...	...	...	...	...	...	0.1
Used merchandise	...	...	...	...	...	...	...	...	0.1	...	...	0.3
Goods imported and returned unchanged	...	...	...	...	...	...	...	...	...	...	...	...
Special classification provisions	...	...	...	...	...	...	0.1	...	0.4	2.1	1.6	0.2

Table D-4. ALASKA: State Exports of Goods by Destination and Industry, 1994–1999–*Continued*

(Millions of dollars.)

Industry	Japan						South Korea					
	1994	1995	1996	1997	1998	1999	1994	1995	1996	1997	1998	1999
ALL GOODS	412.6	327.5	270.0	259.2	214.0	325.8	75.6	93.7	127.6	97.4	60.6	72.5
Manufactured Goods	167.2	109.4	67.3	47.8	22.9	70.3	36.8	21.6	34.2	32.3	13.4	22.4
Food products	4.9	7.2	4.1	3.2	1.7	3.7	0.2	5.4	0.1	0.1	...	0.2
Tobacco products	...	...	...	...	...	...	...	...	...	...	...	...
Textile mill products	...	0.1	...	...	...	...	...	...	...	...	...	...
Apparel	...	0.1	0.3	...	...	...	...	...	...	...	...	...
Lumber and wood products	121.7	44.4	26.6	27.6	8.4	30.7	21.6	13.2	7.8	8.1	3.2	7.1
Furniture and fixtures	...	...	...	...	0.1	0.7	...	...	...	...	...	...
Paper products	14.2	20.3	11.2	6.7	0.4	0.4	0.5	0.1	...	...	...	...
Printing and publishing	0.1	...	...	...	0.1	...	...	...	...	...	...	...
Chemical products	1.4	0.7	4.0	1.1	4.1	5.2	...	0.5	0.8	0.4	...	...
Refined petroleum products	20.0	25.7	12.1	2.0	...	20.9	6.4	...	14.6	15.3	...	6.8
Rubber and plastic products	0.1	4.6	0.6	...	0.1	0.2	...	...	...	...	...	...
Leather products	...	...	...	...	...	...	...	...	...	...	...	...
Stone, clay and glass products	0.2	0.1	0.1	0.7	0.1	0.1	...	...	...	...	...	0.1
Primary metals	...	...	...	...	...	0.1	...	...	...	...	...	...
Fabricated metal products	0.1	...	...	0.2	...	0.2	...	...	...	0.1	...	0.1
Industrial machinery and computers	0.2	0.4	0.5	0.7	1.4	1.7	...	0.1	0.7	...	1.4	0.4
Electric and electronic equipment	0.2	0.2	0.3	1.3	2.0	1.5	...	0.7	1.1	0.1	0.1	0.2
Transportation equipment	2.3	1.2	4.0	2.3	1.7	3.5	7.8	1.3	9.0	8.0	8.5	6.9
Scientific and measuring instruments	1.7	3.9	3.2	1.7	2.5	1.2	...	...	...	...	...	0.5
Miscellaneous manufactures	0.1	0.3	...	0.1	0.1	0.1	...	0.1	...	...	0.1	...
Unidentified manufactures	0.1	...	0.1	0.1	0.1	0.1	...	0.1	0.1	...	...	...
Agricultural And Livestock Products	0.1	0.1	0.2	0.1	0.5	0.1	...	...	0.1	0.1	...	0.1
Agricultural products	...	0.1	0.1	0.1	0.4	0.1	...	...	...	0.1	...	0.1
Livestock and livestock products	0.1	...	...	...	...	...	...	...	...	...	...	...
Other Commodities	245.2	218.0	202.5	211.3	190.6	255.4	38.8	72.1	93.4	65.0	47.2	50.1
Forestry products	...	...	...	...	...	...	...	...	...	...	...	...
Fish and other marine products	87.5	46.1	39.9	22.0	21.7	45.4	10.9	16.4	20.7	15.5	5.9	7.7
Metallic ores and concentrates	17.6	26.2	17.4	46.8	27.2	68.5	4.9	26.1	46.0	24.1	30.6	27.3
Bituminous coal and lignite	...	...	...	...	...	...	22.9	29.5	26.7	25.3	10.5	15.0
Crude petroleum and natural gas	140.0	144.7	144.9	141.0	140.9	140.9	...	...	...	...	...	...
Nonmetallic minerals	0.1	0.9	...	...	...	0.1	...	...	...	...	...	...
Scrap and waste	...	...	...	...	...	...	...	...	...	...	...	...
Used merchandise	...	...	...	...	...	0.3	...	...	...	...	...	...
Goods imported and returned unchanged	...	...	...	...	...	...	...	...	...	...	...	...
Special classification provisions	...	...	0.3	1.4	0.8	0.1	0.1	...	...	0.1	0.1	...

Industry	Taiwan						Singapore					
	1994	1995	1996	1997	1998	1999	1994	1995	1996	1997	1998	1999
ALL GOODS	34.5	61.4	40.7	18.4	7.7	12.5	1.1	5.1	6.1	0.9	2.8	7.8
Manufactured Goods	34.4	61.1	40.7	18.3	7.6	12.2	1.0	5.1	5.9	0.9	2.8	7.8
Food products	...	0.3	0.4	1.3	0.4	1.4	...	...	...	...	...	0.1
Tobacco products	...	...	...	...	...	...	...	...	...	...	...	...
Textile mill products	...	...	...	...	...	...	...	...	...	...	...	...
Apparel	...	...	...	...	...	...	...	...	...	...	...	...
Lumber and wood products	6.8	1.8	1.5	4.0	1.0	1.2	...	...	...	...	...	...
Furniture and fixtures	...	...	...	...	...	...	...	...	...	...	...	...
Paper products	26.8	46.5	37.3	10.3	...	...	...	...	...	...	...	...
Printing and publishing	...	...	...	...	...	...	...	...	...	...	...	...
Chemical products	...	0.1	0.3	0.5	0.4	0.3	0.2	...	...	0.1	...	0.2
Refined petroleum products	...	...	...	...	...	6.6	...	4.8	5.6	...	...	...
Rubber and plastic products	...	0.2	0.3	0.4	0.1	...	...	...	...	...	...	...
Leather products	...	...	...	...	...	...	...	...	...	...	...	...
Stone, clay and glass products	...	...	...	...	...	0.1	...	...	...	...	...	...
Primary metals	0.1	...	...	...	...	0.5	...	...	...	...	...	0.2
Fabricated metal products	...	...	...	...	...	0.2	...	...	...	...	0.3	0.2
Industrial machinery and computers	0.3	0.3	0.2	0.1	0.4	0.3	0.5	0.2	...	...	1.9	2.2
Electric and electronic equipment	0.1	0.2	0.1	0.1	0.1	0.8	0.1	...	...	...	0.3	1.2
Transportation equipment	...	11.7	0.2	1.5	5.1	0.3	0.1	0.1	0.1	0.2	0.2	1.4
Scientific and measuring instruments	0.1	...	0.2	...	0.2	0.4	...	...	...	0.5	...	2.0
Miscellaneous manufactures	0.1	...	0.1	0.1	...	...	...	...	...	...	...	...
Unidentified manufactures	...	...	...	...	...	...	...	...	...	...	...	...
Agricultural And Livestock Products	...	...	...	...	...	0.1	0.1	...	0.1	...	...	...
Agricultural products	...	...	...	...	...	0.1	0.1	...	0.1	...	...	...
Livestock and livestock products	...	...	...	...	...	...	...	...	...	...	...	...
Other Commodities	0.2	0.4	...	...	...	0.2	...	...	0.1	0.1	...	...
Forestry products	...	...	...	...	...	...	...	...	...	...	...	...
Fish and other marine products	0.2	0.4	...	...	...	0.1	...	...	0.1	...	...	...
Metallic ores and concentrates	...	...	...	...	...	...	...	...	...	...	...	...
Bituminous coal and lignite	...	...	...	...	...	...	...	...	...	...	...	...
Crude petroleum and natural gas	...	...	...	...	...	...	...	...	...	...	...	...
Nonmetallic minerals	...	...	...	...	...	...	...	...	...	...	...	...
Scrap and waste	...	...	...	...	...	...	...	...	...	...	...	...
Used merchandise	...	...	...	...	...	...	...	...	...	...	...	...
Goods imported and returned unchanged	...	...	...	...	...	...	...	...	...	...	...	...
Special classification provisions	...	...	...	...	...	...	...	...	...	...	...	...

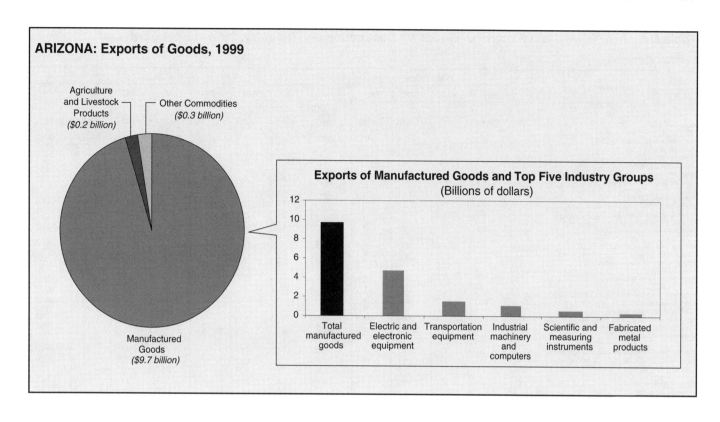

ARIZONA: Exports of Goods, 1999

Agriculture and Livestock Products ($0.2 billion) — Other Commodities ($0.3 billion)

Manufactured Goods ($9.7 billion)

Exports of Manufactured Goods and Top Five Industry Groups
(Billions of dollars)

Total manufactured goods / Electric and electronic equipment / Transportation equipment / Industrial machinery and computers / Scientific and measuring instruments / Fabricated metal products

Table D-5. ARIZONA: State Exports of Goods by Destination and Industry, 1994–1999

(Millions of dollars.)

Industry	All destinations						Canada					
	1994	1995	1996	1997	1998	1999	1994	1995	1996	1997	1998	1999
ALL GOODS	6 970.6	8 402.8	9 937.8	13 556.7	10 753.0	10 123.0	644.2	839.0	970.2	1 072.2	1 058.6	1 159.1
Manufactured Goods	6 632.5	7 910.1	9 561.0	13 138.7	10 382.3	9 657.2	561.8	736.2	858.9	960.8	952.3	1 044.2
Food products	89.1	57.3	63.1	105.9	104.7	120.0	17.4	16.3	14.7	16.0	9.2	7.3
Tobacco products	0.6	0.8	1.5	1.9	1.2	0.2	...	...	0.2	0.4	...	...
Textile mill products	16.6	21.2	24.4	32.2	27.0	43.6	0.5	0.2	0.2	0.4	5.3	16.6
Apparel	87.7	55.3	111.4	114.1	104.1	74.5	21.6	20.9	20.2	20.6	14.3	20.1
Lumber and wood products	6.1	6.5	6.4	7.1	9.0	14.0	0.2	0.3	0.8	0.7	1.2	2.2
Furniture and fixtures	24.0	18.7	38.3	27.7	27.6	19.0	2.9	2.1	4.0	7.3	8.0	4.3
Paper products	76.7	106.5	113.3	128.2	142.9	152.1	1.7	1.7	1.9	1.3	1.4	1.6
Printing and publishing	12.8	22.8	25.8	13.1	14.1	20.0	3.2	3.0	2.8	2.0	2.7	2.3
Chemical products	122.4	201.8	185.3	161.0	162.2	195.8	17.9	21.0	21.8	23.6	26.4	40.4
Refined petroleum products	2.4	2.9	3.9	65.8	54.5	115.8	0.2	0.2	1.0	19.5	13.9	24.2
Rubber and plastic products	119.1	117.4	150.3	177.9	232.9	239.2	4.5	4.6	5.5	8.0	10.6	12.4
Leather products	6.2	5.1	5.1	8.0	8.2	9.6	0.4	0.6	0.6	0.9	1.2	1.4
Stone, clay and glass products	13.9	20.1	21.1	25.4	19.2	22.2	0.8	1.0	1.7	1.5	1.9	2.3
Primary metals	245.0	368.7	420.1	248.6	232.6	221.8	16.7	48.3	34.7	43.3	23.1	24.9
Fabricated metal products	163.7	162.6	239.1	277.5	288.8	333.5	25.6	49.5	75.5	80.4	67.6	74.6
Industrial machinery and computers	826.5	883.9	1 098.3	3 237.6	2 005.3	1 109.1	71.6	89.8	117.5	155.1	157.8	174.0
Electric and electronic equipment	3 636.5	4 503.3	5 428.8	6 539.5	4 651.1	4 730.6	220.6	293.5	339.6	350.7	326.6	365.4
Transportation equipment	655.0	718.2	942.8	1 228.8	1 615.4	1 527.5	86.9	106.7	138.1	145.5	187.0	176.4
Scientific and measuring instruments	431.9	522.2	559.3	622.5	545.8	582.2	47.1	56.2	57.9	64.8	74.9	72.0
Miscellaneous manufactures	75.8	94.2	101.1	90.6	92.3	94.3	15.6	12.2	12.5	9.8	9.6	11.3
Unidentified manufactures	20.5	20.6	21.6	25.1	43.4	32.3	6.5	8.1	7.9	9.4	9.4	10.5
Agricultural And Livestock Products	156.4	181.5	176.9	216.6	222.5	208.1	49.9	66.7	70.7	66.5	73.5	72.1
Agricultural products	145.9	178.5	168.6	196.4	210.0	197.2	49.8	66.4	70.5	66.4	73.3	72.0
Livestock and livestock products	10.5	3.0	8.3	20.1	12.5	10.9	0.1	0.4	0.1	0.1	0.2	0.1
Other Commodities	181.7	311.2	199.8	201.5	148.2	257.7	32.4	36.1	40.6	44.9	32.8	42.8
Forestry products	0.4	0.5	0.8	0.8	0.8	1.6	...	0.2	0.1	0.2	0.2	0.1
Fish and other marine products	0.8	0.8	1.0	0.4	0.9	0.9	0.2	0.8	0.4	...	0.3	0.1
Metallic ores and concentrates	66.6	206.1	80.1	62.5	5.8	34.4	2.7	1.5	2.4	1.4	2.3	2.4
Bituminous coal and lignite	...	...	...	...	...	...	...	...	...	...	...	...
Crude petroleum and natural gas	...	0.3	...	0.2	0.3	5.4	...	0.1	...	0.1	0.1	0.3
Nonmetallic minerals	5.2	6.0	4.9	2.9	3.6	3.7	0.4	0.2	0.2	0.2	0.5	0.2
Scrap and waste	7.8	28.4	13.1	28.4	23.0	25.3	3.1	16.1	4.1	9.3	0.4	0.5
Used merchandise	9.9	8.0	15.4	18.4	12.7	24.2	1.6	1.2	6.9	4.2	2.4	8.3
Goods imported and returned unchanged	14.4	10.9	20.7	23.9	15.2	12.8	14.4	10.9	20.7	23.9	15.2	12.8
Special classification provisions	76.7	50.1	64.0	63.9	86.0	149.2	10.0	5.2	5.9	5.7	11.3	18.0

Table D-5. ARIZONA: State Exports of Goods by Destination and Industry, 1994–1999—*Continued*

(Millions of dollars.)

Industry	South and Central American and Caribbean						Mexico					
	1994	1995	1996	1997	1998	1999	1994	1995	1996	1997	1998	1999
ALL GOODS	92.7	111.8	154.7	218.9	295.9	358.5	1 206.5	1 265.6	1 622.2	1 963.1	1 993.1	2 195.5
Manufactured Goods	80.3	101.3	142.0	213.3	289.8	351.8	1 153.5	1 234.5	1 580.8	1 897.6	1 890.8	2 017.6
Food products	1.6	2.8	2.2	2.7	3.0	3.3	49.6	22.4	30.7	55.2	65.2	91.0
Tobacco products	...	...	...	...	...	...	0.6	0.8	1.5	1.9	1.2	0.2
Textile mill products	0.6	...	0.1	0.1	0.2	0.6	13.7	18.1	22.2	22.6	19.9	24.9
Apparel	0.3	0.1	0.2	0.3	0.3	0.3	60.7	25.8	82.9	85.9	84.4	48.2
Lumber and wood products	0.2	0.1	0.2	...	0.1	0.1	5.1	4.9	3.6	4.8	5.7	9.8
Furniture and fixtures	0.3	0.4	0.6	0.3	1.1	0.3	18.2	13.7	29.0	16.7	14.5	10.4
Paper products	0.3	0.2	1.4	1.7	1.8	1.0	72.1	101.6	106.7	120.8	135.1	145.0
Printing and publishing	0.2	0.6	0.2	0.3	0.5	1.3	2.9	3.5	5.5	5.0	3.9	6.9
Chemical products	5.3	3.8	7.4	5.4	5.3	7.0	34.9	36.3	43.1	52.2	41.8	44.7
Refined petroleum products	0.1	0.1	0.1	7.9	11.2	8.2	1.7	2.3	2.5	25.4	21.8	55.1
Rubber and plastic products	0.7	2.7	1.9	2.8	2.7	2.3	79.6	83.9	111.2	133.6	183.8	197.0
Leather products	...	...	...	0.1	...	0.1	3.0	1.8	1.9	4.4	5.0	5.8
Stone, clay and glass products	0.2	0.3	0.2	0.2	0.2	0.2	5.2	4.2	8.9	9.4	8.2	10.5
Primary metals	1.8	1.7	2.9	1.9	2.0	1.6	41.4	52.1	92.9	103.8	146.2	173.0
Fabricated metal products	1.3	1.0	4.2	2.2	4.0	2.3	86.3	60.6	78.8	117.1	126.0	173.0
Industrial machinery and computers	16.6	21.8	37.0	31.7	60.8	57.1	242.6	227.3	303.4	348.7	312.1	193.1
Electric and electronic equipment	30.3	43.7	57.4	70.0	73.4	155.3	334.9	495.2	528.8	630.0	603.6	705.7
Transportation equipment	15.3	13.0	16.2	72.2	103.2	71.8	41.9	23.1	70.1	74.5	40.7	77.5
Scientific and measuring instruments	4.2	7.4	8.3	10.5	8.4	26.3	36.5	29.3	29.0	51.0	36.1	19.9
Miscellaneous manufactures	0.7	1.4	1.2	2.3	3.4	12.1	17.3	24.2	21.0	27.5	21.7	15.1
Unidentified manufactures	0.4	0.3	0.3	0.6	8.0	0.8	5.2	3.5	7.2	7.2	13.7	10.8
Agricultural And Livestock Products	5.5	0.9	2.7	3.9	5.2	1.9	30.3	14.8	26.7	49.7	64.3	81.0
Agricultural products	5.4	0.9	2.7	3.8	5.2	1.8	20.0	12.9	19.3	29.9	52.2	70.3
Livestock and livestock products	...	...	...	0.1	...	0.1	10.3	1.9	7.4	19.7	12.1	10.7
Other Commodities	6.9	9.7	10.1	1.6	0.9	4.8	22.6	16.3	14.6	15.8	38.0	96.9
Forestry products	...	...	...	...	...	0.6	0.2	0.2	0.2	0.4	0.3	0.8
Fish and other marine products	...	...	...	...	...	...	0.1	0.1	0.2	0.2	0.3	0.5
Metallic ores and concentrates	4.7	8.1	2.6	0.7	...	0.5	1.3	6.1	1.8	...	0.5	18.9
Bituminous coal and lignite	...	...	...	...	...	...	...	0.2	...	...	0.1	...
Crude petroleum and natural gas	...	...	...	...	...	...	...	...	...	...	0.1	5.1
Nonmetallic minerals	0.3	0.5	0.3	0.1	0.2	0.2	0.4	0.4	0.5	0.6	1.6	2.1
Scrap and waste	...	...	0.1	0.1	...	...	2.0	1.5	1.0	1.1	1.2	0.4
Used merchandise	0.1	0.6	0.4	...	0.1	0.4	3.9	1.8	4.9	6.0	4.5	5.0
Goods imported and returned unchanged	...	...	...	...	...	...	...	...	...	...	...	...
Special classification provisions	1.9	0.5	6.7	0.6	0.6	3.2	14.5	6.1	5.9	7.6	29.4	64.2

Industry	European Union						United Kingdom					
	1994	1995	1996	1997	1998	1999	1994	1995	1996	1997	1998	1999
ALL GOODS	1 879.5	2 443.8	2 448.6	3 686.4	2 542.4	2 064.4	906.0	1 085.1	827.2	1 061.5	720.2	752.5
Manufactured Goods	1 787.3	2 238.8	2 346.4	3 548.7	2 464.3	1 969.6	872.9	1 014.4	792.6	1 038.1	711.2	738.7
Food products	5.2	6.4	5.8	7.2	10.0	3.2	1.8	2.0	2.0	2.9	3.5	0.7
Tobacco products	...	...	...	...	...	...	...	...	...	...	...	...
Textile mill products	0.4	0.3	0.3	0.8	0.2	0.3	...	0.1	0.1	0.4	0.1	0.1
Apparel	0.5	1.3	2.9	1.9	1.3	2.1	0.1	0.2	0.3	0.3	0.2	0.7
Lumber and wood products	0.1	0.1	0.7	0.3	0.3	0.5	...	0.1	0.2	0.1	0.1	0.1
Furniture and fixtures	2.1	0.8	1.9	1.5	1.8	3.2	0.2	0.1	0.6	0.6	0.9	2.0
Paper products	1.2	1.2	1.6	1.0	1.6	1.2	0.5	0.4	0.5	0.1	0.3	0.2
Printing and publishing	3.6	3.6	3.9	2.8	3.4	7.4	1.8	1.3	1.7	0.9	1.0	0.9
Chemical products	14.4	48.6	21.1	21.3	36.6	23.1	1.5	1.7	3.7	5.8	5.7	5.9
Refined petroleum products	...	0.1	...	...	0.2	5.9	...	...	...	...	...	...
Rubber and plastic products	10.8	11.0	11.3	15.9	18.1	11.1	2.0	1.5	2.7	3.9	3.2	2.3
Leather products	0.7	0.8	0.8	0.6	0.9	0.5	0.4	0.4	0.4	0.2	0.1	0.1
Stone, clay and glass products	1.2	9.6	1.8	9.0	4.0	4.4	0.2	0.3	0.3	0.7	1.7	2.8
Primary metals	7.3	11.8	18.8	11.1	14.1	9.4	0.9	1.5	3.5	1.6	5.2	4.5
Fabricated metal products	16.3	36.7	51.2	38.9	46.8	40.7	2.1	2.9	6.4	8.8	4.2	12.4
Industrial machinery and computers	249.1	244.5	243.8	1 432.4	738.5	289.4	49.3	40.4	36.7	492.5	196.7	80.2
Electric and electronic equipment	913.4	1 177.5	1 177.1	1 141.3	465.7	433.6	661.4	819.3	555.2	339.6	98.7	120.6
Transportation equipment	322.5	365.0	464.6	556.2	858.4	886.6	110.9	90.3	123.0	127.2	324.3	430.5
Scientific and measuring instruments	222.2	301.2	319.6	289.6	234.1	225.9	32.1	43.0	45.9	46.1	52.5	66.5
Miscellaneous manufactures	13.0	13.9	16.9	14.5	23.5	17.9	6.9	7.9	9.0	5.9	11.3	7.5
Unidentified manufactures	3.3	4.3	2.3	2.4	4.8	3.2	0.7	1.0	0.4	0.4	1.6	0.6
Agricultural And Livestock Products	16.3	22.3	28.7	39.2	32.6	28.9	0.6	1.0	1.6	1.6	1.1	2.9
Agricultural products	16.3	22.3	28.7	39.2	32.5	28.9	0.6	1.0	1.6	1.6	1.1	2.9
Livestock and livestock products	...	...	0.1	0.1	0.1	...	...	...	...	...	...	...
Other Commodities	75.9	182.7	73.5	98.5	45.6	66.0	32.5	69.6	33.0	21.9	7.9	10.9
Forestry products	...	0.1	0.3	0.3	0.2	0.2	...	...	...	0.1	...	0.1
Fish and other marine products	...	...	0.1	...	...	0.1	...	...	...	...	...	0.1
Metallic ores and concentrates	38.0	145.9	38.2	51.7	2.8	9.2	16.9	58.9	25.0	12.1	...	...
Bituminous coal and lignite	...	...	...	...	...	...	...	...	...	...	...	...
Crude petroleum and natural gas	...	...	...	...	...	...	...	...	...	...	...	...
Nonmetallic minerals	1.4	0.3	0.2	0.1	0.3	0.1	1.2	...	0.1	...	0.2	0.1
Scrap and waste	...	7.3	5.1	12.3	14.2	18.3	...	0.2	...	...	...	...
Used merchandise	2.7	2.6	1.1	4.2	1.9	4.3	0.2	0.3	0.2	1.9	0.2	1.4
Goods imported and returned unchanged	...	...	...	...	...	...	...	...	...	...	...	...
Special classification provisions	33.7	26.7	28.4	30.0	26.2	33.7	14.1	10.3	7.7	7.8	7.4	9.2

Table D-5. ARIZONA: State Exports of Goods by Destination and Industry, 1994–1999—*Continued*

(Millions of dollars.)

Industry	Germany						France					
	1994	1995	1996	1997	1998	1999	1994	1995	1996	1997	1998	1999
ALL GOODS	349.8	410.8	392.9	413.7	529.7	454.3	206.7	285.7	324.9	382.2	439.4	381.4
Manufactured Goods	336.1	381.7	380.9	393.8	510.3	431.0	201.6	280.7	313.5	373.0	429.6	367.7
Food products	1.6	1.6	1.0	0.4	1.9	0.5	0.5	0.4	0.5	0.5	0.8	0.9
Tobacco products	...	...	...	...	...	...	...	...	...	...	...	...
Textile mill products	0.3	0.2	...	...	...	0.1	0.1	...	...	...	...	...
Apparel	0.1	0.6	0.4	0.6	0.4	0.3	...	0.1	0.1	0.1	0.1	0.2
Lumber and wood products	...	...	0.2	...	0.1	0.1	...	...	...	...	...	...
Furniture and fixtures	1.0	0.5	0.2	0.2	0.6	0.7	0.2	0.1	0.4	0.3	0.2	0.1
Paper products	0.3	0.1	0.1	0.1	...	0.1	0.2	0.1	...	...	0.1	0.1
Printing and publishing	0.4	0.8	0.6	1.0	0.9	1.5	0.1	0.3	0.2	0.3	0.4	1.3
Chemical products	1.5	2.8	3.1	2.0	4.0	3.8	0.4	0.6	3.0	1.7	1.8	2.9
Refined petroleum products	...	...	...	...	...	0.1	...	...	...	...	...	5.4
Rubber and plastic products	6.0	4.6	1.9	1.3	1.6	1.0	0.3	1.6	3.0	6.5	9.4	3.6
Leather products	0.2	0.3	0.2	0.3	0.5	0.3	...	...	0.2	...	0.1	...
Stone, clay and glass products	0.5	0.7	1.1	1.7	1.5	0.8	0.2	8.2	0.1	0.1	0.2	0.2
Primary metals	4.0	4.0	7.5	1.9	2.8	1.8	0.1	0.3	0.7	0.2	1.1	0.3
Fabricated metal products	5.8	20.6	35.2	14.2	3.3	3.7	3.3	6.1	4.9	8.0	7.9	9.2
Industrial machinery and computers	51.0	52.9	47.9	40.6	57.5	42.5	32.1	39.2	37.7	41.8	38.4	43.6
Electric and electronic equipment	51.9	82.2	86.9	92.3	139.7	104.3	82.9	101.4	82.6	109.0	111.9	129.1
Transportation equipment	163.0	144.0	143.2	194.9	248.1	237.9	24.9	56.2	107.1	127.4	185.9	104.2
Scientific and measuring instruments	44.6	62.4	47.8	39.0	41.0	26.4	55.3	65.1	71.6	75.8	67.9	63.7
Miscellaneous manufactures	3.3	2.8	3.0	2.7	5.2	4.4	0.4	0.3	0.8	0.8	2.2	1.9
Unidentified manufactures	0.7	0.7	0.5	0.5	1.0	0.5	0.5	0.6	0.4	0.5	1.1	1.0
Agricultural And Livestock Products	0.6	1.9	0.8	0.7	0.2	0.7	0.4	0.1	0.2	0.1	0.2	0.4
Agricultural products	0.6	1.9	0.8	0.7	0.2	0.7	0.4	0.1	0.2	0.1	0.2	0.4
Livestock and livestock products	...	...	...	...	...	...	...	...	...	...	...	...
Other Commodities	13.0	27.2	11.1	19.3	19.3	22.7	4.7	4.9	11.2	9.1	9.6	13.3
Forestry products	...	...	...	...	...	...	...	...	...	...	...	...
Fish and other marine products	...	...	...	...	...	...	...	...	0.1	...	...	...
Metallic ores and concentrates	2.3	12.1	1.9	...	...	...	...	...	...	...	...	...
Bituminous coal and lignite	...	...	...	...	...	...	...	...	...	...	...	...
Crude petroleum and natural gas	...	...	...	...	...	...	...	...	...	...	...	...
Nonmetallic minerals	0.1	0.3	...	...	...	...	...	...	...	...	0.1	...
Scrap and waste	...	7.1	5.1	12.2	14.2	18.3	...	...	...	...	...	...
Used merchandise	1.9	1.6	0.3	0.8	0.7	0.6	0.3	0.2	0.1	1.1	0.5	1.4
Goods imported and returned unchanged	...	...	...	...	...	...	...	...	...	...	...	...
Special classification provisions	8.8	6.2	3.8	6.3	4.3	3.7	4.5	4.8	10.9	7.9	9.0	11.8

Industry	The Netherlands						Asian 10					
	1994	1995	1996	1997	1998	1999	1994	1995	1996	1997	1998	1999
ALL GOODS	134.1	291.1	558.5	1 454.6	408.1	100.2	2 859.9	3 437.2	4 451.6	5 975.8	4 129.7	3 810.9
Manufactured Goods	114.8	212.8	541.8	1 407.0	404.4	98.1	2 774.7	3 312.4	4 352.3	5 895.7	4 064.4	3 763.2
Food products	1.0	1.2	1.7	1.9	3.0	0.6	4.2	6.3	7.9	13.7	8.7	12.7
Tobacco products	...	...	...	...	...	...	...	...	...	...	...	...
Textile mill products	...	...	...	0.3	...	...	1.3	2.5	1.4	8.0	1.1	1.1
Apparel	...	0.1	0.2	0.3	0.1	...	4.0	7.0	4.3	4.4	2.5	3.4
Lumber and wood products	...	...	0.1	...	...	...	0.1	0.3	0.8	1.1	1.2	1.0
Furniture and fixtures	...	...	0.4	...	...	...	0.2	1.0	1.3	0.8	0.4	0.4
Paper products	0.1	0.2	0.2	0.3	0.3	0.3	0.8	1.3	1.3	2.6	1.7	1.6
Printing and publishing	0.1	0.1	0.2	0.1	0.5	2.8	2.0	11.5	11.6	2.0	1.9	1.4
Chemical products	6.4	40.4	4.7	3.6	2.0	3.5	42.5	83.2	85.3	43.9	37.8	70.0
Refined petroleum products	...	...	...	...	...	0.1	0.1	0.2	0.2	12.8	7.2	22.1
Rubber and plastic products	0.2	0.2	0.9	0.3	0.2	0.3	19.8	12.7	18.6	13.9	13.3	13.9
Leather products	...	...	...	...	0.2	...	2.0	1.6	1.5	1.6	0.7	1.0
Stone, clay and glass products	...	0.2	0.1	5.8	0.2	0.1	5.8	4.2	8.3	5.0	4.3	4.3
Primary metals	0.9	1.8	0.8	0.3	0.6	0.2	177.0	253.5	263.8	85.3	40.5	9.2
Fabricated metal products	0.6	1.9	1.1	4.6	7.3	5.8	29.1	9.1	21.8	19.2	21.2	31.7
Industrial machinery and computers	22.6	24.3	23.8	733.9	300.5	37.0	169.6	230.7	317.6	1 162.4	592.6	282.1
Electric and electronic equipment	9.0	29.4	374.8	542.3	36.0	11.1	2 048.6	2 403.9	3 246.5	4 102.5	2 961.1	2 955.9
Transportation equipment	3.8	7.3	4.6	7.3	9.1	5.3	159.7	148.5	210.6	243.5	218.7	174.7
Scientific and measuring instruments	69.3	104.3	126.0	103.4	42.6	30.1	80.1	96.3	108.8	142.3	114.5	141.6
Miscellaneous manufactures	0.5	0.8	2.0	2.5	1.5	0.6	24.9	36.3	38.5	28.3	29.5	30.9
Unidentified manufactures	0.3	0.5	0.3	0.1	0.3	0.4	3.0	2.5	2.1	2.4	5.4	4.2
Agricultural And Livestock Products	0.7	2.3	4.6	7.5	0.2	0.3	52.2	65.0	43.7	49.9	42.5	16.1
Agricultural products	0.7	2.3	4.6	7.5	0.2	0.3	52.2	64.3	43.1	49.8	42.4	16.1
Livestock and livestock products	...	...	...	...	...	...	...	0.7	0.6	0.1	0.1	0.1
Other Commodities	18.6	76.0	12.2	40.2	3.4	1.8	33.0	59.7	55.6	30.2	22.8	31.5
Forestry products	...	...	...	...	...	...	0.1	...	0.1	...	...	...
Fish and other marine products	...	...	...	...	...	...	0.4	...	0.2	0.2	0.1	...
Metallic ores and concentrates	18.2	74.8	11.3	39.0	2.8	...	19.2	44.4	35.1	8.6	0.1	3.3
Bituminous coal and lignite	...	...	...	...	...	...	...	...	...	...	...	...
Crude petroleum and natural gas	...	...	...	...	...	...	...	...	...	...	...	...
Nonmetallic minerals	...	...	...	...	...	...	2.6	4.6	3.6	1.8	0.9	0.9
Scrap and waste	...	...	...	...	...	...	2.7	3.5	2.7	5.7	7.1	5.6
Used merchandise	...	...	0.3	0.1	0.1	0.1	0.8	0.8	1.5	2.8	2.6	5.6
Goods imported and returned unchanged	...	...	...	...	...	...	...	...	...	...	...	...
Special classification provisions	0.3	1.1	0.6	1.1	0.6	1.8	7.1	6.4	12.4	11.0	11.9	16.0

Table D-5. ARIZONA: State Exports of Goods by Destination and Industry, 1994–1999—*Continued*

(Millions of dollars.)

Industry	Japan						South Korea					
	1994	1995	1996	1997	1998	1999	1994	1995	1996	1997	1998	1999
ALL GOODS	808.3	1 125.5	1 356.2	1 806.4	679.6	799.7	206.2	230.2	287.8	296.9	352.9	334.6
Manufactured Goods	777.0	1 069.4	1 326.9	1 785.4	666.0	783.4	185.5	202.8	268.0	282.5	326.0	326.6
Food products	1.0	2.2	2.1	5.8	3.4	3.4	1.0	1.4	2.5	2.1	1.4	3.2
Tobacco products	...	...	...	...	...	...	...	...	...	...	...	...
Textile mill products	0.5	0.3	0.5	2.1	...	...	...	0.1	0.2	0.2	0.1	...
Apparel	3.2	4.5	3.6	3.6	1.9	3.0	0.4	2.1	0.1	0.1	0.1	...
Lumber and wood products	0.1	0.2	0.6	0.7	0.3	0.1	...	...	0.1	...	0.4	...
Furniture and fixtures	0.1	0.7	1.1	0.2	0.2	0.3	0.1	0.1	0.1	0.1	0.1	0.1
Paper products	0.1	0.2	0.2	0.3	0.1	0.2	0.1	0.2	0.2	0.3	0.2	0.1
Printing and publishing	0.8	0.8	0.6	0.6	0.4	0.1	0.1	0.1	0.1	0.1	0.1	...
Chemical products	36.2	73.4	72.0	23.7	26.0	57.4	1.3	3.5	3.2	2.8	1.3	2.2
Refined petroleum products	...	...	...	0.8	0.4	12.0	...	...	...	1.0	...	0.7
Rubber and plastic products	1.0	1.4	2.3	1.9	3.1	7.9	3.7	6.2	12.1	3.4	0.6	0.8
Leather products	1.6	1.3	0.6	0.5	0.5	0.7	...	...	0.6	0.6	0.1	...
Stone, clay and glass products	1.7	2.1	1.6	2.3	2.3	2.8	...	0.5	0.3	0.2	0.1	0.1
Primary metals	74.8	101.4	74.1	12.4	1.7	1.0	2.5	13.3	10.1	15.5	9.2	0.3
Fabricated metal products	0.9	2.0	11.7	4.4	4.0	3.2	0.5	0.3	0.3	0.4	0.6	5.3
Industrial machinery and computers	48.5	78.0	92.6	423.9	141.5	60.5	16.7	27.4	33.5	73.5	41.4	41.1
Electric and electronic equipment	555.8	745.7	987.0	1 225.9	402.6	558.4	140.8	126.9	172.8	147.7	245.8	242.7
Transportation equipment	12.6	13.9	17.5	17.2	22.6	12.9	7.9	4.2	14.7	15.8	17.2	15.6
Scientific and measuring instruments	20.2	23.3	31.3	38.2	32.1	39.1	8.5	12.4	13.9	17.0	6.8	12.9
Miscellaneous manufactures	17.2	17.5	26.7	20.5	21.9	19.6	1.7	3.9	3.0	1.6	0.4	1.1
Unidentified manufactures	0.7	0.6	0.6	0.4	1.1	0.9	0.1	0.3	0.2	0.3	0.6	0.4
Agricultural And Livestock Products	7.7	5.4	4.7	4.9	10.1	10.9	18.1	24.7	17.8	9.3	20.3	0.8
Agricultural products	7.6	5.4	4.2	4.8	10.0	10.9	18.1	24.7	17.8	9.3	20.3	0.8
Livestock and livestock products	...	...	0.5	0.1	0.1	...	...	...	...	...	...	...
Other Commodities	23.6	50.7	24.6	16.1	3.5	5.4	2.6	2.7	2.0	5.0	6.5	7.2
Forestry products	...	...	...	...	...	...	0.1	...	...	...	...	...
Fish and other marine products	0.4	...	...	0.1	...	...	...	...	...	...	...	...
Metallic ores and concentrates	19.2	44.4	18.6	8.6	...	2.1	...	...	...	...	...	1.2
Bituminous coal and lignite	...	...	...	...	...	...	...	...	...	...	...	...
Crude petroleum and natural gas	...	...	...	...	...	...	...	...	...	...	...	...
Nonmetallic minerals	2.5	4.4	3.1	1.4	0.2	0.1	0.1	0.1	0.1	...	0.1	...
Scrap and waste	...	...	0.3	0.8	...	0.1	2.3	2.4	1.7	4.2	6.1	4.7
Used merchandise	0.5	0.6	0.6	1.7	0.6	1.0	...	...	...	...	...	...
Goods imported and returned unchanged	...	...	...	...	...	...	...	...	...	...	...	...
Special classification provisions	0.9	1.3	1.9	3.7	2.6	2.1	0.1	0.1	0.3	0.8	0.3	1.2

Industry	Taiwan						Singapore					
	1994	1995	1996	1997	1998	1999	1994	1995	1996	1997	1998	1999
ALL GOODS	604.3	648.2	895.4	1 062.8	624.5	490.3	351.4	302.8	364.6	473.2	301.3	312.2
Manufactured Goods	598.4	639.9	888.0	1 054.8	618.3	482.8	348.8	300.8	359.9	470.1	297.8	310.4
Food products	0.1	0.4	0.9	1.6	0.8	0.8	1.5	1.4	1.1	1.1	0.4	0.7
Tobacco products	...	...	...	...	...	...	...	...	...	...	...	...
Textile mill products	...	0.1	...	...	0.3	0.1	...	0.2	0.1	0.1	...	...
Apparel	0.1	...	...	...	...	...	...	...	0.1	0.2	0.1	0.2
Lumber and wood products	...	0.1	...	0.2	...	0.1	...	...	0.1	...	...	...
Furniture and fixtures	...	...	...	...	...	...	...	0.2	...	...	...	...
Paper products	0.1	0.1	0.1	0.1	0.2	0.1	0.1	0.2	0.1	0.3	...	0.1
Printing and publishing	0.1	0.1	0.2	0.1	0.1	0.3	0.1	0.2	0.9	0.1	0.1	0.2
Chemical products	1.5	1.7	1.1	2.0	1.6	2.0	1.2	2.3	4.3	6.0	1.9	2.8
Refined petroleum products	...	0.1	...	...	0.2	...	...	...	0.1	8.0	...	1.4
Rubber and plastic products	0.3	0.7	0.3	0.5	0.4	0.5	2.1	2.2	1.6	1.5	2.0	1.6
Leather products	...	...	...	0.1	...	...	0.1	...	0.1	0.2	0.1	0.1
Stone, clay and glass products	1.6	0.7	5.2	0.3	0.3	...	1.9	0.5	0.3	0.2	0.4	0.6
Primary metals	63.0	72.5	95.1	32.3	2.7	0.3	1.1	28.4	8.1	6.7	8.6	4.8
Fabricated metal products	24.3	1.0	1.0	6.6	1.8	4.3	2.1	2.9	3.0	2.3	6.5	9.0
Industrial machinery and computers	24.6	24.6	26.6	151.1	71.1	55.7	12.8	17.7	24.0	126.5	81.4	38.3
Electric and electronic equipment	396.0	463.6	663.5	761.7	473.5	372.1	278.9	190.4	236.2	218.0	95.6	162.1
Transportation equipment	71.7	62.2	85.1	85.4	52.9	33.1	39.4	45.5	67.2	83.3	87.3	73.2
Scientific and measuring instruments	14.3	10.9	8.2	11.8	10.9	12.2	5.4	7.0	10.3	14.4	10.2	12.4
Miscellaneous manufactures	0.3	0.8	0.3	0.8	1.0	0.9	1.4	1.3	2.1	1.2	2.9	2.6
Unidentified manufactures	0.4	0.3	0.3	0.2	0.5	0.3	0.7	0.5	0.2	0.2	0.3	0.3
Agricultural And Livestock Products	3.4	5.7	5.1	5.2	2.7	0.4	0.1	...	...	...	...	...
Agricultural products	3.4	5.7	5.1	5.2	2.7	0.4	0.1	...	...	...	...	...
Livestock and livestock products	...	...	...	...	...	...	...	...	...	...	...	...
Other Commodities	2.5	2.7	2.2	2.8	3.5	7.1	2.5	2.0	4.7	3.1	3.4	1.8
Forestry products	...	...	...	...	...	...	...	...	...	...	...	...
Fish and other marine products	...	...	...	...	...	...	...	...	...	...	...	...
Metallic ores and concentrates	...	...	...	...	...	...	...	...	...	...	...	...
Bituminous coal and lignite	...	...	...	...	...	...	...	...	...	...	...	...
Crude petroleum and natural gas	...	...	...	...	...	...	...	...	...	...	...	...
Nonmetallic minerals	...	...	0.3	0.3	0.4	0.7	...	...	...	...	...	...
Scrap and waste	...	0.1	0.4	...	...	...	...	...	...	...	...	...
Used merchandise	0.1	...	0.2	0.5	0.8	3.9	...	...	0.4	0.3	0.1	0.2
Goods imported and returned unchanged	...	...	...	...	...	...	...	...	...	...	...	...
Special classification provisions	2.4	2.5	1.3	1.9	2.3	2.4	2.5	2.0	4.3	2.8	3.3	1.6

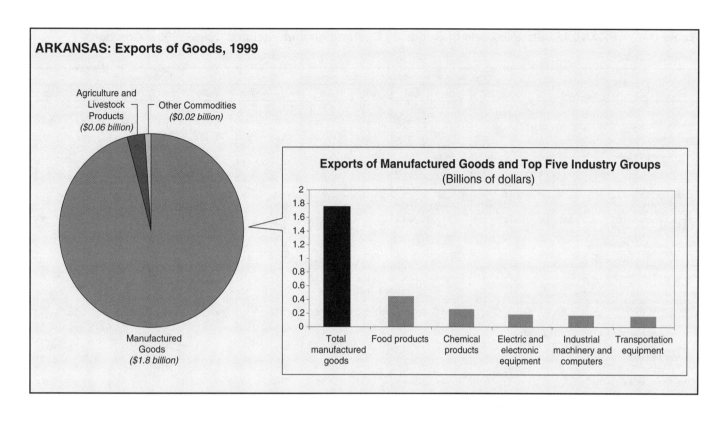

ARKANSAS: Exports of Goods, 1999

Agriculture and Livestock Products ($0.06 billion)

Other Commodities ($0.02 billion)

Manufactured Goods ($1.8 billion)

Exports of Manufactured Goods and Top Five Industry Groups
(Billions of dollars)

Table D-6. ARKANSAS: State Exports of Goods by Destination and Industry, 1994–1999

(Millions of dollars.)

Industry	All destinations						Canada					
	1994	1995	1996	1997	1998	1999	1994	1995	1996	1997	1998	1999
ALL GOODS	1 470.9	1 794.4	1 997.2	2 211.6	1 934.1	1 828.9	521.1	574.1	614.9	820.4	687.5	751.3
Manufactured Goods	1 409.9	1 715.5	1 903.3	2 036.5	1 850.2	1 754.3	497.1	554.0	591.6	710.4	655.0	717.7
Food products	486.8	673.6	811.9	718.3	566.8	450.5	44.9	51.9	53.1	58.4	53.7	56.2
Tobacco products	...	...	...	...	...	...	...	...	...	...	...	...
Textile mill products	9.8	9.6	11.0	8.7	15.6	44.3	7.1	7.3	8.9	5.3	8.3	21.3
Apparel	3.8	6.1	4.9	2.1	5.5	4.1	2.1	1.8	1.0	0.7	0.3	0.4
Lumber and wood products	6.3	7.5	8.7	11.6	12.6	11.8	4.0	5.4	6.5	8.8	9.2	8.9
Furniture and fixtures	31.6	19.9	19.5	22.2	22.7	12.9	28.6	12.8	14.9	14.4	15.6	9.0
Paper products	32.4	43.3	40.0	32.4	34.3	33.7	20.1	18.1	24.1	20.5	17.7	24.2
Printing and publishing	8.7	43.0	43.3	40.8	39.4	30.0	6.6	40.8	41.2	38.6	36.5	26.5
Chemical products	202.3	247.7	228.4	273.7	284.0	263.0	33.9	52.3	39.1	37.0	46.6	66.4
Refined petroleum products	3.1	2.7	2.9	3.3	3.3	4.7	1.8	2.3	2.4	2.6	2.7	2.9
Rubber and plastic products	32.7	33.1	33.9	44.3	55.8	57.4	21.5	24.4	25.2	28.0	38.6	38.2
Leather products	3.3	7.1	9.7	13.5	3.4	2.5	1.2	1.3	0.5	0.9	1.1	1.0
Stone, clay and glass products	7.7	9.9	10.4	9.6	22.8	19.5	1.5	1.8	1.8	1.5	6.2	3.3
Primary metals	63.4	61.1	98.1	164.6	79.2	116.2	54.1	36.1	70.1	136.8	59.9	83.0
Fabricated metal products	63.5	69.6	69.2	78.2	87.7	107.5	39.7	35.1	41.1	47.3	56.1	71.1
Industrial machinery and computers	152.4	172.5	168.1	181.6	166.8	171.6	72.7	77.7	78.5	83.1	78.8	91.9
Electric and electronic equipment	137.2	155.4	168.0	199.7	194.3	186.0	93.8	105.7	96.6	107.7	100.1	79.9
Transportation equipment	100.5	101.9	123.9	168.6	192.0	160.1	49.8	64.8	73.1	102.1	107.5	114.3
Scientific and measuring instruments	47.9	31.8	34.9	44.7	42.8	49.4	7.5	7.4	7.4	9.4	8.5	11.3
Miscellaneous manufactures	13.8	15.6	13.4	14.4	15.5	22.7	5.2	5.4	5.1	6.2	6.3	6.7
Unidentified manufactures	2.9	4.3	3.1	4.2	5.6	6.4	1.1	1.4	1.0	1.4	1.4	1.3
Agricultural And Livestock Products	42.3	39.1	42.2	45.7	62.1	55.6	17.4	10.9	14.8	17.6	27.5	19.5
Agricultural products	16.1	7.8	6.4	3.8	4.6	14.0	2.4	1.3	1.8	1.3	2.4	1.2
Livestock and livestock products	26.3	31.3	35.8	41.9	57.5	41.6	15.0	9.6	13.0	16.3	25.1	18.2
Other Commodities	18.6	39.9	51.7	129.4	21.8	19.0	6.6	9.3	8.4	92.5	5.1	14.1
Forestry products	...	...	...	...	...	0.1	...	...	...	...	...	...
Fish and other marine products	5.6	16.2	33.1	24.3	5.8	0.8	1.4	0.9	0.3	0.1	...	0.4
Metallic ores and concentrates	0.3	0.2	0.3	0.1	0.1	1.4	...	...	0.1	...	0.1	1.2
Bituminous coal and lignite	5.0	4.4	3.3	2.9	0.7	...	...	...	...	...	...	...
Crude petroleum and natural gas	...	...	...	0.2	79.5	...	0.3	...	...	...	79.5	...	0.1
Nonmetallic minerals	1.6	2.2	1.6	2.2	3.7	3.0	0.9	0.4	0.2	0.2	0.2	1.2
Scrap and waste	1.6	2.4	1.7	1.8	1.1	1.1	1.0	1.4	0.6	1.2	0.3	0.2
Used merchandise	0.8	0.8	0.7	0.7	0.5	0.4	0.1	0.3	0.2	0.2	0.2	0.1
Goods imported and returned unchanged	2.7	5.8	6.0	8.9	3.8	4.2	2.7	5.8	6.0	8.9	3.8	4.2
Special classification provisions	0.9	7.9	4.8	8.9	6.1	7.8	0.4	0.4	1.0	2.3	0.5	6.6

Table D-6. ARKANSAS: State Exports of Goods by Destination and Industry, 1994–1999—*Continued*

(Millions of dollars.)

Industry	South and Central American and Caribbean						Mexico					
	1994	1995	1996	1997	1998	1999	1994	1995	1996	1997	1998	1999
ALL GOODS	41.6	80.1	75.6	84.6	90.2	67.5	94.2	59.8	102.2	140.8	179.4	207.9
Manufactured Goods	37.8	71.0	67.8	76.5	81.6	58.0	85.4	46.4	90.5	121.9	155.0	192.3
Food products	11.8	15.5	13.9	15.0	15.7	11.6	6.4	5.3	10.3	10.5	9.0	10.4
Tobacco products	...	...	...	...	...	...	...	...	...	...	...	...
Textile mill products	1.5	1.4	0.6	0.2	0.4	12.7	0.4	0.3	0.7	1.6	4.4	5.3
Apparel	0.5	2.0	1.0	0.4	0.2	1.3	0.2	0.8	1.7	0.1	3.5	1.4
Lumber and wood products	0.1	0.1	0.4	0.1	...	0.3	0.3	0.1	0.1	0.3	0.3	0.8
Furniture and fixtures	0.3	3.2	2.2	3.3	3.2	0.5	0.5	0.2	0.2	0.6	0.8	1.0
Paper products	0.6	0.5	1.2	0.4	0.2	0.8	5.9	3.7	6.2	5.1	7.8	6.0
Printing and publishing	0.1	0.2	0.1	0.2	0.3	0.3	0.5	0.1	0.2	0.3	0.6	0.7
Chemical products	6.3	7.1	9.4	12.5	16.9	7.1	6.1	5.2	5.3	10.8	12.3	22.4
Refined petroleum products	...	0.1	...	0.1	0.1	0.2	0.1	...	0.2	0.4	0.4	1.3
Rubber and plastic products	0.6	1.4	1.6	5.1	5.7	1.0	2.4	0.9	1.1	1.6	1.3	10.2
Leather products	...	0.3	0.1	0.1	0.1	0.2	1.2	4.9	7.8	11.0	1.2	0.4
Stone, clay and glass products	0.1	0.2	0.7	0.6	0.4	0.4	0.6	0.3	0.4	1.2	9.0	6.0
Primary metals	0.6	2.6	8.5	8.3	2.9	1.0	4.2	7.1	7.4	9.8	7.8	26.3
Fabricated metal products	2.2	3.2	2.9	2.3	4.4	1.4	3.7	2.2	2.4	2.9	3.5	6.5
Industrial machinery and computers	5.2	15.4	11.4	11.5	14.2	8.5	16.6	4.2	5.9	10.0	21.7	23.1
Electric and electronic equipment	3.9	10.8	9.2	8.4	5.7	2.9	9.3	5.0	27.7	40.1	41.7	58.5
Transportation equipment	1.3	1.0	0.7	3.5	4.9	2.1	21.8	2.5	10.6	12.6	26.8	9.0
Scientific and measuring instruments	1.3	2.1	1.6	1.9	1.8	1.2	3.2	1.5	0.5	1.2	1.3	0.5
Miscellaneous manufactures	1.1	2.6	1.3	1.4	3.0	3.0	1.8	2.0	1.6	1.6	0.8	1.0
Unidentified manufactures	0.3	1.3	1.1	1.3	1.6	1.5	0.3	0.1	0.2	0.2	0.6	1.7
Agricultural And Livestock Products	3.9	8.9	7.7	7.8	8.3	9.1	8.1	6.1	7.9	12.4	18.8	14.8
Agricultural products	...	...	0.1	0.2	...	0.1	5.9	1.3	0.7	0.3	0.2	3.9
Livestock and livestock products	3.8	8.9	7.6	7.6	8.2	8.9	2.2	4.8	7.2	12.2	18.6	10.8
Other Commodities	...	0.1	0.1	0.4	0.3	0.4	0.6	7.3	3.9	6.5	5.6	0.8
Forestry products	...	...	...	...	...	0.1	...	...	...	...	...	...
Fish and other marine products	...	...	...	...	...	...	...	...	...	...	...	...
Metallic ores and concentrates	...	...	...	...	...	...	0.2	...	...	...	...	0.1
Bituminous coal and lignite	...	...	...	...	...	...	...	...	...	...	...	...
Crude petroleum and natural gas	...	...	...	...	...	0.1	...	...	...	...	...	...
Nonmetallic minerals	...	...	0.1	0.1	0.1	0.1	0.1	0.1	0.1	0.1	...	0.1
Scrap and waste	...	...	...	...	...	...	...	...	0.3	...	0.4	0.5
Used merchandise	...	...	...	0.3	0.2	...	...	0.1	...	...	...	...
Goods imported and returned unchanged	...	...	...	...	...	...	...	...	...	...	...	...
Special classification provisions	...	...	...	...	...	...	0.4	7.2	3.5	6.3	5.2	0.1

Industry	European Union						United Kingdom					
	1994	1995	1996	1997	1998	1999	1994	1995	1996	1997	1998	1999
ALL GOODS	185.8	258.3	268.6	302.9	321.1	274.6	64.4	76.2	74.5	84.8	88.5	72.1
Manufactured Goods	178.5	249.0	260.3	297.2	316.4	271.7	60.4	71.5	71.6	82.0	86.9	71.3
Food products	58.3	42.4	70.1	68.8	71.1	70.7	19.1	15.6	27.0	27.0	26.6	29.6
Tobacco products	...	...	...	...	...	...	...	...	...	...	...	...
Textile mill products	0.4	0.3	0.2	1.2	2.1	3.8	0.1	...	0.1	0.1	0.1	0.2
Apparel	0.3	0.5	0.3	0.3	0.8	0.4	0.1	0.1	...	...	0.3	0.1
Lumber and wood products	1.1	0.9	1.0	1.5	2.2	0.7	0.2	0.4	0.2	0.2	0.1	...
Furniture and fixtures	0.7	1.9	1.0	1.2	1.7	1.1	0.3	0.5	0.5	0.8	0.9	0.5
Paper products	4.0	19.9	7.2	5.9	7.7	1.7	1.3	2.5	0.3	0.8	1.0	1.4
Printing and publishing	0.5	0.7	0.6	0.9	0.7	0.7	0.3	0.5	0.4	0.5	0.4	0.4
Chemical products	41.3	77.7	74.0	88.3	94.2	64.5	11.8	23.7	16.4	20.6	25.3	10.2
Refined petroleum products	0.4	0.2	0.3	0.1	...	0.1	...	0.1	0.1	...	...	...
Rubber and plastic products	1.7	3.5	2.8	4.7	5.2	3.5	0.6	1.1	0.5	1.2	1.4	1.5
Leather products	0.1	0.2	0.8	1.3	0.5	0.1	...	...	...	...	...	0.1
Stone, clay and glass products	3.6	5.1	5.0	4.7	6.0	4.8	0.4	0.7	0.9	1.1	1.8	1.7
Primary metals	2.4	9.6	4.0	5.2	6.8	4.9	1.3	2.8	1.4	1.5	1.4	1.7
Fabricated metal products	8.7	18.0	14.3	16.2	12.5	20.9	4.1	5.0	5.6	5.4	5.9	2.3
Industrial machinery and computers	23.5	32.4	29.8	31.4	27.7	31.6	7.2	9.5	9.5	9.6	10.4	12.8
Electric and electronic equipment	9.8	13.1	18.0	24.2	26.4	24.6	3.2	3.0	3.2	7.4	5.9	3.0
Transportation equipment	15.7	16.8	23.8	32.9	43.4	25.1	8.8	5.0	3.6	3.0	2.9	2.9
Scientific and measuring instruments	3.3	3.2	4.9	6.3	4.6	5.1	0.9	0.5	1.1	1.9	1.3	0.9
Miscellaneous manufactures	2.4	2.0	2.0	2.0	2.3	6.6	0.5	0.4	0.4	0.6	1.0	1.7
Unidentified manufactures	0.5	0.6	0.4	0.4	0.6	0.7	0.2	0.2	0.1	0.2	0.3	0.4
Agricultural And Livestock Products	1.3	2.9	2.3	0.6	1.1	0.6	0.1	0.2	0.1	0.2	...	...
Agricultural products	0.2	2.2	1.6	0.2	0.4	0.4	0.1	0.2	...	...	...	...
Livestock and livestock products	1.1	0.7	0.7	0.5	0.7	0.2	...	...	0.1	0.2	...	...
Other Commodities	6.0	6.5	5.9	5.1	3.7	2.2	3.9	4.5	2.8	2.6	1.5	0.8
Forestry products	...	...	...	...	...	...	...	...	...	...	...	...
Fish and other marine products	...	...	0.4	0.1	0.1	...	...	...	...	...	...	...
Metallic ores and concentrates	0.2	0.1	0.1	...	...	...	...	...	...	...	...	...
Bituminous coal and lignite	5.0	4.4	3.3	2.9	0.7	...	3.9	4.4	1.8	1.1	...	...
Crude petroleum and natural gas	...	...	0.2	...	...	...	...	...	...	...	...	...
Nonmetallic minerals	0.1	0.7	0.9	1.5	2.2	1.0	...	...	0.7	1.4	1.4	0.7
Scrap and waste	0.6	0.7	0.8	0.4	0.4	0.3	...	...	...	...	...	...
Used merchandise	0.1	0.4	0.1	0.1	0.1	0.1	...	...	0.1	0.1	0.1	...
Goods imported and returned unchanged	...	...	...	...	...	...	...	...	...	...	...	...
Special classification provisions	...	0.1	0.2	...	0.1	0.7	...	...	0.2	...	...	0.1

Table D-6. ARKANSAS: State Exports of Goods by Destination and Industry, 1994–1999—*Continued*

(Millions of dollars.)

Industry	Germany						France					
	1994	1995	1996	1997	1998	1999	1994	1995	1996	1997	1998	1999
ALL GOODS	24.4	34.0	43.3	45.4	48.0	40.4	13.0	20.3	30.8	45.8	53.9	37.9
Manufactured Goods	24.2	33.7	41.4	45.2	47.7	40.0	12.3	19.5	30.0	45.3	53.5	37.5
Food products	10.2	6.4	14.3	20.8	21.4	19.4	1.9	2.1	3.5	6.5	9.2	8.5
Tobacco products	...	...	...	...	...	...	...	...	...	...	...	...
Textile mill products	...	...	...	...	0.1	0.1	...	0.2	...	0.1	0.5	0.2
Apparel	0.1	0.1	...	0.1	0.1	0.1	...	0.1	...	...	...	...
Lumber and wood products	0.3	0.3	0.4	1.0	1.2	0.1	0.2	0.2	0.2	0.2	0.1	0.1
Furniture and fixtures	0.2	...	0.1	...	0.1	0.1	0.1	0.1	0.2	0.2	0.3	0.1
Paper products	...	...	...	...	0.1	...	...	1.7	2.7	3.0	5.0	0.1
Printing and publishing	0.1	...	0.1	...	...	...	0.1	0.1	...	...	...	...
Chemical products	1.7	2.6	0.9	1.7	0.7	2.4	0.7	0.7	0.8	1.6	2.2	4.0
Refined petroleum products	...	...	...	...	...	...	0.2	0.1	...	...	...	...
Rubber and plastic products	0.1	0.2	0.1	0.3	0.1	0.1	0.6	0.5	0.4	0.4	0.3	0.3
Leather products	0.1	...	...	...	...	...	...	...	...	...	...	...
Stone, clay and glass products	0.9	1.7	0.5	0.8	1.0	0.8	0.3	0.3	0.5	0.5	0.3	0.4
Primary metals	0.6	5.7	1.2	2.6	4.5	3.0	...	...	0.1	...	...	...
Fabricated metal products	1.6	4.2	1.5	1.7	2.1	1.1	0.7	3.6	3.0	6.9	2.3	0.5
Industrial machinery and computers	3.6	3.9	7.3	4.4	3.9	5.8	1.0	3.3	2.2	2.6	1.1	0.5
Electric and electronic equipment	3.3	6.3	11.9	6.4	6.7	2.4	0.6	0.4	0.8	2.5	4.0	3.4
Transportation equipment	0.4	1.0	2.2	4.7	3.8	3.2	5.4	5.5	14.2	18.5	27.6	15.2
Scientific and measuring instruments	1.0	0.3	0.6	0.3	1.4	0.7	0.3	0.7	1.2	2.0	0.4	1.0
Miscellaneous manufactures	0.1	0.8	0.2	0.3	0.5	0.8	0.2	0.1	...	0.2	0.1	3.2
Unidentified manufactures	0.1	0.1	0.1	0.1	...	0.1	...	...	...	...	0.1	0.1
Agricultural And Livestock Products	0.1	0.2	1.5	...	0.1	0.2	...	0.1	...	0.1	...	...
Agricultural products	0.1	0.2	1.4	...	0.1	0.2	...	0.1	...	...	...	...
Livestock and livestock products	...	...	0.1	...	...	...	...	...	...	0.1	...	...
Other Commodities	0.1	0.1	0.4	0.2	0.3	0.2	0.6	0.8	0.8	0.4	0.4	0.4
Forestry products	...	...	...	...	...	...	...	...	...	...	...	...
Fish and other marine products	...	...	0.3	0.1	0.1	...	...	...	...	...	...	...
Metallic ores and concentrates	...	...	...	...	...	...	0.1	...	...	...	...	...
Bituminous coal and lignite	...	...	...	...	...	...	...	...	...	...	...	...
Crude petroleum and natural gas	...	...	...	...	...	...	...	...	...	...	...	...
Nonmetallic minerals	0.1	0.1	0.1	0.1	0.1	...	...	0.1	...	...	0.1	...
Scrap and waste	...	...	...	...	...	...	0.6	0.7	0.8	0.4	0.3	0.3
Used merchandise	...	...	...	...	...	0.1	...	...	...	...	...	...
Goods imported and returned unchanged	...	...	...	...	...	...	...	...	...	...	...	...
Special classification provisions	...	...	...	...	...	...	...	...	...	...	...	...

Industry	The Netherlands						Asian 10					
	1994	1995	1996	1997	1998	1999	1994	1995	1996	1997	1998	1999
ALL GOODS	23.0	27.6	28.0	31.8	30.1	40.7	361.1	381.8	391.0	417.2	317.6	357.3
Manufactured Goods	23.0	27.0	27.9	31.8	30.1	40.3	349.8	359.1	349.9	388.1	305.5	349.8
Food products	14.3	13.1	11.9	7.7	3.7	6.8	164.7	170.7	167.0	195.6	153.4	194.7
Tobacco products	...	...	...	...	...	...	...	...	...	...	...	...
Textile mill products	...	...	...	1.0	0.9	...	0.2	0.3	0.4	0.4	0.2	0.6
Apparel	...	...	...	...	...	...	0.5	0.8	0.9	0.4	0.1	0.6
Lumber and wood products	...	...	0.1	0.1	0.1	...	0.7	0.9	0.6	0.8	0.6	0.8
Furniture and fixtures	...	1.1	...	...	...	...	1.2	1.3	0.7	0.7	0.6	0.5
Paper products	0.8	...	...	...	...	...	1.5	0.6	0.6	0.2	0.4	0.6
Printing and publishing	...	...	...	...	...	...	0.3	0.5	0.4	0.3	0.5	0.8
Chemical products	3.8	6.4	11.4	9.4	13.6	4.1	100.8	96.4	91.4	97.9	81.4	76.3
Refined petroleum products	...	...	...	...	...	0.1	0.7	...	...	0.1	...	0.2
Rubber and plastic products	...	...	0.1	...	...	0.1	4.8	2.1	2.4	2.4	1.2	1.7
Leather products	...	...	...	...	...	...	0.7	0.3	0.6	0.1	...	0.1
Stone, clay and glass products	0.9	1.1	0.9	0.3	0.4	0.4	1.4	1.9	1.4	1.0	0.2	4.5
Primary metals	...	0.5	0.5	0.9	0.1	...	0.5	2.0	4.4	3.8	1.3	0.7
Fabricated metal products	0.1	0.2	0.2	0.2	0.1	10.6	3.0	8.1	4.9	4.3	5.7	4.9
Industrial machinery and computers	1.0	2.4	1.5	4.0	0.8	0.4	22.1	31.6	31.5	30.5	14.2	10.2
Electric and electronic equipment	1.4	1.5	0.4	6.0	6.9	13.5	14.0	14.1	11.5	14.4	15.0	14.6
Transportation equipment	0.1	0.1	...	1.5	2.8	3.0	2.1	9.4	10.9	9.1	4.0	5.4
Scientific and measuring instruments	0.3	0.5	0.7	0.5	0.5	1.0	27.4	14.9	17.9	23.6	24.3	28.5
Miscellaneous manufactures	0.1	...	0.1	...	0.1	0.1	2.5	2.7	2.3	2.3	1.6	3.6
Unidentified manufactures	...	0.1	...	0.1	...	...	0.5	0.5	0.3	0.4	0.7	0.7
Agricultural And Livestock Products	...	...	0.1	...	...	0.1	7.5	7.2	9.1	5.5	5.5	6.2
Agricultural products	...	...	...	...	...	0.1	4.0	1.5	2.2	0.5	0.7	2.9
Livestock and livestock products	...	...	0.1	...	...	...	3.5	5.7	6.9	5.0	4.7	3.3
Other Commodities	0.1	0.6	...	...	...	0.3	3.9	15.5	32.0	23.5	6.6	1.3
Forestry products	...	...	...	...	...	...	...	...	...	...	...	...
Fish and other marine products	...	...	...	...	...	...	3.3	14.2	31.3	22.9	5.1	0.3
Metallic ores and concentrates	...	0.1	...	...	...	...	...	...	...	...	...	...
Bituminous coal and lignite	...	...	...	...	...	...	...	...	...	...	...	...
Crude petroleum and natural gas	...	...	...	...	...	...	...	...	...	...	...	...
Nonmetallic minerals	...	0.4	...	...	...	0.3	0.3	1.0	0.4	0.4	1.1	0.6
Scrap and waste	...	...	...	...	...	...	...	0.1	...	...	...	...
Used merchandise	...	...	...	...	...	...	0.1	...	0.2	...	...	...
Goods imported and returned unchanged	...	...	...	...	...	...	...	...	...	...	...	...
Special classification provisions	...	0.1	...	...	...	...	...	0.1	0.1	0.2	0.3	0.3

Table D-6. ARKANSAS: State Exports of Goods by Destination and Industry, 1994–1999—Continued

(Millions of dollars.)

Industry	Japan						South Korea					
	1994	1995	1996	1997	1998	1999	1994	1995	1996	1997	1998	1999
ALL GOODS	157.1	139.4	126.9	117.2	90.2	106.0	33.8	37.2	41.4	33.1	24.4	32.1
Manufactured Goods	153.7	130.1	98.8	96.3	84.3	103.1	30.0	32.2	38.1	33.0	24.1	31.2
Food products	90.5	65.7	41.3	41.2	42.5	51.5	0.8	3.0	2.8	1.8	2.9	6.2
Tobacco products	...	...	...	...	...	...	...	...	...	...	...	...
Textile mill products	...	0.1	0.2	0.2	...	0.3	...	0.1	0.1	0.1	...	0.1
Apparel	0.1	0.6	0.2	...	0.1	0.4	...	...	0.3	...	...	0.2
Lumber and wood products	0.5	0.6	0.3	0.4	0.3	0.3	...	...	0.1	0.1	...	0.1
Furniture and fixtures	0.4	0.9	0.2	0.5	0.1	0.2	...	...	0.1	...	0.1	...
Paper products	0.2	...	...	...	...	0.1	0.1	...	0.1	...	...	0.3
Printing and publishing	0.1	0.3	...	...	0.4	...	...	...	0.1	...	...	...
Chemical products	38.2	37.9	36.4	37.2	28.0	32.3	24.1	20.7	23.4	22.0	19.0	18.4
Refined petroleum products	...	...	...	...	...	0.1	...	...	...	...	...	...
Rubber and plastic products	3.0	1.1	1.2	0.7	0.8	0.3	...	0.1	0.5	0.1	...	0.2
Leather products	...	0.1	0.1	...	...	...	...	...	0.2	...	...	0.1
Stone, clay and glass products	0.6	1.2	0.3	...	0.1	4.2	0.1	0.1	0.2	0.4	...	...
Primary metals	0.1	0.1	0.6	0.6	0.1	...	0.4	0.2	0.1	0.2	...	0.1
Fabricated metal products	0.5	1.9	0.8	0.1	0.2	0.5	0.3	1.9	0.4	0.3	0.5	0.1
Industrial machinery and computers	8.3	12.0	9.8	7.7	5.6	3.9	3.3	2.9	3.9	5.7	0.6	1.1
Electric and electronic equipment	6.8	3.3	1.7	2.8	1.4	1.3	0.4	1.5	1.6	1.0	0.3	2.2
Transportation equipment	0.7	2.2	3.0	2.8	2.9	4.7	...	1.1	3.3	0.5	0.2	0.3
Scientific and measuring instruments	2.5	0.9	1.9	1.0	0.6	2.0	0.1	0.1	0.2	0.7	0.3	1.6
Miscellaneous manufactures	1.0	1.2	0.7	0.8	1.1	0.9	0.1	0.1	0.5	0.1	...	0.1
Unidentified manufactures	0.1	0.1	0.1	0.1	0.2	0.3	0.1	0.2	...	...	...	...
Agricultural And Livestock Products	0.6	0.8	0.6	0.8	0.8	2.4	3.5	1.0	2.3	0.1	0.2	0.8
Agricultural products	0.6	0.8	0.5	0.4	0.7	2.3	3.1	0.5	1.6	0.1	...	0.6
Livestock and livestock products	...	...	...	0.4	0.1	0.1	0.4	0.5	0.7	...	0.2	0.3
Other Commodities	2.8	8.5	27.6	20.1	5.1	0.5	0.3	4.0	1.1	...	...	...
Forestry products	...	...	...	...	...	...	...	...	...	...	...	...
Fish and other marine products	2.6	8.3	27.5	20.1	5.1	0.3	0.3	4.0	1.1	...	...	...
Metallic ores and concentrates	...	...	...	...	...	...	...	...	...	...	...	...
Bituminous coal and lignite	...	...	...	...	...	...	...	...	...	...	...	...
Crude petroleum and natural gas	...	...	...	...	...	...	...	...	...	...	...	...
Nonmetallic minerals	0.1	0.1	...	...	...	0.1	...	...	...	...	...	...
Scrap and waste	...	0.1	...	...	...	...	...	...	...	...	...	...
Used merchandise	0.1	...	...	...	...	...	...	...	...	...	...	...
Goods imported and returned unchanged	...	...	...	...	...	...	...	...	...	...	...	...
Special classification provisions	...	...	0.1	...	...	0.1	...	...	...	...	...	...

Industry	Taiwan						Singapore					
	1994	1995	1996	1997	1998	1999	1994	1995	1996	1997	1998	1999
ALL GOODS	32.4	32.8	24.2	30.3	34.1	25.4	25.7	25.4	22.0	20.5	14.1	13.5
Manufactured Goods	31.8	31.5	23.4	29.9	33.7	25.1	25.5	25.1	21.9	20.3	13.2	13.0
Food products	0.1	0.1	0.5	0.3	1.1	1.8	12.2	7.0	6.3	5.0	2.8	3.5
Tobacco products	...	...	...	...	...	...	...	...	...	...	...	...
Textile mill products	...	...	...	...	...	...	0.1	...	0.1	0.1	...	0.1
Apparel	...	...	...	...	...	...	0.1	0.1	0.1	0.1	...	...
Lumber and wood products	0.1	0.2	0.2	0.3	0.1	0.1	...	...	...	...	0.1	0.1
Furniture and fixtures	0.1	...	...	...	0.1	0.2	0.1	...	0.1	...	0.1	...
Paper products	0.3	...	...	...	...	...	0.2	0.2	0.3	...	0.2	...
Printing and publishing	...	...	...	...	...	...	0.1	0.1	0.1	0.1	...	0.5
Chemical products	25.5	22.1	15.8	19.7	23.0	17.1	5.4	7.9	7.3	5.9	2.5	2.3
Refined petroleum products	...	...	...	...	...	...	0.6	...	...	...	...	...
Rubber and plastic products	...	...	0.1	0.1	0.1	0.1	0.7	0.6	0.3	1.0	0.1	0.8
Leather products	...	...	...	...	...	...	0.1	0.1	...	...	...	...
Stone, clay and glass products	0.3	0.1	...	...	0.1	...	0.4	0.5	0.6	0.5	0.1	0.1
Primary metals	...	0.1	0.1	...	0.1	...	...	0.9	0.5	0.6	0.5	0.5
Fabricated metal products	0.1	0.1	0.1	0.5	2.3	0.9	1.0	1.9	1.3	0.7	0.4	1.2
Industrial machinery and computers	2.4	4.0	3.9	4.0	3.1	2.3	1.3	1.7	1.5	1.8	1.3	0.5
Electric and electronic equipment	1.6	3.3	1.9	4.1	3.1	2.0	2.7	2.4	2.0	2.5	4.6	2.9
Transportation equipment	...	0.1	...	0.2	0.1	...	0.2	1.5	1.2	1.8	0.4	0.2
Scientific and measuring instruments	0.7	1.1	0.5	0.4	0.3	0.1	...	0.1	0.1	0.2	0.1	0.1
Miscellaneous manufactures	0.4	0.2	0.3	0.2	0.1	0.2	0.3	0.2	0.2	0.1	0.1	0.1
Unidentified manufactures	...	...	...	0.1	0.2	...	...	0.1	...	...	0.1	...
Agricultural And Livestock Products	0.1	0.7	0.7	0.3	0.1	0.1	...	...	...	...	...	0.1
Agricultural products	...	...	...	...	...	...	...	...	...	...	...	0.1
Livestock and livestock products	0.1	0.7	0.7	0.3	0.1	0.1	...	...	...	...	...	...
Other Commodities	0.5	0.7	0.1	0.1	0.4	0.1	0.1	0.3	0.1	0.3	0.9	0.4
Forestry products	...	...	...	...	...	...	...	...	...	...	...	...
Fish and other marine products	0.3	0.2	...	...	...	...	0.1	0.1	...	...	...	...
Metallic ores and concentrates	...	...	...	...	...	...	...	...	...	...	...	...
Bituminous coal and lignite	...	...	...	...	...	...	...	...	...	...	...	...
Crude petroleum and natural gas	...	...	...	...	...	...	...	...	...	...	...	...
Nonmetallic minerals	0.2	0.5	...	0.1	0.2	0.1	...	0.2	0.1	0.2	0.9	0.4
Scrap and waste	...	...	...	...	...	...	...	...	...	...	...	...
Used merchandise	...	...	...	...	...	...	...	...	...	...	...	...
Goods imported and returned unchanged	...	...	...	...	...	...	...	...	...	...	...	...
Special classification provisions	...	...	...	...	0.1	...	...	...	...	...	...	0.1

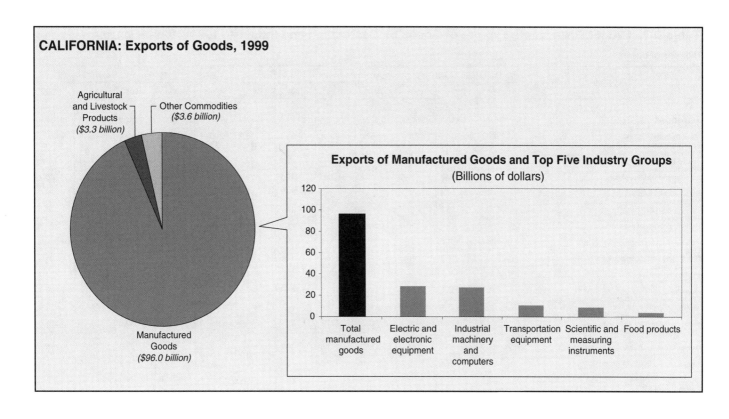

CALIFORNIA: Exports of Goods, 1999

Agricultural and Livestock Products ($3.3 billion)

Other Commodities ($3.6 billion)

Manufactured Goods ($96.0 billion)

Exports of Manufactured Goods and Top Five Industry Groups
(Billions of dollars)

Total manufactured goods / Electric and electronic equipment / Industrial machinery and computers / Transportation equipment / Scientific and measuring instruments / Food products

Table D-7. CALIFORNIA: State Exports of Goods by Destination and Industry, 1994–1999

(Millions of dollars.)

Industry	All destinations						Canada					
	1994	1995	1996	1997	1998	1999	1994	1995	1996	1997	1998	1999
ALL GOODS	78 190.4	92 038.4	98 634.0	103 802.5	98 809.0	102 863.8	8 054.5	9 537.7	10 577.1	11 492.4	12 644.1	13 245.9
Manufactured Goods	72 794.8	85 881.4	92 687.2	97 881.1	93 389.3	95 951.8	7 205.3	8 600.0	9 610.2	10 485.7	11 635.4	11 898.7
Food products	4 531.5	4 953.0	5 246.5	5 096.7	4 709.4	3 979.7	518.6	526.2	591.2	620.8	681.1	669.0
Tobacco products	1.9	11.6	2.3	2.2	5.3	1.8	. . .	. . .	0.1	0.1	. . .	. . .
Textile mill products	352.2	377.0	444.2	473.6	465.8	584.4	21.8	22.8	32.1	40.4	48.5	55.0
Apparel	1 164.4	1 339.0	1 505.8	1 584.8	1 423.4	1 407.2	49.0	65.7	73.0	102.6	131.4	128.9
Lumber and wood products	473.4	425.8	448.6	470.9	444.7	450.8	64.7	59.5	50.8	60.6	50.4	56.3
Furniture and fixtures	246.8	241.6	267.0	316.4	354.7	246.9	47.1	60.0	57.8	64.8	67.6	50.2
Paper products	818.7	1 030.2	1 112.5	1 197.2	1 134.2	1 079.1	45.7	58.7	66.2	63.7	63.7	78.1
Printing and publishing	458.8	487.7	519.9	573.9	624.6	581.2	94.3	94.4	87.4	100.1	98.6	91.5
Chemical products	2 733.0	3 087.4	3 262.0	3 732.8	3 597.4	3 621.1	239.1	269.4	272.8	305.4	321.4	339.7
Refined petroleum products	1 275.5	937.2	1 165.6	1 039.0	757.3	792.5	74.0	70.7	69.2	95.6	86.6	77.2
Rubber and plastic products	975.4	1 065.4	1 280.2	1 408.2	1 225.1	1 347.6	103.3	124.0	125.9	133.5	146.9	166.9
Leather products	214.7	224.6	233.4	210.6	166.5	229.0	19.1	26.2	22.2	22.9	24.2	35.4
Stone, clay and glass products	309.5	543.0	521.4	690.4	620.7	591.7	44.3	57.8	60.6	69.1	72.0	76.2
Primary metals	1 470.9	1 694.5	1 494.3	1 671.5	1 386.0	1 249.1	121.9	112.5	194.3	135.1	182.4	157.8
Fabricated metal products	1 341.8	1 615.5	1 900.7	1 907.3	1 822.5	1 937.4	190.0	207.6	232.1	278.0	321.8	314.2
Industrial machinery and computers	17 651.4	21 216.0	25 491.7	26 899.7	24 400.8	27 393.6	2 382.2	2 765.8	3 048.7	3 240.5	3 375.9	3 552.8
Electric and electronic equipment	19 800.7	25 932.3	27 198.5	27 715.3	27 011.7	28 451.8	1 734.0	2 280.3	2 776.9	2 909.9	3 336.5	3 366.0
Transportation equipment	11 806.7	12 420.0	10 981.8	12 055.7	12 440.4	10 743.3	716.2	1 021.9	1 008.6	1 273.3	1 496.9	1 481.7
Scientific and measuring instruments	5 399.1	6 247.2	7 457.5	8 469.9	8 549.3	8 818.6	473.7	498.5	565.2	613.8	759.6	847.6
Miscellaneous manufactures	1 413.9	1 691.7	1 806.9	1 968.4	1 739.1	1 789.7	202.3	205.0	198.6	264.3	263.3	243.9
Unidentified manufactures	354.5	340.6	346.4	396.5	510.5	655.4	63.9	73.0	76.8	90.9	106.4	110.2
Agricultural And Livestock Products	3 215.5	3 320.9	3 242.6	3 458.1	3 193.8	3 301.0	635.7	707.2	682.6	743.7	732.1	730.0
Agricultural products	3 099.1	3 194.2	3 109.7	3 325.6	3 090.2	3 207.0	630.4	701.9	677.0	739.0	728.5	725.9
Livestock and livestock products	116.4	126.8	132.9	132.5	103.5	94.0	5.3	5.3	5.7	4.7	3.5	4.1
Other Commodities	2 180.0	2 836.1	2 704.2	2 463.3	2 226.0	3 611.1	213.5	230.5	284.3	263.0	276.7	617.2
Forestry products	29.7	32.1	26.1	37.2	27.6	23.3	2.2	2.8	3.7	4.6	5.1	2.5
Fish and other marine products	200.7	238.7	231.9	224.1	157.7	215.0	23.9	25.8	24.7	22.6	28.4	47.5
Metallic ores and concentrates	0.8	3.8	6.4	16.4	13.1	4.9	0.1	2.4	1.4	1.9	1.5	. . .
Bituminous coal and lignite	2.7	0.9	4.0	3.3	0.2	2.4	. . .	. . .	4.0	. . .	. . .	0.1
Crude petroleum and natural gas	5.4	15.0	30.1	34.9	15.7	8.6	1.1	2.0	1.6	0.7	1.5	0.3
Nonmetallic minerals	82.6	77.3	82.7	87.7	71.1	73.5	5.6	4.0	4.2	5.4	4.6	5.7
Scrap and waste	862.3	1 467.6	1 143.4	861.8	676.9	793.7	35.9	39.2	35.2	26.4	24.4	22.4
Used merchandise	260.0	264.3	292.3	251.3	335.1	269.2	11.8	7.1	9.7	6.3	8.4	13.2
Goods imported and returned unchanged	89.2	102.8	128.3	151.0	164.0	135.4	89.2	102.8	128.3	151.0	164.0	135.4
Special classification provisions	646.7	633.6	759.0	795.5	764.7	2 085.1	43.7	44.5	71.6	44.0	38.8	390.2

Table D-7. CALIFORNIA: State Exports of Goods by Destination and Industry, 1994–1999—*Continued*

(Millions of dollars.)

Industry	South and Central American and Caribbean						Mexico					
	1994	1995	1996	1997	1998	1999	1994	1995	1996	1997	1998	1999
ALL GOODS	2 662.7	2 952.3	3 357.7	4 307.0	4 700.5	3 871.6	5 957.0	6 171.6	7 787.3	9 942.0	10 798.2	12 230.9
Manufactured Goods	2 564.6	2 838.6	3 220.7	4 157.3	4 490.1	3 664.1	5 736.2	5 952.6	7 496.0	9 582.4	10 462.9	11 859.6
Food products	87.6	80.2	100.2	142.4	137.7	127.9	252.3	188.8	292.2	332.5	346.8	380.7
Tobacco products	...	0.1	...	0.2	0.4	0.2	...	1.5	1.3	0.2	0.1	0.1
Textile mill products	47.7	30.5	34.4	49.8	44.6	22.9	80.6	110.8	118.4	120.8	148.5	327.6
Apparel	157.1	180.1	201.0	316.9	287.6	237.6	212.9	203.1	309.6	433.2	508.2	598.2
Lumber and wood products	8.6	10.8	11.6	10.9	12.5	10.2	195.7	121.7	139.1	156.5	195.2	210.7
Furniture and fixtures	9.1	9.4	12.1	23.4	23.2	14.1	58.3	31.4	45.7	57.0	80.6	52.0
Paper products	59.6	103.5	100.2	122.7	112.5	109.5	212.2	234.5	295.9	337.2	357.8	380.2
Printing and publishing	9.9	13.2	19.0	17.8	18.9	11.7	47.6	48.2	58.5	72.5	93.7	75.7
Chemical products	153.8	143.2	158.9	206.2	205.6	186.6	277.0	264.5	368.4	476.4	493.7	476.6
Refined petroleum products	168.6	69.0	155.0	114.7	71.0	24.9	273.4	208.6	230.2	267.3	238.9	209.3
Rubber and plastic products	35.5	31.4	51.7	91.8	76.1	68.7	333.7	345.1	472.0	492.2	437.6	529.4
Leather products	16.6	20.5	17.0	11.9	10.9	13.9	15.2	12.3	16.9	18.4	17.4	31.4
Stone, clay and glass products	10.1	10.2	10.8	14.0	18.7	13.8	44.7	39.0	49.3	70.0	95.3	105.8
Primary metals	27.5	32.0	43.7	135.6	91.3	79.3	235.5	291.8	309.0	386.7	362.2	403.5
Fabricated metal products	35.4	41.3	44.0	58.3	58.6	42.5	272.9	302.3	417.3	423.0	541.7	604.0
Industrial machinery and computers	629.8	753.5	907.8	1 293.8	1 389.4	1 167.7	899.5	786.8	1 119.5	1 451.3	1 542.2	1 982.3
Electric and electronic equipment	480.6	530.5	499.2	667.5	747.7	732.1	1 585.0	2 128.4	2 500.5	3 378.6	3 710.5	4 126.0
Transportation equipment	369.1	471.4	511.1	447.2	717.4	367.4	257.6	231.5	228.2	396.3	547.8	615.9
Scientific and measuring instruments	133.2	184.1	214.5	289.2	323.7	292.9	220.3	181.9	239.4	295.5	357.2	321.0
Miscellaneous manufactures	109.3	111.9	116.8	128.1	101.8	89.0	237.9	202.9	261.8	389.8	347.8	370.8
Unidentified manufactures	15.7	11.8	11.5	11.5	40.2	51.2	23.9	17.8	23.0	27.0	39.6	58.2
Agricultural And Livestock Products	69.7	83.5	101.5	112.0	161.5	134.2	97.5	90.2	159.8	189.6	193.0	196.5
Agricultural products	68.0	80.4	98.8	106.8	159.0	131.7	86.2	85.4	154.1	173.7	183.6	189.2
Livestock and livestock products	1.8	3.1	2.7	5.2	2.5	2.5	11.3	4.8	5.7	15.9	9.4	7.2
Other Commodities	28.3	30.3	35.5	37.7	48.9	73.4	123.3	128.7	131.6	169.9	142.3	174.8
Forestry products	3.0	0.3	0.3	0.2	0.4	0.5	3.4	6.5	3.8	6.5	6.2	3.0
Fish and other marine products	1.7	1.3	1.8	1.5	3.5	1.8	11.9	3.4	4.8	6.7	8.7	10.5
Metallic ores and concentrates	...	...	0.9	6.6	5.6	2.0	...	0.1	0.1	0.1	0.4	0.2
Bituminous coal and lignite	...	...	...	...	...	...	...	0.1	...	0.1	0.1	0.1
Crude petroleum and natural gas	...	0.1	0.1	0.1	0.2	...	3.1	12.4	26.4	32.1	12.5	7.9
Nonmetallic minerals	3.8	3.6	3.7	10.7	10.1	4.9	2.3	3.3	4.4	7.6	7.8	12.6
Scrap and waste	2.0	9.1	10.7	2.7	2.4	2.8	14.4	34.6	37.8	37.2	43.2	40.7
Used merchandise	9.0	7.9	9.5	8.9	14.6	8.1	52.4	21.3	19.9	19.5	22.1	14.3
Goods imported and returned unchanged	...	...	...	...	...	...	...	...	...	...	...	...
Special classification provisions	8.9	8.0	8.6	7.1	12.1	53.3	35.6	47.0	34.4	60.2	41.3	85.6

Industry	European Union						United Kingdom					
	1994	1995	1996	1997	1998	1999	1994	1995	1996	1997	1998	1999
ALL GOODS	17 147.1	18 897.0	18 687.0	19 709.4	21 428.1	21 887.4	3 835.4	4 507.1	4 779.0	5 109.8	5 361.8	5 195.5
Manufactured Goods	16 532.8	18 106.4	17 716.5	18 987.3	20 749.1	20 648.0	3 647.2	4 313.5	4 606.4	4 950.0	5 176.7	4 927.5
Food products	951.9	939.4	1 151.7	999.1	1 041.1	590.3	161.7	181.2	223.4	228.4	242.3	207.8
Tobacco products	0.2	9.0	0.1	0.1	0.1	0.4	...	...	...	...	...	...
Textile mill products	89.7	82.5	106.8	110.8	123.4	83.3	25.0	21.0	35.8	30.5	31.1	25.4
Apparel	147.8	204.9	220.8	210.6	124.6	78.4	21.9	22.3	31.2	44.3	27.1	26.9
Lumber and wood products	41.7	45.0	34.4	49.7	44.2	43.4	5.0	5.7	4.0	5.4	4.7	4.2
Furniture and fixtures	31.8	26.7	30.5	38.6	64.1	64.5	8.0	9.8	11.1	15.7	31.8	33.9
Paper products	35.9	38.1	48.1	54.7	81.2	49.5	11.8	9.2	8.8	11.8	16.6	11.2
Printing and publishing	92.8	89.6	104.9	108.1	112.4	134.7	26.6	25.4	39.4	33.8	34.2	38.5
Chemical products	732.4	785.2	703.9	804.4	916.1	851.2	129.6	98.7	108.3	153.6	185.7	180.7
Refined petroleum products	32.0	26.2	30.5	37.5	31.6	23.4	0.9	0.9	0.8	1.9	1.1	2.1
Rubber and plastic products	102.9	112.0	118.5	141.8	151.0	165.4	23.9	28.6	37.7	34.8	39.5	46.3
Leather products	25.7	27.8	25.7	23.8	26.2	36.3	7.1	3.8	2.5	5.2	4.5	5.2
Stone, clay and glass products	38.5	44.7	55.4	80.9	77.6	84.6	10.4	19.5	23.6	31.9	24.6	24.8
Primary metals	520.9	568.3	234.7	308.3	247.3	212.3	40.5	180.3	97.2	136.4	70.4	53.6
Fabricated metal products	179.8	187.6	197.5	217.4	272.3	359.6	45.3	55.0	62.4	71.5	82.5	94.8
Industrial machinery and computers	4 836.0	5 802.7	6 485.6	6 949.8	6 859.1	7 309.9	1 297.4	1 453.8	1 693.9	1 818.3	1 715.7	1 606.4
Electric and electronic equipment	3 388.4	4 078.7	3 659.8	4 036.3	4 560.2	4 439.3	1 021.0	1 303.5	1 198.9	1 249.9	1 441.3	1 301.4
Transportation equipment	3 297.9	2 801.2	2 044.0	1 919.1	2 769.1	2 767.7	396.2	431.7	506.1	492.1	546.9	587.8
Scientific and measuring instruments	1 675.1	1 885.0	2 090.0	2 488.4	2 800.4	2 914.5	318.5	359.5	394.6	449.3	492.8	488.1
Miscellaneous manufactures	233.0	287.6	322.8	358.2	374.8	363.3	76.3	84.6	110.3	119.8	161.8	162.7
Unidentified manufactures	78.3	64.3	51.0	50.0	72.4	76.1	20.0	18.9	16.5	15.3	22.0	25.7
Agricultural And Livestock Products	235.8	262.0	290.3	291.1	289.4	618.4	48.3	44.6	51.7	61.0	53.2	86.3
Agricultural products	208.7	236.8	257.7	258.9	262.8	599.6	42.1	38.2	39.9	49.8	46.3	83.3
Livestock and livestock products	27.2	25.2	32.6	32.2	26.6	18.8	6.2	6.5	11.8	11.2	6.8	3.0
Other Commodities	378.5	528.6	680.2	431.0	389.6	621.0	139.9	149.0	120.8	98.7	132.0	181.7
Forestry products	3.4	2.4	3.4	5.1	4.0	3.2	1.0	1.0	1.1	1.1	1.2	0.8
Fish and other marine products	14.3	13.1	10.1	23.0	8.6	14.2	1.3	0.9	1.1	1.5	1.0	1.6
Metallic ores and concentrates	0.4	0.3	0.5	2.8	0.7	0.2	...	0.3	0.4	0.2	...	0.1
Bituminous coal and lignite	...	...	...	...	...	...	...	...	...	...	...	...
Crude petroleum and natural gas	0.1	...	0.3	0.1	0.2	...	...	...	...	...	0.1	...
Nonmetallic minerals	24.6	26.5	23.8	22.0	14.3	13.2	4.3	6.1	5.0	6.8	3.0	1.7
Scrap and waste	155.2	303.4	421.5	182.6	52.6	47.6	68.8	63.6	10.2	7.3	4.3	4.3
Used merchandise	56.0	67.5	99.3	79.0	180.4	139.0	19.1	27.7	59.3	44.0	73.5	62.3
Goods imported and returned unchanged	...	...	...	...	...	...	...	...	...	...	...	...
Special classification provisions	124.6	115.4	121.4	116.5	128.7	403.6	45.4	49.6	43.7	38.0	49.1	110.7

Table D-7. CALIFORNIA: State Exports of Goods by Destination and Industry, 1994–1999—*Continued*

(Millions of dollars.)

Industry	Germany						France					
	1994	1995	1996	1997	1998	1999	1994	1995	1996	1997	1998	1999
ALL GOODS	3 406.8	3 752.9	3 798.6	3 761.4	4 369.2	4 232.6	2 387.9	2 443.8	2 552.3	2 422.7	2 239.2	2 334.1
Manufactured Goods	3 312.3	3 658.7	3 710.0	3 689.8	4 287.6	3 995.6	2 286.4	2 211.3	2 131.7	2 223.9	2 182.3	2 207.5
Food products	246.7	264.7	326.5	260.5	237.4	63.9	75.6	62.7	86.3	89.2	64.4	18.3
Tobacco products	...	...	...	...	...	...	...	...	...	...	...	...
Textile mill products	6.4	4.2	5.2	4.1	3.0	4.8	4.4	4.2	2.5	6.6	9.0	2.2
Apparel	19.9	29.6	27.2	18.7	13.8	12.2	17.4	29.5	24.0	59.2	33.9	9.8
Lumber and wood products	17.8	14.2	12.5	13.1	14.8	10.3	2.3	2.7	2.2	3.0	4.2	6.0
Furniture and fixtures	4.6	5.2	7.3	8.5	9.3	8.5	7.9	4.8	2.1	5.5	9.2	8.9
Paper products	4.2	5.6	5.6	9.7	16.0	8.3	2.7	2.9	3.1	2.1	2.3	2.2
Printing and publishing	19.1	18.4	18.7	20.0	32.2	27.6	8.5	10.0	12.7	10.2	8.4	8.6
Chemical products	124.4	125.0	145.4	163.6	163.4	172.6	53.4	50.0	51.6	59.1	72.0	81.8
Refined petroleum products	0.5	1.9	0.4	0.4	0.9	0.4	0.1	0.1	0.2	0.4	0.2	...
Rubber and plastic products	15.2	21.5	20.3	29.4	40.0	30.8	11.4	17.6	14.0	14.3	11.2	22.7
Leather products	7.5	7.7	7.4	7.6	14.6	7.5	3.3	2.9	3.1	3.2	2.9	4.0
Stone, clay and glass products	14.1	8.7	15.9	30.8	28.8	32.1	2.7	4.5	4.6	6.2	7.3	10.9
Primary metals	20.9	32.7	37.4	38.7	36.7	37.1	397.6	280.4	17.3	26.5	43.4	30.0
Fabricated metal products	50.7	47.4	37.2	38.4	42.7	49.8	14.9	17.0	20.5	27.3	36.5	54.7
Industrial machinery and computers	916.0	1 301.1	1 409.6	1 329.6	1 317.0	1 237.5	632.5	742.3	903.7	782.0	640.2	639.0
Electric and electronic equipment	797.9	863.0	705.2	749.2	762.7	708.2	395.2	503.8	373.3	480.9	502.7	475.4
Transportation equipment	545.1	321.2	343.9	301.6	861.7	824.6	359.0	163.3	243.1	234.4	272.3	393.2
Scientific and measuring instruments	434.6	513.4	503.8	581.9	619.7	690.6	265.7	271.3	332.6	372.8	419.1	401.2
Miscellaneous manufactures	48.6	58.9	70.1	75.1	64.9	48.6	24.1	34.3	30.1	36.1	35.9	30.5
Unidentified manufactures	18.0	14.2	10.5	8.8	15.1	15.6	7.7	7.3	4.8	5.0	7.3	8.1
Agricultural And Livestock Products	44.7	48.0	47.1	37.3	45.1	142.7	12.8	15.7	13.3	16.0	20.6	46.0
Agricultural products	40.0	44.9	45.4	35.6	41.6	140.7	10.0	13.9	10.3	14.8	18.9	43.9
Livestock and livestock products	4.6	3.1	1.7	1.7	3.5	2.0	2.8	1.8	3.1	1.2	1.6	2.1
Other Commodities	49.9	46.3	41.5	34.3	36.5	94.3	88.6	216.7	407.3	182.8	36.3	80.6
Forestry products	0.3	0.3	0.6	0.9	0.2	0.8	...	0.1	0.1	0.2	0.1	...
Fish and other marine products	1.3	0.8	0.9	1.4	0.8	1.3	1.8	3.1	2.4	2.2	0.8	1.5
Metallic ores and concentrates	...	...	...	1.5	0.7	...	...	...	...	...	...	...
Bituminous coal and lignite	...	...	...	...	...	...	...	...	...	...	...	...
Crude petroleum and natural gas	...	...	...	...	...	...	...	...	...	...	...	...
Nonmetallic minerals	6.2	5.2	7.1	4.5	3.1	3.7	2.0	1.4	0.7	0.5	0.4	0.2
Scrap and waste	2.5	0.8	0.6	0.4	5.7	5.2	64.2	194.6	382.0	152.9	4.7	2.1
Used merchandise	13.0	14.3	15.3	9.7	11.5	17.0	9.3	6.3	8.5	7.9	14.0	29.3
Goods imported and returned unchanged	...	...	...	...	...	...	...	...	...	...	...	...
Special classification provisions	26.6	24.9	16.9	15.9	14.5	66.3	11.3	11.3	13.6	19.2	16.3	47.4

Industry	The Netherlands						Asian 10					
	1994	1995	1996	1997	1998	1999	1994	1995	1996	1997	1998	1999
ALL GOODS	2 624.3	2 914.3	2 138.1	3 096.0	3 569.5	4 165.1	37 949.6	47 427.4	51 192.1	49 784.3	40 385.4	43 550.1
Manufactured Goods	2 574.1	2 857.8	2 078.6	3 032.8	3 507.7	4 006.4	34 673.4	43 733.4	47 953.9	46 520.6	37 625.8	40 377.0
Food products	114.3	103.9	114.6	99.7	145.5	132.2	2 371.4	2 788.3	2 666.3	2 540.5	2 124.1	1 978.5
Tobacco products	0.2	...	...	...	...	0.4	0.9	0.2	0.3	1.3	4.1	0.5
Textile mill products	1.9	1.4	1.3	2.1	1.6	1.9	88.1	101.8	124.2	117.5	73.7	73.3
Apparel	7.6	26.1	24.7	11.3	8.1	7.6	560.2	635.8	641.0	450.9	306.9	314.2
Lumber and wood products	2.6	4.1	2.8	9.5	6.5	6.2	143.7	167.5	186.0	164.1	116.1	106.4
Furniture and fixtures	5.2	2.5	3.0	1.9	3.4	4.2	73.1	79.8	93.5	105.4	92.3	50.1
Paper products	4.7	2.7	4.1	4.0	5.8	4.0	407.4	506.5	514.0	528.8	427.4	386.3
Printing and publishing	21.9	12.3	11.1	13.6	18.9	40.3	145.4	163.6	169.7	167.4	167.3	145.1
Chemical products	175.5	248.3	174.1	175.1	177.3	146.9	1 066.2	1 375.8	1 452.2	1 647.0	1 346.2	1 438.2
Refined petroleum products	15.4	15.3	17.8	22.0	22.6	19.9	654.7	460.4	509.4	390.0	197.8	337.0
Rubber and plastic products	21.5	11.8	13.6	23.4	23.7	20.9	304.2	369.7	420.7	459.5	325.9	326.8
Leather products	2.8	6.8	5.3	2.0	3.4	3.3	125.0	126.1	137.8	120.5	75.7	96.6
Stone, clay and glass products	3.6	2.4	3.1	2.1	3.1	2.1	149.8	357.1	316.7	423.3	320.9	280.5
Primary metals	5.7	6.7	6.3	10.3	15.0	12.6	484.6	622.5	648.2	636.6	414.7	337.4
Fabricated metal products	10.5	9.3	25.0	24.6	20.4	14.0	529.0	734.3	875.0	791.3	506.5	493.6
Industrial machinery and computers	773.4	847.5	929.1	1 466.1	1 709.6	2 233.2	6 972.9	9 154.1	11 774.7	11 748.8	9 111.2	11 060.3
Electric and electronic equipment	277.3	348.8	361.2	471.4	614.5	742.6	11 413.7	15 367.1	16 678.6	15 449.0	13 123.6	14 292.1
Transportation equipment	930.1	985.2	104.3	301.1	286.4	145.5	6 192.4	6 949.6	6 125.5	5 983.1	4 654.6	4 107.7
Scientific and measuring instruments	176.9	195.2	257.0	364.3	411.0	432.4	2 345.2	2 885.2	3 687.3	3 986.9	3 536.8	3 680.3
Miscellaneous manufactures	18.2	21.6	15.4	21.9	22.4	30.3	536.3	766.0	794.0	676.9	523.0	591.2
Unidentified manufactures	4.9	5.5	4.8	6.4	8.2	5.9	109.2	121.9	138.8	131.7	177.1	281.0
Agricultural And Livestock Products	26.5	24.9	32.9	36.7	38.3	75.5	1 978.4	1 909.9	1 813.4	1 871.3	1 555.2	1 332.0
Agricultural products	25.2	23.3	31.0	32.2	35.3	73.2	1 932.2	1 838.7	1 749.9	1 809.6	1 506.8	1 282.7
Livestock and livestock products	1.3	1.6	1.9	4.5	3.0	2.3	46.2	71.2	63.5	61.7	48.4	49.3
Other Commodities	23.8	31.6	26.6	26.6	23.5	83.2	1 297.8	1 784.1	1 424.8	1 392.5	1 204.5	1 841.1
Forestry products	1.6	0.6	0.9	1.7	1.5	0.4	16.3	18.0	13.5	18.4	9.3	11.4
Fish and other marine products	0.9	1.0	1.4	2.8	0.5	1.8	143.7	190.4	184.2	160.5	94.8	120.5
Metallic ores and concentrates	0.1	...	...	0.8	...	...	0.2	0.9	3.5	4.5	4.8	2.1
Bituminous coal and lignite	...	...	...	...	...	...	2.6	0.8	...	3.2	...	2.2
Crude petroleum and natural gas	...	...	...	...	0.1	...	0.6	0.5	1.3	1.1	1.0	0.3
Nonmetallic minerals	1.7	5.0	3.8	3.7	3.1	3.4	36.1	34.8	40.1	31.2	25.0	28.7
Scrap and waste	5.2	18.0	4.1	2.0	1.6	1.6	642.4	1 061.7	619.9	592.8	524.7	646.5
Used merchandise	3.5	2.7	5.3	3.6	3.3	10.1	90.6	132.5	114.9	96.4	66.3	56.6
Goods imported and returned unchanged	...	...	...	...	...	...	...	...	...	...	...	...
Special classification provisions	10.7	4.3	11.2	11.9	13.4	65.9	365.4	344.5	447.3	484.4	478.5	972.7

Table D-7. CALIFORNIA: State Exports of Goods by Destination and Industry, 1994–1999—*Continued*

(Millions of dollars.)

Industry	Japan						South Korea					
	1994	1995	1996	1997	1998	1999	1994	1995	1996	1997	1998	1999
ALL GOODS	14 536.6	18 288.8	19 704.6	17 927.4	14 939.2	14 653.2	4 557.5	6 406.6	7 398.8	6 494.2	4 005.1	5 890.7
Manufactured Goods	13 124.2	16 667.8	18 234.2	16 587.7	13 780.9	13 152.2	4 117.7	5 840.8	6 961.8	6 037.8	3 607.9	5 527.0
Food products	1 473.8	1 680.8	1 580.6	1 445.8	1 405.7	1 190.9	311.0	438.8	347.8	304.2	179.0	233.1
Tobacco products	0.8	0.1	...	1.2	...	...	0.1	0.1	0.2	0.1	0.2	0.4
Textile mill products	36.3	34.7	42.2	36.7	28.5	20.5	9.5	16.7	18.2	17.7	7.9	9.0
Apparel	489.8	556.4	554.1	370.9	265.6	268.2	15.6	21.9	30.2	24.3	4.4	6.8
Lumber and wood products	81.0	107.8	121.8	102.4	67.2	61.5	27.3	32.0	29.2	22.0	10.9	15.0
Furniture and fixtures	36.4	37.2	45.8	54.9	49.2	28.2	7.0	10.8	8.6	12.1	4.1	2.8
Paper products	132.7	172.0	151.6	120.7	114.0	82.0	37.5	59.1	58.4	58.0	24.7	35.0
Printing and publishing	80.7	90.7	80.6	76.5	72.2	52.8	9.8	15.8	20.3	22.8	9.1	17.8
Chemical products	405.8	532.6	517.1	629.5	628.5	578.4	157.3	231.4	245.9	267.0	190.6	205.8
Refined petroleum products	98.4	89.0	116.7	97.2	62.6	57.3	191.4	115.1	114.5	60.1	26.8	42.4
Rubber and plastic products	111.5	120.8	151.1	180.9	125.5	106.8	29.9	41.2	44.3	53.8	27.5	32.6
Leather products	83.3	91.6	90.1	72.2	50.5	60.9	6.4	5.6	15.7	20.3	0.9	2.7
Stone, clay and glass products	50.2	58.2	59.5	63.9	53.0	51.2	19.6	39.3	39.1	35.0	21.8	30.0
Primary metals	138.6	190.9	231.5	167.7	106.3	95.3	54.6	112.2	102.3	98.6	86.1	67.0
Fabricated metal products	298.1	358.2	381.0	221.4	189.2	166.9	51.1	70.7	91.2	74.0	33.3	45.9
Industrial machinery and computers	2 367.1	3 155.7	4 224.6	3 832.2	3 017.5	3 309.5	1 143.9	1 942.1	2 430.5	1 824.4	814.7	1 552.8
Electric and electronic equipment	2 261.2	3 070.2	3 696.6	3 624.4	3 021.8	2 616.0	1 445.5	1 973.9	2 237.6	2 190.7	1 597.8	2 392.7
Transportation equipment	3 376.3	4 253.6	3 767.0	3 241.1	2 540.1	2 307.2	210.9	252.3	432.4	256.1	242.1	294.6
Scientific and measuring instruments	1 228.7	1 546.1	1 894.4	1 780.5	1 575.5	1 613.0	352.0	396.2	586.6	635.6	285.7	484.0
Miscellaneous manufactures	334.4	461.8	447.8	400.4	333.0	341.8	26.9	55.7	97.1	50.7	26.0	32.4
Unidentified manufactures	39.1	59.3	79.1	67.3	74.9	143.9	10.6	10.0	11.7	10.4	14.2	24.1
Agricultural And Livestock Products	912.1	1 053.4	933.3	832.2	733.5	789.7	205.1	203.8	190.1	185.0	204.6	73.3
Agricultural products	881.2	1 002.5	887.6	785.6	693.2	754.0	199.6	197.2	185.1	181.3	203.2	69.8
Livestock and livestock products	30.9	51.0	45.7	46.6	40.4	35.8	5.5	6.6	5.0	3.8	1.3	3.5
Other Commodities	500.3	567.5	537.1	507.4	424.7	711.2	234.7	361.9	246.8	271.5	192.6	290.5
Forestry products	1.4	1.7	2.3	5.5	3.3	5.9	1.8	1.6	1.6	1.3	0.6	0.4
Fish and other marine products	106.1	122.1	106.2	86.0	57.3	75.3	5.1	7.2	10.5	7.3	6.9	8.4
Metallic ores and concentrates	0.1	0.3	1.8	2.4	4.1	0.9	...	...	...	0.1	0.1	0.2
Bituminous coal and lignite	2.6	...	...	3.1	...	2.2	...	0.1	...	...	...	...
Crude petroleum and natural gas	...	...	0.2	0.8	0.1	...	0.2	0.1	0.1	0.1	0.2	0.1
Nonmetallic minerals	21.0	21.1	27.6	17.8	13.5	17.5	2.1	2.0	3.4	2.6	1.5	1.4
Scrap and waste	149.2	213.0	110.2	82.1	64.4	61.9	173.1	276.8	145.3	179.6	143.6	188.1
Used merchandise	49.7	78.2	76.8	58.0	47.9	36.2	16.0	26.6	6.4	6.4	1.8	4.8
Goods imported and returned unchanged	...	...	...	...	...	...	...	...	...	...	...	...
Special classification provisions	170.2	131.0	212.0	251.7	234.1	511.2	36.5	47.5	79.5	74.0	38.1	87.1

Industry	Taiwan						Singapore					
	1994	1995	1996	1997	1998	1999	1994	1995	1996	1997	1998	1999
ALL GOODS	4 923.9	5 503.5	5 396.5	6 184.8	5 577.9	6 528.7	3 993.9	4 647.7	5 559.7	5 336.7	4 368.1	4 515.6
Manufactured Goods	4 577.7	5 162.5	5 100.8	5 869.2	5 305.7	6 194.9	3 918.8	4 592.9	5 495.3	5 279.5	4 315.0	4 411.5
Food products	165.0	182.9	170.3	175.8	135.0	113.9	67.9	63.7	62.9	61.0	49.7	53.2
Tobacco products	...	...	...	...	0.1	...	...	...	...	...	0.3	...
Textile mill products	8.1	10.0	10.2	7.8	7.1	7.1	3.5	4.7	7.4	5.9	2.9	2.0
Apparel	4.8	6.2	6.1	8.8	6.4	6.5	11.0	12.4	23.8	17.6	6.3	7.9
Lumber and wood products	14.8	10.4	9.4	9.5	13.1	4.2	2.6	1.6	1.7	2.2	2.3	1.1
Furniture and fixtures	5.9	8.6	7.3	7.4	8.5	4.1	6.0	6.7	7.2	5.6	4.9	2.9
Paper products	47.3	69.2	56.3	52.1	41.0	42.3	21.3	30.4	38.3	35.4	27.3	26.1
Printing and publishing	10.3	13.9	12.1	11.8	15.5	13.4	8.5	9.6	11.7	11.3	13.5	11.6
Chemical products	138.6	138.4	162.6	222.2	145.0	184.1	88.9	92.4	88.4	79.2	69.9	82.2
Refined petroleum products	131.2	108.8	125.4	34.2	22.6	36.6	146.5	103.7	107.0	112.6	26.9	152.0
Rubber and plastic products	28.5	35.4	30.9	39.8	35.1	39.5	32.0	41.9	54.8	50.9	41.4	47.5
Leather products	3.1	3.7	1.6	3.0	1.6	1.4	2.2	2.1	4.3	4.7	2.1	6.6
Stone, clay and glass products	29.1	31.6	35.6	31.6	17.1	18.0	9.5	21.3	20.1	21.0	13.8	12.9
Primary metals	52.2	78.9	57.1	52.6	34.6	38.9	16.1	18.2	26.3	27.8	23.6	20.3
Fabricated metal products	43.0	49.6	58.1	52.6	37.7	66.0	32.0	36.9	55.1	146.9	75.4	91.2
Industrial machinery and computers	653.6	935.2	1 313.5	1 819.3	1 482.7	2 298.6	1 249.7	1 273.7	1 494.3	1 642.1	1 329.9	1 511.0
Electric and electronic equipment	1 451.2	1 755.1	1 888.2	1 886.9	1 949.4	2 133.2	1 779.7	2 360.5	2 891.6	2 382.5	2 032.4	1 786.6
Transportation equipment	1 533.4	1 426.2	780.9	980.9	787.2	528.4	221.3	243.0	256.2	284.3	303.3	260.4
Scientific and measuring instruments	208.6	232.4	333.3	432.7	518.5	604.6	157.4	209.1	281.8	323.7	239.7	273.5
Miscellaneous manufactures	39.3	53.1	31.3	29.2	27.5	28.3	44.8	50.8	53.0	56.7	36.8	47.7
Unidentified manufactures	9.8	13.1	10.7	10.8	19.7	25.9	18.0	10.1	9.4	8.0	12.6	14.7
Agricultural And Livestock Products	184.0	129.4	129.7	147.7	144.3	152.4	31.5	33.4	25.7	28.8	24.5	29.1
Agricultural products	181.4	125.7	126.9	145.1	143.1	151.3	31.4	33.3	25.4	28.2	24.4	28.8
Livestock and livestock products	2.6	3.7	2.8	2.5	1.2	1.2	0.1	0.1	0.3	0.6	0.1	0.4
Other Commodities	162.2	211.6	166.0	168.0	128.0	181.4	43.5	21.3	38.7	28.4	28.6	75.0
Forestry products	1.9	1.6	0.9	1.6	0.3	0.6	0.2	0.2	0.4	0.2	0.1	0.2
Fish and other marine products	17.9	26.2	28.5	27.1	13.0	7.8	1.4	1.0	1.0	1.9	1.7	0.4
Metallic ores and concentrates	...	0.1	0.3	1.1	0.1	0.5	...	...	...	...	0.1	0.1
Bituminous coal and lignite	...	0.7	...	...	...	...	...	...	...	...	...	...
Crude petroleum and natural gas	0.2	...	0.4	...	0.3	...	...	...	...	...	0.1	...
Nonmetallic minerals	3.9	4.1	3.6	4.7	5.0	2.2	0.8	0.7	0.5	0.8	0.7	0.8
Scrap and waste	96.4	133.8	98.6	97.0	75.7	66.5	2.4	2.6	1.9	0.8	0.7	2.5
Used merchandise	2.4	2.9	1.8	1.6	1.2	6.8	3.0	5.1	5.3	4.5	0.8	0.8
Goods imported and returned unchanged	...	...	...	...	...	...	...	...	...	...	...	...
Special classification provisions	39.4	42.2	32.0	34.8	32.4	97.1	35.7	11.8	29.5	20.2	24.4	70.1

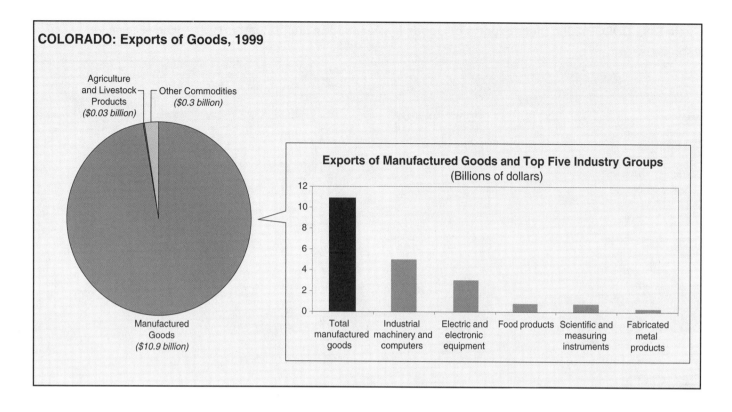

COLORADO: Exports of Goods, 1999

Agriculture and Livestock Products ($0.03 billion)

Other Commodities ($0.3 billion)

Manufactured Goods ($10.9 billion)

Exports of Manufactured Goods and Top Five Industry Groups
(Billions of dollars)

Total manufactured goods | Industrial machinery and computers | Electric and electronic equipment | Food products | Scientific and measuring instruments | Fabricated metal products

Table D-8. COLORADO: State Exports of Goods by Destination and Industry, 1994–1999

(Millions of dollars.)

Industry	All destinations						Canada					
	1994	1995	1996	1997	1998	1999	1994	1995	1996	1997	1998	1999
ALL GOODS	7 802.1	9 688.8	10 064.9	11 329.2	10 733.3	11 171.2	524.2	602.8	609.7	671.6	729.3	920.7
Manufactured Goods	7 641.5	9 423.0	9 824.4	11 056.6	10 476.1	10 863.4	490.1	561.7	559.3	614.1	683.1	876.0
Food products	449.6	539.5	612.2	829.9	678.9	803.8	118.9	107.3	105.4	114.5	116.6	120.3
Tobacco products	0.2	0.2	. . .	. . .	. . .	0.2	. . .	. . .	. . .	. . .	. . .	0.2
Textile mill products	7.0	9.9	11.5	11.6	12.8	15.3	1.6	1.9	1.3	1.4	2.0	4.6
Apparel	21.6	23.8	23.5	27.0	25.1	25.2	6.6	6.7	7.4	9.9	9.0	6.8
Lumber and wood products	5.5	4.0	12.0	6.5	3.6	5.6	0.5	0.2	0.8	1.5	1.0	1.3
Furniture and fixtures	16.8	12.4	13.1	15.0	17.2	18.5	2.7	3.9	3.9	4.7	4.4	6.7
Paper products	10.0	13.2	14.9	12.9	8.6	8.2	2.5	2.7	3.6	2.7	1.9	2.1
Printing and publishing	74.8	69.8	92.3	75.5	78.9	76.7	5.4	5.5	5.3	6.9	6.5	8.5
Chemical products	71.7	109.5	111.8	131.3	135.9	160.6	12.8	28.9	27.2	20.8	19.7	25.0
Refined petroleum products	7.3	4.9	2.8	3.4	5.2	3.9	2.7	1.5	1.2	1.0	1.1	0.7
Rubber and plastic products	86.4	101.3	91.7	97.4	97.1	100.2	8.4	10.1	9.1	10.4	9.0	11.0
Leather products	20.6	17.1	20.1	22.8	19.8	22.1	0.6	1.7	3.1	3.9	4.8	4.0
Stone, clay and glass products	82.8	86.8	76.0	87.0	73.6	85.2	3.8	4.4	3.9	4.3	4.5	8.3
Primary metals	76.6	156.1	121.8	122.2	147.1	80.2	6.3	13.3	48.1	28.4	23.5	24.0
Fabricated metal products	91.9	105.6	167.7	200.1	260.0	306.4	19.5	18.4	51.4	51.8	56.2	46.5
Industrial machinery and computers	4 621.9	5 650.5	5 574.2	5 491.7	5 014.7	5 007.0	146.2	162.7	123.0	130.4	131.3	139.6
Electric and electronic equipment	1 292.8	1 743.4	2 031.1	2 964.6	2 837.5	3 039.5	56.2	89.4	64.9	109.6	163.9	292.6
Transportation equipment	76.5	91.0	96.6	134.6	237.8	260.2	29.8	28.6	25.7	39.9	49.8	85.4
Scientific and measuring instruments	574.5	622.8	691.0	760.0	759.5	779.9	52.1	58.1	60.5	55.6	60.0	70.7
Miscellaneous manufactures	38.5	41.4	47.3	50.4	45.0	44.6	9.3	10.9	8.7	12.0	12.5	11.3
Unidentified manufactures	14.5	19.8	12.7	12.7	18.1	20.3	4.3	5.5	5.0	4.4	5.3	6.2
Agricultural And Livestock Products	33.5	35.4	32.0	41.6	43.2	28.3	5.2	8.5	7.0	7.1	7.0	8.0
Agricultural products	29.5	27.4	22.6	25.8	27.7	20.5	4.8	8.4	6.4	6.0	5.7	7.3
Livestock and livestock products	3.9	8.0	9.5	15.8	15.5	7.8	0.5	0.1	0.5	1.2	1.4	0.7
Other Commodities	127.2	230.3	208.5	231.0	214.0	279.4	28.9	32.6	43.4	50.4	39.2	36.7
Forestry products	0.9	1.0	1.8	2.1	4.2	2.3	0.1	0.5	0.8	0.6	0.5	0.2
Fish and other marine products	0.3	0.6	0.2	1.7	2.5	0.4	. . .	0.3	0.1	. . .	0.6	0.3
Metallic ores and concentrates	22.2	81.5	47.5	64.6	48.5	24.7	0.4	1.0	0.6	1.4	1.9	3.6
Bituminous coal and lignite	32.8	62.4	57.1	59.9	62.3	59.8	. . .	. . .	. . .	. . .	. . .	. . .
Crude petroleum and natural gas	9.5	16.8	24.8	17.5	9.2	0.5	0.5	. . .	4.9	1.6	0.8	. . .
Nonmetallic minerals	18.1	20.5	24.3	25.0	26.2	12.0	3.4	5.1	6.8	7.4	11.2	4.2
Scrap and waste	2.1	11.8	2.9	4.2	1.9	1.7	0.7	2.9	1.9	2.0	1.1	0.3
Used merchandise	11.4	9.8	13.4	12.7	17.1	20.8	4.8	4.2	5.9	8.7	5.4	6.5
Goods imported and returned unchanged	15.6	15.1	17.6	24.3	13.7	12.3	15.6	15.1	17.6	24.3	13.7	12.3
Special classification provisions	14.3	10.9	18.9	19.1	28.4	144.9	3.5	3.5	4.8	4.5	4.1	9.1

Table D-8. COLORADO: State Exports of Goods by Destination and Industry, 1994–1999—*Continued*

(Millions of dollars.)

Industry	South and Central American and Caribbean						Mexico					
	1994	1995	1996	1997	1998	1999	1994	1995	1996	1997	1998	1999
ALL GOODS	521.4	518.4	519.2	516.7	457.0	418.8	636.8	692.7	902.5	1 418.0	1 105.4	868.4
Manufactured Goods	514.5	510.5	511.5	510.4	449.7	413.2	622.4	660.3	851.5	1 359.2	1 036.5	802.2
Food products	1.7	2.1	3.0	7.6	17.8	15.7	52.6	15.7	17.2	42.1	44.5	50.5
Tobacco products	0.1	0.2	...	...	...	...	...	...	...	...	...	...
Textile mill products	1.2	2.2	2.6	2.3	2.6	1.7	1.7	1.6	2.8	3.2	3.5	4.3
Apparel	0.6	3.2	2.5	0.7	0.8	0.4	0.3	0.2	0.8	1.2	2.1	2.2
Lumber and wood products	1.4	0.1	0.2	0.2	0.1	0.3	0.3	0.1	0.3	0.3	0.2	0.1
Furniture and fixtures	2.7	0.6	0.4	0.6	1.2	0.5	1.1	0.5	1.1	0.9	1.2	1.1
Paper products	1.1	0.7	1.3	0.8	0.5	0.9	1.3	2.3	3.2	1.4	1.5	1.5
Printing and publishing	1.7	1.0	1.7	3.3	3.3	3.4	4.1	3.5	17.0	9.9	13.9	22.3
Chemical products	8.0	22.9	17.0	17.0	8.0	6.4	22.6	30.3	16.6	26.7	6.9	4.5
Refined petroleum products	0.1	0.2	0.1	0.1	0.4	0.1	2.8	0.4	0.2	0.3	0.6	...
Rubber and plastic products	9.8	15.3	10.4	8.6	10.5	3.9	6.7	17.7	9.4	7.3	10.4	9.5
Leather products	2.5	2.7	1.5	1.6	0.7	0.7	0.2	0.3	0.4	2.5	4.4	6.4
Stone, clay and glass products	1.6	1.5	1.4	1.3	2.0	3.1	0.9	0.7	0.8	0.8	1.7	1.5
Primary metals	7.0	5.3	5.6	9.9	6.5	2.8	4.6	5.7	4.5	10.7	14.2	9.4
Fabricated metal products	4.9	5.9	17.8	5.9	7.5	7.5	3.9	2.4	2.0	7.5	8.0	5.7
Industrial machinery and computers	391.2	371.1	381.6	371.4	300.4	305.5	454.8	519.8	722.4	1 083.8	832.1	612.1
Electric and electronic equipment	58.9	52.7	34.2	42.2	50.4	28.9	43.2	49.7	38.8	139.1	66.6	48.9
Transportation equipment	3.6	3.3	6.7	5.0	11.0	6.7	2.4	0.9	0.6	3.7	2.9	2.2
Scientific and measuring instruments	14.9	16.2	20.9	27.4	21.6	20.3	15.7	5.9	10.8	13.2	15.9	14.7
Miscellaneous manufactures	0.9	1.0	1.5	2.4	2.8	1.4	2.3	2.2	2.1	3.0	3.0	3.4
Unidentified manufactures	0.8	2.3	1.1	2.1	1.6	2.8	0.7	0.3	0.4	1.4	2.8	2.0
Agricultural And Livestock Products	1.7	2.6	1.9	2.1	2.8	1.5	2.7	1.1	4.1	3.4	8.6	4.4
Agricultural products	1.7	2.6	1.9	2.1	2.7	1.5	2.2	1.1	4.0	3.2	8.5	3.9
Livestock and livestock products	...	...	...	...	...	...	0.4	...	...	0.3	0.1	0.5
Other Commodities	5.2	5.3	5.7	4.1	4.5	4.1	11.7	31.3	46.9	55.4	60.3	61.8
Forestry products	...	...	...	...	...	...	0.3	0.2	0.2	0.1	0.3	0.2
Fish and other marine products	...	...	...	...	...	...	...	...	...	...	...	...
Metallic ores and concentrates	2.2	0.1	0.1	0.2	0.3	...	...	...	0.1	...	...	...
Bituminous coal and lignite	...	...	...	...	...	...	...	13.3	25.3	38.0	50.2	57.6
Crude petroleum and natural gas	...	...	...	...	...	...	9.0	16.7	19.7	15.9	7.9	0.4
Nonmetallic minerals	2.0	4.6	4.9	3.4	1.9	0.3	0.5	0.5	0.5	0.5	0.6	0.1
Scrap and waste	0.3	0.2	...	...	...	...	0.4	0.4	0.2	0.4	0.1	0.4
Used merchandise	0.3	0.2	0.2	0.4	1.6	0.6	0.8	0.1	0.4	0.2	0.8	1.2
Goods imported and returned unchanged	...	...	...	...	...	...	...	...	...	...	...	...
Special classification provisions	0.4	0.1	0.5	0.2	0.7	3.1	0.8	...	0.5	0.1	0.4	2.0

Industry	European Union						United Kingdom					
	1994	1995	1996	1997	1998	1999	1994	1995	1996	1997	1998	1999
ALL GOODS	3 263.6	3 741.7	3 674.0	3 693.1	3 905.4	3 999.1	780.3	811.4	671.6	689.3	714.5	757.2
Manufactured Goods	3 225.6	3 669.8	3 631.9	3 634.4	3 848.8	3 916.0	774.7	802.8	662.0	678.6	705.5	740.9
Food products	16.5	22.6	22.2	35.5	28.2	26.5	6.1	4.0	3.8	6.4	15.3	7.4
Tobacco products	...	...	...	...	...	...	...	...	...	...	...	...
Textile mill products	0.8	1.2	2.4	2.4	1.5	1.8	...	0.1	0.5	0.2	0.2	0.1
Apparel	7.3	8.2	6.2	8.2	7.7	9.0	1.6	2.0	1.6	2.1	1.8	2.5
Lumber and wood products	0.7	0.1	0.8	0.3	0.7	1.6	...	...	0.2	...	0.4	1.3
Furniture and fixtures	7.4	5.3	5.4	6.6	8.0	8.3	3.3	2.0	1.8	2.6	3.2	2.4
Paper products	2.4	4.8	2.6	2.5	1.7	1.8	0.8	3.3	0.6	0.6	0.3	0.4
Printing and publishing	43.7	39.9	39.9	26.4	26.3	28.5	5.6	5.2	5.8	5.0	7.3	8.1
Chemical products	14.2	15.7	21.3	25.6	25.6	34.8	2.2	1.7	2.3	4.7	4.9	6.3
Refined petroleum products	0.8	1.3	0.5	0.8	0.2	0.5	...	0.5	...	0.4	...	...
Rubber and plastic products	30.3	30.0	28.9	27.0	31.5	37.0	4.0	6.6	7.5	7.0	5.8	6.2
Leather products	1.7	2.0	2.1	2.6	1.6	1.1	1.0	0.5	0.4	0.2	0.1	0.3
Stone, clay and glass products	41.5	36.7	38.3	40.4	29.2	29.7	18.7	14.4	13.5	10.8	9.2	9.3
Primary metals	35.3	59.8	26.0	21.0	23.5	27.7	9.1	7.9	6.1	2.8	2.4	1.3
Fabricated metal products	49.1	58.0	69.9	72.5	95.2	166.2	6.2	6.5	6.7	7.7	9.9	5.5
Industrial machinery and computers	2 115.2	2 416.9	2 233.0	1 990.4	2 003.7	2 116.4	500.5	555.1	430.6	383.2	389.1	376.8
Electric and electronic equipment	547.3	658.7	798.8	1 013.8	1 154.7	989.8	172.1	152.9	136.6	198.6	173.0	232.0
Transportation equipment	21.3	25.2	19.8	21.8	61.1	63.2	12.0	9.1	6.8	4.4	31.7	24.3
Scientific and measuring instruments	273.1	266.4	297.0	325.4	336.6	360.6	28.5	28.4	35.4	40.4	48.5	53.1
Miscellaneous manufactures	13.4	12.5	14.9	9.7	9.1	8.9	2.2	1.7	1.6	1.1	1.8	2.5
Unidentified manufactures	3.6	4.4	2.0	1.4	2.8	2.6	0.6	0.8	0.4	0.3	0.5	0.9
Agricultural And Livestock Products	9.9	10.2	6.5	8.4	7.8	2.1	2.6	2.5	1.2	1.7	1.4	0.2
Agricultural products	8.8	9.0	5.9	6.1	5.5	1.2	2.6	2.5	1.0	1.2	1.2	0.1
Livestock and livestock products	1.1	1.2	0.6	2.3	2.3	0.9	...	...	0.2	0.5	0.2	0.1
Other Commodities	28.0	61.6	35.5	50.3	48.8	81.0	2.9	6.1	8.4	9.0	7.6	16.0
Forestry products	...	0.1	0.1	1.0	3.2	0.6	...	...	...	...	...	...
Fish and other marine products	0.1	0.1	0.1	1.4	1.7	...	...	...	...	...	...	...
Metallic ores and concentrates	13.8	39.0	16.6	25.6	21.7	16.3	0.3	2.5	1.7	3.0	1.4	1.5
Bituminous coal and lignite	6.6	13.2	3.3	8.0	1.0	2.2	...	...	...	2.8	0.5	2.2
Crude petroleum and natural gas	...	...	...	...	...	...	...	...	...	...	...	...
Nonmetallic minerals	2.6	3.3	4.6	4.8	6.8	4.3	0.3	1.4	1.4	0.9	2.4	1.1
Scrap and waste	0.1	0.1	...	0.4	0.1	0.3	...	0.1	...	0.1	...	...
Used merchandise	1.0	2.7	4.4	1.3	2.4	6.0	0.4	1.0	3.2	0.3	0.7	1.4
Goods imported and returned unchanged	...	...	...	...	...	...	...	...	...	...	...	...
Special classification provisions	3.9	3.1	6.4	7.7	12.0	51.3	1.8	1.0	2.0	2.1	2.6	9.8

Table D-8. COLORADO: State Exports of Goods by Destination and Industry, 1994–1999—*Continued*

(Millions of dollars.)

Industry	Germany						France					
	1994	1995	1996	1997	1998	1999	1994	1995	1996	1997	1998	1999
ALL GOODS	769.9	900.5	735.0	669.4	678.4	820.7	512.6	715.6	624.2	521.9	567.0	532.0
Manufactured Goods	767.1	898.0	731.7	664.3	669.6	805.9	510.9	713.5	622.3	519.4	564.0	525.4
Food products	1.7	11.1	6.7	1.3	1.0	1.3	0.9	0.6	0.5	0.7	0.3	2.1
Tobacco products	...	...	...	...	...	...	...	...	...	...	...	...
Textile mill products	...	...	0.1	0.5	0.2	0.2	...	...	0.2	0.2	0.1	0.1
Apparel	2.3	1.6	1.6	1.7	0.8	1.2	0.6	0.4	0.1	0.6	0.4	0.5
Lumber and wood products	...	...	...	...	0.1	0.1	0.1	...	0.1	...	...	...
Furniture and fixtures	0.9	0.8	0.6	0.6	1.1	1.8	1.9	1.3	1.8	2.6	2.3	3.3
Paper products	0.9	0.8	1.3	1.1	0.7	0.7	0.3	0.2	0.2	0.1	...	...
Printing and publishing	6.7	8.5	4.5	2.7	2.6	4.2	5.0	3.9	4.2	2.4	2.7	2.3
Chemical products	1.4	1.3	2.1	3.6	4.6	6.8	1.4	2.0	5.9	5.3	4.1	3.6
Refined petroleum products	...	...	...	...	...	0.4	...	...	...	...	0.1	...
Rubber and plastic products	9.6	7.7	8.5	9.0	11.8	11.8	4.1	3.3	1.0	1.3	1.3	1.3
Leather products	0.3	0.1	0.2	0.1	0.1	0.4	...	...	0.1	0.2	0.3	...
Stone, clay and glass products	10.3	7.9	6.2	8.2	7.7	8.9	1.5	1.5	2.0	5.2	4.9	5.1
Primary metals	5.4	19.7	2.5	2.3	4.0	4.2	8.2	20.4	6.7	5.6	7.2	6.5
Fabricated metal products	35.6	47.3	59.1	57.5	76.9	121.5	0.9	1.1	1.6	1.6	1.0	1.1
Industrial machinery and computers	529.1	578.5	433.8	389.8	317.4	424.1	384.9	559.6	459.2	342.1	271.0	276.0
Electric and electronic equipment	106.8	141.8	134.5	110.5	140.5	124.0	66.8	86.6	98.9	109.3	214.9	157.5
Transportation equipment	3.5	4.5	2.6	4.3	12.5	11.9	2.0	2.4	5.8	8.0	9.4	15.6
Scientific and measuring instruments	49.5	61.9	64.4	69.0	84.8	79.5	29.5	28.5	33.6	33.1	42.9	49.4
Miscellaneous manufactures	2.1	3.2	2.8	1.9	2.1	2.3	2.4	1.1	1.0	0.8	0.8	0.5
Unidentified manufactures	1.0	1.1	0.4	0.2	0.5	0.5	0.4	0.6	0.2	0.2	0.4	0.4
Agricultural And Livestock Products	0.7	0.9	0.9	0.8	0.6	0.3	1.2	0.6	0.9	0.6	0.9	0.4
Agricultural products	0.4	0.9	0.9	0.6	0.3	0.2	1.2	0.6	0.9	0.6	0.8	...
Livestock and livestock products	0.3	...	...	0.2	0.3	0.1	...	...	...	...	...	0.4
Other Commodities	2.1	1.6	2.4	4.3	8.3	14.5	0.5	1.5	1.0	1.8	2.2	6.1
Forestry products	...	...	...	0.9	3.2	0.6	...	...	...	...	...	...
Fish and other marine products	...	...	...	0.1	0.2	...	...	0.1	0.1	...	...	...
Metallic ores and concentrates	1.2	0.4	...	...	...	0.2	...	...	...	...	...	0.1
Bituminous coal and lignite	...	...	...	...	...	...	...	...	...	...	...	...
Crude petroleum and natural gas	...	...	...	...	...	...	...	...	...	...	...	...
Nonmetallic minerals	0.1	...	...	0.1	...	...	...	...	0.1	...	...	...
Scrap and waste	...	...	...	...	...	...	...	...	...	...	...	...
Used merchandise	0.2	0.6	0.5	0.3	0.5	0.3	0.2	0.8	0.2	0.3	0.3	0.9
Goods imported and returned unchanged	...	...	...	...	...	...	...	...	...	...	...	...
Special classification provisions	0.6	0.7	1.9	2.8	4.4	13.4	0.3	0.6	0.7	1.5	1.8	5.1

Industry	The Netherlands						Asian 10					
	1994	1995	1996	1997	1998	1999	1994	1995	1996	1997	1998	1999
ALL GOODS	363.0	428.8	548.5	500.2	613.2	619.1	2 299.4	3 400.4	3 574.9	4 098.4	3 746.0	4 296.0
Manufactured Goods	351.7	407.2	541.3	488.3	600.2	597.5	2 248.6	3 305.7	3 497.6	4 024.1	3 681.9	4 212.6
Food products	0.8	1.9	1.2	1.1	1.2	2.3	252.3	379.7	441.2	520.9	419.7	560.8
Tobacco products	...	...	...	...	...	...	...	...	...	...	...	...
Textile mill products	0.2	0.4	0.5	0.7	0.6	0.7	0.8	1.7	1.4	1.4	1.3	1.5
Apparel	0.3	3.3	1.6	1.5	1.7	1.8	3.9	3.4	5.0	3.8	2.7	2.5
Lumber and wood products	0.1	...	0.2	...	...	0.1	1.1	1.8	8.5	3.4	1.2	1.9
Furniture and fixtures	0.6	0.7	0.7	0.3	0.5	0.2	2.1	1.1	1.5	1.1	0.9	1.0
Paper products	0.1	0.1	0.2	0.2	0.1	0.2	2.0	1.5	3.0	4.0	2.5	1.0
Printing and publishing	2.0	1.9	3.1	1.0	2.2	3.3	13.0	14.4	21.6	22.3	23.2	10.4
Chemical products	2.4	1.7	2.6	4.1	2.4	3.1	10.2	8.0	19.8	12.5	11.3	14.0
Refined petroleum products	...	...	...	...	...	...	0.9	1.4	0.6	0.5	2.2	1.9
Rubber and plastic products	1.1	2.6	2.0	1.7	1.6	0.9	21.3	20.6	24.4	32.2	22.9	25.4
Leather products	0.1	0.1	0.1	0.1	0.1	0.3	10.3	7.2	8.3	9.9	7.4	9.3
Stone, clay and glass products	3.0	2.3	3.6	2.6	2.1	1.8	30.9	37.7	26.0	34.2	31.2	38.0
Primary metals	2.3	2.5	3.5	2.8	2.3	6.6	17.7	66.2	20.0	38.3	75.8	13.9
Fabricated metal products	1.0	1.4	1.6	2.4	2.7	2.9	11.4	17.5	20.3	50.1	85.7	76.1
Industrial machinery and computers	277.8	293.5	397.9	325.9	425.0	437.1	1 175.5	1 744.5	1 697.9	1 460.2	1 384.4	1 533.9
Electric and electronic equipment	19.4	45.0	70.7	91.6	107.5	77.4	510.0	748.5	913.4	1 493.2	1 267.0	1 586.5
Transportation equipment	1.5	5.9	2.2	3.0	2.6	6.2	15.5	23.3	36.1	46.4	98.9	89.3
Scientific and measuring instruments	36.6	40.8	43.1	48.3	45.0	51.6	158.7	211.3	230.5	268.2	229.2	232.3
Miscellaneous manufactures	1.8	2.8	6.2	1.0	2.1	0.8	8.8	11.8	15.7	19.6	11.5	9.2
Unidentified manufactures	0.4	0.4	0.4	0.2	0.5	0.3	2.4	4.1	2.4	2.0	2.8	3.8
Agricultural And Livestock Products	0.5	0.4	0.3	0.4	0.2	0.2	3.0	5.7	8.2	9.2	10.9	6.1
Agricultural products	0.5	0.4	0.3	0.4	0.2	0.2	1.7	1.9	2.0	2.6	2.1	1.3
Livestock and livestock products	...	...	...	...	...	0.1	1.3	3.8	6.2	6.6	8.9	4.8
Other Commodities	10.8	21.2	7.0	11.5	12.8	21.4	47.8	89.0	69.1	65.1	53.2	77.3
Forestry products	...	...	...	...	...	...	0.5	...	0.7	0.4	0.3	0.6
Fish and other marine products	...	...	...	...	...	...	0.1	0.1	...	0.2	0.2	0.1
Metallic ores and concentrates	10.4	20.2	5.7	9.0	8.6	8.2	5.5	41.2	29.2	36.7	24.1	3.8
Bituminous coal and lignite	...	...	...	...	...	...	26.2	35.9	26.4	13.8	11.2	...
Crude petroleum and natural gas	...	...	...	...	...	...	...	...	0.1	...	0.4	0.1
Nonmetallic minerals	...	0.8	0.7	2.1	1.9	2.2	8.5	6.7	5.7	8.0	4.3	1.3
Scrap and waste	...	...	...	...	...	...	0.5	0.5	0.7	0.4	0.5	0.6
Used merchandise	...	...	0.1	...	...	0.1	1.3	1.5	1.8	1.0	4.8	1.5
Goods imported and returned unchanged	...	...	...	...	...	...	...	...	...	...	...	...
Special classification provisions	0.4	0.2	0.5	0.4	2.2	10.8	5.1	3.1	4.5	4.6	7.5	69.3

Table D-8. COLORADO: State Exports of Goods by Destination and Industry, 1994–1999—*Continued*

(Millions of dollars.)

Industry	Japan						South Korea					
	1994	1995	1996	1997	1998	1999	1994	1995	1996	1997	1998	1999
ALL GOODS	1 158.7	1 555.6	1 590.1	1 691.4	1 370.8	1 407.9	174.8	250.4	342.2	609.0	365.1	570.2
Manufactured Goods	1 137.2	1 490.7	1 538.7	1 637.5	1 331.6	1 390.5	164.4	238.4	329.8	606.6	362.7	567.9
Food products	226.6	337.4	324.6	342.0	309.7	302.2	7.0	13.3	33.6	82.4	42.7	115.8
Tobacco products	...	...	...	...	...	...	...	...	...	...	...	...
Textile mill products	0.4	0.4	0.3	0.4	0.2	0.2	0.1	0.8	0.2	0.4	0.3	0.3
Apparel	3.3	2.9	3.6	2.8	1.8	1.9	...	...	0.1	0.1	...	0.1
Lumber and wood products	0.6	1.2	7.6	0.3	0.4	0.7	0.3	0.3	0.3	1.9	0.7	0.1
Furniture and fixtures	0.3	0.2	0.8	0.3	0.2	0.2	...	...	0.3	...	0.1	0.1
Paper products	0.3	0.2	0.9	0.8	0.7	0.2	...	0.2	0.1	0.2	0.1	0.1
Printing and publishing	8.8	9.9	16.7	13.7	12.1	6.8	0.4	1.5	1.6	3.3	1.2	0.2
Chemical products	1.4	3.9	6.3	4.1	3.3	3.7	0.7	0.8	2.2	3.1	1.4	2.2
Refined petroleum products	0.1	0.4	0.4	0.3	1.5	0.7	0.6	0.7	0.2	...	0.1	0.2
Rubber and plastic products	4.6	7.2	7.7	8.6	6.0	5.3	7.0	3.8	3.6	5.2	3.7	3.4
Leather products	0.6	1.3	0.8	1.1	0.4	2.0	2.4	2.3	4.2	2.1	0.2	0.6
Stone, clay and glass products	2.9	6.7	4.9	8.9	6.4	9.5	3.1	2.6	2.9	1.8	0.4	1.4
Primary metals	10.6	8.2	9.2	9.2	4.9	5.1	0.7	0.6	0.5	2.2	1.4	1.6
Fabricated metal products	3.6	11.5	15.1	43.1	33.4	9.4	1.0	0.6	0.3	0.6	0.8	0.8
Industrial machinery and computers	629.2	791.1	802.3	640.9	535.6	589.7	64.4	105.4	116.9	95.9	53.9	86.4
Electric and electronic equipment	146.1	180.7	168.1	357.4	213.6	268.9	62.7	84.1	139.9	385.2	242.2	335.0
Transportation equipment	1.1	4.4	21.5	33.8	56.6	53.4	0.2	2.6	2.0	1.3	1.7	1.3
Scientific and measuring instruments	91.5	116.1	140.8	163.4	140.1	123.7	12.8	16.4	18.4	17.0	11.1	17.7
Miscellaneous manufactures	4.5	5.9	6.6	5.8	3.9	6.1	0.6	1.3	1.8	3.4	0.6	0.5
Unidentified manufactures	0.7	1.1	0.4	0.5	0.8	1.1	0.3	1.3	0.6	0.6	0.3	0.3
Agricultural And Livestock Products	1.1	1.3	0.8	1.1	1.1	0.4	0.3	0.4	0.3	0.4	0.9	0.5
Agricultural products	1.1	1.3	0.8	1.0	1.1	0.4	0.1	0.1	0.3	0.4	0.5	...
Livestock and livestock products	...	...	...	0.1	...	...	0.1	0.4	...	...	0.4	0.4
Other Commodities	20.4	63.6	50.6	52.8	38.1	17.0	10.1	11.5	12.1	2.0	1.4	1.8
Forestry products	0.1	...	...	...	...	...	...	...	0.6	0.4	0.3	0.6
Fish and other marine products	0.1	...	...	...	0.1	...	...	0.1	...	0.2	...	...
Metallic ores and concentrates	5.2	41.2	29.1	36.6	24.1	3.8	0.3	...	...	...	...	...
Bituminous coal and lignite	11.4	19.9	16.8	13.8	11.2	...	8.2	10.3	9.7	...	...	...
Crude petroleum and natural gas	...	...	0.1	...	0.4	...	...	...	...	...	...	...
Nonmetallic minerals	...	...	...	...	...	...	0.8	0.8	1.4	1.3	0.4	0.2
Scrap and waste	...	0.1	0.4	0.2	0.2	0.3	0.1	0.1	...	...	...	0.1
Used merchandise	0.9	0.6	1.3	0.4	0.3	0.6	...	...	...	...	0.1	...
Goods imported and returned unchanged	...	...	...	...	...	...	...	...	...	...	...	...
Special classification provisions	2.7	1.8	2.8	1.8	1.8	12.3	0.8	0.2	0.4	0.2	0.7	0.9

Industry	Taiwan						Singapore					
	1994	1995	1996	1997	1998	1999	1994	1995	1996	1997	1998	1999
ALL GOODS	130.4	205.7	197.2	214.2	217.7	357.2	308.6	591.7	638.9	622.5	745.9	736.1
Manufactured Goods	117.2	198.4	195.3	212.4	215.8	354.2	306.8	586.9	638.0	619.8	744.5	691.3
Food products	3.2	6.9	14.5	19.4	15.7	72.7	0.3	0.7	2.2	1.7	0.5	0.7
Tobacco products	...	...	...	...	...	...	...	...	...	...	...	...
Textile mill products	0.1	...	0.2	0.2	0.2	0.2	...	0.3	0.4	0.2	0.1	0.1
Apparel	0.1	0.1	0.3	0.3	0.1	0.1	0.2	...	0.4	0.1	0.1	0.1
Lumber and wood products	...	0.2	0.3	0.1	...	0.3	...	...	0.1	0.1	...	0.5
Furniture and fixtures	0.2	...	...	...	...	0.2	1.3	0.5	0.2	0.1	0.2	0.2
Paper products	...	0.1	0.2	0.3	0.1	0.1	1.0	0.7	0.7	2.2	0.3	0.3
Printing and publishing	0.7	0.5	0.5	0.6	0.5	0.7	1.2	1.1	1.1	2.1	2.0	1.3
Chemical products	0.3	0.7	1.1	0.9	1.6	3.0	1.0	0.6	2.6	0.6	0.8	1.2
Refined petroleum products	0.1	0.1	...	0.2	0.3	0.2	...	...	...	...	0.1	0.7
Rubber and plastic products	2.4	0.7	3.0	4.1	3.7	2.8	5.3	6.3	6.9	8.6	4.9	6.3
Leather products	0.9	0.4	0.3	2.4	2.8	2.9	2.6	1.2	1.3	2.0	0.1	...
Stone, clay and glass products	7.7	7.1	6.6	6.9	10.5	8.5	2.4	3.4	1.9	0.5	0.5	0.6
Primary metals	0.9	1.2	1.4	4.9	1.8	1.0	3.3	24.6	3.9	17.0	49.1	3.6
Fabricated metal products	0.9	0.5	0.4	1.1	1.0	6.6	2.7	2.0	1.2	2.0	45.8	57.2
Industrial machinery and computers	41.7	74.9	46.2	54.2	67.2	76.7	159.4	375.9	374.6	304.8	306.4	340.6
Electric and electronic equipment	45.7	92.3	100.8	96.4	90.9	144.7	104.2	132.6	211.1	252.0	306.7	254.2
Transportation equipment	0.2	0.1	0.8	0.3	1.3	0.2	1.2	1.7	2.0	1.6	1.8	1.0
Scientific and measuring instruments	10.6	11.7	14.8	17.5	16.6	32.9	19.8	33.5	26.0	23.7	24.2	21.7
Miscellaneous manufactures	1.3	0.8	3.7	2.3	1.4	0.3	0.4	1.2	1.3	0.5	0.6	0.6
Unidentified manufactures	0.2	0.3	0.3	0.2	0.3	0.2	0.5	0.6	0.3	0.1	0.3	0.4
Agricultural And Livestock Products	...	...	0.2	0.1	0.1	0.1	...	...	...	...	...	...
Agricultural products	...	...	0.2	0.1	0.1	0.1	...	...	...	...	...	...
Livestock and livestock products	...	...	...	...	...	...	...	...	...	...	...	...
Other Commodities	13.2	7.3	1.8	1.8	1.8	3.0	1.8	4.8	0.9	2.6	1.4	44.8
Forestry products	...	...	...	...	...	0.1	...	...	...	...	...	...
Fish and other marine products	...	...	...	...	...	0.1	...	...	...	...	...	...
Metallic ores and concentrates	...	...	...	...	...	...	...	...	...	...	...	...
Bituminous coal and lignite	6.7	5.7	...	...	...	...	...	...	...	...	...	...
Crude petroleum and natural gas	...	...	...	...	...	...	...	...	...	...	...	0.1
Nonmetallic minerals	6.3	1.0	1.5	1.7	1.3	0.6	0.6	4.3	0.6	1.0	0.6	0.1
Scrap and waste	0.1	...	0.1	...	...	...	...	...	...	...	...	0.1
Used merchandise	...	0.4	...	...	...	...	0.1	...	...	...	...	0.1
Goods imported and returned unchanged	...	...	...	...	...	...	...	...	...	...	...	...
Special classification provisions	...	0.1	0.1	0.1	0.4	2.3	1.1	0.5	0.3	1.5	0.8	44.5

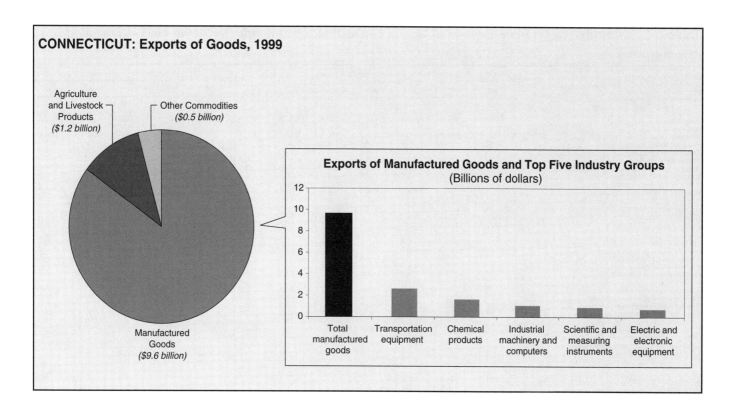

CONNECTICUT: Exports of Goods, 1999

Agriculture and Livestock Products ($1.2 billion)

Other Commodities ($0.5 billion)

Manufactured Goods ($9.6 billion)

Exports of Manufactured Goods and Top Five Industry Groups
(Billions of dollars)

Total manufactured goods / Transportation equipment / Chemical products / Industrial machinery and computers / Scientific and measuring instruments / Electric and electronic equipment

Table D-9. CONNECTICUT: State Exports of Goods by Destination and Industry, 1994–1999

(Millions of dollars.)

Industry	All destinations						Canada					
	1994	1995	1996	1997	1998	1999	1994	1995	1996	1997	1998	1999
ALL GOODS	10 272.0	12 942.1	13 052.5	12 897.1	12 139.7	11 335.1	1 481.1	1 660.2	1 603.9	1 847.7	1 872.8	1 973.5
Manufactured Goods	8 257.5	9 985.7	9 705.0	10 730.2	10 473.4	9 622.4	1 344.3	1 500.1	1 478.0	1 715.3	1 739.7	1 815.9
Food products	313.4	433.6	414.0	404.3	486.0	457.2	19.2	23.8	28.6	29.4	25.2	22.3
Tobacco products	0.4	0.6	3.8	2.2	1.8	4.0	0.1	0.2	0.2	0.3	0.9	1.6
Textile mill products	61.8	58.2	60.7	77.8	68.3	48.6	22.7	23.5	26.9	40.5	37.4	25.8
Apparel	61.0	99.9	115.8	231.5	163.4	128.4	4.8	6.1	5.4	5.9	6.4	5.8
Lumber and wood products	31.7	39.0	27.3	30.4	26.2	22.7	6.2	7.8	7.6	9.1	9.3	5.9
Furniture and fixtures	17.7	20.4	37.4	43.6	49.9	73.5	6.7	9.9	12.9	14.6	16.9	11.3
Paper products	497.6	656.8	641.7	619.2	575.0	294.2	52.0	55.5	53.2	73.2	76.0	92.8
Printing and publishing	127.1	112.0	115.3	105.2	76.6	52.8	55.8	72.9	70.0	72.2	55.4	32.6
Chemical products	2 326.8	2 845.7	2 933.5	3 146.1	2 523.6	1 638.4	361.0	302.0	346.8	383.6	393.4	435.2
Refined petroleum products	460.8	570.1	522.8	452.8	411.5	410.6	34.1	40.3	50.5	34.5	106.2	109.0
Rubber and plastic products	96.8	108.8	113.2	134.9	127.2	129.6	27.0	29.4	32.2	30.8	26.5	35.3
Leather products	9.3	7.8	9.6	6.5	5.3	7.9	1.4	1.5	0.9	1.3	1.0	1.1
Stone, clay and glass products	23.5	27.2	36.1	30.8	25.9	43.9	9.2	9.2	9.3	9.0	8.6	9.8
Primary metals	308.5	485.8	351.3	273.4	336.2	358.0	73.7	103.4	59.8	87.9	80.8	90.5
Fabricated metal products	264.7	277.4	329.4	414.6	367.4	423.8	70.9	78.7	79.0	91.3	92.7	108.6
Industrial machinery and computers	725.6	867.5	865.4	1 019.9	949.3	1 077.9	152.7	177.2	175.5	233.9	206.3	252.5
Electric and electronic equipment	664.0	721.3	770.3	802.0	691.4	744.0	147.8	153.4	159.4	181.7	181.1	168.2
Transportation equipment	1 447.9	1 729.3	1 652.3	2 119.7	2 764.3	2 635.5	161.3	158.6	224.0	261.1	252.7	224.2
Scientific and measuring instruments	683.9	686.0	576.1	677.8	661.8	913.2	99.4	98.1	79.9	97.4	105.0	123.9
Miscellaneous manufactures	76.0	88.2	93.5	101.3	108.9	109.9	30.2	39.6	46.5	47.7	47.6	48.6
Unidentified manufactures	58.9	150.1	35.6	36.4	53.5	48.2	8.1	108.8	9.4	10.0	10.5	10.8
Agricultural And Livestock Products	1 044.6	1 728.4	2 330.8	1 501.0	1 217.6	1 229.3	11.1	27.0	31.6	19.7	32.7	24.0
Agricultural products	1 018.5	1 702.6	2 317.8	1 483.0	1 194.4	1 206.0	6.7	22.4	30.0	19.2	32.0	23.2
Livestock and livestock products	26.1	25.8	13.0	18.0	23.1	23.3	4.3	4.6	1.6	0.5	0.7	0.8
Other Commodities	969.9	1 228.0	1 016.7	666.0	448.8	483.4	125.7	133.2	94.3	112.7	100.4	133.6
Forestry products	5.4	3.7	4.0	4.1	3.9	3.0	2.6	1.7	1.4	1.8	1.7	1.6
Fish and other marine products	8.0	6.6	6.8	9.3	12.3	17.4	1.8	1.2	1.7	2.3	1.5	2.4
Metallic ores and concentrates	42.0	70.4	25.6	28.5	36.2	38.6	35.5	20.6	14.5	27.9	32.2	38.0
Bituminous coal and lignite	530.3	658.2	580.4	309.5	136.7	101.6	15.9	18.8	11.6	11.7	13.5	13.9
Crude petroleum and natural gas	0.2	8.7	10.4	4.3	0.1	0.8	. . .	0.1	. . .	. . .	. . .	0.8
Nonmetallic minerals	48.0	54.6	67.8	58.0	54.4	51.9	1.2	0.8	1.0	1.0	1.3	0.6
Scrap and waste	236.3	316.1	227.6	160.4	101.8	81.6	20.3	56.0	21.7	26.2	17.0	20.0
Used merchandise	15.0	6.3	7.3	8.3	23.0	28.9	0.6	0.4	1.5	1.8	2.1	1.4
Goods imported and returned unchanged	30.6	21.1	28.1	29.8	25.2	47.7	30.6	21.1	28.1	29.8	25.2	47.7
Special classification provisions	54.3	82.4	58.7	53.7	55.2	111.9	17.2	12.5	12.7	10.3	6.0	7.4

Table D-9. CONNECTICUT: State Exports of Goods by Destination and Industry, 1994–1999—*Continued*

(Millions of dollars.)

Industry	South and Central American and Caribbean						Mexico					
	1994	1995	1996	1997	1998	1999	1994	1995	1996	1997	1998	1999
ALL GOODS	1 122.0	1 421.9	1 333.5	1 410.1	1 362.8	1 084.8	441.4	321.9	521.5	529.5	544.1	699.2
Manufactured Goods	965.9	1 224.0	1 190.0	1 248.7	1 165.0	880.3	368.6	275.1	396.7	464.9	498.6	635.1
Food products	62.8	98.6	78.5	77.3	118.5	97.2	3.7	1.4	6.2	5.1	22.7	103.1
Tobacco products	0.1	0.2	0.2	0.3	0.2	0.2	...	...	...	0.2	0.1	0.2
Textile mill products	15.7	2.3	3.1	3.4	3.4	1.7	0.9	0.9	1.0	2.7	3.0	1.1
Apparel	34.9	69.0	80.6	191.4	133.1	99.9	10.1	10.7	13.6	15.3	12.1	11.4
Lumber and wood products	0.2	0.4	0.6	0.4	0.4	0.2	0.1	0.5	...	1.7	2.4	2.6
Furniture and fixtures	1.1	1.4	1.3	3.7	5.8	1.1	0.4	0.3	0.3	0.3	0.7	0.3
Paper products	58.0	80.7	91.3	91.0	82.0	49.6	49.6	58.5	54.8	49.3	54.9	40.0
Printing and publishing	8.8	4.1	2.2	1.3	1.4	4.5	0.8	0.3	0.5	1.5	2.2	2.1
Chemical products	407.3	553.0	510.3	491.2	444.0	306.1	92.8	79.0	109.6	154.6	129.7	116.0
Refined petroleum products	172.3	185.2	138.0	98.8	85.6	50.9	4.6	5.5	38.5	34.6	62.2	80.3
Rubber and plastic products	7.5	8.5	6.4	9.8	9.2	8.9	8.0	7.5	7.4	11.3	11.3	18.3
Leather products	0.4	0.5	0.1	0.6	0.7	0.6	...	...	...	0.3	0.3	2.6
Stone, clay and glass products	1.1	2.2	1.8	1.7	1.7	1.6	0.8	1.3	0.5	1.3	1.1	1.4
Primary metals	10.0	11.8	5.5	17.9	17.2	14.1	15.0	14.9	29.5	22.4	16.5	17.5
Fabricated metal products	16.6	16.1	11.0	24.5	17.5	14.2	16.3	10.9	16.1	26.0	26.8	41.3
Industrial machinery and computers	50.4	64.6	85.1	79.4	76.7	46.8	36.9	17.7	23.4	29.5	37.7	36.8
Electric and electronic equipment	54.7	60.9	74.0	86.6	71.5	78.6	74.7	53.0	59.9	75.2	79.1	76.9
Transportation equipment	25.1	30.6	54.2	18.2	38.3	28.3	44.1	1.6	19.1	3.9	3.4	36.6
Scientific and measuring instruments	24.6	24.6	34.6	43.8	45.6	62.6	7.4	7.3	13.0	20.6	19.4	22.0
Miscellaneous manufactures	6.1	3.8	3.1	3.0	7.3	5.6	1.6	3.0	2.6	8.1	9.1	19.2
Unidentified manufactures	8.2	5.4	5.4	4.4	5.1	7.5	0.7	0.7	0.7	0.9	3.9	5.3
Agricultural And Livestock Products	97.4	123.8	109.1	153.8	193.6	175.2	61.3	38.9	117.4	61.0	42.6	60.0
Agricultural products	92.3	120.4	107.5	150.8	187.3	169.7	59.6	37.0	117.2	60.2	42.5	60.0
Livestock and livestock products	5.1	3.5	1.6	2.9	6.3	5.5	1.7	1.9	0.2	0.8	0.1	...
Other Commodities	58.7	74.0	34.4	7.7	4.2	29.4	11.6	7.9	7.4	3.6	2.9	4.2
Forestry products	0.1	0.3	0.1	0.1	0.2	0.2	1.8	0.1	0.1	0.1	0.1	0.1
Fish and other marine products	...	...	...	...	0.5	...	0.1	...	...	0.2	0.5	...
Metallic ores and concentrates	...	...	...	...	...	...	...	...	...	...	...	0.6
Bituminous coal and lignite	41.2	23.6	11.1	...	...	0.3	...	2.4	3.3	...	...	...
Crude petroleum and natural gas	...	5.7	...	4.1	...	...	...	...	...	...	...	...
Nonmetallic minerals	2.7	3.2	10.2	2.0	2.0	2.1	2.2	0.7	3.5	0.8	1.4	2.3
Scrap and waste	9.2	14.8	12.3	0.4	0.6	0.6	6.3	4.6	0.2	0.9	0.6	0.3
Used merchandise	0.9	0.8	0.3	0.5	0.5	0.4	...	...	...	0.1	...	...
Goods imported and returned unchanged	...	...	...	...	...	...	...	...	...	...	...	...
Special classification provisions	4.5	25.8	0.4	0.5	0.5	25.7	1.1	0.1	0.1	1.6	0.3	0.8

Industry	European Union						United Kingdom					
	1994	1995	1996	1997	1998	1999	1994	1995	1996	1997	1998	1999
ALL GOODS	2 584.7	3 413.6	3 416.0	3 636.7	3 708.2	3 253.8	500.4	604.1	693.7	813.0	773.7	649.2
Manufactured Goods	2 096.9	2 710.2	2 661.0	3 045.7	3 405.9	3 014.7	431.2	533.5	581.8	733.8	703.2	605.7
Food products	36.3	29.7	151.4	216.5	165.7	102.5	5.8	3.8	14.8	28.8	31.2	128.0
Tobacco products	...	...	0.2	0.2	...	0.7	...	...	...	...	...	0.2
Textile mill products	13.7	23.1	20.2	17.0	10.6	9.3	1.4	2.5	3.1	2.6	1.8	1.7
Apparel	5.9	6.5	6.2	7.1	5.6	4.9	1.6	1.6	1.0	1.8	0.9	1.1
Lumber and wood products	18.2	21.9	14.4	13.7	9.7	6.1	2.4	2.0	1.8	1.7	2.3	2.3
Furniture and fixtures	5.1	3.9	5.3	8.0	10.2	47.2	1.4	1.5	1.9	3.0	1.5	27.4
Paper products	134.1	165.0	175.7	192.4	186.7	53.2	20.5	27.4	32.2	48.9	46.3	12.9
Printing and publishing	14.9	13.0	21.6	13.8	8.4	5.8	8.9	7.9	16.5	9.6	4.1	2.6
Chemical products	468.4	572.5	620.9	670.5	568.8	212.0	28.2	29.9	31.7	38.4	28.9	29.4
Refined petroleum products	95.5	114.1	113.7	104.4	71.2	50.2	1.2	2.8	2.4	7.7	0.5	2.2
Rubber and plastic products	27.0	33.2	31.5	45.3	42.7	33.2	8.5	11.9	10.7	13.6	10.1	9.6
Leather products	1.7	1.3	3.8	1.6	1.0	1.8	0.2	0.3	0.9	0.7	0.3	0.5
Stone, clay and glass products	6.0	6.8	10.0	9.7	5.9	14.1	1.6	2.3	2.6	1.7	2.1	6.1
Primary metals	36.6	77.1	96.7	41.6	85.8	57.6	7.8	45.2	29.3	19.0	46.3	11.9
Fabricated metal products	48.1	63.9	70.8	76.0	88.8	94.9	13.4	15.3	26.7	19.7	22.0	23.0
Industrial machinery and computers	234.3	311.5	304.3	337.1	358.7	413.2	80.1	103.8	106.1	117.6	116.7	131.0
Electric and electronic equipment	144.4	181.1	158.9	172.3	164.3	185.1	55.5	72.7	53.7	59.2	55.0	79.2
Transportation equipment	481.5	748.5	643.5	885.2	1 360.0	1 304.8	144.3	150.7	183.7	303.9	276.2	171.7
Scientific and measuring instruments	295.0	307.5	183.4	201.0	226.7	390.0	38.7	39.8	52.4	44.0	44.3	69.8
Miscellaneous manufactures	17.2	16.0	17.0	20.0	19.0	16.3	6.2	5.5	5.8	6.6	6.4	6.7
Unidentified manufactures	13.2	13.7	11.5	12.4	16.0	11.7	3.7	6.4	4.6	5.2	6.2	3.7
Agricultural And Livestock Products	168.9	268.3	368.0	325.0	111.4	75.9	5.7	0.3	1.5	0.9	1.1	1.1
Agricultural products	166.7	264.9	365.2	321.6	108.2	72.6	5.5	0.1	1.5	0.9	0.7	0.3
Livestock and livestock products	2.1	3.4	2.8	3.4	3.3	3.3	0.2	0.2	...	0.1	0.4	0.8
Other Commodities	318.9	435.1	387.0	266.0	190.9	163.2	63.5	70.3	110.5	78.2	69.4	42.4
Forestry products	0.3	1.2	1.5	0.8	0.6	0.4	0.3	0.4	0.5	0.3	0.1	...
Fish and other marine products	5.6	5.1	5.0	6.8	9.5	14.3	...	...	...	...	...	...
Metallic ores and concentrates	2.7	32.4	2.8	0.5	...	...	0.1	1.7	2.1	...	...	...
Bituminous coal and lignite	219.1	308.4	288.3	141.7	52.2	22.2	35.9	51.1	85.8	62.6	38.6	8.6
Crude petroleum and natural gas	...	2.1	0.1	...	...	...	...	...	...	...	...	...
Nonmetallic minerals	27.3	25.9	24.8	26.3	24.1	22.4	1.5	1.1	1.5	1.3	1.3	1.3
Scrap and waste	39.4	41.0	42.1	64.1	60.2	36.4	11.7	6.0	6.7	2.9	2.6	1.9
Used merchandise	7.8	3.2	3.3	3.7	18.2	25.4	5.4	1.3	2.8	2.4	14.2	16.5
Goods imported and returned unchanged	...	...	...	...	...	...	...	...	...	...	...	...
Special classification provisions	16.7	15.8	19.2	22.1	26.0	42.1	8.7	8.6	11.1	8.7	12.6	14.0

Table D-9. CONNECTICUT: State Exports of Goods by Destination and Industry, 1994–1999—*Continued*

(Millions of dollars.)

Industry	Germany						France					
	1994	1995	1996	1997	1998	1999	1994	1995	1996	1997	1998	1999
ALL GOODS	477.8	583.3	658.4	721.9	684.1	509.6	252.7	297.6	298.5	314.6	732.2	810.0
Manufactured Goods	425.8	488.2	537.4	597.1	626.3	447.5	221.5	219.2	240.8	269.0	715.4	797.8
Food products	6.1	3.0	6.4	3.9	3.1	2.0	4.5	3.0	17.8	36.7	24.1	7.3
Tobacco products	...	...	...	0.1	...	0.1	...	...	...	...	...	...
Textile mill products	4.9	14.5	11.7	9.7	4.6	3.2	0.7	0.5	0.5	0.8	0.9	0.3
Apparel	1.6	1.4	2.0	2.2	2.2	1.5	0.4	0.8	0.6	0.3	0.6	0.3
Lumber and wood products	2.7	3.4	1.5	1.1	0.2	0.1	1.8	3.3	2.3	2.3	1.6	0.4
Furniture and fixtures	0.4	0.5	0.9	2.5	6.7	14.5	2.7	0.5	1.6	2.0	0.9	4.3
Paper products	56.5	59.3	75.8	83.6	66.3	8.0	15.1	19.5	16.8	8.7	10.4	2.1
Printing and publishing	0.7	0.6	0.5	0.9	0.7	0.4	0.3	0.9	2.3	0.9	0.9	0.2
Chemical products	75.0	99.2	143.3	165.8	163.2	48.9	10.5	15.3	25.7	17.1	15.1	5.8
Refined petroleum products	4.2	7.3	2.7	6.0	4.5	2.2	6.9	8.2	14.0	9.9	7.8	1.9
Rubber and plastic products	5.0	7.6	6.1	11.4	8.6	6.8	3.6	3.5	3.4	3.9	2.7	3.6
Leather products	0.4	0.1	0.3	0.2	0.2	0.7	0.2	0.6	1.9	0.2	0.2	0.1
Stone, clay and glass products	1.8	1.6	2.5	3.6	1.5	3.8	0.7	1.0	3.3	1.4	1.0	0.8
Primary metals	8.2	10.4	11.1	8.5	8.1	17.0	4.2	3.0	2.7	2.2	7.4	1.6
Fabricated metal products	8.9	9.2	10.8	11.7	17.6	16.3	8.2	6.5	5.0	6.9	9.8	7.8
Industrial machinery and computers	61.3	68.6	77.9	86.7	84.1	107.8	25.9	34.1	32.5	46.2	60.1	36.8
Electric and electronic equipment	24.1	27.2	20.9	25.9	22.6	22.6	11.3	18.6	12.2	9.2	10.2	16.7
Transportation equipment	94.4	109.3	120.4	132.4	186.3	146.6	54.4	19.0	81.0	95.4	539.5	683.3
Scientific and measuring instruments	59.2	59.2	38.1	36.2	39.9	40.9	67.3	77.3	14.6	19.8	18.4	21.0
Miscellaneous manufactures	4.6	3.8	2.6	3.0	3.2	2.1	2.1	3.2	2.0	4.5	3.1	2.7
Unidentified manufactures	5.7	2.0	2.1	1.8	2.7	2.1	0.7	0.6	0.5	0.7	1.0	1.0
Agricultural And Livestock Products	17.1	39.7	83.8	66.2	11.7	27.6	0.1	27.5	11.6	15.2	7.5	0.8
Agricultural products	17.1	39.0	83.7	66.2	11.7	27.6	0.1	27.5	11.6	15.2	7.3	...
Livestock and livestock products	...	0.6	0.2	...	...	...	...	...	...	...	0.3	0.8
Other Commodities	34.9	55.5	37.2	58.6	46.1	34.5	31.1	50.9	46.0	30.4	9.3	11.3
Forestry products	...	0.4	0.6	0.1	...	...	...	0.1	...	0.2	0.1	...
Fish and other marine products	0.1	0.1	...	0.2	...	...	3.7	3.5	2.7	1.2	0.1	4.1
Metallic ores and concentrates	...	...	0.4	...	...	...	...	0.1	0.1	...	...	...
Bituminous coal and lignite	...	28.7	9.7	2.4	...	...	21.8	44.1	38.9	21.7	2.8	...
Crude petroleum and natural gas	...	...	...	...	...	...	...	...	...	...	...	...
Nonmetallic minerals	14.5	9.8	9.3	10.3	8.8	6.7	3.4	2.3	3.9	4.5	4.0	4.6
Scrap and waste	15.8	14.6	15.1	39.2	31.5	18.1	0.4	0.2	0.1	0.1	...	...
Used merchandise	0.7	0.4	0.2	0.1	0.7	2.0	1.3	0.1	...	0.6	0.6	0.6
Goods imported and returned unchanged	...	...	...	...	...	...	...	...	...	...	...	...
Special classification provisions	3.9	1.4	1.9	6.2	5.1	7.7	0.3	0.4	0.3	2.1	1.6	2.0

Industry	The Netherlands						Asian 10					
	1994	1995	1996	1997	1998	1999	1994	1995	1996	1997	1998	1999
ALL GOODS	291.1	378.0	449.8	466.9	346.0	388.9	3 077.2	4 034.5	4 004.2	3 740.2	3 242.1	2 798.9
Manufactured Goods	208.3	234.1	277.1	335.8	291.0	354.0	2 432.0	3 049.6	2 730.9	3 007.0	2 559.7	2 193.6
Food products	4.4	6.0	57.2	72.3	41.3	36.0	73.5	127.4	83.8	39.2	118.2	47.9
Tobacco products	...	...	0.1	...	...	0.3	...	...	0.4	0.8	0.1	0.3
Textile mill products	1.6	1.4	0.8	1.6	0.2	0.3	4.0	4.6	4.6	7.6	7.3	6.8
Apparel	0.8	1.8	1.5	1.4	1.0	0.9	2.2	5.5	7.1	8.4	2.1	1.9
Lumber and wood products	2.0	2.1	1.1	1.1	0.4	0.3	5.4	6.8	3.1	3.6	2.8	6.2
Furniture and fixtures	0.2	0.6	...	...	0.3	0.1	2.2	3.9	15.8	14.0	8.5	9.4
Paper products	12.4	22.0	20.3	18.5	24.9	8.8	183.8	262.5	214.9	181.6	149.0	45.4
Printing and publishing	1.5	0.7	0.9	0.7	0.6	0.5	24.0	16.7	15.7	12.1	5.0	4.1
Chemical products	60.4	58.1	73.1	49.3	33.5	53.0	761.7	974.3	1 027.8	991.7	687.9	412.0
Refined petroleum products	47.7	45.2	41.4	30.3	35.3	27.1	111.3	131.4	100.9	74.6	46.1	96.3
Rubber and plastic products	1.3	1.9	1.3	1.4	1.3	0.9	18.6	19.4	23.1	26.8	18.7	21.4
Leather products	...	0.1	0.1	0.1	0.1	...	5.5	3.9	3.8	2.1	2.0	1.5
Stone, clay and glass products	0.4	0.7	0.2	1.5	0.6	0.5	3.7	4.9	10.0	6.7	4.8	6.5
Primary metals	5.4	2.5	1.9	2.3	3.3	2.7	148.3	244.7	67.3	79.4	44.8	65.7
Fabricated metal products	4.3	4.6	9.8	11.7	9.6	9.0	76.3	69.8	115.0	157.0	113.8	133.9
Industrial machinery and computers	14.9	18.0	18.4	23.1	28.4	31.1	172.5	192.0	182.1	248.0	178.8	231.1
Electric and electronic equipment	11.9	8.7	12.8	14.5	15.8	18.0	183.2	207.8	252.2	219.4	124.6	176.8
Transportation equipment	6.0	27.3	13.0	48.8	42.2	24.2	480.3	585.9	405.0	710.5	836.3	689.4
Scientific and measuring instruments	31.3	31.4	21.3	54.9	50.5	138.1	155.8	161.5	178.8	205.2	187.6	216.5
Miscellaneous manufactures	1.3	0.6	1.2	1.5	1.3	0.9	14.5	18.3	16.4	14.4	14.2	13.7
Unidentified manufactures	0.6	0.4	0.6	0.6	0.6	1.2	5.3	8.4	3.1	4.1	7.1	6.7
Agricultural And Livestock Products	33.6	52.4	108.8	110.3	43.0	21.1	317.8	611.7	990.5	549.1	558.7	473.1
Agricultural products	33.4	50.7	107.5	109.0	41.3	20.2	307.6	601.1	985.4	541.3	550.6	463.1
Livestock and livestock products	0.2	1.8	1.3	1.3	1.7	0.9	10.2	10.6	5.1	7.7	8.1	10.1
Other Commodities	49.2	91.5	63.9	20.8	12.0	13.8	327.5	373.2	282.8	184.1	123.7	132.2
Forestry products	...	0.1	0.3	...	...	...	0.2	...	0.5	0.6	0.6	0.4
Fish and other marine products	0.2	0.1	...	...	...	...	0.2	0.2	...	...	...	...
Metallic ores and concentrates	2.6	30.6	0.2	0.2	...	...	3.7	15.1	5.4	8.3	3.8	...
Bituminous coal and lignite	40.1	50.8	52.9	9.1	...	...	179.7	193.3	118.7	91.2	61.4	59.9
Crude petroleum and natural gas	...	...	...	...	...	...	0.2	0.8	10.4	0.1	...	...
Nonmetallic minerals	5.5	7.7	7.4	8.5	7.5	6.8	9.1	11.3	18.8	18.1	19.7	22.5
Scrap and waste	0.2	0.4	0.1	0.1	0.4	1.1	117.5	127.4	103.5	57.5	21.6	21.5
Used merchandise	0.2	0.1	...	0.1	1.8	3.8	5.1	1.7	1.3	2.2	1.2	0.5
Goods imported and returned unchanged	...	...	...	...	...	...	...	...	...	...	...	...
Special classification provisions	0.5	1.7	3.0	2.8	2.3	2.1	11.8	23.3	21.4	14.4	15.3	27.3

Table D-9. CONNECTICUT: State Exports of Goods by Destination and Industry, 1994–1999—*Continued*

(Millions of dollars.)

Industry	Japan						South Korea					
	1994	1995	1996	1997	1998	1999	1994	1995	1996	1997	1998	1999
ALL GOODS	1 050.2	1 222.5	1 178.6	1 189.8	1 005.9	935.0	577.5	763.3	879.2	812.9	581.4	628.3
Manufactured Goods	771.9	878.7	798.4	855.3	754.2	684.2	361.9	493.1	489.2	616.2	414.7	502.3
Food products	22.3	20.6	11.3	14.0	19.9	13.5	0.8	4.5	1.3	1.3	17.6	8.6
Tobacco products	...	...	...	...	0.1	...	...	...	0.3	0.1	...	...
Textile mill products	0.8	0.9	1.1	2.2	4.4	3.7	0.5	0.4	0.2	0.3	0.1	0.1
Apparel	1.1	4.1	5.7	2.9	0.8	0.8	0.4	0.1	0.1	0.2	...	...
Lumber and wood products	2.1	1.7	0.9	1.9	2.3	5.3	0.7	3.6	1.2	0.9	0.2	0.2
Furniture and fixtures	0.7	1.1	10.1	5.7	3.7	1.9	0.8	1.0	1.6	1.3	0.2	0.5
Paper products	81.7	105.2	89.9	78.5	69.4	11.3	16.9	17.4	13.1	10.4	7.1	5.1
Printing and publishing	4.6	2.5	2.1	1.8	2.4	1.0	0.5	0.6	0.1	0.6	0.2	0.2
Chemical products	199.3	238.6	238.0	237.6	200.4	109.9	119.3	145.7	146.5	135.7	80.8	64.1
Refined petroleum products	43.8	65.7	57.7	43.8	23.8	22.4	23.4	13.2	15.7	20.9	10.9	36.3
Rubber and plastic products	7.7	7.7	9.8	9.0	5.2	6.8	1.6	1.2	0.6	3.2	2.7	3.2
Leather products	2.2	1.9	1.1	1.0	1.4	1.0	1.3	0.4	0.1	0.1	...	0.1
Stone, clay and glass products	1.4	2.3	5.4	3.7	2.4	3.1	0.8	0.8	0.9	0.8	0.4	0.5
Primary metals	93.4	70.5	27.0	24.5	10.4	12.8	28.0	59.4	22.9	32.9	6.6	20.6
Fabricated metal products	3.9	7.6	16.9	29.7	40.9	13.9	21.6	20.7	61.9	19.4	20.6	95.1
Industrial machinery and computers	38.0	58.7	48.0	53.5	47.4	85.8	23.5	23.8	32.4	38.0	12.5	26.3
Electric and electronic equipment	61.4	79.4	66.9	26.0	23.0	19.3	12.0	14.0	46.7	63.0	14.4	29.6
Transportation equipment	102.2	121.2	97.3	201.2	177.3	230.1	92.8	159.9	117.5	251.2	223.5	197.0
Scientific and measuring instruments	95.0	75.9	100.4	109.5	109.5	132.2	14.6	23.9	23.0	32.2	15.2	12.9
Miscellaneous manufactures	9.5	8.5	8.1	8.2	8.7	8.5	2.2	2.1	2.4	2.8	1.1	1.1
Unidentified manufactures	1.0	4.8	0.8	0.6	1.0	1.1	0.3	0.6	0.6	0.6	0.8	0.8
Agricultural And Livestock Products	109.3	163.2	279.8	277.5	207.3	202.9	92.1	137.4	273.1	109.8	107.4	66.5
Agricultural products	108.4	162.3	279.4	277.0	207.0	202.2	91.7	136.5	273.1	109.8	106.6	65.8
Livestock and livestock products	0.9	0.9	0.4	0.5	0.3	0.8	0.4	0.9	...	...	0.7	0.7
Other Commodities	168.9	180.6	100.4	57.0	44.4	47.9	123.5	132.7	116.8	86.8	59.3	59.5
Forestry products	...	...	0.1	...	...	...	...	...	0.3	0.6	0.1	0.3
Fish and other marine products	0.1	0.1	...	...	...	...	...	...	...	...	...	...
Metallic ores and concentrates	3.7	2.5	...	...	3.8	...	...	...	...	...	...	...
Bituminous coal and lignite	108.0	127.2	55.6	16.1	4.8	4.2	70.9	66.1	62.3	65.9	54.4	55.7
Crude petroleum and natural gas	0.1	...	3.1	0.1	...	...	...	0.6	...	...	...	...
Nonmetallic minerals	6.1	7.0	12.1	15.1	17.5	20.4	0.5	1.0	0.5	0.4	0.2	0.3
Scrap and waste	45.6	40.4	26.8	21.4	13.5	17.2	52.0	64.6	53.1	19.6	4.4	0.8
Used merchandise	3.7	0.6	0.5	1.7	1.0	0.2	...	...	...	...	0.1	...
Goods imported and returned unchanged	...	...	...	...	...	...	...	...	...	...	...	...
Special classification provisions	1.6	2.8	2.3	2.5	3.7	5.9	0.1	0.3	0.6	0.3	...	2.4

Industry	Taiwan						Singapore					
	1994	1995	1996	1997	1998	1999	1994	1995	1996	1997	1998	1999
ALL GOODS	333.6	429.2	331.2	364.4	418.8	308.9	349.9	357.3	287.3	270.2	282.9	243.5
Manufactured Goods	271.4	379.4	281.9	283.0	366.3	231.9	347.4	355.6	285.1	263.0	274.4	227.2
Food products	1.8	1.5	1.7	2.7	0.4	1.3	0.7	0.5	0.7	0.9	0.4	0.8
Tobacco products	...	...	...	...	...	...	...	...	...	0.3	...	0.1
Textile mill products	0.3	0.3	0.3	0.6	0.2	0.2	0.7	1.0	0.3	0.6	0.1	0.2
Apparel	0.2	0.4	0.3	0.7	1.1	0.8	0.1	0.1	0.1	0.4	...	0.1
Lumber and wood products	1.9	1.0	0.3	0.4	0.1	0.3	0.1	0.1	...	...	...	...
Furniture and fixtures	...	1.1	1.4	2.7	0.8	1.8	0.4	0.1	1.8	3.5	1.1	3.6
Paper products	18.4	28.3	26.2	18.2	11.1	4.2	3.0	3.9	5.3	7.0	4.6	3.6
Printing and publishing	3.3	1.4	0.8	0.8	0.6	...	3.6	1.5	1.0	0.6	0.3	0.2
Chemical products	136.4	187.6	155.1	150.4	117.5	59.8	44.5	64.8	71.4	45.7	33.9	22.5
Refined petroleum products	4.3	1.2	1.3	1.2	0.8	5.6	22.1	28.4	4.7	1.5	6.0	23.0
Rubber and plastic products	2.9	4.5	3.6	2.6	2.2	3.1	2.8	2.5	3.2	5.2	2.8	1.6
Leather products	...	...	...	...	...	...	0.1	...	...	...	...	...
Stone, clay and glass products	0.3	0.3	1.1	0.3	0.2	0.7	0.1	0.2	0.3	0.4	0.2	0.7
Primary metals	13.2	42.7	3.1	3.3	5.8	20.8	3.1	2.1	1.3	9.2	1.4	1.8
Fabricated metal products	3.7	2.8	1.7	2.4	12.3	12.0	7.5	6.5	6.7	8.3	6.3	4.6
Industrial machinery and computers	13.2	16.6	10.2	11.7	46.6	14.1	22.6	22.9	24.1	20.4	16.3	22.8
Electric and electronic equipment	7.4	12.5	16.0	14.9	17.5	30.3	25.5	36.5	47.6	19.8	9.4	10.9
Transportation equipment	53.4	62.8	44.2	58.5	137.1	58.1	198.9	164.1	105.1	117.7	165.3	107.5
Scientific and measuring instruments	9.5	10.4	12.2	10.5	11.0	16.6	10.1	19.2	10.2	20.3	24.8	22.2
Miscellaneous manufactures	0.6	3.4	2.0	0.6	0.5	1.1	0.9	1.0	0.8	1.0	1.0	0.5
Unidentified manufactures	0.7	0.5	0.3	0.4	0.5	1.2	0.6	0.4	0.3	0.3	0.5	0.6
Agricultural And Livestock Products	58.8	42.6	30.2	56.6	46.4	74.1	...	0.1	0.1	0.1	...	...
Agricultural products	58.2	42.0	30.0	56.2	46.0	73.4	...	...	...	...	...	...
Livestock and livestock products	0.6	0.5	0.2	0.4	0.4	0.7	...	...	0.1	0.1	...	...
Other Commodities	3.4	7.2	19.1	24.8	6.2	2.9	2.5	1.6	2.1	7.1	8.4	16.4
Forestry products	...	...	...	...	...	...	0.1	...	...	...	...	0.1
Fish and other marine products	...	...	...	...	...	...	...	...	...	...	...	...
Metallic ores and concentrates	...	...	...	...	...	...	...	...	...	...	...	...
Bituminous coal and lignite	0.9	...	0.8	9.1	2.2	...	...	...	...	...	...	...
Crude petroleum and natural gas	...	...	...	...	...	...	...	...	...	0.1	...	...
Nonmetallic minerals	1.1	1.1	1.4	0.3	0.5	0.1	0.3	0.7	1.6	0.4	0.4	0.1
Scrap and waste	0.9	1.9	13.3	13.0	2.8	2.0	0.1	0.3	0.2	...	...	0.1
Used merchandise	...	0.5	0.2	...	...	...	0.1	...	0.1	...	...	...
Goods imported and returned unchanged	...	...	...	...	...	...	...	...	...	...	...	...
Special classification provisions	0.5	3.7	3.4	2.2	0.7	0.7	1.8	0.7	0.2	6.6	8.0	16.1

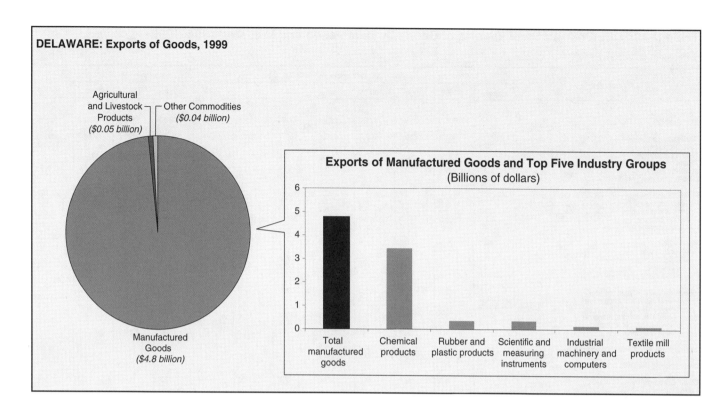

DELAWARE: Exports of Goods, 1999

Agricultural and Livestock Products ($0.05 billion)

Other Commodities ($0.04 billion)

Manufactured Goods ($4.8 billion)

Exports of Manufactured Goods and Top Five Industry Groups
(Billions of dollars)

Total manufactured goods / Chemical products / Rubber and plastic products / Scientific and measuring instruments / Industrial machinery and computers / Textile mill products

Table D-10. DELAWARE: State Exports of Goods by Destination and Industry, 1994–1999

(Millions of dollars.)

Industry	All destinations						Canada					
	1994	1995	1996	1997	1998	1999	1994	1995	1996	1997	1998	1999
ALL GOODS	3 758.1	4 396.8	4 584.5	5 103.9	4 968.6	4 856.8	692.5	717.5	739.7	788.3	937.9	989.5
Manufactured Goods	3 666.9	4 282.6	4 474.2	5 004.4	4 884.2	4 771.0	640.2	652.2	681.2	741.2	899.1	949.4
Food products	21.0	24.4	37.0	46.7	60.8	56.4	13.1	11.6	8.2	21.5	44.8	40.6
Tobacco products	...	...	...	...	...	...	...	...	...	...	...	...
Textile mill products	125.9	133.5	128.7	175.4	128.7	111.1	1.3	1.5	1.2	5.4	14.4	15.3
Apparel	10.2	8.4	3.4	4.5	8.6	7.6	6.1	4.7	0.5	0.7	3.9	5.8
Lumber and wood products	1.1	1.8	1.5	1.7	1.6	1.9	0.2	0.3	0.3	0.2	0.2	...
Furniture and fixtures	3.2	2.0	2.4	3.7	2.2	3.7	2.8	1.7	1.5	2.1	1.7	3.1
Paper products	34.8	45.7	53.7	60.4	61.3	55.6	1.1	2.2	6.9	7.3	7.3	3.6
Printing and publishing	2.0	1.9	2.3	2.3	3.6	11.1	0.6	0.6	0.8	0.7	0.7	1.2
Chemical products	2 614.1	3 124.5	3 251.7	3 649.6	3 471.1	3 446.5	455.9	488.8	504.5	539.0	672.5	709.1
Refined petroleum products	1.8	1.3	2.2	1.7	3.1	9.4	1.0	0.8	0.3	0.4	0.6	7.4
Rubber and plastic products	305.3	359.6	378.9	454.5	390.5	363.3	65.1	65.6	74.7	72.1	76.8	75.5
Leather products	0.9	0.5	0.4	0.8	0.3	0.3	0.5	0.2	0.2	0.2	0.1	0.1
Stone, clay and glass products	32.2	56.8	48.3	56.1	47.4	19.4	0.9	1.0	1.0	0.8	1.7	1.3
Primary metals	28.2	36.1	43.6	29.5	23.3	23.4	23.1	6.6	3.5	20.6	17.7	11.7
Fabricated metal products	34.8	31.5	25.0	14.5	11.4	13.6	10.6	9.0	6.5	2.4	3.6	2.8
Industrial machinery and computers	71.1	71.5	76.1	96.6	127.8	143.8	10.1	11.4	11.2	14.3	13.2	20.5
Electric and electronic equipment	33.6	37.4	33.8	26.2	19.0	29.2	9.6	13.3	14.6	10.0	5.9	13.4
Transportation equipment	58.7	42.0	77.9	89.8	144.2	89.7	13.4	5.8	5.8	3.4	6.4	11.3
Scientific and measuring instruments	273.5	291.1	288.4	269.9	358.0	357.0	23.0	26.1	37.7	39.1	25.9	25.3
Miscellaneous manufactures	11.8	11.0	16.3	18.9	17.9	25.5	0.7	0.2	0.5	0.2	0.6	0.7
Unidentified manufactures	2.7	1.5	2.6	1.6	3.5	2.6	1.1	0.7	0.7	0.8	1.0	0.7
Agricultural And Livestock Products	57.7	68.3	58.5	49.6	45.8	46.5	44.6	50.9	44.5	32.5	25.9	26.7
Agricultural products	57.4	68.0	58.5	49.3	45.8	46.5	44.6	50.8	44.5	32.5	25.9	26.7
Livestock and livestock products	0.3	0.2	0.1	0.3	...	...	...	0.1	...	...	...	...
Other Commodities	33.5	45.9	51.8	49.9	38.5	39.3	7.7	14.4	14.0	14.6	12.9	13.4
Forestry products	0.1	0.1	...	0.1	...	...	...	...	...	0.1	...	...
Fish and other marine products	1.0	1.0	0.3	0.3	0.3	0.4	0.9	1.0	0.2	0.3	0.3	0.3
Metallic ores and concentrates	3.6	6.3	7.5	9.4	7.2	6.9	1.5	2.8	3.6	2.9	2.0	0.7
Bituminous coal and lignite	...	...	...	...	...	...	...	...	...	...	...	...
Crude petroleum and natural gas	...	...	0.3	0.6	...	...	...	...	...	...	...	...
Nonmetallic minerals	5.0	5.0	7.5	11.3	9.4	10.7	0.1	0.3	0.2	0.4	0.2	0.3
Scrap and waste	14.3	21.7	21.0	15.2	10.1	7.1	0.7	3.9	0.3	3.2	5.9	6.3
Used merchandise	0.4	0.3	0.8	1.0	0.6	1.5	0.2	0.1	...	...	0.1	0.7
Goods imported and returned unchanged	4.2	6.0	9.5	7.6	4.3	4.8	4.2	6.0	9.5	7.6	4.3	4.8
Special classification provisions	5.0	5.5	4.8	4.4	6.7	7.9	0.1	0.1	0.2	0.1	0.2	0.3

Table D-10. DELAWARE: State Exports of Goods by Destination and Industry, 1994–1999—*Continued*

(Millions of dollars.)

Industry	South and Central American and Caribbean						Mexico					
	1994	1995	1996	1997	1998	1999	1994	1995	1996	1997	1998	1999
ALL GOODS	414.8	505.9	516.0	611.5	498.9	433.4	212.6	183.1	286.1	308.2	290.2	257.1
Manufactured Goods	411.9	501.1	513.9	607.2	495.2	430.7	204.2	178.0	273.2	290.2	278.6	253.6
Food products	0.4	0.5	1.4	1.0	0.4	0.6	0.4	0.3	0.4	1.0	3.2	2.5
Tobacco products	...	...	...	...	...	...	...	...	...	...	...	...
Textile mill products	9.8	11.8	7.0	13.9	11.0	6.7	4.2	2.0	4.6	7.5	5.2	4.4
Apparel	0.1	1.0	0.8	0.3	0.1	0.1	0.6	0.7	0.4	1.3	2.0	0.7
Lumber and wood products	...	0.1	...	...	...	...	...	...	...	...	...	0.1
Furniture and fixtures	...	...	0.1	...	...	...	...	...	...	...	0.3	0.4
Paper products	1.3	2.0	2.3	3.3	1.6	1.5	0.6	1.5	1.5	1.3	0.2	0.3
Printing and publishing	0.1	0.1	0.2	0.7	0.3	0.1	0.1	...	...	...	...	...
Chemical products	321.0	403.5	418.8	480.5	398.7	350.6	158.3	139.8	185.0	230.4	220.5	201.6
Refined petroleum products	...	...	0.1	0.1	...	...	0.1	...	1.4	...	0.1	...
Rubber and plastic products	17.3	21.9	19.8	29.6	34.9	21.3	10.6	11.9	14.0	27.0	19.5	18.6
Leather products	...	...	...	0.1	...	0.1	0.2	...	...	...	...	...
Stone, clay and glass products	0.3	7.5	9.7	14.5	2.4	0.5	0.2	0.4	0.3	0.2	0.6	0.2
Primary metals	0.3	0.4	0.3	0.4	0.5	0.8	0.3	0.2	0.5	0.7	0.2	1.4
Fabricated metal products	0.6	1.3	1.3	1.1	0.2	1.1	1.5	0.3	1.0	0.7	0.5	1.1
Industrial machinery and computers	3.9	3.6	3.9	15.3	5.9	6.7	2.9	3.0	6.0	1.7	1.1	2.6
Electric and electronic equipment	0.7	1.3	1.6	4.1	1.5	1.7	2.6	0.2	0.8	0.4	0.2	0.5
Transportation equipment	26.5	13.2	6.1	10.7	5.0	4.1	0.6	0.1	41.2	0.2	11.2	5.9
Scientific and measuring instruments	26.5	29.0	33.2	26.2	27.8	25.2	14.2	11.3	9.1	5.5	2.3	1.6
Miscellaneous manufactures	2.8	3.7	7.2	5.5	4.7	9.2	6.7	6.2	6.9	12.1	11.1	11.5
Unidentified manufactures	0.3	0.1	0.2	0.1	0.1	0.2	0.2	0.1	0.1	0.1	0.3	0.5
Agricultural And Livestock Products	...	0.3	...	0.2	0.3	...	2.9	1.1	...	...	0.6	...
Agricultural products	...	0.3	...	0.2	0.3	...	2.9	1.1	...	...	0.6	...
Livestock and livestock products	...	...	...	...	...	...	...	...	...	...	...	...
Other Commodities	2.9	4.6	2.1	4.1	3.4	2.7	5.5	4.1	12.9	18.0	11.0	3.5
Forestry products	...	...	...	...	...	...	...	...	...	...	...	...
Fish and other marine products	...	...	...	...	...	...	...	...	...	...	...	...
Metallic ores and concentrates	0.1	0.9	0.4	1.7	0.5	0.1	0.4	0.4	0.4	1.2	1.7	1.9
Bituminous coal and lignite	...	...	...	...	...	...	...	...	...	0.2	...	...
Crude petroleum and natural gas	...	...	...	...	...	...	...	...	...	...	...	...
Nonmetallic minerals	0.3	0.4	...	0.3	0.7	...	2.2	1.6	2.2	2.9	1.5	0.3
Scrap and waste	0.5	0.3	...	...	...	...	...	0.1	8.1	11.6	3.9	...
Used merchandise	...	...	...	0.3	0.1	0.5	...	...	...	...	...	...
Goods imported and returned unchanged	...	...	...	...	...	...	...	...	...	...	...	...
Special classification provisions	2.0	3.0	1.7	1.9	2.1	2.0	2.9	2.0	2.2	2.1	3.9	1.2

Industry	European Union						United Kingdom					
	1994	1995	1996	1997	1998	1999	1994	1995	1996	1997	1998	1999
ALL GOODS	1 154.7	1 465.6	1 455.8	1 536.6	1 704.4	1 588.1	140.4	160.1	166.5	195.6	229.2	198.2
Manufactured Goods	1 142.6	1 439.7	1 429.8	1 515.3	1 680.1	1 559.6	139.6	159.6	165.9	193.0	227.6	196.7
Food products	0.7	0.5	0.3	0.7	1.7	1.7	0.1	...	...	...	0.1	0.2
Tobacco products	...	...	...	...	...	...	...	...	...	...	...	...
Textile mill products	67.6	71.2	61.8	78.6	62.2	43.8	0.7	0.9	0.9	3.7	3.1	0.3
Apparel	2.4	1.0	0.6	0.5	0.9	0.1	1.2	0.5	0.4	0.1	0.1	...
Lumber and wood products	0.9	1.3	1.0	1.1	0.9	1.6	0.1	0.2	0.2	0.1	0.1	0.3
Furniture and fixtures	0.1	0.1	0.4	0.1	0.1	0.2	...	...	...	...	...	...
Paper products	8.5	14.2	12.1	17.1	18.0	16.5	0.6	2.0	1.4	1.8	1.0	0.8
Printing and publishing	0.4	0.6	0.3	0.2	1.6	8.3	...	0.2	...	...	0.2	0.7
Chemical products	742.2	975.5	1 013.4	1 076.7	1 162.4	1 068.1	102.8	103.3	122.7	154.5	181.0	154.7
Refined petroleum products	0.2	0.2	0.1	0.5	1.0	0.3	...	...	...	0.2	0.1	...
Rubber and plastic products	108.9	144.2	132.9	154.3	152.2	135.3	16.4	21.6	17.5	14.2	16.2	17.3
Leather products	0.1	0.1	0.1	...	0.1	0.1	...	...	...	...	...	...
Stone, clay and glass products	29.3	45.2	32.2	38.8	41.0	14.6	0.5	0.5	0.2	0.4	0.7	0.3
Primary metals	2.7	2.4	2.0	3.5	2.9	6.8	1.4	2.0	1.0	1.7	0.7	4.2
Fabricated metal products	13.3	12.7	7.3	2.2	2.4	2.6	1.3	2.8	1.5	0.8	0.2	0.3
Industrial machinery and computers	28.3	22.6	25.8	26.0	44.0	35.1	3.2	7.8	8.6	7.5	13.7	5.1
Electric and electronic equipment	12.2	10.7	7.3	3.5	3.4	7.6	3.1	3.6	2.3	1.5	1.1	0.9
Transportation equipment	3.5	3.1	3.2	10.9	7.8	53.3	1.1	1.2	0.4	2.7	1.6	1.0
Scientific and measuring instruments	119.5	133.2	126.8	100.0	175.0	160.8	6.9	12.8	7.7	3.5	6.8	9.5
Miscellaneous manufactures	1.2	0.7	0.8	0.3	1.1	2.4	...	0.2	...	0.1	0.6	0.8
Unidentified manufactures	0.6	0.3	1.3	0.2	1.5	0.5	0.2	0.1	1.1	0.1	0.3	0.2
Agricultural And Livestock Products	0.3	11.3	13.7	16.4	19.0	19.8	...	...	...	...	...	...
Agricultural products	...	11.2	13.7	16.4	19.0	19.8	...	...	...	...	...	...
Livestock and livestock products	0.3	0.2	...	...	...	...	...	...	...	...	...	...
Other Commodities	11.8	14.6	12.3	4.9	5.3	8.7	0.8	0.5	0.6	2.6	1.6	1.5
Forestry products	...	...	...	...	...	...	...	...	...	...	...	...
Fish and other marine products	...	...	...	...	...	...	...	...	...	...	...	...
Metallic ores and concentrates	1.3	2.1	2.9	3.2	2.6	3.8	...	0.2	0.1	2.2	0.8	0.6
Bituminous coal and lignite	...	...	...	...	...	...	...	...	...	...	...	...
Crude petroleum and natural gas	...	...	0.3	0.4	...	...	...	...	...	...	...	...
Nonmetallic minerals	1.0	0.9	1.1	0.5	2.2	2.4	0.6	0.3	0.4	0.2	0.6	0.7
Scrap and waste	9.3	11.5	7.7	...	...	...	...	...	...	...	...	...
Used merchandise	0.2	...	0.1	0.6	0.2	0.1	0.2	...	...	0.1	0.1	0.1
Goods imported and returned unchanged	...	...	...	...	...	...	...	...	...	...	...	...
Special classification provisions	0.1	0.2	0.1	0.2	0.3	2.3	...	...	...	...	...	0.1

Table D-10. DELAWARE: State Exports of Goods by Destination and Industry, 1994–1999—*Continued*

(Millions of dollars.)

Industry	Germany						France					
	1994	1995	1996	1997	1998	1999	1994	1995	1996	1997	1998	1999
ALL GOODS	170.0	156.9	178.3	166.2	220.2	185.3	99.7	112.6	89.9	99.9	105.3	119.3
Manufactured Goods	160.6	143.8	168.1	165.7	219.6	184.0	99.4	112.4	89.9	99.7	105.1	119.1
Food products	...	...	...	0.2	0.1	0.3	...	0.1	0.1	0.2	0.2	0.2
Tobacco products	...	...	...	...	...	...	...	...	...	...	...	...
Textile mill products	5.6	5.0	2.4	2.2	1.6	1.2	1.6	1.9	3.0	3.0	0.7	0.8
Apparel	0.9	0.3	...	0.3	0.6	...	...	...	...	0.1	0.1	...
Lumber and wood products	0.3	0.3	0.2	0.2	...	0.2	...	...	...	...	...	0.1
Furniture and fixtures	...	...	...	...	...	...	...	...	...	...	...	...
Paper products	0.6	0.9	1.4	1.8	3.6	4.6	0.2	0.3	0.7	0.2	0.5	0.8
Printing and publishing	0.2	0.1	...	...	0.2	0.1	...	...	...	...	0.1	0.1
Chemical products	36.1	30.5	35.7	62.3	82.1	71.4	50.6	50.3	43.4	46.2	52.9	43.1
Refined petroleum products	0.1	0.1	0.1	0.1	0.1	0.1	...	...	...	...	...	...
Rubber and plastic products	17.4	18.0	24.4	49.1	47.9	28.4	2.9	3.4	2.4	2.6	2.6	1.8
Leather products	...	...	...	...	...	...	...	...	...	...	...	...
Stone, clay and glass products	0.1	...	0.4	0.3	2.1	1.9	26.5	42.9	30.0	37.4	37.9	11.7
Primary metals	0.2	0.1	0.1	0.2	0.5	1.3	...	...	0.6	1.0	1.2	0.6
Fabricated metal products	1.9	2.0	1.9	0.6	1.2	1.3	5.3	4.7	1.2	0.1	0.1	0.2
Industrial machinery and computers	3.3	3.1	1.1	1.4	10.9	7.8	5.6	3.0	3.9	6.5	5.5	4.4
Electric and electronic equipment	1.9	1.2	1.5	0.5	0.8	0.6	2.8	2.2	0.9	0.3	0.3	0.3
Transportation equipment	1.6	0.5	0.8	0.4	0.4	1.4	0.1	0.2	1.8	0.1	...	50.0
Scientific and measuring instruments	90.1	81.4	97.5	46.0	66.5	63.3	3.5	3.2	1.7	2.1	3.0	4.9
Miscellaneous manufactures	0.3	0.4	0.7	...	0.1	...	...	...	...	...	...	...
Unidentified manufactures	...	...	...	0.1	1.0	0.1	0.1	...	...	...	...	...
Agricultural And Livestock Products	...	0.1	...	...	...	...	0.3	0.1	...	...	...	...
Agricultural products	...	...	...	...	...	...	...	...	...	...	...	...
Livestock and livestock products	...	...	...	...	...	...	0.3	0.1	...	...	...	...
Other Commodities	9.4	13.0	10.2	0.5	0.6	1.3	...	...	...	0.1	0.2	0.2
Forestry products	...	...	...	...	...	...	...	...	...	...	...	...
Fish and other marine products	...	...	...	...	...	...	...	...	...	...	...	...
Metallic ores and concentrates	0.5	1.7	2.6	...	0.3	1.0	...	...	...	...	...	...
Bituminous coal and lignite	...	...	...	...	...	...	...	...	...	...	...	...
Crude petroleum and natural gas	...	...	...	...	...	...	...	...	...	...	...	...
Nonmetallic minerals	0.1	...	...	...	0.2	0.1	...	...	...	0.1	0.2	0.2
Scrap and waste	8.8	11.3	7.6	...	...	...	...	...	...	...	...	...
Used merchandise	...	...	...	0.5	0.1	...	...	...	...	...	...	...
Goods imported and returned unchanged	...	...	...	...	...	...	...	...	...	...	...	...
Special classification provisions	...	...	...	...	0.2	0.3	...	...	...	...	...	...

Industry	The Netherlands						Asian 10					
	1994	1995	1996	1997	1998	1999	1994	1995	1996	1997	1998	1999
ALL GOODS	165.0	200.9	210.7	269.9	270.9	253.7	1 004.5	1 173.7	1 263.7	1 514.1	1 198.6	1 274.6
Manufactured Goods	164.8	200.9	210.7	269.3	270.2	251.0	999.1	1 165.8	1 253.6	1 505.9	1 193.2	1 264.3
Food products	0.1	0.1	0.1	...	0.1	0.2	5.1	6.6	9.6	6.5	5.1	6.6
Tobacco products	...	...	...	...	...	...	...	...	...	...	...	...
Textile mill products	0.2	0.2	0.3	0.2	0.1	0.1	39.3	43.0	50.0	64.7	32.3	31.4
Apparel	...	...	...	...	...	...	0.8	0.4	0.5	0.4	0.5	0.2
Lumber and wood products	0.2	0.2	0.1	...	0.1	0.4	...	0.1	0.1	0.3	0.3	0.1
Furniture and fixtures	0.1	...	...	...	...	...	0.2	...	0.1	0.1	0.1	...
Paper products	0.4	0.8	0.9	1.0	0.6	0.7	22.0	25.0	30.4	30.9	33.6	33.1
Printing and publishing	...	...	...	...	0.6	6.9	0.1	0.1	0.2	0.2	0.3	0.8
Chemical products	127.2	148.8	174.4	225.2	231.3	199.8	764.4	887.0	935.7	1 116.1	805.6	925.4
Refined petroleum products	0.1	...	...	0.1	...	...	0.4	0.3	0.3	0.3	1.2	1.5
Rubber and plastic products	25.8	45.0	29.3	40.0	31.3	32.1	77.1	83.3	105.8	130.3	74.2	80.0
Leather products	...	...	...	...	...	...	...	0.1	0.1	0.3	...	...
Stone, clay and glass products	0.7	...	...	...	0.1	0.4	1.1	1.3	1.1	0.6	0.9	2.4
Primary metals	...	0.1	...	...	...	0.1	1.7	26.2	35.1	3.6	1.8	2.1
Fabricated metal products	2.5	0.2	0.4	0.5	0.7	0.4	6.3	4.1	5.8	6.8	4.2	5.8
Industrial machinery and computers	5.0	3.0	3.8	1.0	1.7	1.5	14.3	14.2	11.7	20.2	49.3	54.6
Electric and electronic equipment	0.3	0.1	0.3	0.3	0.1	4.0	5.9	6.7	5.5	4.9	3.2	4.3
Transportation equipment	0.2	0.5	0.1	...	0.4	...	0.3	0.2	0.3	46.8	85.2	0.5
Scientific and measuring instruments	1.9	2.0	1.2	1.1	2.8	4.2	59.7	67.0	60.4	72.1	95.0	115.0
Miscellaneous manufactures	0.1	...	...	...	...	0.2	0.2	0.1	0.8	0.7	0.1	0.3
Unidentified manufactures	...	...	...	...	...	...	0.2	0.1	0.2	0.2	0.2	0.3
Agricultural And Livestock Products	...	...	...	...	...	...	...	...	...	0.5	...	...
Agricultural products	...	...	...	...	...	...	...	...	...	0.2	...	...
Livestock and livestock products	...	...	...	...	...	...	...	...	...	0.3	...	...
Other Commodities	0.2	...	...	0.6	0.8	2.8	5.5	7.9	10.2	7.7	5.5	10.2
Forestry products	...	...	...	...	...	...	...	...	...	...	...	...
Fish and other marine products	...	...	...	...	...	...	...	...	...	...	...	0.1
Metallic ores and concentrates	0.2	...	...	0.6	...	1.1	0.2	0.1	0.3	0.3	0.3	0.3
Bituminous coal and lignite	...	...	...	...	...	...	...	...	...	...	...	...
Crude petroleum and natural gas	...	...	...	...	...	...	...	...	...	...	...	...
Nonmetallic minerals	...	...	...	...	0.8	...	1.4	1.9	3.9	7.2	4.8	7.5
Scrap and waste	...	...	...	...	...	...	3.8	5.9	4.8	0.2	0.2	0.7
Used merchandise	...	...	...	...	...	...	...	...	0.5	...	...	...
Goods imported and returned unchanged	...	...	...	...	...	...	...	...	...	...	...	...
Special classification provisions	...	...	...	...	...	1.7	...	0.1	0.6	...	0.1	1.6

Table D-10. DELAWARE: State Exports of Goods by Destination and Industry, 1994–1999—*Continued*

(Millions of dollars.)

Industry	Japan						South Korea					
	1994	1995	1996	1997	1998	1999	1994	1995	1996	1997	1998	1999
ALL GOODS	370.2	433.0	441.5	556.0	531.5	444.0	155.9	172.5	208.0	190.2	114.8	174.4
Manufactured Goods	368.6	431.4	437.6	550.1	528.5	441.4	152.1	166.3	202.6	189.1	114.8	172.9
Food products	0.1	0.6	1.2	0.4	0.6	0.7	...	2.1	1.4	0.5	...	0.5
Tobacco products	...	...	...	...	...	...	...	...	...	...	...	...
Textile mill products	31.7	30.6	34.2	41.4	22.0	19.3	3.5	4.1	6.2	7.1	3.6	6.7
Apparel	0.3	0.1	0.2	0.4	0.4	0.1	0.1	...	...	...	...	...
Lumber and wood products	...	0.1	...	0.2	0.3	...	...	...	...	...	0.1	...
Furniture and fixtures	0.2	...	...	...	0.1	...	...	...	...	...	...	...
Paper products	13.2	10.4	14.2	11.1	11.3	10.1	0.1	0.6	1.3	1.6	0.8	1.4
Printing and publishing	...	...	...	...	0.1	0.3	...	...	...	...	...	...
Chemical products	265.7	323.2	322.7	348.9	304.2	302.9	118.9	121.4	124.7	137.6	90.5	131.4
Refined petroleum products	...	0.1	...	...	0.1	...	...	...	...	...	...	...
Rubber and plastic products	30.5	27.8	44.3	64.5	30.1	30.8	16.6	21.2	20.2	27.1	12.1	17.6
Leather products	...	...	...	...	...	...	...	...	...	...	...	...
Stone, clay and glass products	0.4	0.2	0.2	0.2	0.6	1.1	0.3	0.1	...	0.2	0.1	0.1
Primary metals	0.1	12.4	0.1	0.1	0.4	0.2	0.1	0.1	33.7	1.6	0.1	0.2
Fabricated metal products	4.2	2.8	2.9	2.1	3.1	4.4	0.2	0.2	0.5	0.5	...	...
Industrial machinery and computers	1.8	1.7	1.8	5.4	25.0	23.0	3.2	4.4	1.2	1.7	1.7	4.5
Electric and electronic equipment	1.8	1.9	0.8	2.1	1.6	1.2	0.7	2.0	1.9	0.5	0.2	0.2
Transportation equipment	...	...	0.1	45.6	83.6	0.1	...	...	...	...	...	0.1
Scientific and measuring instruments	18.6	19.2	14.7	27.5	44.9	46.8	7.8	10.2	11.3	10.3	5.4	10.0
Miscellaneous manufactures	0.1	0.1	0.1	0.1	0.1	0.2	0.1	...	0.3	0.4	...	0.1
Unidentified manufactures	...	...	0.1	0.1	0.1	0.1	0.1	...	...	...	0.1	0.1
Agricultural And Livestock Products	...	...	...	...	...	...	...	...	...	...	...	...
Agricultural products	...	...	...	...	...	...	...	...	...	...	...	...
Livestock and livestock products	...	...	...	...	...	...	...	...	...	...	...	...
Other Commodities	1.6	1.6	3.9	5.9	3.0	2.6	3.8	6.2	5.5	1.1	0.1	1.5
Forestry products	...	...	...	...	...	0.1	...	...	...	...	...	...
Fish and other marine products	...	...	...	...	...	...	...	...	...	...	...	...
Metallic ores and concentrates	0.2	0.1	0.1	0.3	0.3	0.3	...	...	0.2	...	...	...
Bituminous coal and lignite	...	...	...	...	...	...	...	...	...	...	...	...
Crude petroleum and natural gas	...	...	...	...	...	...	...	...	...	...	...	...
Nonmetallic minerals	1.3	1.5	3.3	5.6	2.7	1.4	...	0.4	0.5	1.1	0.1	1.4
Scrap and waste	...	...	...	...	...	0.2	3.8	5.8	4.7	...	...	...
Used merchandise	...	...	0.5	...	...	...	...	...	...	...	...	...
Goods imported and returned unchanged	...	...	...	...	...	0.7	...	...	...	...	...	...
Special classification provisions	...	0.1	...	...	...	...	...	...	...	...	...	...

Industry	Taiwan						Singapore					
	1994	1995	1996	1997	1998	1999	1994	1995	1996	1997	1998	1999
ALL GOODS	149.0	170.4	167.9	205.1	166.5	200.5	74.6	88.8	105.1	147.5	135.4	157.9
Manufactured Goods	148.9	170.3	167.2	204.9	166.2	199.3	74.6	88.7	105.0	147.0	133.4	154.2
Food products	...	...	0.1	0.3	0.2	0.5	...	...	0.2	...	...	...
Tobacco products	...	...	...	...	...	...	...	...	...	...	...	...
Textile mill products	1.0	2.4	1.9	3.5	0.7	0.4	0.6	1.7	3.2	3.4	0.2	0.1
Apparel	...	...	0.1	...	...	...	...	...	...	...	...	...
Lumber and wood products	...	...	0.1	...	...	...	...	...	...	...	...	...
Furniture and fixtures	...	...	...	0.1	...	...	...	...	...	...	...	...
Paper products	0.9	1.1	1.2	4.8	3.7	2.4	0.1	0.3	0.2	0.4	1.1	1.1
Printing and publishing	...	...	...	...	...	...	...	...	0.1	0.1	0.1	0.3
Chemical products	121.5	122.7	137.4	165.4	124.8	145.4	58.5	71.3	86.1	125.4	107.1	126.9
Refined petroleum products	0.1	...	0.2	0.1	0.9	1.4	0.2	0.2	0.1	0.1	0.1	...
Rubber and plastic products	5.6	8.2	8.6	11.0	10.4	9.2	6.2	7.5	7.9	9.0	5.7	9.1
Leather products	...	...	...	...	...	...	...	...	...	...	...	...
Stone, clay and glass products	0.1	0.2	0.3	0.2	0.2	0.8	0.1	0.1	0.1	0.1	...	0.1
Primary metals	0.4	13.4	1.0	1.6	1.1	1.1	0.9	0.3	0.2	0.1	0.1	0.1
Fabricated metal products	0.4	0.2	0.3	1.6	0.4	0.7	0.4	0.4	1.4	2.2	0.5	0.4
Industrial machinery and computers	2.6	2.5	1.7	2.8	5.9	12.5	2.3	3.5	2.2	2.7	12.1	10.0
Electric and electronic equipment	0.8	0.7	0.3	0.4	0.1	1.9	1.0	0.5	0.2	0.3	0.3	0.5
Transportation equipment	0.1	...	0.1	0.1	0.1	0.1	...	...	0.1	0.1	0.1	...
Scientific and measuring instruments	15.5	18.8	13.9	12.9	17.7	22.7	4.3	2.8	2.8	3.0	5.9	5.5
Miscellaneous manufactures	...	...	...	...	...	...	...	...	0.1	0.1	...	...
Unidentified manufactures	...	...	...	...	...	...	...	...	...	...	...	...
Agricultural And Livestock Products	...	...	...	0.1	...	...	...	...	...	...	...	...
Agricultural products	...	...	...	0.1	...	...	...	...	...	...	...	...
Livestock and livestock products	...	...	...	...	...	...	...	...	...	...	...	...
Other Commodities	...	...	0.7	0.1	0.2	1.3	...	...	0.1	0.5	2.1	3.7
Forestry products	...	...	...	...	...	...	...	...	...	...	...	...
Fish and other marine products	...	...	...	...	...	...	...	...	...	...	...	...
Metallic ores and concentrates	...	...	...	...	...	...	...	...	...	...	...	...
Bituminous coal and lignite	...	...	...	...	...	...	...	...	...	...	...	...
Crude petroleum and natural gas	...	...	...	...	...	...	...	...	...	...	...	...
Nonmetallic minerals	...	...	0.1	0.1	0.2	1.2	...	...	...	0.4	1.8	3.4
Scrap and waste	...	...	...	...	...	...	...	...	...	0.1	0.2	0.1
Used merchandise	...	...	...	...	...	...	...	...	...	...	...	...
Goods imported and returned unchanged	...	...	0.6	...	...	...	...	...	...	...	...	0.2
Special classification provisions	...	...	...	...	...	...	...	...	...	...	...	...

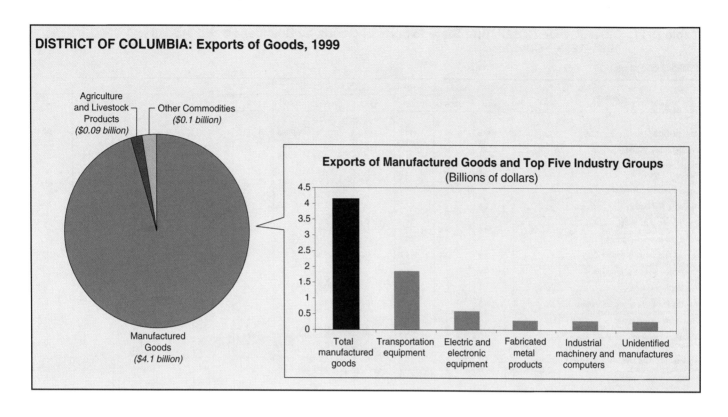

DISTRICT OF COLUMBIA: Exports of Goods, 1999

Agriculture and Livestock Products ($0.09 billion)

Other Commodities ($0.1 billion)

Manufactured Goods ($4.1 billion)

Exports of Manufactured Goods and Top Five Industry Groups (Billions of dollars)

Total manufactured goods / Transportation equipment / Electric and electronic equipment / Fabricated metal products / Industrial machinery and computers / Unidentified manufactures

Table D-11. DISTRICT OF COLUMBIA: State Exports of Goods by Destination and Industry, 1994–1999

(Millions of dollars.)

Industry	All destinations						Canada					
	1994	1995	1996	1997	1998	1999	1994	1995	1996	1997	1998	1999
ALL GOODS	5 150.7	5 323.5	5 084.8	4 881.0	4 392.4	4 344.5	120.9	81.8	102.1	142.1	157.8	113.5
Manufactured Goods	5 003.8	5 126.8	4 897.2	4 766.2	4 249.5	4 147.3	110.3	66.9	82.9	124.7	139.0	95.7
Food products	63.6	47.2	47.2	43.8	77.4	98.9	3.5	3.6	6.4	10.8	7.2	7.2
Tobacco products	...	...	...	...	...	...	...	...	...	...	...	...
Textile mill products	2.4	4.4	7.2	3.3	5.4	3.7	0.2	0.4	0.6	0.5	0.2	0.6
Apparel	7.9	11.5	15.6	14.7	21.2	11.7	...	0.2	0.1	0.2	0.5	0.3
Lumber and wood products	0.7	0.7	0.7	0.5	0.9	1.5	...	...	0.1	0.1	0.1	0.1
Furniture and fixtures	7.8	6.5	11.1	11.3	5.8	4.3	0.2	0.1	0.4	0.2	0.2	0.3
Paper products	9.8	7.8	2.0	4.5	8.0	9.4	9.1	5.7	0.3	2.2	5.7	7.7
Printing and publishing	12.2	10.6	9.5	15.8	24.2	36.9	1.0	0.7	0.9	4.4	6.1	6.7
Chemical products	192.9	299.0	213.6	166.5	142.2	120.3	20.8	7.4	3.5	5.3	2.8	4.2
Refined petroleum products	5.3	2.3	2.7	0.9	1.7	0.7	2.1	0.7	0.8	...	...	...
Rubber and plastic products	29.0	32.1	70.5	74.8	102.9	26.7	0.1	0.1	37.0	45.9	60.7	0.8
Leather products	0.1	0.5	0.3	0.4	0.7	0.4	...	0.1	...	...	0.1	0.2
Stone, clay and glass products	1.1	2.1	2.8	3.3	2.0	3.1	0.1	0.2	0.7	0.3	0.3	0.3
Primary metals	15.5	11.5	8.5	37.4	167.3	255.5	0.3	1.5	0.2	5.7	0.5	0.2
Fabricated metal products	693.0	901.6	344.2	386.5	518.8	308.3	1.7	0.5	0.5	1.3	0.8	1.7
Industrial machinery and computers	275.8	283.0	245.0	371.7	290.9	297.6	2.2	2.0	5.0	8.1	13.0	11.8
Electric and electronic equipment	250.7	337.6	216.8	336.2	491.2	597.3	2.3	4.2	8.2	13.1	17.1	17.0
Transportation equipment	2 766.4	2 520.4	3 283.7	2 549.3	1 857.6	1 857.1	60.3	34.3	12.3	17.3	16.5	28.4
Scientific and measuring instruments	162.1	180.4	80.7	420.4	213.5	207.2	5.9	4.7	5.5	8.7	5.7	6.5
Miscellaneous manufactures	3.8	11.2	3.4	5.8	18.1	22.2	0.1	0.1	0.2	0.2	0.4	0.4
Unidentified manufactures	503.6	456.4	331.7	319.1	299.9	284.2	0.3	0.4	0.4	0.5	1.1	1.4
Agricultural And Livestock Products	60.2	127.0	116.4	33.2	61.3	94.2	7.3	7.4	8.9	9.9	10.5	8.6
Agricultural products	60.0	125.5	115.1	32.7	60.8	94.1	7.3	7.4	8.9	9.9	10.5	8.6
Livestock and livestock products	0.2	1.6	1.4	0.5	0.6	0.1	...	...	...	...	...	...
Other Commodities	86.7	69.7	71.2	81.5	81.5	103.0	3.4	7.5	10.2	7.5	8.3	9.2
Forestry products	...	...	...	0.1	...	...	...	...	...	...	...	...
Fish and other marine products	0.0	0.3	0.1	0.9	0.4	1.1	...	...	...	...	...	0.1
Metallic ores and concentrates	1.5	1.0	0.2	0.1	...	...	...	...	...	...	...	...
Bituminous coal and lignite	...	...	...	...	...	...	...	...	...	...	...	...
Crude petroleum and natural gas	0.2	...	...	...	0.1	...	0.1	...	...	...	...	...
Nonmetallic minerals	...	0.2	0.1	0.4	0.1	0.2	...	...	...	0.2	...	...
Scrap and waste	0.9	0.7	0.5	0.3	0.2	3.1	0.1	0.1	0.2	0.1	0.1	0.1
Used merchandise	58.0	45.5	36.1	30.8	42.3	50.0	...	0.3	0.1	0.3	...	0.1
Goods imported and returned unchanged	1.9	4.5	6.5	5.3	6.2	6.4	1.9	4.5	6.5	5.3	6.2	6.4
Special classification provisions	24.1	17.6	27.7	43.7	32.2	42.2	1.3	1.5	3.4	1.6	2.0	2.6

Table D-11. DISTRICT OF COLUMBIA: State Exports of Goods by Destination and Industry, 1994–1999—Continued

(Millions of dollars.)

Industry	South and Central America and Caribbean						Mexico					
	1994	1995	1996	1997	1998	1999	1994	1995	1996	1997	1998	1999
ALL GOODS	209.6	96.2	141.2	168.5	166.7	185.3	30.0	12.3	8.9	17.1	28.7	29.6
Manufactured Goods	205.2	92.4	135.5	164.0	156.7	131.2	28.6	11.2	4.7	16.8	28.5	28.7
Food products	4.4	4.7	1.9	2.5	9.9	7.5	19.3	7.7	0.3	8.7	18.1	17.4
Tobacco products	...	...	...	...	...	...	...	...	0.3	0.1	0.2	0.1
Textile mill products	0.5	0.1	1.4	0.5	1.1	0.9	...	...	...	...	0.2	0.1
Apparel	0.8	0.9	1.1	3.2	2.9	2.7	0.1	0.1	...	...	0.2	0.1
Lumber and wood products	...	0.1	0.1	...	...	0.1	...	...	...	...	...	...
Furniture and fixtures	2.6	4.9	7.7	7.5	3.3	0.8	...	...	0.1	...	0.1	...
Paper products	...	0.1	0.4	0.2	...	0.3	0.2	0.7	0.2	1.4	1.0	0.3
Printing and publishing	1.4	0.8	1.3	0.8	0.6	0.2	0.2	0.1	0.1	0.1	0.3	0.1
Chemical products	3.5	3.1	3.8	5.8	24.9	4.1	0.7	0.1	0.5	0.1	0.1	0.1
Refined petroleum products	...	0.1	0.9	...	...	...	...	...	...	...	...	...
Rubber and plastic products	3.3	5.2	4.6	5.2	5.6	1.7	0.9	...	...	0.1	0.2	0.1
Leather products	...	0.2	0.1	0.1	0.1	0.1	...	...	...	...	...	...
Stone, clay and glass products	0.2	0.1	0.5	0.2	0.4	0.9	...	...	...	...	...	...
Primary metals	2.9	...	0.1	0.2	0.1	3.2	0.1	...	0.1	0.2	0.2	...
Fabricated metal products	1.5	0.8	0.3	6.2	0.6	1.2	...	...	0.1	0.1	0.1	0.1
Industrial machinery and computers	8.6	8.2	16.1	10.5	12.6	25.9	1.4	0.5	1.0	1.6	2.2	2.3
Electric and electronic equipment	18.7	25.1	13.7	47.8	43.4	21.5	3.2	1.1	1.2	1.0	2.9	3.3
Transportation equipment	125.4	13.2	47.8	52.8	24.2	22.8	0.9	0.3	0.4	0.3	2.0	3.8
Scientific and measuring instruments	5.7	6.9	5.2	4.7	8.4	8.3	1.5	0.3	0.7	1.5	0.7	0.5
Miscellaneous manufactures	0.3	0.3	0.9	0.6	0.2	1.9	...	...	...	1.4	0.2	...
Unidentified manufactures	25.4	17.8	27.7	15.1	18.5	26.9	0.1	0.1	...	0.1	0.2	0.2
Agricultural And Livestock Products	1.9	2.5	0.3	0.1	6.6	50.4	0.9	0.4	0.3	...	0.1	...
Agricultural products	1.9	2.5	0.3	0.1	6.6	50.4	0.9	0.4	0.3	...	0.1	...
Livestock and livestock products	...	...	...	...	...	...	...	...	...	...	...	...
Other Commodities	2.5	1.3	5.4	4.4	3.4	3.7	0.5	0.7	3.9	0.3	0.1	0.9
Forestry products	...	...	...	...	...	...	...	...	...	...	...	...
Fish and other marine products	...	...	...	...	...	...	...	...	...	...	...	...
Metallic ores and concentrates	...	...	...	...	...	...	...	...	...	...	...	...
Bituminous coal and lignite	...	...	...	...	...	...	...	...	...	...	0.1	...
Crude petroleum and natural gas	...	...	...	...	...	...	...	...	...	...	...	...
Nonmetallic minerals	...	...	...	...	...	...	...	0.3	...	...	...	...
Scrap and waste	0.7	...	0.1	0.1	...	...	...	...	...	...	...	...
Used merchandise	0.4	0.2	1.0	2.4	1.2	1.0	0.2	...	3.7	0.1	...	0.5
Goods imported and returned unchanged	...	...	...	...	...	...	...	...	...	...	...	...
Special classification provisions	1.4	1.1	4.3	1.9	2.1	2.7	0.2	0.3	0.2	0.1	...	0.3

Industry	European Union						United Kingdom					
	1994	1995	1996	1997	1998	1999	1994	1995	1996	1997	1998	1999
ALL GOODS	937.8	1 288.2	929.3	1 177.8	1 148.6	1 302.3	513.6	390.5	546.3	500.1	579.5	575.0
Manufactured Goods	917.9	1 257.5	907.6	1 127.4	1 104.2	1 245.9	505.6	384.2	540.1	467.1	565.5	567.8
Food products	9.8	4.3	6.0	2.1	6.1	4.9	1.0	0.1	0.3	0.3	0.3	0.8
Tobacco products	...	...	...	...	...	...	...	...	...	...	...	...
Textile mill products	0.5	0.5	0.3	0.2	1.3	0.6	0.2	0.1	0.1	0.1	0.2	0.1
Apparel	2.9	2.8	4.3	1.8	2.2	2.3	1.9	1.6	1.8	1.3	1.4	0.9
Lumber and wood products	0.1	...	0.2	0.1	...	0.2	...	...	...	...	...	...
Furniture and fixtures	0.4	0.3	0.4	1.1	0.9	1.8	0.3	0.1	0.1	0.1	0.1	0.7
Paper products	0.1	0.4	0.4	0.2	0.4	0.4	...	0.1	...	0.1	0.1	0.1
Printing and publishing	5.1	2.3	1.7	3.5	4.7	5.3	1.6	0.9	1.1	1.0	3.1	4.3
Chemical products	20.6	50.0	26.4	27.9	11.7	8.2	13.6	8.5	15.8	16.0	5.0	4.8
Refined petroleum products	1.8	0.8	0.1	0.1	0.7	0.1	...	...	...	...	0.5	...
Rubber and plastic products	1.4	0.8	1.4	2.1	3.9	2.1	0.6	0.5	0.1	0.2	0.2	0.4
Leather products	...	...	...	0.2	0.5	0.1	...	...	...	0.1	...	...
Stone, clay and glass products	0.3	0.6	0.8	0.3	0.2	0.9	0.2	0.4	0.4	0.1	...	0.1
Primary metals	1.5	2.4	1.9	1.2	1.1	3.2	1.2	0.2	0.5	0.4	0.5	2.1
Fabricated metal products	151.3	223.5	85.1	117.5	119.0	70.1	19.8	56.2	65.9	31.3	68.8	26.2
Industrial machinery and computers	70.1	72.6	40.7	86.5	92.3	82.7	23.5	19.0	14.7	30.4	29.6	28.1
Electric and electronic equipment	57.1	87.8	54.8	78.6	65.3	85.1	18.2	45.3	20.5	24.7	18.2	27.4
Transportation equipment	534.7	766.2	621.0	742.5	732.9	851.9	388.4	232.9	376.4	329.6	422.1	421.1
Scientific and measuring instruments	27.2	28.9	34.1	27.9	42.8	82.6	16.4	16.3	19.0	9.9	12.4	44.1
Miscellaneous manufactures	0.8	1.7	0.8	1.6	6.1	7.7	0.2	0.4	0.2	0.2	0.5	0.8
Unidentified manufactures	32.1	11.6	27.1	32.1	12.1	35.9	18.6	1.6	23.3	21.2	2.3	5.8
Agricultural And Livestock Products	3.5	0.6	1.9	1.6	2.5	1.3	2.3	0.5	0.6	0.3	0.2	0.1
Agricultural products	3.5	0.6	1.4	1.6	2.5	1.3	2.3	0.5	0.6	0.3	0.2	0.1
Livestock and livestock products	...	...	0.5	...	...	...	...	...	...	...	...	...
Other Commodities	16.4	30.1	19.8	48.8	41.9	55.1	5.7	5.7	5.6	32.6	13.8	7.1
Forestry products	...	...	...	...	...	...	...	...	...	...	...	...
Fish and other marine products	...	...	...	0.8	0.3	0.8	...	...	...	...	...	...
Metallic ores and concentrates	1.5	...	0.2	...	...	...	1.5	...	...	...	...	...
Bituminous coal and lignite	...	...	...	...	...	...	...	...	...	...	...	...
Crude petroleum and natural gas	0.1	...	...	...	...	...	...	...	...	...	...	...
Nonmetallic minerals	...	...	...	...	...	...	...	...	...	...	...	...
Scrap and waste	...	0.1	...	0.1	...	0.5	...	...	...	...	...	...
Used merchandise	12.7	27.9	18.0	21.8	30.7	38.4	3.5	4.5	4.5	7.2	5.3	5.6
Goods imported and returned unchanged	...	...	...	...	...	...	...	...	...	...	...	...
Special classification provisions	2.1	2.2	1.6	26.2	10.9	15.3	0.6	1.3	1.1	25.4	8.5	1.5

Table D-11. DISTRICT OF COLUMBIA: State Exports of Goods by Destination and Industry, 1994–1999—*Continued*

(Millions of dollars.)

Industry	Germany						France					
	1994	1995	1996	1997	1998	1999	1994	1995	1996	1997	1998	1999
ALL GOODS	130.9	98.6	96.8	187.2	71.9	103.6	44.7	89.8	43.5	46.9	105.8	264.4
Manufactured Goods	125.5	90.1	92.1	181.5	67.6	95.5	44.0	87.8	38.0	44.0	94.6	257.7
Food products	1.4	0.4	...	...	...	0.4	...	0.1	0.5	0.4	...	0.1
Tobacco products	...	...	...	...	...	...	...	...	...	...	...	...
Textile mill products	...	0.3	0.2	...	0.8	0.5	0.1	...	...	...	...	...
Apparel	...	0.1	0.3	0.2	...	0.1	...	...	...	...	...	...
Lumber and wood products	...	...	...	...	...	0.1	...	...	...	...	...	...
Furniture and fixtures	0.1	0.1	0.3	0.6	0.3	0.2	...	...	...	...	...	...
Paper products	0.1	0.1	0.2	...	...	0.1	...	0.1	...	...	...	...
Printing and publishing	0.2	0.3	0.1	1.4	0.2	0.2	...	...	...	...	...	...
Chemical products	1.5	0.1	0.3	1.2	0.4	0.5	2.9	1.0	0.2	0.6	0.7	0.3
Refined petroleum products	...	...	...	...	...	...	0.2	8.9	0.4	1.2	1.1	0.3
Rubber and plastic products	...	...	0.1	...	0.1	...	...	...	...	0.2	0.2	0.1
Leather products	...	...	...	...	...	...	...	...	...	0.1	0.1	...
Stone, clay and glass products	...	0.1	...	...	...	...	...	...	...	0.1	0.1	0.2
Primary metals	0.1	0.3	0.3	0.3	0.4	0.5	0.1	...	...	0.1	...	0.1
Fabricated metal products	97.3	57.3	0.8	2.4	1.2	11.7	2.3	19.8	2.3	0.5	2.0	1.6
Industrial machinery and computers	6.0	4.5	4.7	18.0	26.7	21.7	3.7	2.8	5.2	4.9	5.4	6.7
Electric and electronic equipment	5.6	6.3	4.4	6.9	7.5	11.9	3.7	3.3	2.6	8.7	11.3	6.3
Transportation equipment	12.1	19.0	79.0	141.5	19.6	24.6	27.7	49.4	24.7	24.5	70.6	240.1
Scientific and measuring instruments	0.5	0.3	0.9	1.9	3.7	9.6	2.9	1.7	2.1	2.5	1.7	1.3
Miscellaneous manufactures	0.2	0.7	0.4	0.8	2.9	2.5	0.2	0.5	0.1	0.2	1.0	0.3
Unidentified manufactures	0.4	0.1	...	6.3	3.8	10.8	0.1	0.1	0.1	0.1	0.2	0.1
Agricultural And Livestock Products	1.0	...	...	...	...	...	...	...	...	...	...	...
Agricultural products	1.0	...	...	...	...	...	...	...	...	...	...	...
Livestock and livestock products	...	...	...	...	...	...	...	...	...	...	...	...
Other Commodities	4.4	8.5	4.7	5.6	4.2	8.2	0.7	2.0	5.5	2.9	11.2	6.7
Forestry products	...	...	...	...	...	...	...	...	...	...	...	...
Fish and other marine products	...	...	...	...	...	0.1	...	...	...	...	...	...
Metallic ores and concentrates	...	...	...	...	...	...	...	...	...	...	...	...
Bituminous coal and lignite	...	...	...	...	...	...	...	...	...	...	...	...
Crude petroleum and natural gas	...	...	...	...	...	...	...	...	...	...	...	...
Nonmetallic minerals	...	...	...	...	...	...	...	...	...	...	...	...
Scrap and waste	...	...	...	...	...	0.5	...	...	...	...	...	...
Used merchandise	4.3	8.1	4.5	5.4	3.4	6.1	0.5	1.9	5.4	2.9	11.1	6.5
Goods imported and returned unchanged	...	...	...	...	...	...	...	...	...	...	...	...
Special classification provisions	0.1	0.4	0.2	0.2	0.8	1.4	0.2	0.1	...	0.1	0.1	0.2

Industry	The Netherlands						Asian 10					
	1994	1995	1996	1997	1998	1999	1994	1995	1996	1997	1998	1999
ALL GOODS	14.6	22.8	18.7	11.3	19.7	20.2	1 037.1	1 144.6	873.0	1 194.8	920.5	1 128.7
Manufactured Goods	12.5	19.8	17.4	9.8	19.0	11.0	992.4	1 122.3	851.6	1 182.2	905.4	1 103.3
Food products	3.9	2.0	3.9	1.2	5.0	0.5	3.9	8.5	11.6	3.4	1.4	8.8
Tobacco products	...	...	...	...	...	...	...	...	...	...	...	...
Textile mill products	...	...	...	...	...	...	0.8	0.3	0.2	0.3	0.1	...
Apparel	...	...	0.1	...	0.1	...	0.8	1.7	1.5	2.3	0.7	0.1
Lumber and wood products	...	...	...	...	...	...	0.3	0.3	...	0.1	0.2	0.2
Furniture and fixtures	...	...	...	...	...	0.1	3.0	0.3	0.2	0.3	...	...
Paper products	...	...	...	...	...	...	0.1	0.3	0.5	0.1	0.2	0.2
Printing and publishing	0.1	...	...	0.1	...	...	1.4	1.6	1.8	2.1	1.8	1.4
Chemical products	4.4	14.8	0.1	0.1	0.7	...	121.8	211.6	100.4	90.0	77.3	74.5
Refined petroleum products	...	...	...	...	...	...	0.1	...	...	0.2	...	...
Rubber and plastic products	0.7	...	...	0.6	2.3	1.0	3.8	2.1	3.0	1.4	3.8	0.8
Leather products	...	...	...	...	...	...	...	0.1	0.2	0.1	...	...
Stone, clay and glass products	...	...	...	...	...	...	...	0.5	0.1	1.9	0.2	0.3
Primary metals	...	...	...	...	0.1	0.1	7.2	4.3	1.8	8.4	9.9	16.5
Fabricated metal products	...	0.1	...	...	0.6	...	187.2	185.6	56.2	35.0	92.7	58.7
Industrial machinery and computers	1.8	0.9	2.0	2.8	2.6	5.4	63.7	86.8	80.7	77.1	55.4	103.6
Electric and electronic equipment	0.9	1.2	1.6	2.2	4.7	1.4	56.9	81.1	49.1	93.4	242.0	377.6
Transportation equipment	0.3	0.6	9.4	2.2	0.5	0.4	416.5	405.8	420.3	721.3	358.0	402.6
Scientific and measuring instruments	0.2	0.1	0.2	0.3	0.3	0.1	11.8	14.5	14.3	108.8	35.4	37.4
Miscellaneous manufactures	0.1	...	...	0.1	0.6	0.7	1.5	0.3	0.4	0.5	9.6	8.9
Unidentified manufactures	0.2	...	...	0.3	1.5	1.2	111.4	116.9	109.4	35.5	16.5	11.7
Agricultural And Livestock Products	...	...	0.5	0.5	0.4	...	0.3	0.9	2.1	2.0	0.3	4.3
Agricultural products	...	...	...	0.5	0.4	...	0.2	0.7	1.8	2.0	0.3	4.3
Livestock and livestock products	...	...	0.5	...	...	...	0.1	0.2	0.3	0.1	...	...
Other Commodities	2.1	2.9	0.8	1.0	0.4	9.2	44.4	21.5	19.3	10.6	14.8	21.0
Forestry products	...	...	...	...	...	...	...	...	...	...	...	...
Fish and other marine products	...	...	...	...	...	...	...	0.2	0.1	0.1	...	...
Metallic ores and concentrates	...	...	...	...	...	...	...	...	...	0.1	...	...
Bituminous coal and lignite	...	...	...	...	...	...	...	...	...	...	...	...
Crude petroleum and natural gas	...	...	...	...	...	...	...	...	...	...	...	...
Nonmetallic minerals	...	...	...	...	...	...	...	...	...	...	...	...
Scrap and waste	...	...	...	...	...	...	...	0.1	0.1	0.1	0.1	...
Used merchandise	2.1	2.9	0.8	0.9	0.3	9.1	28.2	13.3	7.5	2.0	1.5	4.3
Goods imported and returned unchanged	...	...	...	...	...	...	...	0.1	0.3	...	0.1	0.1
Special classification provisions	...	...	0.1	0.1	...	0.1	16.1	7.7	11.3	8.3	13.1	16.6

Table D-11. DISTRICT OF COLUMBIA: State Exports of Goods by Destination and Industry, 1994–1999—Continued

(Millions of dollars.)

Industry	Japan 1994	1995	1996	1997	1998	1999	South Korea 1994	1995	1996	1997	1998	1999
ALL GOODS	127.9	213.9	86.7	116.4	294.0	465.4	39.9	19.2	34.8	37.1	17.0	19.4
Manufactured Goods	105.6	205.2	82.7	115.6	292.4	463.9	34.4	18.0	32.7	37.0	16.9	18.7
Food products	...	...	...	...	...	0.2	2.6	...	...	0.1	0.1	3.1
Tobacco products	...	...	...	...	...	...	...	...	...	...	...	...
Textile mill products	0.1	0.1	0.1	0.1	0.1	...	...	0.1	...	...	...	...
Apparel	0.3	1.3	0.9	1.3	0.3	0.2	...	...	...	...	0.1	...
Lumber and wood products	...	...	...	...	...	...	...	...	...	...	...	...
Furniture and fixtures	2.9	0.2	0.1	0.1	...	...	...	...	...	...	...	0.1
Paper products	...	...	0.2	...	0.2	...	0.2	0.2	0.4	0.3	0.3	0.4
Printing and publishing	0.5	0.6	0.8	0.8	0.9	0.5	0.2	0.2	0.4	0.3	0.3	0.2
Chemical products	93.8	195.9	68.3	80.2	69.4	61.3	23.3	12.0	27.3	6.8	0.2	0.2
Refined petroleum products	...	...	...	...	...	...	...	...	...	...	...	...
Rubber and plastic products	...	0.2	0.2	0.4	0.3	0.1	...	...	0.1	0.1	0.2	0.3
Leather products	...	0.1	0.1	0.1	...	...	...	...	...	0.1	...	...
Stone, clay and glass products	...	...	0.1	...	0.1	0.1	...	...	...	0.1	...	...
Primary metals	0.3	...	0.1	7.9	9.6	15.7	...	...	...	0.1	...	...
Fabricated metal products	...	0.1	0.2	0.2	0.2	0.5	0.1	...	...	0.1	...	0.1
Industrial machinery and computers	3.8	3.1	6.1	16.2	8.9	12.5	1.4	1.7	2.2	6.1	4.4	5.3
Electric and electronic equipment	1.4	1.9	2.2	4.6	195.7	355.7	6.5	2.1	1.9	21.5	4.7	2.2
Transportation equipment	0.5	1.1	1.9	0.8	2.1	12.1	0.2	1.5	0.3	0.3	0.6	0.3
Scientific and measuring instruments	0.5	0.4	1.0	2.7	1.5	2.4	0.1	0.3	0.2	1.1	0.7	0.7
Miscellaneous manufactures	1.4	0.2	0.1	0.1	3.1	2.5	...	...	...	0.2	5.6	6.0
Unidentified manufactures	0.1	0.1	0.3	0.1	0.1	0.2	0.1	...	0.1	0.1	0.1	...
Agricultural And Livestock Products	...	...	...	...	0.3	0.3	...	...	...	...	...	0.1
Agricultural products	...	...	...	...	0.3	...	...	...	...	...	...	0.1
Livestock and livestock products	...	...	...	...	...	...	...	...	...	...	...	...
Other Commodities	22.3	8.7	4.0	0.8	1.3	1.5	5.5	1.2	2.1	0.2	0.1	0.7
Forestry products	...	...	...	...	...	...	...	...	...	...	...	...
Fish and other marine products	...	...	...	...	...	...	...	...	...	...	...	...
Metallic ores and concentrates	...	...	...	0.1	...	...	...	...	...	...	...	...
Bituminous coal and lignite	...	...	...	...	...	...	...	...	...	...	...	...
Crude petroleum and natural gas	...	...	...	...	...	...	...	...	...	...	...	...
Nonmetallic minerals	...	...	...	...	...	...	...	...	0.1	0.1	...	...
Scrap and waste	...	...	...	...	...	...	...	...	...	...	...	0.4
Used merchandise	22.1	8.5	2.7	0.6	1.2	0.7	5.4	1.2	2.0	...	...	...
Goods imported and returned unchanged	...	...	1.2	...	...	...	...	...	0.1	...	...	0.3
Special classification provisions	0.1	0.1	...	...	0.2	0.7	...	...	...	...	...	...

Industry	Taiwan 1994	1995	1996	1997	1998	1999	Singapore 1994	1995	1996	1997	1998	1999
ALL GOODS	676.2	649.7	491.3	602.8	447.9	515.9	29.9	35.6	34.6	41.4	37.1	45.8
Manufactured Goods	660.9	645.3	485.1	600.3	447.1	513.4	29.8	35.0	34.0	41.3	25.8	33.5
Food products	...	...	...	...	...	...	0.2	0.3	0.6	0.3	0.1	...
Tobacco products	...	...	...	...	...	...	...	...	...	...	...	...
Textile mill products	...	0.1	...	0.1	...	...	...	...	...	0.1	0.4	...
Apparel	...	...	...	...	...	...	...	...	...	...	...	...
Lumber and wood products	...	...	...	...	...	...	...	...	...	...	...	...
Furniture and fixtures	...	...	0.1	...	...	...	...	...	...	...	...	...
Paper products	0.1	0.2	0.2	...	...	...	...	...	...	0.3	...	...
Printing and publishing	0.3	0.1	0.2	0.1	...	...	0.1	0.1	...	...	...	...
Chemical products	1.0	0.8	1.2	0.8	1.1	4.1	0.1	...	...	...	...	...
Refined petroleum products	0.1	...	...	0.2	...	...	...	...	...	...	...	...
Rubber and plastic products	0.8	1.1	0.2	0.1	...	...	...	...	...	...	0.6	0.1
Leather products	...	...	...	...	...	0.1	...	...	...	...	...	...
Stone, clay and glass products	...	...	...	...	...	...	...	...	...	...	...	...
Primary metals	6.9	4.1	0.9	...	...	...	0.1	...	...	...	...	...
Fabricated metal products	148.2	145.9	47.3	27.5	73.3	32.2	0.3	0.4	0.7	0.1	0.4	12.6
Industrial machinery and computers	50.9	69.2	64.1	45.6	35.3	79.3	1.8	0.4	1.3	1.2	0.9	0.5
Electric and electronic equipment	17.1	28.4	14.4	19.9	20.2	9.5	2.4	10.4	5.0	4.9	1.6	0.6
Transportation equipment	316.2	271.4	240.2	390.8	273.3	346.9	24.5	23.0	25.7	33.7	20.8	18.0
Scientific and measuring instruments	8.5	8.0	9.4	85.6	27.7	29.8	...	...	0.1	...	...	...
Miscellaneous manufactures	...	...	...	0.1	...	0.1	...	...	...	...	...	...
Unidentified manufactures	110.7	116.1	106.9	29.5	16.1	11.2	...	...	...	...	...	...
Agricultural And Livestock Products	...	...	...	...	...	...	...	...	...	...	...	...
Agricultural products	...	...	...	...	...	...	...	...	...	...	...	...
Livestock and livestock products	...	...	...	...	...	...	...	...	...	...	...	...
Other Commodities	15.3	4.4	6.2	2.5	0.8	2.5	0.2	0.7	0.6	...	11.3	12.3
Forestry products	...	...	...	...	...	...	...	...	...	...	...	...
Fish and other marine products	...	...	...	...	...	...	...	...	...	...	...	...
Metallic ores and concentrates	...	...	...	...	...	...	...	...	...	...	...	...
Bituminous coal and lignite	...	...	...	...	...	...	...	...	...	...	...	...
Crude petroleum and natural gas	...	...	...	...	...	...	...	...	...	...	...	...
Nonmetallic minerals	...	...	...	...	...	...	...	...	...	...	...	...
Scrap and waste	...	...	...	...	...	0.1	0.1	0.3	0.3	...	...	...
Used merchandise	0.4	0.3	0.9	...	...	...	0.1	0.3	0.3	...	...	...
Goods imported and returned unchanged	14.9	4.1	5.3	2.5	0.8	2.4	0.1	0.3	0.3	...	11.3	12.3
Special classification provisions												

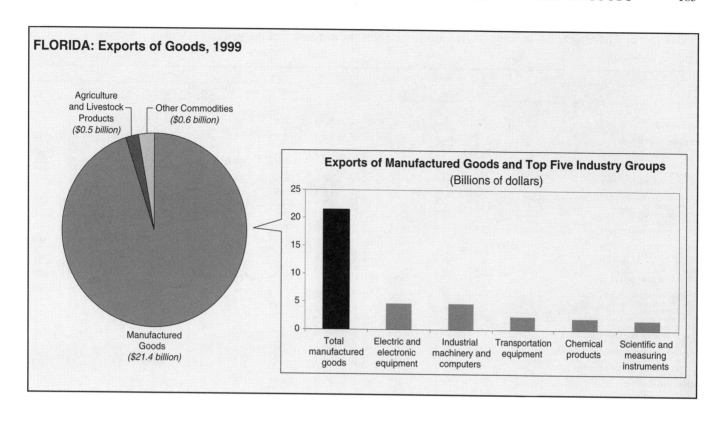

FLORIDA: Exports of Goods, 1999

Agriculture and Livestock Products ($0.5 billion)

Other Commodities ($0.6 billion)

Manufactured Goods ($21.4 billion)

Exports of Manufactured Goods and Top Five Industry Groups
(Billions of dollars)

Total manufactured goods · Electric and electronic equipment · Industrial machinery and computers · Transportation equipment · Chemical products · Scientific and measuring instruments

Table D-12. FLORIDA: State Exports of Goods by Destination and Industry, 1994–1999

(Millions of dollars.)

Industry	All destinations						Canada					
	1994	1995	1996	1997	1998	1999	1994	1995	1996	1997	1998	1999
ALL GOODS	16 559.2	18 564.4	19 618.2	22 888.6	23 172.6	22 544.2	1 504.8	1 608.2	1 631.6	1 928.4	2 057.7	2 094.9
Manufactured Goods	15 235.3	17 495.1	18 467.7	21 715.1	22 072.1	21 432.1	1 169.1	1 251.9	1 285.1	1 531.3	1 695.3	1 713.5
Food products	835.2	882.0	877.2	960.9	926.4	919.7	125.3	131.1	133.5	138.8	140.4	129.2
Tobacco products	9.6	18.9	23.9	28.0	19.7	22.3	0.2	0.3	0.5	0.7	1.1	1.6
Textile mill products	157.9	192.3	247.4	355.8	395.4	340.9	6.1	8.8	8.1	11.2	14.6	12.8
Apparel	541.5	558.8	582.3	713.6	674.7	595.0	6.3	11.1	12.0	15.8	17.2	24.0
Lumber and wood products	171.1	193.8	186.8	229.1	258.1	266.8	5.4	5.3	4.6	4.6	5.0	5.8
Furniture and fixtures	110.5	113.0	136.4	165.3	166.6	122.6	7.4	6.7	7.7	8.2	7.8	9.0
Paper products	381.6	589.3	522.1	544.6	537.2	620.1	16.2	20.1	15.1	24.5	19.6	28.2
Printing and publishing	191.7	206.3	171.5	194.4	215.1	157.9	100.7	100.6	79.6	87.2	72.4	34.0
Chemical products	1 706.0	2 007.9	1 890.4	2 239.3	2 223.4	2 110.5	92.9	130.7	129.2	151.1	160.3	149.5
Refined petroleum products	121.8	99.5	121.3	130.4	93.8	79.5	3.5	0.9	1.2	3.0	3.2	0.9
Rubber and plastic products	385.4	472.4	480.8	582.7	560.5	492.3	33.1	30.6	29.4	32.6	32.2	42.3
Leather products	53.1	63.6	73.7	80.2	81.2	78.6	2.2	3.5	3.8	4.6	4.7	4.9
Stone, clay and glass products	144.7	155.8	157.6	168.7	162.4	166.5	9.5	10.8	15.1	17.2	15.7	14.5
Primary metals	435.4	517.3	409.0	510.2	583.3	511.7	108.7	122.9	80.1	89.2	184.3	142.2
Fabricated metal products	385.4	424.1	451.1	558.3	573.4	496.7	40.3	31.8	36.8	38.3	52.6	57.1
Industrial machinery and computers	3 409.4	4 097.0	4 743.8	5 769.8	5 323.5	4 656.6	151.4	144.5	206.8	263.5	212.7	277.9
Electric and electronic equipment	2 595.1	2 956.4	3 282.0	4 058.5	4 265.1	4 672.3	186.6	187.1	186.9	210.9	227.3	259.8
Transportation equipment	2 011.6	2 144.0	2 185.8	2 245.1	2 622.2	2 420.4	141.2	148.5	154.8	231.8	324.0	267.8
Scientific and measuring instruments	1 164.8	1 341.1	1 453.2	1 571.5	1 642.0	1 767.3	105.9	126.9	151.5	161.6	159.7	208.3
Miscellaneous manufactures	280.5	328.0	329.7	427.3	447.2	562.3	14.0	15.9	13.9	20.2	22.2	24.0
Unidentified manufactures	143.1	133.5	141.8	181.4	300.9	372.2	12.1	13.7	14.3	16.2	18.3	19.8
Agricultural And Livestock Products	910.6	579.8	651.9	640.3	589.6	498.0	248.0	260.4	250.4	267.5	255.8	245.6
Agricultural products	885.6	553.6	624.4	615.5	565.7	474.8	245.8	257.1	245.5	262.8	249.1	242.8
Livestock and livestock products	25.0	26.2	27.5	24.8	23.9	23.3	2.2	3.4	4.9	4.7	6.7	2.9
Other Commodities	413.3	489.5	498.7	533.2	510.9	614.0	87.8	95.8	96.1	129.6	106.7	135.8
Forestry products	33.3	32.9	34.9	35.1	35.9	31.2	1.4	1.7	1.2	1.2	1.2	1.3
Fish and other marine products	67.8	87.7	78.8	81.3	65.8	83.0	21.0	24.8	26.2	28.9	22.5	24.8
Metallic ores and concentrates	2.2	3.5	3.4	3.2	2.3	1.8	...	1.5	...	...	...	...
Bituminous coal and lignite	12.1	7.7	4.2	3.2	0.2	2.5	...	...	0.2	1.1	...	...
Crude petroleum and natural gas	0.6	0.8	1.6	1.6	1.5	2.1	...	...	...	...	...	1.9
Nonmetallic minerals	25.6	12.7	15.2	29.1	36.9	35.6	6.1	0.8	1.4	12.2	19.3	21.1
Scrap and waste	46.8	124.8	72.9	64.5	59.3	54.5	2.9	14.4	4.1	2.5	5.2	4.6
Used merchandise	87.6	78.7	100.3	123.6	138.7	100.7	3.5	2.4	5.7	5.6	3.1	7.2
Goods imported and returned unchanged	47.0	44.2	48.3	69.7	49.2	45.0	47.0	44.2	48.3	69.7	49.2	45.0
Special classification provisions	90.3	96.5	139.2	121.8	121.1	257.4	5.9	6.1	9.1	8.4	6.2	29.7

Table D-12. FLORIDA: State Exports of Goods by Destination and Industry, 1994–1999—*Continued*

(Millions of dollars.)

Industry	South and Central American and Caribbean						Mexico					
	1994	1995	1996	1997	1998	1999	1994	1995	1996	1997	1998	1999
ALL GOODS	9 041.1	10 070.1	10 742.6	12 819.2	12 851.4	11 661.5	993.6	536.2	737.0	1 220.8	1 271.5	1 426.8
Manufactured Goods	8 632.6	9 783.0	10 466.2	12 514.2	12 496.8	11 345.5	786.4	520.2	726.2	1 188.3	1 244.6	1 403.6
Food products	422.7	475.7	479.8	536.1	545.2	519.1	22.5	6.7	8.8	12.0	12.9	17.7
Tobacco products	3.4	6.7	12.2	15.3	8.9	11.4	...	...	0.1	0.4	1.1	0.8
Textile mill products	126.8	150.1	198.8	295.7	320.7	247.4	2.3	4.8	16.4	28.9	43.1	65.1
Apparel	480.0	511.6	521.8	636.2	606.1	520.1	7.1	4.6	8.3	25.6	26.3	29.0
Lumber and wood products	136.3	156.9	151.4	197.3	227.7	236.6	1.5	1.0	1.0	1.4	3.6	3.6
Furniture and fixtures	78.2	88.2	102.8	117.3	131.0	86.4	5.7	1.9	2.6	3.6	4.1	3.2
Paper products	224.5	343.1	339.8	357.9	356.3	387.8	54.3	52.1	49.5	49.0	53.5	73.2
Printing and publishing	46.3	59.2	55.7	69.6	103.5	82.5	21.0	12.2	7.1	6.3	9.0	8.1
Chemical products	528.7	613.3	665.2	718.1	659.8	595.2	74.6	62.3	139.2	298.0	264.0	200.1
Refined petroleum products	70.2	63.9	38.6	46.6	53.9	49.9	6.6	1.0	17.4	14.8	7.9	1.8
Rubber and plastic products	251.7	325.1	307.9	382.2	337.1	305.0	29.8	18.1	19.0	22.9	28.2	38.9
Leather products	41.0	43.3	46.3	58.4	58.1	51.1	1.2	1.1	0.5	1.4	0.8	2.5
Stone, clay and glass products	90.8	99.2	99.9	107.3	109.5	111.5	5.6	2.2	3.0	3.7	6.2	4.7
Primary metals	159.0	175.2	219.8	259.0	262.8	214.8	130.3	51.1	25.7	65.5	80.2	87.8
Fabricated metal products	240.6	270.4	275.6	367.2	341.6	296.7	48.0	30.4	28.6	31.4	41.9	51.9
Industrial machinery and computers	2 293.1	2 759.7	3 218.0	3 852.3	3 674.6	3 076.2	150.5	118.7	198.1	263.8	262.2	227.2
Electric and electronic equipment	1 466.8	1 737.8	1 909.7	2 474.9	2 552.9	2 471.5	115.3	87.6	117.9	248.8	231.8	280.1
Transportation equipment	1 269.7	1 166.5	1 027.6	1 055.1	1 109.0	1 003.6	39.9	22.5	25.5	46.1	79.7	80.7
Scientific and measuring instruments	434.3	429.5	497.4	562.6	537.8	555.1	43.3	29.9	42.2	51.3	60.8	67.5
Miscellaneous manufactures	175.3	218.2	207.8	288.0	313.7	271.2	23.7	10.6	12.7	11.1	18.4	146.2
Unidentified manufactures	93.1	89.4	90.3	117.1	186.5	252.3	3.0	1.5	2.6	2.5	8.9	13.6
Agricultural And Livestock Products	250.9	90.2	98.7	97.4	139.9	73.1	196.2	7.8	3.2	9.8	7.3	6.1
Agricultural products	241.2	77.7	87.1	86.3	128.6	59.8	194.9	7.1	2.5	9.0	6.7	5.4
Livestock and livestock products	9.7	12.5	11.6	11.1	11.3	13.3	1.3	0.6	0.7	0.7	0.6	0.7
Other Commodities	157.6	196.9	177.7	207.6	214.7	243.0	11.0	8.3	7.5	22.7	19.6	17.2
Forestry products	2.0	2.2	3.3	2.9	3.2	4.1	...	...	0.1	0.2	0.1	0.1
Fish and other marine products	13.2	14.2	14.7	15.7	21.0	22.9	0.6	0.8	0.5	1.8	0.7	0.6
Metallic ores and concentrates	...	0.2	0.6	0.1	1.6	0.3	...	...	...	...	...	...
Bituminous coal and lignite	...	0.2	2.3	1.4	0.1	0.1	...	...	...	...	...	...
Crude petroleum and natural gas	0.4	0.7	1.2	1.5	1.4	2.0	...	...	...	...	...	0.1
Nonmetallic minerals	9.2	8.7	10.4	12.4	12.8	9.9	0.5	0.4	0.8	0.8	1.1	1.4
Scrap and waste	30.7	72.9	39.4	39.6	32.7	28.3	1.6	3.8	1.6	6.0	7.7	5.7
Used merchandise	57.1	54.0	58.7	77.5	93.9	63.8	5.5	0.6	2.1	8.8	3.5	3.5
Goods imported and returned unchanged	...	...	...	...	...	...	...	...	...	...	...	...
Special classification provisions	45.1	43.8	47.2	56.6	47.9	111.6	2.7	2.7	2.4	5.1	6.5	5.8

Industry	European Union						United Kingdom					
	1994	1995	1996	1997	1998	1999	1994	1995	1996	1997	1998	1999
ALL GOODS	2 033.6	2 612.9	2 909.9	2 772.9	2 886.1	3 184.2	489.9	560.1	601.3	687.1	742.7	821.7
Manufactured Goods	1 899.4	2 469.0	2 750.3	2 608.5	2 716.2	3 001.9	471.8	539.4	574.2	649.2	697.3	786.6
Food products	144.5	156.6	156.6	158.1	128.0	147.4	28.2	28.2	25.5	18.3	10.6	12.5
Tobacco products	3.5	8.3	7.5	5.1	2.9	2.0	0.5	1.1	0.6	1.1	0.6	0.3
Textile mill products	9.2	11.9	7.5	7.2	7.5	5.8	2.8	3.0	2.1	2.2	1.4	1.7
Apparel	32.0	14.2	17.0	17.6	9.8	10.9	1.7	3.2	6.1	7.4	3.3	3.1
Lumber and wood products	12.9	12.0	10.3	9.9	6.8	7.2	3.3	4.4	4.1	3.5	1.2	1.0
Furniture and fixtures	5.7	5.9	9.9	10.1	8.5	10.6	1.3	1.1	2.6	3.2	1.5	3.2
Paper products	32.3	84.4	49.1	50.2	38.9	39.0	4.5	9.8	8.5	7.6	8.1	9.8
Printing and publishing	8.1	12.3	8.7	14.0	15.8	17.4	2.4	6.1	4.1	5.5	5.7	6.4
Chemical products	209.1	250.1	236.0	204.8	208.8	217.4	54.1	50.8	41.9	59.7	37.6	55.2
Refined petroleum products	22.1	18.2	27.3	34.7	13.7	14.5	0.1	0.5	5.3	1.7	1.6	0.3
Rubber and plastic products	38.3	52.4	72.5	66.6	69.2	45.2	10.5	16.1	43.9	26.8	44.2	14.1
Leather products	3.3	5.9	7.2	5.7	6.7	6.9	0.9	0.8	0.8	1.0	1.2	0.3
Stone, clay and glass products	12.8	16.0	13.2	13.3	13.2	14.4	4.3	5.4	3.5	3.5	3.7	3.9
Primary metals	15.5	20.6	21.0	28.5	30.6	30.4	5.0	7.1	5.6	8.5	6.7	7.4
Fabricated metal products	20.0	29.0	31.3	38.0	28.2	41.5	8.2	8.8	9.9	8.7	7.4	11.7
Industrial machinery and computers	384.7	501.7	522.3	576.1	566.8	503.1	97.2	95.0	103.4	111.7	139.4	146.0
Electric and electronic equipment	275.0	346.2	429.8	359.8	345.4	539.0	102.0	107.4	97.4	122.5	119.1	156.8
Transportation equipment	296.3	491.8	627.6	515.3	679.4	679.8	64.0	100.7	98.7	127.4	176.7	159.4
Scientific and measuring instruments	333.3	383.0	435.3	430.4	462.0	560.9	69.0	79.9	98.6	102.8	91.5	145.8
Miscellaneous manufactures	27.1	34.3	37.0	44.0	41.7	58.5	6.8	7.0	9.2	13.0	16.0	15.6
Unidentified manufactures	13.5	14.4	23.3	19.4	32.2	49.9	4.8	3.0	2.5	13.2	19.6	32.2
Agricultural And Livestock Products	66.3	69.3	73.1	77.4	68.2	71.6	9.1	7.2	8.6	11.2	11.5	9.5
Agricultural products	62.1	66.5	68.5	74.8	65.7	69.1	8.6	6.7	7.3	10.8	11.3	9.1
Livestock and livestock products	4.2	2.9	4.6	2.6	2.5	2.6	0.6	0.6	1.3	0.4	0.3	0.5
Other Commodities	67.9	74.6	86.5	87.0	101.8	110.6	8.9	13.4	18.5	26.7	33.8	25.6
Forestry products	27.2	25.9	27.2	28.2	29.7	23.4	1.2	1.6	2.2	2.6	1.8	1.7
Fish and other marine products	4.8	9.7	9.4	4.8	8.0	15.2	0.7	0.5	0.5	0.5	1.0	1.3
Metallic ores and concentrates	0.8	0.1	0.7	0.8	0.5	1.5	...	...	...	0.3	...	...
Bituminous coal and lignite	...	0.8	0.8	0.8	...	...	...	...	...	...	...	...
Crude petroleum and natural gas	0.1	0.1	0.1	...	...	...	...	...	...	...	...	...
Nonmetallic minerals	7.0	1.9	0.9	1.1	0.8	0.8	0.1	0.1	0.2	0.7	0.1	0.2
Scrap and waste	3.9	6.4	5.6	3.7	5.7	5.0	0.1	0.8	1.0	0.7	0.8	1.1
Used merchandise	10.4	11.6	13.7	23.9	24.5	16.9	2.8	4.7	6.1	13.0	16.0	7.7
Goods imported and returned unchanged	...	...	...	...	...	...	...	...	...	...	...	...
Special classification provisions	13.7	18.0	28.1	23.6	32.6	47.8	4.0	5.7	8.5	8.9	14.1	13.6

Table D-12. FLORIDA: State Exports of Goods by Destination and Industry, 1994–1999—*Continued*

(Millions of dollars.)

Industry	Germany						France					
	1994	1995	1996	1997	1998	1999	1994	1995	1996	1997	1998	1999
ALL GOODS	309.9	399.4	408.1	383.4	450.9	512.4	311.1	395.4	494.2	397.5	348.3	483.0
Manufactured Goods	287.1	377.3	385.7	362.6	431.8	490.1	285.1	369.7	463.6	365.3	320.2	448.0
Food products	10.7	14.0	17.8	11.5	4.8	12.9	26.4	26.2	36.3	33.1	10.4	8.7
Tobacco products	...	...	0.2	0.3	0.4	0.4	...	...	0.1	...	...	0.2
Textile mill products	2.0	2.6	1.3	0.7	0.6	0.8	1.5	2.9	0.5	0.6	0.7	0.4
Apparel	1.4	2.3	2.6	3.6	1.0	1.7	9.9	4.3	1.5	1.3	1.5	1.7
Lumber and wood products	3.7	2.0	2.0	0.9	1.0	0.3	0.7	0.2	0.2	0.2	0.5	1.3
Furniture and fixtures	0.5	1.4	1.4	0.9	0.5	1.2	0.7	1.0	1.7	1.7	1.8	0.8
Paper products	0.7	1.1	1.5	0.6	0.4	1.1	9.6	35.9	14.9	19.0	8.4	5.2
Printing and publishing	1.2	1.1	0.9	2.5	6.1	6.3	0.8	1.9	0.7	0.9	0.5	1.7
Chemical products	42.6	40.3	39.4	27.1	27.8	29.1	23.5	45.6	38.2	24.0	23.1	37.8
Refined petroleum products	0.1	0.3	0.4	3.8	0.6	0.3	2.9	...	2.1	5.3	0.3	0.0
Rubber and plastic products	6.2	7.3	7.4	7.9	4.4	4.9	7.0	7.0	2.0	4.4	3.2	4.9
Leather products	0.5	1.0	2.5	1.9	1.3	1.5	0.6	3.1	2.4	1.2	1.9	0.9
Stone, clay and glass products	1.1	1.4	2.1	1.6	0.9	2.4	2.5	2.4	1.6	1.1	1.0	1.5
Primary metals	1.9	2.4	4.2	5.3	4.5	5.0	2.6	1.5	1.9	5.6	10.2	12.3
Fabricated metal products	3.7	6.3	4.0	4.4	5.5	7.7	1.1	2.7	2.9	8.1	2.3	3.0
Industrial machinery and computers	43.2	67.3	62.9	85.2	76.0	72.4	31.3	38.4	40.0	41.9	63.1	31.6
Electric and electronic equipment	41.2	48.8	43.1	50.5	51.9	91.2	29.1	39.7	156.5	36.2	37.3	108.4
Transportation equipment	71.3	114.5	116.8	89.3	148.8	137.8	56.6	73.2	91.6	107.8	78.5	105.9
Scientific and measuring instruments	47.6	50.6	66.6	56.4	84.3	99.0	72.8	76.8	63.7	64.8	69.3	110.8
Miscellaneous manufactures	5.1	7.0	6.3	6.5	6.4	10.5	4.1	5.9	3.8	6.7	4.4	8.9
Unidentified manufactures	2.4	5.4	2.3	1.5	4.6	3.5	1.6	1.2	1.1	1.4	1.7	2.0
Agricultural And Livestock Products	6.0	8.7	8.8	6.8	6.4	7.9	21.2	19.2	19.9	22.4	18.8	20.5
Agricultural products	5.5	8.3	8.1	6.5	5.7	7.7	20.4	18.8	19.4	22.0	18.4	19.9
Livestock and livestock products	0.5	0.4	0.7	0.4	0.7	0.2	0.8	0.4	0.5	0.4	0.4	0.6
Other Commodities	16.8	13.4	13.6	14.0	12.7	14.4	4.8	6.6	10.7	9.9	9.3	14.5
Forestry products	10.7	9.3	9.2	9.2	7.9	6.1	0.2	0.1	0.2	0.5	1.0	0.4
Fish and other marine products	0.3	0.5	0.3	0.4	0.6	1.2	1.4	2.5	4.5	2.1	1.6	6.1
Metallic ores and concentrates	0.2	0.1	0.4	0.7	...	...	...	...	0.1	...	...	...
Bituminous coal and lignite	...	...	...	...	...	...	...	...	...	...	...	...
Crude petroleum and natural gas	...	...	...	...	...	...	...	...	...	...	...	...
Nonmetallic minerals	0.2	...	0.1	0.1	...	0.5	...	...	...	...	0.1	...
Scrap and waste	0.2	0.3	0.3	0.1	0.8	0.7	0.2	...	0.2	0.1	...	0.2
Used merchandise	1.4	1.1	1.2	2.0	0.9	1.1	1.9	1.8	1.8	3.0	1.4	1.4
Goods imported and returned unchanged	...	...	...	...	...	...	...	...	...	...	...	...
Special classification provisions	4.0	2.1	2.0	1.6	2.4	4.9	1.1	2.1	3.9	4.2	5.2	6.4

Industry	The Netherlands						Asian 10					
	1994	1995	1996	1997	1998	1999	1994	1995	1996	1997	1998	1999
ALL GOODS	247.9	332.6	378.7	399.6	416.2	409.2	1 862.9	2 288.8	2 082.8	2 474.2	2 192.3	2 471.5
Manufactured Goods	214.0	293.7	335.5	360.6	380.6	370.1	1 669.9	2 065.1	1 808.1	2 229.2	2 039.6	2 309.4
Food products	38.7	60.3	53.2	64.5	67.5	80.0	90.0	57.9	67.1	59.6	51.5	72.9
Tobacco products	2.6	4.9	2.1	2.0	0.3	0.1	0.3	1.8	1.6	2.5	1.3	1.0
Textile mill products	1.1	0.5	0.4	0.4	0.9	0.3	6.0	5.8	6.4	5.9	3.4	3.1
Apparel	0.8	1.3	1.5	1.3	0.7	0.7	10.1	10.7	15.6	12.3	5.3	5.9
Lumber and wood products	0.3	1.1	0.6	0.3	0.3	0.3	4.0	4.7	4.8	5.0	4.2	4.0
Furniture and fixtures	0.5	0.2	0.9	1.7	0.8	0.7	5.0	4.2	5.1	4.8	3.9	5.0
Paper products	1.0	0.5	0.5	0.4	2.4	1.1	38.2	55.5	40.2	37.1	28.0	63.6
Printing and publishing	0.8	1.0	0.7	0.3	0.6	0.4	11.3	18.0	18.0	12.8	9.7	9.1
Chemical products	24.0	31.6	46.8	27.3	26.3	35.0	538.5	582.6	324.7	433.1	432.6	438.1
Refined petroleum products	1.3	0.2	0.4	0.1	0.6	0.1	14.7	6.7	17.8	5.8	5.7	3.0
Rubber and plastic products	3.6	6.5	4.6	5.4	4.0	4.3	18.5	27.3	27.4	27.4	15.0	21.6
Leather products	0.4	0.1	0.1	0.3	0.9	2.9	3.6	8.1	13.1	7.6	9.2	11.7
Stone, clay and glass products	0.5	0.7	0.7	0.8	0.8	0.5	18.0	19.6	18.7	20.0	9.4	10.7
Primary metals	0.3	0.9	0.6	0.7	1.2	1.3	13.8	130.4	40.9	37.9	11.6	24.8
Fabricated metal products	1.5	1.5	2.3	1.7	1.6	2.1	17.7	29.8	54.6	48.9	20.8	19.3
Industrial machinery and computers	36.2	38.8	57.7	125.0	114.3	100.1	211.4	329.5	359.0	491.2	311.8	309.6
Electric and electronic equipment	12.0	16.4	17.1	13.0	22.1	37.6	393.5	385.9	413.7	584.2	639.6	890.6
Transportation equipment	25.2	62.3	42.6	27.9	58.3	50.5	77.1	93.2	126.3	115.6	113.3	140.2
Scientific and measuring instruments	60.0	62.3	85.8	84.8	72.7	48.6	171.3	265.8	219.2	264.0	300.1	227.1
Miscellaneous manufactures	2.2	1.7	2.7	2.4	2.8	1.7	22.0	22.5	31.4	37.3	23.6	28.1
Unidentified manufactures	1.0	0.8	14.2	0.5	1.6	1.8	4.8	5.0	4.1	16.1	39.6	20.0
Agricultural And Livestock Products	16.2	18.5	20.6	20.6	15.7	20.9	132.0	132.0	173.0	182.3	111.0	89.8
Agricultural products	15.7	18.0	20.0	20.2	15.3	20.4	124.8	125.6	167.7	177.0	108.5	86.3
Livestock and livestock products	0.5	0.5	0.6	0.4	0.3	0.5	7.2	6.3	5.4	5.3	2.5	3.5
Other Commodities	17.6	20.4	22.6	18.5	19.9	18.2	60.9	91.7	101.7	62.7	41.6	72.3
Forestry products	14.4	14.4	14.9	15.3	15.3	14.3	1.4	1.6	1.8	1.1	0.6	0.7
Fish and other marine products	0.7	2.7	2.4	0.5	2.0	1.3	25.9	35.9	24.4	25.4	8.6	13.5
Metallic ores and concentrates	0.4	...	...	...	...	...	1.3	1.7	1.8	1.3	0.3	0.5
Bituminous coal and lignite	...	0.8	...	...	...	...	...	0.9	0.3	0.9	...	...
Crude petroleum and natural gas	...	...	...	...	...	...	...	...	0.1	...	...	...
Nonmetallic minerals	0.1	0.1	0.3	0.1	0.2	...	1.7	0.3	0.6	0.5	0.3	0.5
Scrap and waste	0.3	0.6	1.2	0.2	0.4	0.2	6.9	24.7	19.7	9.4	6.9	6.7
Used merchandise	0.5	0.7	0.6	0.7	0.5	0.6	5.5	4.3	4.9	2.3	2.6	1.1
Goods imported and returned unchanged	...	...	...	...	...	...	...	...	...	...	...	...
Special classification provisions	1.2	1.0	3.3	1.6	1.5	1.9	18.2	22.3	48.0	21.8	22.4	49.2

Table D-12. FLORIDA: State Exports of Goods by Destination and Industry, 1994–1999—*Continued*

(Millions of dollars.)

Industry	Japan						South Korea					
	1994	1995	1996	1997	1998	1999	1994	1995	1996	1997	1998	1999
ALL GOODS	487.4	584.1	554.2	588.2	541.7	553.2	179.2	357.8	351.6	341.3	216.6	266.4
Manufactured Goods	398.6	493.6	470.5	504.5	495.4	480.9	112.6	268.2	244.4	220.0	153.9	237.7
Food products	68.0	37.3	48.0	40.3	32.1	42.9	10.5	8.0	4.9	5.1	4.4	10.7
Tobacco products	0.3	1.1	0.3	0.5	0.4	0.5	...	...	0.2	...	...	...
Textile mill products	2.0	1.0	2.7	2.1	0.3	0.4	0.3	1.2	0.5	0.3	0.7	0.3
Apparel	5.4	7.3	8.2	5.2	2.6	3.0	0.6	0.6	0.3	0.2	0.2	0.2
Lumber and wood products	1.1	3.3	3.4	3.0	1.7	2.1	0.5	0.3	0.5	0.3	0.5	0.9
Furniture and fixtures	0.7	0.9	1.6	2.5	2.5	4.2	2.3	0.6	0.4	0.3	0.1	0.1
Paper products	13.4	26.5	14.4	8.6	14.0	19.8	12.2	25.0	16.9	18.7	8.1	30.1
Printing and publishing	6.7	10.6	7.9	3.7	3.0	4.3	0.1	0.4	0.3	1.4	0.4	0.4
Chemical products	30.6	42.6	31.9	38.3	25.7	26.6	11.0	23.3	25.8	23.9	11.1	15.7
Refined petroleum products	2.7	5.3	6.1	4.5	4.0	0.6	0.2	...	...	0.2	0.3	1.4
Rubber and plastic products	5.0	7.1	7.9	8.7	2.9	2.8	1.7	2.8	2.0	2.9	0.6	1.1
Leather products	0.9	3.4	5.4	4.5	4.7	4.6	...	...	0.4	0.1	1.9	3.4
Stone, clay and glass products	2.2	2.4	3.2	2.7	2.4	4.5	3.0	1.7	1.7	1.3	0.9	1.0
Primary metals	0.4	1.0	2.2	2.0	3.2	15.7	2.3	35.7	12.5	13.5	1.4	1.6
Fabricated metal products	3.0	4.2	6.9	15.8	8.1	5.9	1.5	5.6	7.3	8.5	2.7	2.9
Industrial machinery and computers	43.2	51.4	71.7	86.2	93.4	114.2	22.6	97.8	86.8	47.3	31.7	42.4
Electric and electronic equipment	98.3	87.5	85.4	85.0	65.4	48.7	24.9	27.3	38.9	44.9	45.3	66.7
Transportation equipment	10.2	18.3	16.9	14.9	14.8	29.2	7.0	14.1	21.7	19.1	24.3	37.3
Scientific and measuring instruments	94.6	173.2	134.1	163.0	204.4	134.4	10.6	20.5	17.7	21.7	16.5	18.5
Miscellaneous manufactures	8.2	7.8	11.1	11.7	7.5	10.7	0.9	2.7	4.9	9.7	2.4	1.6
Unidentified manufactures	1.6	1.7	1.1	1.4	2.4	5.7	0.5	0.5	0.8	0.7	0.7	1.4
Agricultural And Livestock Products	60.5	50.7	53.0	63.2	38.3	42.8	61.4	75.9	99.4	114.0	58.5	25.2
Agricultural products	56.6	46.9	48.8	59.4	36.2	40.9	61.4	75.9	99.3	114.0	58.5	25.2
Livestock and livestock products	3.9	3.8	4.1	3.8	2.1	1.9	...	...	0.1	...	...	...
Other Commodities	28.2	39.8	30.8	20.5	8.0	29.4	5.1	13.6	7.7	7.3	4.2	3.5
Forestry products	0.9	0.9	0.8	0.7	0.4	0.3	0.4	0.6	0.1	0.2	...	0.3
Fish and other marine products	16.5	23.8	15.0	12.1	5.1	4.2	0.2	0.4	...	0.1	...	...
Metallic ores and concentrates	...	...	...	...	...	...	...	...	...	...	...	...
Bituminous coal and lignite	...	0.9	0.3	0.9	...	0.5	...	...	...	...	...	...
Crude petroleum and natural gas	...	...	...	...	...	...	...	...	...	...	...	...
Nonmetallic minerals	0.1	...	...	...	...	0.2	0.9	...	0.1	...	...	...
Scrap and waste	1.0	3.4	2.1	1.7	0.1	0.1	3.5	12.1	6.1	3.9	3.6	2.2
Used merchandise	2.1	0.7	0.6	0.4	0.2	0.4	...	...	0.6	0.6	...	...
Goods imported and returned unchanged	...	...	...	...	...	...	...	...	...	...	...	...
Special classification provisions	7.6	10.1	11.9	4.7	2.2	23.8	0.1	0.5	0.8	2.5	0.5	1.0

Industry	Taiwan						Singapore					
	1994	1995	1996	1997	1998	1999	1994	1995	1996	1997	1998	1999
ALL GOODS	153.4	155.3	122.2	131.2	96.9	167.0	140.1	218.5	236.9	319.9	449.1	474.8
Manufactured Goods	138.8	138.1	104.1	113.7	90.1	148.8	136.4	215.4	232.1	315.7	444.6	470.8
Food products	3.7	2.9	3.6	3.2	3.4	3.9	2.0	2.8	1.8	1.4	1.8	2.8
Tobacco products	...	0.2	0.2	...	0.5	0.1	...	0.1	...	0.4	0.2	0.1
Textile mill products	0.6	1.3	0.8	0.2	0.2	0.2	1.1	0.2	0.4	0.8	0.3	0.4
Apparel	0.4	0.3	1.3	1.0	0.7	0.9	1.0	0.4	1.8	1.1	0.6	0.8
Lumber and wood products	0.5	0.7	0.4	0.5	0.3	0.5	0.1	...	0.1	0.1	0.1	0.1
Furniture and fixtures	0.5	0.5	0.1	0.4	0.2	0.1	1.0	0.3	0.3	0.2	0.2	0.3
Paper products	2.9	1.3	0.3	0.6	0.5	1.5	0.2	0.5	0.2	0.2	0.2	0.6
Printing and publishing	1.2	5.2	6.3	6.3	3.8	3.0	0.8	0.7	0.4	0.4	1.2	0.3
Chemical products	11.6	12.7	10.3	13.3	11.6	9.7	13.0	11.7	9.5	17.4	7.7	8.3
Refined petroleum products	0.5	0.3	1.4	0.3	0.4	0.3	0.1	...	0.1	0.3	0.2	...
Rubber and plastic products	2.9	3.7	3.1	2.3	1.2	3.0	3.9	6.9	8.8	5.2	3.5	3.2
Leather products	...	0.3	0.3	0.9	0.7	0.3	0.1	2.3	3.9	0.9	0.8	1.0
Stone, clay and glass products	1.1	2.3	0.7	0.5	0.3	0.5	1.2	0.8	0.6	1.2	0.6	1.1
Primary metals	4.1	52.4	7.5	4.1	0.4	1.0	1.6	0.5	0.8	0.9	1.3	0.3
Fabricated metal products	6.2	3.3	2.4	2.1	1.8	2.6	1.4	1.6	1.3	1.4	0.9	0.9
Industrial machinery and computers	15.5	20.9	24.2	29.6	23.2	28.4	24.8	38.9	27.3	25.6	19.8	21.0
Electric and electronic equipment	65.5	15.2	18.5	30.1	20.7	68.8	60.2	113.9	135.4	202.9	310.7	379.6
Transportation equipment	6.7	4.7	11.3	4.4	8.3	7.4	14.1	18.7	22.1	25.6	29.8	26.9
Scientific and measuring instruments	12.7	8.6	9.8	12.5	10.8	12.0	8.1	11.7	13.6	17.7	29.7	13.0
Miscellaneous manufactures	1.7	0.7	1.3	1.2	0.5	4.0	1.0	2.9	3.0	2.0	1.6	0.7
Unidentified manufactures	0.5	0.5	0.3	0.2	0.6	0.6	0.7	0.6	0.7	9.9	33.5	9.3
Agricultural And Livestock Products	2.5	2.7	2.5	2.9	0.8	0.8	1.0	0.8	0.5	0.5	0.2	0.2
Agricultural products	0.9	1.5	2.1	2.4	0.8	0.7	0.2	0.4	0.4	0.4	0.2	0.2
Livestock and livestock products	1.5	1.2	0.5	0.5	...	...	0.7	0.4	0.1	...	0.1	0.1
Other Commodities	12.1	14.6	15.5	14.7	6.0	17.5	2.8	2.3	4.4	3.7	4.2	3.9
Forestry products	...	0.1	...	...	...	...	...	...	...	...	...	...
Fish and other marine products	7.9	10.4	7.8	11.2	1.9	8.3	0.1	0.1	...	0.2	0.1	0.1
Metallic ores and concentrates	...	...	...	...	...	...	...	...	...	...	...	...
Bituminous coal and lignite	...	...	...	...	...	...	...	...	...	...	...	...
Crude petroleum and natural gas	...	...	0.1	...	...	...	...	...	...	...	...	...
Nonmetallic minerals	0.7	0.2	0.1	0.2	0.1	0.1	...	...	...	...	...	...
Scrap and waste	0.9	0.9	1.7	1.3	0.3	0.4	0.1	0.1	0.1	0.1	0.1	1.1
Used merchandise	...	0.3	0.1	0.2	0.5	0.3	0.3	0.7	0.4	0.4	1.8	0.1
Goods imported and returned unchanged	...	...	...	...	...	...	...	...	...	...	...	...
Special classification provisions	2.6	2.8	5.8	1.8	3.1	8.4	2.2	1.4	3.8	3.0	2.3	2.5

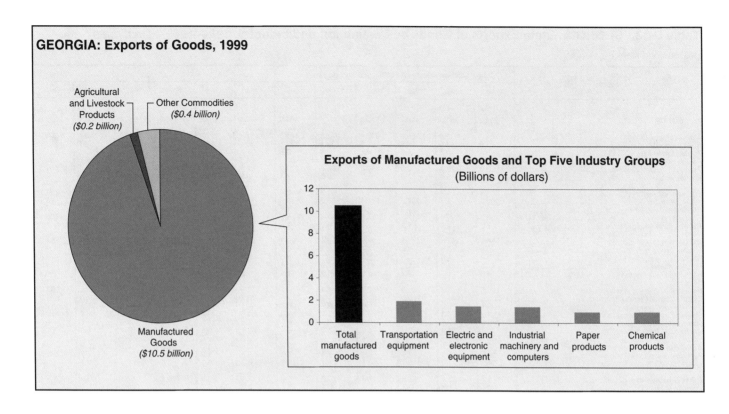

GEORGIA: Exports of Goods, 1999

Agricultural and Livestock Products ($0.2 billion)

Other Commodities ($0.4 billion)

Manufactured Goods ($10.5 billion)

Exports of Manufactured Goods and Top Five Industry Groups
(Billions of dollars)

Total manufactured goods · Transportation equipment · Electric and electronic equipment · Industrial machinery and computers · Paper products · Chemical products

Table D-13. GEORGIA: State Exports of Goods by Destination and Industry, 1994–1999

(Millions of dollars.)

Industry	All destinations						Canada					
	1994	1995	1996	1997	1998	1999	1994	1995	1996	1997	1998	1999
ALL GOODS	7 108.1	8 626.8	8 618.0	9 810.0	11 212.1	11 060.6	1 646.3	1 820.7	1 896.9	1 999.7	2 115.9	2 221.4
Manufactured Goods	6 567.7	8 063.9	8 062.1	9 214.9	10 629.2	10 471.9	1 499.9	1 678.6	1 738.5	1 835.4	1 953.3	2 032.3
Food products	506.4	695.5	836.7	632.2	611.1	570.0	81.0	71.6	86.5	66.9	67.8	68.1
Tobacco products	2.8	4.1	3.6	5.5	11.1	11.4	0.8	0.8	0.9	1.1	1.2	1.5
Textile mill products	618.6	579.9	652.0	708.0	679.7	636.1	199.6	202.3	228.7	274.3	293.7	290.5
Apparel	288.8	332.2	397.6	445.6	527.2	337.1	23.3	22.3	24.5	27.6	29.1	22.9
Lumber and wood products	250.8	230.1	198.9	258.2	183.4	158.2	13.8	11.4	15.8	21.6	22.5	30.6
Furniture and fixtures	36.1	35.0	40.9	54.7	46.5	34.6	12.7	10.1	10.2	11.6	14.5	7.4
Paper products	684.3	1 092.7	915.6	904.7	811.0	973.4	111.3	137.9	153.5	162.3	157.8	151.2
Printing and publishing	44.6	56.3	51.6	52.4	54.1	46.4	10.7	8.9	9.4	8.7	9.2	10.1
Chemical products	584.5	683.0	811.7	1 312.6	1 724.5	971.6	172.5	158.5	171.7	241.5	236.3	222.8
Refined petroleum products	63.1	82.7	78.0	82.6	53.5	44.9	8.4	7.8	1.3	1.5	4.0	3.2
Rubber and plastic products	232.5	230.2	221.7	226.7	242.1	212.4	64.2	62.9	65.9	77.1	74.2	78.4
Leather products	5.3	8.3	6.9	5.9	6.5	10.8	0.8	1.0	1.8	1.0	1.8	1.3
Stone, clay and glass products	45.2	40.3	42.1	50.4	69.7	73.0	11.5	10.6	13.0	15.7	18.2	27.5
Primary metals	191.8	229.1	282.2	306.7	579.9	566.6	47.2	59.5	57.7	58.6	62.0	47.7
Fabricated metal products	121.7	133.0	158.9	177.2	193.0	214.3	51.2	40.3	42.9	51.7	54.1	58.0
Industrial machinery and computers	1 021.1	1 241.5	1 271.4	1 407.6	1 372.5	1 433.2	263.0	287.6	281.9	308.1	350.5	406.2
Electric and electronic equipment	746.1	789.3	852.1	1 079.3	1 288.8	1 467.0	205.8	232.5	259.2	241.2	245.8	280.5
Transportation equipment	653.2	1 028.5	673.0	828.2	1 489.7	1 924.7	139.9	258.1	212.5	153.8	183.5	180.3
Scientific and measuring instruments	389.7	480.4	475.5	568.9	536.5	537.5	62.9	71.4	72.4	83.4	86.3	92.2
Miscellaneous manufactures	57.6	67.4	68.9	81.8	81.0	105.5	11.7	13.5	20.4	18.1	30.0	40.3
Unidentified manufactures	23.5	24.7	22.6	25.6	67.5	143.0	7.6	9.5	8.3	9.6	10.5	11.6
Agricultural And Livestock Products	132.0	164.0	137.1	182.5	181.2	158.6	32.6	38.5	37.5	42.8	42.0	53.7
Agricultural products	106.0	135.1	108.5	150.0	138.5	133.4	28.7	35.7	31.5	36.9	32.5	46.7
Livestock and livestock products	26.0	28.9	28.6	32.6	42.7	25.1	3.9	2.8	6.0	5.8	9.4	7.0
Other Commodities	408.4	398.9	418.9	412.6	401.6	430.1	113.8	103.7	120.9	121.5	120.7	135.5
Forestry products	3.2	3.0	2.2	1.8	2.0	3.0	0.1	. . .	0.1	0.2	0.1	0.4
Fish and other marine products	2.4	4.1	2.1	5.2	2.4	2.5	0.7	0.5	0.3	0.1	0.3	0.2
Metallic ores and concentrates	6.0	5.7	4.4	3.6	4.0	4.0	6.0	5.2	4.1	2.4	3.0	3.1
Bituminous coal and lignite	. . .	. . .	. . .	. . .	0.8	1.3	. . .	. . .	. . .	. . .	0.8	1.3
Crude petroleum and natural gas	0.4	0.2	. . .	0.4	0.2	3.4	0.4	0.2	. . .	. . .	0.1	3.2
Nonmetallic minerals	259.4	265.4	278.9	287.7	277.2	274.8	52.4	56.7	60.6	61.5	66.8	65.2
Scrap and waste	43.6	56.5	40.7	35.8	37.3	27.7	4.7	5.2	11.6	10.6	8.0	3.9
Used merchandise	12.5	15.5	19.5	20.0	18.4	17.5	2.0	2.2	1.9	2.2	2.8	2.5
Goods imported and returned unchanged	45.0	30.5	36.9	41.7	35.9	34.2	45.0	30.5	36.9	41.7	35.9	34.2
Special classification provisions	35.8	18.0	34.2	16.5	23.5	61.7	2.5	3.1	5.4	3.0	2.8	21.7

Table D-13. GEORGIA: State Exports of Goods by Destination and Industry, 1994–1999—*Continued*

(Millions of dollars.)

Industry	South and Central American and Caribbean						Mexico					
	1994	1995	1996	1997	1998	1999	1994	1995	1996	1997	1998	1999
ALL GOODS	1 203.2	1 490.0	1 418.1	1 575.5	1 957.9	1 481.5	469.5	403.8	516.9	685.7	1 135.7	1 327.6
Manufactured Goods	1 153.7	1 435.9	1 380.9	1 532.4	1 911.5	1 441.6	451.7	392.9	503.2	665.0	1 113.4	1 309.2
Food products	73.6	117.4	98.5	101.5	133.1	128.1	36.1	15.4	18.8	23.9	22.1	17.7
Tobacco products	0.4	0.3	0.2	0.1	0.3	0.6	...	...	...	...	...	...
Textile mill products	53.1	61.1	67.3	77.3	87.4	69.0	24.9	26.3	55.1	46.5	59.6	94.1
Apparel	206.7	224.9	279.8	286.3	298.9	182.0	23.0	50.2	60.8	100.5	164.4	101.3
Lumber and wood products	49.1	45.1	36.3	58.5	36.5	42.4	3.9	0.6	0.7	1.8	1.3	1.7
Furniture and fixtures	1.8	4.2	3.4	6.7	3.2	3.7	1.4	0.5	1.5	1.6	0.9	1.2
Paper products	108.3	219.1	174.3	174.3	167.7	168.6	79.1	60.3	52.7	53.8	47.9	78.7
Printing and publishing	3.2	5.2	2.2	5.9	3.8	1.7	9.7	7.3	3.4	3.8	7.0	5.4
Chemical products	85.0	125.4	143.9	215.2	450.6	156.7	40.6	37.0	59.2	75.1	100.5	105.1
Refined petroleum products	7.7	9.4	7.9	11.4	4.7	1.3	1.8	0.9	1.1	1.7	1.4	1.0
Rubber and plastic products	36.4	52.4	31.3	22.3	26.4	22.3	63.0	48.5	40.9	44.5	50.2	51.3
Leather products	0.8	0.9	0.6	...	...	...	0.2	0.2	0.4	0.2	0.2	0.1
Stone, clay and glass products	3.7	4.6	5.8	6.7	11.1	8.0	2.4	1.1	1.6	4.6	5.2	8.6
Primary metals	12.6	18.0	21.2	30.0	127.9	150.4	22.1	20.0	27.6	14.6	18.7	34.0
Fabricated metal products	14.5	21.2	43.7	28.0	29.8	17.9	7.8	6.6	9.0	13.5	25.3	21.9
Industrial machinery and computers	155.5	192.4	206.9	217.7	187.4	134.7	51.9	45.7	54.0	82.1	86.5	103.8
Electric and electronic equipment	202.5	141.6	100.8	131.4	161.2	170.6	33.2	25.4	41.8	118.4	427.5	578.8
Transportation equipment	33.1	26.2	33.3	29.6	83.0	100.7	6.4	10.2	23.5	11.6	25.1	52.6
Scientific and measuring instruments	98.0	156.3	111.9	113.1	81.6	59.0	33.0	23.6	43.9	60.3	58.7	35.8
Miscellaneous manufactures	5.0	7.2	7.9	10.8	8.3	14.5	9.8	12.5	5.6	5.2	4.5	4.6
Unidentified manufactures	2.7	3.0	3.6	4.9	8.0	8.8	1.4	0.9	1.4	1.4	6.4	11.6
Agricultural And Livestock Products	32.9	32.2	23.1	25.2	29.4	23.3	2.8	1.3	2.9	8.6	12.8	4.8
Agricultural products	14.9	13.5	7.5	5.9	5.3	7.0	2.5	1.2	2.5	5.7	4.5	3.6
Livestock and livestock products	17.9	18.6	15.6	19.4	24.1	16.3	0.3	0.1	0.4	3.0	8.3	1.2
Other Commodities	16.7	22.0	14.1	17.9	17.0	16.7	15.1	9.6	10.8	12.1	9.5	13.7
Forestry products	0.4	1.3	0.3	0.5	0.4	0.6	0.3	0.1	0.3	0.3	0.1	0.1
Fish and other marine products	0.6	0.6	0.4	0.3	0.1	0.6	...	...	...	0.4	0.3	0.2
Metallic ores and concentrates	...	...	0.1	0.7	...	...	...	...	...	...	...	...
Bituminous coal and lignite	...	...	...	0.3	0.1	0.1	...	...	...	...	...	...
Crude petroleum and natural gas	...	...	...	...	...	...	...	...	...	...	...	...
Nonmetallic minerals	7.3	10.8	9.2	11.2	11.0	9.0	6.5	3.8	4.7	5.0	4.9	4.2
Scrap and waste	2.2	3.0	0.7	1.8	1.2	0.4	2.8	3.9	4.5	4.6	3.2	2.3
Used merchandise	4.5	4.3	2.6	2.5	2.8	2.0	0.6	0.2	0.1	0.6	...	0.1
Goods imported and returned unchanged	...	...	...	...	...	...	4.5	1.6	1.2	0.9	0.6	6.0
Special classification provisions	1.7	2.0	0.9	0.7	1.4	4.0	...	...	...	...	...	...

Industry	European Union						United Kingdom					
	1994	1995	1996	1997	1998	1999	1994	1995	1996	1997	1998	1999
ALL GOODS	1 578.2	2 010.8	1 818.5	2 351.4	3 048.7	2 898.6	385.8	459.8	426.6	489.3	1 005.7	916.8
Manufactured Goods	1 409.8	1 814.4	1 643.5	2 170.2	2 881.0	2 731.3	364.6	443.9	414.5	472.7	989.5	892.0
Food products	27.7	42.0	51.6	29.5	37.6	27.7	6.3	4.4	3.0	2.2	2.9	3.3
Tobacco products	1.2	1.7	1.9	2.9	7.4	4.4	0.4	0.2	0.2	...	...	0.4
Textile mill products	58.7	65.3	75.3	78.1	68.4	62.2	26.3	32.6	38.7	40.6	39.3	36.1
Apparel	12.5	10.3	8.1	7.0	13.3	18.4	2.4	1.1	1.0	1.6	2.7	1.9
Lumber and wood products	120.5	111.8	79.9	125.5	82.2	45.1	23.9	23.5	16.0	27.9	23.5	10.1
Furniture and fixtures	6.0	6.2	6.9	7.5	7.8	4.1	2.8	2.9	2.8	3.8	3.8	1.8
Paper products	166.1	296.8	221.1	273.9	249.7	293.9	25.5	31.4	27.4	34.8	30.5	43.9
Printing and publishing	13.8	27.5	24.0	17.9	18.3	18.5	2.0	18.0	6.9	10.2	8.6	5.8
Chemical products	88.8	111.8	120.6	270.4	425.5	230.8	30.3	41.1	44.3	45.4	34.8	21.2
Refined petroleum products	29.2	47.9	38.0	31.7	25.0	18.1	0.8	3.7	...	0.6	1.5	...
Rubber and plastic products	35.9	28.7	28.5	22.1	28.8	25.0	11.0	5.5	6.3	5.1	7.8	5.3
Leather products	1.9	2.3	1.6	1.7	1.8	4.4	...	0.2	0.9	1.0	0.5	1.2
Stone, clay and glass products	16.9	13.3	10.3	12.6	14.4	12.5	6.3	1.6	2.0	2.9	2.2	1.9
Primary metals	20.7	17.5	29.3	61.5	151.0	141.5	6.2	3.9	6.2	12.1	37.9	25.8
Fabricated metal products	16.0	18.3	28.4	41.5	44.1	49.2	3.4	6.3	6.7	10.3	16.1	14.4
Industrial machinery and computers	300.7	405.7	410.4	430.6	468.1	471.9	55.7	59.3	60.6	73.0	66.3	77.0
Electric and electronic equipment	148.4	169.5	148.8	241.2	202.5	200.6	68.5	80.4	79.5	57.2	62.4	38.9
Transportation equipment	213.0	277.5	217.4	352.3	848.2	867.1	43.1	59.8	70.8	107.4	597.6	561.4
Scientific and measuring instruments	112.8	142.6	126.3	141.0	157.1	151.5	44.5	62.7	37.7	32.8	46.5	33.2
Miscellaneous manufactures	12.8	12.6	11.9	17.9	12.6	18.9	2.6	3.1	2.6	2.7	1.9	5.2
Unidentified manufactures	6.1	5.2	3.3	3.3	17.5	65.5	2.4	2.1	1.1	1.2	2.8	3.1
Agricultural And Livestock Products	30.1	65.5	33.6	48.5	37.9	40.2	5.0	9.3	4.3	6.4	6.3	11.2
Agricultural products	28.3	64.8	31.4	45.8	37.6	39.9	5.0	9.1	4.2	6.4	6.3	11.1
Livestock and livestock products	1.8	0.7	2.3	2.8	0.2	0.3	...	0.1	0.1	...	...	0.1
Other Commodities	138.4	130.9	141.4	132.7	129.8	127.1	16.2	6.6	7.8	10.2	9.9	13.6
Forestry products	0.8	0.1	0.4	0.1	0.4	0.5	...	...	0.1	...	...	...
Fish and other marine products	...	0.3	0.1	...	0.3	0.1	...	...	0.1	...	...	...
Metallic ores and concentrates	...	0.5	0.1	0.1	0.6	...	...	...	...	...	...	...
Bituminous coal and lignite	...	...	...	...	...	...	...	...	...	...	...	...
Crude petroleum and natural gas	...	...	...	...	...	...	...	...	...	...	...	...
Nonmetallic minerals	109.9	108.0	112.5	116.5	99.4	93.4	13.4	1.6	4.9	6.4	5.9	5.1
Scrap and waste	11.6	14.1	9.7	4.4	16.6	12.4	1.1	1.1	0.2	0.7	0.5	2.0
Used merchandise	1.5	5.7	5.3	4.3	3.8	4.3	0.5	3.4	1.1	1.5	1.7	1.2
Goods imported and returned unchanged	...	...	...	...	...	...	...	...	...	...	...	...
Special classification provisions	14.6	2.1	13.4	7.2	8.8	16.4	1.3	0.5	1.5	1.6	1.7	5.2

Table D-13. GEORGIA: State Exports of Goods by Destination and Industry, 1994–1999—*Continued*

(Millions of dollars.)

Industry	Germany						France					
	1994	1995	1996	1997	1998	1999	1994	1995	1996	1997	1998	1999
ALL GOODS	259.3	298.9	311.5	340.0	338.3	403.8	172.8	243.4	246.2	279.6	291.3	276.1
Manufactured Goods	235.2	282.1	289.4	318.6	330.5	388.9	169.4	239.4	244.2	276.9	288.4	271.5
Food products	2.5	2.6	5.9	3.1	3.5	3.8	2.7	2.5	2.0	1.8	3.6	3.4
Tobacco products	...	0.5	0.6	0.3	1.5	2.2	...	...	...	0.7	4.0	0.2
Textile mill products	8.2	10.4	12.6	10.6	5.4	5.3	2.8	2.2	2.2	2.0	1.7	1.6
Apparel	3.1	2.1	1.5	1.5	1.1	8.1	0.5	0.5	0.2	0.3	0.8	0.5
Lumber and wood products	22.5	17.6	17.9	32.9	14.1	4.6	2.0	1.2	0.7	2.1	1.2	1.0
Furniture and fixtures	2.1	0.5	0.4	1.2	0.7	0.7	0.1	0.3	0.3	0.3	0.5	0.2
Paper products	15.2	19.8	14.9	15.9	17.5	71.3	28.2	58.1	51.4	60.3	48.7	42.3
Printing and publishing	0.4	0.9	4.5	0.7	1.0	1.1	0.4	0.8	0.8	0.5	0.5	0.2
Chemical products	8.0	10.0	11.5	16.0	12.7	33.6	4.8	6.4	10.0	15.8	29.3	26.2
Refined petroleum products	...	...	0.1	...	...	0.1	11.8	18.1	15.9	10.0	9.9	9.1
Rubber and plastic products	5.4	5.3	5.0	6.2	6.5	8.8	3.1	2.5	1.8	1.3	2.3	2.2
Leather products	0.7	0.6	0.2	...	0.2	0.5	0.3	0.2	0.1	0.1	0.2	0.2
Stone, clay and glass products	1.0	1.1	0.9	1.6	2.0	2.9	0.2	0.6	0.8	5.4	4.5	2.8
Primary metals	0.9	4.3	12.5	9.6	19.8	10.5	1.0	1.0	3.2	1.1	2.5	8.9
Fabricated metal products	4.8	3.0	4.1	6.7	6.5	10.3	1.5	1.8	2.2	4.9	2.6	2.8
Industrial machinery and computers	60.9	80.2	74.1	68.6	68.4	73.4	68.0	105.3	110.5	111.8	121.1	115.4
Electric and electronic equipment	9.0	21.3	17.7	43.7	32.2	31.3	19.4	15.1	7.6	6.9	15.6	14.1
Transportation equipment	49.1	61.8	62.0	58.0	87.3	61.3	15.6	12.7	25.0	41.9	23.8	25.5
Scientific and measuring instruments	36.5	36.7	40.3	37.6	40.7	30.8	5.7	9.2	8.3	8.4	14.3	10.3
Miscellaneous manufactures	3.7	2.6	2.2	3.7	3.3	4.1	0.8	0.5	1.1	1.2	0.7	2.0
Unidentified manufactures	1.1	0.7	0.6	0.5	6.3	24.2	0.7	0.4	0.3	0.2	0.6	2.8
Agricultural And Livestock Products	3.7	5.1	2.7	1.8	2.8	1.3	2.4	2.2	0.3	0.9	0.6	1.1
Agricultural products	3.3	5.0	2.3	1.6	2.8	1.2	1.2	1.7	0.3	0.8	0.5	1.0
Livestock and livestock products	0.4	0.1	0.4	0.2	...	0.1	1.2	0.5	...	0.1	0.1	0.1
Other Commodities	20.4	11.7	19.4	19.5	5.0	13.6	1.0	1.8	1.7	1.8	2.3	3.5
Forestry products	...	...	...	...	...	...	...	...	...	...	...	...
Fish and other marine products	...	0.3	...	...	...	...	...	...	...	...	...	...
Metallic ores and concentrates	...	...	...	...	...	...	...	...	...	...	0.1	...
Bituminous coal and lignite	...	...	...	...	...	...	...	...	...	...	...	...
Crude petroleum and natural gas	...	...	...	...	...	...	...	...	...	...	...	...
Nonmetallic minerals	8.1	10.6	8.5	17.3	2.5	0.9	0.7	0.3	0.6	0.5	1.0	1.2
Scrap and waste	0.3	0.2	0.1	...	...	8.2	...	...	...	0.1	...	...
Used merchandise	0.2	0.2	1.6	1.0	0.9	1.1	0.1	1.4	0.8	0.5	0.8	1.0
Goods imported and returned unchanged	...	...	...	...	...	...	...	...	...	...	...	...
Special classification provisions	11.8	0.5	9.2	1.2	1.6	3.4	0.2	0.1	0.1	0.6	0.4	1.3

Industry	The Netherlands						Asian 10					
	1994	1995	1996	1997	1998	1999	1994	1995	1996	1997	1998	1999
ALL GOODS	241.1	282.2	259.5	380.2	367.3	422.8	1 287.8	1 874.8	1 732.9	1 976.8	1 690.3	1 795.7
Manufactured Goods	216.2	229.5	220.0	321.0	320.9	377.8	1 187.0	1 756.2	1 613.4	1 845.8	1 568.0	1 677.4
Food products	7.0	14.4	26.7	9.9	9.4	6.7	126.4	201.6	221.8	171.2	140.4	176.9
Tobacco products	0.7	0.9	1.1	1.5	1.7	1.4	0.3	0.4	0.4	0.3	0.9	3.1
Textile mill products	6.6	4.9	8.2	7.5	5.5	6.6	114.6	103.5	103.1	106.8	67.7	56.3
Apparel	1.3	1.1	1.3	0.6	0.4	0.3	14.7	16.2	17.3	13.9	10.1	5.2
Lumber and wood products	22.9	22.7	11.9	18.4	9.6	5.0	52.0	49.6	51.5	39.9	34.8	33.4
Furniture and fixtures	0.1	0.8	0.2	0.8	1.4	0.5	3.6	4.6	5.2	6.9	4.3	6.2
Paper products	45.7	79.5	59.1	73.0	64.8	44.4	178.7	316.4	228.7	171.1	144.7	243.4
Printing and publishing	3.6	1.2	4.5	3.2	3.0	4.1	2.6	2.8	8.2	8.9	10.2	5.5
Chemical products	8.5	13.4	12.0	70.3	44.2	36.6	130.4	139.6	181.3	381.3	343.7	162.0
Refined petroleum products	1.6	1.9	1.4	1.7	0.7	0.4	9.8	11.9	22.3	27.7	12.7	14.4
Rubber and plastic products	7.8	6.1	5.0	1.9	2.0	2.0	15.8	22.5	32.8	42.3	28.0	16.0
Leather products	0.5	0.6	0.1	0.2	...	0.6	1.3	2.6	1.6	1.6	1.7	2.3
Stone, clay and glass products	2.0	2.8	2.3	0.6	2.3	1.8	8.5	5.8	6.8	7.1	8.0	11.9
Primary metals	1.0	0.4	0.6	3.3	6.1	21.2	82.7	106.8	133.7	125.8	194.0	153.5
Fabricated metal products	1.5	0.7	1.0	1.1	4.1	5.6	22.1	38.4	24.1	25.5	25.8	46.1
Industrial machinery and computers	27.3	37.3	45.7	58.6	56.0	65.7	158.8	179.0	166.1	187.3	126.8	173.8
Electric and electronic equipment	6.2	13.1	6.0	13.9	28.2	40.3	104.7	144.6	216.5	262.3	182.9	160.4
Transportation equipment	61.9	23.4	28.7	41.4	74.6	119.6	103.7	347.2	93.6	127.2	100.9	223.0
Scientific and measuring instruments	8.4	2.9	2.8	10.5	4.7	10.6	39.8	45.8	78.9	117.8	100.3	146.3
Miscellaneous manufactures	1.2	0.8	0.9	2.3	1.7	3.8	13.8	14.0	17.0	18.2	18.7	16.0
Unidentified manufactures	0.3	0.5	0.3	0.2	0.7	0.8	2.6	2.8	2.5	2.8	11.5	21.9
Agricultural And Livestock Products	13.4	29.9	12.9	31.9	22.2	23.6	6.4	13.6	14.6	25.0	23.4	7.2
Agricultural products	13.4	29.9	11.7	29.5	22.1	23.6	5.9	10.2	12.3	24.0	23.2	7.2
Livestock and livestock products	...	...	1.1	2.4	0.1	...	0.5	3.5	2.3	1.0	0.1	...
Other Commodities	11.5	22.8	26.6	27.3	24.2	21.4	94.4	105.0	104.9	106.0	98.9	111.1
Forestry products	...	...	...	...	0.4	0.5	0.6	0.7	0.8	0.4	0.8	1.1
Fish and other marine products	...	...	...	...	0.2	...	0.7	2.4	0.5	1.6	1.2	1.1
Metallic ores and concentrates	...	0.5	0.1	0.1	0.4	...	...	...	...	...	...	...
Bituminous coal and lignite	...	...	...	...	...	...	...	...	...	...	...	...
Crude petroleum and natural gas	...	...	...	...	...	...	...	...	...	...	...	...
Nonmetallic minerals	10.2	18.3	23.7	25.1	21.6	18.7	75.6	81.0	86.7	87.4	86.8	96.8
Scrap and waste	0.8	3.4	2.6	1.4	1.3	0.7	15.6	19.2	9.4	10.7	3.5	4.7
Used merchandise	0.1	0.4	0.1	0.4	0.1	0.5	1.0	0.5	1.6	2.9	1.3	0.3
Goods imported and returned unchanged	...	...	...	...	...	...	...	...	...	...	...	...
Special classification provisions	0.4	0.2	0.1	0.3	0.3	1.0	0.9	1.2	5.8	3.0	5.3	7.1

Table D-13. GEORGIA: State Exports of Goods by Destination and Industry, 1994–1999—*Continued*

(Millions of dollars.)

Industry	Japan						South Korea					
	1994	1995	1996	1997	1998	1999	1994	1995	1996	1997	1998	1999
ALL GOODS	401.8	589.9	567.6	622.3	589.6	708.2	174.1	429.1	236.5	253.5	233.4	132.0
Manufactured Goods	358.2	540.4	512.7	558.5	522.2	647.7	155.4	410.0	217.8	235.0	219.4	113.1
Food products	25.2	46.9	44.7	20.8	11.7	14.6	2.5	4.5	4.8	3.0	4.8	9.8
Tobacco products	0.1	0.2	0.2	0.2	0.6	2.8	...	...	...	...	...	...
Textile mill products	18.5	20.7	16.3	15.4	14.4	11.9	17.2	7.5	5.7	4.4	1.2	4.0
Apparel	5.7	9.8	7.3	6.4	4.7	3.3	0.1	0.6	0.6	0.5	0.2	0.3
Lumber and wood products	25.7	26.8	29.9	17.9	15.7	8.1	2.8	1.3	0.6	3.1	0.8	5.3
Furniture and fixtures	1.0	2.1	2.1	3.5	3.5	5.5	0.5	0.1	0.4	0.6	...	0.1
Paper products	65.8	131.8	83.2	63.3	53.6	98.1	48.1	89.4	53.7	32.9	25.4	24.9
Printing and publishing	1.0	1.1	4.6	5.1	8.0	1.2	...	0.1	0.1	0.1	...	0.2
Chemical products	16.5	18.4	16.3	103.3	39.8	45.8	13.4	22.9	75.4	115.1	142.2	17.8
Refined petroleum products	0.1	0.2	0.2	0.1	0.6	0.3	...	...	0.1	...	...	0.1
Rubber and plastic products	9.6	16.2	21.2	29.4	19.7	10.3	0.2	1.0	0.6	2.7	3.9	1.2
Leather products	0.5	0.2	0.5	0.7	1.1	1.4	0.3	1.9	0.1	0.1	...	...
Stone, clay and glass products	1.5	1.4	1.5	2.4	4.5	2.5	1.4	0.6	0.7	0.6	0.3	0.9
Primary metals	77.8	91.3	109.0	90.5	133.9	108.2	0.5	1.0	9.2	9.2	8.5	8.7
Fabricated metal products	15.6	14.2	7.7	7.6	8.0	6.8	0.8	2.6	1.2	1.7	1.4	1.3
Industrial machinery and computers	41.1	39.0	38.9	45.0	51.8	50.5	9.3	20.8	29.1	18.7	11.5	12.1
Electric and electronic equipment	19.8	36.1	69.7	52.4	45.6	43.1	23.1	20.3	12.7	13.8	5.6	7.3
Transportation equipment	13.9	62.7	31.4	54.6	64.9	175.9	22.5	226.4	5.5	9.7	2.6	6.9
Scientific and measuring instruments	9.1	12.7	20.2	31.8	24.5	33.8	9.8	6.4	12.1	16.0	9.0	8.9
Miscellaneous manufactures	8.8	7.3	7.0	7.7	8.1	6.6	2.2	2.4	4.8	2.7	1.4	1.9
Unidentified manufactures	1.1	1.1	0.7	0.6	7.5	16.9	0.3	0.2	0.3	0.3	0.6	1.2
Agricultural And Livestock Products	0.9	2.3	5.4	15.4	16.0	2.3	0.1	0.3	0.1	0.2	0.1	2.0
Agricultural products	0.9	2.3	5.3	15.1	16.0	2.3	0.1	0.3	0.1	0.2	0.1	2.0
Livestock and livestock products	...	...	0.1	0.3	...	...	...	...	...	...	...	...
Other Commodities	42.7	47.2	49.5	48.4	51.4	58.1	18.5	18.7	18.6	18.4	14.0	16.9
Forestry products	0.1	0.5	0.3	0.1	0.7	1.1	...	...	...	...	...	...
Fish and other marine products	0.3	0.9	0.1	0.3	0.1	0.3	...	...	0.2	0.2	...	0.2
Metallic ores and concentrates	...	...	...	...	...	...	...	...	...	...	...	...
Bituminous coal and lignite	...	...	...	...	...	...	...	...	...	...	...	...
Crude petroleum and natural gas	...	...	...	...	...	...	...	...	...	...	...	...
Nonmetallic minerals	39.9	45.1	47.7	46.8	49.4	54.3	15.7	15.1	13.7	15.4	12.9	14.9
Scrap and waste	1.8	0.2	0.9	...	0.2	0.1	2.7	3.4	1.3	1.2	0.1	0.6
Used merchandise	0.5	0.2	0.2	0.7	0.2	0.1	0.1	...	...	0.4	...	...
Goods imported and returned unchanged	...	...	...	...	...	...	...	...	...	...	...	...
Special classification provisions	0.1	0.1	0.3	0.3	0.8	2.1	...	0.1	3.4	1.1	0.9	1.3

Industry	Taiwan						Singapore					
	1994	1995	1996	1997	1998	1999	1994	1995	1996	1997	1998	1999
ALL GOODS	138.9	138.8	120.9	136.4	149.5	163.4	92.8	134.3	158.2	213.3	134.2	172.6
Manufactured Goods	118.3	119.1	106.1	116.7	133.9	146.5	92.4	133.8	157.6	212.5	132.9	171.8
Food products	1.8	1.4	2.8	1.6	7.0	13.0	10.8	13.6	10.0	7.5	6.2	5.3
Tobacco products	...	...	...	...	0.1	...	0.1	...	...	...	...	...
Textile mill products	11.8	3.8	4.0	4.5	3.5	3.9	25.6	26.6	24.8	24.9	12.6	10.1
Apparel	0.4	0.4	0.1	0.3	0.3	0.2	0.6	0.8	1.1	1.1	0.8	0.2
Lumber and wood products	16.4	10.8	6.5	6.7	6.0	4.9	0.2	...	...	...	...	...
Furniture and fixtures	0.9	0.4	0.3	0.1	0.1	...	0.2	0.8	1.3	1.9	0.2	0.2
Paper products	15.5	28.5	16.5	17.5	13.7	20.2	1.1	5.1	5.6	4.8	2.5	2.2
Printing and publishing	0.2	0.7	1.0	0.6	0.1	0.1	0.4	0.4	1.2	1.4	0.5	0.3
Chemical products	14.9	20.2	29.0	41.7	51.4	22.9	2.4	4.7	5.6	8.6	10.6	12.5
Refined petroleum products	...	0.1	...	0.1	...	...	...	1.1	5.7	0.4	0.7	1.6
Rubber and plastic products	0.4	0.7	1.4	0.9	1.0	1.4	0.9	1.2	2.8	4.7	1.0	0.6
Leather products	...	...	0.1	...	...	...	...	0.1	...	0.1	...	0.1
Stone, clay and glass products	0.8	0.4	1.4	0.6	0.3	0.3	0.2	0.4	0.1	0.5	0.1	...
Primary metals	0.8	1.6	1.2	3.3	9.5	8.0	0.5	1.8	1.5	1.7	2.3	2.0
Fabricated metal products	1.8	1.4	1.6	1.5	1.9	2.2	1.9	0.8	2.1	3.8	3.0	2.3
Industrial machinery and computers	32.8	24.4	18.3	15.4	9.7	48.8	12.1	17.6	15.0	26.5	12.4	14.4
Electric and electronic equipment	11.6	17.3	10.7	14.7	21.1	14.2	10.9	10.0	21.0	27.1	9.7	8.6
Transportation equipment	2.3	1.5	5.8	1.3	1.3	1.4	18.7	38.1	30.8	46.8	20.1	32.7
Scientific and measuring instruments	4.5	3.5	4.5	5.1	4.9	3.7	4.9	10.0	27.9	49.8	49.4	77.3
Miscellaneous manufactures	0.9	1.6	0.8	0.6	1.4	0.6	0.7	0.5	0.5	0.5	0.2	0.4
Unidentified manufactures	0.4	0.4	0.2	0.2	0.5	0.5	0.3	0.3	0.3	0.3	0.5	0.8
Agricultural And Livestock Products	0.1	0.1	1.1	1.9	0.7	0.9	0.1	...	...	0.1	...	0.1
Agricultural products	0.1	0.1	1.1	1.9	0.7	0.9	0.1	...	...	0.1	...	0.1
Livestock and livestock products	...	...	...	...	...	...	...	...	...	...	...	...
Other Commodities	20.5	19.6	13.7	17.8	14.9	16.0	0.3	0.5	0.6	0.7	1.3	0.8
Forestry products	...	...	0.1	...	...	...	...	...	0.1	...	...	...
Fish and other marine products	...	...	...	0.1	0.1	0.1	0.2	0.2	0.1	0.2	0.3	0.2
Metallic ores and concentrates	...	...	...	...	...	...	...	...	...	...	...	...
Bituminous coal and lignite	...	...	...	...	...	...	...	...	...	...	...	...
Crude petroleum and natural gas	...	...	...	...	...	...	...	...	...	...	...	...
Nonmetallic minerals	10.8	11.4	8.4	11.7	13.1	13.2	...	...	...	0.3	0.3	0.3
Scrap and waste	9.5	8.2	4.7	5.1	0.4	0.4	...	...	...	...	0.1	...
Used merchandise	0.1	...	...	...	...	...	...	...	0.1	0.1	0.1	...
Goods imported and returned unchanged	...	...	...	...	...	...	...	...	...	...	...	...
Special classification provisions	...	...	0.5	0.9	1.2	2.2	0.1	0.2	0.3	0.1	0.4	0.3

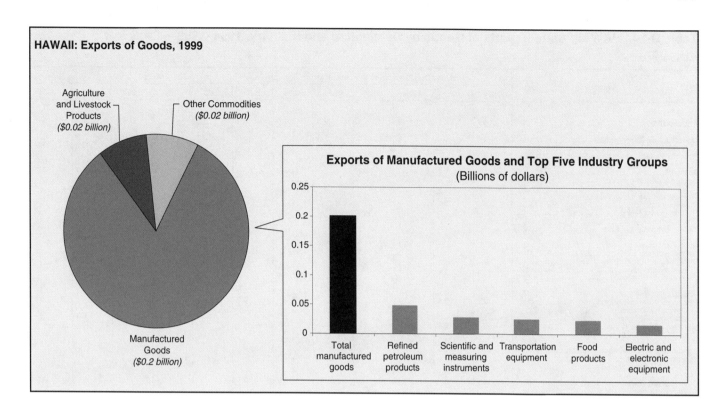

HAWAII: Exports of Goods, 1999

Agriculture and Livestock Products ($0.02 billion)

Other Commodities ($0.02 billion)

Manufactured Goods ($0.2 billion)

Exports of Manufactured Goods and Top Five Industry Groups
(Billions of dollars)

Table D-14. HAWAII: State Exports of Goods by Destination and Industry, 1994–1999

(Millions of dollars.)

Industry	All destinations						Canada					
	1994	1995	1996	1997	1998	1999	1994	1995	1996	1997	1998	1999
ALL GOODS	237.4	255.7	295.2	303.2	211.4	243.5	13.4	53.1	69.8	33.3	16.8	21.5
Manufactured Goods	183.0	210.6	247.3	255.8	156.6	200.4	4.2	43.6	59.2	22.5	10.8	13.7
Food products	44.1	35.7	35.6	30.5	23.6	23.9	1.6	5.4	8.0	3.4	2.1	1.4
Tobacco products	. . .	. . .	0.1	. . .	. . .	. . .	. . .	. . .	0.1	. . .	. . .	. . .
Textile mill products	0.4	1.0	1.3	1.3	0.9	0.9	. . .	0.1	0.3	. . .	. . .	. . .
Apparel	8.0	13.3	11.8	9.2	6.7	8.6	. . .	0.2	0.1	. . .	. . .	. . .
Lumber and wood products	0.4	3.7	4.1	2.5	0.6	1.2	. . .	2.9	3.8	1.5	. . .	. . .
Furniture and fixtures	3.4	1.7	2.4	0.8	0.8	0.3	. . .	0.2	0.6	0.1	. . .	. . .
Paper products	0.4	3.7	4.5	1.6	0.4	0.3	. . .	2.3	3.5	1.0	0.1	0.1
Printing and publishing	12.2	4.4	4.5	3.0	1.0	1.8	. . .	0.3	0.5	. . .	. . .	0.1
Chemical products	5.1	6.0	15.1	6.5	4.2	7.3	0.1	2.9	8.7	2.3	0.3	0.3
Refined petroleum products	49.7	50.4	70.8	99.5	42.9	48.4	. . .	0.4	0.9	0.2	. . .	0.1
Rubber and plastic products	0.4	1.1	2.1	1.3	0.8	0.3	. . .	0.5	1.6	0.7	. . .	. . .
Leather products	4.9	4.0	3.4	2.8	1.5	2.0	. . .	0.2	. . .	. . .	. . .	. . .
Stone, clay and glass products	0.6	1.9	1.3	0.8	0.7	1.6	. . .	0.4	0.7	0.3	. . .	. . .
Primary metals	0.8	3.1	6.5	1.8	0.5	0.8	. . .	2.6	5.7	1.4	. . .	. . .
Fabricated metal products	1.5	2.5	2.1	1.2	0.2	1.1	. . .	1.3	1.3	0.2	0.1	0.5
Industrial machinery and computers	9.2	10.3	13.7	11.0	8.4	9.8	0.2	5.4	7.4	2.6	0.6	1.2
Electric and electronic equipment	5.7	14.7	13.3	9.4	7.8	16.4	0.3	7.9	4.2	1.1	1.6	0.7
Transportation equipment	14.9	19.5	20.7	35.2	17.0	25.9	0.8	8.5	8.7	5.1	3.2	3.1
Scientific and measuring instruments	10.9	16.9	17.8	22.9	20.5	28.5	0.5	1.3	2.0	1.7	1.7	5.0
Miscellaneous manufactures	7.7	13.9	14.1	12.3	14.0	16.4	0.1	0.4	0.2	0.1	0.1	0.1
Unidentified manufactures	2.7	3.0	2.2	2.4	4.0	4.9	0.5	0.6	0.7	0.8	1.0	0.9
Agricultural And Livestock Products	21.6	27.6	25.9	22.2	21.5	20.9	5.8	4.8	2.3	2.0	2.2	4.5
Agricultural products	18.2	23.8	24.0	21.1	20.0	17.7	2.7	1.8	1.8	1.7	1.4	1.7
Livestock and livestock products	3.5	3.7	1.9	1.1	1.5	3.2	3.1	3.0	0.6	0.3	0.8	2.8
Other Commodities	32.7	17.5	22.0	25.2	33.3	22.2	3.4	4.6	8.2	8.8	3.8	3.3
Forestry products	0.1	0.1	0.1	0.1	0.1	0.1	. . .	. . .	. . .	. . .	. . .	0.1
Fish and other marine products	7.4	7.2	5.3	4.1	6.0	6.3	0.5	1.2	2.4	1.4	1.1	0.8
Metallic ores and concentrates	. . .	. . .	. . .	. . .	. . .	. . .	. . .	. . .	. . .	. . .	. . .	. . .
Bituminous coal and lignite	. . .	. . .	. . .	. . .	. . .	. . .	. . .	. . .	. . .	. . .	. . .	. . .
Crude petroleum and natural gas	. . .	. . .	. . .	. . .	0.1	0.1	. . .	. . .	. . .	. . .	. . .	. . .
Nonmetallic minerals	0.1	0.1	0.1	0.1	. . .	0.4	. . .	0.1	0.1	0.1	. . .	. . .
Scrap and waste	1.6	0.7	2.8	0.4	2.3	0.2	. . .	0.1	0.3	. . .	. . .	. . .
Used merchandise	21.0	6.6	8.3	14.1	22.0	12.1	0.7	0.6	0.5	1.3	0.4	0.2
Goods imported and returned unchanged	2.2	2.3	4.6	5.9	2.3	2.2	2.2	2.3	4.6	5.9	2.3	2.2
Special classification provisions	0.4	0.4	0.8	0.4	0.4	0.8	. . .	0.2	0.4	0.1	0.1	0.1

Table D-14. HAWAII: State Exports of Goods by Destination and Industry, 1994–1999—*Continued*

(Millions of dollars.)

Industry	South and Central American and Caribbean						Mexico					
	1994	1995	1996	1997	1998	1999	1994	1995	1996	1997	1998	1999
ALL GOODS	0.7	0.8	1.2	1.1	2.0	1.6	6.0	0.3	0.7	1.0	1.9	0.8
Manufactured Goods	0.6	0.6	1.2	1.0	1.9	1.3	5.9	0.2	0.5	0.8	1.8	0.6
Food products	...	...	...	...	...	...	...	...	...	...	0.1	0.1
Tobacco products	...	...	...	...	...	...	...	...	...	...	...	...
Textile mill products	...	...	...	...	...	0.1	...	...	0.3	0.2	0.1	0.1
Apparel	0.2	0.1	0.1	0.1	...	...	...	...	...	0.1	0.0	0.1
Lumber and wood products	...	...	...	...	...	...	...	...	...	...	...	...
Furniture and fixtures	...	...	...	...	...	...	...	...	...	...	...	...
Paper products	...	0.1	...	...	...	...	...	...	...	...	...	...
Printing and publishing	...	...	...	...	1.2	...	...	...	...	...	...	...
Chemical products	...	...	...	...	0.1	...	...	...	...	...	...	...
Refined petroleum products	...	...	...	...	...	...	...	...	...	...	...	...
Rubber and plastic products	...	...	0.1	0.1	0.1	...	...	...	...	...	...	...
Leather products	...	...	...	0.1	...	...	...	...	...	...	...	...
Stone, clay and glass products	...	...	...	...	...	...	...	...	...	...	...	...
Primary metals	...	...	0.2	...	...	0.1	...	...	...	...	...	...
Fabricated metal products	...	0.1	...	...	...	0.1	...	0.1	...	...	...	...
Industrial machinery and computers	...	...	...	0.1	...	0.1	0.3	...	0.1	0.1	...	...
Electric and electronic equipment	0.1	0.1	...	...	...	0.2	0.1	...	...	...	...	...
Transportation equipment	...	...	0.5	0.1	...	...	5.4	...	...	...	...	...
Scientific and measuring instruments	...	...	...	...	...	0.3	...	...	...	0.3	1.5	...
Miscellaneous manufactures	0.2	0.2	0.2	0.3	0.3	0.2	...	...	...	0.1	0.1	0.1
Unidentified manufactures	...	...	...	...	...	0.1	...	...	...	...	...	0.1
Agricultural And Livestock Products	...	...	...	...	...	...	...	...	...	0.2	...	...
Agricultural products	...	...	...	...	...	...	...	...	...	0.2	...	...
Livestock and livestock products	...	...	...	...	...	...	...	...	...	...	...	...
Other Commodities	0.1	0.1	...	...	...	0.2	0.1	...	...	0.2	0.1	0.1
Forestry products	...	...	...	...	...	...	...	...	...	...	...	...
Fish and other marine products	0.1	...	...	...	...	0.2	...	...	...	0.1	0.1	0.1
Metallic ores and concentrates	...	...	...	...	...	...	...	...	...	...	...	...
Bituminous coal and lignite	...	...	...	...	...	...	...	...	...	...	...	...
Crude petroleum and natural gas	...	...	...	...	...	...	...	...	...	...	...	...
Nonmetallic minerals	...	...	...	...	...	...	...	...	...	...	...	...
Scrap and waste	...	...	...	...	...	...	...	...	...	...	...	...
Used merchandise	...	...	...	...	...	...	...	...	...	...	...	...
Goods imported and returned unchanged	...	...	...	...	...	...	...	...	...	...	...	...
Special classification provisions	...	...	...	...	...	...	...	...	...	...	...	...

Industry	European Union						United Kingdom					
	1994	1995	1996	1997	1998	1999	1994	1995	1996	1997	1998	1999
ALL GOODS	6.5	7.8	9.4	7.1	10.5	11.8	0.9	1.1	2.9	2.0	2.3	3.9
Manufactured Goods	3.9	5.3	6.0	5.6	6.3	9.3	0.5	0.9	1.2	1.8	2.1	3.4
Food products	0.1	0.1	0.5	0.1	0.1	...	...	...	...	...	...	...
Tobacco products	...	...	...	...	...	...	...	...	...	...	...	...
Textile mill products	...	...	...	...	...	...	...	...	...	...	...	...
Apparel	0.3	0.4	0.4	0.2	0.1	0.1	...	0.1	...	...	...	...
Lumber and wood products	...	...	...	...	0.2	0.2	...	...	...	...	...	...
Furniture and fixtures	...	...	...	...	...	...	...	...	...	...	...	...
Paper products	...	0.1	...	...	...	...	...	...	...	...	...	...
Printing and publishing	...	0.1	...	0.3	0.2	0.1	...	...	...	...	...	...
Chemical products	0.1	0.1	0.4	0.1	0.4	0.2	...	0.1	0.3	...	...	...
Refined petroleum products	...	...	...	...	...	...	...	...	...	...	...	...
Rubber and plastic products	...	...	...	...	...	...	...	...	...	...	...	...
Leather products	0.2	0.1	0.1	0.5	...	0.3	...	...	...	...	...	...
Stone, clay and glass products	...	0.4	...	0.1	...	0.2	...	...	...	...	...	...
Primary metals	...	...	...	...	...	...	...	...	...	...	...	...
Fabricated metal products	...	...	0.1	0.1	...	0.1	...	...	...	0.1	...	0.1
Industrial machinery and computers	0.3	0.3	0.6	0.3	0.5	0.9	...	0.3	...	0.3	0.1	0.4
Electric and electronic equipment	0.2	0.5	0.7	1.3	0.8	0.6	0.1	0.1	0.1	0.5	0.5	0.5
Transportation equipment	1.4	1.5	0.6	0.2	0.2	0.1	...	...	...	0.1	0.1	...
Scientific and measuring instruments	0.7	1.2	1.9	1.6	2.5	4.5	0.2	0.2	0.5	0.7	0.7	1.4
Miscellaneous manufactures	0.4	0.4	0.3	0.6	1.0	1.6	0.1	0.1	0.1	0.1	0.4	0.7
Unidentified manufactures	0.1	0.1	0.1	0.1	0.2	0.4	...	...	...	...	0.1	0.1
Agricultural And Livestock Products	1.6	1.8	1.5	0.8	1.5	1.2	0.1	0.1	0.1	0.1	0.1	0.1
Agricultural products	1.5	1.6	1.2	0.6	1.2	1.0	...	...	0.1	...	...	...
Livestock and livestock products	0.1	0.2	0.2	0.2	0.3	0.2	0.1	0.1	0.1	...	0.1	0.1
Other Commodities	1.0	0.7	1.9	0.7	2.7	1.3	0.4	0.2	1.5	0.2	0.1	0.5
Forestry products	...	...	...	...	...	...	...	...	...	...	...	...
Fish and other marine products	0.4	0.4	0.2	0.2	1.3	0.7	...	...	0.1	0.1	...	0.1
Metallic ores and concentrates	...	...	...	...	...	...	...	...	...	...	...	...
Bituminous coal and lignite	...	...	...	...	...	...	...	...	...	...	...	...
Crude petroleum and natural gas	...	...	...	...	...	...	...	...	...	...	...	...
Nonmetallic minerals	...	...	...	...	...	...	...	...	...	...	...	...
Scrap and waste	...	...	...	...	...	...	...	...	...	...	...	...
Used merchandise	0.6	0.3	1.7	0.4	1.2	0.6	0.4	0.1	1.5	0.1	0.1	0.3
Goods imported and returned unchanged	...	...	...	...	...	...	...	...	...	...	...	...
Special classification provisions	...	...	...	0.1	0.1	...	...	...	...	...	...	...

Table D-14. HAWAII: State Exports of Goods by Destination and Industry, 1994–1999—*Continued*

(Millions of dollars.)

Industry	Germany						France					
	1994	1995	1996	1997	1998	1999	1994	1995	1996	1997	1998	1999
ALL GOODS	2.3	2.4	2.5	1.4	3.7	3.1	1.6	1.9	1.5	1.3	1.1	1.5
Manufactured Goods	1.2	1.3	1.5	0.7	1.5	1.9	1.5	1.9	1.5	1.1	0.9	1.2
Food products	...	...	0.4	0.1	...	...	...	0.1	0.1	...	...	...
Tobacco products	...	...	...	...	...	...	...	...	...	...	...	...
Textile mill products	...	...	...	...	...	...	...	...	...	...	...	...
Apparel	...	0.1	0.1	...	...	...	...	0.1	0.1	...	...	...
Lumber and wood products	...	...	...	...	...	...	...	...	...	...	...	...
Furniture and fixtures	...	...	...	...	...	...	...	...	...	...	...	...
Paper products	...	...	...	...	...	...	...	...	...	...	...	...
Printing and publishing	...	...	...	...	0.1	...	...	...	...	0.2	0.1	...
Chemical products	...	...	...	...	...	...	0.1	...	...	0.1	0.4	0.1
Refined petroleum products	...	...	...	...	...	...	...	...	...	...	...	...
Rubber and plastic products	...	...	...	...	...	...	...	...	...	...	...	...
Leather products	...	...	...	...	...	...	0.2	...	0.1	0.1	...	0.2
Stone, clay and glass products	...	...	...	...	...	...	...	...	...	...	...	...
Primary metals	...	...	...	...	...	...	...	...	...	...	...	...
Fabricated metal products	...	...	...	...	...	...	...	...	...	...	...	...
Industrial machinery and computers	0.2	...	0.6	...	0.3	...	...	...	...	...	...	0.2
Electric and electronic equipment	0.1	0.3	0.1	0.1	0.1	...	...	0.1	0.2	0.3	...	...
Transportation equipment	0.7	0.5	...	...	...	...	0.6	0.8	...	...	...	...
Scientific and measuring instruments	0.1	...	0.1	0.3	0.8	1.5	0.3	0.7	0.7	0.2	0.1	0.5
Miscellaneous manufactures	...	0.1	0.2	0.1	0.1	0.2	0.2	0.1	...	0.1	0.2	0.1
Unidentified manufactures	...	...	...	...	0.1	0.1	...	...	...	...	...	0.2
Agricultural And Livestock Products	0.9	1.0	0.9	0.6	1.2	0.9	0.1	...	...	0.1	0.1	...
Agricultural products	0.9	0.9	0.8	0.5	1.0	0.9	0.1	...	...	...	...	...
Livestock and livestock products	...	0.1	...	...	0.1	0.1	...	...	...	...	0.1	...
Other Commodities	0.2	0.2	0.2	0.1	1.0	0.2	...	...	...	0.2	0.2	0.2
Forestry products	...	...	...	...	...	...	...	...	...	...	...	...
Fish and other marine products	...	...	...	...	0.6	...	...	...	...	...	0.1	0.2
Metallic ores and concentrates	...	...	...	...	...	...	...	...	...	...	...	...
Bituminous coal and lignite	...	...	...	...	...	...	...	...	...	...	...	...
Crude petroleum and natural gas	...	...	...	...	...	...	...	...	...	...	...	...
Nonmetallic minerals	...	...	...	...	...	...	...	...	...	...	...	...
Scrap and waste	...	...	...	...	...	...	...	...	...	...	...	...
Used merchandise	0.1	0.2	0.2	0.1	0.5	0.1	...	...	...	0.1	0.1	0.1
Goods imported and returned unchanged	...	...	...	...	...	...	...	...	...	...	...	...
Special classification provisions	...	...	...	...	...	...	...	...	...	...	...	...

Industry	The Netherlands						Asian 10					
	1994	1995	1996	1997	1998	1999	1994	1995	1996	1997	1998	1999
ALL GOODS	0.8	1.1	1.5	0.4	0.9	1.0	180.0	170.8	190.8	217.2	152.3	170.3
Manufactured Goods	0.2	0.3	1.1	0.2	0.1	0.6	138.9	139.5	158.3	183.6	113.6	139.1
Food products	...	...	...	...	...	...	39.6	27.7	25.5	25.7	20.0	20.5
Tobacco products	...	...	...	...	...	...	...	...	...	...	...	...
Textile mill products	...	...	...	...	...	...	0.4	0.6	0.6	0.6	0.4	0.6
Apparel	...	...	...	...	...	...	7.3	12.4	10.4	8.5	6.2	8.2
Lumber and wood products	...	...	...	...	...	...	0.3	0.7	0.2	0.5	0.3	0.6
Furniture and fixtures	...	...	...	...	...	...	3.3	1.4	1.4	0.6	0.6	0.2
Paper products	...	...	...	...	...	...	0.3	1.3	0.8	0.5	0.2	0.2
Printing and publishing	...	...	...	...	...	...	6.2	1.9	2.5	2.4	0.6	1.3
Chemical products	...	...	...	...	...	...	4.0	1.9	4.9	3.1	2.3	3.1
Refined petroleum products	...	...	...	...	...	...	38.8	45.5	65.0	92.1	40.3	40.8
Rubber and plastic products	...	...	...	...	...	...	0.2	0.5	0.3	0.3	0.6	0.2
Leather products	...	...	...	...	...	...	4.6	3.9	3.0	2.1	1.5	1.7
Stone, clay and glass products	...	...	...	...	...	0.1	0.4	0.7	0.5	0.4	0.6	0.7
Primary metals	...	...	...	...	...	...	0.7	0.5	0.6	0.2	0.1	0.2
Fabricated metal products	...	...	0.1	...	...	...	1.2	0.6	0.5	0.7	0.1	0.3
Industrial machinery and computers	...	...	...	...	...	...	6.5	2.3	3.7	6.7	3.9	2.9
Electric and electronic equipment	...	0.1	0.2	...	...	...	4.2	5.6	6.7	6.1	4.2	13.6
Transportation equipment	0.1	0.1	0.5	0.1	...	...	4.7	5.4	5.3	4.0	4.5	9.7
Scientific and measuring instruments	...	...	0.2	...	0.1	0.4	7.9	13.0	13.2	18.1	13.6	17.9
Miscellaneous manufactures	...	...	...	...	...	...	6.5	11.8	12.5	10.1	11.3	13.8
Unidentified manufactures	...	...	...	...	...	...	1.6	1.7	0.9	1.1	2.2	2.8
Agricultural And Livestock Products	0.3	0.4	0.3	0.1	0.1	0.1	13.6	20.4	21.2	19.0	17.5	15.0
Agricultural products	0.2	0.3	0.2	0.1	0.1	0.1	13.3	19.9	20.2	18.4	17.1	14.8
Livestock and livestock products	0.1	0.1	0.1	...	...	...	0.3	0.5	1.0	0.5	0.4	0.2
Other Commodities	0.4	0.4	0.1	0.1	0.7	0.3	27.6	10.9	11.2	14.7	21.2	16.2
Forestry products	...	...	...	...	...	...	0.1	...	0.1	...	0.1	...
Fish and other marine products	0.4	0.4	0.1	0.1	0.6	0.2	6.3	5.4	2.8	2.3	3.2	4.3
Metallic ores and concentrates	...	...	...	...	...	...	...	...	...	...	...	...
Bituminous coal and lignite	...	...	...	...	...	...	...	...	...	...	...	...
Crude petroleum and natural gas	...	...	...	...	...	...	...	...	...	...	...	...
Nonmetallic minerals	...	...	...	...	...	...	0.1	...	...	...	...	...
Scrap and waste	...	...	...	...	...	...	1.6	0.6	2.5	0.4	2.3	0.2
Used merchandise	...	...	...	0.1	...	0.1	19.1	4.7	5.5	11.8	15.3	11.0
Goods imported and returned unchanged	...	...	...	...	...	...	...	...	...	...	...	...
Special classification provisions	...	...	...	...	...	...	0.4	0.2	0.4	0.2	0.3	0.7

Table D-14. HAWAII: State Exports of Goods by Destination and Industry, 1994–1999—*Continued*

(Millions of dollars.)

Industry	Japan						South Korea					
	1994	1995	1996	1997	1998	1999	1994	1995	1996	1997	1998	1999
ALL GOODS	120.1	126.7	161.2	173.0	126.9	136.7	26.2	24.8	9.3	9.7	5.5	10.7
Manufactured Goods	80.6	97.4	133.4	146.1	95.1	109.1	25.6	24.5	8.9	9.6	5.5	10.6
Food products	22.8	19.4	17.5	17.1	14.4	13.0	4.7	4.5	4.3	3.8	1.8	3.0
Tobacco products	...	...	...	...	...	...	...	...	...	...	...	...
Textile mill products	0.2	0.3	0.6	0.6	0.2	0.5	...	...	...	...	...	...
Apparel	7.0	12.1	10.0	7.9	5.9	8.0	0.1	0.2	0.1	...	...	...
Lumber and wood products	0.1	0.7	0.2	0.4	0.3	0.6	...	...	...	...	...	...
Furniture and fixtures	1.3	1.1	1.2	0.5	0.3	0.2	1.9	...	...	...	0.1	...
Paper products	0.3	0.9	0.6	0.4	0.1	0.1	...	...	...	...	...	...
Printing and publishing	6.0	1.7	2.3	2.0	0.5	1.2	...	0.1	...	...	...	...
Chemical products	2.2	1.1	4.4	2.0	1.7	2.7	...	...	0.1	0.1	0.1	...
Refined petroleum products	13.0	21.7	60.2	83.2	40.2	36.5	17.9	17.8	...	...	...	2.0
Rubber and plastic products	0.2	0.5	0.2	0.3	0.5	0.1	...	...	...	...	...	...
Leather products	4.4	3.8	2.8	2.1	1.3	1.6	...	...	...	...	...	...
Stone, clay and glass products	0.4	0.5	0.4	0.3	0.3	0.3	...	...	...	...	0.2	...
Primary metals	...	0.1	0.1	0.1	0.1	0.1	...	...	...	...	...	...
Fabricated metal products	1.1	0.5	0.4	0.4	0.1	0.2	...	...	...	...	...	...
Industrial machinery and computers	2.8	1.2	1.4	2.5	1.8	1.9	...	0.2	0.6	0.4	0.6	0.4
Electric and electronic equipment	3.3	3.7	5.7	3.7	3.5	12.0	0.4	0.3	0.6	2.2	0.4	1.2
Transportation equipment	1.8	4.0	2.7	1.7	1.6	2.0	0.5	0.9	1.8	0.4	0.5	0.5
Scientific and measuring instruments	7.5	12.3	11.6	12.3	12.0	14.7	...	0.5	0.9	2.2	0.7	1.8
Miscellaneous manufactures	5.4	10.5	10.7	7.8	8.5	11.1	...	0.1	0.3	0.4	0.9	1.5
Unidentified manufactures	0.9	1.3	0.6	1.0	1.7	2.2	...	...	...	...	0.1	0.1
Agricultural And Livestock Products	13.3	19.6	20.1	18.4	17.1	14.9	0.1	0.2	...	0.1	0.1	...
Agricultural products	13.1	19.2	19.5	18.0	16.8	14.7	0.1	0.2	...	0.1	0.1	...
Livestock and livestock products	0.2	0.4	0.6	0.4	0.3	0.2	...	...	...	...	...	...
Other Commodities	26.2	9.7	7.7	8.5	14.6	12.8	0.4	...	0.3	0.1	...	0.1
Forestry products	0.1	...	...	...	...	...	...	...	...	...	...	...
Fish and other marine products	6.2	4.8	2.7	1.9	2.3	2.8	...	...	0.1	...	...	...
Metallic ores and concentrates	...	...	...	...	...	...	...	...	...	...	...	...
Bituminous coal and lignite	...	...	...	...	...	...	...	...	...	...	...	...
Crude petroleum and natural gas	...	...	...	...	...	...	...	...	...	...	...	...
Nonmetallic minerals	0.1	...	...	...	...	...	...	...	...	...	...	...
Scrap and waste	0.7	0.4	0.2	0.2	...	...	0.4	...	...	...	...	...
Used merchandise	18.8	4.3	4.7	6.3	12.1	9.4	...	...	...	...	...	...
Goods imported and returned unchanged	...	...	...	...	...	...	...	...	...	...	...	...
Special classification provisions	0.3	0.2	0.1	0.1	0.2	0.6	...	...	0.2	...	...	0.1

Industry	Taiwan						Singapore					
	1994	1995	1996	1997	1998	1999	1994	1995	1996	1997	1998	1999
ALL GOODS	9.6	3.8	4.2	2.1	3.6	2.4	2.1	5.6	5.1	11.9	6.6	7.6
Manufactured Goods	9.3	3.6	1.7	1.6	0.9	1.3	2.1	5.6	4.5	6.6	3.7	6.0
Food products	0.6	0.4	0.2	0.3	0.3	0.2	1.2	1.1	1.1	1.3	0.7	0.8
Tobacco products	...	...	...	...	...	...	...	...	...	...	...	...
Textile mill products	...	0.1	...	...	...	...	...	...	...	...	...	...
Apparel	...	...	...	0.1	...	...	...	...	0.1	0.4	0.2	0.1
Lumber and wood products	...	...	...	...	...	...	...	...	...	...	...	...
Furniture and fixtures	...	0.3	...	...	0.1	...	...	...	...	...	...	...
Paper products	...	...	...	...	...	...	...	...	0.1	...	...	...
Printing and publishing	...	...	...	0.1	...	...	...	...	...	...	...	...
Chemical products	0.1	0.1	0.1	0.1	0.1	...	0.1	...	0.1	0.2	...	0.1
Refined petroleum products	7.9	1.9	...	0.1	...	0.1	...	4.2	2.3	...	...	2.1
Rubber and plastic products	...	...	...	...	...	...	...	...	...	...	...	...
Leather products	...	...	0.1	...	...	...	0.1	...	...	...	...	0.1
Stone, clay and glass products	0.1	0.2	...	0.1	...	0.2	...	...	...	...	...	...
Primary metals	...	...	...	0.2	...	...	...	...	...	...	...	...
Fabricated metal products	...	...	...	...	...	...	...	...	...	...	...	...
Industrial machinery and computers	0.1	0.1	0.7	0.1	0.1	0.1	0.1	...	0.1	...	0.5	0.1
Electric and electronic equipment	...	0.1	...	...	0.1	0.1	0.3	0.1	0.1	...	...	0.1
Transportation equipment	0.2	0.2	0.2	...	...	...	0.1	...	0.1	1.7	1.8	2.4
Scientific and measuring instruments	0.2	0.1	0.1	0.1	...	0.3	0.1	0.1	0.4	2.9	0.4	0.2
Miscellaneous manufactures	0.1	0.1	0.1	0.3	0.1	0.1	0.1	0.1	0.1	...	...	...
Unidentified manufactures	...	...	...	...	0.1	0.1	...	...	...	...	...	...
Agricultural And Livestock Products	...	0.1	0.2	0.1	0.1	...	...	...	...	0.1	...	...
Agricultural products	...	...	...	...	...	...	...	...	...	0.1	...	...
Livestock and livestock products	...	...	0.1	0.1	...	...	...	...	...	...	...	...
Other Commodities	0.3	0.1	2.3	0.3	2.6	1.1	0.1	...	0.6	5.2	2.9	1.5
Forestry products	...	...	...	...	...	...	...	...	...	...	...	...
Fish and other marine products	...	...	...	0.2	0.3	1.1	...	...	...	...	...	0.1
Metallic ores and concentrates	...	...	...	...	...	...	...	...	...	...	...	...
Bituminous coal and lignite	...	...	...	...	...	...	...	...	...	...	...	...
Crude petroleum and natural gas	...	...	...	...	...	...	...	...	...	...	...	...
Nonmetallic minerals	...	...	...	...	...	...	...	...	...	...	...	...
Scrap and waste	0.2	...	2.3	...	2.3	...	...	...	...	...	...	...
Used merchandise	...	0.1	...	0.1	...	...	...	...	0.6	5.2	2.9	1.4
Goods imported and returned unchanged	...	...	...	...	...	...	...	...	...	...	...	...
Special classification provisions	...	...	...	...	...	...	...	...	...	...	...	...

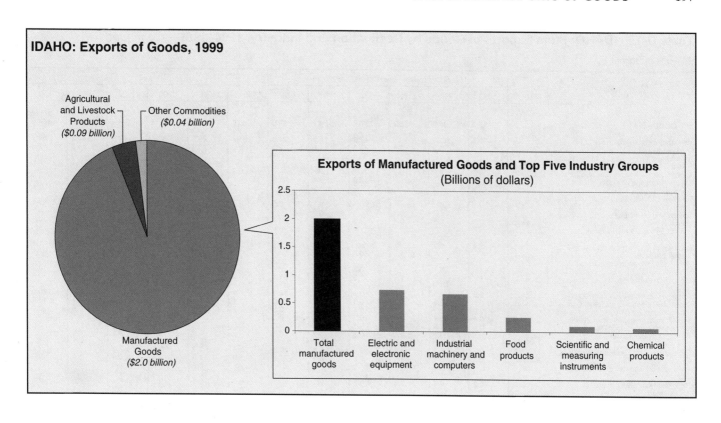

IDAHO: Exports of Goods, 1999

Agricultural and Livestock Products ($0.09 billion)

Other Commodities ($0.04 billion)

Manufactured Goods ($2.0 billion)

Exports of Manufactured Goods and Top Five Industry Groups
(Billions of dollars)

- Total manufactured goods
- Electric and electronic equipment
- Industrial machinery and computers
- Food products
- Scientific and measuring instruments
- Chemical products

Table D-15. IDAHO: State Exports of Goods by Destination and Industry, 1994–1999

(Millions of dollars.)

Industry	All destinations						Canada					
	1994	1995	1996	1997	1998	1999	1994	1995	1996	1997	1998	1999
ALL GOODS	1 530.5	1 892.6	1 610.1	1 716.1	1 460.0	2 116.6	208.7	292.3	276.5	277.9	280.5	280.9
Manufactured Goods	1 469.0	1 831.0	1 539.3	1 634.4	1 362.1	1 989.4	182.8	267.3	245.5	241.5	240.3	230.8
Food products	154.5	213.0	225.5	242.8	252.5	261.9	27.6	29.0	27.2	27.1	37.5	37.6
Tobacco products	...	...	...	...	...	...	...	...	...	...	...	...
Textile mill products	0.3	2.8	0.9	0.3	0.4	0.4	0.1	0.1	...	...	...	...
Apparel	2.8	6.1	1.9	1.0	0.8	0.6	0.3	0.3	0.4	0.5	0.4	0.3
Lumber and wood products	49.6	47.7	46.4	54.6	37.0	41.3	13.2	9.5	10.7	16.8	16.9	18.6
Furniture and fixtures	2.6	2.6	5.1	9.8	3.8	0.5	0.1	0.3	0.3	0.5	0.5	0.3
Paper products	50.9	69.3	35.1	32.6	30.4	17.8	10.0	13.1	12.7	18.5	17.4	7.6
Printing and publishing	2.9	4.4	4.9	3.1	4.2	3.3	2.1	3.3	2.9	1.0	2.8	2.3
Chemical products	49.9	52.4	57.3	57.5	76.2	77.7	40.7	46.3	49.4	48.6	72.2	70.2
Refined petroleum products	0.3	0.2	0.2	0.2	0.3	0.4	...	...	...	...	0.2	0.1
Rubber and plastic products	5.6	4.4	13.7	4.2	3.4	5.4	0.7	0.8	1.0	1.3	0.9	1.1
Leather products	1.2	1.6	3.4	4.9	2.8	2.1	0.1	0.2	0.7	1.8	1.8	1.5
Stone, clay and glass products	0.7	0.7	1.0	1.5	1.2	2.8	0.4	0.1	0.5	1.1	0.7	0.8
Primary metals	2.8	6.1	1.9	2.6	2.4	9.6	1.4	0.5	0.5	0.9	0.9	0.9
Fabricated metal products	17.5	22.9	21.1	19.6	21.6	19.3	5.8	3.8	2.9	3.8	2.9	3.8
Industrial machinery and computers	571.0	676.1	626.5	656.2	529.3	667.1	22.8	28.1	37.3	39.1	32.4	24.4
Electric and electronic equipment	517.8	648.7	438.2	483.8	329.5	734.5	45.6	94.7	79.6	61.5	30.2	44.0
Transportation equipment	16.7	45.2	25.9	20.5	24.6	30.4	7.7	32.6	14.4	14.5	16.0	13.3
Scientific and measuring instruments	16.3	19.6	20.5	31.4	33.6	104.2	2.2	2.3	1.8	1.6	4.4	1.8
Miscellaneous manufactures	3.3	3.7	5.2	3.6	4.5	5.8	0.8	0.7	0.7	0.6	0.7	1.1
Unidentified manufactures	2.2	3.2	4.7	4.2	3.6	4.4	1.3	1.7	2.6	2.1	1.4	1.1
Agricultural And Livestock Products	51.2	49.5	54.5	62.8	69.9	87.0	18.0	16.6	17.8	22.5	26.5	28.4
Agricultural products	46.7	45.7	51.8	59.9	66.0	81.3	13.5	13.2	15.4	19.5	22.8	22.9
Livestock and livestock products	4.5	3.8	2.7	3.0	3.9	5.7	4.5	3.4	2.4	2.9	3.7	5.5
Other Commodities	10.4	12.1	16.3	18.9	27.9	40.2	7.9	8.4	13.2	13.9	13.6	21.7
Forestry products	0.3	0.2	0.2	0.4	0.4	0.2	0.1	0.1	0.1	0.2	0.3	0.2
Fish and other marine products	2.0	1.9	1.8	2.0	1.6	1.4	2.0	1.7	1.8	1.9	1.5	1.3
Metallic ores and concentrates	1.8	0.5	5.8	6.2	17.3	18.8	1.8	0.5	5.8	6.0	7.4	13.2
Bituminous coal and lignite	...	...	...	...	...	2.4	...	...	...	...	...	2.4
Crude petroleum and natural gas	...	...	...	...	...	...	...	...	...	...	...	...
Nonmetallic minerals	2.1	2.2	2.0	3.3	3.4	3.5	0.8	0.9	0.9	1.1	1.0	0.7
Scrap and waste	0.3	0.6	...	0.1	0.2	0.3	0.3	0.6	...	0.1	0.2	0.3
Used merchandise	1.0	0.8	1.8	1.3	0.2	0.5	0.6	0.5	1.2	0.3	...	0.3
Goods imported and returned unchanged	2.1	3.9	3.2	3.9	3.2	2.9	2.1	3.9	3.2	3.9	3.2	2.9
Special classification provisions	0.8	1.8	1.6	1.8	1.7	10.3	0.2	0.2	0.3	0.3	...	0.4

Table D-15. IDAHO: State Exports of Goods by Destination and Industry, 1994–1999—*Continued*

(Millions of dollars.)

Industry	South and Central American and Caribbean						Mexico					
	1994	1995	1996	1997	1998	1999	1994	1995	1996	1997	1998	1999
ALL GOODS	18.7	24.3	18.7	27.0	24.7	43.0	33.7	29.1	37.4	44.2	56.2	64.4
Manufactured Goods	12.4	18.8	13.8	17.8	16.3	21.5	31.4	26.8	34.8	42.9	44.2	54.7
Food products	1.7	3.2	3.9	3.4	1.8	2.7	8.0	10.2	13.6	19.4	15.3	12.2
Tobacco products	...	...	...	...	...	...	...	...	...	...	...	...
Textile mill products	0.1	2.4	0.6	...	...	...	...	...	...	...	0.1	...
Apparel	1.5	4.6	0.4	...	...	...	0.2	...	...	...	...	...
Lumber and wood products	...	...	...	0.6	0.6	1.2	0.7	0.2	0.2	1.2	0.8	1.7
Furniture and fixtures	...	...	...	...	...	...	...	...	...	...	0.1	...
Paper products	...	...	...	...	0.1	0.1	2.4	1.0	1.6	2.3	2.6	1.1
Printing and publishing	...	...	0.1	...	0.1	...	0.2	0.1	0.1	0.1	0.1	0.2
Chemical products	0.2	0.3	0.4	0.3	...	0.4	6.8	3.6	6.0	5.7	1.8	3.1
Refined petroleum products	...	...	...	...	...	...	...	...	...	...	...	...
Rubber and plastic products	2.4	0.1	...	...	0.2	0.1	0.4	1.4	1.4	0.4	0.8	1.1
Leather products	...	...	...	0.2	0.1	...	...	...	...	0.1	...	...
Stone, clay and glass products	...	...	...	...	0.1	0.3	...	...	...	...	...	...
Primary metals	...	0.1	...	0.3	...	...	0.1	0.1	0.1	0.1	0.2	0.4
Fabricated metal products	1.0	2.7	1.6	1.6	1.0	1.1	0.2	0.4	0.3	0.2	2.3	0.5
Industrial machinery and computers	4.3	3.9	4.6	9.5	10.2	12.8	8.8	8.0	9.4	11.3	14.5	20.3
Electric and electronic equipment	0.7	0.6	0.7	0.6	0.7	1.8	1.1	1.0	0.6	1.2	3.1	11.4
Transportation equipment	0.2	0.2	1.0	0.8	0.4	0.2	1.7	0.5	1.1	0.9	1.8	2.0
Scientific and measuring instruments	0.1	0.1	0.1	0.2	0.4	0.3	...	0.2	...	...	0.1	...
Miscellaneous manufactures	0.1	0.5	0.1	0.1	0.2	0.3	0.5	...	0.3	0.1	0.1	0.2
Unidentified manufactures	...	0.1	0.1	0.2	0.2	0.3	...	0.1	0.1	0.1	0.5	0.5
Agricultural And Livestock Products	6.2	5.4	4.6	9.0	8.3	20.8	2.0	2.0	2.5	1.0	1.4	2.1
Agricultural products	6.2	5.4	4.6	9.0	8.3	20.8	1.9	1.9	2.4	0.9	1.4	2.0
Livestock and livestock products	...	...	...	...	...	...	0.1	0.2	...	...	...	...
Other Commodities	0.2	0.1	0.3	0.2	0.1	0.7	0.3	0.3	0.1	0.4	10.6	7.6
Forestry products	...	...	...	...	...	...	0.1	0.2	0.1	0.1	0.1	...
Fish and other marine products	...	...	...	0.1	...	...	...	...	...	...	...	...
Metallic ores and concentrates	...	...	...	...	...	...	...	...	...	0.1	9.9	5.6
Bituminous coal and lignite	...	...	...	...	...	...	...	...	...	...	...	...
Crude petroleum and natural gas	...	...	...	...	...	...	...	...	...	...	...	...
Nonmetallic minerals	0.1	0.1	0.2	0.1	0.1	...	0.1	0.1	...	...	0.6	1.9
Scrap and waste	...	...	...	...	...	...	0.1	0.1	...	0.2	...	...
Used merchandise	...	...	0.1	...	...	...	...	...	...	...	...	...
Goods imported and returned unchanged	...	...	...	...	...	...	...	...	...	...	...	...
Special classification provisions	...	...	...	...	...	0.7	...	...	...	...	...	0.1

Industry	European Union						United Kingdom					
	1994	1995	1996	1997	1998	1999	1994	1995	1996	1997	1998	1999
ALL GOODS	428.5	528.8	384.9	460.9	430.1	571.3	186.6	192.4	116.4	169.8	189.6	294.9
Manufactured Goods	412.1	512.9	367.3	441.8	407.5	546.1	183.9	190.8	114.0	168.8	187.1	292.4
Food products	1.0	6.1	6.7	4.9	5.7	39.2	0.5	2.3	1.3	2.0	0.4	0.1
Tobacco products	...	...	...	...	...	...	...	...	...	...	...	...
Textile mill products	...	0.1	0.1	...	...	0.1	...	...	...	0.1	...	...
Apparel	0.6	0.8	0.9	0.3	0.2	0.1	...	...	...	...	...	...
Lumber and wood products	26.9	25.2	19.1	10.7	4.4	4.4	10.7	7.1	4.4	1.3	0.4	0.9
Furniture and fixtures	2.5	2.2	4.2	7.4	2.0	0.1	2.4	2.0	0.1	...	0.1	...
Paper products	5.3	9.7	1.2	2.3	2.3	0.4	0.2	0.1	...	...	1.2	...
Printing and publishing	0.3	0.5	0.8	1.0	0.1	0.1	0.2	0.3	0.2	0.4	...	...
Chemical products	0.4	0.8	0.4	1.3	1.1	2.4	0.2	0.2	0.2	0.5	0.5	0.6
Refined petroleum products	...	...	...	...	...	0.2	...	...	...	...	...	...
Rubber and plastic products	0.2	0.6	0.2	0.2	0.3	0.3	...	...	...	0.1	0.1	0.1
Leather products	0.1	0.2	0.6	0.9	0.2	0.3	...	0.1	...	...	...	0.2
Stone, clay and glass products	...	0.4	0.2	0.2	0.3	1.1	...	0.3	0.2	...	0.4	0.1
Primary metals	1.0	0.8	0.4	0.7	1.0	0.6	0.8	0.3	0.1	0.2	0.4	0.1
Fabricated metal products	5.5	8.4	6.4	4.8	6.6	5.3	0.6	0.9	0.7	0.6	0.7	0.4
Industrial machinery and computers	232.2	289.2	255.2	330.5	289.0	364.9	114.6	121.6	87.0	131.7	141.8	215.0
Electric and electronic equipment	126.4	155.3	60.9	67.6	68.3	91.0	52.2	51.0	16.4	29.1	40.1	67.2
Transportation equipment	1.6	2.4	2.7	2.0	3.4	8.0	0.2	0.4	0.3	0.3	0.1	6.0
Scientific and measuring instruments	7.0	8.7	4.6	5.7	20.1	23.8	0.9	3.9	1.7	2.3	1.2	0.8
Miscellaneous manufactures	0.7	1.2	1.5	0.9	2.0	2.1	0.2	0.2	0.1	0.1	0.1	0.7
Unidentified manufactures	0.4	0.4	1.4	0.3	0.6	1.6	0.1	0.1	1.2	...	0.1	0.1
Agricultural And Livestock Products	15.7	14.9	16.5	17.2	20.4	19.5	2.7	1.3	1.8	0.6	1.5	1.1
Agricultural products	15.7	14.9	16.5	17.2	20.2	19.3	2.7	1.3	1.8	0.6	1.5	1.1
Livestock and livestock products	...	...	...	...	0.2	0.2	...	...	...	...	...	...
Other Commodities	0.7	1.0	1.1	1.9	2.2	5.7	...	0.3	0.6	0.4	1.1	1.3
Forestry products	...	...	...	...	...	...	...	...	...	...	...	...
Fish and other marine products	...	...	...	...	...	...	...	...	...	...	...	...
Metallic ores and concentrates	...	...	...	...	...	...	...	...	...	...	...	...
Bituminous coal and lignite	...	...	...	...	...	...	...	...	...	...	...	...
Crude petroleum and natural gas	...	...	...	...	...	...	...	...	...	...	...	...
Nonmetallic minerals	0.7	0.4	0.3	1.5	1.1	0.2	...	...	...	0.4	0.3	...
Scrap and waste	...	...	...	...	...	...	...	...	...	...	...	...
Used merchandise	...	0.2	0.1	0.1	...	...	...	...	...	...	...	...
Goods imported and returned unchanged	...	...	...	...	...	...	...	...	...	...	...	...
Special classification provisions	...	0.3	0.7	0.2	1.2	5.4	...	0.3	0.6	...	0.8	1.3

Table D-15. IDAHO: State Exports of Goods by Destination and Industry, 1994–1999—Continued

(Millions of dollars.)

Industry	Germany						France					
	1994	1995	1996	1997	1998	1999	1994	1995	1996	1997	1998	1999
ALL GOODS	82.4	83.0	92.0	132.2	89.6	82.5	49.2	66.7	26.2	17.4	20.6	41.4
Manufactured Goods	81.7	82.7	91.7	131.1	88.6	79.7	47.4	64.4	21.2	12.6	15.5	35.9
Food products	0.1	0.2	0.2	0.1	0.5	0.4	...	...	...	...	...	...
Tobacco products	...	...	...	...	...	...	...	0.7	...	...	...	0.8
Textile mill products	...	...	...	...	...	...	...	...	...	...	...	...
Apparel	...	...	0.2	...	0.1	...	...	...	...	...	...	...
Lumber and wood products	7.7	10.9	10.7	5.5	1.5	0.3	0.2	...	0.1	...	...	0.3
Furniture and fixtures	...	0.2	4.0	7.4	1.8	...	...	...	...	...	...	...
Paper products	...	...	...	...	0.2	0.3	1.3	2.6	...	0.6	...	...
Printing and publishing	0.1	0.1	0.3	0.2	...	...	...	0.1	0.1	0.1	...	...
Chemical products	0.1	0.2	0.1	0.3	0.1	0.1	...	0.2	...	0.1	...	...
Refined petroleum products	...	...	...	...	...	...	...	...	...	...	...	...
Rubber and plastic products	0.1	0.4	0.1	0.1	...	0.1	...	...	...	...	...	...
Leather products	...	...	0.1	...	...	...	...	...	...	0.2	...	...
Stone, clay and glass products	...	0.1	...	...	...	0.8	...	...	...	...	...	...
Primary metals	0.1	0.2	0.2	0.1	0.3	0.3	...	...	...	...	...	0.1
Fabricated metal products	1.9	2.7	2.6	1.1	1.1	2.1	1.2	2.0	1.0	1.1	1.1	1.4
Industrial machinery and computers	53.9	48.7	65.2	104.0	74.9	63.8	23.6	28.5	16.6	8.4	12.8	27.7
Electric and electronic equipment	16.4	17.9	6.4	10.9	5.7	8.2	18.6	29.2	2.9	1.7	0.7	4.9
Transportation equipment	0.4	0.4	1.0	0.4	1.5	1.5	0.5	0.3	0.3	0.3	0.2	0.1
Scientific and measuring instruments	0.6	0.2	0.5	0.9	0.5	1.2	1.9	0.6	0.1	0.1	0.3	0.4
Miscellaneous manufactures	...	0.1	0.1	...	0.1	0.4	0.1	...	0.1	...	0.2	...
Unidentified manufactures	0.1	0.1	...	0.1	0.2	0.1	...	...	...	...	...	...
Agricultural And Livestock Products	0.2	0.1	0.3	0.1	0.3	0.7	1.8	2.2	4.9	4.8	5.1	5.0
Agricultural products	0.2	0.1	0.3	0.1	0.3	0.7	1.8	2.2	4.9	4.8	5.1	5.0
Livestock and livestock products	...	...	...	...	...	...	...	...	...	...	...	...
Other Commodities	0.6	0.2	0.1	0.9	0.7	2.1	...	...	0.1	...	...	0.6
Forestry products	...	...	...	...	...	...	...	...	...	...	...	...
Fish and other marine products	...	...	...	...	...	...	...	...	...	...	...	...
Metallic ores and concentrates	...	...	...	...	...	...	...	...	...	...	...	...
Bituminous coal and lignite	...	...	...	...	...	...	...	...	...	...	...	...
Crude petroleum and natural gas	...	...	...	...	...	...	...	...	...	...	...	...
Nonmetallic minerals	0.6	0.2	0.1	0.8	0.6	0.1	...	...	...	...	...	...
Scrap and waste	...	...	...	...	...	...	...	...	...	...	...	...
Used merchandise	...	...	...	0.1	...	...	...	...	...	...	...	...
Goods imported and returned unchanged	...	...	...	...	...	...	...	...	...	...	...	...
Special classification provisions	...	...	...	0.1	0.1	2.0	...	...	0.1	...	...	0.6

Industry	The Netherlands						Asian 10					
	1994	1995	1996	1997	1998	1999	1994	1995	1996	1997	1998	1999
ALL GOODS	16.0	57.1	71.5	73.1	42.4	17.3	768.1	922.6	805.5	796.5	592.2	1 022.3
Manufactured Goods	10.4	51.5	67.4	67.1	37.4	13.4	759.8	913.3	794.6	785.4	580.7	1 006.6
Food products	0.1	1.5	0.7	1.1	0.8	1.1	111.5	159.0	166.2	180.1	183.4	163.8
Tobacco products	...	...	...	...	...	...	...	...	...	...	...	...
Textile mill products	...	...	0.1	...	...	...	0.1	0.1	0.1	0.2	0.2	0.2
Apparel	0.4	0.6	0.6	0.1	...	...	0.1	0.4	0.2	0.1	0.2	0.1
Lumber and wood products	3.5	3.8	1.9	0.5	...	...	8.6	11.9	15.1	21.6	12.5	13.6
Furniture and fixtures	...	...	...	...	...	...	...	0.1	0.6	1.5	1.2	...
Paper products	...	...	...	0.1	0.9	...	31.5	44.8	19.1	9.0	7.6	6.6
Printing and publishing	...	...	0.1	0.2	...	...	0.1	0.4	0.6	0.2	0.7	0.3
Chemical products	...	0.1	0.1	0.2	0.2	0.1	0.2	0.2	0.5	0.8	0.5	0.5
Refined petroleum products	...	...	...	...	...	...	0.2	0.1	0.1	...	...	...
Rubber and plastic products	...	...	...	...	...	0.1	0.8	0.4	0.7	0.3	0.5	0.3
Leather products	0.1	0.1	0.1	...	...	...	1.0	1.2	2.1	1.8	0.7	0.3
Stone, clay and glass products	...	...	...	0.2	...	0.2	0.2	...	0.1	0.1	0.1	0.3
Primary metals	...	...	...	0.1	...	0.1	0.2	0.6	0.4	0.4	0.1	0.5
Fabricated metal products	0.3	0.3	0.2	0.4	0.5	0.3	3.0	3.2	6.5	7.2	5.4	4.7
Industrial machinery and computers	4.9	43.7	62.6	62.7	31.4	10.2	275.4	314.7	289.7	236.7	144.8	176.0
Electric and electronic equipment	0.5	0.4	0.4	0.5	1.4	0.7	319.3	367.0	278.8	318.8	214.2	569.7
Transportation equipment	0.1	0.7	0.1	0.3	1.1	0.2	0.9	0.6	2.5	0.5	0.5	1.0
Scientific and measuring instruments	0.1	0.2	0.4	0.4	0.6	0.3	5.7	7.1	8.8	3.8	6.3	66.2
Miscellaneous manufactures	...	...	...	...	...	...	0.9	0.9	1.9	1.4	1.2	1.7
Unidentified manufactures	...	...	0.1	0.1	0.2	0.2	0.2	0.6	0.3	0.6	0.6	0.7
Agricultural And Livestock Products	5.5	5.2	3.8	5.8	4.6	3.5	7.2	7.0	9.8	9.4	10.3	12.3
Agricultural products	5.5	5.2	3.8	5.8	4.6	3.5	7.2	7.0	9.8	9.4	10.3	12.3
Livestock and livestock products	...	...	...	...	...	...	...	...	...	...	...	...
Other Commodities	0.1	0.4	0.2	0.2	0.4	0.5	1.2	2.2	1.1	1.7	1.2	3.4
Forestry products	...	...	...	...	...	...	...	...	...	...	...	...
Fish and other marine products	...	...	...	...	...	...	...	...	...	...	...	...
Metallic ores and concentrates	...	...	...	...	...	...	...	0.2	...	...	...	...
Bituminous coal and lignite	...	...	...	...	...	...	...	...	...	...	...	...
Crude petroleum and natural gas	...	...	...	...	...	...	...	...	...	...	...	...
Nonmetallic minerals	0.1	0.2	0.2	0.1	0.1	0.1	0.5	0.7	0.6	0.5	0.6	0.6
Scrap and waste	...	...	...	...	...	...	...	...	...	...	...	...
Used merchandise	...	0.2	...	...	...	...	0.1	...	0.1	0.2	0.1	0.1
Goods imported and returned unchanged	...	...	...	...	...	...	...	...	...	...	...	...
Special classification provisions	...	...	...	0.1	0.3	0.4	0.6	1.3	0.4	1.0	0.5	2.7

Table D-15. IDAHO: State Exports of Goods by Destination and Industry, 1994–1999—*Continued*

(Millions of dollars.)

Industry	Japan						South Korea					
	1994	1995	1996	1997	1998	1999	1994	1995	1996	1997	1998	1999
ALL GOODS	352.8	348.0	309.4	317.1	233.5	229.7	29.2	35.5	36.8	32.5	21.5	41.9
Manufactured Goods	346.7	341.7	302.0	310.5	228.0	220.0	28.6	34.2	36.4	31.6	20.8	40.9
Food products	80.4	95.2	105.1	125.6	135.8	118.4	12.5	25.9	27.1	21.9	14.1	20.8
Tobacco products	...	...	...	...	...	...	...	...	...	...	...	...
Textile mill products	...	0.1	0.1	0.1	0.2	0.2	...	...	...	...	...	...
Apparel	0.1	0.3	0.2	0.1	0.1	0.1	...	...	...	...	...	...
Lumber and wood products	6.3	9.3	13.2	19.3	9.6	8.9	0.5	0.8	0.3	0.6	0.3	...
Furniture and fixtures	...	...	0.5	1.5	1.1	...	...	...	...	...	...	...
Paper products	2.8	7.5	5.0	2.9	0.4	0.1	0.8	0.3	1.0	0.4	0.4	0.4
Printing and publishing	...	...	0.1	...	...	...	...	...	...	...	...	...
Chemical products	0.1	0.2	0.4	0.2	0.1	0.2	...	...	0.1	...	0.3	...
Refined petroleum products	...	...	...	...	...	...	...	...	...	...	...	...
Rubber and plastic products	0.2	0.3	0.4	...	...	0.2	0.2	...	...	0.1	...	...
Leather products	0.2	0.1	0.1	0.1	...	...	0.2	0.3	0.2	0.5	0.1	...
Stone, clay and glass products	0.1	...	0.1	0.1	0.1	0.2	...	...	...	...	...	...
Primary metals	0.1	0.1	0.1	0.2	0.1	0.1	...	...	...	...	...	...
Fabricated metal products	0.2	0.2	0.4	1.1	0.1	0.1	0.9	1.1	1.9	2.3	0.8	0.1
Industrial machinery and computers	225.3	184.1	142.7	131.8	66.1	58.5	3.0	2.1	4.1	3.1	2.9	8.7
Electric and electronic equipment	29.1	41.4	29.9	24.2	12.2	28.8	10.1	3.2	1.4	2.5	1.3	10.4
Transportation equipment	0.3	0.3	0.3	0.3	0.3	0.7	0.1	0.2	0.2	...	0.2	0.1
Scientific and measuring instruments	1.0	1.7	2.1	2.4	1.5	2.6	0.2	...	0.1	0.1	0.4	0.2
Miscellaneous manufactures	0.5	0.7	1.5	0.2	0.2	0.5	...	0.1	0.1	0.1	...	...
Unidentified manufactures	0.1	0.2	...	0.2	0.1	0.3	...	0.2	...	...	...	...
Agricultural And Livestock Products	5.7	5.6	7.0	5.9	5.3	8.7	0.2	...	...	0.3	0.5	0.3
Agricultural products	5.7	5.6	7.0	5.9	5.3	8.7	0.2	...	...	0.3	0.5	0.3
Livestock and livestock products	...	...	...	...	...	...	...	...	...	...	...	...
Other Commodities	0.4	0.7	0.5	0.6	0.2	1.0	0.4	1.2	0.4	0.7	0.3	0.8
Forestry products	...	...	...	...	...	...	...	...	...	...	...	...
Fish and other marine products	...	...	...	...	...	...	...	...	...	...	...	...
Metallic ores and concentrates	...	...	...	...	...	...	...	...	...	...	...	...
Bituminous coal and lignite	...	...	...	...	...	...	...	...	...	...	...	...
Crude petroleum and natural gas	...	...	...	...	...	...	...	...	...	...	...	...
Nonmetallic minerals	0.4	0.5	0.3	0.3	0.2	0.1	...	0.1	...	...	...	...
Scrap and waste	...	...	...	...	...	0.1	...	...	...	...	...	...
Used merchandise	...	...	...	...	...	...	...	...	...	...	...	...
Goods imported and returned unchanged	...	...	...	...	...	...	0.4	1.1	0.3	0.7	0.3	0.7
Special classification provisions	...	...	0.1	0.2	...	0.8	...	...	...	...	...	...

Industry	Taiwan						Singapore					
	1994	1995	1996	1997	1998	1999	1994	1995	1996	1997	1998	1999
ALL GOODS	110.6	132.0	60.4	97.2	77.5	161.8	149.5	208.6	154.8	120.2	99.0	248.9
Manufactured Goods	109.6	131.2	59.7	96.2	76.5	160.6	149.5	208.6	154.7	120.2	99.0	248.5
Food products	10.8	15.6	14.5	11.3	6.8	6.1	0.5	2.3	0.4	0.3	0.3	0.4
Tobacco products	...	...	...	...	...	...	...	...	...	...	...	...
Textile mill products	...	...	...	...	...	...	...	...	...	...	...	...
Apparel	...	...	...	...	...	...	...	...	...	...	...	...
Lumber and wood products	1.6	1.3	1.4	1.0	0.8	0.9	...	...	...	...	...	...
Furniture and fixtures	...	...	...	...	...	...	0.8	0.1	0.1	...	...	0.1
Paper products	11.2	15.2	2.8	1.8	3.0	3.2	0.1	...	...	0.1	...	...
Printing and publishing	...	...	...	...	0.1	...	...	...	...	...	...	...
Chemical products	...	...	0.1	0.3	...	...	...	...	...	...	...	...
Refined petroleum products	0.2	0.1	...	0.1	...	...	...	...	...	...	...	...
Rubber and plastic products	...	...	...	...	...	...	0.3	...	...	...	...	...
Leather products	0.1	0.2	1.5	0.3	0.1	...	...	...	...	...	...	...
Stone, clay and glass products	0.1	...	...	...	...	0.1	...	...	...	...	...	0.3
Primary metals	...	...	...	...	...	0.1	0.5	0.5	0.2	1.1	0.9	0.1
Fabricated metal products	0.4	0.4	0.5	0.4	0.3	...	...	...	...	...	...	...
Industrial machinery and computers	5.6	22.8	6.9	5.1	6.3	11.6	22.0	75.9	97.1	84.1	55.3	64.7
Electric and electronic equipment	79.5	75.5	28.5	75.7	59.0	138.3	124.9	129.7	55.2	34.3	39.8	120.9
Transportation equipment	0.1	...	0.3	...	...	...	0.1	...	1.5	...	...	0.1
Scientific and measuring instruments	...	0.1	3.1	0.1	...	0.2	0.1	0.1	...	0.1	2.4	61.7
Miscellaneous manufactures	...	0.1	...	0.1	...	0.1	0.1	...	...	0.1	0.1	...
Unidentified manufactures	...	...	...	0.1	0.1	0.1	...	0.1	...	0.1	...	...
Agricultural And Livestock Products	0.9	0.6	0.6	0.7	0.8	1.1	...	...	...	...	...	...
Agricultural products	0.9	0.6	0.6	0.7	0.8	1.1	...	...	...	...	...	...
Livestock and livestock products	...	...	...	...	...	...	...	...	...	...	...	...
Other Commodities	0.1	0.1	0.1	0.2	0.2	0.1	...	...	0.1	...	...	0.4
Forestry products	...	...	...	...	...	...	...	...	...	...	...	...
Fish and other marine products	...	...	...	...	...	...	...	...	...	...	...	...
Metallic ores and concentrates	...	...	...	...	...	...	...	...	...	...	...	...
Bituminous coal and lignite	...	...	...	...	...	...	...	...	...	...	...	...
Crude petroleum and natural gas	...	...	...	...	...	...	...	...	...	...	...	...
Nonmetallic minerals	...	0.1	0.1	0.1	0.2	...	...	...	0.1	...	...	...
Scrap and waste	...	...	...	...	...	...	...	...	...	...	...	...
Used merchandise	0.1	...	...	0.1	...	...	...	...	...	...	...	...
Goods imported and returned unchanged	...	...	...	...	...	...	...	...	...	...	...	0.4
Special classification provisions	...	...	...	...	...	0.1	...	...	...	...	...	...

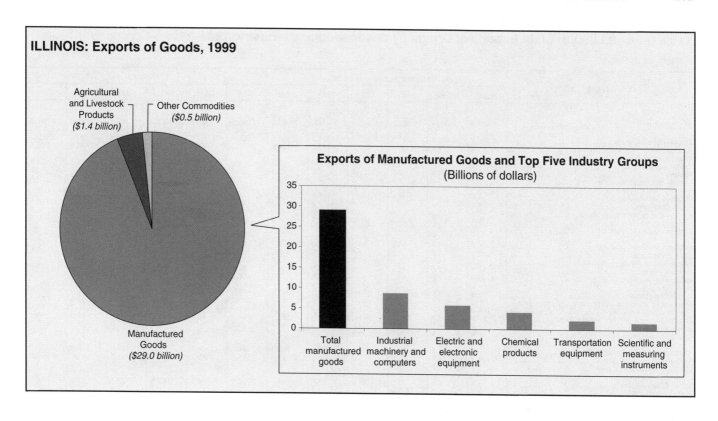

ILLINOIS: Exports of Goods, 1999

Agricultural and Livestock Products ($1.4 billion)

Other Commodities ($0.5 billion)

Manufactured Goods ($29.0 billion)

Exports of Manufactured Goods and Top Five Industry Groups
(Billions of dollars)

Total manufactured goods / Industrial machinery and computers / Electric and electronic equipment / Chemical products / Transportation equipment / Scientific and measuring instruments

Table D-16. ILLINOIS: State Exports of Goods by Destination and Industry, 1994–1999

(Millions of dollars.)

Industry	All destinations						Canada					
	1994	1995	1996	1997	1998	1999	1994	1995	1996	1997	1998	1999
ALL GOODS	24 534.2	30 478.2	32 224.9	34 225.0	33 838.1	30 856.5	5 763.1	6 452.6	6 767.3	8 044.2	7 942.8	7 885.6
Manufactured Goods	22 464.2	27 660.6	28 747.9	31 454.4	31 631.9	28 994.8	5 556.5	6 224.4	6 493.3	7 777.1	7 707.5	7 619.5
Food products	1 279.4	1 677.9	1 629.1	1 919.2	1 892.5	1 449.4	259.3	286.6	305.9	324.7	356.7	356.5
Tobacco products	0.7	7.8	8.3	8.5	8.8	6.5	. . .	2.1	7.9	8.2	8.2	6.4
Textile mill products	51.1	74.4	84.7	97.0	96.7	96.6	14.0	17.3	19.4	22.2	23.8	20.8
Apparel	63.3	69.8	86.5	98.0	107.1	88.1	7.2	10.1	10.7	11.6	10.9	12.7
Lumber and wood products	45.7	54.6	52.4	91.9	95.3	95.3	12.4	14.5	11.2	31.1	48.6	58.7
Furniture and fixtures	89.0	100.5	110.9	117.6	131.2	95.1	50.6	59.7	57.6	60.4	67.6	32.3
Paper products	404.6	549.0	565.0	672.9	675.9	583.0	95.0	117.0	127.1	132.1	138.0	169.2
Printing and publishing	294.4	322.1	314.4	324.6	323.0	356.5	168.6	170.6	155.0	177.8	185.5	214.7
Chemical products	3 484.7	4 152.9	4 156.2	4 337.6	4 289.6	4 223.8	525.7	614.9	640.7	731.1	771.1	761.0
Refined petroleum products	70.2	82.8	179.3	169.4	105.4	96.9	38.3	32.9	31.9	31.9	32.3	22.0
Rubber and plastic products	507.6	627.7	735.5	843.0	897.3	938.7	174.3	196.5	216.0	251.5	265.4	293.5
Leather products	46.6	50.3	55.9	56.9	48.1	42.9	8.7	10.0	10.1	10.6	12.2	12.9
Stone, clay and glass products	168.5	179.0	200.2	237.1	233.4	253.6	64.2	59.4	65.8	70.7	60.4	59.9
Primary metals	467.1	644.6	630.3	833.9	824.5	717.7	226.8	275.1	285.2	383.8	348.0	333.5
Fabricated metal products	658.4	778.4	917.9	922.6	904.1	956.8	268.7	314.1	421.5	336.2	330.4	408.5
Industrial machinery and computers	6 641.5	7 663.1	8 153.1	9 065.8	9 451.3	8 705.5	2 017.3	2 125.8	2 081.9	2 711.6	2 697.3	2 534.4
Electric and electronic equipment	4 830.9	6 822.4	6 560.9	7 006.5	6 695.8	5 800.3	798.2	1 068.8	1 054.9	1 269.2	1 058.1	1 026.6
Transportation equipment	1 725.6	2 023.0	2 289.1	2 470.2	2 479.7	2 206.6	537.3	567.3	674.6	805.7	784.2	792.2
Scientific and measuring instruments	1 112.6	1 274.1	1 467.9	1 593.5	1 753.6	1 665.3	170.2	171.9	209.2	275.3	305.3	314.6
Miscellaneous manufactures	425.7	423.9	448.7	479.9	488.2	476.0	97.9	86.6	83.3	102.1	176.5	160.6
Unidentified manufactures	96.5	82.5	101.6	108.3	130.3	138.0	21.7	23.3	23.4	29.2	27.0	28.5
Agricultural And Livestock Products	1 605.9	2 295.8	2 993.9	2 357.1	1 816.5	1 365.8	22.7	21.6	56.0	43.2	49.8	41.2
Agricultural products	1 588.6	2 275.8	2 964.1	2 314.3	1 774.7	1 334.7	18.4	17.2	50.0	35.9	41.8	36.7
Livestock and livestock products	17.3	20.1	29.9	42.8	41.8	31.1	4.3	4.3	6.0	7.3	8.1	4.5
Other Commodities	464.1	521.8	483.0	413.5	389.7	496.0	183.9	206.6	218.0	223.9	185.5	224.9
Forestry products	2.2	2.2	3.2	3.6	4.4	5.4	0.7	0.6	0.7	1.1	1.8	2.2
Fish and other marine products	2.2	3.3	3.4	5.5	3.4	3.1	1.2	1.6	1.2	0.8	1.0	1.0
Metallic ores and concentrates	3.5	23.7	15.0	2.7	1.9	2.2	0.7	1.2	0.7	0.6	0.5	0.9
Bituminous coal and lignite	55.2	76.8	50.5	2.8	0.8	1.0	. . .	0.5	0.6	. . .	. . .	. . .
Crude petroleum and natural gas	49.9	43.4	46.5	56.5	49.0	38.9	39.1	40.3	44.0	50.4	47.4	33.7
Nonmetallic minerals	117.6	70.2	62.9	66.6	61.8	74.5	23.3	25.2	19.0	22.2	13.5	14.5
Scrap and waste	89.6	131.8	79.4	76.5	79.2	106.4	31.6	48.1	32.5	30.4	24.2	37.0
Used merchandise	36.6	50.2	58.5	45.4	50.0	72.4	6.7	3.9	4.8	7.1	13.0	24.2
Goods imported and returned unchanged	64.4	68.1	76.4	93.7	72.2	63.5	64.4	68.1	76.4	93.7	72.2	63.5
Special classification provisions	42.9	52.2	87.2	60.2	67.1	128.5	16.2	17.2	38.1	17.8	11.8	47.8

Table D-16. ILLINOIS: State Exports of Goods by Destination and Industry, 1994–1999—*Continued*

(Millions of dollars.)

Industry	South and Central American and Caribbean						Mexico					
	1994	1995	1996	1997	1998	1999	1994	1995	1996	1997	1998	1999
ALL GOODS	2 044.2	2 186.9	2 368.8	3 012.3	3 067.7	2 567.3	1 825.4	1 366.1	1 844.7	2 189.7	2 797.9	2 886.2
Manufactured Goods	1 909.4	2 154.8	2 261.5	2 825.7	2 996.2	2 380.1	1 609.2	1 197.2	1 448.7	1 967.9	2 460.4	2 629.7
Food products	81.6	124.2	98.2	137.1	127.7	124.9	177.7	146.9	165.9	171.7	194.4	205.6
Tobacco products	...	...	...	...	...	...	...	...	...	...	...	...
Textile mill products	7.6	9.3	9.1	9.1	6.6	7.4	4.9	5.7	11.0	15.4	14.7	21.4
Apparel	19.4	20.6	38.3	39.9	38.6	22.8	3.7	2.5	3.0	8.2	21.7	21.5
Lumber and wood products	1.9	1.3	4.9	4.8	2.4	1.5	1.9	2.9	7.8	10.2	5.9	5.1
Furniture and fixtures	4.8	6.5	4.4	5.7	9.5	5.6	4.0	1.7	2.0	2.9	3.4	5.0
Paper products	29.4	48.2	61.3	75.4	57.7	41.8	59.9	43.1	52.0	78.0	116.8	110.1
Printing and publishing	4.0	14.9	21.4	19.5	16.2	12.8	13.6	14.8	14.1	9.3	16.1	19.6
Chemical products	371.4	366.0	390.6	409.0	399.4	333.6	104.6	91.3	140.5	178.6	229.8	270.0
Refined petroleum products	2.2	3.7	3.6	23.2	11.0	3.4	3.1	4.1	43.7	26.1	25.8	9.0
Rubber and plastic products	25.9	46.4	55.0	63.5	68.0	58.4	63.5	50.4	74.9	109.1	146.6	177.3
Leather products	3.1	4.8	1.9	3.5	3.2	3.9	10.5	8.0	7.9	7.7	7.7	3.1
Stone, clay and glass products	9.6	14.4	14.4	19.8	19.5	13.4	17.5	11.5	17.7	22.3	33.8	44.5
Primary metals	12.3	21.6	19.8	18.8	26.2	22.2	67.0	65.6	100.8	138.0	182.8	179.5
Fabricated metal products	46.0	72.2	55.7	63.0	56.8	37.0	69.3	53.9	59.3	110.3	135.5	144.3
Industrial machinery and computers	705.5	722.8	779.1	858.6	974.0	646.2	497.9	298.1	334.7	460.9	589.4	569.2
Electric and electronic equipment	319.0	394.1	420.9	739.7	776.1	802.7	372.3	303.4	284.6	435.0	543.5	629.2
Transportation equipment	168.9	147.8	108.6	141.9	155.1	87.2	52.1	32.4	44.1	89.8	79.7	83.8
Scientific and measuring instruments	81.8	115.2	134.7	161.9	209.9	127.5	56.1	40.6	61.6	65.2	73.6	83.0
Miscellaneous manufactures	12.0	16.7	36.5	27.7	31.0	20.4	24.2	17.0	18.1	21.5	19.7	25.5
Unidentified manufactures	2.9	3.9	3.0	3.3	7.4	7.5	5.5	3.0	5.1	7.5	19.6	22.8
Agricultural And Livestock Products	125.0	23.8	98.3	174.6	58.8	168.0	186.2	144.3	378.5	198.7	319.8	231.7
Agricultural products	124.0	22.7	97.2	174.0	58.0	167.6	185.4	143.9	378.1	197.9	319.2	231.3
Livestock and livestock products	1.0	1.1	1.1	0.6	0.7	0.4	0.7	0.4	0.4	0.8	0.6	0.4
Other Commodities	9.9	8.3	9.1	12.0	12.7	19.1	30.0	24.5	17.5	23.1	17.6	24.8
Forestry products	0.3	0.8	0.5	0.2	0.3	0.7	0.3	...	0.2	0.2	0.6	0.3
Fish and other marine products	0.1	0.5	0.8	0.4	0.2	0.2	0.1	...	...	0.2	0.1	...
Metallic ores and concentrates	...	0.2	0.1	...	...	...	2.1	1.0	0.1	0.3	0.1	0.1
Bituminous coal and lignite	3.3	0.1	...	...	...	...	...	...	0.1	0.1	0.1	0.4
Crude petroleum and natural gas	0.3	0.3	0.1	0.7	0.1	0.2	10.1	2.5	2.0	4.8	0.4	3.4
Nonmetallic minerals	2.7	2.3	3.7	6.4	7.3	5.9	1.5	0.8	1.7	1.7	2.4	2.0
Scrap and waste	1.5	2.2	0.9	1.4	1.0	1.3	13.8	17.1	10.1	13.3	10.6	14.9
Used merchandise	0.7	1.5	1.7	0.7	1.1	2.3	1.4	2.3	2.5	1.3	2.2	1.6
Goods imported and returned unchanged	...	...	...	...	...	...	...	...	...	...	...	...
Special classification provisions	0.9	0.5	1.3	2.3	2.7	8.6	0.8	0.7	0.7	1.2	1.2	2.1

Industry	European Union						United Kingdom					
	1994	1995	1996	1997	1998	1999	1994	1995	1996	1997	1998	1999
ALL GOODS	5 970.4	7 419.0	8 062.6	8 713.5	8 715.4	8 112.0	1 276.0	1 572.1	1 641.8	1 830.8	1 826.2	1 689.8
Manufactured Goods	5 535.4	6 699.1	7 345.2	8 075.6	8 283.6	7 783.7	1 244.3	1 527.5	1 612.9	1 802.8	1 798.5	1 647.1
Food products	114.7	147.8	251.5	294.9	205.3	131.6	21.2	13.0	21.1	18.9	37.8	24.9
Tobacco products	0.3	0.1	...	0.1	0.1	...	...	...	...	...	...	...
Textile mill products	10.4	22.4	23.9	27.7	33.0	30.3	3.1	5.6	5.3	5.6	5.9	5.7
Apparel	18.1	20.0	15.6	18.4	18.8	18.1	2.8	3.1	3.7	7.8	4.1	4.5
Lumber and wood products	12.6	17.6	12.9	27.4	23.0	15.6	4.5	7.1	4.5	19.3	13.4	6.3
Furniture and fixtures	17.1	13.8	20.9	18.8	25.1	34.0	10.5	7.0	7.5	7.7	12.1	20.6
Paper products	146.2	222.2	190.4	245.2	250.2	160.6	24.2	40.5	44.8	49.2	50.7	23.5
Printing and publishing	41.6	57.2	59.4	53.0	50.7	63.7	20.0	26.9	28.9	19.1	21.8	32.6
Chemical products	982.0	1 128.3	1 292.4	1 443.9	1 418.7	1 369.4	136.8	232.5	216.4	217.1	193.2	183.4
Refined petroleum products	10.8	16.0	56.7	42.4	7.2	43.2	1.1	0.8	0.9	6.8	1.1	0.7
Rubber and plastic products	144.2	181.0	186.2	211.0	245.3	220.4	40.1	39.9	37.5	39.1	46.0	41.2
Leather products	4.3	5.3	5.2	4.9	4.5	4.4	1.3	2.3	1.3	1.3	0.6	0.6
Stone, clay and glass products	26.3	37.5	34.8	47.2	61.2	57.3	8.8	10.2	9.0	12.5	11.4	12.2
Primary metals	49.6	104.8	73.2	93.7	89.2	77.4	16.4	44.1	24.6	35.0	36.4	23.3
Fabricated metal products	114.9	142.7	157.3	182.9	196.1	191.4	48.5	54.3	52.2	54.7	58.0	63.8
Industrial machinery and computers	1 733.7	2 062.0	2 180.8	2 365.1	2 686.1	2 663.7	334.1	406.0	448.0	489.0	519.7	546.9
Electric and electronic equipment	996.3	1 239.9	1 279.3	1 425.5	1 226.4	1 033.9	354.6	405.3	414.7	547.6	461.4	351.1
Transportation equipment	535.4	630.3	828.0	863.9	997.0	922.5	106.2	111.5	179.8	149.4	178.5	159.8
Scientific and measuring instruments	378.3	452.3	503.2	527.4	576.2	571.9	64.7	76.4	67.8	75.3	92.1	89.7
Miscellaneous manufactures	181.8	179.4	158.0	168.2	150.7	150.8	37.3	34.7	40.3	43.6	48.4	48.0
Unidentified manufactures	17.1	18.4	15.5	14.0	18.9	23.6	8.1	6.5	4.3	3.8	5.9	8.5
Agricultural And Livestock Products	335.6	576.8	594.1	578.9	362.7	241.9	6.6	14.5	9.7	5.4	4.8	2.6
Agricultural products	333.5	573.5	591.1	571.3	355.6	239.5	6.5	13.7	9.3	2.4	2.6	2.1
Livestock and livestock products	2.1	3.3	3.0	7.6	7.0	2.4	0.1	0.8	0.4	3.0	2.3	0.5
Other Commodities	99.5	143.1	123.3	59.0	69.1	86.5	25.1	30.2	19.2	22.5	22.8	40.1
Forestry products	0.3	0.6	1.5	1.8	0.9	1.0	...	...	0.4	0.5	0.3	0.1
Fish and other marine products	0.2	0.1	0.2	0.6	1.1	0.8	0.2	...	...	...	...	...
Metallic ores and concentrates	...	20.5	12.1	1.1	0.3	0.7	...	0.2	...	...	...	0.1
Bituminous coal and lignite	34.6	60.9	42.1	2.3	0.4	0.4	8.9	3.6	...	...	...	...
Crude petroleum and natural gas	...	0.2	0.2	0.4	0.8	1.0	...	0.2	0.2	0.4	0.7	0.8
Nonmetallic minerals	23.6	11.2	13.9	12.5	14.8	11.5	3.0	3.8	5.2	5.2	6.8	3.7
Scrap and waste	9.5	7.8	7.7	7.2	8.7	7.6	0.4	1.4	0.6	0.7	0.4	0.8
Used merchandise	17.2	24.7	29.3	19.0	21.2	33.5	7.6	11.8	5.0	8.4	5.1	19.5
Goods imported and returned unchanged	...	...	...	...	...	...	...	...	...	...	...	...
Special classification provisions	13.9	17.1	16.2	14.2	21.0	29.9	5.0	9.1	7.8	7.2	9.5	15.1

Table D-16. ILLINOIS: State Exports of Goods by Destination and Industry, 1994–1999—*Continued*

(Millions of dollars.)

Industry	Germany						France					
	1994	1995	1996	1997	1998	1999	1994	1995	1996	1997	1998	1999
ALL GOODS	1 224.9	1 491.2	1 597.7	1 643.5	1 769.7	1 587.1	646.1	791.7	811.8	916.1	834.1	717.7
Manufactured Goods	1 177.4	1 368.9	1 497.7	1 551.0	1 719.4	1 573.6	638.2	780.3	803.4	902.5	823.3	707.3
Food products	19.0	28.8	31.7	32.0	34.8	28.4	7.4	10.8	9.8	10.2	5.4	5.8
Tobacco products	0.3	...	...	0.1	...	...	...	...	...	...	...	...
Textile mill products	2.4	4.9	4.4	6.0	8.6	8.8	1.8	5.3	3.9	6.0	7.4	7.9
Apparel	3.5	3.1	3.1	0.9	1.0	1.7	3.9	3.5	3.4	2.2	1.6	2.1
Lumber and wood products	3.7	3.7	3.6	3.1	3.2	1.8	0.1	0.7	0.5	0.6	0.8	1.1
Furniture and fixtures	2.2	1.9	6.2	3.5	4.0	7.2	1.3	2.4	4.5	3.6	4.2	1.4
Paper products	38.6	66.0	44.5	47.5	59.1	49.3	22.5	20.3	12.0	20.7	29.8	32.9
Printing and publishing	6.4	11.2	10.6	9.7	6.5	13.7	2.5	5.4	2.9	4.5	5.2	4.3
Chemical products	284.4	270.1	359.2	356.9	292.4	273.6	84.1	107.4	121.1	104.3	92.7	86.8
Refined petroleum products	0.4	0.3	0.3	0.4	0.3	0.5	0.8	0.3	5.2	0.2	0.4	0.2
Rubber and plastic products	38.3	53.9	40.4	35.4	41.1	38.3	6.9	12.5	14.9	16.8	24.5	29.4
Leather products	0.4	0.6	0.6	0.6	0.4	0.4	0.4	0.4	0.3	0.3	0.6	0.7
Stone, clay and glass products	5.5	8.0	7.7	14.3	17.5	14.3	2.1	3.6	2.8	5.2	8.9	9.3
Primary metals	7.5	9.7	15.3	17.4	20.6	21.9	5.3	7.3	6.8	12.7	6.0	9.3
Fabricated metal products	22.2	24.5	27.6	35.3	31.2	35.3	10.6	14.3	13.1	16.9	16.3	23.8
Industrial machinery and computers	272.1	365.9	387.0	434.3	594.6	494.3	237.6	311.1	277.1	285.7	349.2	279.9
Electric and electronic equipment	160.7	157.0	137.1	186.1	186.6	177.1	96.5	109.5	192.6	274.5	131.3	83.7
Transportation equipment	106.7	120.4	180.7	145.3	221.6	198.1	78.4	93.1	56.1	64.9	63.7	56.9
Scientific and measuring instruments	123.9	162.5	181.2	166.5	154.9	162.1	51.3	50.7	60.0	54.7	57.2	59.3
Miscellaneous manufactures	76.3	73.5	54.6	54.0	37.8	42.5	23.4	20.4	15.8	17.3	16.0	15.0
Unidentified manufactures	2.8	2.8	2.0	1.8	3.0	4.3	1.1	1.3	0.9	1.1	2.0	2.3
Agricultural And Livestock Products	31.1	109.3	78.5	78.3	39.3	3.4	3.5	4.9	3.1	7.1	3.3	3.8
Agricultural products	30.1	108.2	77.2	77.2	38.3	2.3	3.3	4.6	3.1	5.2	1.5	3.7
Livestock and livestock products	1.0	1.2	1.3	1.1	0.9	1.1	0.2	0.3	...	1.8	1.9	0.1
Other Commodities	16.4	13.0	21.5	14.2	11.1	10.1	4.5	6.5	5.2	6.5	7.5	6.6
Forestry products	0.2	0.3	0.2	0.1	0.1	0.1	...	...	0.6	1.1	0.4	...
Fish and other marine products	0.1	...	...	0.2	0.2	0.1	...	...	0.2	...	...	...
Metallic ores and concentrates	...	...	...	...	...	...	...	...	0.1	...	...	...
Bituminous coal and lignite	...	...	...	1.7	...	...	...	...	...	...	...	...
Crude petroleum and natural gas	...	...	...	...	...	0.1	...	...	...	...	...	...
Nonmetallic minerals	5.9	1.4	1.7	1.5	1.9	1.3	1.0	0.3	0.3	0.3	0.4	0.1
Scrap and waste	3.7	2.4	1.7	1.4	2.0	1.4	...	0.2	0.7	1.4	...	0.1
Used merchandise	3.9	4.9	15.0	6.3	4.6	3.3	1.0	3.4	2.1	1.6	2.9	2.7
Goods imported and returned unchanged	...	...	...	...	...	...	...	...	...	...	...	...
Special classification provisions	2.6	3.9	2.8	3.1	2.3	3.7	2.5	2.6	1.3	2.1	3.8	3.6

Industry	The Netherlands						Asian 10					
	1994	1995	1996	1997	1998	1999	1994	1995	1996	1997	1998	1999
ALL GOODS	788.6	915.8	1 171.3	1 369.3	1 030.2	980.6	5 894.1	8 803.2	8 626.1	7 714.3	6 721.0	5 647.8
Manufactured Goods	489.8	590.2	796.3	957.0	781.5	757.6	5 123.7	7 888.1	7 420.6	6 827.9	5 924.5	5 113.1
Food products	24.5	44.4	90.1	93.1	41.1	34.1	356.1	710.0	541.1	612.3	613.0	312.8
Tobacco products	...	...	...	...	...	...	0.2	0.2	0.2	...	0.2	...
Textile mill products	0.5	1.5	3.8	2.6	2.8	1.1	6.1	8.4	10.2	10.1	10.5	11.2
Apparel	4.5	7.2	1.8	1.1	1.3	0.5	10.2	10.5	12.5	8.8	8.7	6.3
Lumber and wood products	0.5	0.4	0.3	0.3	0.9	0.3	13.2	14.3	12.6	13.7	10.6	11.7
Furniture and fixtures	1.9	0.5	0.5	1.3	0.8	0.7	7.4	11.3	18.8	19.0	14.2	6.6
Paper products	6.2	14.7	29.4	54.5	34.0	13.2	51.5	76.4	83.7	90.9	68.1	67.9
Printing and publishing	4.0	3.7	4.9	6.9	7.3	5.5	27.2	32.6	31.6	31.4	23.6	24.2
Chemical products	148.1	157.4	172.6	260.3	213.4	168.7	1 148.9	1 462.0	1 253.7	1 092.6	903.9	895.1
Refined petroleum products	3.0	2.8	36.4	29.2	0.6	13.7	13.9	22.6	37.2	23.1	13.1	13.8
Rubber and plastic products	20.6	25.5	31.6	40.6	39.0	39.1	57.6	97.3	124.3	133.7	108.0	130.8
Leather products	0.2	0.1	0.4	0.6	0.2	0.2	7.7	9.0	14.1	15.8	12.7	9.9
Stone, clay and glass products	2.2	6.3	7.0	7.1	8.0	2.9	32.3	35.8	47.2	55.4	37.1	56.3
Primary metals	4.0	3.4	2.1	4.7	4.4	8.1	80.2	141.4	113.8	158.0	143.1	69.1
Fabricated metal products	8.1	12.3	14.6	11.6	13.4	9.5	106.6	136.7	153.8	164.6	101.7	109.7
Industrial machinery and computers	119.3	114.3	113.9	125.9	137.8	163.2	802.1	1 260.9	1 345.5	1 180.5	815.4	988.0
Electric and electronic equipment	58.4	77.3	72.7	82.0	62.3	68.0	1 820.1	3 138.1	2 823.0	2 427.7	2 374.0	1 706.1
Transportation equipment	52.7	73.7	159.7	174.3	139.8	163.3	189.7	266.1	259.0	256.3	156.6	156.2
Scientific and measuring instruments	19.9	35.6	40.0	45.5	52.7	43.7	304.7	353.6	409.6	408.6	420.9	437.3
Miscellaneous manufactures	10.1	7.6	12.9	14.5	18.4	18.4	76.4	89.4	115.4	114.3	72.7	77.9
Unidentified manufactures	1.2	1.4	1.4	0.8	3.5	3.1	11.7	11.5	13.4	11.0	16.2	22.1
Agricultural And Livestock Products	264.4	291.6	346.1	408.0	243.9	213.7	651.6	792.0	1 113.4	805.2	719.2	423.4
Agricultural products	264.0	291.2	345.8	407.7	243.8	213.7	643.2	784.3	1 103.1	797.8	712.7	416.5
Livestock and livestock products	0.4	0.4	0.3	0.3	0.1	...	8.4	7.7	10.2	7.4	6.5	6.9
Other Commodities	34.4	34.0	28.9	4.3	4.8	9.3	118.8	123.1	92.1	81.2	77.3	111.3
Forestry products	...	...	...	...	0.1	0.4	0.4	0.1	0.2	0.2	0.3	0.7
Fish and other marine products	...	...	...	0.3	0.9	0.7	0.4	1.0	1.0	3.4	0.7	0.5
Metallic ores and concentrates	...	20.2	11.8	0.9	0.1	...	0.6	0.9	2.0	0.6	0.9	0.4
Bituminous coal and lignite	20.3	10.1	12.8	...	...	...	17.3	15.2	7.4	0.1	0.1	...
Crude petroleum and natural gas	...	...	...	...	...	...	0.2	0.1	0.1	0.1	0.2	0.1
Nonmetallic minerals	10.3	2.2	1.3	2.3	3.3	3.8	51.6	24.3	22.6	21.1	20.6	35.3
Scrap and waste	0.1	0.1	0.3	...	...	0.1	31.8	53.5	24.6	22.1	33.0	43.5
Used merchandise	0.6	1.0	2.3	0.6	0.1	1.5	7.3	13.5	14.4	14.2	4.2	5.0
Goods imported and returned unchanged	...	...	...	...	...	...	...	...	...	...	...	...
Special classification provisions	3.1	0.2	0.5	0.2	0.4	2.8	9.3	14.5	19.8	19.4	17.5	25.8

Table D-16. ILLINOIS: State Exports of Goods by Destination and Industry, 1994–1999—*Continued*

(Millions of dollars.)

Industry	Japan						South Korea					
	1994	1995	1996	1997	1998	1999	1994	1995	1996	1997	1998	1999
ALL GOODS	2 121.5	2 940.1	3 024.6	2 437.4	2 953.2	2 304.5	698.1	1 266.2	1 301.0	892.6	626.8	690.0
Manufactured Goods	1 671.5	2 599.1	2 554.6	2 031.4	2 545.8	2 064.0	614.2	1 026.5	1 024.4	785.2	469.2	612.6
Food products	187.7	256.6	254.3	184.2	170.5	131.5	24.8	48.6	34.0	38.1	38.5	25.0
Tobacco products	...	...	...	...	...	...	0.1	0.2	...	...	...	...
Textile mill products	1.3	1.5	4.4	2.4	1.6	1.3	0.8	1.1	1.3	1.4	1.3	0.8
Apparel	7.4	7.3	8.0	5.5	6.0	3.2	0.1	0.4	1.5	0.7	0.3	0.3
Lumber and wood products	8.6	9.8	7.8	8.7	5.8	6.9	2.5	1.9	2.1	2.7	2.8	2.2
Furniture and fixtures	3.6	5.5	10.2	4.3	3.4	2.8	0.4	0.5	1.1	1.7	0.4	0.2
Paper products	9.3	9.9	13.7	13.3	14.0	11.2	8.9	5.9	5.4	4.0	3.6	7.0
Printing and publishing	7.3	7.9	8.1	7.6	8.8	7.1	1.3	1.9	2.6	2.1	0.8	0.9
Chemical products	249.9	370.4	338.2	353.2	296.1	243.7	72.5	166.4	138.5	108.9	64.7	87.1
Refined petroleum products	5.2	6.4	8.1	7.4	6.2	5.3	2.8	3.5	5.5	5.8	1.2	2.2
Rubber and plastic products	26.4	48.8	59.7	64.1	44.2	52.0	7.3	10.5	10.9	9.7	6.6	10.6
Leather products	1.0	1.1	3.2	1.6	1.1	1.2	0.3	0.1	1.1	0.5	...	0.7
Stone, clay and glass products	9.5	6.4	5.2	9.5	6.4	5.4	3.6	7.2	16.3	15.7	6.9	7.5
Primary metals	26.0	50.9	31.9	43.9	34.8	17.1	7.3	10.7	14.8	36.2	29.4	6.5
Fabricated metal products	42.3	40.4	48.2	50.8	29.9	26.6	13.2	21.0	22.0	22.5	12.6	10.9
Industrial machinery and computers	263.5	366.6	386.5	386.7	298.0	378.4	118.8	202.7	230.6	145.4	64.6	93.8
Electric and electronic equipment	562.3	1 058.7	994.1	569.8	1 311.5	872.9	246.8	409.3	408.9	251.8	159.2	267.3
Transportation equipment	73.9	119.1	88.3	76.0	57.6	40.8	52.6	68.1	67.1	82.8	39.4	47.9
Scientific and measuring instruments	145.4	182.7	224.7	185.2	212.0	211.3	40.4	52.7	44.4	45.8	32.2	34.7
Miscellaneous manufactures	37.8	45.1	56.6	54.4	34.5	41.1	8.4	12.4	14.4	8.3	3.6	3.7
Unidentified manufactures	3.1	3.8	3.4	2.8	3.5	4.1	1.4	1.6	1.7	1.2	1.1	3.3
Agricultural And Livestock Products	405.2	294.1	443.1	374.4	375.2	204.2	42.2	218.4	262.1	100.4	151.7	68.8
Agricultural products	401.0	289.7	437.6	371.2	371.3	199.1	41.7	217.7	261.3	98.6	151.6	68.6
Livestock and livestock products	4.2	4.4	5.6	3.2	3.9	5.1	0.6	0.7	0.9	1.8	0.1	0.2
Other Commodities	44.7	47.0	26.8	31.5	32.2	36.3	41.7	21.3	14.5	7.0	5.9	8.6
Forestry products	...	...	0.1	0.1	...	0.4	...	...	...	0.1	0.1	0.1
Fish and other marine products	0.3	0.5	0.6	2.1	0.2	...	0.1	0.1	0.2	...	...	0.1
Metallic ores and concentrates	0.2	...	...	0.2	0.1	0.2	...	...	...	...	...	...
Bituminous coal and lignite	12.7	7.6	4.0	...	...	...	4.6	7.6	3.0	...	...	...
Crude petroleum and natural gas	...	...	...	...	...	...	0.1	0.1	...	...	...	...
Nonmetallic minerals	7.2	7.5	4.3	5.8	7.6	5.6	33.0	7.7	4.0	4.0	2.8	2.8
Scrap and waste	15.3	13.8	3.1	4.4	12.8	10.3	3.3	4.4	5.1	1.6	1.2	4.5
Used merchandise	6.2	11.6	12.5	12.8	2.6	4.2	0.2	0.4	0.5	0.4	0.1	...
Goods imported and returned unchanged	...	...	...	...	...	...	...	...	...	...	...	...
Special classification provisions	2.9	6.0	2.2	6.0	8.8	15.5	0.3	1.0	1.7	1.0	1.7	1.1

Industry	Taiwan						Singapore					
	1994	1995	1996	1997	1998	1999	1994	1995	1996	1997	1998	1999
ALL GOODS	637.8	592.1	512.2	496.1	516.9	443.1	356.3	649.7	744.7	720.6	516.3	581.7
Manufactured Goods	562.6	571.2	454.0	462.1	484.2	357.7	354.1	646.1	740.4	710.2	514.3	578.7
Food products	22.3	28.0	29.2	44.0	37.6	24.8	22.7	30.3	29.3	41.1	26.7	20.3
Tobacco products	...	...	0.2	...	0.2	...	...	...	...	...	...	...
Textile mill products	0.5	0.6	0.4	0.3	0.6	0.4	1.2	1.5	1.0	1.0	0.3	1.0
Apparel	0.3	0.5	0.5	0.3	0.3	0.5	0.4	0.6	0.6	0.7	0.3	0.3
Lumber and wood products	0.6	0.7	0.7	0.3	0.2	0.3	0.2	0.4	0.3	0.2	0.1	0.1
Furniture and fixtures	0.9	1.8	1.4	0.9	1.5	0.4	0.8	1.0	1.5	0.8	5.6	0.5
Paper products	14.4	21.6	19.5	22.6	14.7	15.0	3.1	6.3	6.8	5.3	5.7	5.1
Printing and publishing	1.2	1.6	2.1	2.4	2.5	2.8	3.5	2.4	3.8	5.6	2.2	3.5
Chemical products	250.3	248.9	139.9	75.4	87.5	110.0	39.9	60.0	80.2	42.4	39.1	47.9
Refined petroleum products	1.5	1.6	2.0	1.8	1.2	1.5	0.3	6.0	14.2	1.2	1.2	1.2
Rubber and plastic products	4.7	5.4	4.9	6.8	8.6	6.1	7.6	10.3	21.9	18.8	12.0	16.3
Leather products	0.7	0.5	0.5	0.2	0.7	0.6	0.1	0.3	0.3	1.5	0.2	0.3
Stone, clay and glass products	4.4	5.1	4.0	3.8	2.2	4.0	3.2	4.3	6.1	7.7	6.5	6.4
Primary metals	7.0	9.3	9.1	15.7	15.9	12.0	5.2	7.2	5.2	8.3	6.8	7.9
Fabricated metal products	11.4	22.5	15.2	27.0	11.8	15.0	7.2	13.3	18.2	19.7	9.9	10.3
Industrial machinery and computers	68.9	68.7	68.4	67.6	52.6	57.4	64.1	234.7	216.2	165.0	133.9	182.1
Electric and electronic equipment	102.6	84.8	91.9	126.7	190.4	55.7	146.9	206.9	232.7	278.9	175.7	189.2
Transportation equipment	37.7	31.0	19.8	15.4	7.5	5.8	7.4	20.3	47.4	45.0	29.1	26.2
Scientific and measuring instruments	19.2	23.6	25.8	25.8	30.4	39.8	32.8	33.8	47.2	60.0	55.0	50.5
Miscellaneous manufactures	11.7	14.0	17.6	22.1	15.8	3.5	6.5	5.3	6.3	5.7	2.6	6.5
Unidentified manufactures	2.3	1.0	1.2	1.0	2.1	2.1	1.1	1.1	1.2	1.0	1.2	3.3
Agricultural And Livestock Products	67.6	10.2	53.9	26.7	22.4	61.6	0.2	0.3	0.2	7.1	0.5	0.3
Agricultural products	67.0	9.4	52.6	26.7	22.2	61.3	0.2	0.3	0.1	7.1	0.4	0.3
Livestock and livestock products	0.6	0.8	1.3	0.1	0.1	0.3	...	...	...	...	...	...
Other Commodities	7.6	10.6	4.4	7.3	10.3	23.7	2.0	3.3	4.1	3.3	1.5	2.6
Forestry products	0.1	...	...	...	0.1	...	...	...	0.1	...	...	...
Fish and other marine products	...	...	...	...	0.1	...	0.1	0.1	...	...	...	0.2
Metallic ores and concentrates	...	...	...	...	0.8	...	...	...	...	...	...	...
Bituminous coal and lignite	...	...	...	...	...	...	...	...	...	...	0.1	...
Crude petroleum and natural gas	...	...	...	...	...	...	...	...	...	...	...	...
Nonmetallic minerals	3.0	2.5	2.5	3.6	5.2	19.9	1.2	0.8	0.9	0.8	0.6	1.2
Scrap and waste	4.3	7.8	1.5	3.2	3.2	1.7	0.1	1.6	1.9	0.6	0.2	0.1
Used merchandise	0.1	0.1	...	0.1	0.1	0.1	0.2	0.3	0.5	0.2	0.1	...
Goods imported and returned unchanged	...	...	...	...	...	...	0.4	0.5	0.7	1.7	0.6	...
Special classification provisions	0.1	0.3	0.4	0.4	0.9	1.9	...	...	...	...	...	1.1

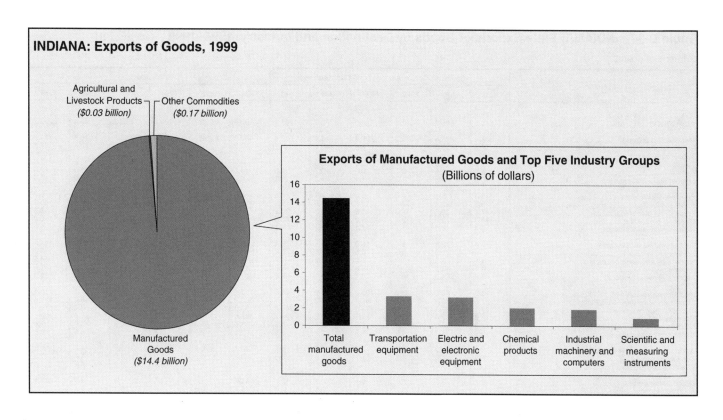

INDIANA: Exports of Goods, 1999

Agricultural and Livestock Products ($0.03 billion)

Other Commodities ($0.17 billion)

Manufactured Goods ($14.4 billion)

Exports of Manufactured Goods and Top Five Industry Groups
(Billions of dollars)

Total manufactured goods · Transportation equipment · Electric and electronic equipment · Chemical products · Industrial machinery and computers · Scientific and measuring instruments

Table D-17. INDIANA: State Exports of Goods by Destination and Industry, 1994–1999

(Millions of dollars.)

Industry	All destinations						Canada					
	1994	1995	1996	1997	1998	1999	1994	1995	1996	1997	1998	1999
ALL GOODS	9 534.0	11 052.0	12 119.0	13 097.3	13 949.1	14 583.9	4 593.6	4 594.8	4 630.3	5 060.3	5 671.6	6 391.4
Manufactured Goods	9 384.0	10 898.3	11 950.8	12 930.8	13 811.1	14 388.2	4 515.2	4 514.4	4 538.8	4 957.4	5 591.7	6 255.5
Food products	182.0	224.7	243.7	248.7	213.4	177.8	49.4	52.8	70.9	60.7	50.9	45.5
Tobacco products	. . .	7.8	. . .	. . .	. . .	. . .	. . .	. . .	. . .	. . .	. . .	. . .
Textile mill products	19.6	32.4	27.1	33.6	33.5	25.6	13.2	22.2	20.2	20.2	19.6	14.5
Apparel	12.5	21.6	20.9	23.7	26.6	28.6	6.0	6.1	5.1	6.5	7.5	11.0
Lumber and wood products	125.6	116.7	116.9	130.5	132.9	127.6	29.6	29.2	31.2	39.8	49.2	57.9
Furniture and fixtures	134.9	92.8	90.1	101.4	141.6	86.5	105.2	59.9	47.0	49.2	52.4	32.8
Paper products	60.8	110.5	121.0	103.1	116.5	118.1	22.7	29.7	34.2	35.8	43.6	54.6
Printing and publishing	70.4	103.9	97.0	122.2	124.6	108.1	24.5	31.9	37.1	62.1	67.1	60.2
Chemical products	1 314.4	1 681.8	1 971.2	2 162.3	2 247.3	2 045.0	212.2	281.2	254.7	261.3	264.2	292.4
Refined petroleum products	24.4	22.2	24.7	23.7	26.8	22.9	11.4	10.7	11.0	12.6	12.2	9.2
Rubber and plastic products	252.9	310.1	401.1	449.3	445.4	474.0	136.3	142.5	146.6	162.7	171.9	194.6
Leather products	10.0	11.1	9.5	10.5	11.6	12.1	1.0	1.1	1.0	1.2	2.7	1.3
Stone, clay and glass products	81.2	104.8	85.0	112.3	104.0	130.5	63.0	64.5	52.0	49.1	59.3	92.1
Primary metals	307.7	445.3	450.1	516.0	750.7	752.8	156.5	212.6	205.9	277.4	477.2	483.7
Fabricated metal products	345.7	371.6	451.8	516.9	708.5	822.2	203.1	192.3	190.9	206.4	387.7	544.3
Industrial machinery and computers	1 509.6	1 700.0	1 866.8	2 082.4	1 940.4	1 903.5	576.0	665.3	678.9	783.4	935.6	1 031.6
Electric and electronic equipment	1 799.5	2 104.6	2 582.5	2 704.4	3 037.9	3 234.7	889.0	602.3	508.5	615.1	713.3	710.8
Transportation equipment	1 918.4	2 364.8	2 504.2	2 692.5	2 847.7	3 342.4	1 583.8	1 787.7	1 940.3	2 020.8	2 101.1	2 398.1
Scientific and measuring instruments	1 130.6	993.1	804.6	813.4	813.4	895.5	402.8	303.4	282.4	265.7	151.4	199.6
Miscellaneous manufactures	54.1	51.4	55.4	60.5	52.3	46.5	14.6	10.3	10.9	15.5	16.2	13.1
Unidentified manufactures	29.5	27.1	27.3	23.3	36.1	33.7	15.1	8.7	9.9	11.8	8.8	8.0
Agricultural And Livestock Products	53.0	52.9	55.8	60.0	44.5	29.8	10.2	9.1	8.6	22.4	9.5	7.3
Agricultural products	47.5	48.6	50.9	55.9	40.4	27.8	5.4	5.6	4.9	19.6	6.8	6.3
Livestock and livestock products	5.5	4.2	4.9	4.1	4.1	2.0	4.9	3.4	3.6	2.9	2.7	1.1
Other Commodities	97.1	100.8	112.4	106.4	93.5	165.9	68.1	71.3	83.0	80.5	70.4	128.5
Forestry products	1.0	1.1	1.0	1.2	1.4	0.4	0.1	. . .	0.1	0.1	0.1	0.2
Fish and other marine products	1.4	1.7	0.7	1.7	1.9	2.2	1.0	1.0	0.3	. . .	. . .	0.1
Metallic ores and concentrates	0.3	0.5	0.8	1.1	2.9	2.9	. . .	. . .	0.1	. . .	. . .	. . .
Bituminous coal and lignite	0.9	3.2	3.6	1.6	0.5	. . .	0.8	. . .	1.3	. . .	. . .	. . .
Crude petroleum and natural gas	. . .	0.2	2.0	0.1	2.8	0.1	. . .	0.1	2.0	. . .	2.8	0.1
Nonmetallic minerals	2.1	3.2	3.2	4.0	4.2	4.1	1.9	2.3	3.0	2.9	3.2	3.3
Scrap and waste	25.3	37.0	35.2	37.2	28.0	24.5	24.2	30.9	33.4	35.6	26.3	21.4
Used merchandise	12.0	9.3	10.3	5.3	5.6	6.3	1.5	0.4	0.6	1.2	1.1	3.5
Goods imported and returned unchanged	31.0	31.7	36.5	35.7	33.1	27.3	31.0	31.7	36.5	35.7	33.1	27.3
Special classification provisions	22.9	12.8	19.0	18.6	13.2	98.1	7.7	5.0	5.6	5.0	3.8	72.6

Table D-17. INDIANA: State Exports of Goods by Destination and Industry, 1994–1999—*Continued*

(Millions of dollars.)

Industry	South and Central American and Caribbean						Mexico					
	1994	1995	1996	1997	1998	1999	1994	1995	1996	1997	1998	1999
ALL GOODS	315.9	486.2	511.1	716.0	778.7	788.1	1 492.6	1 955.7	2 529.3	2 573.3	3 046.4	3 225.7
Manufactured Goods	308.4	478.6	501.8	709.2	775.4	772.4	1 480.8	1 952.3	2 524.5	2 567.7	3 040.3	3 214.2
Food products	11.3	23.5	16.8	8.5	10.1	7.7	10.8	3.0	3.2	21.3	23.5	17.6
Tobacco products	...	...	...	...	...	...	...	...	...	...	...	...
Textile mill products	0.5	0.8	0.4	3.3	2.8	1.7	0.3	0.7	1.1	3.9	5.4	3.0
Apparel	0.3	0.6	0.7	0.9	0.7	0.5	0.5	9.7	9.2	11.4	13.2	12.0
Lumber and wood products	0.6	1.5	1.8	1.1	1.3	1.2	2.8	2.8	2.7	2.6	8.3	16.5
Furniture and fixtures	3.2	5.1	6.6	6.3	6.7	4.6	4.6	2.2	2.1	5.6	29.6	8.7
Paper products	6.3	22.7	22.4	10.3	6.6	1.9	15.7	40.1	43.0	34.7	48.4	50.0
Printing and publishing	7.7	10.7	12.8	18.8	10.3	4.2	6.0	6.4	6.7	7.3	8.9	8.7
Chemical products	80.3	173.2	180.1	229.2	244.4	183.5	28.0	46.9	75.2	82.6	119.1	115.2
Refined petroleum products	0.4	0.6	1.3	1.1	1.1	1.1	0.6	0.5	1.1	1.2	1.1	1.7
Rubber and plastic products	7.4	12.5	9.9	15.0	15.8	26.4	48.9	80.3	136.2	135.1	120.5	143.3
Leather products	0.5	1.0	0.5	0.5	0.5	0.4	1.7	0.9	0.3	0.2	0.4	0.4
Stone, clay and glass products	1.1	1.2	1.0	15.5	2.2	1.7	4.4	22.8	18.1	30.0	27.1	14.5
Primary metals	4.1	14.6	11.6	13.5	12.8	9.6	47.8	76.2	101.0	98.0	125.4	152.5
Fabricated metal products	6.5	9.3	10.3	13.7	13.1	9.0	67.8	81.2	138.7	145.3	177.3	156.9
Industrial machinery and computers	111.2	93.0	98.7	103.2	83.2	68.0	157.5	159.3	164.8	231.1	277.7	218.1
Electric and electronic equipment	27.8	46.9	48.0	64.9	58.2	72.7	662.3	1 144.5	1 711.9	1 643.3	1 886.4	2 111.6
Transportation equipment	22.7	38.1	60.8	178.6	280.3	348.6	33.0	29.3	44.3	47.4	58.6	74.7
Scientific and measuring instruments	13.8	19.4	15.4	22.2	20.8	24.7	383.8	242.5	61.4	63.9	99.0	100.5
Miscellaneous manufactures	2.2	3.0	2.0	1.3	1.4	1.3	1.6	1.0	1.0	0.9	0.9	1.4
Unidentified manufactures	0.8	1.1	0.8	1.2	3.0	3.6	2.9	2.1	2.4	1.9	9.5	6.9
Agricultural And Livestock Products	6.8	4.0	4.3	1.7	0.7	3.3	0.4	0.7	1.3	1.2	1.4	1.0
Agricultural products	6.8	4.0	4.3	1.7	0.6	3.3	0.4	0.7	1.2	1.0	1.2	1.0
Livestock and livestock products	...	...	...	...	...	...	...	...	0.1	0.2	0.2	...
Other Commodities	0.7	3.6	5.1	5.1	2.7	12.4	11.5	2.6	3.5	4.4	4.7	10.4
Forestry products	...	...	...	0.1	0.1	...	0.6	0.8	0.8	0.7	0.4	...
Fish and other marine products	...	...	...	...	0.1	...	...	...	...	1.4	1.7	2.0
Metallic ores and concentrates	...	...	...	...	...	...	...	...	...	0.1	2.3	2.2
Bituminous coal and lignite	...	3.2	2.3	1.6	...	...	...	...	...	...	...	...
Crude petroleum and natural gas	...	...	...	...	...	...	...	...	...	...	...	...
Nonmetallic minerals	...	0.1	...	0.5	0.3	...	...	...	...	0.1	...	...
Scrap and waste	0.4	0.2	...	...	0.1	...	0.1	0.2	0.6	0.6	0.2	1.1
Used merchandise	0.2	0.1	0.2	...	0.1	0.2	0.1	...	...	...	...	0.2
Goods imported and returned unchanged	...	...	...	...	...	...	...	...	...	...	...	...
Special classification provisions	...	0.1	2.5	3.0	2.1	12.1	10.7	1.6	2.1	1.5	0.2	4.9

Industry	European Union						United Kingdom					
	1994	1995	1996	1997	1998	1999	1994	1995	1996	1997	1998	1999
ALL GOODS	1 555.7	1 901.8	2 149.5	2 377.7	2 405.5	2 285.8	495.7	627.5	644.0	704.8	713.1	673.6
Manufactured Goods	1 515.0	1 859.1	2 099.2	2 341.2	2 370.1	2 264.3	486.0	617.7	633.5	699.5	706.5	669.0
Food products	33.8	37.2	37.9	31.9	26.5	18.0	18.7	19.8	14.9	9.8	9.8	7.0
Tobacco products	...	7.7	...	...	...	...	...	...	...	...	...	...
Textile mill products	3.6	3.7	2.4	3.7	3.1	3.2	0.6	1.0	0.8	0.7	0.7	0.5
Apparel	4.0	3.0	2.1	2.4	3.0	3.3	2.0	1.2	0.7	0.5	0.9	1.2
Lumber and wood products	59.9	51.2	49.3	53.2	52.9	35.1	8.1	8.2	7.5	6.0	4.3	3.1
Furniture and fixtures	3.8	5.2	6.5	8.4	21.6	22.8	0.9	1.0	1.3	1.9	4.4	4.1
Paper products	4.3	3.8	5.2	8.9	7.1	2.8	1.3	0.8	1.3	2.3	1.7	1.6
Printing and publishing	19.5	33.5	18.5	16.5	20.5	24.0	8.8	15.3	12.5	11.4	15.2	21.0
Chemical products	537.7	640.8	870.2	999.7	974.7	939.0	108.4	177.7	184.6	191.6	185.6	175.4
Refined petroleum products	2.4	2.6	2.0	1.8	3.6	3.4	0.5	1.2	0.6	0.7	0.8	0.9
Rubber and plastic products	33.5	40.6	59.5	75.5	70.6	52.1	10.3	13.0	24.9	22.4	24.2	20.7
Leather products	2.6	2.6	3.3	3.9	3.2	5.3	1.5	1.8	2.1	2.4	1.8	3.6
Stone, clay and glass products	7.2	9.0	7.0	9.5	9.3	16.0	1.7	2.7	2.4	3.3	2.8	3.7
Primary metals	63.9	76.7	62.5	66.5	78.2	55.9	18.2	26.4	21.5	25.6	25.8	22.4
Fabricated metal products	21.7	32.9	38.5	49.6	48.3	43.2	7.8	9.6	10.9	11.4	13.0	9.9
Industrial machinery and computers	309.6	349.1	343.2	364.4	287.7	253.7	181.7	206.8	203.4	214.8	135.0	114.9
Electric and electronic equipment	93.3	115.6	113.2	133.6	184.4	161.3	26.2	31.5	35.0	39.4	51.9	46.6
Transportation equipment	159.2	260.0	253.7	267.6	232.0	262.1	56.1	63.1	62.2	66.0	96.2	101.2
Scientific and measuring instruments	134.8	163.2	200.4	224.1	319.3	339.6	26.2	30.6	38.2	83.7	122.6	123.8
Miscellaneous manufactures	14.3	13.2	18.0	16.8	17.0	16.8	4.9	3.9	7.5	4.5	7.4	5.0
Unidentified manufactures	5.8	7.7	5.8	3.2	7.0	6.5	2.0	2.2	1.2	1.2	2.5	2.3
Agricultural And Livestock Products	28.6	27.8	35.6	27.7	26.7	13.2	1.7	1.0	1.7	2.2	2.5	1.7
Agricultural products	28.3	27.4	35.1	27.3	26.3	12.7	1.5	1.0	1.7	2.2	2.5	1.7
Livestock and livestock products	0.4	0.4	0.5	0.4	0.5	0.5	0.2	...	...	...	...	...
Other Commodities	12.1	14.9	14.7	8.9	8.7	8.3	8.0	8.8	8.8	3.1	4.1	3.0
Forestry products	0.2	0.1	...	0.1	0.6	0.1	...	...	...	...	0.1	...
Fish and other marine products	0.2	0.4	0.3	0.2	...	...	...	...	...	...	...	...
Metallic ores and concentrates	0.2	0.5	0.7	1.0	0.7	0.7	0.1	0.3	0.5	0.6	0.5	0.5
Bituminous coal and lignite	...	...	...	...	...	...	...	...	...	...	...	...
Crude petroleum and natural gas	...	0.1	...	...	...	...	...	...	...	...	...	...
Nonmetallic minerals	...	0.7	0.1	0.2	0.3	0.5	...	0.2	...	...	0.1	0.2
Scrap and waste	0.6	2.7	0.5	0.2	0.3	0.4	0.1	1.9	0.2	0.1	0.1	0.1
Used merchandise	7.9	8.2	8.4	2.1	3.0	1.9	6.9	5.9	7.0	0.1	2.2	0.7
Goods imported and returned unchanged	...	...	...	...	...	...	...	...	...	...	...	...
Special classification provisions	2.8	2.1	4.8	5.2	3.9	4.7	0.9	0.4	1.2	2.3	1.2	1.6

Table D-17. INDIANA: State Exports of Goods by Destination and Industry, 1994–1999—*Continued*

(Millions of dollars.)

Industry	Germany						France					
	1994	1995	1996	1997	1998	1999	1994	1995	1996	1997	1998	1999
ALL GOODS	294.1	290.3	288.9	337.3	318.2	295.5	170.1	191.2	298.8	389.2	444.0	538.3
Manufactured Goods	291.2	286.9	285.5	333.1	316.0	291.6	169.3	189.0	295.4	386.7	442.7	532.7
Food products	1.9	1.9	2.6	3.0	1.8	0.8	0.5	0.6	1.0	0.7	1.2	1.6
Tobacco products	...	...	...	...	...	...	...	...	...	...	...	...
Textile mill products	2.5	0.8	0.4	0.6	0.9	2.0	0.2	0.1	0.4	0.4	...	...
Apparel	1.3	0.8	0.3	0.7	0.8	0.9	0.1	0.1	0.3	0.3	0.3	0.3
Lumber and wood products	32.4	23.6	20.1	23.3	25.2	14.8	0.7	0.4	0.7	0.8	0.6	0.5
Furniture and fixtures	0.4	0.6	0.6	0.6	1.1	1.3	1.5	2.0	3.2	3.0	4.0	4.1
Paper products	0.1	0.2	0.3	1.1	1.4	0.1	0.4	0.2	1.1	2.1	0.8	0.1
Printing and publishing	1.8	7.3	1.6	1.8	1.4	1.2	0.8	2.3	0.5	0.2	0.4	0.2
Chemical products	117.0	108.1	120.1	145.7	96.2	78.8	73.6	76.1	185.6	261.6	287.6	363.4
Refined petroleum products	...	...	...	0.1	0.1	0.1	0.6	0.5	0.5	0.7	0.7	0.4
Rubber and plastic products	7.6	3.6	4.4	5.5	6.9	7.2	0.7	3.7	3.2	5.0	3.2	3.0
Leather products	0.6	0.4	0.7	0.9	0.7	0.8	0.1	...	...	0.1	...	0.3
Stone, clay and glass products	3.7	3.8	2.5	2.5	2.8	2.9	0.5	1.3	1.1	2.0	1.7	8.4
Primary metals	27.4	24.6	8.2	11.6	13.1	11.9	6.4	8.6	7.7	6.6	5.3	5.2
Fabricated metal products	3.4	5.7	8.5	7.2	6.4	6.8	1.9	2.7	6.0	13.0	7.2	9.9
Industrial machinery and computers	27.7	31.9	33.6	38.9	38.5	29.2	29.5	26.9	22.1	21.0	23.9	20.8
Electric and electronic equipment	21.2	30.2	19.2	26.6	45.0	45.6	9.7	17.8	17.1	21.5	26.3	21.2
Transportation equipment	19.4	20.3	22.8	27.7	24.5	17.4	16.1	20.3	21.0	21.9	31.4	30.1
Scientific and measuring instruments	18.0	18.9	35.3	29.3	43.7	62.5	24.5	23.9	22.2	24.1	46.2	62.1
Miscellaneous manufactures	4.3	3.4	3.7	5.7	4.2	6.0	1.2	1.1	1.4	1.3	1.2	1.1
Unidentified manufactures	0.7	0.8	0.7	0.5	1.4	1.5	0.4	0.4	0.4	0.3	0.6	0.3
Agricultural And Livestock Products	2.4	2.0	1.8	2.2	1.4	1.2	0.4	1.4	2.8	0.4	0.2	4.5
Agricultural products	2.4	1.8	1.6	2.0	1.1	0.9	0.4	1.4	2.8	0.3	0.2	4.5
Livestock and livestock products	...	0.1	0.1	0.2	0.3	0.3	...	...	...	...	0.1	...
Other Commodities	0.6	1.4	1.6	2.0	0.8	2.7	0.3	0.8	0.6	2.1	1.1	1.1
Forestry products	0.2	0.1	...	0.1	0.2	0.1	...	...	...	...	...	...
Fish and other marine products	0.1	...	...	...	...	...	...	...	0.1	...	...	...
Metallic ores and concentrates	...	...	...	...	...	...	0.1	0.2	0.2	0.4	0.1	0.2
Bituminous coal and lignite	...	...	...	...	...	...	...	...	...	...	...	...
Crude petroleum and natural gas	...	...	...	...	...	...	...	...	...	...	...	...
Nonmetallic minerals	...	0.1	...	0.1	0.1	0.1	...	...	...	...	...	...
Scrap and waste	...	0.1	0.2	...	0.1	0.1	0.1	0.5	0.1	0.1	0.1	0.1
Used merchandise	0.2	0.8	0.9	1.6	...	0.9	0.1	0.1	...	0.1	0.6	0.3
Goods imported and returned unchanged	...	...	...	...	...	...	...	...	...	...	...	...
Special classification provisions	0.1	0.2	0.4	0.3	0.4	1.5	...	...	0.2	1.5	0.3	0.5

Industry	The Netherlands						Asian 10					
	1994	1995	1996	1997	1998	1999	1994	1995	1996	1997	1998	1999
ALL GOODS	175.2	250.4	301.9	364.8	279.1	208.8	1 182.1	1 528.6	1 691.4	1 757.0	1 439.0	1 333.5
Manufactured Goods	174.7	249.2	300.2	363.4	278.4	208.0	1 177.2	1 520.1	1 686.1	1 749.9	1 430.1	1 326.7
Food products	9.2	5.8	8.8	10.6	7.5	5.7	71.8	97.1	103.5	117.4	93.6	81.3
Tobacco products	...	...	...	...	...	...	...	...	...	...	...	...
Textile mill products	0.2	0.9	0.1	0.3	0.1	0.1	1.5	2.4	2.6	1.6	1.9	2.8
Apparel	0.1	0.5	0.4	0.1	0.3	0.4	0.7	1.4	1.9	1.0	1.2	1.1
Lumber and wood products	1.5	2.6	1.2	0.7	0.4	0.3	25.4	23.2	23.6	25.1	15.2	12.1
Furniture and fixtures	0.4	0.7	0.4	1.6	9.3	10.0	5.3	6.9	8.5	11.0	9.6	4.1
Paper products	0.2	0.5	0.1	1.1	1.5	0.1	5.1	7.8	11.8	9.5	6.8	5.2
Printing and publishing	3.1	2.8	1.8	1.3	1.5	0.4	6.2	9.6	11.7	9.8	8.3	6.2
Chemical products	71.4	75.1	118.7	150.2	123.6	106.5	376.3	448.0	458.1	424.8	458.5	355.8
Refined petroleum products	...	0.4	0.6	...	...	0.1	7.6	5.8	6.9	5.5	4.7	4.9
Rubber and plastic products	9.9	13.7	16.4	30.6	24.2	8.4	18.3	21.3	32.7	44.6	46.2	44.4
Leather products	...	...	0.1	0.2	0.4	0.1	4.0	5.0	3.7	4.0	4.4	4.2
Stone, clay and glass products	0.1	0.3	0.1	0.2	0.3	0.4	4.3	4.8	5.2	6.9	4.8	4.6
Primary metals	1.4	6.2	12.1	11.6	18.6	2.1	23.1	49.9	51.8	46.9	42.9	36.8
Fabricated metal products	1.1	2.4	3.4	5.1	5.0	1.8	35.2	42.7	55.7	80.9	64.8	51.9
Industrial machinery and computers	22.5	26.5	24.5	35.1	17.5	19.8	238.7	296.6	425.0	440.0	231.5	203.5
Electric and electronic equipment	15.8	9.2	6.5	7.3	9.2	9.5	99.4	142.6	155.7	211.8	152.4	148.4
Transportation equipment	29.8	72.2	64.1	77.3	9.6	31.7	83.4	123.2	116.6	106.8	107.0	172.1
Scientific and measuring instruments	5.9	26.5	38.5	27.8	48.0	8.4	153.2	214.7	190.5	181.0	160.7	171.8
Miscellaneous manufactures	0.9	0.9	0.8	1.9	0.7	1.7	14.7	13.8	16.8	18.0	11.2	9.6
Unidentified manufactures	1.2	2.0	1.8	0.4	0.7	0.4	2.9	3.1	3.8	3.2	4.6	5.8
Agricultural And Livestock Products	0.5	0.6	0.6	0.3	0.2	0.3	1.7	2.8	2.7	3.6	4.0	2.8
Agricultural products	0.3	0.3	0.3	0.2	0.2	0.2	1.7	2.7	2.0	2.9	3.3	2.5
Livestock and livestock products	0.2	0.3	0.3	0.1	...	0.1	...	0.2	0.6	0.7	0.6	0.3
Other Commodities	0.1	0.7	1.1	1.1	0.5	0.5	3.2	5.8	2.6	3.5	4.9	4.1
Forestry products	...	...	...	...	...	...	...	0.1	...	...	0.1	...
Fish and other marine products	...	...	...	...	...	...	0.1	0.2	...	...	...	...
Metallic ores and concentrates	...	...	...	...	...	...	...	...	...	...	...	...
Bituminous coal and lignite	...	...	...	...	...	...	...	...	...	...	...	...
Crude petroleum and natural gas	...	...	...	...	...	...	...	...	...	...	...	...
Nonmetallic minerals	...	...	...	0.1	0.1	0.2	0.1	0.1	0.1	0.4	0.4	0.2
Scrap and waste	...	0.1	...	...	...	...	0.1	2.7	0.5	0.8	0.6	1.3
Used merchandise	...	0.3	0.4	0.2	0.1	0.1	2.0	0.5	0.1	0.1	1.2	...
Goods imported and returned unchanged	...	...	...	...	...	...	...	...	...	...	...	...
Special classification provisions	0.1	0.2	0.7	0.8	0.3	0.2	0.9	2.2	1.9	2.1	2.5	2.5

Table D-17. INDIANA: State Exports of Goods by Destination and Industry, 1994–1999—Continued

(Millions of dollars.)

Industry	Japan						South Korea					
	1994	1995	1996	1997	1998	1999	1994	1995	1996	1997	1998	1999
ALL GOODS	571.0	733.6	747.2	729.9	696.7	687.8	158.7	183.0	199.3	227.1	127.9	132.9
Manufactured Goods	569.5	732.8	745.2	725.7	691.8	685.5	158.6	180.3	198.2	226.0	127.1	131.8
Food products	63.9	86.8	88.0	102.0	82.1	67.0	1.6	1.4	3.5	3.1	2.4	2.6
Tobacco products	...	...	...	...	...	...	...	...	...	...	...	...
Textile mill products	0.3	0.1	1.4	0.4	0.5	0.5	0.2	0.4	0.1	0.1	0.2	0.5
Apparel	0.3	0.5	0.8	0.5	0.4	0.3	...	0.1	0.1	0.1	...	0.1
Lumber and wood products	12.8	11.1	10.6	11.4	6.2	6.3	3.5	3.5	1.8	0.3	0.3	0.3
Furniture and fixtures	1.2	3.4	4.5	5.4	2.7	1.6	0.2	0.4	0.7	0.6	0.1	0.1
Paper products	0.3	0.9	3.6	3.7	2.9	1.0	0.8	0.2	0.6	0.4	0.7	...
Printing and publishing	1.1	2.2	2.2	1.8	1.5	0.9	1.1	1.5	1.6	1.1	0.8	0.5
Chemical products	252.0	296.3	294.8	240.1	243.1	232.7	31.8	32.7	30.8	33.1	37.6	25.2
Refined petroleum products	2.7	2.7	2.3	2.0	1.5	0.3	1.9	0.7	1.1	0.2	0.2	0.1
Rubber and plastic products	3.9	4.0	10.8	7.2	6.0	6.3	1.8	2.0	2.8	8.3	1.6	2.6
Leather products	0.7	0.3	0.4	0.4	0.6	0.3	0.4	0.3	0.2	0.2	0.1	0.3
Stone, clay and glass products	1.1	1.6	1.8	2.7	2.0	1.7	0.2	1.0	0.5	0.6	0.8	1.1
Primary metals	3.8	8.5	12.7	6.6	10.3	5.0	3.0	4.3	3.9	3.0	3.7	5.7
Fabricated metal products	8.8	12.0	17.6	31.0	25.3	22.9	1.7	3.3	3.1	3.9	4.5	1.8
Industrial machinery and computers	36.2	45.1	62.8	69.5	66.5	58.5	42.8	54.3	77.9	109.2	24.9	25.3
Electric and electronic equipment	32.1	32.3	40.7	55.8	51.4	41.3	12.1	10.9	9.5	15.8	19.2	12.0
Transportation equipment	28.4	45.7	46.1	57.7	59.0	109.2	38.4	45.6	35.4	20.7	17.8	36.6
Scientific and measuring instruments	111.5	171.8	134.7	115.6	120.0	120.6	13.5	13.3	20.1	21.1	11.4	15.6
Miscellaneous manufactures	7.9	6.4	8.4	10.8	7.4	6.1	3.3	4.2	3.7	3.9	0.6	1.1
Unidentified manufactures	0.7	0.9	1.1	1.2	2.5	3.0	0.3	0.6	0.9	0.4	0.3	0.3
Agricultural And Livestock Products	0.8	0.5	1.0	2.3	2.4	1.5	0.1	0.2	0.9	1.0	0.7	0.9
Agricultural products	0.8	0.4	0.8	1.8	1.8	1.3	...	0.1	0.8	1.0	0.7	0.9
Livestock and livestock products	...	0.1	0.2	0.6	0.6	0.3	...	...	0.1	...	...	...
Other Commodities	0.6	0.3	1.0	1.9	2.5	0.8	...	2.5	0.3	0.1	0.1	0.1
Forestry products	...	...	...	...	...	...	...	...	...	...	...	...
Fish and other marine products	...	0.1	...	...	...	...	...	...	...	...	...	...
Metallic ores and concentrates	...	...	...	...	...	...	...	...	...	...	...	...
Bituminous coal and lignite	...	...	...	...	...	...	...	...	...	...	...	...
Crude petroleum and natural gas	...	...	...	...	...	...	...	...	...	...	...	...
Nonmetallic minerals	0.1	...	...	0.2	0.4	...	...	...	...	...	...	...
Scrap and waste	...	...	0.3	0.2	...	...	...	2.3	...	...	0.1	0.1
Used merchandise	0.2	...	...	...	1.1	...	...	...	...	...	...	...
Goods imported and returned unchanged	...	...	...	...	...	...	...	...	...	...	...	...
Special classification provisions	0.3	0.1	0.7	1.4	1.0	0.7	...	0.2	0.2	...	...	0.1

Industry	Taiwan						Singapore					
	1994	1995	1996	1997	1998	1999	1994	1995	1996	1997	1998	1999
ALL GOODS	79.0	116.1	140.9	134.4	129.2	101.7	126.5	149.8	188.1	185.2	149.8	134.8
Manufactured Goods	78.4	115.4	140.5	133.8	128.5	100.6	126.4	148.0	188.0	185.2	148.4	134.1
Food products	1.7	2.0	2.4	3.3	2.1	2.3	2.2	1.9	2.5	2.0	1.7	2.6
Tobacco products	...	...	...	...	...	...	...	...	...	...	...	...
Textile mill products	0.4	0.5	0.3	0.5	0.3	0.4	0.1	0.5	0.3	0.1	0.1	0.2
Apparel	0.1	0.1	...	0.1	0.1	0.1	...	0.4	0.3	0.1	0.3	0.1
Lumber and wood products	4.5	3.4	2.6	1.3	1.3	0.5	1.0	0.9	1.5	1.7	1.0	0.1
Furniture and fixtures	1.0	0.5	0.1	0.3	3.9	0.6	0.7	0.7	0.6	1.1	1.0	0.5
Paper products	0.2	0.9	2.2	1.5	1.2	2.3	0.5	0.6	1.2	0.3	0.2	0.4
Printing and publishing	1.0	1.4	1.5	1.6	1.6	1.0	1.6	2.5	4.4	2.7	2.4	1.5
Chemical products	20.5	22.0	19.9	23.4	28.5	19.5	16.3	33.5	35.7	34.3	37.5	11.3
Refined petroleum products	2.1	1.6	1.9	1.6	1.8	2.4	0.1	0.2	0.1	0.2	0.1	0.1
Rubber and plastic products	0.3	2.1	4.8	13.9	27.0	27.6	3.6	3.4	4.6	5.8	2.5	2.3
Leather products	0.3	1.3	0.9	1.1	1.4	0.7	0.1	...	...	0.3	0.1	...
Stone, clay and glass products	0.3	0.3	0.4	0.2	0.3	0.4	0.1	0.2	0.2	0.3	0.1	0.1
Primary metals	2.4	8.3	18.8	12.0	6.8	3.2	3.6	3.1	7.7	13.5	7.2	8.0
Fabricated metal products	1.2	1.3	1.8	2.2	1.8	1.4	18.9	17.5	22.1	25.3	23.9	20.1
Industrial machinery and computers	17.4	23.3	23.5	30.3	22.9	12.5	46.5	44.0	55.8	43.9	34.1	41.6
Electric and electronic equipment	14.0	32.9	44.4	28.2	15.8	17.5	13.7	16.6	22.7	23.3	11.8	20.8
Transportation equipment	3.2	7.9	7.2	3.0	6.5	1.9	3.6	9.9	12.2	13.2	8.9	7.8
Scientific and measuring instruments	6.6	4.6	6.7	8.4	4.3	5.7	12.4	10.7	13.7	16.4	14.3	15.2
Miscellaneous manufactures	1.0	0.9	1.0	0.7	0.6	0.4	0.6	0.8	2.3	0.8	0.8	0.6
Unidentified manufactures	0.2	0.2	0.3	0.4	0.3	0.3	0.7	0.5	0.2	0.2	0.4	0.7
Agricultural And Livestock Products	0.2	...	...	...	0.5	0.2	...	...	...	...	...	...
Agricultural products	0.2	...	...	...	0.5	0.2	...	...	...	...	...	...
Livestock and livestock products	...	...	...	...	...	...	...	...	...	...	...	...
Other Commodities	0.5	0.7	0.4	0.6	0.3	0.9	0.1	1.8	0.1	...	1.4	0.8
Forestry products	...	0.1	...	...	...	...	...	...	...	...	...	...
Fish and other marine products	0.1	...	...	...	...	...	...	0.1	...	...	...	...
Metallic ores and concentrates	...	...	...	...	...	...	...	...	...	...	...	...
Bituminous coal and lignite	...	...	...	...	...	...	...	...	...	...	...	...
Crude petroleum and natural gas	...	...	...	...	...	...	...	...	...	...	...	...
Nonmetallic minerals	...	...	...	...	...	...	...	...	...	...	0.1	...
Scrap and waste	...	0.2	0.1	...	0.2	0.4	...	...	...	...	...	...
Used merchandise	...	...	...	...	...	...	0.1	0.4	...	...	...	...
Goods imported and returned unchanged	...	...	...	...	...	...	...	...	...	...	...	...
Special classification provisions	0.3	0.4	0.2	0.5	...	0.5	...	1.3	...	...	1.3	0.7

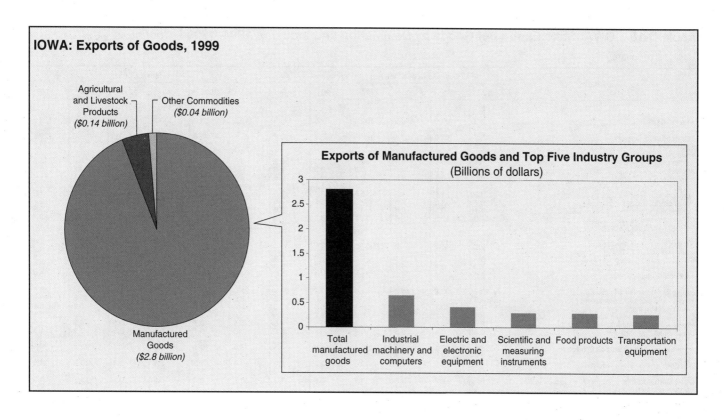

IOWA: Exports of Goods, 1999

Agricultural and Livestock Products ($0.14 billion)

Other Commodities ($0.04 billion)

Manufactured Goods ($2.8 billion)

Exports of Manufactured Goods and Top Five Industry Groups
(Billions of dollars)

Total manufactured goods | Industrial machinery and computers | Electric and electronic equipment | Scientific and measuring instruments | Food products | Transportation equipment

Table D-18. IOWA: State Exports of Goods by Destination and Industry, 1994–1999

(Millions of dollars.)

Industry	All destinations						Canada					
	1994	1995	1996	1997	1998	1999	1994	1995	1996	1997	1998	1999
ALL GOODS	2 331.4	2 577.8	2 695.1	3 116.7	3 411.7	2 985.2	1 152.8	1 220.5	1 277.2	1 569.1	1 742.2	1 439.2
Manufactured Goods	2 137.3	2 387.9	2 484.8	2 892.1	3 185.8	2 800.3	1 117.4	1 178.9	1 247.2	1 532.5	1 708.1	1 404.2
Food products	235.3	295.9	296.3	337.8	321.6	297.7	111.0	119.9	135.8	166.7	183.6	148.1
Tobacco products	...	...	0.2	...	0.1	...	...	...	0.2	...	0.1	...
Textile mill products	4.8	4.4	5.2	5.7	24.0	20.9	2.4	1.7	1.6	1.9	1.9	1.8
Apparel	6.2	8.5	10.1	10.8	9.2	10.1	2.4	1.9	0.7	1.6	2.0	2.3
Lumber and wood products	28.1	23.6	19.2	24.2	20.2	21.3	21.6	17.9	13.6	17.9	14.5	13.8
Furniture and fixtures	43.2	46.9	56.8	63.1	70.4	38.0	36.6	39.5	48.1	52.1	58.3	25.1
Paper products	20.7	29.8	34.9	36.5	36.1	36.4	4.1	6.0	6.7	5.7	8.7	14.3
Printing and publishing	37.3	39.6	33.5	34.9	26.4	19.5	28.7	23.6	25.3	29.5	20.0	14.1
Chemical products	119.4	136.4	160.6	174.3	210.3	184.9	38.0	44.7	57.6	67.5	67.5	71.7
Refined petroleum products	0.5	0.6	8.9	1.3	6.1	2.5	0.2	0.2	8.2	0.5	3.8	1.5
Rubber and plastic products	121.9	121.9	135.6	151.5	138.7	118.2	63.0	61.4	57.2	60.8	61.7	60.4
Leather products	14.0	13.0	8.1	6.8	4.9	4.8	0.5	0.9	1.3	0.8	1.4	0.7
Stone, clay and glass products	6.6	6.1	13.4	14.1	9.4	6.2	1.7	2.3	5.0	7.8	5.5	3.4
Primary metals	51.1	57.7	65.6	103.0	144.1	140.9	13.8	13.3	16.4	53.7	100.6	107.0
Fabricated metal products	123.3	114.1	114.9	121.6	161.1	176.2	56.1	40.4	38.7	48.9	80.8	91.7
Industrial machinery and computers	635.5	744.8	745.7	934.4	887.6	650.1	398.6	456.0	437.1	572.3	538.6	317.9
Electric and electronic equipment	320.5	311.4	297.0	375.1	443.4	415.4	162.2	148.9	153.2	193.7	229.1	237.0
Transportation equipment	144.2	189.9	187.1	227.0	310.0	269.1	122.2	143.7	151.4	194.6	271.1	230.1
Scientific and measuring instruments	153.8	163.1	208.7	193.2	284.1	300.8	29.8	31.6	64.6	32.6	32.0	33.6
Miscellaneous manufactures	63.0	73.3	77.2	68.7	66.7	75.9	21.6	22.1	21.5	20.4	24.0	25.5
Unidentified manufactures	7.9	6.8	6.0	8.0	11.4	11.3	2.9	3.0	3.2	3.4	3.0	4.2
Agricultural And Livestock Products	145.4	145.1	165.0	178.2	182.8	141.4	8.1	13.7	8.7	14.8	16.2	17.9
Agricultural products	129.8	129.4	147.0	158.7	164.1	119.4	6.5	10.6	6.6	12.2	13.5	15.2
Livestock and livestock products	15.6	15.7	18.0	19.4	18.7	21.9	1.6	3.1	2.0	2.6	2.7	2.7
Other Commodities	48.6	44.8	45.2	46.4	43.2	43.5	27.3	27.9	21.3	21.8	17.9	17.1
Forestry products	0.3	0.5	0.2	0.4	0.3	0.4	0.2	0.4	0.2	0.3	0.3	0.4
Fish and other marine products	4.6	7.1	6.3	8.1	7.4	7.0	...	0.3	0.3	0.5	0.3	0.2
Metallic ores and concentrates	2.9	1.1	...	1.0	...	...	...	1.0	...	0.3	...	...
Bituminous coal and lignite	...	0.1	2.7	0.7	0.2	0.7	...	...	1.8	0.1	0.2	0.2
Crude petroleum and natural gas	0.1	...	...	0.1	0.1	0.8	0.1	...	...	...	...	...
Nonmetallic minerals	0.2	0.3	1.2	0.7	0.2	0.2	...	0.1	0.6	0.2	0.1	0.1
Scrap and waste	18.7	12.9	7.2	7.8	4.7	4.6	13.7	11.2	6.8	6.8	3.9	3.4
Used merchandise	1.8	1.7	7.6	8.3	11.7	8.4	0.1	0.4	0.5	0.6	0.7	0.7
Goods imported and returned unchanged	12.5	12.9	7.9	11.5	11.4	8.9	12.5	12.9	7.9	11.5	11.4	8.9
Special classification provisions	7.5	8.2	12.2	7.8	7.0	12.4	0.7	1.5	3.2	1.4	0.9	3.2

Table D-18. IOWA: State Exports of Goods by Destination and Industry, 1994–1999—*Continued*

(Millions of dollars.)

Industry	South and Central America and Caribbean						Mexico					
	1994	1995	1996	1997	1998	1999	1994	1995	1996	1997	1998	1999
ALL GOODS	83.3	108.0	140.5	182.8	169.0	132.8	99.2	81.9	110.3	167.7	158.2	153.0
Manufactured Goods	72.8	101.3	125.6	163.2	155.4	120.2	82.5	72.6	90.8	140.0	138.8	129.9
Food products	4.6	7.1	7.8	11.1	9.6	6.9	12.0	11.5	21.4	41.6	13.7	13.7
Tobacco products	...	...	...	...	...		...	...	...	...		
Textile mill products	0.1	0.4	0.2	0.2	0.1	0.9	0.1	...	0.1	0.2	19.2	15.6
Apparel	0.4	1.0	0.9	0.5	0.3	2.6	0.2	0.2	0.6	0.1	0.2	0.4
Lumber and wood products	0.2	0.1	0.1	0.3	0.6	0.6	0.1	0.2	0.3	0.4	1.1	1.7
Furniture and fixtures	0.9	1.1	1.8	1.6	2.4	2.5	1.7	0.8	0.6	1.0	1.2	1.5
Paper products	0.7	1.3	2.5	3.3	5.5	2.5	4.0	3.4	5.8	6.0	4.7	2.7
Printing and publishing	0.1	0.4	0.1	0.2	0.2	0.3	1.0	0.9	1.8	2.0	1.9	0.9
Chemical products	11.0	12.0	13.6	11.7	18.0	17.6	8.2	6.3	8.4	10.3	17.8	13.5
Refined petroleum products	...	...	...	...	1.7	0.4	...	...	0.1	...	...	...
Rubber and plastic products	13.2	13.0	16.2	19.7	19.6	17.9	6.1	6.0	4.8	6.9	6.1	5.0
Leather products	0.1	0.1	...	...			0.3	0.8	0.4	0.7	0.3	0.2
Stone, clay and glass products	0.3	0.1	0.3	0.2	0.6	0.3	0.5	0.4	1.0	0.6	0.1	0.3
Primary metals	1.9	3.7	5.4	6.1	1.8	0.3	2.3	1.5	2.2	4.2	5.3	5.0
Fabricated metal products	3.6	5.1	6.1	11.3	7.4	7.0	4.0	2.6	3.6	5.4	5.1	8.0
Industrial machinery and computers	23.3	33.8	40.8	51.9	47.2	36.3	25.0	12.0	22.3	24.5	24.4	35.5
Electric and electronic equipment	4.6	11.3	16.8	32.0	21.0	9.8	8.9	5.3	6.1	19.1	19.5	10.7
Transportation equipment	1.7	2.1	2.4	4.1	5.4	1.5	3.2	12.5	3.7	3.2	6.6	8.1
Scientific and measuring instruments	3.1	4.4	5.7	5.7	9.6	9.8	2.6	7.5	5.5	8.0	6.0	5.1
Miscellaneous manufactures	2.8	3.8	4.4	2.9	3.5	2.6	2.1	0.7	2.0	5.2	4.3	1.1
Unidentified manufactures	0.3	0.4	0.3	0.4	0.7	0.5	0.3	0.1	0.2	0.5	1.2	1.1
Agricultural And Livestock Products	9.8	6.2	12.7	18.8	12.8	11.3	16.0	9.1	18.9	27.2	17.6	22.5
Agricultural products	7.9	4.3	10.7	15.8	10.6	8.4	12.3	7.8	16.1	23.9	15.8	17.8
Livestock and livestock products	1.9	1.9	2.0	3.0	2.1	2.9	3.8	1.3	2.8	3.3	1.8	4.8
Other Commodities	0.7	0.6	2.2	0.8	0.8	1.3	0.7	0.2	0.6	0.5	1.7	0.5
Forestry products	0.1	...	...	...	...		...	...	...	...		
Fish and other marine products	0.1	0.4	0.6	0.3	0.4	...	...	...	...	...	...	...
Metallic ores and concentrates	...	...	...	...	...	...	...	...	...	...	...	...
Bituminous coal and lignite	...	...	0.9	...	...	0.5	...	...	...	...	...	...
Crude petroleum and natural gas	...	...	...	...	...	...	...	...	...	...	0.1	...
Nonmetallic minerals	...	...	0.3	...	...	...	...	...	...	0.1	...	...
Scrap and waste	...	...	...	...	...	...	...	...	...	...	...	...
Used merchandise	...	...	0.4	0.3	0.2	0.2	0.5	...	...	0.1	1.5	0.3
Goods imported and returned unchanged	...	...	...	...	...		...	...	...	...		
Special classification provisions	0.5	0.1	0.1	0.2	0.2	0.5	0.1	0.1	0.6	0.3	0.1	0.2

Industry	European Union						United Kingdom					
	1994	1995	1996	1997	1998	1999	1994	1995	1996	1997	1998	1999
ALL GOODS	430.0	483.4	507.3	524.9	718.6	641.5	85.0	87.9	93.2	114.1	150.3	156.2
Manufactured Goods	345.3	390.9	404.8	438.7	609.3	571.1	80.7	85.5	87.4	109.8	144.1	149.0
Food products	12.7	18.3	11.9	18.2	22.2	19.1	3.4	8.1	5.0	7.7	4.2	6.3
Tobacco products	...	...	...	...	...		...	...	...	...		
Textile mill products	1.1	1.0	1.4	1.5	1.2	1.8	0.1	0.1	0.2	0.2	0.2	0.3
Apparel	2.1	2.8	3.4	3.9	3.1	1.8	0.1	0.2	0.1	...	0.7	0.3
Lumber and wood products	2.2	2.2	2.5	3.2	1.9	2.4	...	0.1	0.1	0.2	0.1	...
Furniture and fixtures	3.4	4.4	5.1	5.5	5.6	5.1	1.8	3.1	3.3	3.8	4.3	2.8
Paper products	8.8	14.4	15.2	15.1	9.8	6.3	0.6	0.6	0.5	0.8	0.5	0.6
Printing and publishing	4.2	4.0	2.0	1.3	1.7	2.1	3.2	3.2	1.0	0.9	1.1	1.3
Chemical products	23.9	32.2	37.7	32.7	49.8	26.4	4.0	3.8	7.6	9.3	4.3	5.3
Refined petroleum products	...	...	...	...	0.1	0.1	...	...	...	...	...	...
Rubber and plastic products	18.5	16.2	24.7	28.2	28.2	15.0	4.6	3.4	0.6	1.1	1.4	1.2
Leather products	1.6	0.5	0.7	0.7	0.7	0.6	...	0.1	0.1	0.2	...	0.1
Stone, clay and glass products	2.7	2.5	6.0	4.0	2.6	1.5	0.4	0.6	1.0	0.6	0.9	0.9
Primary metals	2.1	2.8	5.1	7.0	21.6	20.8	0.4	1.0	1.1	1.7	2.9	0.6
Fabricated metal products	16.1	13.9	13.2	12.6	8.8	15.5	7.2	6.5	4.9	5.7	4.2	7.8
Industrial machinery and computers	93.0	103.1	101.5	114.1	153.2	142.1	14.9	16.7	16.8	22.7	32.0	30.0
Electric and electronic equipment	66.0	66.1	60.7	75.2	110.9	96.2	19.9	16.3	15.1	23.0	34.8	32.5
Transportation equipment	8.2	12.8	18.4	14.3	15.1	20.2	1.4	1.5	4.1	3.6	4.8	12.5
Scientific and measuring instruments	59.9	71.3	73.8	79.9	152.5	165.6	10.5	10.3	15.9	18.7	38.9	38.1
Miscellaneous manufactures	16.2	20.5	20.5	19.7	17.5	26.7	7.5	9.6	9.5	9.0	7.5	7.7
Unidentified manufactures	2.7	1.8	1.1	1.6	2.6	1.7	0.5	0.5	0.6	0.7	1.3	0.7
Agricultural And Livestock Products	78.3	88.3	92.0	78.7	96.9	57.6	0.2	0.2	1.0	1.0	0.5	0.9
Agricultural products	77.0	86.7	90.8	77.2	94.7	54.5	...	...	0.9	0.9	0.1	...
Livestock and livestock products	1.3	1.7	1.2	1.5	2.3	3.1	0.2	0.2	0.1	0.2	0.4	0.8
Other Commodities	6.3	4.3	10.5	7.4	12.4	12.8	4.1	2.2	4.7	3.3	5.7	6.3
Forestry products	...	...	...	0.1	...		...	...	...	...		
Fish and other marine products	0.1	0.6	0.5	...	2.7	2.8	...	0.1	...	...	...	...
Metallic ores and concentrates	2.9	...	...	0.7	...	...	2.9	...	...	...	...	...
Bituminous coal and lignite	...	...	...	...	...	...	...	...	...	...	...	...
Crude petroleum and natural gas	...	...	...	...	...	...	...	...	...	...	...	...
Nonmetallic minerals	...	...	0.1	...	...	...	...	...	...	...	...	...
Scrap and waste	...	0.5	0.1	0.6	0.3	0.3	...	0.4	...	...	...	...
Used merchandise	0.3	0.2	5.7	3.5	6.7	4.6	...	0.1	1.4	1.7	3.6	2.7
Goods imported and returned unchanged	...	...	...	...	...		...	...	...	...		
Special classification provisions	3.0	2.9	4.2	2.6	2.7	5.1	1.2	1.5	3.4	1.6	2.0	3.5

Table D-18. IOWA: State Exports of Goods by Destination and Industry, 1994–1999—*Continued*

(Millions of dollars.)

Industry	Germany						France					
	1994	1995	1996	1997	1998	1999	1994	1995	1996	1997	1998	1999
ALL GOODS	52.6	71.4	84.1	86.2	117.6	136.9	54.7	46.6	63.1	81.0	119.1	109.6
Manufactured Goods	49.6	67.3	82.0	83.8	115.9	134.3	38.5	28.4	48.9	74.5	105.5	98.3
Food products	1.3	1.9	2.7	3.9	6.9	2.2	0.5	0.5	0.2	0.9	1.8	0.5
Tobacco products	...	...	...	...	...	...	...	...	...	...	...	...
Textile mill products	0.1	0.2	0.6	0.8	0.6	1.1	...	...	...	...	0.1	...
Apparel	0.1	0.2	0.3	0.1	0.8	1.4	0.3	0.3	...	...	...	0.1
Lumber and wood products	...	0.1	0.1	0.1	0.1	...	0.1	0.1	...	...	...	0.3
Furniture and fixtures	0.2	0.2	0.3	0.5	0.5	0.6	...	0.1	...	...	...	0.1
Paper products	1.5	2.0	4.3	3.9	1.8	4.0	0.2	0.5	0.4	5.5	3.5	0.1
Printing and publishing	0.2	0.1	0.1	0.1	0.1	0.1	0.3	...	0.1	0.1	0.1	0.1
Chemical products	3.9	9.9	8.0	3.7	3.2	2.1	1.8	2.1	1.5	2.4	2.0	1.2
Refined petroleum products	...	...	...	...	...	...	...	...	...	...	...	0.1
Rubber and plastic products	0.7	1.7	4.8	9.7	8.4	3.8	1.0	0.4	0.2	4.7	4.0	0.7
Leather products	...	...	0.1	...	0.1	...	0.1	...	...	...	...	0.1
Stone, clay and glass products	0.9	0.5	0.5	0.9	0.6	0.3	...	0.1	...	...	...	0.1
Primary metals	...	...	1.4	2.9	12.0	15.4	0.6	...	0.1	0.3	1.5	2.0
Fabricated metal products	2.2	1.2	1.1	1.2	1.1	1.5	2.0	1.0	1.0	1.4	0.7	3.0
Industrial machinery and computers	22.5	30.8	25.3	29.2	38.9	30.0	7.2	8.0	10.0	8.6	8.1	5.7
Electric and electronic equipment	7.6	9.6	7.8	7.6	9.0	7.1	9.8	4.9	11.4	15.5	24.0	20.1
Transportation equipment	3.6	3.2	8.6	7.4	1.5	1.0	1.0	0.8	0.6	0.9	2.1	2.7
Scientific and measuring instruments	2.0	3.2	12.4	8.3	29.4	55.9	12.0	7.7	21.3	32.1	55.9	58.2
Miscellaneous manufactures	2.2	2.4	3.2	3.1	0.7	7.5	1.5	1.6	1.9	2.0	1.6	3.1
Unidentified manufactures	0.4	0.2	0.2	0.3	0.3	0.2	0.2	0.1	0.1	0.1	0.1	0.1
Agricultural And Livestock Products	2.6	3.5	1.0	0.4	1.0	1.6	14.9	17.9	13.8	6.0	13.1	10.7
Agricultural products	2.5	3.2	0.9	0.3	0.9	1.6	14.9	17.9	13.8	6.0	13.1	10.6
Livestock and livestock products	0.1	0.3	0.1	...	0.1	...	...	...	...	...	...	0.1
Other Commodities	0.5	0.6	1.2	2.0	0.7	1.0	1.3	0.4	0.3	0.5	0.4	0.6
Forestry products	...	...	...	...	0.1	...	...	...	...	...	...	...
Fish and other marine products	...	...	...	...	...	...	...	0.2	...	...	0.1	...
Metallic ores and concentrates	...	...	...	0.7	...	...	...	...	0.2	...	...	...
Bituminous coal and lignite	...	...	...	...	...	...	...	...	...	...	...	...
Crude petroleum and natural gas	...	...	...	...	...	...	...	...	...	...	...	...
Nonmetallic minerals	...	...	...	...	...	...	...	...	...	...	...	...
Scrap and waste	...	...	...	...	0.2	...	...	...	...	...	...	...
Used merchandise	0.2	0.1	0.7	1.0	0.3	0.5	...	...	...	...	...	...
Goods imported and returned unchanged	...	...	...	...	...	...	...	...	...	...	...	...
Special classification provisions	0.2	0.5	0.5	0.3	0.2	0.5	1.3	0.2	0.1	0.5	0.3	0.6

Industry	The Netherlands						Asian 10					
	1994	1995	1996	1997	1998	1999	1994	1995	1996	1997	1998	1999
ALL GOODS	82.8	108.0	92.0	84.5	116.8	71.0	394.7	486.5	465.6	464.2	401.2	402.2
Manufactured Goods	82.2	107.8	91.7	83.8	114.2	67.8	370.7	460.4	438.4	437.3	376.4	379.0
Food products	0.7	0.6	1.1	2.1	4.0	6.3	86.4	129.6	110.8	91.2	85.8	99.8
Tobacco products	...	...	...	...	...	...	...	...	...	...	...	...
Textile mill products	0.8	0.5	0.6	0.4	0.2	...	0.7	1.2	1.9	1.7	1.3	0.7
Apparel	1.3	2.0	2.9	3.4	1.5	...	0.9	2.4	4.1	4.1	3.3	2.9
Lumber and wood products	0.1	0.1	0.2	0.7	0.1	...	3.5	3.0	2.6	2.3	1.5	2.6
Furniture and fixtures	0.2	0.1	0.1	0.2	0.2	0.7	0.1	0.5	0.4	1.1	0.7	1.6
Paper products	6.1	7.5	8.1	4.5	3.4	1.1	1.9	2.8	3.5	5.2	6.1	9.3
Printing and publishing	0.2	0.1	...	0.1	0.1	0.4	2.3	8.7	2.2	1.2	1.3	1.4
Chemical products	6.3	8.2	14.0	9.8	23.3	9.7	30.2	30.8	33.3	43.2	44.5	39.5
Refined petroleum products	...	...	...	...	...	...	0.3	0.3	0.4	0.6	0.3	0.4
Rubber and plastic products	3.1	2.8	7.8	10.9	12.1	6.9	16.5	15.7	21.5	24.2	12.5	10.8
Leather products	0.1	0.1	0.1	0.1	0.2	0.1	11.6	10.7	5.6	4.3	2.5	3.2
Stone, clay and glass products	1.0	1.1	2.5	2.3	0.9	...	1.2	0.4	0.7	1.2	0.3	0.3
Primary metals	0.3	0.4	0.7	1.8	4.4	0.2	30.7	35.0	35.6	31.3	14.1	6.3
Fabricated metal products	2.1	2.6	3.3	2.2	1.1	1.1	36.4	46.3	45.7	35.8	47.0	45.7
Industrial machinery and computers	22.2	23.7	26.3	26.1	35.1	33.2	58.2	75.4	81.3	94.8	57.2	54.0
Electric and electronic equipment	5.6	6.1	2.6	2.3	3.4	2.6	43.4	46.9	35.5	29.5	28.0	33.1
Transportation equipment	0.5	4.9	0.9	0.1	0.3	0.3	3.6	6.1	3.5	5.9	7.1	4.4
Scientific and measuring instruments	30.1	45.8	19.9	16.1	22.1	3.6	29.6	29.1	31.7	45.3	51.2	48.8
Miscellaneous manufactures	1.5	1.1	0.7	0.6	1.7	1.2	12.3	14.6	17.2	13.2	9.3	12.1
Unidentified manufactures	0.1	0.1	...	0.1	0.2	0.2	1.0	0.9	0.7	1.0	2.4	2.2
Agricultural And Livestock Products	0.4	0.1	...	...	0.1	0.4	11.9	16.7	18.6	18.8	19.9	16.1
Agricultural products	0.3	...	...	...	...	0.1	7.9	13.3	14.9	14.6	16.5	12.8
Livestock and livestock products	0.1	0.1	...	...	0.1	0.3	3.9	3.5	3.8	4.2	3.4	3.3
Other Commodities	0.2	0.1	0.3	0.7	2.6	2.8	12.1	9.3	8.6	8.1	5.0	7.1
Forestry products	...	...	...	...	...	...	...	...	...	...	...	...
Fish and other marine products	0.1	...	...	...	2.5	2.8	4.2	5.4	4.6	5.3	3.4	3.8
Metallic ores and concentrates	...	...	...	...	...	...	...	0.2	...	...	...	...
Bituminous coal and lignite	...	...	...	...	...	...	...	...	...	0.5	...	...
Crude petroleum and natural gas	...	...	...	...	...	...	...	...	...	...	...	0.8
Nonmetallic minerals	...	...	0.1	...	...	...	0.1	0.2	0.2	0.3	0.1	0.1
Scrap and waste	...	...	0.1	0.6	...	...	4.4	0.2	0.1	0.1	0.2	0.8
Used merchandise	...	...	0.1	0.1	...	...	0.6	0.8	0.2	1.2	0.8	0.6
Goods imported and returned unchanged	...	...	...	...	...	...	...	...	...	...	...	...
Special classification provisions	0.1	0.1	...	...	...	...	2.7	2.7	3.5	0.6	0.5	1.1

Table D-18. IOWA: State Exports of Goods by Destination and Industry, 1994–1999—Continued

(Millions of dollars.)

Industry	Japan						South Korea					
	1994	1995	1996	1997	1998	1999	1994	1995	1996	1997	1998	1999
ALL GOODS	111.1	145.1	159.3	161.5	176.7	162.0	83.0	87.3	82.8	90.8	46.9	54.2
Manufactured Goods	100.3	130.0	142.1	146.9	161.8	147.7	75.9	82.9	79.7	88.2	44.3	52.0
Food products	24.3	53.2	57.3	50.1	51.9	52.4	19.0	16.6	13.1	12.9	11.7	15.2
Tobacco products	...	...	...	...	...	...	...	...	...	...	...	...
Textile mill products	0.5	0.7	1.6	1.5	1.1	0.6	...	0.2	0.1	0.1	...	...
Apparel	0.7	2.3	3.9	3.6	3.2	2.7	...	...	...	0.1	...	...
Lumber and wood products	0.9	0.7	0.6	0.4	0.7	0.7	2.1	1.8	1.4	1.2	0.1	0.5
Furniture and fixtures	0.1	0.3	0.3	0.6	0.2	1.1	...	0.1	0.1	0.4	0.2	...
Paper products	0.1	0.2	0.7	0.6	0.9	0.9	0.7	0.8	1.0	0.6	0.2	0.4
Printing and publishing	0.5	0.6	0.5	0.3	0.7	0.1	0.7	0.8	0.4	0.1	0.1	0.1
Chemical products	16.0	13.2	14.1	22.9	28.9	19.1	3.8	3.8	5.0	5.5	3.0	3.9
Refined petroleum products	0.1	0.1	0.1	0.2	0.1	0.1	0.1	0.1	...	0.1	...	0.1
Rubber and plastic products	5.7	5.1	5.9	6.2	4.7	4.7	0.8	1.2	2.3	3.0	0.3	0.6
Leather products	...	0.1	0.1	0.1	...	...	4.6	6.6	3.9	4.0	2.0	2.6
Stone, clay and glass products	0.3	...	0.1	0.1	0.1	0.1	0.3	0.1	0.2	0.2	0.2	0.2
Primary metals	1.0	0.2	1.6	2.6	1.0	0.4	24.6	24.6	23.7	22.9	11.3	5.3
Fabricated metal products	5.3	5.4	6.5	6.2	6.5	6.0	1.2	4.1	3.4	2.5	0.4	1.4
Industrial machinery and computers	22.1	18.5	20.1	20.0	18.4	16.9	8.9	13.5	17.8	17.8	5.9	6.9
Electric and electronic equipment	11.5	10.6	10.6	6.1	12.3	5.7	4.6	3.2	2.2	4.6	2.1	8.0
Transportation equipment	1.8	2.6	1.4	2.8	2.7	3.0	0.5	0.7	0.2	0.5	3.1	0.2
Scientific and measuring instruments	6.2	12.5	13.2	19.9	26.1	28.6	3.2	3.5	3.7	9.2	3.1	5.2
Miscellaneous manufactures	2.9	3.5	3.4	2.5	1.5	3.8	0.7	1.2	1.0	2.4	0.2	1.0
Unidentified manufactures	0.2	0.4	0.2	0.2	1.0	0.6	0.1	0.1	0.1	0.1	0.3	0.3
Agricultural And Livestock Products	7.7	11.2	12.1	11.6	12.4	11.1	1.2	2.7	1.5	1.2	2.0	0.7
Agricultural products	7.1	10.3	11.1	10.7	11.9	10.7	0.6	2.2	0.8	0.4	1.3	0.1
Livestock and livestock products	0.6	0.8	1.0	0.9	0.5	0.4	0.6	0.5	0.7	0.8	0.6	0.6
Other Commodities	3.2	4.0	5.1	3.0	2.5	3.2	5.9	1.7	1.6	1.5	0.6	1.5
Forestry products	...	...	...	...	...	...	...	...	...	...	...	...
Fish and other marine products	2.1	2.5	2.7	2.3	2.2	2.4	1.8	1.3	1.6	1.3	0.5	0.5
Metallic ores and concentrates	...	...	...	...	...	...	...	...	...	...	...	...
Bituminous coal and lignite	...	...	...	...	...	...	...	...	...	...	...	...
Crude petroleum and natural gas	...	...	...	...	...	...	...	...	...	...	...	0.8
Nonmetallic minerals	...	...	...	...	...	...	...	...	...	0.1	...	0.1
Scrap and waste	0.1	...	...	...	...	0.4	4.0	0.1	...	...	0.1	...
Used merchandise	0.2	...	0.1	0.5	0.2	0.3	...	...	...	...	...	...
Goods imported and returned unchanged	...	...	...	...	...	...	...	...	...	...	...	...
Special classification provisions	0.7	1.4	2.4	0.2	0.1	0.1	0.1	0.2	...	...	...	0.1

Industry	Taiwan						Singapore					
	1994	1995	1996	1997	1998	1999	1994	1995	1996	1997	1998	1999
ALL GOODS	56.9	61.3	41.3	35.1	26.4	28.7	50.1	65.8	61.6	55.0	56.8	51.5
Manufactured Goods	56.0	60.9	40.5	34.3	25.5	27.5	48.6	64.2	60.5	53.6	55.1	50.8
Food products	26.7	32.5	21.1	13.0	7.5	11.8	2.4	3.3	1.9	1.5	1.1	1.3
Tobacco products	...	...	...	...	...	...	...	...	...	...	...	...
Textile mill products	...	0.1	...	...	...	...	...	...	...	...	...	...
Apparel	0.1	0.1	...	...	0.1	0.1	...	...	...	...	...	...
Lumber and wood products	0.4	0.4	0.6	0.7	0.5	1.0	...	...	...	...	...	...
Furniture and fixtures	...	...	...	...	...	...	...	...	...	...	...	0.2
Paper products	0.1	0.3	0.3	0.8	0.8	0.4	0.7	0.7	0.8	1.0	0.9	1.4
Printing and publishing	0.7	1.3	0.3	0.2	0.2	...	0.2	4.6	0.3	0.5	0.2	1.0
Chemical products	2.2	2.6	3.1	3.1	2.0	2.2	0.2	0.4	0.7	1.2	0.5	0.6
Refined petroleum products	...	0.2	0.2	0.2	0.1	0.1	...	...	...	...	...	...
Rubber and plastic products	2.0	0.7	0.7	1.2	0.4	0.1	0.3	0.8	0.8	0.9	0.9	0.5
Leather products	6.3	4.0	1.2	0.1	0.2	0.1	...	...	...	...	...	0.1
Stone, clay and glass products	0.4	...	...	...	...	...	0.1	...	...	...	...	...
Primary metals	0.9	1.6	1.0	...	0.1	0.1	0.2	0.1	0.4	0.4	...	0.1
Fabricated metal products	2.4	1.8	1.0	0.5	0.7	3.1	20.1	26.8	30.2	22.1	29.3	25.6
Industrial machinery and computers	5.8	8.9	5.5	7.8	5.0	3.2	6.1	8.2	9.2	14.8	8.8	4.7
Electric and electronic equipment	4.5	3.7	2.1	2.4	3.2	2.2	10.6	13.4	8.2	4.3	4.7	6.2
Transportation equipment	...	0.2	0.1	1.4	0.4	0.5	0.3	0.2	0.4	0.2	0.4	0.5
Scientific and measuring instruments	2.1	1.4	1.7	1.3	2.7	0.9	4.7	3.6	5.1	5.4	7.2	6.7
Miscellaneous manufactures	1.0	1.2	1.4	1.5	1.3	1.3	2.4	1.8	2.2	0.9	0.9	1.4
Unidentified manufactures	0.2	0.1	0.1	0.2	0.3	0.3	0.2	0.1	0.1	0.1	0.3	0.4
Agricultural And Livestock Products	0.1	0.2	0.6	0.5	0.7	0.7	...	...	0.3	0.3	1.0	...
Agricultural products	...	...	...	...	...	0.2	...	...	0.3	0.3	1.0	...
Livestock and livestock products	...	0.1	0.6	0.4	0.5	0.7	...	...	...	...	...	...
Other Commodities	0.8	0.3	0.2	0.3	0.2	0.5	1.4	1.6	0.8	1.1	0.6	0.6
Forestry products	...	...	...	...	...	...	...	...	...	...	...	...
Fish and other marine products	0.1	0.2	0.1	0.3	0.2	0.2	...	0.1	...	...	0.1	...
Metallic ores and concentrates	...	...	...	...	...	...	...	...	...	...	...	...
Bituminous coal and lignite	...	...	...	...	...	...	...	...	...	0.5	...	...
Crude petroleum and natural gas	...	...	...	...	...	...	...	...	...	...	...	...
Nonmetallic minerals	0.1	0.1	...	...	...	...	...	...	...	...	...	...
Scrap and waste	0.3	...	0.1	...	...	0.2	...	...	...	...	...	...
Used merchandise	...	...	...	...	...	0.1	0.2	0.5	0.2	0.4	0.4	0.2
Goods imported and returned unchanged	...	...	...	...	...	...	1.2	1.0	0.6	0.1	0.1	0.4
Special classification provisions	0.3	...	...	...	...	...	...	...	...	...	...	...

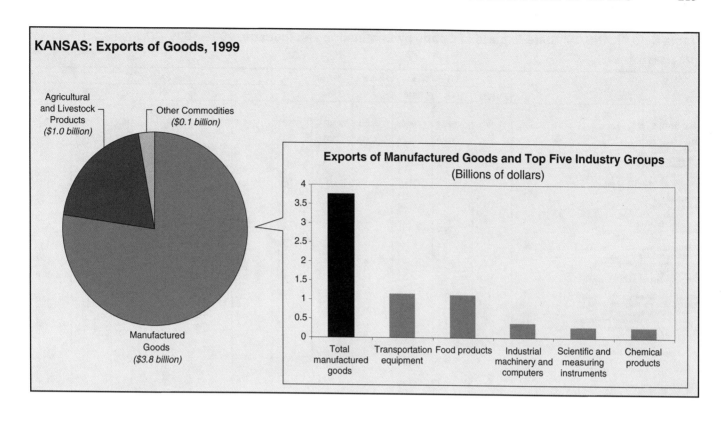

KANSAS: Exports of Goods, 1999

Agricultural and Livestock Products ($1.0 billion)

Other Commodities ($0.1 billion)

Manufactured Goods ($3.8 billion)

Exports of Manufactured Goods and Top Five Industry Groups
(Billions of dollars)

Total manufactured goods · Transportation equipment · Food products · Industrial machinery and computers · Scientific and measuring instruments · Chemical products

Table D-19. KANSAS: State Exports of Goods by Destination and Industry, 1994–1999

(Millions of dollars.)

Industry	All destinations						Canada					
	1994	1995	1996	1997	1998	1999	1994	1995	1996	1997	1998	1999
ALL GOODS	3 498.3	4 461.5	4 971.3	5 133.2	4 402.8	4 856.3	571.2	687.0	696.0	834.4	878.9	847.5
Manufactured Goods	2 450.3	2 803.6	3 192.7	3 846.1	3 303.2	3 754.3	541.8	667.8	651.5	795.7	853.4	817.9
Food products	681.5	854.8	887.3	912.6	890.2	1 118.6	97.3	102.5	90.8	113.0	103.0	115.6
Tobacco products	...	...	...	...	...	...	...	...	...	...	...	...
Textile mill products	2.3	2.9	10.1	25.8	7.8	3.5	0.8	1.0	0.7	0.8	1.2	1.3
Apparel	36.6	49.6	65.3	84.1	12.9	8.7	0.4	0.7	0.7	1.7	1.6	1.5
Lumber and wood products	6.7	5.7	4.0	3.7	5.6	5.7	1.4	2.5	1.2	0.9	1.9	1.8
Furniture and fixtures	7.9	7.8	9.0	7.5	5.1	6.1	1.5	1.4	1.6	1.9	1.7	2.5
Paper products	13.4	17.6	16.9	13.9	15.7	14.4	4.4	5.7	5.1	4.4	4.7	4.4
Printing and publishing	18.8	15.5	16.4	11.2	13.6	17.2	13.0	9.6	9.2	8.5	10.1	12.2
Chemical products	141.7	166.1	253.0	269.7	330.2	273.8	28.2	32.7	34.5	34.4	52.4	53.3
Refined petroleum products	87.5	101.3	157.5	250.5	127.9	134.3	3.5	2.8	4.6	5.2	7.3	1.1
Rubber and plastic products	64.5	64.4	52.2	51.1	66.9	49.4	26.7	29.4	31.1	34.4	37.9	29.5
Leather products	2.2	1.3	1.1	1.6	11.7	23.6	0.3	0.3	0.3	0.3	4.6	21.2
Stone, clay and glass products	14.7	16.8	25.1	15.6	22.2	21.3	5.6	6.0	7.4	6.9	11.3	13.6
Primary metals	18.6	20.0	14.4	22.1	23.8	21.8	5.9	9.4	9.4	14.7	12.8	13.5
Fabricated metal products	54.7	70.2	61.5	67.2	82.7	60.7	17.0	28.3	19.3	25.3	34.7	33.5
Industrial machinery and computers	309.1	348.5	398.6	457.5	490.2	390.0	136.4	144.3	144.6	168.2	178.6	158.8
Electric and electronic equipment	141.3	156.5	140.4	148.4	143.8	140.1	52.2	58.5	55.3	56.9	60.8	65.7
Transportation equipment	688.1	735.9	883.8	1 287.9	799.8	1 147.1	114.9	195.3	192.8	274.6	271.4	229.6
Scientific and measuring instruments	128.5	145.3	158.8	183.6	216.0	284.1	26.2	30.4	34.5	35.1	46.5	47.4
Miscellaneous manufactures	11.3	10.4	17.4	16.5	22.0	17.8	2.2	2.9	3.4	3.9	5.5	5.9
Unidentified manufactures	21.0	12.9	20.0	15.6	15.2	16.3	4.0	4.0	4.8	4.8	5.6	5.7
Agricultural And Livestock Products	945.9	1 565.2	1 639.4	1 203.4	1 050.6	963.8	1.0	1.1	3.0	2.7	1.9	1.1
Agricultural products	944.9	1 564.6	1 637.4	1 202.3	1 049.3	963.0	0.7	0.7	2.1	2.1	1.0	0.8
Livestock and livestock products	1.0	0.6	1.9	1.1	1.4	0.8	0.3	0.4	0.9	0.6	0.8	0.3
Other Commodities	102.1	92.7	139.2	83.6	49.0	138.3	28.4	18.1	41.5	36.0	23.6	28.5
Forestry products	0.1	0.1	0.2	0.2	0.2	0.1	...	0.1	0.2	0.2	0.1	...
Fish and other marine products	2.2	0.7	1.9	5.3	1.4	5.3	...	...	...	...	...	...
Metallic ores and concentrates	...	...	...	0.2	...	0.1	...	...	...	...	...	...
Bituminous coal and lignite	...	3.0	0.3	2.3	1.5	...	...	...	0.3	2.3	1.5	...
Crude petroleum and natural gas	3.6	3.1	4.8	3.8	4.6	6.2	3.6	3.0	4.8	3.6	4.6	6.2
Nonmetallic minerals	3.9	4.5	2.0	2.4	1.8	3.2	1.4	1.1	1.4	1.4	0.7	0.6
Scrap and waste	2.0	1.3	0.6	1.0	0.7	3.5	0.6	0.9	0.3	0.6	0.3	0.1
Used merchandise	1.8	4.4	7.2	2.4	2.4	3.3	0.1	0.1	0.4	0.3	0.4	0.3
Goods imported and returned unchanged	18.0	6.9	22.7	21.4	9.8	8.9	18.0	6.9	22.7	21.4	9.8	8.9
Special classification provisions	70.5	68.7	99.6	44.6	26.5	107.7	4.7	5.9	11.5	6.2	6.1	12.4

Table D-19. KANSAS: State Exports of Goods by Destination and Industry, 1994–1999—*Continued*

(Millions of dollars.)

Industry	South and Central American and Caribbean						Mexico					
	1994	1995	1996	1997	1998	1999	1994	1995	1996	1997	1998	1999
ALL GOODS	407.3	580.5	699.7	931.2	597.6	583.5	366.0	348.8	643.1	449.2	484.9	489.6
Manufactured Goods	265.1	329.9	388.8	620.3	360.0	327.5	177.0	106.2	201.5	240.7	249.8	320.3
Food products	68.9	73.1	120.8	112.3	79.7	55.9	30.4	25.4	30.1	28.7	72.7	123.1
Tobacco products	. . .	. . .	. . .	. . .	. . .	. . .	. . .	. . .	. . .	. . .	. . .	. . .
Textile mill products	0.6	0.4	0.1	0.2	0.2	0.3	0.2	0.6	7.0	24.1	5.9	0.6
Apparel	31.1	39.9	57.4	72.2	6.5	5.2	0.3	1.5	0.4	7.3	2.8	. . .
Lumber and wood products	. . .	. . .	0.1	0.1	. . .	0.2	. . .	0.1	0.1	0.1	0.1	0.7
Furniture and fixtures	0.4	0.1	0.1	0.9	0.3	0.2	1.3	0.5	0.2	0.7	0.3	0.1
Paper products	1.4	1.0	1.1	1.2	0.6	0.6	3.2	4.1	5.4	3.3	5.3	3.6
Printing and publishing	0.2	0.4	1.6	0.3	0.6	0.6	0.8	1.5	2.6	0.8	0.3	0.9
Chemical products	8.3	12.5	28.4	24.6	28.2	23.4	28.6	14.5	40.2	28.2	31.9	33.2
Refined petroleum products	5.6	24.2	14.5	54 7	67.8	24.7	0.0	17.3	59.6	71.4	15.3	42.1
Rubber and plastic products	12.7	7.4	1.5	1.4	1.5	0.6	5.2	4.3	4.6	4.9	4.9	11.3
Leather products	0.1	0.1	0.2	0.3	0.2	0.1	0.2	0.1	. . .	0.2	5.6	0.9
Stone, clay and glass products	4.5	7.4	14.1	4.4	6.0	0.6	1.4	0.2	0.2	0.1	0.2	0.3
Primary metals	2.5	2.8	0.7	1.5	1.9	0.5	0.6	0.1	0.6	0.5	1.6	3.0
Fabricated metal products	2.9	3.7	8.1	11.2	3.0	1.7	3.0	1.6	2.2	4.2	4.8	6.0
Industrial machinery and computers	25.9	24.2	35.2	75.2	52.3	22.0	14.7	16.9	14.3	21.3	38.7	25.7
Electric and electronic equipment	6.0	8.7	10.2	26.9	9.8	2.5	6.7	5.6	3.7	11.8	15.6	10.2
Transportation equipment	88.3	117.9	87.2	226.1	90.8	176.6	72.3	8.7	27.3	28.4	37.9	47.5
Scientific and measuring instruments	4.7	4.7	5.0	4.7	8.7	10 4	6.3	2.6	2.3	3.0	4.1	9.3
Miscellaneous manufactures	0.6	0.9	2.1	1.8	1.5	0.8	1.1	0.3	0.4	1.1	0.6	0.3
Unidentified manufactures	0.3	0.4	0.2	0.3	0.4	0.7	0.6	0.4	0.4	0.6	1.3	1.6
Agricultural And Livestock Products	141.2	249.9	308.0	308.6	236.5	247.3	187.9	242.4	440.9	206.9	234.5	157.0
Agricultural products	141.2	249.9	307.9	308.5	236.3	247.3	187.3	242.4	440.8	206.9	234.5	156.9
Livestock and livestock products	. . .	. . .	0.1	. . .	0.2	. . .	0.6	. . .	0.1	. . .	. . .	0.2
Other Commodities	1.0	0.7	3.0	2.3	1.1	8.7	1.1	0.2	0.7	1.7	0.7	12.3
Forestry products	. . .	. . .	. . .	. . .	. . .	. . .	. . .	. . .	. . .	. . .	. . .	. . .
Fish and other marine products	0.1	. . .	. . .	0.9	0.2	0.5	. . .	. . .	. . .	. . .	. . .	0.2
Metallic ores and concentrates	. . .	. . .	. . .	. . .	. . .	. . .	. . .	. . .	. . .	. . .	. . .	. . .
Bituminous coal and lignite	. . .	. . .	. . .	. . .	. . .	. . .	. . .	. . .	. . .	. . .	. . .	. . .
Crude petroleum and natural gas	. . .	. . .	. . .	. . .	. . .	. . .	. . .	. . .	. . .	. . .	. . .	. . .
Nonmetallic minerals	. . .	. . .	. . .	. . .	. . .	0.1	. . .	0.1	. . .	. . .	. . .	2.5
Scrap and waste	. . .	. . .	. . .	. . .	. . .	0.1	0.7	. . .	. . .	. . .	. . .	0.3
Used merchandise	. . .	. . .	. . .	0.1	. . .	0.1	0.2	0.1	. . .	0.2	0.3	0.3
Goods imported and returned unchanged	. . .	. . .	. . .	. . .	. . .	. . .	. . .	. . .	. . .	. . .	. . .	. . .
Special classification provisions	0.9	0.6	2.9	1.3	0.8	8.0	0.2	0.1	0.6	1.4	0.4	9.3

Industry	European Union						United Kingdom					
	1994	1995	1996	1997	1998	1999	1994	1995	1996	1997	1998	1999
ALL GOODS	488.4	483.8	636.9	744.6	693.1	914.4	92.7	90.5	129.6	173.4	189.3	273.4
Manufactured Goods	449.8	442.4	597.0	710.0	677.9	894.1	92.0	87.0	128.4	169.0	184.3	269.0
Food products	55.8	50.8	63.5	37.1	36.7	27.2	18.2	13.8	15.7	6.9	4.3	3.5
Tobacco products	. . .	. . .	. . .	. . .	. . .	. . .	. . .	0.2	0.1	0.2	0.3	0.4
Textile mill products	0.2	0.4	0.3	0.2	0.4	0.5	0.3	0.7	0.8	0.5	0.4	0.3
Apparel	0.9	1.3	1.2	1.0	0.9	0.8	. . .	0.1	0.3	. . .	0.8	. . .
Lumber and wood products	2.5	2.1	1.7	1.5	2.7	1.6	. . .	. . .	. . .	. . .	. . .	. . .
Furniture and fixtures	0.6	0.4	0.6	0.7	0.7	0.3	0.4	0.3	0.3	0.3	0.6	0.2
Paper products	2.5	5.0	3.0	2.4	2.7	2.8	0.6	0.5	0.6	0.6	0.7	1.0
Printing and publishing	1.2	1.0	0.8	0.6	1.4	1.0	0.9	0.5	0.5	0.4	1.2	0.7
Chemical products	45.6	52.1	72.8	115.7	121.1	101.3	1.8	4.2	10.4	16.2	28.7	21.8
Refined petroleum products	30.7	29.5	51.2	61.9	26.0	55.2	0.9	0.4	1.0	0.7	1.2	2.9
Rubber and plastic products	5.7	7.8	6.1	3.7	7.6	4.1	1.4	1.3	1.7	0.9	0.9	0.7
Leather products	0.3	0.2	0.2	0.1	0.2	0.1	. . .	. . .	. . .	. . .	. . .	. . .
Stone, clay and glass products	0.8	1.5	1.9	2.2	2.9	4.4	0.1	0.4	0.9	1.2	2.0	3.2
Primary metals	2.9	2.8	1.5	1.5	2.3	2.5	1.5	0.6	0.4	0.6	1.1	1.3
Fabricated metal products	7.0	9.4	5.6	8.9	9.9	7.1	2.2	2.2	3.3	5.7	7.2	4.3
Industrial machinery and computers	45.1	58.3	64.0	80.3	90.5	105.7	13.9	11.9	17.1	22.9	33.6	43.3
Electric and electronic equipment	15.7	18.9	19.3	21.8	26.4	28.1	4.8	4.7	6.9	6.6	6.9	6.5
Transportation equipment	185.1	145.2	234.8	299.8	238.1	413.2	33.6	33.4	37.7	80.3	61.5	142.4
Scientific and measuring instruments	43.9	51.9	50.9	65.9	95.2	130.9	9.8	10.6	14.6	21.9	28.2	31.6
Miscellaneous manufactures	2.0	2.5	4.8	3.7	9.2	4.0	1.2	0.9	3.9	2.6	3.2	2.8
Unidentified manufactures	1.2	1.2	12.7	0.9	2.7	3.3	0.3	0.3	12.2	0.5	1.5	2.2
Agricultural And Livestock Products	32.4	30.9	34.2	24.0	5.1	2.8	0.1	. . .	. . .	. . .	. . .	. . .
Agricultural products	32.4	30.9	34.1	24.0	5.0	2.8	0.1	. . .	. . .	. . .	. . .	. . .
Livestock and livestock products	. . .	. . .	. . .	. . .	. . .	. . .	. . .	. . .	. . .	. . .	. . .	. . .
Other Commodities	6.2	10.4	5.8	10.6	10.1	17.5	0.7	3.4	1.2	4.4	5.0	4.4
Forestry products	. . .	. . .	. . .	. . .	. . .	. . .	. . .	. . .	. . .	. . .	. . .	. . .
Fish and other marine products	1.9	0.3	0.4	0.4	0.6	1.0	. . .	. . .	. . .	. . .	0.1	0.1
Metallic ores and concentrates	. . .	. . .	. . .	. . .	. . .	. . .	. . .	1.9	. . .	. . .	. . .	. . .
Bituminous coal and lignite	. . .	2.2	. . .	. . .	. . .	. . .	. . .	. . .	. . .	. . .	. . .	. . .
Crude petroleum and natural gas	. . .	. . .	. . .	. . .	. . .	. . .	. . .	. . .	. . .	. . .	. . .	. . .
Nonmetallic minerals	. . .	0.5	0.1	. . .	. . .	1.2	. . .	. . .	. . .	. . .	. . .	. . .
Scrap and waste	. . .	0.1	0.1	0.1	0.4	0.7	. . .	. . .	. . .	. . .	. . .	. . .
Used merchandise	1.2	3.7	2.6	1.1	1.1	1.6	0.1	0.1	. . .	0.3	0.6	0.2
Goods imported and returned unchanged	. . .	. . .	. . .	. . .	. . .	. . .	. . .	. . .	. . .	. . .	. . .	. . .
Special classification provisions	3.1	3.7	2.8	9.0	7.9	12.9	0.6	1.4	1.2	4.1	4.3	4.1

Table D-19. KANSAS: State Exports of Goods by Destination and Industry, 1994–1999—*Continued*

(Millions of dollars.)

Industry	Germany						France					
	1994	1995	1996	1997	1998	1999	1994	1995	1996	1997	1998	1999
ALL GOODS	121.5	98.0	94.9	114.8	125.0	178.5	52.3	64.3	108.1	98.2	98.1	124.8
Manufactured Goods	120.7	97.1	94.4	111.1	123.8	176.1	51.2	63.7	107.3	97.3	95.8	119.1
Food products	5.6	7.0	7.5	3.0	4.3	4.7	8.2	8.7	6.3	. . .	1.6	1.6
Tobacco products	. . .	. . .	. . .	. . .	. . .	. . .	. . .	. . .	. . .	. . .	. . .	. . .
Textile mill products	. . .	. . .	. . .	. . .	. . .	. . .	. . .	0.1	. . .	. . .	. . .	. . .
Apparel	0.1	0.1	. . .	0.1	. . .	. . .	. . .	0.1	. . .	. . .	0.1	. . .
Lumber and wood products	0.8	0.3	. . .	. . .	0.2	. . .	. . .	. . .	. . .	. . .	0.1	0.1
Furniture and fixtures	0.1	0.1	0.2	0.1	0.1	0.1	0.1	. . .	. . .	. . .	. . .	. . .
Paper products	. . .	0.1	0.1	0.3	0.1	. . .	1.4	4.1	1.7	1.3	1.3	1.4
Printing and publishing	0.1	. . .	. . .	0.1	0.1	. . .	0.1	0.2	. . .	. . .	. . .	0.1
Chemical products	9.2	8.1	9.6	5.7	6.0	5.7	1.0	4.3	1.7	2.4	1.2	1.6
Refined petroleum products	2.8	. . .	1.5	5.1	. . .	. . .	0.1	0.8	0.2	. . .	. . .	0.2
Rubber and plastic products	0.4	1.0	0.5	0.3	0.4	0.4	0.3	0.6	0.5	0.5	0.9	0.2
Leather products	0.1	0.1	. . .	. . .	0.1	. . .	. . .	. . .	. . .	. . .	0.1	. . .
Stone, clay and glass products	0.4	0.1	0.1	0.2	0.3	0.4	0.1	0.2	0.3	0.5	0.3	0.4
Primary metals	0.3	0.3	0.1	0.1	0.1	0.1	0.2	0.1	. . .	0.2	0.1	0.1
Fabricated metal products	0.3	0.5	0.4	0.6	0.8	1.1	0.7	2.9	0.7	0.2	0.5	0.2
Industrial machinery and computers	9.4	10.6	9.5	7.6	11.7	8.1	2.6	4.0	3.8	7.6	6.0	9.3
Electric and electronic equipment	2.8	2.3	3.3	2.0	6.3	4.8	2.8	2.7	2.4	4.1	6.5	8.7
Transportation equipment	73.4	51.7	49.6	71.8	66.3	126.8	25.6	21.7	79.7	62.6	45.2	47.4
Scientific and measuring instruments	14.3	14.4	11.5	13.6	21.3	23.1	7.6	12.2	9.3	17.2	31.2	47.5
Miscellaneous manufactures	0.3	0.1	0.2	0.2	5.4	0.7	0.1	1.0	0.3	0.5	0.5	0.2
Unidentified manufactures	0.3	0.4	0.1	0.2	0.3	0.1	0.2	0.1	0.1	0.1	0.4	0.2
Agricultural And Livestock Products	0.1	. . .	0.1	. . .	0.1	. . .	0.3	. . .	. . .	. . .	. . .	0.1
Agricultural products	0.1	. . .	. . .	. . .	. . .	. . .	0.3	. . .	. . .	. . .	. . .	0.1
Livestock and livestock products	. . .	. . .	. . .	. . .	. . .	. . .	. . .	. . .	. . .	. . .	. . .	. . .
Other Commodities	0.7	0.9	0.5	3.6	1.1	2.4	0.8	0.6	0.7	0.8	2.3	5.6
Forestry products	. . .	. . .	. . .	. . .	. . .	. . .	. . .	. . .	. . .	. . .	. . .	. . .
Fish and other marine products	. . .	. . .	. . .	. . .	. . .	. . .	. . .	. . .	. . .	. . .	. . .	. . .
Metallic ores and concentrates	. . .	. . .	. . .	. . .	. . .	. . .	. . .	. . .	. . .	. . .	. . .	. . .
Bituminous coal and lignite	. . .	. . .	. . .	. . .	. . .	. . .	. . .	. . .	. . .	. . .	. . .	. . .
Crude petroleum and natural gas	. . .	. . .	. . .	. . .	. . .	. . .	. . .	. . .	. . .	. . .	. . .	. . .
Nonmetallic minerals	. . .	. . .	. . .	. . .	. . .	. . .	. . .	. . .	. . .	. . .	. . .	. . .
Scrap and waste	. . .	0.1	. . .	0.1	0.4	0.7	. . .	. . .	. . .	. . .	. . .	. . .
Used merchandise	0.1	. . .	. . .	. . .	0.2	. . .	0.1	0.1	0.3	. . .	. . .	0.1
Goods imported and returned unchanged	. . .	. . .	. . .	. . .	. . .	. . .	. . .	. . .	. . .	. . .	. . .	. . .
Special classification provisions	0.6	0.8	0.4	3.4	0.5	1.7	0.7	0.5	0.5	0.8	2.2	5.5

Industry	The Netherlands						Asian 10					
	1994	1995	1996	1997	1998	1999	1994	1995	1996	1997	1998	1999
ALL GOODS	36.1	32.6	73.1	102.0	52.7	83.8	1 125.3	1 827.4	1 761.2	1 501.7	1 219.5	1 485.1
Manufactured Goods	34.2	32.3	72.8	101.8	52.3	83.5	645.9	877.1	923.3	971.3	800.0	981.2
Food products	5.5	4.6	2.5	0.7	0.2	0.2	357.1	540.6	567.0	594.9	554.9	766.4
Tobacco products	. . .	. . .	. . .	. . .	. . .	. . .	0.2	0.3	1.3	0.2	0.1	0.7
Textile mill products	. . .	. . .	. . .	. . .	. . .	. . .	. . .	. . .	. . .	. . .	. . .	. . .
Apparel	0.2	0.1	. . .	0.1	. . .	0.1	3.5	5.6	4.9	1.0	0.4	0.7
Lumber and wood products	. . .	. . .	0.1	0.1	. . .	. . .	2.5	0.9	0.7	0.9	0.7	1.1
Furniture and fixtures	. . .	. . .	. . .	. . .	. . .	. . .	3.3	2.7	2.8	2.4	0.4	1.9
Paper products	. . .	. . .	0.1	0.1	0.4	0.1	0.2	0.3	1.1	1.1	0.7	1.7
Printing and publishing	. . .	. . .	0.2	0.1	. . .	0.2	2.5	2.2	1.3	0.5	0.6	1.1
Chemical products	11.8	10.0	31.9	57.0	32.5	36.2	19.6	45.3	59.1	42.8	56.0	44.3
Refined petroleum products	. . .	0.5	17.7	15.6	2.8	23.9	37.5	20.8	21.1	52.8	7.4	9.8
Rubber and plastic products	0.6	0.6	0.2	0.4	0.3	0.1	7.0	10.2	6.3	5.1	13.5	3.3
Leather products	0.1	. . .	. . .	. . .	. . .	. . .	1.0	0.7	0.4	0.6	0.8	1.2
Stone, clay and glass products	0.1	0.1	0.2	0.1	0.1	0.1	1.4	0.8	1.0	1.2	0.9	1.1
Primary metals	0.3	0.1	0.1	0.2	0.5	0.3	1.5	1.2	1.6	2.7	3.0	1.3
Fabricated metal products	0.2	0.8	0.5	0.2	0.1	0.2	16.5	18.1	18.6	13.7	19.0	6.0
Industrial machinery and computers	5.8	7.4	7.3	11.8	4.4	8.0	42.9	56.7	70.1	61.8	44.8	33.4
Electric and electronic equipment	1.0	2.8	2.3	3.3	2.2	2.4	49.0	55.8	36.8	24.7	23.0	21.0
Transportation equipment	6.1	1.7	5.4	7.4	4.4	6.8	69.7	87.0	92.2	113.3	38.8	39.2
Scientific and measuring instruments	2.3	3.4	4.0	4.8	4.2	4.7	25.9	23.9	31.7	39.5	27.7	39.8
Miscellaneous manufactures	0.1	0.1	. . .	. . .	0.1	0.1	3.7	2.4	4.7	4.0	3.2	4.2
Unidentified manufactures	0.1	0.1	0.1	. . .	. . .	0.1	1.0	1.5	0.8	8.1	4.0	2.9
Agricultural And Livestock Products	. . .	. . .	0.1	0.1	0.1	. . .	417.9	890.7	753.6	521.9	411.0	440.5
Agricultural products	. . .	. . .	0.1	0.1	0.1	. . .	417.8	890.7	753.2	521.9	411.0	440.5
Livestock and livestock products	. . .	. . .	. . .	. . .	. . .	. . .	. . .	. . .	0.4	. . .	. . .	. . .
Other Commodities	1.9	0.3	0.2	0.1	0.2	0.3	61.6	59.6	84.4	8.4	8.6	63.5
Forestry products	. . .	. . .	. . .	. . .	. . .	. . .	0.1	. . .	. . .	. . .	. . .	. . .
Fish and other marine products	1.9	0.2	0.1	. . .	. . .	. . .	0.3	0.3	0.9	4.0	0.2	2.3
Metallic ores and concentrates	. . .	. . .	. . .	. . .	. . .	. . .	. . .	. . .	. . .	0.2	. . .	. . .
Bituminous coal and lignite	. . .	. . .	. . .	. . .	. . .	. . .	. . .	. . .	. . .	. . .	. . .	. . .
Crude petroleum and natural gas	. . .	. . .	. . .	. . .	. . .	. . .	. . .	. . .	. . .	0.2	. . .	. . .
Nonmetallic minerals	. . .	. . .	. . .	. . .	. . .	. . .	. . .	. . .	. . .	. . .	. . .	. . .
Scrap and waste	. . .	. . .	. . .	. . .	. . .	. . .	2.4	2.6	0.4	0.9	0.9	1.4
Used merchandise	. . .	. . .	. . .	. . .	. . .	. . .	0.6	0.2	0.2	0.2	. . .	0.1
Goods imported and returned unchanged	. . .	. . .	. . .	. . .	0.1	. . .	0.2	0.3	3.7	0.2	0.1	0.1
Special classification provisions	. . .	. . .	0.1	0.1	0.1	0.2	57.9	56.2	79.1	2.8	7.4	59.7

Table D-19. KANSAS: State Exports of Goods by Destination and Industry, 1994–1999—*Continued*

(Millions of dollars.)

Industry	Japan						South Korea					
	1994	1995	1996	1997	1998	1999	1994	1995	1996	1997	1998	1999
ALL GOODS	697.4	1 057.3	1 075.0	921.8	830.3	947.7	107.7	341.5	239.3	179.1	127.3	186.5
Manufactured Goods	386.4	510.6	542.0	573.2	512.6	660.6	56.6	145.8	132.8	127.5	84.6	158.8
Food products	280.0	408.3	427.5	432.6	442.3	581.7	31.5	77.9	78.3	101.3	57.7	130.6
Tobacco products	...	...	...	...	...	...	...	...	0.1	...	...	0.1
Textile mill products	0.1	0.2	0.7	0.2	...	0.5	...	...	0.4	...	...	...
Apparel	3.3	4.8	4.8	0.9	0.3	0.6	...	0.2	...	...	...	...
Lumber and wood products	1.2	0.6	0.6	0.7	0.6	0.6	1.1	...	...	...	...	...
Furniture and fixtures	3.0	2.4	2.1	1.2	0.1	1.5	...	...	...	0.3	...	...
Paper products	0.1	0.1	...	0.2	0.2	1.5	...	...	0.3	...	...	...
Printing and publishing	0.1	0.1	0.4	0.2	0.2	0.2	0.1	...	...	...	...	0.1
Chemical products	11.5	14.0	18.4	25.9	22.0	17.8	1.8	21.9	30.7	2.5	15.1	13.7
Refined petroleum products	29.2	20.3	20.1	44.6	6.3	3.9	1.9	0.2	0.2	7.6	0.2	1.3
Rubber and plastic products	1.8	4.3	2.5	1.5	0.5	1.1	2.0	2.8	2.8	1.9	1.9	0.6
Leather products	...	0.1	0.2	0.1	0.1	0.1	...	...	...	0.3	...	0.2
Stone, clay and glass products	0.2	0.2	0.3	0.1	0.1	0.2	0.6	0.1	0.3	0.1	0.1	...
Primary metals	0.1	0.7	0.6	0.2	0.5	0.4	0.1	...	0.5	0.2	...	...
Fabricated metal products	5.2	7.7	7.1	6.6	0.8	3.2	1.3	1.8	2.6	0.2	0.7	0.1
Industrial machinery and computers	7.4	14.9	16.3	17.3	9.9	9.5	4.9	7.5	6.1	5.5	2.0	1.4
Electric and electronic equipment	21.3	24.2	18.3	6.1	3.8	5.6	2.6	2.9	2.8	1.5	0.3	0.5
Transportation equipment	15.3	2.4	14.5	25.8	18.9	14.9	2.1	23.3	0.6	0.7	2.8	0.9
Scientific and measuring instruments	4.9	3.0	5.1	6.2	3.3	14.1	6.2	6.3	6.7	3.1	3.2	8.1
Miscellaneous manufactures	1.7	1.6	2.2	2.6	2.2	2.7	0.2	0.3	0.6	0.8	0.4	0.8
Unidentified manufactures	0.3	0.4	0.2	0.2	0.4	0.6	0.1	0.1	0.1	1.4	0.1	0.2
Agricultural And Livestock Products	262.0	511.1	528.5	347.7	316.7	252.7	50.8	195.6	106.5	51.6	42.6	27.5
Agricultural products	262.0	511.1	528.5	347.7	316.7	252.7	50.8	195.6	106.5	51.6	42.6	27.5
Livestock and livestock products	...	...	...	...	...	...	...	...	...	...	...	...
Other Commodities	49.0	35.7	4.5	0.8	1.0	34.4	0.3	0.1	...	0.1	0.1	0.1
Forestry products	0.1	...	...	...	...	...	...	...	...	...	...	...
Fish and other marine products	0.1	0.1	...	...	0.1	0.4	...	...	...	...	...	0.1
Metallic ores and concentrates	...	...	...	0.2	...	...	...	...	...	...	...	...
Bituminous coal and lignite	...	...	...	...	...	...	...	...	...	...	...	...
Crude petroleum and natural gas	...	...	...	...	...	...	...	...	...	...	...	...
Nonmetallic minerals	1.1	1.0	0.1	0.1	0.3	0.2	0.1	...	...	...	...	...
Scrap and waste	...	...	...	...	...	...	...	...	...	...	...	...
Used merchandise	0.1	0.2	3.7	0.1	0.1	0.1	0.1	0.1	...	...	...	...
Goods imported and returned unchanged	...	...	...	...	...	...	0.1	...	...	...	...	...
Special classification provisions	47.7	34.3	0.6	0.4	0.5	33.7	0.1	...	...	...	...	...

Industry	Taiwan						Singapore					
	1994	1995	1996	1997	1998	1999	1994	1995	1996	1997	1998	1999
ALL GOODS	159.5	216.3	171.6	153.3	85.9	182.3	25.3	24.0	51.2	33.5	24.5	42.4
Manufactured Goods	53.5	75.4	71.8	59.0	47.8	37.7	25.1	23.6	50.7	32.8	24.1	35.6
Food products	24.9	43.0	43.2	34.9	14.6	21.4	0.6	0.4	0.7	0.5	0.6	0.6
Tobacco products	...	...	...	...	...	...	...	...	...	...	...	...
Textile mill products	...	...	...	...	0.1	0.1	...	...	...	...	...	...
Apparel	0.1	...	...	...	0.1	0.1	...	...	...	...	...	...
Lumber and wood products	0.1	...	...	0.1	0.1	0.3	...	...	...	...	...	...
Furniture and fixtures	0.1	0.1	...	0.1	0.1	...	...	0.1	0.2	0.1	0.1	0.3
Paper products	...	...	0.1	0.1	0.1	...	0.5	0.2	0.1	...	0.1	...
Printing and publishing	0.5	...	0.5	...	...	...	0.1	1.0	1.2	0.8	0.4	0.6
Chemical products	0.9	4.8	0.3	5.8	11.4	4.1	...	...	0.2	0.1	0.7	3.0
Refined petroleum products	0.1	0.2	0.3	0.1	...	0.2	...	...	...	...	...	...
Rubber and plastic products	0.4	1.0	0.3	0.8	0.4	0.4	0.7	0.5	0.3	0.3	0.4	0.6
Leather products	...	...	...	...	...	0.1	0.1	0.1	...	...	0.2	0.2
Stone, clay and glass products	0.4	0.2	0.1	0.1	...	0.1	0.1	0.1	0.1	0.1	0.3	0.1
Primary metals	0.9	0.1	...	0.1	0.2	0.3	0.1	...	0.1	0.1	0.8	0.3
Fabricated metal products	4.0	4.5	3.1	1.2	3.5	0.2	0.8	0.5	1.7	1.1	0.8	0.3
Industrial machinery and computers	5.3	6.4	9.3	4.4	4.6	2.8	5.6	3.8	9.4	11.5	6.4	6.4
Electric and electronic equipment	7.9	8.3	3.9	6.4	6.1	2.8	7.7	6.1	7.1	4.3	3.5	4.5
Transportation equipment	1.6	3.7	6.0	1.5	1.2	0.5	2.5	4.5	20.3	6.1	4.0	14.7
Scientific and measuring instruments	4.7	2.9	4.3	3.2	4.9	4.0	6.0	5.9	8.5	7.4	6.3	3.8
Miscellaneous manufactures	1.4	0.1	0.4	0.1	0.3	0.2	0.1	0.1	0.7	0.1	0.2	0.2
Unidentified manufactures	0.1	0.1	...	0.1	0.2	0.3	0.3	0.4	0.1	0.2	0.2	0.2
Agricultural And Livestock Products	104.6	122.3	99.0	93.5	37.5	120.3	0.1	...	0.1	0.1	0.1	6.3
Agricultural products	104.6	122.3	99.0	93.5	37.5	120.3	0.1	...	0.1	0.1	0.1	6.3
Livestock and livestock products	...	...	...	...	...	...	...	...	...	...	...	...
Other Commodities	1.3	18.7	0.8	0.8	0.5	24.3	0.1	0.4	0.4	0.6	0.3	0.5
Forestry products	...	...	...	...	...	...	...	...	...	...	...	...
Fish and other marine products	...	...	...	...	...	...	...	...	...	...	...	...
Metallic ores and concentrates	...	...	...	...	...	...	...	...	...	...	...	...
Bituminous coal and lignite	...	...	...	...	...	...	...	...	...	...	...	...
Crude petroleum and natural gas	...	...	...	...	...	...	...	...	...	0.1	...	...
Nonmetallic minerals	1.2	1.5	0.3	0.8	0.5	0.2	...	...	...	...	...	...
Scrap and waste	...	...	0.1	...	...	...	...	...	...	...	...	...
Used merchandise	...	...	...	...	...	...	...	...	...	...	...	...
Goods imported and returned unchanged	...	...	...	...	...	...	...	...	...	...	...	...
Special classification provisions	0.1	17.1	0.3	0.1	0.1	24.0	0.1	0.4	0.4	0.4	0.3	0.5

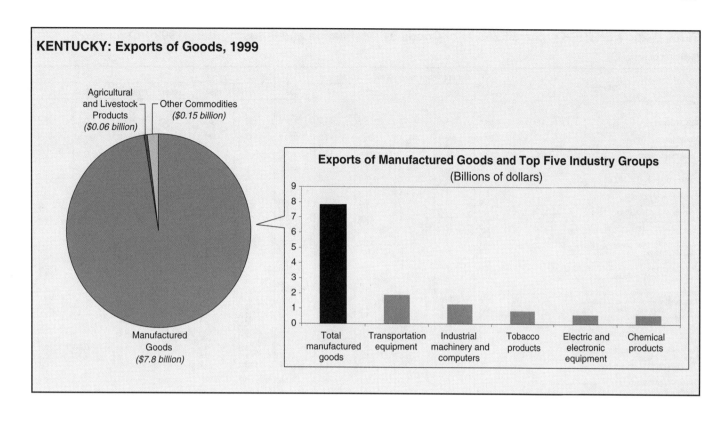

KENTUCKY: Exports of Goods, 1999

Agricultural and Livestock Products ($0.06 billion)

Other Commodities ($0.15 billion)

Manufactured Goods ($7.8 billion)

Exports of Manufactured Goods and Top Five Industry Groups
(Billions of dollars)

Total manufactured goods | Transportation equipment | Industrial machinery and computers | Tobacco products | Electric and electronic equipment | Chemical products

Table D-20. KENTUCKY: State Exports of Goods by Destination and Industry, 1994–1999

(Millions of dollars.)

Industry	All destinations						Canada					
	1994	1995	1996	1997	1998	1999	1994	1995	1996	1997	1998	1999
ALL GOODS	4 188.2	5 030.1	5 824.2	6 904.1	7 440.0	8 016.2	1 571.1	1 804.7	1 905.3	2 368.9	2 325.0	2 801.4
Manufactured Goods	4 051.8	4 810.5	5 581.7	6 664.3	7 253.7	7 805.8	1 528.9	1 751.9	1 846.2	2 309.7	2 277.2	2 726.1
Food products	222.2	305.6	305.5	312.2	301.1	339.1	50.1	57.1	54.7	38.8	43.1	45.8
Tobacco products	809.2	967.5	862.1	868.9	886.5	854.4	1.6	1.4	1.8	1.2	0.9	0.8
Textile mill products	46.7	52.9	59.7	57.3	71.6	74.0	26.5	34.5	33.3	30.6	26.7	19.2
Apparel	61.0	169.8	311.8	495.6	835.4	598.3	18.2	29.5	20.8	24.4	22.9	24.0
Lumber and wood products	33.9	35.0	37.8	53.1	46.8	58.2	5.1	5.0	6.4	9.3	8.0	12.8
Furniture and fixtures	44.5	48.0	58.6	62.4	91.9	13.9	38.3	40.1	45.0	51.8	77.0	4.9
Paper products	53.6	66.0	91.1	81.9	98.5	98.3	25.7	35.2	44.3	47.0	54.9	59.6
Printing and publishing	51.0	78.4	77.2	97.3	85.5	93.9	27.3	60.1	58.8	77.8	71.2	75.7
Chemical products	176.8	260.7	333.0	365.7	516.1	605.9	99.5	134.0	136.5	154.0	142.8	207.2
Refined petroleum products	13.0	14.4	14.4	10.5	7.1	8.5	7.5	8.9	8.8	6.8	3.8	6.1
Rubber and plastic products	86.5	104.2	120.0	148.0	194.2	250.4	54.9	60.5	63.9	84.3	101.6	113.2
Leather products	8.5	11.6	14.7	9.6	7.4	54.8	3.0	4.3	3.2	2.3	2.3	3.4
Stone, clay and glass products	72.7	63.3	80.6	118.1	91.9	137.6	23.2	15.1	16.5	19.8	18.9	23.0
Primary metals	240.7	240.4	280.1	296.7	279.9	293.4	162.3	111.8	114.2	194.2	182.8	193.7
Fabricated metal products	68.2	87.4	96.3	128.5	152.5	331.9	32.5	42.8	51.1	69.6	76.4	234.1
Industrial machinery and computers	609.2	690.4	950.6	1 182.1	1 247.2	1 285.7	221.7	264.7	274.5	366.6	368.7	418.4
Electric and electronic equipment	428.5	479.1	545.8	620.0	586.4	607.3	121.3	138.0	168.9	187.1	211.3	242.7
Transportation equipment	879.3	958.8	1 133.8	1 544.3	1 553.0	1 888.5	576.4	664.8	696.4	892.4	806.6	976.2
Scientific and measuring instruments	77.0	105.0	128.3	136.1	125.8	112.6	17.1	21.3	23.5	25.7	22.4	29.0
Miscellaneous manufactures	61.5	64.1	65.7	65.9	62.4	58.8	13.4	19.3	20.0	21.3	29.5	30.4
Unidentified manufactures	7.9	7.9	14.5	10.2	12.5	40.3	3.4	3.7	3.6	4.8	5.2	5.9
Agricultural And Livestock Products	50.8	74.3	45.8	67.9	59.6	55.6	10.5	7.9	8.1	7.6	8.8	9.5
Agricultural products	31.2	27.7	31.9	51.4	49.6	42.0	2.7	1.9	3.6	3.4	5.4	4.8
Livestock and livestock products	19.6	46.6	13.8	16.5	10.0	13.6	7.8	5.9	4.4	4.3	3.4	4.7
Other Commodities	85.7	145.3	196.8	171.9	126.6	154.8	31.7	44.9	51.1	51.6	39.0	65.7
Forestry products	0.1	0.4	0.2	0.3	0.1	0.2	...	0.1	0.1	...	...	...
Fish and other marine products	0.1	1.7	1.4	1.7	2.0	0.2	...	0.2	0.4	0.2	0.2	0.1
Metallic ores and concentrates	0.4	4.8	0.1	0.1	0.2	0.2	0.4	4.7	...	0.1	0.1	0.1
Bituminous coal and lignite	52.2	84.5	136.3	105.1	73.5	81.4	9.0	6.0	8.6	6.4	4.7	10.7
Crude petroleum and natural gas	0.7	0.3	0.5	0.3	0.4	0.3	0.4	0.1	...	...	0.1	...
Nonmetallic minerals	7.0	8.1	11.5	13.3	11.1	8.6	0.7	1.4	2.1	1.9	1.1	0.9
Scrap and waste	7.1	12.8	8.7	8.9	9.9	6.9	5.7	8.8	7.8	6.8	8.1	5.2
Used merchandise	2.8	2.1	3.7	4.6	1.4	4.5	1.2	0.2	0.9	0.8	0.3	0.9
Goods imported and returned unchanged	13.6	21.8	30.3	35.1	23.6	15.7	13.6	21.8	30.3	35.1	23.6	15.7
Special classification provisions	1.7	8.7	4.1	2.4	4.4	36.8	0.6	1.6	0.9	0.3	0.8	32.0

Table D-20. KENTUCKY: State Exports of Goods by Destination and Industry, 1994–1999—Continued

(Millions of dollars.)

Industry	South and Central American and Caribbean						Mexico					
	1994	1995	1996	1997	1998	1999	1994	1995	1996	1997	1998	1999
ALL GOODS	156.5	304.0	446.6	573.0	849.1	819.3	232.1	188.0	280.1	345.1	450.7	566.6
Manufactured Goods	152.9	296.2	438.1	566.5	842.2	814.8	224.6	179.2	274.0	337.9	443.5	561.5
Food products	5.7	6.1	6.7	9.7	10.8	10.1	6.3	9.0	11.2	7.4	6.3	6.5
Tobacco products	22.4	19.1	13.4	13.4	13.2	14.3	1.3	0.7	0.2	0.2	0.1	0.7
Textile mill products	4.5	5.0	11.3	2.7	1.6	19.7	0.8	1.5	2.9	10.3	17.7	14.1
Apparel	21.2	120.4	236.2	317.1	581.5	539.2	0.2	0.2	9.2	31.4	41.9	21.7
Lumber and wood products	0.5	1.3	0.2	1.0	1.0	2.6	0.5	0.3	0.4	0.8	0.5	1.3
Furniture and fixtures	0.3	1.8	1.2	1.6	2.5	0.9	0.6	0.3	0.3	0.2	1.8	0.7
Paper products	0.8	2.5	4.0	2.4	2.5	2.9	15.5	17.7	23.5	17.2	20.3	17.2
Printing and publishing	0.6	0.8	1.6	1.9	1.3	1.5	10.8	1.2	1.4	0.9	0.9	1.7
Chemical products	7.3	16.3	19.2	21.5	23.9	26.9	6.7	6.3	6.4	9.7	10.6	19.9
Refined petroleum products	2.7	2.1	2.6	1.4	1.4	1.1	0.1	0.1	. . .	0.1	0.1	0.2
Rubber and plastic products	2.4	4.2	4.3	10.1	15.8	12.7	14.3	16.9	18.9	18.9	34.7	77.9
Leather products	0.4	0.4	0.5	0.5	0.1	0.2	. . .	. . .	0.2	1.3	0.6	0.4
Stone, clay and glass products	2.3	4.2	4.9	7.1	2.4	2.0	5.9	4.6	4.2	4.2	5.8	18.3
Primary metals	2.3	7.5	10.5	8.4	8.4	11.7	30.6	15.8	36.8	37.1	53.3	56.2
Fabricated metal products	3.1	3.4	5.5	8.0	11.5	16.1	4.6	6.0	11.1	14.7	19.6	34.8
Industrial machinery and computers	38.4	49.1	73.4	88.0	112.0	89.6	31.7	20.7	44.7	78.5	123.0	154.1
Electric and electronic equipment	24.6	35.6	24.8	42.3	28.5	29.2	73.8	52.3	76.1	78.9	82.3	79.2
Transportation equipment	4.3	5.6	6.9	16.2	8.6	20.9	10.6	12.3	16.2	16.6	14.1	16.7
Scientific and measuring instruments	3.6	4.8	4.9	8.6	9.3	7.0	2.8	4.0	3.5	4.5	4.3	8.6
Miscellaneous manufactures	5.2	5.8	5.5	3.6	5.0	5.0	6.9	9.1	6.0	4.3	2.8	4.0
Unidentified manufactures	0.3	0.4	0.4	1.1	0.9	1.4	0.7	0.4	0.6	0.8	2.7	27.3
Agricultural And Livestock Products	2.6	2.4	1.3	2.8	3.7	2.7	3.8	0.6	0.8	2.4	0.8	0.4
Agricultural products	1.1	1.7	0.4	1.6	2.0	1.0	1.5	0.5	0.8	0.9	0.3	0.4
Livestock and livestock products	1.5	0.7	0.8	1.1	1.7	1.6	2.3	0.2	. . .	1.5	0.5	0.1
Other Commodities	1.1	5.4	7.2	3.7	3.2	1.8	3.7	8.2	5.3	4.8	6.5	4.7
Forestry products	0.1	0.1	. . .	0.1	. . .	. . .	. . .	. . .	. . .	. . .	. . .	. . .
Fish and other marine products	. . .	1.5	0.8	0.1	. . .	. . .	. . .	. . .	. . .	. . .	0.9	. . .
Metallic ores and concentrates	. . .	0.1	. . .	. . .	. . .	. . .	. . .	. . .	. . .	. . .	. . .	. . .
Bituminous coal and lignite	. . .	1.5	4.6	. . .	. . .	. . .	. . .	. . .	. . .	. . .	. . .	. . .
Crude petroleum and natural gas	. . .	0.1	0.3	0.2	0.1	0.1	. . .	. . .	. . .	0.1	. . .	. . .
Nonmetallic minerals	0.9	1.8	1.2	2.7	2.0	1.3	3.2	2.1	3.5	4.4	5.4	4.5
Scrap and waste	. . .	. . .	. . .	0.1	. . .	0.2	. . .	. . .	. . .	0.2	0.1	. . .
Used merchandise	. . .	0.2	0.3	0.6	0.5	0.1	0.4	0.2	. . .	. . .	. . .	. . .
Goods imported and returned unchanged	. . .	. . .	. . .	. . .	. . .	. . .	. . .	. . .	. . .	. . .	. . .	. . .
Special classification provisions	. . .	. . .	. . .	. . .	0.6	0.2	0.1	5.9	1.8	0.1	0.1	0.1

Industry	European Union						United Kingdom					
	1994	1995	1996	1997	1998	1999	1994	1995	1996	1997	1998	1999
ALL GOODS	718.4	790.2	1 099.0	1 202.7	1 455.1	1 547.5	114.7	167.2	283.9	255.2	309.0	349.7
Manufactured Goods	672.6	719.5	998.9	1 092.4	1 369.5	1 468.4	99.7	136.5	249.2	210.3	287.7	325.0
Food products	84.7	98.6	106.0	114.4	103.4	141.7	17.2	21.0	28.7	27.9	24.7	30.9
Tobacco products	92.7	70.1	35.4	45.2	54.8	48.1	. . .	. . .	1.2	0.4	2.6	1.8
Textile mill products	8.3	6.6	10.9	7.1	9.3	2.5	0.9	0.3	0.2	0.3	1.2	1.7
Apparel	6.6	3.3	3.0	2.2	4.1	3.4	0.6	0.1	0.2	0.3	1.2	1.7
Lumber and wood products	21.8	21.8	23.5	37.5	33.4	36.4	5.3	6.0	10.9	16.2	19.9	19.1
Furniture and fixtures	4.0	4.6	5.4	3.7	6.0	4.6	1.6	1.4	1.8	2.2	1.9	1.1
Paper products	2.4	4.3	8.0	5.2	7.2	7.9	0.7	1.1	1.8	1.3	4.5	4.6
Printing and publishing	6.4	8.5	9.2	9.7	6.3	6.9	5.7	7.5	7.1	7.7	5.1	6.0
Chemical products	19.2	41.4	91.0	114.0	273.9	282.3	4.8	6.9	24.4	29.1	33.7	44.3
Refined petroleum products	0.4	0.3	0.5	0.6	0.4	0.4	. . .	. . .	. . .	. . .	. . .	. . .
Rubber and plastic products	6.7	13.7	17.6	14.3	18.0	21.0	2.0	6.0	9.9	7.7	8.2	8.6
Leather products	2.7	1.7	2.7	1.6	1.5	1.0	0.2	0.4	1.4	1.1	0.8	0.6
Stone, clay and glass products	7.1	6.8	5.2	4.2	4.8	15.3	3.3	1.6	1.4	1.1	0.8	1.2
Primary metals	6.0	12.7	12.6	15.1	16.3	17.6	1.2	2.1	4.0	6.0	3.9	3.4
Fabricated metal products	12.1	11.3	11.1	13.1	23.6	25.6	5.5	3.6	4.5	5.2	4.8	5.7
Industrial machinery and computers	162.8	188.2	341.1	388.9	400.9	358.7	22.2	42.3	97.0	53.8	90.3	107.7
Electric and electronic equipment	74.9	74.9	85.5	85.0	86.9	103.9	15.2	19.2	24.4	13.4	16.8	30.6
Transportation equipment	100.0	86.4	144.3	146.7	262.8	346.3	9.0	11.9	24.1	30.9	60.4	53.2
Scientific and measuring instruments	32.6	46.5	66.8	64.3	42.3	31.7	2.3	3.3	4.2	3.6	4.8	2.1
Miscellaneous manufactures	19.9	16.2	17.3	17.8	12.0	10.3	1.6	1.3	1.9	2.1	2.9	1.8
Unidentified manufactures	1.5	1.7	1.8	1.6	1.6	2.7	0.4	0.4	0.4	0.4	0.5	0.7
Agricultural And Livestock Products	12.3	16.2	11.3	15.6	13.2	3.7	0.4	6.0	0.2	1.0	0.3	0.3
Agricultural products	10.3	10.0	10.7	15.5	13.0	3.6	0.1	0.1	0.2	1.0	0.2	0.3
Livestock and livestock products	2.0	6.2	0.6	. . .	0.1	0.1	0.3	5.9	. . .	. . .	0.1	. . .
Other Commodities	33.4	54.6	88.8	94.7	72.5	75.4	14.6	24.6	34.5	43.9	21.0	24.4
Forestry products	. . .	. . .	. . .	. . .	0.1	0.1	. . .	. . .	. . .	. . .	. . .	0.1
Fish and other marine products	. . .	. . .	. . .	0.5	0.5	0.1	. . .	. . .	. . .	. . .	. . .	. . .
Metallic ores and concentrates	. . .	. . .	. . .	. . .	0.1	0.1	. . .	. . .	. . .	. . .	0.1	0.1
Bituminous coal and lignite	31.7	51.3	84.0	89.7	68.8	70.7	14.1	24.2	34.3	42.9	20.6	23.7
Crude petroleum and natural gas	. . .	. . .	0.1	. . .	. . .	0.2	. . .	. . .	. . .	. . .	. . .	. . .
Nonmetallic minerals	0.1	0.7	1.8	1.0	0.8	1.1	. . .	. . .	. . .	. . .	. . .	. . .
Scrap and waste	1.0	1.3	0.2	1.1	1.5	1.3	. . .	. . .	. . .	. . .	0.2	. . .
Used merchandise	0.4	0.9	1.7	1.6	0.2	0.4	0.2	0.3	. . .	0.8	0.1	0.2
Goods imported and returned unchanged	. . .	. . .	. . .	. . .	. . .	. . .	. . .	. . .	. . .	. . .	. . .	. . .
Special classification provisions	0.3	0.3	1.1	0.7	0.4	1.4	0.2	. . .	0.1	0.1	0.2	0.4

Table D-20. KENTUCKY: State Exports of Goods by Destination and Industry, 1994–1999—Continued

(Millions of dollars.)

Industry	Germany						France					
	1994	1995	1996	1997	1998	1999	1994	1995	1996	1997	1998	1999
ALL GOODS	136.6	228.6	229.6	232.7	327.1	351.6	166.8	151.6	258.9	366.5	359.4	338.9
Manufactured Goods	135.2	213.0	215.0	231.0	321.7	344.2	161.8	144.9	247.5	355.0	353.7	337.1
Food products	27.9	27.8	25.7	28.3	25.8	43.4	7.9	11.5	15.8	14.2	13.0	20.6
Tobacco products	4.3	54.8	25.4	32.4	33.7	28.0	. . .	0.2	0.1	0.1	. . .	. . .
Textile mill products	0.2	0.4	0.7	0.1	0.3	0.3	. . .	0.2	0.6	0.1	. . .	0.1
Apparel	1.0	1.1	1.6	1.1	1.4	0.8	0.2	0.4	0.1	0.1	0.1	0.1
Lumber and wood products	5.9	5.2	3.5	11.2	3.3	4.1	0.2	0.2	0.8	1.5	1.1	1.9
Furniture and fixtures	0.7	1.3	0.9	0.6	1.1	0.2	0.1	0.1	0.8	0.2	. . .	0.1
Paper products	0.2	0.2	0.4	0.3	0.9	1.6	1.3	2.7	5.0	2.8	0.8	0.8
Printing and publishing	0.2	0.3	0.3	0.3	0.1	0.2	0.2	0.1	1.0	1.0	0.6	0.2
Chemical products	3.9	13.4	19.6	20.6	85.8	64.9	3.2	3.7	10.8	21.1	9.2	17.1
Refined petroleum products	. . .	. . .	. . .	0.1	. . .	0.1	. . .	. . .	. . .	. . .	. . .	. . .
Rubber and plastic products	1.7	1.9	1.1	1.7	2.1	1.9	1.0	0.5	0.9	1.1	3.0	3.4
Leather products	1.3	0.2	0.3	. . .	0.1	0.1	. . .	0.2	0.2	. . .	0.1	. . .
Stone, clay and glass products	1.8	3.3	1.5	1.5	1.7	4.9	0.7	0.3	0.8	0.6	0.8	5.9
Primary metals	1.0	0.5	0.8	2.4	4.9	8.4	0.4	0.4	0.6	0.4	1.4	0.2
Fabricated metal products	1.9	1.5	2.1	3.2	13.0	11.9	1.6	1.4	1.1	1.9	1.8	1.2
Industrial machinery and computers	9.5	25.3	26.4	41.0	31.4	45.2	84.1	75.9	157.5	251.9	226.6	144.6
Electric and electronic equipment	12.5	5.4	4.4	8.1	6.6	7.6	18.7	15.0	17.4	16.3	19.6	22.7
Transportation equipment	57.9	58.9	87.0	71.8	104.0	117.1	7.0	1.2	3.8	10.2	51.6	97.8
Scientific and measuring instruments	2.6	10.9	10.6	3.0	3.0	1.3	18.0	17.6	18.2	19.4	17.6	14.7
Miscellaneous manufactures	0.4	0.2	2.4	2.7	2.0	1.9	17.1	13.2	11.6	11.9	6.2	5.3
Unidentified manufactures	0.3	0.4	0.2	0.5	0.4	0.6	0.1	0.2	0.3	0.1	0.2	0.3
Agricultural And Livestock Products	. . .	0.1	. . .	0.1	0.5	. . .	1.0	0.2	0.6	0.1	0.1	. . .
Agricultural products	. . .	0.1	. . .	0.1	0.5	. . .	0.8	0.1	0.1	0.1	0.1	. . .
Livestock and livestock products	. . .	. . .	. . .	. . .	. . .	. . .	0.2	0.1	0.5	. . .	. . .	. . .
Other Commodities	1.4	15.5	14.6	1.6	4.9	7.3	4.0	6.5	10.8	11.3	5.6	1.8
Forestry products	. . .	. . .	. . .	. . .	. . .	. . .	. . .	. . .	. . .	. . .	. . .	. . .
Fish and other marine products	. . .	. . .	. . .	. . .	. . .	. . .	. . .	. . .	. . .	. . .	. . .	. . .
Metallic ores and concentrates	. . .	. . .	. . .	. . .	. . .	. . .	. . .	. . .	. . .	. . .	. . .	. . .
Bituminous coal and lignite	0.3	13.8	14.1	0.4	3.5	5.9	4.0	6.5	10.8	10.6	5.6	1.3
Crude petroleum and natural gas	. . .	. . .	. . .	. . .	. . .	. . .	. . .	. . .	. . .	. . .	. . .	. . .
Nonmetallic materials	. . .	. . .	. . .	. . .	. . .	. . .	. . .	. . .	. . .	. . .	. . .	. . .
Scrap and waste	0.9	1.2	0.2	1.0	1.3	1.2	. . .	. . .	. . .	. . .	. . .	. . .
Used merchandise	0.1	0.3	. . .	. . .	. . .	0.1	. . .	. . .	. . .	0.7	. . .	. . .
Goods imported and returned unchanged	. . .	. . .	. . .	. . .	. . .	. . .	. . .	. . .	. . .	. . .	. . .	. . .
Special classification provisions	. . .	0.2	0.2	0.1	. . .	0.2	. . .	. . .	. . .	. . .	. . .	0.5

Industry	The Netherlands						Asian 10					
	1994	1995	1996	1997	1998	1999	1994	1995	1996	1997	1998	1999
ALL GOODS	56.7	60.3	114.3	132.6	121.2	117.2	1 109.8	1 478.6	1 605.4	1 816.8	1 719.0	1 676.4
Manufactured Goods	54.3	51.4	96.5	101.0	91.3	91.3	1 089.1	1 416.3	1 552.5	1 791.6	1 708.7	1 651.5
Food products	2.4	3.7	1.4	2.6	3.2	3.6	38.7	84.4	81.3	93.6	77.9	80.7
Tobacco products	. . .	. . .	0.5	. . .	0.7	. . .	546.6	708.1	654.9	638.9	611.0	659.0
Textile mill products	0.1	0.1	. . .	. . .	. . .	. . .	6.4	5.2	0.8	5.2	12.4	12.9
Apparel	0.9	0.4	0.3	0.1	0.3	0.2	11.3	13.5	40.6	118.2	183.2	9.2
Lumber and wood products	1.9	1.5	1.3	1.2	0.7	0.4	5.0	5.6	5.2	3.2	2.3	2.7
Furniture and fixtures	. . .	0.1	. . .	0.1	0.3	0.2	0.8	0.5	3.1	4.5	2.9	1.5
Paper products	. . .	0.1	0.1	0.1	0.4	0.3	8.2	5.3	9.2	8.4	9.3	7.9
Printing and publishing	0.1	0.2	0.4	0.3	0.2	0.2	4.7	5.5	5.6	5.2	3.1	4.7
Chemical products	2.5	4.6	18.0	22.9	25.5	24.9	22.3	44.1	67.1	44.8	43.3	45.0
Refined petroleum products	0.2	0.1	0.4	0.4	0.3	0.2	1.4	1.3	1.3	0.3	0.3	0.1
Rubber and plastic products	0.5	0.8	1.6	1.4	0.7	0.5	5.3	6.2	9.5	16.6	16.3	17.4
Leather products	0.1	. . .	0.2	. . .	. . .	. . .	1.3	1.6	6.4	3.0	2.3	49.6
Stone, clay and glass products	0.6	0.4	0.3	0.2	0.2	2.3	32.8	30.1	47.9	73.1	56.0	76.9
Primary metals	0.4	1.5	0.8	1.4	1.9	1.1	37.4	90.7	102.5	37.7	16.8	9.5
Fabricated metal products	0.6	0.6	0.4	0.6	1.2	2.0	10.1	13.8	9.1	12.2	11.1	15.7
Industrial machinery and computers	30.0	22.5	33.4	24.6	22.6	28.4	81.2	104.5	138.1	156.5	122.2	120.3
Electric and electronic equipment	5.6	6.6	7.4	7.1	6.7	5.0	83.1	114.2	115.5	147.0	115.5	91.1
Transportation equipment	6.9	6.5	10.2	13.8	23.2	20.9	163.3	154.6	221.9	384.3	372.9	414.6
Scientific and measuring instruments	1.1	0.9	18.9	23.8	2.8	0.4	14.9	13.9	18.6	22.5	38.4	23.4
Miscellaneous manufactures	0.3	0.6	0.5	0.4	0.4	0.5	13.3	10.6	13.6	15.5	10.5	7.4
Unidentified manufactures	0.1	0.2	0.3	0.3	0.1	0.1	1.2	1.1	1.1	1.2	1.1	1.9
Agricultural And Livestock Products	1.2	2.6	0.1	. . .	. . .	. . .	6.0	35.5	10.3	11.9	7.7	20.0
Agricultural products	1.2	2.6	0.1	. . .	. . .	. . .	0.7	2.0	2.4	2.4	3.4	13.0
Livestock and livestock products	. . .	. . .	. . .	. . .	. . .	. . .	5.3	33.5	7.8	9.5	4.3	7.0
Other Commodities	1.3	6.3	17.8	31.6	30.0	25.8	14.6	26.8	42.7	13.2	2.6	4.9
Forestry products	. . .	. . .	. . .	. . .	. . .	. . .	. . .	0.3	. . .	0.1	. . .	. . .
Fish and other marine products	. . .	. . .	. . .	. . .	. . .	. . .	. . .	. . .	. . .	0.6	0.1	. . .
Metallic ores and concentrates	. . .	. . .	. . .	. . .	. . .	. . .	. . .	. . .	. . .	. . .	. . .	. . .
Bituminous coal and lignite	1.2	6.3	17.8	31.6	29.9	25.7	11.6	22.0	39.1	8.7	. . .	. . .
Crude petroleum and natural gas	. . .	. . .	. . .	. . .	. . .	0.1	0.2	. . .	0.1	. . .	. . .	. . .
Nonmetallic materials	0.1	. . .	. . .	. . .	. . .	. . .	2.1	2.0	2.6	2.3	1.4	0.6
Scrap and waste	. . .	. . .	. . .	. . .	. . .	. . .	0.3	2.3	0.6	0.7	0.1	0.1
Used merchandise	. . .	. . .	. . .	. . .	. . .	. . .	0.1	0.1	0.1	. . .	0.1	2.9
Goods imported and returned unchanged	. . .	. . .	. . .	. . .	. . .	. . .	. . .	. . .	. . .	. . .	. . .	. . .
Special classification provisions	. . .	. . .	. . .	. . .	. . .	. . .	0.3	0.3	0.2	0.8	0.9	1.2

Table D-20. KENTUCKY: State Exports of Goods by Destination and Industry, 1994–1999—Continued

(Millions of dollars.)

Industry	Japan						South Korea					
	1994	1995	1996	1997	1998	1999	1994	1995	1996	1997	1998	1999
ALL GOODS	752.3	1 041.8	1 143.0	1 385.0	1 436.1	1 372.2	72.2	107.0	116.1	99.6	45.1	72.7
Manufactured Goods	736.7	985.8	1 105.0	1 368.7	1 429.6	1 363.1	70.5	106.8	116.0	98.7	44.8	72.3
Food products	24.8	30.8	25.1	33.2	33.9	32.1	4.2	11.8	19.5	17.9	16.9	18.9
Tobacco products	383.7	563.7	529.2	537.8	554.4	631.8	11.5	21.4	19.3	19.5	8.9	8.1
Textile mill products	5.2	4.5	0.4	4.9	11.3	11.1	0.1	0.1	0.1	0.1	0.1	0.1
Apparel	10.6	12.7	40.0	117.5	182.5	9.0	...	0.1	...	0.2	...	...
Lumber and wood products	2.7	3.8	2.4	0.6	1.3	0.6	0.3	0.2	0.3	0.6	0.1	0.2
Furniture and fixtures	0.4	0.2	2.9	4.1	2.3	0.5	...	...	...	...	...	0.5
Paper products	6.5	3.8	7.0	6.9	6.5	5.5	0.1	0.1	0.3	0.2	0.1	0.3
Printing and publishing	1.3	0.9	0.8	1.1	0.8	1.7	0.7	1.2	0.8	1.0	0.5	0.4
Chemical products	13.1	20.4	25.2	27.7	27.0	24.5	1.5	2.2	6.0	3.9	1.9	3.9
Refined petroleum products	0.7	0.8	0.6	0.1	0.2	...	0.1	...	...	...	...	...
Rubber and plastic products	3.0	3.5	6.3	8.6	5.4	4.9	0.5	0.9	1.0	4.2	4.8	6.5
Leather products	0.1	0.8	2.3	0.9	0.1	47.6	0.3	0.4	0.1	...	...	...
Stone, clay and glass products	31.5	28.3	43.0	70.8	54.5	73.0	0.6	0.6	2.1	0.7	0.2	2.4
Primary metals	26.9	64.0	88.9	12.3	7.3	2.4	2.2	14.0	2.3	6.6	1.1	0.9
Fabricated metal products	2.2	7.5	4.3	6.0	7.5	9.9	0.8	2.1	1.1	1.6	0.4	0.5
Industrial machinery and computers	37.8	49.4	58.0	56.0	73.0	53.4	12.2	18.5	31.0	25.8	7.2	13.6
Electric and electronic equipment	26.9	43.0	43.3	94.2	80.5	49.4	23.8	25.5	21.1	5.5	0.6	11.6
Transportation equipment	148.5	138.6	209.4	366.1	347.2	386.4	6.3	3.5	6.3	5.5	0.8	2.9
Scientific and measuring instruments	7.8	6.3	10.9	13.3	30.8	16.1	1.8	2.8	1.9	2.3	1.0	0.8
Miscellaneous manufactures	2.5	2.2	4.5	6.0	2.5	2.2	3.3	1.3	2.6	3.1	0.3	0.5
Unidentified manufactures	0.5	0.6	0.4	0.6	0.5	1.0	0.3	0.1	0.1	0.2	0.1	0.3
Agricultural And Livestock Products	3.7	33.6	8.7	10.9	5.5	8.3	1.3	0.1	...	...	0.2	0.3
Agricultural products	...	0.2	0.9	1.5	1.4	1.7	...	...	...	...	...	...
Livestock and livestock products	3.7	33.4	7.8	9.4	4.1	6.6	1.2	0.1	...	...	0.2	0.3
Other Commodities	11.9	22.5	29.3	5.4	1.0	0.8	0.4	...	0.1	0.8	0.1	0.1
Forestry products	...	...	...	...	...	...	...	...	...	...	...	...
Fish and other marine products	...	...	...	0.3	...	...	...	...	...	0.3	...	...
Metallic ores and concentrates	...	...	...	...	...	...	...	...	...	...	...	...
Bituminous coal and lignite	11.6	22.0	28.7	4.4	...	...	...	...	...	...	...	...
Crude petroleum and natural gas	0.1	...	...	...	...	...	0.1	...	...	...	...	...
Nonmetallic materials	...	0.1	0.3	0.4	0.3	0.3	...	...	0.1	0.1	0.1	...
Scrap and waste	0.1	0.1	...	...	...	...	...	...	...	0.4	...	...
Used merchandise	0.1	...	...	...	...	...	...	...	...	...	...	...
Goods imported and returned unchanged	...	...	...	...	...	...	...	...	...	...	...	...
Special classification provisions	...	0.2	0.2	0.2	0.6	0.4	0.3	...	...	...	...	0.1

Industry	Taiwan						Singapore					
	1994	1995	1996	1997	1998	1999	1994	1995	1996	1997	1998	1999
ALL GOODS	38.6	53.6	66.5	58.2	40.7	42.7	90.3	88.6	96.0	91.6	57.6	35.9
Manufactured Goods	36.3	50.0	52.6	55.7	37.9	35.9	90.3	88.6	96.0	91.5	57.5	35.7
Food products	3.8	23.4	15.3	20.0	9.3	10.2	1.0	1.7	2.2	1.4	1.1	1.6
Tobacco products	2.3	0.9	1.8	1.0	1.4	0.9	64.5	56.6	59.4	38.4	28.7	10.8
Textile mill products	...	...	...	...	0.2	...	...	...	...	...	...	0.1
Apparel	0.1	...	...	...	0.2	0.1	0.2	...	0.1	0.1	0.1	0.1
Lumber and wood products	0.1	0.4	0.7	1.1	0.2	0.6	...	...	...	...	...	...
Furniture and fixtures	...	...	...	...	...	...	...	0.3	0.1	0.2	0.1	0.1
Paper products	0.1	0.1	0.1	...	0.1	0.3	0.3	0.5	0.2	0.3	0.2	0.3
Printing and publishing	1.0	0.6	0.5	0.5	0.4	1.5	1.0	2.2	1.5	1.6	0.9	0.5
Chemical products	3.6	4.2	3.8	4.5	4.4	4.7	1.5	3.3	4.3	3.9	1.9	1.2
Refined petroleum products	...	...	0.1	...	...	...	...	...	...	...	...	...
Rubber and plastic products	0.2	0.1	0.3	0.3	0.6	0.5	0.8	0.7	0.5	0.3	0.3	0.8
Leather products	...	0.3	1.1	0.1	0.1	...	0.1	0.4	0.5	0.3	0.1	...
Stone, clay and glass products	0.1	0.2	0.3	0.3	0.5	0.3	...	...	0.2	...	0.1	...
Primary metals	3.4	5.6	3.4	6.5	1.4	...	0.4	0.4	0.3	5.2	1.3	1.1
Fabricated metal products	0.4	0.3	0.6	0.5	0.4	1.2	1.1	0.7	1.1	0.8	0.4	0.5
Industrial machinery and computers	1.9	5.1	10.1	10.0	6.9	7.2	8.3	8.7	11.4	20.2	11.0	9.3
Electric and electronic equipment	12.0	6.0	10.5	8.8	8.4	6.8	5.8	6.0	7.1	8.6	4.5	3.1
Transportation equipment	3.3	0.8	1.3	0.7	1.0	0.2	0.8	2.4	2.9	4.1	2.4	2.8
Scientific and measuring instruments	0.8	0.4	1.3	0.6	1.1	0.8	1.9	2.2	2.0	3.1	2.4	1.8
Miscellaneous manufactures	3.1	1.6	1.4	0.6	1.2	0.6	2.4	2.3	2.2	2.7	1.7	1.2
Unidentified manufactures	0.1	0.1	...	0.1	0.1	0.1	0.1	0.1	0.1	0.1	0.1	...
Agricultural And Livestock Products	...	1.7	1.4	0.7	2.0	6.5	...	...	...	...	...	...
Agricultural products	...	1.7	1.4	0.7	2.0	6.5	...	...	...	...	...	...
Livestock and livestock products	...	...	...	...	...	...	...	...	...	...	...	...
Other Commodities	2.2	1.9	12.6	1.8	0.8	0.3	...	...	...	...	0.1	0.2
Forestry products	...	...	...	...	0.1	...	...	...	...	...	...	...
Fish and other marine products	...	...	...	...	0.1	...	...	...	...	...	...	...
Metallic ores and concentrates	...	...	...	...	...	...	...	...	...	...	...	...
Bituminous coal and lignite	...	...	10.4	...	...	...	...	...	...	...	...	...
Crude petroleum and natural gas	...	...	...	...	...	...	...	...	...	...	...	...
Nonmetallic materials	2.0	1.8	2.1	1.6	0.7	...	...	...	...	...	...	...
Scrap and waste	0.2	0.1	...	...	...	...	...	...	...	...	...	...
Used merchandise	...	...	...	...	...	...	...	...	...	...	...	...
Goods imported and returned unchanged	...	...	...	...	...	...	...	...	...	...	0.1	0.2
Special classification provisions	...	...	...	...	...	0.1	...	...	...	...	...	...

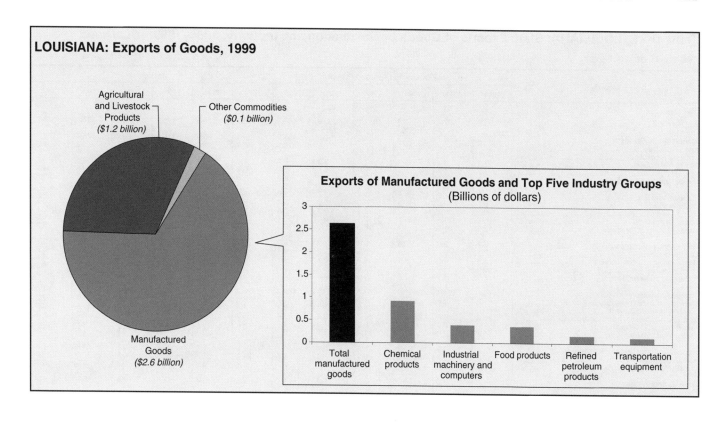

LOUISIANA: Exports of Goods, 1999

Agricultural and Livestock Products ($1.2 billion)

Other Commodities ($0.1 billion)

Manufactured Goods ($2.6 billion)

Exports of Manufactured Goods and Top Five Industry Groups
(Billions of dollars)

Total manufactured goods | Chemical products | Industrial machinery and computers | Food products | Refined petroleum products | Transportation equipment

Table D-21. LOUISIANA: State Exports of Goods by Destination and Industry, 1994–1999

(Millions of dollars.)

Industry	All destinations						Canada					
	1994	1995	1996	1997	1998	1999	1994	1995	1996	1997	1998	1999
ALL GOODS	3 576.9	4 580.7	4 730.8	4 373.5	4 391.9	3 947.3	449.1	557.4	542.9	663.1	735.9	745.0
Manufactured Goods	2 464.6	2 953.5	2 613.6	2 730.5	2 970.4	2 622.4	419.9	518.1	512.3	601.7	680.6	702.5
Food products	459.2	559.3	344.9	361.2	480.2	368.3	15.4	26.9	25.4	36.1	45.4	35.1
Tobacco products	...	10.6	...	...	...	0.1	...	...	...	...	...	...
Textile mill products	22.1	20.7	20.8	24.9	23.9	24.4	7.8	6.2	6.6	7.3	5.8	4.9
Apparel	3.9	4.9	11.7	17.2	31.9	44.3	0.4	0.5	0.2	1.3	2.4	8.1
Lumber and wood products	46.0	37.4	40.4	30.7	31.3	30.3	4.6	3.5	5.2	5.0	3.3	5.0
Furniture and fixtures	9.3	4.7	4.2	6.2	6.4	4.7	0.2	0.5	0.7	1.0	0.7	0.6
Paper products	120.9	186.2	141.8	100.9	77.1	70.2	21.8	26.8	22.2	24.6	18.9	21.4
Printing and publishing	1.5	6.1	2.1	2.3	2.5	3.1	0.4	0.9	0.7	0.7	0.6	0.7
Chemical products	642.6	827.4	813.2	839.1	856.6	923.0	227.9	254.8	265.5	305.4	354.1	332.3
Refined petroleum products	92.6	146.6	158.6	133.4	71.0	165.7	8.6	15.9	17.9	23.9	21.5	39.3
Rubber and plastic products	40.7	35.6	39.7	50.9	59.7	51.1	6.1	7.7	9.5	10.0	13.9	12.0
Leather products	3.4	1.6	1.0	4.5	7.0	6.8	0.1	0.1	0.1	0.2	0.2	0.3
Stone, clay and glass products	13.8	17.9	20.1	12.5	17.3	17.5	0.6	1.0	2.3	1.1	1.9	4.7
Primary metals	73.0	180.9	88.4	152.2	139.5	71.4	18.2	30.0	26.5	35.5	39.6	34.1
Fabricated metal products	67.6	57.7	78.2	89.5	88.6	75.8	12.4	16.9	13.7	18.0	30.5	30.3
Industrial machinery and computers	498.7	466.8	480.0	520.1	519.9	397.9	47.6	52.1	46.8	57.8	75.6	79.7
Electric and electronic equipment	118.0	128.1	131.9	145.9	107.8	120.9	18.0	43.8	40.6	40.0	27.5	41.5
Transportation equipment	140.5	137.2	106.9	105.4	319.8	128.1	6.1	9.4	4.6	8.2	8.9	26.0
Scientific and measuring instruments	95.2	103.7	116.7	113.7	111.9	97.7	21.0	18.9	21.7	23.5	25.7	23.6
Miscellaneous manufactures	10.7	13.2	8.1	15.2	8.7	9.8	1.7	1.1	0.8	1.0	2.6	1.3
Unidentified manufactures	5.1	6.9	4.6	4.7	9.1	11.3	1.0	1.2	1.4	1.4	1.5	1.8
Agricultural And Livestock Products	1 027.6	1 508.6	2 002.6	1 510.8	1 334.8	1 233.1	7.0	5.8	5.6	7.4	8.0	6.0
Agricultural products	1 023.3	1 501.3	1 992.8	1 497.4	1 327.1	1 228.5	6.9	5.7	5.4	6.9	7.5	5.8
Livestock and livestock products	4.3	7.3	9.8	13.4	7.6	4.6	0.1	0.1	0.2	0.5	0.5	0.2
Other Commodities	84.7	118.7	114.6	132.1	86.7	91.8	22.2	33.4	25.0	53.9	47.4	36.4
Forestry products	...	0.1	0.1	0.5	0.2	0.7	...	0.1	...	...	...	...
Fish and other marine products	26.0	24.9	20.2	26.2	18.4	23.0	6.7	9.3	8.4	10.2	9.6	11.1
Metallic ores and concentrates	2.0	0.6	0.7	...	0.1	0.2	2.0	0.2	0.6	...	...	...
Bituminous coal and lignite	22.2	34.8	35.9	37.3	10.8	15.0	...	...	...	...	0.9	...
Crude petroleum and natural gas	3.8	0.6	2.5	21.7	19.2	14.7	...	...	2.0	20.6	15.9	13.9
Nonmetallic minerals	4.4	10.5	9.0	12.0	13.0	15.3	1.9	1.2	0.7	1.4	3.9	0.7
Scrap and waste	8.6	17.7	10.0	5.8	5.1	5.9	3.0	0.7	0.4	1.3	1.9	1.3
Used merchandise	8.6	8.3	21.7	7.4	3.1	3.7	1.1	2.1	1.1	1.6	0.1	0.4
Goods imported and returned unchanged	7.3	19.0	10.8	18.4	14.5	8.6	7.3	19.0	10.8	18.4	14.5	8.6
Special classification provisions	1.7	2.1	3.7	2.8	2.4	4.7	0.2	0.7	1.0	0.4	0.5	0.6

Table D-21. LOUISIANA: State Exports of Goods by Destination and Industry, 1994–1999—*Continued*

(Millions of dollars.)

Industry	South and Central American and Caribbean						Mexico					
	1994	1995	1996	1997	1998	1999	1994	1995	1996	1997	1998	1999
ALL GOODS	391.8	537.4	517.6	597.1	799.9	463.6	108.9	79.8	145.5	132.6	196.1	246.2
Manufactured Goods	374.9	522.7	468.5	562.3	790.5	454.2	82.4	69.9	116.9	128.7	175.4	221.3
Food products	32.0	50.8	40.1	52.7	62.6	73.7	6.6	12.8	5.0	10.7	5.2	19.8
Tobacco products	...	...	...	...	...	...	...	...	...	...	...	...
Textile mill products	7.2	7.4	7.2	7.8	9.9	9.7	1.2	0.7	2.9	3.1	3.5	5.8
Apparel	1.7	1.7	1.4	2.9	16.4	19.9	0.7	0.4	5.1	11.9	12.0	14.1
Lumber and wood products	4.0	3.5	5.5	7.1	6.9	5.6	1.5	0.2	0.1	1.1	5.2	5.6
Furniture and fixtures	4.0	2.2	1.5	2.9	2.7	2.0	4.3	0.6	0.1	0.4	1.3	0.3
Paper products	8.2	17.0	10.3	8.0	10.0	8.4	8.2	5.8	10.0	8.9	16.8	20.7
Printing and publishing	0.3	0.3	0.7	0.3	0.3	0.4	0.1	0.1	0.2	0.1	0.6	0.1
Chemical products	68.8	131.6	131.7	119.1	116.2	97.4	13.4	13.5	20.9	32.2	33.6	52.0
Refined petroleum products	19.1	31.1	34.1	16.3	16.1	12.3	0.5	0.4	0.4	0.5	1.0	0.2
Rubber and plastic products	7.2	9.0	10.5	10.3	12.1	9.8	2.9	2.7	3.6	5.4	6.2	5.5
Leather products	0.1	...	0.1	0.3	0.2	0.4	...	...	...	0.1	0.2	0.2
Stone, clay and glass products	3.4	5.1	4.4	4.9	3.7	4.7	4.0	1.0	2.6	1.8	7.7	5.1
Primary metals	16.5	48.1	15.9	81.9	68.5	12.3	1.7	2.8	4.1	6.8	11.4	6.3
Fabricated metal products	11.5	14.4	17.4	24.6	23.8	16.8	3.2	2.0	3.8	3.3	3.7	2.3
Industrial machinery and computers	116.1	124.7	119.6	150.8	173.8	120.0	20.2	14.1	19.6	16.0	29.9	51.9
Electric and electronic equipment	15.3	12.8	18.2	17.0	21.6	13.4	4.5	4.7	6.5	8.0	10.0	11.2
Transportation equipment	40.8	42.8	31.1	35.3	224.7	29.4	4.5	3.2	24.2	4.9	16.5	9.2
Scientific and measuring instruments	16.2	16.4	15.5	18.2	16.8	13.4	3.9	4.5	7.3	12.3	8.3	6.4
Miscellaneous manufactures	1.2	0.8	1.4	0.9	1.3	1.7	0.6	0.1	0.2	0.5	0.6	1.1
Unidentified manufactures	1.6	2.8	1.7	1.2	2.9	2.7	0.4	0.3	0.3	0.5	1.6	3.3
Agricultural And Livestock Products	12.6	10.9	30.2	28.8	5.4	4.7	24.3	5.7	20.7	1.3	14.8	18.6
Agricultural products	12.5	10.7	30.1	28.5	5.3	4.7	24.1	5.7	20.4	0.5	13.9	18.3
Livestock and livestock products	...	0.2	...	0.3	0.2	...	0.2	0.1	0.3	0.8	0.9	0.3
Other Commodities	4.4	3.8	18.9	6.1	4.0	4.7	2.2	4.2	7.9	2.5	5.9	6.3
Forestry products	...	...	...	...	...	0.1	...	...	...	...	0.1	0.3
Fish and other marine products	...	...	0.2	...	0.1	0.1	...	...	0.1	0.1	0.1	0.1
Metallic ores and concentrates	...	...	...	...	...	0.2	...	...	0.1	...	...	...
Bituminous coal and lignite	...	...	...	...	...	...	...	...	...	...	...	...
Crude petroleum and natural gas	2.6	0.5	0.4	0.2	0.3	0.3	1.2	...	...	0.8	2.9	0.1
Nonmetallic minerals	0.9	1.9	3.8	3.2	2.8	2.3	...	...	...	0.2	0.3	3.8
Scrap and waste	0.2	0.3	0.5	0.9	0.1	...	0.6	3.9	7.6	1.4	2.4	1.9
Used merchandise	0.3	0.9	13.7	1.6	0.5	0.3	0.4	0.1	...	...	...	...
Goods imported and returned unchanged	...	...	...	...	...	...	...	...	...	...	...	...
Special classification provisions	0.3	0.2	0.3	0.2	0.3	1.3	...	...	...	...	...	0.1

Industry	European Union						United Kingdom					
	1994	1995	1996	1997	1998	1999	1994	1995	1996	1997	1998	1999
ALL GOODS	785.6	1 072.2	976.6	841.6	711.3	525.3	73.0	113.6	97.2	97.9	108.8	96.0
Manufactured Goods	589.8	811.8	621.0	551.6	494.7	432.0	72.5	112.9	96.0	96.3	107.9	94.2
Food products	216.1	277.6	112.9	73.4	68.9	63.6	12.5	12.8	4.8	4.7	5.1	10.9
Tobacco products	...	10.5	...	...	...	...	...	...	...	...	...	...
Textile mill products	0.7	1.2	1.0	2.7	1.8	2.0	0.4	0.5	0.3	1.3	1.0	0.7
Apparel	0.4	0.7	0.3	0.5	0.2	0.7	...	0.1	...	0.3	0.1	0.1
Lumber and wood products	8.1	8.8	9.3	10.7	11.6	10.5	0.2	0.3	0.3	0.3	0.8	0.8
Furniture and fixtures	0.1	0.8	1.2	0.7	0.6	0.9	...	0.1	...	0.1	0.2	0.4
Paper products	43.2	72.3	56.1	37.1	22.3	15.3	14.6	15.0	16.1	8.3	8.4	4.5
Printing and publishing	0.5	3.6	0.2	0.6	0.5	0.5	0.2	1.9	0.1	0.2	0.2	0.2
Chemical products	160.9	196.9	214.4	186.6	185.8	179.3	13.5	23.5	20.4	24.8	27.9	31.5
Refined petroleum products	16.6	28.0	27.7	22.4	2.7	13.2	3.0	10.2	9.2	4.3	1.2	5.9
Rubber and plastic products	6.2	7.7	8.1	17.5	20.2	17.1	0.9	2.1	1.6	2.9	7.5	4.7
Leather products	2.6	0.9	0.6	3.9	5.6	5.6	...	...	...	...	0.3	0.4
Stone, clay and glass products	2.2	5.2	4.2	0.1	0.9	1.3	...	0.4	0.1	...	0.3	0.4
Primary metals	5.7	22.4	17.0	5.6	8.5	4.5	1.2	1.2	1.8	2.9	5.2	1.8
Fabricated metal products	7.9	6.4	6.6	8.6	9.8	12.2	3.0	2.3	2.1	4.1	3.4	4.7
Industrial machinery and computers	63.7	105.1	98.3	102.8	73.8	42.0	13.0	25.0	23.6	24.0	23.4	13.6
Electric and electronic equipment	25.6	21.4	26.7	26.8	20.2	20.2	2.5	4.0	3.4	5.9	2.9	3.3
Transportation equipment	4.5	8.1	5.9	17.5	28.7	12.9	1.9	4.3	1.7	3.5	6.4	2.7
Scientific and measuring instruments	21.9	27.6	28.4	24.3	29.2	25.9	5.4	8.2	10.3	8.4	13.4	7.4
Miscellaneous manufactures	2.2	5.9	1.8	9.6	2.0	3.4	...	0.9	0.1	0.1	0.3	0.4
Unidentified manufactures	0.4	0.6	0.2	0.3	1.4	1.0	0.1	0.2	0.1	0.1	0.4	0.4
Agricultural And Livestock Products	150.8	198.1	307.2	234.8	199.5	67.5	0.2	0.1	0.3	...	...	0.1
Agricultural products	149.8	195.6	305.4	232.9	198.5	66.5	0.1	0.1	0.2	...	...	0.1
Livestock and livestock products	1.0	2.5	1.8	1.9	1.0	1.0	0.1	0.1	...	...	...	...
Other Commodities	45.0	62.3	48.4	55.2	17.1	25.7	0.3	0.6	0.9	1.6	0.9	1.7
Forestry products	...	...	...	...	0.5	0.1	...	...	...	...	...	...
Fish and other marine products	14.7	9.6	5.5	10.6	2.9	2.4	...	...	...	...	...	0.1
Metallic ores and concentrates	...	0.3	...	...	...	...	...	...	...	...	...	...
Bituminous coal and lignite	22.2	33.1	35.8	37.3	9.9	15.0	...	...	...	...	...	...
Crude petroleum and natural gas	...	...	...	...	...	0.1	...	...	...	...	...	...
Nonmetallic minerals	0.9	4.5	2.1	2.2	2.0	3.6	...	0.1	...	0.1	...	0.3
Scrap and waste	4.8	12.4	1.2	2.1	0.2	0.8	...	0.1	...	0.6	...	...
Used merchandise	2.3	2.2	2.6	2.3	1.4	2.0	0.2	0.2	0.8	0.6	0.7	0.8
Goods imported and returned unchanged	...	...	...	...	...	...	...	...	...	...	...	...
Special classification provisions	0.1	0.3	1.2	0.3	0.5	1.7	0.1	0.2	0.1	0.2	0.3	0.5

Table D-21. LOUISIANA: State Exports of Goods by Destination and Industry, 1994–1999—*Continued*

(Millions of dollars.)

Industry	Germany						France					
	1994	1995	1996	1997	1998	1999	1994	1995	1996	1997	1998	1999
ALL GOODS	70.4	63.6	122.1	90.1	71.3	67.4	82.4	110.9	60.2	65.1	44.1	28.2
Manufactured Goods	37.8	49.9	52.1	58.4	56.3	50.9	68.7	92.1	58.5	46.2	33.8	27.3
Food products	2.7	2.9	2.5	2.0	5.2	6.8	44.7	54.0	24.1	8.0	7.0	5.5
Tobacco products	...	...	...	...	...	...	...	...	...	...	...	...
Textile mill products	...	...	...	...	0.1	...	...	...	0.1	0.4	0.1	...
Apparel	...	...	0.1	0.1	...	...	0.1	0.1	...	...	...	0.4
Lumber and wood products	1.4	1.4	1.7	1.2	0.9	1.3	0.9	1.0	0.6	0.4	0.5	0.4
Furniture and fixtures	...	...	0.9	0.3	0.1	0.1	...	0.5	...	0.1	0.1	...
Paper products	4.7	6.6	8.4	7.5	6.8	8.1	0.8	1.1	1.9	4.3	0.8	...
Printing and publishing	0.1	0.2	...	...	...	...	...	...	1.3	0.1	0.2	0.1
Chemical products	2.3	7.9	4.6	11.3	19.2	10.7	4.5	9.6	9.8	4.7	5.4	6.3
Refined petroleum products	0.1	1.9	3.2	3.3	...	3.3	1.5	...	3.5	1.3	...	...
Rubber and plastic products	0.1	0.1	0.1	0.1	0.1	0.7	0.1	0.1	0.1	0.4	0.2	0.2
Leather products	...	...	...	...	...	...	1.3	0.9	0.1	2.9	4.2	3.8
Stone, clay and glass products	...	0.1	...	...	...	...	...	...	0.1	...	...	...
Primary metals	1.0	2.1	0.8	0.6	0.8	0.9	0.4	0.6	1.9	0.4	0.4	0.3
Fabricated metal products	0.8	0.8	0.8	0.8	0.9	0.8	0.1	0.2	0.7	0.2	0.5	1.2
Industrial machinery and computers	17.5	20.2	23.2	23.4	12.4	10.3	8.3	11.3	8.4	8.8	7.2	1.8
Electric and electronic equipment	4.2	2.8	3.5	1.4	2.3	2.7	4.0	6.2	4.2	3.8	3.8	3.1
Transportation equipment	0.6	1.2	1.2	5.3	6.5	4.0	0.8	0.8	0.9	0.5	1.1	0.3
Scientific and measuring instruments	1.8	1.0	0.6	0.9	0.6	0.7	0.5	1.0	1.6	0.9	1.6	3.5
Miscellaneous manufactures	0.2	0.5	0.5	0.2	0.1	0.2	0.8	3.2	0.4	8.8	0.4	0.2
Unidentified manufactures	0.1	0.1	...	0.1	0.1	0.1	...	0.1	0.1	0.1	0.1	...
Agricultural And Livestock Products	31.4	13.5	69.8	31.4	14.7	15.2	12.9	18.3	1.4	18.7	10.1	0.1
Agricultural products	31.3	12.5	69.7	31.1	14.5	15.1	12.8	18.2	1.3	18.5	10.0	...
Livestock and livestock products	0.1	1.1	0.1	0.3	0.2	0.1	0.1	0.2	0.2	0.2	...	0.1
Other Commodities	1.2	0.2	0.2	0.3	0.3	1.4	0.7	0.5	0.3	0.1	0.3	0.8
Forestry products	...	...	...	...	...	...	...	...	...	...	...	...
Fish and other marine products	...	...	...	...	...	...	0.1	0.1	...	...	...	0.2
Metallic ores and concentrates	...	...	...	...	...	...	...	...	...	...	...	...
Bituminous coal and lignite	...	...	...	...	...	...	...	...	...	...	...	...
Crude petroleum and natural gas	...	...	...	...	...	...	...	...	...	...	...	...
Nonmetallic minerals	0.8	...	...	...	...	0.5	...	...	...	...	...	...
Scrap and waste	...	...	...	...	0.1	0.3	...	...	...	...	...	...
Used merchandise	0.4	0.2	0.2	0.2	0.1	0.5	0.7	0.3	0.3	0.1	0.2	0.5
Goods imported and returned unchanged	...	...	...	...	...	...	...	...	...	...	...	...
Special classification provisions	...	...	0.1	0.1	0.1	0.1	...	...	...	...	0.1	...

Industry	The Netherlands						Asian 10					
	1994	1995	1996	1997	1998	1999	1994	1995	1996	1997	1998	1999
ALL GOODS	155.8	288.6	226.8	180.0	141.8	102.3	1 272.7	1 701.7	1 978.3	1 568.4	1 398.9	1 360.7
Manufactured Goods	153.4	247.5	199.2	150.3	123.2	99.8	530.2	565.4	426.0	405.9	381.0	383.1
Food products	75.5	108.9	48.3	45.3	42.2	26.1	64.6	86.6	52.1	61.7	138.4	67.3
Tobacco products	...	...	...	...	...	...	...	...	...	...	...	...
Textile mill products	...	...	...	0.3	...	0.4	3.7	3.7	1.7	2.1	1.4	0.6
Apparel	...	0.2	0.1	0.1	...	0.1	0.4	1.1	4.3	0.2	0.3	0.2
Lumber and wood products	0.4	0.8	1.5	1.4	1.3	0.7	24.4	20.2	19.1	5.4	2.3	2.8
Furniture and fixtures	...	0.1	0.1	...	...	...	0.2	0.2	0.2	0.4	0.7	0.6
Paper products	8.2	26.9	19.1	5.8	2.5	1.3	17.7	26.9	27.4	11.6	0.9	1.7
Printing and publishing	...	0.2	...	...	...	...	0.2	...	0.8	0.3	0.4	0.6
Chemical products	39.6	53.7	87.0	55.1	42.5	38.8	126.8	174.2	126.3	147.2	121.2	209.9
Refined petroleum products	2.1	2.6	3.9	4.2	0.3	2.6	14.0	17.9	7.2	2.6	1.9	4.0
Rubber and plastic products	4.5	4.5	5.5	12.2	5.4	5.7	15.3	5.5	4.5	4.0	2.5	3.7
Leather products	...	...	...	...	...	0.1	0.5	...	...	0.1	0.1	0.1
Stone, clay and glass products	2.0	4.1	0.1	...	...	0.1	1.3	0.6	2.6	2.6	1.8	0.8
Primary metals	0.5	2.1	0.9	1.0	0.5	0.1	22.3	65.7	16.2	11.8	2.9	4.3
Fabricated metal products	0.9	0.9	0.5	0.7	3.2	0.6	21.5	9.1	24.5	18.5	9.1	7.5
Industrial machinery and computers	6.2	25.0	15.5	8.8	9.5	6.1	128.6	84.3	73.5	74.1	56.4	34.5
Electric and electronic equipment	1.5	2.4	3.1	5.6	2.6	4.8	43.8	33.9	23.1	30.3	16.2	21.0
Transportation equipment	0.3	1.1	0.3	0.3	3.4	0.8	22.7	12.9	14.8	11.0	2.9	4.4
Scientific and measuring instruments	11.7	13.7	13.1	9.6	8.8	9.8	18.1	16.8	25.4	19.7	19.5	16.8
Miscellaneous manufactures	0.1	0.3	0.1	0.1	0.8	1.7	3.5	4.3	2.5	2.0	1.4	1.2
Unidentified manufactures	...	...	...	...	0.2	0.1	0.6	0.6	0.4	0.4	0.7	0.9
Agricultural And Livestock Products	1.6	24.9	24.6	25.8	16.5	0.2	733.8	1 127.7	1 543.4	1 155.3	1 010.6	966.1
Agricultural products	1.6	24.9	24.5	25.7	16.4	0.1	731.6	1 124.2	1 537.5	1 147.0	1 007.6	964.4
Livestock and livestock products	0.1	...	0.1	0.1	0.1	0.1	2.2	3.5	5.9	8.2	3.1	1.6
Other Commodities	0.7	16.2	2.9	3.8	2.1	2.3	8.7	8.6	9.0	7.3	7.2	11.5
Forestry products	...	...	...	0.4	...	...	...	...	...	...	...	...
Fish and other marine products	...	...	...	...	...	...	4.6	5.9	6.0	5.3	5.7	8.8
Metallic ores and concentrates	...	0.3	...	...	...	...	...	...	...	...	...	...
Bituminous coal and lignite	...	...	...	...	...	...	...	...	...	...	...	...
Crude petroleum and natural gas	...	...	...	...	...	...	...	...	...	0.1	0.1	0.3
Nonmetallic minerals	...	4.0	1.7	2.1	1.7	1.6	...	0.3	0.2	0.2	0.2	0.5
Scrap and waste	0.6	11.9	1.1	0.9	0.1	0.6	...	0.4	0.1	0.1	0.2	1.1
Used merchandise	0.1	0.1	0.2	0.4	0.3	0.1	3.5	1.5	2.1	1.0	0.3	0.4
Goods imported and returned unchanged	...	...	...	...	...	...	...	...	...	...	...	...
Special classification provisions	...	...	...	...	...	...	0.5	0.5	0.4	0.5	0.8	0.5

Table D-21. LOUISIANA: State Exports of Goods by Destination and Industry, 1994–1999—*Continued*

(Millions of dollars.)

Industry	Japan						South Korea					
	1994	1995	1996	1997	1998	1999	1994	1995	1996	1997	1998	1999
ALL GOODS	800.5	879.8	1 111.3	974.2	792.9	746.1	61.1	98.9	144.8	127.0	126.0	155.9
Manufactured Goods	90.4	110.7	111.1	127.7	90.9	95.4	49.5	84.3	54.1	56.7	32.3	58.5
Food products	12.6	13.7	33.8	43.4	31.7	14.2	2.1	2.0	3.3	3.8	3.8	12.3
Tobacco products	...	...	...	...	...	...	...	...	...	...	...	...
Textile mill products	0.7	0.4	0.9	0.5	0.5	0.3	...	0.1	...	0.1	0.1	0.1
Apparel	0.1	0.7	4.1	0.1	0.2	0.1	0.2	0.1	...	...	...	...
Lumber and wood products	2.0	2.1	3.3	3.5	1.9	2.2	18.9	16.5	7.3	0.4	...	...
Furniture and fixtures	...	...	...	0.1	0.2	...	...	...	...	...	...	...
Paper products	2.3	6.6	5.7	3.1	...	...	0.1	...	0.6	0.6	0.2	...
Printing and publishing	...	0.1	...	0.1	...	0.1	...	...	...	...	...	0.1
Chemical products	52.4	63.5	48.2	44.7	40.9	61.6	18.9	32.6	26.7	39.5	24.0	37.0
Refined petroleum products	1.5	0.1	0.2	...	...	1.4	2.6	2.8	1.3	0.1	...	...
Rubber and plastic products	0.7	0.8	1.2	2.3	1.0	0.8	0.3	0.7	0.7	0.6	0.1	0.1
Leather products	0.1	...	...	...	...	0.1	0.1	...	...	...	...	...
Stone, clay and glass products	0.6	...	0.1	0.3	0.7	0.2	0.1	...	...	...	0.5	0.1
Primary metals	3.1	4.1	...	4.9	0.5	0.2	0.2	19.8	0.2	0.4	0.5	0.4
Fabricated metal products	0.7	0.8	0.9	3.1	1.2	1.3	0.2	1.0	2.0	1.8	0.7	0.4
Industrial machinery and computers	4.8	3.8	3.2	11.0	4.0	3.0	2.5	2.5	4.8	2.9	0.8	4.9
Electric and electronic equipment	1.4	4.5	4.3	2.9	2.3	4.5	2.2	4.4	1.1	2.8	0.7	1.6
Transportation equipment	0.9	2.5	0.7	1.1	0.7	1.7	0.2	0.6	0.1	1.5	...	0.1
Scientific and measuring instruments	5.9	6.0	3.4	6.1	4.4	3.3	0.8	1.0	5.5	1.2	0.9	1.3
Miscellaneous manufactures	0.3	0.6	0.9	0.5	0.6	0.2	...	0.1	0.6	0.7	...	0.2
Unidentified manufactures	0.2	0.1	0.1	0.1	0.2	0.2	0.1	0.2	...	0.1	0.1	0.1
Agricultural And Livestock Products	708.3	767.9	997.6	845.0	701.4	649.9	11.4	14.4	90.7	70.3	93.7	97.3
Agricultural products	707.9	767.4	997.1	844.4	701.1	649.5	10.8	13.1	89.7	69.6	93.5	97.0
Livestock and livestock products	0.4	0.6	0.5	0.6	0.4	0.4	0.6	1.3	0.9	0.6	0.2	0.3
Other Commodities	1.8	1.2	2.7	1.5	0.6	0.8	0.1	0.2	0.1	...	...	0.2
Forestry products	...	...	...	...	...	...	...	...	...	...	...	...
Fish and other marine products	1.1	0.6	0.4	0.7	0.1	0.3	...	...	...	...	...	...
Metallic ores and concentrates	...	...	...	...	...	...	...	...	...	...	...	...
Bituminous coal and lignite	...	...	...	...	...	...	...	...	...	...	...	...
Crude petroleum and natural gas	...	...	...	...	...	...	...	...	...	...	...	...
Nonmetallic minerals	...	...	0.2	0.2	0.2	0.1	...	0.2	...	...	...	0.1
Scrap and waste	...	0.1	...	...	...	...	...	...	...	...	...	...
Used merchandise	0.4	0.3	2.0	0.6	0.3	0.4	...	...	...	...	...	...
Goods imported and returned unchanged	...	...	...	...	...	...	...	...	...	...	...	...
Special classification provisions	0.3	0.1	...	0.1	...	...	0.1	...	0.1	...	...	...

Industry	Taiwan						Singapore					
	1994	1995	1996	1997	1998	1999	1994	1995	1996	1997	1998	1999
ALL GOODS	50.2	247.3	324.3	173.4	172.4	189.3	47.9	37.8	51.8	45.6	48.8	43.9
Manufactured Goods	34.3	63.7	46.4	43.3	57.6	64.1	47.5	37.2	51.0	44.6	48.0	42.4
Food products	0.6	4.8	0.7	5.4	12.4	10.5	3.5	1.9	4.6	2.6	3.4	3.5
Tobacco products	...	...	...	...	...	...	...	...	...	...	...	...
Textile mill products	0.1	...	0.1	...	0.1	...	0.1	0.1	...	0.1	0.3	0.1
Apparel	...	0.2	...	...	...	...	...	...	0.1	...	...	...
Lumber and wood products	0.4	0.7	7.5	1.2	0.4	0.3	0.5	0.3	0.2	...	...	...
Furniture and fixtures	...	...	...	...	...	...	...	...	...	...	...	...
Paper products	...	0.8	2.0	0.1	...	0.6	0.3	0.5	0.5	0.8	0.2	...
Printing and publishing	...	0.2	0.1	0.2	0.3	0.3	...	...	...	...	...	...
Chemical products	20.9	40.2	20.3	22.8	30.5	40.6	12.1	12.7	9.4	8.3	6.8	18.3
Refined petroleum products	2.4	2.7	1.8	0.2	0.5	1.4	...	0.5	...	0.2	...	...
Rubber and plastic products	0.3	0.3	0.2	0.3	0.1	0.5	7.3	0.2	0.3	0.2	0.5	0.9
Leather products	...	...	...	...	...	...	0.2	...	...	...	0.1	...
Stone, clay and glass products	0.1	0.2	...	0.1	...	...	0.1	0.2	0.4	0.1	...	0.3
Primary metals	1.0	2.0	0.1	0.1	0.7	0.3	0.9	0.9	0.8	2.8	0.2	0.3
Fabricated metal products	0.6	0.7	2.0	0.4	2.6	1.3	1.1	0.8	2.0	2.3	1.8	1.8
Industrial machinery and computers	1.7	2.1	3.2	3.7	3.4	2.1	11.1	11.5	15.3	17.8	23.6	9.2
Electric and electronic equipment	0.8	1.3	1.3	1.1	0.5	1.1	4.4	4.1	6.1	5.3	4.4	4.2
Transportation equipment	2.1	3.5	3.0	3.0	0.8	0.1	4.1	1.2	2.4	0.3	0.3	0.9
Scientific and measuring instruments	3.1	3.8	4.0	4.6	5.0	4.7	1.6	1.9	8.7	3.8	6.0	2.3
Miscellaneous manufactures	...	...	...	...	...	...	0.2	0.1	0.1	0.1	0.1	0.6
Unidentified manufactures	0.1	0.1	...	0.1	0.1	0.1	...	0.1	0.1	...	0.1	0.1
Agricultural And Livestock Products	12.5	177.7	272.3	125.4	109.3	116.4	0.3	0.4	0.6	0.4	0.2	1.0
Agricultural products	12.5	177.4	271.8	125.1	109.1	116.4	...	...	...	...	...	0.9
Livestock and livestock products	...	0.3	0.5	0.3	0.1	...	0.3	0.4	0.6	0.4	0.2	0.2
Other Commodities	3.4	5.9	5.6	4.7	5.6	8.8	0.1	0.2	0.2	0.6	0.6	0.5
Forestry products	...	...	...	...	...	...	...	...	...	...	...	...
Fish and other marine products	3.4	5.2	5.5	4.6	5.4	8.1	0.1	...	...	...	...	...
Metallic ores and concentrates	...	...	...	...	...	...	...	...	...	...	...	...
Bituminous coal and lignite	...	...	...	...	...	...	...	...	...	...	...	...
Crude petroleum and natural gas	...	...	...	...	...	0.3	...	...	...	...	...	...
Nonmetallic minerals	...	0.2	...	0.1	...	0.2	...	...	...	...	...	...
Scrap and waste	...	0.1	0.1	...	0.2	0.3	...	...	...	...	...	0.1
Used merchandise	...	0.4	...	...	...	...	...	...	...	0.3	...	...
Goods imported and returned unchanged	...	...	...	...	...	...	...	0.1	0.2	0.3	0.6	0.4
Special classification provisions	...	0.1	...	...	...	...	...	...	...	...	...	...

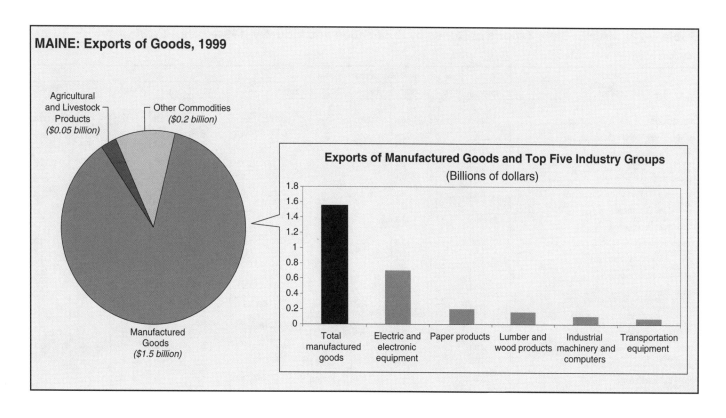

MAINE: Exports of Goods, 1999

Agricultural and Livestock Products ($0.05 billion)

Other Commodities ($0.2 billion)

Manufactured Goods ($1.5 billion)

Exports of Manufactured Goods and Top Five Industry Groups
(Billions of dollars)

Total manufactured goods | Electric and electronic equipment | Paper products | Lumber and wood products | Industrial machinery and computers | Transportation equipment

Table D-22. MAINE: State Exports of Goods by Destination and Industry, 1994–1999

(Millions of dollars.)

Industry	All destinations						Canada					
	1994	1995	1996	1997	1998	1999	1994	1995	1996	1997	1998	1999
ALL GOODS	1 138.9	1 318.2	1 248.8	1 590.2	1 664.3	1 785.2	406.2	469.8	489.0	557.4	528.3	639.7
Manufactured Goods	983.6	1 138.5	1 051.6	1 361.0	1 492.1	1 548.3	327.2	369.3	376.5	415.1	415.5	473.4
Food products	38.8	43.2	44.7	50.8	49.9	36.6	21.6	27.0	28.2	33.5	31.5	22.9
Tobacco products	. . .	. . .	. . .	. . .	. . .	. . .	. . .	. . .	. . .	. . .	. . .	. . .
Textile mill products	6.0	7.8	7.9	7.6	9.6	9.3	2.8	3.8	3.7	4.2	4.9	5.8
Apparel	7.3	8.8	9.7	10.7	9.1	9.5	1.4	1.7	2.7	3.3	3.3	5.2
Lumber and wood products	114.0	121.2	112.8	126.6	129.0	163.4	107.8	115.7	105.4	118.3	122.2	152.8
Furniture and fixtures	6.2	6.3	4.0	5.2	7.1	4.3	2.1	3.2	2.1	3.2	4.9	2.2
Paper products	179.1	245.6	258.3	239.1	194.8	201.5	62.4	64.1	67.1	71.8	78.0	82.1
Printing and publishing	3.4	4.0	5.3	3.8	2.8	2.5	2.2	2.4	2.1	2.9	1.8	1.8
Chemical products	29.3	25.9	39.3	38.8	32.1	37.2	7.5	9.4	11.5	11.2	12.8	9.4
Refined petroleum products	3.3	7.0	2.2	14.9	1.6	4.8	3.2	6.9	2.2	14.2	1.1	2.2
Rubber and plastic products	18.1	22.6	25.0	23.9	24.6	23.2	13.3	14.5	16.4	14.1	15.9	14.0
Leather products	160.2	124.4	62.7	84.9	75.4	74.0	10.4	8.6	5.4	7.1	6.9	6.7
Stone, clay and glass products	5.3	3.1	4.4	3.7	5.3	5.9	3.5	2.0	1.9	1.4	1.8	2.2
Primary metals	12.4	18.1	20.2	13.6	13.9	17.5	5.0	8.6	6.4	4.3	4.5	4.4
Fabricated metal products	38.6	33.6	16.3	25.8	32.4	37.5	6.1	6.8	8.8	7.7	9.4	11.5
Industrial machinery and computers	57.6	68.4	78.0	86.1	95.0	107.2	25.3	29.3	36.2	36.0	33.5	50.4
Electric and electronic equipment	241.3	316.9	259.8	522.7	695.1	701.6	29.5	32.4	33.6	33.9	42.1	43.3
Transportation equipment	29.4	37.5	55.5	68.9	77.0	77.9	14.7	23.2	30.6	37.8	32.5	46.1
Scientific and measuring instruments	23.4	31.4	36.2	22.3	27.1	21.3	4.8	6.0	9.0	6.9	4.2	5.7
Miscellaneous manufactures	5.5	8.5	5.7	8.2	6.7	8.6	2.2	2.0	1.7	2.0	3.0	3.3
Unidentified manufactures	4.4	4.1	3.4	3.4	3.6	4.6	1.5	1.8	1.5	1.2	1.1	1.4
Agricultural And Livestock Products	45.1	50.6	55.8	70.1	43.4	46.8	14.8	18.1	24.4	32.7	23.6	28.9
Agricultural products	5.4	4.9	6.8	31.0	11.3	14.4	4.6	3.8	5.0	12.7	10.2	12.2
Livestock and livestock products	39.8	45.7	48.9	39.1	32.0	32.4	10.2	14.3	19.3	20.0	13.4	16.6
Other Commodities	110.2	129.1	141.4	159.1	128.9	190.1	64.3	82.4	88.2	109.6	89.2	137.5
Forestry products	4.2	0.2	1.8	0.7	0.4	. . .	3.7	. . .	0.3	0.2	. . .	. . .
Fish and other marine products	88.7	95.5	107.1	125.1	98.2	147.5	44.2	51.3	61.4	79.6	59.6	101.8
Metallic ores and concentrates	. . .	. . .	0.2	. . .	. . .	. . .	. . .	. . .	. . .	. . .	. . .	. . .
Bituminous coal and lignite	. . .	. . .	. . .	0.8	. . .	. . .	. . .	. . .	. . .	0.8	. . .	. . .
Crude petroleum and natural gas	. . .	. . .	. . .	1.4	. . .	. . .	. . .	. . .	. . .	1.4	. . .	. . .
Nonmetallic minerals	0.6	0.2	0.6	0.5	0.6	0.7	0.5	0.2	0.4	0.3	0.4	0.1
Scrap and waste	6.3	19.6	7.8	5.6	3.5	6.8	5.9	19.0	3.2	5.3	3.5	6.0
Used merchandise	0.9	2.0	0.9	3.7	1.1	1.7	0.5	0.5	0.3	0.9	0.8	0.4
Goods imported and returned unchanged	8.8	11.2	21.6	20.9	24.3	27.3	8.8	11.2	21.6	20.9	24.3	27.3
Special classification provisions	0.7	0.3	1.3	0.3	0.7	5.9	0.6	0.2	1.0	0.2	0.6	1.8

Table D-22. MAINE: State Exports of Goods by Destination and Industry, 1994–1999—Continued

(Millions of dollars.)

Industry	South and Central America and Caribbean						Mexico					
	1994	1995	1996	1997	1998	1999	1994	1995	1996	1997	1998	1999
ALL GOODS	39.2	36.7	40.6	52.0	59.3	58.7	36.0	10.7	12.3	18.4	17.2	30.4
Manufactured Goods	36.0	32.7	37.1	47.5	52.6	54.1	35.3	9.5	10.0	17.3	16.7	30.0
Food products	1.0	1.3	1.6	2.1	1.8	1.7	0.1	0.2	0.3	...	0.1	2.1
Tobacco products	...	...	...	...	...	...	...	...	...	...	...	...
Textile mill products	0.6	0.2	0.5	0.3	0.4	0.4	0.6	0.8	0.2	0.1	0.4	0.6
Apparel	4.2	5.2	5.2	5.7	4.2	2.6	...	...	...	...	...	0.1
Lumber and wood products	0.1	...	0.1	...	0.1	0.1	0.1	0.1	...	0.1	0.1	...
Furniture and fixtures	0.5	0.4	0.2	0.1	0.6	0.4	0.2	...	...	...	0.1	0.4
Paper products	2.9	1.9	4.4	9.2	5.5	9.5	0.9	0.8	0.9	1.2	0.7	2.5
Printing and publishing	...	0.1	...	...	0.1	0.1	0.1	0.1	0.1	0.1	0.1	...
Chemical products	0.8	1.1	1.9	1.7	1.5	1.7	0.9	0.6	1.5	1.8	2.0	2.2
Refined petroleum products	...	...	...	...	...	...	0.1	...	...	...	...	...
Rubber and plastic products	0.5	1.5	0.8	0.3	0.1	0.3	0.1	0.1	0.4	0.4	0.3	0.3
Leather products	11.8	10.2	4.2	5.2	6.7	6.4	13.0	4.6	0.7	1.1	0.7	0.3
Stone, clay and glass products	0.2	0.1	0.4	0.7	0.9	0.4	0.6	...	0.3	0.9	0.8	2.3
Primary metals	0.1	0.2	0.1	0.3	0.3	0.1	0.1	...	0.6	0.9	0.1	0.1
Fabricated metal products	0.3	0.2	1.5	1.8	3.2	0.4	13.5	0.2	0.1	0.4	0.3	0.4
Industrial machinery and computers	1.7	1.4	2.1	2.7	6.0	3.2	1.3	0.3	0.9	3.4	1.8	1.5
Electric and electronic equipment	10.4	8.2	12.4	16.1	19.1	24.4	2.9	1.0	3.2	6.1	6.7	15.2
Transportation equipment	0.2	0.2	0.3	0.1	0.7	0.8	0.4	0.5	0.4	0.2	0.2	0.7
Scientific and measuring instruments	0.2	0.3	0.8	0.6	0.8	0.7	0.1	0.2	0.4	0.3	2.3	0.9
Miscellaneous manufactures	0.4	0.2	0.3	0.4	0.3	0.4	0.1	0.1	...	...	...	...
Unidentified manufactures	0.2	0.2	0.5	0.3	0.4	0.5	...	...	0.1	0.1	0.2	0.2
Agricultural And Livestock Products	2.8	3.4	3.2	4.1	6.1	3.4	0.6	0.8	1.8	0.8	0.5	0.4
Agricultural products	0.1	0.7	0.3	...	0.5	0.5	...	...	0.6	...	...	0.4
Livestock and livestock products	2.7	2.8	2.9	4.1	5.6	2.9	0.6	0.8	1.2	0.8	0.5	...
Other Commodities	0.4	0.5	0.3	0.4	0.6	1.2	0.1	0.4	0.5	0.3	...	...
Forestry products	...	0.1	...	...	...	...	...	...	...	...	...	...
Fish and other marine products	0.2	0.3	0.2	0.3	0.4	0.7	...	...	0.1	...	...	...
Metallic ores and concentrates	...	...	...	...	...	...	...	...	...	...	...	...
Bituminous coal and lignite	...	...	...	...	...	...	...	...	...	...	...	...
Crude petroleum and natural gas	...	...	...	...	...	...	...	...	...	...	...	...
Nonmetallic minerals	...	...	...	...	...	...	0.1	0.4	0.4	0.3	...	...
Scrap and waste	0.1	...	...	...	...	...						
Used merchandise	...	0.1	...	0.1	0.1	0.5	...	...	...	...	...	...
Goods imported and returned unchanged	...	...	...	...	...	...	...	...	...	...	...	...
Special classification provisions	...	...	...	...	...	...	...	...	...	...	...	...

Industry	European Union						United Kingdom					
	1994	1995	1996	1997	1998	1999	1994	1995	1996	1997	1998	1999
ALL GOODS	204.5	228.3	208.0	220.8	212.1	196.6	43.8	62.4	44.5	59.1	52.1	47.3
Manufactured Goods	196.8	219.6	197.7	197.9	205.6	184.1	43.3	60.1	43.0	58.2	51.6	46.2
Food products	8.7	11.6	11.3	10.3	10.8	3.4	0.7	1.3	1.5	0.7	0.5	0.6
Tobacco products	...	...	...	...	...	...	...	...	...	...	...	...
Textile mill products	0.5	0.8	0.6	0.6	0.7	0.5	0.2	0.3	0.2	0.2	0.3	0.1
Apparel	0.5	0.8	1.0	1.0	0.7	0.8	...	0.2	0.2	0.3	0.4	0.5
Lumber and wood products	2.6	2.4	3.1	3.8	2.4	1.1	0.4	0.5	0.8	0.8	0.1	0.1
Furniture and fixtures	0.3	0.8	0.4	0.4	0.5	1.0	0.2	0.3	0.4	0.4	0.4	0.7
Paper products	48.3	65.9	59.5	57.3	40.7	27.7	15.2	36.5	23.3	28.0	11.1	12.5
Printing and publishing	0.7	0.7	2.4	0.4	0.5	0.3	0.4	0.3	0.2	0.1	0.1	0.2
Chemical products	6.0	7.4	16.9	13.0	9.0	11.4	0.3	0.3	0.4	1.3	0.5	1.4
Refined petroleum products	...	...	...	...	0.1	2.6	...	...	...	...	...	...
Rubber and plastic products	1.5	2.8	2.5	2.9	3.4	2.2	0.5	0.9	0.5	0.3	0.3	0.3
Leather products	51.6	35.8	17.1	21.5	16.8	16.7	11.9	4.2	3.1	6.9	5.6	5.7
Stone, clay and glass products	0.3	0.4	0.9	0.3	0.6	0.3	...	0.2	0.2	0.1	0.1	0.1
Primary metals	4.9	6.8	4.1	4.6	5.5	4.2	0.2	0.3	1.5	0.5	0.1	0.2
Fabricated metal products	4.5	4.0	3.2	3.5	2.5	2.1	1.5	2.4	1.3	2.0	1.0	0.7
Industrial machinery and computers	17.5	20.8	17.6	22.3	36.1	34.7	2.8	3.6	2.7	6.4	18.5	14.1
Electric and electronic equipment	21.6	26.7	21.9	29.4	30.5	37.9	7.0	7.1	4.9	7.4	8.8	6.1
Transportation equipment	11.4	10.8	17.6	20.4	34.8	25.8	0.3	0.5	0.6	1.8	1.2	0.9
Scientific and measuring instruments	13.2	18.3	15.5	3.8	8.0	7.7	0.2	0.3	0.3	0.4	1.7	0.5
Miscellaneous manufactures	1.1	1.8	1.3	1.5	1.0	2.6	0.4	0.2	0.4	0.4	0.4	1.1
Unidentified manufactures	1.7	1.2	0.7	0.8	1.0	1.2	1.1	0.7	0.3	0.2	0.3	0.4
Agricultural And Livestock Products	4.9	3.8	3.2	19.4	2.9	0.9	0.2	0.3	0.4	0.3	0.2	...
Agricultural products	0.6	0.3	0.7	18.0	0.4	0.1	0.1	0.3	0.4	0.3	0.1	...
Livestock and livestock products	4.3	3.5	2.5	1.4	2.5	0.8	...	...	...	...	0.1	...
Other Commodities	2.7	4.9	7.1	3.5	3.6	11.6	0.3	2.1	1.1	0.6	0.3	1.1
Forestry products	0.3	0.1	1.6	0.5	0.3	...	...	...	0.3	0.2	0.1	...
Fish and other marine products	2.1	3.3	4.7	2.4	3.2	7.9	0.1	0.8	0.6	0.4	0.2	...
Metallic ores and concentrates	...	...	...	...	...	...	...	...	...	...	...	...
Bituminous coal and lignite	...	...	...	...	...	...	...	...	...	...	...	...
Crude petroleum and natural gas	...	...	...	...	...	...	...	...	...	...	...	...
Nonmetallic minerals	...	...	0.2	0.1	...	0.6	...	...	0.1	...	...	...
Scrap and waste	...	0.2	...	...	...	...	...	0.2	...	...	...	...
Used merchandise	0.3	1.2	0.4	0.4	0.1	0.8	0.2	1.1	0.1	0.1	...	0.2
Goods imported and returned unchanged	...	...	...	...	...	...	...	...	...	...	...	...
Special classification provisions	0.1	0.1	0.2	...	0.1	2.4	...	...	...	...	...	0.9

Table D-22. MAINE: State Exports of Goods by Destination and Industry, 1994–1999—*Continued*

(Millions of dollars.)

Industry	Germany						France					
	1994	1995	1996	1997	1998	1999	1994	1995	1996	1997	1998	1999
ALL GOODS	27.6	30.9	34.0	28.4	47.3	34.5	36.9	56.5	61.3	46.1	35.5	25.3
Manufactured Goods	27.0	30.2	32.8	28.2	46.9	33.5	36.5	56.2	61.1	45.6	35.0	24.1
Food products	2.7	5.5	5.0	2.3	1.5	0.9	0.3	0.2	0.9	0.9	1.1	0.5
Tobacco products	...	...	...	...	...	...	...	...	...	...	...	...
Textile mill products	0.1	0.1	...	...	...	...	0.1	0.3	0.2	0.1	0.1	0.1
Apparel	0.1	0.2	0.1	0.2	0.2	0.2	0.1	0.1	0.2	0.2	0.1	...
Lumber and wood products	...	0.3	0.2	1.3	0.9	0.2	0.1	...	...	0.1	...	...
Furniture and fixtures	...	...	...	...	...	0.1	...	...	...	...	0.1	...
Paper products	2.3	4.9	2.3	0.1	2.4	0.4	2.0	11.3	15.0	21.6	15.1	8.1
Printing and publishing	0.1	0.1	...	0.1	...	...	0.2	0.2	0.1	...	...	...
Chemical products	0.3	0.4	0.7	1.3	0.4	0.9	3.7	5.0	12.0	7.9	4.1	1.0
Refined petroleum products	...	...	...	...	...	...	...	...	...	...	...	...
Rubber and plastic products	0.1	0.4	0.1	0.3	0.4	0.4	0.5	1.0	1.3	1.5	2.0	0.6
Leather products	5.6	1.5	0.1	0.2	0.1	0.3	9.8	8.9	5.9	5.4	5.7	5.8
Stone, clay and glass products	0.1	...	...	...	...	...	...	...	...	...	0.2	0.1
Primary metals	0.4	0.3	0.2	0.5	0.4	0.6	0.2	0.2	0.2	0.1	0.1	1.1
Fabricated metal products	0.6	0.9	0.8	0.6	0.6	0.4	0.5	0.1	0.1	...	0.5	...
Industrial machinery and computers	5.3	4.6	5.8	3.0	5.5	4.1	3.6	4.6	3.3	2.1	1.5	1.5
Electric and electronic equipment	1.6	2.3	2.5	4.4	5.0	5.1	3.4	7.8	7.2	4.3	3.4	4.2
Transportation equipment	6.0	8.2	14.0	13.0	28.6	18.7	0.9	0.2	0.4	0.1	0.2	0.5
Scientific and measuring instruments	1.1	0.4	0.4	0.2	0.5	0.7	11.0	16.3	14.2	1.1	0.8	0.4
Miscellaneous manufactures	0.5	0.2	0.3	0.3	0.1	0.1	...	...	0.1	0.1	...	...
Unidentified manufactures	0.1	0.1	0.1	0.3	0.3	0.3	0.1	...	...	...	0.1	0.1
Agricultural And Livestock Products	0.3	0.1	0.2	0.1	0.2	0.1	0.2	...	...	0.1	...	...
Agricultural products	0.3	...	0.2	0.1	0.2	0.1	...	...	...	...	...	...
Livestock and livestock products	...	...	...	...	...	...	0.1	...	...	0.1	...	...
Other Commodities	0.3	0.7	1.1	0.1	0.2	1.0	0.2	0.4	0.3	0.4	0.4	1.2
Forestry products	0.1	...	1.0	...	0.1	...	...	...	...	...	...	...
Fish and other marine products	0.1	0.6	...	...	...	...	0.2	0.3	0.2	0.4	0.4	0.6
Metallic ores and concentrates	...	...	...	...	...	...	...	...	...	...	...	...
Bituminous coal and lignite	...	...	...	...	...	...	...	...	...	...	...	...
Crude petroleum and natural gas	...	...	...	...	...	...	...	...	...	...	...	...
Nonmetallic minerals	...	...	...	...	...	0.6	...	...	...	...	...	...
Scrap and waste	...	...	...	...	...	...	...	...	...	...	...	...
Used merchandise	...	...	...	...	...	...	...	...	...	...	...	0.2
Goods imported and returned unchanged	...	...	...	...	...	...	...	...	...	...	...	...
Special classification provisions	...	0.1	...	...	...	0.3	...	...	...	...	...	0.4

Industry	The Netherlands						Asian 10					
	1994	1995	1996	1997	1998	1999	1994	1995	1996	1997	1998	1999
ALL GOODS	19.1	16.7	11.8	11.2	18.9	28.5	364.7	489.8	400.5	668.6	783.6	794.2
Manufactured Goods	16.2	14.9	9.2	9.5	16.1	27.3	308.0	432.7	339.2	616.0	741.2	746.7
Food products	1.0	1.4	0.6	0.5	0.5	0.3	5.7	1.8	2.4	3.5	5.0	5.3
Tobacco products	...	...	...	...	...	...	...	...	...	...	...	...
Textile mill products	...	...	...	...	...	...	1.2	1.8	2.7	1.8	2.3	1.6
Apparel	...	...	0.1	...	...	...	1.0	0.9	0.6	0.6	0.5	0.6
Lumber and wood products	0.4	0.5	0.7	0.1	0.2	0.1	3.2	2.4	4.2	3.9	3.8	9.2
Furniture and fixtures	...	...	...	...	...	...	2.6	1.1	0.8	1.0	0.7	...
Paper products	2.3	3.0	0.9	...	0.9	1.4	44.6	92.7	102.8	87.3	56.7	67.5
Printing and publishing	...	...	2.0	...	0.1	...	0.1	0.3	0.3	0.2	0.2	0.2
Chemical products	0.1	0.3	0.9	0.8	2.3	5.7	12.4	5.1	4.6	7.6	4.6	7.4
Refined petroleum products	...	...	...	...	0.1	2.6	...	...	...	0.4	0.2	...
Rubber and plastic products	0.1	0.1	...	0.1	...	0.1	1.6	2.3	3.0	4.6	3.4	4.4
Leather products	2.2	1.1	0.1	0.3	0.2	0.2	62.5	57.0	28.6	39.8	36.2	34.1
Stone, clay and glass products	...	...	...	...	0.1	...	0.6	0.2	0.4	0.1	0.3	0.2
Primary metals	3.9	5.1	1.6	3.3	4.5	2.0	1.5	0.9	1.2	3.0	3.0	1.7
Fabricated metal products	0.3	0.3	0.3	0.3	0.2	0.2	1.2	19.3	1.8	10.9	13.4	22.5
Industrial machinery and computers	1.4	0.8	0.8	1.0	0.5	3.8	5.9	11.5	9.2	11.0	10.0	10.5
Electric and electronic equipment	0.4	0.3	0.4	1.2	0.3	2.7	158.8	227.7	165.0	427.9	587.3	572.6
Transportation equipment	3.7	1.4	0.5	1.4	3.5	3.1	1.0	1.3	2.2	0.9	1.1	2.4
Scientific and measuring instruments	0.2	0.5	...	0.4	2.5	3.9	2.3	4.2	7.0	8.1	10.5	4.2
Miscellaneous manufactures	...	...	0.1	0.2	0.2	1.0	1.2	2.1	2.1	3.1	1.6	1.7
Unidentified manufactures	0.1	0.1	...	0.1	0.1	0.1	0.5	0.4	0.3	0.4	0.5	0.7
Agricultural And Livestock Products	2.4	1.5	1.5	1.1	2.2	0.6	16.7	19.5	19.6	11.1	8.2	9.9
Agricultural products	...	...	0.1	...	0.1	...	0.1	...	0.1	0.2	0.1	1.0
Livestock and livestock products	2.4	1.5	1.5	1.1	2.1	0.6	16.6	19.4	19.6	10.9	8.0	8.9
Other Commodities	0.5	0.2	1.1	0.5	0.5	0.6	40.1	37.6	41.6	41.5	34.3	37.6
Forestry products	0.2	...	0.2	0.3	...	...	0.1	...	...	...	...	...
Fish and other marine products	0.3	0.2	0.6	0.1	0.5	0.2	39.7	37.3	37.4	39.7	34.0	35.5
Metallic ores and concentrates	...	...	...	...	...	...	...	...	...	...	...	...
Bituminous coal and lignite	...	...	...	...	...	...	...	...	...	...	...	...
Crude petroleum and natural gas	...	...	...	...	...	...	...	...	...	...	...	...
Nonmetallic minerals	...	...	0.1	0.1	...	...	...	...	...	...	0.1	...
Scrap and waste	...	...	...	...	...	...	0.1	0.1	4.1	...	0.1	0.8
Used merchandise	...	...	...	0.1	...	0.3	0.1	0.1	...	1.8	0.1	...
Goods imported and returned unchanged	...	...	...	...	...	...	...	...	...	...	...	...
Special classification provisions	...	...	0.2	...	...	0.2	0.1	...	...	...	...	1.2

Table D-22. MAINE: State Exports of Goods by Destination and Industry, 1994–1999—*Continued*

(Millions of dollars.)

Industry	Japan						South Korea					
	1994	1995	1996	1997	1998	1999	1994	1995	1996	1997	1998	1999
ALL GOODS	109.1	102.1	99.6	88.2	68.8	79.1	18.2	49.2	69.2	65.6	42.7	44.4
Manufactured Goods	71.1	68.9	65.8	53.6	35.9	43.9	16.6	46.4	67.6	64.9	42.2	42.3
Food products	4.6	1.4	1.8	2.4	4.2	4.8	0.1	0.2	0.1	0.2	0.1	0.1
Tobacco products	...	...	...	...	...	...	...	...	...	...	...	...
Textile mill products	0.7	0.2	0.1	...	...	0.1	...	0.5	0.7	0.1	0.5	0.3
Apparel	0.7	0.5	0.4	0.2	0.2	0.5	...	...	...	0.1	...	...
Lumber and wood products	1.5	0.6	2.3	1.7	1.0	2.0	0.2	0.1	0.1	0.1	0.1	...
Furniture and fixtures	1.9	0.3	0.3	0.1	0.1	...	...	...	0.1	0.1	...	...
Paper products	30.4	43.6	34.5	29.7	15.6	19.8	7.7	38.3	57.6	48.2	34.8	30.6
Printing and publishing	...	...	0.1	...	0.1	0.1	...	...	0.1	0.1	...	...
Chemical products	10.5	3.0	2.9	4.0	3.2	5.4	...	...	0.3	1.0	0.1	0.4
Refined petroleum products	...	...	...	...	...	...	...	...	...	...	...	...
Rubber and plastic products	0.3	0.8	0.6	0.7	0.5	0.4	...	0.1	...	...	...	0.2
Leather products	1.9	1.1	1.1	0.8	1.2	0.5	4.5	2.3	1.2	1.5	..	0.1
Stone, clay and glass products	0.2	0.1	0.1	0.1	...	...	0.1	...	...	...	...	...
Primary metals	0.7	0.1	0.2	1.4	2.2	1.0	...	0.1	0.3	0.2	0.1	0.2
Fabricated metal products	0.7	0.9	0.7	0.8	0.4	0.3	...	...	0.4	...	...	...
Industrial machinery and computers	3.3	6.8	4.5	1.9	1.1	1.3	0.6	0.6	0.8	2.7	0.3	1.5
Electric and electronic equipment	12.0	7.3	11.6	5.9	3.4	5.1	2.0	4.1	4.4	6.3	5.7	8.2
Transportation equipment	0.4	0.3	1.0	0.5	0.6	0.3	0.1	...	...	0.2	...	0.2
Scientific and measuring instruments	0.3	0.6	2.0	1.6	0.6	0.7	1.2	...	1.3	3.5	0.1	0.2
Miscellaneous manufactures	0.9	1.1	1.5	1.5	1.2	1.3	0.1	...	0.1	0.7	...	0.1
Unidentified manufactures	0.1	0.2	0.1	0.1	0.1	0.1	...	...	...	...	0.1	0.1
Agricultural And Livestock Products	0.2	0.1	0.1	1.3	1.3	2.5	0.3	0.6	0.6	0.3	0.3	0.3
Agricultural products	0.1	...	0.1	0.1	0.1	1.0	...	...	...	...	...	...
Livestock and livestock products	0.1	...	0.1	1.2	1.2	1.5	0.3	0.6	0.6	0.3	0.3	0.3
Other Commodities	37.9	33.1	33.8	33.3	31.6	32.7	1.4	2.2	0.9	0.3	0.2	1.8
Forestry products	0.1	...	...	...	...	...	...	...	...	...	...	...
Fish and other marine products	37.7	33.0	32.5	33.0	31.4	32.6	1.3	2.1	0.5	0.3	0.2	1.4
Metallic ores and concentrates	...	...	...	...	...	...	...	...	...	...	...	...
Bituminous coal and lignite	...	...	...	...	...	...	...	...	...	...	...	...
Crude petroleum and natural gas	...	...	...	...	...	...	...	...	...	...	...	...
Nonmetallic minerals	...	...	...	...	0.1	...	...	...	...	...	...	...
Scrap and waste	...	...	1.3	...	...	...	...	...	0.4	...	0.1	0.2
Used merchandise	...	0.1	...	0.3	0.1	...	...	...	...	...	...	...
Goods imported and returned unchanged	...	...	...	...	...	0.1	...	...	...	...	...	...
Special classification provisions	...	...	...	...	...	...	...	...	...	...	...	0.1

Industry	Taiwan						Singapore					
	1994	1995	1996	1997	1998	1999	1994	1995	1996	1997	1998	1999
ALL GOODS	28.9	37.5	19.6	21.3	27.5	28.7	36.5	46.3	47.9	166.1	290.5	389.9
Manufactured Goods	28.4	34.4	18.0	20.6	27.3	28.5	36.5	46.2	47.8	164.6	290.5	389.7
Food products	0.2	...	0.1	0.1	0.2	0.2	0.1	...	...	...	...	...
Tobacco products	...	...	...	...	...	...	...	...	...	...	...	...
Textile mill products	...	0.1	0.1	0.1	0.1	0.1	0.1	...	...	...	...	...
Apparel	...	0.1	...	...	0.2	...	...	0.1	...	...	0.1	...
Lumber and wood products	1.1	1.4	0.6	0.4	0.1	0.3	...	0.1	0.1	...	0.1	...
Furniture and fixtures	...	0.4	0.1	0.3	0.3	...	0.1	...	...	...	...	...
Paper products	0.2	0.7	3.5	1.3	0.2	0.2	4.0	3.4	0.6	0.2	0.1	...
Printing and publishing	...	...	...	...	...	...	...	...	...	...	...	...
Chemical products	0.7	0.6	0.5	0.4	0.6	0.4	...	0.1	0.1	0.4	0.2	0.2
Refined petroleum products	...	...	...	...	...	...	...	...	...	0.1	0.1	...
Rubber and plastic products	0.1	0.6	0.3	0.4	0.3	0.5	1.0	0.5	1.7	2.8	2.0	2.2
Leather products	15.3	9.4	0.3	0.3	0.5	0.1	0.2	0.1	0.4	0.1	0.1	0.3
Stone, clay and glass products	...	...	0.1	...	0.1	...	...	...	0.1	...	0.1	...
Primary metals	0.2	0.3	0.2	0.4	0.1	0.1	0.1	0.1	0.1	0.2	0.2	0.1
Fabricated metal products	...	9.0	...	4.1	12.1	20.7	0.1	0.2	0.1	...	...	...
Industrial machinery and computers	0.5	0.4	0.7	1.9	0.4	1.5	0.2	0.5	1.2	0.7	4.2	2.1
Electric and electronic equipment	9.3	10.7	9.3	9.4	4.9	3.5	30.2	37.6	42.0	159.6	282.8	382.4
Transportation equipment	0.4	0.3	0.2	...	0.1	...	...	0.1	0.6	0.2	0.3	1.6
Scientific and measuring instruments	0.2	0.3	2.0	1.4	7.1	0.8	0.1	2.5	0.6	0.1	0.2	0.7
Miscellaneous manufactures	...	...	...	...	...	0.1	0.1	0.9	...	0.1	...	...
Unidentified manufactures	0.1	...	0.1	...	0.1	...	0.1	0.1	0.1	0.1	...	...
Agricultural And Livestock Products	0.4	1.7	1.4	0.7	0.2	0.2	...	...	...	...	...	...
Agricultural products	...	...	...	0.1	...	...	...	...	...	...	...	...
Livestock and livestock products	0.4	1.7	1.4	0.5	0.2	0.2	...	...	...	...	...	...
Other Commodities	0.1	1.4	0.2	...	...	...	...	0.1	0.1	1.5	...	0.2
Forestry products	...	...	...	...	...	...	...	...	...	...	...	...
Fish and other marine products	...	1.4	0.2	...	...	...	...	0.1	0.1	...	...	...
Metallic ores and concentrates	...	...	...	...	...	...	...	...	...	...	...	...
Bituminous coal and lignite	...	...	...	...	...	...	...	...	...	...	...	...
Crude petroleum and natural gas	...	...	...	...	...	...	...	...	...	...	...	...
Nonmetallic minerals	0.1	...	...	...	...	...	...	...	...	...	...	...
Scrap and waste	...	...	...	...	...	...	...	...	...	1.5	...	...
Used merchandise	...	...	...	...	...	...	...	...	...	...	...	...
Goods imported and returned unchanged	...	...	...	...	...	...	...	...	...	...	...	0.1
Special classification provisions	...	...	...	...	...	...	...	...	...	...	...	...

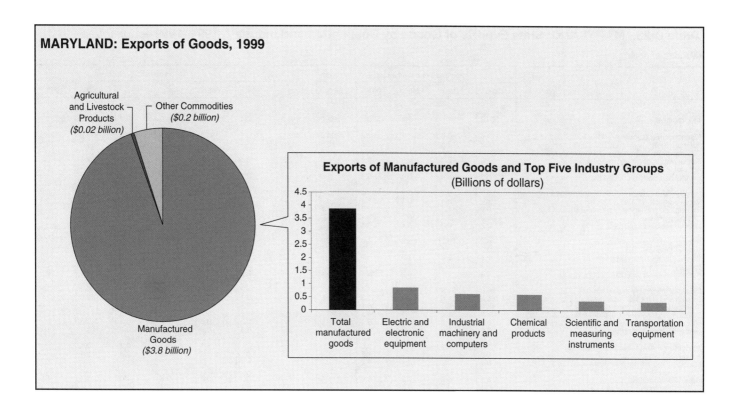

MARYLAND: Exports of Goods, 1999

Agricultural and Livestock Products ($0.02 billion)

Other Commodities ($0.2 billion)

Manufactured Goods ($3.8 billion)

Exports of Manufactured Goods and Top Five Industry Groups
(Billions of dollars)

Total manufactured goods / Electric and electronic equipment / Industrial machinery and computers / Chemical products / Scientific and measuring instruments / Transportation equipment

Table D-23. MARYLAND: State Exports of Goods by Destination and Industry, 1994–1999

(Millions of dollars.)

Industry	All destinations						Canada					
	1994	1995	1996	1997	1998	1999	1994	1995	1996	1997	1998	1999
ALL GOODS	2 848.5	3 439.0	3 509.9	3 861.0	4 013.7	4 068.3	621.4	551.9	553.3	653.2	690.4	847.6
Manufactured Goods	2 575.6	2 976.7	3 054.9	3 412.3	3 667.7	3 846.8	570.7	495.8	492.2	584.5	639.4	797.9
Food products	131.6	147.2	193.8	246.6	180.7	153.1	26.7	20.4	12.0	21.4	33.6	41.1
Tobacco products	. . .	5.8	0.2	0.3	0.2	0.2	. . .	. . .	. . .	. . .	. . .	. . .
Textile mill products	58.0	52.4	61.7	108.8	116.8	121.0	14.9	11.8	12.8	14.3	14.5	17.0
Apparel	22.2	25.2	30.0	32.1	31.4	21.2	5.6	6.9	7.7	6.1	5.9	5.2
Lumber and wood products	27.1	32.2	37.4	37.3	41.4	53.7	3.2	3.2	4.2	4.9	5.0	6.8
Furniture and fixtures	13.0	10.0	20.1	13.1	20.7	18.9	6.0	1.2	2.2	3.4	2.6	2.4
Paper products	34.5	37.2	40.2	34.2	30.1	40.9	26.5	20.7	20.1	21.0	14.3	17.4
Printing and publishing	131.9	133.4	129.6	135.9	146.3	111.0	24.6	29.5	29.1	27.6	30.5	32.3
Chemical products	316.0	379.8	393.9	384.3	485.3	601.8	91.1	77.4	68.4	84.4	150.3	235.7
Refined petroleum products	28.9	20.4	31.7	37.3	19.8	13.7	3.8	1.9	4.6	2.2	2.8	2.1
Rubber and plastic products	73.3	79.9	79.8	95.7	106.9	120.3	17.1	15.0	14.8	16.1	16.4	20.3
Leather products	4.4	5.3	7.2	5.2	12.4	7.7	2.3	2.7	1.6	1.1	1.0	1.1
Stone, clay and glass products	27.6	40.0	35.9	33.6	30.1	33.8	10.7	12.9	12.4	15.0	12.0	14.3
Primary metals	50.4	66.5	106.4	111.0	62.9	83.5	19.8	22.0	35.8	49.6	16.9	28.4
Fabricated metal products	182.0	168.5	189.1	162.8	232.1	228.5	22.7	24.4	18.9	26.2	53.9	58.4
Industrial machinery and computers	455.1	568.2	618.2	619.9	594.8	618.9	135.7	119.4	128.6	158.5	160.6	175.5
Electric and electronic equipment	345.7	498.6	485.6	662.8	806.0	853.8	58.5	56.3	52.2	57.6	58.6	64.1
Transportation equipment	360.8	312.0	268.2	310.8	347.7	323.1	48.9	26.6	27.1	34.2	22.7	31.9
Scientific and measuring instruments	254.7	310.6	255.3	309.8	327.9	353.6	41.6	33.6	30.4	28.4	28.0	32.7
Miscellaneous manufactures	23.6	33.5	31.3	33.8	34.2	32.0	8.5	6.6	6.3	8.6	5.8	7.1
Unidentified manufactures	34.8	50.0	39.2	37.1	40.0	56.3	2.6	3.1	3.0	3.8	4.0	4.4
Agricultural And Livestock Products	76.4	149.8	151.9	119.5	64.0	19.8	8.1	5.9	3.5	5.1	3.4	3.6
Agricultural products	74.9	149.0	150.3	115.9	62.6	18.9	7.0	5.8	3.2	3.8	2.8	3.5
Livestock and livestock products	1.5	0.9	1.6	3.5	1.3	0.9	1.1	0.1	0.4	1.3	0.6	0.1
Other Commodities	196.4	312.4	303.1	329.2	282.1	201.6	42.6	50.2	57.5	63.5	47.6	46.2
Forestry products	2.4	3.4	2.5	2.5	2.8	3.4	0.8	0.6	0.9	0.4	0.1	0.2
Fish and other marine products	5.0	4.2	3.8	8.7	9.6	12.5	2.2	2.3	1.9	5.6	7.6	9.7
Metallic ores and concentrates	0.6	3.7	6.8	12.7	14.4	2.2	. . .	. . .	. . .	0.1	0.9	. . .
Bituminous coal and lignite	94.6	143.5	176.3	178.2	153.3	72.6	3.8	5.1	3.2	5.3	3.4	3.4
Crude petroleum and natural gas	0.5	. . .	1.6	1.4	0.1	. . .	0.5	. . .	1.5	1.4	. . .	. . .
Nonmetallic minerals	25.6	33.4	26.1	40.3	34.4	30.8	1.0	2.4	2.1	2.0	1.9	0.8
Scrap and waste	26.7	34.4	26.3	27.0	13.9	14.1	16.3	22.9	18.5	19.9	9.2	8.4
Used merchandise	13.9	12.3	15.1	17.4	18.8	12.8	3.4	0.6	2.3	5.7	7.1	3.2
Goods imported and returned unchanged	13.7	14.7	25.5	21.4	15.3	14.3	13.7	14.7	25.5	21.4	15.3	14.3
Special classification provisions	13.5	62.8	19.1	19.6	19.4	38.9	1.0	1.6	1.4	1.7	2.0	6.2

Table D-23. MARYLAND: State Exports of Goods by Destination and Industry, 1994–1999—Continued

(Millions of dollars.)

Industry	South and Central American and Caribbean						Mexico					
	1994	1995	1996	1997	1998	1999	1994	1995	1996	1997	1998	1999
ALL GOODS	250.8	288.8	262.4	270.1	301.9	191.3	100.4	94.5	174.9	199.2	337.2	330.2
Manufactured Goods	243.8	280.6	252.1	262.5	294.9	183.0	100.1	93.1	174.0	198.0	334.8	328.4
Food products	16.2	17.3	13.4	15.6	15.3	12.0	14.3	8.4	13.2	12.9	13.0	10.6
Tobacco products	...	...	...	...	0.2	...	...	...	...	...	...	...
Textile mill products	2.6	2.3	2.3	3.9	6.0	5.8	2.1	2.2	2.2	2.7	2.5	2.2
Apparel	6.2	5.7	5.1	11.0	9.1	4.3	0.7	0.5	1.2	0.9	3.1	0.3
Lumber and wood products	0.2	0.4	0.4	0.7	1.5	0.2	0.1	0.1	0.4	0.2	0.4	4.3
Furniture and fixtures	0.5	0.8	0.7	1.0	0.7	0.6	0.1	2.8	12.1	3.7	4.3	0.2
Paper products	1.7	5.4	6.1	5.8	6.8	5.8	1.1	1.6	7.7	1.1	3.6	9.1
Printing and publishing	0.9	1.1	0.5	0.6	1.7	1.4	0.6	0.4	0.5	0.2	0.8	2.8
Chemical products	23.3	33.7	36.0	36.4	33.4	28.6	16.4	9.5	13.9	11.4	11.3	14.8
Refined petroleum products	0.2	0.2	0.1	0.1	0.8	0.4	...	...	...	...	...	...
Rubber and plastic products	6.8	9.7	6.2	6.8	7.9	5.9	4.5	5.9	10.0	6.5	13.8	15.2
Leather products	0.2	0.1	1.0	0.3	1.3	0.9	...	...	...	0.5	5.8	1.9
Stone, clay and glass products	2.4	2.3	1.0	3.9	2.5	1.2	0.5	1.0	3.2	0.9	1.5	1.0
Primary metals	7.3	2.3	5.0	7.0	3.4	4.4	2.0	4.0	6.9	5.9	0.7	1.7
Fabricated metal products	4.4	7.7	13.2	6.8	9.4	5.8	2.5	4.9	8.1	12.8	42.5	18.3
Industrial machinery and computers	56.2	98.9	85.4	82.1	84.5	41.3	25.0	16.2	16.6	14.8	30.3	33.7
Electric and electronic equipment	46.6	34.8	28.3	31.5	56.6	32.6	9.1	23.3	64.9	112.7	182.8	189.9
Transportation equipment	42.6	26.1	21.7	18.1	22.3	11.7	2.7	1.3	1.0	0.7	0.4	0.9
Scientific and measuring instruments	21.9	21.4	13.4	24.3	23.0	8.9	17.5	9.7	11.6	9.8	16.0	19.9
Miscellaneous manufactures	0.6	4.6	4.5	5.4	2.5	1.5	0.2	0.9	0.3	0.1	0.3	0.4
Unidentified manufactures	2.8	5.8	7.7	1.4	5.9	9.7	0.5	0.5	0.2	0.3	1.7	1.1
Agricultural And Livestock Products	1.9	2.0	3.1	2.0	1.3	1.5	...	1.1	0.1	0.2	0.1	...
Agricultural products	1.8	1.9	3.0	1.8	1.2	1.5	...	1.1	0.1	0.2	0.1	...
Livestock and livestock products	0.1	0.2	0.1	0.2	0.1	...	...	...	...	...	...	...
Other Commodities	5.1	6.2	7.2	5.6	5.6	6.7	0.3	0.2	0.8	1.0	2.3	1.8
Forestry products	0.1	0.2	0.3	0.2	0.2	0.2	0.1	0.1	0.3	0.8	1.4	1.1
Fish and other marine products	0.4	...	...	...	...	...	...	...	...	0.1	...	...
Metallic ores and concentrates	0.1	0.3	0.8	1.3	1.4	0.1	...	...	...	...	...	...
Bituminous coal and lignite	1.3	1.5	3.2	...	...	...	...	...	...	...	...	...
Crude petroleum and natural gas	...	...	...	...	...	...	...	...	0.1	...	...	...
Nonmetallic minerals	0.9	1.9	1.5	1.2	0.6	0.5	...	...	...	...	...	...
Scrap and waste	0.9	0.6	0.3	0.5	0.5	1.5	...	0.1	...	...	0.1	0.1
Used merchandise	1.3	1.1	0.9	1.9	2.0	1.0	...	...	...	0.1	...	...
Goods imported and returned unchanged	...	...	...	...	...	...	...	...	...	...	...	...
Special classification provisions	0.3	0.7	0.3	0.4	1.0	3.4	0.1	...	0.3	0.1	0.8	0.5

Industry	European Union						United Kingdom					
	1994	1995	1996	1997	1998	1999	1994	1995	1996	1997	1998	1999
ALL GOODS	886.9	1 167.7	1 076.3	1 077.5	1 200.0	1 274.5	189.9	329.9	308.6	286.7	313.5	274.1
Manufactured Goods	804.9	969.7	963.8	962.3	1 093.2	1 208.1	180.7	318.3	295.0	278.2	303.5	264.6
Food products	8.4	8.3	10.2	12.8	10.0	15.0	0.9	2.0	1.7	4.4	2.2	3.5
Tobacco products	...	5.7	...	...	...	...	...	...	...	...	...	...
Textile mill products	21.4	20.4	26.5	38.9	32.6	36.3	6.0	9.2	12.1	16.3	14.9	13.0
Apparel	3.6	4.5	6.1	5.1	4.9	4.4	1.1	0.8	0.7	1.7	1.7	0.9
Lumber and wood products	16.7	21.3	21.5	21.2	28.6	31.7	1.9	3.2	3.4	2.0	1.3	1.1
Furniture and fixtures	1.7	2.5	2.0	2.2	8.1	10.7	0.3	0.2	0.4	0.5	1.6	0.4
Paper products	1.0	1.6	1.6	1.8	1.6	1.5	0.3	0.8	0.6	0.9	0.5	0.7
Printing and publishing	97.5	87.4	75.7	89.0	88.2	55.0	54.7	71.5	68.2	71.4	71.4	42.2
Chemical products	106.6	161.0	167.2	130.3	149.6	169.4	21.0	45.0	54.0	28.2	34.6	37.4
Refined petroleum products	16.9	11.4	18.4	21.9	11.4	7.7	2.4	2.0	4.0	5.5	1.3	1.8
Rubber and plastic products	18.8	16.6	18.1	24.9	34.4	40.1	6.3	6.0	4.7	5.1	6.4	10.0
Leather products	0.8	1.7	4.0	2.4	3.4	1.2	0.2	0.1	...	...	0.3	0.3
Stone, clay and glass products	4.2	5.7	5.8	6.5	5.8	8.3	1.0	1.4	1.9	2.8	2.3	2.3
Primary metals	7.3	13.1	36.9	26.2	22.2	20.5	2.0	2.8	10.5	7.4	3.7	3.9
Fabricated metal products	86.3	70.9	90.6	28.6	44.6	100.6	4.0	5.2	3.3	6.1	6.4	5.5
Industrial machinery and computers	83.9	146.8	132.9	115.6	110.7	135.1	22.8	46.1	44.8	28.5	26.7	29.1
Electric and electronic equipment	84.2	119.6	116.5	145.8	225.6	275.3	25.5	56.5	51.8	65.5	81.6	58.7
Transportation equipment	164.1	131.7	129.8	189.9	199.4	160.6	13.3	9.3	10.3	11.4	12.7	21.8
Scientific and measuring instruments	71.5	121.1	87.2	88.5	97.8	116.4	14.6	53.4	17.0	16.2	30.5	26.6
Miscellaneous manufactures	5.4	8.4	8.6	7.7	9.1	11.3	1.5	2.3	5.3	3.8	2.2	3.3
Unidentified manufactures	4.5	10.0	4.1	3.0	5.4	6.9	0.8	0.7	0.4	0.5	1.4	2.2
Agricultural And Livestock Products	7.2	41.8	5.8	0.5	0.5	0.7	0.2	0.2	0.2	0.1	0.3	0.3
Agricultural products	6.8	41.5	5.6	0.4	0.3	0.5	...	0.1	0.1	...	0.1	0.1
Livestock and livestock products	0.3	0.3	0.2	0.1	0.2	0.2	0.2	0.1	0.1	0.1	0.1	0.2
Other Commodities	74.8	156.1	106.8	114.7	106.3	65.6	9.1	11.4	13.4	8.4	9.8	9.2
Forestry products	0.7	1.6	0.2	0.2	0.2	0.3	0.5	1.6	0.1	0.2	0.1	0.2
Fish and other marine products	0.5	0.3	0.2	0.4	0.6	0.5	0.3	0.3	0.2	0.3	0.4	0.3
Metallic ores and concentrates	0.5	3.3	3.5	8.9	10.1	1.7	...	0.1	1.7	2.8	3.4	0.6
Bituminous coal and lignite	59.3	87.2	85.7	87.3	76.8	42.6	6.8	7.5	9.6	2.6	...	...
Crude petroleum and natural gas	...	...	...	...	...	...	...	...	...	...	...	...
Nonmetallic minerals	1.1	1.6	2.9	5.2	5.6	1.7	0.2	0.2	0.1	0.1	0.2	...
Scrap and waste	1.1	1.3	0.7	0.2	0.3	0.3	0.3	0.1	...	...	...	0.1
Used merchandise	3.0	3.0	4.9	3.7	4.6	5.6	0.7	0.9	0.7	1.4	3.5	4.4
Goods imported and returned unchanged	...	...	...	...	...	...	...	...	...	...	...	...
Special classification provisions	8.7	57.9	8.8	9.0	8.1	12.8	0.3	0.6	1.0	1.1	2.1	3.7

Table D-23. MARYLAND: State Exports of Goods by Destination and Industry, 1994–1999—*Continued*

(Millions of dollars.)

Industry	Germany						France					
	1994	1995	1996	1997	1998	1999	1994	1995	1996	1997	1998	1999
ALL GOODS	87.9	121.7	138.5	165.3	139.4	196.9	89.4	107.8	84.2	108.8	114.1	118.4
Manufactured Goods	86.9	119.9	135.7	155.8	135.4	194.5	85.5	104.2	75.4	98.1	101.5	109.1
Food products	2.0	1.2	1.1	1.5	2.3	2.7	...	...	0.2	...	0.1	...
Tobacco products	...	...	...	...	...	...	...	...	...	...	...	...
Textile mill products	3.1	1.6	6.1	12.3	5.7	8.4	1.5	1.4	1.6	1.4	2.3	3.3
Apparel	0.4	1.1	1.6	0.7	0.5	0.7	0.3	0.3	0.4	0.4	0.4	0.5
Lumber and wood products	3.1	4.5	3.2	4.5	9.7	13.4	0.4	0.1	0.4	0.1	0.3	0.3
Furniture and fixtures	0.3	1.4	1.0	0.8	1.5	2.0	0.3	0.2	0.1	0.1	0.2	...
Paper products	0.2	0.1	0.3	0.3	0.4	0.2	0.1	0.1	...	...	0.2	0.1
Printing and publishing	9.2	3.0	1.6	7.4	4.0	4.6	14.6	6.3	3.8	7.6	4.7	1.5
Chemical products	18.7	34.5	38.5	33.6	32.6	46.2	5.6	13.7	8.6	6.2	5.8	26.3
Refined petroleum products	...	...	0.1	0.1	...	...	...	...	...	...	...	0.2
Rubber and plastic products	5.5	3.3	5.1	5.6	3.8	8.4	1.6	1.4	2.4	1.6	5.8	3.0
Leather products	...	0.4	0.8	1.1	1.2	0.7	0.1	0.4	2.4	0.1	0.4	...
Stone, clay and glass products	0.3	0.7	0.6	0.6	0.5	0.5	1.6	2.7	2.4	0.7	0.6	0.4
Primary metals	0.6	0.4	5.2	5.2	2.1	1.5	0.2	0.4	0.4	0.3	0.5	1.8
Fabricated metal products	0.9	0.5	4.2	1.0	0.9	2.2	0.2	1.1	0.3	0.4	1.4	2.5
Industrial machinery and computers	13.6	26.3	27.3	37.6	25.0	50.3	8.7	15.1	14.4	15.6	9.7	9.6
Electric and electronic equipment	14.8	19.1	15.8	13.1	19.8	27.4	11.3	15.0	15.1	9.4	16.8	12.6
Transportation equipment	4.1	8.9	8.5	17.3	12.2	10.2	31.1	37.3	13.1	35.6	44.4	30.3
Scientific and measuring instruments	7.8	10.5	11.8	11.4	10.2	12.8	7.1	7.5	9.0	17.9	5.9	14.4
Miscellaneous manufactures	1.7	1.7	1.1	1.3	2.4	1.7	0.4	1.0	0.4	0.4	1.5	1.4
Unidentified manufactures	0.6	0.6	1.8	0.3	0.6	0.7	0.4	0.3	0.2	0.2	0.6	0.6
Agricultural And Livestock Products	0.1	0.3	0.3	0.1	0.2	0.1	...	0.1	...	...	...	0.1
Agricultural products	...	0.3	0.2	0.1	0.2	0.1	...	...	...	...	...	0.1
Livestock and livestock products	0.1	...	...	...	...	...	...	0.1	...	...	...	...
Other Commodities	0.9	1.5	2.6	9.4	3.8	2.4	3.9	3.5	8.7	10.7	12.5	9.2
Forestry products	0.1	...	...	...	...	...	...	...	...	...	...	...
Fish and other marine products	...	...	...	...	...	0.1	...	...	...	...	...	...
Metallic ores and concentrates	...	...	...	2.9	0.1	0.2	0.1	...	0.2	0.1	...	0.7
Bituminous coal and lignite	...	0.5	...	4.0	...	...	2.2	2.0	6.6	8.8	11.2	6.6
Crude petroleum and natural gas	...	...	...	...	...	...	...	...	...	...	...	...
Nonmetallic minerals	0.1	0.1	0.2	1.5	3.0	0.2	...	...	...	0.1	...	...
Scrap and waste	...	0.3	0.3	...	...	...	...	0.3	...	...	...	0.1
Used merchandise	0.6	0.4	1.7	0.9	0.3	0.4	0.5	0.4	0.2	0.9	0.3	0.2
Goods imported and returned unchanged	...	...	...	...	...	...	...	...	...	...	...	...
Special classification provisions	0.2	0.3	0.3	0.2	0.4	1.5	1.0	0.8	1.6	0.9	0.9	1.6

Industry	The Netherlands						Asian 10					
	1994	1995	1996	1997	1998	1999	1994	1995	1996	1997	1998	1999
ALL GOODS	167.9	226.6	201.8	128.3	174.4	196.6	448.6	608.8	663.8	766.2	675.6	698.7
Manufactured Goods	152.9	162.1	185.3	101.7	156.0	190.5	411.8	564.1	628.7	723.1	641.3	654.5
Food products	0.3	0.9	1.4	2.2	0.1	1.1	30.9	35.0	37.3	36.2	36.6	39.0
Tobacco products	...	...	...	...	...	...	...	...	0.2	0.2	...	0.1
Textile mill products	0.7	0.3	0.4	1.5	3.3	2.7	11.1	8.5	11.8	37.1	47.2	51.6
Apparel	0.6	0.2	0.5	0.7	0.4	0.7	3.5	5.7	7.4	6.0	5.0	2.3
Lumber and wood products	1.3	1.3	2.4	1.5	1.4	1.8	5.4	4.4	8.7	8.5	4.0	7.0
Furniture and fixtures	0.2	0.2	0.2	...	3.8	7.5	1.3	0.7	0.8	0.9	1.4	3.3
Paper products	0.1	0.1	0.2	...	0.1	0.3	3.2	3.1	2.9	2.1	2.5	3.1
Printing and publishing	18.0	5.5	0.9	0.5	2.3	2.5	3.9	7.6	9.3	3.3	3.6	4.6
Chemical products	15.9	16.4	14.5	8.1	13.0	12.0	50.3	64.4	74.6	85.1	83.2	56.6
Refined petroleum products	1.8	1.8	3.7	9.1	5.5	2.7	0.2	0.6	2.0	2.0	1.2	1.4
Rubber and plastic products	0.5	0.9	1.5	1.5	1.8	4.3	12.1	13.8	9.6	16.4	10.6	17.6
Leather products	0.2	0.3	0.3	0.6	0.8	...	0.4	0.5	0.3	0.5	0.7	2.2
Stone, clay and glass products	1.0	0.6	0.5	0.8	0.2	0.4	7.3	14.7	11.4	5.4	4.3	3.5
Primary metals	1.4	5.3	10.0	2.7	0.6	0.4	10.2	16.2	12.6	10.4	7.0	18.3
Fabricated metal products	44.4	45.1	75.8	12.0	23.3	52.3	27.4	22.5	40.4	38.0	51.4	15.5
Industrial machinery and computers	16.4	19.7	14.1	7.0	11.2	15.3	83.9	110.9	165.2	132.1	99.0	140.4
Electric and electronic equipment	3.3	6.4	8.6	22.2	30.6	23.0	76.9	167.1	135.1	189.3	109.3	133.4
Transportation equipment	43.5	49.3	41.4	26.5	52.7	54.9	20.9	21.7	19.3	17.9	38.9	26.9
Scientific and measuring instruments	2.5	5.1	7.8	4.0	3.5	6.2	54.6	54.7	67.6	116.6	112.6	109.7
Miscellaneous manufactures	0.6	2.0	1.0	0.5	0.4	0.7	5.9	8.0	9.4	8.4	11.5	4.2
Unidentified manufactures	0.2	0.5	0.1	0.1	0.8	1.5	2.5	3.7	3.0	6.7	11.4	13.8
Agricultural And Livestock Products	...	0.1	...	0.2	...	0.1	1.3	3.7	1.1	2.1	0.5	0.8
Agricultural products	...	0.1	...	0.2	...	0.1	1.3	3.6	0.2	0.4	0.2	0.4
Livestock and livestock products	...	...	...	...	...	...	...	0.1	0.9	1.8	0.3	0.5
Other Commodities	14.9	64.4	16.4	26.4	18.4	6.0	35.6	41.1	34.0	40.9	33.8	43.4
Forestry products	...	...	...	...	...	0.1	0.6	0.6	0.7	0.6	0.6	1.1
Fish and other marine products	...	...	...	0.1	0.2	0.1	1.8	1.6	1.3	1.8	1.4	2.1
Metallic ores and concentrates	0.2	2.9	1.3	1.4	5.5	...	...	0.1	2.2	1.1	0.5	0.3
Bituminous coal and lignite	7.3	5.5	7.7	17.8	8.9	0.9	1.1	0.6	1.0	...	0.8	...
Crude petroleum and natural gas	...	...	...	...	...	...	...	...	...	...	0.1	...
Nonmetallic minerals	...	0.1	0.4	0.6	0.6	0.2	22.3	26.6	18.7	31.6	25.7	27.6
Scrap and waste	0.3	0.1	0.1	...	0.1	0.1	6.0	6.3	2.4	1.5	1.3	1.8
Used merchandise	0.3	...	1.7	0.2	0.1	0.1	2.2	3.8	1.9	0.5	0.8	0.6
Goods imported and returned unchanged	...	...	...	...	...	...	...	...	...	...	...	...
Special classification provisions	6.9	55.8	5.2	6.4	3.0	4.6	1.4	1.4	5.8	3.9	2.6	9.8

Table D-23. MARYLAND: State Exports of Goods by Destination and Industry, 1994–1999—*Continued*

(Millions of dollars.)

Industry	Japan						South Korea					
	1994	1995	1996	1997	1998	1999	1994	1995	1996	1997	1998	1999
ALL GOODS	134.3	153.1	171.1	158.6	189.0	179.5	48.1	60.8	74.6	95.4	67.0	88.7
Manufactured Goods	122.7	138.8	160.0	148.4	178.7	169.8	41.9	53.9	70.5	88.0	63.2	78.1
Food products	10.7	13.2	15.6	6.8	5.8	4.3	1.5	2.2	3.5	4.1	4.2	6.4
Tobacco products	...	...	0.2	...	...	...	...	...	...	0.2	...	...
Textile mill products	2.4	2.8	3.2	3.0	3.7	3.9	1.5	1.2	1.6	4.2	2.1	4.4
Apparel	2.9	4.9	6.2	3.0	3.4	0.6	0.1	...	0.4	1.2	0.2	0.4
Lumber and wood products	3.1	2.2	1.2	2.0	1.4	1.2	0.1	0.2	1.1	0.9	...	0.2
Furniture and fixtures	0.6	0.1	0.3	0.3	0.3	0.2	...	...	0.2	0.1	0.3	...
Paper products	0.3	0.9	0.5	0.5	0.3	0.5	...	0.1	0.2	0.1	0.1	0.2
Printing and publishing	1.7	3.4	1.9	0.9	1.5	0.7	0.6	0.7	1.5	0.7	0.7	1.1
Chemical products	30.5	28.7	32.9	37.8	33.6	24.5	3.9	7.2	10.6	12.3	12.8	6.8
Refined petroleum products	...	...	0.1	0.2	0.1	0.1	...	0.1	0.2	0.2	...	0.2
Rubber and plastic products	6.2	7.5	1.6	4.3	1.9	4.6	2.2	2.0	1.9	1.5	0.5	1.6
Leather products	0.2	0.2	0.2	0.1	...	1.7	...	...	...	0.1	...	...
Stone, clay and glass products	0.1	0.8	0.6	0.4	0.5	0.5	0.8	1.2	1.2	1.2	1.4	1.9
Primary metals	4.1	2.1	4.8	2.5	1.0	1.0	0.1	1.7	0.7	0.4	0.9	6.4
Fabricated metal products	3.8	1.9	20.2	3.7	2.6	1.1	2.2	2.8	3.1	3.9	0.6	0.7
Industrial machinery and computers	8.2	10.2	16.4	20.6	27.4	34.8	12.8	12.8	18.1	22.7	6.2	5.4
Electric and electronic equipment	23.0	22.2	26.4	25.1	26.7	29.6	8.6	12.7	10.3	18.6	11.7	13.4
Transportation equipment	3.6	16.7	6.8	3.3	16.7	7.8	0.3	0.5	4.8	0.9	1.0	0.6
Scientific and measuring instruments	18.5	15.4	15.8	27.6	41.9	40.1	6.6	7.0	10.0	13.2	19.5	27.3
Miscellaneous manufactures	2.2	3.1	3.1	1.5	1.1	1.3	0.4	1.1	1.0	0.9	0.6	0.7
Unidentified manufactures	0.5	2.4	1.9	5.0	8.8	11.4	0.2	0.2	0.2	0.6	0.4	0.3
Agricultural And Livestock Products	...	1.2	0.3	0.2	0.2	0.1	0.1	...	...	1.1	...	0.1
Agricultural products	...	1.1	0.2	0.2	0.2	...	0.1	...	...	...	...	0.1
Livestock and livestock products	...	0.1	0.1	...	...	...	...	...	...	1.1	...	...
Other Commodities	11.5	13.1	10.8	10.0	10.1	9.6	6.1	7.0	4.0	6.3	3.8	10.5
Forestry products	0.3	0.1	0.2	0.3	0.3	0.2	0.3	0.5	0.2	0.1	0.1	0.4
Fish and other marine products	1.4	1.5	1.3	1.6	1.3	0.9	0.4	...	...	0.1	...	...
Metallic ores and concentrates	...	0.1	1.3	0.2	0.1	...	...	...	0.6	0.2	0.2	0.1
Bituminous coal and lignite	1.1	0.6	1.0	...	0.7	...	...	...	...	...	...	...
Crude petroleum and natural gas	...	...	...	...	...	...	...	...	...	...	...	...
Nonmetallic minerals	6.6	7.1	5.1	7.0	6.5	6.9	5.2	6.1	3.0	5.6	3.4	4.2
Scrap and waste	...	0.1	...	0.1	0.1	0.5	...	...	...	...	...	0.1
Used merchandise	1.8	3.2	1.2	0.3	0.6	0.4	...	...	...	...	...	...
Goods imported and returned unchanged	...	...	...	...	...	...	...	...	...	...	...	...
Special classification provisions	0.4	0.5	0.7	0.6	0.5	0.7	0.1	0.3	0.1	0.3	0.1	5.8

Industry	Taiwan						Singapore					
	1994	1995	1996	1997	1998	1999	1994	1995	1996	1997	1998	1999
ALL GOODS	67.2	66.0	57.4	64.7	67.0	74.3	31.6	64.5	72.5	51.4	44.0	51.3
Manufactured Goods	54.2	52.4	47.8	48.9	53.0	60.2	30.7	63.1	71.7	51.1	43.2	50.5
Food products	0.4	0.2	0.4	0.2	0.5	0.5	1.1	0.7	0.6	1.4	1.5	2.2
Tobacco products	...	...	...	...	...	...	...	...	...	...	...	...
Textile mill products	0.5	0.3	0.7	2.1	2.8	2.1	2.7	1.2	1.0	1.0	0.4	0.3
Apparel	...	0.2	0.2	0.6	0.7	0.2	...	0.3	0.1	...	...	...
Lumber and wood products	1.1	0.7	2.9	0.3	0.1	0.2	0.1	0.1	...	0.1	...	0.1
Furniture and fixtures	...	0.4	...	...	0.1	0.3	...	...	0.1	0.2	0.1	0.5
Paper products	...	0.2	...	...	0.1	0.2	0.1	0.1	0.1	0.1	0.1	0.1
Printing and publishing	...	0.1	0.2	0.3	0.4	1.0	...	0.1	0.4	0.4	0.2	0.5
Chemical products	3.0	4.4	5.3	5.1	4.4	6.5	7.3	15.2	15.8	14.5	13.1	3.6
Refined petroleum products	...	...	0.1	0.1	0.1	...	...	...	0.6	0.6	0.1	0.2
Rubber and plastic products	1.3	0.9	0.5	0.7	0.3	0.6	0.3	1.1	0.7	0.9	0.9	0.8
Leather products	0.1	...	...	...	...	...	...	...	...	...	...	...
Stone, clay and glass products	3.5	3.0	0.2	0.3	0.2	0.2	...	0.1	1.1	0.5	0.1	0.2
Primary metals	2.4	6.5	0.3	0.3	0.4	1.5	0.1	0.5	0.1	0.3	0.1	1.2
Fabricated metal products	14.6	4.2	6.0	5.3	1.2	0.4	1.6	3.2	2.0	1.6	0.8	1.4
Industrial machinery and computers	7.2	15.5	18.3	12.8	18.0	13.7	8.3	22.1	39.4	18.0	14.4	21.1
Electric and electronic equipment	10.6	8.9	6.4	12.1	14.3	22.4	2.4	6.1	3.9	5.5	6.1	14.4
Transportation equipment	1.5	1.1	2.2	2.8	3.6	4.5	1.4	0.6	0.7	0.5	1.8	1.5
Scientific and measuring instruments	6.8	5.4	3.8	5.2	5.4	5.2	4.7	11.6	4.4	3.6	3.2	2.3
Miscellaneous manufactures	0.5	0.2	0.1	0.3	0.1	0.2	0.6	0.2	0.6	1.8	0.4	0.1
Unidentified manufactures	0.6	0.2	0.1	0.2	0.4	0.3	0.2	0.1	0.2	0.1	...	0.1
Agricultural And Livestock Products	...	0.1	...	...	...	...	...	...	...	...	...	...
Agricultural products	...	0.1	...	...	...	...	...	...	...	...	...	...
Livestock and livestock products	...	...	...	...	...	...	...	...	...	...	...	...
Other Commodities	13.1	13.6	9.6	15.8	14.0	14.1	0.9	1.4	0.8	0.3	0.8	0.8
Forestry products	...	...	0.1	...	...	...	...	...	...	...	...	0.1
Fish and other marine products	...	...	...	...	...	...	...	...	...	...	...	...
Metallic ores and concentrates	...	...	0.1	0.1	0.2	...	...	...	...	...	...	...
Bituminous coal and lignite	...	...	...	...	...	...	...	...	...	...	...	...
Crude petroleum and natural gas	...	...	...	...	...	...	...	...	...	...	...	...
Nonmetallic minerals	7.7	9.3	8.6	15.4	13.5	13.3	0.4	1.2	0.4	0.2	0.1	0.2
Scrap and waste	4.9	3.7	0.8	...	...	...	...	...	0.3	...	...	...
Used merchandise	...	0.4	...	0.1	...	...	0.3	0.1	0.1	...	...	0.2
Goods imported and returned unchanged	...	...	...	...	...	...	...	...	...	...	...	...
Special classification provisions	0.4	0.1	0.1	0.2	0.3	0.7	0.1	0.1	0.1	0.1	0.6	0.4

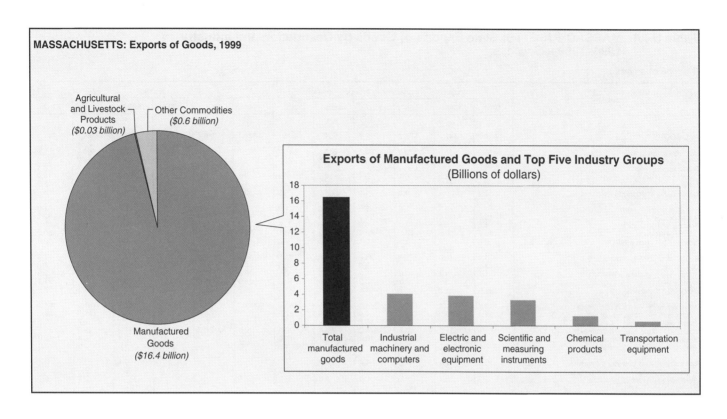

MASSACHUSETTS: Exports of Goods, 1999

Agricultural and Livestock Products ($0.03 billion)

Other Commodities ($0.6 billion)

Manufactured Goods ($16.4 billion)

Exports of Manufactured Goods and Top Five Industry Groups
(Billions of dollars)

Total manufactured goods | Industrial machinery and computers | Electric and electronic equipment | Scientific and measuring instruments | Chemical products | Transportation equipment

Table D-24. MASSACHUSETTS: State Exports of Goods by Destination and Industry, 1994–1999

(Millions of dollars.)

Industry	All destinations						Canada					
	1994	1995	1996	1997	1998	1999	1994	1995	1996	1997	1998	1999
ALL GOODS	12 586.0	14 396.4	15 368.4	17 368.1	16 467.3	17 105.8	2 860.4	3 339.9	3 486.8	3 677.5	3 387.6	3 256.8
Manufactured Goods	12 132.8	13 930.7	14 864.6	16 918.9	16 049.5	16 430.9	2 696.4	3 140.3	3 294.5	3 507.6	3 224.6	3 041.1
Food products	162.0	199.8	276.1	300.8	289.4	282.2	35.4	44.4	46.6	70.0	71.6	72.2
Tobacco products	0.1	. . .	. . .	0.1	0.1	0.1	. . .	. . .	. . .	0.1	. . .	. . .
Textile mill products	216.5	227.5	215.8	263.9	247.9	223.7	58.7	75.4	96.7	114.9	98.0	82.2
Apparel	77.0	106.1	100.9	88.6	57.9	65.1	30.6	54.5	46.4	36.2	12.2	9.1
Lumber and wood products	79.2	92.1	100.7	129.9	123.3	130.5	7.8	9.2	12.5	17.2	14.7	15.7
Furniture and fixtures	22.3	23.6	23.9	31.5	39.4	41.2	9.6	13.3	10.3	11.2	25.4	27.9
Paper products	271.4	359.2	398.3	431.1	402.3	418.0	104.4	123.9	141.8	148.4	157.1	151.7
Printing and publishing	148.1	167.3	178.7	201.9	180.8	136.0	59.5	66.6	75.2	86.7	66.0	67.1
Chemical products	716.7	896.2	1 023.9	1 225.1	1 168.3	1 278.7	180.1	183.2	227.2	226.4	183.3	212.0
Refined petroleum products	25.9	45.1	60.6	32.5	19.1	20.6	3.2	13.1	19.4	19.1	9.6	2.9
Rubber and plastic products	470.2	466.0	404.4	453.2	419.9	477.7	71.1	87.1	84.1	83.3	84.3	98.8
Leather products	123.4	111.6	99.4	118.3	98.2	86.9	19.8	21.3	19.1	18.2	17.6	10.8
Stone, clay and glass products	77.7	91.1	90.9	100.2	95.4	145.5	23.7	26.1	25.4	23.5	23.9	25.7
Primary metals	193.6	219.9	252.9	345.0	426.9	335.3	51.5	58.3	56.6	86.9	96.5	76.1
Fabricated metal products	448.6	476.2	550.4	705.8	618.5	584.9	125.3	143.3	160.1	150.8	146.3	138.8
Industrial machinery and computers	3 908.0	4 318.7	4 599.4	5 017.7	4 380.8	4 057.5	900.5	941.9	998.7	1 012.9	827.1	664.6
Electric and electronic equipment	2 688.4	3 262.7	3 214.1	3 779.6	3 711.0	3 847.8	584.3	759.2	672.0	708.6	674.8	597.6
Transportation equipment	308.2	393.6	498.3	553.4	529.6	603.2	191.7	262.4	351.5	420.9	408.2	471.7
Scientific and measuring instruments	1 909.6	2 159.2	2 470.6	2 809.0	2 870.2	3 320.4	164.8	174.0	165.0	179.4	210.8	201.4
Miscellaneous manufactures	201.8	233.8	237.0	264.6	279.5	282.1	56.8	63.0	66.0	69.3	71.9	90.3
Unidentified manufactures	84.1	81.1	68.1	66.8	91.2	93.6	17.5	20.0	19.6	23.7	25.1	24.4
Agricultural And Livestock Products	50.3	46.3	42.3	37.7	39.1	34.6	33.3	29.9	25.2	23.9	26.6	23.2
Agricultural products	42.9	39.1	36.6	30.4	29.9	22.9	32.3	28.1	22.2	20.5	19.7	14.6
Livestock and livestock products	7.4	7.2	5.6	7.3	9.2	11.7	1.0	1.8	2.9	3.4	6.9	8.7
Other Commodities	402.9	419.3	461.6	411.5	378.7	640.3	130.7	169.7	167.1	146.0	136.5	192.5
Forestry products	9.0	5.5	3.4	3.0	5.5	6.1	0.4	0.4	0.7	0.8	1.3	1.9
Fish and other marine products	171.2	180.6	186.0	162.1	158.6	174.7	45.0	52.0	54.4	42.2	45.4	53.0
Metallic ores and concentrates	0.6	2.8	0.7	1.0	0.3	0.3	0.2	2.6	0.3	. . .	. . .	. . .
Bituminous coal and lignite	1.8	. . .	0.6	1.9	0.1	. . .	. . .	. . .	0.6	. . .	0.1	. . .
Crude petroleum and natural gas	0.3	0.3	1.0	1.4	2.5	2.8	0.1	. . .	0.8	1.0	1.8	2.7
Nonmetallic minerals	7.4	8.9	6.9	7.9	11.6	6.6	1.2	1.9	1.5	1.9	2.2	2.5
Scrap and waste	86.7	95.3	66.2	71.5	67.4	55.0	29.6	51.2	29.8	34.1	30.1	31.3
Used merchandise	17.3	18.7	28.0	30.1	38.7	22.2	4.1	3.6	5.7	3.9	4.6	3.7
Goods imported and returned unchanged	43.9	40.9	57.1	54.5	46.2	33.1	43.9	40.9	57.1	54.5	46.2	33.1
Special classification provisions	64.6	66.3	111.7	78.0	47.8	339.3	6.3	17.0	16.3	7.7	4.6	64.2

Table D-24. MASSACHUSETTS: State Exports of Goods by Destination and Industry, 1994–1999—Continued

(Millions of dollars.)

Industry	South and Central American and Caribbean						Mexico					
	1994	1995	1996	1997	1998	1999	1994	1995	1996	1997	1998	1999
ALL GOODS	464.7	542.7	582.9	677.4	651.3	630.7	535.1	316.7	388.8	467.6	564.5	715.5
Manufactured Goods	455.5	538.0	573.5	668.9	643.6	615.7	522.0	308.9	383.3	465.0	560.9	708.6
Food products	17.7	24.5	25.7	27.7	33.5	22.4	4.8	3.6	5.6	8.3	8.7	4.8
Tobacco products	...	...	...	...	...	...	...	...	...	...	...	0.1
Textile mill products	9.1	5.8	6.1	9.4	10.7	10.3	9.1	4.2	5.9	9.4	11.6	18.9
Apparel	13.8	12.6	12.5	10.2	15.1	23.6	1.3	0.8	2.0	1.9	3.1	2.2
Lumber and wood products	0.4	0.4	0.3	1.0	1.2	0.5	0.3	0.1	0.1	1.3	1.7	3.5
Furniture and fixtures	1.4	1.3	1.0	1.5	1.6	1.2	0.8	0.5	0.7	0.6	1.0	1.0
Paper products	18.9	35.6	30.7	24.7	24.0	20.1	14.6	15.3	9.5	13.3	19.2	32.7
Printing and publishing	4.2	6.8	3.6	5.9	8.0	5.6	2.6	1.9	3.1	2.2	3.7	3.0
Chemical products	40.7	79.6	79.2	98.4	76.0	70.1	38.4	41.7	49.3	75.1	88.3	59.2
Refined petroleum products	0.8	0.2	0.3	0.4	4.6	9.6	0.2	0.4	0.4	0.7	0.5	0.5
Rubber and plastic products	15.8	18.6	25.3	25.6	14.8	13.5	9.9	8.5	11.8	14.7	15.1	17.4
Leather products	12.2	11.7	13.0	8.9	4.5	2.3	10.9	6.4	8.3	11.5	10.4	6.8
Stone, clay and glass products	3.1	4.4	3.6	5.2	4.2	6.1	2.6	3.9	2.9	3.0	2.8	3.9
Primary metals	3.5	3.9	4.0	3.9	10.6	10.9	24.0	13.8	5.3	3.6	7.7	21.1
Fabricated metal products	39.9	52.2	44.7	34.5	23.4	39.4	25.2	21.6	22.8	29.1	39.1	53.0
Industrial machinery and computers	152.6	141.8	166.0	215.2	181.9	160.4	143.8	83.1	123.3	144.9	161.2	185.0
Electric and electronic equipment	55.0	69.2	75.9	94.9	95.5	87.3	183.7	62.0	82.6	96.2	118.6	208.0
Transportation equipment	6.8	7.3	8.0	10.1	35.2	36.5	3.6	0.2	2.2	1.7	8.7	10.2
Scientific and measuring instruments	47.1	51.8	60.6	78.2	85.4	79.9	39.5	36.7	43.0	41.2	49.1	65.4
Miscellaneous manufactures	10.0	7.0	10.1	10.9	10.4	11.6	6.0	3.7	3.5	5.4	8.4	9.0
Unidentified manufactures	2.4	3.1	2.7	2.2	2.2	4.3	1.0	0.8	1.0	1.0	2.0	3.0
Agricultural And Livestock Products	0.8	1.4	4.2	4.4	4.2	2.7	0.1	...	...	0.1	0.5	0.1
Agricultural products	0.5	0.8	2.9	2.5	3.9	2.5	...	...	...	0.1	0.4	...
Livestock and livestock products	0.3	0.7	1.3	1.9	0.4	0.2	0.1	...	...	...	0.1	0.1
Other Commodities	8.4	3.3	5.1	4.1	3.5	12.3	13.0	7.8	5.5	2.5	3.1	6.8
Forestry products	1.9	0.8	0.3	0.1	0.5	0.5	0.1	...	0.1	...	...	...
Fish and other marine products	0.5	0.3	0.3	0.6	0.5	0.3	0.3	0.1	0.1	0.1	0.4	0.5
Metallic ores and concentrates	...	...	...	...	...	...	...	...	...	...	...	...
Bituminous coal and lignite	...	...	...	...	...	...	...	...	...	...	...	...
Crude petroleum and natural gas	...	...	...	...	...	...	...	...	...	...	...	...
Nonmetallic minerals	0.4	0.1	0.1	0.3	0.2	0.1	1.5	0.2	0.3	0.1	0.1	...
Scrap and waste	4.9	0.6	0.3	0.4	...	0.2	0.1	3.0	3.0	1.2	1.4	0.1
Used merchandise	0.5	1.3	0.9	0.7	0.5	0.5	0.1	...	...	0.1	0.8	0.1
Goods imported and returned unchanged	...	...	...	...	...	...	...	...	...	...	...	...
Special classification provisions	0.2	0.1	3.2	2.1	1.7	10.8	10.8	4.5	2.1	0.9	0.3	6.0

Industry	European Union						United Kingdom					
	1994	1995	1996	1997	1998	1999	1994	1995	1996	1997	1998	1999
ALL GOODS	4 629.8	5 288.6	5 353.1	5 889.3	6 200.1	6 304.9	1 245.0	1 479.0	1 415.2	1 706.4	1 794.5	1 826.5
Manufactured Goods	4 457.0	5 126.0	5 154.8	5 733.9	6 055.5	6 042.4	1 210.0	1 453.1	1 383.1	1 680.2	1 772.7	1 770.9
Food products	51.3	64.2	79.7	65.3	77.0	72.1	4.5	6.4	10.2	13.5	18.5	29.2
Tobacco products	...	...	...	...	...	...	...	...	...	...	...	...
Textile mill products	77.9	75.3	49.9	69.8	71.3	56.3	20.2	18.7	14.7	17.1	17.0	14.3
Apparel	15.9	11.3	12.5	14.6	8.8	10.7	6.3	5.5	5.1	9.6	4.8	5.0
Lumber and wood products	37.3	37.0	50.3	68.2	66.7	69.6	4.4	3.6	6.5	9.6	11.2	13.1
Furniture and fixtures	5.4	5.1	5.9	8.8	6.1	5.9	2.4	1.9	1.3	1.8	1.2	1.6
Paper products	52.9	91.5	104.3	121.9	115.2	105.8	16.1	18.0	13.6	19.4	24.0	21.4
Printing and publishing	43.1	57.9	49.5	50.8	54.2	37.2	12.6	21.9	15.2	15.1	19.1	9.1
Chemical products	233.1	328.5	359.5	466.9	546.4	669.0	72.0	113.4	132.6	140.5	179.7	214.2
Refined petroleum products	6.4	1.1	25.4	2.7	1.0	1.6	1.6	0.2	1.2	2.3	0.5	0.1
Rubber and plastic products	250.9	208.5	163.7	177.6	172.5	208.7	49.4	49.3	44.9	51.2	57.7	62.7
Leather products	24.5	24.6	19.9	23.6	20.3	16.4	4.9	6.1	3.2	3.0	3.5	4.5
Stone, clay and glass products	27.4	29.0	31.7	36.4	40.4	61.1	6.9	7.5	7.4	7.0	6.1	17.6
Primary metals	65.2	87.4	99.3	130.6	228.8	118.1	18.8	31.4	31.0	56.7	138.7	41.4
Fabricated metal products	152.8	141.1	146.9	153.0	206.9	179.5	27.8	21.2	24.8	25.1	97.6	109.4
Industrial machinery and computers	1 470.2	1 619.4	1 509.8	1 696.8	1 650.4	1 526.2	312.2	363.6	406.4	566.8	487.9	466.2
Electric and electronic equipment	859.4	1 138.7	1 116.7	1 230.2	1 279.2	1 250.8	368.9	481.5	339.8	392.9	346.7	368.6
Transportation equipment	45.4	64.3	60.3	53.9	44.4	59.2	6.2	7.1	8.3	11.9	8.9	10.3
Scientific and measuring instruments	952.1	1 042.3	1 175.8	1 263.1	1 341.4	1 470.8	243.6	252.4	279.4	306.2	313.8	326.5
Miscellaneous manufactures	59.9	77.2	77.9	86.3	94.0	98.7	22.7	36.7	32.6	26.5	29.4	48.6
Unidentified manufactures	25.9	21.9	16.0	13.3	30.5	24.5	8.4	6.7	5.2	4.0	6.2	7.1
Agricultural And Livestock Products	9.9	10.6	10.1	6.6	5.4	6.9	4.8	3.0	2.9	2.7	2.1	2.5
Agricultural products	8.0	8.4	9.4	5.7	4.2	4.4	3.8	2.3	2.7	2.7	2.0	2.5
Livestock and livestock products	1.8	2.2	0.8	0.9	1.3	2.5	1.0	0.7	0.2	...	0.1	...
Other Commodities	162.9	152.0	188.2	148.8	139.2	255.6	30.1	22.9	29.2	23.5	19.7	53.1
Forestry products	4.4	2.4	0.9	0.8	1.6	0.6	0.2	0.3	0.3	0.2	0.1	0.3
Fish and other marine products	74.3	76.8	83.7	66.4	69.8	72.5	2.4	3.3	3.2	4.9	4.3	8.2
Metallic ores and concentrates	0.4	0.1	0.3	0.9	0.1	...	0.2	...	...	0.8	...	...
Bituminous coal and lignite	1.8	...	...	1.9	...	...	...	...	...	1.9	...	...
Crude petroleum and natural gas	0.1	...	0.1	0.2	0.1	0.1	...	...	...	0.1	0.1	...
Nonmetallic minerals	3.1	3.5	3.5	4.3	4.9	1.5	1.6	2.4	2.2	1.8	2.2	0.2
Scrap and waste	39.1	27.8	24.0	27.4	27.4	17.3	6.8	4.9	3.1	2.0	2.4	0.8
Used merchandise	9.3	10.6	15.9	13.9	15.1	11.5	3.0	4.5	7.8	5.1	4.7	5.1
Goods imported and returned unchanged	...	...	...	...	...	...	...	...	...	...	...	...
Special classification provisions	30.5	30.6	59.7	32.9	20.1	152.1	15.9	7.5	12.6	6.7	6.0	38.5

Table D-24. MASSACHUSETTS: State Exports of Goods by Destination and Industry, 1994–1999—Continued

(Millions of dollars.)

Industry	Germany						France					
	1994	1995	1996	1997	1998	1999	1994	1995	1996	1997	1998	1999
ALL GOODS	851.8	1 040.5	1 098.8	1 019.4	1 163.8	1 057.9	542.0	528.2	562.8	626.7	673.5	761.1
Manufactured Goods	829.1	1 014.4	1 068.7	998.6	1 138.9	1 019.8	505.8	491.9	514.4	587.5	639.6	719.0
Food products	1.2	1.8	1.7	3.1	2.2	2.0	1.3	1.4	2.4	2.2	0.6	1.5
Tobacco products	...	...	...	...	...	...	...	...	...	...	...	...
Textile mill products	22.1	21.6	6.1	20.3	24.6	21.7	8.6	6.0	3.8	5.4	4.8	3.4
Apparel	2.8	1.3	3.1	0.5	0.6	0.6	0.8	0.7	0.6	0.6	0.4	0.2
Lumber and wood products	11.6	11.5	9.6	10.1	10.2	10.9	5.0	1.5	2.8	2.2	4.7	6.3
Furniture and fixtures	1.2	1.3	1.2	1.2	1.2	1.6	0.1	...	0.4	0.4	0.2	0.4
Paper products	5.4	6.9	16.6	11.4	8.3	8.8	3.3	2.3	2.5	2.0	1.7	1.9
Printing and publishing	11.6	12.5	14.5	12.7	8.3	6.6	2.1	3.7	2.5	3.0	2.1	0.9
Chemical products	46.4	70.2	69.2	72.6	71.5	59.2	24.9	32.1	36.6	51.0	106.0	165.9
Refined petroleum products	...	...	...	...	0.1	0.7	...	...	15.9			
Rubber and plastic products	27.9	21.5	19.7	28.7	24.3	32.2	18.1	16.1	8.1	12.8	17.4	13.6
Leather products	5.8	5.6	5.7	7.2	3.8	5.1	3.4	2.1	1.0	2.7	1.9	1.2
Stone, clay and glass products	7.5	6.2	7.7	6.1	10.3	20.2	4.3	4.8	4.5	6.2	5.5	6.9
Primary metals	19.9	28.9	33.2	24.5	27.6	39.3	9.8	8.3	8.7	12.3	26.1	10.5
Fabricated metal products	90.7	76.1	73.5	54.7	32.9	14.8	8.2	8.3	7.1	19.5	14.1	18.1
Industrial machinery and computers	234.4	273.2	240.6	239.6	371.4	223.9	190.7	184.1	187.9	212.9	178.3	189.4
Electric and electronic equipment	137.0	221.8	266.3	240.5	273.6	278.1	77.9	81.4	97.7	127.1	148.6	123.9
Transportation equipment	6.7	8.3	9.7	8.5	5.9	6.8	3.6	6.8	5.3	4.7	6.9	8.7
Scientific and measuring instruments	180.9	231.5	273.2	238.8	242.3	271.5	138.9	126.5	120.6	114.0	110.7	156.7
Miscellaneous manufactures	10.2	9.8	13.9	14.7	16.3	10.5	2.4	3.8	4.7	7.3	8.1	7.8
Unidentified manufactures	5.8	4.4	3.4	3.3	3.3	5.3	2.3	2.0	1.3	1.1	1.6	1.6
Agricultural And Livestock Products	0.7	1.1	1.3	0.5	0.2	0.2	1.0	0.9	1.1	0.8	0.1	0.1
Agricultural products	0.7	1.1	1.2	0.4	0.1	0.2	0.5	0.9	0.7	0.4	0.1	
Livestock and livestock products	...	0.1	...	0.1	0.2	0.1	0.5	...	0.4	0.3	0.1	...
Other Commodities	22.0	24.9	28.9	20.3	24.7	37.8	35.2	35.4	47.3	38.4	33.8	42.1
Forestry products	0.6	0.2	0.1	0.2	0.3	0.1	0.2	...	...	...		
Fish and other marine products	4.5	10.0	10.6	4.3	3.2	4.0	29.7	32.6	37.7	29.9	27.9	22.2
Metallic ores and concentrates	0.1	0.1	...	...	...	...	0.1	...	0.1	...	...	...
Bituminous coal and lignite	...	...	...	...	...	...	0.6	...	...	...	...	...
Crude petroleum and natural gas	...	...	...	...	...	...	...	...	...	...	...	...
Nonmetallic minerals	0.8	0.4	0.5	0.9	1.4	0.3	0.2	0.2	0.1	0.4	0.6	0.5
Scrap and waste	9.6	8.4	7.9	7.2	9.4	3.5	...	0.1	...	...	0.8	0.1
Used merchandise	2.9	3.3	2.3	1.6	6.8	1.3	1.0	0.6	2.3	3.6	1.9	1.8
Goods imported and returned unchanged	...	...	...	...	...	...	...	...	...	...	...	...
Special classification provisions	3.4	2.5	7.5	6.1	3.7	28.7	3.4	1.9	7.0	4.5	2.5	17.4

Industry	The Netherlands						Asian 10					
	1994	1995	1996	1997	1998	1999	1994	1995	1996	1997	1998	1999
ALL GOODS	710.1	763.4	692.3	928.9	903.9	1 013.3	3 023.8	3 713.9	4 316.5	5 323.4	4 419.6	4 878.9
Manufactured Goods	703.0	744.5	664.7	914.9	897.2	987.6	2 949.5	3 636.7	4 237.4	5 233.6	4 346.5	4 752.6
Food products	0.6	0.8	1.4	1.2	1.3	2.2	46.1	50.7	100.7	107.1	84.0	80.4
Tobacco products	...	...	...	...	...	...	...	...	...	...	0.1	...
Textile mill products	3.1	3.6	1.1	3.7	3.0	2.4	36.8	43.4	39.8	39.8	34.9	37.2
Apparel	1.8	0.4	0.4	1.2	1.7	2.0	7.4	16.6	18.7	18.9	16.1	16.1
Lumber and wood products	1.7	2.3	3.1	5.6	3.1	2.2	31.8	36.9	34.5	37.0	28.2	30.4
Furniture and fixtures	0.2	0.2	1.0	2.4	0.9	0.1	1.9	2.0	2.8	2.7	3.4	3.4
Paper products	10.9	24.3	20.4	29.6	43.6	57.6	63.4	63.5	80.3	98.8	70.5	84.0
Printing and publishing	4.0	4.8	5.3	7.1	6.6	7.5	21.0	23.5	36.1	43.0	37.7	14.1
Chemical products	26.9	39.6	35.8	120.1	111.2	146.6	158.1	186.8	225.5	255.8	182.5	184.0
Refined petroleum products	3.6	0.6	7.9	...	...	...	4.9	15.1	5.5	5.0	1.9	3.8
Rubber and plastic products	122.8	86.2	54.2	51.3	54.2	74.6	86.6	92.4	77.9	97.1	103.5	109.8
Leather products	1.7	2.0	2.6	1.8	2.5	1.4	47.3	41.8	35.3	50.4	41.3	46.4
Stone, clay and glass products	1.7	4.3	4.5	5.1	6.3	6.0	16.5	21.5	20.5	22.5	17.1	32.6
Primary metals	3.1	1.9	3.3	8.1	5.2	1.6	36.5	43.2	50.1	70.5	36.2	41.9
Fabricated metal products	4.1	3.7	12.4	19.5	14.4	7.9	70.2	85.8	140.2	282.6	137.4	101.2
Industrial machinery and computers	253.1	264.2	249.0	264.3	174.1	180.2	864.0	1 125.4	1 397.1	1 542.7	1 194.7	1 165.1
Electric and electronic equipment	74.3	93.4	93.3	133.6	138.8	126.2	824.7	1 032.5	1 066.1	1 424.9	1 315.7	1 507.1
Transportation equipment	3.8	11.3	6.8	4.1	2.8	2.8	39.1	23.6	27.7	42.1	16.5	5.7
Scientific and measuring instruments	175.8	189.9	151.0	243.4	317.1	358.4	531.7	658.9	809.3	1 014.4	942.0	1 227.8
Miscellaneous manufactures	8.3	9.6	10.1	12.2	9.3	7.0	52.7	64.7	62.2	72.0	73.1	47.8
Unidentified manufactures	1.5	1.4	1.0	0.8	1.2	1.2	8.8	8.7	7.2	6.3	9.8	13.6
Agricultural And Livestock Products	0.9	0.7	2.6	0.6	0.6	0.7	1.7	1.1	1.6	1.2	1.9	1.1
Agricultural products	0.9	0.6	2.6	0.6	0.6	0.6	0.8	0.4	1.3	0.8	1.5	0.9
Livestock and livestock products	...	...	...	...	...	...	0.9	0.8	0.3	0.4	0.3	0.2
Other Commodities	6.2	18.2	25.0	13.4	6.1	25.0	72.6	76.1	77.5	88.6	71.2	125.2
Forestry products	...	...	...	...	...	...	1.2	1.2	1.3	0.9	1.9	2.7
Fish and other marine products	1.3	1.6	2.0	0.7	0.6	0.4	47.1	48.3	43.9	49.8	38.0	43.7
Metallic ores and concentrates	...	...	0.2	0.1	0.1	...	...	...	...	...	0.1	...
Bituminous coal and lignite	...	...	...	...	...	...	...	...	...	...	...	...
Crude petroleum and natural gas	...	...	...	...	...	...	...	0.1	0.1	0.1	0.1	...
Nonmetallic minerals	0.1	...	...	0.6	0.2	0.2	0.8	2.2	0.9	0.9	2.0	0.3
Scrap and waste	0.8	0.7	0.3	0.5	0.7	0.3	9.5	11.5	8.2	8.2	7.8	5.1
Used merchandise	0.4	0.2	1.1	0.4	0.3	0.5	2.5	1.5	3.9	2.1	6.5	3.6
Goods imported and returned unchanged	...	...	...	...	...	...	...	...	...	...	...	...
Special classification provisions	3.6	15.7	21.3	11.2	4.3	23.6	11.4	11.1	19.2	26.6	14.9	69.7

Table D-24. MASSACHUSETTS: State Exports of Goods by Destination and Industry, 1994–1999—Continued

(Millions of dollars.)

Industry	Japan						South Korea					
	1994	1995	1996	1997	1998	1999	1994	1995	1996	1997	1998	1999
ALL GOODS	1 155.1	1 396.4	1 680.5	1 969.0	1 859.3	1 793.0	348.4	432.5	530.7	616.5	320.1	464.4
Manufactured Goods	1 109.7	1 349.7	1 633.9	1 917.0	1 818.5	1 733.9	340.3	425.6	520.8	607.1	312.2	440.5
Food products	3.7	6.1	30.2	25.8	32.5	30.3	26.9	25.1	32.3	48.1	25.8	22.8
Tobacco products	...	...	...	...	...	...	...	...	...	...	...	...
Textile mill products	4.0	6.0	6.1	6.0	5.3	4.3	4.5	5.3	3.0	4.9	1.6	3.1
Apparel	4.1	10.6	12.4	11.2	5.3	7.4	0.2	0.7	0.2	0.4	0.1	0.1
Lumber and wood products	7.8	10.5	10.5	8.3	4.8	3.8	5.6	5.6	7.6	10.3	2.8	6.0
Furniture and fixtures	0.4	1.1	1.1	1.6	0.8	2.4	0.1	0.2	0.5	0.2	...	0.2
Paper products	8.4	13.3	12.2	11.1	11.6	13.6	3.9	4.5	5.0	6.4	2.7	2.9
Printing and publishing	7.6	10.3	14.6	24.2	25.6	5.6	3.1	4.2	6.3	3.5	3.4	1.4
Chemical products	54.3	58.0	72.4	110.8	99.4	90.7	23.0	35.9	31.5	27.5	15.0	15.4
Refined petroleum products	3.2	3.1	3.4	2.3	0.4	0.5	0.3	3.0	0.5	0.7	0.4	0.3
Rubber and plastic products	54.0	62.7	55.3	56.8	71.0	67.7	6.8	5.9	3.7	4.2	2.3	2.6
Leather products	12.5	9.4	9.3	14.9	17.6	28.2	2.7	3.8	3.7	8.9	1.1	1.3
Stone, clay and glass products	7.5	7.3	9.0	7.3	6.9	18.1	3.7	4.1	3.4	3.0	1.2	2.9
Primary metals	19.8	21.5	18.9	15.6	15.1	15.4	2.4	6.6	4.7	14.3	3.3	3.5
Fabricated metal products	26.3	19.1	22.0	24.0	28.1	30.3	7.1	16.1	13.4	8.6	2.8	11.8
Industrial machinery and computers	389.6	499.5	653.7	697.0	585.1	499.5	91.7	105.7	155.4	175.8	78.5	101.5
Electric and electronic equipment	223.1	309.0	303.7	375.4	370.6	382.8	67.5	91.2	120.1	198.4	107.5	197.3
Transportation equipment	4.1	2.2	2.4	3.6	3.2	1.5	26.8	12.8	10.0	8.0	1.9	0.3
Scientific and measuring instruments	249.0	264.2	365.1	476.4	480.2	506.7	60.0	89.4	106.0	79.1	58.9	59.5
Miscellaneous manufactures	27.5	33.1	30.0	42.4	51.9	22.1	2.9	4.8	4.8	4.2	2.0	4.1
Unidentified manufactures	2.8	2.7	1.6	2.1	3.2	3.1	1.0	0.8	0.7	0.7	1.0	3.5
Agricultural And Livestock Products	0.4	0.2	1.3	0.6	0.3	0.3	0.2	0.1	...	...	...	...
Agricultural products	0.3	0.2	1.1	0.4	0.1	0.2	0.1	0.1	...	...	...	...
Livestock and livestock products	0.1	...	0.2	0.1	0.2	0.2	0.1	...	...	...	...	...
Other Commodities	45.1	46.5	45.3	51.4	40.6	58.8	7.8	6.7	9.8	9.4	7.9	23.9
Forestry products	...	...	0.1	...	0.2	0.3	...	...	0.1	...	...	...
Fish and other marine products	35.7	39.2	33.6	36.5	28.9	30.4	7.0	5.4	6.5	6.6	6.7	11.6
Metallic ores and concentrates	...	...	...	...	...	...	...	...	...	...	...	...
Bituminous coal and lignite	...	...	...	...	...	...	...	...	...	...	...	...
Crude petroleum and natural gas	...	...	...	...	...	...	...	...	...	...	...	...
Nonmetallic minerals	0.6	1.8	0.4	0.4	0.8	0.2	0.1	0.1	...	...	0.1	0.1
Scrap and waste	0.4	0.4	0.2	0.1	0.1	0.1	...	...	0.1	1.5	...	0.1
Used merchandise	2.2	0.5	1.8	0.9	5.0	2.3	...	0.6	1.6	0.3	...	0.1
Goods imported and returned unchanged	...	...	...	...	...	...	...	...	...	...	...	...
Special classification provisions	6.1	4.5	9.2	13.5	5.6	25.5	0.6	0.7	1.5	0.9	1.1	12.0

Industry	Taiwan						Singapore					
	1994	1995	1996	1997	1998	1999	1994	1995	1996	1997	1998	1999
ALL GOODS	427.6	489.6	592.3	789.0	557.2	697.8	329.0	352.4	409.0	544.8	430.4	583.9
Manufactured Goods	425.2	488.4	590.1	782.6	553.1	689.2	324.8	346.4	402.9	537.9	426.2	574.2
Food products	8.3	12.3	24.7	21.7	14.2	9.7	0.1	...	0.2	0.6	0.2	0.4
Tobacco products	...	...	...	...	...	...	...	...	...	...	...	...
Textile mill products	5.3	3.1	3.5	3.3	2.9	2.3	2.3	2.5	1.9	2.4	0.7	0.8
Apparel	0.2	0.4	1.3	1.5	0.8	0.2	1.3	1.6	0.8	0.6	0.4	0.4
Lumber and wood products	10.4	7.8	4.6	4.5	3.9	3.8	0.5	0.8	0.5	0.4	0.1	...
Furniture and fixtures	0.1	0.1	0.1	...	...	0.1	0.2	0.1	0.2	0.1	1.1	0.3
Paper products	5.7	5.2	5.1	6.0	3.8	3.6	8.6	6.8	7.0	7.0	6.2	5.6
Printing and publishing	4.0	2.4	5.2	4.0	2.7	2.0	2.4	2.9	2.9	2.5	1.0	1.4
Chemical products	11.6	12.3	18.9	19.9	18.6	26.3	17.3	18.2	27.3	22.9	14.6	11.7
Refined petroleum products	0.3	0.2	0.3	0.4	0.3	0.3	0.2	0.3	0.3	0.3	0.2	0.1
Rubber and plastic products	6.7	4.8	3.9	4.8	5.0	11.8	5.1	3.0	2.6	4.6	5.8	9.5
Leather products	3.6	1.9	1.7	3.6	1.9	1.4	1.5	0.9	0.8	0.9	0.3	0.3
Stone, clay and glass products	1.2	3.2	2.5	3.8	3.5	6.8	0.4	1.7	1.2	1.7	1.3	1.4
Primary metals	2.6	2.6	6.5	6.3	3.2	4.6	2.9	3.1	3.8	12.0	6.3	8.9
Fabricated metal products	10.3	4.7	58.7	161.3	38.7	6.4	9.0	12.5	13.2	15.0	7.1	7.0
Industrial machinery and computers	70.2	108.4	145.5	168.2	97.0	160.6	67.7	88.3	131.2	179.3	140.5	186.6
Electric and electronic equipment	228.2	235.8	172.2	224.6	221.6	242.8	129.6	113.5	108.9	134.4	122.6	143.3
Transportation equipment	1.3	0.4	6.2	5.8	7.9	0.9	0.6	0.5	1.0	19.4	1.2	1.2
Scientific and measuring instruments	52.0	78.0	123.7	138.5	123.0	201.9	68.6	83.4	93.9	127.3	111.6	191.2
Miscellaneous manufactures	1.9	3.7	3.7	3.2	2.7	2.1	5.4	5.3	4.2	6.0	3.8	3.2
Unidentified manufactures	1.1	1.0	1.9	1.0	1.3	1.7	0.9	1.1	0.7	0.6	1.2	1.0
Agricultural And Livestock Products	0.1	0.2	0.1	0.1	0.4	...	0.1	...	0.1	...	...	...
Agricultural products	0.1	...	0.1	0.1	0.3	...	0.1	...	...	0.1	...	...
Livestock and livestock products	...	0.2	...	...	0.1	...	...	...	...	...	...	...
Other Commodities	2.3	1.0	2.1	6.3	3.7	8.6	4.1	6.0	6.0	6.9	4.2	9.7
Forestry products	...	...	...	0.1	0.2	...	0.3	0.3	0.2	0.1	0.3	0.1
Fish and other marine products	0.8	0.2	0.1	...	0.3	...	0.1	0.2	0.2	1.3	0.5	0.3
Metallic ores and concentrates	...	...	...	...	...	...	...	...	...	...	...	...
Bituminous coal and lignite	...	...	...	...	...	...	...	...	...	...	...	...
Crude petroleum and natural gas	...	...	...	...	...	...	...	...	...	...	...	...
Nonmetallic minerals	...	0.1	0.3	0.1	0.6	...	...	0.1	0.1	0.1	...	0.1
Scrap and waste	1.0	...	0.1	0.3	0.1	0.5	0.9	1.1	0.6	0.2	0.4	...
Used merchandise	...	...	0.1	...	...	0.2	...	0.3	0.1	0.2	...	...
Goods imported and returned unchanged	...	...	...	...	...	...	...	...	...	...	...	...
Special classification provisions	0.4	0.6	1.3	5.7	2.5	7.8	2.8	4.1	4.9	5.0	2.9	9.1

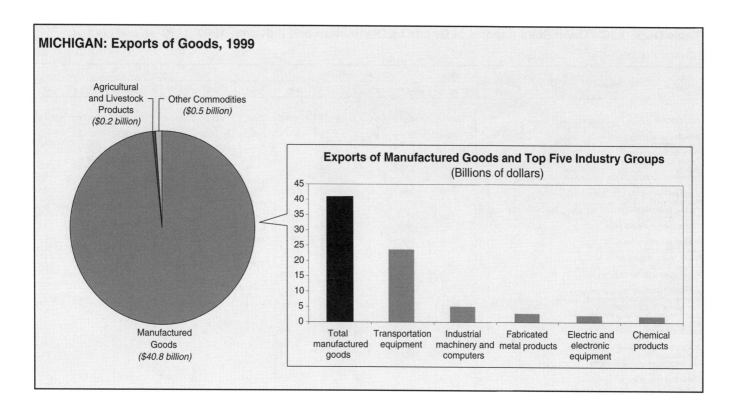

MICHIGAN: Exports of Goods, 1999

Agricultural and Livestock Products ($0.2 billion)

Other Commodities ($0.5 billion)

Manufactured Goods ($40.8 billion)

Exports of Manufactured Goods and Top Five Industry Groups
(Billions of dollars)

Total manufactured goods / Transportation equipment / Industrial machinery and computers / Fabricated metal products / Electric and electronic equipment / Chemical products

Table D-25. MICHIGAN: State Exports of Goods by Destination and Industry, 1994–1999

(Millions of dollars.)

Industry	All destinations						Canada					
	1994	1995	1996	1997	1998	1999	1994	1995	1996	1997	1998	1999
ALL GOODS	36 812.1	37 102.3	38 128.2	37 920.1	39 268.8	41 489.9	20 809.1	21 935.9	21 949.6	19 760.2	19 665.9	21 992.1
Manufactured Goods	36 196.2	36 392.8	37 498.5	37 240.6	38 683.2	40 796.1	20 329.5	21 369.5	21 465.3	19 228.9	19 229.3	21 444.9
Food products	346.1	396.7	463.0	468.6	405.6	357.9	154.2	157.5	163.7	173.1	146.5	126.7
Tobacco products	0.3	2.3	. . .	. . .	. . .	. . .	. . .	0.1	. . .	. . .	. . .	. . .
Textile mill products	89.2	96.1	57.0	72.7	77.1	92.8	18.0	22.1	22.7	28.3	25.4	28.9
Apparel	121.3	155.9	187.9	176.5	142.0	88.2	28.8	95.8	101.2	94.1	91.0	64.5
Lumber and wood products	90.6	88.1	80.7	82.4	85.4	101.0	55.7	46.5	50.4	49.6	50.8	57.2
Furniture and fixtures	700.1	793.5	695.4	735.3	831.3	250.9	291.7	368.6	435.4	449.4	575.7	112.3
Paper products	146.3	168.9	184.9	181.4	161.0	170.2	86.3	103.7	121.9	104.7	107.7	117.1
Printing and publishing	92.9	93.6	81.3	87.8	76.8	75.2	66.9	67.3	59.9	53.7	48.1	41.0
Chemical products	1 156.7	1 315.2	1 669.3	1 930.1	1 793.4	1 968.3	257.6	352.7	617.7	717.8	681.1	718.6
Refined petroleum products	56.9	53.8	80.6	78.1	48.5	63.8	42.7	39.1	66.8	58.1	34.0	39.4
Rubber and plastic products	573.8	576.5	629.1	705.8	733.3	906.3	156.8	184.3	235.5	266.1	321.7	387.3
Leather products	79.5	116.2	133.0	172.4	170.8	172.7	2.4	2.8	3.5	5.2	3.8	28.5
Stone, clay and glass products	381.7	405.3	470.8	481.4	505.9	570.7	227.9	257.7	296.9	301.7	318.2	387.2
Primary metals	719.5	811.7	735.4	801.6	864.6	756.8	423.6	486.2	427.0	461.6	548.3	490.3
Fabricated metal products	1 367.5	1 158.1	1 299.7	1 251.6	2 006.2	2 933.8	419.3	502.1	504.1	553.5	1 411.0	2 109.0
Industrial machinery and computers	3 991.2	4 169.3	4 281.4	5 332.6	4 778.0	5 103.3	2 297.3	2 144.4	2 270.0	2 988.0	2 555.0	2 790.5
Electric and electronic equipment	1 870.3	1 777.9	1 805.3	1 961.7	1 985.3	2 221.0	573.1	690.6	746.4	728.8	813.8	967.1
Transportation equipment	23 546.7	23 241.0	23 688.9	21 588.0	22 790.5	23 725.8	15 000.7	15 532.6	15 030.2	11 777.4	11 021.6	12 479.3
Scientific and measuring instruments	635.1	736.7	743.4	909.1	1 016.5	1 060.4	182.3	275.2	274.4	378.7	436.0	454.2
Miscellaneous manufactures	179.9	187.2	175.6	185.3	133.2	114.1	27.8	25.1	22.2	24.5	25.7	31.9
Unidentified manufactures	50.6	48.9	35.8	38.1	77.7	63.0	16.2	15.0	15.3	14.4	13.8	13.9
Agricultural And Livestock Products	171.4	181.4	173.8	197.8	185.7	184.8	72.7	70.3	70.2	96.8	82.7	122.4
Agricultural products	152.2	168.6	164.3	190.3	172.4	168.3	55.1	58.5	62.7	90.8	70.9	106.6
Livestock and livestock products	19.3	12.8	9.5	7.5	13.3	16.5	17.6	11.8	7.5	5.9	11.8	15.9
Other Commodities	444.5	528.1	455.9	481.7	399.8	509.1	406.9	496.1	414.1	434.5	353.8	424.7
Forestry products	0.4	1.5	1.6	1.5	1.0	0.9	0.2	0.3	0.4	1.4	0.4	0.3
Fish and other marine products	3.1	3.6	2.9	3.4	3.4	6.1	2.9	3.1	2.7	2.8	3.3	5.9
Metallic ores and concentrates	4.9	78.8	8.1	0.4	64.3	115.0	4.6	78.8	7.8	0.3	63.9	115.0
Bituminous coal and lignite	1.4	1.1	0.8	. . .	. . .	0.7	1.4	1.1	0.8	. . .	. . .	0.7
Crude petroleum and natural gas	33.5	51.3	36.8	27.2	36.3	35.5	33.3	51.2	36.8	27.2	36.3	35.4
Nonmetallic minerals	19.5	21.4	21.0	19.4	17.5	18.5	18.7	20.5	19.9	16.8	15.7	17.1
Scrap and waste	81.8	107.4	97.5	107.2	83.3	128.3	72.2	90.0	75.1	83.3	65.0	88.4
Used merchandise	10.3	10.3	11.3	12.8	16.8	12.4	4.0	5.6	4.8	5.3	3.8	4.3
Goods imported and returned unchanged	248.8	216.7	235.1	277.0	145.1	117.5	248.8	216.7	235.1	277.0	145.1	117.5
Special classification provisions	40.9	36.0	41.0	32.7	32.1	74.2	20.8	28.8	30.9	18.8	20.3	40.2

Table D-25. MICHIGAN: State Exports of Goods by Destination and Industry, 1994–1999—*Continued*

(Millions of dollars.)

Industry	South and Central America and Caribbean						Mexico					
	1994	1995	1996	1997	1998	1999	1994	1995	1996	1997	1998	1999
ALL GOODS	752.5	1 028.8	1 209.6	1 613.9	1 684.9	1 013.5	7 088.5	5 002.8	4 686.8	6 458.0	7 888.1	9 294.9
Manufactured Goods	744.9	1 019.2	1 195.0	1 609.7	1 679.0	1 009.3	7 082.3	4 994.8	4 664.4	6 424.9	7 831.6	9 256.9
Food products	18.4	27.1	33.5	18.2	17.3	14.1	14.6	5.1	6.7	10.7	23.0	10.7
Tobacco products	...	...	...	...	...	...	0.3	...	...	...	...	...
Textile mill products	3.6	14.0	2.1	2.6	2.1	2.1	59.7	50.9	24.6	26.6	39.6	53.9
Apparel	0.9	0.5	0.8	2.4	1.2	1.9	52.2	31.7	40.6	51.9	36.7	14.0
Lumber and wood products	0.7	0.5	3.1	0.9	2.7	2.9	7.4	9.9	1.0	0.7	3.0	9.9
Furniture and fixtures	6.2	17.6	28.6	43.4	47.2	23.1	302.1	285.2	95.6	79.9	61.5	30.0
Paper products	3.7	3.5	4.6	2.6	1.6	1.8	26.1	24.5	18.8	29.5	19.3	27.5
Printing and publishing	1.3	1.5	1.2	2.7	2.3	2.7	1.4	1.4	1.2	2.1	3.0	2.8
Chemical products	58.6	56.4	53.4	62.5	86.5	112.0	128.1	89.4	108.9	163.1	158.3	251.2
Refined petroleum products	0.3	0.5	0.6	1.8	0.6	1.3	7.1	7.4	7.2	10.8	7.1	15.4
Rubber and plastic products	11.4	10.9	17.6	28.9	26.4	12.3	335.2	302.4	287.5	298.4	292.6	395.3
Leather products	14.6	10.2	4.9	5.1	1.8	1.9	48.8	94.2	110.9	138.1	141.1	110.5
Stone, clay and glass products	4.1	3.2	3.2	4.5	5.8	4.3	76.2	74.8	69.7	60.7	64.5	64.6
Primary metals	2.7	4.2	10.9	12.2	6.4	3.9	205.9	122.8	126.0	118.4	103.6	104.4
Fabricated metal products	9.8	10.2	27.2	17.8	12.7	23.2	732.1	410.7	495.1	449.1	352.0	501.8
Industrial machinery and computers	148.4	179.8	146.3	183.2	181.2	193.4	449.8	555.0	590.4	736.4	714.2	912.6
Electric and electronic equipment	11.6	23.8	30.2	24.6	26.3	32.7	785.6	459.6	449.5	656.7	628.0	669.0
Transportation equipment	435.2	639.6	811.0	1 176.8	1 229.6	545.1	3 624.6	2 265.0	2 058.0	3 351.1	4 883.8	5 787.1
Scientific and measuring instruments	8.0	9.7	11.0	13.2	18.5	20.9	211.5	198.5	166.3	223.2	258.0	276.0
Miscellaneous manufactures	3.8	4.4	3.9	4.9	6.3	6.3	9.0	2.5	1.9	13.4	6.7	4.5
Unidentified manufactures	1.6	1.5	1.2	1.5	2.5	3.5	4.7	3.9	4.3	4.2	35.6	15.7
Agricultural And Livestock Products	6.7	9.4	12.2	3.3	3.3	1.4	3.6	4.1	12.8	13.8	42.6	10.1
Agricultural products	6.6	9.4	12.2	3.2	3.3	1.4	3.1	4.1	12.8	13.5	42.6	10.0
Livestock and livestock products	...	...	...	...	...	...	0.4	...	...	0.3	0.1	0.1
Other Commodities	0.9	0.2	2.4	0.8	2.6	2.9	2.6	3.9	9.6	19.4	13.8	27.9
Forestry products	0.1	...	...	...	0.1	...	...	...	...	...	...	0.3
Fish and other marine products	...	...	...	...	...	...	...	...	...	...	...	0.1
Metallic ores and concentrates	...	...	...	...	...	...	...	...	...	...	...	...
Bituminous coal and lignite	...	...	...	...	...	...	...	...	...	...	...	...
Crude petroleum and natural gas	...	...	...	...	...	...	0.2	...	...	...	...	...
Nonmetallic minerals	...	...	...	0.1	...	0.2	0.4	0.2	0.5	0.6	0.5	0.3
Scrap and waste	0.3	0.1	2.0	0.2	0.1	0.4	1.2	3.4	8.4	16.7	12.3	24.4
Used merchandise	0.3	0.1	0.1	0.3	2.2	0.4	0.1	...	0.2	1.0	0.2	0.2
Goods imported and returned unchanged	...	...	...	...	...	...	...	...	...	...	...	...
Special classification provisions	0.3	0.1	0.3	0.3	0.2	1.8	0.7	0.2	0.6	1.0	0.8	2.6

Industry	European Union						United Kingdom					
	1994	1995	1996	1997	1998	1999	1994	1995	1996	1997	1998	1999
ALL GOODS	3 553.2	4 193.2	4 155.6	4 745.7	5 110.0	4 944.4	688.7	588.6	633.8	742.8	934.0	1 329.2
Manufactured Goods	3 473.9	4 111.7	4 071.1	4 658.7	5 045.7	4 878.5	652.6	551.1	592.6	699.8	901.5	1 298.4
Food products	31.1	39.4	44.3	61.2	46.1	48.5	7.9	6.8	8.2	27.1	8.9	14.1
Tobacco products	...	0.4	...	...	...	...	...	...	...	...	...	...
Textile mill products	1.9	3.1	3.6	4.5	6.1	4.3	0.5	0.9	0.8	1.1	1.6	1.7
Apparel	3.8	4.7	12.6	11.1	7.6	4.4	0.6	0.4	0.3	0.4	0.9	0.6
Lumber and wood products	19.3	19.6	13.9	17.8	18.6	19.5	1.8	1.4	0.7	0.7	1.5	1.4
Furniture and fixtures	27.5	34.2	49.1	49.6	49.6	21.6	14.6	11.8	20.8	22.0	26.5	13.4
Paper products	17.5	21.0	24.9	31.0	22.0	13.6	7.2	8.0	7.9	9.5	3.5	2.1
Printing and publishing	11.3	7.7	7.2	15.3	8.3	9.5	3.4	2.5	2.6	7.5	3.2	4.9
Chemical products	375.2	370.6	352.0	402.3	439.0	343.3	60.7	70.6	65.0	76.5	83.6	73.1
Refined petroleum products	1.1	0.9	1.3	1.7	1.4	1.2	0.3	0.2	0.3	0.4	0.1	0.4
Rubber and plastic products	26.6	27.2	29.8	34.9	33.9	63.2	8.2	7.0	8.7	9.4	8.7	20.1
Leather products	1.8	1.8	1.9	4.6	2.5	2.5	0.6	0.7	1.0	2.7	1.4	0.9
Stone, clay and glass products	20.8	22.3	55.8	59.3	78.1	75.5	1.8	1.6	1.3	1.5	1.3	6.0
Primary metals	29.4	86.5	73.5	87.2	67.5	46.4	10.0	18.0	16.0	17.1	17.8	14.9
Fabricated metal products	96.2	105.9	110.6	125.6	131.1	164.8	17.6	24.1	26.9	32.3	28.1	50.2
Industrial machinery and computers	435.6	547.2	525.1	655.4	632.1	662.1	92.6	126.7	130.7	151.1	153.1	140.0
Electric and electronic equipment	194.0	250.6	194.0	192.3	206.5	198.9	26.0	37.6	32.7	39.2	40.0	49.1
Transportation equipment	2 033.4	2 403.4	2 398.4	2 703.9	3 091.9	2 974.4	369.9	200.2	234.2	261.2	478.5	846.5
Scientific and measuring instruments	101.4	117.5	137.3	159.0	160.2	182.3	17.4	22.8	26.2	28.5	28.8	48.4
Miscellaneous manufactures	35.5	36.7	29.8	35.3	33.7	32.5	6.5	5.2	5.4	7.8	10.7	7.0
Unidentified manufactures	10.6	10.9	6.3	6.9	9.6	10.1	4.9	4.5	2.7	3.9	3.3	3.7
Agricultural And Livestock Products	63.7	74.7	69.0	75.3	48.1	41.7	30.9	35.2	37.1	39.2	28.4	26.2
Agricultural products	63.5	74.5	68.6	74.7	47.8	41.6	30.9	35.2	37.1	39.2	28.4	26.2
Livestock and livestock products	0.2	0.2	0.4	0.6	0.3	0.1	...	...	...	...	...	...
Other Commodities	15.6	6.7	15.4	11.7	16.1	24.2	5.3	2.3	4.1	3.8	4.1	4.6
Forestry products	0.1	0.6	0.3	...	0.5	0.2	...	0.1	0.2	...	...	...
Fish and other marine products	0.1	...	0.1	0.1	...	0.1	...	...	0.1	...	...	...
Metallic ores and concentrates	...	...	0.3	0.1	...	...	...	...	0.1	...	...	...
Bituminous coal and lignite	...	...	...	...	...	...	...	...	...	...	...	...
Crude petroleum and natural gas	...	0.1	...	...	...	...	...	...	...	...	...	...
Nonmetallic minerals	0.3	0.4	0.3	...	...	0.4	...	...	...	...	...	...
Scrap and waste	1.1	1.9	6.7	1.7	1.6	1.1	0.9	1.3	0.5	1.4	1.2	0.5
Used merchandise	3.0	1.5	3.7	3.3	7.8	4.6	1.2	0.1	2.0	0.6	1.8	1.1
Goods imported and returned unchanged	...	...	...	...	...	...	...	...	...	...	...	...
Special classification provisions	11.0	2.2	4.1	6.5	6.2	17.8	3.2	0.7	1.4	1.8	1.0	3.0

Table D-25. MICHIGAN: State Exports of Goods by Destination and Industry, 1994–1999—*Continued*

(Millions of dollars.)

Industry	Germany						France					
	1994	1995	1996	1997	1998	1999	1994	1995	1996	1997	1998	1999
ALL GOODS	893.6	1 054.5	999.4	1 057.0	1 047.9	900.9	392.3	345.9	283.7	297.6	314.4	274.5
Manufactured Goods	886.7	1 047.0	990.5	1 052.0	1 043.1	895.3	386.0	341.7	280.1	292.4	307.0	272.6
Food products	12.7	15.6	19.9	19.0	16.3	4.7	0.8	1.2	0.8	1.6	5.5	1.0
Tobacco products	...	...	...	...	...	...	...	...	...	...	...	...
Textile mill products	0.8	1.3	1.2	1.0	0.7	1.0	0.1	0.4	0.4	0.3	0.4	0.2
Apparel	1.9	3.3	10.6	2.5	3.8	2.3	0.9	0.2	0.1	0.1	0.1	0.2
Lumber and wood products	10.0	11.3	7.1	8.8	10.2	7.6	0.3	0.6	0.3	0.4	0.2	0.3
Furniture and fixtures	1.1	1.9	2.2	2.9	2.8	1.4	5.5	5.1	4.1	8.4	3.6	4.1
Paper products	1.6	2.6	2.8	2.4	2.0	0.9	2.2	3.8	2.7	3.4	1.5	2.6
Printing and publishing	2.6	1.5	1.2	1.9	2.0	1.7	0.5	0.6	0.4	1.0	0.9	0.7
Chemical products	29.1	27.7	24.7	30.1	32.2	22.9	99.7	36.5	31.3	22.1	26.8	15.0
Refined petroleum products	0.2	0.2	0.3	0.3	0.3	0.1	...	...	...	0.1	0.1	...
Rubber and plastic products	3.1	4.1	5.4	5.3	5.4	16.1	1.4	3.4	5.6	5.8	3.7	9.1
Leather products	0.3	0.1	0.2	0.2	...	0.2	0.3	0.3	0.2	0.5	0.2	0.1
Stone, clay and glass products	8.6	14.0	26.1	39.7	53.3	37.7	3.6	0.6	1.1	0.5	0.5	0.7
Primary metals	3.3	26.8	6.6	11.8	10.2	11.2	6.5	10.2	8.7	15.3	16.3	11.6
Fabricated metal products	44.3	43.6	42.1	37.5	48.3	38.4	9.2	8.2	9.4	13.7	8.6	7.0
Industrial machinery and computers	108.0	139.0	115.8	147.6	153.0	163.8	99.3	108.4	63.1	89.0	83.2	99.0
Electric and electronic equipment	34.1	37.6	24.2	25.0	50.5	45.4	23.2	34.0	16.5	17.6	23.4	16.1
Transportation equipment	591.7	674.8	648.3	633.9	582.2	472.2	121.1	113.0	122.0	100.5	109.7	83.3
Scientific and measuring instruments	24.2	29.2	41.8	66.4	56.7	58.9	7.8	11.3	11.1	9.6	18.3	19.4
Miscellaneous manufactures	6.9	10.1	9.0	14.7	10.5	6.9	2.9	2.6	1.5	2.1	2.5	1.2
Unidentified manufactures	2.4	2.3	1.1	0.9	2.5	1.9	0.8	1.4	0.7	0.5	1.5	0.9
Agricultural And Livestock Products	3.4	6.2	6.7	4.2	3.5	2.8	2.9	3.5	2.6	3.2	2.1	0.1
Agricultural products	3.4	6.1	6.6	4.0	3.3	2.7	2.8	3.5	2.5	3.0	1.9	0.1
Livestock and livestock products	...	...	0.1	0.2	0.2	0.1	0.1	...	0.1	0.2	0.2	...
Other Commodities	3.4	1.4	2.2	0.8	1.4	2.8	3.3	0.7	1.0	2.0	5.3	1.8
Forestry products	...	...	...	...	...	...	...	...	...	...	...	...
Fish and other marine products	...	...	...	...	...	...	...	...	...	...	...	...
Metallic ores and concentrates	...	...	...	...	...	...	...	...	0.1	...	...	...
Bituminous coal and lignite	...	...	...	...	...	...	...	...	...	...	...	...
Crude petroleum and natural gas	...	...	...	...	...	...	...	...	...	...	...	...
Nonmetallic minerals	...	...	...	...	...	0.2	0.1	0.2	0.3	...	...	...
Scrap and waste	0.1	0.2	0.1	...	0.3	0.3	0.1	0.1	...	0.1	0.1	0.1
Used merchandise	0.1	0.2	0.7	...	0.2	0.1	0.9	0.2	0.4	1.7	4.7	0.8
Goods imported and returned unchanged	...	...	...	...	...	...	...	...	...	...	...	...
Special classification provisions	3.2	0.9	1.4	0.8	0.9	2.1	2.2	0.1	0.2	0.1	0.5	0.9

Industry	The Netherlands						Asian 10					
	1994	1995	1996	1997	1998	1999	1994	1995	1996	1997	1998	1999
ALL GOODS	155.3	175.6	205.8	238.7	217.0	233.9	2 471.6	2 822.0	3 300.4	3 083.8	2 550.0	2 426.2
Manufactured Goods	153.6	170.3	201.7	235.0	216.3	230.8	2 445.8	2 804.1	3 290.2	3 074.0	2 541.0	2 402.0
Food products	3.4	5.1	3.8	5.3	6.1	22.8	113.4	144.2	188.6	161.2	132.6	140.0
Tobacco products	...	...	...	...	...	...	...	...	...	...	...	...
Textile mill products	...	0.2	0.1	0.1	0.4	0.5	4.1	2.8	2.0	8.3	2.1	2.3
Apparel	0.1	0.1	0.2	0.1	0.2	0.1	34.6	21.6	28.6	15.3	4.7	2.8
Lumber and wood products	0.1	0.3	0.1	0.3	...	0.4	5.5	7.5	8.2	10.5	6.8	8.9
Furniture and fixtures	2.2	1.1	0.6	0.2	0.5	0.2	48.5	69.1	62.5	71.2	55.3	40.3
Paper products	1.4	1.5	5.7	10.4	11.0	6.0	5.7	5.9	5.9	5.3	4.5	6.2
Printing and publishing	1.0	0.4	0.8	0.9	0.4	0.3	5.2	8.6	6.1	8.2	9.6	10.9
Chemical products	18.5	14.3	26.6	32.4	32.5	56.3	276.0	372.1	448.7	488.5	360.4	462.5
Refined petroleum products	0.1	0.2	0.1	0.2	0.1	0.1	4.6	4.5	3.6	4.0	3.0	3.7
Rubber and plastic products	4.2	5.6	4.6	5.9	4.8	4.5	30.5	38.9	43.0	56.7	34.7	24.9
Leather products	0.2	0.1	...	0.2	0.1	0.4	8.7	5.2	10.3	16.9	17.0	23.1
Stone, clay and glass products	1.2	1.6	1.1	1.6	2.9	3.6	30.9	28.0	31.5	39.9	26.0	25.1
Primary metals	1.2	1.2	1.4	1.4	1.0	1.1	48.3	97.2	82.0	110.3	127.3	102.6
Fabricated metal products	2.1	4.0	4.9	7.2	14.5	8.0	91.4	105.1	135.1	80.5	72.4	98.0
Industrial machinery and computers	36.4	43.7	72.7	82.1	68.9	63.2	435.4	522.8	519.6	515.3	459.8	364.6
Electric and electronic equipment	5.2	7.0	10.0	17.5	15.6	19.3	219.6	238.0	264.7	260.0	225.2	275.3
Transportation equipment	63.5	60.9	44.0	39.9	31.4	26.1	880.2	917.8	1 229.8	1 021.6	845.9	688.8
Scientific and measuring instruments	11.3	20.5	23.4	26.0	21.5	13.4	98.2	96.6	109.5	94.7	96.6	83.5
Miscellaneous manufactures	1.3	1.9	1.2	2.9	3.8	4.0	96.2	109.7	107.8	99.5	51.1	28.9
Unidentified manufactures	0.5	0.7	0.4	0.4	0.6	0.5	8.6	8.5	2.7	6.0	5.7	9.4
Agricultural And Livestock Products	1.4	4.3	3.4	2.6	0.2	0.2	15.7	5.0	3.6	3.0	3.2	3.9
Agricultural products	1.4	4.2	3.2	2.5	0.2	0.2	14.7	4.5	2.1	2.6	2.4	3.7
Livestock and livestock products	...	0.1	0.2	0.1	...	...	0.9	0.5	1.4	0.5	0.9	0.3
Other Commodities	0.3	1.1	0.7	1.1	0.4	2.9	10.2	12.9	6.6	6.8	5.8	20.3
Forestry products	...	0.2	...	...	...	0.1	...	...	0.2	...	...	...
Fish and other marine products	...	...	...	...	...	...	...	0.5	...	0.3	...	...
Metallic ores and concentrates	...	...	...	...	...	...	0.3	0.1	...	...	0.4	...
Bituminous coal and lignite	...	...	...	...	...	...	...	...	...	...	...	...
Crude petroleum and natural gas	...	...	...	...	...	...	...	...	...	...	...	0.1
Nonmetallic minerals	0.1	...	...	...	...	0.1	0.1	0.1	0.2	0.4	1.2	0.4
Scrap and waste	...	0.1	0.2	0.1	...	...	3.6	7.5	2.1	1.2	0.7	12.3
Used merchandise	0.1	0.6	0.4	0.8	0.1	2.3	2.1	1.2	1.3	1.2	0.3	0.6
Goods imported and returned unchanged	...	...	...	...	...	...	...	...	...	...	...	...
Special classification provisions	0.1	...	0.2	0.3	0.3	0.4	4.0	3.6	2.8	3.8	3.2	6.9

Table D-25. MICHIGAN: State Exports of Goods by Destination and Industry, 1994–1999—Continued

(Millions of dollars.)

Industry	Japan						South Korea					
	1994	1995	1996	1997	1998	1999	1994	1995	1996	1997	1998	1999
ALL GOODS	1 223.4	1 451.8	1 789.5	1 444.3	1 394.3	1 120.9	243.0	367.2	435.7	369.3	148.8	241.9
Manufactured Goods	1 218.6	1 443.3	1 784.2	1 440.0	1 389.7	1 102.9	242.1	366.0	434.5	368.2	147.3	241.3
Food products	63.6	83.3	93.0	80.1	75.1	58.8	8.9	24.4	45.4	27.0	15.8	24.0
Tobacco products	...	...	...	...	...	...	...	...	...	...	...	...
Textile mill products	3.3	1.1	1.0	7.1	0.9	0.8	0.2	0.3	0.4	0.1	0.1	0.7
Apparel	33.9	17.8	23.2	11.6	3.2	1.8	0.2	3.0	4.2	3.3	0.6	...
Lumber and wood products	3.3	4.7	5.1	6.2	3.2	3.0	0.6	0.4	0.7	0.4	0.3	0.5
Furniture and fixtures	17.8	19.1	20.6	21.5	19.0	20.0	1.2	5.2	2.9	2.5	0.9	2.5
Paper products	2.5	1.3	2.7	1.0	1.0	2.0	1.3	2.7	1.4	1.5	0.8	1.5
Printing and publishing	2.2	5.7	1.1	2.0	1.5	1.3	0.4	0.5	0.7	0.7	0.4	0.4
Chemical products	136.8	184.1	213.4	267.5	200.1	185.0	22.9	69.7	100.6	62.9	31.9	69.1
Refined petroleum products	0.4	0.4	0.6	0.6	1.0	1.2	0.5	0.8	0.3	0.4	0.3	0.7
Rubber and plastic products	17.1	29.3	24.9	31.2	22.1	13.3	3.6	3.1	8.4	14.1	5.1	3.2
Leather products	5.9	2.3	2.3	2.5	2.2	2.2	0.7	0.3	0.1	0.1	0.2	0.4
Stone, clay and glass products	16.4	11.9	17.6	27.5	17.0	16.0	7.6	6.5	5.2	7.2	3.2	4.5
Primary metals	28.9	45.9	39.8	71.0	101.3	68.4	2.9	26.4	22.9	21.1	7.1	3.1
Fabricated metal products	46.8	62.2	72.4	49.0	47.7	45.8	4.1	10.0	26.0	6.0	2.6	6.8
Industrial machinery and computers	147.1	156.9	174.8	160.5	143.1	117.4	49.7	70.3	47.7	69.1	19.6	56.0
Electric and electronic equipment	40.5	66.1	67.1	70.7	60.9	50.8	17.7	15.4	23.7	24.8	6.6	17.0
Transportation equipment	601.4	690.6	950.8	566.5	637.7	459.9	70.1	88.6	115.2	96.1	31.2	35.0
Scientific and measuring instruments	43.3	48.3	61.2	39.6	35.8	41.5	20.8	17.6	19.4	25.3	18.6	11.7
Miscellaneous manufactures	6.0	10.6	11.7	22.5	14.9	10.9	27.8	20.1	8.8	5.2	1.7	3.1
Unidentified manufactures	1.3	1.4	1.0	1.4	2.2	2.9	0.8	0.8	0.4	0.4	0.7	0.9
Agricultural And Livestock Products	1.6	2.0	1.9	2.4	2.7	3.0	0.1	0.3	0.3	0.2	0.2	0.1
Agricultural products	1.5	1.7	1.1	2.4	2.2	2.8	...	0.1	0.2	...	...	0.1
Livestock and livestock products	0.1	0.3	0.8	...	0.5	0.2	...	0.2	0.2	0.1	0.2	...
Other Commodities	3.2	6.5	3.5	1.8	1.9	15.0	0.9	1.0	0.9	0.9	1.3	0.5
Forestry products	...	...	0.2	...	...	...	...	...	...	...	...	...
Fish and other marine products	...	0.4	...	...	...	...	...	...	...	...	...	...
Metallic ores and concentrates	0.2	...	...	...	0.4	...	...	0.1	...	...	...	...
Bituminous coal and lignite	...	...	...	...	...	...	...	...	...	...	...	...
Crude petroleum and natural gas	...	...	...	...	...	0.1	...	...	...	...	...	...
Nonmetallic minerals	...	...	0.1	0.1	0.1	0.2	...	...	...	...	0.9	0.1
Scrap and waste	0.2	4.9	0.7	0.3	0.1	11.9	...	...	...	...	0.1	0.1
Used merchandise	1.6	0.2	1.2	0.6	0.2	0.4	0.3	0.1	...	...	...	...
Goods imported and returned unchanged	...	...	...	...	...	...	...	...	...	...	...	...
Special classification provisions	1.1	1.0	1.3	0.8	1.1	2.4	0.5	0.7	0.8	0.9	0.2	0.3

Industry	Taiwan						Singapore					
	1994	1995	1996	1997	1998	1999	1994	1995	1996	1997	1998	1999
ALL GOODS	359.6	293.3	198.8	207.6	174.0	168.3	84.0	119.0	110.5	117.5	105.4	132.0
Manufactured Goods	357.9	291.7	197.9	205.2	172.1	165.5	83.5	118.8	110.3	117.1	105.3	131.3
Food products	20.6	12.8	12.8	16.2	18.5	16.2	0.5	1.0	0.9	0.7	0.2	0.3
Tobacco products	...	...	...	...	...	...	...	...	...	...	...	...
Textile mill products	0.2	0.2	...	0.3	0.1	...	0.1	0.2	0.2	0.2	0.1	0.1
Apparel	0.1	0.1	...	...	...	0.1	0.1	0.3	...	...	...	...
Lumber and wood products	1.2	1.4	1.2	1.2	0.8	1.1	0.2	0.3	0.5	0.6	0.4	0.3
Furniture and fixtures	2.1	1.7	1.7	2.8	0.7	1.1	9.3	13.9	14.7	12.5	7.0	4.2
Paper products	0.6	0.5	0.4	0.9	1.3	0.5	0.2	0.2	0.2	0.5	0.5	0.2
Printing and publishing	0.6	0.6	0.8	0.6	0.3	0.6	0.4	0.6	2.4	3.6	6.4	6.8
Chemical products	43.8	37.7	33.2	35.1	36.5	50.5	8.0	9.1	7.2	19.0	24.6	43.0
Refined petroleum products	1.5	1.0	0.8	0.7	0.5	0.7	0.4	0.1	0.3	0.1	0.1	0.1
Rubber and plastic products	2.9	1.2	1.0	1.7	1.4	1.7	1.1	1.7	3.0	2.5	0.7	1.5
Leather products	0.4	0.1	0.2	0.1	0.2	...	...	...	0.1	...	...	0.1
Stone, clay and glass products	1.0	1.3	1.4	0.8	0.6	0.8	1.0	2.1	0.5	0.9	0.3	0.3
Primary metals	5.3	14.9	5.8	7.8	8.7	10.6	1.1	1.0	0.8	1.3	1.2	0.6
Fabricated metal products	15.0	13.6	13.4	8.2	4.6	6.2	6.8	4.3	2.6	2.3	4.0	3.4
Industrial machinery and computers	40.9	48.7	35.9	36.8	30.7	24.1	33.8	61.2	45.4	50.7	33.8	31.5
Electric and electronic equipment	37.4	37.3	35.7	25.8	14.0	14.1	8.3	11.8	15.5	11.0	4.6	11.9
Transportation equipment	123.6	78.0	43.6	55.8	44.3	29.3	8.5	7.6	11.7	7.1	12.7	21.6
Scientific and measuring instruments	8.0	5.5	5.8	6.3	7.6	6.4	2.0	1.6	2.8	2.8	7.5	4.0
Miscellaneous manufactures	50.2	31.7	3.9	1.8	0.9	0.7	1.2	1.3	1.2	1.1	0.7	1.3
Unidentified manufactures	2.7	3.3	0.3	2.3	0.3	0.6	0.3	0.3	0.3	0.1	0.1	0.2
Agricultural And Livestock Products	0.9	0.4	0.5	0.4	0.1	0.2	0.1	...	0.1	...	...	...
Agricultural products	0.1	0.4	0.4	0.1	0.1	0.2	0.1	...	0.1	...	...	...
Livestock and livestock products	0.8	...	0.1	0.3	...	0.1	...	...	...	...	...	...
Other Commodities	0.9	1.2	0.3	2.1	1.7	2.6	0.5	0.2	0.1	0.4	0.1	0.6
Forestry products	...	...	...	...	...	...	...	...	...	...	...	...
Fish and other marine products	...	...	...	...	...	...	...	...	...	...	...	...
Metallic ores and concentrates	0.1	...	...	...	...	...	...	...	...	...	...	...
Bituminous coal and lignite	...	...	...	...	...	...	...	...	...	...	...	...
Crude petroleum and natural gas	...	...	...	...	...	...	...	...	...	...	...	...
Nonmetallic minerals	...	...	...	0.1	0.1	...	...	...	...	...	...	...
Scrap and waste	...	0.1	...	0.2	0.2	0.3	...	...	...	...	...	...
Used merchandise	0.1	0.5	0.1	0.5	...	0.2	...	...	...	...	...	...
Goods imported and returned unchanged	...	...	...	...	...	...	...	...	...	...	...	...
Special classification provisions	0.6	0.5	0.2	1.3	1.4	2.1	0.4	0.1	0.1	0.4	0.1	0.6

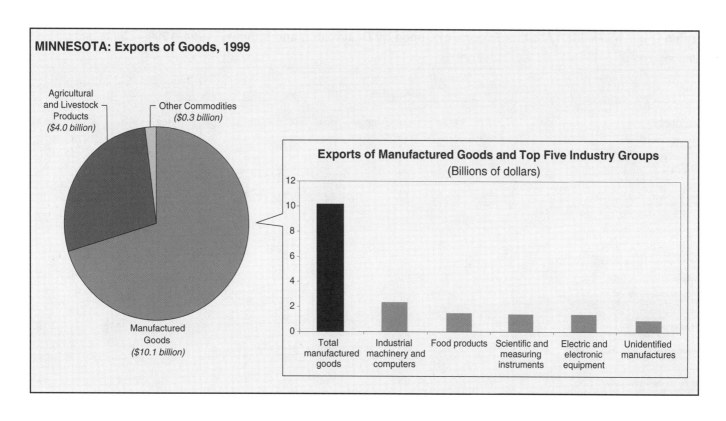

MINNESOTA: Exports of Goods, 1999

Agricultural and Livestock Products ($4.0 billion)

Other Commodities ($0.3 billion)

Manufactured Goods ($10.1 billion)

Exports of Manufactured Goods and Top Five Industry Groups
(Billions of dollars)

Total manufactured goods · Industrial machinery and computers · Food products · Scientific and measuring instruments · Electric and electronic equipment · Unidentified manufactures

Table D-26. MINNESOTA: State Exports of Goods by Destination and Industry, 1994–1999

(Millions of dollars.)

Industry	All destinations						Canada					
	1994	1995	1996	1997	1998	1999	1994	1995	1996	1997	1998	1999
ALL GOODS	10 011.1	12 404.3	13 884.1	13 793.3	13 499.4	14 400.8	2 108.5	2 442.2	2 860.6	3 190.2	3 389.5	3 443.4
Manufactured Goods	7 201.1	8 115.4	8 811.6	9 590.0	9 827.6	10 136.3	1 971.1	2 331.6	2 715.7	2 936.4	3 146.8	3 173.0
Food products	1 508.1	1 718.4	1 714.5	1 801.4	1 762.3	1 498.6	208.3	230.8	251.5	314.0	345.4	338.1
Tobacco products	. . .	. . .	0.3	. . .	. . .	0.2	. . .	. . .	. . .	. . .	. . .	0.2
Textile mill products	19.9	24.0	24.2	26.9	26.0	38.2	7.2	8.1	8.4	12.0	11.5	13.6
Apparel	24.6	17.5	19.7	24.0	23.1	24.8	8.9	10.5	10.6	11.8	13.0	12.6
Lumber and wood products	42.8	53.5	56.2	56.1	51.8	66.1	21.4	22.0	25.3	24.6	27.0	36.5
Furniture and fixtures	24.1	24.7	26.9	35.0	31.4	27.9	10.2	11.1	13.1	15.4	15.7	11.9
Paper products	153.6	154.7	170.1	194.7	205.3	300.0	72.9	91.3	97.9	113.0	133.4	158.9
Printing and publishing	54.2	67.2	68.5	71.7	61.8	58.4	23.7	24.6	25.1	27.9	27.8	30.2
Chemical products	206.5	223.7	266.7	332.6	373.0	384.5	65.1	67.5	78.1	96.1	131.2	147.2
Refined petroleum products	6.5	10.7	18.4	28.2	9.8	21.2	4.7	9.3	17.0	9.7	7.8	12.7
Rubber and plastic products	194.3	188.5	208.6	237.6	267.9	314.2	37.9	43.2	51.0	58.2	59.7	67.0
Leather products	32.8	31.5	32.9	40.3	47.5	44.0	1.4	2.0	2.6	4.0	4.0	3.7
Stone, clay and glass products	175.1	107.6	100.0	116.4	112.2	143.1	35.3	40.7	34.2	35.5	44.0	47.1
Primary metals	64.4	93.3	74.9	91.8	84.3	69.3	23.6	27.5	28.1	28.9	28.4	26.7
Fabricated metal products	234.7	208.6	233.3	269.8	253.1	300.2	85.2	90.8	122.2	119.0	134.8	143.0
Industrial machinery and computers	1 562.5	1 787.1	1 974.7	2 181.5	2 252.1	2 359.7	309.9	350.5	413.6	473.2	457.3	449.4
Electric and electronic equipment	891.6	988.3	1 008.1	1 089.6	1 189.5	1 408.7	164.9	168.0	200.6	209.0	234.2	266.6
Transportation equipment	424.8	485.8	517.5	577.3	697.7	624.3	277.7	345.5	361.5	340.2	392.9	332.8
Scientific and measuring instruments	1 021.3	1 166.9	1 354.0	1 415.7	1 349.9	1 421.8	108.8	100.1	109.5	121.0	132.6	139.7
Miscellaneous manufactures	82.4	119.6	114.4	114.7	105.8	102.0	38.7	57.9	50.1	51.1	46.9	41.0
Unidentified manufactures	477.0	643.8	827.7	884.7	923.1	928.7	465.2	630.2	815.1	871.9	899.1	894.3
Agricultural And Livestock Products	2 672.5	4 177.6	4 949.9	3 981.6	3 459.1	4 002.0	37.2	39.7	54.6	63.8	63.7	67.7
Agricultural products	2 662.8	4 171.1	4 942.9	3 973.8	3 451.1	3 998.2	31.7	34.7	49.3	57.2	56.5	64.8
Livestock and livestock products	9.7	6.5	7.0	7.8	8.1	3.8	5.5	5.0	5.2	6.6	7.2	2.9
Other Commodities	137.4	111.3	122.6	221.6	212.7	262.5	100.3	71.0	90.3	189.9	179.0	202.8
Forestry products	0.9	1.4	1.9	0.9	1.3	1.8	0.6	1.1	0.8	0.3	0.4	0.9
Fish and other marine products	7.7	5.7	5.1	4.3	6.5	6.5	6.0	3.7	2.6	2.7	3.5	4.1
Metallic ores and concentrates	21.7	2.3	23.2	112.7	110.5	94.6	19.3	0.2	21.5	111.2	110.2	94.4
Bituminous coal and lignite	. . .	0.3	0.8	. . .	. . .	0.1	. . .	. . .	0.8	. . .	. . .	. . .
Crude petroleum and natural gas	2.0	1.1	0.1	. . .	. . .	0.2	2.0	1.1	. . .	. . .	. . .	0.2
Nonmetallic minerals	18.2	10.8	7.5	14.9	15.7	19.2	4.5	3.7	4.6	8.7	6.7	12.2
Scrap and waste	29.3	28.6	18.8	20.1	14.2	18.0	28.9	27.2	17.8	17.8	11.9	15.3
Used merchandise	10.3	9.5	8.2	10.8	6.4	8.2	1.4	1.8	1.8	2.6	2.3	2.4
Goods imported and returned unchanged	31.3	26.6	35.0	42.4	40.8	39.6	31.3	26.6	35.0	42.4	40.8	39.6
Special classification provisions	15.8	25.2	21.9	15.5	17.4	74.5	6.3	5.6	5.4	4.3	3.1	33.8

Table D-26. MINNESOTA: State Exports of Goods by Destination and Industry, 1994–1999—*Continued*

(Millions of dollars.)

Industry	South and Central American and Caribbean						Mexico					
	1994	1995	1996	1997	1998	1999	1994	1995	1996	1997	1998	1999
ALL GOODS	450.7	686.6	762.1	780.8	787.0	687.1	329.8	505.7	846.3	822.8	870.4	974.1
Manufactured Goods	278.8	327.4	354.3	433.9	436.6	376.5	274.5	243.2	292.7	352.0	387.7	481.0
Food products	65.1	116.9	116.3	154.5	155.7	134.8	69.2	66.8	60.2	61.0	47.4	34.6
Tobacco products	...	...	...	...	...	...	...	...	...	...	...	...
Textile mill products	1.8	0.6	1.5	0.9	0.9	1.2	0.6	0.2	0.4	1.7	2.5	2.9
Apparel	4.2	2.2	2.4	1.3	0.6	0.8	0.9	0.5	0.4	2.2	0.3	0.8
Lumber and wood products	0.6	1.0	1.0	0.9	1.9	1.0	1.1	0.4	0.2	0.3	2.8	4.7
Furniture and fixtures	1.1	1.3	1.3	1.4	1.3	1.3	2.0	0.7	1.2	3.1	1.8	1.6
Paper products	14.3	6.9	5.7	6.2	6.0	9.7	7.0	8.8	10.0	12.2	13.3	30.9
Printing and publishing	1.2	2.0	1.3	1.6	1.8	1.0	7.4	10.0	17.3	20.8	14.1	7.6
Chemical products	19.5	14.2	18.8	17.0	15.9	13.1	4.0	3.8	4.8	5.3	6.0	9.5
Refined petroleum products	0.1	...	...	0.1	0.3	...	0.1	0.2	0.1	...	...	...
Rubber and plastic products	7.8	6.5	7.2	8.9	8.6	7.3	4.0	4.5	5.2	6.9	14.5	17.5
Leather products	7.2	3.8	2.4	1.9	2.9	0.8	0.3	...	...	0.1	6.0	2.6
Stone, clay and glass products	3.9	3.5	2.8	5.3	2.8	5.0	1.5	1.0	2.3	3.5	2.7	5.7
Primary metals	0.3	1.8	1.8	1.8	0.9	0.7	2.7	7.7	11.3	5.0	7.4	17.7
Fabricated metal products	6.3	6.7	8.5	10.8	10.0	6.8	7.3	9.5	8.0	9.0	18.9	15.4
Industrial machinery and computers	57.6	68.5	89.4	102.0	93.9	65.8	65.1	36.4	50.9	54.8	64.9	102.0
Electric and electronic equipment	46.1	48.9	40.1	46.6	55.6	53.2	58.7	52.3	78.5	110.7	115.3	175.0
Transportation equipment	3.3	3.5	5.5	13.3	17.6	18.3	4.3	2.5	3.2	4.2	3.6	4.7
Scientific and measuring instruments	34.9	34.3	43.1	54.9	53.4	50.1	35.3	31.4	36.7	48.0	61.3	41.6
Miscellaneous manufactures	2.8	4.1	4.4	3.7	5.3	4.1	2.5	6.0	1.2	1.8	1.2	1.8
Unidentified manufactures	0.6	0.7	0.6	0.8	1.4	1.4	0.6	0.4	0.7	1.3	3.6	4.3
Agricultural And Livestock Products	171.2	358.0	407.3	345.7	349.5	308.4	53.5	261.1	552.2	468.6	480.4	489.7
Agricultural products	171.2	357.6	407.3	345.7	349.4	308.4	50.1	260.6	551.6	468.1	480.1	489.5
Livestock and livestock products	...	0.4	...	...	0.1	...	3.4	0.5	0.7	0.5	0.3	0.2
Other Commodities	0.7	1.2	0.5	1.2	0.9	2.2	1.8	1.5	1.4	2.2	2.3	3.4
Forestry products	...	...	...	...	...	0.1	...	...	0.6	...	...	...
Fish and other marine products	...	...	...	...	...	...	0.1	0.1	...	0.2	0.1	0.1
Metallic ores and concentrates	...	...	...	...	...	...	...	...	...	...	...	...
Bituminous coal and lignite	...	0.3	...	...	...	...	...	...	...	...	...	...
Crude petroleum and natural gas	...	...	...	...	...	...	...	...	...	...	...	...
Nonmetallic minerals	0.1	...	...	0.2	0.4	0.5	1.3	0.8	0.2	0.2	0.4	0.4
Scrap and waste	...	...	...	...	...	...	0.1	...	0.3	1.6	1.3	1.3
Used merchandise	0.5	0.6	0.2	0.7	0.3	0.7	0.2	0.5	0.1	0.1	...	...
Goods imported and returned unchanged	...	...	...	...	...	...	...	...	...	...	...	...
Special classification provisions	0.1	0.4	0.2	0.2	0.2	0.9	0.2	0.1	0.2	0.1	0.5	1.6

Industry	European Union						United Kingdom					
	1994	1995	1996	1997	1998	1999	1994	1995	1996	1997	1998	1999
ALL GOODS	3 393.6	4 049.7	4 075.7	4 025.2	3 785.0	3 732.3	448.3	540.9	599.3	703.8	638.8	688.4
Manufactured Goods	2 378.2	2 661.6	2 814.4	2 910.1	2 809.0	3 023.3	410.6	465.8	499.4	550.8	520.5	620.6
Food products	764.6	844.8	832.8	793.4	614.7	545.5	94.0	105.1	126.2	129.9	84.8	79.5
Tobacco products	...	...	...	...	...	...	...	...	...	...	...	...
Textile mill products	6.8	7.8	8.5	6.0	6.4	12.0	1.9	1.0	2.0	1.4	1.4	1.0
Apparel	7.8	1.5	2.5	4.6	6.5	5.7	1.4	0.1	0.5	0.6	0.4	0.4
Lumber and wood products	4.4	5.5	5.2	6.7	5.2	7.5	1.5	3.1	3.2	3.8	3.2	5.6
Furniture and fixtures	3.9	5.3	5.6	6.4	6.0	5.9	1.2	1.5	1.2	2.4	1.9	2.0
Paper products	38.5	26.4	32.2	30.6	27.6	43.9	5.8	5.2	7.8	7.2	8.0	7.6
Printing and publishing	14.1	20.3	14.9	12.9	9.9	9.1	5.9	9.4	5.6	6.0	3.5	2.6
Chemical products	64.2	60.8	78.5	88.9	97.7	117.1	15.9	13.8	20.7	29.7	38.6	44.3
Refined petroleum products	0.4	0.4	0.4	16.9	0.9	6.8	0.2	...	...	...	...	0.1
Rubber and plastic products	55.9	51.8	55.4	63.8	74.8	75.8	11.8	8.9	8.7	12.5	14.9	14.4
Leather products	6.1	9.4	9.3	8.1	10.3	10.3	0.5	1.0	1.4	1.6	1.0	1.4
Stone, clay and glass products	23.2	15.1	18.4	22.2	21.1	36.4	8.4	2.0	2.3	2.7	2.6	11.4
Primary metals	14.2	32.0	11.0	14.3	11.8	8.7	2.0	1.6	1.6	3.5	3.7	1.0
Fabricated metal products	39.2	43.8	46.3	47.5	36.0	85.6	15.0	14.5	12.9	15.8	10.3	53.2
Industrial machinery and computers	513.0	572.4	645.9	729.1	726.1	741.8	98.5	114.5	112.7	135.6	160.1	164.8
Electric and electronic equipment	239.8	287.5	263.3	252.7	303.8	382.4	73.1	88.7	74.3	62.3	60.7	59.9
Transportation equipment	91.5	80.1	77.0	116.4	173.1	203.9	11.3	18.4	10.3	14.9	19.4	72.5
Scientific and measuring instruments	466.1	567.4	669.3	655.4	641.9	684.5	54.0	69.0	97.2	108.9	95.9	89.2
Miscellaneous manufactures	18.8	23.4	32.9	30.2	27.7	30.6	6.6	6.4	9.6	10.6	8.5	7.0
Unidentified manufactures	5.7	5.7	5.2	4.1	7.5	9.7	1.8	1.5	1.3	1.4	1.4	2.8
Agricultural And Livestock Products	998.6	1 373.3	1 244.3	1 099.4	956.4	677.1	33.4	72.7	95.0	148.6	115.3	63.0
Agricultural products	998.3	1 373.2	1 243.8	1 099.1	956.3	676.9	33.3	72.7	94.9	148.6	115.3	63.0
Livestock and livestock products	0.3	0.1	0.5	0.3	0.1	0.2	...	...	0.1	...	...	...
Other Commodities	16.9	14.7	17.0	15.8	19.5	31.9	4.3	2.4	4.8	4.3	3.1	4.9
Forestry products	0.2	0.2	0.4	0.3	0.6	0.5	...	0.1	...	...	...	0.1
Fish and other marine products	1.1	1.6	2.3	1.3	2.5	1.7	...	...	...	...	...	...
Metallic ores and concentrates	...	...	...	...	...	0.1	...	...	...	...	...	...
Bituminous coal and lignite	...	...	...	...	...	...	...	...	...	...	...	...
Crude petroleum and natural gas	...	...	...	...	...	...	...	...	...	...	...	...
Nonmetallic minerals	3.9	3.6	1.2	0.8	4.3	2.2	...	...	...	0.1	0.1	...
Scrap and waste	0.1	...	0.2	0.3	0.3	0.6	...	...	...	...	...	...
Used merchandise	5.6	1.5	2.9	5.6	3.0	3.3	1.2	0.5	1.0	2.3	1.2	0.5
Goods imported and returned unchanged	...	...	...	...	...	...	...	...	...	...	...	...
Special classification provisions	5.9	7.7	10.1	7.4	8.8	23.5	3.0	1.9	3.8	1.9	1.7	4.3

Table D-26. MINNESOTA: State Exports of Goods by Destination and Industry, 1994–1999—*Continued*

(Millions of dollars.)

Industry	Germany						France					
	1994	1995	1996	1997	1998	1999	1994	1995	1996	1997	1998	1999
ALL GOODS	473.8	514.1	658.7	593.4	577.8	550.2	236.7	265.4	280.2	362.9	420.8	400.6
Manufactured Goods	349.4	402.0	470.3	422.9	422.9	434.6	205.2	212.3	224.7	308.2	346.0	362.0
Food products	55.9	62.6	66.3	54.4	55.9	39.4	20.8	13.9	18.8	42.2	26.5	5.4
Tobacco products	...	...	...	...	...	...	...	...	...	...	...	...
Textile mill products	1.5	4.6	3.4	1.3	1.2	3.4	1.4	0.7	0.8	0.9	1.6	5.3
Apparel	0.8	0.5	0.4	1.9	2.2	1.2	0.4	0.3	0.3	0.5	1.9	3.1
Lumber and wood products	1.1	1.4	0.9	2.2	1.5	0.6	0.4	0.1	0.2	0.1	...	...
Furniture and fixtures	0.9	1.3	1.0	1.3	1.2	1.2	0.3	0.5	0.3	0.1	0.4	0.1
Paper products	9.9	5.7	6.8	4.1	4.9	11.6	8.5	6.0	6.6	5.8	6.3	9.7
Printing and publishing	4.0	5.1	3.4	1.6	1.9	1.4	1.7	1.7	1.2	0.9	0.7	0.8
Chemical products	11.4	10.0	11.2	10.9	8.5	11.5	11.4	12.6	16.4	18.4	15.4	19.8
Refined petroleum products	...	0.1	0.1	0.1	0.1	0.1	...	...	...	...	...	6.4
Rubber and plastic products	16.6	17.3	21.6	20.3	24.6	27.9	5.7	5.6	5.7	7.9	7.5	11.9
Leather products	0.6	0.9	3.2	0.4	0.9	0.9	...	...	0.1	0.1	0.1	0.1
Stone, clay and glass products	7.0	7.5	9.7	13.9	13.7	16.0	2.0	1.4	1.8	2.5	2.1	5.5
Primary metals	2.6	3.6	4.4	5.5	2.9	2.6	0.8	2.6	1.1	0.7	0.8	5.5
Fabricated metal products	8.5	10.6	10.0	11.9	9.7	13.3	2.1	2.4	3.3	3.1	3.7	3.9
Industrial machinery and computers	77.3	84.5	113.1	98.0	86.1	91.3	66.9	59.1	63.3	75.5	85.4	109.2
Electric and electronic equipment	24.2	35.5	43.3	40.4	31.4	28.9	15.5	21.4	21.6	32.9	23.3	24.1
Transportation equipment	9.7	13.5	12.9	6.5	18.6	7.8	6.5	3.4	3.3	34.3	81.3	64.3
Scientific and measuring instruments	113.2	131.3	153.2	143.9	153.3	167.4	59.0	78.7	77.6	80.1	86.3	86.6
Miscellaneous manufactures	3.2	4.8	4.5	3.6	2.9	6.7	1.4	1.4	1.9	1.8	1.9	3.8
Unidentified manufactures	1.0	1.3	1.0	0.7	1.4	1.4	0.5	0.4	0.4	0.4	0.7	0.9
Agricultural And Livestock Products	122.2	110.1	186.4	168.2	153.1	111.3	28.6	52.1	54.1	52.8	73.1	35.7
Agricultural products	122.1	110.0	186.0	168.1	153.1	111.3	28.6	52.1	54.1	52.8	73.1	35.7
Livestock and livestock products	0.1	0.1	0.4	0.1	...	...	...	...	...	...	...	...
Other Commodities	2.2	1.9	2.0	2.3	1.8	4.3	3.0	1.0	1.5	1.8	1.8	2.9
Forestry products	...	0.1	...	0.1	0.1	0.3	...	...	0.1	0.2	0.5	0.1
Fish and other marine products	0.2	0.1	0.1	0.1	0.1	0.1	...	...	...	...	...	...
Metallic ores and concentrates	...	...	...	...	...	...	...	...	...	...	...	...
Bituminous coal and lignite	...	...	...	...	...	...	...	...	...	...	...	...
Crude petroleum and natural gas	...	...	...	...	...	...	...	...	...	...	...	...
Nonmetallic minerals	0.3	0.4	0.1	0.1	...	...	...	...	0.1	...	...	...
Scrap and waste	...	...	...	...	...	...	...	...	...	...	...	...
Used merchandise	1.1	0.2	1.1	0.9	...	0.2	2.2	0.2	...	1.0	...	...
Goods imported and returned unchanged	...	...	...	...	...	...	...	...	...	...	...	...
Special classification provisions	0.6	1.2	0.7	1.2	1.7	3.7	0.7	0.8	1.2	0.7	1.3	2.7

Industry	The Netherlands						Asian 10					
	1994	1995	1996	1997	1998	1999	1994	1995	1996	1997	1998	1999
ALL GOODS	968.5	1 072.8	989.1	846.2	758.5	641.2	2 292.4	2 935.4	3 126.2	3 027.7	2 984.5	3 639.5
Manufactured Goods	635.6	582.2	609.9	574.6	516.6	481.7	1 606.0	1 779.9	1 844.3	2 109.5	2 238.1	2 259.7
Food products	279.2	281.8	277.0	211.1	168.2	136.7	145.3	198.3	205.1	182.9	370.0	203.9
Tobacco products	...	...	...	...	...	...	...	...	...	...	...	...
Textile mill products	0.7	0.1	0.2	0.2	0.3	0.2	2.2	6.3	4.4	4.7	3.4	6.2
Apparel	4.1	0.2	0.5	0.5	0.6	0.2	1.7	2.1	2.7	3.1	1.5	3.4
Lumber and wood products	0.2	...	0.1	0.1	0.1	0.1	15.0	23.9	23.7	22.6	14.0	15.6
Furniture and fixtures	0.6	0.8	1.7	1.3	1.3	1.2	3.3	3.4	3.1	5.7	3.0	3.1
Paper products	6.0	3.1	5.6	6.6	3.0	3.5	10.9	15.1	16.3	22.7	16.6	41.3
Printing and publishing	0.7	2.1	2.8	1.8	2.0	1.2	3.4	4.9	5.8	4.7	3.0	7.1
Chemical products	6.3	6.4	9.7	6.2	11.2	13.0	41.4	47.2	66.4	94.9	77.5	65.6
Refined petroleum products	...	0.1	...	16.6	...	...	1.0	0.7	0.7	0.9	0.5	0.9
Rubber and plastic products	10.3	5.9	6.1	8.5	13.3	4.1	81.2	76.0	81.7	88.1	96.9	129.3
Leather products	0.8	0.6	0.4	1.5	1.7	2.4	13.0	12.3	14.5	21.4	18.5	20.4
Stone, clay and glass products	2.9	0.8	1.4	1.0	1.2	0.6	105.6	40.6	35.4	39.5	29.4	37.1
Primary metals	6.5	3.4	1.6	1.0	1.3	2.1	20.9	18.7	18.0	35.4	27.3	11.5
Fabricated metal products	1.8	2.1	10.3	2.9	4.9	4.8	86.8	35.5	39.6	50.5	35.0	27.7
Industrial machinery and computers	70.9	63.8	58.9	68.4	57.5	69.8	422.1	558.0	570.6	628.3	709.5	828.6
Electric and electronic equipment	83.3	68.4	45.0	21.9	64.6	121.7	323.1	354.4	328.7	401.4	401.6	465.5
Transportation equipment	41.3	22.9	24.0	19.9	14.6	11.6	29.8	24.6	26.7	51.3	64.4	25.5
Scientific and measuring instruments	116.9	116.2	160.5	202.5	167.4	105.9	282.3	333.8	381.0	432.4	345.1	348.6
Miscellaneous manufactures	2.3	2.7	3.3	2.3	2.9	1.8	14.0	19.3	16.2	15.3	13.0	12.1
Unidentified manufactures	0.7	0.6	0.8	0.4	0.7	1.0	2.8	4.7	3.8	3.5	7.8	6.4
Agricultural And Livestock Products	331.7	487.3	375.9	268.4	238.1	154.7	673.2	1 138.7	1 273.6	910.4	738.2	1 365.0
Agricultural products	331.7	487.3	375.9	268.4	238.0	154.7	672.7	1 138.2	1 273.0	910.1	737.9	1 364.8
Livestock and livestock products	...	...	...	...	0.1	...	0.5	0.5	0.6	0.4	0.4	0.2
Other Commodities	1.1	3.3	3.3	3.2	3.8	4.8	13.2	16.8	8.3	7.8	8.1	14.8
Forestry products	...	...	...	...	...	0.1	...	...	...	0.1	0.1	0.1
Fish and other marine products	0.3	0.1	0.1	0.2	0.3	0.2	0.1	0.1	0.1	...	0.2	0.2
Metallic ores and concentrates	...	...	...	...	...	...	...	0.1	0.1	...	...	0.2
Bituminous coal and lignite	...	...	...	...	...	...	...	...	...	...	...	...
Crude petroleum and natural gas	...	...	...	...	...	...	...	...	0.1	...	...	...
Nonmetallic minerals	...	...	0.1	...	0.3	...	8.1	2.5	1.4	4.4	3.7	3.8
Scrap and waste	...	...	...	...	...	...	0.3	1.2	0.4	0.3	0.1	0.5
Used merchandise	...	0.3	0.2	...	0.1	0.1	2.3	2.9	1.8	0.8	0.3	1.1
Goods imported and returned unchanged	...	...	...	...	...	...	...	...	...	...	...	...
Special classification provisions	0.8	3.0	2.9	2.9	3.0	4.4	2.4	9.9	4.3	2.2	3.7	8.9

Table D-26. MINNESOTA: State Exports of Goods by Destination and Industry, 1994–1999—*Continued*

(Millions of dollars.)

Industry	Japan						South Korea					
	1994	1995	1996	1997	1998	1999	1994	1995	1996	1997	1998	1999
ALL GOODS	761.6	863.6	1 047.8	1 089.8	822.3	894.7	261.2	435.4	488.3	268.4	301.3	570.2
Manufactured Goods	390.4	464.2	574.3	636.2	523.0	571.3	187.1	261.0	207.8	200.5	160.5	155.9
Food products	33.4	35.8	46.6	38.5	36.5	57.2	30.3	33.2	31.0	40.8	56.1	30.2
Tobacco products	...	...	...	...	...	...	...	...	...	...	...	...
Textile mill products	0.8	0.7	1.1	0.5	0.8	1.8	...	1.0	0.4	0.9	0.1	0.5
Apparel	1.1	1.4	1.4	0.9	1.0	1.6	0.1	0.1	0.2	0.1	0.1	0.6
Lumber and wood products	13.0	21.2	20.3	19.0	11.8	14.2	0.8	0.7	1.7	0.8	0.5	0.4
Furniture and fixtures	0.8	1.4	1.5	2.1	1.3	1.1	0.2	0.6	0.6	0.6	0.1	0.1
Paper products	3.8	5.1	5.6	6.1	3.8	13.7	2.0	3.5	2.5	1.9	0.5	3.6
Printing and publishing	1.2	1.7	1.8	1.5	1.2	1.3	0.3	0.6	0.5	0.4	0.1	0.6
Chemical products	11.0	15.9	30.2	35.1	27.2	20.3	4.6	11.1	9.3	11.7	3.8	5.6
Refined petroleum products	...	...	...	...	...	...	0.9	0.6	0.3	0.5	0.1	...
Rubber and plastic products	32.2	25.4	23.0	24.1	18.6	20.5	4.3	4.2	3.6	3.9	1.3	5.5
Leather products	4.4	5.9	7.1	9.3	7.8	8.1	0.3	0.4	0.2	0.2	0.9	0.3
Stone, clay and glass products	5.8	6.8	6.0	7.2	4.6	7.1	1.7	3.8	7.8	3.8	1.4	2.2
Primary metals	1.2	1.2	2.5	3.0	2.0	0.5	0.7	0.7	0.5	0.9	1.0	0.1
Fabricated metal products	7.2	7.0	11.1	10.9	10.2	7.9	6.5	4.7	6.1	10.1	3.1	4.2
Industrial machinery and computers	87.9	133.8	131.3	138.3	119.5	176.3	81.4	119.5	85.1	63.1	52.7	56.9
Electric and electronic equipment	42.1	37.0	43.0	41.2	45.6	39.7	22.6	43.2	23.3	23.3	10.7	17.6
Transportation equipment	7.8	8.0	6.8	7.2	8.5	5.8	2.3	1.7	3.1	2.0	3.1	3.1
Scientific and measuring instruments	130.6	146.6	228.0	287.3	216.7	190.1	26.6	28.8	29.7	34.1	23.7	22.5
Miscellaneous manufactures	5.3	7.7	5.6	2.6	4.4	2.9	1.0	1.9	1.8	1.0	0.8	1.0
Unidentified manufactures	0.8	1.6	1.3	1.2	1.5	1.3	0.4	0.5	0.3	0.3	0.6	0.7
Agricultural And Livestock Products	368.6	397.8	470.9	451.8	296.7	317.8	71.7	173.3	280.2	67.5	140.4	413.0
Agricultural products	368.2	397.5	470.8	451.5	296.4	317.7	71.7	173.3	279.8	67.5	140.4	412.9
Livestock and livestock products	0.4	0.3	0.1	0.2	0.2	0.1	...	...	0.4	...	...	0.1
Other Commodities	2.6	1.6	2.7	1.8	2.6	5.6	2.3	1.1	0.3	0.4	0.4	1.3
Forestry products	...	...	...	...	...	0.1	...	...	...	...	...	...
Fish and other marine products	...	...	...	...	...	...	...	...	...	...	...	...
Metallic ores and concentrates	...	...	...	...	...	...	...	...	...	...	0.2	0.2
Bituminous coal and lignite	...	...	...	...	...	...	...	...	...	...	...	...
Crude petroleum and natural gas	...	...	...	...	...	...	...	...	...	...	...	...
Nonmetallic minerals	1.5	0.2	0.1	0.2	0.3	0.3	2.1	...	...	0.2	0.1	0.1
Scrap and waste	...	...	...	...	...	...	0.2	0.3	0.1	...	...	...
Used merchandise	0.8	0.5	1.0	0.4	0.3	1.0	...	0.8	0.1	...	...	...
Goods imported and returned unchanged	...	...	...	...	...	...	...	...	...	...	...	...
Special classification provisions	0.3	0.9	1.6	1.3	2.0	4.3	...	0.1	0.1	0.1	0.1	1.0

Industry	Taiwan						Singapore					
	1994	1995	1996	1997	1998	1999	1994	1995	1996	1997	1998	1999
ALL GOODS	262.9	255.8	449.9	257.1	269.0	364.2	190.0	230.2	259.2	245.4	317.7	295.8
Manufactured Goods	134.1	147.5	134.2	147.6	162.2	154.4	189.1	228.8	257.9	244.7	316.7	290.0
Food products	18.7	24.4	19.6	12.6	34.0	33.5	5.0	6.9	4.5	3.6	2.8	3.8
Tobacco products	...	...	...	...	...	...	0.4	4.0	1.3	0.9	0.9	1.0
Textile mill products	0.1	0.1	...	...	0.3	0.2	0.1	0.1	0.1	0.3	...	0.3
Apparel	...	0.1	0.1	0.1	0.1	0.2	...	0.1	0.2	...	0.1	...
Lumber and wood products	0.9	0.5	0.9	0.5	0.1	0.4	...	0.1	0.2	...	...	...
Furniture and fixtures	0.4	0.2	0.1	0.2	0.1	0.5	0.4	0.3	0.5	0.8	0.3	0.2
Paper products	1.0	1.4	1.1	3.0	2.0	3.2	0.8	2.1	3.6	4.9	2.4	4.8
Printing and publishing	0.3	0.3	1.4	0.4	0.1	0.3	0.9	1.0	0.7	0.8	0.2	0.4
Chemical products	3.4	5.1	4.2	6.1	8.5	8.7	1.6	2.3	3.1	6.6	6.8	8.0
Refined petroleum products	...	...	...	0.1	...	0.1	...	...	0.1	...	0.1	0.2
Rubber and plastic products	10.4	13.1	10.9	15.4	12.6	17.9	19.6	20.5	31.1	21.4	35.5	39.3
Leather products	1.6	1.0	1.2	0.6	0.6	0.2	0.5	1.3	1.0	1.6	1.0	0.8
Stone, clay and glass products	2.2	2.6	3.2	1.7	1.1	1.7	3.0	2.6	1.5	4.0	3.4	4.0
Primary metals	0.4	0.4	0.4	0.5	0.5	0.6	2.3	2.8	2.8	3.0	2.4	2.6
Fabricated metal products	5.2	2.8	5.4	6.5	7.2	3.9	5.8	5.4	5.5	5.3	3.6	3.9
Industrial machinery and computers	30.6	34.9	28.0	39.7	35.0	40.3	36.7	48.2	88.4	91.2	113.2	83.8
Electric and electronic equipment	31.5	32.4	28.9	28.9	28.4	17.4	73.5	78.6	57.9	29.5	71.8	75.4
Transportation equipment	1.4	2.3	2.1	3.8	13.3	1.0	9.7	7.0	8.2	31.4	31.5	12.0
Scientific and measuring instruments	23.9	23.3	24.1	25.3	16.4	22.9	25.5	40.3	44.3	36.0	38.1	47.2
Miscellaneous manufactures	1.8	1.6	2.2	2.0	1.2	0.8	2.9	4.7	2.7	2.6	1.7	1.1
Unidentified manufactures	0.3	0.9	0.4	0.3	0.5	0.7	0.4	0.6	0.7	0.7	0.9	1.2
Agricultural And Livestock Products	124.9	106.2	314.4	106.1	103.3	207.0	...	0.8	0.7	0.2	0.2	2.7
Agricultural products	124.9	106.2	314.4	106.0	103.3	207.0	...	0.8	0.7	0.2	0.2	2.7
Livestock and livestock products	0.1	...	...	...	...	...	...	...	...	...	...	...
Other Commodities	3.8	2.1	1.3	3.4	3.6	2.8	0.8	0.6	0.6	0.5	0.7	3.1
Forestry products	...	...	...	...	...	...	...	...	...	...	0.1	0.1
Fish and other marine products	...	...	...	...	...	...	...	...	...	...	...	...
Metallic ores and concentrates	...	...	...	...	0.1	...	...	...	...	...	...	...
Bituminous coal and lignite	...	...	...	...	...	...	...	...	...	...	...	...
Crude petroleum and natural gas	...	...	...	...	...	...	...	...	...	...	...	...
Nonmetallic minerals	3.7	2.1	1.2	3.2	3.2	1.7	...	...	...	...	...	1.5
Scrap and waste	...	...	...	...	...	...	...	...	...	...	...	0.1
Used merchandise	...	...	...	...	...	...	...	...	...	0.1	...	...
Goods imported and returned unchanged	...	...	...	0.1	0.4	1.0	0.8	0.6	0.5	0.4	0.6	1.4
Special classification provisions	0.1	...	...	0.1	0.4	1.0	0.8	0.6	0.5	0.4	0.6	1.4

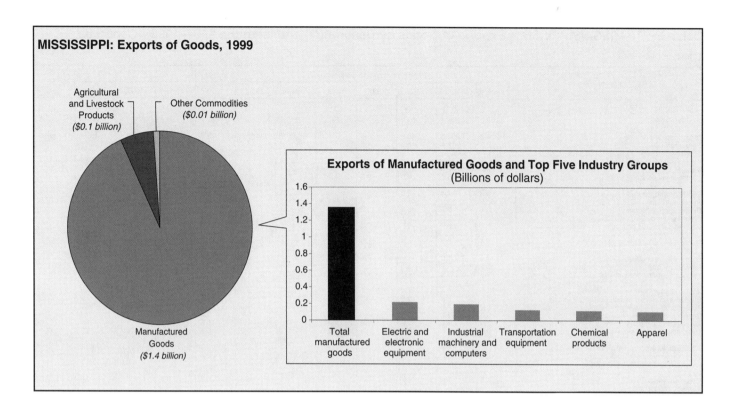

MISSISSIPPI: Exports of Goods, 1999

Agricultural and Livestock Products ($0.1 billion)

Other Commodities ($0.01 billion)

Manufactured Goods ($1.4 billion)

Exports of Manufactured Goods and Top Five Industry Groups
(Billions of dollars)

Table D-27. MISSISSIPPI: State Exports of Goods by Destination and Industry, 1994–1999

(Millions of dollars.)

Industry	All destinations						Canada					
	1994	1995	1996	1997	1998	1999	1994	1995	1996	1997	1998	1999
ALL GOODS	1 099.9	1 368.7	1 221.7	1 421.3	1 414.0	1 454.3	352.1	372.7	387.8	430.4	492.8	520.7
Manufactured Goods	1 055.1	1 261.1	1 145.5	1 307.5	1 281.3	1 352.2	342.9	354.4	366.8	408.9	476.3	507.0
Food products	76.7	138.5	159.6	203.5	96.5	53.4	18.1	21.5	18.7	12.5	16.9	13.3
Tobacco products	0.1	0.1	0.2	0.1	0.1	0.2	. . .	. . .	. . .	. . .	. . .	. . .
Textile mill products	50.6	59.9	76.6	81.9	75.8	66.3	21.7	22.9	28.3	24.6	23.8	12.2
Apparel	28.3	54.6	89.7	111.1	113.5	109.1	4.8	6.7	8.5	5.6	3.1	5.6
Lumber and wood products	26.4	30.5	34.8	54.2	43.9	31.3	5.9	4.8	9.8	11.2	4.2	5.1
Furniture and fixtures	56.7	47.6	45.7	66.4	71.3	57.1	41.7	29.5	25.9	38.2	42.3	31.6
Paper products	122.3	169.4	119.0	91.2	99.6	88.2	15.7	23.3	18.0	28.8	35.1	39.9
Printing and publishing	20.1	18.8	15.5	17.0	14.5	16.3	8.6	5.9	5.2	4.5	3.4	2.6
Chemical products	62.9	70.7	79.5	71.9	128.6	117.8	28.3	23.4	27.6	38.1	62.4	57.5
Refined petroleum products	6.1	13.3	9.4	10.9	4.7	22.6	1.0	1.1	1.0	1.1	1.0	1.9
Rubber and plastic products	33.8	37.2	36.3	43.3	51.4	65.1	12.7	17.3	20.3	29.5	34.9	37.9
Leather products	0.7	0.6	1.2	0.8	2.4	7.1	0.1	0.4	0.2	. . .	0.1	0.2
Stone, clay and glass products	14.3	14.6	16.7	20.1	16.1	15.3	7.7	7.4	7.2	7.0	6.9	7.0
Primary metals	25.9	27.4	18.6	33.8	42.4	43.7	12.3	10.1	8.5	8.7	16.5	15.5
Fabricated metal products	28.0	35.1	51.1	62.4	57.1	73.6	10.4	11.7	16.5	20.2	25.3	40.2
Industrial machinery and computers	105.2	106.8	131.7	190.3	205.5	194.6	53.7	58.9	63.2	71.7	91.1	92.9
Electric and electronic equipment	160.5	178.7	162.8	139.1	130.1	218.8	59.0	68.4	71.7	76.1	67.8	97.6
Transportation equipment	208.8	216.8	70.0	52.9	80.2	127.2	32.6	29.6	29.3	16.9	26.3	32.9
Scientific and measuring instruments	10.0	13.5	13.1	35.4	24.4	24.7	2.6	3.0	2.3	6.0	7.3	5.3
Miscellaneous manufactures	15.7	24.8	11.7	15.4	15.4	12.3	5.4	7.8	4.0	5.9	7.1	6.5
Unidentified manufactures	2.1	2.2	2.4	5.7	8.0	7.6	0.6	0.8	0.6	2.3	1.0	1.3
Agricultural And Livestock Products	28.5	81.1	52.5	65.0	118.2	87.3	1.1	1.8	3.4	1.6	5.3	6.2
Agricultural products	27.5	80.4	51.2	63.0	115.9	85.5	0.4	1.7	3.2	0.7	3.8	4.6
Livestock and livestock products	1.0	0.7	1.3	2.1	2.3	1.8	0.7	0.1	0.2	0.9	1.5	1.6
Other Commodities	16.3	26.5	23.7	48.8	14.6	14.8	8.1	16.5	17.6	19.9	11.2	7.5
Forestry products	. . .	. . .	. . .	0.1	0.4	0.4	. . .	. . .	. . .	. . .	. . .	. . .
Fish and other marine products	3.6	6.0	6.3	4.5	3.7	3.1	3.1	4.7	4.4	3.4	3.4	2.7
Metallic ores and concentrates	. . .	. . .	. . .	0.8	. . .	. . .	. . .	. . .	. . .	. . .	. . .	. . .
Bituminous coal and lignite	. . .	. . .	. . .	. . .	. . .	. . .	. . .	. . .	. . .	. . .	. . .	. . .
Crude petroleum and natural gas	2.8	3.0	. . .	0.4	0.7	2.3	0.1	. . .	. . .	. . .	. . .	. . .
Nonmetallic minerals	2.3	2.6	4.0	2.1	1.1	0.9	0.5	1.7	2.4	1.3	0.3	0.3
Scrap and waste	1.6	6.9	5.0	8.4	2.5	0.6	0.6	5.5	4.8	8.1	1.9	0.5
Used merchandise	1.1	1.8	1.4	0.7	1.1	2.2	0.2	1.0	0.3	0.1	0.7	0.1
Goods imported and returned unchanged	3.5	3.5	5.5	6.9	4.5	3.4	3.5	3.5	5.5	6.9	4.5	3.4
Special classification provisions	1.2	2.7	1.5	25.0	0.5	1.8	0.1	0.2	0.1	0.1	0.3	0.5

Table D-27. MISSISSIPPI: State Exports of Goods by Destination and Industry, 1994–1999—*Continued*

(Millions of dollars.)

Industry	South and Central American and Caribbean						Mexico					
	1994	1995	1996	1997	1998	1999	1994	1995	1996	1997	1998	1999
ALL GOODS	208.5	245.1	254.0	232.5	242.6	272.9	65.7	87.9	91.3	127.4	242.4	293.0
Manufactured Goods	204.4	238.3	248.8	228.5	239.7	269.7	59.2	79.5	87.1	80.4	159.5	237.5
Food products	2.5	12.4	8.9	4.7	3.9	2.5	14.0	7.2	6.3	4.6	4.6	7.0
Tobacco products	...	...	...	...	...	...	...	...	...	...	...	...
Textile mill products	26.8	33.4	42.6	46.8	34.2	26.3	0.3	0.7	2.8	6.6	13.6	23.1
Apparel	22.2	42.3	65.0	81.4	83.4	70.4	0.2	3.5	13.5	20.1	23.5	29.3
Lumber and wood products	4.0	5.4	4.0	3.3	2.9	2.2	0.8	0.4	0.3	2.6	3.2	2.3
Furniture and fixtures	0.8	1.4	2.0	2.9	3.0	2.6	3.1	0.9	0.2	0.9	0.9	1.2
Paper products	58.8	58.9	47.9	17.9	17.3	17.7	1.8	1.8	1.6	1.8	5.6	6.6
Printing and publishing	0.4	0.5	0.3	0.2	1.0	0.5	0.2	0.3	0.3	1.4	0.4	0.5
Chemical products	22.2	22.9	23.2	15.9	43.1	32.7	2.4	2.7	4.8	4.0	5.1	6.4
Refined petroleum products	0.7	0.7	0.6	0.3	0.1	19.1	...	...	...	0.1	0.1	...
Rubber and plastic products	7.4	5.3	4.3	2.0	1.5	1.6	5.2	0.6	2.3	3.5	7.5	16.3
Leather products	...	...	0.2	...	0.1	...	...	...	...	...	0.1	0.7
Stone, clay and glass products	1.3	1.9	1.8	2.4	2.3	1.7	0.9	0.2	0.1	0.3	0.2	0.4
Primary metals	5.3	5.7	3.3	1.7	1.8	1.8	3.1	2.5	2.2	10.2	16.4	20.2
Fabricated metal products	2.9	3.2	4.3	4.2	2.9	3.9	5.4	1.1	2.2	4.2	13.2	10.7
Industrial machinery and computers	13.5	16.5	17.9	14.1	18.6	12.8	2.8	1.9	4.5	13.3	34.1	26.7
Electric and electronic equipment	25.9	9.8	8.6	12.2	5.4	7.2	16.6	48.5	43.1	3.4	17.2	77.9
Transportation equipment	6.9	12.5	6.6	9.7	9.4	58.1	1.0	0.3	0.5	1.1	10.3	3.1
Scientific and measuring instruments	0.8	3.7	5.8	7.1	4.8	6.0	0.2	0.3	0.2	0.4	0.4	1.1
Miscellaneous manufactures	1.4	1.2	1.0	0.9	1.8	0.8	1.0	6.3	2.1	1.7	1.9	1.6
Unidentified manufactures	0.5	0.6	0.5	0.8	2.3	1.9	0.2	0.1	0.2	0.4	1.1	2.4
Agricultural And Livestock Products	2.7	4.9	4.5	3.4	1.9	1.7	2.1	3.2	3.7	21.3	82.2	53.0
Agricultural products	2.7	4.9	4.3	3.4	1.9	1.7	2.1	3.2	3.7	21.1	81.5	53.0
Livestock and livestock products	...	...	0.1	...	...	...	...	...	...	0.2	0.7	...
Other Commodities	1.5	1.9	0.7	0.6	1.0	1.5	4.3	5.2	0.5	25.6	0.7	2.5
Forestry products	...	...	...	...	0.2	0.4	...	...	...	...	...	...
Fish and other marine products	...	...	...	...	...	...	...	...	...	...	...	0.1
Metallic ores and concentrates	...	...	...	0.1	...	...	...	...	...	0.6	...	...
Bituminous coal and lignite	...	...	...	...	...	...	...	...	...	...	...	...
Crude petroleum and natural gas	...	...	...	...	...	...	2.8	3.0	...	0.4	0.6	2.3
Nonmetallic minerals	0.4	0.1	0.4	0.1	...	0.2	0.6	...	...	...	...	...
Scrap and waste	0.7	1.2	...	...	0.4	...	...	...	...	...	...	...
Used merchandise	0.3	0.6	0.2	0.3	0.3	0.8	0.2	...	...	0.1	...	0.1
Goods imported and returned unchanged	...	...	...	...	...	0.1	0.8	2.2	0.5	24.5	...	...
Special classification provisions	0.1	...	0.1	...	...	...						

Industry	European Union						United Kingdom					
	1994	1995	1996	1997	1998	1999	1994	1995	1996	1997	1998	1999
ALL GOODS	169.8	223.3	208.1	266.9	254.3	208.9	68.5	91.3	75.2	80.9	70.4	57.0
Manufactured Goods	151.0	201.3	184.0	240.3	227.4	195.7	52.7	71.5	56.8	68.0	70.2	56.9
Food products	9.6	7.1	16.3	7.5	7.2	9.2	...	0.4	0.6	2.4	0.7	6.3
Tobacco products	0.1	0.1	0.1	0.1	0.1	0.1	0.1	0.1	0.1	0.1	0.1	0.1
Textile mill products	0.8	1.0	1.2	2.6	2.1	2.8	0.3	0.3	0.4	0.9	0.9	0.9
Apparel	0.4	1.4	1.2	1.5	1.1	0.9	0.1	0.5	0.5	0.4	0.4	0.2
Lumber and wood products	8.3	9.4	12.1	21.9	24.8	13.6	0.5	0.4	1.4	3.4	4.6	0.9
Furniture and fixtures	6.4	8.1	8.7	15.2	15.4	10.3	0.5	1.1	0.9	3.5	4.8	5.0
Paper products	43.9	84.0	50.2	41.5	40.5	23.6	10.1	29.8	13.0	9.2	4.7	2.1
Printing and publishing	7.2	8.4	6.9	8.2	7.1	8.9	4.2	3.7	3.2	3.4	3.5	3.9
Chemical products	4.0	8.7	12.3	4.7	7.3	8.6	1.1	1.4	2.3	1.1	1.2	1.1
Refined petroleum products	2.3	7.4	1.1	3.5	0.4	0.1	0.7	1.8	0.5	1.4	...	...
Rubber and plastic products	4.1	5.7	5.4	2.7	2.6	4.0	0.9	2.4	2.6	0.6	0.4	0.5
Leather products	0.5	...	...	0.3	1.1	5.3	0.2	...	...	...	...	0.2
Stone, clay and glass products	2.4	2.0	2.6	3.2	3.3	2.0	0.9	0.1	0.2	0.2	0.6	0.2
Primary metals	0.4	2.0	1.6	1.2	1.6	1.3	...	0.4	0.3	1.0	1.5	1.1
Fabricated metal products	1.8	3.0	7.0	16.4	9.3	12.1	0.9	1.5	4.9	12.9	6.6	5.0
Industrial machinery and computers	15.6	16.9	27.0	62.0	45.9	41.5	4.0	5.0	9.0	9.2	15.6	13.5
Electric and electronic equipment	25.4	18.7	13.9	14.0	18.9	17.2	17.4	11.3	6.8	7.0	10.5	9.1
Transportation equipment	10.1	10.8	11.4	15.1	26.7	26.8	7.3	7.7	8.8	10.1	12.7	5.7
Scientific and measuring instruments	3.9	3.4	2.3	15.8	8.9	5.3	1.5	1.8	0.8	0.8	0.3	0.4
Miscellaneous manufactures	3.5	2.9	2.0	2.3	2.1	1.1	2.1	1.8	0.2	0.4	0.8	0.4
Unidentified manufactures	0.3	0.3	0.7	0.7	1.1	0.9	0.1	0.2	0.3	0.2	0.4	0.3
Agricultural And Livestock Products	17.8	20.6	21.7	25.0	26.0	12.4	15.5	19.6	18.2	12.6	...	...
Agricultural products	17.8	20.6	21.6	24.8	26.0	12.4	15.5	19.6	18.1	12.6	...	...
Livestock and livestock products	...	...	0.1	0.2	...	...	...	...	0.1	...	...	...
Other Commodities	1.0	1.4	2.4	1.5	0.9	0.7	0.3	0.1	0.2	0.3	0.2	0.2
Forestry products	...	...	...	...	0.2	...	...	...	...	...	...	...
Fish and other marine products	0.4	0.8	1.6	0.8	0.3	0.2	...	...	...	...	...	...
Metallic ores and concentrates	...	...	...	...	...	...	...	...	...	...	...	...
Bituminous coal and lignite	...	...	...	...	...	...	...	...	...	...	...	...
Crude petroleum and natural gas	...	...	...	...	...	...	...	...	...	...	...	...
Nonmetallic minerals	...	...	0.1	0.2	0.2	0.1	...	...	...	...	...	...
Scrap and waste	0.4	0.2	...	0.2	0.2	...	0.1	...	...	0.1	0.1	...
Used merchandise	0.1	0.2	0.3	0.1	0.1	0.2	0.1	0.1	0.1	0.1	...	0.1
Goods imported and returned unchanged	...	...	...	...	...	...	...	...	...	0.1	...	...
Special classification provisions	0.1	0.1	0.5	0.2	0.1	0.2	0.1	...	...	0.1	...	0.1

Table D-27. MISSISSIPPI: State Exports of Goods by Destination and Industry, 1994–1999—*Continued*

(Millions of dollars.)

Industry	Germany						France					
	1994	1995	1996	1997	1998	1999	1994	1995	1996	1997	1998	1999
ALL GOODS	20.2	20.2	17.3	17.4	26.1	29.4	17.7	24.0	17.5	12.0	12.7	6.5
Manufactured Goods	19.8	19.2	15.5	16.5	25.9	29.1	17.6	23.9	17.2	11.9	12.7	6.5
Food products	0.1	...	2.2	0.4	0.6	1.6	...	...	0.2	...	...	...
Tobacco products	...	...	...	...	...	...	...	...	...	...	...	...
Textile mill products	...	...	0.1	0.1	0.2	0.4	0.2	0.2	0.1	...	0.3	0.6
Apparel	0.1	0.1	0.2	0.2	...	...	0.1	0.6	...	0.1	0.2	0.1
Lumber and wood products	1.0	0.9	0.8	0.9	1.0	0.3	0.4	0.3	0.8	0.7	0.8	0.5
Furniture and fixtures	2.4	1.0	0.6	0.5	0.2	0.3	0.5	0.6	0.9	1.3	0.1	...
Paper products	3.1	1.3	1.3	1.4	1.5	0.1	8.8	15.3	4.0	2.6	3.9	0.2
Printing and publishing	...	...	...	0.1	...	...	...	...	...	...	...	0.2
Chemical products	1.2	3.1	0.3	1.1	1.6	2.0	...	...	1.8	0.1	0.3	0.1
Refined petroleum products	...	...	...	...	...	...	...	...	...	0.4	0.2	...
Rubber and plastic products	1.6	1.3	0.6	0.6	0.2	0.4	0.5	0.9	1.0	0.2	0.4	0.3
Leather products	...	...	...	...	...	...	...	...	...	...	...	...
Stone, clay and glass products	...	...	...	0.2	0.2	...	0.4	0.4	0.8	1.0	0.6	0.1
Primary metals	...	1.3	0.2	...	...	...	...	0.2	...	...	...	...
Fabricated metal products	0.3	0.3	0.6	0.6	0.6	0.5	0.1	0.1	0.2	0.1	0.5	...
Industrial machinery and computers	4.4	4.9	5.4	7.0	8.5	7.2	4.9	4.4	6.3	3.5	3.8	1.4
Electric and electronic equipment	2.7	1.9	1.2	1.0	1.0	1.0	0.2	0.2	0.4	0.6	0.5	0.9
Transportation equipment	2.1	2.3	1.7	1.7	9.6	13.8	0.2	0.2	0.3	0.6	0.6	1.8
Scientific and measuring instruments	0.4	0.3	0.2	0.3	0.4	1.1	0.5	0.4	0.1	0.3	0.1	0.1
Miscellaneous manufactures	0.1	0.4	0.2	0.4	0.1	0.2	0.6	0.1	0.2	0.3	0.1	0.1
Unidentified manufactures	...	...	0.1	0.1	...	0.1	...	...	...	0.1	0.2	...
Agricultural And Livestock Products	...	...	...	...	...	...	...	...	...	...	...	...
Agricultural products	...	...	...	...	...	...	...	...	...	...	...	...
Livestock and livestock products	...	...	...	...	...	...	...	...	...	...	...	...
Other Commodities	0.4	1.0	1.8	0.9	0.3	0.3	0.1	0.1	0.3	0.1	...	...
Forestry products	...	...	...	...	...	...	...	...	...	...	...	...
Fish and other marine products	0.4	0.8	1.6	0.8	0.2	0.2	...	...	...	...	...	...
Metallic ores and concentrates	...	...	...	...	...	...	...	...	...	...	...	...
Bituminous coal and lignite	...	...	...	...	...	...	...	...	...	...	...	...
Crude petroleum and natural gas	...	...	...	...	...	...	...	...	...	...	...	...
Nonmetallic minerals	...	...	...	...	...	...	...	...	...	...	...	...
Scrap and waste	...	0.1	...	0.1	...	...	0.1	0.1	...	...	...	...
Used merchandise	...	0.1	0.1	...	...	0.1	...	...	...	...	...	...
Goods imported and returned unchanged	...	...	...	...	...	...	...	...	...	...	...	...
Special classification provisions	...	...	0.1	...	...	...	...	...	0.3	0.1	...	...

Industry	The Netherlands						Asian 10					
	1994	1995	1996	1997	1998	1999	1994	1995	1996	1997	1998	1999
ALL GOODS	22.1	32.8	26.3	26.1	22.2	27.8	78.4	177.8	127.9	139.8	88.0	84.5
Manufactured Goods	21.9	32.7	26.2	25.7	22.1	27.8	74.6	126.9	107.5	129.4	84.8	69.7
Food products	7.9	5.0	6.9	3.0	1.7	0.2	7.4	24.7	19.2	17.6	19.2	6.2
Tobacco products	...	...	...	...	...	...	...	...	...	...	...	0.1
Textile mill products	0.1	0.3	0.5	1.3	0.4	0.4	0.4	1.0	0.7	0.6	1.3	0.8
Apparel	...	0.1	0.3	0.2	0.1	0.1	0.3	0.5	0.9	2.0	2.1	1.2
Lumber and wood products	0.2	0.1	0.1	0.3	0.3	0.3	6.0	7.4	6.4	8.9	6.6	5.5
Furniture and fixtures	0.2	0.7	1.0	1.2	1.6	1.4	0.9	2.4	1.6	1.9	2.9	4.2
Paper products	6.0	11.2	6.9	4.0	1.4	1.4	1.3	1.3	1.2	1.1	0.7	0.2
Printing and publishing	2.8	4.6	3.6	4.7	3.4	4.8	1.4	1.2	0.5	0.5	0.6	1.0
Chemical products	0.7	3.7	1.7	1.5	2.4	4.1	2.2	10.5	7.8	6.4	9.3	9.3
Refined petroleum products	1.6	4.6	0.3	0.3	...	0.1	1.9	3.8	6.5	5.5	1.6	1.1
Rubber and plastic products	...	0.1	0.2	0.2	0.2	0.6	1.5	1.4	0.9	1.9	1.4	1.6
Leather products	...	...	...	...	0.7	5.1	...	0.1	0.6	0.4	1.1	0.8
Stone, clay and glass products	0.8	0.8	1.1	1.4	1.4	1.4	1.2	2.0	3.3	5.9	2.0	2.1
Primary metals	...	...	0.5	0.1	...	...	4.0	4.7	1.3	7.6	2.5	3.1
Fabricated metal products	...	0.1	0.1	0.1	0.8	0.2	4.9	14.7	15.8	13.1	2.9	3.9
Industrial machinery and computers	0.2	0.4	1.2	0.8	0.6	1.0	6.0	9.8	13.5	19.0	9.0	8.4
Electric and electronic equipment	0.7	0.6	1.1	1.4	1.7	0.5	23.6	21.8	14.8	24.6	13.8	14.1
Transportation equipment	0.1	0.2	0.3	2.4	3.1	3.7	6.3	12.0	9.7	5.6	3.7	2.4
Scientific and measuring instruments	0.4	0.2	0.3	2.4	2.2	2.3	1.2	1.7	1.2	3.8	2.3	2.5
Miscellaneous manufactures	0.1	...	0.1	0.3	0.4	...	3.8	5.8	1.5	2.7	1.4	0.7
Unidentified manufactures	0.1	...	0.1	0.1	0.1	...	0.2	0.2	0.3	0.4	0.4	0.4
Agricultural And Livestock Products	...	...	...	0.3	...	...	2.9	49.6	18.7	9.4	2.6	13.0
Agricultural products	...	...	...	0.1	...	...	2.5	49.1	17.8	9.0	2.4	12.9
Livestock and livestock products	...	...	...	0.2	...	...	0.4	0.5	0.8	0.4	0.2	0.1
Other Commodities	0.2	0.1	...	0.1	0.1	...	0.9	1.3	1.7	1.0	0.6	1.7
Forestry products	...	...	...	...	...	...	...	...	...	...	...	...
Fish and other marine products	...	...	...	...	...	...	0.1	0.5	0.2	0.3	0.1	0.1
Metallic ores and concentrates	...	...	...	...	...	...	...	...	...	...	...	...
Bituminous coal and lignite	...	...	...	...	...	...	...	...	...	...	...	...
Crude petroleum and natural gas	...	...	...	...	...	...	...	...	...	...	...	...
Nonmetallic minerals	...	...	...	0.1	0.1	...	0.7	0.6	0.6	0.4	0.4	0.3
Scrap and waste	0.2	...	...	...	...	...	...	...	...	...	0.1	...
Used merchandise	...	...	...	...	...	...	0.1	...	0.5	0.1	...	0.9
Goods imported and returned unchanged	...	...	...	...	...	...	...	...	...	...	...	...
Special classification provisions	...	0.1	...	...	...	...	...	0.1	0.2	0.2	0.1	0.4

Table D-27. MISSISSIPPI: State Exports of Goods by Destination and Industry, 1994–1999—*Continued*

(Millions of dollars.)

Industry	Japan						South Korea					
	1994	1995	1996	1997	1998	1999	1994	1995	1996	1997	1998	1999
ALL GOODS	17.9	26.5	39.0	49.2	44.3	24.3	16.0	29.3	19.7	11.2	4.6	9.7
Manufactured Goods	16.6	20.0	30.2	43.9	41.5	22.8	15.6	28.4	19.2	10.5	4.5	4.4
Food products	1.5	3.3	10.3	11.4	15.4	0.8	...	0.1	0.1	0.3	0.2	0.2
Tobacco products	...	...	...	...	...	...	...	...	...	...	...	...
Textile mill products	0.2	0.4	0.2	0.1	...	...	...	0.1	...	...	...	0.2
Apparel	0.2	0.4	0.8	1.6	0.6	1.2	...	...	0.1	0.4	0.0	...
Lumber and wood products	1.6	1.3	0.3	3.8	2.9	4.1	2.9	4.2	3.4	3.3	2.3	0.4
Furniture and fixtures	0.3	0.4	0.6	1.3	2.7	3.6	0.2	0.1	0.5	0.1	...	0.1
Paper products	0.9	1.0	0.7	0.2	0.4	...	0.3	0.3	0.1	0.1	...	0.1
Printing and publishing	...	...	0.1	0.1	...	...	0.1	0.1	...	...	...	0.3
Chemical products	1.7	1.9	0.3	0.2	2.2	3.5	0.1	6.4	0.2	0.4	0.4	0.7
Refined petroleum products	1.8	2.6	4.4	3.6	1.4	...	0.1	0.5	1.2	0.8	0.1	0.1
Rubber and plastic products	0.4	0.4	0.1	0.2	0.4	0.4	0.2	0.8	0.4	0.2	...	0.1
Leather products	...	...	...	0.1	0.1	...	...	...	...	...	...	0.2
Stone, clay and glass products	0.3	1.2	1.3	1.6	1.1	1.2	0.5	0.1	0.1	0.2	0.2	...
Primary metals	0.3	0.1	0.1	...	0.3	0.3	0.8	0.6	0.3	0.1	0.1	...
Fabricated metal products	0.6	1.1	0.8	1.4	1.3	1.0	2.1	5.6	5.4	0.8	0.1	...
Industrial machinery and computers	2.2	2.7	2.7	5.9	4.2	0.8	0.6	0.9	2.0	0.5	0.3	0.4
Electric and electronic equipment	2.2	1.8	1.0	5.4	3.7	3.5	2.1	1.2	2.3	2.2	0.4	1.3
Transportation equipment	1.4	0.2	5.8	3.4	2.3	1.3	2.0	2.0	1.8	0.2	...	0.2
Scientific and measuring instruments	0.5	0.8	0.4	2.4	1.9	0.7	0.1	0.2	0.4	0.1	...	...
Miscellaneous manufactures	0.4	0.3	0.4	1.3	0.4	0.3	3.2	5.1	0.9	0.9	0.4	...
Unidentified manufactures	0.1	...	0.1	...	0.1	0.2	...	...	...	0.1	...	...
Agricultural And Livestock Products	0.7	5.9	7.7	4.9	2.3	0.3	0.1	0.4	0.5	0.6	...	5.2
Agricultural products	0.7	5.9	7.6	4.7	2.3	0.3	...	0.4	0.5	0.6	...	5.2
Livestock and livestock products	...	0.1	0.1	0.2	...	...	0.1	...	...	...	...	0.1
Other Commodities	0.6	0.6	1.1	0.4	0.4	1.1	0.2	0.5	0.1	0.1	...	0.1
Forestry products	...	...	...	...	...	...	...	...	...	...	...	...
Fish and other marine products	0.1	0.4	0.2	0.1	0.1	0.1	...	...	...	...	...	...
Metallic ores and concentrates	...	...	...	...	...	...	...	...	...	...	...	...
Bituminous coal and lignite	...	...	...	...	...	...	...	...	...	...	...	...
Crude petroleum and natural gas	...	...	...	...	...	...	...	...	...	...	...	...
Nonmetallic minerals	0.5	0.3	0.4	0.3	0.4	0.1	0.1	0.3	0.1	0.1	...	0.1
Scrap and waste	...	...	...	...	...	...	...	...	...	...	...	...
Used merchandise	...	...	0.5	...	...	0.8	0.1	...	...	...	...	...
Goods imported and returned unchanged	...	...	...	...	...	...	...	...	...	...	...	...
Special classification provisions	...	...	...	...	...	0.1	...	0.1	...	...	...	...

Industry	Taiwan						Singapore					
	1994	1995	1996	1997	1998	1999	1994	1995	1996	1997	1998	1999
ALL GOODS	8.1	19.9	8.8	7.0	3.4	7.1	12.1	10.6	12.1	9.2	8.4	8.3
Manufactured Goods	6.8	11.3	5.8	6.6	3.3	5.2	12.1	10.5	11.9	9.1	8.3	8.3
Food products	...	0.2	0.7	0.9	0.3	0.2	...	...	...	0.2	0.1	0.2
Tobacco products	...	...	...	...	...	...	...	...	...	...	...	0.1
Textile mill products	...	...	...	...	...	...	...	0.1	0.1	...	...	...
Apparel	...	...	...	...	...	...	...	...	...	...	1.5	...
Lumber and wood products	1.1	0.8	1.2	0.1	0.1	0.1	0.1	0.2	0.2	0.1	...	...
Furniture and fixtures	0.3	1.5	0.4	0.2	...	0.1	...	0.3	...	...	...	0.1
Paper products	0.1	...	0.1	0.3	...	...	...	0.1	...	...	...	...
Printing and publishing	...	...	...	...	...	...	...	...	0.3	0.4	0.4	0.5
Chemical products	0.1	0.1	0.1	0.3	0.2	1.0	...	1.6	5.5	3.1	1.8	0.8
Refined petroleum products	...	0.6	0.9	1.1	...	...	...	...	...	...	...	...
Rubber and plastic products	0.2	...	...	0.2	0.4	0.1	...	...	0.1	...	0.4	0.5
Leather products	...	...	...	...	0.1	0.1	...	...	...	...	...	...
Stone, clay and glass products	...	...	...	...	0.4	1.3	0.1	0.2	1.0	0.3	0.4	0.4
Primary metals	1.3	2.2	0.1	0.2	0.4	1.3	0.1	...	0.1	0.1	0.2	0.3
Fabricated metal products	0.1	0.1	0.1	0.2	0.3	0.1	0.1	0.1	0.1	0.3	0.1	0.1
Industrial machinery and computers	2.0	0.9	0.2	0.8	0.6	0.5	0.2	0.8	1.4	1.3	0.8	0.9
Electric and electronic equipment	0.7	1.9	0.9	1.1	0.4	1.4	9.4	6.8	2.8	2.2	2.0	3.0
Transportation equipment	0.5	2.5	0.8	0.2	0.1	0.1	1.9	...	0.2	0.3	0.3	0.1
Scientific and measuring instruments	0.3	0.2	...	0.8	0.1	0.1	...	0.1	0.1	0.4	0.1	1.3
Miscellaneous manufactures	...	0.2	0.1	0.2	0.2	0.2	...	...	0.1	...	0.1	...
Unidentified manufactures	...	...	...	0.1	...	...	...	...	...	...	0.1	...
Agricultural And Livestock Products	1.2	8.6	3.0	0.2	...	1.7	...	...	0.1	...	...	...
Agricultural products	1.1	8.6	2.5	...	...	1.7	...	...	...	...	...	...
Livestock and livestock products	0.2	0.1	0.5	0.2	...	...	...	...	0.1	...	...	...
Other Commodities	...	...	...	0.2	...	0.2	...	...	0.1	0.1	...	...
Forestry products	...	...	...	...	...	...	...	...	...	...	...	...
Fish and other marine products	...	...	...	0.2	...	...	...	...	0.1	...	...	...
Metallic ores and concentrates	...	...	...	...	...	...	...	...	...	...	...	...
Bituminous coal and lignite	...	...	...	...	...	...	...	...	...	...	...	...
Crude petroleum and natural gas	...	...	...	...	...	...	...	...	...	...	...	...
Nonmetallic minerals	...	...	...	...	...	0.1	...	...	0.1	...	...	...
Scrap and waste	...	...	...	...	...	...	...	...	...	...	...	...
Used merchandise	...	...	...	...	...	...	...	...	...	...	...	...
Goods imported and returned unchanged	...	...	...	...	...	...	...	...	...	...	...	...
Special classification provisions	...	...	...	...	...	...	...	...	...	...	...	...

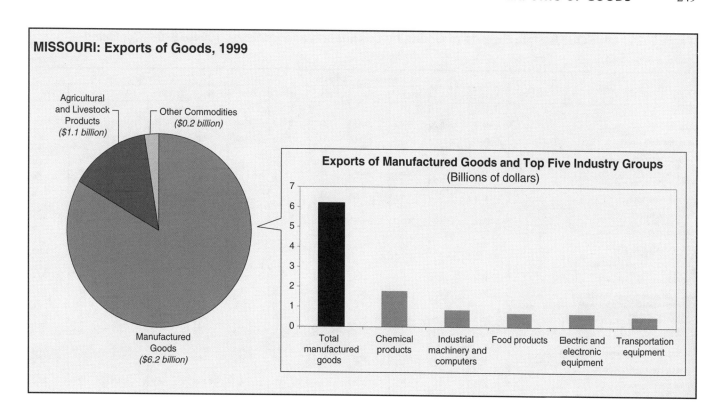

MISSOURI: Exports of Goods, 1999

Agricultural and Livestock Products ($1.1 billion)

Other Commodities ($0.2 billion)

Manufactured Goods ($6.2 billion)

Exports of Manufactured Goods and Top Five Industry Groups
(Billions of dollars)

Total manufactured goods | Chemical products | Industrial machinery and computers | Food products | Electric and electronic equipment | Transportation equipment

Table D-28. MISSOURI: State Exports of Goods by Destination and Industry, 1994–1999

(Millions of dollars.)

Industry	All destinations						Canada					
	1994	1995	1996	1997	1998	1999	1994	1995	1996	1997	1998	1999
ALL GOODS	5 234.8	5 689.9	6 590.5	7 043.0	6 832.4	7 431.1	1 347.9	1 369.7	1 288.1	1 490.1	1 570.3	1 570.2
Manufactured Goods	4 392.8	4 857.7	5 122.3	5 711.9	5 632.8	6 184.1	1 305.0	1 319.3	1 237.2	1 432.7	1 523.6	1 526.1
Food products	287.7	391.7	369.5	493.2	716.7	702.5	60.9	78.2	57.3	73.4	75.9	76.5
Tobacco products	. . .	. . .	. . .	. . .	. . .	. . .	. . .	. . .	. . .	. . .	. . .	. . .
Textile mill products	12.2	21.8	24.3	21.8	23.8	25.0	4.1	7.5	8.4	7.0	7.4	7.9
Apparel	40.8	49.8	58.4	58.8	86.5	78.0	2.8	4.6	3.9	3.9	4.0	4.9
Lumber and wood products	45.0	45.3	47.0	56.1	66.8	67.1	11.9	11.4	13.5	15.7	22.8	21.4
Furniture and fixtures	44.5	37.0	40.9	47.0	53.5	35.8	33.2	25.1	21.8	27.8	28.9	13.4
Paper products	44.5	49.7	47.7	50.3	49.1	51.6	20.7	16.5	12.8	19.9	19.2	23.3
Printing and publishing	84.7	103.3	99.1	132.0	121.4	129.2	36.6	46.1	45.6	63.9	54.3	59.1
Chemical products	1 389.3	1 524.8	1 593.7	1 529.7	1 216.3	1 798.1	293.2	325.2	293.6	285.8	391.9	391.3
Refined petroleum products	73.7	71.4	108.8	154.4	81.6	149.0	10.3	7.0	3.7	11.0	4.4	4.2
Rubber and plastic products	129.4	143.1	144.7	207.3	211.4	216.5	53.5	49.2	41.2	57.0	71.5	78.6
Leather products	8.6	9.3	12.6	20.9	19.5	15.8	3.2	3.0	6.4	13.9	12.4	7.5
Stone, clay and glass products	49.4	56.7	49.1	41.8	40.7	41.2	19.1	14.8	13.9	16.8	18.8	15.9
Primary metals	119.5	159.6	179.3	266.9	257.6	181.9	42.9	46.7	44.7	75.7	62.1	55.0
Fabricated metal products	275.8	249.8	229.7	302.9	292.6	272.0	148.6	90.3	81.6	80.9	86.6	93.2
Industrial machinery and computers	543.4	616.2	666.4	825.0	811.7	854.2	197.0	214.6	209.1	266.2	269.5	266.6
Electric and electronic equipment	522.7	490.1	583.9	618.5	596.8	680.3	126.2	126.9	143.4	157.1	147.3	133.9
Transportation equipment	469.5	569.1	564.3	570.3	667.8	544.4	199.6	207.9	180.5	199.0	182.7	208.0
Scientific and measuring instruments	203.3	218.9	250.1	257.6	248.5	271.6	29.2	28.3	38.4	38.6	43.1	45.3
Miscellaneous manufactures	34.1	35.2	39.1	43.4	48.3	45.4	7.5	9.8	11.8	15.1	16.1	15.3
Unidentified manufactures	14.7	14.8	13.7	14.2	22.1	24.6	4.5	6.0	5.6	4.3	4.6	5.0
Agricultural And Livestock Products	738.1	697.3	1 354.9	1 182.1	1 014.2	1 065.8	4.0	4.4	5.6	7.1	7.3	5.4
Agricultural products	734.8	694.4	1 351.4	1 178.9	1 009.6	1 063.2	2.4	2.9	3.6	5.4	4.2	4.4
Livestock and livestock products	3.3	3.0	3.5	3.2	4.6	2.6	1.5	1.4	2.0	1.7	3.2	1.1
Other Commodities	104.0	134.9	113.2	149.0	185.4	181.1	39.0	46.1	45.4	50.3	39.3	38.7
Forestry products	5.2	4.6	4.0	3.6	2.0	2.3	0.1	. . .	0.1	0.1	0.1	0.1
Fish and other marine products	0.6	1.0	0.6	0.8	0.5	1.1	0.3	0.3	0.3	0.5	0.2	0.9
Metallic ores and concentrates	11.9	16.9	14.3	11.7	3.7	5.8	11.9	16.4	13.7	10.8	3.7	3.0
Bituminous coal and lignite	19.1	8.8	5.2	42.6	82.4	70.9	1.1	. . .	0.7	. . .	. . .	. . .
Crude petroleum and natural gas	. . .	0.1	0.1	0.1	0.2	0.1	. . .	. . .	. . .	. . .	0.1	. . .
Nonmetallic minerals	4.5	5.3	4.9	5.3	5.2	3.4	2.7	2.8	2.3	2.8	2.1	2.0
Scrap and waste	19.1	45.2	32.5	37.4	36.7	39.8	3.3	7.0	3.8	10.1	10.1	11.1
Used merchandise	8.5	4.9	5.5	14.2	7.4	9.9	1.9	1.6	1.4	4.1	0.5	1.4
Goods imported and returned unchanged	14.0	16.0	20.9	20.1	20.4	16.3	14.0	16.0	20.9	20.1	20.4	16.3
Special classification provisions	21.1	32.1	25.2	13.1	26.9	31.4	3.5	1.8	2.3	1.9	2.2	3.8

Table D-28. MISSOURI: State Exports of Goods by Destination and Industry, 1994–1999—Continued

(Millions of dollars.)

Industry	South and Central America and Caribbean						Mexico					
	1994	1995	1996	1997	1998	1999	1994	1995	1996	1997	1998	1999
ALL GOODS	498.6	660.2	788.2	797.1	733.7	875.3	773.4	699.0	1 089.0	1 042.4	1 189.6	1 272.5
Manufactured Goods	434.8	576.7	666.9	739.1	639.7	794.9	480.4	448.7	533.8	594.2	687.8	728.7
Food products	39.2	48.9	60.3	78.4	134.5	111.5	30.3	41.0	47.3	32.7	59.8	74.1
Tobacco products	...	...	...	...	...	...	...	...	...	...	...	...
Textile mill products	2.9	4.1	4.8	3.6	4.1	3.0	1.5	2.6	1.5	2.0	2.0	5.9
Apparel	19.2	27.1	35.7	42.1	65.1	54.6	7.8	7.6	3.6	3.4	8.2	11.1
Lumber and wood products	0.6	0.9	1.6	2.2	2.9	1.8	0.3	0.8	0.7	1.5	2.4	1.9
Furniture and fixtures	1.5	1.4	1.6	2.3	4.8	3.4	2.5	0.7	1.7	3.3	4.4	2.9
Paper products	1.3	2.5	2.7	5.0	3.3	3.0	11.9	13.3	21.6	14.1	11.8	10.3
Printing and publishing	3.1	4.2	3.0	4.0	4.4	1.9	18.2	17.3	19.6	21.0	15.3	23.5
Chemical products	208.6	263.0	305.2	265.5	140.7	329.3	128.8	89.2	86.2	101.1	93.5	91.7
Refined petroleum products	43.1	50.3	89.3	129.8	69.4	118.4	0.4	0.5	0.5	0.5	4.3	6.5
Rubber and plastic products	7.1	14.6	18.3	18.4	17.8	11.7	17.5	12.0	11.2	16.4	22.2	32.1
Leather products	0.6	3.0	2.4	0.9	1.8	1.3	0.6	0.3	0.1	0.7	0.7	1.2
Stone, clay and glass products	3.3	6.3	4.8	4.8	3.8	2.6	1.7	1.6	2.0	2.4	2.9	4.1
Primary metals	2.8	5.3	6.1	11.2	8.0	2.4	30.7	49.4	64.3	85.4	93.8	89.2
Fabricated metal products	10.4	23.7	21.9	21.5	35.0	19.4	17.7	20.0	18.1	37.4	49.7	60.2
Industrial machinery and computers	44.8	64.7	60.7	84.4	77.7	72.8	46.1	47.1	49.5	54.3	62.3	68.0
Electric and electronic equipment	18.7	22.6	18.4	25.6	30.9	20.5	86.7	86.4	126.4	140.4	178.1	175.6
Transportation equipment	6.6	12.3	9.2	15.9	16.1	19.9	22.8	12.8	18.5	22.5	29.8	31.8
Scientific and measuring instruments	15.4	18.6	18.9	19.2	14.0	12.2	50.1	43.4	57.3	49.7	36.7	26.9
Miscellaneous manufactures	4.7	2.3	1.2	2.7	3.6	2.9	3.1	2.1	2.4	4.0	5.6	6.9
Unidentified manufactures	0.7	0.9	0.7	1.6	1.8	2.2	1.7	0.7	1.3	1.7	4.2	4.8
Agricultural And Livestock Products	46.3	76.8	120.3	57.4	92.3	75.6	284.5	234.7	542.7	438.9	481.9	520.6
Agricultural products	46.0	76.4	120.2	57.3	92.2	75.6	283.8	234.7	542.7	438.3	481.4	519.4
Livestock and livestock products	0.3	0.4	0.1	0.2	0.1	0.1	0.8	...	...	0.6	0.5	1.2
Other Commodities	17.5	6.6	1.0	0.6	1.6	4.8	8.5	15.6	12.5	9.3	19.9	23.2
Forestry products	...	...	...	0.1	0.1	0.1	...	...	...	...	...	...
Fish and other marine products	...	...	...	...	...	...	0.1	...	...	...	...	0.1
Metallic ores and concentrates	...	...	...	...	...	...	...	...	...	...	...	...
Bituminous coal and lignite	16.8	6.0	...	...	0.9	3.0	...	...	...	...	...	...
Crude petroleum and natural gas	...	...	...	...	...	...	...	...	...	...	...	...
Nonmetallic minerals	0.3	0.3	0.1	0.1	0.2	0.4	0.2	0.9	1.0	1.0	0.4	0.2
Scrap and waste	0.1	0.1	...	0.1	...	0.3	0.4	0.4	0.8	4.6	4.6	5.5
Used merchandise	0.3	...	0.1	0.1	0.3	0.2	0.3	0.1	...	0.1	0.1	0.2
Goods imported and returned unchanged	...	...	...	...	...	...	7.5	14.1	10.6	3.6	14.7	17.3
Special classification provisions	...	0.2	0.7	0.3	0.1	0.8	...	...	...	...	...	...

Industry	European Union						United Kingdom					
	1994	1995	1996	1997	1998	1999	1994	1995	1996	1997	1998	1999
ALL GOODS	1 123.4	1 330.8	1 493.0	1 701.7	1 527.4	1 689.4	262.5	195.6	193.7	235.8	293.5	345.8
Manufactured Goods	977.5	1 195.4	1 262.0	1 316.9	1 340.7	1 559.5	256.5	189.8	182.7	225.6	289.2	338.8
Food products	34.0	52.6	47.3	64.1	59.0	63.1	5.2	9.5	5.7	6.1	7.3	5.6
Tobacco products	...	...	...	...	...	...	...	...	...	...	...	...
Textile mill products	1.5	3.3	3.5	4.2	5.1	3.7	0.5	0.9	1.0	1.7	2.4	2.0
Apparel	6.8	6.7	8.4	4.4	6.1	5.0	1.2	1.7	3.5	1.5	3.6	3.8
Lumber and wood products	23.7	22.9	22.9	27.3	30.4	32.2	7.2	6.2	7.9	9.7	10.8	9.1
Furniture and fixtures	3.8	4.9	7.9	8.4	8.3	10.4	1.3	1.9	3.4	3.9	4.8	6.3
Paper products	4.0	8.0	5.5	7.1	7.4	8.8	0.4	0.9	0.5	0.7	1.3	0.8
Printing and publishing	11.7	15.7	11.2	20.3	25.4	25.4	7.5	10.2	6.7	12.3	21.8	21.8
Chemical products	364.8	451.6	482.0	511.6	350.3	576.5	56.8	37.4	40.9	48.9	41.1	65.9
Refined petroleum products	17.7	10.1	7.2	5.2	0.5	13.7	1.9	1.9	2.6	1.5	0.1	2.1
Rubber and plastic products	32.1	38.2	42.1	56.5	51.7	51.7	6.0	6.1	6.8	12.7	9.9	10.0
Leather products	0.9	0.8	0.5	0.8	0.7	0.5	0.3	0.2	0.2	0.3	0.1	0.1
Stone, clay and glass products	19.0	23.0	19.5	9.9	8.9	7.3	3.1	3.7	3.3	4.0	3.9	2.4
Primary metals	10.0	12.5	23.8	26.4	54.4	12.6	1.1	2.1	9.2	8.6	33.6	4.1
Fabricated metal products	22.2	27.9	24.3	26.5	30.2	35.7	6.4	5.6	6.6	4.8	8.1	5.2
Industrial machinery and computers	97.7	106.9	126.8	142.3	185.0	223.6	32.9	32.6	37.5	51.1	71.5	104.8
Electric and electronic equipment	87.6	79.6	96.1	83.5	74.5	134.2	21.2	18.0	17.0	18.6	16.3	47.8
Transportation equipment	174.6	254.6	257.1	236.8	350.4	224.0	95.2	40.8	17.1	24.8	31.4	32.3
Scientific and measuring instruments	55.1	65.0	65.0	72.8	78.1	119.8	5.0	6.8	9.5	11.5	16.1	11.9
Miscellaneous manufactures	7.5	8.5	8.6	6.9	10.5	7.1	2.3	2.4	2.5	2.2	3.6	2.0
Unidentified manufactures	2.7	2.7	2.3	1.9	3.9	4.3	0.7	0.9	0.9	0.6	1.5	0.8
Agricultural And Livestock Products	137.2	126.7	218.0	341.1	133.9	106.9	3.9	3.1	7.5	5.7	3.3	4.5
Agricultural products	136.5	126.1	216.9	340.9	133.7	106.8	3.9	3.0	7.5	5.7	3.2	4.5
Livestock and livestock products	0.7	0.6	1.1	0.2	0.3	0.1	...	...	0.1	0.1	0.1	...
Other Commodities	8.7	8.7	13.1	43.7	52.7	22.9	2.1	2.7	3.4	4.4	1.0	2.5
Forestry products	...	...	...	0.2	...	...	...	...	...	...	...	...
Fish and other marine products	0.1	0.3	0.2	0.1	0.1	0.1	...	0.4	0.3	0.3	...	...
Metallic ores and concentrates	...	0.4	0.3	0.7	...	...	...	...	...	...	...	...
Bituminous coal and lignite	1.2	2.8	4.6	30.5	45.6	14.4	...	...	...	...	...	...
Crude petroleum and natural gas	...	...	...	...	0.1	...	...	...	...	...	...	...
Nonmetallic minerals	0.7	0.6	0.6	0.7	1.5	0.6	0.3	0.2	0.2	0.2	...	0.4
Scrap and waste	...	0.1	0.2	0.1	0.1	0.3	...	0.1	0.1	...	0.3	0.2
Used merchandise	3.2	0.9	2.6	7.1	0.7	3.5	0.1	0.2	1.3	3.3	0.2	1.5
Goods imported and returned unchanged	...	...	...	...	...	...	...	...	...	...	...	...
Special classification provisions	3.4	3.6	4.6	4.3	4.6	4.0	1.7	1.8	1.5	0.6	0.6	0.5

Table D-28. MISSOURI: State Exports of Goods by Destination and Industry, 1994–1999—*Continued*

(Millions of dollars.)

Industry	Germany						France					
	1994	1995	1996	1997	1998	1999	1994	1995	1996	1997	1998	1999
ALL GOODS	117.3	156.5	171.6	202.7	217.8	216.9	77.6	91.6	72.1	81.2	119.9	90.9
Manufactured Goods	114.7	148.4	170.1	198.7	200.7	215.1	75.4	83.8	66.7	70.7	97.7	82.7
Food products	2.0	1.7	1.6	1.4	2.1	1.0	1.8	2.2	0.6	0.6	0.8	1.0
Tobacco products	...	...	...	...	...	...	...	...	...	...	...	...
Textile mill products	0.3	1.5	1.3	1.0	1.1	0.5	0.2	0.2	0.3	0.3	0.4	0.5
Apparel	2.2	1.8	1.5	1.0	0.9	0.4	0.3	1.1	1.3	0.1	0.2	...
Lumber and wood products	2.9	6.0	1.7	1.7	1.6	1.0	1.2	2.4	3.2	4.4	5.4	4.2
Furniture and fixtures	0.6	0.4	0.3	0.2	0.1	0.8	0.9	0.9	1.7	2.0	1.4	0.9
Paper products	0.9	1.5	1.4	2.0	2.6	2.0	0.1	0.1	0.1	0.2	0.4	0.8
Printing and publishing	1.7	1.9	1.4	4.5	1.3	1.0	0.9	1.3	0.8	0.8	0.5	0.6
Chemical products	41.7	53.4	55.5	91.3	101.8	92.8	21.2	27.3	16.8	19.1	37.8	25.5
Refined petroleum products	0.2	0.2	0.1	0.3	0.1	0.1	0.1	0.2	0.1	...	0.1	0.1
Rubber and plastic products	2.6	2.7	1.5	4.3	5.5	4.4	1.2	2.1	2.0	1.6	1.7	2.7
Leather products	0.4	0.3	0.1	0.3	0.3	0.2	0.1	...	...	...	...	...
Stone, clay and glass products	3.3	4.4	2.0	2.1	1.4	0.8	0.4	0.5	0.6	0.8	0.5	0.5
Primary metals	1.2	1.6	1.5	1.2	2.8	0.8	0.4	0.6	0.3	0.6	1.5	0.7
Fabricated metal products	1.6	1.6	1.9	5.3	7.0	14.7	0.7	0.7	1.5	1.2	1.1	0.9
Industrial machinery and computers	18.2	20.4	28.7	31.4	30.6	37.3	7.4	11.8	13.3	10.5	15.7	11.1
Electric and electronic equipment	14.9	20.6	49.5	27.0	9.5	9.1	19.7	11.7	6.5	8.4	11.2	5.4
Transportation equipment	5.6	8.7	4.6	5.5	8.0	3.4	4.8	6.6	5.6	5.6	6.4	5.3
Scientific and measuring instruments	12.6	18.6	14.0	16.9	22.0	43.1	13.4	11.9	11.1	13.5	11.1	21.3
Miscellaneous manufactures	1.1	0.7	1.0	0.9	1.5	1.0	0.3	1.9	0.9	0.9	1.0	0.5
Unidentified manufactures	0.6	0.5	0.6	0.3	0.5	0.6	0.3	0.3	0.2	0.1	0.6	0.7
Agricultural And Livestock Products	0.7	7.7	0.2	0.3	15.6	...	...	4.3	...	0.1	5.9	0.1
Agricultural products	0.7	7.6	0.2	0.3	15.6	...	...	4.3	...	0.1	5.8	0.1
Livestock and livestock products	...	0.2	...	...	...	...	...	...	...	...	0.1	...
Other Commodities	1.8	0.3	1.2	3.6	1.4	1.8	2.1	3.5	5.4	10.3	16.3	8.1
Forestry products	...	...	...	...	...	...	...	...	...	...	...	...
Fish and other marine products	...	...	...	...	...	0.1	0.1	0.3	0.2	0.1	...	...
Metallic ores and concentrates	...	...	...	...	...	...	...	...	...	...	...	...
Bituminous coal and lignite	...	...	...	...	...	...	1.2	2.8	4.6	9.4	15.1	6.1
Crude petroleum and natural gas	...	...	...	...	...	...	...	...	...	...	...	...
Nonmetallic minerals	0.2	0.1	0.1	0.2	0.1	...	0.1	0.1	0.1	0.2	0.1	0.2
Scrap and waste	...	...	...	...	...	...	...	...	...	...	...	...
Used merchandise	1.6	0.1	0.5	2.4	0.1	1.1	0.7	0.3	0.5	0.5	0.3	0.7
Goods imported and returned unchanged	...	...	...	...	...	...	...	...	...	...	...	...
Special classification provisions	...	0.1	0.6	1.0	1.2	0.5	...	...	...	0.1	0.9	1.0

Industry	The Netherlands						Asian 10					
	1994	1995	1996	1997	1998	1999	1994	1995	1996	1997	1998	1999
ALL GOODS	122.7	117.3	137.7	129.7	78.6	108.1	945.5	986.8	1 152.2	1 205.3	1 059.6	1 240.8
Manufactured Goods	50.7	64.2	61.1	50.8	54.6	75.2	858.5	915.8	990.6	1 072.3	920.1	1 018.9
Food products	9.4	23.0	17.6	15.5	7.0	8.7	81.0	105.9	138.3	202.1	253.5	256.1
Tobacco products	...	...	...	...	...	...	...	...	...	...	...	...
Textile mill products	0.1	0.3	0.3	0.1	0.1	0.2	1.4	2.2	4.8	2.8	3.9	2.8
Apparel	1.3	0.5	0.5	0.3	0.5	0.2	2.3	2.4	4.9	2.1	2.0	1.6
Lumber and wood products	3.2	0.1	0.4	0.1	0.1	0.2	7.2	7.1	6.1	5.7	3.6	5.2
Furniture and fixtures	0.6	0.5	0.3	0.3	0.7	0.5	1.7	2.8	4.6	3.3	4.4	2.4
Paper products	0.8	0.2	0.4	0.6	0.8	0.4	5.1	7.2	2.9	2.7	5.2	3.7
Printing and publishing	0.2	0.1	0.3	0.6	0.6	0.6	10.8	13.9	12.4	13.9	13.3	10.1
Chemical products	11.9	9.5	10.0	8.2	16.3	4.6	287.0	278.8	270.3	232.9	127.7	258.2
Refined petroleum products	...	0.1	0.1	0.1	...	7.7	1.6	2.8	3.5	2.3	0.7	2.1
Rubber and plastic products	1.1	1.0	2.2	1.9	1.8	4.0	9.9	19.0	24.3	47.4	37.9	30.7
Leather products	...	0.1	...	...	...	...	2.8	1.9	2.6	2.9	2.7	3.6
Stone, clay and glass products	0.2	0.3	0.2	0.4	0.3	0.1	3.8	7.2	6.2	4.5	4.1	9.3
Primary metals	0.2	1.0	2.4	0.5	0.7	0.4	28.4	39.7	33.9	49.3	34.3	19.3
Fabricated metal products	3.6	4.9	2.7	2.9	3.5	2.0	62.9	64.4	65.1	78.2	71.4	47.2
Industrial machinery and computers	9.0	8.1	15.4	12.7	9.9	18.6	80.2	105.2	115.3	124.2	102.4	96.4
Electric and electronic equipment	5.7	8.4	4.9	2.1	3.6	4.6	181.2	146.4	166.6	172.6	133.2	180.1
Transportation equipment	0.5	1.4	0.8	1.6	1.5	1.5	44.6	50.5	70.6	60.2	52.0	31.7
Scientific and measuring instruments	1.9	3.2	1.6	2.2	6.2	20.2	38.6	47.3	46.2	55.1	57.0	45.2
Miscellaneous manufactures	0.7	1.4	0.9	0.4	0.8	0.5	6.1	9.2	10.5	8.7	8.4	9.8
Unidentified manufactures	0.2	0.2	0.1	0.1	0.2	0.1	2.0	1.8	1.7	1.6	2.6	3.4
Agricultural And Livestock Products	71.3	52.7	76.2	73.4	11.0	28.5	58.2	14.5	122.3	91.9	71.7	135.7
Agricultural products	71.3	52.7	76.2	73.4	10.9	28.5	58.1	14.1	122.0	91.5	71.1	135.4
Livestock and livestock products	...	...	...	...	0.1	...	0.1	0.5	0.3	0.4	0.6	0.3
Other Commodities	0.7	0.4	0.4	5.4	13.0	4.4	28.9	56.5	39.4	41.1	67.8	86.2
Forestry products	...	...	...	...	0.1	...	5.1	4.4	3.9	3.3	1.8	1.9
Fish and other marine products	...	...	...	...	...	...	...	0.4	0.1	0.3	0.2	0.1
Metallic ores and concentrates	...	...	...	...	...	...	...	...	0.2	0.2	...	2.6
Bituminous coal and lignite	...	...	...	5.3	12.3	3.8	...	...	...	9.8	35.8	53.5
Crude petroleum and natural gas	...	...	...	...	...	...	...	0.1	...	0.1	...	0.1
Nonmetallic minerals	...	...	0.1	...	0.5	...	0.4	0.5	0.5	0.5	0.4	0.1
Scrap and waste	...	...	...	...	...	...	15.2	37.1	27.4	22.5	21.6	22.1
Used merchandise	0.4	0.1	...	...	0.2	0.1	1.9	1.9	1.1	1.8	3.7	1.2
Goods imported and returned unchanged	...	...	...	...	...	...	...	...	...	...	...	...
Special classification provisions	0.2	0.4	0.3	...	...	0.6	6.4	12.1	6.0	2.7	4.1	4.7

Table D-28. MISSOURI: State Exports of Goods by Destination and Industry, 1994–1999—*Continued*

(Millions of dollars.)

Industry	Japan						South Korea					
	1994	1995	1996	1997	1998	1999	1994	1995	1996	1997	1998	1999
ALL GOODS	259.4	282.0	275.5	307.6	367.8	317.7	104.9	131.0	152.1	151.7	72.5	135.8
Manufactured Goods	245.9	253.7	260.3	269.2	310.0	233.5	102.7	119.0	134.9	136.8	66.1	121.2
Food products	48.1	57.0	42.6	40.7	91.8	74.0	5.3	6.6	6.8	24.7	11.8	33.3
Tobacco products	...	...	...	...	...	...	...	...	...	...	...	...
Textile mill products	0.6	1.3	2.7	1.6	0.6	0.8	0.4	0.4	0.3	0.1	...	0.1
Apparel	1.6	1.7	4.3	1.2	0.9	1.0	0.2	0.1	0.1	0.1	...	...
Lumber and wood products	4.3	3.8	3.6	3.6	2.2	3.2	2.8	2.9	2.1	1.5	0.7	1.2
Furniture and fixtures	0.4	0.9	1.3	1.0	3.3	1.6	0.1	0.4	0.4	0.1	...	0.1
Paper products	0.5	0.1	0.2	0.4	0.2	0.4	3.1	3.9	0.9	0.7	2.9	2.0
Printing and publishing	2.8	3.1	3.9	2.4	1.2	1.2	2.1	2.7	2.4	2.8	2.2	1.5
Chemical products	78.2	55.8	44.1	46.7	36.3	45.1	24.6	26.9	31.9	20.5	13.3	34.5
Refined petroleum products	0.2	0.5	0.8	0.5	0.1	0.3	0.1	0.2	0.2	0.1	...	...
Rubber and plastic products	2.7	4.1	4.5	5.7	10.2	5.1	2.7	4.8	7.6	6.8	1.2	5.3
Leather products	0.3	0.3	0.3	0.3	0.3	0.2	1.4	...	0.2	0.6	0.3	0.2
Stone, clay and glass products	0.8	2.2	0.6	0.4	0.6	0.6	0.8	1.7	0.6	0.9	0.8	1.3
Primary metals	2.8	12.2	6.4	5.8	3.5	4.2	1.4	6.8	7.1	2.2	1.3	0.3
Fabricated metal products	3.9	7.5	3.8	5.0	19.1	12.4	5.5	10.1	11.7	11.9	2.6	7.3
Industrial machinery and computers	21.9	21.1	21.2	28.7	29.3	23.5	15.1	19.3	16.5	19.7	10.8	10.7
Electric and electronic equipment	23.8	20.5	36.2	42.8	29.6	15.2	25.2	23.6	33.7	34.5	12.9	14.2
Transportation equipment	35.7	42.9	59.8	48.8	42.0	21.6	1.5	1.3	3.3	2.6	1.7	2.9
Scientific and measuring instruments	13.8	14.3	20.2	30.1	35.1	20.0	9.9	6.5	7.8	5.9	3.0	5.7
Miscellaneous manufactures	2.7	3.6	3.2	3.1	3.2	2.4	0.2	0.5	1.1	0.7	0.2	0.3
Unidentified manufactures	0.8	0.6	0.5	0.3	0.6	0.7	0.3	0.3	0.3	0.2	0.2	0.4
Agricultural And Livestock Products	2.6	5.7	0.5	16.6	13.8	22.1	0.6	8.0	12.2	8.7	1.1	5.9
Agricultural products	2.5	5.6	0.5	16.5	13.7	22.0	0.6	7.6	12.1	8.6	0.9	5.9
Livestock and livestock products	0.1	...	...	0.1	0.1	0.1	...	0.3	0.1	0.1	0.2	...
Other Commodities	10.9	22.6	14.7	21.8	44.0	62.1	1.6	4.1	5.0	6.2	5.4	8.7
Forestry products	0.1	0.1	...	...	...	...	...	...	...	...	...	...
Fish and other marine products	...	0.3	0.1	0.3	0.2	0.1	...	...	...	...	...	...
Metallic ores and concentrates	...	...	0.2	0.2	...	...	...	...	...	...	...	2.6
Bituminous coal and lignite	...	...	...	9.8	35.8	53.5	...	...	...	0.1	...	...
Crude petroleum and natural gas	...	...	...	...	...	...	...	...	...	...	...	...
Nonmetallic minerals	0.1	0.1	0.1	0.1	0.1	...	...	...	...	0.1	...	...
Scrap and waste	7.6	14.7	12.8	9.6	4.4	6.8	1.2	3.8	2.8	5.9	5.2	6.0
Used merchandise	1.5	1.7	1.1	1.6	3.3	1.1	...	...	...	0.1	...	...
Goods imported and returned unchanged	...	...	...	...	...	...	...	...	...	...	...	...
Special classification provisions	1.5	5.7	0.4	0.3	0.3	0.6	0.4	0.1	2.2	0.1	0.2	0.1

Industry	Taiwan						Singapore					
	1994	1995	1996	1997	1998	1999	1994	1995	1996	1997	1998	1999
ALL GOODS	137.1	106.7	163.4	166.4	113.9	143.4	81.5	103.9	104.2	102.1	108.7	137.6
Manufactured Goods	92.1	101.5	91.0	97.8	80.0	113.7	76.5	97.3	101.7	99.5	106.8	136.4
Food products	14.1	14.9	8.5	16.6	17.6	14.6	1.1	0.4	0.4	0.8	1.4	1.3
Tobacco products	...	...	...	...	...	...	...	...	...	...	...	...
Textile mill products	...	0.1	0.3	0.1	0.4	0.6	...	...	0.2	...	0.1	0.1
Apparel	...	0.1	0.1	0.2	...	0.1	0.1	...	0.1	0.2	0.2	0.1
Lumber and wood products	...	0.2	...	0.3	...	0.3	...	...	0.1	0.1	0.4	...
Furniture and fixtures	0.1	0.1	...	0.2	0.1	...	0.3	0.1	0.3	0.3	0.2	0.1
Paper products	0.5	1.0	...	0.1	0.5	0.1	0.2	0.7	0.6	0.2	...	...
Printing and publishing	0.8	0.7	0.8	0.9	0.8	0.9	1.3	2.1	1.7	3.7	3.5	1.3
Chemical products	33.2	36.8	29.6	25.1	9.7	39.7	40.1	46.6	51.8	43.2	35.9	36.6
Refined petroleum products	0.2	0.2	0.3	0.1	0.2	0.3	0.6	0.8	1.1	0.7	0.1	0.7
Rubber and plastic products	0.5	0.9	1.0	1.3	2.2	2.3	0.2	0.4	0.7	1.8	7.2	11.3
Leather products	...	0.1	...	...	0.1	0.1	0.1	...	...	...	...	...
Stone, clay and glass products	0.5	0.4	2.7	0.8	0.3	6.2	0.2	0.3	0.2	0.2	0.3	0.2
Primary metals	2.1	1.3	1.8	0.5	2.9	4.2	0.5	1.1	1.4	2.3	5.4	0.8
Fabricated metal products	5.3	5.9	3.8	4.3	3.0	2.5	4.4	4.3	4.4	8.8	3.6	4.0
Industrial machinery and computers	7.4	10.3	10.7	9.6	11.1	9.1	7.3	10.0	13.0	12.7	13.2	13.1
Electric and electronic equipment	22.3	24.9	27.5	33.2	25.4	27.6	16.2	23.5	18.5	17.9	28.8	59.2
Transportation equipment	0.5	0.5	0.8	0.5	1.2	0.6	0.9	2.4	2.8	4.0	3.7	2.8
Scientific and measuring instruments	3.6	2.4	2.1	3.5	3.3	3.5	2.1	3.2	2.7	2.0	1.7	3.7
Miscellaneous manufactures	0.7	0.5	0.8	0.4	0.7	0.5	0.6	1.0	1.6	0.5	0.6	0.7
Unidentified manufactures	0.2	0.2	0.2	0.3	0.3	0.3	0.3	0.3	0.2	0.2	0.3	0.3
Agricultural And Livestock Products	42.2	0.3	69.1	66.2	26.4	25.5	...	0.1	0.1	0.1	...	0.8
Agricultural products	42.2	0.2	69.0	66.2	26.4	25.4	...	0.1	0.1	...	...	0.8
Livestock and livestock products	...	0.1	...	...	...	0.1	...	...	...	0.1	...	...
Other Commodities	2.8	4.9	3.3	2.4	7.5	4.3	5.0	6.5	2.5	2.5	1.9	0.3
Forestry products	0.1	...	0.2	...	0.1	...	1.7	1.4	1.0	0.9	0.3	...
Fish and other marine products	...	...	...	...	...	...	...	...	...	...	...	...
Metallic ores and concentrates	...	...	...	...	...	...	...	...	...	...	...	...
Bituminous coal and lignite	...	...	...	...	...	...	...	...	...	...	...	...
Crude petroleum and natural gas	...	...	...	...	...	...	...	...	...	...	...	...
Nonmetallic minerals	0.1	0.1	0.4	0.2	0.2	...	...	...	...	...	...	...
Scrap and waste	2.6	4.6	2.6	2.1	7.0	3.3	...	...	...	...	0.3	...
Used merchandise	...	...	...	...	...	...	0.1	0.1	...	...	0.4	...
Goods imported and returned unchanged	...	...	...	...	...	...	3.1	4.8	1.5	1.6	0.8	0.3
Special classification provisions	...	0.1	0.1	0.1	0.3	0.9	...	...	...	...	...	...

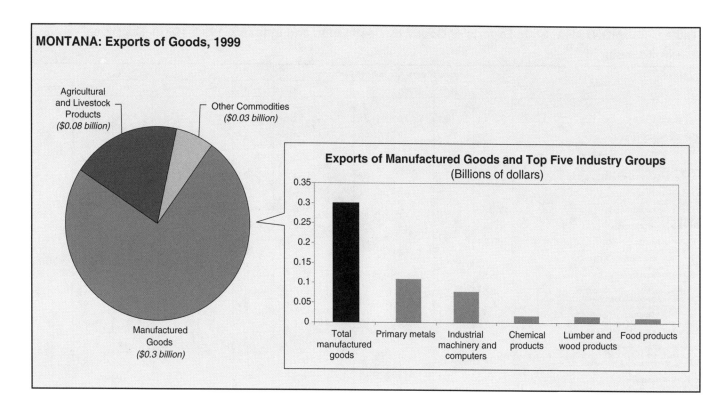

MONTANA: Exports of Goods, 1999

Agricultural and Livestock Products ($0.08 billion)

Other Commodities ($0.03 billion)

Manufactured Goods ($0.3 billion)

Exports of Manufactured Goods and Top Five Industry Groups
(Billions of dollars)

Table D-29. MONTANA: State Exports of Goods by Destination and Industry, 1994–1999

(Millions of dollars.)

Industry	All destinations						Canada					
	1994	1995	1996	1997	1998	1999	1994	1995	1996	1997	1998	1999
ALL GOODS	260.0	279.2	340.9	429.8	390.0	404.0	140.1	140.2	160.6	236.5	192.8	200.1
Manufactured Goods	192.0	206.0	263.7	339.9	304.2	299.7	80.0	78.4	100.5	165.5	121.6	106.7
Food products	4.7	6.6	6.3	4.6	7.3	12.2	2.1	3.5	4.2	3.6	5.8	9.8
Tobacco products	. . .	. . .	. . .	. . .	. . .	. . .	. . .	. . .	. . .	. . .	. . .	. . .
Textile mill products	0.4	0.1	0.6	0.9	0.5	0.2	0.2	0.1	0.1	0.2	0.1	. . .
Apparel	0.4	1.0	1.2	0.8	1.0	0.6	0.1	0.2	0.2	0.1	0.1	0.1
Lumber and wood products	13.7	15.9	13.6	16.5	16.0	16.9	11.3	14.0	12.5	15.3	15.1	15.9
Furniture and fixtures	0.3	0.3	0.2	0.5	0.6	0.8	0.2	0.2	0.2	0.2	0.2	0.6
Paper products	6.2	4.1	4.3	4.4	5.2	3.8	6.1	3.9	4.3	4.3	4.9	3.4
Printing and publishing	2.1	1.0	0.8	0.6	0.4	0.7	0.8	0.7	0.8	0.5	0.3	0.3
Chemical products	13.0	17.5	16.3	41.4	30.0	17.6	11.4	12.3	12.3	37.6	22.9	14.1
Refined petroleum products	1.5	1.2	1.7	1.4	0.3	0.4	1.4	1.1	1.6	1.3	0.3	0.4
Rubber and plastic products	2.8	3.2	4.6	4.1	3.9	3.8	2.3	2.6	2.8	3.5	3.2	3.1
Leather products	0.8	1.0	2.1	2.0	1.5	0.9	0.5	0.7	1.1	1.3	0.9	0.4
Stone, clay and glass products	4.2	4.0	3.7	5.7	5.0	9.8	4.0	4.0	3.0	5.5	4.9	9.7
Primary metals	54.0	49.7	97.1	146.0	114.4	108.9	1.5	1.3	26.6	62.6	32.0	16.6
Fabricated metal products	1.7	1.6	1.5	2.1	1.5	2.7	1.1	1.1	1.0	0.9	0.9	1.3
Industrial machinery and computers	41.5	70.1	72.5	71.1	73.7	77.6	14.9	20.2	18.8	17.7	16.7	13.4
Electric and electronic equipment	3.4	6.5	7.3	9.6	12.0	9.5	1.0	3.5	2.0	1.9	2.9	1.9
Transportation equipment	8.8	5.3	5.5	7.6	9.1	11.0	7.2	3.7	3.2	3.2	6.1	9.3
Scientific and measuring instruments	4.7	6.1	10.8	9.2	9.1	11.1	0.6	0.8	1.2	1.6	1.4	2.9
Miscellaneous manufactures	26.5	9.4	12.8	10.6	12.0	8.7	12.7	3.7	4.4	3.7	2.6	2.8
Unidentified manufactures	1.2	1.4	0.8	0.8	0.7	2.5	0.6	0.7	0.5	0.5	0.4	0.5
Agricultural And Livestock Products	22.1	28.2	33.4	28.8	45.7	76.8	18.1	21.3	20.2	23.6	34.2	68.3
Agricultural products	7.1	13.1	24.2	19.2	23.3	15.0	3.6	6.5	11.8	14.7	12.9	7.9
Livestock and livestock products	15.0	15.1	9.2	9.5	22.4	61.8	14.5	14.8	8.4	9.0	21.3	60.4
Other Commodities	45.8	45.0	43.8	61.2	40.2	27.5	42.1	40.5	39.8	47.3	36.9	25.1
Forestry products	0.3	0.1	0.2	0.1	. . .	. . .	0.2	0.1	0.1	0.1	. . .	. . .
Fish and other marine products	. . .	0.1	0.4	. . .	0.6	. . .	. . .	. . .	. . .	. . .	. . .	. . .
Metallic ores and concentrates	14.3	12.2	7.8	22.6	9.4	7.9	14.3	11.9	7.8	11.3	9.4	7.9
Bituminous coal and lignite	0.2	0.7	0.1	1.5	2.9	2.5	0.2	0.7	0.1	1.5	2.9	2.5
Crude petroleum and natural gas	0.2	1.4	. . .	. . .	. . .	0.1	0.2	1.4	. . .	. . .	. . .	0.1
Nonmetallic minerals	9.8	9.2	9.3	8.6	7.2	3.3	6.9	6.3	6.6	7.0	5.4	1.7
Scrap and waste	10.4	9.9	7.8	7.7	5.6	2.9	10.0	9.9	7.8	7.7	5.6	2.9
Used merchandise	2.8	2.4	3.5	2.3	1.9	2.2	2.7	2.2	3.0	2.2	1.8	1.8
Goods imported and returned unchanged	7.5	7.9	14.3	17.5	11.6	7.9	7.5	7.9	14.3	17.5	11.6	7.9
Special classification provisions	0.4	1.2	0.4	0.9	1.0	0.6	0.1	0.2	0.1	0.1	0.3	0.2

Table D-29. MONTANA: State Exports of Goods by Destination and Industry, 1994–1999—*Continued*

(Millions of dollars.)

Industry	South and Central American and Caribbean						Mexico					
	1994	1995	1996	1997	1998	1999	1994	1995	1996	1997	1998	1999
ALL GOODS	4.3	5.7	3.8	3.5	7.4	6.4	5.1	8.1	46.2	20.6	59.5	76.6
Manufactured Goods	3.0	4.8	3.0	3.2	6.4	5.3	1.7	1.7	34.1	16.4	49.5	71.3
Food products	0.6	1.1	0.4	0.3	0.1	0.3	...	0.1	...	...	...	0.9
Tobacco products	...	...	...	...	...	...	...	...	...	...	...	...
Textile mill products	...	...	...	...	0.1	...	...	...	0.2	0.1	...	0.1
Apparel	...	...	...	...	0.1	0.1	...	...	0.1	...	...	0.1
Lumber and wood products	...	...	...	0.3	0.1	...	0.1	...	...	0.5	0.6	0.4
Furniture and fixtures	...	...	...	...	0.2	...	...	...	...	...	...	...
Paper products	...	...	...	...	0.1	0.1	...	...	...	...	0.1	...
Printing and publishing	...	...	...	...	...	...	...	...	...	...	...	0.1
Chemical products	0.2	1.8	1.1	0.1	0.2	0.4	...	...	...	0.1	2.0	0.2
Refined petroleum products	...	...	...	...	...	...	...	...	...	...	...	...
Rubber and plastic products	0.1	0.1	...	0.1	...	...	0.1	...	1.0	0.1	...	0.1
Leather products	...	...	0.1	...	...	0.1	...	...	...	...	...	...
Stone, clay and glass products	...	...	...	...	...	0.1	...	...	...	...	...	...
Primary metals	...	...	...	...	...	...	0.1	1.0	27.8	11.2	44.1	69.0
Fabricated metal products	0.1	...	...	...	...	0.1	...	...	...	0.1	...	...
Industrial machinery and computers	1.5	1.3	1.0	1.1	1.0	3.2	1.0	0.3	3.7	3.1	1.5	0.2
Electric and electronic equipment	...	0.1	0.2	0.5	0.5	0.2	0.1	...	...	0.1	1.0	0.1
Transportation equipment	0.1	...	...	0.1	0.8	0.1	0.2	0.1	1.0	1.0	0.1	...
Scientific and measuring instruments	0.1	0.1	0.1	0.4	0.1	0.2	0.1	0.1	0.1	0.2	0.1	...
Miscellaneous manufactures	0.2	0.2	...	0.2	3.0	0.4	...	...	0.1	...	...	...
Unidentified manufactures	...	...	...	...	...	0.1	...	...	...	...	...	...
Agricultural And Livestock Products	0.3	0.2	0.1	0.2	0.8	1.1	3.4	6.4	12.1	4.2	10.0	5.3
Agricultural products	...	...	...	...	...	0.1	3.2	6.3	12.1	4.2	9.7	5.2
Livestock and livestock products	0.3	0.2	0.1	0.2	0.7	1.1	0.1	...	...	...	0.3	...
Other Commodities	1.0	0.7	0.7	0.1	0.1	...	...	...	...	...	...	0.1
Forestry products	...	...	...	...	...	...	...	...	...	...	...	...
Fish and other marine products	...	...	...	...	...	...	...	...	...	...	...	...
Metallic ores and concentrates	...	...	...	...	...	...	...	...	...	...	...	...
Bituminous coal and lignite	...	...	...	...	...	...	...	...	...	...	...	...
Crude petroleum and natural gas	...	...	...	...	...	...	...	...	...	...	...	...
Nonmetallic minerals	0.9	0.7	0.7	...	0.1	...	...	...	...	...	...	...
Scrap and waste	...	...	...	...	...	...	...	...	...	...	...	...
Used merchandise	...	...	...	0.1	...	...	...	...	...	...	...	...
Goods imported and returned unchanged	...	...	...	...	...	...	...	...	...	...	...	...
Special classification provisions	...	...	...	...	...	...	...	...	...	...	...	...

Industry	European Union						United Kingdom					
	1994	1995	1996	1997	1998	1999	1994	1995	1996	1997	1998	1999
ALL GOODS	84.1	88.0	82.5	106.9	83.1	50.8	14.3	11.1	8.3	9.1	12.0	13.9
Manufactured Goods	83.6	87.4	81.9	106.3	82.1	49.6	14.2	11.0	8.1	8.8	12.0	13.9
Food products	0.2	0.1	...	0.3	0.4	0.6	0.2	0.1	...	0.2	0.4	0.5
Tobacco products	...	...	...	...	...	...	...	...	...	...	...	...
Textile mill products	...	...	...	...	...	...	...	...	...	...	...	...
Apparel	...	0.2	0.6	0.5	0.6	0.2	...	0.1	0.3	0.2	0.1	0.1
Lumber and wood products	...	...	0.1	...	...	0.1	...	...	...	...	...	...
Furniture and fixtures	...	0.1	...	...	...	0.1	...	0.1	...	...	...	...
Paper products	...	...	...	...	...	0.1	...	...	...	...	...	...
Printing and publishing	0.1	0.1	...	...	...	0.1	...	...	...	...	...	0.1
Chemical products	0.9	1.0	1.7	2.4	3.4	2.1	0.2	0.1	0.3	0.1	0.4	0.6
Refined petroleum products	...	...	...	0.1	...	...	...	...	...	...	...	...
Rubber and plastic products	0.1	0.2	0.1	0.2	0.4	0.2	...	0.1	0.1	0.1	0.3	0.1
Leather products	0.1	0.1	0.4	0.5	0.7	0.4	0.1	...	0.4	0.4	0.6	0.4
Stone, clay and glass products	...	0.1	0.1	0.1	...	...	...	...	...	...	...	...
Primary metals	52.4	47.1	42.4	71.5	35.7	8.0	0.1	0.1	0.1	0.8	3.0	0.6
Fabricated metal products	0.2	0.2	0.2	0.4	0.1	0.2	...	...	...	0.1	0.1	0.1
Industrial machinery and computers	15.5	31.1	26.0	18.6	27.4	25.4	2.9	8.8	5.0	4.3	3.5	5.9
Electric and electronic equipment	1.5	1.8	2.7	4.8	6.5	5.4	0.6	0.5	0.9	0.7	0.7	2.9
Transportation equipment	0.5	0.8	0.7	1.9	1.2	0.7	0.4	0.5	0.2	0.8	0.9	0.5
Scientific and measuring instruments	2.1	2.7	5.7	3.1	4.7	4.6	0.6	0.2	0.3	0.4	1.5	1.3
Miscellaneous manufactures	9.6	1.7	0.9	1.8	0.8	1.2	9.2	0.4	0.4	0.5	0.3	0.7
Unidentified manufactures	0.3	0.3	0.1	0.1	...	0.2	0.1	0.1	...	...	...	...
Agricultural And Livestock Products	0.1	0.1	0.1	0.4	0.2	0.9	...	...	0.1	0.3	...	...
Agricultural products	...	0.1	0.1	0.2	0.2	0.8	...	...	...	0.1	...	...
Livestock and livestock products	0.1	...	0.1	0.2	...	0.1	...	...	0.1	0.2	...	...
Other Commodities	0.3	0.4	0.5	0.1	0.8	0.4	...	0.1	0.1	...	...	...
Forestry products	...	0.1	0.1	...	...	...	...	...	...	...	...	...
Fish and other marine products	...	...	...	...	0.6	...	...	...	...	...	...	...
Metallic ores and concentrates	...	0.3	...	...	...	...	...	...	...	...	...	...
Bituminous coal and lignite	...	...	...	...	...	...	...	...	...	...	...	...
Crude petroleum and natural gas	...	...	...	...	...	...	...	...	...	...	...	...
Nonmetallic minerals	...	...	...	...	...	...	...	...	...	...	...	...
Scrap and waste	0.3	...	...	...	...	...	...	...	...	...	...	...
Used merchandise	...	0.1	0.4	...	...	0.3	...	0.1	0.1	...	...	...
Goods imported and returned unchanged	...	...	0.1	0.1	0.1	0.1	...	...	...	...	...	...
Special classification provisions	...	...	...	...	...	...	...	...	...	...	...	...

Table D-29. MONTANA: State Exports of Goods by Destination and Industry, 1994–1999—*Continued*

(Millions of dollars.)

Industry	Germany						France					
	1994	1995	1996	1997	1998	1999	1994	1995	1996	1997	1998	1999
ALL GOODS	7.0	16.5	13.0	8.0	21.9	21.4	3.4	3.8	8.0	9.6	6.0	4.8
Manufactured Goods	6.8	16.1	12.9	7.9	21.8	21.0	3.4	3.8	7.9	9.6	5.9	4.3
Food products	...	...	...	...	...	...	...	...	...	...	...	...
Tobacco products	...	...	...	...	...	...	...	...	...	...	...	...
Textile mill products	...	...	...	...	...	...	...	...	...	...	...	...
Apparel	...	...	0.2	0.1	...	...	...	...	0.1	0.1	0.5	0.1
Lumber and wood products	...	...	...	...	...	...	...	...	...	...	...	...
Furniture and fixtures	...	...	...	...	...	...	...	...	...	...	...	...
Paper products	...	...	...	...	...	...	...	...	...	...	...	...
Printing and publishing	...	0.1	...	...	...	...	...	...	...	...	...	...
Chemical products	0.2	0.4	0.1	0.3	0.1	0.6	0.3	0.2	0.1	...	...	...
Refined petroleum products	...	...	...	...	...	...	...	...	...	...	...	...
Rubber and plastic products	...	...	0.1	0.1	0.1	...	0.1	...	...	...	...	...
Leather products	...	0.1	...	...	...	...	...	...	...	...	...	...
Stone, clay and glass products	...	...	...	...	...	...	...	...	...	...	0.1	...
Primary metals	...	...	...	...	2.9	7.2	...	...	...	...	...	...
Fabricated metal products	0.1	0.1	0.1	0.2	...	0.1	...	...	...	...	...	...
Industrial machinery and computers	5.7	13.7	8.6	5.2	12.3	11.7	2.2	2.6	6.7	6.2	4.6	2.7
Electric and electronic equipment	0.1	0.1	1.1	1.0	5.4	0.3	0.1	0.1	0.2	1.9	0.3	0.6
Transportation equipment	...	0.1	0.1	...	...	0.1	...	...	...	0.4	0.5	...
Scientific and measuring instruments	0.6	0.7	2.7	0.8	0.8	0.8	0.4	0.7	0.3	0.4	0.3	0.7
Miscellaneous manufactures	...	0.6	0.1	0.2	0.1	0.1	...	0.1	...	0.4	0.1	0.1
Unidentified manufactures	0.1	0.1	...	...	...	...	0.1	...	...	...	...	...
Agricultural And Livestock Products	0.1	0.1	...	0.1	0.1	0.1	...	...	...	...	...	0.6
Agricultural products	...	0.1	...	0.1	0.1	0.1	...	...	...	...	...	0.6
Livestock and livestock products	0.1	...	...	...	...	...	...	...	...	...	...	...
Other Commodities	...	0.3	0.1	...	...	0.3	...	0.1	0.1	0.1	0.1	...
Forestry products	...	...	...	...	...	...	...	0.1	0.1	...	...	...
Fish and other marine products	...	...	...	...	...	...	...	...	...	...	...	...
Metallic ores and concentrates	...	0.3	...	...	...	...	...	...	...	...	...	...
Bituminous coal and lignite	...	...	...	...	...	...	...	...	...	...	...	...
Crude petroleum and natural gas	...	...	...	...	...	...	...	...	...	...	...	...
Nonmetallic minerals	...	...	...	...	...	...	...	...	...	...	...	...
Scrap and waste	...	...	...	...	...	...	...	...	...	...	...	...
Used merchandise	...	...	0.1	...	...	0.3	...	...	...	...	...	...
Goods imported and returned unchanged	...	...	...	...	...	...	...	...	...	...	...	...
Special classification provisions	...	...	...	...	...	...	...	...	...	0.1	...	...

Industry	The Netherlands						Asian 10					
	1994	1995	1996	1997	1998	1999	1994	1995	1996	1997	1998	1999
ALL GOODS	1.7	5.7	3.6	2.4	4.7	4.1	17.3	26.5	32.8	54.5	36.4	47.0
Manufactured Goods	1.7	5.6	3.6	2.3	4.7	4.0	14.9	23.6	30.4	40.9	33.9	44.4
Food products	...	...	...	...	...	...	1.6	1.5	1.2	0.3	0.4	0.4
Tobacco products	...	...	...	...	...	...	...	...	...	...	...	...
Textile mill products	...	...	...	...	...	...	0.1	...	0.3	0.6	0.2	...
Apparel	...	...	...	...	...	...	0.2	0.6	0.2	0.1	0.1	0.1
Lumber and wood products	...	...	...	...	...	...	2.2	1.8	0.9	0.4	0.3	0.2
Furniture and fixtures	...	...	...	...	...	...	...	...	...	0.1	0.1	...
Paper products	...	...	...	...	...	...	...	0.1	...	...	...	0.2
Printing and publishing	...	...	...	...	...	...	...	...	...	...	...	0.1
Chemical products	...	...	0.1	0.1	0.1	0.2	0.3	1.2	0.8	0.7	0.6	0.6
Refined petroleum products	...	...	...	...	...	...	0.1	...	...	...	...	...
Rubber and plastic products	...	...	...	...	...	...	...	0.1	0.5	0.2	0.2	0.2
Leather products	...	...	...	...	...	...	0.2	0.2	0.5	0.1	...	...
Stone, clay and glass products	...	...	...	...	...	...	0.1	...	0.4	0.1	...	...
Primary metals	...	...	...	...	...	...	...	0.3	0.3	0.4	0.5	0.7
Fabricated metal products	...	...	...	...	...	...	...	0.1	0.2	0.5	0.3	0.6
Industrial machinery and computers	1.1	4.1	1.4	1.2	4.1	2.0	7.0	11.9	17.5	28.5	25.3	32.8
Electric and electronic equipment	0.1	0.2	0.2	0.5	0.1	1.4	0.5	0.8	1.2	1.7	0.5	1.2
Transportation equipment	0.1	0.1	...	...	0.1	...	0.5	0.3	0.1	0.4	0.2	0.6
Scientific and measuring instruments	0.2	0.6	1.7	0.3	0.2	0.3	1.2	1.8	3.0	3.1	2.0	2.7
Miscellaneous manufactures	0.2	0.5	0.1	0.1	...	...	0.6	2.6	3.2	3.7	2.9	2.2
Unidentified manufactures	...	...	...	...	...	...	0.2	0.2	0.1	0.1	0.2	1.8
Agricultural And Livestock Products	...	...	...	...	...	...	0.2	0.1	0.7	0.1	0.2	0.8
Agricultural products	...	...	...	...	...	...	0.2	0.1	0.2	0.1	0.2	0.8
Livestock and livestock products	...	...	...	...	...	...	...	...	0.5	...	...	...
Other Commodities	...	...	...	...	...	...	2.2	2.8	1.7	13.5	2.3	1.9
Forestry products	...	...	...	...	...	...	0.2	...	...	...	...	...
Fish and other marine products	...	...	...	...	...	...	...	0.1	...	...	...	...
Metallic ores and concentrates	...	...	...	...	...	...	...	...	...	11.4	...	...
Bituminous coal and lignite	...	...	...	...	...	...	...	...	...	...	...	...
Crude petroleum and natural gas	...	...	...	...	...	...	...	...	...	...	...	...
Nonmetallic minerals	...	...	...	...	...	...	1.7	1.7	1.4	1.4	1.6	1.6
Scrap and waste	...	...	...	...	...	...	...	...	...	...	0.1	...
Used merchandise	...	...	...	...	...	...	...	0.1	0.1	...	...	0.1
Goods imported and returned unchanged	...	...	...	...	...	...	...	...	...	...	...	...
Special classification provisions	...	...	...	...	...	...	0.3	0.9	0.2	0.7	0.6	0.2

Table D-29. MONTANA: State Exports of Goods by Destination and Industry, 1994–1999—*Continued*

(Millions of dollars.)

Industry	Japan						South Korea					
	1994	1995	1996	1997	1998	1999	1994	1995	1996	1997	1998	1999
ALL GOODS	10.9	16.8	20.5	23.1	19.4	28.5	3.9	4.7	4.5	4.3	3.1	2.5
Manufactured Goods	10.0	16.0	19.7	22.5	18.9	27.3	3.1	3.4	3.8	3.4	1.8	1.6
Food products	0.1	0.1	0.3	0.1	0.3	0.3	1.5	1.3	0.6	...	...	...
Tobacco products	...	...	...	...	...	...	...	...	...	...	...	...
Textile mill products	...	...	...	...	...	...	...	...	...	...	...	...
Apparel	0.2	0.5	0.2	0.1	...	0.1	...	...	...	...	...	...
Lumber and wood products	2.0	1.6	0.7	0.3	0.2	0.1	0.1	0.2	0.2	0.1	...	...
Furniture and fixtures	...	...	...	...	...	...	...	...	...	...	...	...
Paper products	...	...	...	...	...	...	...	...	...	...	...	...
Printing and publishing	...	...	...	...	...	...	...	...	...	0.1	...	0.1
Chemical products	0.1	0.2	0.1	0.2	0.1	0.2	...	...	...	...	...	...
Refined petroleum products	0.1	...	...	...	...	...	...	...	...	...	...	...
Rubber and plastic products	...	0.1	0.1	0.1	0.1	...	...	...	0.1	0.1	...	...
Leather products	0.2	0.2	0.3	0.1	...	...	...	...	...	...	...	...
Stone, clay and glass products	...	...	...	0.1	...	...	...	...	...	...	...	...
Primary metals	...	...	...	...	...	...	...	...	...	...	...	...
Fabricated metal products	...	...	0.1	...	0.1	0.1	...	...	...	...	...	...
Industrial machinery and computers	5.3	9.0	13.0	16.4	13.3	20.3	1.1	1.4	2.0	2.8	1.4	1.2
Electric and electronic equipment	0.2	0.2	0.6	1.3	0.2	0.3	0.1	0.1	0.1	...	...	0.1
Transportation equipment	0.2	0.1	0.1	0.1	0.2	...	0.1	...	...	...	...	...
Scientific and measuring instruments	0.9	1.4	1.8	2.0	1.7	2.0	0.1	0.1	0.7	0.2	0.1	0.2
Miscellaneous manufactures	0.5	2.3	2.4	1.8	2.7	2.1	...	0.2	...	0.1	0.2	...
Unidentified manufactures	0.2	0.1	...	...	...	1.7	...	...	...	...	...	...
Agricultural And Livestock Products	0.1	...	0.5	0.1	0.2	0.8	0.1	0.1	0.2	...	...	...
Agricultural products	0.1	...	0.1	...	0.2	0.8	0.1	0.1	0.1	...	...	...
Livestock and livestock products	...	...	0.4	...	...	...	...	...	0.1	...	...	...
Other Commodities	0.8	0.8	0.3	0.5	0.3	0.4	0.7	1.2	0.5	0.9	1.3	0.9
Forestry products	...	...	...	...	...	...	0.2	...	...	...	...	...
Fish and other marine products	...	0.1	...	...	...	...	...	...	...	...	...	...
Metallic ores and concentrates	...	...	...	...	...	...	...	...	...	...	...	...
Crude petroleum and natural gas	...	...	...	...	...	...	...	...	...	...	...	...
Nonmetallic minerals	0.8	0.6	0.3	0.4	0.3	0.4	0.2	0.3	0.3	0.3	0.9	0.7
Scrap and waste	...	...	...	...	...	...	...	...	...	...	...	...
Used merchandise	...	0.1	0.1	...	...	...	...	...	...	...	...	...
Goods imported and returned unchanged	...	...	...	0.1	...	...	0.3	0.9	0.2	0.6	0.4	0.1
Special classification provisions	...	...	...	...	...	...	...	...	...	...	...	...

Industry	Taiwan						Singapore					
	1994	1995	1996	1997	1998	1999	1994	1995	1996	1997	1998	1999
ALL GOODS	1.2	1.2	1.1	5.3	5.2	8.6	0.4	0.9	1.9	4.0	6.1	3.9
Manufactured Goods	0.7	0.7	0.8	4.9	4.8	8.5	0.3	0.8	1.9	3.9	6.1	3.5
Food products	...	...	...	...	...	0.1	...	...	...	...	...	...
Tobacco products	...	...	...	...	...	...	...	...	...	...	...	...
Textile mill products	0.1	...	...	0.2	0.2	...	...	...	...	...	...	...
Apparel	...	...	...	...	...	...	...	...	...	...	...	...
Lumber and wood products	...	...	...	...	...	...	...	...	...	...	...	...
Furniture and fixtures	...	...	...	...	...	...	...	...	...	...	...	...
Paper products	...	...	...	...	...	...	...	...	...	...	...	...
Printing and publishing	...	...	...	...	...	...	...	...	...	...	...	...
Chemical products	...	0.3	0.1	0.2	0.3	0.2	...	...	0.3	0.2	0.1	...
Refined petroleum products	...	...	...	...	...	...	...	...	...	...	...	...
Rubber and plastic products	...	...	...	...	...	...	...	...	0.2	...	...	...
Leather products	...	...	...	...	...	...	...	...	...	...	...	...
Stone, clay and glass products	...	...	...	...	...	...	0.1	...	0.1	0.3	0.5	0.7
Primary metals	...	...	...	...	...	...	...	...	...	...	...	...
Fabricated metal products	...	...	...	...	...	...	...	...	...	...	...	...
Industrial machinery and computers	0.4	0.3	0.4	4.2	4.1	8.0	0.1	0.5	0.9	3.1	5.4	2.1
Electric and electronic equipment	...	...	0.1	0.1	0.1	...	0.1	0.1	0.3	0.2	...	0.1
Transportation equipment	...	...	...	0.2	...	...	...	...	...	...	...	0.4
Scientific and measuring instruments	0.1	0.1	0.1	0.1	...	0.1	...	0.1	...	0.1	...	...
Miscellaneous manufactures	...	...	...	...	...	...	...	...	...	0.1	...	...
Unidentified manufactures	...	...	...	...	...	...	...	...	...	...	...	...
Agricultural And Livestock Products	...	...	...	...	...	...	...	...	...	...	...	...
Agricultural products	...	...	...	...	...	...	...	...	...	...	...	...
Livestock and livestock products	...	...	...	...	...	...	...	...	...	...	...	...
Other Commodities	0.5	0.5	0.3	0.4	0.3	0.1	0.1	0.1	...	...	0.1	0.5
Forestry products	...	...	...	...	...	...	...	...	...	...	...	...
Fish and other marine products	...	...	...	...	...	...	...	...	...	...	...	...
Metallic ores and concentrates	...	...	...	...	...	...	...	...	...	...	...	...
Crude petroleum and natural gas	...	...	...	...	...	...	...	...	...	...	...	...
Nonmetallic minerals	0.5	0.5	0.3	0.4	0.3	0.1	0.1	0.1	...	...	0.1	0.4
Scrap and waste	...	...	...	...	0.1	...	...	...	...	...	...	...
Used merchandise	...	...	...	...	...	...	...	...	...	...	...	0.1
Goods imported and returned unchanged	...	...	...	...	...	...	...	...	...	...	...	...
Special classification provisions	...	...	...	...	...	...	...	...	...	...	...	...

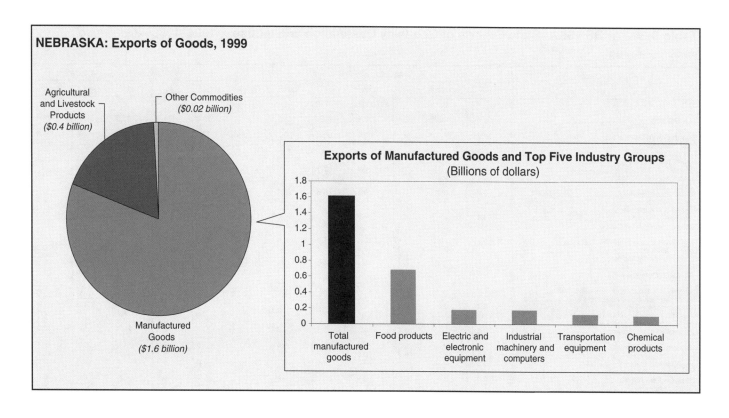

NEBRASKA: Exports of Goods, 1999

Agricultural and Livestock Products ($0.4 billion)

Other Commodities ($0.02 billion)

Manufactured Goods ($1.6 billion)

Exports of Manufactured Goods and Top Five Industry Groups
(Billions of dollars)

Table D-30. NEBRASKA: State Exports of Goods by Destination and Industry, 1994–1999

(Millions of dollars.)

Industry	All destinations						Canada					
	1994	1995	1996	1997	1998	1999	1994	1995	1996	1997	1998	1999
ALL GOODS	1 957.9	2 255.3	2 452.8	2 493.7	2 471.6	1 991.4	327.1	352.3	418.7	529.0	523.9	502.3
Manufactured Goods	1 860.3	2 148.8	2 201.1	2 247.5	2 251.4	1 609.2	315.3	340.7	397.4	504.6	512.4	488.4
Food products	1 209.6	1 477.4	1 427.0	1 324.8	1 249.0	683.4	105.5	111.4	134.1	151.7	141.5	131.9
Tobacco products	0.1	0.1	. . .	. . .	0.1	. . .	. . .	. . .	. . .	. . .	. . .	. . .
Textile mill products	0.8	1.8	1.6	1.8	1.1	1.3	0.1	0.1	0.4	0.1	0.1	0.1
Apparel	5.0	6.1	8.5	8.3	6.2	5.5	0.2	0.1	0.3	0.3	0.3	0.3
Lumber and wood products	0.6	1.5	2.6	3.0	1.5	5.1	0.4	0.1	0.4	0.5	0.5	3.2
Furniture and fixtures	6.6	8.0	10.4	23.3	28.0	5.9	4.2	5.9	6.3	19.6	23.5	4.0
Paper products	3.8	3.5	3.2	4.5	8.1	14.4	1.4	2.0	1.9	2.7	4.8	4.6
Printing and publishing	5.4	4.9	4.6	5.6	5.1	11.9	3.8	4.0	4.1	4.7	4.2	8.5
Chemical products	36.7	40.9	46.8	68.7	112.2	107.9	14.6	19.4	18.2	24.7	38.6	27.2
Refined petroleum products	0.6	0.5	1.2	0.7	1.9	0.8	0.5	0.3	0.6	0.3	0.3	0.1
Rubber and plastic products	16.3	19.3	24.1	21.7	25.8	28.3	11.7	11.8	10.1	10.4	15.2	17.5
Leather products	69.2	69.6	81.0	92.6	103.2	44.9	1.5	0.6	. . .	0.1	0.5	0.9
Stone, clay and glass products	3.2	3.6	2.7	2.5	4.1	2.6	0.4	0.8	0.7	0.8	0.9	1.5
Primary metals	44.5	43.3	39.2	64.3	70.6	55.8	13.2	13.9	21.9	31.5	24.5	22.1
Fabricated metal products	38.4	39.1	40.2	41.2	48.2	59.8	17.2	18.1	15.5	16.3	19.0	41.8
Industrial machinery and computers	137.0	140.1	192.7	245.6	212.2	179.6	63.0	66.4	90.7	124.1	100.3	85.5
Electric and electronic equipment	117.3	122.6	130.8	138.1	159.3	181.8	17.6	17.2	19.0	27.3	42.9	54.0
Transportation equipment	122.0	110.5	119.3	121.9	122.1	126.4	48.2	55.8	58.9	70.3	70.5	64.8
Scientific and measuring instruments	35.8	48.8	58.0	69.1	83.5	83.4	8.5	10.0	11.6	15.8	22.0	17.3
Miscellaneous manufactures	5.1	4.8	4.5	6.4	4.6	3.5	2.5	1.8	1.3	2.1	1.3	1.3
Unidentified manufactures	2.4	2.5	2.6	3.3	4.8	6.8	0.9	1.1	1.4	1.6	1.4	1.7
Agricultural And Livestock Products	85.3	94.3	228.9	222.5	197.9	366.9	1.7	1.6	1.9	3.1	2.2	4.8
Agricultural products	81.4	93.2	227.4	219.5	196.6	365.9	0.9	1.2	1.6	2.1	1.7	4.5
Livestock and livestock products	3.9	1.1	1.4	3.0	1.3	1.0	0.7	0.4	0.2	1.0	0.5	0.3
Other Commodities	12.3	12.2	22.8	23.7	22.3	15.3	10.0	10.0	19.5	21.3	9.3	9.1
Forestry products	0.1	0.2	0.2	0.2	. . .	. . .	0.1	. . .	. . .	. . .	. . .	. . .
Fish and other marine products	0.4	. . .	1.3	0.6	0.4	0.8	0.3	. . .	0.2	0.6	0.3	0.7
Metallic ores and concentrates	0.2	. . .	. . .	. . .	. . .	0.3	. . .	. . .	. . .	. . .	. . .	. . .
Bituminous coal and lignite	. . .	. . .	0.6	0.4	11.8	2.1	. . .	. . .	. . .	. . .	0.2	1.4
Crude petroleum and natural gas	0.6	0.8	10.1	8.5	1.4	. . .	0.6	0.8	10.1	8.5	1.4	. . .
Nonmetallic minerals	0.6	0.6	0.6	0.4	0.4	0.2	0.5	0.5	0.3	0.3	0.3	0.1
Scrap and waste	7.5	6.3	3.7	3.5	1.4	1.2	6.0	5.6	3.7	3.3	1.2	0.9
Used merchandise	0.6	1.7	2.5	3.1	1.8	4.4	0.3	1.1	1.7	2.0	1.2	1.1
Goods imported and returned unchanged	1.5	1.7	3.3	6.4	4.7	3.9	1.5	1.7	3.3	6.4	4.7	3.9
Special classification provisions	0.8	0.7	0.5	0.6	0.5	2.3	0.8	0.2	0.1	0.3	0.2	1.0

Table D-30. NEBRASKA: State Exports of Goods by Destination and Industry, 1994–1999—Continued

(Millions of dollars.)

Industry	South and Central American and Caribbean						Mexico					
	1994	1995	1996	1997	1998	1999	1994	1995	1996	1997	1998	1999
ALL GOODS	66.5	74.8	123.1	176.4	131.5	133.9	108.8	80.0	168.0	142.0	142.9	178.4
Manufactured Goods	32.7	27.1	53.7	102.9	96.3	68.2	78.9	57.3	61.7	80.1	114.6	129.6
Food products	20.3	7.4	19.6	54.0	41.9	14.5	34.1	27.3	32.0	35.7	69.5	71.4
Tobacco products	...	...	...	...	...	...	0.1	0.1	...	...	0.1	...
Textile mill products	...	0.1	0.1	...	...	0.2	...	0.1	...	0.3	0.1	0.1
Apparel	...	...	...	0.3	0.4	0.6	...	0.2	0.2	...	0.2	...
Lumber and wood products	...	0.3	...	...	0.2	0.1	...	...	...	...	...	0.1
Furniture and fixtures	0.2	0.4	0.2	0.6	0.6	0.2	1.7	0.1	0.1	...	0.2	0.1
Paper products	0.4	0.1	0.4	0.5	0.6	1.1	0.7	0.4	0.3	0.6	1.2	7.1
Printing and publishing	...	...	0.1	...	0.1	0.8	0.4	0.5	...	0.1	0.1	...
Chemical products	3.1	3.1	4.5	7.0	9.6	14.0	5.4	5.5	4.3	4.9	7.8	8.0
Refined petroleum products	...	...	...	...	0.3	0.5	...	...	...	...	...	...
Rubber and plastic products	0.3	2.1	0.8	0.4	1.0	0.4	0.9	0.4	1.7	1.9	1.4	1.1
Leather products	...	3.1	4.1	6.4	5.1	1.3	...	...	...	...	0.3	0.2
Stone, clay and glass products	0.1	...	0.1	0.1	0.1	...	0.9	...	...	0.1	0.2	0.3
Primary metals	0.2	0.3	0.7	0.4	0.7	0.3	4.5	0.7	1.2	1.5	2.6	1.8
Fabricated metal products	0.9	0.7	1.1	2.7	3.6	4.2	3.1	1.2	1.5	1.4	2.6	1.6
Industrial machinery and computers	3.4	6.0	18.6	21.7	18.0	10.2	10.3	5.0	5.7	13.3	11.2	10.1
Electric and electronic equipment	1.8	1.3	0.7	4.4	8.9	16.3	11.0	11.9	11.0	13.4	12.5	15.7
Transportation equipment	0.7	0.5	0.4	2.1	2.3	1.9	1.7	1.4	1.7	1.7	1.9	7.4
Scientific and measuring instruments	0.9	1.2	1.5	1.4	1.7	1.0	3.8	2.3	1.8	4.7	1.8	2.1
Miscellaneous manufactures	0.2	0.3	0.7	0.7	0.7	0.4	0.1	0.1	0.1	0.2	0.1	0.1
Unidentified manufactures	0.1	0.1	0.1	0.1	0.2	0.2	0.1	0.1	0.2	0.4	1.0	2.0
Agricultural And Livestock Products	33.7	47.4	69.2	73.4	35.2	65.4	29.6	22.6	105.3	61.0	27.8	48.1
Agricultural products	33.4	47.0	68.7	72.8	34.9	65.1	27.2	22.4	105.1	59.6	27.5	47.8
Livestock and livestock products	0.3	0.4	0.5	0.5	0.4	0.2	2.5	0.2	0.3	1.4	0.3	0.2
Other Commodities	0.2	0.3	0.2	0.1	...	0.4	0.2	0.1	0.9	0.9	0.5	0.8
Forestry products	...	...	...	...	...	...	...	...	0.1	...	...	...
Fish and other marine products	...	...	...	...	...	...	...	...	...	...	...	...
Metallic ores and concentrates	...	...	...	...	...	...	...	0.2	...	...	...	...
Bituminous coal and lignite	...	...	...	...	...	...	...	...	...	0.6	...	...
Crude petroleum and natural gas	...	...	...	...	...	...	...	...	...	...	...	...
Nonmetallic minerals	...	...	...	...	...	...	...	...	0.2	...	...	...
Scrap and waste	...	...	...	...	...	...	...	...	...	0.1	...	...
Used merchandise	0.2	...	0.1	0.1	...	0.1	...	...	...	0.7	0.4	0.8
Goods imported and returned unchanged	...	...	...	...	...	...	...	...	...	...	...	...
Special classification provisions	...	0.3	...	...	...	0.2	...	...	...	...	...	...

Industry	European Union						United Kingdom					
	1994	1995	1996	1997	1998	1999	1994	1995	1996	1997	1998	1999
ALL GOODS	221.8	213.1	237.8	285.7	407.7	343.8	30.5	27.9	30.2	40.7	58.7	51.2
Manufactured Goods	204.3	200.0	207.4	220.1	287.6	215.9	30.4	27.6	26.7	39.4	48.6	39.3
Food products	21.3	31.0	25.7	29.5	32.2	14.5	2.5	2.9	0.5	0.3	0.7	0.4
Tobacco products	...	...	...	...	...	...	...	...	...	...	...	...
Textile mill products	0.1	0.2	0.6	0.7	0.3	0.4	...	...	...	...	...	0.2
Apparel	0.2	0.3	1.3	1.0	0.9	0.5	...	0.1	0.2	0.2	0.2	0.2
Lumber and wood products	...	0.3	0.2	...	0.1	0.1	...	...	0.2	...	...	...
Furniture and fixtures	0.3	0.3	1.7	1.4	0.6	0.2	0.3	0.1	0.5	0.3	0.1	...
Paper products	0.1	0.3	0.1	0.1	0.8	0.3	...	0.1	0.1	...	0.6	...
Printing and publishing	0.4	0.1	0.1	0.1	0.1	0.9	0.1	...	...	...	0.1	0.1
Chemical products	3.4	4.3	9.0	17.8	27.2	28.8	0.3	0.3	0.4	4.7	4.8	5.7
Refined petroleum products	0.1	0.1	0.1	...	0.4	...	...	...	...	...	...	...
Rubber and plastic products	1.0	2.7	4.1	2.6	5.6	3.4	0.4	0.2	0.3	0.3	0.3	0.6
Leather products	27.1	20.6	25.4	12.8	23.6	8.0	...	...	...	...	0.5	...
Stone, clay and glass products	0.2	0.4	0.5	0.5	0.7	0.3	...	0.3	0.2	...	0.5	...
Primary metals	19.2	18.8	6.9	17.2	32.0	13.9	0.2	0.1	0.5	0.4	0.3	0.1
Fabricated metal products	6.1	7.7	6.1	6.7	7.3	4.8	0.4	1.1	0.5	0.3	0.7	0.5
Industrial machinery and computers	23.9	21.5	25.0	29.4	34.3	27.2	11.3	10.6	11.0	15.8	17.6	7.1
Electric and electronic equipment	43.7	48.0	52.6	48.3	55.5	49.0	4.0	3.2	3.9	4.5	8.1	9.9
Transportation equipment	44.0	22.1	22.5	23.9	26.3	21.8	9.0	6.1	4.8	7.2	6.1	7.1
Scientific and measuring instruments	11.5	19.3	24.3	26.4	37.7	40.1	1.7	2.1	3.1	4.8	8.1	7.0
Miscellaneous manufactures	1.3	1.5	0.7	1.4	1.0	0.9	0.1	0.3	0.2	0.4	0.2	0.2
Unidentified manufactures	0.5	0.5	0.4	0.4	1.0	0.8	0.1	0.1	0.2	0.2	0.2	0.1
Agricultural And Livestock Products	17.5	12.7	30.0	65.2	113.0	124.9	...	0.2	3.2	1.2	10.0	11.0
Agricultural products	17.5	12.7	30.0	65.2	112.9	124.9	...	0.2	3.2	1.2	10.0	11.0
Livestock and livestock products	...	...	...	...	...	...	...	...	...	...	...	...
Other Commodities	0.1	0.4	0.3	0.3	7.2	3.0	...	0.2	0.2	0.1	0.1	0.9
Forestry products	...	...	...	0.1	...	...	...	...	...	...	...	...
Fish and other marine products	...	...	...	...	...	...	...	...	...	...	...	...
Metallic ores and concentrates	...	...	...	...	...	0.2	...	...	...	...	...	...
Bituminous coal and lignite	...	...	...	...	6.9	0.7	...	...	...	...	...	...
Crude petroleum and natural gas	...	...	...	...	...	...	...	...	...	...	...	...
Nonmetallic minerals	...	...	...	...	...	...	...	...	...	...	...	...
Scrap and waste	...	0.1	...	...	...	...	...	0.1	...	...	...	...
Used merchandise	...	0.3	0.1	...	0.2	1.6	...	0.1	0.1	...	...	0.7
Goods imported and returned unchanged	...	...	...	...	...	...	...	...	...	...	...	...
Special classification provisions	...	...	0.2	0.2	0.1	0.5	...	...	0.1	0.1	...	0.3

Table D-30. NEBRASKA: State Exports of Goods by Destination and Industry, 1994–1999—*Continued*

(Millions of dollars.)

Industry	Germany						France					
	1994	1995	1996	1997	1998	1999	1994	1995	1996	1997	1998	1999
ALL GOODS	30.8	29.0	35.8	39.0	44.3	37.4	18.3	16.2	20.5	22.2	29.8	27.6
Manufactured Goods	30.2	27.4	34.3	37.7	39.6	30.2	18.1	15.7	20.0	15.9	23.6	25.0
Food products	7.3	7.5	10.0	10.0	7.9	3.2	6.4	5.3	4.1	2.6	8.1	4.8
Tobacco products	...	...	...	...	...	...	...	...	...	...	...	...
Textile mill products	...	...	...	...	...	0.1	...	0.1	...	...	...	0.1
Apparel	0.1	0.1	0.1	0.1	...	...	...	...	...	...	0.1	0.2
Lumber and wood products	...	0.1	...	...	...	...	...	...	...	...	...	...
Furniture and fixtures	...	...	...	...	...	...	...	...	0.3	...	0.4	0.1
Paper products	...	...	...	...	0.1	...	...	0.1	...	...	0.1	0.2
Printing and publishing	0.1	...	...	...	...	...	...	...	0.1	...	...	...
Chemical products	0.9	0.9	1.5	1.6	1.9	1.4	...	0.1	0.4	0.4	0.4	0.2
Refined petroleum products	...	...	...	...	...	...	...	...	...	...	...	...
Rubber and plastic products	0.1	1.0	0.3	0.1	0.7	0.8	0.1	0.7	2.4	1.1	2.5	0.8
Leather products	...	...	0.2	...	...	...	...	...	0.1	0.1	...	...
Stone, clay and glass products	...	...	0.2	...	...	...	...	...	0.1	0.1	0.1	0.2
Primary metals	0.1	0.2	0.3	0.1	0.2	0.3	...	...	...	0.1	...	...
Fabricated metal products	0.9	2.3	3.4	3.5	2.3	1.6	0.5	0.1	0.1	0.3	1.4	1.1
Industrial machinery and computers	2.8	1.5	3.4	1.5	2.2	2.9	1.5	1.5	3.6	3.8	1.4	2.2
Electric and electronic equipment	3.1	4.8	3.8	9.4	9.7	6.1	1.2	1.8	1.4	1.8	1.1	1.5
Transportation equipment	10.8	2.6	5.0	3.9	5.2	2.8	6.1	1.4	1.2	1.4	3.3	3.3
Scientific and measuring instruments	2.8	5.5	5.7	7.0	9.1	10.3	1.9	4.2	6.0	4.1	4.4	10.3
Miscellaneous manufactures	0.9	0.6	0.3	0.4	0.3	0.2	0.3	0.3	0.1	0.2	0.2	0.1
Unidentified manufactures	0.1	0.1	...	...	0.2	0.2	...	0.1	0.1	...	0.2	0.1
Agricultural And Livestock Products	0.6	1.3	1.5	1.1	4.7	7.1	0.1	0.5	0.5	6.3	2.8	2.0
Agricultural products	0.6	1.3	1.5	1.1	4.7	7.1	0.1	0.5	0.5	6.3	2.8	2.0
Livestock and livestock products	...	...	...	...	...	...	...	...	...	...	...	...
Other Commodities	...	0.3	0.1	0.2	...	0.1	...	...	...	...	3.4	0.6
Forestry products	...	...	...	0.1	...	...	...	...	...	...	...	...
Fish and other marine products	...	...	...	...	...	...	...	...	...	...	...	...
Metallic ores and concentrates	...	...	...	...	...	...	...	...	...	...	...	...
Bituminous coal and lignite	...	...	...	...	...	...	...	...	...	...	3.4	...
Crude petroleum and natural gas	...	...	...	...	...	...	...	...	...	...	...	...
Nonmetallic minerals	...	...	...	...	...	...	...	...	...	...	...	...
Scrap and waste	...	...	...	...	...	...	...	...	...	...	...	...
Used merchandise	...	0.2	...	...	...	...	...	...	...	...	...	0.6
Goods imported and returned unchanged	...	...	...	...	...	...	...	...	...	...	...	...
Special classification provisions	...	...	...	...	...	0.1	...	...	...	...	...	...

Industry	The Netherlands						Asian 10					
	1994	1995	1996	1997	1998	1999	1994	1995	1996	1997	1998	1999
ALL GOODS	62.3	73.6	58.7	60.4	73.9	52.3	1 137.3	1 426.7	1 366.0	1 206.4	1 115.4	619.3
Manufactured Goods	62.0	73.3	58.5	57.6	64.1	43.2	1 133.3	1 422.6	1 360.7	1 195.1	1 101.8	555.7
Food products	2.8	11.9	2.2	5.0	5.4	2.7	996.5	1 259.3	1 168.0	990.1	911.6	386.5
Tobacco products	...	...	...	...	...	...	...	...	...	...	...	...
Textile mill products	...	0.1	0.5	0.6	0.3	...	0.5	0.9	0.4	0.5	0.6	0.5
Apparel	...	0.1	0.9	0.7	0.5	...	4.6	5.0	6.5	6.4	4.2	3.4
Lumber and wood products	...	...	...	...	...	...	0.2	0.5	1.8	1.3	0.6	1.5
Furniture and fixtures	...	...	...	...	...	...	0.1	1.1	1.9	1.6	2.2	0.9
Paper products	...	...	...	...	...	...	1.2	0.4	0.1	0.3	0.6	1.1
Printing and publishing	...	...	...	...	...	...	0.7	0.2	0.2	0.6	0.5	1.4
Chemical products	0.1	...	0.3	0.5	0.8	1.6	5.6	4.6	7.5	9.6	17.7	20.6
Refined petroleum products	0.1	...	...	...	...	...	...	...	0.5	0.3	0.9	0.1
Rubber and plastic products	0.1	0.3	0.1	...	0.2	...	1.4	1.9	6.0	3.4	2.0	1.3
Leather products	...	...	...	...	...	...	40.6	45.2	51.5	73.3	73.4	34.4
Stone, clay and glass products	...	...	...	...	...	...	1.7	2.1	1.2	1.0	2.1	0.3
Primary metals	18.5	18.3	5.5	15.5	25.7	11.2	7.0	9.2	7.6	13.6	9.8	17.1
Fabricated metal products	3.4	3.1	0.7	0.9	0.8	0.7	8.0	8.2	12.6	7.7	4.7	4.7
Industrial machinery and computers	0.6	1.2	1.9	0.8	1.6	1.6	13.7	18.7	24.1	18.9	16.4	13.4
Electric and electronic equipment	20.5	27.6	36.5	21.9	16.4	18.0	29.9	32.8	36.4	37.8	27.9	36.7
Transportation equipment	15.3	9.3	7.7	9.3	9.1	5.7	13.3	20.0	19.0	11.7	10.4	13.1
Scientific and measuring instruments	0.6	1.2	2.1	2.4	3.2	1.7	7.5	11.5	13.7	15.1	14.7	16.7
Miscellaneous manufactures	...	...	...	...	...	...	0.6	0.6	1.4	1.7	0.8	0.7
Unidentified manufactures	0.1	...	...	...	0.1	0.1	0.3	0.3	0.3	0.4	0.8	1.4
Agricultural And Livestock Products	0.3	0.2	0.2	2.7	9.7	8.8	2.2	3.7	4.0	10.9	13.3	62.7
Agricultural products	0.3	0.2	0.2	2.7	9.7	8.8	2.1	3.6	3.7	10.9	13.3	62.4
Livestock and livestock products	...	...	...	...	...	...	0.2	0.1	0.3	...	...	0.3
Other Commodities	...	...	...	...	0.1	0.2	1.7	0.4	1.3	0.4	0.3	0.9
Forestry products	...	...	...	...	...	...	...	...	...	0.1	...	...
Fish and other marine products	...	...	...	...	...	...	0.1	...	0.9	...	...	0.1
Metallic ores and concentrates	...	...	...	...	...	...	...	...	...	...	0.2	0.2
Bituminous coal and lignite	...	...	...	...	...	...	...	...	...	...	...	...
Crude petroleum and natural gas	...	...	...	...	...	...	...	...	...	...	...	...
Nonmetallic minerals	...	...	...	...	...	...	...	...	0.1	...	...	0.1
Scrap and waste	...	...	...	...	...	...	1.6	0.1	...	0.2	0.1	0.2
Used merchandise	...	...	...	...	0.1	...	...	0.1	0.2	...	...	0.1
Goods imported and returned unchanged	...	...	...	...	...	...	...	...	...	...	...	...
Special classification provisions	...	...	...	...	...	...	...	0.2	0.2	0.1	0.1	0.2

Table D-30. NEBRASKA: State Exports of Goods by Destination and Industry, 1994–1999—*Continued*

(Millions of dollars.)

Industry	Japan						South Korea					
	1994	1995	1996	1997	1998	1999	1994	1995	1996	1997	1998	1999
ALL GOODS	912.8	1 162.7	1 103.1	870.8	808.3	309.0	146.1	160.8	134.3	184.7	111.4	106.1
Manufactured Goods	911.7	1 160.2	1 098.7	866.5	800.5	304.0	144.3	160.7	134.1	184.5	111.3	77.4
Food products	874.4	1 114.8	1 041.3	820.4	755.3	256.4	111.3	124.7	97.0	121.0	50.2	38.1
Tobacco products	...	...	...	...	...	...	...	...	...	...	...	...
Textile mill products	...	...	...	0.1	0.1	...	0.3	0.5	0.4	0.3	0.2	0.2
Apparel	4.4	4.3	6.1	4.8	4.1	3.3	0.1	0.7	0.2	0.4	...	0.1
Lumber and wood products	...	...	0.1	0.2	0.3	1.2	...	...	...	0.4	0.2	...
Furniture and fixtures	...	0.1	0.1	0.2	1.2	0.6	...	...	...	0.4	...	...
Paper products	1.1	...	...	...	0.5	1.0	...	...	...	...	...	...
Printing and publishing	0.6	0.1	0.1	0.1	0.1	0.2	...	...	...	0.1	...	0.5
Chemical products	3.0	2.1	2.5	4.7	7.7	8.5	0.7	0.5	1.3	1.7	1.7	3.4
Refined petroleum products	...	...	...	...	0.5	...	...	...	...	...	...	...
Rubber and plastic products	0.9	1.0	2.6	2.7	1.3	0.9	0.1	0.2	...	0.2	...	...
Leather products	1.8	1.6	2.3	4.2	1.6	0.4	23.8	22.4	23.0	47.5	52.8	24.8
Stone, clay and glass products	0.5	1.3	0.7	0.7	1.7	0.2	0.8	0.5	0.5	0.3	0.1	...
Primary metals	...	...	...	0.1	0.1	0.2	...	...	0.9	0.8	0.5	0.8
Fabricated metal products	2.2	0.6	0.7	0.5	1.0	1.4	2.1	2.8	2.8	2.0	0.9	0.4
Industrial machinery and computers	5.6	5.3	10.0	4.6	3.5	3.4	2.2	5.1	2.4	1.8	0.9	1.1
Electric and electronic equipment	1.9	5.7	8.6	5.4	2.7	2.7	1.0	1.1	2.7	3.8	1.6	4.6
Transportation equipment	11.5	17.5	14.3	9.4	8.4	12.1	0.3	0.3	0.7	0.6	0.6	0.3
Scientific and measuring instruments	3.5	5.2	9.0	8.3	9.7	10.1	1.6	1.8	1.8	3.1	1.4	2.9
Miscellaneous manufactures	0.3	0.4	0.3	0.3	0.5	0.4	...	...	0.1	0.1	...	0.1
Unidentified manufactures	0.1	0.2	0.1	0.1	0.3	1.0	0.1	...	...	0.1	...	0.1
Agricultural And Livestock Products	1.0	2.4	3.1	4.2	7.8	4.5	0.2	0.1	0.2	0.2	0.1	28.6
Agricultural products	1.0	2.4	3.0	4.2	7.8	4.5	0.2	0.1	0.2	0.2	0.1	28.6
Livestock and livestock products	...	...	0.1	...	...	...	...	...	...	...	...	...
Other Commodities	...	...	1.3	0.2	...	0.5	1.5	...	...	...	...	0.1
Forestry products	...	...	...	...	...	...	...	...	...	...	...	...
Fish and other marine products	...	...	0.9	...	...	...	0.1	...	...	...	...	...
Metallic ores and concentrates	...	...	...	...	...	0.2	...	...	...	...	...	...
Bituminous coal and lignite	...	...	...	...	...	...	...	...	...	...	...	...
Crude petroleum and natural gas	...	...	...	...	...	...	...	...	...	...	...	...
Nonmetallic minerals	...	...	...	...	...	...	1.5	...	...	...	...	0.1
Scrap and waste	...	...	...	...	...	...	...	...	...	...	...	...
Used merchandise	...	...	0.1	...	...	0.1	...	...	...	...	...	...
Goods imported and returned unchanged	...	...	...	...	...	...	...	...	...	...	...	...
Special classification provisions	...	...	0.2	0.1	...	0.2	...	...	...	...	...	...

Industry	Taiwan						Singapore					
	1994	1995	1996	1997	1998	1999	1994	1995	1996	1997	1998	1999
ALL GOODS	10.8	13.2	16.8	24.9	34.3	30.2	16.7	23.8	23.8	29.0	25.1	34.9
Manufactured Goods	10.6	13.1	16.4	24.0	33.7	24.3	16.6	23.8	23.8	29.0	25.1	34.8
Food products	5.5	7.5	7.7	12.7	19.6	12.4	0.2	0.4	0.5	0.4	2.0	0.8
Tobacco products	...	...	...	...	...	...	...	...	...	...	...	...
Textile mill products	...	...	...	...	...	0.1	0.1	0.1	...	...	...	...
Apparel	...	...	0.1	0.2	0.1	...	...	...	...	0.1	...	...
Lumber and wood products	0.1	...	...	...	...	...	...	...	...	...	...	0.3
Furniture and fixtures	...	...	...	0.2	0.2	...	0.1	...	...	...	0.1	0.1
Paper products	0.1	...	0.1	...	...	...	...	...	...	...	...	...
Printing and publishing	...	...	...	...	...	...	0.1	0.1	...	...	...	...
Chemical products	0.5	0.6	1.6	1.0	2.0	1.8	...	0.1	0.1	...	0.3	0.6
Refined petroleum products	...	...	...	0.3	0.1	...	...	...	...	...	...	...
Rubber and plastic products	...	0.2	0.8	0.1	0.5	0.1	...	0.1	0.1	...	...	0.1
Leather products	...	...	...	0.1	5.0	4.7	...	...	...	...	...	...
Stone, clay and glass products	...	...	...	...	0.1	...	0.1	0.1	...	...	0.1	...
Primary metals	0.2	0.5	0.4	0.6	0.1	0.1	6.5	8.2	5.7	11.3	7.4	12.7
Fabricated metal products	0.1	0.7	0.2	0.1	0.2	0.1	0.1	0.3	0.1	0.2	0.2	0.4
Industrial machinery and computers	1.4	0.5	0.8	1.5	1.3	0.8	0.6	0.7	1.6	2.4	5.6	2.9
Electric and electronic equipment	1.5	1.8	2.8	4.0	2.9	2.9	7.9	12.3	14.4	13.4	8.5	15.9
Transportation equipment	...	0.1	1.0	0.9	0.7	...	0.6	0.4	0.5	0.4	0.2	0.2
Scientific and measuring instruments	1.0	0.9	0.7	1.4	0.9	1.1	0.3	0.9	0.8	0.7	0.4	0.6
Miscellaneous manufactures	0.1	...	...	1.0	...	...	...	...	...	0.1	...	0.1
Unidentified manufactures	...	...	0.1	...	...	0.1	...	...	...	...	0.1	0.1
Agricultural And Livestock Products	0.1	0.1	0.4	0.9	0.6	5.9	...	...	...	0.1	...	0.1
Agricultural products	0.1	0.1	0.4	0.9	0.6	5.9	...	...	...	0.1	...	0.1
Livestock and livestock products	...	...	...	...	...	...	...	...	...	...	...	...
Other Commodities	0.1	...	...	...	...	...	...	0.1	...	...	...	...
Forestry products	...	...	...	...	...	...	...	...	...	...	...	...
Fish and other marine products	...	...	...	...	...	...	...	...	...	...	...	...
Metallic ores and concentrates	...	...	...	...	...	...	...	...	...	...	...	...
Bituminous coal and lignite	...	...	...	...	...	...	...	...	...	...	...	...
Crude petroleum and natural gas	...	...	...	...	...	...	...	...	...	...	...	...
Nonmetallic minerals	...	...	...	...	...	...	...	...	...	...	...	...
Scrap and waste	0.1	...	...	...	...	...	...	...	...	...	...	...
Used merchandise	...	...	...	...	...	...	...	...	...	...	...	...
Goods imported and returned unchanged	...	...	...	...	...	...	...	...	...	...	...	...
Special classification provisions	...	...	...	...	...	...	...	...	...	...	...	...

NEVADA: Exports of Goods, 1999

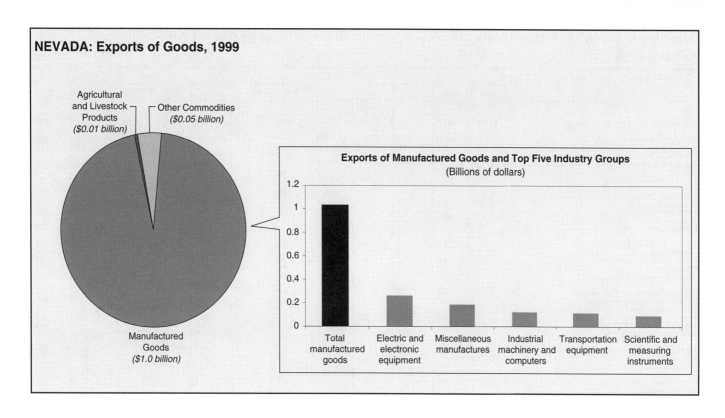

Table D-31. NEVADA: State Exports of Goods by Destination and Industry, 1994–1999

(Millions of dollars.)

Industry	All destinations						Canada					
	1994	1995	1996	1997	1998	1999	1994	1995	1996	1997	1998	1999
ALL GOODS	458.5	711.1	691.6	807.1	764.9	1 083.4	148.9	211.8	265.6	272.1	300.7	549.4
Manufactured Goods	420.4	659.4	631.7	732.3	720.2	1 030.9	131.0	190.1	240.7	243.6	278.5	520.7
Food products	7.2	15.0	15.2	6.4	8.8	24.0	2.1	3.3	2.0	2.6	3.1	15.9
Tobacco products	. . .	. . .	. . .	. . .	. . .	. . .	. . .	. . .	. . .	. . .	. . .	. . .
Textile mill products	1.2	3.1	1.4	1.9	2.0	1.4	0.1	0.3	0.3	0.4	0.4	0.1
Apparel	6.4	13.6	14.4	12.8	12.7	17.9	3.3	3.5	3.0	1.2	3.2	2.9
Lumber and wood products	4.8	3.2	2.0	3.8	2.9	2.0	2.3	1.6	1.4	2.6	0.6	0.4
Furniture and fixtures	1.5	2.0	3.6	1.8	1.4	2.7	0.5	0.4	0.8	0.3	0.4	0.6
Paper products	2.4	3.0	5.0	5.5	5.2	7.1	0.8	1.0	2.7	2.6	2.7	3.4
Printing and publishing	7.4	7.4	8.2	10.8	8.7	11.3	4.5	3.7	5.7	7.5	4.7	7.2
Chemical products	10.6	21.7	22.8	19.3	37.3	72.4	5.8	7.0	7.4	10.8	24.1	56.6
Refined petroleum products	0.8	0.5	0.5	0.4	0.1	0.2	0.6	0.4	0.4	0.2	0.1	0.1
Rubber and plastic products	9.7	11.0	17.4	27.0	18.4	21.4	3.0	3.5	7.1	9.7	8.9	8.6
Leather products	1.0	4.2	4.8	2.8	3.2	5.5	0.2	1.2	0.4	0.4	0.2	0.4
Stone, clay and glass products	6.8	6.2	5.7	5.8	3.8	5.1	3.1	2.9	2.1	1.5	1.4	2.1
Primary metals	50.7	47.2	23.8	33.8	33.7	31.9	17.7	18.8	11.3	4.7	2.4	5.8
Fabricated metal products	28.8	69.1	22.7	44.2	23.9	30.6	7.3	11.9	11.2	21.3	10.5	12.8
Industrial machinery and computers	68.8	130.8	94.7	119.3	114.8	124.6	16.0	17.7	22.3	34.0	42.1	57.1
Electric and electronic equipment	55.4	92.7	102.0	117.3	99.7	262.9	28.2	40.4	58.0	62.3	59.1	167.0
Transportation equipment	14.7	50.4	54.7	72.7	85.9	117.9	3.7	38.3	27.4	33.5	56.2	81.3
Scientific and measuring instruments	67.0	81.0	70.6	88.2	90.5	94.2	10.9	13.2	11.9	12.3	11.0	12.2
Miscellaneous manufactures	70.3	94.0	158.3	153.6	161.6	188.5	19.5	19.3	63.5	34.0	44.4	80.6
Unidentified manufactures	4.8	3.4	3.9	5.0	5.5	9.5	1.6	1.6	2.0	2.4	3.1	5.6
Agricultural And Livestock Products	6.8	4.5	6.0	4.9	4.5	5.8	2.9	2.7	3.9	3.6	3.2	4.6
Agricultural products	6.1	3.3	5.2	3.4	3.5	5.0	2.7	2.4	3.3	2.9	2.6	3.8
Livestock and livestock products	0.7	1.3	0.8	1.5	1.0	0.8	0.2	0.4	0.6	0.7	0.6	0.8
Other Commodities	31.3	47.1	53.9	70.0	40.2	46.6	15.0	19.0	21.0	24.9	19.0	24.0
Forestry products	0.2	0.1	0.1	0.1	0.1	. . .	0.1	. . .	. . .	. . .	. . .	. . .
Fish and other marine products	0.6	0.1	0.4	0.1	0.3	0.7	0.4	0.1	. . .	. . .	0.2	0.1
Metallic ores and concentrates	. . .	. . .	. . .	1.0	. . .	. . .	. . .	. . .	. . .	1.0	. . .	. . .
Bituminous coal and lignite	. . .	. . .	. . .	. . .	. . .	. . .	. . .	. . .	. . .	. . .	. . .	. . .
Crude petroleum and natural gas	. . .	. . .	0.4	. . .	0.5	. . .	. . .	. . .	. . .	. . .	0.5	. . .
Nonmetallic minerals	12.9	14.5	15.3	15.7	16.4	14.8	2.8	2.5	2.7	2.7	2.4	2.2
Scrap and waste	1.3	1.1	1.2	1.0	1.1	1.9	1.0	0.2	0.4	0.3	. . .	0.1
Used merchandise	6.1	16.0	20.5	30.8	4.8	4.0	0.6	1.3	2.4	1.2	1.3	1.0
Goods imported and returned unchanged	10.0	13.9	14.6	19.5	14.2	18.2	10.0	13.9	14.6	19.5	14.2	18.2
Special classification provisions	0.2	1.4	1.4	1.8	2.7	7.0	0.1	0.9	0.7	0.1	0.2	2.5

Table D-31. NEVADA: State Exports of Goods by Destination and Industry, 1994–1999—*Continued*

(Millions of dollars.)

Industry	South and Central America and Caribbean						Mexico					
	1994	1995	1996	1997	1998	1999	1994	1995	1996	1997	1998	1999
ALL GOODS	22.5	34.6	44.7	34.3	38.0	39.2	14.5	12.8	9.2	59.9	22.5	57.3
Manufactured Goods	21.9	34.0	43.0	33.7	36.3	37.4	12.8	12.6	9.0	59.7	22.3	56.8
Food products	0.5	0.4	1.9	0.1	0.2	0.3	1.8	0.8	0.4	0.2	0.5	0.8
Tobacco products	...	...	...	...	...	...	...	...	...	...	...	...
Textile mill products	...	...	0.1	...	0.1	...	0.3	1.8	0.1	0.2	0.3	0.3
Apparel	0.1	...	0.2	0.2	0.2	0.2	0.6	0.2	0.1	0.1	0.2	0.2
Lumber and wood products	1.2	...	0.1	0.2	...	0.6	0.2	0.4	...	0.2	0.3	0.2
Furniture and fixtures	0.1	...	0.2	0.5	0.1	0.8	...	...	...	...	0.1	...
Paper products	0.6	0.9	0.8	1.4	1.1	1.8	0.3	0.7	0.3	0.4	0.3	0.6
Printing and publishing	0.1	...	0.1	0.1	0.1	0.1	0.6	0.9	0.2	0.2	0.1	0.8
Chemical products	0.2	0.5	0.8	0.7	0.7	1.5	0.6	0.7	1.2	1.8	1.2	4.3
Refined petroleum products	...	...	...	...	...	...	...	...	...	...	...	0.1
Rubber and plastic products	0.4	0.6	0.8	0.6	0.5	4.9	0.9	0.7	1.2	0.8	1.1	1.3
Leather products	...	...	0.4	...	...	...	...	...	...	...	...	...
Stone, clay and glass products	0.3	0.3	0.3	0.4	0.2	0.1	...	0.1	...	0.1	0.1	0.1
Primary metals	2.0	2.5	0.7	0.7	0.5	0.4	0.3	0.6	0.3	2.6	0.8	0.9
Fabricated metal products	1.4	1.8	1.6	2.3	1.0	1.8	0.1	0.2	0.1	3.1	0.8	1.0
Industrial machinery and computers	4.4	8.6	7.2	5.6	6.7	3.3	2.3	2.4	1.4	2.9	4.4	2.3
Electric and electronic equipment	1.1	1.8	2.7	2.1	2.8	3.2	2.0	1.8	1.7	2.9	4.6	39.2
Transportation equipment	0.4	0.3	1.1	1.4	1.5	0.9	0.4	0.2	0.3	0.7	0.5	0.8
Scientific and measuring instruments	1.7	2.2	2.5	3.7	3.4	3.8	1.3	0.5	1.0	2.1	1.9	2.0
Miscellaneous manufactures	7.1	13.9	21.4	13.5	17.0	13.4	0.4	0.5	0.5	41.4	5.0	1.5
Unidentified manufactures	0.3	0.1	0.1	0.1	0.2	0.2	0.4	0.1	0.2	0.2	0.2	0.6
Agricultural And Livestock Products	...	...	0.6	...	0.6	0.5	1.4	0.2	0.1	0.1	0.1	0.1
Agricultural products	...	...	0.5	...	0.6	0.5	1.4	0.2	0.1	0.1	0.1	0.1
Livestock and livestock products	...	...	...	...	...	...	...	...	...	...	...	...
Other Commodities	0.6	0.6	1.1	0.6	1.2	1.3	0.3	0.1	0.1	0.1	0.1	0.4
Forestry products	...	...	...	...	...	...	...	...	...	...	...	...
Fish and other marine products	...	...	...	...	...	...	...	...	...	...	...	...
Metallic ores and concentrates	...	...	...	...	...	...	...	...	...	...	...	...
Bituminous coal and lignite	...	...	...	...	...	...	...	...	...	...	...	...
Crude petroleum and natural gas	...	...	0.4	...	...	...	...	...	...	...	...	...
Nonmetallic minerals	0.6	0.5	0.6	0.5	0.6	0.9	0.2	...	0.1	...	...	0.1
Scrap and waste	...	...	...	...	...	...	...	...	...	...	...	...
Used merchandise	...	0.1	...	...	0.4	...	0.1	...	0.1	...	...	0.2
Goods imported and returned unchanged	...	...	...	...	...	...	...	...	...	...	...	...
Special classification provisions	...	...	0.1	0.1	0.1	0.3	...	...	...	...	...	0.2

Industry	European Union						United Kingdom					
	1994	1995	1996	1997	1998	1999	1994	1995	1996	1997	1998	1999
ALL GOODS	97.3	103.6	114.2	181.5	174.9	190.8	45.2	28.1	32.6	64.5	49.1	53.0
Manufactured Goods	91.6	94.5	105.7	153.3	166.1	181.4	44.1	25.5	30.2	43.3	47.9	50.5
Food products	0.1	0.1	1.1	0.8	2.5	2.1	...	...	...	...	...	...
Tobacco products	...	...	...	...	...	...	...	...	...	...	...	...
Textile mill products	0.1	0.3	0.2	0.1	...	0.1	...	0.1	0.1	...	...	...
Apparel	0.5	0.6	2.0	3.4	3.2	2.7	0.1	0.2	0.2	0.9	0.8	0.7
Lumber and wood products	...	0.1	0.1	0.1	0.1	0.5	...	...	...	...	...	...
Furniture and fixtures	0.2	0.2	0.2	0.5	0.5	1.0	...	...	0.1	0.1	0.1	0.2
Paper products	0.2	0.1	0.2	0.1	0.1	0.8	0.1	0.1	0.1	...	...	0.8
Printing and publishing	0.3	0.5	0.8	1.0	0.7	1.2	0.1	0.1	0.6	0.6	0.5	0.3
Chemical products	0.5	0.8	1.4	2.5	2.3	3.5	...	0.2	0.3	0.3	0.9	1.6
Refined petroleum products	...	...	...	...	...	...	...	...	...	...	...	...
Rubber and plastic products	1.4	1.2	1.3	1.4	1.1	2.1	0.4	0.5	0.8	0.4	0.5	0.3
Leather products	0.1	0.2	0.1	0.5	0.2	0.3	...	...	...	0.1	...	0.2
Stone, clay and glass products	0.8	0.9	0.9	0.9	0.9	1.0	0.2	...	...	0.2	0.3	0.2
Primary metals	21.3	2.4	3.0	15.9	21.0	17.0	20.2	0.8	1.0	10.3	15.7	12.9
Fabricated metal products	1.7	1.6	3.0	3.4	4.8	3.7	0.1	0.4	1.7	1.4	2.2	0.8
Industrial machinery and computers	13.8	15.1	19.4	20.7	21.6	13.2	4.3	5.7	5.9	6.9	5.3	4.6
Electric and electronic equipment	9.5	10.9	11.2	14.0	14.9	24.1	3.4	3.1	2.7	3.4	4.0	8.4
Transportation equipment	5.0	5.5	10.0	23.4	18.7	26.2	3.3	2.5	3.1	4.4	2.5	4.4
Scientific and measuring instruments	18.0	35.2	23.1	30.1	34.4	33.4	9.3	10.1	11.3	11.0	10.9	10.6
Miscellaneous manufactures	17.6	18.0	26.9	33.4	38.1	47.3	2.5	1.5	2.2	2.0	3.7	4.3
Unidentified manufactures	0.5	0.7	0.6	1.3	0.8	1.0	0.1	0.3	0.1	1.1	0.4	0.2
Agricultural And Livestock Products	...	0.2	0.1	...	...	0.2	...	...	0.1	...	...	...
Agricultural products	...	0.2	...	...	...	0.2	...	...	...	...	...	...
Livestock and livestock products	...	...	0.1	...	...	...	...	...	0.1	...	...	...
Other Commodities	5.7	8.8	8.4	28.2	8.9	9.3	1.1	2.5	2.3	21.2	1.2	2.6
Forestry products	...	...	...	...	...	...	...	...	...	...	...	...
Fish and other marine products	...	...	...	...	...	...	...	...	...	...	...	...
Metallic ores and concentrates	...	...	...	...	...	...	...	...	...	...	...	...
Bituminous coal and lignite	...	...	...	...	...	...	...	...	...	...	...	...
Crude petroleum and natural gas	...	...	...	...	...	...	...	...	...	...	...	...
Nonmetallic minerals	5.4	6.7	6.4	6.8	7.2	6.3	1.0	1.2	0.9	0.8	0.8	1.0
Scrap and waste	...	...	...	...	0.1	0.8	...	...	...	...	...	0.7
Used merchandise	0.2	2.1	1.7	20.6	0.6	1.0	0.1	1.3	1.3	20.3	0.4	0.7
Goods imported and returned unchanged	...	...	...	...	...	...	...	...	...	...	...	...
Special classification provisions	0.1	0.1	0.3	0.7	1.0	1.2	...	...	0.2	0.1	...	0.2

Table D-31. NEVADA: State Exports of Goods by Destination and Industry, 1994–1999—*Continued*

(Millions of dollars.)

Industry	Germany						France					
	1994	1995	1996	1997	1998	1999	1994	1995	1996	1997	1998	1999
ALL GOODS	12.6	19.7	22.1	20.2	29.1	34.5	14.7	12.1	18.0	24.1	23.3	30.2
Manufactured Goods	11.0	16.0	19.7	18.2	27.2	32.4	12.5	9.9	15.7	23.8	22.2	29.6
Food products	0.1	...	0.4	0.2	...	0.5	...	...	...	...	...	...
Tobacco products	...	...	...	...	...	...	...	...	...	...	...	...
Textile mill products	...	...	...	...	...	...	...	...	...	...	...	...
Apparel	0.2	0.1	0.2	0.1	0.1	0.1	0.1	0.1	0.3	0.1	0.1	0.1
Lumber and wood products	...	...	...	...	...	...	...	...	...	...	...	...
Furniture and fixtures	0.1	...	...	...	0.2	0.2	0.1	0.1	...	0.2	0.1	0.5
Paper products	...	...	0.1	...	...	...	...	...	...	...	...	...
Printing and publishing	0.1	0.3	0.1	0.2	0.1	0.1	...	...	...	...	...	0.1
Chemical products	...	...	0.1	0.1	0.1	0.2	0.3	0.4	0.4	0.4	0.9	1.0
Refined petroleum products	...	...	...	...	...	...	...	...	...	...	...	...
Rubber and plastic products	...	0.1	0.2	0.3	0.2	0.3	...	...	0.1	0.1	0.1	...
Leather products	...	...	...	...	...	...	...	...	...	...	...	...
Stone, clay and glass products	0.2	0.2	0.3	0.5	0.2	0.1	0.2	0.1	0.1	0.1	0.1	0.1
Primary metals	0.1	0.2	0.4	1.4	1.6	2.8	0.3	0.4	0.7	0.4	0.2	0.2
Fabricated metal products	0.2	0.2	0.6	0.6	1.5	1.8	0.4	0.2	0.1	0.2	0.2	0.2
Industrial machinery and computers	1.9	4.6	1.6	1.9	6.7	1.9	4.0	1.0	2.9	1.5	3.5	2.0
Electric and electronic equipment	1.1	2.0	2.3	1.6	2.2	4.7	0.8	0.8	1.3	0.9	1.3	1.3
Transportation equipment	0.9	0.7	0.7	1.2	2.2	6.3	0.5	1.6	5.6	7.9	7.6	11.7
Scientific and measuring instruments	3.0	4.4	4.1	5.2	6.4	6.4	1.0	1.3	1.5	3.5	3.1	3.6
Miscellaneous manufactures	2.8	3.0	8.4	4.8	5.6	7.0	4.8	3.8	2.7	8.5	4.9	8.8
Unidentified manufactures	0.1	0.1	0.1	0.1	0.1	0.1	0.1	0.1	0.1	...	0.1	0.1
Agricultural And Livestock Products	...	...	...	...	...	0.2	...	...	...	...	...	...
Agricultural products	...	...	...	...	...	0.2	...	...	...	...	...	...
Livestock and livestock products	...	...	...	...	...	...	...	...	...	...	...	...
Other Commodities	1.6	3.7	2.5	2.0	1.9	2.0	2.2	2.2	2.3	0.3	1.1	0.6
Forestry products	...	...	...	...	...	...	...	...	...	...	...	...
Fish and other marine products	...	...	...	...	...	...	...	...	...	...	...	...
Metallic ores and concentrates	...	...	...	...	...	...	...	...	...	...	...	...
Bituminous coal and lignite	...	...	...	...	...	...	...	...	...	...	...	...
Crude petroleum and natural gas	...	...	...	...	...	...	...	...	...	...	...	...
Nonmetallic minerals	1.5	2.9	2.3	1.8	1.5	1.8	2.2	2.2	2.3	0.1	0.5	0.5
Scrap and waste	...	...	...	...	...	...	...	...	...	...	...	...
Used merchandise	0.1	0.8	0.1	...	...	...	...	...	...	...	0.1	...
Goods imported and returned unchanged	...	...	...	...	...	...	...	...	...	...	...	...
Special classification provisions	...	...	0.1	0.1	0.3	0.2	...	...	0.1	0.2	0.5	0.1

Industry	The Netherlands						Asian 10					
	1994	1995	1996	1997	1998	1999	1994	1995	1996	1997	1998	1999
ALL GOODS	10.3	9.1	13.4	17.2	17.4	17.8	109.7	269.3	176.6	197.0	135.0	153.1
Manufactured Goods	10.3	9.0	13.1	16.6	17.3	17.4	99.9	251.8	156.6	182.8	127.4	145.8
Food products	...	...	...	0.2	0.1	0.1	0.9	6.4	8.9	1.9	2.1	4.2
Tobacco products	...	...	...	...	...	...	...	...	...	...	...	...
Textile mill products	0.1	0.1	0.1	...	...	...	0.5	0.5	0.5	0.7	0.6	0.8
Apparel	...	...	...	...	...	...	1.7	8.4	7.5	6.7	4.6	4.6
Lumber and wood products	...	...	...	...	...	0.5	0.1	...	0.3	0.5	1.5	0.3
Furniture and fixtures	...	...	...	...	...	0.1	0.1	0.7	1.3	0.1	0.2	0.1
Paper products	0.1	...	...	...	...	...	0.5	0.3	0.7	0.9	0.5	0.2
Printing and publishing	0.1	...	0.1	...	0.1	0.6	1.1	1.9	1.0	1.5	2.4	0.9
Chemical products	0.1	0.1	0.1	0.1	...	0.1	2.7	12.2	11.3	2.6	8.1	4.8
Refined petroleum products	...	...	...	...	...	...	0.1	0.1	0.1	0.2	...	...
Rubber and plastic products	0.8	0.1	0.1	0.1	0.1	0.1	2.5	3.3	5.3	13.5	4.7	2.9
Leather products	...	...	...	0.1	0.1	...	0.4	2.5	3.7	1.7	2.8	4.6
Stone, clay and glass products	0.1	0.3	0.3	...	0.1	...	1.6	0.9	1.7	2.5	1.0	1.2
Primary metals	...	0.1	0.1	...	0.1	0.1	4.1	9.3	5.1	7.2	5.9	4.6
Fabricated metal products	0.7	0.2	0.3	0.1	0.1	0.1	16.1	51.8	4.2	11.5	4.5	7.0
Industrial machinery and computers	1.8	0.4	0.3	1.3	1.1	0.8	22.3	70.2	31.1	46.3	19.7	34.8
Electric and electronic equipment	0.6	1.3	1.2	2.3	1.6	2.8	10.5	30.5	21.3	28.2	13.2	23.9
Transportation equipment	0.2	0.3	0.3	0.8	1.2	1.2	3.1	3.8	5.7	9.1	4.5	4.8
Scientific and measuring instruments	1.4	1.7	1.7	3.2	3.2	2.4	14.5	19.8	21.7	27.9	27.4	28.7
Miscellaneous manufactures	4.4	4.3	8.5	8.2	9.7	8.4	16.8	28.8	24.7	19.6	22.9	15.8
Unidentified manufactures	0.1	...	...	...	...	0.1	0.3	0.4	0.6	0.4	0.7	1.5
Agricultural And Livestock Products	...	0.1	...	...	...	...	1.8	1.4	0.8	1.0	0.2	0.3
Agricultural products	...	0.1	...	...	...	...	1.4	0.5	0.8	0.3	0.1	0.3
Livestock and livestock products	...	...	...	...	...	...	0.4	0.9	...	0.7	...	...
Other Commodities	...	...	0.3	0.5	0.1	0.4	8.0	16.1	19.2	13.1	7.4	7.1
Forestry products	...	...	...	...	...	...	0.1	0.1	...	0.1	...	...
Fish and other marine products	...	...	...	...	...	...	0.1	...	0.4	...	...	0.5
Metallic ores and concentrates	...	...	...	...	...	...	...	...	...	...	...	...
Bituminous coal and lignite	...	...	...	...	...	...	...	...	...	...	...	...
Crude petroleum and natural gas	...	...	...	...	...	...	...	...	...	...	...	...
Nonmetallic minerals	...	...	...	0.1	...	0.1	2.6	2.9	3.5	3.7	3.3	3.1
Scrap and waste	...	...	...	...	...	...	0.3	0.8	0.7	0.4	1.0	1.0
Used merchandise	...	...	0.3	0.3	...	...	4.8	11.9	14.5	8.4	2.4	1.0
Goods imported and returned unchanged	...	...	...	...	...	...	...	...	...	...	...	...
Special classification provisions	...	...	...	0.1	...	0.3	...	0.4	0.2	0.6	0.8	1.4

Table D-31. NEVADA: State Exports of Goods by Destination and Industry, 1994–1999—*Continued*

(Millions of dollars.)

Industry	Japan						South Korea					
	1994	1995	1996	1997	1998	1999	1994	1995	1996	1997	1998	1999
ALL GOODS	34.6	82.6	77.7	82.9	63.8	60.6	11.0	13.3	24.7	21.8	10.9	28.3
Manufactured Goods	28.4	69.8	62.4	72.8	60.2	57.8	10.3	12.0	24.3	21.4	10.0	27.8
Food products	0.7	0.2	0.6	0.2	0.6	0.9	0.1	0.3	0.8	...	0.1	0.2
Tobacco products	...	...	...	...	...	...	...	...	...	...	...	...
Textile mill products	0.1	0.4	0.3	0.4	0.5	0.5	...	...	...	0.1	...	...
Apparel	1.5	7.6	7.1	5.9	4.3	4.3	...	0.1	0.2	0.3	0.1	0.1
Lumber and wood products	...	...	0.2	0.4	0.1	0.2	...	...	0.1	...	1.4	...
Furniture and fixtures	0.1	0.6	0.2	...	...	0.1	...	...	...	...	0.1	...
Paper products	0.3	0.1	0.2	0.1	0.1	...	...	0.1	0.1	0.7	0.1	...
Printing and publishing	0.7	1.5	0.6	0.4	1.2	0.6	0.1	...	...	...	...	...
Chemical products	0.3	8.3	5.7	0.9	0.5	1.0	0.5	0.3	0.4	0.4	0.3	2.0
Refined petroleum products	...	...	...	...	...	...	...	...	...	...	...	...
Rubber and plastic products	0.9	0.8	0.2	1.3	0.5	1.1	0.2	0.2	0.2	0.2	0.1	...
Leather products	0.3	2.3	3.4	1.5	2.7	4.4	...	0.1	0.1	...	...	...
Stone, clay and glass products	0.7	0.6	1.0	1.9	0.6	0.8	0.1	...	0.1	0.3	0.1	0.1
Primary metals	0.2	1.0	1.7	1.1	0.7	0.4	0.2	0.3	0.9	3.0	0.8	0.9
Fabricated metal products	0.7	0.8	0.8	3.3	2.6	5.3	0.2	0.3	0.2	0.8	0.2	0.2
Industrial machinery and computers	4.7	5.9	8.9	20.1	12.9	9.4	3.7	3.1	8.8	4.8	2.2	17.0
Electric and electronic equipment	2.5	5.3	5.5	4.5	3.1	4.2	0.2	1.3	6.3	5.0	1.3	1.3
Transportation equipment	2.2	3.1	3.6	8.0	3.1	4.0	0.1	...	0.6	0.1	0.2	0.4
Scientific and measuring instruments	4.0	7.6	5.4	8.9	11.6	11.7	2.7	4.2	3.7	5.0	1.7	4.2
Miscellaneous manufactures	8.5	23.4	16.8	13.7	14.5	8.2	2.1	1.5	1.7	0.6	1.3	1.1
Unidentified manufactures	0.1	0.2	0.2	0.2	0.2	0.5	...	0.1	0.1	0.1	0.1	0.2
Agricultural And Livestock Products	1.3	0.3	...	0.7	0.1	0.1	0.4	0.9	0.3	0.3	...	...
Agricultural products	1.3	0.3	...	0.3	0.1	0.1	...	0.1	0.3	...	...	...
Livestock and livestock products	...	...	...	0.4	...	...	0.4	0.9	...	0.3	...	...
Other Commodities	4.9	12.6	15.2	9.4	3.5	2.6	0.3	0.3	0.2	0.1	0.9	0.5
Forestry products	...	...	...	...	...	...	0.1	0.1	...	...	...	...
Fish and other marine products	0.1	...	0.1	...	...	0.4	...	...	...	...	...	...
Metallic ores and concentrates	...	...	...	...	...	...	...	...	...	...	...	...
Bituminous coal and lignite	...	...	...	...	...	...	...	...	...	...	...	...
Crude petroleum and natural gas	...	...	...	...	...	...	...	...	...	...	...	...
Nonmetallic minerals	1.0	1.1	1.3	1.4	1.3	1.2	0.3	0.2	0.1	...	0.2	0.2
Scrap and waste	...	0.2	...	...	...	...	...	...	...	...	0.1	...
Used merchandise	3.7	10.9	13.7	7.5	2.1	0.9	...	...	...	...	...	...
Goods imported and returned unchanged	...	...	...	...	...	...	...	...	...	...	...	...
Special classification provisions	...	0.4	0.1	0.5	0.1	0.2	...	...	...	0.1	0.5	0.3

Industry	Taiwan						Singapore					
	1994	1995	1996	1997	1998	1999	1994	1995	1996	1997	1998	1999
ALL GOODS	7.6	8.5	13.6	10.6	14.9	13.1	5.9	7.0	7.5	10.6	10.6	8.2
Manufactured Goods	7.0	8.0	12.5	9.8	13.8	11.7	5.6	6.6	7.1	10.0	10.5	7.9
Food products	...	0.7	2.7	...	0.6	0.6	...	1.8	...	...	0.1	0.1
Tobacco products	...	...	...	...	...	...	...	...	...	...	...	...
Textile mill products	...	...	...	...	0.1	0.1	...	...	0.1	0.3	...	...
Apparel	...	...	...	...	...	...	...	...	...	...	...	...
Lumber and wood products	...	...	...	...	...	...	...	...	...	...	...	...
Furniture and fixtures	...	...	...	...	...	...	0.1	...	0.1	...	...	...
Paper products	...	...	...	...	...	...	...	0.1	...	0.7	0.9	0.1
Printing and publishing	...	...	0.1	...	...	...	0.2	0.5	0.3	0.2	0.2	0.1
Chemical products	0.9	0.4	0.3	0.1	0.7	0.2	...	...	...	...	...	...
Refined petroleum products	...	...	...	...	...	...	...	...	...	...	...	...
Rubber and plastic products	...	...	0.1	...	1.5	0.1	0.1	0.1	0.2	...	...	0.1
Leather products	...	...	...	...	...	0.1	...	0.1	...	0.1	...	...
Stone, clay and glass products	...	0.2	0.1	...	...	...	...	...	...	0.1	0.2	0.2
Primary metals	1.1	1.0	1.0	1.6	2.0	1.2	0.4	0.1	0.5	0.4	0.8	0.2
Fabricated metal products	0.4	0.6	0.3	0.2	0.2	0.2	0.6	0.3	0.6	0.4	0.6	0.4
Industrial machinery and computers	1.4	1.7	4.6	1.1	0.9	2.0	1.3	0.8	1.6	2.1	1.2	2.0
Electric and electronic equipment	0.7	0.6	0.3	0.9	1.0	2.3	0.9	0.7	0.6	1.9	1.5	1.5
Transportation equipment	0.1	...	0.1	0.1	0.1	...	0.2	0.3	0.3	0.2	0.4	...
Scientific and measuring instruments	1.0	1.6	2.1	5.0	4.8	3.8	0.7	1.1	1.2	1.7	1.0	2.1
Miscellaneous manufactures	1.3	1.0	0.5	0.6	1.7	0.9	0.9	0.7	1.5	1.8	3.5	0.8
Unidentified manufactures	...	...	...	...	...	0.2	0.1	...	0.1	...	...	0.1
Agricultural And Livestock Products	...	...	0.1	...	...	0.1	...	...	...	...	...	...
Agricultural products	...	...	0.1	...	...	0.1	...	...	...	...	...	...
Livestock and livestock products	...	...	...	...	...	...	...	...	...	...	...	...
Other Commodities	0.6	0.5	1.0	0.7	1.1	1.3	0.3	0.5	0.4	0.6	0.1	0.3
Forestry products	...	...	...	...	...	...	...	...	...	...	...	...
Fish and other marine products	...	...	0.3	...	...	...	...	...	...	...	...	...
Metallic ores and concentrates	...	...	...	...	...	...	...	...	...	...	...	...
Bituminous coal and lignite	...	...	...	...	...	...	...	...	...	...	...	...
Crude petroleum and natural gas	...	...	...	...	...	...	...	...	...	...	...	...
Nonmetallic minerals	0.4	0.4	0.7	0.4	0.4	0.4	0.1	0.1	0.1	...	0.1	0.1
Scrap and waste	0.1	...	...	0.2	0.6	0.7	...	...	0.1	0.1	...	...
Used merchandise	...	...	0.1	0.1	0.1	...	0.1	0.3	0.3	0.4	...	...
Goods imported and returned unchanged	...	...	...	...	...	...	...	...	...	...	...	...
Special classification provisions	...	...	...	...	...	0.2	...	...	...	...	...	0.2

NEW HAMPSHIRE: Exports of Goods, 1999

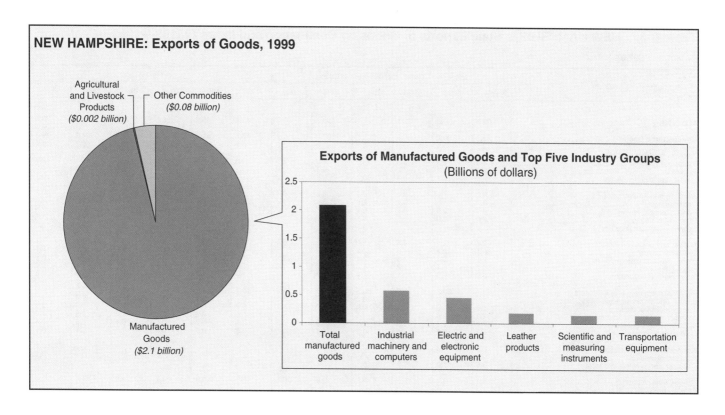

Agricultural and Livestock Products ($0.002 billion)

Other Commodities ($0.08 billion)

Manufactured Goods ($2.1 billion)

Exports of Manufactured Goods and Top Five Industry Groups
(Billions of dollars)

Total manufactured goods · Industrial machinery and computers · Electric and electronic equipment · Leather products · Scientific and measuring instruments · Transportation equipment

Table D-32. NEW HAMPSHIRE: State Exports of Goods by Destination and Industry, 1994–1999

(Millions of dollars.)

Industry	All destinations						Canada					
	1994	1995	1996	1997	1998	1999	1994	1995	1996	1997	1998	1999
ALL GOODS	1 247.9	1 478.6	1 744.9	1 931.0	1 986.5	2 159.1	422.4	494.4	642.4	672.2	643.4	726.3
Manufactured Goods	1 198.3	1 419.7	1 674.4	1 859.3	1 925.2	2 077.6	399.4	465.8	609.1	639.9	611.5	686.6
Food products	5.9	7.9	18.5	33.9	10.8	12.4	3.6	4.5	3.5	15.2	7.3	7.6
Tobacco products	0.1	. . .	. . .	. . .	. . .	. . .	0.1	. . .	. . .	. . .	. . .	. . .
Textile mill products	20.7	26.3	28.1	29.4	29.9	35.4	8.2	9.5	9.2	11.8	11.7	14.7
Apparel	16.8	15.3	12.8	13.8	11.5	13.9	2.0	2.3	2.4	3.4	3.0	2.9
Lumber and wood products	43.5	49.2	45.5	64.6	60.7	66.1	21.3	24.3	26.3	32.1	34.5	39.8
Furniture and fixtures	2.2	6.4	3.3	5.2	4.2	2.8	1.3	5.0	1.3	2.9	2.6	1.5
Paper products	27.5	40.2	28.3	38.2	39.2	38.4	19.5	29.8	22.6	25.1	27.3	25.1
Printing and publishing	7.2	10.3	11.9	16.1	12.3	17.2	1.9	2.8	4.7	8.3	5.0	4.8
Chemical products	86.8	60.4	49.1	89.5	83.9	74.4	30.1	22.0	13.4	48.5	43.1	37.9
Refined petroleum products	4.6	2.1	2.0	3.2	2.3	3.5	3.9	1.1	1.3	1.5	1.3	1.6
Rubber and plastic products	45.7	57.0	63.6	65.4	65.8	87.3	19.6	26.0	29.7	34.7	28.8	41.5
Leather products	64.4	69.5	145.0	143.6	162.5	185.9	5.5	6.5	8.1	10.6	8.9	4.8
Stone, clay and glass products	31.2	34.2	45.6	50.0	44.6	38.3	3.6	3.6	4.0	4.7	4.9	5.5
Primary metals	22.6	22.7	31.0	24.6	29.6	43.0	12.6	11.2	10.4	9.9	12.2	18.3
Fabricated metal products	43.0	50.0	60.8	72.3	72.5	83.3	13.3	14.3	16.2	20.9	22.1	32.0
Industrial machinery and computers	424.5	493.0	550.0	583.5	632.0	575.3	119.8	88.0	144.7	116.5	129.3	110.8
Electric and electronic equipment	160.7	232.3	265.2	332.7	369.9	454.2	53.3	87.3	139.2	136.9	134.4	170.4
Transportation equipment	70.7	110.1	156.5	142.1	118.2	149.0	56.2	98.6	143.2	126.7	100.6	124.6
Scientific and measuring instruments	93.9	100.1	131.6	117.7	117.6	150.9	15.4	18.8	19.6	20.1	20.0	25.4
Miscellaneous manufactures	11.2	17.4	13.4	14.2	20.1	19.0	4.8	6.3	5.6	5.6	9.5	12.2
Unidentified manufactures	15.1	15.4	12.2	19.0	37.7	27.1	3.2	3.8	3.7	4.2	4.9	5.1
Agricultural And Livestock Products	16.8	19.8	21.3	23.0	8.9	2.2	1.2	1.8	2.8	2.7	2.6	1.3
Agricultural products	0.5	1.2	1.7	1.0	1.4	1.5	0.5	0.8	1.2	0.9	0.6	0.7
Livestock and livestock products	16.3	18.6	19.6	22.0	7.5	0.8	0.7	1.0	1.6	1.8	2.0	0.6
Other Commodities	32.9	39.1	49.2	48.7	52.5	79.2	21.8	26.8	30.6	29.7	29.3	38.5
Forestry products	. . .	. . .	0.1	0.1	0.1	0.1	. . .	. . .	. . .	. . .	. . .	. . .
Fish and other marine products	12.9	16.4	19.1	17.9	22.9	32.5	4.8	8.1	4.0	4.7	6.8	14.7
Metallic ores and concentrates	. . .	. . .	0.1	0.2	. . .	. . .	. . .	. . .	. . .	. . .	. . .	. . .
Bituminous coal and lignite	. . .	. . .	. . .	. . .	0.7	. . .	. . .	. . .	. . .	. . .	0.7	. . .
Crude petroleum and natural gas	. . .	0.1	. . .	. . .	. . .	. . .	. . .	0.1	. . .	. . .	. . .	. . .
Nonmetallic minerals	0.8	1.0	0.9	1.7	3.8	3.9	0.4	0.3	0.1	0.4	2.2	2.5
Scrap and waste	8.2	6.5	4.0	4.7	5.2	4.8	6.5	6.1	3.7	4.7	5.1	4.3
Used merchandise	0.6	1.4	1.4	4.4	1.0	1.0	0.3	0.8	0.9	2.0	0.2	0.6
Goods imported and returned unchanged	9.0	9.7	19.5	16.8	12.9	10.2	9.0	9.7	19.5	16.8	12.9	10.2
Special classification provisions	1.3	4.0	4.2	2.9	5.9	26.7	0.8	1.7	2.3	1.1	1.4	6.2

Table D-32. NEW HAMPSHIRE: State Exports of Goods by Destination and Industry, 1994–1999—*Continued*

(Millions of dollars.)

Industry	South and Central American and Caribbean						Mexico					
	1994	1995	1996	1997	1998	1999	1994	1995	1996	1997	1998	1999
ALL GOODS	92.3	97.3	92.7	117.1	109.7	102.5	43.4	45.2	63.6	73.8	86.1	78.3
Manufactured Goods	85.7	90.2	86.3	108.3	107.0	101.9	42.4	44.3	61.9	72.1	84.2	76.8
Food products	0.6	0.4	0.3	2.6	1.2	1.8	0.1	...	9.7	5.7	0.2	1.2
Tobacco products	...	...	...	...	...	...	...	...	...	...	...	...
Textile mill products	5.9	3.3	3.5	3.6	2.9	2.0	0.8	1.5	3.2	3.6	4.0	2.9
Apparel	2.7	3.4	2.2	1.9	0.7	2.8	3.5	3.6	3.8	3.6	4.8	4.0
Lumber and wood products	...	0.1	0.3	0.7	0.8	0.3	...	...	...	0.1	0.1	0.1
Furniture and fixtures	0.2	...	0.3	0.1	0.2	0.1	...	...	0.1	...	...	0.1
Paper products	2.7	1.8	0.7	2.0	1.4	1.2	0.8	2.1	1.5	1.8	2.3	1.6
Printing and publishing	0.1	0.9	0.2	0.4	0.6	0.2	0.3	0.5	0.6	0.6	0.6	0.6
Chemical products	2.0	2.0	3.7	4.1	2.7	1.7	6.5	6.3	4.9	5.9	7.2	5.7
Refined petroleum products	...	...	...	0.1	...	0.1	0.3	0.6	0.2	0.3	0.5	0.9
Rubber and plastic products	2.3	2.1	2.8	5.0	4.8	5.1	1.4	1.7	2.6	3.4	4.6	3.2
Leather products	30.1	20.9	21.8	27.7	31.9	27.5	0.1	0.2	2.0	2.9	2.3	2.1
Stone, clay and glass products	2.2	2.6	2.6	2.4	3.2	2.1	3.5	2.4	5.3	8.2	7.0	5.9
Primary metals	0.2	0.4	2.2	1.6	2.7	1.8	1.3	0.7	0.8	1.0	1.0	2.6
Fabricated metal products	0.9	1.0	0.5	1.9	1.7	1.9	1.7	1.7	1.1	2.1	2.5	1.5
Industrial machinery and computers	23.1	38.2	26.5	30.5	21.5	16.9	14.2	12.3	14.2	16.9	33.2	24.0
Electric and electronic equipment	8.0	7.0	14.5	18.3	23.6	28.5	6.2	8.1	7.7	12.2	7.9	14.7
Transportation equipment	0.3	0.3	0.5	0.9	0.9	1.1	0.2	0.1	0.3	0.3	0.5	0.3
Scientific and measuring instruments	2.9	2.8	2.3	3.1	4.3	5.6	1.0	2.2	3.0	2.8	4.5	4.4
Miscellaneous manufactures	1.2	2.7	1.3	1.0	0.9	0.6	0.1	0.2	0.6	0.4	0.6	0.4
Unidentified manufactures	0.3	0.2	0.1	0.3	1.1	0.6	0.3	0.1	0.4	0.3	0.4	0.6
Agricultural And Livestock Products	6.5	7.0	6.3	8.1	2.3	...	...	...	...	...	0.5	0.2
Agricultural products	...	...	...	...	...	...	...	...	...	...	0.5	0.1
Livestock and livestock products	6.5	7.0	6.3	8.1	2.3	...	...	...	...	...	...	0.1
Other Commodities	0.1	0.1	0.1	0.8	0.4	0.6	0.9	0.9	1.7	1.6	1.4	1.4
Forestry products	...	...	...	...	...	...	...	...	...	...	...	...
Fish and other marine products	...	...	...	...	...	...	0.5	0.2	0.5	0.3	...	...
Metallic ores and concentrates	...	...	...	...	...	...	...	...	...	...	...	...
Bituminous coal and lignite	...	...	...	...	...	...	...	...	...	...	...	...
Crude petroleum and natural gas	...	...	...	...	...	...	...	...	...	...	...	...
Nonmetallic materials	...	...	...	...	...	...	0.4	0.6	0.6	1.2	1.4	1.0
Scrap and waste	...	...	...	...	...	...	...	...	...	...	...	...
Used merchandise	...	0.1	0.1	0.4	0.2	0.1	...	...	...	0.1	...	...
Goods imported and returned unchanged	...	...	...	...	...	...	...	...	0.5	...	...	...
Special classification provisions	0.1	...	0.1	0.4	0.2	0.5	...	...	0.5	0.1	...	0.3

Industry	European Union						United Kingdom					
	1994	1995	1996	1997	1998	1999	1994	1995	1996	1997	1998	1999
ALL GOODS	349.8	459.5	500.3	580.1	652.6	695.2	95.7	104.7	102.7	132.5	147.0	168.6
Manufactured Goods	339.7	448.1	485.3	562.9	634.5	667.7	94.0	102.9	100.6	129.4	144.0	164.3
Food products	0.2	0.5	0.8	0.8	0.6	0.6	0.1	0.1	0.4	0.1	0.1	0.2
Tobacco products	...	...	...	...	...	...	...	...	...	...	...	...
Textile mill products	4.2	6.4	6.3	5.5	4.9	5.8	1.2	2.3	2.4	1.6	2.0	2.7
Apparel	5.5	3.9	2.8	2.6	1.7	2.8	0.6	0.7	0.2	0.3	0.1	0.1
Lumber and wood products	11.5	10.6	7.6	15.4	14.4	14.1	6.0	5.1	4.1	9.6	5.8	7.4
Furniture and fixtures	0.4	0.7	0.7	1.8	1.0	0.3	0.1	0.1	0.2	0.4	0.2	0.3
Paper products	3.1	4.8	2.3	7.6	6.0	7.3	1.2	2.8	0.6	4.3	3.5	4.2
Printing and publishing	1.5	2.2	2.9	2.2	1.2	3.8	0.4	0.9	1.1	0.6	0.6	0.6
Chemical products	10.2	12.3	12.2	14.4	15.2	14.3	1.7	2.2	2.4	3.7	3.1	4.1
Refined petroleum products	0.1	0.1	...	0.2	0.1	0.2	...	...	...	...	...	0.2
Rubber and plastic products	10.8	11.1	12.6	11.0	15.1	20.2	2.9	5.1	5.4	3.6	3.9	6.3
Leather products	18.4	18.0	35.0	27.3	21.6	30.5	2.4	5.1	10.8	7.4	4.4	10.0
Stone, clay and glass products	10.0	12.8	18.2	18.5	14.5	13.9	1.3	2.4	4.8	3.8	2.7	1.8
Primary metals	5.6	5.1	6.7	7.5	8.2	14.6	1.8	1.9	3.1	3.4	2.5	2.1
Fabricated metal products	15.4	17.9	28.5	26.7	31.7	37.4	3.4	3.2	5.1	4.9	6.4	8.2
Industrial machinery and computers	150.7	219.8	234.6	282.8	315.1	301.2	48.4	42.0	34.2	42.5	55.6	61.6
Electric and electronic equipment	39.2	56.4	57.9	78.9	105.0	109.3	11.2	12.9	16.8	27.3	35.4	32.8
Transportation equipment	7.0	8.6	8.7	8.6	9.3	13.4	1.1	3.0	1.4	1.5	2.5	3.7
Scientific and measuring instruments	36.6	43.6	39.6	44.3	43.8	59.8	8.3	11.6	6.8	13.2	12.3	15.1
Miscellaneous manufactures	3.0	6.7	2.8	2.8	4.9	3.7	0.6	0.3	0.2	0.2	0.9	1.2
Unidentified manufactures	6.3	6.6	5.2	4.2	20.1	14.4	1.2	1.2	0.6	0.9	1.8	1.8
Agricultural And Livestock Products	2.9	2.7	2.7	3.4	0.7	0.1	...	...	...	...	...	...
Agricultural products	...	0.1	...	...	0.1	0.1	...	...	...	...	...	...
Livestock and livestock products	2.9	2.7	2.7	3.4	0.7	...	...	...	...	...	...	...
Other Commodities	7.2	8.7	12.2	13.8	17.3	27.4	1.7	1.8	2.1	3.1	3.0	4.3
Forestry products	...	...	...	...	...	...	...	...	...	...	...	...
Fish and other marine products	5.2	6.4	11.0	11.7	13.9	12.6	0.2	0.5	1.5	2.3	1.9	1.2
Metallic ores and concentrates	...	...	0.1	...	...	...	...	...	...	...	...	...
Bituminous coal and lignite	...	...	...	...	...	...	...	...	...	...	...	...
Crude petroleum and natural gas	...	...	...	...	...	...	...	...	...	...	...	...
Nonmetallic materials	...	0.2	...	0.1	...	0.4	...	...	...	...	...	0.2
Scrap and waste	1.7	0.3	0.2	...	...	0.3	1.2	...	...	...	...	0.2
Used merchandise	0.2	0.3	0.3	1.2	0.3	0.3	0.2	0.1	0.3	0.3	0.1	0.3
Goods imported and returned unchanged	...	...	...	...	3.0	13.8	0.1	1.2	0.4	0.4	0.9	...
Special classification provisions	0.1	1.5	0.7	0.7	3.0	13.8	0.1	1.2	0.4	0.4	0.9	2.6

Table D-32. NEW HAMPSHIRE: State Exports of Goods by Destination and Industry, 1994–1999—*Continued*

(Millions of dollars.)

Industry	Germany						France					
	1994	1995	1996	1997	1998	1999	1994	1995	1996	1997	1998	1999
ALL GOODS	60.4	95.3	93.5	144.9	135.5	118.0	36.9	38.1	48.3	50.0	45.1	44.0
Manufactured Goods	59.6	93.6	91.0	142.2	131.6	113.7	34.2	34.5	45.0	47.3	41.0	39.8
Food products	...	...	...	...	...	...	...	0.1	0.2	0.3	0.2	0.2
Tobacco products	...	...	...	...	...	...	...	...	...	...	...	...
Textile mill products	1.1	2.1	1.6	1.6	1.2	1.0	0.4	0.2	0.3	0.4	0.4	0.6
Apparel	0.4	0.4	...	0.4	0.2	0.2	0.6	0.2	...	...	...	...
Lumber and wood products	0.6	0.9	0.5	1.2	1.2	0.8	0.3	0.2	...	0.1	0.1	0.1
Furniture and fixtures	0.1	0.1	...	0.1	0.5	...	...	0.1	0.1	...	...	...
Paper products	0.2	0.4	0.2	1.0	0.8	1.2	0.3	0.5	0.4	0.3	0.2	0.4
Printing and publishing	0.4	0.2	0.2	0.1	0.1	0.3	0.1	0.1	0.1	...	0.1	...
Chemical products	3.2	2.6	1.0	2.0	2.6	2.1	0.5	1.1	0.5	1.2	1.4	0.6
Refined petroleum products	...	0.1	...	0.1	...	...	...	...	...	...	...	...
Rubber and plastic products	1.7	2.6	2.9	2.7	3.1	3.4	2.9	1.5	1.4	1.3	2.0	3.9
Leather products	3.3	1.6	3.5	0.4	0.2	0.3	6.0	3.0	3.6	3.0	2.4	1.8
Stone, clay and glass products	2.9	3.2	3.6	6.1	4.3	3.3	1.3	2.5	3.8	2.7	2.1	1.6
Primary metals	0.7	1.0	1.2	1.2	0.8	3.4	1.1	0.3	0.8	1.3	0.8	0.5
Fabricated metal products	1.1	1.4	2.4	1.9	3.2	8.7	0.7	1.0	1.4	1.0	0.9	1.4
Industrial machinery and computers	26.6	52.1	48.8	99.2	80.4	47.1	8.6	11.3	21.0	25.2	20.5	15.4
Electric and electronic equipment	5.5	7.3	8.9	8.7	16.3	17.2	3.7	5.4	5.1	5.0	3.7	6.6
Transportation equipment	1.7	2.4	2.1	2.5	2.3	2.8	0.5	0.5	0.3	0.7	1.2	2.3
Scientific and measuring instruments	8.7	9.2	12.5	11.3	11.8	20.3	6.5	5.9	5.6	4.1	4.1	3.6
Miscellaneous manufactures	1.0	5.3	1.0	1.0	2.0	0.8	0.4	0.3	0.3	0.5	0.6	0.4
Unidentified manufactures	0.5	0.8	0.6	0.4	0.7	0.9	0.4	0.4	0.3	0.3	0.3	0.3
Agricultural And Livestock Products	...	...	...	...	...	...	0.1	...	...	...	...	...
Agricultural products	...	...	...	...	...	...	...	...	...	...	...	...
Livestock and livestock products	...	...	...	...	...	...	0.1	...	...	...	...	...
Other Commodities	0.8	1.7	2.5	2.7	3.9	4.4	2.7	3.6	3.4	2.7	4.1	4.2
Forestry products	...	...	...	...	...	...	...	...	...	...	...	...
Fish and other marine products	0.8	1.5	2.4	1.9	2.3	1.2	2.6	3.6	3.3	2.5	4.1	2.6
Metallic ores and concentrates	...	...	...	...	...	...	...	...	...	...	...	...
Bituminous coal and lignite	...	...	...	...	...	...	...	...	...	...	...	...
Crude petroleum and natural gas	...	...	...	...	...	...	...	...	...	...	...	...
Nonmetallic materials	...	0.2	...	...	...	0.3	...	...	...	...	...	...
Scrap and waste	...	...	...	...	...	...	...	...	...	...	...	...
Used merchandise	...	...	...	0.7	...	...	...	...	...	...	...	...
Goods imported and returned unchanged	...	...	...	...	...	...	...	...	...	...	...	...
Special classification provisions	...	0.1	0.1	0.1	1.5	2.8	...	...	0.1	0.1	...	1.5

Industry	The Netherlands						Asian 10					
	1994	1995	1996	1997	1998	1999	1994	1995	1996	1997	1998	1999
ALL GOODS	46.2	50.2	58.4	62.5	65.8	85.4	242.8	289.3	344.9	360.2	374.4	417.7
Manufactured Goods	44.0	48.5	56.8	59.4	62.8	81.5	236.2	283.7	337.3	353.6	370.7	408.5
Food products	...	0.2	0.1	0.2	0.2	0.2	0.9	2.0	4.2	8.8	0.8	0.8
Tobacco products	...	...	...	...	...	...	...	...	...	...	...	...
Textile mill products	...	0.2	...	0.1	0.1	0.3	1.2	5.0	5.3	3.3	2.6	1.8
Apparel	2.8	1.6	2.3	1.7	1.3	2.2	1.5	1.4	1.2	2.1	0.9	1.0
Lumber and wood products	0.7	0.6	0.4	0.6	0.4	0.3	7.5	12.3	8.8	13.0	6.7	6.9
Furniture and fixtures	...	0.3	0.1	0.1	...	...	0.2	0.1	0.5	0.2	0.2	0.7
Paper products	1.1	0.8	0.5	0.8	0.3	0.5	0.4	1.3	0.6	1.5	1.6	2.3
Printing and publishing	0.5	0.5	0.8	0.4	0.2	2.4	3.1	3.6	3.2	4.0	3.7	5.2
Chemical products	3.0	3.1	4.6	4.1	3.9	5.0	28.5	13.5	11.4	12.7	12.4	12.8
Refined petroleum products	...	0.1	...	...	...	...	0.2	0.2	0.4	0.8	0.3	0.6
Rubber and plastic products	0.1	0.1	0.7	0.5	1.4	1.9	11.1	14.8	14.5	8.3	10.0	14.3
Leather products	0.5	0.1	2.3	5.3	2.8	7.9	3.6	18.8	72.5	68.4	90.8	109.1
Stone, clay and glass products	2.3	2.9	2.3	3.7	3.4	4.1	10.3	11.1	13.6	14.3	11.1	9.4
Primary metals	0.8	0.2	0.1	0.1	0.8	0.6	0.9	1.9	3.4	3.2	3.6	4.4
Fabricated metal products	3.5	9.9	14.3	13.2	14.5	13.3	8.6	10.6	10.3	14.2	8.1	6.3
Industrial machinery and computers	16.3	17.1	18.3	18.5	21.7	29.9	83.5	99.8	97.6	91.8	98.3	82.1
Electric and electronic equipment	3.0	2.4	1.9	2.9	2.9	4.3	42.4	62.7	37.6	72.3	85.7	108.8
Transportation equipment	1.5	1.3	0.9	0.3	0.1	1.3	2.2	0.6	1.9	2.8	1.3	2.9
Scientific and measuring instruments	7.3	6.8	6.0	6.2	7.3	6.6	27.4	21.8	46.7	27.9	27.6	34.4
Miscellaneous manufactures	0.2	0.1	0.6	0.2	0.3	...	1.4	0.7	2.4	3.0	3.1	1.7
Unidentified manufactures	0.5	0.4	0.5	0.6	1.1	0.7	1.3	1.5	1.0	1.1	2.0	2.9
Agricultural And Livestock Products	1.9	1.7	1.5	2.1	0.6	...	4.0	3.8	4.1	4.6	0.7	0.1
Agricultural products	...	...	...	...	...	...	...	0.2	0.5	0.1	0.2	0.1
Livestock and livestock products	1.9	1.7	1.5	2.1	0.5	...	4.0	3.5	3.6	4.6	0.5	...
Other Commodities	0.3	...	0.1	1.1	2.4	3.8	2.6	1.8	3.5	2.0	3.0	9.1
Forestry products	...	...	...	...	...	...	...	...	...	...	...	...
Fish and other marine products	0.3	...	...	1.0	2.4	2.7	2.4	1.3	3.0	1.3	2.0	5.2
Metallic ores and concentrates	...	...	...	...	...	...	...	...	...	0.1	...	...
Bituminous coal and lignite	...	...	...	...	...	...	...	...	...	...	...	...
Crude petroleum and natural gas	...	...	...	...	...	...	...	...	...	...	...	...
Nonmetallic materials	...	...	...	0.1	...	...	...	...	...	...	0.1	...
Scrap and waste	...	...	...	...	...	...	...	0.1	0.1	...	...	0.1
Used merchandise	...	...	...	...	...	...	0.1	0.1	0.1	0.1	...	...
Goods imported and returned unchanged	...	...	...	...	...	...	...	...	...	...	...	...
Special classification provisions	...	...	...	...	...	1.1	0.1	0.3	0.3	0.4	0.9	3.7

Table D-32. NEW HAMPSHIRE: State Exports of Goods by Destination and Industry, 1994–1999—*Continued*

(Millions of dollars.)

Industry	Japan						South Korea					
	1994	1995	1996	1997	1998	1999	1994	1995	1996	1997	1998	1999
ALL GOODS	60.4	59.0	81.8	109.0	96.3	88.7	40.7	52.5	48.3	31.7	14.7	28.0
Manufactured Goods	57.9	57.6	78.3	107.4	93.8	81.7	40.2	52.0	47.8	31.7	14.7	27.7
Food products	0.2	0.8	0.2	0.5	0.1	0.3	0.6	0.5	0.3	0.5	0.2	0.1
Tobacco products	...	...	...	...	...	...	...	...	...	...	...	...
Textile mill products	0.2	0.2	0.1	0.1	0.2	0.6	...	0.4	...	0.5	0.1	...
Apparel	0.4	0.5	0.7	0.4	0.6	0.6	0.1	0.2	0.2	...	...	...
Lumber and wood products	2.9	5.6	3.1	3.9	1.8	1.6	...	0.6	1.8	1.8	1.0	0.9
Furniture and fixtures	0.1	...	0.2	0.1	0.1	0.6	...	0.1	0.1	...	...	...
Paper products	0.1	0.2	0.2	0.4	0.1	0.2	...	0.1	0.1	0.1	0.1	0.3
Printing and publishing	0.2	0.2	0.2	0.6	0.1	0.2	0.2	0.2	0.1	0.3	0.2	0.4
Chemical products	1.9	1.9	1.7	2.3	1.9	2.1	6.4	2.0	1.2	1.2	1.1	1.2
Refined petroleum products	...	...	0.1	0.2	0.1	0.2	0.1	0.1	0.2	0.4	0.2	0.2
Rubber and plastic products	1.4	1.8	2.2	1.4	1.5	3.2	6.7	10.1	9.5	2.0	0.1	3.5
Leather products	0.3	1.8	6.1	8.5	5.7	5.9	0.2	0.7	5.8	3.0	0.8	4.3
Stone, clay and glass products	7.1	7.1	8.9	8.6	6.6	5.2	1.2	1.9	1.8	1.8	0.8	0.5
Primary metals	0.5	0.7	1.8	0.4	0.2	0.5	0.1	0.3	0.3	0.2	0.1	0.3
Fabricated metal products	1.7	1.3	1.8	2.5	2.3	2.6	4.4	5.9	5.4	5.6	0.5	0.2
Industrial machinery and computers	20.0	18.5	29.0	44.3	39.5	25.6	13.2	22.5	13.7	6.6	4.3	6.0
Electric and electronic equipment	7.1	8.4	10.7	21.7	22.0	19.5	3.3	4.3	4.6	4.4	2.2	7.0
Transportation equipment	0.2	0.2	0.6	0.2	0.3	0.4	...	...	0.1	0.4	0.3	...
Scientific and measuring instruments	12.6	7.8	9.2	9.6	9.5	10.8	3.6	1.9	2.5	2.8	2.6	2.6
Miscellaneous manufactures	0.9	0.4	1.6	1.3	0.8	0.6	...	...	0.1	0.1	...	0.2
Unidentified manufactures	0.4	0.4	0.2	0.2	0.5	0.7	0.1	0.1	0.1	0.1	0.1	0.2
Agricultural And Livestock Products	...	0.1	0.5	0.1	0.2	0.1	0.5	0.4	0.4	...	...	...
Agricultural products	...	0.1	0.5	0.1	0.2	0.1	...	0.1	...	...	...	...
Livestock and livestock products	...	...	...	...	...	...	0.5	0.3	0.4	...	...	...
Other Commodities	2.5	1.3	3.0	1.5	2.3	6.9	...	0.2	0.1	...	...	0.3
Forestry products	...	...	...	...	...	...	...	0.1	...	...	...	...
Fish and other marine products	2.4	1.1	2.8	1.1	2.0	4.8	...	...	...	...	...	...
Metallic ores and concentrates	...	...	...	0.1	...	...	...	...	...	...	...	...
Bituminous coal and lignite	...	...	...	...	...	...	...	...	...	...	...	...
Crude petroleum and natural gas	...	...	...	...	...	...	...	...	...	...	...	...
Nonmetallic materials	...	...	...	...	0.1	...	...	...	...	...	...	...
Scrap and waste	...	...	...	...	...	...	...	...	...	...	...	...
Used merchandise	0.1	0.1	0.1	0.1	...	...	...	...	...	...	...	...
Goods imported and returned unchanged	...	...	...	...	...	...	...	...	...	...	...	0.3
Special classification provisions	0.1	0.1	0.1	0.1	0.2	2.1	...	...	0.1	...	...	0.3

Industry	Taiwan						Singapore					
	1994	1995	1996	1997	1998	1999	1994	1995	1996	1997	1998	1999
ALL GOODS	34.8	36.0	57.4	49.5	79.8	56.3	60.5	76.1	50.3	56.7	68.9	93.5
Manufactured Goods	34.4	35.6	56.9	49.0	79.6	56.1	60.5	75.9	50.2	56.5	68.3	92.8
Food products	...	0.4	0.5	0.3	...	...	...	...	...	...	...	0.1
Tobacco products	...	...	...	...	...	...	...	...	...	...	...	...
Textile mill products	0.1	0.1	0.1	0.1	...	...	0.4	0.7	0.1	0.1	0.1	...
Apparel	0.3	0.4	0.2	0.4	0.1	...	0.2	...	...	0.1	...	...
Lumber and wood products	2.8	3.7	1.3	3.1	1.3	1.4	0.1	0.2	0.1	0.2	...	0.3
Furniture and fixtures	...	...	0.1	...	...	0.1	0.1	...	0.1	0.1	...	0.2
Paper products	0.1	0.2	...	0.3	0.2	0.3	0.1	0.2	...	0.3	0.4	0.2
Printing and publishing	0.4	0.5	0.7	0.6	0.3	0.2	0.7	0.4	0.6	0.8	0.5	0.5
Chemical products	9.5	2.7	2.3	1.8	1.4	1.1	3.5	3.8	4.0	4.4	2.2	2.9
Refined petroleum products	...	...	0.1	0.1	...	...	...	...	0.1	0.1	...	...
Rubber and plastic products	1.5	1.9	1.3	0.6	0.5	0.9	0.4	0.3	0.7	3.1	6.2	3.4
Leather products	0.3	4.2	23.1	20.3	36.7	27.7	0.7	1.4	3.0	3.4	2.1	0.6
Stone, clay and glass products	0.2	0.4	0.7	0.6	0.9	0.9	0.8	0.6	0.9	1.4	1.8	1.4
Primary metals	0.1	0.3	0.2	0.5	0.7	0.9	0.2	0.2	0.3	0.5	0.4	0.6
Fabricated metal products	0.4	1.3	1.3	2.7	1.9	0.7	1.3	0.7	0.5	1.6	1.6	1.2
Industrial machinery and computers	11.8	11.4	17.9	9.6	26.8	11.1	21.3	23.5	17.0	9.1	7.2	13.2
Electric and electronic equipment	3.1	6.2	4.8	6.4	6.3	8.0	26.8	38.4	13.2	23.2	37.8	55.3
Transportation equipment	1.1	0.3	1.0	0.4	0.1	0.1	0.1	0.1	0.1	0.1	0.1	0.5
Scientific and measuring instruments	2.3	1.4	1.0	1.0	1.4	2.5	3.7	5.1	9.2	8.0	7.4	12.0
Miscellaneous manufactures	...	...	0.2	0.1	1.0	...	0.1	0.1	0.3	0.1	0.1	...
Unidentified manufactures	0.3	0.2	0.2	0.1	0.2	0.3	0.1	0.1	0.1	0.3	0.6	0.6
Agricultural And Livestock Products	0.3	0.4	0.4	0.5	0.1	...	...	...	...	0.1	...	...
Agricultural products	...	...	...	...	...	...	...	...	...	...	...	...
Livestock and livestock products	0.3	0.4	0.4	0.5	0.1	...	...	...	...	0.1	...	...
Other Commodities	...	...	0.1	0.1	...	0.2	...	0.2	0.1	0.1	0.6	0.7
Forestry products	...	...	...	...	...	...	...	...	...	...	...	...
Fish and other marine products	...	...	...	0.1	...	...	...	...	...	...	...	...
Metallic ores and concentrates	...	...	...	...	...	...	...	...	...	...	...	...
Bituminous coal and lignite	...	...	...	...	...	...	...	...	...	...	...	...
Crude petroleum and natural gas	...	...	...	...	...	...	...	...	...	...	...	...
Nonmetallic materials	...	...	...	...	...	...	...	...	...	...	...	...
Scrap and waste	...	...	...	...	...	...	...	0.1	...	...	...	...
Used merchandise	...	...	...	...	...	...	...	...	0.1	...	...	...
Goods imported and returned unchanged	...	...	...	...	...	...	...	...	...	...	...	...
Special classification provisions	...	...	0.1	...	...	0.2	...	0.1	0.1	0.1	0.6	0.7

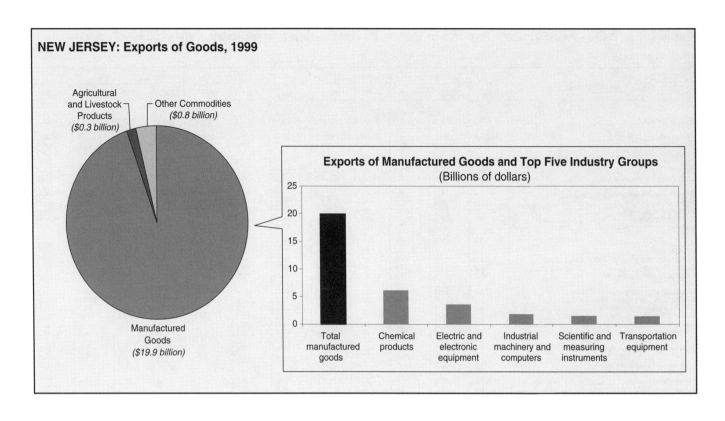

NEW JERSEY: Exports of Goods, 1999

Agricultural and Livestock Products ($0.3 billion)

Other Commodities ($0.8 billion)

Manufactured Goods ($19.9 billion)

Exports of Manufactured Goods and Top Five Industry Groups
(Billions of dollars)

Total manufactured goods | Chemical products | Electric and electronic equipment | Industrial machinery and computers | Scientific and measuring instruments | Transportation equipment

Table D-33. NEW JERSEY: State Exports of Goods by Destination and Industry, 1994–1999

(Millions of dollars.)

Industry	All destinations						Canada					
	1994	1995	1996	1997	1998	1999	1994	1995	1996	1997	1998	1999
ALL GOODS	16 760.8	18 368.6	18 458.4	20 815.4	20 032.9	21 007.6	2 943.7	3 167.2	3 379.1	3 836.8	3 872.7	3 902.1
Manufactured Goods	15 646.3	17 119.1	17 283.0	19 688.6	19 059.1	19 917.1	2 741.2	2 940.3	3 144.0	3 569.9	3 611.6	3 645.6
Food products	1 146.1	1 114.0	1 120.7	1 134.9	1 034.6	967.0	256.5	277.3	304.3	301.7	320.4	296.5
Tobacco products	1.7	14.1	4.8	1.9	1.3	1.1	1.2	1.1	0.8	0.8	0.9	1.0
Textile mill products	163.6	165.4	173.9	227.5	206.0	193.5	24.5	31.3	37.6	42.1	42.8	39.4
Apparel	191.0	216.1	249.2	266.1	238.2	190.5	19.7	15.3	22.5	35.1	41.4	38.9
Lumber and wood products	27.4	30.2	56.2	49.9	38.4	46.2	5.2	5.5	6.6	8.7	11.7	11.8
Furniture and fixtures	91.7	85.6	79.5	148.6	91.2	42.9	26.2	37.8	28.5	96.2	36.8	10.6
Paper products	523.0	826.4	642.3	545.8	434.5	368.5	84.7	105.2	86.4	97.0	104.1	114.0
Printing and publishing	412.7	455.7	495.7	532.7	483.1	469.3	199.6	199.6	204.8	200.2	190.7	180.8
Chemical products	3 974.9	4 642.6	4 858.5	6 160.8	5 830.8	6 114.3	807.1	930.3	1 003.1	1 179.7	1 128.2	1 231.7
Refined petroleum products	150.8	180.4	149.5	108.6	114.8	146.1	18.6	10.2	18.6	16.4	10.9	13.6
Rubber and plastic products	326.0	338.0	343.0	414.7	367.3	411.2	110.9	116.0	122.6	148.0	141.2	157.0
Leather products	52.6	57.3	47.4	59.9	70.4	64.6	6.6	7.0	11.2	13.1	12.5	11.6
Stone, clay and glass products	143.7	153.9	192.7	211.9	223.4	237.0	27.6	29.4	38.4	47.3	47.1	61.9
Primary metals	690.8	753.5	674.5	790.2	1 067.4	1 001.1	161.0	196.7	182.9	189.7	162.8	164.1
Fabricated metal products	388.6	561.4	590.4	591.6	669.0	644.1	71.5	70.7	75.5	79.4	92.3	95.8
Industrial machinery and computers	1 901.0	2 002.4	1 824.1	2 101.3	1 919.3	1 836.0	308.7	303.8	302.4	333.7	340.5	351.7
Electric and electronic equipment	2 693.4	2 678.9	2 622.7	2 991.6	2 753.1	3 606.1	203.6	224.6	220.6	292.3	322.8	231.5
Transportation equipment	1 259.8	1 312.1	1 509.8	1 551.0	1 569.0	1 454.6	142.9	133.1	219.7	227.9	259.5	238.1
Scientific and measuring instruments	1 229.3	1 249.0	1 349.4	1 463.5	1 549.3	1 541.3	187.6	163.3	179.4	172.0	204.1	224.7
Miscellaneous manufactures	172.4	198.7	191.8	223.3	259.4	351.3	64.8	67.7	63.7	72.5	123.8	151.1
Unidentified manufactures	105.6	83.6	106.7	112.8	138.6	230.4	12.7	14.4	14.5	15.9	16.9	19.8
Agricultural And Livestock Products	269.2	308.3	395.0	343.7	293.2	320.3	94.8	84.6	87.8	108.0	121.0	126.9
Agricultural products	248.3	283.6	368.5	307.1	265.3	299.6	82.4	71.6	71.3	81.8	101.8	114.1
Livestock and livestock products	20.9	24.7	26.5	36.6	27.8	20.8	12.4	13.0	16.4	26.2	19.2	12.8
Other Commodities	845.3	941.1	780.4	783.1	680.7	770.1	107.7	142.4	147.3	158.8	140.1	129.6
Forestry products	11.1	11.3	18.0	17.4	25.2	19.2	1.9	2.1	2.1	3.9	6.3	4.0
Fish and other marine products	30.7	43.8	46.1	31.0	20.3	22.8	7.4	13.1	15.6	13.6	7.8	7.6
Metallic ores and concentrates	13.2	4.6	4.5	3.8	3.0	4.5	0.6	1.2	1.6	2.1	1.2	2.4
Bituminous coal and lignite	24.4	20.2	37.7	33.0	4.2	15.1	. . .	. . .	. . .	0.4	. . .	. . .
Crude petroleum and natural gas	1.6	2.8	1.8	2.5	22.6	8.2	0.6	1.3	. . .	0.1	19.4	6.5
Nonmetallic minerals	223.8	256.7	262.0	285.9	284.5	267.4	15.1	17.5	17.8	17.6	22.9	26.5
Scrap and waste	446.9	474.5	290.8	283.2	173.6	254.2	36.3	53.7	57.1	62.6	22.1	18.2
Used merchandise	31.2	54.4	30.6	38.5	57.1	46.6	1.4	1.4	1.9	4.6	3.2	4.1
Goods imported and returned unchanged	37.4	44.3	43.2	44.6	48.8	35.5	37.4	44.3	43.2	44.6	48.8	35.5
Special classification provisions	25.1	28.7	45.7	43.3	41.3	96.5	6.8	7.8	7.9	9.3	8.5	24.8

Table D-33. NEW JERSEY: State Exports of Goods by Destination and Industry, 1994–1999—*Continued*

(Millions of dollars.)

Industry	South and Central American and Caribbean						Mexico					
	1994	1995	1996	1997	1998	1999	1994	1995	1996	1997	1998	1999
ALL GOODS	1 433.6	1 808.6	1 932.9	2 107.8	1 997.2	1 921.0	1 068.1	583.8	679.2	883.8	953.7	1 079.5
Manufactured Goods	1 294.8	1 627.0	1 675.3	1 920.9	1 851.0	1 768.0	1 052.5	569.0	663.4	865.0	940.7	1 066.2
Food products	98.7	142.0	146.7	159.1	152.6	164.5	57.8	23.2	28.8	19.1	42.6	58.6
Tobacco products	...	1.0	0.4	0.9	0.3	...	...	...	...	...	...	...
Textile mill products	38.2	41.1	41.9	53.0	47.7	25.1	20.8	8.1	11.7	20.5	23.1	34.6
Apparel	69.6	61.7	76.8	87.1	70.0	52.8	12.9	20.5	19.3	17.4	28.0	22.7
Lumber and wood products	0.8	1.9	4.1	6.3	4.6	4.1	4.8	0.8	0.2	0.4	0.5	1.0
Furniture and fixtures	2.8	3.9	7.0	7.1	5.8	6.8	12.4	4.6	6.4	11.9	12.2	1.9
Paper products	53.3	80.0	73.9	66.4	69.4	41.3	16.1	21.6	16.5	17.5	19.2	34.6
Printing and publishing	12.9	23.3	30.0	25.6	21.5	18.4	20.8	12.6	17.4	14.6	16.1	22.8
Chemical products	434.1	599.5	667.7	831.1	793.9	738.4	172.8	171.4	215.6	283.1	338.7	426.8
Refined petroleum products	25.0	14.0	10.4	7.1	5.7	12.3	0.8	1.4	1.5	3.1	3.2	4.5
Rubber and plastic products	19.7	30.0	28.5	37.7	27.3	25.3	51.1	24.9	15.7	28.3	28.8	43.3
Leather products	4.4	7.1	4.6	10.9	17.5	14.4	1.2	0.4	0.3	0.5	1.2	3.6
Stone, clay and glass products	17.9	17.0	15.6	18.7	20.8	18.6	4.1	1.9	7.6	8.1	8.4	10.2
Primary metals	38.9	32.9	23.1	23.0	24.2	34.9	38.2	24.2	71.8	35.0	30.7	20.2
Fabricated metal products	16.0	22.9	23.1	24.1	24.8	64.0	20.9	17.0	21.1	24.5	26.3	34.8
Industrial machinery and computers	173.6	224.8	175.9	244.8	198.4	184.9	97.4	47.8	46.5	114.0	89.2	95.3
Electric and electronic equipment	172.5	133.4	158.4	136.6	134.8	192.4	452.0	153.9	140.0	162.6	207.9	194.5
Transportation equipment	24.0	64.4	77.1	53.0	44.9	33.4	9.9	3.5	2.9	2.2	2.7	3.1
Scientific and measuring instruments	65.2	95.3	82.5	98.5	157.7	103.2	45.2	25.0	33.0	90.3	43.0	33.3
Miscellaneous manufactures	17.3	22.6	19.5	20.7	18.0	19.5	10.2	5.0	5.6	8.2	11.2	12.2
Unidentified manufactures	9.1	8.3	8.5	9.2	11.2	13.7	3.1	1.0	1.4	3.9	7.8	8.3
Agricultural And Livestock Products	111.9	156.1	228.9	164.0	122.4	135.5	7.2	5.6	2.3	8.6	5.9	1.0
Agricultural products	111.7	153.3	228.8	163.7	122.3	135.5	6.5	5.5	2.3	8.6	5.8	0.8
Livestock and livestock products	0.2	2.8	...	0.3	0.1	...	0.7	...	...	...	...	0.2
Other Commodities	27.0	25.5	28.7	22.9	23.7	17.5	8.4	9.2	13.4	10.1	7.1	12.3
Forestry products	1.5	2.0	2.4	2.4	2.5	2.8	0.6	1.1	1.1	1.4	0.6	0.9
Fish and other marine products	1.2	1.2	1.9	0.4	0.3	1.3	0.1	0.1	0.1	1.8	0.1	0.7
Metallic ores and concentrates	0.2	0.1	...	0.1	0.3	0.2	...	...	...	0.1	...	0.1
Bituminous coal and lignite	3.1	0.2	1.9	1.1	0.2	0.2	...	...	0.1	0.1	0.1	...
Crude petroleum and natural gas	0.1	0.1	...	...	...	0.1	...	...	...	...	...	...
Nonmetallic minerals	4.6	5.9	12.0	10.3	7.9	4.8	1.9	1.5	1.6	1.5	1.5	2.4
Scrap and waste	10.4	7.0	4.8	2.8	7.1	3.4	3.8	2.5	6.7	0.7	0.7	3.4
Used merchandise	5.2	7.9	4.5	3.3	4.7	1.6	0.1	0.4	...	0.1	...	0.1
Goods imported and returned unchanged	...	...	...	...	...	...	...	...	...	...	...	...
Special classification provisions	0.6	1.0	1.2	2.5	0.6	3.0	1.8	3.7	3.9	4.3	4.1	4.6

Industry	European Union						United Kingdom					
	1994	1995	1996	1997	1998	1999	1994	1995	1996	1997	1998	1999
ALL GOODS	4 350.9	4 792.2	4 499.6	5 269.0	5 700.7	6 011.2	999.0	955.7	854.9	901.1	1 026.1	1 146.8
Manufactured Goods	3 898.1	4 388.2	4 184.7	5 000.3	5 453.1	5 713.5	807.6	829.3	774.2	861.7	983.1	1 016.3
Food products	100.7	98.4	91.7	100.8	103.6	65.4	16.3	16.5	15.6	14.9	32.1	14.2
Tobacco products	0.3	9.6	0.7	0.1	...	...	...	0.5	0.4	...	...	...
Textile mill products	14.9	21.2	17.6	23.1	18.9	18.8	4.0	7.8	4.1	5.7	5.8	4.9
Apparel	26.6	32.8	33.6	36.4	33.8	28.8	4.2	5.8	5.3	7.5	4.6	7.3
Lumber and wood products	4.9	6.6	7.0	7.6	9.4	10.0	1.7	2.3	1.7	4.1	3.4	2.8
Furniture and fixtures	4.2	7.0	6.2	9.1	8.6	7.4	1.6	2.2	1.6	2.1	2.1	1.4
Paper products	194.6	332.6	224.5	157.1	120.5	58.2	55.4	93.1	57.7	43.0	25.2	14.5
Printing and publishing	95.8	118.9	132.6	179.5	149.1	138.6	60.1	57.1	65.9	108.5	79.0	87.5
Chemical products	1 320.5	1 463.9	1 502.4	2 164.8	2 176.0	2 019.0	181.1	167.2	202.3	220.3	235.6	211.7
Refined petroleum products	38.3	63.3	36.0	18.3	19.4	19.7	4.1	34.1	2.9	3.5	2.9	3.9
Rubber and plastic products	65.3	68.1	67.9	88.2	81.6	73.9	21.0	16.2	13.6	19.1	21.5	20.3
Leather products	9.6	7.8	7.1	10.9	11.4	11.6	3.9	2.4	1.6	2.7	1.8	2.0
Stone, clay and glass products	39.2	47.9	55.8	54.0	68.0	74.8	11.8	14.0	17.4	13.7	13.8	13.2
Primary metals	176.5	145.7	137.8	216.8	404.9	339.7	77.2	45.6	56.2	52.0	113.9	115.8
Fabricated metal products	86.9	88.0	80.5	88.3	96.2	94.9	20.8	20.6	17.1	20.7	24.8	21.8
Industrial machinery and computers	445.3	448.2	396.8	457.3	474.7	498.8	116.1	113.6	96.8	107.0	116.6	119.8
Electric and electronic equipment	437.3	540.2	445.2	501.6	664.2	1 063.7	72.0	88.2	93.4	112.6	118.8	163.8
Transportation equipment	310.5	332.6	414.3	332.1	391.7	509.2	42.2	30.8	35.9	40.9	53.4	44.6
Scientific and measuring instruments	476.6	501.8	468.5	491.6	548.0	575.4	100.6	98.2	70.5	64.9	102.5	116.7
Miscellaneous manufactures	32.7	34.6	33.5	41.5	43.1	50.2	8.7	8.8	9.3	14.9	15.7	26.5
Unidentified manufactures	17.5	18.9	24.9	21.1	30.0	55.5	4.5	4.0	4.8	3.6	9.6	23.7
Agricultural And Livestock Products	32.6	31.6	50.1	23.4	20.3	12.1	0.8	2.6	29.6	8.4	3.5	2.1
Agricultural products	29.0	26.3	44.5	20.2	16.3	7.4	0.8	2.5	28.8	7.8	3.2	1.9
Livestock and livestock products	3.6	5.3	5.6	3.2	4.0	4.7	0.1	0.1	0.7	0.6	0.3	0.2
Other Commodities	420.1	372.4	264.8	245.3	227.3	285.6	190.6	123.9	51.1	31.0	39.5	128.5
Forestry products	3.5	2.3	4.4	5.7	4.1	5.5	1.6	0.2	0.9	1.4	1.5	2.4
Fish and other marine products	13.5	12.3	13.1	7.1	6.3	5.9	0.1	...	0.6	0.4	0.2	0.1
Metallic ores and concentrates	10.8	3.1	2.1	0.6	0.8	1.2	5.4	0.7	0.6	0.4	0.3	0.8
Bituminous coal and lignite	21.2	19.9	24.5	13.4	1.5	3.6	0.8	3.3	2.5	0.9	...	...
Crude petroleum and natural gas	0.1	0.4	0.6	0.9	0.9	0.3	...	0.1	0.4	0.6	0.6	...
Nonmetallic minerals	78.6	93.0	78.7	94.2	102.0	91.8	5.9	8.4	6.0	11.6	13.0	12.0
Scrap and waste	269.8	208.3	115.0	103.8	69.6	126.4	166.7	96.6	30.2	9.1	4.8	84.6
Used merchandise	14.2	25.9	8.6	10.1	33.7	25.8	8.6	13.0	4.5	4.0	16.6	21.3
Goods imported and returned unchanged	...	...	...	...	...	...	...	...	...	...	...	...
Special classification provisions	8.5	7.3	17.6	9.3	8.5	25.1	1.5	1.6	5.6	2.6	2.6	7.3

Table D-33. NEW JERSEY: State Exports of Goods by Destination and Industry, 1994–1999—*Continued*

(Millions of dollars.)

Industry	Germany						France					
	1994	1995	1996	1997	1998	1999	1994	1995	1996	1997	1998	1999
ALL GOODS	798.3	920.8	871.5	912.4	904.6	924.6	488.6	525.3	493.0	577.6	610.1	736.2
Manufactured Goods	716.1	834.6	800.3	841.7	859.6	881.6	477.7	515.8	478.4	560.9	593.8	731.3
Food products	14.0	7.5	15.7	18.4	24.1	18.7	19.4	12.6	10.8	4.5	5.0	2.6
Tobacco products	...	...	...	...	...	...	0.2	0.2	0.1	...	...	...
Textile mill products	1.7	2.0	2.0	4.1	4.0	3.3	2.1	1.2	2.4	1.6	1.1	0.7
Apparel	4.8	6.9	6.2	4.1	4.4	2.7	2.9	3.0	5.3	4.8	5.8	1.6
Lumber and wood products	1.2	1.6	2.2	0.5	1.2	0.8	0.8	1.0	0.8	0.8	1.3	1.6
Furniture and fixtures	1.2	1.1	1.1	1.0	0.4	1.1	0.3	1.0	0.7	0.7	0.4	0.7
Paper products	22.2	43.1	30.3	20.4	15.2	8.4	10.6	19.0	13.9	4.9	25.4	4.6
Printing and publishing	10.9	14.7	21.9	15.4	18.2	14.7	6.5	5.4	6.6	12.0	4.4	7.1
Chemical products	198.1	216.4	227.3	274.9	219.0	183.6	154.9	159.4	109.7	244.6	229.4	194.7
Refined petroleum products	2.9	2.9	2.1	2.1	2.0	2.2	1.2	1.5	7.8	2.6	3.4	2.3
Rubber and plastic products	5.5	9.0	7.4	9.9	9.5	6.4	7.0	7.5	6.7	8.8	8.8	7.5
Leather products	0.7	1.1	2.6	3.1	5.0	4.9	1.2	1.1	1.1	2.5	0.7	0.4
Stone, clay and glass products	5.5	7.9	4.3	4.8	9.6	20.0	3.7	5.9	5.9	6.3	7.1	7.4
Primary metals	46.6	22.8	15.7	12.2	14.5	28.5	4.5	13.8	5.5	9.7	11.7	9.5
Fabricated metal products	26.9	28.3	33.2	31.1	25.8	29.9	5.5	7.0	6.6	6.5	8.0	8.6
Industrial machinery and computers	92.7	108.7	95.7	105.7	149.4	149.9	44.1	50.5	43.2	49.5	48.7	82.3
Electric and electronic equipment	76.1	113.9	88.4	96.0	120.2	179.5	39.4	43.2	40.9	42.9	62.6	115.3
Transportation equipment	59.1	77.0	61.4	52.0	47.9	34.7	104.2	109.1	146.3	91.9	105.1	222.7
Scientific and measuring instruments	134.6	159.1	172.8	174.6	181.4	182.1	62.8	67.5	56.6	60.7	56.5	50.5
Miscellaneous manufactures	6.1	6.5	5.2	8.0	5.1	5.2	4.9	4.5	6.6	4.9	5.9	7.4
Unidentified manufactures	5.5	4.2	4.9	3.3	2.7	4.6	1.7	1.5	1.0	0.9	2.6	3.7
Agricultural And Livestock Products	0.4	1.6	0.5	1.9	3.5	2.6	7.8	0.6	3.4	2.6	1.0	0.3
Agricultural products	0.2	0.3	0.1	1.7	3.1	1.9	7.8	0.6	3.4	2.6	1.0	0.3
Livestock and livestock products	0.3	1.3	0.4	0.3	0.4	0.7	...	...	...	...	...	...
Other Commodities	81.7	84.5	70.7	68.8	41.5	40.5	3.0	8.9	11.2	14.1	15.2	4.5
Forestry products	0.8	0.6	0.4	1.6	0.7	1.9	0.4	0.5	0.4	0.3	1.3	0.2
Fish and other marine products	0.1	...	...	...	0.1	...	0.1	0.5	1.4	...	0.2	...
Metallic ores and concentrates	0.3	0.4	0.8	...	0.1	...	...	...	...	0.1	0.3	0.3
Bituminous coal and lignite	...	...	...	...	...	...	0.3	3.5	4.9	8.6	...	...
Crude petroleum and natural gas	...	...	0.1	...	...	...	...	...	...	...	...	...
Nonmetallic minerals	5.1	6.4	5.8	5.9	5.9	4.3	0.6	0.5	1.7	1.4	0.6	0.9
Scrap and waste	72.2	74.8	61.9	59.9	31.4	29.9	0.6	0.7	0.6	0.2	0.4	0.3
Used merchandise	1.8	1.6	0.5	0.8	2.4	1.1	0.2	2.3	1.3	2.4	11.4	0.8
Goods imported and returned unchanged	...	...	...	...	...	...	...	...	...	...	...	...
Special classification provisions	1.3	0.8	1.3	0.4	1.0	3.4	0.9	0.8	0.9	0.9	1.0	2.0

Industry	The Netherlands						Asian 10					
	1994	1995	1996	1997	1998	1999	1994	1995	1996	1997	1998	1999
ALL GOODS	566.0	648.1	747.2	1 016.1	1 057.0	1 051.3	4 410.9	5 154.1	4 862.1	5 264.4	4 205.9	4 954.0
Manufactured Goods	542.6	620.6	711.6	992.4	1 038.9	1 028.2	4 208.3	4 880.8	4 619.9	4 992.1	3 973.6	4 693.5
Food products	6.7	15.2	12.5	19.8	14.8	11.1	498.4	435.9	416.0	417.7	293.9	290.2
Tobacco products	...	0.4	0.2	0.1	...	...	...	1.6	0.4	...	...	...
Textile mill products	3.6	2.2	2.0	1.9	1.5	1.5	31.0	37.0	36.4	49.8	43.3	46.1
Apparel	5.3	7.5	9.0	9.7	9.4	9.1	36.2	59.6	63.8	61.5	39.0	29.4
Lumber and wood products	0.1	0.1	0.5	0.2	0.1	0.3	6.8	7.2	26.2	10.7	4.6	12.5
Furniture and fixtures	0.3	0.5	0.4	0.8	0.8	1.3	14.6	6.2	11.0	8.9	8.4	6.9
Paper products	32.6	38.7	31.6	19.5	18.2	6.4	125.8	197.7	178.4	145.7	83.4	89.5
Printing and publishing	2.8	22.2	20.0	27.6	32.9	14.2	38.9	59.7	60.6	64.2	61.5	66.9
Chemical products	165.2	226.2	373.9	627.5	666.2	591.4	772.4	916.4	943.9	1 106.0	806.7	1 073.3
Refined petroleum products	4.4	6.5	19.8	3.5	6.2	5.4	8.6	12.6	10.1	9.5	9.2	18.3
Rubber and plastic products	4.9	9.4	7.2	6.6	8.0	5.3	50.3	60.5	67.8	65.9	44.9	53.8
Leather products	0.6	0.4	0.5	0.8	1.7	1.9	25.3	29.0	17.9	20.1	17.4	9.1
Stone, clay and glass products	3.4	3.2	7.3	12.5	10.7	8.5	35.2	35.2	40.7	55.7	56.2	42.1
Primary metals	25.7	11.2	17.5	18.9	20.4	18.6	205.4	269.6	178.3	202.3	218.0	279.6
Fabricated metal products	11.7	7.8	7.0	5.1	6.9	7.3	86.4	198.4	151.7	140.3	198.1	243.6
Industrial machinery and computers	75.6	66.8	50.0	81.2	57.1	29.4	549.9	621.2	593.8	585.9	458.9	347.2
Electric and electronic equipment	142.3	145.6	85.4	71.6	98.4	239.5	1 167.0	1 298.0	1 103.3	1 233.3	1 021.4	1 368.6
Transportation equipment	31.5	21.5	21.5	20.6	18.6	10.0	218.6	290.3	251.8	315.1	191.5	166.7
Scientific and measuring instruments	19.8	29.4	40.7	62.0	63.1	64.1	298.1	287.3	411.7	436.8	360.9	391.2
Miscellaneous manufactures	4.4	3.9	3.0	2.1	2.9	1.8	27.3	43.2	43.9	49.8	37.3	82.7
Unidentified manufactures	1.5	1.9	1.3	0.9	1.2	1.3	12.0	14.2	12.3	12.7	19.1	75.9
Agricultural And Livestock Products	3.2	5.3	4.5	1.5	1.5	1.4	6.1	7.7	6.3	14.1	14.8	14.4
Agricultural products	1.1	2.2	1.9	0.4	0.9	0.5	3.7	5.2	2.7	8.6	10.8	13.6
Livestock and livestock products	2.1	3.0	2.6	1.1	0.6	0.9	2.4	2.5	3.6	5.6	4.0	0.8
Other Commodities	20.2	22.2	31.2	22.2	16.6	21.6	196.5	265.5	235.8	258.1	217.5	246.1
Forestry products	0.1	0.3	0.4	0.1	...	0.4	3.3	3.2	6.9	3.1	8.3	5.2
Fish and other marine products	0.1	...	0.2	0.5	0.1	0.1	6.4	14.6	12.6	6.2	3.4	3.3
Metallic ores and concentrates	4.9	1.6	0.5	...	0.1	...	0.5	...	0.5	0.8	0.6	0.4
Bituminous coal and lignite	0.7	...	9.7	...	...	0.6	...	...	...	...	...	...
Crude petroleum and natural gas	...	...	...	...	0.1	0.1	0.8	1.0	1.1	1.2	1.9	1.1
Nonmetallic minerals	12.3	10.5	17.7	19.9	13.8	17.7	108.8	118.8	133.7	142.7	131.9	125.8
Scrap and waste	0.3	1.2	1.3	0.3	1.6	0.6	70.4	117.7	69.4	91.0	56.8	83.2
Used merchandise	0.5	8.2	0.9	1.1	0.5	0.4	2.8	4.3	4.1	4.0	3.0	6.2
Goods imported and returned unchanged	...	...	...	...	...	...	...	...	...	...	...	...
Special classification provisions	1.3	0.3	0.5	0.3	0.4	1.6	3.6	5.8	7.6	8.9	11.6	20.9

Table D-33. NEW JERSEY: State Exports of Goods by Destination and Industry, 1994–1999—*Continued*

(Millions of dollars.)

Industry	Japan						South Korea					
	1994	1995	1996	1997	1998	1999	1994	1995	1996	1997	1998	1999
ALL GOODS	1 357.7	1 470.2	1 577.5	1 648.2	1 432.0	1 880.1	1 260.9	1 359.6	1 279.5	1 356.7	693.2	861.1
Manufactured Goods	1 253.0	1 372.9	1 462.2	1 529.5	1 323.3	1 774.8	1 220.5	1 278.0	1 238.8	1 295.6	666.9	813.6
Food products	238.0	123.5	152.9	146.7	120.1	135.8	177.6	213.2	166.9	155.3	80.0	80.1
Tobacco products	...	...	0.4	...	...	...	...	...	...	...	...	...
Textile mill products	5.1	4.7	5.0	8.2	6.4	5.2	5.7	7.7	6.4	6.5	7.2	5.5
Apparel	21.7	40.2	44.8	35.0	19.2	12.4	2.5	6.9	6.2	7.5	1.3	1.0
Lumber and wood products	4.7	4.8	4.4	3.8	2.5	8.0	1.2	1.0	4.6	3.5	1.1	2.3
Furniture and fixtures	0.4	1.0	2.4	1.2	1.5	4.8	0.6	2.0	6.3	1.4	0.4	0.4
Paper products	39.8	64.1	38.9	14.2	10.6	7.6	5.8	4.8	5.8	5.6	1.0	2.6
Printing and publishing	13.5	17.2	16.7	18.4	19.2	20.4	2.8	3.6	6.0	3.4	1.3	4.7
Chemical products	256.0	288.9	316.9	412.7	311.1	426.8	109.1	117.6	137.6	143.9	113.9	123.9
Refined petroleum products	0.9	1.2	1.0	1.6	2.8	6.7	1.7	3.1	2.8	2.5	1.9	1.8
Rubber and plastic products	18.8	20.6	17.8	15.7	14.0	11.8	11.3	12.9	13.5	10.8	5.0	8.3
Leather products	6.6	8.0	6.5	6.2	3.7	3.2	7.1	4.9	3.4	4.2	1.8	0.9
Stone, clay and glass products	13.3	15.1	16.4	12.7	10.0	23.6	5.6	6.2	8.2	8.9	5.3	5.8
Primary metals	86.1	110.7	85.5	96.4	117.9	140.7	31.1	47.1	34.0	31.6	28.4	63.5
Fabricated metal products	11.6	9.7	12.5	13.5	11.5	17.3	24.2	21.3	23.8	27.8	9.4	13.7
Industrial machinery and computers	94.6	110.1	116.1	167.2	110.5	92.4	232.5	271.4	217.5	192.8	95.9	54.5
Electric and electronic equipment	245.2	356.9	378.9	282.1	288.6	504.2	381.8	283.4	302.9	358.9	134.3	237.3
Transportation equipment	8.8	12.4	10.0	15.6	32.7	24.7	157.6	209.2	187.9	247.0	117.2	128.4
Scientific and measuring instruments	172.8	160.6	219.0	262.1	225.2	228.7	56.8	50.1	92.8	71.5	45.7	55.6
Miscellaneous manufactures	11.7	19.1	12.6	11.6	9.8	41.3	3.4	9.9	10.5	10.2	12.5	18.0
Unidentified manufactures	3.4	4.3	3.5	4.5	6.0	59.3	2.3	1.7	1.9	2.4	3.2	5.3
Agricultural And Livestock Products	0.6	0.5	1.0	0.6	1.0	1.2	1.7	1.3	1.0	4.1	3.6	0.5
Agricultural products	0.4	0.4	0.8	0.4	0.9	1.1	0.4	0.1	0.1	0.4	0.5	0.2
Livestock and livestock products	0.2	0.1	0.2	0.2	0.1	0.1	1.3	1.2	0.8	3.7	3.1	0.3
Other Commodities	104.0	96.7	114.4	118.2	107.7	104.2	38.7	80.2	39.7	57.0	22.7	46.9
Forestry products	1.5	1.6	2.7	2.1	1.6	2.9	...	0.1	0.1	0.2	0.1	...
Fish and other marine products	4.2	4.0	3.8	4.5	2.4	0.5	1.0	7.6	4.1	0.9	0.2	1.9
Metallic ores and concentrates	0.5	...	0.2	0.7	0.1	0.1	...	...	...	...	0.4	...
Bituminous coal and lignite	...	...	...	...	...	...	...	...	...	...	...	...
Crude petroleum and natural gas	0.6	0.7	0.5	0.6	0.6	0.2	0.1	0.1	0.1	0.1	0.1	0.1
Nonmetallic minerals	80.9	80.7	97.7	99.8	96.3	85.7	13.4	14.7	12.0	12.8	8.2	10.2
Scrap and waste	12.9	7.1	6.7	6.2	2.6	7.1	23.4	55.7	20.0	41.2	11.0	28.9
Used merchandise	1.8	0.9	1.3	2.2	1.2	2.9	0.3	0.8	0.7	0.6	0.4	0.1
Goods imported and returned unchanged	...	...	...	...	...	...	...	...	...	...	...	...
Special classification provisions	1.7	1.7	1.5	2.2	2.9	4.8	0.5	1.2	2.7	1.3	2.4	5.7

Industry	Taiwan						Singapore					
	1994	1995	1996	1997	1998	1999	1994	1995	1996	1997	1998	1999
ALL GOODS	517.6	519.0	440.3	484.7	443.6	467.0	262.1	249.6	231.4	304.0	214.9	373.7
Manufactured Goods	507.0	502.8	425.4	463.5	418.1	448.0	260.0	246.3	228.7	301.0	212.5	369.3
Food products	13.2	16.7	16.4	22.5	15.2	11.5	7.0	8.1	6.4	5.9	8.2	6.8
Tobacco products	...	...	...	...	...	...	...	...	...	...	...	...
Textile mill products	1.1	2.1	0.7	0.8	1.5	3.2	3.5	3.3	2.3	6.3	1.5	1.7
Apparel	0.8	1.2	0.5	0.8	0.9	0.9	1.7	1.9	2.5	2.7	1.0	1.4
Lumber and wood products	0.4	0.7	0.9	0.6	0.4	0.4	...	0.1	7.3	0.2	0.1	1.3
Furniture and fixtures	0.1	0.1	0.4	0.8	1.0	0.2	12.0	1.4	0.7	1.6	1.1	0.2
Paper products	7.3	10.2	10.9	11.1	8.5	13.1	13.6	14.8	11.7	11.3	7.6	7.4
Printing and publishing	3.8	8.0	10.2	9.7	6.9	7.9	9.1	8.6	8.6	7.7	7.0	10.4
Chemical products	142.1	197.6	174.3	162.9	97.5	131.1	81.8	93.2	83.5	125.9	83.3	131.0
Refined petroleum products	2.8	3.0	2.1	2.0	2.1	2.4	1.3	1.5	0.9	1.1	0.9	1.6
Rubber and plastic products	3.6	2.7	5.5	5.4	4.1	5.6	4.1	3.3	3.3	3.7	5.3	10.2
Leather products	0.2	0.2	0.2	0.3	0.7	0.4	4.8	2.2	0.3	1.4	1.1	1.5
Stone, clay and glass products	2.1	2.6	2.8	3.1	2.5	4.3	3.3	1.8	2.1	1.8	2.1	2.5
Primary metals	32.3	33.0	13.9	23.2	32.3	28.2	15.4	4.2	4.1	7.4	7.2	11.6
Fabricated metal products	9.0	6.5	4.4	8.5	8.3	32.1	3.4	3.6	5.7	27.4	12.0	28.6
Industrial machinery and computers	57.9	37.4	37.2	48.2	64.8	65.8	29.4	42.1	33.4	30.4	25.8	34.9
Electric and electronic equipment	192.7	129.8	96.2	124.1	119.6	98.3	48.5	32.9	22.3	27.2	23.7	92.1
Transportation equipment	18.6	25.0	21.1	11.4	24.3	5.1	3.6	5.1	9.8	12.7	4.6	3.6
Scientific and measuring instruments	15.3	22.6	24.5	24.8	22.6	31.1	14.7	16.0	19.3	22.8	17.5	16.0
Miscellaneous manufactures	2.3	2.0	2.1	2.2	2.3	4.3	1.7	1.3	3.7	2.9	1.6	4.7
Unidentified manufactures	1.3	1.6	1.1	1.1	2.5	2.1	1.0	0.7	0.7	0.7	1.0	1.9
Agricultural And Livestock Products	0.6	1.0	0.4	1.1	3.9	5.8	0.7	0.6	0.5	0.6	0.3	0.3
Agricultural products	0.6	0.9	0.2	1.0	3.7	5.7	0.5	0.4	0.1	0.2	0.2	0.3
Livestock and livestock products	...	0.1	0.1	0.1	0.2	...	0.2	0.1	0.4	0.4	0.1	...
Other Commodities	10.0	15.1	14.5	20.1	21.6	13.3	1.3	2.8	2.2	2.5	2.1	4.1
Forestry products	0.1	0.1	0.1	0.2	0.7	...	0.1	0.1	...	...	...	...
Fish and other marine products	0.1	...	0.2	0.1	0.2	0.2	...	...	0.9	...	...	...
Metallic ores and concentrates	...	...	...	...	...	...	...	...	...	...	...	...
Bituminous coal and lignite	...	...	...	...	...	...	...	...	...	...	...	...
Crude petroleum and natural gas	...	0.2	0.4	0.5	1.1	0.7	...	...	0.1	0.1	0.1	0.1
Nonmetallic minerals	6.9	5.6	6.3	5.3	4.6	4.0	0.4	0.7	0.7	1.2	0.6	0.6
Scrap and waste	2.0	8.2	6.5	11.9	12.1	4.9	0.2	...	...	0.5	0.8	0.7
Used merchandise	...	0.1	...	0.1	...	0.4	0.4	0.6	0.1	0.1	...	0.1
Goods imported and returned unchanged	...	...	...	...	...	...	...	...	...	...	...	...
Special classification provisions	0.7	0.9	1.0	2.1	2.8	3.0	0.2	1.4	0.5	0.6	0.5	2.6

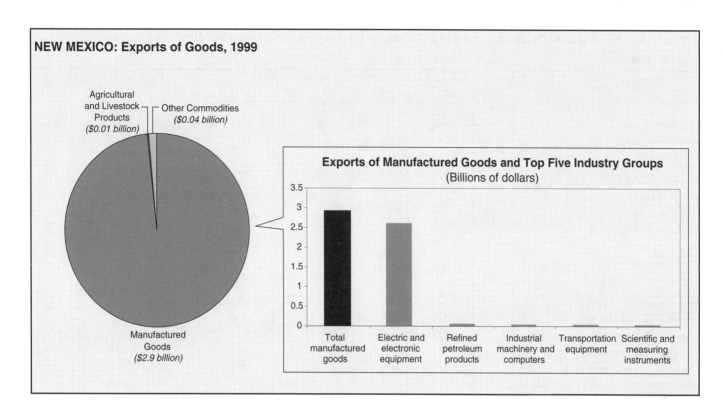

NEW MEXICO: Exports of Goods, 1999

Agricultural and Livestock Products ($0.01 billion)

Other Commodities ($0.04 billion)

Manufactured Goods ($2.9 billion)

Exports of Manufactured Goods and Top Five Industry Groups
(Billions of dollars)

Total manufactured goods / Electric and electronic equipment / Refined petroleum products / Industrial machinery and computers / Transportation equipment / Scientific and measuring instruments

Table D-34. NEW MEXICO: State Exports of Goods by Destination and Industry, 1994–1999

(Millions of dollars.)

Industry	All destinations						Canada					
	1994	1995	1996	1997	1998	1999	1994	1995	1996	1997	1998	1999
ALL GOODS	488.5	426.6	917.4	1 779.9	1 896.2	2 964.9	47.5	41.7	51.2	55.6	67.8	75.8
Manufactured Goods	450.7	385.4	892.6	1 739.3	1 865.8	2 916.2	35.7	30.4	40.6	43.6	57.7	64.6
Food products	5.2	2.0	4.5	8.9	6.8	11.0	1.4	0.5	2.4	2.2	1.6	0.8
Tobacco products	. . .	. . .	0.1	. . .	. . .	. . .	. . .	. . .	. . .	. . .	. . .	. . .
Textile mill products	0.5	1.0	3.7	4.0	2.3	1.8	. . .	0.1	. . .	0.2	0.4	0.7
Apparel	7.6	9.3	1.8	2.8	2.3	2.1	0.1	0.3	0.3	0.1	0.3	0.2
Lumber and wood products	6.9	2.5	5.3	4.0	4.5	4.0	0.9	0.8	1.2	2.3	3.5	2.8
Furniture and fixtures	2.2	0.8	0.6	0.9	1.5	0.9	0.3	0.3	0.1	0.2	0.1	0.1
Paper products	0.8	0.9	1.8	1.5	1.7	1.9	0.1	0.2	0.3	0.5	0.3	0.2
Printing and publishing	3.8	1.0	1.4	1.6	2.4	1.7	0.3	0.3	0.3	0.3	0.4	0.3
Chemical products	15.2	15.0	11.3	16.8	24.0	17.7	5.0	5.9	3.6	5.2	6.3	4.2
Refined petroleum products	50.2	37.9	54.2	68.3	65.5	65.7	0.8	. . .	. . .	. . .	. . .	. . .
Rubber and plastic products	5.0	4.4	4.3	5.3	9.0	8.0	0.7	0.6	0.5	0.3	0.7	1.1
Leather products	0.2	0.2	0.3	0.2	0.5	0.4	. . .	. . .	. . .	. . .	0.1	. . .
Stone, clay and glass products	21.0	4.5	2.5	2.5	8.7	5.2	0.2	0.3	0.4	0.4	0.2	0.5
Primary metals	2.7	3.3	3.8	5.3	10.9	12.2	1.0	1.2	1.1	1.9	5.0	6.0
Fabricated metal products	1.1	2.6	1.6	3.5	3.9	8.4	0.3	0.5	0.4	0.7	1.0	3.4
Industrial machinery and computers	69.2	37.9	39.8	55.2	54.4	50.3	9.7	5.3	7.9	12.7	8.2	11.2
Electric and electronic equipment	203.0	214.7	686.5	1 450.3	1 575.5	2 612.9	8.3	8.5	7.2	8.1	10.9	20.7
Transportation equipment	25.7	13.0	29.5	55.0	42.0	48.2	3.5	3.1	11.6	5.4	15.5	6.0
Scientific and measuring instruments	17.2	21.4	27.4	33.3	36.3	40.8	1.8	1.4	1.7	1.7	1.7	4.4
Miscellaneous manufactures	10.7	11.0	10.4	16.7	10.6	14.2	0.9	0.8	0.8	0.6	0.8	0.7
Unidentified manufactures	2.5	2.2	1.9	3.3	3.1	8.9	0.6	0.6	0.6	0.6	0.8	1.2
Agricultural And Livestock Products	16.0	20.9	12.0	10.3	9.9	9.5	4.4	4.7	2.9	2.3	2.2	2.9
Agricultural products	15.6	20.1	11.4	9.8	8.6	6.5	4.3	4.7	2.8	2.2	2.0	2.8
Livestock and livestock products	0.4	0.7	0.6	0.5	1.3	3.0	0.1	0.1	0.2	. . .	0.3	0.2
Other Commodities	21.8	20.3	12.9	30.2	20.5	39.2	7.4	6.5	7.7	9.8	7.9	8.2
Forestry products	0.1	. . .	0.1	0.1	0.1	0.2	. . .	. . .	0.1	0.1	0.1	0.1
Fish and other marine products	0.3	0.5	0.1	0.5	0.8	0.4	0.1	0.3	0.1	. . .	0.5	0.3
Metallic ores and concentrates	. . .	0.1	0.8	3.0	5.2	6.2	. . .	. . .	. . .	. . .	. . .	. . .
Bituminous coal and lignite	. . .	. . .	. . .	. . .	. . .	. . .	. . .	. . .	. . .	. . .	. . .	. . .
Crude petroleum and natural gas	. . .	3.1	. . .	. . .	. . .	. . .	. . .	. . .	. . .	. . .	. . .	. . .
Nonmetallic minerals	4.9	4.9	4.0	4.2	4.5	5.5	2.3	2.4	2.6	2.8	3.0	4.0
Scrap and waste	0.9	2.9	0.5	0.6	0.1	11.8	0.1	0.1	0.2	0.2	. . .	0.2
Used merchandise	10.5	4.8	2.4	14.5	4.7	7.8	0.3	0.3	0.8	0.1	0.4	0.4
Goods imported and returned unchanged	4.6	3.4	3.3	6.3	3.8	2.7	4.6	3.4	3.3	6.3	3.8	2.7
Special classification provisions	0.5	0.7	1.5	1.1	1.4	4.7	. . .	0.1	0.6	0.2	0.1	0.5

Table D-34. NEW MEXICO: State Exports of Goods by Destination and Industry, 1994–1999—*Continued*

(Millions of dollars.)

Industry	South and Central American and Caribbean						Mexico					
	1994	1995	1996	1997	1998	1999	1994	1995	1996	1997	1998	1999
ALL GOODS	7.2	10.7	8.9	13.8	29.0	53.4	93.9	77.1	100.0	86.6	86.6	114.0
Manufactured Goods	5.6	9.8	6.8	13.4	28.4	52.9	87.6	64.9	96.1	80.5	76.8	97.2
Food products	0.2	...	0.1	0.1	0.7	0.5	2.7	0.8	0.5	1.2	2.8	2.1
Tobacco products	...	...	...	...	...	...	...	...	...	...	...	...
Textile mill products	...	...	...	0.1	0.1	0.2	0.1	0.5	3.4	3.0	1.3	0.2
Apparel	...	0.1	0.1	0.1	0.2	...	6.6	7.8	0.3	1.2	0.7	0.4
Lumber and wood products	0.1	...	...	...	...	0.1	1.6	0.4	0.5	0.2	0.2	0.3
Furniture and fixtures	0.1	...	...	...	...	...	0.1	0.2	0.2	0.2	...	...
Paper products	0.1	0.1	0.1	0.1	0.2	0.1	0.3	0.4	0.3	0.5	0.4	1.0
Printing and publishing	0.1	...	0.2	0.2	0.1	0.2	0.1	...	...	...	0.1	...
Chemical products	0.6	0.3	0.2	0.3	0.4	1.5	0.6	1.2	3.9	2.7	2.7	4.1
Refined petroleum products	...	...	...	...	2.5	...	49.3	37.8	54.0	56.6	46.2	65.6
Rubber and plastic products	0.1	0.2	0.1	0.2	0.3	0.3	0.7	0.9	0.7	1.3	5.1	3.7
Leather products	0.1	...	0.1	...	...	0.1	...	0.1	...	...	...	0.1
Stono, clay and glass products	...	0.2	0.1	0.1	0.9	0.1	0.4	0.3	0.3	0.4	0.5	0.5
Primary metals	0.1	0.1	0.1	0.1	0.3	0.1	0.4	0.4	1.6	1.9	3.8	4.7
Fabricated metal products	0.1	...	...	0.4	0.3	0.2	0.3	0.5	0.3	0.6	0.7	1.2
Industrial machinery and computers	1.2	5.3	3.3	2.8	12.8	1.5	9.0	2.4	4.2	4.2	4.3	3.7
Electric and electronic equipment	0.7	1.2	0.5	5.4	4.5	40.4	13.5	9.5	23.7	1.6	2.6	4.5
Transportation equipment	0.7	0.2	0.2	0.5	0.3	0.2	0.1	0.4	0.4	2.1	2.5	0.7
Scientific and measuring instruments	0.6	0.9	0.7	1.0	2.9	5.4	1.0	0.9	1.0	2.3	1.6	0.6
Miscellaneous manufactures	0.8	0.8	0.8	2.1	2.0	2.0	0.2	0.1	0.1	0.1	0.1	0.2
Unidentified manufactures	0.1	0.1	...	...	0.1	0.1	0.6	0.4	0.7	0.5	1.3	3.4
Agricultural And Livestock Products	1.5	0.8	1.9	0.2	0.4	0.2	4.2	5.5	2.8	3.3	3.9	4.9
Agricultural products	1.5	0.8	1.9	0.2	0.4	0.2	4.0	5.4	2.4	2.9	3.2	2.2
Livestock and livestock products	...	...	...	...	...	...	0.1	...	0.3	0.5	0.7	2.7
Other Commodities	0.1	0.1	0.2	0.1	0.2	0.3	2.1	6.7	1.1	2.8	5.8	12.0
Forestry products	...	...	...	...	...	...	...	...	...	...	...	...
Fish and other marine products	...	...	...	...	0.1	...	...	...	...	...	0.1	...
Metallic ores and concentrates	...	...	...	...	...	...	...	...	0.5	2.2	5.2	...
Bituminous coal and lignite	...	...	...	...	...	...	...	...	...	...	...	...
Crude petroleum and natural gas	...	...	...	...	...	...	...	3.1	...	...	...	...
Nonmetallic materials	...	...	...	...	...	0.1	1.1	1.0	0.1	0.1	0.2	...
Scrap and waste	...	...	...	...	...	...	0.7	2.5	0.3	0.3	0.1	11.6
Used merchandise	0.1	...	0.1	0.1	0.1	...	0.2	...	0.1	0.1	0.3	0.2
Goods imported and returned unchanged	...	...	...	...	...	...	...	...	0.1	...	...	...
Special classification provisions	...	...	...	...	...	0.1	...	...	...	...	...	0.1

Industry	European Union						United Kingdom					
	1994	1995	1996	1997	1998	1999	1994	1995	1996	1997	1998	1999
ALL GOODS	114.3	112.6	103.2	153.8	110.0	206.4	46.4	26.7	10.7	13.4	15.8	23.2
Manufactured Goods	110.9	105.1	99.5	148.8	103.8	194.5	46.0	25.9	9.9	12.8	13.4	22.4
Food products	0.3	0.1	0.2	2.3	1.0	1.0	0.1	0.1	...	1.8	0.2	0.2
Tobacco products	...	...	...	...	...	...	...	...	...	...	...	...
Textile mill products	0.1	0.1	...	0.1	0.1	...	...	...	...	...	...	...
Apparel	0.2	0.6	0.1	0.2	0.7	1.0	...	0.3	...	...	0.1	...
Lumber and wood products	1.8	0.5	1.1	0.2	0.3	0.4	...	...	...	...	0.1	...
Furniture and fixtures	0.2	0.1	...	0.3	0.4	0.2	...	...	...	...	...	...
Paper products	...	...	...	...	0.4	0.2	...	...	...	...	...	0.1
Printing and publishing	3.1	0.2	0.6	0.5	0.6	0.7	0.5	0.1	0.4	0.4	0.4	0.3
Chemical products	7.5	6.2	1.5	6.6	10.0	5.3	0.5	0.2	0.3	0.4	1.5	1.9
Refined petroleum products	...	...	...	0.1	...	...	...	...	...	...	...	...
Rubber and plastic products	1.0	0.8	1.4	1.2	1.8	1.9	0.2	0.2	0.8	0.7	0.9	0.6
Leather products	0.1	0.1	...	0.1	0.3	0.2	...	...	...	...	...	...
Stone, clay and glass products	13.0	1.0	0.8	0.5	0.3	0.8	9.0	0.4	0.1	0.1	0.1	0.4
Primary metals	0.5	0.4	0.5	0.4	0.5	0.7	0.2	...	0.1	0.1	0.1	0.2
Fabricated metal products	0.2	0.7	0.3	1.0	0.6	1.2	...	...	0.2	0.4	0.3	0.5
Industrial machinery and computers	20.5	15.6	10.9	9.0	10.8	14.3	15.2	0.5	1.3	2.1	2.7	2.6
Electric and electronic equipment	49.4	60.4	55.3	71.3	48.5	121.3	18.9	20.7	4.0	3.3	4.1	9.3
Transportation equipment	2.0	5.2	12.3	42.0	14.4	26.0	0.1	0.4	0.2	0.6	0.9	1.8
Scientific and measuring instruments	5.2	8.1	7.9	8.6	8.9	11.8	0.8	2.1	1.7	2.4	1.2	3.6
Miscellaneous manufactures	5.2	4.4	6.4	4.2	3.9	3.8	0.2	0.7	0.6	0.3	0.5	0.6
Unidentified manufactures	0.7	0.6	0.1	0.3	0.4	3.6	0.2	0.1	...	...	0.2	0.2
Agricultural And Livestock Products	1.0	2.8	1.6	2.9	2.3	1.1	0.2	0.4	...	...	0.1	0.1
Agricultural products	0.8	2.5	1.6	2.9	2.1	1.0	...	0.1	...	...	...	...
Livestock and livestock products	0.2	0.3	...	...	0.1	...	0.2	0.3	...	...	...	...
Other Commodities	2.4	4.7	2.0	2.1	4.0	10.8	0.2	0.4	0.8	0.7	2.3	0.7
Forestry products	...	...	...	...	...	...	...	...	...	...	...	...
Fish and other marine products	...	...	...	0.1	0.1	...	...	...	...	...	...	...
Metallic ores and concentrates	...	...	0.3	0.8	...	6.2	...	...	0.3	...	...	0.1
Bituminous coal and lignite	...	...	...	...	...	...	...	...	...	...	...	...
Crude petroleum and natural gas	...	...	...	...	...	...	...	...	...	...	...	...
Nonmetallic materials	0.2	0.6	0.5	0.1	...	0.2	0.1	0.1	...	...	...	0.1
Scrap and waste	...	0.1	...	...	...	...	...	...	...	...	...	...
Used merchandise	2.1	3.8	0.8	0.5	3.0	2.2	0.1	0.2	0.3	0.2	2.2	0.2
Goods imported and returned unchanged	...	...	...	...	...	...	...	...	...	...	...	...
Special classification provisions	0.1	0.2	0.4	0.6	0.9	2.2	...	0.1	0.1	0.4	0.1	0.3

Table D-34. NEW MEXICO: State Exports of Goods by Destination and Industry, 1994–1999—*Continued*

(Millions of dollars.)

Industry	Germany						France					
	1994	1995	1996	1997	1998	1999	1994	1995	1996	1997	1998	1999
ALL GOODS	32.9	26.1	19.1	18.8	13.4	47.2	12.1	20.8	27.6	32.3	30.5	41.5
Manufactured Goods	32.4	22.2	18.5	18.2	12.8	45.3	10.4	20.2	27.0	32.1	30.3	41.2
Food products	...	...	...	0.1	0.3	...	...	...	...	...	0.1	0.3
Tobacco products	...	...	...	...	...	...	...	...	...	...	...	...
Textile mill products	...	...	...	...	...	...	...	...	...	...	...	...
Apparel	0.1	0.1	...	...	...	...	...	...	...	...	...	...
Lumber and wood products	0.5	0.2	0.8	...	0.2	0.3	0.3	0.2	0.2	...	...	...
Furniture and fixtures	...	...	...	0.1	...	0.2	...	...	...	...	...	...
Paper products	...	...	...	...	0.1	...	...	...	...	...	0.3	...
Printing and publishing	2.5	...	...	...	0.1	...	...	...	...	0.1	...	...
Chemical products	0.1	0.4	0.4	1.0	1.0	0.8	0.4	0.7	...	0.9	7.4	2.4
Refined petroleum products	...	...	...	...	...	...	...	...	...	0.1	...	...
Rubber and plastic products	0.3	0.5	0.4	0.2	0.4	1.0	...	...	...	0.1	0.1	0.1
Leather products	...	...	...	0.1	0.1	0.1	...	...	...	...	...	...
Stone, clay and glass products	3.9	0.3	0.2	0.1	...	...	...	0.1	...	0.1	...	...
Primary metals	0.1	0.2	...	...	0.1	0.3	...	...	...	...	0.3	0.1
Fabricated metal products	0.1	0.1	...	0.1	0.1	0.1	...	0.5	...	...	...	0.3
Industrial machinery and computers	0.8	2.0	2.1	1.0	1.4	3.7	2.9	4.3	2.4	1.2	1.1	1.3
Electric and electronic equipment	19.7	9.7	7.3	9.7	4.2	12.7	5.0	11.9	21.5	28.0	19.7	34.8
Transportation equipment	0.2	3.4	0.7	1.8	0.5	20.1	0.4	0.1	0.7	...	0.1	0.5
Scientific and measuring instruments	0.8	2.5	1.9	1.2	2.3	1.0	0.5	1.7	1.7	1.3	0.7	0.8
Miscellaneous manufactures	2.9	2.6	4.5	2.6	1.9	1.9	0.7	0.4	0.3	0.3	0.5	0.5
Unidentified manufactures	0.2	0.2	...	0.2	0.1	3.0	0.1	0.1	...	...	0.1	...
Agricultural And Livestock Products	0.3	1.5	0.2	0.4	0.4	0.2	...	...	...	...	...	0.1
Agricultural products	0.3	1.5	0.2	0.4	0.3	0.2	...	...	...	...	...	0.1
Livestock and livestock products	...	...	...	...	0.1	...	...	...	...	...	...	...
Other Commodities	0.2	2.4	0.4	0.2	0.2	1.7	1.8	0.7	0.6	0.1	0.2	0.3
Forestry products	...	...	...	...	...	...	...	...	...	...	...	...
Fish and other marine products	...	...	...	0.1	...	...	...	...	...	...	...	...
Metallic ores and concentrates	...	...	...	...	...	...	...	...	...	...	...	...
Bituminous coal and lignite	...	...	...	...	...	...	...	...	...	...	...	...
Crude petroleum and natural gas	...	...	...	...	...	...	...	...	...	...	...	...
Nonmetallic materials	0.1	...	...	...	...	...	...	0.5	0.4	0.1	...	...
Scrap and waste	...	...	...	...	...	...	...	...	...	...	...	...
Used merchandise	0.1	2.4	0.3	0.1	0.1	1.5	1.8	0.1	...	...	0.2	0.2
Goods imported and returned unchanged	...	...	...	...	...	...	...	...	...	...	...	...
Special classification provisions	0.1	...	0.1	...	...	0.2	...	0.1	0.1	...	...	0.1

Industry	The Netherlands						Asian 10					
	1994	1995	1996	1997	1998	1999	1994	1995	1996	1997	1998	1999
ALL GOODS	4.4	16.3	4.9	21.3	6.3	24.4	186.5	165.9	630.8	1 426.6	1 570.8	2 450.3
Manufactured Goods	4.2	15.9	4.7	20.4	6.1	18.2	181.5	160.5	628.0	1 424.1	1 568.4	2 448.1
Food products	0.1	...	...	0.1	...	...	0.3	0.4	0.4	0.7	0.6	6.2
Tobacco products	...	...	...	...	...	...	...	...	0.1	...	...	...
Textile mill products	...	...	...	0.1	0.1	...	0.2	0.1	0.2	0.5	0.2	0.2
Apparel	...	...	...	...	0.3	...	0.7	0.5	1.0	1.0	0.4	0.5
Lumber and wood products	0.1	...	...	...	...	...	2.2	0.5	2.0	1.3	0.4	0.5
Furniture and fixtures	0.1	...	...	...	...	...	0.1	0.1	0.2	0.2	0.8	0.2
Paper products	...	...	...	...	...	...	0.4	0.1	0.8	0.4	0.4	0.1
Printing and publishing	...	...	...	...	...	...	0.1	0.2	0.2	0.5	0.5	0.2
Chemical products	...	0.2	0.1	0.2	...	0.1	0.6	0.6	1.2	0.7	1.0	2.0
Refined petroleum products	...	...	...	...	...	...	0.1	...	...	11.6	16.7	...
Rubber and plastic products	0.2	...	...	...	...	...	2.1	1.2	0.9	0.8	0.4	0.3
Leather products	...	...	...	...	...	...	0.1	0.1	0.1	...	0.1	0.1
Stone, clay and glass products	...	...	0.1	0.1	...	...	6.8	2.0	0.7	0.8	6.6	3.1
Primary metals	0.1	0.1	0.2	0.1	0.1	...	0.3	1.1	0.4	0.7	1.1	0.6
Fabricated metal products	...	...	...	0.3	...	0.1	0.1	0.6	0.3	0.4	0.9	1.7
Industrial machinery and computers	0.6	0.6	0.7	0.4	0.7	2.9	25.3	7.2	9.7	20.4	12.7	12.8
Electric and electronic equipment	2.7	14.6	3.4	4.0	4.3	12.8	128.5	130.3	593.9	1 360.1	1 502.1	2 392.6
Transportation equipment	...	0.1	...	14.1	...	1.4	5.9	3.9	3.6	4.3	5.6	9.3
Scientific and measuring instruments	0.1	0.2	0.2	1.1	0.3	0.5	4.7	7.3	10.4	11.7	14.8	10.4
Miscellaneous manufactures	...	...	...	...	0.1	0.1	2.9	4.1	1.7	8.1	2.8	6.7
Unidentified manufactures	...	...	...	...	0.1	0.1	0.3	0.3	0.3	0.2	0.3	0.4
Agricultural And Livestock Products	0.1	0.3	0.2	0.3	0.1	0.1	2.4	3.7	1.6	0.8	0.6	0.3
Agricultural products	0.1	0.3	0.2	0.3	0.1	0.1	2.4	3.4	1.5	0.7	0.6	0.3
Livestock and livestock products	...	...	...	...	...	...	...	0.3	0.1	0.1	...	...
Other Commodities	0.1	...	...	0.5	0.1	6.2	2.6	1.6	1.2	1.7	1.8	1.9
Forestry products	...	...	...	...	...	...	0.1	...	...	...	...	0.1
Fish and other marine products	...	...	...	...	0.1	...	0.2	0.2	...	0.3	...	...
Metallic ores and concentrates	...	...	...	0.5	...	6.1	...	...	...	...	...	...
Bituminous coal and lignite	...	...	...	...	...	...	...	...	...	...	...	...
Crude petroleum and natural gas	...	...	...	...	...	...	...	...	...	...	...	...
Nonmetallic materials	...	...	...	...	...	...	1.2	0.8	0.8	1.2	1.2	1.1
Scrap and waste	...	...	...	...	...	...	...	...	...	...	0.1	...
Used merchandise	0.1	...	...	...	...	...	1.0	0.4	0.3	0.1	0.5	0.1
Goods imported and returned unchanged	...	...	...	...	...	...	...	...	...	...	...	...
Special classification provisions	...	...	...	...	...	...	...	0.1	0.1	0.1	0.1	0.6

Table D-34. NEW MEXICO: State Exports of Goods by Destination and Industry, 1994–1999—Continued

(Millions of dollars.)

Industry	Japan						South Korea					
	1994	1995	1996	1997	1998	1999	1994	1995	1996	1997	1998	1999
ALL GOODS	44.2	21.2	45.7	60.1	26.1	30.9	68.7	59.1	184.4	197.2	375.9	784.9
Manufactured Goods	40.6	18.9	43.6	58.5	24.7	29.6	67.8	57.1	184.2	196.8	375.7	784.7
Food products	0.3	0.1	...	0.3	0.6	2.6	...	...	0.1	0.1	...	1.9
Tobacco products	...	...	0.1	...	...	...	...	...	...	...	...	...
Textile mill products	0.2	0.1	0.1	0.3	0.2	0.1	...	...	...	...	...	...
Apparel	0.7	0.4	0.7	0.9	0.2	0.5	...	...	...	...	...	...
Lumber and wood products	2.2	0.4	2.0	1.0	0.3	0.3	...	...	...	0.1	0.1	0.1
Furniture and fixtures	...	0.1	...	...	0.7	0.2	...	...	...	0.1	...	...
Paper products	0.3	...	0.2	0.2	...	...	...	...	...	...	...	...
Printing and publishing	0.1	0.1	0.1	0.1	0.2	0.1	...	...	...	...	...	...
Chemical products	0.3	0.3	0.5	0.4	0.2	0.1	...	...	...	...	...	0.1
Refined petroleum products	...	...	...	...	...	...	...	...	...	...	...	...
Rubber and plastic products	0.2	0.2	0.4	0.4	0.2	0.2	0.1	0.1	0.1	...	...	...
Leather products	0.1	0.1	...	...	0.1	0.1	...	...	...	...	...	...
Stone, clay and glass products	0.2	0.1	0.1	0.1	0.1	...	0.1	0.1	0.2	0.2	0.3	0.1
Primary metals	0.1	1.0	0.1	0.1	0.1	0.1	...	...	...	...	0.3	0.1
Fabricated metal products	...	0.2	0.2	0.3	0.2	0.2	...	...	...	...	0.1	...
Industrial machinery and computers	20.6	0.7	2.1	3.7	1.0	3.2	0.2	0.3	0.6	0.4	0.6	2.1
Electric and electronic equipment	7.1	6.5	28.4	38.6	6.7	5.4	65.0	55.4	181.4	194.8	372.5	778.0
Transportation equipment	4.1	3.4	3.0	3.9	5.4	8.3	1.4	0.4	0.4	0.1	0.1	0.2
Scientific and measuring instruments	2.0	3.9	4.4	4.7	6.2	5.5	0.5	0.5	1.3	0.8	1.7	1.9
Miscellaneous manufactures	2.1	1.3	1.1	3.4	2.2	2.6	0.3	0.2	...	0.1	...	...
Unidentified manufactures	0.1	0.1	0.1	...	0.1	0.1	...	...	...	...	...	0.1
Agricultural And Livestock Products	1.5	1.1	1.3	0.7	0.2	0.2	0.9	2.0	0.1	...	...	...
Agricultural products	1.5	1.0	1.3	0.7	0.2	0.2	0.9	1.8	...	...	...	...
Livestock and livestock products	...	0.1	...	...	...	...	...	0.2	0.1	...	...	...
Other Commodities	2.2	1.2	0.7	1.0	1.2	1.1	...	0.1	0.1	0.4	0.1	0.1
Forestry products	...	...	...	...	...	...	...	...	...	...	...	...
Fish and other marine products	0.1	0.2	...	...	...	...	...	...	...	0.3	...	...
Metallic ores and concentrates	...	...	...	...	...	...	...	...	...	...	...	...
Bituminous coal and lignite	...	...	...	...	...	...	...	...	...	...	...	...
Crude petroleum and natural gas	...	...	...	...	...	...	...	...	...	...	...	...
Nonmetallic materials	1.1	0.6	0.5	0.7	0.7	0.8	...	0.1	0.1	...	0.1	...
Scrap and waste	...	...	...	0.1	...	...	...	...	...	...	...	...
Used merchandise	1.0	0.3	0.1	0.1	0.4	0.1	...	...	0.1	...	0.1	...
Goods imported and returned unchanged	...	...	...	...	...	...	...	...	...	...	...	0.1
Special classification provisions	...	0.1	0.1	0.1	...	0.2	...	...	...	...	...	0.1

Industry	Taiwan						Singapore					
	1994	1995	1996	1997	1998	1999	1994	1995	1996	1997	1998	1999
ALL GOODS	6.9	13.6	53.4	115.7	67.5	66.9	2.8	8.1	5.4	2.6	1.8	7.8
Manufactured Goods	6.7	13.4	53.4	115.6	67.3	66.8	2.7	8.0	5.4	2.5	1.6	7.5
Food products	...	0.1	0.1	0.1	...	0.2	...	0.2	0.1	0.1	...	...
Tobacco products	...	...	...	...	...	...	...	...	...	0.1	...	0.1
Textile mill products	...	...	...	0.1	...	...	...	...	...	0.1	0.2	...
Apparel	...	...	0.1	...	...	...	...	...	...	...	...	...
Lumber and wood products	...	...	...	0.1	...	...	...	...	...	...	...	...
Furniture and fixtures	...	...	...	...	...	...	...	...	...	0.1	...	...
Paper products	...	...	0.1	...	...	...	...	...	...	...	...	...
Printing and publishing	...	0.1	...	0.4	0.2	...	...	0.1	...	...	...	0.1
Chemical products	0.1	0.1	0.1	0.2	0.1	...	...	0.1	0.2	...	...	...
Refined petroleum products	...	...	...	11.5	16.7	...	...	...	...	...	...	...
Rubber and plastic products	...	...	...	...	...	...	0.1	0.1	0.1	0.2	...	...
Leather products	...	...	...	...	...	...	...	...	...	...	...	...
Stone, clay and glass products	0.1	0.9	0.3	0.3	0.2	...	0.3	0.2	...	...	...	...
Primary metals	0.1	...	...	0.1	0.1	0.1	...	0.1	0.1	...	0.1	0.1
Fabricated metal products	...	...	...	...	0.1	0.7	...	...	0.1	0.1	...	...
Industrial machinery and computers	0.7	0.4	0.2	2.1	1.4	1.6	1.4	3.5	4.1	1.3	0.3	1.8
Electric and electronic equipment	5.2	11.4	51.5	99.0	47.2	60.6	0.6	1.0	0.2	0.3	0.3	4.9
Transportation equipment	0.1	...	...	...	...	0.2	...	...	...	...	...	0.1
Scientific and measuring instruments	0.2	0.3	0.5	1.6	1.1	0.4	0.1	0.7	0.2	0.1	0.5	0.4
Miscellaneous manufactures	0.1	0.1	0.2	0.1	...	3.0	0.2	2.0	0.1	0.1	0.1	...
Unidentified manufactures	...	...	0.2	0.1	0.1	0.1	...	...	...	...	...	...
Agricultural And Livestock Products	...	...	...	...	0.1	...	...	...	...	...	...	...
Agricultural products	...	...	...	...	0.1	...	...	...	...	...	...	...
Livestock and livestock products	...	...	...	...	...	...	...	...	...	...	...	...
Other Commodities	0.1	0.2	0.1	0.1	0.1	...	0.1	0.1	...	0.1	0.2	0.3
Forestry products	0.1	...	...	...	...	...	...	...	...	...	...	...
Fish and other marine products	...	...	...	...	...	...	...	...	...	...	...	...
Metallic ores and concentrates	...	...	...	...	...	...	...	...	...	...	...	...
Bituminous coal and lignite	...	...	...	...	...	...	...	...	...	...	...	...
Crude petroleum and natural gas	...	...	...	...	...	...	...	...	...	...	...	...
Nonmetallic materials	0.1	0.1	0.1	0.1	0.1	...	0.1	...	...	0.1	0.1	...
Scrap and waste	...	...	...	...	...	...	...	...	...	...	...	...
Used merchandise	...	...	...	...	...	...	...	...	...	...	...	...
Goods imported and returned unchanged	...	...	...	...	...	...	...	...	...	...	...	...
Special classification provisions	...	...	...	...	...	...	...	...	...	...	...	0.2

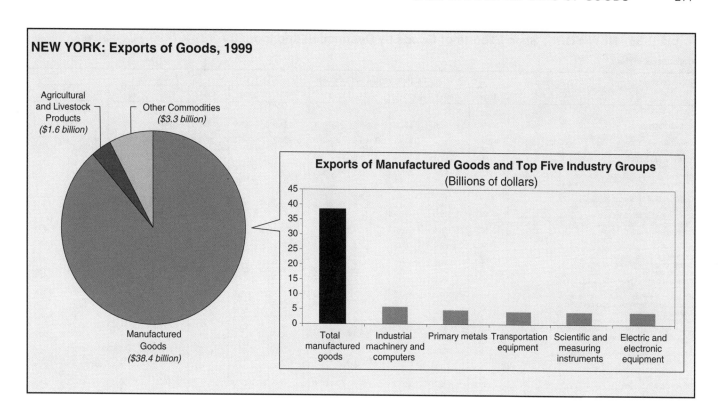

NEW YORK: Exports of Goods, 1999

Agricultural and Livestock Products ($1.6 billion)

Other Commodities ($3.3 billion)

Manufactured Goods ($38.4 billion)

Exports of Manufactured Goods and Top Five Industry Groups
(Billions of dollars)

Total manufactured goods | Industrial machinery and computers | Primary metals | Transportation equipment | Scientific and measuring instruments | Electric and electronic equipment

Table D-35. NEW YORK: State Exports of Goods by Destination and Industry, 1994–1999

(Millions of dollars.)

Industry	All destinations						Canada					
	1994	1995	1996	1997	1998	1999	1994	1995	1996	1997	1998	1999
ALL GOODS	37 259.7	44 080.1	44 964.7	48 885.3	45 564.5	43 296.8	7 487.2	9 243.7	8 956.7	10 616.0	9 957.1	9 735.9
Manufactured Goods	32 145.7	38 094.9	38 794.8	42 577.2	39 552.1	38 376.0	6 580.3	8 337.9	8 003.9	9 363.9	8 664.5	8 663.9
Food products	1 917.3	2 186.1	2 264.2	2 685.6	2 280.6	1 534.4	242.8	225.9	254.8	283.8	297.8	324.6
Tobacco products	248.8	196.2	70.7	73.4	25.1	20.3	0.1	. . .	0.1	0.1	0.1	0.1
Textile mill products	705.5	748.1	741.1	775.2	666.9	551.1	150.2	161.0	174.1	183.3	180.3	165.3
Apparel	620.8	607.1	597.8	669.0	643.8	632.8	65.1	73.1	89.3	112.1	126.3	103.9
Lumber and wood products	352.1	375.8	354.5	413.9	389.6	503.6	148.7	183.1	164.1	225.9	218.0	216.3
Furniture and fixtures	98.3	113.5	96.0	106.6	100.1	76.4	29.3	47.8	35.4	28.0	30.0	25.3
Paper products	1 273.9	1 783.4	1 547.1	1 589.8	1 553.7	1 427.3	236.8	300.1	314.6	341.1	317.5	321.6
Printing and publishing	729.6	769.1	700.2	697.1	782.2	788.5	356.7	373.6	386.8	393.1	420.1	383.0
Chemical products	3 335.8	3 544.1	3 459.0	3 443.2	3 351.8	3 535.8	484.9	528.4	680.4	653.7	616.2	689.0
Refined petroleum products	292.0	317.1	373.0	410.9	298.3	155.7	38.1	66.2	81.2	99.1	67.7	33.6
Rubber and plastic products	554.2	664.9	675.7	818.9	679.8	679.0	172.6	198.7	210.5	201.9	196.5	214.1
Leather products	147.4	147.9	154.3	153.7	145.5	151.0	24.5	26.4	31.6	36.1	33.3	32.8
Stone, clay and glass products	375.5	408.4	428.8	518.1	442.2	467.5	83.5	86.5	89.6	92.1	106.3	128.1
Primary metals	3 047.9	4 671.2	6 013.9	5 426.5	4 689.6	4 725.4	690.7	940.5	887.2	1 264.5	956.5	803.2
Fabricated metal products	499.9	604.4	655.1	753.7	879.2	730.3	131.9	150.0	165.8	178.9	223.2	221.3
Industrial machinery and computers	5 234.6	6 255.7	5 777.6	7 217.5	6 072.4	5 785.0	876.6	1 193.4	1 104.8	1 380.5	1 307.9	1 360.1
Electric and electronic equipment	3 567.8	4 058.0	3 587.4	4 387.1	4 126.9	4 088.2	1 433.3	1 715.5	1 233.7	1 574.0	1 431.6	1 486.0
Transportation equipment	2 969.6	3 887.4	3 808.1	4 345.9	4 486.8	4 261.6	529.1	1 087.2	1 050.8	1 226.8	1 152.4	1 094.6
Scientific and measuring instruments	3 311.7	3 706.5	4 203.3	4 535.5	4 322.3	4 121.6	629.0	709.3	739.2	754.3	683.9	738.2
Miscellaneous manufactures	2 530.6	2 815.4	3 045.7	3 240.5	3 269.8	3 839.0	147.5	158.5	173.2	196.2	199.6	233.0
Unidentified manufactures	332.4	234.7	241.4	315.1	345.4	301.6	109.0	112.7	136.8	138.5	99.3	90.0
Agricultural And Livestock Products	1 784.1	2 520.3	2 921.3	2 477.1	1 942.8	1 607.7	173.8	163.6	170.3	173.2	167.2	138.2
Agricultural products	1 620.9	2 328.6	2 733.1	2 277.3	1 688.9	1 378.7	157.4	149.3	145.7	151.0	144.9	115.3
Livestock and livestock products	163.2	191.7	188.1	199.8	253.8	229.1	16.3	14.3	24.6	22.2	22.2	22.9
Other Commodities	3 329.9	3 464.9	3 248.6	3 831.0	4 069.7	3 313.0	733.1	742.2	782.5	1 078.9	1 125.4	933.7
Forestry products	33.5	31.2	21.4	13.3	12.2	16.6	5.9	5.7	3.8	3.6	1.8	3.1
Fish and other marine products	62.7	61.5	59.3	55.8	62.7	63.0	11.6	10.7	13.3	15.0	18.1	21.0
Metallic ores and concentrates	34.6	49.3	48.6	54.8	40.4	34.7	19.0	22.7	9.9	37.1	30.8	18.7
Bituminous coal and lignite	215.5	285.2	264.4	282.0	241.1	165.4	18.2	43.9	49.5	83.6	114.5	106.6
Crude petroleum and natural gas	34.2	14.3	107.5	364.7	401.1	155.0	32.7	1.7	78.2	334.0	400.8	154.6
Nonmetallic minerals	107.2	92.6	77.2	75.0	64.0	60.0	7.7	9.4	15.7	8.6	9.2	9.8
Scrap and waste	950.3	1 326.7	994.1	895.4	614.7	552.9	368.4	427.3	320.1	275.5	260.7	254.5
Used merchandise	1 382.6	1 191.7	1 150.9	1 558.1	2 078.8	1 658.6	17.2	16.7	23.9	27.4	21.9	20.8
Goods imported and returned unchanged	179.7	187.9	237.7	272.7	251.1	238.0	179.7	187.9	237.7	272.7	251.1	238.0
Special classification provisions	329.7	224.5	287.6	259.3	303.5	368.8	72.7	16.4	30.4	21.5	16.5	106.5

Table D-35. NEW YORK: State Exports of Goods by Destination and Industry, 1994–1999—*Continued*

(Millions of dollars.)

Industry	South and Central American and Caribbean						Mexico					
	1994	1995	1996	1997	1998	1999	1994	1995	1996	1997	1998	1999
ALL GOODS	3 054.5	3 401.8	3 536.8	4 088.6	4 046.1	3 111.3	1 323.9	994.0	1 303.1	1 804.9	1 936.0	2 031.1
Manufactured Goods	2 835.7	3 015.9	2 913.7	3 496.1	3 573.0	2 938.5	1 226.3	877.5	1 103.3	1 633.5	1 824.7	1 926.9
Food products	236.6	232.0	274.9	388.9	361.7	174.7	91.4	109.2	91.4	139.5	165.8	50.0
Tobacco products	46.0	60.1	50.4	28.8	5.8	1.2	. . .	. . .	. . .	. . .	. . .	. . .
Textile mill products	131.0	141.9	130.1	141.5	119.1	89.2	32.9	14.3	29.2	43.3	55.0	79.3
Apparel	294.8	252.5	240.7	300.3	302.8	320.6	24.9	15.9	23.8	29.2	37.6	26.4
Lumber and wood products	5.1	6.3	6.6	9.5	14.9	24.7	1.7	2.9	4.0	5.1	2.6	2.2
Furniture and fixtures	9.9	12.8	11.5	16.8	15.0	12.3	2.9	2.7	2.0	3.0	3.4	4.2
Paper products	152.5	248.4	229.7	262.8	259.9	168.8	75.5	84.8	83.9	92.7	124.7	137.5
Printing and publishing	22.2	16.5	15.3	19.8	32.4	28.6	11.8	8.8	14.1	8.7	10.2	10.0
Chemical products	295.2	358.4	304.8	292.6	366.0	319.5	99.2	77.8	144.6	141.4	169.4	201.9
Refined petroleum products	62.4	58.2	76.3	42.1	68.5	26.3	12.8	5.4	16.9	45.4	42.8	35.4
Rubber and plastic products	55.3	86.9	80.3	87.4	72.2	43.7	71.2	65.5	54.4	68.5	72.6	96.7
Leather products	9.4	14.7	12.6	12.5	13.0	20.0	1.9	1.2	0.8	1.4	1.4	3.8
Stone, clay and glass products	28.5	32.5	30.5	40.8	30.2	49.0	11.4	10.8	14.4	12.8	19.1	22.9
Primary metals	74.9	112.1	62.4	76.2	70.7	64.1	136.6	70.2	96.4	129.0	212.1	186.3
Fabricated metal products	34.9	40.3	41.0	56.2	42.2	29.7	23.0	20.7	33.8	47.9	50.3	67.4
Industrial machinery and computers	442.4	387.6	466.3	604.3	571.3	417.8	113.0	70.3	91.3	242.6	198.4	231.4
Electric and electronic equipment	262.7	252.3	226.0	295.0	403.8	328.2	220.2	98.8	140.3	233.6	228.8	288.7
Transportation equipment	273.1	222.4	157.4	303.2	268.1	340.1	61.3	10.8	7.8	37.5	10.9	10.4
Scientific and measuring instruments	296.8	379.9	383.4	401.9	400.9	310.6	202.3	191.4	237.3	318.6	375.6	408.8
Miscellaneous manufactures	73.1	84.6	96.9	91.8	119.9	138.7	25.2	14.2	12.0	16.4	19.7	25.1
Unidentified manufactures	28.8	15.6	16.4	23.8	34.4	30.7	7.0	1.8	5.0	17.0	24.6	38.5
Agricultural And Livestock Products	132.9	283.3	512.5	469.3	381.5	124.9	68.6	75.4	136.3	118.1	87.2	69.3
Agricultural products	131.1	281.7	504.0	461.1	379.4	122.4	67.7	75.1	136.2	117.8	86.6	68.7
Livestock and livestock products	1.7	1.6	8.5	8.2	2.1	2.4	0.9	0.3	0.2	0.3	0.6	0.6
Other Commodities	85.9	102.7	110.7	123.1	91.6	48.0	29.0	41.2	63.5	53.3	24.1	34.9
Forestry products	2.9	4.1	3.1	0.9	1.8	1.0	3.2	0.5	0.8	1.0	0.8	1.3
Fish and other marine products	0.9	0.7	0.8	1.2	1.4	1.4	0.1	. . .	0.1	0.1	0.3	0.2
Metallic ores and concentrates	0.6	1.8	1.7	0.8	1.7	0.5	0.7	0.1	0.5	. . .	. . .	1.7
Bituminous coal and lignite	38.9	53.5	68.9	75.4	34.3	5.4	7.4	12.8	14.0	9.3	3.8	0.5
Crude petroleum and natural gas	0.3	0.1	0.1	0.3	. . .	. . .	. . .	11.6	29.1	8.3	. . .	. . .
Nonmetallic minerals	5.6	6.7	2.9	2.4	2.9	1.7	1.8	1.9	2.4	1.5	0.5	1.0
Scrap and waste	15.5	18.8	12.0	13.1	10.7	4.8	5.8	10.4	6.2	16.6	1.1	20.3
Used merchandise	11.7	12.2	15.8	24.2	31.9	21.5	8.4	1.5	8.7	13.5	10.8	3.3
Goods imported and returned unchanged	. . .	. . .	. . .	. . .	. . .	. . .	. . .	. . .	. . .	. . .	. . .	. . .
Special classification provisions	9.5	4.9	5.3	4.8	6.9	11.7	1.6	2.3	1.8	3.0	6.9	6.6

Industry	European Union						United Kingdom					
	1994	1995	1996	1997	1998	1999	1994	1995	1996	1997	1998	1999
ALL GOODS	8 152.9	9 474.6	9 958.1	10 108.2	11 210.5	10 362.3	2 703.6	2 744.8	3 593.4	3 140.1	3 898.6	3 344.3
Manufactured Goods	6 984.5	8 133.0	8 912.3	8 853.1	9 802.5	8 811.4	2 323.1	2 397.6	3 295.5	2 609.8	3 457.5	2 752.0
Food products	147.5	143.5	158.9	262.0	265.8	127.1	39.8	37.0	31.5	33.8	40.6	47.1
Tobacco products	125.3	86.2	0.1	6.6	0.2	1.2	. . .	. . .	. . .	. . .	. . .	0.1
Textile mill products	129.2	153.5	136.8	131.4	103.8	64.2	29.4	41.3	36.3	38.9	35.9	19.3
Apparel	48.4	58.4	55.9	55.4	54.3	68.6	8.9	9.6	10.1	16.8	18.3	33.8
Lumber and wood products	49.0	64.5	54.1	55.2	63.7	94.3	7.9	11.0	8.2	10.0	13.9	19.3
Furniture and fixtures	25.5	19.4	14.4	20.2	22.2	17.0	8.8	6.2	5.6	9.6	11.1	10.6
Paper products	253.4	395.3	302.4	319.8	357.0	330.0	42.0	58.2	57.2	75.8	67.8	70.9
Printing and publishing	107.7	143.2	92.0	106.7	112.3	165.1	53.6	79.3	49.1	56.3	60.3	80.8
Chemical products	606.7	735.7	591.7	704.2	858.3	917.4	81.2	84.8	96.5	137.9	152.0	174.3
Refined petroleum products	69.6	82.4	94.1	142.1	70.9	32.4	4.3	4.6	6.1	6.1	5.8	0.8
Rubber and plastic products	96.6	144.6	130.5	207.6	156.4	163.5	19.7	25.3	28.0	40.8	34.1	38.1
Leather products	21.7	20.5	16.3	18.7	19.2	19.4	2.8	3.0	1.9	2.5	5.3	3.4
Stone, clay and glass products	71.0	69.1	65.9	84.5	94.8	90.8	14.7	16.7	16.3	16.2	12.0	22.4
Primary metals	1 029.5	1 112.6	2 050.9	952.8	1 595.8	857.8	915.5	902.0	1 858.4	798.4	1 470.0	728.4
Fabricated metal products	90.5	84.2	105.3	140.3	121.6	150.1	29.0	23.0	27.8	43.4	41.3	36.5
Industrial machinery and computers	1 211.0	1 308.2	1 203.8	1 446.1	1 509.5	1 306.8	501.6	412.4	320.2	475.8	549.4	461.1
Electric and electronic equipment	566.5	665.5	718.4	803.8	796.1	771.4	149.6	173.8	198.4	243.9	261.8	254.2
Transportation equipment	799.3	972.0	924.3	956.2	1 071.9	1 282.4	112.6	103.9	97.5	107.2	121.2	185.9
Scientific and measuring instruments	821.4	1 123.4	1 401.9	1 521.0	1 520.5	1 317.3	194.2	275.6	330.5	331.8	348.7	345.4
Miscellaneous manufactures	686.9	715.3	773.5	886.2	964.3	988.0	99.8	114.2	109.2	155.8	198.8	205.7
Unidentified manufactures	28.0	35.8	21.2	27.9	43.9	46.7	7.6	15.8	6.6	8.7	9.4	13.7
Agricultural And Livestock Products	348.6	474.2	302.6	272.1	458.6	404.1	68.9	65.9	46.2	58.8	83.2	57.7
Agricultural products	245.6	353.0	214.1	161.7	296.9	288.5	11.8	9.4	7.5	7.1	13.4	16.2
Livestock and livestock products	103.0	121.2	88.5	110.4	161.7	115.6	57.1	56.4	38.7	51.7	69.8	41.5
Other Commodities	819.8	867.4	743.2	983.0	949.5	1 146.9	311.6	281.3	251.6	471.5	357.8	534.6
Forestry products	0.6	0.6	0.6	1.0	1.6	2.8	. . .	. . .	0.2	0.2	0.9	2.1
Fish and other marine products	4.2	5.8	9.0	6.1	15.4	8.0	1.5	1.0	0.8	0.8	0.8	1.5
Metallic ores and concentrates	4.3	7.8	8.9	4.8	3.5	3.1	0.4	1.1	1.8	2.4	0.1	0.1
Bituminous coal and lignite	51.4	51.9	64.4	58.6	51.5	33.7	. . .	. . .	10.3	12.5	8.3	7.7
Crude petroleum and natural gas	0.9	0.7	. . .	. . .	0.2	0.2	. . .	. . .	. . .	. . .	. . .	. . .
Nonmetallic minerals	11.7	10.2	9.4	13.9	15.4	11.5	1.8	1.9	1.3	1.5	1.4	1.7
Scrap and waste	88.2	202.1	93.3	39.4	43.8	72.7	7.0	10.1	4.9	3.1	9.5	27.8
Used merchandise	609.0	535.5	475.9	806.6	750.0	906.8	296.4	256.0	199.9	442.2	326.3	472.0
Goods imported and returned unchanged	. . .	. . .	. . .	. . .	. . .	. . .	. . .	. . .	. . .	. . .	. . .	. . .
Special classification provisions	49.6	52.7	81.8	52.6	68.2	108.1	4.4	11.0	32.4	8.8	10.6	21.7

Table D-35. NEW YORK: State Exports of Goods by Destination and Industry, 1994–1999—*Continued*

(Millions of dollars.)

Industry	Germany						France					
	1994	1995	1996	1997	1998	1999	1994	1995	1996	1997	1998	1999
ALL GOODS	1 212.8	1 577.1	1 503.8	1 684.7	1 768.7	1 801.8	826.0	929.9	1 057.9	1 270.4	1 345.3	1 299.4
Manufactured Goods	1 002.4	1 307.1	1 310.5	1 451.8	1 422.0	1 529.2	684.0	769.6	928.1	1 115.7	1 174.2	1 113.9
Food products	10.8	17.5	24.0	28.3	16.6	11.1	7.7	9.0	11.9	10.1	9.8	10.5
Tobacco products	0.5	0.3	. . .	0.7	0.1	0.5	. . .	. . .	. . .	. . .	. . .	. . .
Textile mill products	35.7	44.6	27.8	27.3	21.9	11.2	13.0	11.0	9.3	6.9	6.8	4.9
Apparel	9.8	14.2	12.1	7.8	8.5	6.3	5.2	6.7	3.9	4.1	5.0	5.9
Lumber and wood products	5.1	7.5	6.7	8.4	8.6	15.3	2.8	3.6	4.3	3.6	3.3	6.8
Furniture and fixtures	5.2	3.9	2.2	3.1	1.7	1.1	5.6	3.5	1.8	1.6	1.7	1.1
Paper products	57.6	71.5	70.8	53.3	78.6	49.0	27.1	28.1	26.4	23.6	36.0	29.7
Printing and publishing	25.9	19.1	17.7	22.9	23.9	19.5	6.4	10.0	6.5	5.4	6.7	25.8
Chemical products	51.7	82.4	53.0	79.2	90.0	187.8	102.0	83.7	123.1	111.7	152.3	105.5
Refined petroleum products	4.2	4.4	5.2	27.8	14.1	0.9	9.0	9.7	3.4	3.5	4.9	1.8
Rubber and plastic products	13.2	19.6	13.6	39.4	35.0	24.0	30.3	47.7	38.6	54.0	37.4	30.7
Leather products	5.1	1.6	1.7	2.8	1.3	1.7	1.5	3.6	2.0	2.8	1.4	3.0
Stone, clay and glass products	12.8	17.7	15.7	27.9	37.6	32.0	22.4	18.9	16.1	18.6	25.6	12.0
Primary metals	38.4	50.9	59.4	71.1	34.8	43.2	11.5	30.8	22.3	29.3	24.3	29.0
Fabricated metal products	18.4	13.3	20.3	28.8	22.3	21.4	6.4	7.1	8.7	18.0	15.9	24.0
Industrial machinery and computers	189.1	241.8	222.8	245.1	254.3	239.2	124.6	143.8	153.1	146.2	178.8	178.7
Electric and electronic equipment	94.8	117.1	143.2	154.6	129.0	128.3	70.0	74.7	72.0	90.9	84.6	80.9
Transportation equipment	215.0	290.6	271.4	265.5	350.4	475.1	45.7	50.3	53.7	95.2	72.2	115.3
Scientific and measuring instruments	173.7	250.2	295.0	320.0	253.3	210.0	136.1	160.3	303.2	424.7	453.2	374.9
Miscellaneous manufactures	29.9	33.7	43.3	34.4	34.5	46.1	53.2	64.3	66.0	64.1	51.5	69.3
Unidentified manufactures	5.4	5.1	4.5	3.4	5.5	5.6	3.3	2.9	1.8	1.3	2.7	3.9
Agricultural And Livestock Products	93.3	147.4	77.6	77.0	142.4	78.4	21.0	39.1	28.4	18.1	25.1	38.8
Agricultural products	88.5	139.0	74.3	73.9	137.1	75.8	6.2	10.3	12.6	0.5	3.9	6.1
Livestock and livestock products	4.9	8.4	3.3	3.2	5.3	2.5	14.7	28.8	15.7	17.5	21.2	32.6
Other Commodities	117.1	122.6	115.7	155.9	204.4	194.2	121.0	121.2	101.4	136.6	146.0	146.8
Forestry products	0.2	0.1	0.2	0.2	0.1	0.2	. . .	0.2	. . .	0.4	0.1	0.3
Fish and other marine products	0.5	0.7	. . .	0.1	7.3	. . .	0.1	0.7	1.8	0.3	0.6	0.2
Metallic ores and concentrates	0.2	0.1	0.1	1.1	0.2	1.7	0.2	0.1	0.4	0.4	0.4	0.4
Bituminous coal and lignite	2.0	6.1	4.0	22.3	12.7	. . .	17.6	5.6	1.4	1.4	4.4	. . .
Crude petroleum and natural gas	. . .	. . .	. . .	. . .	0.1	0.2	. . .	. . .	. . .	. . .	. . .	. . .
Nonmetallic minerals	4.2	3.9	4.0	3.7	3.4	3.0	0.7	0.7	1.0	1.4	0.9	0.8
Scrap and waste	2.9	10.3	4.4	4.2	9.5	7.7	1.6	4.5	2.0	1.4	1.0	0.5
Used merchandise	94.9	81.2	81.6	99.1	129.7	133.1	99.0	106.0	89.9	128.4	134.1	134.4
Goods imported and returned unchanged	. . .	. . .	. . .	. . .	. . .	. . .	. . .	. . .	. . .	. . .	. . .	. . .
Special classification provisions	12.1	20.0	21.3	25.1	41.2	48.4	1.8	3.4	4.9	3.0	4.6	10.2

Industry	The Netherlands						Asian 10					
	1994	1995	1996	1997	1998	1999	1994	1995	1996	1997	1998	1999
ALL GOODS	846.6	1 090.9	906.5	874.9	1 019.1	1 054.8	10 724.2	13 013.6	12 191.5	12 122.7	9 275.2	8 880.4
Manufactured Goods	702.5	933.6	753.9	774.8	848.2	855.8	9 073.6	10 853.6	9 822.1	10 086.9	7 990.4	7 767.4
Food products	12.4	16.9	12.7	21.5	15.0	10.5	628.6	819.8	928.5	1 022.5	683.8	539.2
Tobacco products	0.2	31.7	. . .	0.1	. . .	0.5	23.7	24.7	10.8	20.8	2.4	2.1
Textile mill products	8.2	7.2	8.1	6.6	7.4	3.7	119.7	118.8	110.1	105.2	77.0	60.1
Apparel	2.3	4.0	1.9	1.8	2.6	1.7	105.7	143.3	131.0	114.7	80.0	77.2
Lumber and wood products	2.9	3.6	2.0	3.2	4.2	7.5	120.9	96.3	100.8	90.4	58.5	133.2
Furniture and fixtures	0.1	0.6	0.8	0.5	0.8	0.5	13.3	15.5	17.9	17.6	13.1	7.4
Paper products	46.4	91.0	63.2	80.7	66.4	66.6	381.9	493.1	391.5	367.1	301.4	309.7
Printing and publishing	6.8	6.9	4.9	3.9	3.5	4.8	125.2	90.1	81.3	97.7	85.9	93.8
Chemical products	106.5	91.1	78.4	110.1	126.3	187.6	1 562.8	1 512.2	1 415.8	1 329.3	1 006.0	1 109.9
Refined petroleum products	21.2	24.4	21.7	11.1	8.1	3.6	64.6	30.3	48.3	46.3	31.3	15.8
Rubber and plastic products	11.6	13.3	18.4	27.3	9.9	28.0	89.6	100.1	127.5	161.5	103.8	115.1
Leather products	1.0	0.6	0.7	0.6	0.4	1.3	79.1	73.2	82.5	77.1	68.7	65.4
Stone, clay and glass products	3.3	1.6	1.0	2.2	2.4	2.7	133.6	164.9	184.6	234.7	146.5	134.3
Primary metals	7.7	12.3	9.4	11.1	26.3	14.3	723.3	1 048.7	696.6	507.3	308.1	207.8
Fabricated metal products	9.3	6.6	7.2	13.8	8.1	8.7	168.5	250.9	259.6	256.6	364.9	178.2
Industrial machinery and computers	120.4	192.1	150.1	138.9	135.6	106.1	1 753.8	2 470.8	2 038.5	2 256.2	1 668.2	1 580.7
Electric and electronic equipment	59.8	71.7	65.4	50.6	49.9	52.0	603.8	727.0	750.2	916.6	763.2	743.2
Transportation equipment	133.2	161.7	93.8	116.0	122.8	155.0	525.7	768.9	539.1	606.2	726.9	657.1
Scientific and measuring instruments	136.3	182.8	204.8	165.8	249.3	187.7	912.6	944.1	1 021.3	1 020.7	840.5	917.0
Miscellaneous manufactures	11.1	10.7	8.3	8.6	6.9	10.3	820.9	937.1	869.6	818.4	624.0	790.4
Unidentified manufactures	1.7	2.7	1.2	1.1	2.9	2.9	116.0	232.7	16.4	19.8	36.3	29.9
Agricultural And Livestock Products	74.8	90.1	90.9	26.4	106.2	147.9	798.3	1 226.4	1 536.2	1 203.8	670.5	611.8
Agricultural products	73.4	89.7	90.0	26.2	105.8	147.1	774.4	1 189.3	1 481.8	1 149.7	642.1	582.4
Livestock and livestock products	1.4	0.4	0.8	0.2	0.4	0.8	23.9	37.1	54.4	54.1	28.4	29.4
Other Commodities	69.4	67.2	61.8	73.7	64.7	51.1	852.3	933.6	833.2	832.0	614.3	501.2
Forestry products	. . .	. . .	. . .	. . .	0.1	. . .	20.5	19.5	12.7	6.3	5.8	7.1
Fish and other marine products	0.1	0.1	0.1	0.1	. . .	0.1	42.7	41.0	29.9	29.6	25.2	31.2
Metallic ores and concentrates	0.2	0.7	0.6	0.6	1.4	0.4	3.2	16.6	25.8	12.0	4.1	9.4
Bituminous coal and lignite	7.2	20.1	28.1	13.1	11.5	2.4	2.3	2.6	4.5	3.8	1.5	0.1
Crude petroleum and natural gas	0.1	0.6	. . .	. . .	. . .	. . .	0.2	0.2	. . .	22.0	0.1	0.1
Nonmetallic minerals	0.5	0.8	0.5	0.9	1.2	0.3	70.1	57.5	40.3	45.3	31.1	31.1
Scrap and waste	11.6	21.5	4.0	2.0	1.9	1.6	329.4	493.2	433.5	454.1	230.4	174.2
Used merchandise	39.7	14.2	16.4	47.6	46.7	33.7	241.8	201.2	158.2	135.9	146.5	131.0
Goods imported and returned unchanged	. . .	. . .	. . .	. . .	. . .	. . .	. . .	. . .	. . .	. . .	. . .	. . .
Special classification provisions	10.0	9.3	12.0	9.4	1.9	12.6	142.2	101.8	128.2	123.2	169.6	117.0

Table D-35. NEW YORK: State Exports of Goods by Destination and Industry, 1994–1999—*Continued*

(Millions of dollars.)

Industry	Japan						South Korea					
	1994	1995	1996	1997	1998	1999	1994	1995	1996	1997	1998	1999
ALL GOODS	4 634.8	5 463.9	5 422.1	5 369.3	4 536.0	4 224.3	1 344.7	1 954.8	1 793.2	1 423.3	747.9	944.2
Manufactured Goods	3 696.1	4 260.7	4 061.0	4 195.2	3 733.2	3 524.4	1 033.5	1 486.5	1 299.3	1 079.6	564.3	781.5
Food products	156.8	209.5	241.1	255.8	204.2	201.4	150.6	198.2	174.6	168.5	68.8	72.4
Tobacco products	0.2	0.1	...	0.1	1.4	0.2	0.3	0.1	1.0	0.1	...	...
Textile mill products	24.0	30.8	31.0	24.2	16.4	15.4	10.0	8.2	12.9	6.9	6.8	4.4
Apparel	77.2	99.2	95.4	85.0	58.9	58.8	2.1	7.8	8.1	3.3	1.8	1.9
Lumber and wood products	64.6	34.4	34.9	26.6	16.6	67.3	21.3	25.2	21.3	21.9	6.3	15.0
Furniture and fixtures	8.9	10.0	9.8	9.6	7.2	4.1	0.6	1.2	2.6	1.7	0.3	0.4
Paper products	82.4	126.0	88.3	117.4	109.5	80.0	104.7	139.4	75.8	66.8	22.7	36.4
Printing and publishing	42.1	45.0	46.1	57.7	60.0	58.6	3.0	5.0	4.2	4.0	2.4	1.8
Chemical products	1 011.7	836.1	855.0	825.4	642.2	652.0	125.5	158.5	104.6	86.9	59.4	100.3
Refined petroleum products	14.1	13.8	18.4	25.8	14.4	9.5	7.4	1.2	1.5	0.5	0.7	0.8
Rubber and plastic products	56.9	64.8	78.4	101.7	63.3	66.7	7.1	7.2	11.6	14.4	8.1	9.5
Leather products	37.3	34.3	51.1	36.7	35.7	28.5	1.0	1.5	3.5	4.5	4.7	10.3
Stone, clay and glass products	49.3	52.9	81.4	113.7	73.8	57.1	31.8	37.4	26.6	23.7	17.8	27.2
Primary metals	134.5	299.9	251.2	192.9	132.8	102.6	23.5	103.1	131.8	51.3	33.2	34.5
Fabricated metal products	97.6	158.9	117.8	95.1	266.7	93.7	17.4	23.9	26.9	19.0	11.6	15.3
Industrial machinery and computers	703.7	1 005.9	749.8	890.2	611.6	641.1	303.5	561.1	446.9	317.7	147.1	211.6
Electric and electronic equipment	157.8	230.8	227.8	261.3	263.8	245.5	79.5	89.2	102.2	105.0	60.2	79.7
Transportation equipment	272.9	276.2	284.5	353.4	508.8	420.5	72.3	37.0	43.5	72.4	45.4	59.7
Scientific and measuring instruments	442.1	489.9	542.0	521.7	466.3	502.0	51.9	62.7	84.1	91.8	56.8	87.4
Miscellaneous manufactures	197.6	234.1	249.7	194.7	161.8	209.4	16.1	14.9	12.9	15.7	6.4	8.7
Unidentified manufactures	64.5	7.9	7.2	6.3	18.0	10.0	3.7	3.8	2.6	3.8	3.6	4.5
Agricultural And Livestock Products	554.1	853.1	1 054.5	892.6	517.6	485.1	119.6	229.7	290.9	114.4	80.8	37.2
Agricultural products	545.8	830.6	1 012.4	849.7	497.2	462.5	115.0	225.0	286.0	112.2	80.1	36.4
Livestock and livestock products	8.3	22.5	42.1	42.9	20.3	22.5	4.6	4.7	4.9	2.2	0.6	0.8
Other Commodities	384.5	350.1	306.6	281.5	285.2	214.8	191.7	238.6	203.0	229.3	102.9	125.5
Forestry products	0.1	1.6	0.2	0.6	0.8	1.0	0.6	0.1	0.1	...	...	...
Fish and other marine products	34.1	30.3	23.1	21.4	18.3	22.2	2.0	4.4	1.9	3.2	4.5	6.7
Metallic ores and concentrates	0.1	4.2	7.3	11.0	0.3	7.2	2.1	0.1	0.1	0.5	3.8	2.0
Bituminous coal and lignite	2.3	1.0	1.4	0.3	...	...	...	1.6	3.1	3.4	1.5	...
Crude petroleum and natural gas	0.1	...	...	...	...	...	...	0.2	...	...	0.1	0.1
Nonmetallic minerals	49.0	40.4	34.5	39.9	28.1	27.2	4.3	3.1	1.7	1.2	0.3	0.4
Scrap and waste	71.3	112.4	71.1	61.4	41.2	24.4	116.7	163.0	164.0	179.0	53.8	69.7
Used merchandise	156.6	120.9	103.5	77.6	104.1	93.9	17.7	35.1	12.7	15.0	0.8	5.0
Goods imported and returned unchanged	...	...	...	...	...	...	...	...	...	...	...	...
Special classification provisions	71.0	39.3	65.4	69.2	92.4	38.8	48.2	31.0	19.4	26.8	38.1	41.6

Industry	Taiwan						Singapore					
	1994	1995	1996	1997	1998	1999	1994	1995	1996	1997	1998	1999
ALL GOODS	1 082.3	1 442.7	956.0	944.7	784.0	623.6	613.1	628.0	563.1	609.1	423.3	459.2
Manufactured Goods	940.5	1 333.7	823.2	778.6	681.2	554.3	574.4	610.2	552.1	596.2	413.0	454.5
Food products	80.6	94.5	80.8	84.8	89.7	44.0	17.1	20.2	25.0	22.4	5.7	4.8
Tobacco products	0.2	0.1	0.3	14.9	0.1	0.2	...	...	...	0.1	0.1	...
Textile mill products	11.2	10.8	7.6	8.9	5.0	2.8	7.1	5.6	5.7	4.7	1.2	1.5
Apparel	2.0	3.5	3.3	2.0	1.3	2.0	4.4	3.9	5.0	3.2	1.3	2.0
Lumber and wood products	11.4	11.6	11.5	8.9	7.9	10.9	4.4	4.4	3.4	3.6	3.1	4.0
Furniture and fixtures	0.2	0.8	0.7	0.5	0.7	0.5	1.0	0.7	1.5	0.6	0.5	0.3
Paper products	34.5	36.8	22.4	19.1	9.8	19.7	11.9	19.6	16.0	19.3	12.0	7.0
Printing and publishing	46.4	4.2	2.2	2.6	2.1	2.5	14.0	12.9	10.7	12.4	8.8	14.5
Chemical products	115.6	177.7	167.5	133.6	81.8	71.8	26.1	39.2	31.4	42.6	32.4	63.5
Refined petroleum products	3.9	4.5	1.4	2.4	6.1	2.0	30.5	8.1	23.1	8.1	7.6	0.2
Rubber and plastic products	3.1	5.5	5.7	8.4	4.4	4.8	6.0	5.6	6.2	3.7	3.4	3.3
Leather products	1.8	0.9	0.5	1.7	3.7	2.8	0.6	0.7	0.2	0.4	0.5	1.3
Stone, clay and glass products	14.8	15.1	13.8	14.2	16.1	12.9	9.0	12.4	10.4	12.3	6.5	4.0
Primary metals	187.2	249.3	119.2	67.1	68.1	20.7	20.3	56.6	23.6	12.2	13.2	12.9
Fabricated metal products	20.0	11.5	14.5	17.1	21.3	11.7	6.0	5.6	7.7	16.6	6.3	6.1
Industrial machinery and computers	107.5	137.3	103.6	152.7	114.8	137.8	106.0	110.0	109.5	125.1	117.4	104.2
Electric and electronic equipment	94.1	129.3	137.2	149.5	150.8	110.3	53.4	51.4	75.8	103.2	66.1	60.7
Transportation equipment	42.1	331.4	62.8	37.4	46.4	43.1	3.9	9.1	9.7	15.5	10.0	26.2
Scientific and measuring instruments	102.8	91.4	56.0	42.7	41.9	43.0	203.3	165.3	124.4	128.3	89.2	98.1
Miscellaneous manufactures	21.6	15.0	10.5	8.4	6.9	8.8	47.6	75.1	61.4	60.4	26.2	37.6
Unidentified manufactures	39.4	2.5	1.6	1.5	2.3	2.1	2.0	3.8	1.2	1.5	1.5	2.1
Agricultural And Livestock Products	78.9	42.7	77.1	65.6	49.1	27.9	3.7	5.7	1.6	0.1	...	...
Agricultural products	78.8	42.3	76.8	65.3	48.7	27.5	3.7	5.6	1.5	0.1	...	...
Livestock and livestock products	0.1	0.3	0.3	0.2	0.3	0.3	...	0.1	...	...	...	...
Other Commodities	63.0	66.4	55.8	100.5	53.7	41.5	35.0	12.1	9.4	12.8	10.2	4.7
Forestry products	...	...	0.6	0.2	0.1	0.5	0.3	0.2	...	0.5	0.2	0.2
Fish and other marine products	0.2	0.3	0.1	...	0.1	0.1	0.3	...	...	0.5	...	0.2
Metallic ores and concentrates	...	...	...	...	...	...	0.1	...	...	...	...	0.1
Bituminous coal and lignite	...	...	...	...	...	...	...	...	...	...	...	...
Crude petroleum and natural gas	...	...	...	21.9	...	...	...	...	...	...	...	...
Nonmetallic minerals	0.6	1.1	1.1	1.5	1.7	1.9	0.4	1.1	0.1	0.1	0.1	0.1
Scrap and waste	33.2	48.3	32.1	62.7	34.2	23.4	0.4	0.6	0.9	1.3	0.3	0.2
Used merchandise	16.7	6.8	10.7	6.5	4.9	4.3	30.3	8.4	7.2	9.4	8.4	1.8
Goods imported and returned unchanged	...	...	...	...	...	...	...	...	...	...	...	...
Special classification provisions	12.3	9.8	11.3	7.7	12.8	11.3	3.2	1.8	1.2	1.0	1.2	2.0

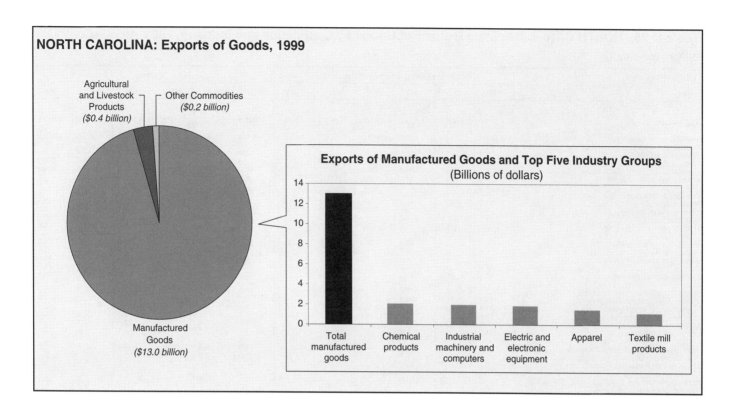

NORTH CAROLINA: Exports of Goods, 1999

Table D-36. NORTH CAROLINA: State Exports of Goods by Destination and Industry, 1994–1999

(Millions of dollars.)

Industry	All destinations						Canada					
	1994	1995	1996	1997	1998	1999	1994	1995	1996	1997	1998	1999
ALL GOODS	8 968.8	10 567.4	11 586.6	13 102.1	12 919.9	13 571.4	2 782.8	3 168.5	3 520.4	3 748.2	3 719.3	4 006.8
Manufactured Goods	8 224.7	9 773.5	10 743.7	12 169.9	12 114.4	12 986.6	2 706.4	3 090.0	3 435.6	3 655.1	3 638.0	3 941.9
Food products	150.8	183.8	183.6	158.8	169.8	167.3	26.5	34.8	33.2	33.1	37.4	35.8
Tobacco products	703.1	650.4	471.2	350.3	384.8	291.6	8.2	7.5	6.8	9.8	13.3	11.5
Textile mill products	742.7	910.4	997.5	1 074.8	1 174.7	1 177.5	220.2	274.9	299.0	350.1	404.3	402.2
Apparel	698.1	1 097.8	1 233.4	1 449.1	1 353.0	1 506.1	77.8	96.1	102.9	125.1	136.3	131.6
Lumber and wood products	171.9	187.0	189.7	199.5	197.5	214.0	14.8	16.8	20.3	28.6	35.6	38.8
Furniture and fixtures	170.3	166.1	174.5	196.1	176.9	180.9	75.3	64.3	58.9	73.0	68.7	64.5
Paper products	159.1	200.1	205.7	243.7	217.2	218.6	57.5	63.8	59.0	58.3	49.8	57.5
Printing and publishing	40.5	41.0	39.6	44.5	54.0	46.5	23.1	23.0	21.3	22.1	25.8	17.8
Chemical products	1 134.8	1 418.9	1 610.0	1 952.5	1 875.4	2 063.3	280.6	309.7	401.1	482.9	457.4	481.2
Refined petroleum products	3.8	4.7	5.4	10.3	6.3	6.4	0.6	0.6	0.3	1.1	1.2	1.2
Rubber and plastic products	152.3	174.8	215.7	305.5	324.3	450.2	39.0	46.8	63.4	103.3	121.6	194.1
Leather products	23.8	32.9	37.0	39.9	38.8	51.1	13.1	17.6	16.9	19.4	21.2	26.6
Stone, clay and glass products	69.0	78.9	67.4	107.4	85.3	706.4	35.7	37.1	35.6	40.7	39.1	305.4
Primary metals	403.1	508.6	652.1	782.5	771.4	335.1	129.7	122.8	180.1	166.9	215.4	82.2
Fabricated metal products	202.3	212.8	234.8	327.8	357.2	370.8	104.8	105.2	92.0	147.9	145.3	185.8
Industrial machinery and computers	1 451.1	1 796.0	2 016.0	2 089.7	2 069.2	1 969.4	708.4	877.3	918.7	922.3	941.1	731.8
Electric and electronic equipment	1 084.2	1 182.3	1 385.7	1 552.5	1 579.0	1 883.4	490.1	591.3	690.7	516.5	451.2	621.2
Transportation equipment	473.9	489.1	524.6	692.9	599.9	695.1	328.3	323.3	340.0	459.3	356.0	423.9
Scientific and measuring instruments	283.7	339.2	380.2	450.3	504.5	489.6	51.6	56.9	65.9	66.4	89.4	97.9
Miscellaneous manufactures	86.3	76.2	97.7	115.7	129.3	105.2	13.5	12.4	19.4	18.4	17.5	17.4
Unidentified manufactures	19.9	22.5	21.8	26.2	45.8	58.1	7.7	7.8	10.1	9.9	10.5	13.1
Agricultural And Livestock Products	634.6	687.7	715.0	764.5	654.7	433.4	13.1	17.6	20.8	17.3	13.7	10.3
Agricultural products	630.5	681.4	709.5	759.8	647.4	426.9	11.8	14.6	18.0	16.3	11.2	7.9
Livestock and livestock products	4.1	6.4	5.5	4.7	7.3	6.5	1.3	3.0	2.8	1.1	2.5	2.4
Other Commodities	109.6	106.2	127.9	167.7	150.8	151.4	63.3	61.0	64.0	75.8	67.5	54.6
Forestry products	1.6	4.3	4.8	6.5	3.8	3.8	0.1	0.8	0.1	0.2	0.4	0.3
Fish and other marine products	10.0	12.2	13.7	38.7	29.3	31.2	5.0	6.0	3.2	4.2	6.2	9.8
Metallic ores and concentrates	0.2	. . .	0.3	0.7	2.3	7.9	. . .	. . .	. . .	. . .	. . .	0.2
Bituminous coal and lignite	. . .	. . .	. . .	. . .	. . .	. . .	. . .	. . .	. . .	. . .	. . .	. . .
Crude petroleum and natural gas	1.8	2.2	3.8	1.7	0.6	0.1	1.6	2.1	3.2	1.5	0.3	. . .
Nonmetallic minerals	29.3	15.1	18.9	13.6	13.8	9.5	6.9	1.5	1.1	1.3	1.6	0.5
Scrap and waste	14.6	20.5	22.5	22.8	28.7	24.9	5.7	9.3	5.1	6.1	7.0	4.6
Used merchandise	3.2	6.5	2.5	5.8	7.5	6.6	0.6	0.8	0.2	1.0	1.2	2.1
Goods imported and returned unchanged	40.9	38.4	45.6	54.3	46.4	25.6	40.9	38.4	45.6	54.3	46.4	25.6
Special classification provisions	8.0	7.1	15.8	23.6	18.4	41.9	2.7	2.0	5.4	7.2	4.5	11.5

Table D-36. NORTH CAROLINA: State Exports of Goods by Destination and Industry, 1994–1999—Continued

(Millions of dollars.)

Industry	South and Central America and Caribbean						Mexico					
	1994	1995	1996	1997	1998	1999	1994	1995	1996	1997	1998	1999
ALL GOODS	1 072.2	1 490.6	1 589.0	1 814.6	1 667.3	1 716.7	493.1	653.8	922.2	1 320.5	1 564.7	1 843.6
Manufactured Goods	1 064.8	1 484.0	1 580.3	1 805.4	1 658.5	1 709.8	490.6	650.6	919.4	1 309.8	1 531.8	1 829.6
Food products	8.0	9.5	18.4	23.2	22.0	15.6	1.6	4.1	4.8	6.4	10.3	10.7
Tobacco products	8.1	10.5	11.5	18.7	31.4	15.3	0.1	0.1	0.1	0.1	0.1	0.1
Textile mill products	152.8	220.7	174.8	150.8	179.9	199.9	51.4	48.1	118.6	150.2	176.5	226.3
Apparel	418.7	589.6	685.5	750.4	630.1	720.8	100.9	291.8	373.4	511.2	528.3	613.2
Lumber and wood products	9.3	10.2	14.0	15.5	18.0	20.0	3.6	0.7	1.2	1.6	1.9	2.8
Furniture and fixtures	4.6	6.8	7.5	10.6	7.2	5.3	7.5	3.3	2.2	2.1	3.9	4.6
Paper products	17.0	39.1	41.2	52.6	37.9	30.0	13.2	9.0	12.1	32.8	39.5	35.8
Printing and publishing	2.4	3.1	3.6	4.8	7.8	3.7	6.6	3.1	3.1	7.2	8.3	8.6
Chemical products	151.9	215.8	223.0	283.4	271.9	269.8	42.6	69.7	95.7	110.9	120.4	140.6
Refined petroleum products	0.6	1.2	0.6	0.7	0.5	0.3	0.1	0.2	0.5	3.0	1.0	0.5
Rubber and plastic products	16.0	21.8	17.8	28.1	22.6	38.4	22.4	16.0	12.8	36.6	52.2	79.8
Leather products	2.4	2.1	4.7	6.9	3.3	2.8	0.2	0.2	0.1	0.4	1.4	3.8
Stone, clay and glass products	3.2	5.9	4.9	3.1	4.2	16.2	9.4	1.9	2.7	4.8	4.3	18.3
Primary metals	47.9	44.8	50.2	69.1	40.9	28.5	13.5	13.6	14.3	22.5	41.0	26.9
Fabricated metal products	13.3	16.5	23.2	28.0	38.9	23.4	22.4	15.7	19.5	22.2	30.7	33.4
Industrial machinery and computers	106.9	164.8	157.4	171.5	168.4	133.4	58.9	49.7	78.1	107.3	132.7	159.2
Electric and electronic equipment	64.1	76.5	98.3	123.1	90.7	117.2	117.1	109.8	158.9	244.2	310.2	321.6
Transportation equipment	21.6	24.8	14.7	20.9	31.7	16.5	3.4	2.1	2.0	11.1	21.3	96.1
Scientific and measuring instruments	10.3	15.0	21.0	29.0	28.8	28.3	11.3	9.5	15.9	19.1	28.8	28.9
Miscellaneous manufactures	3.9	3.9	6.5	11.9	14.6	16.2	3.0	1.1	2.5	13.9	14.3	6.9
Unidentified manufactures	1.9	1.5	1.8	3.3	7.9	8.3	1.4	1.1	1.0	2.1	4.6	11.5
Agricultural And Livestock Products	2.2	3.0	4.1	4.8	4.8	1.9	1.0	2.8	1.9	8.8	19.4	8.5
Agricultural products	1.8	2.5	3.2	4.4	4.1	1.6	1.0	2.6	1.9	8.6	19.1	8.1
Livestock and livestock products	0.5	0.5	0.9	0.4	0.7	0.3	...	0.2	...	0.2	0.3	0.4
Other Commodities	5.2	3.6	4.6	4.3	3.9	5.0	1.5	0.4	0.9	1.9	13.5	5.4
Forestry products	0.1	0.2	0.1	0.2	0.6	0.7	...	...	...	0.1	0.2	0.1
Fish and other marine products	...	0.1	0.1	0.1	0.3	0.1	...	0.1	...	...	...	0.1
Metallic ores and concentrates	0.1	...	...	...	...	...	...	...	...	...	...	...
Bituminous coal and lignite	...	...	...	...	...	...	...	...	...	...	...	...
Crude petroleum and natural gas	...	...	...	...	...	...	0.2	...	...	...	...	...
Nonmetallic minerals	4.2	1.9	0.4	0.6	0.8	0.6	0.1	0.1	0.2	0.6	0.8	0.5
Scrap and waste	0.1	0.2	0.2	0.3	0.4	2.1	0.3	0.1	0.4	0.5	12.1	3.1
Used merchandise	0.2	0.8	0.8	0.7	0.9	0.3	0.2	0.1	...	...	...	0.1
Goods imported and returned unchanged	...	...	...	...	...	...	...	...	...	...	...	...
Special classification provisions	0.4	0.4	2.9	2.5	0.9	1.1	0.7	0.1	0.3	0.7	0.4	1.5

Industry	European Union						United Kingdom					
	1994	1995	1996	1997	1998	1999	1994	1995	1996	1997	1998	1999
ALL GOODS	1 994.4	2 300.0	2 533.0	2 870.7	2 877.7	2 935.0	391.4	446.8	552.8	716.5	708.6	762.4
Manufactured Goods	1 810.7	2 091.0	2 237.0	2 570.1	2 613.3	2 711.5	366.0	422.4	497.5	667.9	668.0	731.5
Food products	5.8	7.4	10.0	6.8	13.4	11.2	1.8	1.1	1.5	3.1	0.7	0.2
Tobacco products	273.9	231.9	163.3	74.4	80.3	40.8	...	...	...	...	0.1	...
Textile mill products	179.3	206.2	220.8	203.7	212.4	151.1	31.2	38.4	43.4	42.7	45.6	32.4
Apparel	28.7	29.2	17.0	18.8	23.1	22.5	4.2	6.7	7.3	7.2	6.9	4.8
Lumber and wood products	75.4	82.3	77.0	92.0	88.7	92.2	12.7	10.8	21.0	17.0	14.9	21.1
Furniture and fixtures	29.8	36.7	31.3	39.3	33.8	47.7	11.8	19.1	12.9	16.2	12.3	24.4
Paper products	34.5	45.0	46.6	47.3	46.1	51.8	8.8	13.6	10.3	11.1	8.5	10.6
Printing and publishing	3.9	5.3	5.6	4.7	5.4	6.7	1.1	1.9	2.2	2.0	2.3	4.0
Chemical products	325.8	363.5	430.9	555.7	545.4	555.7	96.6	62.1	73.0	102.0	98.9	85.8
Refined petroleum products	0.1	0.2	0.6	2.2	0.5	0.9	...	0.1	0.1	0.3	0.1	0.1
Rubber and plastic products	42.1	56.3	65.9	73.6	66.8	74.0	10.6	12.3	13.8	16.6	21.0	23.2
Leather products	4.7	3.5	5.6	5.6	3.8	2.6	0.7	0.4	2.5	2.5	0.3	0.5
Stone, clay and glass products	9.2	20.1	11.9	39.5	22.5	143.1	1.3	1.6	1.3	22.1	1.7	22.9
Primary metals	80.2	104.0	131.8	174.1	165.1	122.0	26.4	21.1	36.1	56.8	52.2	40.1
Fabricated metal products	26.2	29.2	44.5	53.3	68.4	52.1	6.6	8.8	11.4	7.8	10.7	12.1
Industrial machinery and computers	289.7	405.5	464.5	505.0	496.4	612.7	43.0	88.7	100.1	148.9	142.7	186.3
Electric and electronic equipment	166.3	192.3	198.1	304.4	345.8	358.2	37.6	62.3	63.9	88.9	129.0	166.4
Transportation equipment	64.5	76.1	107.9	152.4	133.6	107.7	25.4	26.6	43.0	61.6	47.6	33.6
Scientific and measuring instruments	128.2	159.1	157.5	174.6	198.4	212.5	26.2	31.6	37.4	45.0	46.2	48.0
Miscellaneous manufactures	39.0	33.4	43.5	39.8	56.1	37.9	18.9	14.0	15.3	15.0	24.5	12.8
Unidentified manufactures	3.4	3.7	2.7	2.8	7.3	7.9	1.1	1.2	0.8	1.1	1.9	2.1
Agricultural And Livestock Products	170.2	193.0	270.0	253.8	223.5	164.4	23.1	20.6	49.2	38.6	35.8	15.8
Agricultural products	168.5	190.8	268.4	251.8	220.8	161.8	23.1	20.5	49.1	38.6	35.8	15.8
Livestock and livestock products	1.7	2.2	1.6	2.0	2.7	2.6	...	...	...	...	...	...
Other Commodities	13.5	16.0	26.0	46.7	40.9	59.1	2.4	3.9	6.1	10.1	4.8	15.1
Forestry products	0.3	0.3	0.6	0.6	1.1	2.0	...	...	...	...	...	0.1
Fish and other marine products	3.3	2.9	7.9	27.7	20.8	19.6	...	...	...	0.8	1.2	0.6
Metallic ores and concentrates	...	...	...	0.2	0.6	2.0	1.6	...	...	0.2	0.4	0.7
Bituminous coal and lignite	...	...	...	...	...	...	...	...	...	...	...	...
Crude petroleum and natural gas	0.1	...	0.4	...	...	...	...	...	0.3	...	...	...
Nonmetallic minerals	6.1	7.0	10.8	6.3	6.2	4.5	1.9	2.4	3.2	1.9	1.0	0.7
Scrap and waste	0.3	2.5	2.3	1.1	1.5	10.9	...	0.8	0.7	0.3	0.4	1.2
Used merchandise	0.9	0.8	0.7	2.3	3.5	2.9	0.1	0.4	0.3	1.7	0.4	0.6
Goods imported and returned unchanged	...	...	...	...	...	...	...	...	...	...	...	...
Special classification provisions	2.6	2.4	3.2	8.1	5.8	17.5	0.3	0.3	1.4	5.0	1.2	12.0

Table D-36. NORTH CAROLINA: State Exports of Goods by Destination and Industry, 1994–1999—Continued

(Millions of dollars.)

Industry	Germany						France					
	1994	1995	1996	1997	1998	1999	1994	1995	1996	1997	1998	1999
ALL GOODS	396.0	476.5	482.9	550.1	515.4	591.1	131.1	165.4	191.9	298.3	315.7	317.7
Manufactured Goods	334.6	428.2	430.8	488.3	453.4	532.4	124.8	152.6	182.4	263.7	295.1	301.7
Food products	0.6	0.6	0.9	0.4	0.3	0.3	0.1	0.1	0.3	0.4	2.9	0.5
Tobacco products	12.8	6.1	1.9	...	0.2	0.1	...	...	...	...	...	...
Textile mill products	49.9	50.1	47.3	41.8	39.9	22.5	13.1	15.4	15.0	13.6	13.8	13.1
Apparel	1.7	1.9	1.1	1.8	3.7	1.9	1.1	1.2	0.9	0.4	0.4	0.4
Lumber and wood products	18.1	21.7	14.1	13.3	9.2	6.4	2.1	1.8	2.0	2.8	1.6	4.0
Furniture and fixtures	6.4	8.1	6.6	9.5	6.8	7.3	1.4	1.2	2.3	0.7	1.3	3.3
Paper products	6.8	12.0	10.7	8.3	6.7	7.2	4.4	3.7	4.7	8.7	8.5	7.3
Printing and publishing	0.9	1.0	1.1	0.8	0.6	0.9	0.5	0.3	0.6	0.4	0.3	0.4
Chemical products	53.6	63.0	72.0	84.9	124.7	171.2	21.1	19.2	20.9	30.9	29.0	32.8
Refined petroleum products	...	...	0.1	0.1	...	0.1	...	...	...	1.2	...	...
Rubber and plastic products	6.2	10.1	13.4	15.6	11.6	16.3	5.4	7.9	5.7	10.1	7.2	6.3
Leather products	0.8	1.4	1.1	0.2	0.7	0.3	1.7	0.2	...	...	0.1	0.1
Stone, clay and glass products	2.9	5.7	2.5	2.4	5.8	48.4	0.7	1.3	1.1	1.5	2.1	38.3
Primary metals	10.3	16.3	22.3	24.6	25.3	16.1	13.1	12.0	22.0	45.6	52.0	35.7
Fabricated metal products	5.6	7.9	10.9	15.1	22.0	14.5	2.3	2.6	2.8	3.8	6.9	4.9
Industrial machinery and computers	56.2	84.7	95.7	103.2	57.1	82.5	26.3	48.8	50.8	62.6	62.8	66.3
Electric and electronic equipment	23.6	38.8	34.0	47.3	54.1	65.8	6.5	12.3	16.7	35.7	39.8	30.7
Transportation equipment	16.4	21.1	21.1	44.7	18.4	16.2	7.1	8.4	13.8	22.0	31.8	25.3
Scientific and measuring instruments	56.9	72.7	64.7	68.7	58.4	50.0	15.0	12.6	16.1	17.2	26.4	25.6
Miscellaneous manufactures	4.2	4.4	8.5	5.0	7.1	3.7	2.5	3.2	6.3	6.0	7.8	6.3
Unidentified manufactures	0.8	0.6	0.6	0.6	1.1	0.7	0.3	0.4	0.2	0.2	0.6	0.4
Agricultural And Livestock Products	59.7	46.0	50.3	54.7	52.1	47.2	5.7	11.9	8.5	20.7	11.3	11.2
Agricultural products	59.6	45.1	50.0	54.0	50.7	45.5	5.3	11.9	8.5	20.7	11.2	11.2
Livestock and livestock products	0.1	0.9	0.2	0.7	1.4	1.7	0.4	...	...	...	...	...
Other Commodities	1.7	2.4	1.9	7.0	9.9	11.5	0.6	0.9	0.9	13.9	9.3	4.7
Forestry products	...	0.1	0.3	0.5	0.6	0.5	...	...	...	...	0.1	...
Fish and other marine products	...	...	...	5.0	4.5	2.1	0.1	0.1	0.2	13.3	8.3	3.4
Metallic ores and concentrates	...	...	...	...	...	...	...	...	...	...	...	...
Bituminous coal and lignite	...	...	...	...	...	...	...	...	...	...	...	...
Crude petroleum and natural gas	...	...	...	...	...	...	...	...	...	...	...	...
Nonmetallic minerals	0.3	0.5	0.7	0.6	0.8	0.7	0.3	0.5	0.5	...	0.1	0.1
Scrap and waste	...	0.3	0.2	0.2	0.1	6.5	...	0.1	...	0.3	0.4	0.4
Used merchandise	...	...	...	0.1	2.7	0.5	...	0.1	0.1	0.2	0.2	0.1
Goods imported and returned unchanged	...	...	...	...	...	...	...	...	...	...	...	...
Special classification provisions	1.3	1.4	0.6	0.8	1.2	1.2	0.2	0.1	0.1	0.1	0.2	0.8

Industry	The Netherlands						Asian 10					
	1994	1995	1996	1997	1998	1999	1994	1995	1996	1997	1998	1999
ALL GOODS	215.5	225.7	237.6	291.5	282.0	289.5	1 652.3	1 904.2	1 984.5	2 175.2	1 951.9	1 984.9
Manufactured Goods	203.3	210.1	233.0	284.8	273.9	284.7	1 271.7	1 498.5	1 621.4	1 803.2	1 671.2	1 797.1
Food products	1.6	2.4	0.5	0.5	0.8	0.6	76.3	79.4	77.5	69.6	62.5	69.5
Tobacco products	...	0.1	...	...	...	...	135.1	125.3	116.5	107.8	102.4	99.0
Textile mill products	21.5	27.4	50.0	55.0	48.3	32.4	84.9	93.0	98.1	120.5	92.0	92.3
Apparel	0.5	0.9	0.9	1.3	1.7	1.6	53.8	68.0	29.9	17.8	11.3	8.4
Lumber and wood products	2.1	4.2	2.4	2.2	3.1	2.9	54.3	63.6	62.4	46.5	41.8	44.1
Furniture and fixtures	5.9	3.8	3.8	6.0	6.7	5.1	23.5	29.3	35.8	31.2	22.7	23.6
Paper products	6.4	5.2	8.3	10.4	8.8	10.3	21.5	24.2	29.0	31.6	22.6	24.1
Printing and publishing	0.3	0.3	0.3	0.2	0.4	0.1	2.7	3.5	3.5	3.5	4.0	3.4
Chemical products	16.3	28.7	24.0	56.3	49.9	59.1	199.8	292.2	289.9	273.6	303.8	393.0
Refined petroleum products	...	...	...	0.2	...	...	0.9	1.1	0.3	0.7	0.8	0.9
Rubber and plastic products	10.3	13.6	16.4	16.3	9.1	11.9	24.5	26.1	41.8	50.7	48.1	47.4
Leather products	0.3	0.1	0.2	...	0.5	...	1.8	6.9	4.8	2.0	5.5	13.0
Stone, clay and glass products	1.4	5.4	2.5	10.0	8.7	1.2	6.9	7.7	7.1	9.6	8.9	183.5
Primary metals	2.2	4.0	8.1	8.2	1.3	0.5	96.3	165.4	204.5	294.2	251.3	44.9
Fabricated metal products	1.7	1.7	1.6	1.5	1.6	2.0	25.3	30.5	36.9	52.8	41.2	40.4
Industrial machinery and computers	97.3	83.4	79.8	61.5	81.6	125.9	185.1	200.7	283.6	270.4	211.3	204.3
Electric and electronic equipment	16.0	12.3	18.1	42.7	30.8	9.7	191.3	167.8	175.5	275.3	308.8	388.3
Transportation equipment	6.4	4.6	5.9	1.9	4.8	3.0	21.1	32.0	23.8	19.8	18.6	24.0
Scientific and measuring instruments	7.9	8.5	8.9	9.0	13.6	14.1	48.5	61.6	78.6	100.2	91.2	70.8
Miscellaneous manufactures	4.9	3.1	1.2	1.5	1.7	4.0	16.2	17.7	19.4	22.4	14.9	15.6
Unidentified manufactures	0.2	0.3	0.2	0.2	0.6	0.4	1.8	2.5	2.4	2.9	7.5	6.6
Agricultural And Livestock Products	10.9	14.7	4.1	5.6	5.7	0.7	365.6	385.4	335.8	341.1	262.1	168.0
Agricultural products	10.6	14.5	3.7	5.0	5.0	0.2	365.2	385.0	335.7	340.4	261.8	167.8
Livestock and livestock products	0.3	0.2	0.3	0.6	0.7	0.5	0.4	0.4	0.1	0.7	0.3	0.2
Other Commodities	1.3	0.9	0.6	1.1	2.4	4.2	15.0	20.3	27.2	31.0	18.7	19.8
Forestry products	0.2	0.1	0.2	0.1	0.3	1.2	0.9	2.6	3.9	5.3	1.3	0.6
Fish and other marine products	...	...	...	0.2	0.9	0.8	1.6	2.4	2.2	5.9	1.6	1.2
Metallic ores and concentrates	...	...	...	...	...	...	0.1	...	...	...	0.1	5.8
Bituminous coal and lignite	...	...	...	...	...	...	...	...	...	...	...	...
Crude petroleum and natural gas	...	...	...	...	...	...	...	...	...	...	0.1	...
Nonmetallic minerals	0.1	0.4	...	0.4	0.1	...	3.4	3.5	6.1	4.5	4.1	3.1
Scrap and waste	...	...	...	...	0.2	0.4	7.4	7.9	12.0	12.4	6.2	3.5
Used merchandise	0.3	...	...	0.1	...	1.2	0.4	2.0	...	0.2	0.4	0.1
Goods imported and returned unchanged	...	...	...	...	...	...	...	...	...	...	...	...
Special classification provisions	0.7	0.4	0.3	0.3	0.8	0.6	1.3	1.8	3.0	2.7	4.8	5.5

Table D-36. NORTH CAROLINA: State Exports of Goods by Destination and Industry, 1994–1999—*Continued*

(Millions of dollars.)

Industry	Japan						South Korea					
	1994	1995	1996	1997	1998	1999	1994	1995	1996	1997	1998	1999
ALL GOODS	743.4	760.7	824.0	811.0	779.6	731.0	132.2	183.2	201.9	202.8	151.4	200.0
Manufactured Goods	562.0	577.7	692.2	688.9	662.2	654.4	113.7	145.2	155.7	158.3	121.5	167.5
Food products	34.5	33.9	43.5	30.0	34.3	35.4	4.7	2.5	1.6	2.6	0.5	1.4
Tobacco products	78.5	78.2	91.4	85.3	74.7	69.4	12.3	7.2	4.9	3.6	2.3	2.3
Textile mill products	31.9	28.3	31.4	28.7	24.7	23.0	12.6	14.9	10.5	7.3	8.3	12.3
Apparel	43.5	52.4	19.2	8.7	5.1	5.0	0.2	0.2	0.8	0.8	0.2	0.3
Lumber and wood products	32.5	40.1	34.2	13.5	16.1	11.6	7.0	6.2	5.0	4.2	0.6	2.2
Furniture and fixtures	17.0	22.2	29.5	21.9	17.1	16.3	1.6	3.0	2.5	3.1	0.1	1.3
Paper products	7.5	7.6	7.2	9.8	8.8	7.5	0.8	2.8	2.2	4.2	0.9	3.3
Printing and publishing	0.7	1.0	0.7	0.7	0.9	0.6	0.3	0.2	0.2	0.1	0.2	0.6
Chemical products	34.8	54.5	55.2	44.6	50.0	129.1	25.0	31.3	49.6	43.9	37.0	43.1
Refined petroleum products	...	...	0.1	0.2	...	0.1	0.6	0.9	...	0.1	0.1	...
Rubber and plastic products	16.9	19.4	30.4	39.0	33.9	30.1	1.3	1.7	2.3	2.7	1.7	2.2
Leather products	0.5	0.4	1.0	0.4	3.4	1.8	...	...	1.2	0.6	...	...
Stone, clay and glass products	1.4	2.3	3.3	3.8	1.8	121.0	1.1	...	0.6	1.4	0.4	1.0
Primary metals	40.6	75.9	106.5	138.7	127.7	8.0	0.7	14.8	9.8	12.3	2.2	4.2
Fabricated metal products	8.5	6.9	8.0	20.4	15.9	16.2	2.8	2.5	8.1	4.1	1.6	3.9
Industrial machinery and computers	44.6	42.6	95.2	88.3	92.1	55.0	28.1	27.0	30.3	26.6	12.9	12.5
Electric and electronic equipment	115.4	50.9	64.1	69.9	69.9	61.8	5.5	6.9	7.3	25.5	42.2	64.9
Transportation equipment	13.7	15.2	9.6	7.1	8.8	11.8	2.8	12.2	8.6	2.8	4.3	3.7
Scientific and measuring instruments	28.8	35.0	50.5	62.8	66.4	41.8	4.4	6.0	7.0	9.9	3.9	6.5
Miscellaneous manufactures	10.1	9.8	10.2	14.2	8.9	6.6	1.6	3.5	4.2	2.3	0.7	0.7
Unidentified manufactures	0.7	1.0	1.1	0.8	1.7	2.1	0.2	0.2	0.2	0.7	1.4	1.1
Agricultural And Livestock Products	179.4	175.4	124.5	116.5	115.0	74.7	18.0	37.3	45.7	44.0	29.5	31.8
Agricultural products	179.4	175.4	124.4	116.3	114.8	74.5	18.0	37.3	45.7	44.0	29.5	31.7
Livestock and livestock products	...	...	0.1	0.1	0.3	0.2	...	...	...	...	...	...
Other Commodities	2.0	7.6	7.3	5.7	2.3	1.9	0.5	0.6	0.4	0.5	0.4	0.7
Forestry products	...	0.5	...	...	...	...	...	...	...	...	...	...
Fish and other marine products	0.9	2.0	1.8	4.3	0.9	0.7	...	0.1	0.2	0.2	0.2	0.3
Metallic ores and concentrates	...	...	...	...	...	...	...	...	...	...	...	...
Bituminous coal and lignite	...	...	...	...	...	...	...	...	...	...	...	...
Crude petroleum and natural gas	...	...	...	...	...	...	...	...	...	...	...	...
Nonmetallic minerals	0.7	3.2	4.8	0.5	0.7	0.3	0.2	0.2	0.2	0.1	...	0.1
Scrap and waste	...	0.1	0.3	0.7	0.3	0.2	...	...	...	...	...	...
Used merchandise	0.4	1.7	...	...	...	0.1	...	...	...	0.1	...	...
Goods imported and returned unchanged	...	...	...	...	...	...	...	...	...	...	...	...
Special classification provisions	0.1	0.1	0.4	0.2	0.4	0.7	0.2	0.3	...	0.1	0.1	0.4

Industry	Taiwan						Singapore					
	1994	1995	1996	1997	1998	1999	1994	1995	1996	1997	1998	1999
ALL GOODS	120.7	126.8	115.1	166.1	168.5	122.1	91.4	96.2	119.3	111.9	109.7	166.5
Manufactured Goods	90.4	105.0	90.6	137.6	150.1	118.8	68.1	70.2	93.5	98.6	101.9	159.6
Food products	3.3	3.4	2.0	1.5	2.0	1.1	0.9	1.8	1.1	0.6	0.7	1.7
Tobacco products	6.0	4.9	4.1	5.3	3.0	3.5	6.8	3.4	1.3	2.6	9.3	11.2
Textile mill products	8.2	6.2	7.8	12.8	8.7	4.2	7.5	4.7	5.1	4.8	2.4	2.4
Apparel	1.2	2.8	1.8	1.5	0.8	0.5	2.4	2.6	1.3	1.7	1.6	0.7
Lumber and wood products	8.5	7.0	6.0	7.4	8.0	8.4	0.1	0.3	0.4	0.4	0.5	0.3
Furniture and fixtures	1.2	0.8	0.4	0.5	0.6	0.4	0.3	0.4	0.7	1.1	0.6	0.4
Paper products	1.8	2.0	1.8	2.7	1.5	0.4	2.3	2.7	8.3	4.1	2.6	1.8
Printing and publishing	0.2	0.2	0.5	0.6	0.2	0.2	0.2	0.7	0.1	0.1	0.2	0.1
Chemical products	11.4	20.7	14.5	22.6	23.5	22.1	2.2	4.0	6.7	7.8	10.2	21.0
Refined petroleum products	0.1	0.1	...	0.1	0.3	0.5	...	...	0.1	0.1	0.1	...
Rubber and plastic products	2.4	1.6	1.5	1.8	0.6	2.9	1.1	0.7	3.8	1.6	2.6	2.3
Leather products	...	0.1	...	...	...	...	0.1	...	...	...	...	0.1
Stone, clay and glass products	1.8	1.2	0.8	0.8	0.9	3.5	0.3	0.1	0.1	0.2	0.4	0.3
Primary metals	9.9	14.2	11.8	9.9	19.2	16.8	1.3	1.7	1.9	2.3	4.4	6.3
Fabricated metal products	2.4	6.2	5.2	8.9	11.1	4.2	2.2	2.0	3.4	2.1	3.0	3.5
Industrial machinery and computers	18.8	18.2	17.1	21.4	17.7	15.6	15.3	20.0	34.7	29.5	22.2	46.8
Electric and electronic equipment	6.2	8.1	7.7	28.3	41.7	25.7	20.4	20.3	17.7	29.6	35.5	51.8
Transportation equipment	0.9	0.7	1.5	2.8	1.6	1.5	0.6	0.6	1.9	2.6	1.9	3.3
Scientific and measuring instruments	5.1	5.4	4.8	7.6	7.1	5.4	3.1	3.7	4.0	6.3	2.0	3.8
Miscellaneous manufactures	1.0	1.2	1.1	0.9	1.4	1.2	0.7	0.5	0.7	0.9	1.1	1.3
Unidentified manufactures	0.2	0.2	0.2	0.3	0.4	0.6	0.3	0.2	0.2	0.3	0.5	0.6
Agricultural And Livestock Products	29.7	21.3	22.6	25.7	16.3	0.7	23.2	25.7	25.4	12.7	6.5	0.2
Agricultural products	29.4	21.1	22.6	25.7	16.3	0.7	23.2	25.7	25.4	12.7	6.5	0.2
Livestock and livestock products	0.3	0.3	...	...	...	...	...	...	...	...	...	...
Other Commodities	0.6	0.5	1.8	2.8	2.1	2.6	0.1	0.3	0.3	0.6	1.3	6.7
Forestry products	...	...	...	...	0.1	...	...	0.2	0.1	...	...	0.3
Fish and other marine products	0.2	0.1	...	0.1	...	...	...	...	...	...	0.1	5.8
Metallic ores and concentrates	...	...	...	...	...	...	0.1	...	...	...	...	...
Bituminous coal and lignite	...	...	...	...	...	...	...	...	...	...	...	...
Crude petroleum and natural gas	...	...	...	...	...	...	...	...	...	...	...	...
Nonmetallic minerals	0.1	0.1	0.1	2.4	1.7	1.1	...	...	...	0.4	0.8	0.1
Scrap and waste	...	...	1.1	0.1	0.1	0.3	...	...	...	...	...	...
Used merchandise	...	...	...	...	...	...	...	...	...	...	...	...
Goods imported and returned unchanged	...	...	...	...	...	...	...	...	...	...	...	...
Special classification provisions	0.3	0.3	0.6	0.2	0.2	1.2	...	...	0.1	0.1	0.3	0.5

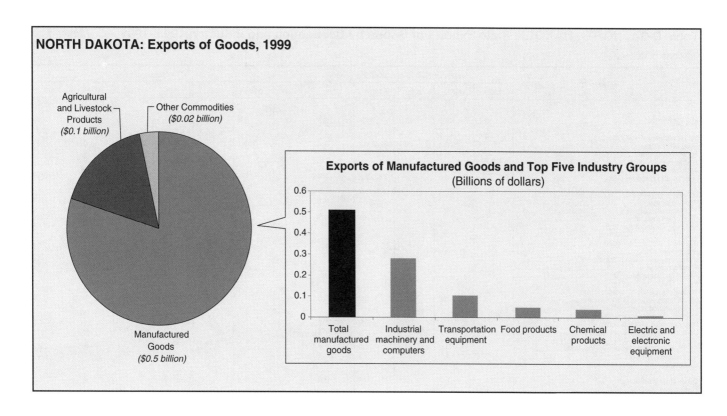

NORTH DAKOTA: Exports of Goods, 1999

Agricultural and Livestock Products ($0.1 billion)

Other Commodities ($0.02 billion)

Manufactured Goods ($0.5 billion)

Exports of Manufactured Goods and Top Five Industry Groups
(Billions of dollars)

Total manufactured goods / Industrial machinery and computers / Transportation equipment / Food products / Chemical products / Electric and electronic equipment

Table D-37. NORTH DAKOTA: State Exports of Goods by Destination and Industry, 1994–1999

(Millions of dollars.)

Industry	All destinations						Canada					
	1994	1995	1996	1997	1998	1999	1994	1995	1996	1997	1998	1999
ALL GOODS	388.9	488.6	576.2	623.1	657.4	634.6	250.6	315.3	378.8	427.6	386.8	345.3
Manufactured Goods	319.5	402.1	470.1	525.6	537.6	507.6	207.6	263.5	320.6	376.0	323.0	274.5
Food products	25.3	31.8	74.0	93.8	37.0	47.9	21.3	24.8	67.2	83.7	30.6	34.0
Tobacco products	. . .	. . .	. . .	. . .	. . .	. . .	. . .	. . .	. . .	. . .	. . .	. . .
Textile mill products	0.3	0.5	0.3	1.1	1.0	0.2	0.3	0.4	0.3	0.5	0.2	0.1
Apparel	0.5	0.3	0.2	0.1	0.3	0.2	0.2	0.1	0.1	. . .	0.1	0.1
Lumber and wood products	1.3	0.8	0.9	1.5	1.4	0.9	0.9	0.6	0.6	0.7	0.8	0.5
Furniture and fixtures	11.0	6.4	1.7	1.7	1.8	1.6	10.5	6.3	1.6	1.5	1.6	1.1
Paper products	2.3	0.4	2.1	2.9	1.0	1.6	0.3	0.3	0.4	0.3	0.4	0.6
Printing and publishing	0.7	1.2	0.8	0.6	0.6	0.5	0.6	0.7	0.8	0.5	0.3	0.4
Chemical products	6.4	13.7	16.3	21.1	22.3	39.3	3.0	9.7	10.8	16.3	18.2	36.4
Refined petroleum products	1.4	0.2	0.4	3.2	0.2	0.2	1.4	0.2	0.4	3.1	0.1	0.2
Rubber and plastic products	7.7	7.2	4.6	7.5	7.4	7.0	5.2	4.8	4.1	6.0	5.9	6.0
Leather products	0.4	0.5	0.3	0.1	0.1	0.3	0.2	0.4	0.1	0.1	0.1	0.1
Stone, clay and glass products	0.4	0.5	0.5	0.4	0.8	0.9	0.3	0.3	0.2	0.2	0.6	0.6
Primary metals	1.9	2.4	4.8	2.2	1.4	1.6	1.7	2.2	1.3	1.7	1.0	0.7
Fabricated metal products	4.4	5.4	5.8	7.2	5.4	5.0	3.6	3.4	3.8	5.9	4.0	3.4
Industrial machinery and computers	195.3	227.2	258.9	278.1	319.5	280.9	104.0	110.2	139.8	167.5	143.9	82.4
Electric and electronic equipment	7.8	9.0	9.8	12.1	21.6	9.5	5.8	6.8	6.0	7.3	9.2	6.7
Transportation equipment	48.3	90.6	83.9	86.4	110.9	104.2	46.0	89.4	80.7	77.8	104.5	100.0
Scientific and measuring instruments	1.8	1.5	2.6	2.7	1.9	3.2	0.6	1.0	1.2	1.6	0.6	0.5
Miscellaneous manufactures	1.3	1.6	1.4	1.9	1.5	0.6	1.0	1.1	0.7	0.8	0.7	0.4
Unidentified manufactures	1.0	1.0	1.0	1.0	1.6	2.0	0.7	0.7	0.7	0.4	0.3	0.3
Agricultural And Livestock Products	36.6	50.6	72.5	65.3	93.5	105.3	13.7	17.9	27.1	23.7	41.6	54.3
Agricultural products	31.7	45.5	67.0	57.7	80.7	96.3	8.9	12.9	21.9	16.3	28.8	45.4
Livestock and livestock products	4.9	5.2	5.5	7.6	12.9	9.0	4.8	5.0	5.2	7.3	12.8	8.9
Other Commodities	32.8	35.8	33.6	32.1	26.3	21.8	29.3	34.0	31.0	27.9	22.2	16.5
Forestry products	. . .	. . .	. . .	. . .	. . .	. . .	. . .	. . .	. . .	. . .	. . .	. . .
Fish and other marine products	0.1	0.3	0.1	0.1	2.6	3.0	0.1	0.3	0.1	0.1	2.5	2.6
Metallic ores and concentrates	2.3	5.2	. . .	. . .	. . .	. . .	2.3	5.2	. . .	. . .	. . .	. . .
Bituminous coal and lignite	0.1	. . .	. . .	. . .	. . .	. . .	. . .	. . .	. . .	. . .	. . .	. . .
Crude petroleum and natural gas	5.0	3.1	2.3	2.8	4.4	1.1	5.0	3.1	2.3	2.8	4.4	1.1
Nonmetallic minerals	0.1	0.1	0.6	0.4	0.5	0.2	0.1	0.1	0.6	0.4	0.4	0.1
Scrap and waste	8.8	7.8	7.4	8.6	4.8	3.6	8.3	6.5	6.1	5.8	2.2	1.0
Used merchandise	6.6	2.2	4.9	6.0	3.0	3.9	3.7	1.8	3.8	4.8	2.0	2.0
Goods imported and returned unchanged	9.7	16.6	17.8	13.7	10.6	5.4	9.7	16.6	17.8	13.7	10.6	5.4
Special classification provisions	0.2	0.5	0.5	0.5	0.3	4.7	0.1	0.4	0.3	0.4	. . .	4.2

Table D-37. NORTH DAKOTA: State Exports of Goods by Destination and Industry, 1994–1999—*Continued*

(Millions of dollars.)

Industry	South and Central American and Caribbean						Mexico					
	1994	1995	1996	1997	1998	1999	1994	1995	1996	1997	1998	1999
ALL GOODS	10.7	15.0	10.3	14.7	14.2	12.1	1.8	16.8	11.5	17.6	17.6	12.5
Manufactured Goods	9.5	13.0	10.2	14.3	13.2	11.8	1.6	15.2	10.1	16.7	8.7	9.1
Food products	1.6	0.4	0.1	0.1	0.1	...	0.1	3.0	0.8	2.6	0.9	5.1
Tobacco products	...	...	...	...	...	...	...	...	...	...	...	...
Textile mill products	...	...	...	...	...	...	...	...	...	0.5	0.8	...
Apparel	0.3	...	...	...	...	...	...	...	...	...	...	...
Lumber and wood products	...	0.1	...	0.2	0.3	0.2	...	...	0.2	0.3	0.1	0.1
Furniture and fixtures	...	0.1	...	...	...	0.4	...	...	...	...	0.3	...
Paper products	...	...	...	...	0.1	0.1	...	...	1.6	2.4	0.1	...
Printing and publishing	...	0.2	...	...	...	...	...	...	...	...	...	...
Chemical products	...	...	...	0.1	0.3	1.3	...	0.1	1.6	0.4	0.5	0.2
Refined petroleum products	...	...	...	...	...	...	...	...	...	0.1	0.1	...
Rubber and plastic products	...	...	...	...	0.3	0.2	...	0.1	0.2	0.2	0.1	0.2
Leather products	...	...	...	...	...	...	...	0.1	...	...	...	...
Stone, clay and glass products	...	...	...	...	...	...	...	...	...	...	...	...
Primary metals	...	...	...	...	...	...	0.1	...	...	...	...	0.1
Fabricated metal products	0.1	...	...	...	0.6	0.1	0.1	1.5	0.2	0.3	0.5	0.3
Industrial machinery and computers	6.9	11.7	9.0	13.3	10.3	7.8	1.1	9.9	4.4	6.8	3.5	2.4
Electric and electronic equipment	0.1	0.2	...	0.2	0.5	0.5	...	0.3	0.2	0.6	1.0	0.2
Transportation equipment	0.3	0.3	0.3	...	0.5	0.3	0.1	...	0.5	2.1	...	0.2
Scientific and measuring instruments	...	...	0.6	...	0.1	0.8	...	...	0.1	0.2	0.5	0.2
Miscellaneous manufactures	...	...	...	0.3	0.2	...	...	...	0.1	...	...	...
Unidentified manufactures	0.1	0.1	...	...	0.1	0.1	...	...	0.1	0.1	0.3	0.1
Agricultural And Livestock Products	0.1	1.9	...	0.3	0.4	0.1	...	1.6	0.8	0.7	8.8	2.2
Agricultural products	0.1	1.9	...	0.3	0.4	0.1	...	1.6	0.7	0.6	8.8	2.2
Livestock and livestock products	...	...	...	...	...	...	...	...	0.1	0.1	...	...
Other Commodities	1.1	0.1	0.1	0.1	0.6	0.2	0.1	...	0.6	0.1	0.1	1.2
Forestry products	...	...	...	...	...	...	...	...	...	...	...	...
Fish and other marine products	...	...	...	...	...	...	...	...	...	...	...	...
Metallic ores and concentrates	...	...	...	...	...	...	...	...	...	...	...	...
Bituminous coal and lignite	...	...	...	...	...	...	0.1	...	...	...	...	...
Crude petroleum and natural gas	...	...	...	...	...	...	...	...	...	...	...	...
Nonmetallic materials	...	...	...	...	...	...	...	...	...	...	...	...
Scrap and waste	...	...	...	...	...	...	...	...	...	...	...	...
Used merchandise	1.1	0.1	0.1	0.1	0.5	0.2	0.1	...	0.6	0.1	0.1	1.1
Goods imported and returned unchanged	...	...	...	...	...	...	...	...	...	...	...	...
Special classification provisions	...	...	...	...	...	...	...	...	...	...	...	...

Industry	European Union						United Kingdom					
	1994	1995	1996	1997	1998	1999	1994	1995	1996	1997	1998	1999
ALL GOODS	98.1	106.1	127.7	110.7	188.1	216.8	4.2	7.2	8.7	12.6	13.7	12.6
Manufactured Goods	75.9	80.2	86.3	74.7	156.3	173.6	3.3	5.7	4.9	7.6	8.1	4.1
Food products	1.5	2.1	3.5	3.8	3.3	4.7	0.3	0.6	0.6	0.6	0.6	0.5
Tobacco products	...	...	...	...	...	...	...	...	...	...	...	...
Textile mill products	...	...	...	...	...	...	...	...	...	...	...	...
Apparel	...	0.1	0.1	...	0.1	...	...	...	...	...	0.1	...
Lumber and wood products	...	...	0.1	0.1	0.1	...	...	...	...	...	...	...
Furniture and fixtures	0.4	...	...	0.1	0.1	0.1	0.4	...	...	...	0.1	...
Paper products	...	...	...	...	0.1	...	...	...	...	...	...	...
Printing and publishing	...	0.3	...	...	0.1	0.2	...	0.2	...	...	...	0.2
Chemical products	1.8	2.9	3.1	3.3	2.0	0.3	1.5	2.7	3.0	3.1	1.9	...
Refined petroleum products	...	...	...	...	...	...	...	...	...	...	...	...
Rubber and plastic products	1.0	1.4	0.1	0.1	0.6	0.3	...	1.3	...	...	0.4	0.1
Leather products	0.2	...	0.2	...	...	0.1	...	...	...	...	...	...
Stone, clay and glass products	...	...	...	...	...	...	...	...	...	...	...	...
Primary metals	...	0.1	...	0.1	0.2	0.3	...	0.1	...	...	...	...
Fabricated metal products	0.1	0.1	0.3	0.2	0.1	0.3	...	...	...	...	0.1	0.1
Industrial machinery and computers	69.4	71.0	74.4	60.0	136.6	161.6	0.5	0.7	0.7	2.1	1.6	1.6
Electric and electronic equipment	0.6	1.0	2.4	2.4	8.2	1.6	0.2	...	0.3	0.3	0.1	0.3
Transportation equipment	0.5	0.6	1.4	3.9	4.1	1.9	0.2	0.1	0.2	1.2	3.0	0.9
Scientific and measuring instruments	0.2	0.2	0.5	0.3	0.2	1.4	...	...	...	0.1	...	0.2
Miscellaneous manufactures	0.1	0.2	0.1	0.2	0.1	0.1	...	...	...	0.1	...	...
Unidentified manufactures	0.1	0.1	0.1	0.1	0.4	0.7	...	...	...	...	0.1	0.1
Agricultural And Livestock Products	20.9	25.5	41.1	35.4	31.2	42.3	0.9	1.5	3.7	5.0	5.4	8.3
Agricultural products	20.9	25.5	41.1	35.4	31.2	42.3	0.9	1.5	3.7	5.0	5.4	8.3
Livestock and livestock products	...	...	...	...	...	0.1	...	...	...	...	...	...
Other Commodities	1.4	0.4	0.2	0.6	0.6	0.9	...	...	0.1	...	0.2	0.2
Forestry products	...	...	...	...	...	...	...	...	...	...	...	...
Fish and other marine products	...	...	...	...	...	0.1	...	...	...	...	...	...
Metallic ores and concentrates	...	...	...	...	...	...	...	...	...	...	...	...
Bituminous coal and lignite	...	...	...	...	...	...	...	...	...	...	...	...
Crude petroleum and natural gas	...	...	...	...	...	...	...	...	...	...	...	...
Nonmetallic materials	...	...	...	...	...	...	...	...	...	...	...	...
Scrap and waste	...	...	...	...	...	...	...	...	...	...	...	...
Used merchandise	1.3	0.3	0.1	0.5	0.3	0.5	...	...	...	...	0.1	...
Goods imported and returned unchanged	...	...	...	...	...	...	...	...	...	...	...	...
Special classification provisions	...	0.1	0.1	...	0.2	0.3	...	...	0.1	...	0.1	0.2

Table D-37. NORTH DAKOTA: State Exports of Goods by Destination and Industry, 1994–1999—*Continued*

(Millions of dollars.)

Industry	Germany						France					
	1994	1995	1996	1997	1998	1999	1994	1995	1996	1997	1998	1999
ALL GOODS	12.7	14.7	17.9	20.7	15.8	18.4	1.6	1.3	2.8	5.0	3.3	4.1
Manufactured Goods	3.1	2.8	2.7	3.7	2.2	2.6	1.6	1.2	2.8	4.9	3.2	3.8
Food products	0.7	1.0	1.2	1.6	0.9	1.0	0.1	...	...	...	...	0.2
Tobacco products	...	...	...	...	...	...	...	...	...	...	...	...
Textile mill products	...	...	...	...	...	...	...	...	...	...	...	...
Apparel	...	...	...	...	...	...	...	...	...	...	...	...
Lumber and wood products	...	...	...	...	...	...	...	...	...	...	...	...
Furniture and fixtures	...	...	...	...	...	...	...	...	...	...	...	...
Paper products	...	...	...	...	...	...	...	...	...	...	...	...
Printing and publishing	...	...	...	...	...	...	...	...	...	...	...	...
Chemical products	...	...	...	...	...	0.1	0.1	...	...	0.1	...	...
Refined petroleum products	...	...	...	...	...	...	...	...	...	...	...	...
Rubber and plastic products	0.9	0.1	0.1	...	...	...	...	...	...	...	0.1	...
Leather products	...	...	...	...	...	...	...	...	...	...	...	...
Stone, clay and glass products	...	...	...	...	...	...	...	...	...	...	...	...
Primary metals	...	...	...	0.1	...	0.1	...	...	...	...	...	...
Fabricated metal products	...	...	0.1	0.1	...	0.1	...	...	0.1	...	...	0.1
Industrial machinery and computers	0.9	1.2	0.9	1.2	0.8	0.7	1.2	1.0	1.3	1.6	2.0	1.5
Electric and electronic equipment	0.2	0.2	0.1	0.2	...	...	0.1	...	0.5	1.5	0.9	0.7
Transportation equipment	0.2	0.2	0.2	0.5	0.2	0.1	0.1	...	0.5	1.3	0.1	0.2
Scientific and measuring instruments	0.1	0.1	...	...	...	...	...	0.1	0.4	0.1	0.1	1.0
Miscellaneous manufactures	...	...	...	...	...	...	...	...	...	0.1	...	...
Unidentified manufactures	...	...	...	...	0.1	0.2	...	...	...	...	...	0.1
Agricultural And Livestock Products	9.6	11.8	15.2	17.0	13.7	15.6	...	...	...	0.1	0.1	0.2
Agricultural products	9.6	11.8	15.2	17.0	13.7	15.6	...	...	...	0.1	0.1	0.2
Livestock and livestock products	...	...	...	...	...	...	...	...	...	...	...	...
Other Commodities	...	...	...	0.1	...	0.2	...	0.1	...	...	...	...
Forestry products	...	...	...	...	...	...	...	...	...	...	...	...
Fish and other marine products	...	...	...	...	...	...	...	...	...	...	...	...
Metallic ores and concentrates	...	...	...	...	...	...	...	...	...	...	...	...
Bituminous coal and lignite	...	...	...	...	...	...	...	...	...	...	...	...
Crude petroleum and natural gas	...	...	...	...	...	...	...	...	...	...	...	...
Nonmetallic materials	...	...	...	...	...	...	...	...	...	...	...	...
Scrap and waste	...	...	...	...	...	...	...	...	...	...	...	...
Used merchandise	...	...	...	0.1	...	0.2	...	...	...	...	...	...
Goods imported and returned unchanged	...	...	...	...	...	...	...	...	...	...	...	...
Special classification provisions	...	...	...	...	...	...	...	0.1	...	...	...	...

Industry	The Netherlands						Asian 10					
	1994	1995	1996	1997	1998	1999	1994	1995	1996	1997	1998	1999
ALL GOODS	1.7	2.8	11.9	4.2	9.0	3.9	22.2	20.4	26.8	30.1	27.6	21.2
Manufactured Goods	0.6	0.7	1.9	0.6	6.9	1.6	20.5	18.0	24.5	24.2	15.3	16.4
Food products	...	0.1	0.2	0.1	0.2	0.8	0.8	1.4	2.2	3.3	1.7	3.1
Tobacco products	...	...	...	...	...	...	...	...	...	...	...	...
Textile mill products	...	...	...	...	...	...	...	...	...	...	...	...
Apparel	...	...	...	...	...	...	...	...	0.1	...	...	...
Lumber and wood products	...	...	0.1	...	...	...	0.3	0.2	...	0.2	0.1	0.1
Furniture and fixtures	...	...	...	...	...	...	...	...	...	...	0.1	...
Paper products	...	...	...	...	...	...	2.0	...	...	...	...	0.9
Printing and publishing	...	...	...	...	...	...	...	...	...	...	0.1	...
Chemical products	0.1	0.2	0.1	...	0.1	...	1.4	1.0	0.9	0.9	1.1	0.7
Refined petroleum products	...	...	...	...	...	...	...	...	...	...	...	...
Rubber and plastic products	...	...	...	...	...	0.1	1.5	0.8	0.1	0.8	0.3	0.2
Leather products	0.2	...	0.2	...	...	...	...	...	...	...	...	0.2
Stone, clay and glass products	...	...	...	...	...	...	0.1	...	0.3	...	...	...
Primary metals	...	...	...	0.1	...	0.1	0.1	...	3.5	0.3	0.2	0.5
Fabricated metal products	...	...	...	0.1	...	...	0.5	0.3	0.1	0.3	0.3	0.4
Industrial machinery and computers	0.2	0.2	0.2	...	0.3	0.1	10.8	13.5	15.3	14.5	6.0	8.6
Electric and electronic equipment	...	...	1.2	0.1	6.1	0.2	0.8	0.2	0.8	1.0	2.5	0.5
Transportation equipment	...	...	...	0.2	0.1	0.2	1.3	0.1	0.7	1.6	1.5	0.9
Scientific and measuring instruments	...	...	...	...	...	...	0.8	0.1	0.1	0.1	0.6	0.1
Miscellaneous manufactures	...	...	...	...	...	...	...	0.2	0.2	0.6	0.4	...
Unidentified manufactures	...	...	...	...	...	0.1	...	...	0.1	0.3	0.3	0.2
Agricultural And Livestock Products	1.1	2.1	9.9	3.6	2.1	2.3	0.9	1.0	1.0	2.8	9.4	1.9
Agricultural products	1.1	2.1	9.9	3.6	2.1	2.2	0.9	1.0	0.8	2.8	9.4	1.9
Livestock and livestock products	...	...	...	...	...	0.1	...	...	0.2	...	...	...
Other Commodities	...	...	...	...	...	...	0.8	1.4	1.3	3.2	2.8	2.9
Forestry products	...	...	...	...	...	...	...	...	...	...	...	...
Fish and other marine products	...	...	...	...	...	...	...	...	...	...	0.1	0.2
Metallic ores and concentrates	...	...	...	...	...	...	...	...	...	...	...	...
Bituminous coal and lignite	...	...	...	...	...	...	...	...	...	...	...	...
Crude petroleum and natural gas	...	...	...	...	...	...	...	...	...	...	...	...
Nonmetallic materials	...	...	...	...	...	...	...	...	...	...	...	0.1
Scrap and waste	...	...	...	...	...	...	0.5	1.4	1.3	2.8	2.7	2.5
Used merchandise	...	...	...	...	...	...	0.3	...	...	0.3	...	...
Goods imported and returned unchanged	...	...	...	...	...	...	...	...	...	...	...	...
Special classification provisions	...	...	...	...	...	...	...	...	...	...	...	0.1

Table D-37. NORTH DAKOTA: State Exports of Goods by Destination and Industry, 1994–1999—*Continued*

(Millions of dollars.)

Industry	Japan						South Korea					
	1994	1995	1996	1997	1998	1999	1994	1995	1996	1997	1998	1999
ALL GOODS	7.4	5.3	6.1	9.7	6.1	6.6	1.1	2.9	7.5	4.5	1.0	2.2
Manufactured Goods	6.3	4.6	5.6	7.1	4.6	5.6	1.0	2.7	7.1	4.2	1.0	1.7
Food products	0.5	...	0.9	2.0	0.2	1.5	0.3	1.0	0.9	0.6	0.2	0.3
Tobacco products	...	...	...	...	...	...	...	...	...	...	...	...
Textile mill products	...	...	...	...	...	...	...	...	...	...	...	...
Apparel	...	...	...	...	...	...	...	...	...	...	...	...
Lumber and wood products	0.2	0.2	...	0.2	0.1	0.1	...	...	...	...	...	...
Furniture and fixtures	...	...	...	...	...	...	...	...	...	...	...	...
Paper products	...	...	...	...	...	...	...	...	...	...	...	...
Printing and publishing	...	...	...	...	...	...	...	...	...	...	...	...
Chemical products	1.3	1.0	0.8	0.8	0.7	0.6	0.1	...	...	...	...	...
Refined petroleum products	...	...	...	...	...	...	...	...	...	...	...	...
Rubber and plastic products	1.2	0.5	0.1	...	...	0.1	...	...	...	...	...	...
Leather products	...	...	...	...	...	...	...	...	...	...	...	...
Stone, clay and glass products	...	...	...	...	...	...	...	...	...	...	...	...
Primary metals	0.1	...	...	...	...	...	...	...	1.9	...	0.1	0.4
Fabricated metal products	...	0.2	...	0.1	0.2	0.3	...	...	0.1	...	...	...
Industrial machinery and computers	1.4	2.4	2.6	3.2	2.0	2.5	0.2	1.5	4.0	3.2	0.5	0.9
Electric and electronic equipment	0.1	...	0.8	0.2	0.2	...	0.5	...	...	...	...	...
Transportation equipment	0.6	...	0.2	0.4	0.7	0.4	...	...	...	...	...	...
Scientific and measuring instruments	0.8	0.1	0.1	...	0.4	0.1	...	...	...	0.1	0.2	...
Miscellaneous manufactures	...	0.2	...	0.1	0.2	...	...	...	0.2	0.2	...	...
Unidentified manufactures	...	...	...	...	0.1	0.1	...	...	...	...	...	...
Agricultural And Livestock Products	0.8	0.7	0.5	2.4	1.4	0.7	...	0.1	0.4	0.2	0.1	0.5
Agricultural products	0.8	0.7	0.5	2.4	1.4	0.7	...	0.1	0.2	0.2	0.1	0.5
Livestock and livestock products	...	...	...	...	...	...	...	...	0.2	...	...	...
Other Commodities	0.3	...	...	0.1	0.1	0.3	...	...	...	0.2	...	0.1
Forestry products	...	...	...	...	...	...	...	...	...	...	...	...
Fish and other marine products	...	...	...	...	0.1	0.2	...	...	...	...	...	...
Metallic ores and concentrates	...	...	...	...	...	...	...	...	...	...	...	...
Bituminous coal and lignite	...	...	...	...	...	...	...	...	...	...	...	...
Crude petroleum and natural gas	...	...	...	...	...	...	...	...	...	...	...	...
Nonmetallic materials	...	...	...	...	...	...	...	...	...	...	...	0.1
Scrap and waste	...	...	...	...	...	...	...	...	...	...	...	...
Used merchandise	0.3	...	...	0.1	...	...	...	...	...	0.2	...	...
Goods imported and returned unchanged	...	...	...	...	...	...	...	...	...	...	...	...
Special classification provisions	...	...	...	...	...	...	...	...	...	...	...	...

Industry	Taiwan						Singapore					
	1994	1995	1996	1997	1998	1999	1994	1995	1996	1997	1998	1999
ALL GOODS	10.2	2.9	2.4	4.4	3.5	4.2	0.6	1.9	1.4	1.8	1.6	0.7
Manufactured Goods	10.1	2.8	2.2	4.4	3.5	4.1	0.6	1.9	1.4	1.8	1.6	0.7
Food products	0.1	0.3	0.2	0.3	0.8	0.7	...	...	...	...	...	...
Tobacco products	...	...	...	...	...	...	...	...	...	...	...	...
Textile mill products	...	...	...	...	...	...	...	...	...	...	...	...
Apparel	...	...	...	...	...	...	...	...	...	...	...	...
Lumber and wood products	...	...	...	...	...	...	...	...	...	...	...	...
Furniture and fixtures	...	...	...	...	...	...	...	...	...	...	...	...
Paper products	0.9	...	...	...	...	...	...	...	...	...	...	...
Printing and publishing	...	...	...	...	...	...	...	...	...	...	...	...
Chemical products	...	...	...	...	0.4	...	...	...	...	...	...	...
Refined petroleum products	...	...	...	...	...	...	...	...	...	...	...	...
Rubber and plastic products	...	...	...	0.5	0.3	...	0.3	...	...	...	...	...
Leather products	...	...	...	...	...	...	...	...	...	...	...	...
Stone, clay and glass products	...	...	...	...	...	...	...	...	...	...	...	...
Primary metals	...	...	...	...	...	...	...	...	...	...	0.1	...
Fabricated metal products	0.1	...	...	0.1	...	...	...	...	...	...	...	...
Industrial machinery and computers	8.4	2.4	1.7	2.5	1.6	3.2	0.2	1.8	1.3	1.5	0.6	0.3
Electric and electronic equipment	0.1	...	...	0.1	0.1	0.1	0.1	...	...	0.1	0.7	0.1
Transportation equipment	0.6	...	0.3	0.8	0.3	...	...	...	...	...	0.3	0.1
Scientific and measuring instruments	...	...	...	...	...	...	...	...	...	...	...	...
Miscellaneous manufactures	...	...	...	0.1	...	...	...	...	...	0.2	...	...
Unidentified manufactures	...	...	...	...	...	...	...	...	...	...	...	...
Agricultural And Livestock Products	0.1	0.1	0.2	...	...	...	...	...	...	...	...	...
Agricultural products	0.1	0.1	0.2	...	...	...	...	...	...	...	...	...
Livestock and livestock products	...	...	...	...	...	...	...	...	...	...	...	...
Other Commodities	...	...	...	...	...	...	...	...	...	...	...	0.1
Forestry products	...	...	...	...	...	...	...	...	...	...	...	...
Fish and other marine products	...	...	...	...	...	...	...	...	...	...	...	...
Metallic ores and concentrates	...	...	...	...	...	...	...	...	...	...	...	...
Bituminous coal and lignite	...	...	...	...	...	...	...	...	...	...	...	...
Crude petroleum and natural gas	...	...	...	...	...	...	...	...	...	...	...	...
Nonmetallic materials	...	...	...	...	...	...	...	...	...	...	...	...
Scrap and waste	...	...	...	...	...	...	...	...	...	...	...	...
Used merchandise	...	...	...	...	...	...	...	...	...	...	...	...
Goods imported and returned unchanged	...	...	...	...	...	...	...	...	...	...	...	...
Special classification provisions	...	...	...	...	...	...	...	...	...	...	...	...

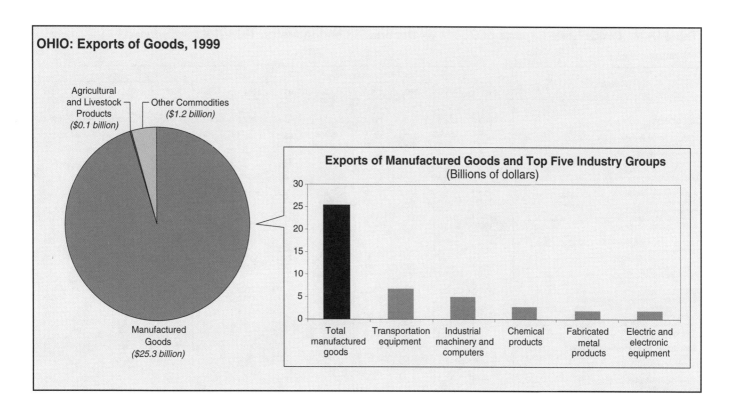

OHIO: Exports of Goods, 1999

Agricultural and Livestock Products ($0.1 billion)

Other Commodities ($1.2 billion)

Manufactured Goods ($25.3 billion)

Exports of Manufactured Goods and Top Five Industry Groups
(Billions of dollars)

Total manufactured goods / Transportation equipment / Industrial machinery and computers / Chemical products / Fabricated metal products / Electric and electronic equipment

Table D-38. OHIO: State Exports of Goods by Destination and Industry, 1994–1999

(Millions of dollars.)

Industry	All destinations						Canada					
	1994	1995	1996	1997	1998	1999	1994	1995	1996	1997	1998	1999
ALL GOODS	19 478.2	20 926.5	22 555.2	25 106.5	24 814.8	26 561.7	8 501.4	8 881.3	9 580.4	10 471.6	10 669.1	11 963.4
Manufactured Goods	18 836.5	20 241.1	21 523.0	24 039.5	23 988.1	25 296.5	8 094.0	8 422.9	9 036.0	10 050.4	10 329.6	11 559.7
Food products	373.5	418.3	445.2	547.7	598.3	605.8	117.8	129.3	157.8	221.1	232.0	254.5
Tobacco products	...	0.9	0.1	0.1	...	...	...	...	...	...	...	...
Textile mill products	103.5	129.3	162.1	213.2	168.6	173.4	66.7	74.3	92.5	111.1	106.5	101.0
Apparel	29.8	31.5	43.2	62.3	84.4	94.3	11.5	8.6	21.6	39.4	52.8	51.7
Lumber and wood products	158.0	163.5	161.3	174.3	174.7	211.5	45.5	44.0	41.0	48.0	48.7	78.0
Furniture and fixtures	136.2	145.0	136.2	142.1	144.2	78.8	100.0	105.1	92.0	96.0	101.1	46.3
Paper products	277.7	394.7	455.7	457.1	451.7	498.9	107.7	177.6	217.7	220.9	250.1	297.2
Printing and publishing	81.6	130.3	140.6	139.6	140.0	154.6	45.7	61.0	57.8	64.3	64.2	74.4
Chemical products	2 421.0	2 861.1	2 957.3	3 119.2	2 545.9	2 792.0	667.7	743.4	835.9	909.2	836.5	911.0
Refined petroleum products	87.0	75.7	109.2	82.4	81.4	83.2	32.8	35.3	32.0	33.5	42.3	35.5
Rubber and plastic products	1 102.3	1 251.2	1 227.8	1 336.5	1 502.6	1 618.8	499.7	557.7	541.2	619.3	733.8	884.0
Leather products	33.1	41.3	70.5	76.3	66.5	60.4	8.4	10.5	13.3	12.0	9.7	8.4
Stone, clay and glass products	542.4	521.4	580.6	661.6	590.1	559.5	211.1	205.7	207.2	245.2	241.3	265.1
Primary metals	787.5	886.2	920.6	1 177.5	1 253.7	1 265.4	381.0	439.6	440.1	523.4	495.3	612.8
Fabricated metal products	846.9	1 033.9	1 144.0	1 123.9	1 606.9	1 914.1	445.2	530.8	595.8	514.1	1 027.9	1 222.3
Industrial machinery and computers	4 208.2	4 575.8	4 932.8	5 460.1	5 178.0	4 976.8	1 727.4	1 638.6	1 769.7	2 066.8	2 144.5	2 108.6
Electric and electronic equipment	1 938.1	1 860.7	1 880.0	1 977.7	1 974.8	1 885.9	701.2	550.2	635.3	675.4	653.5	740.2
Transportation equipment	4 752.6	4 721.1	5 089.7	6 046.8	6 088.0	6 762.1	2 621.9	2 837.2	3 000.8	3 279.2	2 939.4	3 522.2
Scientific and measuring instruments	738.2	754.7	826.5	1 002.8	1 070.7	1 211.3	205.9	168.1	178.1	252.9	222.1	213.0
Miscellaneous manufactures	163.2	188.8	188.8	193.5	196.2	216.5	77.9	88.6	88.1	101.1	108.0	112.0
Unidentified manufactures	55.5	55.7	50.9	45.0	71.3	133.4	18.7	17.1	18.1	17.6	19.8	21.4
Agricultural And Livestock Products	181.1	137.6	124.8	97.4	113.2	75.8	76.2	97.8	80.6	72.2	62.2	50.6
Agricultural products	170.5	124.2	113.9	82.6	95.1	54.4	66.7	85.6	70.8	63.6	49.6	34.5
Livestock and livestock products	10.6	13.4	10.9	14.8	18.1	21.4	9.5	12.2	9.8	8.6	12.6	16.1
Other Commodities	460.6	547.8	907.4	969.5	713.5	1 189.4	331.2	360.6	463.8	349.1	277.3	353.1
Forestry products	6.7	11.3	15.0	12.8	10.0	7.9	1.9	1.8	2.3	3.8	3.8	2.1
Fish and other marine products	1.7	2.5	1.4	1.3	1.8	4.0	1.0	1.7	0.9	0.5	0.8	2.4
Metallic ores and concentrates	63.1	78.0	119.4	51.2	20.3	21.1	62.7	76.8	115.8	30.3	5.2	17.0
Bituminous coal and lignite	150.0	133.9	132.3	81.0	93.4	184.2	114.8	87.7	130.7	79.5	92.8	183.7
Crude petroleum and natural gas	3.6	2.8	266.8	428.7	234.1	498.1	3.2	1.8	3.8	0.7	0.1	0.8
Nonmetallic minerals	16.2	17.1	18.8	17.4	23.0	21.5	8.6	8.3	10.5	8.1	12.2	7.3
Scrap and waste	56.2	105.5	137.0	149.7	90.7	76.9	33.7	66.9	65.8	74.6	36.9	35.5
Used merchandise	11.4	8.0	20.0	12.7	16.9	22.7	1.5	1.5	1.6	4.3	3.1	3.5
Goods imported and returned unchanged	91.1	99.9	120.8	139.2	112.8	76.4	91.1	99.9	120.8	139.2	112.8	76.4
Special classification provisions	60.7	88.9	75.8	75.6	110.5	276.5	12.8	14.2	11.6	7.9	9.5	24.5

Table D-38. OHIO: State Exports of Goods by Destination and Industry, 1994–1999—*Continued*

(Millions of dollars.)

Industry	South and Central America and Caribbean						Mexico					
	1994	1995	1996	1997	1998	1999	1994	1995	1996	1997	1998	1999
ALL GOODS	1 003.1	1 249.0	1 226.7	1 624.6	1 621.2	1 283.9	1 423.2	1 362.2	1 345.1	1 583.7	1 958.6	2 251.8
Manufactured Goods	988.8	1 227.3	1 217.4	1 611.4	1 603.0	1 263.0	1 406.5	1 329.2	1 289.8	1 486.2	1 884.4	2 214.2
Food products	12.1	20.6	19.0	23.8	22.6	33.3	26.9	18.6	17.4	25.5	39.9	28.9
Tobacco products	...	...	...	...	...	...	...	...	...	...	...	...
Textile mill products	14.8	28.7	20.7	28.8	18.6	11.5	2.1	3.0	6.7	11.7	15.0	28.4
Apparel	5.8	6.2	2.8	3.3	4.8	8.1	1.8	0.5	1.3	4.2	8.8	15.2
Lumber and wood products	1.8	2.1	1.8	4.0	3.9	4.9	4.0	3.4	2.6	3.9	8.3	7.2
Furniture and fixtures	5.1	8.3	8.5	9.9	8.2	5.8	11.1	4.0	3.7	9.2	11.0	9.5
Paper products	53.2	83.4	65.1	69.7	56.8	49.6	40.6	36.7	32.4	41.2	55.2	67.0
Printing and publishing	1.8	4.7	5.9	5.4	5.4	4.5	5.0	3.6	6.8	5.2	5.3	8.4
Chemical products	288.0	375.7	352.1	350.5	266.6	246.2	165.8	144.1	157.5	213.7	213.6	227.6
Refined petroleum products	19.3	9.6	7.9	7.1	17.9	1.9	15.1	17.8	6.4	3.9	5.8	1.7
Rubber and plastic products	51.6	68.3	73.7	81.0	87.1	60.7	177.8	174.6	147.2	161.8	227.8	283.1
Leather products	18.5	23.9	41.7	51.7	44.8	27.7	1.1	0.4	0.7	0.7	0.9	2.6
Stone, clay and glass products	18.9	26.4	31.3	33.7	26.5	24.2	20.2	22.7	29.6	60.7	44.2	38.4
Primary metals	26.0	48.2	48.7	97.4	131.2	72.8	102.2	59.6	94.8	121.8	233.5	260.8
Fabricated metal products	26.9	31.4	31.5	47.6	53.6	36.2	93.3	106.6	99.0	109.8	137.4	253.5
Industrial machinery and computers	255.0	299.3	324.6	392.6	374.2	260.3	221.3	226.0	236.2	319.1	400.4	399.9
Electric and electronic equipment	87.8	81.1	76.4	123.7	141.5	71.7	432.0	432.0	359.5	311.8	349.1	318.5
Transportation equipment	59.2	64.7	46.9	178.7	243.2	278.2	54.8	51.7	57.7	45.6	61.7	78.9
Scientific and measuring instruments	31.9	28.7	40.4	88.3	78.1	52.9	22.7	19.1	23.5	26.7	45.2	97.4
Miscellaneous manufactures	8.1	12.7	14.8	10.7	11.0	6.1	6.8	3.5	4.4	6.7	9.3	13.9
Unidentified manufactures	2.9	3.3	3.5	3.7	6.8	6.6	1.8	1.4	2.5	3.2	12.0	73.2
Agricultural And Livestock Products	7.6	3.7	2.7	4.4	3.6	2.9	0.8	11.0	0.6	8.5	11.5	2.3
Agricultural products	7.4	3.6	2.7	0.6	0.4	0.3	0.6	10.9	0.4	7.2	9.9	0.4
Livestock and livestock products	0.1	0.2	...	3.8	3.2	2.6	0.2	...	0.2	1.3	1.6	1.9
Other Commodities	6.8	17.9	6.6	8.8	14.6	18.0	15.9	22.0	54.8	89.0	62.6	35.3
Forestry products	3.3	4.9	2.8	1.6	0.9	0.7	0.4	3.7	6.3	4.4	3.0	2.1
Fish and other marine products	0.4	0.3	...	...	...	...	...	...	...	...	...	...
Metallic ores and concentrates	...	...	0.1	...	0.4	0.1	...	...	0.7	20.0	13.4	0.7
Bituminous coal and lignite	...	7.9	...	...	...	...	...	...	...	...	...	0.1
Crude petroleum and natural gas	...	0.1	...	...	...	0.1	0.4	0.2	0.3	0.1	0.1	0.4
Nonmetallic minerals	0.6	1.0	0.8	1.4	1.0	0.7	0.9	0.6	0.8	1.2	0.5	2.0
Scrap and waste	0.2	0.8	...	0.3	3.6	2.2	13.2	16.8	44.0	62.8	42.7	20.5
Used merchandise	1.0	1.0	1.4	1.2	1.7	1.8	0.2	...	...	0.1	1.0	0.3
Goods imported and returned unchanged	...	...	...	...	...	...	...	...	...	...	...	...
Special classification provisions	1.3	1.8	1.4	4.2	7.0	12.4	0.7	0.7	2.7	0.4	1.9	9.3

Industry	European Union						United Kingdom					
	1994	1995	1996	1997	1998	1999	1994	1995	1996	1997	1998	1999
ALL GOODS	4 369.4	4 472.4	4 725.6	5 380.7	5 732.9	5 833.9	730.7	942.2	1 089.5	1 173.5	1 290.0	1 512.7
Manufactured Goods	4 296.7	4 400.1	4 626.9	5 324.4	5 631.6	5 628.3	721.2	928.7	1 052.5	1 143.1	1 237.0	1 426.7
Food products	71.4	105.5	122.2	133.3	138.9	66.4	15.3	22.0	17.0	17.1	20.0	14.4
Tobacco products	...	0.6	...	...	...	...	...	...	...	...	...	...
Textile mill products	6.1	9.5	23.1	38.1	16.3	20.8	1.4	1.4	2.4	2.6	1.6	3.3
Apparel	7.1	7.2	7.6	6.0	9.1	13.8	2.1	1.4	1.3	0.8	3.4	4.3
Lumber and wood products	68.6	67.0	62.5	61.9	73.2	73.4	17.9	16.0	14.7	12.1	10.8	8.4
Furniture and fixtures	6.2	6.4	9.8	8.4	8.6	8.0	2.5	1.9	2.1	3.0	4.2	3.7
Paper products	18.9	29.1	32.5	35.8	37.0	40.9	6.1	9.1	10.8	11.2	12.7	15.9
Printing and publishing	12.9	31.5	25.0	25.8	33.1	26.8	4.6	13.8	13.1	14.9	18.8	9.8
Chemical products	567.8	611.9	642.4	672.4	513.3	547.9	108.0	127.6	119.4	126.0	99.4	126.1
Refined petroleum products	2.0	4.5	9.6	19.6	7.7	19.0	0.2	0.4	0.5	8.1	0.8	14.8
Rubber and plastic products	171.3	204.9	220.3	213.3	210.6	188.9	28.2	39.7	43.2	42.7	32.2	30.1
Leather products	1.7	2.3	3.2	3.9	6.1	15.8	0.9	1.1	1.2	0.9	4.7	4.7
Stone, clay and glass products	122.1	116.7	125.8	137.6	136.5	88.7	10.1	18.2	11.1	11.5	9.3	11.5
Primary metals	148.5	175.4	156.6	189.0	200.6	156.3	40.6	56.0	57.1	66.8	69.7	64.4
Fabricated metal products	82.4	87.6	112.5	141.0	150.2	163.4	19.2	23.1	25.3	37.0	41.9	46.4
Industrial machinery and computers	880.5	1 055.4	1 047.7	1 072.4	1 085.8	1 100.3	224.3	244.2	251.0	282.5	263.0	303.7
Electric and electronic equipment	264.0	296.8	307.3	299.8	350.0	321.0	75.6	84.6	94.7	95.2	96.2	72.9
Transportation equipment	1 612.5	1 291.6	1 394.9	1 923.3	2 204.2	2 247.3	107.6	205.7	319.1	344.5	477.0	602.2
Scientific and measuring instruments	208.1	249.0	285.5	300.0	406.0	478.4	39.6	45.8	55.2	52.8	58.2	75.9
Miscellaneous manufactures	32.2	32.5	28.9	34.8	31.0	38.4	13.4	13.1	11.1	11.7	9.8	10.1
Unidentified manufactures	12.4	14.7	9.6	8.1	13.4	12.8	3.6	3.5	2.1	1.7	3.3	4.3
Agricultural And Livestock Products	11.5	7.3	29.9	2.6	20.7	14.9	0.6	1.9	1.2	0.8	1.6	1.4
Agricultural products	11.2	7.2	29.4	1.8	20.2	14.8	0.6	1.9	1.2	0.8	1.6	1.4
Livestock and livestock products	0.3	0.1	0.4	0.7	0.5	0.1	...	...	...	0.1	...	...
Other Commodities	61.2	65.0	68.9	53.7	80.6	190.8	8.8	11.6	35.8	29.6	51.4	84.5
Forestry products	0.2	0.3	1.6	2.2	1.0	2.4	...	...	...	0.4	...	...
Fish and other marine products	...	0.2	0.2	0.6	0.8	1.1	...	...	0.2	0.3	0.1	0.1
Metallic ores and concentrates	0.3	1.0	1.4	0.5	0.9	2.7	...	...	0.2	...	...	0.1
Bituminous coal and lignite	26.2	28.6	1.7	1.5	0.6	...	...	...	...	...	...	...
Crude petroleum and natural gas	...	...	...	0.1	...	...	...	...	...	...	...	...
Nonmetallic minerals	2.2	3.2	1.9	1.8	5.3	7.4	0.2	0.2	0.2	0.4	3.8	0.5
Scrap and waste	3.7	6.5	18.5	6.6	1.7	11.3	1.1	4.0	17.4	5.8	0.7	0.5
Used merchandise	5.5	3.8	14.3	3.8	5.5	8.1	1.5	0.8	3.7	1.4	1.5	1.6
Goods imported and returned unchanged	...	...	...	...	...	...	...	...	...	...	...	...
Special classification provisions	23.1	21.4	29.2	36.6	64.8	157.8	6.1	6.7	14.0	21.2	45.2	81.8

Table D-38. OHIO: State Exports of Goods by Destination and Industry, 1994–1999—*Continued*

(Millions of dollars.)

Industry	Germany						France					
	1994	1995	1996	1997	1998	1999	1994	1995	1996	1997	1998	1999
ALL GOODS	604.5	727.9	725.6	737.9	712.3	740.8	1 794.2	1 344.3	1 331.9	1 757.2	1 947.9	1 949.0
Manufactured Goods	595.4	721.3	714.3	731.3	704.2	710.1	1 776.4	1 328.6	1 327.1	1 754.9	1 935.5	1 928.5
Food products	13.6	14.9	26.4	36.6	30.1	15.0	6.6	9.9	10.7	4.8	2.4	1.2
Tobacco products	. . .	. . .	. . .	. . .	. . .	. . .	. . .	. . .	. . .	. . .	. . .	. . .
Textile mill products	2.0	4.8	17.6	28.6	6.1	10.2	0.7	0.3	0.4	0.3	0.5	1.0
Apparel	1.2	1.2	1.2	1.1	1.3	0.7	0.5	1.0	1.0	0.8	0.4	1.4
Lumber and wood products	22.6	23.5	18.2	19.2	25.6	19.9	3.0	3.2	3.8	3.2	3.1	3.5
Furniture and fixtures	0.8	1.7	1.8	1.4	1.9	1.2	1.8	1.4	3.9	2.2	0.8	0.5
Paper products	1.4	2.2	2.3	3.5	2.3	3.9	1.2	1.5	1.3	1.0	1.0	2.0
Printing and publishing	2.6	4.4	2.6	3.4	3.5	9.7	2.0	5.2	3.1	1.2	2.5	1.3
Chemical products	58.2	64.7	60.0	56.1	54.8	61.5	104.6	130.7	114.0	106.9	97.3	127.3
Refined petroleum products	0.1	0.4	0.3	0.4	0.6	0.5	0.1	0.2	0.2	7.0	3.4	1.7
Rubber and plastic products	37.6	47.2	46.3	40.6	40.7	40.3	19.0	23.3	23.8	16.2	12.8	18.0
Leather products	0.3	0.2	0.2	1.8	0.5	0.3	. . .	0.6	1.2	0.1	0.1	0.1
Stone, clay and glass products	33.1	39.2	38.0	23.0	15.9	14.6	5.3	7.0	6.1	7.0	5.4	4.6
Primary metals	26.2	31.5	28.3	37.7	28.6	34.2	38.7	40.0	41.3	58.1	61.9	36.7
Fabricated metal products	18.6	18.2	14.0	17.2	19.8	31.7	12.8	12.1	25.7	27.5	34.7	38.1
Industrial machinery and computers	213.6	281.6	278.4	260.3	220.6	220.6	118.4	139.9	130.3	101.9	146.2	137.3
Electric and electronic equipment	57.7	61.8	61.2	66.0	79.5	78.7	45.3	28.8	27.1	25.7	35.7	36.6
Transportation equipment	36.8	53.1	42.2	70.0	80.2	68.6	1 386.8	896.3	900.3	1 360.4	1 485.2	1 440.9
Scientific and measuring instruments	60.6	62.8	68.8	59.8	87.8	94.0	26.8	24.6	30.0	25.9	37.4	72.8
Miscellaneous manufactures	5.9	3.8	4.1	2.3	2.4	2.3	1.8	1.8	2.4	4.2	2.5	2.1
Unidentified manufactures	2.6	4.1	2.4	2.3	2.1	2.2	1.1	0.8	0.6	0.6	2.0	1.5
Agricultural And Livestock Products	0.7	1.2	2.5	0.6	0.4	0.5	. . .	0.1	0.1	. . .	5.1	. . .
Agricultural products	0.5	1.1	2.4	0.2	0.4	0.5	. . .	0.1	0.1	. . .	5.1	. . .
Livestock and livestock products	0.2	0.1	0.1	0.3	. . .	. . .	. . .	. . .	. . .	. . .	. . .	. . .
Other Commodities	8.4	5.4	8.7	6.0	7.6	30.3	17.7	15.6	4.7	2.2	7.3	20.5
Forestry products	. . .	. . .	0.8	0.2	0.4	1.4	0.1	0.1	. . .	. . .	0.1	. . .
Fish and other marine products	. . .	. . .	. . .	. . .	. . .	0.1	. . .	. . .	. . .	0.1	0.1	0.1
Metallic ores and concentrates	0.2	. . .	0.6	0.1	0.1	0.1	. . .	. . .	. . .	0.1	. . .	. . .
Bituminous coal and lignite	. . .	. . .	. . .	. . .	. . .	. . .	12.8	11.9	. . .	. . .	. . .	. . .
Crude petroleum and natural gas	. . .	. . .	. . .	0.1	. . .	. . .	. . .	. . .	. . .	. . .	. . .	. . .
Nonmetallic minerals	1.3	2.5	1.2	1.2	1.3	4.9	0.3	0.2	0.1	0.1	0.1	. . .
Scrap and waste	0.3	0.1	0.2	0.2	0.3	0.1	0.1	. . .	. . .	0.1	. . .	0.2
Used merchandise	0.8	0.9	2.8	1.1	0.4	2.7	0.8	0.1	1.9	0.4	2.1	2.5
Goods imported and returned unchanged	. . .	. . .	. . .	. . .	. . .	. . .	. . .	. . .	. . .	. . .	. . .	. . .
Special classification provisions	5.7	1.9	3.2	3.2	5.2	21.0	3.6	3.3	2.6	1.5	4.8	17.7

Industry	The Netherlands						Asian 10					
	1994	1995	1996	1997	1998	1999	1994	1995	1996	1997	1998	1999
ALL GOODS	208.4	247.3	290.3	330.6	331.1	369.2	2 723.4	3 326.4	3 927.3	4 233.4	3 229.0	3 726.3
Manufactured Goods	203.8	244.2	286.5	326.7	324.9	339.4	2 671.0	3 255.7	3 631.8	3 780.6	2 964.2	3 180.4
Food products	5.5	4.4	5.9	7.9	4.7	11.3	122.3	114.7	96.0	101.4	117.2	185.1
Tobacco products	. . .	. . .	. . .	. . .	. . .	. . .	. . .	0.3	. . .	. . .	. . .	. . .
Textile mill products	0.3	0.8	0.5	0.6	0.9	1.0	6.5	6.2	11.3	14.1	6.1	5.5
Apparel	0.4	0.5	0.8	0.3	0.2	0.1	1.8	5.7	6.3	6.4	4.6	3.6
Lumber and wood products	1.6	1.4	3.9	2.3	1.9	3.0	24.4	29.1	34.8	37.1	26.7	33.3
Furniture and fixtures	0.4	0.5	0.6	0.2	0.5	0.4	6.9	11.5	13.2	10.2	6.2	3.2
Paper products	5.0	5.7	8.3	8.9	8.2	9.1	47.4	56.5	69.2	70.5	36.4	27.2
Printing and publishing	1.4	2.5	1.9	1.1	3.0	1.2	10.2	22.1	37.9	27.6	21.6	26.6
Chemical products	42.6	40.1	60.7	56.6	42.5	52.0	460.9	679.8	684.1	678.5	507.3	636.8
Refined petroleum products	0.2	0.3	7.2	2.7	0.3	0.3	13.9	3.1	51.8	10.7	5.2	21.9
Rubber and plastic products	21.1	24.1	17.1	9.0	10.8	21.9	120.8	143.4	132.3	167.2	134.9	131.4
Leather products	0.2	0.1	0.1	0.1	0.1	. . .	2.6	3.1	6.5	3.5	3.1	4.9
Stone, clay and glass products	6.5	2.3	2.4	3.1	5.2	9.4	143.2	119.7	150.0	152.9	109.1	107.9
Primary metals	7.8	8.4	8.7	9.0	9.0	5.7	89.6	128.6	128.4	165.5	132.7	128.6
Fabricated metal products	5.7	7.9	14.5	16.1	19.4	15.5	115.7	180.0	187.1	216.8	133.6	131.2
Industrial machinery and computers	58.2	67.7	81.1	129.1	143.6	124.2	704.8	884.2	992.5	978.3	685.1	604.1
Electric and electronic equipment	22.2	32.4	33.2	32.5	34.3	33.6	364.9	377.4	404.3	455.2	348.5	338.3
Transportation equipment	11.2	20.8	17.9	18.3	10.5	12.1	226.0	253.7	377.6	423.1	440.5	479.2
Scientific and measuring instruments	11.3	19.8	19.6	26.1	26.2	32.7	179.5	200.8	216.2	233.4	215.6	275.5
Miscellaneous manufactures	0.9	1.6	1.4	1.9	2.8	4.9	21.8	29.5	26.8	22.7	21.5	27.3
Unidentified manufactures	1.3	2.8	0.5	0.9	1.0	1.1	8.0	6.5	5.5	5.3	8.4	8.7
Agricultural And Livestock Products	0.2	0.2	1.0	0.4	0.1	12.0	17.4	1.8	0.7	1.3	6.4	3.9
Agricultural products	0.2	0.2	0.8	0.3	0.1	12.0	17.4	1.7	0.7	1.2	6.3	3.7
Livestock and livestock products	. . .	. . .	0.2	0.1	. . .	. . .	. . .	0.1	. . .	0.1	0.1	0.2
Other Commodities	4.5	2.9	2.8	3.5	6.1	17.7	34.9	68.9	294.7	451.5	258.3	542.0
Forestry products	. . .	. . .	. . .	. . .	. . .	. . .	0.5	0.1	1.2	0.2	0.7	0.3
Fish and other marine products	. . .	. . .	. . .	. . .	. . .	0.2	0.1	0.1	0.4	0.1	0.1	0.4
Metallic ores and concentrates	. . .	0.6	0.1	. . .	0.5	0.4	. . .	0.1	1.4	0.3	0.4	0.7
Bituminous coal and lignite	. . .	. . .	. . .	. . .	. . .	. . .	8.9	9.8	. . .	. . .	. . .	. . .
Crude petroleum and natural gas	. . .	. . .	. . .	. . .	. . .	. . .	. . .	0.7	262.7	427.7	233.8	496.8
Nonmetallic minerals	. . .	. . .	0.2	0.1	0.1	0.5	2.5	2.5	1.7	1.5	1.9	3.3
Scrap and waste	0.3	0.8	0.3	0.2	0.4	0.1	4.9	13.4	6.7	4.0	4.9	5.7
Used merchandise	0.3	0.2	0.5	0.2	0.7	. . .	2.4	1.1	1.3	1.6	1.9	1.3
Goods imported and returned unchanged	. . .	. . .	. . .	. . .	. . .	. . .	. . .	. . .	. . .	. . .	. . .	. . .
Special classification provisions	3.8	1.3	1.7	2.9	4.5	16.3	15.5	41.2	19.5	16.1	14.8	33.5

Table D-38. OHIO: State Exports of Goods by Destination and Industry, 1994–1999—Continued

(Millions of dollars.)

Industry	Japan						South Korea					
	1994	1995	1996	1997	1998	1999	1994	1995	1996	1997	1998	1999
ALL GOODS	1 033.0	1 124.0	1 254.0	1 190.9	976.5	1 206.9	374.2	538.0	773.0	804.9	445.6	662.2
Manufactured Goods	1 001.4	1 084.2	1 227.3	1 136.5	955.2	1 001.0	371.0	532.9	596.1	565.8	329.5	430.4
Food products	67.3	64.9	61.1	52.8	55.1	89.1	10.2	18.5	5.5	12.0	11.4	19.0
Tobacco products	...	...	...	...	...	...	...	0.3	...	...	...	...
Textile mill products	2.5	2.3	2.3	1.6	1.2	1.7	1.6	0.7	1.0	1.9	1.0	0.3
Apparel	0.6	2.8	1.0	3.0	0.9	0.5	0.2	0.7	1.4	0.8	...	0.1
Lumber and wood products	8.2	11.5	11.9	14.9	9.6	11.4	2.2	3.3	4.8	1.6	1.0	2.3
Furniture and fixtures	3.1	5.1	6.1	3.2	2.2	1.3	0.3	1.7	1.8	1.3	0.1	0.3
Paper products	3.1	4.6	7.7	7.2	6.9	4.5	7.6	6.9	5.9	6.3	4.0	3.1
Printing and publishing	3.7	10.3	26.6	12.9	10.3	10.2	0.7	1.5	2.7	2.2	1.1	1.3
Chemical products	174.5	217.9	207.0	199.7	153.8	190.4	86.7	142.1	162.9	154.7	107.0	136.4
Refined petroleum products	5.5	0.9	25.1	0.9	0.2	0.4	3.9	0.9	0.9	7.0	3.3	8.7
Rubber and plastic products	85.1	90.6	78.7	101.2	80.0	62.0	8.3	17.4	12.4	13.2	4.0	7.1
Leather products	0.5	1.0	1.7	0.7	0.5	0.7	0.1	0.4	2.5	1.2	0.1	0.1
Stone, clay and glass products	87.6	65.8	83.6	99.0	69.4	74.3	23.1	22.3	29.9	19.2	9.7	9.5
Primary metals	60.3	51.8	58.5	64.9	46.5	39.7	9.3	14.0	9.4	10.1	9.3	12.7
Fabricated metal products	56.8	90.0	75.2	25.6	35.8	52.8	12.8	19.6	19.7	42.5	5.6	14.9
Industrial machinery and computers	155.1	178.7	255.2	242.4	225.0	154.0	115.9	179.0	203.2	173.1	75.5	79.8
Electric and electronic equipment	118.9	105.0	115.7	97.7	81.9	70.2	37.2	49.0	51.7	40.6	38.3	73.5
Transportation equipment	66.5	67.6	105.8	108.2	84.6	96.4	20.4	17.3	38.8	35.9	33.8	34.2
Scientific and measuring instruments	93.1	102.5	97.0	93.6	79.6	127.2	22.4	28.3	32.7	34.9	20.2	20.4
Miscellaneous manufactures	5.8	7.3	5.2	5.0	8.3	11.3	6.0	8.1	7.8	6.2	3.1	4.7
Unidentified manufactures	3.2	2.8	1.9	1.9	3.4	2.9	2.2	0.9	0.9	0.8	1.1	1.9
Agricultural And Livestock Products	16.8	0.3	0.1	0.6	6.1	2.1	...	...	...	0.2	...	0.1
Agricultural products	16.8	0.3	0.1	0.5	6.0	1.9	...	...	...	0.2	...	0.1
Livestock and livestock products	...	...	...	0.1	0.1	0.2	...	...	...	...	...	...
Other Commodities	14.8	39.5	26.6	53.8	15.1	203.8	3.2	5.1	176.9	239.0	116.0	231.7
Forestry products	0.2	...	0.8	...	0.4	0.2	...	...	...	...	...	...
Fish and other marine products	0.1	0.1	0.2	0.1	...	...	...	...	0.1	...	...	...
Metallic ores and concentrates	...	...	...	...	...	0.1	...	...	...	...	...	...
Bituminous coal and lignite	8.9	9.8	...	...	...	...	...	...	...	...	...	...
Crude petroleum and natural gas	...	...	16.1	45.0	7.3	190.9	...	0.1	173.2	237.5	114.7	227.6
Nonmetallic minerals	1.2	1.1	0.7	0.2	0.3	0.9	0.2	0.3	0.3	0.5	0.2	0.4
Scrap and waste	1.6	3.8	3.2	2.4	2.3	1.7	0.5	0.9	0.6	0.5	0.3	1.5
Used merchandise	1.7	0.1	0.5	0.9	1.2	1.0	0.3	0.3	...	0.1	0.3	...
Goods imported and returned unchanged	...	...	...	...	...	...	...	...	...	...	...	...
Special classification provisions	1.2	24.6	5.0	5.2	3.7	9.0	2.2	3.5	2.5	0.4	0.5	2.2

Industry	Taiwan						Singapore					
	1994	1995	1996	1997	1998	1999	1994	1995	1996	1997	1998	1999
ALL GOODS	294.7	379.3	384.6	368.9	379.5	301.5	329.3	395.5	454.4	488.6	432.0	523.4
Manufactured Goods	293.3	373.4	324.0	341.2	342.6	277.2	327.9	393.8	453.3	487.0	429.9	520.7
Food products	19.4	14.7	11.7	13.7	18.8	31.1	3.9	2.0	1.8	1.8	2.3	4.1
Tobacco products	...	...	...	...	...	...	...	...	...	...	...	...
Textile mill products	0.2	0.2	0.1	0.7	0.5	0.4	0.5	0.5	2.2	2.9	1.0	0.3
Apparel	0.1	0.2	0.5	0.1	0.2	0.2	0.1	0.1	0.3	0.5	0.1	0.2
Lumber and wood products	6.8	5.1	6.0	5.3	3.7	5.5	0.7	1.0	0.9	0.9	0.7	1.4
Furniture and fixtures	0.7	0.9	0.7	0.8	0.3	0.5	0.9	1.0	1.6	1.6	0.9	0.3
Paper products	22.1	19.4	23.1	30.3	7.6	1.9	1.1	1.8	4.4	8.5	7.7	5.8
Printing and publishing	0.7	0.6	0.6	0.9	1.1	0.8	2.7	3.5	5.1	7.8	6.5	9.2
Chemical products	58.9	96.1	81.8	89.8	85.4	78.4	71.9	112.1	99.6	118.0	72.1	92.2
Refined petroleum products	0.5	0.4	24.2	0.4	0.6	1.8	0.1	0.2	0.2	0.5	...	4.1
Rubber and plastic products	9.6	8.9	5.9	6.1	6.5	11.8	7.2	8.9	11.6	10.1	7.2	9.4
Leather products	1.1	0.4	0.1	0.1	0.1	0.1	0.1	...	0.2	0.2	...	0.2
Stone, clay and glass products	8.9	7.4	6.5	8.3	7.4	6.5	5.0	4.2	4.9	5.0	2.8	3.1
Primary metals	6.0	7.6	11.9	15.7	19.0	14.7	5.0	12.6	16.2	18.3	8.5	9.9
Fabricated metal products	11.1	21.5	10.9	14.3	11.3	12.6	15.8	15.8	17.7	10.0	9.4	17.2
Industrial machinery and computers	74.9	119.0	84.4	91.6	99.3	49.7	52.1	70.6	74.0	61.8	49.4	52.0
Electric and electronic equipment	27.5	25.7	19.6	23.9	18.2	13.7	51.4	38.9	37.8	43.6	32.6	33.7
Transportation equipment	27.3	25.5	16.9	6.5	30.1	4.4	96.3	110.6	158.5	179.9	213.0	268.3
Scientific and measuring instruments	14.4	15.9	17.4	29.7	29.8	38.5	10.7	8.0	14.8	14.4	14.2	7.8
Miscellaneous manufactures	2.4	3.3	1.2	2.0	1.7	3.4	1.7	1.2	0.9	0.9	0.9	1.0
Unidentified manufactures	0.6	0.7	0.6	0.8	1.1	1.1	0.6	0.7	0.5	0.4	0.7	0.6
Agricultural And Livestock Products	...	...	...	...	...	...	...	0.1	...	...	...	...
Agricultural products	...	...	...	...	...	...	...	0.1	...	...	...	...
Livestock and livestock products	...	...	...	...	...	...	...	...	...	...	...	...
Other Commodities	1.4	5.8	60.6	27.7	36.8	24.3	1.4	1.6	1.1	1.6	2.0	2.7
Forestry products	0.2	...	0.1	0.1	...	...	...	...	...	...	...	0.1
Fish and other marine products	...	...	...	...	...	...	...	...	...	...	...	...
Metallic ores and concentrates	...	...	...	0.1	...	...	...	...	...	...	...	0.2
Bituminous coal and lignite	...	...	...	...	...	...	...	...	...	...	...	...
Crude petroleum and natural gas	...	0.6	57.0	26.4	33.7	21.7	...	...	...	...	...	...
Nonmetallic minerals	0.2	0.3	0.3	0.3	0.3	0.5	0.1	0.1	...	...	0.1	...
Scrap and waste	0.4	1.5	1.4	0.1	0.9	...	0.1	...	0.1	0.3	...	...
Used merchandise	...	...	0.3	0.3	...	...	0.3	0.5	0.4	0.1	...	...
Goods imported and returned unchanged	...	...	...	...	...	...	...	...	...	...	...	...
Special classification provisions	0.6	3.3	1.6	0.5	2.0	2.1	1.0	1.0	0.6	1.2	1.9	2.3

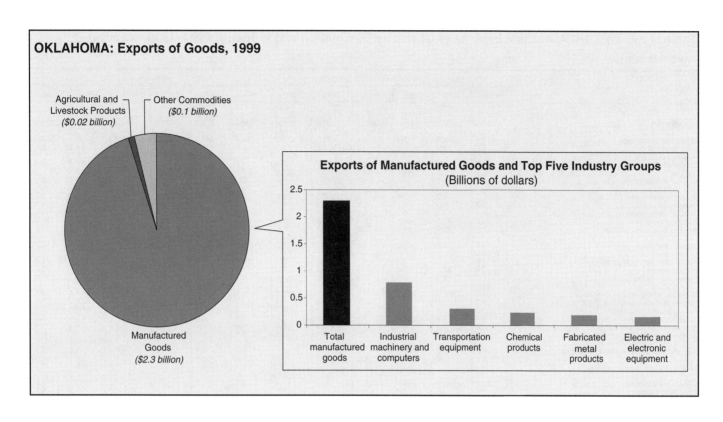

OKLAHOMA: Exports of Goods, 1999

Agricultural and Livestock Products ($0.02 billion)

Other Commodities ($0.1 billion)

Manufactured Goods ($2.3 billion)

Exports of Manufactured Goods and Top Five Industry Groups
(Billions of dollars)

Total manufactured goods | Industrial machinery and computers | Transportation equipment | Chemical products | Fabricated metal products | Electric and electronic equipment

Table D-39. OKLAHOMA: State Exports of Goods by Destination and Industry, 1994–1999

(Millions of dollars.)

Industry	All destinations						Canada					
	1994	1995	1996	1997	1998	1999	1994	1995	1996	1997	1998	1999
ALL GOODS	2 172.0	2 467.3	2 537.6	2 721.6	2 623.2	2 405.3	497.1	492.4	570.9	669.9	656.1	663.7
Manufactured Goods	1 990.3	2 178.3	2 285.0	2 489.1	2 410.3	2 285.3	476.8	468.2	538.3	629.1	623.0	632.9
Food products	59.5	59.4	56.7	71.6	28.8	35.5	5.4	5.3	6.0	9.1	10.9	11.2
Tobacco products	0.3	6.1	. . .	. . .	. . .	. . .	. . .	. . .	. . .	. . .	. . .	. . .
Textile mill products	5.3	6.6	4.1	8.0	7.8	7.6	1.0	1.3	1.6	0.4	0.3	0.5
Apparel	22.8	16.8	19.1	16.8	20.4	20.8	1.6	0.9	3.0	2.9	3.3	4.5
Lumber and wood products	0.5	3.2	1.5	3.1	3.2	5.8	0.1	0.2	0.4	0.2	1.5	4.5
Furniture and fixtures	2.4	2.8	5.0	6.3	7.8	4.8	1.1	1.2	1.3	1.7	2.6	2.2
Paper products	8.0	9.3	6.9	9.4	10.7	16.3	2.6	2.5	2.5	2.2	2.3	8.1
Printing and publishing	4.9	4.7	4.6	8.9	11.1	26.0	1.1	1.1	1.2	1.6	1.9	2.8
Chemical products	239.4	280.1	309.3	309.7	252.3	237.8	51.1	40.2	41.7	40.8	40.2	41.6
Refined petroleum products	91.9	49.3	117.8	129.4	100.9	87.8	7.5	6.2	4.4	7.8	3.7	2.4
Rubber and plastic products	57.0	59.2	61.1	71.7	62.2	65.2	44.0	43.2	42.7	47.3	41.1	39.2
Leather products	1.3	1.4	1.1	0.8	0.9	1.3	0.3	0.3	0.3	0.2	0.3	0.4
Stone, clay and glass products	30.0	47.3	34.7	36.3	41.1	44.9	14.4	14.9	14.9	14.7	14.5	7.4
Primary metals	92.9	125.1	90.6	94.2	121.5	128.7	30.8	26.0	30.2	35.2	29.5	34.8
Fabricated metal products	151.0	148.8	164.6	212.6	187.2	195.5	74.4	56.9	68.0	102.1	88.7	90.2
Industrial machinery and computers	689.1	816.8	820.8	869.5	941.0	788.8	144.4	144.6	176.4	208.9	217.7	197.6
Electric and electronic equipment	258.6	216.5	213.8	271.9	212.2	163.3	27.3	37.0	35.7	52.8	51.5	55.3
Transportation equipment	152.7	158.3	234.9	189.8	229.1	306.7	35.9	52.7	73.4	65.4	77.5	99.6
Scientific and measuring instruments	106.5	131.9	114.4	154.4	146.5	124.0	26.6	24.2	26.6	28.4	26.7	23.2
Miscellaneous manufactures	9.0	13.2	14.4	16.0	14.1	11.0	4.2	6.3	4.9	4.6	5.5	4.1
Unidentified manufactures	7.1	21.5	9.8	8.8	11.5	13.5	2.9	3.3	3.3	2.9	3.3	3.4
Agricultural And Livestock Products	37.3	30.5	19.7	27.1	21.4	24.3	7.5	10.4	8.2	10.6	8.3	8.0
Agricultural products	36.4	29.3	18.5	26.3	20.4	23.5	6.9	9.8	7.8	10.2	8.1	7.9
Livestock and livestock products	0.9	1.2	1.2	0.8	1.0	0.9	0.6	0.6	0.5	0.4	0.2	0.1
Other Commodities	144.4	258.5	232.9	205.4	191.6	95.7	12.9	13.7	24.5	30.3	24.7	22.8
Forestry products	0.2	0.5	0.5	0.3	0.2	0.2	. . .	. . .	. . .	. . .	. . .	. . .
Fish and other marine products	0.6	0.2	0.2	. . .	0.1	. . .	. . .	. . .	0.2	. . .	. . .	. . .
Metallic ores and concentrates	5.8	8.1	3.2	8.3	3.6	3.5	0.9	0.3	. . .	0.2	1.0	0.5
Bituminous coal and lignite	95.8	168.9	133.5	99.7	94.4	23.2	. . .	. . .	. . .	. . .	. . .	. . .
Crude petroleum and natural gas	20.1	54.6	56.0	47.2	15.4	8.8	. . .	1.1	6.5	5.8	2.4	0.7
Nonmetallic minerals	3.2	3.2	5.2	4.4	40.8	13.8	0.3	0.2	0.3	0.2	0.1	0.2
Scrap and waste	0.8	0.7	1.8	1.4	1.9	1.9	0.4	0.3	0.8	0.5	1.5	1.5
Used merchandise	4.4	3.9	4.9	14.0	7.4	11.7	1.2	0.9	1.6	3.4	1.6	2.0
Goods imported and returned unchanged	8.4	7.9	13.4	18.2	15.2	15.0	8.4	7.9	13.4	18.2	15.2	15.0
Special classification provisions	5.3	10.5	14.3	12.0	12.6	17.7	1.7	2.9	1.8	2.0	3.1	3.0

Table D-39. OKLAHOMA: State Exports of Goods by Destination and Industry, 1994–1999—*Continued*

(Millions of dollars.)

Industry	South and Central American and Caribbean						Mexico					
	1994	1995	1996	1997	1998	1999	1994	1995	1996	1997	1998	1999
ALL GOODS	360.3	498.6	433.3	453.2	507.6	306.9	139.3	120.3	178.7	239.6	294.6	283.0
Manufactured Goods	330.5	444.7	377.8	406.6	470.6	289.9	118.9	110.7	170.3	232.8	246.3	264.2
Food products	1.8	1.4	1.1	2.1	1.3	1.7	1.9	1.0	0.9	1.9	2.5	2.7
Tobacco products	...	...	...	...	...	...	...	...	...	...	...	...
Textile mill products	0.7	0.4	0.5	1.4	1.2	0.9	1.6	0.4	0.2	4.4	5.7	5.4
Apparel	10.7	7.5	12.1	12.1	15.4	13.9	1.9	2.2	0.8	0.4	0.3	1.3
Lumber and wood products	0.1	0.2	...	0.2	0.1	0.2	0.2	0.1	0.1	0.2	1.1	0.3
Furniture and fixtures	0.1	0.2	0.4	0.2	0.2	0.2	0.1	0.5	1.8	3.6	3.6	0.3
Paper products	0.2	0.3	0.3	0.5	0.3	0.2	2.2	1.2	1.1	2.0	1.8	4.3
Printing and publishing	0.1	0.1	0.1	0.9	0.3	0.4	0.2	0.1	0.2	0.8	0.3	0.4
Chemical products	28.0	51.3	59.5	38.4	23.2	33.0	36.8	52.6	71.3	45.3	58.2	53.2
Refined petroleum products	41.5	20.8	21.3	10.6	36.7	36.6	6.4	0.3	0.3	1.5	7.9	24.6
Rubber and plastic products	2.4	3.3	3.0	3.2	3.1	2.2	3.2	2.4	2.8	8.4	5.2	10.7
Leather products	0.1	...	...	...	...	...	0.1	...	0.1	...	...	...
Stone, clay and glass products	0.7	2.9	1.3	1.1	0.6	3.1	10.8	7.8	9.9	16.8	20.6	19.7
Primary metals	5.4	17.3	12.0	16.5	30.2	4.0	11.3	10.7	14.7	20.3	24.0	43.6
Fabricated metal products	7.3	9.2	13.0	23.4	14.2	17.0	3.9	2.8	5.8	6.6	7.7	15.4
Industrial machinery and computers	207.3	306.9	226.4	247.2	295.5	149.2	18.5	10.3	20.0	30.1	43.1	19.1
Electric and electronic equipment	11.2	5.3	7.1	25.2	20.3	7.4	12.8	14.5	25.9	46.7	43.0	36.2
Transportation equipment	7.9	7.4	12.1	14.4	18.6	9.7	2.8	1.4	2.0	5.6	14.3	17.6
Scientific and measuring instruments	3.4	7.4	5.5	5.9	6.1	7.9	3.4	1.6	8.1	35.6	5.3	5.2
Miscellaneous manufactures	0.6	1.3	1.5	1.6	0.9	0.4	0.4	0.4	0.6	0.7	0.6	0.5
Unidentified manufactures	1.2	1.5	0.8	1.7	2.3	2.1	0.4	0.3	3.7	2.2	1.0	3.5
Agricultural And Livestock Products	0.2	0.2	0.3	0.5	0.6	0.6	18.2	6.4	0.8	3.6	1.4	3.0
Agricultural products	0.1	0.2	0.3	0.5	0.5	0.6	18.0	6.3	0.7	3.5	1.0	2.5
Livestock and livestock products	...	...	...	...	0.1	...	0.1	0.1	0.2	0.1	0.5	0.4
Other Commodities	29.6	53.7	55.2	46.1	36.4	16.4	2.3	3.3	7.5	3.3	47.0	15.8
Forestry products	...	...	0.1	...	...	...	...	...	0.1	0.1	0.1	0.1
Fish and other marine products	...	...	...	...	...	...	...	...	...	...	...	...
Metallic ores and concentrates	...	0.1	0.3	0.3	...	...	...	...	...	0.1	...	0.3
Bituminous coal and lignite	18.3	29.3	35.1	28.7	27.9	5.7	...	...	...	...	...	...
Crude petroleum and natural gas	8.6	22.4	17.5	7.4	1.9	0.9	0.3	2.3	5.8	...	9.8	2.8
Nonmetallic minerals	2.1	1.4	1.9	1.2	2.9	0.5	0.3	0.2	0.8	1.7	36.6	12.4
Scrap and waste	...	...	...	...	0.1	0.1	0.3	0.2	0.8	0.4	0.1	...
Used merchandise	0.6	0.3	0.3	8.3	3.4	8.4	0.7	0.2	...	0.4	0.2	0.2
Goods imported and returned unchanged	...	...	...	...	...	...	...	...	...	...	...	...
Special classification provisions	0.1	0.1	0.1	0.2	0.2	0.7	0.7	0.3	...	0.5	0.1	0.1

Industry	European Union						United Kingdom					
	1994	1995	1996	1997	1998	1999	1994	1995	1996	1997	1998	1999
ALL GOODS	477.2	540.1	500.1	535.7	450.0	444.4	86.1	109.9	98.1	100.7	100.6	95.7
Manufactured Goods	415.2	433.6	414.1	471.3	392.3	416.3	77.6	95.0	84.7	83.5	83.7	84.2
Food products	2.2	5.3	3.9	5.1	3.4	5.1	0.3	0.8	1.1	0.7	0.5	0.7
Tobacco products	...	6.1	...	...	...	...	...	...	...	...	...	...
Textile mill products	0.8	3.5	0.7	0.7	0.1	0.1	0.1	1.2	0.7	0.3	...	...
Apparel	6.8	5.0	1.8	0.6	0.6	0.6	0.3	0.4	0.6	0.3	0.4	0.4
Lumber and wood products	0.1	2.1	0.2	0.4	0.1	0.2	...	0.6	...	...	...	...
Furniture and fixtures	0.3	0.3	0.7	0.1	0.4	0.4	0.1	0.2	0.3	...	0.3	0.2
Paper products	1.4	3.3	1.8	3.5	5.6	2.7	0.1	0.3	0.1	0.3	0.2	0.1
Printing and publishing	0.6	0.7	1.2	2.2	7.2	20.3	0.5	0.5	0.7	1.8	0.6	1.0
Chemical products	49.0	52.3	77.3	104.1	56.1	37.7	2.2	4.0	5.2	4.4	5.4	3.4
Refined petroleum products	21.4	8.1	31.2	36.6	11.5	20.0	0.8	0.5	0.4	0.5	0.4	0.1
Rubber and plastic products	2.8	3.6	2.3	2.1	3.5	3.1	1.0	1.3	0.7	0.7	0.9	1.1
Leather products	0.4	0.6	0.4	0.2	0.6	0.8	...	0.1	0.2	0.1	0.2	...
Stone, clay and glass products	3.1	5.2	2.8	1.9	2.2	3.1	0.2	1.4	0.8	0.8	0.8	0.7
Primary metals	3.8	5.7	5.8	6.5	3.7	4.8	1.3	1.6	3.3	2.5	1.1	0.8
Fabricated metal products	15.5	18.6	18.8	20.1	22.4	22.7	2.2	2.6	4.5	4.6	3.5	6.1
Industrial machinery and computers	73.5	108.3	93.2	92.4	84.6	87.4	25.4	33.6	29.7	29.1	21.4	19.1
Electric and electronic equipment	157.5	113.8	89.3	98.0	64.5	35.7	14.8	12.4	11.5	10.3	21.3	16.5
Transportation equipment	43.9	36.3	46.4	47.6	55.5	123.2	20.1	10.3	14.2	14.2	15.8	23.0
Scientific and measuring instruments	28.9	38.4	33.4	45.6	67.7	43.7	7.7	10.3	10.4	12.4	10.5	10.3
Miscellaneous manufactures	2.2	3.0	2.4	2.9	1.8	3.3	0.2	0.3	0.1	0.5	0.4	0.4
Unidentified manufactures	0.9	13.3	0.6	0.7	0.9	1.4	0.3	12.6	0.2	0.1	0.2	0.3
Agricultural And Livestock Products	10.0	11.6	8.7	10.0	8.9	10.9	2.1	4.2	3.0	1.7	2.4	5.6
Agricultural products	9.9	11.3	8.4	9.9	8.7	10.7	2.1	4.0	3.0	1.7	2.4	5.6
Livestock and livestock products	0.1	0.3	0.3	0.1	0.1	0.2	...	0.2	...	...	...	...
Other Commodities	52.0	94.9	77.4	54.4	48.8	17.2	6.4	10.6	10.4	15.5	14.5	5.8
Forestry products	...	0.3	0.2	0.1	...	...	...	0.1	0.1	...	...	...
Fish and other marine products	...	...	...	...	...	...	...	...	...	...	...	...
Metallic ores and concentrates	4.7	4.0	0.4	...	...	0.2	...	...	...	...	...	...
Bituminous coal and lignite	43.9	87.0	73.4	49.5	45.5	12.7	5.4	8.8	8.9	14.3	13.2	4.5
Crude petroleum and natural gas	1.4	...	...	...	...	...	...	...	...	...	...	...
Nonmetallic minerals	...	0.1	0.4	0.4	0.2	...	...	...	0.1	0.1	0.1	...
Scrap and waste	0.1	0.1	0.1	0.1	0.1	0.3	...	0.1	...	...	...	...
Used merchandise	0.7	0.5	0.3	1.1	0.6	0.2	...	0.1	0.1	...	0.2	0.1
Goods imported and returned unchanged	...	...	...	...	...	...	...	...	...	...	...	...
Special classification provisions	1.3	2.7	2.5	3.0	2.4	3.8	0.9	1.5	1.3	1.0	1.0	1.3

Table D-39. OKLAHOMA: State Exports of Goods by Destination and Industry, 1994–1999—*Continued*

(Millions of dollars.)

Industry	Germany						France					
	1994	1995	1996	1997	1998	1999	1994	1995	1996	1997	1998	1999
ALL GOODS	63.2	80.1	64.2	60.0	64.2	127.6	42.0	49.1	58.0	80.6	63.5	48.9
Manufactured Goods	60.0	73.2	61.9	56.9	63.5	126.4	40.0	45.3	56.2	79.1	59.5	46.0
Food products	0.1	0.6	0.3	0.4	0.3	0.3	0.8	2.6	1.5	2.8	0.9	0.6
Tobacco products	...	...	...	...	...	...	...	...	...	...	...	...
Textile mill products	0.5	0.1	...	0.1	...	...	...	...	...	...	...	...
Apparel	0.9	1.0	0.5	0.1	0.1	...	2.5	0.4	...	...	0.1	...
Lumber and wood products	...	0.4	...	...	...	0.1	...	0.1	...	...	...	...
Furniture and fixtures	...	0.1	...	...	...	...	...	...	...	...	...	...
Paper products	0.2	...	...	...	0.2	0.3	...	0.2	0.1	0.1	0.1	0.2
Printing and publishing	...	...	0.1	0.1	0.1	6.4	...	...	...	0.2	6.3	7.9
Chemical products	7.1	6.9	10.2	13.4	18.2	17.6	9.0	8.6	15.6	41.2	4.1	4.6
Refined petroleum products	3.8	2.8	1.5	1.6	1.3	...	8.4	2.4	3.3	3.0	2.3	...
Rubber and plastic products	1.0	0.2	0.4	0.4	0.8	0.3	0.1	0.2	0.1	...	0.2	0.1
Leather products	0.2	0.2	0.1	...	0.1	0.4	0.1	0.2	...	...	...	...
Stone, clay and glass products	1.7	1.4	0.9	0.9	0.9	0.2	0.3	1.3	0.1	...	0.3	0.1
Primary metals	0.4	2.2	0.8	0.8	0.2	0.1	0.4	1.1	0.6	1.0	1.4	2.8
Fabricated metal products	2.8	2.5	2.8	1.7	1.9	1.7	0.7	1.2	0.5	1.3	1.7	0.4
Industrial machinery and computers	11.5	16.6	16.0	14.5	15.2	16.2	5.1	7.9	9.8	7.4	7.5	7.2
Electric and electronic equipment	12.5	19.9	8.5	4.5	3.8	8.2	6.1	12.2	8.2	9.8	14.4	2.5
Transportation equipment	10.8	11.9	12.4	10.7	12.6	67.1	2.4	2.8	11.0	7.7	13.8	12.3
Scientific and measuring instruments	6.1	6.0	6.5	7.2	7.1	6.2	3.5	3.1	4.5	4.0	5.9	6.4
Miscellaneous manufactures	0.4	0.4	0.7	0.3	0.5	1.2	0.3	0.7	0.7	0.5	0.3	0.1
Unidentified manufactures	0.2	0.2	0.1	0.1	0.1	0.1	0.2	0.1	0.1	0.1	0.2	0.6
Agricultural And Livestock Products	2.9	2.5	2.0	2.1	0.4	0.7	0.4	0.6	0.4	1.1	1.1	1.2
Agricultural products	2.9	2.5	2.0	2.1	0.3	0.7	0.4	0.6	0.4	1.1	1.1	1.0
Livestock and livestock products	...	...	...	...	...	...	...	...	...	...	...	0.2
Other Commodities	0.4	4.4	0.3	1.0	0.4	0.5	1.6	3.2	1.4	0.4	3.0	1.6
Forestry products	...	...	...	...	...	...	...	...	...	...	...	...
Fish and other marine products	...	...	...	...	...	...	...	...	...	...	...	...
Metallic ores and concentrates	...	...	...	...	...	0.2	...	...	...	...	...	...
Bituminous coal and lignite	...	3.7	...	...	...	...	1.4	2.9	0.9	...	2.6	1.3
Crude petroleum and natural gas	...	...	...	...	...	...	...	...	...	...	...	...
Nonmetallic minerals	...	...	...	0.3	...	...	...	...	0.3	0.1	...	...
Scrap and waste	...	...	0.1	...	...	...	...	...	...	...	...	...
Used merchandise	0.3	0.1	...	...	0.3	...	0.2	0.2	0.1	0.3	0.1	0.1
Goods imported and returned unchanged	...	...	...	...	...	...	...	...	...	...	...	...
Special classification provisions	0.1	0.7	0.2	0.6	0.1	0.2	...	0.1	0.1	...	0.2	0.2

Industry	The Netherlands						Asian 10					
	1994	1995	1996	1997	1998	1999	1994	1995	1996	1997	1998	1999
ALL GOODS	161.0	145.9	130.7	151.6	87.3	56.9	399.3	458.9	473.7	446.4	300.1	271.0
Manufactured Goods	146.6	111.5	123.0	150.1	85.3	55.5	372.2	413.3	428.8	391.0	285.0	253.9
Food products	0.8	0.5	0.5	0.4	0.7	0.8	45.9	42.1	43.8	49.5	9.6	11.0
Tobacco products	...	...	...	...	...	...	...	...	...	...	...	...
Textile mill products	...	0.4	...	...	...	...	0.5	0.5	0.6	0.4	0.1	0.3
Apparel	0.8	2.8	0.6	...	...	...	0.9	0.5	0.5	0.3	0.2	0.2
Lumber and wood products	...	...	...	...	...	...	0.1	0.4	0.7	0.3	0.3	0.3
Furniture and fixtures	...	...	...	...	...	...	0.4	...	0.7	0.3	0.1	0.3
Paper products	1.1	2.5	1.4	2.9	4.3	2.1	1.2	0.9	1.0	0.5	0.5	0.7
Printing and publishing	...	0.1	0.2	...	0.1	4.5	2.6	2.2	1.5	2.8	0.4	1.1
Chemical products	4.8	12.4	20.5	20.2	7.7	4.2	53.8	63.0	39.3	33.9	38.0	48.3
Refined petroleum products	6.1	0.8	24.7	29.9	6.1	19.4	12.8	11.6	53.3	71.1	39.6	2.9
Rubber and plastic products	0.4	1.6	0.4	0.3	0.4	0.5	2.1	3.7	6.0	7.1	2.8	5.9
Leather products	...	...	...	0.1	...	...	0.3	0.3	0.3	0.1	...	0.1
Stone, clay and glass products	...	0.2	0.7	...	...	0.1	0.8	12.5	3.4	1.4	2.7	7.2
Primary metals	1.0	0.2	0.5	0.2	0.3	0.2	8.2	14.7	7.0	4.4	6.0	9.9
Fabricated metal products	0.5	1.6	1.5	0.8	0.6	1.0	36.2	48.3	40.4	39.7	31.1	33.1
Industrial machinery and computers	12.5	15.9	11.6	14.3	14.2	9.4	118.7	107.1	109.1	106.7	96.2	67.9
Electric and electronic equipment	113.9	64.2	56.1	65.4	19.4	0.3	36.8	26.7	44.3	27.8	17.4	21.6
Transportation equipment	0.5	1.5	0.7	0.6	0.9	1.1	28.9	36.4	54.3	22.8	18.6	14.5
Scientific and measuring instruments	3.6	5.9	2.9	14.5	30.3	11.6	20.2	40.0	18.5	16.5	16.7	25.4
Miscellaneous manufactures	0.6	0.9	0.1	0.4	0.2	0.2	1.3	1.6	3.6	5.0	4.1	2.0
Unidentified manufactures	...	0.2	0.1	...	0.1	0.1	0.6	0.9	0.4	0.4	0.8	1.0
Agricultural And Livestock Products	0.1	0.4	0.5	0.7	0.4	0.6	0.3	0.1	0.4	0.9	0.2	0.2
Agricultural products	0.1	0.3	0.3	0.6	0.3	0.6	0.2	...	0.2	0.8	0.1	0.1
Livestock and livestock products	...	0.1	0.3	0.1	...	...	...	0.1	0.2	0.1	0.1	0.1
Other Commodities	14.3	34.0	7.2	0.8	1.7	0.9	26.9	45.4	44.6	54.4	14.9	16.9
Forestry products	...	0.2	0.1	...	...	...	0.1	0.1	...	0.1	...	0.1
Fish and other marine products	...	...	...	...	...	...	0.6	0.2	...	...	...	...
Metallic ores and concentrates	4.7	4.0	...	...	...	...	0.2	3.7	2.4	7.5	2.6	2.5
Bituminous coal and lignite	9.4	29.5	7.0	0.4	1.4	0.4	15.0	8.6	7.4	6.3	5.7	2.1
Crude petroleum and natural gas	...	...	...	...	...	...	9.9	28.7	26.3	33.9	1.3	4.4
Nonmetallic minerals	...	...	...	...	0.1	...	0.3	0.8	1.1	0.7	0.9	0.5
Scrap and waste	...	...	...	0.1	...	0.2	0.1	...	0.1	0.3	0.1	...
Used merchandise	...	...	...	...	...	...	0.2	0.4	0.3	0.5	0.4	0.3
Goods imported and returned unchanged	...	...	...	...	...	...	...	...	...	...	...	...
Special classification provisions	0.2	0.2	0.1	0.2	0.1	0.2	0.7	3.1	6.9	5.1	3.9	6.9

Table D-39. OKLAHOMA: State Exports of Goods by Destination and Industry, 1994–1999—*Continued*

(Millions of dollars.)

Industry	Japan						South Korea					
	1994	1995	1996	1997	1998	1999	1994	1995	1996	1997	1998	1999
ALL GOODS	129.6	133.6	194.9	178.7	97.8	75.3	45.8	66.8	66.0	45.3	11.3	28.6
Manufactured Goods	113.9	120.2	170.5	155.9	87.5	67.8	43.8	57.1	60.8	25.9	11.2	23.6
Food products	27.2	26.6	29.9	40.6	8.4	2.7	8.4	5.1	4.7	2.1	0.2	3.2
Tobacco products	...	...	...	...	...	...	...	0.1	0.3	0.1	...	...
Textile mill products	0.1	0.1	0.1	0.1	...	0.1	...	...	...	...	...	...
Apparel	0.5	0.3	0.3	0.2	0.2	0.1	...	...	...	0.1	...	...
Lumber and wood products	...	...	0.1	0.1	0.1	0.2	...	...	...	...	...	...
Furniture and fixtures	0.1	...	0.4	...	...	0.2	...	...	0.1	0.1	...	...
Paper products	0.3	0.3	...	...	...	0.1	...	...	0.1	...	...	0.1
Printing and publishing	2.5	1.4	0.6	2.3	0.1	0.1	...	...	...	...	...	...
Chemical products	24.9	21.2	16.9	15.2	17.0	25.2	9.1	0.7	3.1	2.2	0.2	6.4
Refined petroleum products	7.5	6.0	49.0	55.3	29.6	1.1	1.0	0.3	0.6	0.6	0.3	...
Rubber and plastic products	0.6	0.3	0.7	0.4	0.9	2.2	0.5	0.7	3.4	2.5	0.7	0.9
Leather products	0.3	0.2	0.3	0.1	...	0.1	...	...	...	...	...	...
Stone, clay and glass products	0.1	0.3	0.3	0.3	1.1	2.4	0.1	9.9	2.7	0.1	0.1	1.2
Primary metals	0.9	1.4	1.7	1.5	1.1	0.8	3.8	1.8	0.4	0.2	0.1	0.6
Fabricated metal products	2.8	4.5	4.8	5.9	3.9	3.3	6.8	16.3	13.4	5.3	4.3	4.2
Industrial machinery and computers	20.7	21.6	21.6	13.3	10.8	9.6	6.6	10.8	14.7	5.1	2.3	3.0
Electric and electronic equipment	3.5	6.8	6.7	6.9	4.4	2.3	2.5	3.4	2.5	3.7	0.8	0.3
Transportation equipment	16.2	18.5	31.2	6.7	2.9	1.7	3.0	4.5	9.2	1.3	0.2	1.2
Scientific and measuring instruments	4.7	9.1	3.4	4.0	4.3	14.3	1.7	3.1	5.1	2.0	1.9	1.8
Miscellaneous manufactures	0.9	1.3	2.5	2.9	2.7	1.3	0.1	0.1	0.4	0.5	0.1	0.5
Unidentified manufactures	0.2	0.3	0.1	0.1	0.1	0.1	0.1	0.1	...	...	0.1	0.1
Agricultural And Livestock Products	...	...	0.2	0.2	0.1	0.1	...	...	0.2	0.1	0.1	0.1
Agricultural products	...	...	...	0.2	0.1	0.1	...	...	0.2	0.1	0.1	...
Livestock and livestock products	...	...	0.1	...	...	...	...	...	...	...	...	...
Other Commodities	15.7	13.4	24.2	22.6	10.3	7.4	2.0	9.8	5.1	19.3	...	4.9
Forestry products	...	...	...	...	...	...	0.1	...	...	...	...	...
Fish and other marine products	0.6	0.1	...	...	...	...	...	...	...	...	...	...
Metallic ores and concentrates	...	0.1	2.4	7.5	2.6	2.5	...	...	...	...	...	...
Bituminous coal and lignite	15.0	8.6	7.4	6.3	5.7	2.1	...	...	...	...	...	...
Crude petroleum and natural gas	...	4.6	13.2	8.6	1.3	...	1.9	9.5	5.1	18.9	...	4.4
Nonmetallic minerals	...	...	...	...	0.1	0.3	...	0.1	...	...	...	...
Scrap and waste	...	...	...	...	...	...	...	...	...	...	...	...
Used merchandise	...	0.1	0.3	...	0.1	...	...	...	...	...	...	...
Goods imported and returned unchanged	...	...	...	...	...	...	...	...	...	...	...	...
Special classification provisions	...	...	1.0	0.1	0.5	2.5	...	0.1	...	0.4	...	0.6

Industry	Taiwan						Singapore					
	1994	1995	1996	1997	1998	1999	1994	1995	1996	1997	1998	1999
ALL GOODS	20.1	27.7	16.4	15.6	29.5	20.7	55.2	56.7	56.3	70.4	66.3	56.0
Manufactured Goods	17.1	18.9	14.8	15.5	29.4	20.4	54.8	53.7	52.8	68.4	64.6	53.6
Food products	1.4	1.2	1.9	1.8	0.2	0.3	0.1	0.4	0.1	0.1	0.1	...
Tobacco products	...	...	...	...	...	0.1	0.1	...	0.1	...	...	...
Textile mill products	0.1	...	...	...	...	...	0.3	0.1	0.1	...	...	...
Apparel	...	0.1	...	...	...	...	...	0.1	...	...	...	...
Lumber and wood products	...	...	0.2	...	...	0.1	...	0.1	...	...	...	...
Furniture and fixtures	...	...	0.1	...	...	...	0.7	0.5	0.6	0.3	0.3	0.5
Paper products	...	...	...	...	...	...	...	...	0.3	0.4	0.3	0.5
Printing and publishing	0.1	...	...	...	...	...	10.9	10.1	8.9	9.2	9.6	4.2
Chemical products	4.0	5.1	2.4	0.2	0.3	0.7	1.3	0.6	0.5	0.5	0.3	0.1
Refined petroleum products	0.8	0.5	0.7	0.9	1.0	1.0	...	...	...	...	...	...
Rubber and plastic products	0.3	0.8	0.2	0.4	0.2	1.7	0.2	0.2	0.3	0.2	0.3	0.3
Leather products	...	...	...	...	...	...	...	...	...	...	...	...
Stone, clay and glass products	0.1	0.2	0.2	0.6	1.1	1.2	0.1	0.5	0.1	0.2	0.1	0.6
Primary metals	0.6	0.6	0.4	0.4	0.2	0.3	1.5	2.6	2.2	0.9	1.1	1.1
Fabricated metal products	3.0	2.2	1.0	2.4	1.8	6.8	5.0	4.4	4.1	7.7	7.2	4.8
Industrial machinery and computers	2.2	3.5	2.9	4.4	16.7	3.1	20.8	20.6	28.1	40.2	34.6	23.9
Electric and electronic equipment	3.7	3.4	3.6	1.9	1.9	3.0	6.9	6.2	2.0	3.0	3.8	9.1
Transportation equipment	0.1	0.2	0.1	0.2	0.9	0.4	2.7	3.0	1.8	2.9	4.0	6.1
Scientific and measuring instruments	0.8	0.9	1.0	2.3	4.8	1.5	3.9	3.9	3.2	2.4	2.1	2.0
Miscellaneous manufactures	...	0.1	0.1	...	0.1	...	0.1	0.1	0.5	0.3	0.8	0.1
Unidentified manufactures	...	0.1	...	...	0.1	0.2	0.2	0.2	0.1	0.1	0.2	0.2
Agricultural And Livestock Products	...	...	...	...	...	...	...	...	...	...	...	...
Agricultural products	...	...	...	...	...	...	...	...	...	...	...	...
Livestock and livestock products	...	...	...	...	...	...	...	...	...	...	...	...
Other Commodities	3.0	8.8	1.5	0.1	0.1	0.3	0.4	3.0	3.5	2.0	1.7	2.4
Forestry products	...	...	...	...	...	...	...	...	...	...	...	...
Fish and other marine products	...	0.1	...	...	...	...	...	...	...	...	...	...
Metallic ores and concentrates	...	3.6	...	...	...	...	...	...	...	...	...	...
Bituminous coal and lignite	...	...	...	...	...	...	...	...	...	...	...	...
Crude petroleum and natural gas	2.8	5.1	1.3	...	...	...	...	...	...	...	...	...
Nonmetallic minerals	...	...	...	...	...	...	0.1	0.1	0.2	0.1	...	0.1
Scrap and waste	...	...	...	0.1	...	...	...	...	0.1	0.2	0.1	...
Used merchandise	...	...	...	...	...	0.1	...	...	...	...	0.3	...
Goods imported and returned unchanged	...	...	...	...	...	...	0.1	0.2	...	...	...	...
Special classification provisions	0.2	...	0.2	...	...	0.2	0.1	2.7	3.2	1.6	1.3	2.3

OREGON: Exports of Goods, 1999

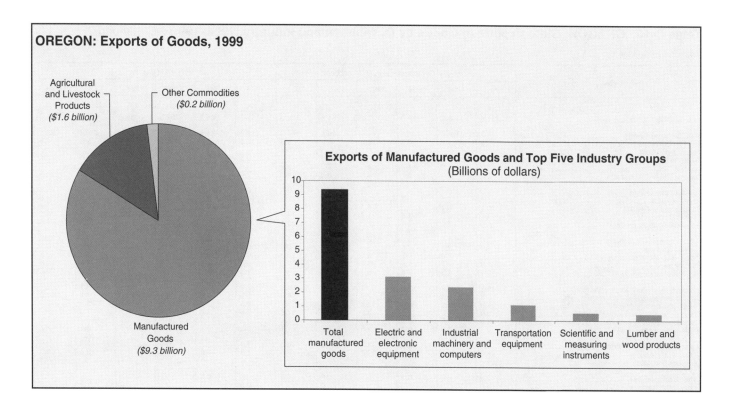

Agricultural and Livestock Products ($1.6 billion)

Other Commodities ($0.2 billion)

Manufactured Goods ($9.3 billion)

Exports of Manufactured Goods and Top Five Industry Groups
(Billions of dollars)

Table D-40. OREGON: State Exports of Goods by Destination and Industry, 1994–1999

(Millions of dollars.)

Industry	All destinations						Canada					
	1994	1995	1996	1997	1998	1999	1994	1995	1996	1997	1998	1999
ALL GOODS	6 987.4	9 902.1	8 481.3	8 358.6	8 143.5	11 164.3	1 020.9	1 097.5	890.2	1 081.7	1 328.6	1 675.2
Manufactured Goods	4 552.4	6 410.1	5 005.4	5 419.9	6 181.7	9 349.6	951.8	1 022.7	831.0	1 012.5	1 255.9	1 578.0
Food products	187.7	209.9	190.0	212.2	209.0	222.0	42.3	47.0	37.5	38.3	51.3	63.1
Tobacco products	0.1	0.1	0.2	0.5	0.1	0.6	...	0.1	0.2	0.1	0.1	...
Textile mill products	7.3	9.8	8.3	7.3	10.4	10.8	1.5	2.2	0.9	1.0	1.1	3.1
Apparel	17.3	27.2	14.8	18.7	18.4	36.3	4.7	8.0	1.7	6.7	8.4	17.7
Lumber and wood products	762.0	735.2	506.5	534.9	411.0	469.7	133.0	120.9	117.4	135.7	134.4	131.6
Furniture and fixtures	14.8	13.5	11.8	12.9	13.9	20.9	10.2	6.4	6.0	6.8	6.7	6.6
Paper products	185.7	287.1	286.7	294.4	250.8	333.5	35.3	34.2	26.6	35.1	47.6	56.6
Printing and publishing	32.0	26.9	26.5	27.9	25.7	25.7	6.4	7.6	7.9	11.0	8.9	7.7
Chemical products	62.3	82.2	64.0	75.9	197.6	301.5	41.0	46.2	41.0	40.2	42.7	54.8
Refined petroleum products	22.1	22.9	21.8	17.8	20.5	31.9	21.4	20.5	19.5	15.8	19.5	23.5
Rubber and plastic products	48.2	67.8	51.1	47.7	54.4	80.8	19.7	20.4	16.6	16.2	17.2	18.9
Leather products	49.5	73.0	23.4	30.2	37.0	144.8	1.8	2.0	1.3	1.5	1.9	6.9
Stone, clay and glass products	25.9	24.5	31.3	35.2	35.4	79.6	9.8	9.8	9.8	9.9	11.5	15.1
Primary metals	124.0	162.0	120.9	194.9	236.0	165.5	58.9	43.6	38.1	46.8	61.7	67.8
Fabricated metal products	84.3	101.7	103.1	131.6	143.8	164.2	35.6	41.7	33.0	39.1	36.7	41.6
Industrial machinery and computers	1 162.1	2 001.1	1 335.7	1 542.9	1 547.5	2 383.1	190.3	217.6	146.7	146.6	136.7	216.0
Electric and electronic equipment	858.6	1 506.9	1 627.5	1 540.3	2 017.0	3 118.0	66.0	82.5	66.8	102.2	134.7	157.7
Transportation equipment	411.9	437.9	357.3	453.9	742.5	1 127.2	213.6	246.0	223.4	317.2	489.2	619.8
Scientific and measuring instruments	425.9	538.4	163.5	179.0	155.1	564.8	41.4	46.0	19.8	25.7	33.0	57.9
Miscellaneous manufactures	53.7	67.3	42.9	40.1	28.6	30.2	11.0	14.3	11.3	13.0	8.3	5.3
Unidentified manufactures	16.9	14.5	18.2	21.6	27.2	38.6	8.0	5.4	3.7	3.6	4.3	6.3
Agricultural And Livestock Products	2 265.3	3 253.3	3 308.8	2 768.6	1 819.1	1 602.8	42.5	46.0	33.1	42.0	41.4	56.9
Agricultural products	2 264.0	3 251.9	3 306.6	2 765.5	1 817.0	1 600.6	41.5	45.0	31.0	39.3	39.5	54.9
Livestock and livestock products	1.4	1.4	2.2	3.1	2.1	2.2	1.0	1.0	2.1	2.7	2.0	2.0
Other Commodities	169.7	238.7	167.1	170.1	142.7	212.0	26.6	28.8	26.1	27.2	31.4	40.3
Forestry products	2.8	2.9	2.1	2.3	3.4	2.7	2.0	2.0	1.3	0.9	1.8	1.8
Fish and other marine products	18.9	20.4	10.8	14.6	7.2	18.0	2.9	3.6	4.6	4.6	3.8	3.6
Metallic ores and concentrates	0.2	0.2	0.1	0.1	0.2	0.5	0.2	0.2	...	...	...	...
Bituminous coal and lignite	...	1.0	...	...	...	...	...	...	...	...	...	...
Crude petroleum and natural gas	...	...	...	...	0.2	0.1	...	...	...	...	0.2	0.1
Nonmetallic minerals	2.1	2.9	1.1	0.8	2.2	3.4	0.7	0.7	0.4	0.5	0.7	0.7
Scrap and waste	107.7	175.4	126.9	126.1	96.8	94.1	3.0	6.4	1.5	1.9	3.4	1.0
Used merchandise	13.1	6.4	6.7	5.7	7.0	18.9	5.4	2.2	2.3	3.2	5.9	5.8
Goods imported and returned unchanged	10.2	10.8	14.0	14.9	12.1	13.1	10.2	10.8	14.0	14.9	12.1	13.1
Special classification provisions	14.8	18.7	5.5	5.5	13.7	61.1	2.2	2.9	2.0	1.3	3.4	14.1

Table D-40. OREGON: State Exports of Goods by Destination and Industry, 1994–1999—*Continued*

(Millions of dollars.)

Industry	South and Central American and Caribbean						Mexico					
	1994	1995	1996	1997	1998	1999	1994	1995	1996	1997	1998	1999
ALL GOODS	123.9	196.2	122.0	193.4	181.9	154.6	120.6	86.1	52.8	88.8	452.0	991.2
Manufactured Goods	115.6	164.7	108.6	179.6	159.5	147.3	117.9	84.4	50.7	84.8	446.4	969.5
Food products	1.0	4.3	3.2	3.8	5.0	9.0	1.5	1.7	1.7	4.4	1.8	3.6
Tobacco products	...	...	...	...	...	0.6	...	...	...	...	...	...
Textile mill products	2.6	2.9	4.4	2.5	3.8	1.9	0.3	0.6	0.6	1.8	3.5	2.4
Apparel	0.6	1.6	1.3	2.5	2.0	5.6	0.4	1.3	1.2	1.7	2.1	3.9
Lumber and wood products	2.5	4.7	9.7	9.4	8.8	4.9	2.7	1.1	2.8	6.9	7.2	4.4
Furniture and fixtures	0.2	0.3	...	0.2	0.1	0.3	0.2	0.1	...	...	2.6	9.6
Paper products	7.7	11.6	5.3	10.5	3.4	3.3	11.2	9.6	3.9	5.8	7.5	8.3
Printing and publishing	0.1	0.1	...	0.4	0.2	0.2	6.5	0.1	1.0	0.2	1.0	1.7
Chemical products	0.7	1.0	1.6	1.7	3.9	13.2	1.4	6.1	0.5	0.8	1.4	4.0
Refined petroleum products	...	0.1	0.1	...	0.1	0.1	0.1	0.2	...	...	0.1	4.8
Rubber and plastic products	1.5	1.1	0.3	0.8	1.3	1.8	3.9	4.3	1.4	3.3	12.9	32.2
Leather products	1.9	2.1	0.3	0.4	0.5	0.6	0.1	...	...	0.1	1.0	0.3
Stone, clay and glass products	0.1	0.6	0.2	0.1	0.1	0.3	0.1	0.1	0.1	0.4	2.0	3.8
Primary metals	2.9	2.6	1.0	23.6	16.9	1.3	0.3	0.2	0.1	0.2	7.6	11.8
Fabricated metal products	3.1	4.3	2.8	5.4	3.8	3.2	1.3	1.9	1.3	2.9	21.7	29.2
Industrial machinery and computers	45.2	43.2	37.5	59.1	48.2	60.5	28.9	48.0	25.6	35.1	208.1	408.3
Electric and electronic equipment	3.2	9.1	3.0	7.9	9.4	16.5	2.3	1.6	2.7	15.7	34.1	56.0
Transportation equipment	31.3	61.8	34.0	45.9	44.7	13.7	48.5	3.5	4.8	1.5	120.2	369.2
Scientific and measuring instruments	8.0	11.2	2.6	3.0	3.7	7.8	6.6	2.7	2.4	2.5	7.9	9.2
Miscellaneous manufactures	2.6	1.9	0.7	1.0	1.2	1.4	1.2	1.0	0.4	1.1	0.7	3.2
Unidentified manufactures	0.3	0.3	0.4	1.5	2.6	1.1	0.3	0.2	0.2	0.3	3.1	3.7
Agricultural And Livestock Products	8.0	31.3	13.3	13.2	21.8	6.5	1.8	1.2	0.7	2.6	3.8	19.9
Agricultural products	8.0	31.2	13.3	13.2	21.8	6.5	1.8	1.2	0.6	2.5	3.8	19.9
Livestock and livestock products	...	...	...	...	...	...	...	...	...	0.1	...	0.1
Other Commodities	0.3	0.2	0.1	0.6	0.6	0.8	0.8	0.5	1.5	1.3	1.9	1.7
Forestry products	...	...	...	...	...	0.1	0.5	0.3	0.5	1.0	1.1	0.5
Fish and other marine products	...	...	...	...	...	...	...	...	...	0.2	0.2	...
Metallic ores and concentrates	...	...	...	...	...	...	...	...	...	...	...	...
Bituminous coal and lignite	...	...	...	...	...	...	...	...	...	...	...	...
Crude petroleum and natural gas	...	...	...	...	...	...	...	...	...	...	...	...
Nonmetallic minerals	...	...	...	...	...	...	...	...	...	...	...	0.5
Scrap and waste	0.2	0.2	...	0.1	0.5	0.3	0.1	...	...	...	...	0.5
Used merchandise	0.1	...	0.1	0.2	...	0.2	0.2	0.1	...	0.1	0.1	0.2
Goods imported and returned unchanged	...	...	...	...	...	...	...	...	...	...	...	...
Special classification provisions	...	0.1	...	0.2	0.1	0.2	...	...	1.0	0.1	0.5	0.5

Industry	European Union						United Kingdom					
	1994	1995	1996	1997	1998	1999	1994	1995	1996	1997	1998	1999
ALL GOODS	1 164.3	1 725.3	952.9	1 061.8	1 077.2	1 726.1	304.9	352.4	161.6	191.0	225.5	325.1
Manufactured Goods	1 124.6	1 683.6	922.8	1 031.1	1 051.3	1 667.2	294.0	344.5	155.2	186.7	221.5	298.7
Food products	8.1	15.4	11.3	9.5	6.6	14.0	1.5	3.5	1.3	1.4	2.2	4.3
Tobacco products	...	...	...	0.5	...	...	...	...	...	...	...	...
Textile mill products	0.4	0.5	0.4	0.5	0.4	2.2	0.2	0.2	...	0.1	0.2	0.4
Apparel	2.9	2.3	0.9	1.3	1.5	3.7	0.2	0.4	0.2	0.3	0.5	0.8
Lumber and wood products	153.1	99.3	70.0	102.1	85.3	75.2	14.4	9.3	8.5	24.4	18.5	7.9
Furniture and fixtures	1.3	1.2	0.9	0.9	0.8	0.4	0.4	0.4	0.5	0.5	0.4	0.2
Paper products	31.0	65.2	7.8	11.9	10.7	32.0	1.0	0.9	0.4	1.1	0.6	0.4
Printing and publishing	5.1	5.8	2.6	3.7	3.8	5.4	2.4	2.9	1.0	1.3	1.2	2.7
Chemical products	8.2	10.5	7.4	11.3	14.1	34.0	3.2	2.5	2.5	4.6	3.4	5.9
Refined petroleum products	0.1	0.1	0.4	0.5	0.2	0.3	...	...	...	...	...	...
Rubber and plastic products	5.4	10.6	3.1	10.9	11.6	9.4	0.4	0.6	0.6	4.2	4.9	3.6
Leather products	2.0	2.1	1.0	0.5	0.3	1.9	0.6	0.4	0.5	0.1	0.1	0.1
Stone, clay and glass products	8.0	4.9	7.3	10.4	13.8	13.8	2.3	1.9	3.4	4.7	5.2	4.5
Primary metals	30.9	55.8	28.6	46.8	49.0	52.6	3.7	4.0	4.0	5.9	5.1	8.7
Fabricated metal products	13.9	17.1	22.2	27.4	32.4	37.9	1.4	2.8	3.8	3.0	5.2	5.3
Industrial machinery and computers	436.8	831.8	515.0	518.3	540.2	897.1	157.9	172.0	56.6	62.9	101.8	162.2
Electric and electronic equipment	223.7	305.5	168.1	178.7	192.0	215.2	57.1	92.3	53.5	50.3	57.4	60.2
Transportation equipment	18.4	28.8	21.0	19.6	35.8	70.3	9.4	13.2	6.9	7.3	4.2	7.0
Scientific and measuring instruments	159.8	209.7	46.3	70.1	47.3	189.7	35.2	34.5	10.1	13.2	9.2	22.6
Miscellaneous manufactures	12.6	13.9	6.9	4.5	3.3	8.6	2.0	2.1	0.9	0.9	0.8	1.1
Unidentified manufactures	2.8	3.2	1.7	1.5	2.3	3.6	0.6	0.6	0.2	0.4	0.5	0.9
Agricultural And Livestock Products	27.1	28.9	23.9	27.2	20.3	21.2	3.5	3.2	3.8	3.3	3.1	3.5
Agricultural products	27.1	28.8	23.9	27.2	20.3	21.2	3.5	3.2	3.8	3.3	3.1	3.5
Livestock and livestock products	...	0.1	...	...	...	...	...	...	...	...	...	...
Other Commodities	12.6	12.7	6.2	3.5	5.7	37.7	7.5	4.8	2.7	1.0	1.0	22.9
Forestry products	...	0.4	0.1	0.1	0.1	0.2	...	0.3	0.1	...	...	0.1
Fish and other marine products	2.5	0.7	0.7	0.6	0.3	3.0	0.2	...	0.1	0.2	0.1	0.3
Metallic ores and concentrates	...	...	0.1	0.1	...	...	...	...	...	...	...	...
Bituminous coal and lignite	...	...	...	...	...	...	...	...	...	...	...	...
Crude petroleum and natural gas	...	...	...	...	...	...	...	...	...	...	...	...
Nonmetallic minerals	...	...	0.3	...	0.2	...	...	...	...	...	...	...
Scrap and waste	...	0.5	4.6	1.5	1.7	0.9	0.2	...	...	0.4	0.3	0.4
Used merchandise	1.1	0.5	2.5	0.2	0.1	11.6	0.5	0.1	2.3	0.1	...	10.8
Goods imported and returned unchanged	...	...	...	...	...	...	...	...	...	...	...	...
Special classification provisions	8.5	6.5	1.0	0.9	3.2	22.0	6.5	4.3	0.2	0.3	0.5	11.3

Table D-40. OREGON: State Exports of Goods by Destination and Industry, 1994–1999—*Continued*

(Millions of dollars.)

Industry	Germany						France					
	1994	1995	1996	1997	1998	1999	1994	1995	1996	1997	1998	1999
ALL GOODS	305.7	414.2	306.1	213.0	171.2	238.5	115.5	242.6	117.5	81.2	95.0	142.5
Manufactured Goods	298.0	406.8	300.5	208.6	163.8	231.8	112.6	239.5	115.1	78.8	93.6	138.1
Food products	0.7	1.3	0.8	1.2	2.0	3.6	0.4	1.2	0.3	0.1	0.2	0.4
Tobacco products	...	...	...	...	...	...	...	...	...	...	...	...
Textile mill products	0.1	...	0.1	0.1	0.1	0.2	...	...	...	...	...	0.2
Apparel	1.3	0.7	0.2	0.2	0.1	0.3	0.6	0.2	...	0.1	...	...
Lumber and wood products	51.8	41.2	20.8	29.3	18.2	18.6	3.4	2.1	1.2	2.3	4.3	3.2
Furniture and fixtures	0.2	0.2	0.1	0.1	0.1	...	0.3	0.1	...	0.1	0.1	...
Paper products	13.2	15.1	4.2	1.0	1.5	0.3	1.1	0.1	...	1.1	...	0.5
Printing and publishing	1.1	0.4	0.1	0.8	0.4	1.0	0.3	1.1	0.1	0.2	0.1	0.2
Chemical products	0.6	1.1	1.2	1.4	1.4	1.1	1.4	0.6	0.3	0.6	1.4	4.1
Refined petroleum products	...	...	...	...	...	...	0.1	0.1	0.4	0.4	0.1	...
Rubber and plastic products	1.1	0.7	0.5	0.3	0.1	0.8	1.2	0.4	0.1	0.1	0.1	0.3
Leather products	0.4	0.4	0.3	0.1	...	0.2	0.1	0.1	...	...	...	...
Stone, clay and glass products	0.6	0.6	1.2	3.9	6.5	5.7	4.4	1.7	1.9	0.8	0.8	0.8
Primary metals	13.6	31.3	3.8	8.6	16.8	11.2	5.0	7.0	5.6	14.1	7.3	14.2
Fabricated metal products	2.0	3.4	5.5	7.3	8.1	9.4	1.3	1.2	0.8	2.3	2.8	3.4
Industrial machinery and computers	126.3	204.9	221.1	114.4	67.2	95.8	43.0	136.1	80.0	26.9	37.7	64.7
Electric and electronic equipment	33.8	33.7	26.7	25.4	23.9	36.3	25.0	54.5	16.1	20.8	22.6	21.2
Transportation equipment	4.1	3.6	5.3	4.3	4.8	11.5	0.7	3.6	2.8	3.1	11.0	13.6
Scientific and measuring instruments	45.3	65.8	6.9	9.3	11.6	34.1	23.3	28.3	4.4	5.3	4.5	9.5
Miscellaneous manufactures	1.2	1.7	1.2	0.6	0.4	1.1	0.4	0.9	0.9	0.2	0.2	1.4
Unidentified manufactures	0.5	0.8	0.4	0.2	0.4	0.5	0.6	0.4	0.2	0.2	0.2	0.4
Agricultural And Livestock Products	6.8	6.4	4.8	4.2	5.0	2.9	1.7	2.7	1.8	2.2	1.1	1.3
Agricultural products	6.8	6.4	4.8	4.2	5.0	2.9	1.7	2.7	1.8	2.2	1.1	1.3
Livestock and livestock products	...	...	...	...	...	...	...	...	...	...	...	...
Other Commodities	0.8	1.0	0.7	0.3	2.4	3.9	1.2	0.4	0.5	0.1	0.3	3.2
Forestry products	...	...	0.1	...	0.1	...	...	...	...	...	...	...
Fish and other marine products	...	...	0.1	0.1	0.1	...	0.1	...	...	...	...	0.2
Metallic ores and concentrates	...	...	...	...	...	...	...	...	0.1	...	...	...
Bituminous coal and lignite	...	...	...	...	...	...	...	...	...	...	...	...
Crude petroleum and natural gas	...	...	...	...	...	...	...	...	...	...	...	...
Nonmetallic minerals	...	...	...	...	...	...	...	...	0.3	...	0.2	...
Scrap and waste	...	0.4	0.1	0.1	...	...	0.1	...	...	...	...	...
Used merchandise	0.1	0.1	0.1	0.1	...	...	0.4	0.2	0.1	...	...	0.5
Goods imported and returned unchanged	...	...	...	...	...	...	...	...	...	...	...	...
Special classification provisions	0.6	0.4	0.3	...	2.1	3.8	0.7	0.2	...	0.1	0.1	2.4

Industry	The Netherlands						Asian 10					
	1994	1995	1996	1997	1998	1999	1994	1995	1996	1997	1998	1999
ALL GOODS	106.9	178.9	46.1	198.3	200.7	535.6	3 654.0	5 675.0	5 419.7	5 147.9	4 544.2	6 033.1
Manufactured Goods	100.6	171.6	41.4	192.5	195.4	526.9	1 848.7	2 919.9	2 603.6	2 713.2	2 954.8	4 507.8
Food products	2.3	3.3	0.3	0.2	0.9	1.9	112.9	127.2	124.1	144.6	128.1	119.3
Tobacco products	...	...	...	0.5	...	...	0.1	...	...	...	...	...
Textile mill products	...	0.1	0.1	0.1	...	...	1.4	1.9	1.2	1.0	0.8	0.8
Apparel	0.2	0.2	0.3	0.3	0.7	0.8	8.1	9.8	7.2	5.6	3.6	3.8
Lumber and wood products	6.9	3.7	3.2	2.8	3.3	2.9	414.3	450.6	276.0	243.2	151.5	215.8
Furniture and fixtures	0.1	0.1	...	0.1	0.1	0.1	2.5	4.6	4.5	3.8	2.8	2.9
Paper products	1.0	4.8	1.2	1.4	3.2	4.7	96.8	159.1	234.5	223.3	174.4	222.9
Printing and publishing	0.6	1.1	0.2	0.2	0.8	1.0	9.7	9.3	10.5	8.1	7.8	7.0
Chemical products	1.0	4.8	0.2	0.3	0.9	8.7	8.1	14.5	9.8	16.5	106.3	155.7
Refined petroleum products	...	...	...	...	...	0.1	0.2	1.7	1.2	1.2	0.4	0.3
Rubber and plastic products	1.1	7.1	0.1	0.2	0.3	2.8	15.3	28.2	28.5	14.5	9.8	14.2
Leather products	...	0.2	...	...	...	0.4	42.7	65.0	17.0	25.3	30.8	105.5
Stone, clay and glass products	...	...	0.1	0.1	0.2	0.4	5.3	7.6	12.6	13.0	6.7	44.4
Primary metals	0.8	0.2	0.3	0.3	0.7	3.5	27.4	53.6	33.7	51.9	91.9	26.2
Fabricated metal products	0.5	0.5	0.5	0.8	0.9	3.8	25.3	29.7	33.3	43.7	38.6	34.2
Industrial machinery and computers	39.7	89.5	22.0	155.2	151.1	365.4	340.2	702.2	505.7	626.2	504.8	634.2
Electric and electronic equipment	23.9	25.2	6.9	22.5	16.0	26.6	512.9	974.9	1 192.9	1 196.6	1 622.1	2 635.3
Transportation equipment	2.1	1.8	0.6	1.0	10.9	3.7	35.8	28.6	19.9	26.9	16.6	20.6
Scientific and measuring instruments	13.8	21.7	4.9	5.9	4.7	97.0	167.2	217.7	71.5	49.0	38.4	251.3
Miscellaneous manufactures	6.2	6.8	0.3	0.4	0.3	2.9	20.4	30.7	18.1	16.3	13.3	8.5
Unidentified manufactures	0.4	0.4	0.2	0.1	0.4	0.6	2.0	3.0	1.6	2.2	6.1	5.0
Agricultural And Livestock Products	5.7	6.1	4.4	5.5	4.7	7.1	1 686.3	2 571.5	2 685.2	2 300.0	1 497.2	1 410.1
Agricultural products	5.7	6.1	4.4	5.5	4.7	7.1	1 686.0	2 571.3	2 685.1	2 299.8	1 497.2	1 410.1
Livestock and livestock products	...	...	...	...	...	...	0.2	0.1	...	0.2	0.1	0.1
Other Commodities	0.6	1.2	0.3	0.3	0.6	1.6	119.0	183.7	130.9	134.7	92.2	115.2
Forestry products	...	0.1	...	...	...	...	0.2	0.2	0.1	0.1	0.2	0.2
Fish and other marine products	...	...	0.2	0.1	...	...	13.1	14.9	5.4	9.1	2.9	9.6
Metallic ores and concentrates	...	...	...	...	...	...	...	...	...	...	0.1	0.2
Bituminous coal and lignite	...	...	...	...	...	...	...	...	...	...	...	...
Crude petroleum and natural gas	...	...	...	...	...	...	...	...	...	...	...	...
Nonmetallic minerals	...	...	...	...	...	...	1.3	2.1	0.3	0.3	1.2	2.6
Scrap and waste	...	0.2	...	0.1	0.5	...	99.7	157.1	122.6	121.2	81.4	84.8
Used merchandise	...	...	...	...	...	...	1.9	1.6	1.0	1.3	0.6	0.4
Goods imported and returned unchanged	...	...	...	...	...	...	...	...	...	...	...	...
Special classification provisions	0.5	1.0	...	0.1	...	1.5	2.9	7.9	1.4	2.7	5.8	17.5

Table D-40. OREGON: State Exports of Goods by Destination and Industry, 1994–1999—Continued

(Millions of dollars.)

Industry	Japan						South Korea					
	1994	1995	1996	1997	1998	1999	1994	1995	1996	1997	1998	1999
ALL GOODS	1 389.1	1 778.7	1 487.2	1 271.8	1 145.2	1 603.0	550.9	936.5	905.5	1 037.8	1 353.5	1 910.8
Manufactured Goods	792.6	1 058.9	751.5	633.2	593.3	919.7	249.2	355.6	355.1	609.8	1 052.2	1 696.5
Food products	68.5	78.0	75.7	89.9	94.5	95.5	11.1	10.1	8.0	9.3	4.8	6.3
Tobacco products	...	...	...	...	...	...	...	...	...	...	...	...
Textile mill products	0.4	1.5	0.8	0.6	0.3	0.4	...	0.1	0.1	0.1	0.2	0.1
Apparel	6.9	9.3	4.8	5.0	3.2	3.3	0.3	0.1	2.2	0.3	0.1	0.2
Lumber and wood products	337.4	379.9	232.1	182.3	120.4	165.2	29.9	22.4	9.3	13.8	4.4	12.9
Furniture and fixtures	2.3	3.7	4.2	3.0	1.7	2.6	0.1	0.7	...	...	0.1	...
Paper products	5.3	6.0	19.3	9.4	7.7	11.9	27.2	32.8	32.4	29.4	27.6	50.2
Printing and publishing	3.8	4.0	2.9	1.5	0.9	1.6	0.2	1.4	1.1	0.8	0.6	0.5
Chemical products	2.8	6.9	5.2	7.1	37.8	53.7	1.4	2.5	0.9	2.0	31.0	43.9
Refined petroleum products	0.2	1.6	1.1	1.1	0.1	0.2	...	...	...	...	...	...
Rubber and plastic products	8.7	21.5	17.0	7.8	5.7	5.6	0.8	1.8	1.1	0.5	0.4	4.6
Leather products	1.9	1.5	1.3	1.8	3.1	2.4	13.8	22.4	12.3	9.8	5.1	5.9
Stone, clay and glass products	3.2	3.7	5.6	8.0	4.7	7.1	1.4	2.6	4.5	2.7	0.5	33.3
Primary metals	21.4	13.0	7.9	21.3	28.2	21.0	1.1	9.0	0.7	1.0	19.8	1.6
Fabricated metal products	10.4	9.8	10.8	15.1	9.9	13.2	2.4	1.0	1.3	2.4	3.9	8.1
Industrial machinery and computers	122.7	257.2	194.6	161.9	174.1	209.6	31.1	52.8	24.3	47.8	13.5	43.8
Electric and electronic equipment	94.5	127.8	101.9	88.1	69.4	207.8	100.3	163.9	247.5	466.8	933.7	1 439.1
Transportation equipment	10.8	9.4	8.0	4.1	5.4	4.4	1.7	3.3	2.3	11.8	4.4	8.2
Scientific and measuring instruments	77.0	99.3	44.4	12.5	13.3	106.6	24.2	26.4	5.0	9.8	0.7	36.1
Miscellaneous manufactures	13.6	23.2	13.2	11.6	11.6	5.5	1.8	2.0	2.0	1.5	0.5	1.2
Unidentified manufactures	0.8	1.5	0.8	1.0	1.2	2.3	0.3	0.3	0.2	0.1	0.9	0.5
Agricultural And Livestock Products	559.5	669.7	711.2	612.3	535.4	650.9	255.1	506.0	482.2	354.5	264.6	179.6
Agricultural products	559.5	669.7	711.2	612.2	535.3	650.8	255.1	506.0	482.1	354.5	264.6	179.6
Livestock and livestock products	...	...	...	0.1	0.1	0.1	...	...	...	...	...	...
Other Commodities	37.0	50.0	24.6	26.3	16.6	32.5	46.7	74.8	68.2	73.5	36.7	34.6
Forestry products	0.1	0.1	0.1	0.1	0.1	0.1	...	...	...	...	...	...
Fish and other marine products	10.7	10.9	3.5	5.8	2.1	8.3	0.7	2.5	0.7	1.2	0.1	0.9
Metallic ores and concentrates	...	...	...	...	...	...	...	...	...	...	0.1	...
Bituminous coal and lignite	...	...	...	...	...	...	...	...	...	...	...	...
Crude petroleum and natural gas	...	...	...	...	...	...	...	...	...	...	...	...
Nonmetallic minerals	0.2	0.2	0.3	0.3	0.7	0.6	...	...	...	...	...	...
Scrap and waste	23.5	36.4	19.5	17.9	12.2	12.6	45.4	71.1	67.5	72.2	36.3	32.0
Used merchandise	1.9	1.2	0.8	1.2	0.5	0.3	...	...	...	...	0.1	0.1
Goods imported and returned unchanged	...	...	...	...	...	...	...	...	...	...	...	...
Special classification provisions	0.7	1.3	0.5	1.0	1.0	10.6	0.5	1.2	0.1	...	0.1	1.5

Industry	Taiwan						Singapore					
	1994	1995	1996	1997	1998	1999	1994	1995	1996	1997	1998	1999
ALL GOODS	688.4	1 057.7	1 047.0	1 063.4	593.8	585.9	252.0	507.3	560.8	449.8	284.4	298.4
Manufactured Goods	147.3	202.7	159.3	206.9	186.4	247.1	249.0	499.6	550.9	444.4	277.4	292.6
Food products	8.0	10.1	6.7	7.3	6.1	5.0	3.1	5.5	3.3	2.9	1.9	1.0
Tobacco products	...	...	...	...	...	...	...	...	0.1	...	...	...
Textile mill products	0.2	...	0.1	...	...	0.2	0.1	0.1	0.1	...	...	0.1
Apparel	0.5	...	...	...	...	...	1.0	1.7	0.8	0.9	0.3	0.8
Lumber and wood products	27.1	20.9	13.4	18.6	10.2	7.4	1.0	1.7	0.8	0.9	0.3	0.8
Furniture and fixtures	...	...	...	0.1	0.1	...	...	0.1	...	0.1	0.1	0.1
Paper products	9.8	24.7	15.2	21.4	12.6	16.3	4.0	15.3	15.1	14.3	11.8	8.0
Printing and publishing	0.6	0.5	0.6	0.4	0.2	0.3	1.9	0.6	1.4	1.7	1.5	1.6
Chemical products	1.5	1.5	0.5	0.3	4.9	20.5	0.6	0.7	0.5	2.1	3.1	1.5
Refined petroleum products	...	...	...	...	...	0.1	...	...	...	...	...	...
Rubber and plastic products	0.2	0.7	0.6	0.5	0.3	0.3	3.6	2.8	4.0	2.3	1.8	2.0
Leather products	9.3	8.2	0.1	0.1	...	1.6	0.1	...	...	0.1	...	0.1
Stone, clay and glass products	0.4	0.3	0.6	0.6	0.6	1.3	0.1	0.2	1.2	0.3	0.4	0.7
Primary metals	1.7	2.8	19.8	26.6	8.1	0.8	1.4	25.8	1.1	0.5	13.4	0.4
Fabricated metal products	1.0	0.6	1.2	1.2	0.3	1.5	4.5	9.2	2.3	2.9	15.4	4.1
Industrial machinery and computers	20.0	36.7	30.7	84.2	101.7	73.1	86.4	155.7	164.3	190.0	100.8	174.1
Electric and electronic equipment	44.9	69.1	63.0	39.6	38.0	87.5	130.8	260.2	350.3	217.1	120.3	80.7
Transportation equipment	2.8	1.5	0.4	0.4	0.3	0.5	0.4	0.4	1.0	0.8	1.4	0.7
Scientific and measuring instruments	16.9	22.4	5.6	4.9	2.7	30.2	10.2	20.5	4.8	7.8	4.9	16.1
Miscellaneous manufactures	1.9	2.3	0.8	0.4	0.1	0.1	0.8	0.6	0.3	0.4	0.1	0.2
Unidentified manufactures	0.3	0.3	0.1	0.1	0.3	0.4	0.2	0.2	0.2	0.2	0.2	0.2
Agricultural And Livestock Products	532.3	839.5	878.8	846.2	396.1	327.2	2.0	5.4	9.3	4.4	5.2	2.3
Agricultural products	532.3	839.5	878.8	846.2	396.1	327.2	2.0	5.4	9.3	4.4	5.2	2.3
Livestock and livestock products	...	...	...	...	...	...	...	...	...	...	...	...
Other Commodities	8.8	15.5	8.9	10.4	11.2	11.7	1.0	2.3	0.6	1.1	1.8	3.5
Forestry products	...	...	...	...	0.1	...	...	...	...	...	...	...
Fish and other marine products	0.2	0.1	0.3	0.4	0.2	...	...	...	0.1	0.1	0.1	0.1
Metallic ores and concentrates	...	...	...	...	...	...	...	...	...	...	...	...
Bituminous coal and lignite	...	...	...	...	...	...	...	...	...	...	...	...
Crude petroleum and natural gas	...	...	...	...	...	...	...	...	...	...	...	...
Nonmetallic minerals	...	...	...	...	...	0.1	...	0.1	...	...	...	0.1
Scrap and waste	8.2	14.3	8.6	9.4	8.3	10.0	0.3	0.4	0.1	...	0.1	1.8
Used merchandise	...	...	...	...	...	...	...	...	0.1	...	...	...
Goods imported and returned unchanged	...	...	...	...	...	...	...	...	...	...	...	...
Special classification provisions	0.4	1.1	0.1	0.5	2.6	1.6	0.6	1.6	0.4	0.9	1.5	1.4

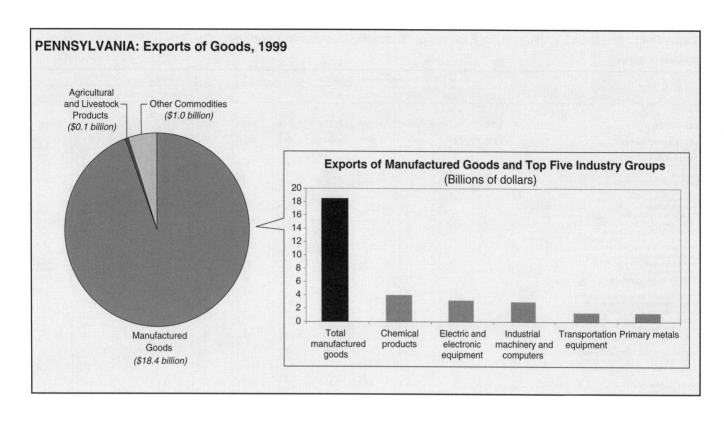

PENNSYLVANIA: Exports of Goods, 1999

Agricultural and Livestock Products ($0.1 billion)

Other Commodities ($1.0 billion)

Manufactured Goods ($18.4 billion)

Exports of Manufactured Goods and Top Five Industry Groups
(Billions of dollars)

Total manufactured goods / Chemical products / Electric and electronic equipment / Industrial machinery and computers / Transportation equipment / Primary metals

Table D-41. PENNSYLVANIA: State Exports of Goods by Destination and Industry, 1994–1999

(Millions of dollars.)

Industry	All destinations						Canada					
	1994	1995	1996	1997	1998	1999	1994	1995	1996	1997	1998	1999
ALL GOODS	14 698.6	17 680.2	17 445.6	19 298.4	19 138.8	19 527.7	4 066.5	4 671.8	4 773.7	5 615.7	5 856.9	5 927.2
Manufactured Goods	13 755.6	16 551.0	16 400.2	18 172.0	17 890.1	18 437.1	3 838.7	4 387.9	4 494.8	5 303.9	5 538.5	5 608.3
Food products	425.9	378.9	512.7	516.5	487.7	493.8	122.3	126.9	152.8	160.2	175.7	187.2
Tobacco products	0.3	9.7	5.9	1.1	2.6	3.1	0.1	. . .	0.1	0.5	0.7	0.8
Textile mill products	164.1	185.5	232.5	220.6	186.3	213.8	43.7	50.0	65.6	70.5	70.9	84.5
Apparel	153.9	236.8	251.3	221.8	239.0	177.5	17.7	56.5	55.8	48.3	51.7	25.2
Lumber and wood products	281.3	288.8	285.6	325.3	299.0	319.6	116.9	105.4	111.2	126.1	118.6	129.9
Furniture and fixtures	74.7	75.0	71.6	87.7	77.2	53.0	42.8	45.0	40.6	49.4	43.0	28.6
Paper products	182.3	289.2	250.1	308.6	289.7	302.9	111.8	179.2	143.8	179.2	191.7	214.5
Printing and publishing	183.9	204.8	225.4	230.4	241.0	251.8	126.9	148.5	159.5	175.2	183.5	198.7
Chemical products	2 731.0	3 570.6	3 335.7	3 537.2	3 872.1	3 994.5	533.8	602.9	670.6	771.3	888.4	991.5
Refined petroleum products	143.1	151.7	156.1	192.4	210.3	161.8	72.9	77.8	84.2	92.6	97.4	85.9
Rubber and plastic products	438.7	501.4	565.5	601.8	668.0	691.2	122.6	140.3	159.4	177.6	169.2	178.1
Leather products	59.3	31.8	45.9	56.9	57.7	139.9	23.7	8.6	11.3	10.4	10.7	36.4
Stone, clay and glass products	483.4	553.3	556.5	606.3	548.3	528.8	235.9	251.5	251.5	250.5	281.6	288.2
Primary metals	921.2	1 741.4	1 459.6	1 500.8	1 336.4	1 318.1	360.7	485.8	497.3	644.9	635.7	645.1
Fabricated metal products	533.6	618.2	581.9	663.0	714.6	712.3	154.8	179.4	202.1	255.0	245.3	268.9
Industrial machinery and computers	2 519.9	2 941.6	3 079.8	3 443.6	2 951.6	2 984.7	584.4	585.1	652.7	748.4	827.1	854.1
Electric and electronic equipment	2 337.5	2 455.1	2 424.0	2 841.1	2 570.6	3 204.1	394.3	438.3	425.4	419.2	436.1	552.4
Transportation equipment	1 030.2	1 201.1	1 131.7	1 480.4	1 753.7	1 377.2	461.0	579.3	467.3	749.9	747.3	466.4
Scientific and measuring instruments	747.9	772.4	839.5	924.1	984.8	1 154.9	189.0	206.5	217.9	245.2	234.4	250.7
Miscellaneous manufactures	277.0	295.4	340.8	356.9	319.1	263.1	110.1	105.6	110.0	113.8	112.0	102.4
Unidentified manufactures	66.3	48.4	48.4	55.5	80.3	91.1	13.5	15.2	15.6	15.8	17.5	18.9
Agricultural And Livestock Products	86.4	78.7	93.4	120.2	129.5	126.2	58.4	55.5	60.6	71.5	71.1	76.2
Agricultural products	59.2	59.4	74.4	99.0	112.7	113.0	47.6	46.8	50.9	59.4	59.8	68.0
Livestock and livestock products	27.2	19.3	19.1	21.2	16.8	13.2	10.8	8.8	9.7	12.1	11.3	8.2
Other Commodities	856.7	1 050.5	951.9	1 006.2	1 119.2	964.4	169.4	228.3	218.4	240.3	247.3	242.6
Forestry products	30.0	34.7	28.3	30.4	26.6	25.1	0.4	0.5	0.9	0.8	3.0	2.3
Fish and other marine products	10.7	11.1	10.8	13.5	7.9	8.6	3.9	2.0	5.0	1.9	0.8	1.0
Metallic ores and concentrates	21.7	27.7	26.0	24.8	18.7	23.3	6.8	8.4	7.6	7.4	7.1	6.8
Bituminous coal and lignite	388.5	437.6	423.5	428.7	489.3	285.7	47.6	45.8	52.6	71.8	87.2	77.2
Crude petroleum and natural gas	9.8	16.7	19.3	21.5	15.2	7.5	6.0	11.2	6.1	9.4	6.0	4.2
Nonmetallic minerals	34.9	44.5	42.2	37.8	33.4	29.0	2.7	4.1	4.9	3.8	2.4	3.8
Scrap and waste	68.5	241.4	264.3	314.8	409.6	367.4	48.4	88.3	53.6	57.4	65.3	68.0
Used merchandise	73.2	49.7	44.1	38.6	32.4	80.3	3.1	2.9	6.0	5.3	3.5	4.3
Goods imported and returned unchanged	40.9	51.9	71.4	72.3	62.7	55.5	40.9	51.9	71.4	72.3	62.7	55.5
Special classification provisions	178.4	135.2	22.0	23.7	23.5	82.0	9.6	13.2	10.4	10.0	9.4	19.5

Table D-41. PENNSYLVANIA: State Exports of Goods by Destination and Industry, 1994–1999—*Continued*

(Millions of dollars.)

Industry	South and Central American and Caribbean						Mexico					
	1994	1995	1996	1997	1998	1999	1994	1995	1996	1997	1998	1999
ALL GOODS	1 363.6	1 689.8	1 550.3	1 820.8	1 567.0	1 377.6	866.4	741.2	879.0	1 140.3	1 425.2	2 306.2
Manufactured Goods	1 298.1	1 611.4	1 446.3	1 696.5	1 452.9	1 302.3	835.9	734.4	870.7	1 116.9	1 409.9	2 290.0
Food products	16.2	20.3	36.1	45.2	38.7	35.8	23.9	16.1	31.2	22.4	35.0	34.4
Tobacco products	...	0.1	0.4	0.2	0.4	0.6	...	...	...	...	1.2	1.5
Textile mill products	10.0	12.1	27.8	39.0	34.1	35.9	36.5	34.8	35.9	28.7	29.8	45.4
Apparel	48.4	81.1	100.6	88.5	93.6	98.4	7.0	13.1	21.9	20.7	36.3	22.0
Lumber and wood products	2.8	2.4	3.4	4.3	5.8	5.9	5.3	1.2	2.3	3.6	2.8	2.8
Furniture and fixtures	2.6	3.2	4.2	5.0	6.5	4.8	3.7	3.5	2.2	4.4	4.1	1.8
Paper products	7.6	11.9	16.8	16.7	16.4	13.4	16.5	30.3	19.5	24.8	22.8	27.1
Printing and publishing	5.8	3.8	2.0	2.5	2.9	4.1	2.0	2.2	2.5	4.2	2.6	8.8
Chemical products	323.7	436.9	355.2	349.6	448.6	411.1	217.6	207.0	225.9	319.2	359.5	361.5
Refined petroleum products	25.2	22.3	16.1	24.8	29.5	20.3	2.6	1.9	0.9	1.0	1.2	3.5
Rubber and plastic products	16.4	37.2	34.5	42.3	46.9	45.4	36.6	30.4	29.2	31.3	80.7	121.9
Leather products	10.4	1.9	2.5	3.4	3.3	2.2	0.5	0.1	...	0.3	10.3	50.3
Stone, clay and glass products	40.5	48.2	40.8	45.4	33.8	21.9	34.7	22.5	26.2	31.4	34.7	53.3
Primary metals	67.6	76.9	67.6	101.1	54.2	53.2	79.6	93.2	91.3	113.2	135.4	153.5
Fabricated metal products	62.7	85.6	39.8	51.8	82.2	36.3	34.9	26.0	24.4	31.1	41.0	97.6
Industrial machinery and computers	276.4	269.0	241.0	332.9	245.6	165.1	156.6	96.0	125.1	183.2	221.5	240.2
Electric and electronic equipment	294.8	375.9	349.5	390.4	171.8	131.3	118.5	114.5	178.8	231.1	272.0	879.2
Transportation equipment	32.8	58.6	49.0	76.4	60.6	146.1	14.8	12.0	7.1	11.3	30.7	77.5
Scientific and measuring instruments	41.6	48.0	41.5	60.0	57.3	55.1	34.1	24.6	37.0	45.6	61.6	79.4
Miscellaneous manufactures	8.9	12.9	13.7	13.0	13.5	7.5	8.4	3.1	6.4	7.1	12.0	6.1
Unidentified manufactures	3.8	3.1	3.6	4.2	7.1	8.0	2.2	2.0	3.1	2.5	14.9	22.1
Agricultural And Livestock Products	7.6	4.9	15.3	29.0	38.6	28.6	3.4	1.2	2.3	4.7	4.0	5.1
Agricultural products	4.0	2.0	12.7	27.6	37.1	27.3	0.9	0.6	1.1	2.3	2.9	4.0
Livestock and livestock products	3.6	2.9	2.6	1.4	1.5	1.3	2.5	0.7	1.2	2.4	1.1	1.2
Other Commodities	57.8	73.5	88.8	95.3	75.6	46.8	27.1	5.6	5.9	18.7	11.3	11.1
Forestry products	3.5	3.3	3.9	3.3	2.8	2.7	...	0.2	0.1	0.1	...	0.2
Fish and other marine products	1.1	2.3	1.4	0.5	1.2	0.9	...	...	0.2	0.1	0.4	...
Metallic ores and concentrates	3.5	4.0	5.1	3.7	4.5	4.4	1.8	2.9	2.2	2.0	1.4	1.3
Bituminous coal and lignite	45.1	58.6	65.9	70.4	53.9	30.3	0.6	0.1	0.1	12.4	2.8	...
Crude petroleum and natural gas	0.9	1.3	6.8	5.6	4.8	1.6	...	...	...	...	...	0.1
Nonmetallic materials	1.5	2.5	2.5	4.8	5.4	3.3	1.4	1.0	1.3	1.6	1.8	2.7
Scrap and waste	0.9	0.7	1.5	3.7	1.4	0.9	0.5	1.2	1.4	1.7	1.9	3.8
Used merchandise	1.0	0.5	0.5	2.3	1.0	0.9	22.7	0.1	0.2	0.1	2.5	0.7
Goods imported and returned unchanged	...	...	...	...	...		...	...	...	...	...	
Special classification provisions	0.3	0.3	1.2	1.1	0.6	1.8	0.1	0.2	0.4	0.5	0.7	2.3

Industry	European Union						United Kingdom					
	1994	1995	1996	1997	1998	1999	1994	1995	1996	1997	1998	1999
ALL GOODS	3 277.5	4 365.0	4 373.1	4 487.9	4 698.5	4 513.7	812.3	1 146.9	1 369.9	1 436.3	1 405.5	1 270.1
Manufactured Goods	2 816.5	3 780.7	3 879.9	3 952.0	4 094.1	3 972.3	663.4	888.2	1 132.3	1 150.3	1 047.2	997.3
Food products	29.5	50.5	50.7	39.9	25.1	20.5	4.5	7.7	9.0	4.6	3.3	6.6
Tobacco products	0.1	2.6	0.3	0.2	0.2	0.1	...	...	0.2	0.1	...	...
Textile mill products	17.2	19.3	20.8	18.4	19.8	14.0	5.9	6.6	7.0	5.6	6.4	4.6
Apparel	25.0	27.6	24.9	22.8	23.5	23.1	6.5	6.8	5.8	6.4	5.3	4.6
Lumber and wood products	93.4	111.4	103.1	119.8	111.4	115.9	31.9	38.9	39.4	28.1	16.7	17.6
Furniture and fixtures	9.1	7.7	10.9	11.9	11.4	10.7	1.1	1.0	3.7	2.3	3.4	4.4
Paper products	22.1	28.6	34.0	36.7	30.9	17.7	9.4	11.8	14.5	16.9	14.0	7.2
Printing and publishing	18.9	25.0	21.1	23.8	21.4	19.0	8.4	8.2	7.3	10.4	8.2	8.1
Chemical products	716.9	967.7	993.3	992.9	1 004.3	885.4	92.8	162.1	295.0	255.7	149.8	149.0
Refined petroleum products	15.2	22.1	19.6	15.0	19.9	12.4	1.0	0.7	3.5	1.2	1.5	0.9
Rubber and plastic products	116.9	142.2	156.8	167.2	194.0	167.4	29.7	29.4	44.6	50.8	64.5	59.3
Leather products	12.6	12.6	18.1	11.6	8.7	10.0	2.7	2.0	1.6	1.2	1.4	2.0
Stone, clay and glass products	79.3	110.7	113.3	125.1	114.8	92.0	15.1	19.3	19.6	15.1	18.1	10.3
Primary metals	154.3	367.4	370.0	316.3	293.9	269.4	47.7	90.1	100.3	100.0	90.3	91.1
Fabricated metal products	75.2	100.4	123.2	131.0	159.6	148.2	22.0	32.4	48.0	54.8	72.8	63.7
Industrial machinery and computers	425.6	696.7	749.0	747.3	694.1	783.6	141.3	196.7	206.3	246.0	220.9	228.4
Electric and electronic equipment	460.8	501.9	394.5	446.8	500.1	461.5	132.6	144.4	167.5	193.1	175.0	119.6
Transportation equipment	257.2	290.4	327.6	343.4	413.6	432.5	44.2	50.0	53.8	53.4	67.0	54.2
Scientific and measuring instruments	209.0	209.4	241.2	263.2	341.5	408.3	42.9	50.5	67.0	60.9	84.8	136.1
Miscellaneous manufactures	65.7	75.2	99.0	111.8	91.3	64.0	19.4	25.9	35.4	40.7	36.9	23.4
Unidentified manufactures	12.4	11.2	8.5	7.1	15.3	16.8	4.3	3.7	2.8	3.0	6.9	6.1
Agricultural And Livestock Products	7.4	10.2	9.0	8.3	8.3	7.7	0.9	3.2	3.2	3.5	1.8	1.0
Agricultural products	2.2	4.5	4.9	4.0	6.3	6.0	0.3	2.2	2.4	2.7	1.4	0.7
Livestock and livestock products	5.2	5.7	4.1	4.3	2.0	1.8	0.6	1.0	0.7	0.8	0.4	0.3
Other Commodities	453.5	574.1	484.2	527.6	595.5	533.6	148.0	255.5	234.4	282.5	356.5	271.7
Forestry products	10.1	12.9	10.6	13.3	10.0	9.8	...	0.1	...	0.5	0.1	0.1
Fish and other marine products	0.8	0.2	0.6	8.8	4.8	5.9	...	...	...	0.5	...	...
Metallic ores and concentrates	6.9	8.2	6.5	6.8	3.3	3.4	0.9	2.3	1.8	2.0	0.6	0.3
Bituminous coal and lignite	215.3	239.9	217.0	213.6	221.9	148.6	41.7	42.7	33.8	39.0	46.5	20.2
Crude petroleum and natural gas	2.7	4.0	6.1	6.1	4.1	1.4	2.7	3.9	5.9	6.1	4.0	1.1
Nonmetallic materials	12.1	13.3	15.5	13.8	13.4	8.5	0.2	0.3	0.7	0.4	0.9	0.3
Scrap and waste	10.9	140.9	201.2	242.3	317.5	243.2	3.7	122.5	186.2	223.5	297.2	235.9
Used merchandise	30.0	36.8	22.3	19.4	16.6	70.6	6.1	18.8	3.6	8.3	5.8	10.1
Goods imported and returned unchanged	...	...	...	...	...		...	...	...	...	...	
Special classification provisions	164.7	117.9	4.3	3.5	3.7	42.2	92.7	64.8	2.4	2.2	1.4	3.8

Table D-41. PENNSYLVANIA: State Exports of Goods by Destination and Industry, 1994–1999—*Continued*

(Millions of dollars.)

Industry	Germany						France					
	1994	1995	1996	1997	1998	1999	1994	1995	1996	1997	1998	1999
ALL GOODS	583.8	692.1	631.1	652.4	681.1	753.7	278.0	388.4	411.8	446.8	457.3	459.0
Manufactured Goods	567.7	666.7	604.8	630.1	648.1	723.7	255.3	354.8	392.3	417.6	426.6	429.9
Food products	5.4	6.0	5.7	5.3	5.3	2.7	1.4	2.0	1.9	1.3	0.8	0.5
Tobacco products	. . .	. . .	. . .	. . .	. . .	. . .	. . .	. . .	. . .	. . .	0.2	. . .
Textile mill products	2.7	4.6	6.6	4.0	4.9	2.9	0.9	1.1	0.7	0.8	1.1	0.7
Apparel	5.6	5.3	5.0	3.2	8.3	4.9	2.0	2.3	2.1	2.8	2.4	2.3
Lumber and wood products	13.8	23.9	20.4	24.2	20.2	19.8	12.4	10.0	6.8	9.1	10.6	8.8
Furniture and fixtures	3.4	2.8	1.5	3.0	2.0	1.2	1.4	0.4	1.0	1.6	1.0	0.2
Paper products	3.9	6.0	7.3	7.0	2.8	3.0	1.6	3.3	5.8	6.2	5.5	2.7
Printing and publishing	2.4	3.4	1.7	2.2	1.2	1.6	2.0	5.7	4.1	3.2	2.8	1.4
Chemical products	89.9	86.4	81.8	111.7	103.8	159.4	49.1	58.3	70.2	68.7	83.6	97.9
Refined petroleum products	1.0	1.2	1.1	0.8	1.9	0.8	0.2	0.1	0.4	0.3	0.4	1.0
Rubber and plastic products	39.7	46.3	43.4	40.1	39.2	40.5	8.8	23.5	24.1	29.6	33.8	29.5
Leather products	1.2	1.5	4.3	0.7	1.2	1.2	0.9	1.7	3.0	0.6	0.7	0.8
Stone, clay and glass products	17.3	28.4	27.0	24.4	17.0	16.7	17.7	20.1	17.4	25.9	33.4	21.4
Primary metals	20.1	30.3	19.7	31.9	36.0	34.6	21.2	25.3	30.1	33.1	33.6	44.0
Fabricated metal products	10.4	15.8	16.6	21.8	19.3	19.5	5.6	6.6	8.9	7.2	10.6	10.0
Industrial machinery and computers	76.7	135.8	137.3	112.5	108.8	141.7	47.2	111.0	128.1	113.0	82.6	75.7
Electric and electronic equipment	111.3	121.5	60.7	70.5	101.5	107.0	38.9	42.2	36.0	37.9	35.6	52.5
Transportation equipment	76.7	78.5	74.5	67.5	68.1	52.1	9.9	9.4	16.3	36.1	38.7	35.3
Scientific and measuring instruments	68.9	53.5	65.2	70.6	83.2	98.9	23.5	21.5	22.9	21.6	34.4	34.9
Miscellaneous manufactures	15.7	13.3	23.2	27.9	21.5	12.2	9.4	9.3	11.9	18.1	14.1	8.8
Unidentified manufactures	1.6	2.2	1.8	1.0	1.7	3.2	1.1	1.0	0.6	0.6	0.9	1.3
Agricultural And Livestock Products	0.1	0.4	0.8	0.4	3.8	0.4	1.1	0.9	0.9	0.7	0.5	0.7
Agricultural products	. . .	0.3	0.7	. . .	3.5	0.2	0.3	0.3	0.4	0.3	0.2	0.3
Livestock and livestock products	0.1	0.1	0.1	0.4	0.3	0.2	0.8	0.6	0.4	0.4	0.3	0.4
Other Commodities	15.9	25.0	25.5	21.9	29.2	29.6	21.7	32.7	18.6	28.5	30.1	28.5
Forestry products	7.3	8.4	6.8	8.8	6.4	5.0	. . .	1.3	. . .	0.2	. . .	. . .
Fish and other marine products	0.3	0.1	0.3	0.1	. . .	0.1	. . .	0.1	0.1	. . .	. . .	0.1
Metallic ores and concentrates	1.3	2.6	4.2	4.1	2.0	2.7	0.7	0.5	. . .	. . .	0.2	0.1
Bituminous coal and lignite	0.8	4.7	2.5	2.5	11.4	10.3	4.2	18.4	12.3	21.6	24.2	15.3
Crude petroleum and natural gas	. . .	. . .	. . .	. . .	. . .	0.2	. . .	. . .	. . .	. . .	. . .	. . .
Nonmetallic materials	0.7	1.0	0.7	0.8	0.4	0.3	0.1	0.2	0.8	0.2	0.3	. . .
Scrap and waste	1.6	3.6	1.0	0.9	5.7	3.9	0.1	. . .	0.3	3.2	0.1	. . .
Used merchandise	3.3	3.6	9.1	4.3	2.5	4.8	16.4	11.5	4.9	3.2	5.1	12.1
Goods imported and returned unchanged	. . .	. . .	. . .	. . .	. . .	. . .	. . .	. . .	. . .	. . .	. . .	. . .
Special classification provisions	0.6	1.0	0.8	0.4	0.8	2.4	0.2	0.7	0.1	0.2	0.3	0.9

Industry	The Netherlands						Asian 10					
	1994	1995	1996	1997	1998	1999	1994	1995	1996	1997	1998	1999
ALL GOODS	500.7	725.6	647.8	664.7	767.3	667.5	3 676.7	4 416.3	4 030.3	4 429.7	3 818.0	3 976.1
Manufactured Goods	473.8	679.2	594.5	624.3	726.6	641.3	3 582.2	4 309.2	3 945.4	4 361.6	3 740.2	3 897.9
Food products	11.0	21.1	9.7	10.7	5.6	3.8	200.2	126.9	144.0	176.8	144.2	158.2
Tobacco products	. . .	. . .	. . .	. . .	. . .	. . .	0.1	0.1	1.1	0.1	. . .	. . .
Textile mill products	2.6	2.6	2.3	2.2	1.6	1.2	46.8	52.4	57.2	37.1	15.7	19.6
Apparel	2.2	4.0	2.3	4.0	2.6	2.5	44.2	47.1	34.5	34.6	23.8	4.6
Lumber and wood products	2.0	1.2	2.1	2.7	2.9	2.6	42.3	48.7	46.9	49.9	39.0	49.8
Furniture and fixtures	0.2	0.4	0.3	0.5	0.4	2.4	10.2	10.6	8.3	10.0	6.9	3.4
Paper products	1.3	1.5	1.7	2.4	2.0	1.3	12.1	20.6	22.4	26.2	16.8	16.6
Printing and publishing	2.9	3.1	4.5	5.0	4.8	4.7	13.1	12.3	28.5	9.4	9.5	11.6
Chemical products	236.5	360.2	276.4	284.9	316.0	221.3	746.0	1 067.2	832.3	817.8	862.2	1 059.2
Refined petroleum products	4.9	8.2	5.4	1.5	1.7	1.7	19.3	19.4	25.4	40.8	41.8	31.4
Rubber and plastic products	18.0	19.5	15.4	15.1	16.5	9.5	106.9	104.0	130.2	134.4	131.3	124.5
Leather products	2.7	2.5	5.6	4.2	2.9	1.8	10.7	5.4	11.0	27.0	22.8	37.0
Stone, clay and glass products	6.4	5.4	9.1	8.6	6.0	4.7	57.2	75.0	88.2	111.6	57.1	49.0
Primary metals	8.6	32.9	34.2	27.0	47.1	24.2	166.4	551.6	304.7	244.2	123.4	130.1
Fabricated metal products	9.2	9.2	9.0	9.7	10.1	7.5	147.4	186.1	145.1	118.6	112.3	108.9
Industrial machinery and computers	32.5	61.5	75.2	82.3	94.4	121.7	710.9	802.6	778.8	918.2	519.8	623.3
Electric and electronic equipment	73.5	74.8	37.9	65.4	66.4	58.2	883.1	822.7	862.1	1 138.1	992.6	987.9
Transportation equipment	34.5	43.0	69.0	56.2	99.8	120.4	102.6	110.0	153.4	174.1	374.5	160.4
Scientific and measuring instruments	15.3	18.8	25.1	33.6	38.8	45.7	181.2	170.3	183.8	200.0	167.7	245.8
Miscellaneous manufactures	8.5	8.3	8.7	7.8	5.7	5.0	59.8	69.4	80.9	79.6	62.8	61.1
Unidentified manufactures	0.9	1.0	0.8	0.6	1.1	1.0	21.9	6.8	6.6	13.3	16.2	15.6
Agricultural And Livestock Products	2.5	1.7	1.4	1.4	0.6	4.3	7.1	4.0	3.4	3.6	1.2	1.0
Agricultural products	1.4	0.1	0.3	0.2	0.2	3.8	2.8	3.4	2.1	3.0	1.0	0.5
Livestock and livestock products	1.2	1.6	1.1	1.2	0.4	0.5	4.3	0.5	1.2	0.6	0.3	0.4
Other Commodities	24.3	44.7	51.9	39.0	40.1	21.9	87.4	103.1	81.6	64.6	76.5	77.3
Forestry products	1.3	1.4	1.9	1.7	1.5	1.7	15.5	17.1	11.4	12.0	10.0	9.3
Fish and other marine products	. . .	. . .	0.1	0.3	0.8	0.1	3.6	4.0	1.4	0.3	0.2	0.3
Metallic ores and concentrates	1.9	0.2	0.1	0.1	0.4	0.2	1.6	3.3	3.7	4.4	2.0	6.8
Bituminous coal and lignite	7.8	22.6	37.0	24.6	25.1	12.1	42.7	48.8	39.0	24.5	42.0	5.9
Crude petroleum and natural gas	. . .	0.1	0.2	. . .	. . .	. . .	0.2	0.2	0.3	0.1	0.1	0.2
Nonmetallic materials	9.8	9.8	11.9	10.5	9.6	6.1	14.2	18.6	13.5	12.4	8.2	9.2
Scrap and waste	0.5	0.6	0.2	0.8	2.1	0.4	5.6	6.9	4.7	5.1	10.0	33.1
Used merchandise	2.8	0.7	0.3	0.9	0.5	0.2	1.7	1.7	3.7	1.6	0.9	1.5
Goods imported and returned unchanged	. . .	. . .	. . .	. . .	. . .	. . .	. . .	. . .	. . .	. . .	. . .	. . .
Special classification provisions	0.2	9.4	0.1	0.2	0.2	1.1	2.3	2.5	3.9	4.2	3.1	11.0

Table D-41. PENNSYLVANIA: State Exports of Goods by Destination and Industry, 1994–1999—*Continued*

(Millions of dollars.)

Industry	Japan						South Korea					
	1994	1995	1996	1997	1998	1999	1994	1995	1996	1997	1998	1999
ALL GOODS	861.7	1 098.6	1 119.4	1 162.0	961.1	956.1	641.1	694.9	593.3	593.8	459.9	415.0
Manufactured Goods	812.6	1 044.0	1 078.7	1 128.9	912.6	936.9	627.7	680.6	580.2	584.5	455.1	401.1
Food products	35.3	34.9	36.7	33.3	32.2	23.0	40.3	17.4	17.3	16.3	7.8	17.9
Tobacco products	...	0.1	1.0	...	...	...	...	...	...	...	...	...
Textile mill products	3.4	5.8	5.5	5.8	4.9	6.0	3.8	3.9	4.2	3.2	3.9	2.2
Apparel	35.0	40.1	24.5	25.1	20.9	1.7	0.7	0.7	1.1	4.0	0.1	0.5
Lumber and wood products	8.6	13.4	14.4	15.0	13.5	8.8	10.5	9.9	10.7	8.8	1.1	5.1
Furniture and fixtures	4.3	4.0	2.4	2.2	2.8	0.8	0.5	0.7	0.3	0.6	...	0.3
Paper products	2.4	3.5	5.0	6.8	3.8	2.8	2.6	4.2	3.3	2.7	2.2	1.8
Printing and publishing	5.7	6.2	22.6	2.3	2.5	3.8	0.8	1.5	0.9	1.2	0.2	1.2
Chemical products	181.3	229.3	275.6	272.8	209.0	247.3	124.8	146.8	122.0	115.5	114.8	113.6
Refined petroleum products	7.6	8.9	12.0	11.9	15.0	10.6	2.3	1.6	1.7	4.6	11.0	12.7
Rubber and plastic products	76.0	69.7	84.7	83.4	82.4	72.2	7.4	4.3	11.5	9.3	7.5	10.7
Leather products	8.7	1.1	7.9	23.5	20.6	34.9	0.7	1.9	0.6	0.2	0.1	0.1
Stone, clay and glass products	14.3	28.5	35.5	52.1	19.6	12.5	16.3	10.5	13.3	11.1	9.1	10.7
Primary metals	70.7	162.0	133.5	99.2	34.7	46.1	14.3	112.8	39.0	35.3	12.4	14.4
Fabricated metal products	28.0	44.7	31.3	25.7	33.2	22.2	62.8	79.7	48.0	22.8	10.4	17.2
Industrial machinery and computers	90.8	105.5	98.5	115.2	79.7	89.1	197.9	151.8	144.1	174.4	50.7	60.6
Electric and electronic equipment	106.8	147.9	132.9	160.8	124.6	110.8	65.3	59.2	73.8	99.1	30.7	48.7
Transportation equipment	30.5	46.7	57.1	85.6	110.1	98.8	30.3	25.2	30.1	24.5	167.4	44.3
Scientific and measuring instruments	65.7	51.4	53.1	65.9	60.4	99.1	33.1	35.0	41.9	37.2	21.5	32.7
Miscellaneous manufactures	36.4	38.2	43.5	40.5	40.1	39.4	7.9	11.3	15.1	12.7	2.8	4.4
Unidentified manufactures	1.1	1.3	1.1	1.7	2.7	7.0	5.4	2.1	1.5	0.7	1.4	2.0
Agricultural And Livestock Products	0.7	0.8	0.5	0.5	0.4	0.6	...	...	...	2.0	...	0.1
Agricultural products	0.5	0.4	0.1	0.1	0.2	0.2	...	...	...	2.0	...	...
Livestock and livestock products	0.2	0.4	0.4	0.5	0.2	0.3	...	...	...	...	...	...
Other Commodities	48.4	53.7	40.2	32.6	48.1	18.7	13.3	14.3	13.1	7.3	4.8	13.8
Forestry products	6.9	5.8	5.7	5.4	5.2	3.2	...	0.2	0.1	0.4	...	0.1
Fish and other marine products	0.1	...	0.1	...	0.2	...	0.1	0.1	0.1	...	...	...
Metallic ores and concentrates	...	...	0.1	0.1	...	...	0.2	0.2	0.3	0.1	...	...
Bituminous coal and lignite	28.8	33.3	24.4	19.4	38.4	5.9	9.1	9.8	8.4	3.5	2.7	...
Crude petroleum and natural gas	...	...	...	...	...	0.1	0.1	0.1	0.3	...	...	...
Nonmetallic materials	6.2	9.1	4.8	3.8	2.1	1.4	3.3	3.3	3.0	1.2	1.1	0.9
Scrap and waste	4.5	3.9	2.0	2.1	1.1	4.3	0.2	0.3	0.4	...	0.6	11.2
Used merchandise	1.2	0.9	2.2	1.3	0.7	1.3	0.1	0.2	0.5	0.1	...	...
Goods imported and returned unchanged	...	...	...	...	...	...	...	...	...	...	...	...
Special classification provisions	0.8	0.7	0.9	0.4	0.4	2.4	0.2	0.1	0.1	1.9	0.2	1.5

Industry	Taiwan						Singapore					
	1994	1995	1996	1997	1998	1999	1994	1995	1996	1997	1998	1999
ALL GOODS	565.3	727.6	428.1	521.3	591.3	645.4	486.8	592.9	627.8	675.0	548.7	462.2
Manufactured Goods	553.4	714.2	416.8	514.5	580.7	626.4	483.9	588.9	623.7	671.0	545.4	456.1
Food products	64.1	40.8	41.2	55.2	48.1	31.5	1.5	2.1	3.7	5.4	4.5	6.4
Tobacco products	...	...	0.1	...	...	...	...	...	...	...	...	...
Textile mill products	3.9	3.1	3.8	2.1	0.7	2.2	0.7	0.9	0.7	0.8	0.5	0.5
Apparel	0.3	0.3	1.3	1.6	0.2	...	0.3	0.5	1.0	1.1	0.2	0.4
Lumber and wood products	12.2	11.3	7.2	9.3	8.1	8.2	0.9	1.4	0.8	0.6	0.6	0.4
Furniture and fixtures	0.9	0.8	0.8	0.5	0.3	0.7	1.3	1.7	2.3	2.6	1.2	0.6
Paper products	2.2	2.8	3.4	5.7	2.8	3.0	0.7	1.3	2.2	3.0	1.8	1.8
Printing and publishing	0.4	0.8	0.4	0.5	2.4	0.3	0.5	0.6	0.9	1.0	0.5	1.0
Chemical products	197.6	286.7	96.3	94.0	185.4	290.6	89.4	138.9	109.6	117.6	108.8	110.2
Refined petroleum products	6.0	5.8	3.0	3.5	2.2	1.5	0.2	0.4	0.7	0.7	3.7	0.5
Rubber and plastic products	8.1	6.0	5.9	8.4	9.5	7.6	4.5	5.9	6.3	10.7	8.2	12.2
Leather products	0.1	0.1	0.2	0.1	0.1	0.1	0.1	0.1	0.4	0.2	0.3	0.2
Stone, clay and glass products	9.4	8.0	13.6	15.2	10.3	9.5	4.5	4.5	5.6	8.7	4.8	3.3
Primary metals	22.0	114.3	50.4	27.8	19.4	20.6	12.0	41.4	15.5	9.5	8.9	5.7
Fabricated metal products	17.9	15.4	15.2	15.4	17.6	14.0	10.0	11.0	14.8	19.4	15.2	20.0
Industrial machinery and computers	79.7	140.8	107.3	169.6	109.0	126.3	54.0	59.0	76.3	72.8	54.2	91.8
Electric and electronic equipment	62.5	46.7	42.2	67.8	76.7	71.0	281.5	294.4	340.9	383.8	285.7	166.5
Transportation equipment	27.2	6.6	3.6	3.7	59.9	3.5	2.9	4.0	18.8	12.8	24.9	3.8
Scientific and measuring instruments	25.4	20.0	18.0	22.3	20.1	32.3	13.6	14.5	16.1	14.6	16.6	25.5
Miscellaneous manufactures	2.9	3.5	2.5	3.7	5.2	2.2	4.4	5.1	6.1	5.3	3.8	4.4
Unidentified manufactures	10.7	0.5	0.6	8.1	2.7	1.3	1.0	1.2	1.0	0.6	0.9	1.0
Agricultural And Livestock Products	1.8	0.9	0.7	0.1	0.1	...	...	...	...	...	...	0.1
Agricultural products	1.7	0.9	0.6	0.1	0.1	...	...	...	...	...	...	0.1
Livestock and livestock products	0.2	...	0.1	...	...	...	...	...	...	...	...	...
Other Commodities	10.1	12.5	10.5	6.8	10.5	19.0	2.9	4.1	4.0	4.1	3.3	6.0
Forestry products	0.3	0.4	0.8	0.1	0.3	0.2	1.0	0.9	1.0	1.3	0.9	1.5
Fish and other marine products	0.9	1.0	0.3	...	...	...	0.1	0.4	0.1	...	...	...
Metallic ores and concentrates	0.3	0.2	0.2	0.1	0.1	0.7	0.3	0.1	0.3	...	...	1.6
Bituminous coal and lignite	4.8	5.8	6.0	1.5	0.9	...	...	...	...	...	...	...
Crude petroleum and natural gas	0.1	...	...	...	0.1	0.1	0.1	...	...	0.1	...	...
Nonmetallic materials	3.3	3.5	2.9	3.9	2.7	3.1	1.1	2.3	2.0	2.4	1.9	2.1
Scrap and waste	0.3	0.7	0.1	0.9	5.8	13.7	0.1	0.1	0.1	0.1	0.1	...
Used merchandise	...	0.2	0.3	...	0.1	0.1	0.2	0.1	0.2	...	0.1	...
Goods imported and returned unchanged	...	...	...	...	...	...	...	...	...	...	...	...
Special classification provisions	0.2	0.7	0.1	0.3	0.5	1.1	0.1	0.1	0.4	0.1	0.3	0.7

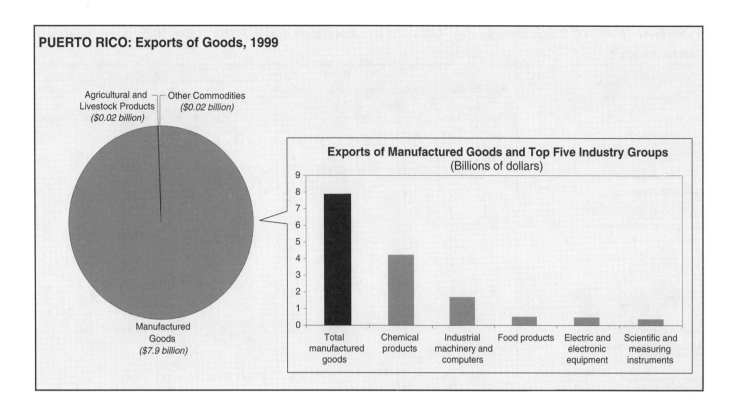

PUERTO RICO: Exports of Goods, 1999

Agricultural and Livestock Products ($0.02 billion)

Other Commodities ($0.02 billion)

Manufactured Goods ($7.9 billion)

Exports of Manufactured Goods and Top Five Industry Groups
(Billions of dollars)

Total manufactured goods — Chemical products — Industrial machinery and computers — Food products — Electric and electronic equipment — Scientific and measuring instruments

Table D-42. PUERTO RICO: State Exports of Goods by Destination and Industry, 1994–1999

(Millions of dollars.)

Industry	All destinations						Canada					
	1994	1995	1996	1997	1998	1999	1994	1995	1996	1997	1998	1999
ALL GOODS	4 618.9	4 704.5	5 188.4	5 528.1	6 126.5	7 893.6	671.3	535.9	575.8	689.5	657.4	798.8
Manufactured Goods	4 557.2	4 648.6	5 141.4	5 470.7	6 082.6	7 854.8	665.8	533.7	573.5	686.5	653.4	796.1
Food products	475.2	262.4	287.1	616.1	299.9	529.2	175.9	30.2	31.1	47.7	42.9	44.7
Tobacco products	42.8	88.5	86.7	73.6	38.3	14.7	...	...	...	...	...	...
Textile mill products	44.1	66.7	73.6	64.0	41.8	47.8	0.1	0.2	...	0.2	0.1	...
Apparel	46.3	77.9	73.7	93.4	109.5	146.0	8.6	12.7	7.5	4.6	2.8	3.4
Lumber and wood products	4.8	5.3	4.2	4.3	4.3	5.1	0.1	0.1	0.3	0.2	0.2	0.2
Furniture and fixtures	2.3	2.4	5.3	4.1	2.8	2.2	0.3	0.1	0.9	0.6	0.6	1.4
Paper products	14.3	12.4	13.9	8.6	10.7	23.1	0.7	0.4	0.5	0.5	0.4	0.6
Printing and publishing	3.2	2.7	3.5	2.6	17.8	3.8	0.6	0.4	0.1	0.4	0.3	0.4
Chemical products	2 390.3	2 070.9	2 049.5	2 411.8	3 255.8	4 239.6	369.9	375.5	407.0	491.0	464.7	585.1
Refined petroleum products	47.9	32.4	34.5	31.8	30.8	35.5	0.1	0.2	0.5	1.0	3.2	0.3
Rubber and plastic products	22.6	21.6	21.4	24.8	29.5	37.1	4.2	4.4	3.9	5.2	5.9	5.4
Leather products	36.3	23.0	20.8	45.7	43.4	49.3	...	...	0.2	0.2	0.2	0.1
Stone, clay and glass products	5.9	6.2	11.2	31.6	20.1	20.7	3.4	0.4	0.5	0.4	0.2	0.2
Primary metals	11.5	12.2	12.7	31.7	47.0	45.5	2.1	5.7	1.6	1.8	0.6	2.8
Fabricated metal products	19.5	20.0	18.0	18.5	17.2	30.8	1.2	0.7	1.0	1.0	0.5	0.1
Industrial machinery and computers	667.7	1 161.6	1 685.3	1 212.9	1 257.1	1 696.3	22.3	30.2	45.9	48.3	55.0	51.0
Electric and electronic equipment	398.6	403.7	350.5	454.6	462.2	492.4	56.2	43.6	45.8	66.3	57.4	62.0
Transportation equipment	22.3	17.4	13.3	16.1	27.0	24.8	0.8	0.5	0.7	1.0	0.8	6.2
Scientific and measuring instruments	271.9	344.0	361.8	310.1	339.3	383.0	17.8	26.4	23.9	13.9	14.8	28.7
Miscellaneous manufactures	24.0	12.5	9.9	9.8	14.0	15.4	0.6	1.1	1.1	1.0	1.3	2.0
Unidentified manufactures	5.8	4.8	4.5	4.7	14.1	12.5	1.1	1.0	1.1	1.3	1.5	1.6
Agricultural And Livestock Products	12.4	12.5	20.8	30.2	22.2	22.6	0.4	0.4	0.2	0.2	0.3	0.8
Agricultural products	12.4	12.3	20.7	30.1	22.1	22.6	0.4	0.2	0.2	0.2	0.3	0.8
Livestock and livestock products	0.1	0.2	...	...	...	...	...	0.2	...	...	...	...
Other Commodities	49.3	43.4	26.2	27.2	21.8	16.1	5.1	1.8	2.1	2.8	3.6	2.0
Forestry products	0.5	1.2	3.6	1.5	0.9	1.1	...	...	...	...	...	0.2
Fish and other marine products	0.7	1.8	3.0	1.0	0.5	1.0	...	...	0.1	...	...	...
Metallic ores and concentrates	...	...	...	...	...	...	...	...	...	...	...	...
Bituminous coal and lignite	...	...	...	...	...	...	...	...	...	...	...	...
Crude petroleum and natural gas	1.4	0.2	0.1	1.6	1.1	0.2	...	...	...	...	...	...
Nonmetallic minerals	0.2	0.2	0.2	0.3	0.1	0.2	0.1	...	...	...	...	...
Scrap and waste	19.9	26.9	15.6	17.6	13.6	8.1	0.1	0.1	0.1	0.3	1.3	0.6
Used merchandise	1.7	2.3	0.5	0.2	2.9	1.8	0.2	0.1	...	...	...	...
Goods imported and returned unchanged	4.8	1.7	1.7	2.5	2.3	0.9	4.8	1.7	1.7	2.5	2.3	0.9
Special classification provisions	20.1	9.0	1.6	2.5	0.4	2.8	...	...	0.1	...	...	0.2

Table D-42. PUERTO RICO: State Exports of Goods by Destination and Industry, 1994–1999—*Continued*

(Millions of dollars.)

Industry	South and Central America and Caribbean						Mexico					
	1994	1995	1996	1997	1998	1999	1994	1995	1996	1997	1998	1999
ALL GOODS	852.6	950.1	981.7	1 097.1	1 089.8	1 156.9	137.0	205.5	226.9	216.8	160.2	164.2
Manufactured Goods	809.7	913.2	961.1	1 077.2	1 075.7	1 146.7	136.6	205.2	226.7	216.7	159.3	162.6
Food products	117.4	121.6	119.1	145.6	162.3	160.7	6.5	2.7	17.4	9.5	3.0	1.2
Tobacco products	0.2	7.9	4.7	1.8	0.4	...	...	...	...	...	...	...
Textile mill products	43.5	65.6	72.8	62.3	41.0	47.0	0.1	...	0.2	0.8	0.5	0.4
Apparel	34.6	61.3	62.2	86.3	101.6	135.3	0.9	0.7	0.4	0.2	0.3	5.3
Lumber and wood products	4.4	4.6	3.2	3.4	3.2	4.2	...	0.1	...	...	...	...
Furniture and fixtures	1.7	1.8	2.0	1.0	1.2	0.8	...	...	0.1	...	0.1	...
Paper products	12.6	10.4	11.7	7.4	9.3	20.9	0.7	0.7	1.0	0.4	0.3	0.5
Printing and publishing	1.9	1.2	1.1	1.4	2.8	2.3	...	0.1	0.1	0.1	0.2	0.5
Chemical products	226.7	234.2	256.1	284.2	247.8	291.9	100.9	116.3	89.2	98.9	103.5	123.7
Refined petroleum products	36.6	24.6	24.3	18.8	19.2	14.6	0.8	0.4	0.3	0.2	...	0.7
Rubber and plastic products	12.6	11.2	9.8	13.8	17.1	21.6	0.9	0.8	1.6	0.6	1.6	0.9
Leather products	8.9	11.8	14.3	22.1	21.8	16.8	...	...	0.1	...	0.1	...
Stone, clay and glass products	1.5	3.7	10.3	30.3	15.7	15.4	0.2	...	...	0.2	1.9	1.3
Primary metals	2.9	4.4	2.9	6.1	6.5	2.6	0.1	...	...	...	0.2	0.6
Fabricated metal products	12.8	13.3	14.5	15.4	12.0	10.8	0.4	0.4	0.1	0.2	0.2	2.6
Industrial machinery and computers	29.2	37.7	42.7	44.9	32.3	50.9	6.2	67.2	103.5	60.9	12.7	7.2
Electric and electronic equipment	129.1	133.2	156.4	183.2	230.8	220.9	11.4	10.3	5.6	31.5	27.3	11.4
Transportation equipment	19.4	14.1	9.0	14.1	17.4	15.6	0.1	0.5	0.2	...	0.1	0.4
Scientific and measuring instruments	105.2	143.4	136.1	126.5	117.2	100.3	5.8	4.6	6.9	12.9	6.0	3.8
Miscellaneous manufactures	6.0	4.6	5.6	6.5	8.4	6.0	1.5	0.3	0.1	0.2	1.0	1.7
Unidentified manufactures	2.7	2.6	2.2	2.1	7.8	8.0	0.2	...	0.1	0.2	0.4	0.4
Agricultural And Livestock Products	1.1	0.6	0.4	1.0	0.5	0.3	...	...	0.2	0.1	0.1	...
Agricultural products	1.0	0.6	0.4	1.0	0.5	0.3	...	...	0.2	...	0.1	...
Livestock and livestock products	0.1	...	...	...	...	...	...	...	...	...	...	...
Other Commodities	41.8	36.2	20.2	18.9	13.5	9.9	0.4	0.2	0.1	...	0.8	1.6
Forestry products	0.5	1.2	3.6	1.5	0.8	0.9	...	...	0.1	...	...	...
Fish and other marine products	0.6	0.7	1.7	0.4	0.4	1.0	...	...	...	...	...	...
Metallic ores and concentrates	...	...	...	...	...	...	...	...	...	...	...	...
Bituminous coal and lignite	...	...	...	...	...	...	...	...	...	...	...	...
Crude petroleum and natural gas	1.4	0.2	0.1	0.1	...	0.2	...	...	...	...	...	...
Nonmetallic minerals	0.1	0.2	0.2	0.2	0.1	0.1	...	...	...	...	...	...
Scrap and waste	19.0	25.8	13.8	16.2	11.2	5.7	0.1	0.2	...	...	0.7	1.0
Used merchandise	0.6	0.5	0.4	0.2	0.8	0.7	0.3	...	...	...	0.1	...
Goods imported and returned unchanged	...	...	...	...	...	...	...	...	...	...	...	...
Special classification provisions	19.7	7.6	0.5	0.3	0.2	1.4	...	...	...	...	...	0.6

Industry	European Union						United Kingdom					
	1994	1995	1996	1997	1998	1999	1994	1995	1996	1997	1998	1999
ALL GOODS	1 787.3	2 042.1	2 277.3	2 115.0	2 944.1	4 139.8	249.9	238.3	148.4	179.4	279.2	499.6
Manufactured Goods	1 775.0	2 027.8	2 255.4	2 083.5	2 919.8	4 117.2	245.2	235.3	146.6	175.0	276.5	498.0
Food products	4.1	4.5	3.7	6.1	2.8	5.2	...	...	...	0.1	0.1	0.9
Tobacco products	36.3	78.2	66.4	35.1	24.5	10.8	...	...	...	...	...	...
Textile mill products	0.1	0.6	0.3	0.4	0.1	0.2	...	...	0.3	0.1	...	0.1
Apparel	0.4	1.0	0.4	0.1	1.3	0.8	...	...	...	...	1.1	0.1
Lumber and wood products	...	...	0.1	0.1	0.1	0.2	...	...	...	...	...	...
Furniture and fixtures	0.2	0.5	2.0	2.4	0.6	...	...	0.2	0.2	0.3	...	...
Paper products	0.1	0.6	0.4	0.2	0.3	0.8	...	...	...	...	...	...
Printing and publishing	0.2	0.6	0.6	0.1	0.9	0.3	...	...	0.1	...	...	...
Chemical products	972.6	895.6	925.7	1 093.3	1 790.8	2 410.8	87.1	77.9	56.0	93.3	143.5	373.5
Refined petroleum products	10.2	7.1	8.4	10.4	6.1	9.8	...	...	...	...	0.1	0.1
Rubber and plastic products	4.3	4.8	4.8	4.3	4.3	6.8	3.6	2.8	3.1	2.9	2.9	1.9
Leather products	20.4	7.8	4.8	19.7	20.7	30.6	3.2	0.8	0.2	0.6	...	...
Stone, clay and glass products	0.4	1.9	0.2	0.5	0.4	1.7	0.1	0.1	0.1	0.1	0.3	0.3
Primary metals	3.1	0.5	3.5	4.4	4.3	1.9	2.9	0.3	2.4	2.1	2.5	0.9
Fabricated metal products	2.5	2.2	1.1	1.0	3.9	13.6	1.7	1.5	0.6	0.4	0.2	0.3
Industrial machinery and computers	459.3	790.2	1 051.2	712.0	815.5	1 294.4	81.9	93.0	50.6	44.2	88.3	40.8
Electric and electronic equipment	159.2	134.9	91.9	113.4	97.4	157.0	27.4	35.0	11.5	14.4	11.7	36.8
Transportation equipment	1.4	1.2	2.5	0.4	8.1	0.7	...	0.2	2.0	0.1	0.2	0.2
Scientific and measuring instruments	83.6	88.7	84.2	77.3	132.2	166.0	22.4	18.0	16.9	14.8	23.5	41.6
Miscellaneous manufactures	15.3	6.2	2.6	1.8	2.6	3.8	14.6	5.1	2.5	1.5	1.9	0.3
Unidentified manufactures	1.1	0.8	0.5	0.5	3.1	1.8	0.3	0.3	0.1	0.1	0.2	0.2
Agricultural And Livestock Products	11.0	11.4	19.8	28.7	20.9	21.3	4.5	3.0	1.7	4.3	2.5	1.6
Agricultural products	11.0	11.4	19.8	28.7	20.9	21.3	4.5	3.0	1.7	4.3	2.5	1.6
Livestock and livestock products	...	...	...	...	...	...	...	...	...	...	...	...
Other Commodities	1.3	2.9	2.1	2.8	3.3	1.3	0.2	...	...	0.1	0.2	...
Forestry products	...	...	...	...	...	...	...	...	...	...	...	...
Fish and other marine products	0.1	0.2	0.6	0.2	0.1	...	...	...	...	...	...	...
Metallic ores and concentrates	...	...	...	...	...	...	...	...	...	...	...	...
Bituminous coal and lignite	...	...	...	...	...	...	...	...	...	...	...	...
Crude petroleum and natural gas	...	...	...	1.6	1.0	...	...	...	...	...	...	...
Nonmetallic minerals	...	...	...	...	...	...	...	...	...	...	...	...
Scrap and waste	0.4	0.8	1.2	0.8	0.1	0.5	0.1	...	...	...	...	...
Used merchandise	0.6	1.7	...	...	2.0	0.2	...	...	...	...	0.1	...
Goods imported and returned unchanged	...	...	...	...	...	...	...	...	...	...	...	...
Special classification provisions	0.3	0.2	0.2	0.2	0.1	0.6	0.1	...	...	...	...	...

Table D-42. PUERTO RICO: State Exports of Goods by Destination and Industry, 1994–1999—*Continued*

(Millions of dollars.)

Industry	Germany						France					
	1994	1995	1996	1997	1998	1999	1994	1995	1996	1997	1998	1999
ALL GOODS	652.5	781.6	935.6	532.8	667.7	1 233.8	209.9	309.9	309.8	318.2	407.2	590.0
Manufactured Goods	652.0	780.7	935.2	530.3	666.3	1 233.0	209.4	309.8	309.3	318.0	406.7	589.9
Food products	1.5	1.8	1.1	0.7	0.1	2.6	0.4	0.3	0.3	0.3	0.2	...
Tobacco products	...	...	...	...	...	...	...	...	...	...	...	...
Textile mill products	...	0.6	...	...	...	...	...	...	...	...	...	...
Apparel	0.1	0.2	0.1	...	0.1	...	...	...	...	...	...	0.3
Lumber and wood products	...	...	...	...	...	...	...	...	...	...	...	...
Furniture and fixtures	...	...	...	...	0.1	...	...	...	...	...	...	...
Paper products	...	0.5	0.1	...	0.1	0.3	...	...	...	...	...	...
Printing and publishing	...	...	...	0.1	...	...	...	...	...	...	...	...
Chemical products	277.9	222.7	221.7	171.0	224.7	272.9	146.6	150.1	137.9	162.5	302.6	494.5
Refined petroleum products	8.3	7.1	8.4	9.4	4.8	9.5	...	...	...	...	0.1	...
Rubber and plastic products	0.1	0.3	0.2	0.1	0.1	0.3	0.1	0.2	0.1	0.1	...	0.1
Leather products	7.6	2.3	1.8	9.3	11.8	15.8	5.5	1.5	0.9	0.4	1.7	3.5
Stone, clay and glass products	0.1	...	...	...	...	...	0.1	0.1	...	0.2	...	...
Primary metals	0.2	...	...	...	0.4	...	...	...	...	...	0.2	...
Fabricated metal products	0.2	0.1	0.1	...	3.0	0.1	...	...	...	0.1	0.2	...
Industrial machinery and computers	295.8	520.6	683.7	320.6	366.8	880.0	43.9	145.2	151.3	118.6	78.0	78.9
Electric and electronic equipment	49.4	13.6	8.2	6.7	35.9	42.9	9.6	9.2	16.2	31.6	8.8	9.0
Transportation equipment	0.3	0.8	0.1	0.2	0.1	0.3	0.5	...	...	...	7.7	...
Scientific and measuring instruments	9.8	9.0	9.6	11.9	15.7	7.2	2.5	3.0	2.5	3.9	6.8	3.1
Miscellaneous manufactures	0.5	1.0	...	0.1	...	0.8	...	...	...	...	0.2	0.2
Unidentified manufactures	0.1	0.1	0.1	...	2.5	0.4	0.1	0.1	...	...	...	0.1
Agricultural And Livestock Products	0.3	0.3	...	0.4	0.2	0.5	0.3	...	...	0.1	0.2	...
Agricultural products	0.3	0.3	...	0.4	0.2	0.5	0.3	...	...	0.1	0.2	...
Livestock and livestock products	...	...	...	...	...	...	...	...	...	...	...	...
Other Commodities	0.2	0.7	0.4	2.2	1.2	0.3	0.2	0.1	0.5	0.1	0.3	...
Forestry products	...	...	...	...	...	...	...	...	...	...	...	...
Fish and other marine products	...	...	...	...	...	...	...	...	0.5	...	...	...
Metallic ores and concentrates	...	...	...	...	...	...	...	...	...	...	...	...
Bituminous coal and lignite	...	...	...	...	...	...	...	...	...	...	...	...
Crude petroleum and natural gas	...	...	...	1.6	1.0	...	...	...	...	...	...	...
Nonmetallic minerals	...	...	...	...	...	...	...	...	...	...	...	...
Scrap and waste	0.1	0.6	0.3	0.5	0.1	0.2	...	...	...	...	...	...
Used merchandise	...	...	...	...	...	0.1	0.2	...	...	...	0.3	...
Goods imported and returned unchanged	...	...	...	...	...	...	...	...	...	...	...	...
Special classification provisions	0.1	0.1	0.1	...	...	...	...	0.1	...	0.1	...	...

Industry	The Netherlands						Asian 10					
	1994	1995	1996	1997	1998	1999	1994	1995	1996	1997	1998	1999
ALL GOODS	164.9	206.8	235.5	415.6	686.1	629.9	611.0	697.5	841.5	797.8	788.5	934.3
Manufactured Goods	159.1	205.8	233.7	413.6	684.9	627.3	610.6	695.5	840.6	796.9	787.8	933.8
Food products	2.0	2.0	1.9	1.6	1.7	1.1	35.0	19.6	46.4	56.0	34.3	60.3
Tobacco products	5.7	...	0.2	...	...	0.5	2.8	0.2	0.1	0.4	2.9	1.1
Textile mill products	...	...	...	0.1	...	...	0.1	0.1	0.2	0.3	0.1	...
Apparel	0.1	...	...	...	...	...	0.1	0.3	0.2	0.3	1.2	0.2
Lumber and wood products	...	...	...	...	...	...	...	...	...	0.1	0.3	...
Furniture and fixtures	...	...	1.7	2.0	0.5	...	0.1	...	0.1	0.1	0.2	...
Paper products	...	...	0.2	0.1	0.1	...	0.2	0.1	0.3	...	0.3	0.1
Printing and publishing	...	...	0.1	...	0.7	0.3	0.1	0.4	1.1	0.5	12.7	0.3
Chemical products	96.5	143.0	77.3	164.2	367.0	250.6	348.4	317.1	231.8	274.9	304.4	459.7
Refined petroleum products	1.9	...	...	0.4	1.1	0.1	...	...	...	0.4	0.7	0.7
Rubber and plastic products	0.2	0.8	0.1	0.3	0.6	0.9	0.4	0.3	0.7	0.5	0.5	1.1
Leather products	0.1	0.2	0.7	5.3	1.7	...	1.7	2.0	0.3	1.8	0.3	1.2
Stone, clay and glass products	...	1.4	...	...	...	1.1	...	...	0.1	0.2	0.5	0.8
Primary metals	...	...	...	...	...	0.5	1.2	0.1	3.5	17.9	33.2	37.2
Fabricated metal products	0.4	...	...	0.1	0.1	4.9	2.2	3.3	1.0	0.2	0.1	2.9
Industrial machinery and computers	7.9	7.4	106.1	199.0	230.6	236.1	131.4	216.9	420.1	324.4	302.1	261.8
Electric and electronic equipment	1.5	3.9	5.1	1.5	9.5	37.9	35.5	66.1	41.5	50.6	40.9	34.8
Transportation equipment	0.5	0.1	...	...	...	0.1	0.2	0.2	0.7	0.3	0.4	0.7
Scientific and measuring instruments	42.2	46.8	40.1	39.0	71.1	92.9	50.4	68.0	91.8	67.8	52.1	69.2
Miscellaneous manufactures	...	...	...	...	0.2	0.2	0.5	0.4	0.2	0.1	0.3	1.3
Unidentified manufactures	0.1	...	...	0.1	0.1	0.1	0.3	0.1	0.5	0.2	0.2	0.2
Agricultural And Livestock Products	5.6	0.8	0.9	1.7	1.1	2.4	...	...	0.2	0.2	0.3	0.2
Agricultural products	5.6	0.8	0.9	1.7	1.1	2.4	...	...	0.2	0.2	0.3	0.2
Livestock and livestock products	...	...	...	...	...	...	...	...	...	...	...	...
Other Commodities	0.2	0.2	0.9	0.2	...	0.2	0.4	2.0	0.7	0.8	0.4	0.3
Forestry products	...	...	...	...	...	...	...	...	...	...	...	...
Fish and other marine products	...	...	...	...	...	...	...	...	0.9	0.1	0.4	...
Metallic ores and concentrates	...	...	...	...	...	...	...	...	...	...	...	...
Bituminous coal and lignite	...	...	...	...	...	...	...	...	...	...	...	...
Crude petroleum and natural gas	...	...	...	...	...	...	...	...	...	...	...	...
Nonmetallic minerals	...	...	...	...	...	...	...	...	...	...	...	...
Scrap and waste	0.2	0.2	0.9	0.2	...	0.1	0.3	0.1	0.5	0.2	0.3	0.3
Used merchandise	...	...	...	...	...	0.1	...	...	...	...	...	...
Goods imported and returned unchanged	...	...	...	0.1	...	...	0.1	1.0	0.2	0.2	...	...
Special classification provisions	...	...	...	0.1	...	...	...	...	0.2	0.2	...	...

Table D-42. PUERTO RICO: State Exports of Goods by Destination and Industry, 1994–1999—Continued

(Millions of dollars.)

Industry	Japan						South Korea					
	1994	1995	1996	1997	1998	1999	1994	1995	1996	1997	1998	1999
ALL GOODS	397.3	400.5	413.1	448.7	428.0	547.8	43.1	61.7	51.5	35.0	32.5	32.9
Manufactured Goods	397.2	399.5	412.8	448.5	427.7	547.7	43.0	61.7	51.5	35.0	32.5	32.8
Food products	0.5	0.2	0.5	0.3	0.2	0.5	0.1	...	...	0.3	0.3	0.2
Tobacco products	...	...	...	...	0.1	0.1	...	...	...	...	...	...
Textile mill products	...	...	...	0.1	...	...	...	...	...	...	...	...
Apparel	0.1	0.3	0.2	0.2	1.2	0.1	...	...	...	...	...	...
Lumber and wood products	...	...	...	...	0.3	...	...	...	...	...	...	...
Furniture and fixtures	0.1	...	...	0.1	...	...	...	...	...	...	...	...
Paper products	...	...	0.2	...	0.2	0.1	...	0.1	...	...	...	...
Printing and publishing	0.1	...	1.1	...	0.3	0.3	...	...	...	0.1	0.3	...
Chemical products	269.7	221.5	150.7	194.1	222.3	357.4	33.3	51.5	38.0	21.9	23.0	20.2
Refined petroleum products	...	...	...	0.3	0.7	0.6	...	...	...	...	...	...
Rubber and plastic products	0.3	0.2	0.3	0.3	0.3	0.5	...	...	...	...	...	0.1
Leather products	0.3	0.2	0.2	...	0.1	0.1	0.1	...	0.1	1.8	...	0.9
Stone, clay and glass products	...	...	...	0.1	0.5	0.7	...	...	...	...	...	...
Primary metals	1.2	0.1	0.1	0.7	2.0	2.5	...	...	...	...	0.2	0.1
Fabricated metal products	2.0	2.9	0.9	0.1	0.1	...	...	...	...	...	...	0.3
Industrial machinery and computers	65.2	92.9	168.5	184.3	139.8	113.0	6.1	7.2	8.2	8.7	7.4	7.9
Electric and electronic equipment	12.7	18.7	7.6	5.8	17.6	16.1	0.8	0.6	1.2	0.9	0.5	0.9
Transportation equipment	0.1	0.2	0.3	0.3	0.1	0.2	...	...	0.3	...	0.3	0.2
Scientific and measuring instruments	44.8	62.2	82.1	61.5	42.0	54.3	2.5	2.2	3.5	1.0	0.6	2.0
Miscellaneous manufactures	0.2	...	...	...	0.1	1.2	...	...	...	0.1	...	...
Unidentified manufactures	0.1	...	...	...	0.1	...	...	...	...	0.1	...	...
Agricultural And Livestock Products	...	...	0.2	0.2	0.3	0.2	...	...	...	...	...	...
Agricultural products	...	...	0.2	0.2	0.3	0.2	...	...	...	...	...	...
Livestock and livestock products	...	...	...	...	...	...	...	...	...	...	...	...
Other Commodities	0.1	1.0	0.1	0.1	...	...	0.1	...	...	...	...	0.1
Forestry products	...	...	...	...	...	...	...	...	...	...	...	...
Fish and other marine products	...	0.9	0.1	...	...	...	...	...	...	...	...	...
Metallic ores and concentrates	...	...	...	...	...	...	...	...	...	...	...	...
Bituminous coal and lignite	...	...	...	...	...	...	...	...	...	...	...	...
Crude petroleum and natural gas	...	...	...	...	...	...	...	...	...	...	...	...
Nonmetallic minerals	...	...	...	...	...	...	...	...	...	...	...	...
Scrap and waste	0.1	...	...	...	...	...	0.1	...	...	...	...	0.1
Used merchandise	...	...	...	...	...	...	...	...	...	...	...	...
Goods imported and returned unchanged	...	...	...	...	...	...	...	...	...	...	...	...
Special classification provisions	...	0.1	...	0.1	...	...	...	...	...	...	...	...

Industry	Taiwan						Singapore					
	1994	1995	1996	1997	1998	1999	1994	1995	1996	1997	1998	1999
ALL GOODS	29.5	23.0	37.7	56.4	63.4	97.2	71.4	140.9	244.8	149.8	125.2	147.6
Manufactured Goods	29.5	23.0	37.6	56.4	63.2	97.2	71.3	140.8	244.5	149.7	125.1	147.6
Food products	6.5	4.8	9.6	9.2	6.6	32.9	6.8	3.3	6.5	10.5	8.9	9.4
Tobacco products	...	...	...	...	...	...	2.8	0.2	0.1	0.4	2.8	0.9
Textile mill products	...	...	...	...	...	...	...	...	0.1	...	...	...
Apparel	...	...	...	...	...	...	...	...	...	...	...	0.1
Lumber and wood products	...	...	...	...	...	...	...	...	...	...	...	...
Furniture and fixtures	...	...	...	...	...	...	...	...	0.1	...	...	...
Paper products	...	...	...	...	0.1	...	...	...	...	...	...	...
Printing and publishing	...	...	...	...	0.2	...	...	...	...	...	0.2	...
Chemical products	17.6	14.4	20.2	21.7	20.7	29.0	6.6	4.5	2.5	10.3	17.8	23.1
Refined petroleum products	...	...	...	...	...	...	...	...	...	...	...	...
Rubber and plastic products	...	...	...	...	...	0.1	...	...	0.1	...	0.1	0.2
Leather products	...	...	...	...	...	...	0.2	...	...	...	...	...
Stone, clay and glass products	...	...	...	...	...	...	...	...	...	...	...	...
Primary metals	...	...	3.3	15.0	25.7	27.2	...	...	...	0.3	0.2	...
Fabricated metal products	...	...	...	...	...	0.5	0.1	0.1	...	0.1	...	0.1
Industrial machinery and computers	4.5	1.8	1.7	4.6	5.0	3.7	45.6	103.9	219.0	105.3	87.5	108.9
Electric and electronic equipment	0.8	1.8	1.3	5.1	2.3	1.9	8.3	28.5	15.5	22.1	6.9	4.3
Transportation equipment	...	...	...	...	0.1	0.3	...	...	...	...	...	...
Scientific and measuring instruments	...	0.2	1.5	0.7	2.3	1.3	0.9	0.4	0.5	0.5	0.6	0.5
Miscellaneous manufactures	...	...	...	...	...	...	...	...	...	...	...	...
Unidentified manufactures	...	...	...	...	...	...	0.1	...	0.1	...	...	...
Agricultural And Livestock Products	...	...	...	...	...	...	...	...	...	...	...	...
Agricultural products	...	...	...	...	...	...	...	...	...	...	...	...
Livestock and livestock products	...	...	...	...	...	...	...	...	...	...	...	...
Other Commodities	...	...	...	...	0.2	0.1	0.1	0.1	0.3	0.1	...	...
Forestry products	...	...	...	...	...	...	...	...	...	...	...	...
Fish and other marine products	...	...	...	...	...	...	...	...	...	...	...	...
Metallic ores and concentrates	...	...	...	...	...	...	...	...	...	...	...	...
Bituminous coal and lignite	...	...	...	...	...	...	...	...	...	...	...	...
Crude petroleum and natural gas	...	...	...	...	...	...	...	...	...	...	...	...
Nonmetallic minerals	...	...	...	...	...	...	...	...	...	...	...	...
Scrap and waste	...	...	...	...	0.2	0.1	...	...	0.3	...	...	...
Used merchandise	...	...	...	...	...	...	...	...	...	...	...	...
Goods imported and returned unchanged	...	...	...	...	...	...	0.1	0.1	...	0.1	...	...
Special classification provisions	...	...	...	...	...	...	...	...	...	...	...	...

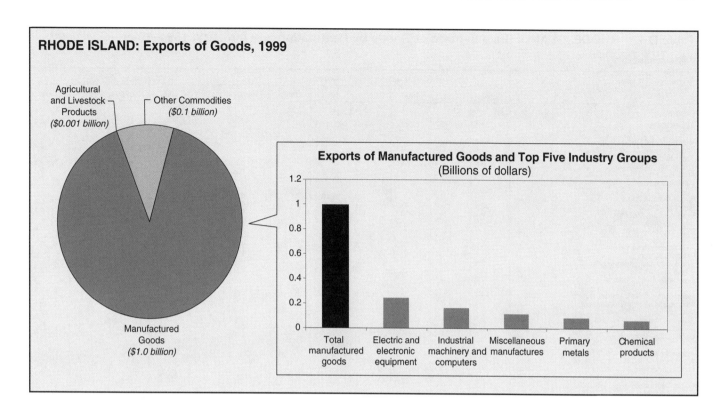

RHODE ISLAND: Exports of Goods, 1999

Agricultural and Livestock Products ($0.001 billion)

Other Commodities ($0.1 billion)

Manufactured Goods ($1.0 billion)

Exports of Manufactured Goods and Top Five Industry Groups
(Billions of dollars)

Table D-43. RHODE ISLAND: State Exports of Goods by Destination and Industry, 1994–1999

(Millions of dollars.)

Industry	All destinations						Canada					
	1994	1995	1996	1997	1998	1999	1994	1995	1996	1997	1998	1999
ALL GOODS	1 011.5	956.8	954.8	1 126.5	1 113.1	1 104.7	268.8	294.3	322.6	329.6	371.5	360.5
Manufactured Goods	884.6	793.7	811.7	1 005.8	990.8	993.6	216.1	234.8	260.2	275.1	301.9	301.8
Food products	6.3	8.9	11.0	5.8	4.3	5.2	4.8	7.0	5.8	3.4	3.2	3.0
Tobacco products	...	...	0.1	...	...	...	...	...	0.1	...	...	...
Textile mill products	26.3	31.8	34.8	36.2	34.9	36.8	13.6	14.8	14.6	18.1	15.4	17.2
Apparel	2.1	2.5	1.8	2.8	3.4	5.1	0.9	1.0	0.7	1.4	1.3	1.2
Lumber and wood products	1.2	1.4	1.6	1.9	3.4	2.6	0.5	0.8	1.1	1.3	1.2	2.0
Furniture and fixtures	2.4	2.5	1.8	2.6	2.2	2.7	0.7	0.7	0.8	0.9	1.3	1.5
Paper products	7.9	10.3	10.4	18.8	18.5	22.4	3.7	5.2	5.7	4.9	5.0	6.6
Printing and publishing	4.3	5.8	5.9	3.9	12.7	5.2	1.0	1.1	1.7	0.8	9.0	0.7
Chemical products	51.5	51.4	38.7	88.6	63.1	66.8	19.1	17.7	15.5	17.1	20.0	23.7
Refined petroleum products	0.7	0.8	0.6	0.5	0.1	0.4	0.1	0.2	...	0.1	...	...
Rubber and plastic products	50.4	53.0	53.6	61.0	54.7	63.9	16.2	17.3	23.8	21.7	22.7	21.4
Leather products	1.0	1.8	3.0	2.1	1.7	2.6	0.5	0.7	1.1	1.1	0.5	1.0
Stone, clay and glass products	6.8	7.8	6.7	6.3	11.4	19.7	5.3	4.8	3.9	4.5	9.0	17.1
Primary metals	72.3	61.4	59.0	73.3	92.3	86.6	30.5	33.0	35.6	40.3	45.9	34.4
Fabricated metal products	32.3	35.6	37.8	46.5	40.2	37.6	10.3	12.4	12.9	15.5	17.7	18.2
Industrial machinery and computers	229.9	142.6	169.0	185.7	143.0	164.6	26.2	29.8	38.5	34.6	38.1	32.8
Electric and electronic equipment	153.6	146.9	156.6	200.7	265.6	244.6	24.2	31.4	41.4	52.8	54.7	62.1
Transportation equipment	32.7	34.9	35.3	40.7	41.6	33.5	16.5	20.1	21.0	20.4	21.8	21.4
Scientific and measuring instruments	55.2	57.7	63.3	70.2	66.7	65.9	14.3	15.9	18.4	12.5	10.6	15.4
Miscellaneous manufactures	142.1	130.8	115.5	153.0	123.0	117.9	26.0	19.1	15.5	21.4	22.2	19.4
Unidentified manufactures	5.5	6.0	5.3	5.6	8.0	9.4	1.8	1.9	2.1	2.3	2.3	2.8
Agricultural And Livestock Products	0.7	1.5	1.2	1.4	1.3	1.2	0.1	0.1	0.3	0.4	0.8	1.0
Agricultural products	0.2	0.2	0.4	0.4	0.9	1.0	...	0.1	0.3	0.3	0.7	0.9
Livestock and livestock products	0.5	1.3	0.9	1.1	0.4	0.2	...	...	...	0.1	0.1	0.1
Other Commodities	126.2	161.6	141.8	119.3	120.9	109.9	52.6	59.5	62.1	54.0	68.8	57.7
Forestry products	0.1	...	0.1	0.1	0.1	0.1	0.1	...	0.1	0.1	0.1	0.1
Fish and other marine products	26.6	36.3	33.3	24.5	18.6	19.3	6.8	10.8	11.2	7.3	7.3	10.1
Metallic ores and concentrates	...	0.1	0.1	0.1	0.1	...	...	0.1	0.1	...	0.1	...
Bituminous coal and lignite	...	...	...	...	...	...	...	...	...	...	...	...
Crude petroleum and natural gas	...	...	...	...	...	...	...	...	...	...	...	...
Nonmetallic minerals	1.0	1.1	0.9	0.2	0.4	0.4	0.2	0.2	0.1	0.1	0.2	0.1
Scrap and waste	93.4	117.1	95.7	82.1	93.5	75.8	42.0	43.3	44.7	40.8	55.2	39.1
Used merchandise	1.0	1.4	4.3	5.7	1.4	2.0	...	0.1	0.5	0.3	0.1	0.2
Goods imported and returned unchanged	3.4	4.7	4.9	5.0	5.5	7.3	3.4	4.7	4.9	5.0	5.5	7.3
Special classification provisions	0.6	0.8	2.7	1.6	1.2	4.9	0.1	0.1	0.5	0.4	0.3	0.8

Table D-43. RHODE ISLAND: State Exports of Goods by Destination and Industry, 1994–1999—*Continued*

(Millions of dollars.)

Industry	South and Central American and Caribbean						Mexico					
	1994	1995	1996	1997	1998	1999	1994	1995	1996	1997	1998	1999
ALL GOODS	53.1	42.7	28.7	64.8	47.1	41.0	27.6	15.4	23.2	77.3	68.1	80.9
Manufactured Goods	52.4	42.0	27.7	63.5	45.7	40.3	27.6	15.4	23.1	77.2	68.0	80.6
Food products	0.2	0.1	0.1	. . .	0.1	0.2	. . .	. . .	. . .	. . .	. . .	0.4
Tobacco products	. . .	. . .	. . .	. . .	. . .	. . .	. . .	. . .	. . .	. . .	. . .	. . .
Textile mill products	0.3	0.5	0.7	1.0	1.3	0.5	0.2	0.5	0.7	0.9	3.1	2.1
Apparel	. . .	0.2	0.1	0.1	0.3	0.1	0.2	0.1	. . .	. . .	0.5	0.3
Lumber and wood products	. . .	. . .	. . .	0.1	0.1	0.1	. . .	. . .	. . .	. . .	. . .	. . .
Furniture and fixtures	0.1	0.2	0.3	0.5	0.1	0.1	0.1	. . .	. . .	0.1	. . .	. . .
Paper products	0.5	0.2	0.1	0.1	0.3	0.4	0.3	. . .	0.1	6.3	2.7	2.3
Printing and publishing	0.5	0.7	0.2	0.2	0.2	0.3	0.2	0.2	0.2	0.3	0.1	0.7
Chemical products	3.6	4.8	2.1	4.2	6.3	5.7	1.9	0.7	1.5	2.4	3.4	4.3
Refined petroleum products	. . .	. . .	. . .	0.1	. . .	. . .	. . .	. . .	. . .	0.1	. . .	0.2
Rubber and plastic products	2.2	2.2	2.3	3.3	3.2	2.0	1.3	2.5	0.7	2.0	1.7	3.1
Leather products	. . .	. . .	. . .	. . .	0.1	0.2	. . .	. . .	. . .	0.1	. . .	. . .
Stone, clay and glass products	0.4	. . .	0.1	0.2	0.2	0.1	0.1	0.2	0.9	0.2	0.2	0.8
Primary metals	1.1	0.7	1.1	1.0	1.3	1.3	6.6	1.0	3.3	17.2	27.5	30.4
Fabricated metal products	0.9	2.1	1.3	2.4	1.4	0.6	0.8	1.5	2.9	6.8	6.0	6.7
Industrial machinery and computers	14.7	5.1	3.2	24.3	9.7	5.5	4.2	2.5	4.0	12.1	6.8	11.4
Electric and electronic equipment	11.6	8.1	3.1	4.7	6.2	9.6	2.8	1.9	3.0	5.5	6.5	8.9
Transportation equipment	8.2	7.0	5.6	8.6	5.5	5.2	0.9	0.6	1.3	1.5	1.9	2.1
Scientific and measuring instruments	1.8	1.3	1.9	4.1	3.5	3.1	1.1	0.6	1.4	1.2	2.2	1.9
Miscellaneous manufactures	6.1	8.3	5.4	8.3	5.6	4.4	6.7	2.9	2.9	20.2	4.4	4.4
Unidentified manufactures	0.3	0.5	0.2	0.3	0.5	0.8	0.1	0.1	0.1	0.2	0.8	0.6
Agricultural And Livestock Products	. . .	. . .	. . .	. . .	. . .	. . .	. . .	. . .	. . .	. . .	. . .	. . .
Agricultural products	. . .	. . .	. . .	. . .	. . .	. . .	. . .	. . .	. . .	. . .	. . .	. . .
Livestock and livestock products	. . .	. . .	. . .	. . .	. . .	. . .	. . .	. . .	. . .	. . .	. . .	. . .
Other Commodities	0.6	0.7	1.0	1.4	1.4	0.7	0.1	. . .	0.1	0.1	0.1	0.3
Forestry products	. . .	. . .	. . .	. . .	. . .	. . .	. . .	. . .	. . .	. . .	. . .	. . .
Fish and other marine products	0.5	0.6	0.8	1.3	1.2	0.5	. . .	. . .	. . .	. . .	. . .	0.1
Metallic ores and concentrates	. . .	. . .	. . .	. . .	. . .	. . .	. . .	. . .	. . .	. . .	. . .	. . .
Bituminous coal and lignite	. . .	. . .	. . .	. . .	. . .	. . .	. . .	. . .	. . .	. . .	. . .	. . .
Crude petroleum and natural gas	. . .	. . .	. . .	. . .	. . .	. . .	. . .	. . .	. . .	. . .	. . .	. . .
Nonmetallic materials	. . .	. . .	. . .	. . .	. . .	. . .	. . .	. . .	. . .	. . .	. . .	. . .
Scrap and waste	. . .	. . .	0.1	. . .	. . .	. . .	. . .	. . .	. . .	. . .	. . .	. . .
Used merchandise	0.1	. . .	. . .	0.1	0.1	. . .	. . .	. . .	. . .	. . .	. . .	. . .
Goods imported and returned unchanged	. . .	. . .	. . .	. . .	. . .	. . .	. . .	. . .	. . .	. . .	. . .	. . .
Special classification provisions	. . .	. . .	0.1	. . .	0.1	0.1	. . .	. . .	0.1	. . .	0.1	0.1

Industry	European Union						United Kingdom					
	1994	1995	1996	1997	1998	1999	1994	1995	1996	1997	1998	1999
ALL GOODS	387.9	324.8	296.6	342.1	285.1	265.3	147.0	84.0	64.1	91.7	66.0	60.3
Manufactured Goods	327.7	240.3	234.8	292.5	241.6	222.7	144.4	80.1	58.7	84.6	64.5	58.3
Food products	0.6	0.3	0.2	0.2	0.1	0.4	0.2	0.1	0.2	0.1	. . .	0.3
Tobacco products	. . .	. . .	. . .	. . .	. . .	. . .	. . .	. . .	. . .	. . .	. . .	. . .
Textile mill products	7.9	9.3	12.2	9.9	8.5	7.8	3.0	3.8	4.9	4.1	3.0	3.0
Apparel	0.3	0.4	0.3	0.4	0.2	0.6	. . .	0.1	0.2	0.2	0.1	0.2
Lumber and wood products	. . .	0.1	0.2	0.2	1.8	0.5	. . .	. . .	. . .	0.2	0.2	. . .
Furniture and fixtures	0.9	0.5	0.4	0.7	0.6	0.7	0.7	0.4	0.3	0.4	0.3	0.5
Paper products	1.7	2.4	1.4	3.0	3.0	1.7	0.3	0.5	0.2	1.0	1.6	0.3
Printing and publishing	1.1	2.3	2.5	1.7	2.0	1.4	0.6	1.8	1.3	1.4	0.9	1.1
Chemical products	21.8	18.8	9.7	52.7	26.3	16.7	16.3	13.2	4.6	34.4	20.6	12.7
Refined petroleum products	0.4	0.3	0.1	0.1	. . .	0.1	. . .	. . .	. . .	. . .	. . .	. . .
Rubber and plastic products	20.2	17.7	13.8	15.7	10.7	19.1	2.1	3.0	2.8	4.7	4.3	6.2
Leather products	0.1	0.3	0.4	0.2	0.2	0.1	. . .	0.1	0.2	0.2	0.1	. . .
Stone, clay and glass products	0.4	1.6	0.6	0.4	1.0	0.9	0.1	0.1	0.1	0.1	0.1	0.1
Primary metals	28.6	20.5	12.3	7.9	10.2	12.0	4.8	6.2	3.7	1.3	1.8	3.6
Fabricated metal products	11.6	13.4	13.5	14.3	7.7	6.2	2.4	5.7	5.9	6.1	3.7	2.1
Industrial machinery and computers	134.2	69.3	80.7	75.9	44.1	53.1	91.0	23.4	13.0	7.3	8.5	7.8
Electric and electronic equipment	45.2	30.0	31.4	39.8	58.6	37.9	10.2	8.0	4.9	4.9	5.3	8.4
Transportation equipment	2.5	2.5	3.7	5.9	9.2	3.5	0.8	0.7	1.8	2.0	2.7	0.9
Scientific and measuring instruments	18.5	17.3	20.8	31.5	27.0	23.2	3.6	3.4	3.7	4.6	3.8	3.6
Miscellaneous manufactures	29.8	31.0	28.9	30.4	27.8	34.0	7.8	9.0	10.4	11.1	6.8	6.5
Unidentified manufactures	2.0	2.3	1.9	1.6	2.5	2.8	0.5	0.6	0.6	0.6	0.9	0.9
Agricultural And Livestock Products	0.5	0.7	0.7	0.9	0.2	0.1	0.1	. . .	0.1	0.5	. . .	. . .
Agricultural products	. . .	. . .	. . .	. . .	0.1	. . .	. . .	. . .	. . .	. . .	. . .	. . .
Livestock and livestock products	0.5	0.7	0.7	0.9	0.2	0.1	0.1	. . .	0.1	0.5	. . .	. . .
Other Commodities	59.6	83.9	61.0	48.7	43.2	42.4	2.5	3.9	5.3	6.6	1.5	2.0
Forestry products	0.1	. . .	. . .	. . .	0.1	. . .	. . .	. . .	. . .	. . .	. . .	. . .
Fish and other marine products	9.6	9.1	5.7	2.1	3.7	3.3	1.3	0.3	0.1	0.1	0.6	1.1
Metallic ores and concentrates	. . .	. . .	. . .	0.1	. . .	. . .	. . .	. . .	. . .	. . .	. . .	. . .
Bituminous coal and lignite	. . .	. . .	. . .	. . .	. . .	. . .	. . .	. . .	. . .	. . .	. . .	. . .
Crude petroleum and natural gas	. . .	. . .	. . .	. . .	. . .	. . .	. . .	. . .	. . .	. . .	. . .	. . .
Nonmetallic materials	0.3	0.6	0.1	. . .	0.1	. . .	0.1	. . .	. . .	. . .	. . .	. . .
Scrap and waste	48.8	72.9	50.4	40.8	38.2	35.2	0.5	3.4	1.2	1.7	0.3	0.4
Used merchandise	0.8	1.0	3.8	5.3	0.8	0.9	0.6	0.1	3.5	4.7	0.4	. . .
Goods imported and returned unchanged	. . .	. . .	. . .	. . .	. . .	. . .	. . .	. . .	. . .	. . .	. . .	. . .
Special classification provisions	0.1	0.3	1.0	0.4	0.5	2.9	. . .	. . .	0.4	0.1	0.3	0.4

Table D-43. RHODE ISLAND: State Exports of Goods by Destination and Industry, 1994–1999—*Continued*

(Millions of dollars.)

Industry	Germany						France					
	1994	1995	1996	1997	1998	1999	1994	1995	1996	1997	1998	1999
ALL GOODS	25.2	30.2	38.6	41.2	29.3	30.5	19.2	18.3	16.4	18.3	17.7	19.6
Manufactured Goods	24.9	29.9	38.3	40.5	27.9	29.6	16.9	16.3	14.9	17.6	16.6	17.1
Food products	0.1	...	...	...	...	...	...	...	...	...	...	...
Tobacco products	...	...	...	...	...	...	...	...	...	...	...	...
Textile mill products	1.4	2.6	3.5	2.4	1.3	1.8	...	...	0.1	0.1	0.1	0.3
Apparel	0.1	0.2	...	...	0.1	0.1	...	...	...	...	...	...
Lumber and wood products	...	...	...	...	...	...	...	...	...	...	1.5	...
Furniture and fixtures	...	...	...	...	...	...	...	...	0.1	0.1	...	0.1
Paper products	0.4	0.3	0.2	0.8	0.2	0.2	0.3	...	0.2	0.4	0.3	0.7
Printing and publishing	0.3	0.1	0.2	0.1	0.3	...	0.1	...	...	...	...	...
Chemical products	1.1	1.5	1.3	10.6	1.7	1.0	0.2	0.2	0.2	0.4	0.5	0.3
Refined petroleum products	...	0.1	...	...	...	...	...	...	...	...	...	...
Rubber and plastic products	1.7	2.1	2.1	0.8	1.7	2.2	0.4	0.3	0.2	0.3	0.4	0.5
Leather products	0.1	...	...	...	0.1	...	...	0.1	0.1	...	...	...
Stone, clay and glass products	...	0.5	...	...	0.1	0.2	...	...	...	0.1	...	0.4
Primary metals	0.3	1.3	1.0	1.8	1.9	1.1	0.3	0.5	0.5	1.3	0.9	1.9
Fabricated metal products	0.9	0.8	0.6	0.7	0.4	0.7	1.8	1.9	2.2	3.4	0.7	0.8
Industrial machinery and computers	8.1	11.4	16.9	10.8	9.0	10.4	3.7	4.8	4.6	5.9	5.4	6.7
Electric and electronic equipment	2.1	2.4	3.8	3.8	4.1	6.1	2.7	1.9	2.4	1.5	1.0	1.6
Transportation equipment	0.5	0.2	0.3	0.5	0.2	0.2	0.2	0.2	0.1	0.4	1.9	0.3
Scientific and measuring instruments	5.2	3.9	5.2	6.6	5.5	3.7	2.5	2.1	1.7	2.3	1.9	1.9
Miscellaneous manufactures	2.5	2.4	3.0	1.3	1.2	1.6	4.5	3.7	2.4	1.1	1.6	1.2
Unidentified manufactures	0.2	0.2	0.1	0.1	0.2	0.3	0.2	0.4	0.1	0.2	0.3	0.3
Agricultural And Livestock Products	...	...	...	...	...	...	...	...	...	...	...	...
Agricultural products	...	...	...	...	...	...	...	...	...	...	...	...
Livestock and livestock products	...	...	...	...	...	...	...	...	...	...	...	...
Other Commodities	0.3	0.2	0.3	0.7	1.4	1.0	2.3	2.0	1.4	0.7	1.1	2.5
Forestry products	...	...	...	...	...	...	...	...	...	...	...	...
Fish and other marine products	0.2	0.2	0.1	...	0.4	0.1	2.1	1.3	1.1	0.6	0.9	0.8
Metallic ores and concentrates	...	...	...	...	...	...	...	...	...	...	...	...
Bituminous coal and lignite	...	...	...	...	...	...	...	...	...	...	...	...
Crude petroleum and natural gas	...	...	...	...	...	...	...	...	...	...	...	...
Nonmetallic materials	...	...	...	...	...	...	...	...	...	...	...	...
Scrap and waste	...	...	0.1	0.5	0.9	0.5	...	...	...	0.1	0.1	0.5
Used merchandise	...	...	...	...	...	...	0.2	0.7	0.2	0.1	...	0.8
Goods imported and returned unchanged	...	...	...	...	...	...	...	...	...	...	...	...
Special classification provisions	...	...	0.2	0.2	0.1	0.3	...	...	0.2	...	...	0.5

Industry	The Netherlands						Asian 10					
	1994	1995	1996	1997	1998	1999	1994	1995	1996	1997	1998	1999
ALL GOODS	48.4	29.1	24.7	20.8	16.9	22.7	191.6	209.9	216.9	236.1	273.2	270.5
Manufactured Goods	48.2	28.8	24.1	20.6	16.8	22.6	180.9	193.4	200.1	222.6	268.5	263.1
Food products	0.1	...	...	...	...	...	0.4	0.8	3.0	0.5	0.6	0.5
Tobacco products	...	...	...	...	...	...	...	...	...	...	...	...
Textile mill products	0.1	0.4	1.8	1.2	1.3	0.8	2.9	5.0	4.4	4.5	5.0	7.1
Apparel	0.1	...	...	...	...	...	0.6	0.6	0.6	0.6	0.7	0.4
Lumber and wood products	...	...	...	...	...	...	0.4	0.4	0.3	0.3	0.2	...
Furniture and fixtures	...	...	...	...	0.1	...	0.2	0.7	0.1	0.1	0.1	0.1
Paper products	0.5	0.7	0.4	0.7	0.6	0.2	1.3	2.3	2.6	4.1	6.8	9.6
Printing and publishing	...	...	...	...	...	0.1	1.1	1.0	0.7	0.6	1.2	1.0
Chemical products	...	0.1	0.2	0.6	0.1	0.2	3.5	5.8	6.1	8.6	5.4	14.3
Refined petroleum products	...	...	...	...	...	...	0.1	0.2	0.5	0.2	0.1	...
Rubber and plastic products	12.4	9.0	4.7	3.6	0.9	0.5	8.3	11.0	10.9	15.8	13.7	14.7
Leather products	...	...	...	...	...	...	0.3	0.2	0.1	0.5	0.7	1.3
Stone, clay and glass products	0.1	...	...	0.2	0.3	...	0.5	1.0	1.0	0.6	0.7	0.5
Primary metals	19.2	7.5	2.8	0.1	0.1	0.7	3.9	4.6	4.6	4.6	6.2	6.3
Fabricated metal products	0.1	0.4	1.7	0.9	0.3	0.1	6.0	4.2	5.4	5.3	5.4	3.9
Industrial machinery and computers	6.1	1.8	2.9	4.4	2.4	3.9	28.9	21.3	24.6	19.2	26.0	26.2
Electric and electronic equipment	7.0	6.0	7.6	5.9	6.6	10.4	61.7	67.0	71.6	92.3	132.7	117.0
Transportation equipment	0.5	0.3	0.3	0.7	1.7	0.5	1.4	1.1	1.4	1.7	1.6	0.6
Scientific and measuring instruments	1.0	0.8	1.0	1.5	2.1	2.8	14.7	16.6	15.4	15.5	15.0	13.8
Miscellaneous manufactures	0.9	1.6	0.7	0.7	0.3	2.2	43.8	48.8	46.1	47.0	45.3	44.0
Unidentified manufactures	0.1	0.1	...	...	...	0.1	0.9	0.7	0.7	0.8	1.3	1.8
Agricultural And Livestock Products	...	...	...	...	...	...	...	0.6	0.2	...	0.1	...
Agricultural products	...	...	...	...	...	...	...	...	...	...	...	...
Livestock and livestock products	...	...	...	...	...	...	...	0.6	0.2	...	0.1	...
Other Commodities	0.2	0.3	0.6	0.2	0.1	0.1	10.7	16.0	16.6	13.4	4.7	7.4
Forestry products	...	...	...	...	...	...	...	...	...	...	...	...
Fish and other marine products	0.2	0.1	0.5	0.2	0.1	...	9.0	15.0	14.8	12.2	4.3	5.2
Metallic ores and concentrates	...	...	...	...	...	...	...	...	...	...	...	...
Bituminous coal and lignite	...	...	...	...	...	...	...	...	...	...	...	...
Crude petroleum and natural gas	...	...	...	...	...	...	...	...	...	...	...	...
Nonmetallic materials	...	...	...	...	...	...	0.3	0.3	0.7	0.1	...	0.1
Scrap and waste	...	...	...	...	...	...	1.0	0.3	0.4	0.4	0.1	1.1
Used merchandise	...	...	...	...	...	0.1	0.1	0.1	...	...	0.1	0.1
Goods imported and returned unchanged	...	...	...	...	...	...	...	...	...	...	...	...
Special classification provisions	...	0.2	0.1	...	...	...	0.3	0.3	0.7	0.7	0.2	1.0

Table D-43. RHODE ISLAND: State Exports of Goods by Destination and Industry, 1994–1999—*Continued*

(Millions of dollars.)

Industry	Japan						South Korea					
	1994	1995	1996	1997	1998	1999	1994	1995	1996	1997	1998	1999
ALL GOODS	46.7	65.8	61.8	89.4	114.9	83.1	24.8	28.6	26.8	20.2	11.6	18.8
Manufactured Goods	40.0	59.3	57.1	86.5	112.7	80.6	22.2	19.7	18.8	15.6	10.6	16.0
Food products	0.3	...	0.1	0.2	0.3	0.2	...	0.2	...	...	...	...
Tobacco products	...	...	...	...	...	...	...	...	...	...	...	...
Textile mill products	0.4	0.2	0.2	0.2	0.2	0.2	...	0.5	1.0	1.1	0.9	1.1
Apparel	0.1	0.1	0.2	0.3	0.1	...	...	0.1	0.1	...	...	...
Lumber and wood products	...	0.3	0.2	0.2	...	...	...	...	...	...	...	...
Furniture and fixtures	0.1	...	...	...	...	...	...	...	...	...	...	...
Paper products	0.2	0.1	0.1	0.2	0.3	0.2	...	0.1	0.1	0.1	0.2	0.2
Printing and publishing	0.1	0.2	0.2	0.2	0.5	0.4	...	...	...	...	...	...
Chemical products	0.5	0.9	1.0	1.5	0.9	0.6	0.7	0.5	0.8	0.4	0.1	0.5
Refined petroleum products	0.1	0.2	0.1	0.2	...	...	...	...	...	...	...	...
Rubber and plastic products	3.8	4.1	4.2	7.6	6.9	6.8	1.1	1.7	1.8	1.7	0.9	1.1
Leather products	...	0.1	...	0.1	...	0.1	...	0.1	...	...	...	0.1
Stone, clay and glass products	0.2	0.7	0.5	0.1	...	...	...	...	0.2	0.1	...	...
Primary metals	1.0	0.8	1.8	0.9	1.1	1.2	0.1	0.2	0.1	0.1	0.1	0.1
Fabricated metal products	0.9	0.4	0.5	1.4	1.1	1.1	0.7	0.7	0.7	0.6	0.7	0.4
Industrial machinery and computers	1.2	3.7	4.8	5.5	4.5	3.8	2.3	2.8	2.7	1.2	0.9	2.1
Electric and electronic equipment	6.1	17.0	20.5	36.5	63.9	42.2	10.0	7.6	4.8	4.3	2.7	5.0
Transportation equipment	0.3	0.2	0.4	0.7	1.4	0.3	0.4	0.2	0.6	0.1	...	0.1
Scientific and measuring instruments	6.8	8.6	6.7	6.7	4.5	4.8	1.9	1.6	1.1	1.2	0.6	0.9
Miscellaneous manufactures	17.7	21.6	15.4	24.0	26.6	18.4	4.8	3.4	4.7	4.5	3.4	4.3
Unidentified manufactures	0.4	0.2	0.1	0.1	0.3	0.2	0.1	0.1	0.1	0.1	0.1	0.2
Agricultural And Livestock Products	...	0.6	0.2	...	0.1	...	...	...	...	...	...	...
Agricultural products	...	...	...	...	...	...	...	...	...	...	...	...
Livestock and livestock products	...	0.6	0.2	...	0.1	...	...	...	...	...	...	...
Other Commodities	6.6	5.9	4.5	2.9	2.1	2.5	2.6	8.9	8.0	4.6	0.9	2.8
Forestry products	...	...	...	...	...	...	...	...	...	...	...	...
Fish and other marine products	5.4	5.7	3.8	2.3	2.0	2.2	2.6	8.8	8.0	4.5	0.9	2.7
Metallic ores and concentrates	...	...	...	...	...	...	...	...	...	...	...	...
Bituminous coal and lignite	...	...	...	...	...	...	...	...	...	...	...	...
Crude petroleum and natural gas	...	...	...	...	...	...	...	...	...	...	...	...
Nonmetallic materials	0.2	0.2	...	0.1	...	...	...	...	...	...	...	...
Scrap and waste	1.0	...	0.3	0.4	0.1	...	...	...	...	...	...	...
Used merchandise	0.1	...	...	...	0.1	...	...	...	...	...	...	...
Goods imported and returned unchanged	...	...	0.4	0.1	...	0.2	...	...	...	0.1	...	...
Special classification provisions	...	...	...	...	...	...	...	...	...	...	...	...

Industry	Taiwan						Singapore					
	1994	1995	1996	1997	1998	1999	1994	1995	1996	1997	1998	1999
ALL GOODS	13.3	14.3	12.4	20.0	19.0	22.2	22.1	23.9	19.7	18.4	16.9	24.8
Manufactured Goods	13.3	14.3	12.4	19.4	18.9	22.0	22.1	23.9	19.6	18.4	16.8	24.4
Food products	...	...	...	...	0.1	...	...	...	...	...	...	...
Tobacco products	...	...	...	...	...	...	...	...	...	...	...	...
Textile mill products	0.2	0.2	0.1	0.6	0.3	0.2	0.4	0.5	0.1	...	0.1	0.2
Apparel	...	...	0.1	0.1	0.2	...	0.1	...	0.1	...	0.1	...
Lumber and wood products	...	...	...	...	...	...	...	...	...	...	0.1	...
Furniture and fixtures	...	...	...	...	...	0.1	...	...	...	...	...	...
Paper products	0.1	...	0.1	0.2	0.2	0.2	0.8	1.3	0.1	0.2	0.3	0.4
Printing and publishing	0.1	...	...	...	...	...	0.1	0.1	0.1	0.1	0.1	0.1
Chemical products	0.8	0.6	0.3	0.8	1.0	2.2	0.6	1.0	1.1	2.7	0.8	8.0
Refined petroleum products	...	...	...	...	...	...	...	...	0.3	...	...	...
Rubber and plastic products	0.3	0.9	1.1	1.1	0.9	1.2	1.3	1.3	1.2	1.9	1.1	1.5
Leather products	...	...	...	0.1	0.1	...	...	...	...	...	0.1	0.1
Stone, clay and glass products	...	...	0.1	...	0.1	...	...	...	...	...	...	0.1
Primary metals	0.8	1.0	0.5	1.1	1.1	0.6	0.5	0.8	0.4	0.6	0.6	0.5
Fabricated metal products	0.9	0.9	1.3	0.9	1.2	0.3	0.4	0.8	1.0	0.8	0.6	0.4
Industrial machinery and computers	2.2	2.4	2.9	3.2	1.8	5.9	7.3	4.6	5.3	3.3	2.6	4.0
Electric and electronic equipment	1.8	3.5	1.8	6.2	7.7	8.2	5.9	6.3	3.2	2.6	6.5	5.2
Transportation equipment	0.3	0.5	0.1	0.1	...	...	...	...	0.1	0.7	...	...
Scientific and measuring instruments	1.4	1.4	1.1	1.5	1.3	0.6	1.2	1.4	1.7	2.0	2.6	1.9
Miscellaneous manufactures	4.2	2.8	2.8	3.1	2.8	2.4	3.3	5.5	4.7	3.2	1.0	1.8
Unidentified manufactures	0.1	0.1	0.1	0.2	0.2	0.1	0.1	0.1	0.1	0.1	0.2	0.2
Agricultural And Livestock Products	...	...	...	...	...	...	...	...	...	...	...	...
Agricultural products	...	...	...	...	...	...	...	...	...	...	...	...
Livestock and livestock products	...	...	...	...	...	...	...	...	...	...	...	...
Other Commodities	0.1	...	...	0.7	0.1	0.2	...	0.1	0.1	0.1	...	0.4
Forestry products	...	...	...	...	...	...	...	...	...	...	...	...
Fish and other marine products	0.1	...	...	0.4	...	0.1	...	...	...	...	...	...
Metallic ores and concentrates	...	...	...	...	...	...	...	...	...	...	...	...
Bituminous coal and lignite	...	...	...	...	...	...	...	...	...	...	...	...
Crude petroleum and natural gas	...	...	...	...	...	...	...	...	...	...	...	...
Nonmetallic materials	...	...	...	...	...	...	...	...	...	...	...	...
Scrap and waste	...	...	...	...	...	...	...	0.1	...	...	...	...
Used merchandise	...	...	...	...	...	...	...	...	...	...	...	...
Goods imported and returned unchanged	...	...	...	0.2	...	...	...	...	...	0.1	...	...
Special classification provisions	...	...	...	...	...	...	...	...	...	...	...	0.3

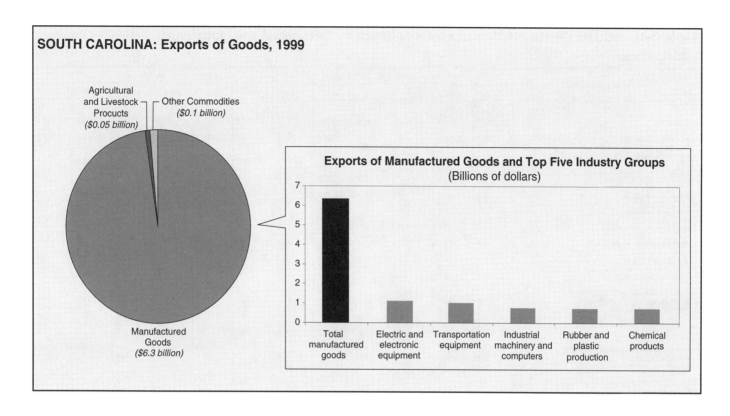

SOUTH CAROLINA: Exports of Goods, 1999

Agricultural and Livestock Procucts ($0.05 billion)

Other Commodities ($0.1 billion)

Manufactured Goods ($6.3 billion)

Exports of Manufactured Goods and Top Five Industry Groups
(Billions of dollars)

Total manufactured goods / Electric and electronic equipment / Transportation equipment / Industrial machinery and computers / Rubber and plastic production / Chemical products

Table D-44. SOUTH CAROLINA: State Exports of Goods by Destination and Industry, 1994–1999

(Millions of dollars.)

Industry	All destinations						Canada					
	1994	1995	1996	1997	1998	1999	1994	1995	1996	1997	1998	1999
ALL GOODS	3 510.1	4 497.9	4 924.9	5 673.8	5 856.9	6 476.5	1 252.7	1 538.5	1 478.2	1 620.7	1 710.8	1 989.7
Manufactured Goods	3 398.3	4 353.5	4 799.2	5 540.9	5 734.9	6 327.5	1 190.1	1 450.2	1 384.9	1 521.1	1 626.2	1 875.7
Food products	47.2	42.3	47.0	56.9	63.5	42.8	21.7	17.9	21.4	25.5	26.9	20.6
Tobacco products	0.3	0.1	...	...	1.9	1.8	...	...	...	...	...	...
Textile mill products	308.1	377.2	374.2	402.9	401.8	468.2	140.4	169.0	182.4	192.8	185.8	164.4
Apparel	111.5	140.9	166.6	215.5	318.9	236.8	23.6	32.9	38.4	47.6	65.3	55.1
Lumber and wood products	19.0	20.3	29.2	54.5	53.4	46.7	5.5	6.1	7.2	8.0	6.7	7.2
Furniture and fixtures	15.4	13.5	14.3	16.2	21.5	13.9	7.5	4.9	3.3	3.7	4.7	3.2
Paper products	191.4	282.7	299.6	319.0	275.3	274.3	29.1	51.8	57.1	48.6	47.6	48.2
Printing and publishing	4.5	8.9	7.7	10.7	9.2	8.3	2.3	3.5	4.0	4.4	5.5	4.0
Chemical products	442.8	608.2	583.0	606.9	540.6	749.8	161.2	182.8	162.1	181.6	156.9	180.7
Refined petroleum products	1.1	8.1	15.2	13.0	11.4	19.1	0.2	0.3	0.3	1.1	0.7	6.7
Rubber and plastic products	278.7	373.7	339.1	341.8	395.5	750.7	220.1	307.0	234.7	225.2	248.0	442.5
Leather products	3.0	3.0	1.9	1.4	4.4	6.7	0.1	0.2	0.2	0.2	0.1	0.1
Stone, clay and glass products	40.1	57.3	49.4	65.2	61.4	96.0	22.9	24.3	27.4	35.0	32.3	35.0
Primary metals	92.3	113.2	119.0	166.7	119.6	133.0	43.7	46.9	48.5	53.9	51.1	43.4
Fabricated metal products	130.5	152.6	138.2	182.5	196.5	214.9	84.9	95.7	70.8	115.3	128.3	129.5
Industrial machinery and computers	596.8	755.6	710.6	695.0	745.7	770.5	147.5	170.2	184.7	195.8	239.5	273.4
Electric and electronic equipment	754.9	954.9	904.4	1 119.6	1 115.6	1 123.3	120.2	140.6	140.5	146.2	167.2	172.9
Transportation equipment	227.3	314.3	828.7	1 005.7	1 077.9	1 026.1	121.5	151.3	149.1	166.7	190.8	199.4
Scientific and measuring instruments	94.5	93.8	131.2	226.0	265.9	289.0	27.6	34.7	41.5	56.3	53.7	73.6
Miscellaneous manufactures	30.7	25.0	31.4	31.8	42.0	41.6	6.9	7.1	7.6	9.1	10.4	10.9
Unidentified manufactures	8.2	7.9	8.2	9.3	12.7	14.2	3.2	3.3	3.8	4.2	4.8	5.1
Agricultural And Livestock Products	54.6	69.9	64.0	76.6	63.1	50.6	34.2	49.5	52.5	70.0	56.5	37.2
Agricultural products	51.3	63.1	59.1	74.2	61.8	49.0	33.9	47.4	50.2	69.5	56.2	36.9
Livestock and livestock products	3.4	6.8	5.0	2.5	1.3	1.6	0.3	2.1	2.4	0.5	0.3	0.3
Other Commodities	57.2	74.5	61.7	56.3	59.0	98.4	28.4	38.8	40.8	29.6	28.1	76.9
Forestry products	0.7	2.4	1.0	3.1	1.7	1.9	0.6	2.1	0.8	2.6	0.5	1.3
Fish and other marine products	5.9	6.7	3.9	3.5	8.2	4.1	5.5	5.6	3.5	2.1	1.8	3.0
Metallic ores and concentrates	0.1	0.1	0.3	0.1	3.6	1.2	...	...	...	...	...	...
Bituminous coal and lignite	...	...	0.1	...	...	...	...	...	...	...	...	...
Crude petroleum and natural gas	0.4	0.6	0.3	0.4	0.1	0.5	...	...	...	...	...	...
Nonmetallic minerals	10.5	11.7	8.1	5.3	4.1	4.0	7.5	7.8	5.2	2.5	1.1	0.8
Scrap and waste	13.0	13.0	8.6	4.6	6.8	6.5	2.3	6.6	3.8	1.3	1.7	2.0
Used merchandise	2.8	6.8	3.8	3.0	3.0	1.5	0.8	0.1	0.2	1.0	1.1	0.3
Goods imported and returned unchanged	8.2	12.7	22.2	17.8	18.9	21.4	8.2	12.7	22.2	17.8	18.9	21.4
Special classification provisions	15.6	20.5	13.4	18.4	12.7	57.3	3.5	3.8	5.3	2.3	2.9	48.1

Table D-44. SOUTH CAROLINA: State Exports of Goods by Destination and Industry, 1994–1999—*Continued*

(Millions of dollars.)

Industry	South and Central America and Caribbean						Mexico					
	1994	1995	1996	1997	1998	1999	1994	1995	1996	1997	1998	1999
ALL GOODS	237.7	337.9	309.2	439.6	528.3	536.8	450.0	641.4	661.8	935.9	1 054.3	1 296.8
Manufactured Goods	236.7	334.5	305.9	437.6	526.4	531.5	444.3	631.8	658.1	929.4	1 048.9	1 292.7
Food products	0.8	1.7	1.8	5.3	12.1	9.8	0.2	0.1	0.8	0.3	0.5	0.1
Tobacco products	. . .	. . .	. . .	. . .	. . .	. . .	. . .	. . .	. . .	. . .	. . .	. . .
Textile mill products	28.7	57.4	45.5	43.2	73.9	140.9	18.6	23.0	27.7	53.5	49.9	74.1
Apparel	61.6	71.2	71.4	111.2	154.7	115.5	10.0	18.3	33.7	33.1	77.2	44.0
Lumber and wood products	1.4	0.6	0.7	0.8	1.4	0.6	0.5	. . .	0.2	0.1	0.2	0.5
Furniture and fixtures	0.6	0.7	0.8	1.7	1.3	1.1	0.3	0.2	0.9	0.4	2.1	1.5
Paper products	14.7	17.5	18.3	22.7	21.1	17.6	9.1	12.0	9.9	21.9	30.1	43.5
Printing and publishing	0.3	0.3	0.5	1.2	1.9	0.8	0.2	3.0	0.3	0.5	0.4	1.8
Chemical products	20.5	43.0	37.5	50.2	58.0	50.4	12.6	17.0	19.5	20.0	44.7	42.1
Refined petroleum products	0.1	0.9	1.6	1.3	1.0	0.7	0.1	. . .	0.2	0.1	0.6	0.6
Rubber and plastic products	9.5	11.0	18.5	22.2	22.2	22.7	8.4	14.0	19.6	25.1	41.6	171.1
Leather products	. . .	0.3	0.2	0.1	2.9	3.7	. . .	. . .	0.1	0.1	0.2	. . .
Stone, clay and glass products	2.9	2.3	1.6	2.9	2.4	2.7	1.7	1.9	2.7	0.8	1.3	1.1
Primary metals	6.8	23.5	11.9	44.9	7.8	4.3	8.2	13.7	12.5	15.5	17.5	38.2
Fabricated metal products	11.2	8.0	8.2	9.5	8.1	12.5	8.0	12.7	7.3	7.4	8.6	12.8
Industrial machinery and computers	43.0	62.1	54.3	76.5	60.1	42.0	50.9	65.6	58.0	61.7	66.6	86.8
Electric and electronic equipment	17.6	17.1	12.7	21.0	42.6	44.2	294.9	433.6	432.3	635.2	643.0	728.4
Transportation equipment	10.4	10.5	11.2	6.1	13.9	12.8	10.4	4.8	9.1	18.5	15.6	0.8
Scientific and measuring instruments	3.5	3.5	5.7	12.3	33.2	44.6	8.8	10.3	21.3	32.8	46.1	33.1
Miscellaneous manufactures	2.4	2.3	3.0	4.1	7.0	3.6	0.9	1.2	1.3	1.8	1.6	2.4
Unidentified manufactures	0.6	0.6	0.5	0.5	0.8	1.0	0.6	0.4	0.7	0.7	1.3	1.9
Agricultural And Livestock Products	0.1	0.6	1.1	0.3	0.6	2.2	0.9	2.0	0.1	0.1	0.2	0.4
Agricultural products	0.1	0.4	0.1	0.3	0.4	1.4	. . .	0.4	0.1	0.1	0.2	0.4
Livestock and livestock products	. . .	0.1	1.1	. . .	0.1	0.8	0.8	1.6	. . .	. . .	. . .	. . .
Other Commodities	1.0	2.9	2.2	1.7	1.4	3.1	4.8	7.6	3.6	6.4	5.1	3.7
Forestry products	. . .	0.1	0.1	0.2	0.7	0.1	. . .	0.1	. . .	. . .	. . .	0.1
Fish and other marine products	. . .	. . .	. . .	. . .	0.1	. . .	. . .	. . .	. . .	. . .	. . .	. . .
Metallic ores and concentrates	. . .	. . .	. . .	. . .	. . .	. . .	. . .	. . .	0.1	. . .	. . .	. . .
Bituminous coal and lignite	. . .	. . .	0.1	. . .	. . .	. . .	. . .	. . .	. . .	. . .	. . .	. . .
Crude petroleum and natural gas	0.4	0.5	0.3	0.4	. . .	. . .	. . .	. . .	. . .	. . .	. . .	. . .
Nonmetallic minerals	0.1	. . .	0.1	0.1	. . .	1.7	0.1	. . .	0.1	. . .	0.4	0.6
Scrap and waste	. . .	0.4	0.5	0.3	0.2	0.5	0.1	0.4	0.1	0.9	0.8	0.4
Used merchandise	0.4	1.2	0.4	0.4	0.2	0.2	0.1	. . .	. . .	. . .	0.2	. . .
Goods imported and returned unchanged	. . .	. . .	. . .	. . .	. . .	. . .	. . .	. . .	. . .	. . .	. . .	. . .
Special classification provisions	0.1	0.6	0.6	0.2	0.2	0.6	4.6	7.0	3.3	5.4	3.6	2.6

Industry	European Union						United Kingdom					
	1994	1995	1996	1997	1998	1999	1994	1995	1996	1997	1998	1999
ALL GOODS	786.2	926.8	1 452.0	1 592.9	1 618.4	1 569.4	177.3	225.5	210.0	212.9	337.1	295.6
Manufactured Goods	764.7	909.6	1 439.5	1 576.6	1 598.5	1 555.4	173.6	223.1	207.2	210.5	333.9	293.7
Food products	14.3	16.7	15.3	16.5	13.5	5.3	3.2	3.0	4.3	5.3	4.3	1.7
Tobacco products	0.3	0.1	. . .	. . .	1.8	0.1	. . .	. . .	. . .	. . .	. . .	0.1
Textile mill products	55.2	46.8	49.4	50.9	52.7	45.5	29.1	24.0	28.2	23.6	16.8	15.6
Apparel	5.2	5.3	3.2	5.0	4.0	5.8	1.5	3.1	2.0	2.0	1.9	2.9
Lumber and wood products	6.6	7.3	9.3	7.7	8.1	9.4	0.6	0.4	1.1	0.6	0.6	1.2
Furniture and fixtures	1.5	2.4	2.8	3.6	4.3	2.5	0.2	0.4	0.4	0.5	1.3	1.0
Paper products	75.9	143.9	137.8	123.6	118.8	106.0	8.1	16.1	11.2	10.8	10.2	11.4
Printing and publishing	1.2	1.0	2.2	3.6	0.6	0.8	0.3	0.4	0.2	0.3	0.3	0.4
Chemical products	136.8	134.2	165.5	152.5	147.8	143.6	20.7	35.9	37.9	35.5	33.6	28.4
Refined petroleum products	0.1	3.5	6.4	5.6	4.7	4.5	. . .	0.3	0.1	0.2	0.1	0.1
Rubber and plastic products	25.2	25.4	32.8	45.9	50.2	59.6	12.5	13.9	13.9	15.6	16.0	13.4
Leather products	2.2	0.9	0.4	0.5	0.3	1.1	1.0	0.2	. . .	0.1	. . .	0.3
Stone, clay and glass products	6.1	15.7	5.9	8.3	17.4	42.1	0.6	0.5	0.7	0.9	1.3	1.1
Primary metals	22.9	13.4	15.4	23.4	14.6	23.4	8.9	7.7	5.9	2.0	3.1	5.7
Fabricated metal products	15.9	17.4	27.4	29.7	30.6	38.8	5.4	4.0	9.3	10.4	14.8	10.1
Industrial machinery and computers	187.0	202.5	165.0	162.9	173.8	210.0	27.9	45.4	31.8	40.7	53.2	40.7
Electric and electronic equipment	109.0	133.5	128.5	130.1	121.5	92.2	25.0	32.9	29.0	25.2	20.8	15.8
Transportation equipment	51.2	107.5	619.9	704.2	711.0	633.8	20.6	28.1	22.7	26.7	141.4	127.5
Scientific and measuring instruments	36.3	25.5	41.6	94.2	112.2	115.0	3.5	4.6	5.2	6.4	9.0	9.6
Miscellaneous manufactures	10.0	4.8	8.9	6.6	8.7	13.4	4.0	1.4	2.6	3.0	4.4	6.1
Unidentified manufactures	1.8	2.0	1.8	1.7	2.0	2.5	0.5	0.6	0.5	0.6	0.7	0.8
Agricultural And Livestock Products	6.0	3.7	5.2	4.0	4.7	9.2	0.2	0.8	0.6	0.3	0.2	0.8
Agricultural products	6.0	3.4	5.0	3.7	4.6	9.2	0.1	0.5	0.5	0.3	0.2	0.8
Livestock and livestock products	. . .	0.2	0.2	0.3	0.1	. . .	. . .	0.2	0.1	. . .	. . .	. . .
Other Commodities	15.4	13.5	7.3	12.3	15.1	4.8	3.6	1.6	2.1	2.1	3.0	1.1
Forestry products	. . .	. . .	0.1	0.1	0.2	0.1	. . .	. . .	. . .	. . .	0.1	. . .
Fish and other marine products	. . .	0.4	. . .	1.4	5.3	1.0	. . .	. . .	. . .	1.2	1.9	0.3
Metallic ores and concentrates	0.1	0.1	0.2	0.1	2.8	0.1	0.1	. . .	. . .	0.1	. . .	0.1
Bituminous coal and lignite	. . .	. . .	. . .	. . .	. . .	. . .	. . .	. . .	. . .	. . .	. . .	. . .
Crude petroleum and natural gas	. . .	. . .	. . .	. . .	. . .	. . .	. . .	. . .	. . .	. . .	. . .	. . .
Nonmetallic minerals	2.3	2.8	2.2	2.3	1.8	0.4	. . .	0.2	. . .	. . .	0.2	. . .
Scrap and waste	9.4	4.8	2.2	1.1	1.4	0.9	3.3	1.3	1.9	0.5	0.6	0.1
Used merchandise	0.3	0.3	0.5	0.5	0.3	0.6	0.1	0.1	. . .	0.1	0.1	0.2
Goods imported and returned unchanged	. . .	. . .	. . .	. . .	. . .	. . .	. . .	. . .	. . .	. . .	. . .	. . .
Special classification provisions	3.3	5.0	2.1	6.8	3.3	1.7	. . .	0.1	0.2	0.3	0.1	0.5

Table D-44. SOUTH CAROLINA: State Exports of Goods by Destination and Industry, 1994–1999—*Continued*

(Millions of dollars.)

Industry	Germany						France					
	1994	1995	1996	1997	1998	1999	1994	1995	1996	1997	1998	1999
ALL GOODS	214.8	233.6	727.4	854.7	748.4	654.4	73.0	86.0	92.8	108.0	94.3	103.9
Manufactured Goods	209.8	229.7	724.9	852.8	743.7	652.4	72.9	85.5	92.1	101.4	93.7	101.8
Food products	6.4	6.1	3.7	4.2	1.0	1.2	0.7	1.8	1.2	0.7	1.2	0.3
Tobacco products	. . .	. . .	. . .	. . .	. . .	. . .						
Textile mill products	8.3	5.4	5.3	7.4	7.8	7.3	2.3	2.0	1.5	4.3	5.9	4.7
Apparel	1.3	0.6	0.3	0.4	0.5	0.3	0.8	0.2	0.1	0.1	0.4	0.3
Lumber and wood products	2.5	3.0	1.9	1.9	1.7	2.0	0.1	0.2	0.2	0.1	0.3	0.4
Furniture and fixtures	0.8	1.0	1.5	0.9	1.0	0.5	0.4	0.4	0.2	0.1	0.3	0.1
Paper products	5.7	12.7	8.0	9.1	9.6	13.5	12.8	24.2	21.4	18.3	9.3	6.9
Printing and publishing	0.1	0.1	0.3	0.2	0.1	0.2	0.3	0.1	. . .	. . .		
Chemical products	56.0	17.8	27.9	15.7	32.4	26.4	6.4	9.4	12.2	12.2	7.4	5.5
Refined petroleum products	. . .	1.1	2.3	2.2	2.1	2.0	. . .	0.9	1.3	1.4	1.1	1.2
Rubber and plastic products	3.9	4.1	4.5	3.6	6.3	20.0	1.8	2.2	2.2	2.1	5.2	11.9
Leather products	1.0	0.5	0.3	0.2	0.1	0.1	. . .	0.1	0.1	. . .	. . .	0.1
Stone, clay and glass products	1.4	2.1	3.4	4.0	1.7	1.6	0.3	0.2	1.1	0.4	1.3	0.6
Primary metals	2.5	1.5	1.8	18.5	3.8	4.9	0.7	1.7	1.2	1.2	1.8	2.1
Fabricated metal products	2.9	8.2	8.8	9.0	6.8	15.9	1.4	1.2	2.6	2.0	1.6	1.3
Industrial machinery and computers	38.5	45.5	28.2	31.6	31.8	38.0	27.3	22.1	23.5	20.4	18.3	26.2
Electric and electronic equipment	38.8	48.2	42.4	38.7	34.1	20.6	10.9	12.6	17.4	17.1	14.4	5.7
Transportation equipment	11.0	56.1	571.7	655.5	543.7	457.9	4.1	3.6	2.9	6.0	8.1	1.8
Scientific and measuring instruments	27.4	15.3	11.4	48.0	58.1	37.7	1.9	1.9	2.6	14.4	16.2	31.5
Miscellaneous manufactures	0.9	0.3	0.9	0.9	0.5	1.7	0.5	0.5	0.2	0.4	0.7	1.0
Unidentified manufactures	0.5	0.5	0.5	0.8	0.5	0.5	0.2	0.2	0.2	0.1	0.2	0.3
Agricultural And Livestock Products	1.2	0.9	1.0	0.6	0.1	0.5	. . .	. . .	0.1	0.2	0.5	1.7
Agricultural products	1.2	0.9	1.0	0.5	. . .	0.5	. . .	. . .	0.1	0.1	0.5	1.7
Livestock and livestock products	. . .	. . .	. . .	0.2	0.1	. . .	. . .	. . .	. . .	. . .	. . .	. . .
Other Commodities	3.8	2.9	1.5	1.3	4.6	1.6	0.1	0.5	0.6	6.5	0.2	0.3
Forestry products	. . .	. . .	. . .	. . .	0.1	. . .	. . .	. . .	. . .	. . .	. . .	. . .
Fish and other marine products	. . .	. . .	. . .	. . .	3.4	0.7	. . .	0.4	. . .	. . .	. . .	. . .
Metallic ores and concentrates	. . .	. . .	. . .	. . .	. . .	. . .	. . .	. . .	. . .	. . .	. . .	. . .
Bituminous coal and lignite	. . .	. . .	. . .	. . .	. . .	. . .	. . .	. . .	. . .	. . .	. . .	. . .
Crude petroleum and natural gas	. . .	. . .	. . .	. . .	. . .	. . .	. . .	. . .	. . .	. . .	. . .	. . .
Nonmetallic minerals	0.2	. . .	0.7	0.8	0.4	0.2	. . .	. . .	. . .	. . .	. . .	. . .
Scrap and waste	3.5	2.0	0.1	0.4	0.5	0.4	. . .	0.1	. . .	. . .	. . .	0.1
Used merchandise	. . .	. . .	0.1	. . .	. . .	. . .	0.1	. . .	0.4	0.3	0.1	0.2
Goods imported and returned unchanged	. . .	. . .	. . .	. . .	. . .	. . .	. . .	. . .	. . .	. . .	. . .	. . .
Special classification provisions	0.1	0.8	0.6	0.1	0.2	0.2	. . .	. . .	0.1	6.2	0.1	. . .

Industry	The Netherlands						Asian 10					
	1994	1995	1996	1997	1998	1999	1994	1995	1996	1997	1998	1999
ALL GOODS	88.6	102.4	121.9	96.7	88.1	119.7	585.5	760.5	712.9	773.0	647.9	721.0
Manufactured Goods	88.2	101.8	121.5	95.8	87.3	115.6	570.3	738.2	702.3	768.9	641.3	715.4
Food products	2.7	4.7	4.4	2.7	3.8	0.2	7.3	3.5	1.9	6.9	6.7	4.1
Tobacco products	0.2	0.1	. . .	. . .	. . .	. . .						
Textile mill products	2.3	1.6	1.0	1.2	1.1	3.0	49.7	57.7	42.4	36.6	19.6	24.1
Apparel	0.2	0.6	0.1	1.3	0.1	0.7	7.2	9.8	17.8	15.3	15.2	13.9
Lumber and wood products	0.4	0.3	1.3	0.7	0.3	0.3	4.9	5.7	11.3	36.9	36.3	27.7
Furniture and fixtures	. . .	0.3	0.2	0.3	. . .	0.1	0.2	0.4	0.6	0.7	0.7	0.3
Paper products	19.4	31.4	31.6	14.0	13.8	14.7	52.2	38.8	49.4	78.7	41.7	45.0
Printing and publishing	0.1	0.1	. . .	0.1	. . .	. . .	0.4	0.8	0.3	0.3	0.3	0.4
Chemical products	14.3	17.3	21.9	28.3	12.6	12.6	79.2	185.1	161.1	166.9	87.7	227.4
Refined petroleum products	. . .	0.2	0.5	0.4	0.3	0.3	0.1	2.1	3.5	3.3	2.5	4.6
Rubber and plastic products	1.2	0.9	6.8	11.5	15.3	6.4	8.4	7.6	23.7	16.8	24.0	39.0
Leather products	. . .	. . .	. . .	. . .	0.1	0.5	0.5	1.1	0.6	0.2	0.3	1.6
Stone, clay and glass products	1.7	0.1	0.3	0.6	0.8	0.7	5.0	9.7	7.5	14.8	5.7	12.2
Primary metals	2.5	0.1	1.6	0.3	1.6	1.1	8.4	11.1	17.4	21.5	15.4	14.5
Fabricated metal products	1.5	0.9	1.4	1.8	1.2	4.9	7.0	11.6	16.8	13.2	10.0	11.3
Industrial machinery and computers	24.7	24.6	15.8	7.1	5.9	10.4	107.5	152.1	137.4	99.5	136.3	96.0
Electric and electronic equipment	7.1	6.2	4.4	4.4	11.2	23.8	201.9	215.0	176.5	172.6	118.4	66.9
Transportation equipment	5.1	8.0	5.9	3.3	3.4	22.8	10.1	8.2	12.5	56.4	94.6	100.3
Scientific and measuring instruments	1.3	2.1	20.1	16.6	13.5	9.1	9.2	9.4	11.8	19.3	14.8	15.9
Miscellaneous manufactures	3.0	2.1	4.1	1.3	2.0	3.6	9.8	7.7	9.1	8.3	9.4	8.4
Unidentified manufactures	0.3	0.1	0.2	0.1	0.2	0.2	1.0	0.9	0.8	0.6	1.7	1.8
Agricultural And Livestock Products	. . .	0.1	0.3	0.4	0.7	3.8	10.3	12.6	4.4	1.7	0.8	0.7
Agricultural products	. . .	0.1	0.3	0.4	0.7	3.8	8.2	9.8	3.1	. . .	0.1	0.2
Livestock and livestock products	. . .	. . .	. . .	. . .	. . .	. . .	2.0	2.8	1.3	1.7	0.7	0.4
Other Commodities	0.4	0.4	0.1	0.4	0.1	0.3	4.9	9.6	6.2	2.4	5.8	5.0
Forestry products	. . .	. . .	. . .	. . .	. . .	. . .	. . .	. . .	. . .	. . .	0.2	. . .
Fish and other marine products	. . .	. . .	. . .	0.2	. . .	. . .	0.4	0.7	0.4	. . .	1.0	. . .
Metallic ores and concentrates	. . .	. . .	. . .	. . .	. . .	. . .	. . .	. . .	. . .	. . .	. . .	0.1
Bituminous coal and lignite	. . .	. . .	. . .	. . .	. . .	. . .	. . .	. . .	. . .	. . .	. . .	. . .
Crude petroleum and natural gas	. . .	. . .	. . .	. . .	. . .	. . .	. . .	. . .	. . .	. . .	. . .	0.5
Nonmetallic minerals	0.3	. . .	. . .	. . .	. . .	0.1	0.5	0.9	0.1	0.2	0.4	0.4
Scrap and waste	0.1	0.3	. . .	0.2	. . .	. . .	0.7	0.3	1.6	0.3	1.6	1.4
Used merchandise	. . .	. . .	. . .	. . .	. . .	. . .	1.1	4.9	2.5	0.4	. . .	0.1
Goods imported and returned unchanged	. . .	. . .	. . .	. . .	. . .	. . .	. . .	. . .	. . .	. . .	. . .	. . .
Special classification provisions	0.1	0.1	0.1	. . .	0.1	0.2	2.1	2.9	1.6	1.5	2.5	2.5

Table D-44. SOUTH CAROLINA: State Exports of Goods by Destination and Industry, 1994–1999—*Continued*

(Millions of dollars.)

Industry	Japan						South Korea					
	1994	1995	1996	1997	1998	1999	1994	1995	1996	1997	1998	1999
ALL GOODS	180.5	181.5	201.6	273.1	247.8	236.0	112.4	115.2	69.9	67.5	44.9	164.3
Manufactured Goods	179.4	178.7	200.5	272.8	246.9	235.4	110.8	110.2	66.2	67.0	44.2	163.2
Food products	0.8	0.4	0.7	1.4	1.1	1.4	...	...	0.3	0.1	0.1	0.1
Tobacco products	...	...	...	...	...	...	...	...	...	...	...	...
Textile mill products	2.5	4.6	1.6	5.3	4.1	5.9	25.4	24.1	11.5	12.5	2.6	8.6
Apparel	5.8	8.2	16.0	13.1	14.2	13.1	...	0.1	0.2	...	0.1	...
Lumber and wood products	2.9	2.9	10.0	35.9	35.7	27.0	0.1	0.9	0.4	0.6	...	...
Furniture and fixtures	0.1	0.2	0.5	0.5	0.5	0.1	...	0.1	...	...	...	...
Paper products	23.4	8.4	11.4	18.0	4.6	4.2	1.9	7.5	8.1	9.2	4.1	9.7
Printing and publishing	0.2	0.4	...	...	...	0.1	...	...	...	...	...	0.1
Chemical products	15.3	21.9	24.2	21.5	16.6	17.4	6.2	10.6	8.0	10.2	4.6	116.9
Refined petroleum products	...	1.5	2.9	2.3	1.8	3.4	...	0.3	0.4	0.4	0.2	0.3
Rubber and plastic products	3.8	4.4	11.4	9.4	15.5	29.4	2.6	0.8	3.0	1.9	2.3	2.5
Leather products	0.1	...	0.1	0.1	0.1	1.4	...	...	0.2	...	...	...
Stone, clay and glass products	0.8	1.3	1.2	5.4	1.8	3.1	0.1	0.9	1.3	2.9	1.3	1.9
Primary metals	4.6	6.1	10.2	15.0	12.4	11.6	1.9	0.7	0.9	0.4	0.2	0.6
Fabricated metal products	2.0	2.9	3.4	4.4	4.5	3.5	1.2	0.8	0.6	3.2	0.5	0.5
Industrial machinery and computers	26.5	31.5	35.0	25.9	17.0	17.8	29.9	30.5	17.7	15.8	24.2	13.5
Electric and electronic equipment	77.3	73.0	62.6	51.7	21.1	8.7	37.4	30.6	11.3	7.9	2.5	5.0
Transportation equipment	3.8	3.2	2.0	50.9	86.0	80.1	2.3	0.6	0.7	0.8	0.7	2.3
Scientific and measuring instruments	4.2	3.8	4.4	10.5	8.1	5.8	1.4	1.5	0.9	0.6	0.2	0.7
Miscellaneous manufactures	5.2	3.5	2.8	1.4	1.2	0.8	0.1	0.1	0.7	0.2	0.3	0.1
Unidentified manufactures	0.2	0.4	0.3	0.2	0.5	0.5	0.3	0.1	0.2	0.1	0.3	0.3
Agricultural And Livestock Products	0.6	1.8	1.0	0.1	0.2	0.2	...	0.1	...	...	...	...
Agricultural products	0.6	1.7	1.0	...	0.1	0.2	...	...	...	...	...	...
Livestock and livestock products	...	0.2	...	0.1	...	...	...	0.1	...	...	...	...
Other Commodities	0.5	0.9	0.1	0.3	0.8	0.5	1.6	5.0	3.7	0.5	0.7	1.1
Forestry products	...	...	...	...	...	...	...	...	...	...	...	...
Fish and other marine products	0.4	0.5	...	...	...	...	...	...	...	...	...	...
Metallic ores and concentrates	...	...	...	...	...	...	...	...	...	...	...	...
Bituminous coal and lignite	...	...	...	...	...	...	...	...	...	...	...	...
Crude petroleum and natural gas	...	...	...	...	...	...	...	...	...	...	...	...
Nonmetallic minerals	0.1	0.3	...	0.2	0.2	0.1	...	...	...	...	...	...
Scrap and waste	...	...	...	...	0.5	0.3	0.1	...	0.8	...	0.7	1.0
Used merchandise	...	...	...	...	...	...	1.1	4.4	2.5	0.4	...	...
Goods imported and returned unchanged	...	...	...	...	...	...	...	...	...	...	...	...
Special classification provisions	...	0.1	0.1	0.1	0.1	0.1	0.4	0.5	0.3	0.1	...	...

Industry	Taiwan						Singapore					
	1994	1995	1996	1997	1998	1999	1994	1995	1996	1997	1998	1999
ALL GOODS	71.0	154.1	165.8	160.3	135.6	113.3	55.5	50.6	49.8	44.7	32.6	36.2
Manufactured Goods	66.0	146.2	162.9	159.7	134.1	112.7	55.4	50.5	49.7	44.7	32.5	36.1
Food products	0.1	0.1	0.1	0.3	0.2	0.4	...	...	0.2	0.5	0.7	0.1
Tobacco products	...	...	...	...	...	...	...	...	...	...	...	...
Textile mill products	2.2	3.2	3.5	1.5	1.2	1.2	1.9	1.0	0.7	2.1	0.5	1.0
Apparel	...	0.1	0.1	0.3	0.2	...	0.5	0.2	0.3	0.3	0.2	0.2
Lumber and wood products	0.8	0.8	0.1	0.1	0.2	0.3	0.1	0.1	...	0.1	...	...
Furniture and fixtures	0.1	...	...	0.1	0.1	...	...	...	...	...	...	...
Paper products	9.8	9.6	11.6	14.9	13.9	13.6	1.1	3.3	0.9	2.4	0.9	1.7
Printing and publishing	...	0.2	...	...	...	0.1	...	...	0.1	0.1	0.1	...
Chemical products	21.4	83.8	102.2	110.0	47.1	64.6	1.4	0.6	2.1	1.5	1.9	5.2
Refined petroleum products	...	...	...	0.1	0.1	0.1	...	...	...	0.1	0.1	0.1
Rubber and plastic products	0.5	0.6	3.0	0.8	1.2	1.2	0.6	0.3	1.4	0.6	0.5	0.6
Leather products	...	0.1	...	0.1	...	...	0.1	0.1	...	...	0.1	...
Stone, clay and glass products	0.5	0.6	0.7	2.0	0.9	2.0	0.5	2.1	0.8	0.7	...	0.1
Primary metals	0.3	0.7	0.9	1.2	0.5	0.5	0.4	0.2	0.2	0.1	0.2	0.1
Fabricated metal products	0.2	0.4	3.9	0.8	0.9	3.8	2.2	0.8	1.5	1.0	0.6	0.9
Industrial machinery and computers	16.3	28.3	15.0	5.4	51.3	11.1	5.9	7.8	7.4	4.9	4.6	3.7
Electric and electronic equipment	11.4	15.7	16.6	18.7	12.8	6.1	39.1	32.7	33.0	28.5	20.6	21.0
Transportation equipment	0.9	0.8	2.7	0.7	0.9	3.1	0.8	0.7	0.2	0.7	0.6	0.8
Scientific and measuring instruments	1.1	0.9	2.0	2.5	2.2	3.9	0.3	0.4	0.6	0.5	0.3	0.2
Miscellaneous manufactures	0.1	0.2	0.1	0.3	0.1	0.4	0.4	0.2	0.2	0.5	0.6	0.3
Unidentified manufactures	0.1	0.1	0.1	0.1	0.3	0.3	0.1	0.1	0.1	...	0.1	0.1
Agricultural And Livestock Products	4.1	6.1	1.7	0.5	0.1	0.1	...	...	...	...	...	...
Agricultural products	3.3	4.0	1.0	...	...	...	...	...	...	...	...	...
Livestock and livestock products	0.8	2.0	0.7	0.5	0.1	0.1	...	...	...	...	...	...
Other Commodities	0.9	1.8	1.3	0.2	1.4	0.5	0.1	...	0.1	...	0.1	0.1
Forestry products	...	...	...	...	0.2	...	...	...	...	...	...	...
Fish and other marine products	...	...	0.1	...	1.0	...	...	...	...	...	...	...
Metallic ores and concentrates	...	...	...	...	...	...	...	...	...	...	...	...
Bituminous coal and lignite	...	...	...	...	...	...	...	...	...	...	...	...
Crude petroleum and natural gas	...	...	...	...	...	...	...	...	...	...	...	...
Nonmetallic minerals	...	0.1	...	...	0.2	0.3	0.1	...	...	...	...	...
Scrap and waste	...	...	0.6	0.1	0.1	0.1	...	...	...	...	...	...
Used merchandise	...	...	...	...	...	...	...	...	...	...	...	...
Goods imported and returned unchanged	...	...	...	...	...	...	...	...	0.1	...	...	...
Special classification provisions	0.9	1.7	0.6	...	...	...	...	...	...	...	...	0.1

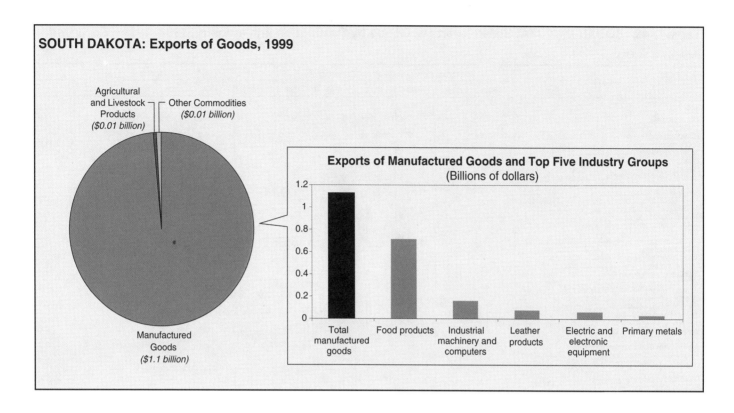

SOUTH DAKOTA: Exports of Goods, 1999

Agricultural and Livestock Products ($0.01 billion)

Other Commodities ($0.01 billion)

Manufactured Goods ($1.1 billion)

Exports of Manufactured Goods and Top Five Industry Groups (Billions of dollars)

Table D-45. SOUTH DAKOTA: State Exports of Goods by Destination and Industry, 1994–1999

(Millions of dollars.)

Industry	All destinations						Canada					
	1994	1995	1996	1997	1998	1999	1994	1995	1996	1997	1998	1999
ALL GOODS	263.9	348.6	397.3	435.3	373.5	1 143.4	130.8	142.1	164.1	167.3	165.9	178.9
Manufactured Goods	252.4	334.1	382.5	418.1	358.5	1 126.4	122.9	131.5	151.2	152.6	153.7	166.8
Food products	5.7	9.3	15.3	31.5	34.4	714.2	4.3	7.0	11.1	28.1	30.6	26.6
Tobacco products	. . .	. . .	. . .	. . .	. . .	. . .	. . .	. . .	. . .	. . .	. . .	. . .
Textile mill products	1.4	2.8	4.9	4.4	3.3	2.4	0.3	0.1	0.2	0.2	0.2	0.1
Apparel	2.7	3.0	5.8	5.1	2.1	1.9	0.2	0.2	0.4	0.4	0.3	0.6
Lumber and wood products	0.3	0.2	0.6	0.5	0.7	0.4	0.2	0.1	0.4	0.4	0.5	0.3
Furniture and fixtures	0.3	0.3	0.4	0.7	0.1	0.4	0.2	0.2	0.2	0.3	0.1	0.2
Paper products	3.0	4.4	8.2	10.4	9.9	10.7	1.2	2.0	4.4	5.4	6.3	7.3
Printing and publishing	2.1	2.8	3.5	7.2	5.5	3.1	2.0	2.2	2.1	2.9	1.7	1.6
Chemical products	2.2	2.9	3.9	4.3	4.6	7.4	1.4	1.5	1.3	0.9	1.1	2.2
Refined petroleum products	0.4	0.5	0.6	1.2	0.7	0.3	0.4	0.5	0.6	1.2	0.6	0.2
Rubber and plastic products	3.0	4.0	4.5	5.9	6.5	6.6	1.4	2.5	1.6	2.0	2.0	1.5
Leather products	0.2	0.2	0.2	0.4	0.2	77.6	0.1	0.2	0.1	0.1	. . .	0.1
Stone, clay and glass products	0.4	0.3	0.2	0.5	0.4	0.5	0.3	0.2	0.1	0.3	0.3	0.3
Primary metals	43.2	36.1	56.1	37.3	34.9	32.2	42.8	35.9	55.9	37.0	34.7	31.7
Fabricated metal products	2.7	3.5	4.9	6.6	4.4	6.3	1.7	2.7	2.6	4.5	3.3	4.2
Industrial machinery and computers	95.8	161.5	144.6	159.6	140.9	160.2	38.0	42.9	38.1	38.6	34.7	37.2
Electric and electronic equipment	24.5	31.0	41.8	65.1	60.8	62.1	10.7	12.0	10.4	9.9	14.5	29.3
Transportation equipment	16.2	18.3	23.6	22.1	22.2	21.2	13.2	15.9	13.3	15.6	17.3	18.6
Scientific and measuring instruments	43.3	44.4	52.7	50.8	21.5	13.7	1.6	1.4	2.0	2.2	2.6	2.1
Miscellaneous manufactures	2.4	4.9	8.0	2.2	2.2	2.7	0.9	0.9	3.8	0.9	1.0	1.1
Unidentified manufactures	2.7	3.7	2.9	2.6	3.3	2.5	2.1	3.2	2.7	2.1	1.8	1.4
Agricultural And Livestock Products	4.4	7.3	9.9	8.5	8.4	8.6	3.4	4.6	8.9	7.9	8.0	7.0
Agricultural products	2.7	5.2	7.6	5.8	5.7	7.3	2.3	3.3	7.3	5.7	5.4	6.1
Livestock and livestock products	1.6	2.1	2.3	2.7	2.7	1.3	1.1	1.3	1.5	2.3	2.6	0.9
Other Commodities	7.2	7.2	4.9	8.7	6.6	8.4	4.4	5.9	4.0	6.7	4.2	5.1
Forestry products	1.2	0.4	. . .	. . .	. . .	. . .	. . .	. . .	. . .	. . .	. . .	. . .
Fish and other marine products	. . .	. . .	0.1	. . .	. . .	. . .	. . .	. . .	0.1	. . .	. . .	. . .
Metallic ores and concentrates	. . .	. . .	. . .	. . .	. . .	. . .	. . .	. . .	. . .	. . .	. . .	. . .
Bituminous coal and lignite	. . .	. . .	. . .	. . .	. . .	. . .	. . .	. . .	. . .	. . .	. . .	. . .
Crude petroleum and natural gas	0.2	. . .	. . .	. . .	. . .	. . .	0.2	. . .	. . .	. . .	. . .	. . .
Nonmetallic minerals	0.9	1.2	1.3	2.3	3.4	3.7	0.5	0.6	0.8	0.7	1.3	1.8
Scrap and waste	0.8	1.0	0.5	0.3	0.3	0.2	0.7	1.0	0.4	0.2	0.3	0.2
Used merchandise	2.1	0.7	0.4	0.7	0.7	1.5	1.5	0.4	0.2	0.6	0.6	1.1
Goods imported and returned unchanged	1.5	3.6	2.3	5.1	2.0	1.9	1.5	3.6	2.3	5.1	2.0	1.9
Special classification provisions	0.5	0.4	0.4	0.2	0.1	1.1	. . .	0.4	0.3	0.2	. . .	0.2

Table D-45. SOUTH DAKOTA: State Exports of Goods by Destination and Industry, 1994–1999—Continued

(Millions of dollars.)

Industry	South and Central American and Caribbean						Mexico					
	1994	1995	1996	1997	1998	1999	1994	1995	1996	1997	1998	1999
ALL GOODS	5.8	11.9	17.4	14.8	16.7	15.7	5.5	5.3	7.8	11.5	18.6	17.9
Manufactured Goods	5.8	11.8	17.4	14.8	16.6	15.6	5.1	4.9	7.1	11.0	18.3	17.5
Food products	...	...	...	...	...	5.1	0.4	1.8	3.0	2.0	1.0	1.2
Tobacco products	...	...	...	...	...	...	...	...	...	...	...	...
Textile mill products	...	0.7	0.6	0.9	0.9	1.1	0.1	0.2	0.2	0.1	...	...
Apparel	0.2	0.5	0.9	0.6	0.7	0.3	0.1	0.3	0.4	0.5	...	...
Lumber and wood products	...	...	...	...	0.1	...	...	...	...	...	...	...
Furniture and fixtures	...	...	...	0.1	...	0.1	...	...	...	0.1	...	...
Paper products	...	...	0.1	0.5	0.5	...	0.1	0.2	0.1	0.4	0.2	2.2
Printing and publishing	...	0.1	...	0.1	...	...	...	...	0.1	0.3	1.3	1.1
Chemical products	0.2	0.2	0.1	0.4	0.1	0.1	0.1	0.1	0.1	0.1	0.3	0.3
Refined petroleum products	...	...	...	...	...	...	...	...	...	...	...	0.1
Rubber and plastic products	...	0.1	0.1	0.4	...	0.3	0.1	...	0.1	1.0	0.9	1.2
Leather products	...	...	...	...	...	2.0	...	...	...	0.1	...	...
Stone, clay and glass products	...	...	...	...	...	...	...	...	...	...	...	...
Primary metals	...	...	...	...	...	...	0.1	...	...	...	...	0.2
Fabricated metal products	0.1	0.1	0.2	0.1	0.1	0.2	...	...	0.2	0.1	0.1	1.3
Industrial machinery and computers	3.7	6.1	9.8	8.6	10.4	5.3	2.3	1.1	1.7	3.8	7.0	4.5
Electric and electronic equipment	0.3	0.8	1.2	2.2	3.0	0.6	0.3	0.2	0.3	1.3	6.4	3.8
Transportation equipment	0.2	0.2	0.6	0.3	0.5	0.2	1.3	0.3	0.3	0.6	0.5	0.7
Scientific and measuring instruments	0.8	0.1	0.2	0.1	0.1	0.2	0.1	0.5	0.7	0.4	0.5	0.4
Miscellaneous manufactures	0.1	2.8	3.3	0.3	0.1	0.1	...	...	...	...	0.1	0.2
Unidentified manufactures	0.1	...	...	...	0.1	...	0.1	0.1	...	...	0.1	0.2
Agricultural And Livestock Products	...	0.1	...	...	...	...	0.4	0.4	0.6	0.3	0.1	0.3
Agricultural products	...	0.1	...	...	...	...	0.1	...	...	...	...	...
Livestock and livestock products	...	...	...	...	...	...	0.3	0.4	0.6	0.3	0.1	0.3
Other Commodities	...	...	...	...	...	0.1	...	...	0.1	0.2	0.2	0.2
Forestry products	...	...	...	...	...	...	...	...	...	...	...	...
Fish and other marine products	...	...	...	...	...	...	...	...	...	...	...	...
Metallic ores and concentrates	...	...	...	...	...	...	...	...	...	...	...	...
Bituminous coal and lignite	...	...	...	...	...	...	...	...	...	...	...	...
Crude petroleum and natural gas	...	...	...	...	...	...	...	...	...	...	...	...
Nonmetallic materials	...	...	...	...	...	...	...	...	0.1	0.1	0.1	0.1
Scrap and waste	...	...	...	...	...	...	...	...	...	...	...	...
Used merchandise	...	...	...	...	...	...	...	...	...	...	...	0.1
Goods imported and returned unchanged	...	...	...	...	...	...	...	...	...	...	...	...
Special classification provisions	...	...	...	...	...	0.1	...	...	...	...	...	...

Industry	European Union						United Kingdom					
	1994	1995	1996	1997	1998	1999	1994	1995	1996	1997	1998	1999
ALL GOODS	69.5	111.2	105.8	121.7	92.6	114.7	8.7	35.5	29.6	35.7	27.4	25.5
Manufactured Goods	68.9	108.8	105.3	120.9	91.3	113.2	8.6	35.2	29.4	35.4	27.3	25.4
Food products	0.3	0.1	0.1	...	0.2	8.7	...	...	...	...	...	0.1
Tobacco products	...	...	...	...	...	...	...	...	...	...	...	...
Textile mill products	0.7	1.8	3.3	2.9	2.0	1.1	...	0.3	...	0.2	...	...
Apparel	1.6	1.7	2.7	2.0	0.7	0.1	0.1	0.1	1.3	0.9	0.1	...
Lumber and wood products	...	0.1	0.1	...	0.1	0.1	...	...	...	...	0.1	0.1
Furniture and fixtures	...	0.1	...	...	...	...	...	...	...	...	...	...
Paper products	1.2	1.9	3.0	3.4	2.6	0.7	0.3	0.1	0.1	...	...	...
Printing and publishing	...	0.3	1.2	3.4	2.0	0.2	...	...	0.1	0.2	0.4	0.1
Chemical products	0.3	0.6	1.0	1.4	2.4	3.9	...	0.2	0.2	0.3	0.9	0.7
Refined petroleum products	...	...	...	...	...	...	...	...	...	...	...	...
Rubber and plastic products	0.8	0.7	1.6	1.7	2.8	3.2	...	0.1	0.7	0.7	2.0	0.8
Leather products	...	...	...	0.1	0.1	10.6	...	...	...	...	...	...
Stone, clay and glass products	...	...	...	...	...	0.1	...	...	...	...	...	...
Primary metals	0.1	...	...	0.2	0.2	0.1	0.1	...	...	...	...	0.1
Fabricated metal products	0.2	0.3	0.6	0.5	0.3	0.3	...	0.1	0.3	0.1	0.1	0.2
Industrial machinery and computers	31.3	66.2	46.3	51.3	48.2	63.4	4.9	33.4	23.7	31.2	21.7	17.3
Electric and electronic equipment	2.9	4.4	7.4	19.3	16.0	11.0	1.0	0.6	0.8	1.0	1.0	4.6
Transportation equipment	0.5	1.4	3.5	1.4	0.9	0.8	0.1	...	1.6	0.2	0.1	0.3
Scientific and measuring instruments	28.1	28.7	33.8	32.4	11.3	7.5	1.6	0.1	0.3	0.1	0.1	0.1
Miscellaneous manufactures	0.6	0.5	0.5	0.5	0.8	1.0	0.4	0.3	0.3	0.3	0.6	0.8
Unidentified manufactures	0.1	0.1	0.1	0.2	0.7	0.3	0.1	0.1	...	...	0.1	...
Agricultural And Livestock Products	0.5	1.9	0.2	0.1	0.1	0.2	...	0.1	...	...	...	...
Agricultural products	0.3	1.8	0.2	0.1	0.1	0.1	...	...	...	...	...	...
Livestock and livestock products	0.1	0.1	...	...	...	0.1	...	0.1	...	...	...	...
Other Commodities	0.1	0.5	0.3	0.8	1.2	1.3	0.1	0.2	0.2	0.3	0.1	0.1
Forestry products	...	...	...	...	...	...	...	...	...	...	...	...
Fish and other marine products	...	...	...	...	...	...	...	...	...	...	...	...
Metallic ores and concentrates	...	...	...	...	...	...	...	...	...	...	...	...
Bituminous coal and lignite	...	...	...	...	...	...	...	...	...	...	...	...
Crude petroleum and natural gas	...	...	...	...	...	...	...	...	...	...	...	...
Nonmetallic materials	0.1	0.4	0.3	0.6	1.1	1.0	0.1	0.2	0.2	0.2	0.1	0.1
Scrap and waste	...	...	...	...	...	...	...	...	...	...	...	...
Used merchandise	0.1	0.1	...	0.1	0.1	0.1	...	...	...	...	...	...
Goods imported and returned unchanged	...	...	...	...	...	...	...	...	...	...	...	...
Special classification provisions	...	...	...	0.1	...	0.2	...	...	...	...	...	0.1

Table D-45. SOUTH DAKOTA: State Exports of Goods by Destination and Industry, 1994–1999—Continued

(Millions of dollars.)

Industry	Germany						France					
	1994	1995	1996	1997	1998	1999	1994	1995	1996	1997	1998	1999
ALL GOODS	8.3	10.6	17.1	18.2	22.9	15.7	4.2	6.7	7.2	7.4	5.0	6.1
Manufactured Goods	8.3	10.6	17.1	18.1	22.8	15.5	4.2	6.6	7.2	7.4	5.0	6.0
Food products	0.2	...	0.1	...	...	1.6	...	...	...	...	...	3.4
Tobacco products	...	...	...	...	...	...	...	...	...	...	...	...
Textile mill products	0.3	0.1	1.6	1.5	1.1	0.5	0.1	...	...	...	...	...
Apparel	0.3	0.1	0.1	0.2	0.4	...	...	...	...	...	...	...
Lumber and wood products	...	...	...	...	...	...	...	...	...	...	...	...
Furniture and fixtures	...	...	...	...	...	...	...	...	...	...	...	...
Paper products	...	0.3	1.3	1.3	0.8	0.5	...	...	...	...	...	...
Printing and publishing	...	...	0.8	2.9	1.4	...	...	...	0.2	0.2	...	...
Chemical products	0.2	0.1	...	0.2	0.9	1.5	...	0.2	0.2	0.2	0.2	0.2
Refined petroleum products	...	...	...	...	...	...	...	...	...	...	...	...
Rubber and plastic products	...	...	0.2	0.3	0.3	0.1	...	...	0.1	0.1	...	...
Leather products	...	...	...	...	...	...	...	...	...	...	0.1	...
Stone, clay and glass products	...	...	...	...	...	...	...	...	...	...	...	...
Primary metals	...	...	...	...	...	...	...	...	...	...	...	...
Fabricated metal products	0.1	...	...	...	...	...	...	...	0.1	0.1	...	...
Industrial machinery and computers	5.5	6.8	7.7	6.1	5.4	2.4	0.6	0.7	0.8	0.7	1.1	1.2
Electric and electronic equipment	0.2	0.3	0.5	1.0	5.7	1.9	0.1	1.2	2.3	2.3	2.1	0.8
Transportation equipment	0.1	0.9	1.5	0.9	0.2	0.1	0.1	...	0.1	...	0.4	0.2
Scientific and measuring instruments	1.2	1.8	3.3	3.6	6.4	6.7	3.2	4.2	3.4	3.5	0.4	0.1
Miscellaneous manufactures	0.1	...	...	...	0.1	0.1	...	...	...	...	...	...
Unidentified manufactures	...	...	...	...	...	...	...	...	...	0.1	0.6	0.2
Agricultural And Livestock Products	...	...	...	0.1	0.1	0.1	...	...	...	...	...	...
Agricultural products	...	...	...	0.1	0.1	0.1	...	...	...	...	...	...
Livestock and livestock products	...	...	...	...	...	...	...	...	...	...	...	...
Other Commodities	...	...	...	...	...	...	...	0.1	...	...	...	...
Forestry products	...	...	...	...	...	...	...	...	...	...	...	...
Fish and other marine products	...	...	...	...	...	...	...	...	...	...	...	...
Metallic ores and concentrates	...	...	...	...	...	...	...	...	...	...	...	...
Bituminous coal and lignite	...	...	...	...	...	...	...	...	...	...	...	...
Crude petroleum and natural gas	...	...	...	...	...	...	...	...	...	...	...	...
Nonmetallic materials	...	...	...	...	...	...	...	...	...	...	...	...
Scrap and waste	...	...	...	...	...	...	...	...	...	...	...	...
Used merchandise	...	...	...	...	...	...	...	0.1	...	...	...	...
Goods imported and returned unchanged	...	...	...	...	...	...	...	...	...	...	...	...
Special classification provisions	...	...	...	...	...	...	...	...	...	...	...	...

Industry	The Netherlands						Asian 10					
	1994	1995	1996	1997	1998	1999	1994	1995	1996	1997	1998	1999
ALL GOODS	25.7	26.6	31.7	29.6	6.4	14.8	38.2	58.4	81.9	104.5	66.5	798.3
Manufactured Goods	25.6	26.6	31.7	29.6	6.3	14.7	36.4	57.4	81.3	103.5	65.3	795.7
Food products	...	...	...	...	0.1	...	0.3	0.1	0.6	0.9	2.0	671.2
Tobacco products	...	...	...	...	...	...	...	...	...	...	...	...
Textile mill products	...	0.1	...	...	...	...	0.3	0.1	0.5	0.3	0.1	0.1
Apparel	1.2	1.4	1.3	0.9	0.1	...	0.7	0.3	1.0	1.6	0.4	0.7
Lumber and wood products	...	0.1	...	...	...	...	...	...	0.1	...	...	...
Furniture and fixtures	...	...	...	...	...	...	...	...	0.1	0.2	...	...
Paper products	0.8	0.9	1.1	0.9	0.2	...	0.2	0.3	0.6	0.6	0.3	0.1
Printing and publishing	...	0.2	...	...	0.1	...	...	0.1	0.1	0.1	0.2	0.1
Chemical products	...	...	0.1	...	...	0.7	0.2	0.3	1.2	1.2	0.3	0.3
Refined petroleum products	...	...	...	...	...	...	...	...	...	...	...	...
Rubber and plastic products	0.5	0.4	0.6	0.6	0.2	...	0.7	0.6	0.9	0.5	0.5	0.2
Leather products	...	...	...	...	...	...	...	...	...	0.1	0.1	64.8
Stone, clay and glass products	...	...	...	...	...	...	...	...	...	0.1	...	...
Primary metals	...	...	...	...	...	...	0.1	0.1	0.1	0.1	0.1	0.1
Fabricated metal products	...	...	0.1	0.2	...	...	0.3	0.2	1.1	1.1	0.2	0.1
Industrial machinery and computers	1.8	0.6	0.8	0.7	1.4	13.1	12.6	30.5	39.2	51.4	34.9	43.2
Electric and electronic equipment	0.5	1.2	1.6	1.9	0.3	0.7	8.8	11.3	19.5	30.0	19.0	11.5
Transportation equipment	0.1	0.1	...	...	...	...	0.3	0.1	0.3	0.5	0.3	0.2
Scientific and measuring instruments	20.7	21.6	26.0	24.3	3.9	0.1	11.1	12.8	15.6	14.8	6.5	2.8
Miscellaneous manufactures	0.1	0.1	0.1	0.1	...	...	0.7	0.6	0.2	...	0.2	...
Unidentified manufactures	...	...	...	...	...	...	0.2	0.1	0.1	0.1	0.1	0.2
Agricultural And Livestock Products	...	...	...	...	...	...	...	0.3	0.2	...	0.2	1.1
Agricultural products	...	...	...	...	...	...	...	...	...	...	0.2	0.9
Livestock and livestock products	...	...	...	...	...	...	...	0.3	0.1	...	...	0.1
Other Commodities	...	...	...	...	...	...	1.8	0.7	0.4	1.0	1.0	1.5
Forestry products	...	...	...	...	...	...	1.2	0.4	...	...	...	...
Fish and other marine products	...	...	...	...	...	...	...	...	...	...	...	...
Metallic ores and concentrates	...	...	...	...	...	...	...	...	...	...	...	...
Bituminous coal and lignite	...	...	...	...	...	...	...	...	...	...	...	...
Crude petroleum and natural gas	...	...	...	...	...	...	...	...	...	...	...	...
Nonmetallic materials	...	...	...	...	...	...	0.3	0.1	0.1	0.9	0.9	0.7
Scrap and waste	...	...	...	...	...	...	0.1	...	0.1	...	...	...
Used merchandise	...	...	...	...	...	...	0.1	0.2	0.2	0.1	0.1	0.2
Goods imported and returned unchanged	...	...	...	...	...	...	...	...	...	...	...	...
Special classification provisions	...	...	...	...	...	...	0.1	...	...	...	...	0.6

Table D-45. SOUTH DAKOTA: State Exports of Goods by Destination and Industry, 1994–1999—Continued

(Millions of dollars.)

Industry	Japan						South Korea					
	1994	1995	1996	1997	1998	1999	1994	1995	1996	1997	1998	1999
ALL GOODS	22.1	38.6	28.0	22.0	14.7	580.7	2.6	1.0	3.2	4.7	0.7	125.9
Manufactured Goods	20.8	37.9	27.7	21.2	13.7	578.9	2.5	1.0	3.2	4.7	0.7	125.2
Food products	0.2	...	0.6	0.6	1.6	570.1	...	0.1	...	...	...	76.8
Tobacco products	...	...	...	...	...	...	0.3	0.1	...	0.1	...	...
Textile mill products	...	...	...	...	...	...	...	...	...	...	...	...
Apparel	0.7	0.2	0.2	0.1	...	...	...	...	0.8	1.3	0.3	0.7
Lumber and wood products	...	...	0.1	...	...	...	...	...	...	...	...	...
Furniture and fixtures	...	...	0.1	...	...	...	...	...	...	...	...	...
Paper products	0.2	0.2	0.2	0.4	0.1	...	...	...	0.1	0.1	...	...
Printing and publishing	...	...	...	...	0.1	...	...	...	...	...	...	0.1
Chemical products	0.1	0.1	0.9	0.2	0.1	...	...	...	0.1	0.1	0.1	0.3
Refined petroleum products	...	...	...	...	...	...	...	...	...	...	...	...
Rubber and plastic products	0.2	0.3	0.3	0.3	0.3	0.1	0.2	0.1	...	...	...	...
Leather products	...	...	...	0.1	...	1.2	...	...	...	...	...	45.6
Stone, clay and glass products	...	...	...	...	...	...	...	...	...	...	...	...
Primary metals	...	...	...	...	...	...	...	...	...	...	...	...
Fabricated metal products	...	0.1	...	0.2	0.1	...	0.2	...	1.0	0.8	...	...
Industrial machinery and computers	6.8	21.7	7.8	2.3	3.9	4.4	1.3	0.6	0.9	1.5	0.1	0.5
Electric and electronic equipment	1.0	2.6	2.1	2.1	0.9	0.3	0.4	...	0.1	0.3	0.1	1.0
Transportation equipment	0.2	0.1	0.2	0.3	0.2	0.2	...	...	...	...	...	...
Scientific and measuring instruments	10.8	12.0	14.8	14.4	6.0	2.3	...	0.1	0.2	0.2	...	0.1
Miscellaneous manufactures	0.5	0.4	0.1	...	...	...	...	...	...	...	...	...
Unidentified manufactures	0.1	0.1	...	...	0.1	0.1	...	...	...	...	...	...
Agricultural And Livestock Products	...	0.1	...	...	0.2	0.9	...	...	...	...	...	0.1
Agricultural products	...	...	...	...	0.2	0.9	...	...	...	...	...	0.1
Livestock and livestock products	...	...	...	...	...	...	...	...	...	...	...	...
Other Commodities	1.4	0.6	0.3	0.8	0.8	0.8	0.1	...	0.1	...	...	0.6
Forestry products	1.1	0.4	...	...	...	...	0.1	...	...	...	...	...
Fish and other marine products	...	...	...	...	...	...	...	...	...	...	...	...
Metallic ores and concentrates	...	...	...	...	...	...	...	...	...	...	...	...
Bituminous coal and lignite	...	...	...	...	...	...	...	...	...	...	...	...
Crude petroleum and natural gas	...	...	...	...	...	...	...	...	...	...	...	...
Nonmetallic materials	0.1	...	...	0.7	0.8	0.6	0.1	...	0.1	...	...	...
Scrap and waste	...	...	...	...	...	...	...	...	...	...	...	...
Used merchandise	0.1	0.2	0.2	0.1	...	0.2	...	...	...	...	...	...
Goods imported and returned unchanged	...	...	...	...	...	...	...	...	...	...	...	0.6
Special classification provisions	...	...	...	...	...	...	...	...	...	...	...	...

Industry	Taiwan						Singapore					
	1994	1995	1996	1997	1998	1999	1994	1995	1996	1997	1998	1999
ALL GOODS	4.2	6.2	14.0	32.0	9.4	25.8	3.9	3.9	2.9	4.7	4.1	13.7
Manufactured Goods	3.9	6.1	14.0	31.9	9.4	25.8	3.9	3.9	2.9	4.7	4.0	13.7
Food products	0.1	...	...	...	0.1	16.7	...	...	...	...	...	0.1
Tobacco products	...	...	...	...	...	...	...	...	...	...	...	...
Textile mill products	...	...	...	...	0.1	...	...	...	...	0.2	...	...
Apparel	...	...	0.1	...	...	...	...	...	...	...	...	...
Lumber and wood products	...	...	...	...	...	...	...	...	...	...	...	...
Furniture and fixtures	...	...	...	0.1	...	...	...	...	...	...	...	...
Paper products	...	...	0.3	...	...	...	...	...	...	...	...	...
Printing and publishing	...	...	...	...	0.1	...	...	...	...	...	...	...
Chemical products	...	...	...	0.3	...	...	...	0.2	...	0.3	0.1	...
Refined petroleum products	...	...	...	...	...	...	...	...	...	...	...	...
Rubber and plastic products	0.1	0.1	0.1	...	...	...	0.1	...	...	0.1	0.1	0.1
Leather products	...	...	...	...	...	1.6	...	...	...	...	...	...
Stone, clay and glass products	...	...	...	...	...	...	...	...	...	...	...	...
Primary metals	...	...	0.1	...	...	...	...	...	...	...	...	...
Fabricated metal products	0.1	...	...	...	0.1	...	...	...	...	...	...	...
Industrial machinery and computers	0.2	0.8	6.1	19.7	3.0	2.8	0.8	2.0	1.6	1.7	2.1	11.0
Electric and electronic equipment	3.5	4.9	7.3	11.5	6.1	4.6	2.9	1.6	1.2	2.4	1.6	2.4
Transportation equipment	...	...	...	0.1	...	...	...	...	...	...	...	...
Scientific and measuring instruments	...	0.2	...	...	...	...	...	...	...	...	...	...
Miscellaneous manufactures	...	0.1	...	...	...	...	...	...	...	...	...	...
Unidentified manufactures	...	...	...	...	...	...	...	...	...	...	...	0.1
Agricultural And Livestock Products	...	...	...	...	...	...	...	...	...	...	...	...
Agricultural products	...	...	...	...	...	...	...	...	...	...	...	...
Livestock and livestock products	...	...	...	...	...	...	...	...	...	...	...	...
Other Commodities	0.2	...	...	0.1	0.1	...	...	...	...	...	...	...
Forestry products	...	...	...	...	...	...	...	...	...	...	...	...
Fish and other marine products	...	...	...	...	...	...	...	...	...	...	...	...
Metallic ores and concentrates	...	...	...	...	...	...	...	...	...	...	...	...
Bituminous coal and lignite	...	...	...	...	...	...	...	...	...	...	...	...
Crude petroleum and natural gas	...	...	...	...	...	...	...	...	...	...	...	...
Nonmetallic materials	0.2	...	...	0.1	...	...	...	...	...	...	...	...
Scrap and waste	...	...	...	...	...	...	...	...	...	...	...	...
Used merchandise	...	...	...	...	...	...	...	...	...	...	...	...
Goods imported and returned unchanged	...	...	...	...	...	...	...	...	...	...	...	...
Special classification provisions	0.1	...	...	...	...	...	...	...	...	...	...	...

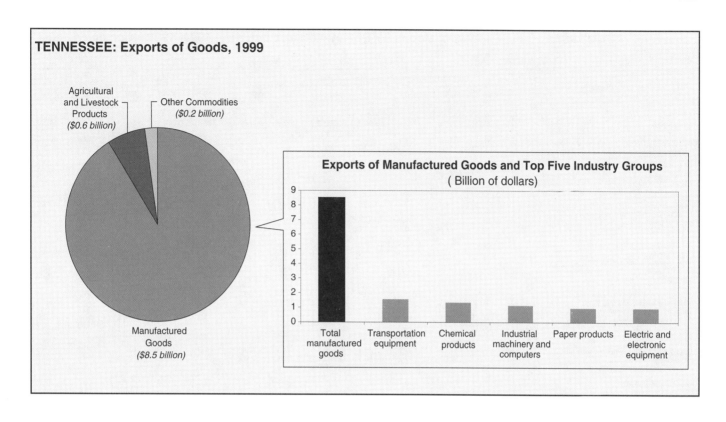

TENNESSEE: Exports of Goods, 1999

Agricultural and Livestock Products ($0.6 billion)

Other Commodities ($0.2 billion)

Manufactured Goods ($8.5 billion)

Exports of Manufactured Goods and Top Five Industry Groups
(Billion of dollars)

Total manufactured goods

Transportation equipment

Chemical products

Industrial machinery and computers

Paper products

Electric and electronic equipment

Table D-46. TENNESSEE: State Exports of Goods by Destination and Industry, 1994–1999

(Millions of dollars.)

Industry	All destinations						Canada					
	1994	1995	1996	1997	1998	1999	1994	1995	1996	1997	1998	1999
ALL GOODS	7 506.2	9 460.5	9 328.3	9 916.9	9 872.5	9 342.7	1 976.2	2 101.0	2 199.9	2 389.4	2 589.1	2 919.3
Manufactured Goods	6 103.7	6 974.4	7 298.0	8 357.7	8 474.8	8 504.6	1 913.4	1 992.7	2 081.1	2 268.6	2 443.7	2 782.3
Food products	113.9	159.7	197.3	156.0	192.9	158.9	34.7	44.0	44.6	61.0	76.5	56.4
Tobacco products	6.8	6.2	0.4	0.3	1.8	0.4	6.7	5.4	0.2	0.2	0.1	0.1
Textile mill products	118.6	125.2	139.6	197.0	216.5	196.4	42.9	39.8	40.0	51.2	64.4	63.0
Apparel	121.5	130.6	159.8	196.2	249.9	189.3	12.4	8.4	15.3	19.2	24.7	23.2
Lumber and wood products	87.4	94.5	86.7	74.6	62.3	68.8	12.5	13.2	17.9	21.4	13.6	20.9
Furniture and fixtures	113.9	111.3	118.9	139.2	164.2	61.2	96.0	93.8	100.9	109.1	134.3	48.1
Paper products	760.2	971.2	897.5	995.0	948.2	971.1	71.3	92.4	95.7	101.5	111.0	119.2
Printing and publishing	58.8	72.8	74.2	80.2	94.2	120.1	37.6	40.8	43.9	38.7	41.9	55.6
Chemical products	1 317.6	1 453.1	1 362.7	1 502.5	1 426.6	1 347.4	231.1	248.9	251.9	268.0	312.1	293.5
Refined petroleum products	4.9	8.8	3.6	5.5	7.0	7.7	1.2	1.8	0.7	1.3	1.4	2.1
Rubber and plastic products	205.9	239.7	256.6	359.5	394.6	368.9	98.6	117.4	119.2	138.8	159.3	193.5
Leather products	22.6	16.7	15.6	15.1	15.6	16.3	9.0	7.1	6.6	5.5	5.7	6.1
Stone, clay and glass products	78.9	101.7	118.8	125.3	119.2	135.5	54.5	69.5	75.1	76.7	65.2	72.0
Primary metals	98.1	141.5	117.7	175.1	153.3	142.9	25.5	36.1	34.7	63.5	45.1	47.5
Fabricated metal products	222.9	247.8	186.9	218.6	225.8	431.3	68.8	68.7	76.8	96.9	109.1	259.1
Industrial machinery and computers	724.1	878.7	992.2	1 095.0	1 115.0	1 155.2	272.0	307.0	335.3	372.4	433.9	461.8
Electric and electronic equipment	558.0	649.6	817.5	986.7	996.4	959.5	258.8	237.1	245.8	275.7	296.9	355.4
Transportation equipment	1 110.3	1 175.0	1 296.4	1 493.5	1 476.1	1 564.2	468.5	471.1	454.7	448.4	409.3	536.9
Scientific and measuring instruments	254.3	257.2	323.0	378.2	456.1	456.4	73.3	50.0	75.9	68.3	86.1	112.8
Miscellaneous manufactures	110.4	119.3	116.7	143.9	131.0	120.1	31.2	33.5	38.9	43.8	44.2	45.1
Unidentified manufactures	14.6	13.6	16.0	20.0	28.2	33.1	6.8	6.5	6.9	7.1	9.1	10.1
Agricultural And Livestock Products	1 226.8	2 314.4	1 852.2	1 293.9	1 179.6	633.2	38.9	56.2	56.3	54.3	59.9	25.1
Agricultural products	1 225.3	2 313.8	1 850.1	1 292.7	1 171.3	621.5	38.8	55.9	55.9	54.1	59.4	24.4
Livestock and livestock products	1.5	0.6	2.0	1.2	8.3	11.7	0.1	0.3	0.4	0.3	0.5	0.7
Other Commodities	175.8	171.7	178.2	265.3	218.0	204.8	23.9	52.1	62.6	66.4	85.5	111.9
Forestry products	1.5	0.6	1.7	0.7	1.4	1.4	0.2	0.1	0.2	0.1	1.0	0.3
Fish and other marine products	21.5	29.1	25.5	10.9	3.4	3.4	0.3	0.5	0.5	0.7	0.4	0.4
Metallic ores and concentrates	0.2	4.1	15.5	15.4	18.1	10.0	. . .	0.1	0.1	0.1	0.1	. . .
Bituminous coal and lignite	94.7	54.6	47.9	72.3	71.9	38.5	0.8	1.0	1.2	0.9	1.0	0.9
Crude petroleum and natural gas	. . .	. . .	0.3	. . .	0.1	0.3	. . .	. . .	. . .	. . .	. . .	. . .
Nonmetallic minerals	8.4	9.2	10.3	9.8	7.8	5.8	0.2	0.1	0.3	0.4	0.3	0.4
Scrap and waste	8.8	13.5	8.0	11.3	8.7	9.5	1.9	6.4	3.8	3.5	2.4	3.0
Used merchandise	18.1	7.5	2.4	52.9	1.8	7.9	0.9	0.5	0.5	0.7	0.5	1.9
Goods imported and returned unchanged	16.4	39.5	45.5	54.5	73.5	67.1	16.4	39.5	45.5	54.5	73.5	67.1
Special classification provisions	6.3	13.6	21.0	37.5	31.3	60.8	3.3	3.9	10.6	5.5	6.4	38.0

Table D-46. TENNESSEE: State Exports of Goods by Destination and Industry, 1994–1999—*Continued*

(Millions of dollars.)

Industry	South and Central American and Caribbean						Mexico					
	1994	1995	1996	1997	1998	1999	1994	1995	1996	1997	1998	1999
ALL GOODS	492.1	707.9	771.9	894.1	982.2	769.9	752.4	839.4	913.6	1 188.1	1 288.3	975.0
Manufactured Goods	360.1	516.6	571.1	708.1	771.1	674.1	645.2	748.7	808.6	1 048.5	1 017.4	892.0
Food products	12.9	15.4	22.5	22.1	47.1	47.6	27.6	10.4	23.4	11.3	8.0	5.0
Tobacco products	...	0.8	...	...	0.2	...	...	...	...	...	...	...
Textile mill products	6.7	8.5	12.1	20.1	30.1	26.2	7.7	12.7	13.7	23.5	19.6	23.8
Apparel	54.1	77.4	94.8	122.2	112.0	56.4	11.1	12.0	18.4	25.4	74.5	70.3
Lumber and wood products	1.8	3.2	0.8	1.1	3.1	4.1	2.5	3.1	3.4	3.9	3.5	3.6
Furniture and fixtures	1.7	1.8	2.5	2.5	2.5	1.6	3.2	3.2	3.2	6.2	3.3	0.8
Paper products	55.6	72.3	83.3	118.9	110.0	136.8	49.4	64.5	42.9	37.5	30.8	36.0
Printing and publishing	1.8	4.8	6.2	7.7	10.4	8.2	2.1	4.1	4.9	6.0	4.1	2.9
Chemical products	106.7	140.2	141.9	139.6	134.5	110.4	72.6	84.6	88.8	98.8	99.7	108.8
Refined petroleum products	0.1	0.3	0.1	0.2	0.8	1.2	3.0	5.8	2.2	1.2	0.8	1.6
Rubber and plastic products	5.9	12.0	17.8	41.0	68.1	42.5	23.5	22.3	25.4	85.7	91.1	75.6
Leather products	5.1	1.6	0.4	0.9	1.6	2.2	0.7	0.3	0.4	0.5	0.5	0.5
Stone, clay and glass products	2.5	3.1	5.2	4.7	5.0	4.6	7.8	2.1	10.1	5.2	8.8	6.3
Primary metals	7.9	12.6	13.0	15.3	10.1	3.6	44.3	51.0	20.0	38.4	35.0	44.4
Fabricated metal products	5.9	9.2	7.8	10.2	13.3	12.7	106.8	116.9	25.9	33.3	32.1	33.0
Industrial machinery and computers	39.4	49.1	38.0	49.4	67.3	56.3	50.1	62.6	42.4	68.6	94.1	83.7
Electric and electronic equipment	10.4	20.0	39.9	74.1	62.1	80.8	108.5	162.4	269.7	330.6	275.7	142.9
Transportation equipment	21.2	53.4	60.7	52.4	66.7	56.3	101.1	116.7	197.2	234.5	208.2	221.6
Scientific and measuring instruments	9.3	16.3	10.7	11.6	11.5	11.0	6.9	8.7	9.2	15.2	12.3	18.9
Miscellaneous manufactures	10.2	13.6	12.3	12.8	11.0	8.3	5.8	3.2	3.1	8.2	9.3	6.5
Unidentified manufactures	0.7	1.1	1.0	1.4	3.6	3.5	1.4	1.9	4.4	5.5	6.1	5.7
Agricultural And Livestock Products	127.5	186.1	197.7	180.1	205.1	89.8	104.1	88.0	100.6	131.0	260.8	71.0
Agricultural products	127.3	186.1	197.7	180.1	202.3	85.1	103.2	87.9	100.4	130.3	260.6	69.8
Livestock and livestock products	0.2	...	...	...	2.9	4.8	0.9	0.2	0.1	0.7	0.2	1.2
Other Commodities	4.5	5.2	3.1	6.0	5.9	5.9	3.1	2.6	4.4	8.6	10.1	12.0
Forestry products	...	...	...	0.1	0.1	0.2	...	...	...	0.1	0.1	0.4
Fish and other marine products	...	...	...	...	...	...	...	...	...	...	...	...
Metallic ores and concentrates	...	...	...	0.2	...	...	...	...	...	...	0.4	3.0
Bituminous coal and lignite	0.9	2.6	0.3	1.3	1.4	1.3	...	...	...	...	...	...
Crude petroleum and natural gas	...	...	...	...	...	...	...	...	...	...	...	...
Nonmetallic minerals	1.9	2.0	1.9	1.5	1.4	0.8	2.6	2.3	4.2	3.8	3.1	2.1
Scrap and waste	0.1	...	...	1.1	0.8	0.4	0.3	0.1	...	0.1	...	0.4
Used merchandise	0.2	0.1	0.2	0.3	0.3	0.7	0.1	...	...	...	...	0.1
Goods imported and returned unchanged	...	...	...	...	...	...	...	...	...	...	...	...
Special classification provisions	1.3	0.4	0.6	1.5	1.9	2.4	0.1	0.1	0.1	4.5	6.4	6.0

Industry	European Union						United Kingdom					
	1994	1995	1996	1997	1998	1999	1994	1995	1996	1997	1998	1999
ALL GOODS	1 708.0	1 898.8	1 869.1	2 132.4	2 314.2	2 290.6	378.4	422.9	395.5	531.7	619.9	604.5
Manufactured Goods	1 612.0	1 780.4	1 772.4	2 015.0	2 216.2	2 220.3	373.4	408.1	384.7	502.9	585.3	594.4
Food products	15.0	45.5	52.3	20.7	12.1	8.2	0.7	0.7	2.0	1.3	0.8	0.5
Tobacco products	...	...	...	...	1.0	0.1	...	...	...	...	...	...
Textile mill products	43.9	37.5	45.2	68.6	70.1	58.8	25.7	22.7	32.1	53.3	56.3	47.3
Apparel	8.4	12.3	13.6	11.8	8.4	18.8	0.7	1.7	1.8	2.0	1.9	2.6
Lumber and wood products	43.2	45.7	41.1	29.4	31.0	28.0	7.0	8.5	8.0	6.3	5.7	5.1
Furniture and fixtures	4.6	4.0	5.3	9.2	15.2	5.0	1.5	1.2	2.9	4.6	9.9	2.5
Paper products	256.0	307.6	324.6	370.1	336.8	326.0	45.4	56.8	74.0	88.8	59.1	55.9
Printing and publishing	11.3	14.6	12.6	16.3	24.0	34.4	7.8	9.2	8.7	10.7	16.1	21.7
Chemical products	425.1	462.2	388.8	465.0	460.6	447.2	67.4	71.0	36.3	70.9	74.2	62.3
Refined petroleum products	0.3	0.1	0.1	1.7	0.7	0.5	...	...	...	0.1	...	...
Rubber and plastic products	21.4	22.4	18.6	23.7	26.7	28.4	13.4	13.4	8.8	11.5	10.9	11.7
Leather products	3.8	4.3	3.8	2.8	2.7	3.9	0.6	0.3	0.4	0.2	0.3	0.7
Stone, clay and glass products	6.4	10.7	12.3	16.0	16.8	14.3	3.6	4.3	6.5	8.9	10.7	8.1
Primary metals	8.1	13.2	13.0	25.6	30.8	29.4	2.0	2.3	3.2	5.1	3.9	4.4
Fabricated metal products	16.5	14.2	21.1	25.4	27.5	64.3	3.8	6.3	6.6	8.2	8.6	35.7
Industrial machinery and computers	180.6	229.5	233.7	240.8	276.0	300.7	25.6	41.1	48.9	55.7	56.2	43.4
Electric and electronic equipment	101.4	114.9	118.8	120.2	182.4	203.4	19.4	25.1	23.8	27.0	60.8	59.8
Transportation equipment	339.8	302.4	316.3	381.8	457.1	432.8	117.7	113.7	92.9	111.1	172.2	194.4
Scientific and measuring instruments	91.0	98.6	118.6	146.3	195.1	178.8	18.7	14.5	16.8	17.7	16.3	21.3
Miscellaneous manufactures	33.6	38.9	31.5	37.3	37.1	32.2	11.8	14.8	10.7	18.7	20.1	16.2
Unidentified manufactures	1.6	1.6	1.4	2.1	4.1	5.2	0.5	0.4	0.3	0.8	1.2	1.0
Agricultural And Livestock Products	67.1	95.8	61.3	51.5	35.3	36.5	3.6	12.6	6.7	3.4	1.4	...
Agricultural products	67.0	95.6	61.1	51.3	33.3	35.1	3.6	12.5	6.6	3.3	1.3	...
Livestock and livestock products	0.1	0.2	0.2	0.2	2.0	1.4	0.1	0.1	0.1	0.1	0.1	...
Other Commodities	28.9	22.6	35.3	66.0	62.7	33.8	1.5	2.2	4.1	25.5	33.2	10.0
Forestry products	1.1	0.4	0.4	...	...	...	...	...	...	...	...	...
Fish and other marine products	0.1	0.1	0.1	...	0.1	0.1	...	0.1	...	...	...	...
Metallic ores and concentrates	0.1	3.9	15.2	15.1	17.6	7.0	...	...	0.2	0.1	0.5	0.7
Bituminous coal and lignite	2.2	...	6.7	23.3	28.7	7.4	...	...	...	17.8	28.7	7.4
Crude petroleum and natural gas	...	...	0.3	...	...	...	...	...	0.3	...	...	...
Nonmetallic minerals	1.9	1.5	1.6	1.8	1.3	0.9	0.9	0.8	0.8	0.7	0.1	0.1
Scrap and waste	5.9	5.8	3.1	4.8	3.5	3.6	0.1	0.2	0.3	0.4	...	0.1
Used merchandise	16.4	2.6	1.2	1.1	0.8	4.5	0.2	0.6	0.4	0.3	0.2	0.8
Goods imported and returned unchanged	...	...	...	...	...	...	...	...	...	...	...	...
Special classification provisions	1.3	8.3	6.7	19.8	10.7	10.4	0.3	0.5	2.0	6.2	3.8	1.0

Table D-46. TENNESSEE: State Exports of Goods by Destination and Industry, 1994–1999—*Continued*

(Millions of dollars.)

Industry	Germany						France					
	1994	1995	1996	1997	1998	1999	1994	1995	1996	1997	1998	1999
ALL GOODS	334.8	323.5	371.8	403.1	366.7	377.5	209.7	202.3	240.5	283.6	298.9	246.9
Manufactured Goods	328.3	315.1	365.9	396.0	364.0	375.2	204.4	198.6	236.1	280.3	290.5	238.4
Food products	0.3	0.4	0.2	0.2	0.1	...	1.6	0.8	0.1	0.1	0.5	0.3
Tobacco products	...	...	...	...	...	...	...	...	...	...	1.0	...
Textile mill products	1.7	1.7	2.7	2.4	1.2	3.7	1.2	1.3	5.0	4.1	1.8	1.6
Apparel	2.6	3.6	4.2	3.7	0.6	1.3	1.0	0.4	0.2	0.8	1.1	0.9
Lumber and wood products	9.2	10.6	6.5	5.8	5.3	2.8	3.5	3.9	5.1	2.4	2.2	2.4
Furniture and fixtures	0.8	0.7	0.8	0.7	1.7	0.4	0.1	0.1	...	0.2	0.2	0.2
Paper products	34.8	31.7	43.8	51.3	48.8	44.7	17.3	18.6	36.5	55.8	34.3	29.2
Printing and publishing	1.0	0.9	1.5	1.6	3.3	6.8	1.1	1.3	0.9	1.7	2.8	3.0
Chemical products	58.9	68.3	65.7	82.2	81.5	83.5	18.1	19.7	22.1	22.8	22.5	17.9
Refined petroleum products	0.1	...	...	...	...	...	...	...	...	0.9	...	...
Rubber and plastic products	4.3	3.3	2.4	4.1	4.4	3.3	0.7	0.9	1.7	1.7	6.0	4.3
Leather products	1.9	1.5	1.7	1.6	1.2	0.8	0.3	1.0	0.7	0.1	0.2	0.1
Stone, clay and glass products	1.1	2.3	2.4	3.0	1.9	3.0	0.2	1.3	0.7	0.5	0.5	0.6
Primary metals	3.5	6.0	6.4	9.4	8.6	4.6	0.3	0.2	0.2	0.5	2.2	3.3
Fabricated metal products	4.9	1.0	4.1	2.4	4.9	3.5	0.6	1.5	1.8	2.2	2.3	4.6
Industrial machinery and computers	37.3	50.7	52.5	63.4	51.9	66.2	48.9	50.4	42.7	30.8	29.0	32.3
Electric and electronic equipment	29.2	35.2	31.0	32.8	28.2	34.6	19.9	15.3	17.8	12.4	19.2	20.3
Transportation equipment	113.3	79.1	124.1	115.6	90.2	86.9	65.3	48.2	43.0	80.8	111.3	54.1
Scientific and measuring instruments	16.6	11.5	11.0	11.1	24.9	23.7	20.5	30.6	52.3	58.5	51.0	59.5
Miscellaneous manufactures	6.7	6.1	4.6	4.0	4.7	4.4	3.6	3.1	5.1	3.9	1.8	3.3
Unidentified manufactures	0.4	0.4	0.3	0.4	0.6	1.2	0.2	0.1	0.2	0.3	0.5	0.6
Agricultural And Livestock Products	4.8	5.9	4.3	1.6	0.3	0.3	2.4	2.8	3.1	1.2	6.6	4.1
Agricultural products	4.8	5.8	4.2	1.5	0.1	0.2	2.4	2.8	3.1	1.2	6.5	2.8
Livestock and livestock products	...	0.1	0.1	0.1	0.2	0.1	...	...	...	...	0.1	1.3
Other Commodities	1.6	2.5	1.7	5.6	2.4	2.1	2.9	0.9	1.3	2.1	1.8	4.4
Forestry products	1.1	0.2	...	...	...	...	...	...	...	...	...	...
Fish and other marine products	...	...	...	...	...	...	...	...	...	...	...	0.1
Metallic ores and concentrates	...	...	0.5	1.1	...	0.1	...	...	...	...	...	...
Bituminous coal and lignite	...	...	...	...	...	...	2.2	...	...	...	...	...
Crude petroleum and natural gas	...	...	...	...	...	...	...	...	...	...	...	...
Nonmetallic minerals	0.3	0.2	0.3	0.3	0.5	0.1	...	...	0.1	0.1	...	...
Scrap and waste	...	...	...	...	...	...	...	...	0.2	...	...	...
Used merchandise	0.1	0.5	...	0.1	...	0.3	...	...	...	...	0.4	2.3
Goods imported and returned unchanged	...	...	...	...	...	...	...	...	...	...	...	...
Special classification provisions	0.1	1.5	0.8	4.0	1.9	1.5	0.7	0.9	1.0	2.0	1.3	2.0

Industry	The Netherlands						Asian 10					
	1994	1995	1996	1997	1998	1999	1994	1995	1996	1997	1998	1999
ALL GOODS	372.8	413.1	343.1	385.7	417.0	430.2	1 949.4	2 984.1	2 693.9	2 247.4	1 744.3	1 561.2
Manufactured Goods	352.9	397.6	326.1	361.9	402.0	407.8	1 114.0	1 367.0	1 465.4	1 577.3	1 368.0	1 334.1
Food products	2.6	1.2	1.6	3.4	1.9	0.5	17.8	37.5	46.5	35.7	19.9	18.6
Tobacco products	...	...	...	...	...	...	...	...	...	...	...	...
Textile mill products	2.5	3.3	2.1	2.0	2.3	2.6	10.3	16.5	18.3	19.0	19.5	16.1
Apparel	0.6	1.7	2.1	2.2	1.8	4.6	30.1	15.9	14.6	13.3	21.9	11.5
Lumber and wood products	2.8	2.2	1.9	1.3	1.2	1.5	22.9	23.8	18.4	13.9	7.6	9.1
Furniture and fixtures	0.7	0.6	0.7	0.4	0.6	0.5	3.5	5.3	3.4	4.0	3.8	1.7
Paper products	63.7	87.6	60.4	56.5	69.9	74.6	217.6	278.1	214.7	234.7	211.0	205.6
Printing and publishing	0.6	0.9	0.1	0.3	0.2	0.2	1.5	3.4	2.5	5.3	5.5	7.2
Chemical products	221.0	228.3	205.2	222.0	225.9	228.3	392.9	409.0	380.2	426.5	348.7	319.6
Refined petroleum products	...	...	...	0.1	...	...	0.1	0.6	0.1	0.1	1.4	0.6
Rubber and plastic products	0.6	1.0	0.7	1.0	2.0	1.5	48.4	53.5	64.3	55.5	28.7	15.2
Leather products	0.1	0.1	0.2	0.2	0.2	0.6	3.4	2.7	3.6	3.6	4.3	2.7
Stone, clay and glass products	0.4	0.1	0.2	0.2	0.2	0.5	5.9	11.8	10.4	19.0	20.6	23.5
Primary metals	0.1	0.5	0.5	0.8	1.0	0.6	5.4	13.8	15.6	17.4	23.3	10.1
Fabricated metal products	1.1	0.7	1.0	4.3	0.9	0.5	17.8	26.9	37.9	35.6	28.8	43.6
Industrial machinery and computers	15.0	13.8	13.4	16.1	21.0	44.8	107.7	166.8	262.2	176.6	117.5	147.9
Electric and electronic equipment	6.8	7.6	9.1	12.4	23.6	21.3	51.1	78.8	105.7	129.6	131.2	138.7
Transportation equipment	11.6	12.8	6.2	5.2	5.3	5.9	108.1	145.7	171.2	270.5	251.9	251.3
Scientific and measuring instruments	19.4	26.5	17.3	32.1	42.5	17.8	48.7	55.5	75.3	91.3	103.8	88.6
Miscellaneous manufactures	3.3	8.6	3.2	1.3	1.1	1.3	19.3	20.5	19.3	24.7	16.0	17.7
Unidentified manufactures	0.1	0.2	0.2	0.2	0.4	0.3	1.2	1.0	1.1	0.9	2.5	5.0
Agricultural And Livestock Products	19.9	15.0	15.9	20.9	13.3	22.1	720.8	1 529.6	1 162.4	560.6	328.1	191.7
Agricultural products	19.9	15.0	15.9	20.9	12.2	22.1	720.8	1 529.6	1 161.1	560.6	327.3	191.2
Livestock and livestock products	...	...	...	...	1.1	...	...	...	1.2	...	0.8	0.5
Other Commodities	...	0.4	1.2	2.9	1.7	0.4	114.6	87.6	66.2	109.5	48.3	35.4
Forestry products	...	0.1	...	...	...	...	0.2	0.1	1.2	0.3	0.3	0.4
Fish and other marine products	...	...	...	...	...	...	21.1	28.4	24.6	9.8	2.9	3.0
Metallic ores and concentrates	...	...	...	...	...	...	...	0.1	...	...	...	...
Bituminous coal and lignite	...	...	...	...	...	...	90.8	51.0	35.9	44.0	39.3	26.3
Crude petroleum and natural gas	...	...	...	...	...	...	...	...	...	...	...	0.2
Nonmetallic minerals	...	...	...	...	0.1	...	1.8	2.8	2.0	1.7	1.3	1.3
Scrap and waste	...	...	...	...	...	...	0.3	1.0	0.9	1.8	1.9	2.1
Used merchandise	...	...	0.1	...	...	0.1	0.4	3.9	0.1	50.4	0.1	0.3
Goods imported and returned unchanged	...	...	...	...	...	...	...	...	...	...	...	...
Special classification provisions	...	0.2	1.1	2.9	1.6	0.2	0.1	0.2	1.5	1.4	2.6	1.8

Table D-46. TENNESSEE: State Exports of Goods by Destination and Industry, 1994–1999—*Continued*

(Millions of dollars.)

Industry	Japan						South Korea					
	1994	1995	1996	1997	1998	1999	1994	1995	1996	1997	1998	1999
ALL GOODS	563.3	674.3	727.7	692.8	614.7	555.0	230.4	284.4	320.6	279.2	187.6	157.0
Manufactured Goods	478.2	566.4	645.0	625.2	541.1	500.5	175.9	206.2	199.5	236.5	136.1	124.1
Food products	11.6	18.1	18.0	16.7	11.0	13.9	0.6	3.6	3.4	2.7	3.0	0.4
Tobacco products	...	...	...	...	...	...	...	...	...	...	...	...
Textile mill products	3.5	7.9	4.3	2.0	1.4	1.1	2.2	2.1	4.0	5.6	4.1	4.8
Apparel	29.3	14.4	12.1	11.2	15.0	9.8	...	0.1	0.7	0.8	4.9	0.3
Lumber and wood products	9.7	12.7	10.5	8.4	4.4	6.2	8.0	5.4	3.2	2.3	0.9	...
Furniture and fixtures	1.2	1.0	1.3	1.5	1.1	0.7	0.3	0.6	0.4	0.4	0.1	...
Paper products	112.9	184.0	118.4	119.6	103.7	109.4	39.5	40.8	43.5	53.9	38.6	28.4
Printing and publishing	0.2	0.3	0.3	0.7	1.4	1.2	0.1	0.3	0.1	0.4	0.1	0.2
Chemical products	118.5	77.7	83.8	75.9	53.7	59.4	65.9	54.5	28.4	68.9	44.3	50.2
Refined petroleum products	0.1	0.5	0.1	...	0.7	0.4	...	...	...	0.1	0.3	...
Rubber and plastic products	44.0	44.2	55.7	44.8	22.3	10.0	1.2	2.2	3.8	4.7	1.2	1.4
Leather products	0.7	0.7	0.7	0.5	0.7	0.5	0.2	0.1	...	...	0.1	0.1
Stone, clay and glass products	5.1	5.6	4.9	16.4	18.4	21.2	0.2	4.3	4.0	0.4	0.2	0.1
Primary metals	0.8	3.5	5.6	5.2	4.0	3.1	1.2	1.0	1.2	1.8	8.1	2.9
Fabricated metal products	7.0	8.1	6.7	6.8	8.6	9.6	0.9	3.6	4.1	3.1	1.2	1.2
Industrial machinery and computers	53.7	80.9	167.0	80.1	33.0	40.0	10.9	13.5	31.4	31.2	5.6	5.7
Electric and electronic equipment	13.9	24.2	24.6	21.5	28.7	19.8	1.6	4.8	18.9	16.8	4.5	7.4
Transportation equipment	22.4	30.8	70.8	139.9	158.6	125.8	36.2	62.4	41.7	32.4	0.6	9.0
Scientific and measuring instruments	28.7	36.8	48.0	56.9	61.4	52.1	6.3	6.6	9.8	10.4	10.2	11.3
Miscellaneous manufactures	13.4	14.6	11.7	16.6	12.2	13.2	0.7	0.6	0.7	0.7	0.1	0.2
Unidentified manufactures	0.5	0.4	0.6	0.4	0.8	3.1	0.1	0.1	0.1	0.1	0.2	0.4
Agricultural And Livestock Products	62.4	75.3	56.8	52.6	65.0	45.1	53.9	77.6	120.7	42.6	51.2	32.3
Agricultural products	62.3	75.3	56.7	52.5	65.0	45.1	53.9	77.6	119.6	42.6	51.2	32.3
Livestock and livestock products	...	...	0.2	...	...	...	...	...	1.0	...	...	...
Other Commodities	22.7	32.5	26.0	15.0	8.6	9.4	0.5	0.6	0.4	0.2	0.3	0.6
Forestry products	...	...	0.1	...	...	...	...	...	...	...	0.1	0.4
Fish and other marine products	20.6	27.8	24.1	9.6	2.5	2.8	0.2	0.1	...	...	...	...
Metallic ores and concentrates	...	0.1	...	...	...	...	...	...	...	...	...	...
Bituminous coal and lignite	1.1	...	0.5	3.8	3.7	3.7	...	...	...	...	...	...
Crude petroleum and natural gas	...	...	...	...	...	0.2	...	...	...	...	...	...
Nonmetallic minerals	0.4	0.5	0.3	0.1	...	...	0.3	0.5	0.3	0.1	...	0.1
Scrap and waste	0.3	0.2	0.5	0.9	1.7	2.0	...	...	...	...	0.1	...
Used merchandise	0.3	3.8	0.1	0.1	...	0.2	...	...	...	...	...	...
Goods imported and returned unchanged	...	...	...	...	...	...	...	...	...	...	...	...
Special classification provisions	...	0.1	0.4	0.6	0.7	0.5	...	...	0.1	...	0.1	0.1

Industry	Taiwan						Singapore					
	1994	1995	1996	1997	1998	1999	1994	1995	1996	1997	1998	1999
ALL GOODS	249.4	213.1	176.6	226.2	200.7	202.9	87.0	85.1	83.2	165.7	152.2	170.1
Manufactured Goods	119.4	111.6	108.8	123.6	121.0	128.1	86.0	82.7	81.6	164.2	150.6	168.9
Food products	1.3	1.9	1.1	0.6	0.4	0.5	0.1	0.3	0.3	0.7	0.6	0.1
Tobacco products	...	...	...	...	...	...	...	...	...	...	...	...
Textile mill products	2.1	2.7	5.5	4.4	3.7	3.8	0.2	0.6	1.2	1.1	1.0	1.2
Apparel	0.1	0.4	0.2	0.2	0.5	0.2	0.4	0.5	0.8	0.3	0.4	0.4
Lumber and wood products	1.4	0.5	0.5	0.2	0.3	0.1	0.2	0.8	0.6	0.5	0.1	0.5
Furniture and fixtures	0.3	...	...	0.2	...	0.2	0.5	1.9	0.4	0.5	0.2	0.1
Paper products	19.0	17.0	11.4	20.5	24.5	16.3	3.4	2.7	2.5	2.8	2.4	4.8
Printing and publishing	0.2	0.5	0.5	1.3	1.2	1.3	0.4	1.5	0.9	0.6	0.5	2.1
Chemical products	37.3	31.1	30.1	28.6	29.8	22.9	34.5	26.5	14.2	57.4	48.9	44.2
Refined petroleum products	...	...	...	...	...	0.1	...	...	...	...	...	...
Rubber and plastic products	0.4	0.3	0.2	0.4	0.4	0.9	1.1	1.2	1.5	1.8	1.3	0.6
Leather products	0.1	...	0.1	0.4	...	...	0.2	0.3	0.1	0.2	0.1	0.2
Stone, clay and glass products	0.2	0.4	0.3	1.3	0.2	0.3	...	0.2	0.2	0.1	0.1	0.1
Primary metals	2.1	2.2	1.2	1.2	2.5	1.8	0.5	0.9	0.8	0.6	0.1	0.1
Fabricated metal products	0.5	2.2	8.0	8.6	8.0	8.6	1.2	1.8	2.1	2.5	1.3	0.7
Industrial machinery and computers	8.2	9.2	11.9	13.2	7.3	8.6	11.5	12.4	15.0	12.7	38.8	54.9
Electric and electronic equipment	6.8	11.0	16.8	24.0	21.3	22.4	15.7	14.2	15.0	19.5	12.7	14.2
Transportation equipment	33.5	27.7	14.0	9.3	11.6	33.1	10.6	11.5	21.1	57.6	36.3	38.8
Scientific and measuring instruments	4.2	3.9	5.7	7.5	8.0	6.3	4.2	3.2	3.6	4.4	5.4	5.4
Miscellaneous manufactures	1.6	0.4	1.2	1.5	0.7	0.5	1.2	2.0	1.3	0.7	0.2	0.5
Unidentified manufactures	0.2	0.1	0.1	0.1	0.3	0.2	0.2	0.1	0.2	0.1	0.2	0.2
Agricultural And Livestock Products	40.0	50.0	31.7	62.0	43.3	51.7	0.2	0.8	0.2	...	...	...
Agricultural products	40.0	50.0	31.7	62.0	43.3	51.7	0.2	0.8	0.2	...	...	...
Livestock and livestock products	...	...	...	...	...	...	...	...	...	...	...	...
Other Commodities	90.0	51.5	36.0	40.6	36.4	23.1	0.9	1.6	1.4	1.5	1.5	1.2
Forestry products	...	0.1	0.1	0.1	0.1	0.1	...	...	...	...	...	...
Fish and other marine products	...	...	...	...	...	...	...	...	...	...	...	...
Metallic ores and concentrates	...	...	...	...	...	...	...	...	...	...	...	...
Bituminous coal and lignite	89.7	51.0	35.4	40.1	35.6	22.5	...	...	...	...	...	...
Crude petroleum and natural gas	...	...	...	...	...	...	...	...	...	...	...	...
Nonmetallic minerals	0.2	0.3	0.3	0.3	0.3	0.2	0.8	1.5	1.1	1.2	0.8	0.7
Scrap and waste	...	...	...	...	...	...	...	...	...	...	...	...
Used merchandise	...	...	...	...	...	...	...	...	...	...	...	...
Goods imported and returned unchanged	...	...	...	...	...	...	...	...	...	...	...	...
Special classification provisions	...	...	0.2	0.1	0.3	0.2	...	0.1	0.3	0.3	0.7	0.5

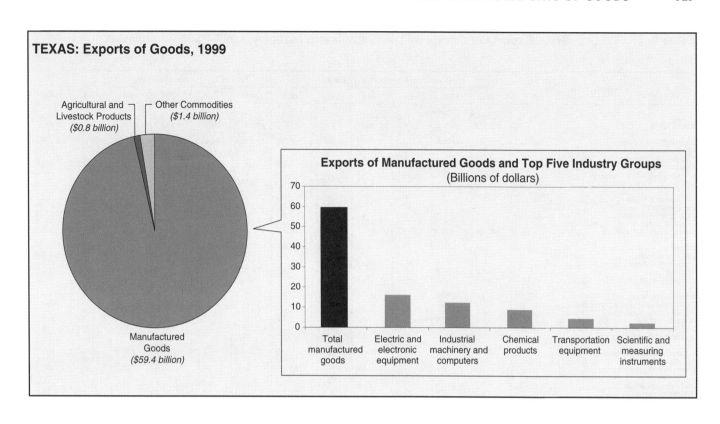

TEXAS: Exports of Goods, 1999

Agricultural and Livestock Products ($0.8 billion)

Other Commodities ($1.4 billion)

Manufactured Goods ($59.4 billion)

Exports of Manufactured Goods and Top Five Industry Groups
(Billions of dollars)

Total manufactured goods / Electric and electronic equipment / Industrial machinery and computers / Chemical products / Transportation equipment / Scientific and measuring instruments

Table D-47. TEXAS: State Exports of Goods by Destination and Industry, 1994–1999

(Millions of dollars.)

Industry	All destinations						Canada					
	1994	1995	1996	1997	1998	1999	1994	1995	1996	1997	1998	1999
ALL GOODS	40 489.0	45 192.6	48 252.1	56 292.9	59 029.3	61 705.6	4 830.4	6 142.0	6 616.4	8 117.6	8 505.9	9 295.9
Manufactured Goods	38 295.3	42 779.2	45 988.3	53 805.8	56 686.1	59 440.2	4 563.3	5 849.2	6 250.4	7 705.2	8 159.9	8 884.9
Food products	1 466.8	1 257.3	1 396.0	1 518.9	1 709.7	1 594.5	83.5	93.1	90.8	91.4	105.6	97.6
Tobacco products	36.6	19.4	33.1	19.6	7.0	6.5	. . .	. . .	. . .	. . .	. . .	. . .
Textile mill products	409.9	433.2	487.5	537.5	763.9	1 053.8	8.2	7.5	9.0	13.4	13.6	18.7
Apparel	1 005.1	957.5	1 009.1	1 075.2	1 185.7	1 057.9	75.7	98.9	85.5	106.4	100.1	117.4
Lumber and wood products	223.3	165.5	153.8	181.1	156.4	137.3	8.6	8.1	7.8	9.3	13.3	14.2
Furniture and fixtures	308.8	278.8	391.9	524.8	622.8	113.7	103.7	106.8	66.5	100.8	77.6	18.9
Paper products	713.6	724.7	695.8	824.7	887.7	959.2	33.6	49.8	54.1	75.0	83.8	92.3
Printing and publishing	129.2	126.2	142.6	145.1	153.2	177.0	25.7	33.0	32.0	30.8	25.0	18.5
Chemical products	7 105.3	8 993.6	7 916.3	8 390.0	7 740.8	8 879.8	971.5	1 029.9	1 114.3	1 279.7	1 318.1	1 452.6
Refined petroleum products	1 677.1	2 052.3	2 364.9	2 683.8	2 315.3	2 376.3	125.1	151.6	181.9	226.7	256.5	171.4
Rubber and plastic products	811.2	769.6	1 084.9	1 480.4	1 838.6	2 062.4	71.6	84.2	104.6	151.5	168.1	178.5
Leather products	93.5	103.9	105.1	141.7	145.3	350.8	8.3	7.9	11.0	15.9	13.0	8.8
Stone, clay and glass products	288.8	304.2	315.4	340.7	418.3	490.2	50.7	56.4	58.4	61.2	67.8	74.2
Primary metals	1 118.3	1 476.5	1 811.6	2 067.4	2 082.7	1 810.3	163.2	191.9	201.9	270.0	223.7	222.9
Fabricated metal products	1 194.1	1 180.4	1 745.7	1 686.0	1 855.1	2 162.4	218.4	225.3	276.1	339.8	369.2	461.6
Industrial machinery and computers	8 631.6	9 287.7	10 194.4	11 882.9	13 285.7	12 329.0	1 034.7	1 354.1	1 522.5	1 835.7	2 110.6	2 217.8
Electric and electronic equipment	7 888.8	10 036.1	10 661.3	13 566.2	14 056.5	16 070.2	845.2	1 470.7	1 543.9	2 055.0	2 029.9	2 337.9
Transportation equipment	3 186.7	2 510.4	3 039.5	3 918.0	4 255.8	4 670.0	425.0	443.0	509.3	585.5	710.8	916.0
Scientific and measuring instruments	1 594.1	1 742.5	2 026.2	2 396.4	2 597.1	2 428.2	252.1	364.4	310.7	374.4	383.0	364.6
Miscellaneous manufactures	300.7	248.5	311.0	309.8	357.5	370.8	37.5	50.2	44.9	53.0	57.4	63.6
Unidentified manufactures	111.4	110.8	102.1	115.8	251.1	340.0	21.0	22.7	25.3	29.8	32.9	37.3
Agricultural And Livestock Products	1 015.0	1 143.0	1 025.8	1 123.0	1 164.4	785.2	52.0	72.1	68.8	78.3	84.3	82.0
Agricultural products	923.2	1 106.6	956.9	969.6	1 055.1	704.5	50.4	68.1	66.4	76.6	82.9	80.9
Livestock and livestock products	91.8	36.4	68.9	153.4	109.3	80.8	1.6	4.0	2.4	1.7	1.4	1.1
Other Commodities	1 178.7	1 270.5	1 238.0	1 364.2	1 178.7	1 480.1	215.1	220.7	297.2	334.1	261.7	328.9
Forestry products	21.1	26.0	26.9	26.8	23.9	22.3	0.6	0.6	0.8	1.4	0.7	1.5
Fish and other marine products	33.6	27.3	27.4	25.7	26.3	23.3	1.2	0.4	0.9	0.7	0.3	0.3
Metallic ores and concentrates	92.0	104.2	105.9	75.4	64.2	17.8	81.3	86.3	97.8	68.2	51.3	5.7
Bituminous coal and lignite	0.9	6.2	5.1	18.0	17.8	3.6	. . .	. . .	0.6	. . .	. . .	. . .
Crude petroleum and natural gas	171.7	291.0	271.5	323.0	243.4	456.6	12.1	6.7	45.6	89.5	60.1	161.0
Nonmetallic minerals	69.7	86.7	73.1	82.8	84.3	71.4	4.9	4.7	4.1	3.7	4.3	4.4
Scrap and waste	238.3	365.1	238.2	306.4	227.7	234.7	8.0	9.2	10.1	14.0	9.6	13.1
Used merchandise	127.6	87.3	87.0	109.5	119.6	114.7	9.4	8.3	10.9	11.3	11.1	7.1
Goods imported and returned unchanged	77.0	82.9	104.7	129.5	106.5	97.2	77.0	82.9	104.7	129.5	106.5	97.2
Special classification provisions	346.7	193.8	298.2	267.2	265.0	438.6	20.5	21.6	21.5	15.8	17.9	38.6

Table D-47. TEXAS: State Exports of Goods by Destination and Industry, 1994–1999—Continued

(Millions of dollars.)

Industry	South and Central American and Caribbean						Mexico					
	1994	1995	1996	1997	1998	1999	1994	1995	1996	1997	1998	1999
ALL GOODS	3 976.2	5 073.2	5 180.2	6 402.8	6 180.0	5 846.5	14 364.9	12 589.0	15 586.7	18 864.1	21 626.6	23 329.6
Manufactured Goods	3 862.4	4 884.1	5 032.0	6 223.1	6 029.6	5 729.3	13 275.9	11 563.2	14 547.8	17 727.9	20 489.7	22 299.9
Food products	78.7	131.7	125.4	100.4	144.7	109.8	861.1	566.0	701.4	899.6	1 017.6	976.0
Tobacco products	. . .	. . .	0.3	0.1	. . .		36.6	19.3	32.7	18.8	6.4	5.3
Textile mill products	7.2	12.6	10.2	14.2	14.1	19.4	360.4	368.6	420.9	465.3	697.9	985.7
Apparel	124.8	97.8	80.6	91.0	80.6	89.3	766.6	717.0	786.8	814.1	940.9	795.9
Lumber and wood products	4.5	3.4	4.1	8.6	9.9	12.4	120.9	48.2	41.8	50.4	66.4	62.7
Furniture and fixtures	6.1	7.4	8.4	10.0	15.7	8.9	166.7	133.7	276.4	372.3	465.6	33.7
Paper products	6.8	7.5	10.1	16.4	12.2	8.3	619.2	617.2	602.8	701.8	762.8	818.6
Printing and publishing	4.0	5.6	8.0	6.3	5.7	8.9	69.8	48.1	57.2	62.4	75.3	100.0
Chemical products	1 025.5	1 326.5	1 172.1	1 239.6	1 182.5	1 187.1	1 276.5	1 377.0	1 511.1	1 739.7	1 879.1	1 929.3
Refined petroleum products	363.8	466.0	635.1	841.8	558.5	433.4	371.1	489.8	590.2	942.8	965.4	1 266.2
Rubber and plastic products	28.8	50.6	40.3	46.6	53.3	58.7	566.4	491.7	785.9	1 119.1	1 449.9	1 612.2
Leather products	2.0	5.1	4.7	2.7	2.7	2.7	68.1	69.6	69.3	97.9	110.0	319.6
Stone, clay and glass products	31.0	41.6	54.3	52.9	49.0	36.1	131.1	111.3	108.4	109.2	151.6	222.4
Primary metals	112.8	137.3	135.4	171.3	146.8	88.8	632.7	763.0	1 067.5	1 229.5	1 366.6	1 263.6
Fabricated metal products	95.9	89.9	89.9	184.4	132.2	132.3	582.1	509.1	898.7	646.8	827.7	1 062.7
Industrial machinery and computers	1 413.7	1 906.3	1 960.0	2 304.0	2 467.8	1 956.7	1 735.3	1 035.5	1 303.9	1 867.3	2 409.4	2 962.0
Electric and electronic equipment	170.9	304.9	394.9	639.8	729.1	886.9	3 038.2	3 158.8	3 699.2	4 508.2	4 869.6	5 460.1
Transportation equipment	295.5	167.8	166.7	338.3	257.4	559.2	1 308.3	663.9	1 085.6	1 413.1	1 524.4	1 434.8
Scientific and measuring instruments	70.4	92.1	112.4	128.2	138.7	104.8	350.4	245.1	352.8	482.9	565.0	578.7
Miscellaneous manufactures	8.4	11.0	11.6	18.3	12.3	12.5	162.1	90.6	120.3	133.9	186.1	174.6
Unidentified manufactures	11.6	19.1	7.6	8.2	16.2	13.0	52.0	39.8	35.0	52.8	152.0	235.9
Agricultural And Livestock Products	46.6	81.2	55.0	100.9	81.4	20.3	607.6	429.5	576.4	584.3	684.7	480.7
Agricultural products	42.8	78.3	52.6	97.5	78.4	18.0	548.3	419.0	524.9	447.1	589.9	423.6
Livestock and livestock products	3.9	2.9	2.4	3.4	3.0	2.3	59.3	10.5	51.5	137.2	94.8	57.1
Other Commodities	67.2	107.8	93.2	78.8	69.0	97.0	481.4	596.3	462.4	551.9	452.2	549.0
Forestry products	1.3	0.7	2.3	2.8	1.3	1.4	11.3	16.3	18.2	17.5	16.3	14.2
Fish and other marine products	0.2	0.2	0.1	0.3	0.4	1.3	31.2	24.0	24.2	22.1	24.2	20.8
Metallic ores and concentrates	. . .	0.2	0.2	0.7	0.6	0.5	6.1	5.1	5.0	5.4	5.7	4.3
Bituminous coal and lignite	0.1	0.3	1.2	11.7	6.5	0.6	0.6	5.8	2.7	3.0	2.0	2.8
Crude petroleum and natural gas	26.4	60.2	25.9	18.9	23.4	46.2	120.7	216.5	185.8	177.2	131.3	214.0
Nonmetallic minerals	12.2	23.1	18.4	21.6	13.9	11.1	27.2	30.8	27.2	27.0	39.4	27.7
Scrap and waste	4.3	12.7	25.7	3.8	0.9	2.9	167.5	240.8	133.4	223.6	161.5	134.1
Used merchandise	7.1	8.4	13.0	15.0	16.3	12.5	56.5	19.2	20.8	27.8	39.7	53.6
Goods imported and returned unchanged	. . .	. . .	. . .	. . .	. . .		. . .	. . .	. . .	. . .	. . .	
Special classification provisions	15.5	2.0	6.4	4.1	5.7	20.5	60.3	37.8	45.3	48.3	32.0	77.6

Industry	European Union						United Kingdom					
	1994	1995	1996	1997	1998	1999	1994	1995	1996	1997	1998	1999
ALL GOODS	4 957.7	5 803.7	5 419.8	6 162.9	7 118.6	6 723.6	1 674.6	1 915.5	1 717.1	1 979.3	2 236.7	1 672.9
Manufactured Goods	4 833.7	5 662.6	5 285.9	6 033.2	6 984.9	6 581.2	1 623.2	1 876.8	1 683.8	1 954.0	2 209.5	1 631.9
Food products	128.0	124.6	123.0	97.1	115.9	71.0	10.6	8.8	16.5	14.9	17.4	9.7
Tobacco products	. . .	. . .	. . .	. . .	. . .	0.6	. . .	. . .	. . .	. . .	. . .	. . .
Textile mill products	8.3	9.7	8.2	9.1	10.2	9.3	2.6	2.0	2.3	2.1	1.8	2.7
Apparel	15.2	19.7	27.1	32.3	33.1	30.5	3.6	2.9	4.3	4.2	3.5	3.9
Lumber and wood products	63.2	73.6	54.0	72.0	30.1	12.1	18.5	15.6	19.4	18.7	6.4	1.6
Furniture and fixtures	11.2	8.0	14.6	15.3	31.6	20.7	4.5	3.3	8.4	1.9	1.9	1.8
Paper products	24.8	19.3	9.9	9.8	7.5	10.9	1.3	1.1	0.9	1.4	2.2	2.7
Printing and publishing	10.4	14.4	20.6	17.2	20.5	18.4	5.0	4.8	7.0	7.5	8.2	8.4
Chemical products	1 093.0	1 427.1	989.8	1 076.2	1 292.1	1 505.3	143.3	182.7	114.9	138.0	162.7	185.3
Refined petroleum products	222.6	242.9	329.7	301.7	214.2	198.8	17.4	11.9	10.4	18.0	17.1	16.8
Rubber and plastic products	51.4	57.6	43.2	54.8	62.7	89.3	6.0	9.6	11.1	18.9	16.6	22.6
Leather products	6.6	9.7	8.0	10.6	8.0	8.4	0.9	1.5	1.2	3.5	1.1	3.1
Stone, clay and glass products	22.5	23.8	24.2	27.2	44.3	55.7	4.1	3.4	5.0	5.0	7.9	7.9
Primary metals	64.4	98.4	83.3	102.2	87.3	56.0	11.0	19.9	24.7	31.8	24.3	12.8
Fabricated metal products	56.4	97.1	102.5	124.8	129.8	124.7	17.6	48.4	55.8	64.2	55.9	50.2
Industrial machinery and computers	1 486.7	1 730.9	1 606.8	1 816.1	1 980.9	1 820.1	680.5	927.8	806.2	889.9	921.8	591.7
Electric and electronic equipment	931.1	986.2	910.3	1 166.7	1 377.6	1 148.6	515.0	441.5	373.8	452.4	455.7	326.5
Transportation equipment	308.3	326.0	405.1	532.6	887.7	820.9	75.8	66.7	77.1	136.2	319.7	226.1
Scientific and measuring instruments	292.1	352.4	478.5	517.2	586.8	514.3	95.2	110.4	130.1	129.0	164.9	139.6
Miscellaneous manufactures	27.7	29.8	38.6	43.5	50.4	49.3	7.3	11.0	11.8	14.5	17.2	13.6
Unidentified manufactures	10.0	11.6	8.5	6.8	14.3	16.3	2.8	3.5	3.0	1.9	3.3	4.8
Agricultural And Livestock Products	48.8	57.1	45.4	35.5	38.3	48.6	19.7	13.1	7.0	4.8	5.5	11.6
Agricultural products	27.7	42.1	39.6	30.3	32.9	39.6	1.9	2.4	3.2	1.3	1.2	5.4
Livestock and livestock products	21.0	15.0	5.8	5.2	5.3	9.0	17.7	10.7	3.7	3.4	4.3	6.2
Other Commodities	75.2	84.0	88.4	94.2	95.5	93.9	31.7	25.7	26.3	20.6	21.7	29.4
Forestry products	3.8	3.9	3.2	2.2	1.5	2.2	0.4	0.5	0.5	1.6	0.5	0.5
Fish and other marine products	0.2	0.1	0.1	0.3	0.1	0.2	. . .	. . .	. . .	. . .	. . .	. . .
Metallic ores and concentrates	3.7	9.7	1.7	0.8	2.8	2.4	0.4	0.5	0.1	0.2	0.5	0.1
Bituminous coal and lignite	. . .	. . .	0.4	1.3	1.9		. . .	. . .	. . .	. . .	. . .	
Crude petroleum and natural gas	6.5	4.9	0.1	10.2	7.7	3.0	6.4	. . .	. . .	0.1	1.8	0.2
Nonmetallic minerals	7.7	8.0	7.4	8.3	7.3	9.9	2.9	3.4	3.9	4.3	3.5	5.0
Scrap and waste	12.8	21.8	23.7	23.7	23.8	10.9	0.9	2.3	3.5	1.8	1.2	4.3
Used merchandise	24.7	25.6	16.1	17.9	23.2	12.7	11.6	14.6	7.8	4.0	5.9	4.7
Goods imported and returned unchanged	. . .	. . .	. . .	. . .	. . .		. . .	. . .	. . .	. . .	. . .	
Special classification provisions	15.8	10.1	35.7	29.5	27.2	52.4	9.1	4.4	10.5	8.5	8.3	14.7

Table D-47. TEXAS: State Exports of Goods by Destination and Industry, 1994–1999—*Continued*

(Millions of dollars.)

Industry	Germany						France					
	1994	1995	1996	1997	1998	1999	1994	1995	1996	1997	1998	1999
ALL GOODS	563.2	722.2	719.0	882.7	970.0	1 056.6	539.8	557.1	570.8	584.5	737.3	727.5
Manufactured Goods	545.0	707.7	701.8	864.4	952.4	1 031.5	531.7	541.9	558.1	576.4	726.1	717.9
Food products	12.6	11.3	10.7	11.0	7.2	8.3	17.2	21.9	25.6	24.8	17.4	12.5
Tobacco products	...	...	...	...	...	...	...	...	...	...	...	...
Textile mill products	0.8	1.4	2.3	1.1	1.2	1.2	0.5	0.8	0.4	0.3	0.6	0.7
Apparel	3.0	2.8	4.1	10.1	11.1	10.6	1.1	1.6	3.7	5.6	5.4	4.5
Lumber and wood products	10.1	7.5	6.7	13.8	5.8	2.8	1.2	1.7	1.6	1.5	1.0	0.9
Furniture and fixtures	3.3	1.2	1.6	8.2	19.9	11.4	1.3	1.9	2.2	3.4	7.1	5.5
Paper products	5.8	5.6	3.2	2.7	1.5	4.6	2.6	0.6	1.7	1.8	1.0	1.4
Printing and publishing	1.8	2.4	2.5	3.1	2.7	2.1	1.1	1.0	1.3	1.5	2.5	2.4
Chemical products	73.4	90.2	76.8	75.8	106.0	114.4	111.6	128.2	122.0	126.7	132.5	147.1
Refined petroleum products	9.8	8.1	12.1	13.5	9.6	6.0	64.5	72.2	96.6	63.0	76.2	27.6
Rubber and plastic products	5.9	6.3	6.1	5.7	10.0	18.0	2.0	2.8	3.2	2.8	4.0	5.8
Leather products	2.3	2.9	2.0	1.9	2.0	2.0	0.9	2.3	0.9	0.8	1.1	0.4
Stone, clay and glass products	9.4	11.8	12.7	12.0	14.1	14.5	5.6	1.3	1.5	1.1	4.7	5.2
Primary metals	3.2	2.4	2.2	2.6	7.1	4.3	2.2	2.7	2.8	4.1	5.2	5.8
Fabricated metal products	6.9	8.4	13.9	20.8	21.1	18.0	13.7	16.0	8.5	7.9	17.5	14.9
Industrial machinery and computers	134.6	179.3	150.0	217.5	257.6	257.1	135.3	93.0	91.4	117.1	125.0	207.4
Electric and electronic equipment	106.2	155.8	159.3	223.5	216.2	237.6	80.6	96.9	74.8	94.8	182.0	137.7
Transportation equipment	44.9	65.7	41.8	61.9	55.2	123.5	46.7	66.9	59.4	50.1	64.1	68.3
Scientific and measuring instruments	99.2	133.2	179.4	164.5	185.4	173.7	40.2	32.2	56.2	65.4	75.1	65.5
Miscellaneous manufactures	9.1	9.0	13.3	13.8	16.6	18.6	2.4	2.5	3.4	3.2	2.0	2.9
Unidentified manufactures	2.6	2.3	1.1	1.0	2.0	2.7	0.9	1.4	0.8	0.8	1.6	1.6
Agricultural And Livestock Products	6.4	6.1	10.0	8.0	8.8	8.9	2.8	6.2	0.6	1.5	0.5	3.6
Agricultural products	5.8	4.5	8.8	7.0	8.2	6.9	1.8	5.2	0.6	1.5	0.5	3.6
Livestock and livestock products	0.6	1.6	1.2	1.0	0.6	2.0	1.0	1.0	...	...	0.1	0.1
Other Commodities	11.8	8.4	7.2	10.4	8.8	16.1	5.3	9.0	12.2	6.7	10.7	5.9
Forestry products	2.0	1.9	0.6	0.2	0.3	1.5	0.1	0.3	0.7	0.1	0.1	0.1
Fish and other marine products	...	...	...	...	...	...	0.1	...	...	...	...	0.1
Metallic ores and concentrates	...	...	...	...	...	...	1.9	...	...	...	...	...
Bituminous coal and lignite	...	...	...	...	...	...	...	...	0.4	...	...	...
Crude petroleum and natural gas	...	...	...	...	...	...	...	2.4	...	2.2	...	...
Nonmetallic minerals	1.0	0.7	0.4	0.8	1.0	1.1	0.6	0.6	0.4	0.7	0.7	0.6
Scrap and waste	0.6	1.8	0.8	0.7	1.1	0.3	0.2	0.5	0.3	0.1	0.6	0.2
Used merchandise	6.8	2.3	1.6	3.8	3.5	2.5	1.3	4.5	3.7	0.9	6.5	1.5
Goods imported and returned unchanged	...	...	...	...	...	...	...	...	...	...	...	...
Special classification provisions	1.3	1.7	3.8	4.8	2.9	10.7	1.1	0.6	6.6	2.7	2.8	3.5

Industry	The Netherlands						Asian 10					
	1994	1995	1996	1997	1998	1999	1994	1995	1996	1997	1998	1999
ALL GOODS	934.3	1 128.6	1 105.2	1 161.0	1 364.2	1 099.8	8 159.0	10 826.5	9 981.2	11 006.0	9 707.5	11 408.0
Manufactured Goods	922.4	1 112.0	1 087.4	1 147.0	1 346.9	1 073.9	7 866.9	10 307.9	9 680.2	10 677.6	9 441.8	11 182.0
Food products	16.9	19.5	13.4	10.8	17.0	14.5	108.4	88.2	99.6	123.4	112.3	126.4
Tobacco products	...	...	...	...	...	0.4	...	...	...	0.2	...	0.1
Textile mill products	0.6	0.9	0.6	0.6	1.5	1.1	10.4	12.2	12.8	15.5	9.8	7.2
Apparel	0.7	1.9	3.2	4.3	2.6	1.7	11.1	11.4	12.4	15.1	13.2	11.7
Lumber and wood products	12.9	23.0	10.8	14.4	7.4	2.0	19.8	23.3	39.4	32.1	28.5	26.3
Furniture and fixtures	0.9	0.4	0.4	0.2	0.4	0.4	4.3	5.9	9.1	9.5	6.8	5.2
Paper products	7.5	6.5	0.6	0.4	1.7	1.1	21.4	21.3	13.7	13.3	8.7	8.2
Printing and publishing	0.8	2.0	1.8	1.9	2.1	1.5	5.3	10.8	11.6	11.0	10.2	14.9
Chemical products	383.9	521.9	330.8	379.9	453.9	429.5	2 238.7	3 003.2	2 433.3	2 329.4	1 391.9	1 996.3
Refined petroleum products	29.6	35.0	129.8	117.2	46.5	88.1	538.6	592.9	456.4	192.4	171.2	208.9
Rubber and plastic products	5.3	6.4	7.1	13.9	15.6	17.7	51.2	50.9	64.4	61.0	50.3	68.1
Leather products	1.0	1.3	1.3	0.8	1.0	0.1	6.7	8.5	8.8	10.7	8.0	8.0
Stone, clay and glass products	1.4	2.3	2.3	2.3	4.3	4.0	28.9	43.5	33.7	43.7	40.1	55.0
Primary metals	7.7	12.3	23.3	41.6	35.3	14.9	70.4	130.6	137.9	115.9	89.9	88.6
Fabricated metal products	8.1	6.2	8.6	6.6	10.9	4.9	151.0	161.7	210.2	174.1	202.6	140.7
Industrial machinery and computers	252.8	271.3	252.1	300.8	263.4	194.6	1 327.2	1 600.4	1 507.3	1 711.4	1 739.8	1 598.0
Electric and electronic equipment	81.0	101.0	132.4	135.6	210.4	159.6	2 645.7	3 756.8	3 691.2	4 801.9	4 613.3	5 842.4
Transportation equipment	96.5	80.3	142.7	68.3	230.2	93.7	275.9	337.7	415.9	475.6	407.7	378.1
Scientific and measuring instruments	11.0	16.4	21.2	43.5	37.4	36.3	290.3	390.7	448.0	490.3	491.6	531.3
Miscellaneous manufactures	2.7	2.6	4.1	3.2	3.3	6.3	53.1	49.7	56.9	43.6	30.6	49.0
Unidentified manufactures	0.9	0.9	0.9	0.9	2.0	1.3	8.4	8.3	17.6	7.6	15.2	17.6
Agricultural And Livestock Products	3.4	5.1	7.0	3.0	3.8	11.9	218.5	407.1	213.0	219.9	171.9	73.6
Agricultural products	3.4	5.1	6.9	3.0	3.8	11.8	215.4	404.7	208.0	216.6	170.2	71.3
Livestock and livestock products	...	...	...	0.1	...	...	3.0	2.4	5.0	3.4	1.7	2.3
Other Commodities	8.5	11.6	10.8	11.0	13.4	14.0	73.7	111.5	88.0	108.4	93.8	152.4
Forestry products	0.9	0.5	0.9	0.2	0.2	0.1	4.0	4.2	2.3	1.6	1.9	2.4
Fish and other marine products	...	...	...	...	...	...	0.8	2.5	1.8	1.9	1.1	0.5
Metallic ores and concentrates	...	2.2	1.4	0.2	0.5	0.7	0.1	0.7	0.7	0.2	2.2	4.8
Bituminous coal and lignite	...	...	...	1.3	1.2	...	0.1	0.1	0.1	0.1	0.3	0.2
Crude petroleum and natural gas	0.1	...	...	...	0.1	...	2.9	0.5	13.1	26.8	19.1	20.2
Nonmetallic minerals	1.3	1.5	1.7	1.4	0.8	1.3	10.4	14.4	9.6	17.5	12.4	9.5
Scrap and waste	3.1	3.7	1.0	0.8	0.5	0.6	32.1	62.5	30.6	24.2	19.8	54.0
Used merchandise	0.8	1.6	1.0	1.4	3.3	0.9	10.8	6.7	12.7	13.0	13.9	5.6
Goods imported and returned unchanged	...	...	...	...	...	...	...	...	...	...	...	...
Special classification provisions	2.3	2.1	4.7	5.7	6.8	10.4	12.5	20.1	16.9	23.2	23.2	55.3

Table D-47. TEXAS: State Exports of Goods by Destination and Industry, 1994–1999—*Continued*

(Millions of dollars.)

Industry	Japan						South Korea					
	1994	1995	1996	1997	1998	1999	1994	1995	1996	1997	1998	1999
ALL GOODS	1 558.4	2 181.0	2 073.9	2 218.4	1 846.4	2 109.5	923.6	1 474.0	1 354.2	1 352.6	1 084.4	1 841.4
Manufactured Goods	1 526.5	2 099.5	2 025.9	2 155.8	1 773.8	2 036.8	868.7	1 386.6	1 297.1	1 306.1	1 036.3	1 785.3
Food products	78.7	37.5	49.3	69.9	48.0	57.0	5.6	6.5	9.0	10.9	14.8	15.3
Tobacco products	...	...	...	...	...	...	...	...	...	...	...	...
Textile mill products	3.3	3.0	4.3	4.6	3.7	2.2	1.4	1.2	3.3	1.3	0.5	2.4
Apparel	6.5	7.4	9.6	9.8	9.6	8.1	2.8	1.4	0.6	0.6	0.4	1.6
Lumber and wood products	13.8	20.6	26.7	17.3	20.6	13.9	0.3	0.9	7.1	10.3	3.0	9.6
Furniture and fixtures	1.7	2.5	3.9	5.5	3.3	2.8	0.4	1.2	1.0	0.5	0.2	0.1
Paper products	5.2	6.5	4.1	2.0	2.2	2.0	1.8	3.1	1.7	1.6	0.7	0.6
Printing and publishing	1.3	3.4	2.9	2.9	3.5	4.5	0.2	0.7	1.7	0.6	0.3	0.6
Chemical products	528.2	651.4	483.8	435.7	346.4	389.3	356.0	595.1	505.0	493.3	178.6	340.1
Refined petroleum products	45.2	78.2	104.4	54.2	44.0	33.4	124.8	258.9	132.5	28.5	14.9	55.6
Rubber and plastic products	12.4	12.6	12.6	11.8	15.6	18.4	4.1	5.7	9.8	8.6	2.4	4.9
Leather products	2.5	4.1	4.8	3.1	3.0	5.7	1.5	1.0	0.5	0.3	0.2	0.3
Stone, clay and glass products	6.5	16.7	7.9	12.9	12.4	20.6	4.1	8.7	4.7	3.3	3.2	3.1
Primary metals	19.8	25.2	24.9	23.2	21.7	9.0	15.9	27.2	33.5	28.1	16.2	16.6
Fabricated metal products	47.9	29.5	37.3	40.5	50.5	42.1	26.2	60.2	73.4	44.0	14.9	18.0
Industrial machinery and computers	188.0	243.9	219.2	314.3	219.4	247.9	80.0	82.9	103.6	130.6	204.4	167.9
Electric and electronic equipment	323.0	619.7	653.7	805.3	617.6	736.2	153.9	240.8	255.9	353.8	453.8	1 088.6
Transportation equipment	113.3	174.8	184.5	149.3	124.0	208.6	28.3	36.5	93.0	133.7	84.3	21.6
Scientific and measuring instruments	104.7	135.5	156.1	175.4	210.0	206.0	55.2	49.0	52.6	50.2	41.7	34.7
Miscellaneous manufactures	22.6	24.9	23.5	16.4	14.8	23.6	5.3	4.9	7.4	5.2	0.9	2.2
Unidentified manufactures	1.7	2.0	12.6	1.7	3.5	5.5	0.9	0.8	0.9	0.8	1.0	1.4
Agricultural And Livestock Products	18.5	63.3	34.7	18.6	33.1	15.7	43.4	68.5	35.4	40.7	43.3	20.3
Agricultural products	18.4	62.9	34.1	17.5	32.6	15.4	42.5	68.5	35.3	40.4	43.2	19.9
Livestock and livestock products	0.1	0.4	0.5	1.1	0.5	0.3	0.9	...	0.1	0.2	0.1	0.4
Other Commodities	13.5	18.2	13.3	44.0	39.6	57.0	11.5	18.8	21.7	5.9	4.8	35.8
Forestry products	1.0	0.9	0.2	0.3	0.2	0.7	2.2	2.5	1.2	0.4	...	1.0
Fish and other marine products	0.2	1.4	1.0	0.3	0.1	0.2	...	0.1	0.1	...	...	...
Metallic ores and concentrates	0.1	0.7	0.6	...	1.5	2.5	...	...	...	...	...	...
Bituminous coal and lignite	...	...	...	...	...	...	...	...	...	...	...	...
Crude petroleum and natural gas	0.4	0.1	...	26.2	18.8	15.4	2.4	0.3	12.9	0.4	0.1	4.4
Nonmetallic minerals	4.5	5.0	2.2	4.7	2.4	2.4	1.3	2.7	2.1	1.9	0.9	1.1
Scrap and waste	3.4	3.0	2.4	2.7	5.2	8.1	3.8	12.6	4.1	0.9	0.1	23.0
Used merchandise	1.9	3.0	2.4	3.5	5.4	1.8	1.3	0.3	0.3	1.2	...	...
Goods imported and returned unchanged	...	...	...	...	...	...	...	...	...	...	...	...
Special classification provisions	1.9	4.2	4.4	6.3	6.0	26.0	0.5	0.3	1.1	1.1	3.6	6.2

Industry	Taiwan						Singapore					
	1994	1995	1996	1997	1998	1999	1994	1995	1996	1997	1998	1999
ALL GOODS	1 200.4	1 371.4	1 179.0	1 348.3	1 211.8	1 539.8	1 529.3	1 755.5	1 528.7	2 015.8	1 964.4	1 629.6
Manufactured Goods	1 181.9	1 323.4	1 152.9	1 305.1	1 170.5	1 521.5	1 519.6	1 742.2	1 512.6	2 003.0	1 954.0	1 618.1
Food products	16.9	16.7	14.0	14.3	16.9	13.1	1.8	3.8	4.0	3.0	1.8	2.1
Tobacco products	...	...	...	0.2	...	...	...	...	...	...	...	...
Textile mill products	2.6	3.2	0.6	2.0	0.8	0.2	0.3	1.5	1.3	1.1	0.5	0.4
Apparel	0.2	0.2	0.2	1.0	0.4	0.1	0.8	0.5	0.8	1.2	0.7	0.4
Lumber and wood products	0.8	0.2	0.1	0.7	0.4	0.5	0.4	0.3	0.4	1.2	0.4	1.5
Furniture and fixtures	0.7	0.8	0.5	0.4	0.3	0.4	0.3	0.2	1.1	0.4	0.9	0.6
Paper products	5.0	3.4	3.9	2.1	0.5	0.4	1.1	1.2	0.3	0.8	0.4	0.5
Printing and publishing	0.9	1.7	1.2	0.6	0.5	0.4	0.9	0.9	1.1	1.1	1.3	1.4
Chemical products	677.0	748.4	529.9	483.8	282.5	414.1	186.6	272.1	240.4	340.3	195.8	223.7
Refined petroleum products	45.2	42.7	20.3	25.4	27.8	19.7	250.0	136.4	85.9	35.7	49.7	59.2
Rubber and plastic products	7.3	8.7	10.1	10.1	4.3	10.1	6.1	6.8	8.1	9.5	8.9	11.1
Leather products	0.9	0.7	0.5	0.6	...	...	0.3	0.4	0.4	0.3	0.2	0.2
Stone, clay and glass products	2.5	1.5	1.0	2.0	4.0	3.3	4.5	6.8	6.4	6.9	7.2	21.2
Primary metals	4.9	18.2	4.0	12.4	3.6	4.1	6.6	11.0	13.7	14.3	16.8	24.7
Fabricated metal products	27.8	11.7	5.2	9.0	21.8	9.3	10.4	15.6	22.4	21.8	27.7	29.0
Industrial machinery and computers	53.9	60.5	89.0	121.6	117.4	114.2	532.6	537.2	495.5	611.4	660.1	578.2
Electric and electronic equipment	283.8	356.0	381.7	551.3	613.2	860.4	430.2	627.9	514.3	772.2	770.3	553.6
Transportation equipment	16.0	20.0	5.1	26.1	29.5	12.9	45.8	45.1	64.2	88.5	117.7	62.3
Scientific and measuring instruments	18.7	21.8	78.0	36.7	41.4	52.6	38.1	72.0	48.9	84.7	87.0	41.0
Miscellaneous manufactures	15.9	6.2	6.7	3.8	2.3	2.0	1.2	1.3	2.4	7.4	4.1	5.1
Unidentified manufactures	0.8	0.8	0.8	1.1	2.7	2.5	1.6	1.1	1.0	1.0	2.7	2.0
Agricultural And Livestock Products	10.7	27.6	15.9	31.4	30.5	7.7	0.4	0.5	0.2	...	0.4	0.1
Agricultural products	10.5	26.5	15.8	31.4	30.4	7.3	0.4	0.5	0.2	...	0.3	0.1
Livestock and livestock products	0.2	1.0	0.1	...	0.1	0.4	...	...	...	...	0.1	...
Other Commodities	7.8	20.5	10.3	11.8	10.8	10.6	9.3	12.7	15.8	12.8	10.1	11.4
Forestry products	...	0.1	0.1	0.1	...	0.1	...	0.1	0.1	...	0.1	...
Fish and other marine products	0.7	0.4	0.4	...	1.0	0.4	...	...	...	...	...	...
Metallic ores and concentrates	...	...	...	...	...	...	...	...	0.1	...	...	...
Bituminous coal and lignite	...	...	...	...	...	...	0.1	...	...	0.1	0.3	0.2
Crude petroleum and natural gas	...	...	...	...	...	0.3	...	0.1	...	0.1	...	...
Nonmetallic minerals	1.0	1.8	1.6	4.0	2.2	0.9	1.7	2.8	1.5	2.7	4.2	1.9
Scrap and waste	5.3	17.2	7.6	5.3	4.1	4.8	0.4	0.3	0.5	0.5	0.1	0.3
Used merchandise	0.2	0.2	...	0.1	...	0.1	1.2	0.9	5.6	2.6	2.4	2.6
Goods imported and returned unchanged	...	...	...	...	...	...	...	...	...	...	...	...
Special classification provisions	0.7	0.7	0.5	2.2	3.5	4.0	6.0	8.5	7.9	6.8	2.8	6.4

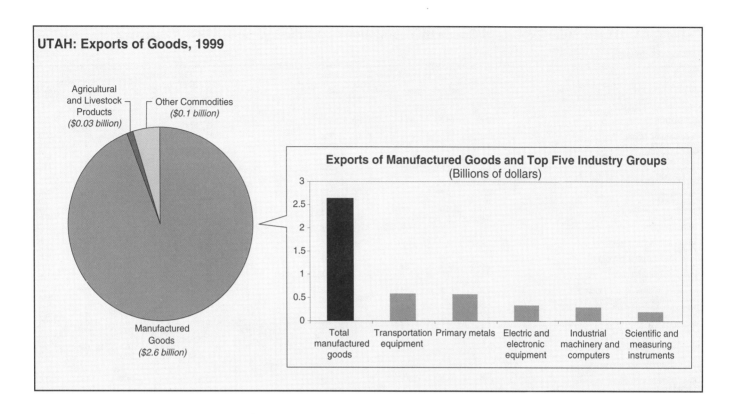

UTAH: Exports of Goods, 1999

Agricultural and Livestock Products ($0.03 billion)

Other Commodities ($0.1 billion)

Manufactured Goods ($2.6 billion)

Exports of Manufactured Goods and Top Five Industry Groups
(Billions of dollars)

Total manufactured goods | Transportation equipment | Primary metals | Electric and electronic equipment | Industrial machinery and computers | Scientific and measuring instruments

Table D-48. UTAH: State Exports of Goods by Destination and Industry, 1994–1999

(Millions of dollars.)

Industry	All destinations						Canada					
	1994	1995	1996	1997	1998	1999	1994	1995	1996	1997	1998	1999
ALL GOODS	2 233.1	2 313.4	2 768.5	3 293.3	3 099.4	2 789.3	342.9	413.1	443.3	514.5	505.2	563.2
Manufactured Goods	1 851.8	1 793.3	2 379.0	2 968.1	2 949.2	2 630.0	300.6	381.3	415.7	487.4	486.9	536.4
Food products	56.9	116.9	126.6	141.0	141.1	156.9	21.8	33.0	21.8	24.4	28.3	28.2
Tobacco products	. . .	. . .	. . .	. . .	. . .	. . .	. . .	. . .	. . .	. . .	. . .	. . .
Textile mill products	2.3	3.0	2.2	3.5	3.7	5.0	1.1	1.0	0.6	0.6	0.4	0.9
Apparel	8.7	8.5	8.8	8.2	6.0	8.6	1.0	1.5	1.1	1.4	1.2	1.1
Lumber and wood products	0.8	2.5	1.4	1.6	1.6	4.5	0.4	0.5	0.2	0.4	0.4	1.1
Furniture and fixtures	3.3	3.6	3.9	5.1	7.3	6.8	1.8	1.5	1.7	2.5	3.3	3.2
Paper products	3.3	5.0	6.9	6.1	15.4	43.5	0.4	1.4	2.3	1.1	8.1	35.3
Printing and publishing	24.8	28.4	35.3	33.5	25.1	26.6	8.0	9.7	9.9	8.0	5.7	6.0
Chemical products	141.4	124.7	201.6	222.1	191.5	158.2	31.0	38.7	48.5	45.1	42.7	45.0
Refined petroleum products	0.8	1.0	1.1	0.6	0.6	1.4	. . .	0.2	0.1	0.1	. . .	0.3
Rubber and plastic products	11.3	25.7	26.1	35.7	38.8	49.3	2.0	2.1	3.3	4.3	5.2	10.4
Leather products	3.5	4.5	5.4	5.5	7.9	14.9	0.8	1.6	1.4	1.2	1.3	1.6
Stone, clay and glass products	4.6	5.2	6.7	8.0	7.5	11.5	1.6	1.1	1.1	1.1	0.9	1.3
Primary metals	752.4	363.8	438.8	784.1	935.9	576.9	22.1	51.9	52.9	64.2	42.8	36.2
Fabricated metal products	31.3	38.0	51.2	63.2	49.5	49.9	10.6	10.9	16.3	18.6	15.7	10.7
Industrial machinery and computers	194.4	317.1	447.9	398.8	281.1	298.6	34.6	51.3	60.5	81.1	77.6	59.2
Electric and electronic equipment	222.2	319.5	362.4	462.9	462.8	339.9	53.2	48.3	42.9	48.4	55.4	37.7
Transportation equipment	212.6	230.8	418.8	497.1	511.2	588.9	76.8	89.8	114.1	126.4	145.9	194.5
Scientific and measuring instruments	109.4	118.6	146.0	177.8	169.4	201.6	15.3	17.5	17.2	26.0	27.4	43.2
Miscellaneous manufactures	59.6	67.1	76.0	103.3	78.9	74.7	15.8	16.2	16.9	29.5	21.3	17.3
Unidentified manufactures	7.9	9.3	11.8	10.1	14.0	12.4	2.3	3.2	2.9	3.1	3.5	3.3
Agricultural And Livestock Products	5.3	5.0	24.4	23.3	20.8	26.7	3.4	1.8	1.6	1.2	1.2	2.3
Agricultural products	5.2	4.9	23.9	23.3	20.6	26.4	3.3	1.8	1.4	1.1	1.2	2.3
Livestock and livestock products	0.1	0.1	0.5	. . .	0.2	0.3	0.1	. . .	0.2	. . .	. . .	. . .
Other Commodities	376.1	515.2	365.1	302.0	129.4	132.5	38.9	30.0	26.0	25.9	17.2	24.5
Forestry products	0.1	0.2	0.1	0.5	0.5	0.6	. . .	. . .	. . .	0.1	0.3	0.3
Fish and other marine products	1.8	3.3	6.8	6.2	0.9	0.8	0.1	0.1	. . .	. . .	. . .	. . .
Metallic ores and concentrates	281.4	387.8	190.3	162.8	32.1	34.7	31.6	4.8	3.2	. . .	2.9	2.5
Bituminous coal and lignite	66.2	81.9	115.1	86.1	68.3	39.4	. . .	. . .	. . .	. . .	0.3	. . .
Crude petroleum and natural gas	0.3	. . .	. . .	. . .	. . .	. . .	0.3	. . .	. . .	. . .	. . .	. . .
Nonmetallic minerals	6.7	7.3	8.1	6.5	5.3	3.9	0.5	0.6	0.9	1.0	1.0	1.2
Scrap and waste	10.0	22.5	15.5	4.8	1.6	2.0	0.5	18.2	10.0	4.3	0.3	0.5
Used merchandise	1.3	4.2	3.8	7.0	4.5	2.6	0.6	0.5	1.3	2.1	1.6	0.5
Goods imported and returned unchanged	4.6	5.1	7.9	17.1	9.2	5.9	4.6	5.1	7.9	17.1	9.2	5.9
Special classification provisions	3.7	2.9	17.3	10.9	6.9	42.7	0.6	0.7	2.5	1.2	1.5	13.6

Table D-48. UTAH: State Exports of Goods by Destination and Industry, 1994–1999—*Continued*

(Millions of dollars.)

Industry	South and Central America and Caribbean						Mexico					
	1994	1995	1996	1997	1998	1999	1994	1995	1996	1997	1998	1999
ALL GOODS	50.2	86.3	96.4	109.8	102.9	107.7	82.7	66.7	76.4	73.0	87.5	113.6
Manufactured Goods	39.2	55.0	69.1	96.7	93.6	104.2	78.0	33.2	50.4	71.9	85.7	110.3
Food products	2.5	6.4	9.6	9.7	14.2	20.9	3.6	2.4	2.5	2.0	2.5	5.8
Tobacco products	...	...	...	...	...	...	...	...	...	...	...	...
Textile mill products	0.2	0.6	0.3	1.1	1.2	1.7	0.1	0.2	0.2	0.6	0.6	0.5
Apparel	0.4	0.2	0.2	0.3	0.2	0.6	0.2	0.3	0.1	0.1	0.1	0.2
Lumber and wood products	...	...	...	...	...	0.3	...	...	0.1	0.1	0.1	2.3
Furniture and fixtures	0.1	0.2	0.3	0.2	1.4	1.8	0.2	0.1	0.1	0.2	0.3	0.4
Paper products	0.6	1.1	0.7	0.8	0.6	0.5	0.6	0.9	2.5	2.6	4.3	5.5
Printing and publishing	1.9	0.8	2.0	3.2	3.3	3.6	2.1	1.1	0.6	2.2	2.7	4.1
Chemical products	4.6	4.1	13.4	13.4	9.2	6.6	8.6	2.9	6.9	8.4	8.3	3.5
Refined petroleum products	0.1	0.3	0.5	0.5	0.5	0.2	0.6	0.6	0.2	...	...	...
Rubber and plastic products	0.2	0.3	0.4	0.6	0.8	1.1	3.0	5.0	8.5	12.7	15.0	20.3
Leather products	...	...	...	...	0.1	0.1	...	0.1	0.1	0.2	0.2	0.6
Stone, clay and glass products	0.6	0.5	0.3	0.2	0.6	0.4	0.1	...	0.9	1.1	1.1	1.6
Primary metals	2.0	2.5	2.3	1.5	1.3	0.9	26.4	0.4	0.6	2.1	3.0	2.0
Fabricated metal products	4.6	2.2	1.8	4.0	1.5	1.3	0.7	1.3	1.2	1.8	3.6	4.2
Industrial machinery and computers	10.2	20.5	12.4	25.1	14.7	14.0	12.2	6.5	6.7	10.3	8.0	12.4
Electric and electronic equipment	2.6	4.4	2.1	4.6	7.6	10.0	4.0	4.3	4.9	4.4	11.9	16.8
Transportation equipment	0.2	0.4	3.9	14.7	25.0	29.3	1.6	1.6	9.4	11.7	18.7	21.4
Scientific and measuring instruments	5.7	8.0	15.2	8.2	6.3	7.4	12.9	5.1	4.4	10.8	4.5	6.3
Miscellaneous manufactures	2.2	2.1	3.2	7.8	3.9	2.8	0.9	0.2	0.6	0.5	0.3	1.3
Unidentified manufactures	0.4	0.3	0.6	0.5	1.2	0.5	0.2	0.1	0.1	0.2	0.2	1.0
Agricultural And Livestock Products	...	...	0.1	...	0.1	0.1	0.1	...	5.1	0.1	0.2	0.2
Agricultural products	...	...	...	...	...	...	0.1	...	5.1	0.1	0.1	0.2
Livestock and livestock products	...	...	0.1	...	0.1	0.1	...	...	...	...	0.1	...
Other Commodities	11.0	31.3	27.1	13.0	9.1	3.4	4.5	33.5	20.9	1.0	1.6	3.2
Forestry products	...	...	...	...	...	...	...	...	...	...	...	...
Fish and other marine products	...	0.2	0.2	0.2	...	...	...	...	0.1	0.2	0.1	...
Metallic ores and concentrates	10.6	27.9	18.7	12.0	7.9	...	2.9	33.0	19.9	...	...	0.1
Bituminous coal and lignite	...	2.5	7.5	...	...	...	...	...	0.4	...	...	...
Crude petroleum and natural gas	...	...	...	...	...	...	...	...	...	...	...	...
Nonmetallic minerals	0.3	0.4	0.4	0.4	0.2	0.2	...	0.1	0.1	...	0.1	0.1
Scrap and waste	...	...	...	...	...	...	...	...	...	0.5	1.2	1.0
Used merchandise	...	...	...	0.1	0.2	0.2	...	...	...	...	...	0.1
Goods imported and returned unchanged	...	...	...	...	...	...	...	...	...	...	...	...
Special classification provisions	0.1	0.2	0.2	0.3	0.8	2.9	1.6	0.3	0.4	0.3	0.3	1.9

Industry	European Union						United Kingdom					
	1994	1995	1996	1997	1998	1999	1994	1995	1996	1997	1998	1999
ALL GOODS	522.5	619.2	895.1	1 257.1	1 132.4	1 122.2	60.8	108.8	365.9	735.1	697.7	626.5
Manufactured Goods	432.1	499.5	829.2	1 169.4	1 107.0	1 086.2	50.6	103.4	359.6	733.9	696.2	622.1
Food products	4.9	7.5	9.8	9.6	10.0	10.7	1.8	2.2	1.8	1.5	1.9	1.4
Tobacco products	...	...	...	...	...	...	...	...	...	...	...	...
Textile mill products	0.3	0.5	0.2	0.3	0.4	0.3	0.1	0.1	0.1	0.1	0.1	0.1
Apparel	1.6	2.6	2.1	1.6	1.5	2.9	0.3	0.2	0.4	0.4	0.6	0.9
Lumber and wood products	...	0.1	0.1	0.1	0.2	0.3	...	0.1	...	0.1	0.2	0.1
Furniture and fixtures	0.5	0.5	0.4	1.3	1.8	0.5	0.4	0.2	0.2	0.4	0.9	0.3
Paper products	0.8	0.6	0.4	0.6	0.4	0.4	0.1	0.3	0.1	0.4	0.2	0.2
Printing and publishing	5.0	5.5	6.9	4.3	3.9	3.1	3.3	4.4	3.0	2.9	1.7	1.6
Chemical products	10.3	12.1	13.5	28.9	29.9	28.8	0.5	2.1	0.9	3.9	3.9	5.5
Refined petroleum products	...	...	...	...	...	0.1	...	...	...	...	...	...
Rubber and plastic products	2.4	5.9	7.4	6.8	7.4	5.9	0.4	2.0	2.2	1.7	1.8	2.0
Leather products	0.3	0.5	0.5	0.9	1.7	6.5	0.1	0.2	0.3	0.2	0.3	0.2
Stone, clay and glass products	1.1	2.1	2.2	2.5	3.5	3.5	0.1	0.1	0.2	0.4	1.4	1.5
Primary metals	130.3	114.1	290.5	652.3	611.0	525.2	5.8	37.6	280.1	646.1	596.9	515.8
Fabricated metal products	5.1	5.4	7.9	19.2	8.1	11.0	2.6	1.8	3.2	3.8	2.6	3.4
Industrial machinery and computers	83.9	100.9	139.9	94.6	76.8	80.0	14.6	18.7	16.6	17.1	14.3	10.4
Electric and electronic equipment	33.7	58.1	119.9	84.0	91.7	97.1	9.5	12.6	24.6	14.8	32.8	22.5
Transportation equipment	89.1	109.6	145.0	158.4	164.2	200.8	0.7	6.8	7.9	12.4	14.0	30.7
Scientific and measuring instruments	42.9	49.5	54.6	73.0	67.3	77.3	6.4	8.6	9.5	19.5	16.6	14.2
Miscellaneous manufactures	18.0	22.0	26.5	29.6	24.9	28.8	3.3	5.2	8.3	8.1	5.3	11.0
Unidentified manufactures	1.9	2.0	1.5	1.5	2.2	3.0	0.5	0.4	0.4	0.3	0.7	0.4
Agricultural And Livestock Products	0.3	0.3	0.2	0.2	1.1	0.3	...	0.1	...	0.1	0.5	0.1
Agricultural products	0.3	0.3	0.2	0.2	1.1	0.3	...	0.1	...	0.1	0.5	0.1
Livestock and livestock products	...	0.1	...	...	...	...	...	...	...	...	...	...
Other Commodities	90.0	119.4	65.7	87.5	24.3	35.6	10.1	5.3	6.2	1.1	1.0	4.4
Forestry products	...	...	...	0.1	...	0.1	...	...	...	...	...	...
Fish and other marine products	0.2	0.2	0.4	0.2	0.3	0.1	...	...	...	...	...	...
Metallic ores and concentrates	75.7	110.4	51.6	78.2	19.7	22.8	...	...	...	...	...	...
Bituminous coal and lignite	...	...	...	...	...	...	...	...	...	...	...	...
Crude petroleum and natural gas	...	...	...	...	...	...	...	...	...	...	...	...
Nonmetallic minerals	4.4	3.7	3.5	3.4	2.2	0.6	0.7	0.4	0.5	0.7	...	0.2
Scrap and waste	9.1	4.1	5.4	...	...	...	9.1	3.9	5.4	...	...	...
Used merchandise	0.3	0.1	0.3	0.1	0.3	0.1	0.1	...	...	...	0.1	0.1
Goods imported and returned unchanged	...	...	...	...	...	...	...	...	...	...	...	...
Special classification provisions	0.4	0.9	4.5	5.5	1.9	12.0	0.2	0.4	0.4	0.5	0.8	4.1

Table D-48. UTAH: State Exports of Goods by Destination and Industry, 1994–1999—*Continued*

(Millions of dollars.)

Industry	Germany						France					
	1994	1995	1996	1997	1998	1999	1994	1995	1996	1997	1998	1999
ALL GOODS	187.9	196.7	210.2	146.5	114.5	120.8	16.1	26.8	42.2	41.1	37.2	48.7
Manufactured Goods	186.3	195.1	207.8	127.2	111.9	117.5	15.5	26.1	40.7	40.3	36.5	48.1
Food products	0.5	0.4	0.4	0.8	0.7	0.8	0.2	0.5	0.5	0.6	0.6	0.5
Tobacco products	...	...	...	...	...	...	...	...	...	...	...	...
Textile mill products	...	0.1	0.1	...	...	...	0.1	0.2	...	...	0.1	...
Apparel	0.3	1.0	1.2	0.6	0.3	0.9	0.2	0.1	0.1	0.1	0.1	0.1
Lumber and wood products	...	...	...	...	...	...	...	...	...	...	...	...
Furniture and fixtures	0.1	0.3	0.1	...	...	...	...	...	...	...	...	...
Paper products	...	...	0.1	...	...	...	...	...	...	...	...	...
Printing and publishing	0.2	0.3	1.5	0.6	0.8	0.6	0.1	0.1	0.3	0.1	0.1	0.1
Chemical products	1.5	1.9	1.9	4.4	4.8	4.2	1.2	0.4	0.6	3.5	1.2	1.4
Refined petroleum products	...	...	...	...	...	...	...	...	...	...	...	...
Rubber and plastic products	0.2	1.0	0.1	0.1	0.2	0.2	0.5	0.2	1.0	0.2	0.2	0.4
Leather products	...	0.1	0.1	...	...	0.1	...	...	...	0.2	0.4	...
Stone, clay and glass products	0.6	0.2	1.1	0.8	0.8	0.8	0.1	0.3	0.4	0.5	0.3	0.2
Primary metals	117.6	61.8	1.3	0.6	0.9	0.5	0.4	0.6	0.8	0.1	6.1	...
Fabricated metal products	0.8	1.1	0.7	4.6	0.9	0.9	0.1	0.5	0.5	1.0	2.1	1.3
Industrial machinery and computers	25.4	39.5	65.9	15.8	7.4	5.3	2.8	7.9	13.6	7.4	5.5	4.4
Electric and electronic equipment	8.0	17.2	45.2	13.3	10.9	17.7	2.5	6.4	12.0	12.3	8.5	11.6
Transportation equipment	19.6	55.4	75.0	68.1	69.5	70.5	0.2	0.2	1.6	4.1	2.9	17.0
Scientific and measuring instruments	7.5	9.6	8.7	12.5	9.7	11.1	4.8	5.5	5.7	6.1	4.8	6.7
Miscellaneous manufactures	3.7	4.5	4.3	4.9	4.7	3.5	2.0	3.1	3.4	4.1	3.7	4.1
Unidentified manufactures	0.3	0.8	0.2	0.1	0.3	0.3	0.2	0.2	0.1	0.1	0.1	0.1
Agricultural And Livestock Products	0.2	0.1	...	...	...	...	...	0.1	0.1	...	0.3	...
Agricultural products	0.2	...	...	...	...	...	...	0.1	0.1	...	0.3	...
Livestock and livestock products	...	0.1	...	...	...	...	...	...	...	...	...	...
Other Commodities	1.4	1.5	2.4	19.2	2.6	3.3	0.6	0.6	1.4	0.7	0.4	0.6
Forestry products	...	...	...	...	...	...	...	...	...	...	...	...
Fish and other marine products	0.1	...	...	0.1	...	...	...	...	...	...	...	...
Metallic ores and concentrates	...	...	...	17.4	1.6	...	...	...	0.2	...	...	...
Bituminous coal and lignite	...	...	...	...	...	...	...	...	...	...	...	...
Crude petroleum and natural gas	...	...	...	...	...	...	...	...	...	...	...	...
Nonmetallic minerals	1.3	1.4	1.4	1.4	0.7	...	0.5	0.6	0.6	0.5	...	...
Scrap and waste	...	...	...	...	...	...	...	...	...	...	...	...
Used merchandise	...	...	0.1	0.1	...	...	0.1	...	0.2	...	0.1	...
Goods imported and returned unchanged	...	...	...	...	...	...	...	...	...	...	...	...
Special classification provisions	...	0.1	0.8	0.2	0.2	3.2	...	...	0.5	0.2	0.2	0.6

Industry	The Netherlands						Asian 10					
	1994	1995	1996	1997	1998	1999	1994	1995	1996	1997	1998	1999
ALL GOODS	117.6	90.9	116.1	118.1	106.9	120.3	1 086.8	1 021.0	1 116.0	1 204.5	857.7	718.8
Manufactured Goods	115.1	89.9	113.0	112.1	104.9	110.9	855.8	721.5	890.4	1 014.5	767.3	642.0
Food products	1.6	3.0	4.8	4.5	4.0	3.7	22.7	63.3	77.3	85.1	76.2	77.9
Tobacco products	...	...	...	...	...	...	...	...	...	...	...	...
Textile mill products	0.1	0.1	...	...	...	...	0.3	0.4	0.5	0.5	0.7	1.1
Apparel	0.1	0.8	0.2	0.3	0.2	0.4	4.7	3.0	3.7	3.5	1.5	2.0
Lumber and wood products	...	...	...	...	...	0.2	0.3	0.9	1.1	0.7	0.6	0.3
Furniture and fixtures	...	...	...	...	...	...	0.3	1.2	1.0	0.6	0.4	0.6
Paper products	0.6	0.2	0.1	...	...	0.1	0.5	0.5	0.9	0.5	1.0	1.2
Printing and publishing	0.9	0.5	0.6	0.3	0.8	0.3	4.7	8.2	11.7	12.7	6.3	6.4
Chemical products	2.2	3.1	6.2	9.9	9.1	3.8	76.6	55.7	108.4	114.5	84.7	61.1
Refined petroleum products	...	...	...	...	...	...	0.1	...	0.3	...	...	0.7
Rubber and plastic products	0.8	0.7	0.2	0.4	0.3	0.5	3.0	11.7	5.5	8.3	8.2	9.5
Leather products	0.1	0.1	...	0.2	0.4	3.1	2.0	2.1	3.2	2.6	4.3	5.1
Stone, clay and glass products	...	...	...	...	...	...	1.0	1.3	2.0	2.4	1.1	4.3
Primary metals	5.4	3.5	5.6	4.4	5.2	7.2	495.9	193.9	91.2	63.0	11.9	10.8
Fabricated metal products	0.1	0.6	0.6	1.2	0.3	0.5	5.9	10.4	12.4	13.3	9.0	13.0
Industrial machinery and computers	19.9	15.9	20.3	14.6	15.3	11.6	38.0	116.9	209.5	163.8	82.0	101.3
Electric and electronic equipment	4.4	6.3	14.8	15.2	8.4	8.0	121.4	192.4	181.1	306.2	277.9	160.5
Transportation equipment	67.8	43.9	47.7	52.7	51.1	60.3	41.9	16.7	123.8	178.5	144.2	124.7
Scientific and measuring instruments	7.5	8.5	9.5	5.6	7.1	7.4	18.4	21.4	34.9	33.9	39.1	44.0
Miscellaneous manufactures	3.5	2.3	2.1	2.2	2.1	1.9	16.9	19.8	20.3	23.2	14.2	14.7
Unidentified manufactures	0.2	0.1	0.2	0.5	0.7	1.8	1.2	1.5	1.7	1.4	3.9	2.7
Agricultural And Livestock Products	...	...	...	...	...	0.1	0.6	0.6	4.7	17.0	14.6	15.8
Agricultural products	...	...	...	...	...	0.1	0.6	0.6	4.5	17.0	14.6	15.8
Livestock and livestock products	...	...	...	...	...	...	...	...	0.2	...	...	0.1
Other Commodities	2.4	1.0	3.1	5.9	1.9	9.3	230.4	299.0	221.0	173.1	75.8	61.0
Forestry products	...	...	...	...	...	...	...	0.2	...	0.4	0.2	0.1
Fish and other marine products	...	...	...	...	...	...	1.5	2.8	6.0	5.2	0.4	0.6
Metallic ores and concentrates	1.4	...	0.5	1.9	0.5	8.4	160.4	211.7	93.5	72.7	1.5	9.4
Bituminous coal and lignite	...	...	...	...	...	...	66.2	79.4	107.3	86.1	67.8	39.4
Crude petroleum and natural gas	...	...	...	...	...	...	...	...	...	...	...	...
Nonmetallic minerals	0.9	0.9	0.4	0.3	1.2	0.2	1.1	2.2	2.8	1.4	1.7	1.2
Scrap and waste	...	...	...	...	...	...	...	0.1	0.1	...	0.1	0.4
Used merchandise	...	0.1	...	...	...	...	0.3	2.1	2.1	4.4	2.2	1.4
Goods imported and returned unchanged	...	...	...	...	...	...	...	...	...	...	...	...
Special classification provisions	0.1	...	2.2	3.6	0.2	0.7	0.8	0.6	9.1	2.9	1.8	8.6

Table D-48. UTAH: State Exports of Goods by Destination and Industry, 1994–1999—*Continued*

(Millions of dollars.)

Industry	Japan						South Korea					
	1994	1995	1996	1997	1998	1999	1994	1995	1996	1997	1998	1999
ALL GOODS	296.1	404.8	468.9	516.8	387.9	281.0	89.6	159.4	140.7	107.1	46.3	92.5
Manufactured Goods	143.8	196.4	297.2	400.6	319.6	252.6	65.0	139.5	135.2	74.5	45.9	90.9
Food products	2.9	11.4	25.9	53.4	49.7	40.1	5.0	7.1	7.7	7.4	3.2	6.9
Tobacco products	...	...	...	...	...	...	...	...	...	...	...	...
Textile mill products	0.1	0.2	...	0.1	...	0.1	0.1	...	...	0.1	...	...
Apparel	4.6	2.8	2.7	2.5	1.0	1.4	...	0.1	0.6	0.6	0.3	0.3
Lumber and wood products	0.3	0.9	0.7	0.6	0.6	0.3	...	...	0.3	...	...	...
Furniture and fixtures	0.2	0.5	0.4	0.1	0.1	0.4	0.1	...	0.1	...	...	...
Paper products	0.3	0.3	0.3	0.1	0.4	0.6	...	0.1	...	...	...	0.1
Printing and publishing	1.7	3.7	7.2	8.3	2.8	2.9	0.2	0.9	0.1	0.4	0.1	0.1
Chemical products	42.3	26.7	37.9	67.0	62.4	45.6	0.9	1.5	36.6	13.0	1.0	2.9
Refined petroleum products	...	...	...	...	...	...	...	...	...	...	...	...
Rubber and plastic products	1.6	1.9	2.2	3.7	4.7	6.4	0.1	0.6	0.4	0.3	0.3	0.5
Leather products	1.3	1.6	2.2	1.4	3.7	4.2	0.1	0.1	0.1	0.3	0.3	...
Stone, clay and glass products	0.8	0.4	0.3	0.4	0.2	1.6	...	...	0.1	0.2	0.8	0.2
Primary metals	13.3	70.2	10.3	16.2	3.8	1.1	4.0	24.0	36.0	8.6	2.7	4.6
Fabricated metal products	0.6	2.1	0.7	3.0	1.4	1.5	0.3	1.2	1.8	2.0	0.7	0.5
Industrial machinery and computers	13.8	24.3	35.2	21.5	11.3	27.8	2.5	7.8	6.8	3.1	1.0	6.0
Electric and electronic equipment	7.3	19.2	30.9	37.5	24.6	17.7	45.1	87.0	29.1	14.4	5.8	6.7
Transportation equipment	37.4	8.3	111.4	157.7	117.2	64.6	0.2	2.7	7.3	14.0	25.1	56.9
Scientific and measuring instruments	9.1	11.8	21.0	17.2	25.6	26.8	3.1	4.3	4.0	4.2	1.7	2.7
Miscellaneous manufactures	6.1	9.7	7.6	9.7	9.4	8.5	3.3	1.9	3.9	5.6	1.0	2.2
Unidentified manufactures	0.4	0.5	0.2	0.2	0.9	1.0	0.1	0.1	0.1	0.2	1.7	0.3
Agricultural And Livestock Products	0.1	0.2	0.1	0.4	0.1	0.2	0.1	0.1	0.7	...	...	0.7
Agricultural products	0.1	0.2	0.1	0.4	0.1	0.2	0.1	0.1	0.7	...	...	0.7
Livestock and livestock products	...	...	...	...	...	...	...	...	...	...	...	...
Other Commodities	152.1	208.2	171.6	115.7	68.1	28.1	24.5	19.8	4.8	32.6	0.4	0.9
Forestry products	...	0.1	...	0.2	0.2	...	...	...	...	...	...	...
Fish and other marine products	0.1	...	0.3	0.7	...	...	...	...	0.6	0.2	...	0.2
Metallic ores and concentrates	106.1	143.5	83.7	49.4	0.8	...	24.2	19.3	3.6	23.1	...	...
Bituminous coal and lignite	44.8	61.9	80.1	58.9	63.0	24.8	...	...	...	8.8	...	...
Crude petroleum and natural gas	...	...	...	...	...	...	...	...	...	...	...	...
Nonmetallic minerals	0.4	0.3	0.3	0.5	0.6	0.4	0.2	0.4	0.5	0.4	0.4	0.4
Scrap and waste	...	...	...	...	...	...	...	...	...	...	...	...
Used merchandise	0.3	2.0	2.0	4.4	2.2	1.3	...	...	...	...	...	...
Goods imported and returned unchanged	...	...	...	...	...	...	...	...	...	...	...	...
Special classification provisions	0.5	0.3	5.2	1.7	1.3	1.5	...	0.1	0.1	0.1	...	0.3

Industry	Taiwan						Singapore					
	1994	1995	1996	1997	1998	1999	1994	1995	1996	1997	1998	1999
ALL GOODS	172.6	144.9	138.8	112.8	54.1	54.7	24.1	82.5	131.9	64.6	41.0	46.8
Manufactured Goods	150.5	127.1	108.8	87.8	44.9	33.7	23.7	80.8	129.4	63.8	40.7	44.4
Food products	7.8	10.8	10.9	7.8	8.6	4.1	0.4	1.7	1.6	1.3	0.7	1.4
Tobacco products	...	...	...	...	...	...	...	0.1	...	...	0.2	0.9
Textile mill products	...	...	...	...	...	...	...	...	...	0.1	...	0.1
Apparel	...	...	0.1	...	...	...	...	...	...	...	...	...
Lumber and wood products	...	...	...	...	...	...	...	...	...	...	...	...
Furniture and fixtures	...	...	0.3	0.1	...	...	...	0.4	0.1	0.1	0.1	...
Paper products	...	...	...	...	0.1	...	0.1	0.1	0.2	0.1	0.1	...
Printing and publishing	1.0	2.4	1.8	2.0	0.2	0.3	0.9	0.5	0.7	0.6	0.7	0.2
Chemical products	28.7	20.3	25.8	19.2	13.4	5.7	0.6	1.1	2.9	3.7	2.9	1.3
Refined petroleum products	0.1	...	...	...	...	...	...	...	...	...	...	0.7
Rubber and plastic products	0.7	7.4	1.6	1.9	0.6	0.2	0.2	0.8	...	0.1	0.7	0.1
Leather products	0.3	0.2	0.6	0.4	...	...	...	...	...	0.3	0.1	0.3
Stone, clay and glass products	...	0.5	1.5	0.1	0.1	0.1	0.2	...	...	...	...	0.2
Primary metals	96.8	59.1	27.2	22.0	0.3	4.2	8.4	7.3	2.6	1.6	0.8	0.1
Fabricated metal products	1.1	2.9	2.2	2.1	2.7	5.6	0.8	0.2	0.4	0.9	1.2	0.9
Industrial machinery and computers	2.6	9.0	17.3	11.9	11.0	6.6	4.7	52.5	96.7	30.7	10.1	18.9
Electric and electronic equipment	5.1	7.3	15.6	15.3	4.5	2.9	4.4	12.9	21.5	20.5	20.1	12.8
Transportation equipment	2.7	3.7	1.1	1.8	0.3	0.9	0.4	0.8	0.3	1.0	0.6	0.3
Scientific and measuring instruments	1.7	1.5	1.4	1.6	1.4	1.8	1.2	1.1	1.0	1.5	2.1	5.1
Miscellaneous manufactures	1.5	1.5	1.4	1.4	1.3	0.8	1.2	1.1	1.0	1.1	0.3	0.9
Unidentified manufactures	0.2	0.2	0.2	0.3	0.3	0.3	0.1	0.1	0.3	0.2	0.1	0.1
Agricultural And Livestock Products	0.3	...	1.6	6.1	4.2	5.1	...	...	...	...	0.3	1.4
Agricultural products	0.3	...	1.6	6.1	4.2	5.0	...	...	...	...	0.3	1.4
Livestock and livestock products	...	...	...	...	...	...	...	...	...	...	...	...
Other Commodities	21.8	17.8	28.4	18.9	5.1	16.0	0.4	1.7	2.5	0.8	0.1	1.0
Forestry products	...	...	...	...	...	...	...	...	...	...	...	...
Fish and other marine products	0.2	0.1	0.2	0.1	...	0.2	...	0.4	0.4	0.3	...	...
Metallic ores and concentrates	...	0.1	...	...	...	...	...	...	...	...	...	...
Bituminous coal and lignite	21.4	17.5	27.2	18.4	4.8	14.6	...	...	...	...	...	...
Crude petroleum and natural gas	...	...	...	...	...	...	...	...	...	...	...	...
Nonmetallic minerals	...	...	...	...	0.1	0.1	0.3	1.2	0.5	0.1	0.1	0.1
Scrap and waste	...	...	...	...	...	...	...	...	...	...	...	...
Used merchandise	...	...	...	...	...	...	...	...	...	...	...	...
Goods imported and returned unchanged	...	...	...	...	...	...	...	...	1.6	0.3	...	0.9
Special classification provisions	0.1	0.1	0.9	0.4	0.2	1.1	...	...	1.6	0.3	...	0.9

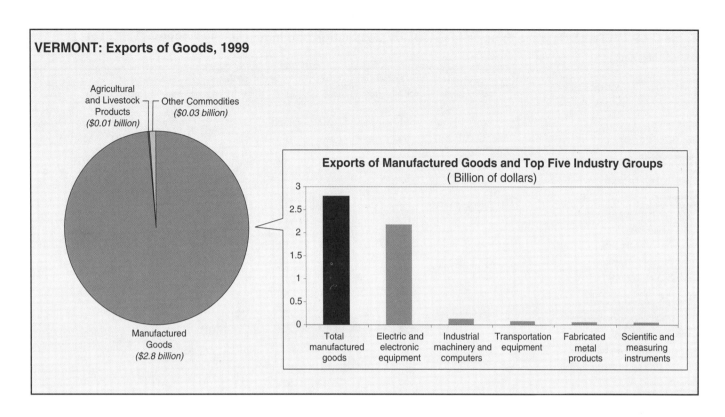

VERMONT: Exports of Goods, 1999

Agricultural and Livestock Products ($0.01 billion)

Other Commodities ($0.03 billion)

Manufactured Goods ($2.8 billion)

Exports of Manufactured Goods and Top Five Industry Groups
(Billion of dollars)

Total manufactured goods / Electric and electronic equipment / Industrial machinery and computers / Transportation equipment / Fabricated metal products / Scientific and measuring instruments

Table D-49. VERMONT: State Exports of Goods by Destination and Industry, 1994–1999

(Millions of dollars.)

Industry	All destinations						Canada					
	1994	1995	1996	1997	1998	1999	1994	1995	1996	1997	1998	1999
ALL GOODS	2 304.3	2 683.6	2 610.8	2 592.1	2 757.7	2 826.7	2 064.5	2 509.9	2 377.6	2 310.3	2 486.3	2 477.4
Manufactured Goods	2 210.9	2 625.7	2 534.7	2 538.0	2 712.6	2 789.2	1 983.5	2 461.1	2 314.0	2 266.6	2 446.8	2 451.6
Food products	12.0	11.6	14.6	24.6	28.0	37.4	8.6	7.9	10.3	19.5	22.2	20.6
Tobacco products	. . .	. . .	0.1	. . .	. . .	. . .	. . .	. . .	. . .	. . .	. . .	. . .
Textile mill products	9.4	11.7	14.2	12.5	10.9	19.9	4.1	3.1	3.2	4.2	4.2	4.3
Apparel	4.9	5.2	14.1	18.4	18.0	24.8	3.4	3.3	6.3	6.7	8.3	13.2
Lumber and wood products	29.7	34.8	35.8	43.9	41.7	42.1	26.4	31.5	32.9	41.1	38.1	38.7
Furniture and fixtures	4.4	2.5	1.3	1.4	1.6	1.9	0.8	1.0	0.6	0.9	0.5	0.9
Paper products	26.7	35.4	35.0	41.7	23.9	23.8	18.2	26.5	28.0	30.7	17.5	17.5
Printing and publishing	6.9	7.3	8.9	7.2	8.7	7.3	4.5	5.2	5.4	4.0	6.0	4.1
Chemical products	27.1	27.5	34.8	35.4	33.0	32.9	21.3	21.9	26.2	27.3	25.2	21.5
Refined petroleum products	0.2	0.2	0.9	0.1	0.3	0.4	0.2	0.2	0.9	0.1	0.1	0.3
Rubber and plastic products	16.7	18.3	18.1	19.7	14.0	16.0	10.6	12.7	11.0	10.5	8.5	10.0
Leather products	1.9	5.2	5.0	3.6	2.5	2.6	0.6	2.1	1.9	2.2	0.6	0.6
Stone, clay and glass products	4.0	4.6	5.0	4.6	6.0	6.1	3.0	3.1	2.7	3.8	3.0	4.3
Primary metals	5.8	6.8	8.9	11.1	14.7	12.1	1.9	2.6	3.3	5.4	6.3	6.0
Fabricated metal products	50.5	25.8	59.0	51.2	59.6	61.6	18.0	17.9	22.9	22.8	33.6	35.5
Industrial machinery and computers	144.8	136.0	121.4	138.0	116.2	132.0	82.4	99.5	78.0	73.6	41.9	43.4
Electric and electronic equipment	1 775.2	2 202.3	2 055.7	1 983.1	2 188.2	2 180.0	1 738.7	2 181.1	2 037.8	1 951.9	2 164.6	2 150.3
Transportation equipment	28.7	27.6	37.8	54.3	50.8	81.4	19.0	20.9	22.4	38.3	36.1	52.7
Scientific and measuring instruments	35.7	29.0	33.0	42.7	49.9	52.8	15.3	11.0	12.2	14.9	20.2	18.1
Miscellaneous manufactures	22.4	31.1	28.6	41.8	41.2	49.7	5.7	8.5	7.0	7.6	8.5	8.4
Unidentified manufactures	3.9	2.7	2.6	2.6	3.5	4.5	0.8	1.1	1.1	1.2	1.4	1.3
Agricultural And Livestock Products	12.7	10.5	12.3	9.4	8.5	9.7	9.2	8.6	6.5	6.2	6.4	6.8
Agricultural products	0.9	1.0	3.3	2.2	2.3	3.5	0.4	0.6	0.6	0.6	0.9	0.6
Livestock and livestock products	11.8	9.5	9.1	7.2	6.2	6.2	8.8	7.9	5.9	5.7	5.5	6.2
Other Commodities	80.7	47.4	63.8	44.7	36.7	27.8	71.7	40.2	57.1	37.5	33.2	19.0
Forestry products	0.3	0.3	1.2	2.5	0.2	0.6	. . .	0.1	0.1	0.4	0.1	0.2
Fish and other marine products	0.7	1.0	0.8	1.1	1.6	2.3	0.7	1.0	0.8	1.1	1.6	2.3
Metallic ores and concentrates	. . .	0.1	. . .	. . .	. . .	. . .	. . .	. . .	. . .	. . .	. . .	. . .
Bituminous coal and lignite	. . .	. . .	. . .	. . .	. . .	. . .	. . .	. . .	. . .	. . .	. . .	. . .
Crude petroleum and natural gas	. . .	. . .	. . .	. . .	. . .	. . .	. . .	. . .	. . .	. . .	. . .	. . .
Nonmetallic minerals	14.3	14.1	10.9	11.3	10.1	7.4	7.4	8.8	7.0	8.1	7.9	2.1
Scrap and waste	2.6	5.6	2.2	2.5	3.1	2.3	2.3	5.1	2.1	2.3	2.7	2.0
Used merchandise	1.0	2.2	1.5	1.9	0.9	0.8	0.2	1.8	0.7	1.3	0.7	0.6
Goods imported and returned unchanged	60.0	22.3	44.2	22.3	19.1	9.2	60.0	22.3	44.2	22.3	19.1	9.2
Special classification provisions	1.8	1.8	3.0	3.1	1.7	5.2	1.1	1.2	2.3	2.0	1.1	2.6

Table D-49. VERMONT: State Exports of Goods by Destination and Industry, 1994–1999—*Continued*

(Millions of dollars.)

Industry	South and Central American and Caribbean						Mexico					
	1994	1995	1996	1997	1998	1999	1994	1995	1996	1997	1998	1999
ALL GOODS	8.0	10.0	16.8	22.8	23.2	25.3	15.9	10.4	8.5	8.7	10.8	14.7
Manufactured Goods	7.9	9.6	16.4	22.4	23.0	25.2	15.1	10.3	8.3	8.6	10.4	14.6
Food products	0.3	0.1	0.1	...	0.4	1.0	0.1	0.1	0.2	0.5	0.3	0.5
Tobacco products	...	...	0.1	...	...	...	...	...	...	...	...	...
Textile mill products	0.6	0.1	0.5	0.7	1.1	1.8	0.2	0.3	0.5	0.2	0.1	...
Apparel	...	0.1	5.1	9.9	7.9	9.7	...	...	...	0.1	0.1	0.1
Lumber and wood products	...	...	0.1	...	...	...	...	0.1	0.1	...	0.3	1.2
Furniture and fixtures	...	...	...	...	0.1	...	...	...	...	...	...	...
Paper products	1.7	2.3	1.4	1.8	1.0	1.1	3.0	1.8	2.0	2.4	1.2	1.5
Printing and publishing	0.3	0.3	1.3	0.4	0.2	0.1	0.5	0.3	0.6	0.9	0.3	0.3
Chemical products	0.4	0.2	0.7	0.6	0.4	0.2	0.3	0.2	0.3	0.5	0.7	3.2
Refined petroleum products	...	...	...	...	...	...	...	...	...	...	...	0.1
Rubber and plastic products	0.1	0.2	0.1	0.3	0.2	0.2	0.4	0.4	0.2	0.2	0.8	0.6
Leather products	0.2	0.2	0.1	...	0.1	...	...	...	0.1	...	...	...
Stone, clay and glass products	0.1	...	0.1	0.1	0.1	0.1	0.2	0.1	0.2	0.1	0.1	...
Primary metals	0.4	0.8	1.2	0.7	0.8	0.7	0.9	0.2	0.6	0.5	0.5	0.6
Fabricated metal products	0.1	0.8	0.5	3.2	5.0	1.4	0.2	0.1	0.4	0.3	1.0	0.2
Industrial machinery and computers	1.0	1.5	2.5	2.6	2.0	4.0	2.6	0.9	1.1	0.9	1.9	4.5
Electric and electronic equipment	1.3	1.8	0.7	0.8	1.1	1.3	5.6	5.2	0.9	1.6	0.9	0.8
Transportation equipment	0.9	0.1	1.2	0.4	1.5	1.7	0.1	...	0.7	0.1	0.2	0.2
Scientific and measuring instruments	0.4	0.8	0.7	0.6	0.7	1.3	1.0	0.5	0.4	0.2	1.7	0.6
Miscellaneous manufactures	...	0.3	0.2	0.3	0.3	0.3	...	0.1	...	...	0.1	0.1
Unidentified manufactures	...	0.1	0.1	...	0.1	0.2	0.1	...	...	...	0.2	0.3
Agricultural And Livestock Products	0.1	0.2	0.1	0.3	...	...	0.8	...	0.1	...	0.3	0.1
Agricultural products	...	0.1	0.1	0.1	...	...	...	...	0.1	...	0.3	...
Livestock and livestock products	0.1	0.1	...	0.2	...	...	0.8	...	...	...	...	...
Other Commodities	...	0.1	0.2	0.1	0.2	...	...	0.1	0.1	0.1	...	...
Forestry products	...	...	...	...	...	...	...	...	...	...	...	...
Fish and other marine products	...	...	...	...	...	...	...	...	...	...	...	...
Metallic ores and concentrates	...	...	...	...	...	...	...	...	...	...	...	...
Bituminous coal and lignite	...	...	...	...	...	...	...	...	...	...	...	...
Crude petroleum and natural gas	...	...	...	...	...	...	...	...	...	...	...	...
Nonmetallic materials	...	...	0.1	...	0.2	...	...	...	...	...	...	...
Scrap and waste	...	...	...	...	...	...	...	...	...	...	...	...
Used merchandise	...	...	...	0.1	...	...	...	...	...	...	...	...
Goods imported and returned unchanged	...	...	...	...	...	...	...	...	...	...	...	...
Special classification provisions	...	0.1	0.1	...	...	...	...	...	...	...	...	...

Industry	European Union						United Kingdom					
	1994	1995	1996	1997	1998	1999	1994	1995	1996	1997	1998	1999
ALL GOODS	123.7	73.9	96.6	136.6	139.1	168.0	29.5	29.7	32.8	49.1	47.6	69.3
Manufactured Goods	120.5	71.2	90.9	133.3	136.2	162.7	29.3	29.3	32.5	48.8	47.4	68.6
Food products	2.0	2.4	2.8	3.4	4.2	5.3	1.8	2.1	2.2	3.0	2.7	5.1
Tobacco products	...	...	...	...	...	...	...	...	...	...	...	...
Textile mill products	0.8	0.7	0.6	1.6	1.6	1.4	...	0.1	0.1	0.1	0.2	0.3
Apparel	1.0	1.4	1.9	1.0	1.3	1.1	0.3	0.5	0.4	0.4	0.3	0.2
Lumber and wood products	1.8	1.7	1.4	1.8	1.9	1.6	1.2	0.9	1.2	1.4	1.3	1.3
Furniture and fixtures	3.6	1.3	0.1	0.2	0.3	0.8	3.5	1.3	0.1	0.2	0.2	0.4
Paper products	0.9	1.0	1.0	1.3	1.9	1.7	0.2	0.2	...	0.2	0.5	0.2
Printing and publishing	0.6	0.5	1.0	1.4	1.6	1.5	0.4	0.4	0.6	1.0	0.8	0.7
Chemical products	3.3	3.2	4.8	5.5	5.2	4.0	2.0	2.2	2.7	2.9	2.5	1.9
Refined petroleum products	...	...	...	...	0.1	...	...	...	...	...	...	...
Rubber and plastic products	2.9	3.2	5.5	7.0	2.9	3.3	1.4	1.9	3.1	4.8	1.5	1.4
Leather products	0.5	1.9	1.9	0.8	1.0	1.4	0.1	0.5	0.3	0.3	0.3	0.3
Stone, clay and glass products	0.4	0.5	0.5	0.4	2.2	0.4	0.1	0.3	0.3	0.2	2.0	0.2
Primary metals	1.2	1.4	2.3	1.6	1.4	1.2	0.5	0.5	1.6	0.9	0.5	0.3
Fabricated metal products	19.7	3.0	14.1	9.2	8.9	9.0	0.9	1.1	3.3	5.4	0.4	1.7
Industrial machinery and computers	39.8	16.8	15.7	38.6	47.8	58.4	6.6	9.5	6.0	15.1	19.9	28.4
Electric and electronic equipment	18.9	7.0	6.0	16.2	9.1	8.9	3.5	1.5	1.9	5.5	2.9	4.2
Transportation equipment	2.9	3.0	6.2	7.3	7.2	17.0	0.3	0.3	1.3	1.1	2.1	11.4
Scientific and measuring instruments	9.9	9.6	13.4	20.4	21.3	24.7	3.5	2.5	2.7	3.3	5.5	6.1
Miscellaneous manufactures	9.5	11.7	11.2	15.0	15.4	20.0	2.5	3.2	4.3	2.8	3.5	4.2
Unidentified manufactures	0.8	0.8	0.5	0.4	0.9	0.9	0.3	0.3	0.3	0.2	0.3	0.2
Agricultural And Livestock Products	0.1	0.1	2.1	1.4	0.9	0.9	...	...	...	0.1	...	...
Agricultural products	...	0.1	2.1	1.2	0.6	0.9	...	...	...	0.1	...	...
Livestock and livestock products	0.1	...	0.1	0.2	0.3	...	...	...	...	...	...	...
Other Commodities	3.1	2.5	3.6	1.9	2.0	4.4	0.2	0.4	0.3	0.2	0.2	0.7
Forestry products	...	...	...	...	...	0.1	...	...	...	...	...	...
Fish and other marine products	...	...	...	...	...	...	...	...	...	...	...	...
Metallic ores and concentrates	...	...	...	...	...	...	...	...	...	...	...	...
Bituminous coal and lignite	...	...	...	...	...	...	...	...	...	...	...	...
Crude petroleum and natural gas	...	...	...	...	...	...	...	...	...	...	...	...
Nonmetallic materials	2.4	1.7	2.8	1.6	1.4	2.3	...	...	...	0.1	...	...
Scrap and waste	0.2	0.3	...	...	0.1	0.1	0.1	0.1	...	...	...	0.1
Used merchandise	0.5	0.4	0.6	0.2	0.2	0.2	0.1	0.3	0.3	0.1	0.1	0.1
Goods imported and returned unchanged	...	...	...	...	...	...	...	...	...	...	...	...
Special classification provisions	0.1	0.1	0.2	0.1	0.4	1.8	...	...	...	...	...	0.5

Table D-49. VERMONT: State Exports of Goods by Destination and Industry, 1994–1999—*Continued*

(Millions of dollars.)

Industry	Germany						France					
	1994	1995	1996	1997	1998	1999	1994	1995	1996	1997	1998	1999
ALL GOODS	16.4	12.0	13.5	27.8	25.6	22.6	8.4	7.1	11.3	19.7	14.3	17.4
Manufactured Goods	16.3	11.7	13.0	27.4	25.1	22.0	8.3	7.0	11.2	19.6	14.3	17.3
Food products	0.1	...	0.1	0.1	0.3	...	...	...	0.1	...	...	...
Tobacco products	...	...	...	...	...	...	...	...	...	...	...	...
Textile mill products	...	0.2	0.2	0.2	...	...	...	0.1	...	0.2	0.1	...
Apparel	0.1	0.2	0.5	0.1	0.2	0.2	...	0.1	...	...	0.1	0.1
Lumber and wood products	0.1	0.2	0.1	0.1	0.4	0.2	0.1	...	0.1	...	...	...
Furniture and fixtures	0.1	...	...	...	...	0.1	0.1	0.1	...	...	...	...
Paper products	0.1	0.1	0.1	0.1	0.3	0.2	0.3	0.1	0.2	0.1	0.1	0.1
Printing and publishing	...	...	0.1	0.1	...	0.1	...	...	0.1	...	...	0.1
Chemical products	0.5	0.5	0.4	1.8	1.7	0.8	0.3	0.1	0.1	...	0.1	...
Refined petroleum products	...	...	...	...	0.1	...	...	...	...	...	...	...
Rubber and plastic products	0.4	0.3	0.4	0.4	0.2	0.3	0.4	0.2	0.3	0.6	0.3	0.3
Leather products	0.1	0.2	0.1	0.1	0.2	0.2	0.1	0.1	0.1	0.1	0.2	0.3
Stone, clay and glass products	...	...	...	...	0.1	0.1	...	...	...	...	...	...
Primary metals	0.3	0.4	0.2	0.3	0.1	0.1	...	...	0.1	...	...	...
Fabricated metal products	0.5	0.8	0.1	1.6	0.2	0.6	0.3	0.2	0.2	0.1	0.2	0.2
Industrial machinery and computers	6.6	2.0	3.0	8.9	10.7	7.4	2.3	1.8	1.8	4.3	3.7	6.6
Electric and electronic equipment	2.7	1.6	1.2	2.0	1.8	0.5	1.0	0.6	0.7	5.2	0.6	0.9
Transportation equipment	0.5	0.3	0.4	1.4	0.7	0.7	1.0	1.7	3.8	3.5	3.3	3.0
Scientific and measuring instruments	2.9	3.0	5.4	8.7	7.2	9.4	1.6	1.2	1.8	4.5	4.4	4.5
Miscellaneous manufactures	1.2	1.9	0.7	1.6	0.8	1.0	1.0	0.7	1.7	0.8	1.1	0.9
Unidentified manufactures	0.1	0.1	0.1	0.1	0.1	0.2	...	0.1	...	...	...	0.1
Agricultural And Livestock Products	...	...	0.1	0.3	0.1	0.1	...	...	...	0.2	...	...
Agricultural products	...	...	0.1	0.3	0.1	0.1	...	...	...	0.2	...	...
Livestock and livestock products	...	...	...	...	...	...	...	...	...	...	...	...
Other Commodities	0.1	0.3	0.4	0.1	0.4	0.5	0.1	0.1	0.1	...	...	0.1
Forestry products	...	...	...	...	...	...	...	...	...	...	...	...
Fish and other marine products	...	...	...	...	...	...	...	...	...	...	...	...
Metallic ores and concentrates	...	...	...	...	...	...	...	...	...	...	...	...
Bituminous coal and lignite	...	...	...	...	...	...	...	...	...	...	...	...
Crude petroleum and natural gas	...	...	...	...	...	...	...	...	...	...	...	...
Nonmetallic materials	...	...	...	...	...	...	...	...	...	...	...	...
Scrap and waste	...	0.2	...	...	...	...	...	...	...	...	...	...
Used merchandise	...	...	0.3	...	...	...	0.1	...	...	...	...	...
Goods imported and returned unchanged	...	...	...	...	...	...	...	...	...	...	...	...
Special classification provisions	...	...	0.1	...	0.3	0.4	...	...	0.1	...	...	0.1

Industry	The Netherlands						Asian 10					
	1994	1995	1996	1997	1998	1999	1994	1995	1996	1997	1998	1999
ALL GOODS	20.4	3.1	15.4	6.0	9.2	11.1	65.8	54.3	78.7	80.3	63.8	95.1
Manufactured Goods	20.0	2.9	15.4	5.8	9.2	10.9	59.8	50.2	75.1	74.9	62.5	91.0
Food products	0.1	0.1	...	0.2	0.1	0.1	0.4	0.7	1.0	1.0	0.4	8.7
Tobacco products	...	...	...	...	...	...	...	...	...	...	...	...
Textile mill products	...	...	...	...	...	...	3.1	6.9	8.8	5.1	2.8	4.0
Apparel	...	0.2	0.1	...	...	...	0.4	0.2	0.5	0.5	0.2	0.5
Lumber and wood products	0.1	...	...	0.1	...	...	1.4	1.2	1.2	0.8	0.9	0.6
Furniture and fixtures	...	...	...	...	...	...	...	...	0.4	0.2	0.4	0.1
Paper products	...	...	0.2	...	...	0.1	1.7	2.2	1.4	2.4	1.4	1.3
Printing and publishing	...	...	...	...	0.2	...	0.7	0.8	0.4	0.4	0.5	1.0
Chemical products	0.1	0.1	...	0.1	0.1	...	1.5	1.0	1.0	0.9	0.5	3.6
Refined petroleum products	...	...	...	...	...	...	...	...	...	...	0.1	...
Rubber and plastic products	0.2	0.1	0.1	0.4	0.3	0.4	1.7	0.5	0.4	0.7	0.9	0.8
Leather products	...	0.1	0.1	0.1	...	0.1	0.4	0.7	0.8	0.4	0.6	0.4
Stone, clay and glass products	0.1	...	...	...	...	...	0.3	0.8	1.6	0.2	0.5	1.1
Primary metals	...	0.1	0.1	0.1	...	...	0.4	0.4	0.9	2.3	2.0	2.7
Fabricated metal products	16.6	0.1	9.8	0.1	2.4	4.8	12.0	3.0	10.5	12.2	7.7	12.6
Industrial machinery and computers	0.5	0.6	1.8	0.8	3.4	1.9	14.8	12.5	20.0	16.1	15.5	15.8
Electric and electronic equipment	0.3	0.2	0.4	0.2	0.5	0.2	7.5	4.9	7.7	9.3	8.6	13.3
Transportation equipment	1.0	0.1	0.4	0.8	0.3	1.0	1.8	1.7	5.9	4.2	2.9	2.1
Scientific and measuring instruments	0.7	0.8	1.4	1.2	1.0	1.2	5.2	4.2	3.9	3.6	3.3	4.7
Miscellaneous manufactures	0.3	0.4	0.7	1.7	0.8	1.2	4.8	8.1	8.3	14.1	12.7	16.9
Unidentified manufactures	0.1	0.1	...	...	0.1	...	1.9	0.4	0.6	0.7	0.5	1.0
Agricultural And Livestock Products	...	...	...	0.2	...	...	0.3	...	1.1	0.4	0.3	0.2
Agricultural products	...	...	...	0.2	...	...	0.2	...	0.1	0.1	0.1	0.2
Livestock and livestock products	...	...	...	...	...	...	0.1	...	1.0	0.3	0.2	...
Other Commodities	0.3	0.1	...	...	...	0.2	5.7	4.1	2.4	5.0	1.1	3.9
Forestry products	...	...	...	...	...	...	0.3	0.2	1.0	2.0	0.1	0.3
Fish and other marine products	...	...	...	...	...	...	...	...	...	...	...	...
Metallic ores and concentrates	...	...	...	...	...	...	...	0.1	...	...	...	...
Bituminous coal and lignite	...	...	...	...	...	...	...	...	...	...	...	...
Crude petroleum and natural gas	...	...	...	...	...	...	...	...	...	...	...	...
Nonmetallic materials	...	...	...	...	...	...	4.5	3.3	0.9	1.5	0.6	3.0
Scrap and waste	...	...	...	...	...	...	...	0.1	...	0.2	0.3	0.1
Used merchandise	0.3	...	...	...	...	...	0.4	0.1	0.2	0.3	...	...
Goods imported and returned unchanged	...	...	...	...	...	...	...	...	...	...	...	...
Special classification provisions	...	0.1	...	...	...	0.2	0.5	0.4	0.3	0.9	0.2	0.4

Table D-49. VERMONT: State Exports of Goods by Destination and Industry, 1994–1999—Continued

(Millions of dollars.)

Industry	Japan						South Korea					
	1994	1995	1996	1997	1998	1999	1994	1995	1996	1997	1998	1999
ALL GOODS	18.0	26.0	33.5	31.3	26.4	35.8	5.4	5.7	9.3	17.6	13.2	5.8
Manufactured Goods	14.3	22.2	31.5	29.1	25.8	34.8	5.3	5.7	9.3	17.6	13.1	5.7
Food products	0.1	0.1	0.2	0.6	0.3	0.2	...	...	...	...	...	0.2
Tobacco products	...	...	...	...	...	...	...	...	...	...	...	...
Textile mill products	2.2	6.7	7.7	4.3	2.4	3.5	0.1	...	0.8	0.3	0.1	0.1
Apparel	0.3	0.2	0.3	0.3	0.1	0.3	...	...	0.1	0.1	...	...
Lumber and wood products	...	0.2	0.1	0.2	0.1	...	...	...	...	...	...	...
Furniture and fixtures	...	...	0.1	0.1	0.4	0.1	...	...	0.2	...	...	...
Paper products	0.1	0.4	0.1	0.1	0.2	0.1	0.7	0.7	0.5	1.0	0.1	0.3
Printing and publishing	0.1	0.6	0.2	0.1	0.2	0.4	...	...	0.1	...	...	...
Chemical products	0.2	0.3	0.3	0.5	0.2	0.1	...	0.1	0.2	0.1	...	0.3
Refined petroleum products	...	...	...	...	...	...	...	...	...	...	...	...
Rubber and plastic products	1.5	0.3	0.2	0.2	0.5	0.4	...	0.1	...	0.1	...	0.1
Leather products	0.1	0.2	0.5	0.2	0.1	0.1	...	0.1	...	...	...	...
Stone, clay and glass products	0.1	0.5	1.4	0.1	0.3	0.9	0.2	...	...	...	...	0.1
Primary metals	0.1	0.1	0.1	0.1	0.2	0.2	...	0.1	0.2	1.2	0.6	1.3
Fabricated metal products	0.7	0.2	0.2	0.3	0.4	0.5	0.2	0.8	1.7	9.5	4.0	0.3
Industrial machinery and computers	0.8	1.5	3.7	4.5	3.6	6.6	1.8	1.7	2.8	2.0	2.9	1.8
Electric and electronic equipment	1.5	1.9	2.1	1.3	2.3	1.3	1.6	1.0	1.1	2.0	3.1	0.6
Transportation equipment	0.2	0.8	5.3	1.8	1.1	1.4	0.1	...	0.1	0.4	1.6	...
Scientific and measuring instruments	1.6	1.0	1.4	1.2	1.0	2.4	0.4	0.5	1.3	0.6	0.4	0.5
Miscellaneous manufactures	4.4	7.1	7.6	13.4	12.3	16.2	0.1	0.6	0.1	0.2	...	0.1
Unidentified manufactures	0.1	0.1	...	0.1	0.1	0.1	...	...	...	0.1	0.1	0.1
Agricultural And Livestock Products	0.1	...	1.1	0.4	0.2	0.1	...	...	...	...	...	...
Agricultural products	...	...	0.1	0.1	...	0.1	...	...	...	...	...	...
Livestock and livestock products	0.1	...	1.0	0.3	0.2	...	...	...	...	...	...	...
Other Commodities	3.7	3.8	1.0	1.7	0.4	0.9	0.1	...	...	...	0.1	0.1
Forestry products	...	...	...	...	...	...	...	...	...	...	...	...
Fish and other marine products	...	...	...	...	...	...	...	...	...	...	...	...
Metallic ores and concentrates	...	0.1	...	...	...	...	...	...	...	...	...	...
Bituminous coal and lignite	...	...	...	...	...	...	...	...	...	...	...	...
Crude petroleum and natural gas	...	...	...	...	...	...	...	...	...	...	...	...
Nonmetallic materials	3.6	3.3	0.7	1.4	0.4	0.6	...	...	...	...	...	...
Scrap and waste	...	...	...	...	...	...	...	...	...	...	0.1	0.1
Used merchandise	...	0.1	0.2	0.3	...	...	...	...	...	...	...	...
Goods imported and returned unchanged	...	...	...	...	...	...	...	...	...	...	...	...
Special classification provisions	...	0.3	...	...	...	0.3	...	...	...	...	...	...

Industry	Taiwan						Singapore					
	1994	1995	1996	1997	1998	1999	1994	1995	1996	1997	1998	1999
ALL GOODS	17.0	3.4	12.1	6.3	7.0	19.0	13.2	8.5	8.1	10.5	4.7	6.9
Manufactured Goods	17.0	3.4	12.1	6.3	6.9	18.8	12.6	8.5	7.5	9.0	4.6	6.4
Food products	...	0.1	...	...	...	4.1	...	...	0.1	...	0.1	0.3
Tobacco products	...	...	...	...	...	...	...	...	...	...	...	...
Textile mill products	0.3	0.1	0.1	0.1	0.1	0.1	...	...	...	0.1	...	...
Apparel	...	...	...	...	...	0.1	...	...	...	...	...	...
Lumber and wood products	1.1	0.7	0.9	0.2	0.7	0.3	...	...	...	...	...	...
Furniture and fixtures	...	...	...	...	...	...	...	...	...	...	...	...
Paper products	0.2	...	0.1	0.1	0.2	0.3	0.4	0.6	0.4	0.6	0.1	0.2
Printing and publishing	0.4	...	...	...	0.1	...	0.1	...	...	0.1	0.2	0.4
Chemical products	...	...	...	0.1	...	3.1	0.1	...	...	...	...	...
Refined petroleum products	...	...	...	...	...	...	...	...	...	...	...	...
Rubber and plastic products	...	...	0.1	0.1	0.2	0.1	...	...	...	...	...	0.1
Leather products	...	...	...	0.1	...	0.1	...	...	...	...	...	...
Stone, clay and glass products	...	0.1	...	0.1	...	0.1	...	...	...	...	...	...
Primary metals	0.2	0.1	0.1	0.4	0.7	0.7	...	0.1	...	0.2	0.1	...
Fabricated metal products	10.6	0.7	7.5	1.9	1.8	6.2	...	...	0.3	0.1	0.4	1.1
Industrial machinery and computers	0.6	0.3	1.4	0.6	2.0	2.3	9.7	6.8	5.6	2.2	2.4	2.6
Electric and electronic equipment	0.9	0.6	0.8	0.2	0.6	0.9	1.5	0.4	0.5	4.9	0.8	0.4
Transportation equipment	0.5	...	0.3	1.8	0.1	0.1	0.1	0.1	...	...	...	0.4
Scientific and measuring instruments	0.3	0.3	0.2	0.2	0.3	0.2	0.5	0.2	0.3	0.7	0.4	0.6
Miscellaneous manufactures	...	0.1	...	...	0.1	0.1	0.2	0.1	0.4	0.1	...	0.1
Unidentified manufactures	1.6	0.2	0.5	0.4	0.1	0.2	...	...	...	...	0.1	0.1
Agricultural And Livestock Products	...	...	...	...	...	...	...	...	...	...	...	0.1
Agricultural products	...	...	...	...	...	...	...	...	...	...	...	0.1
Livestock and livestock products	...	...	...	...	...	...	...	...	...	...	...	...
Other Commodities	...	...	...	0.1	0.1	0.2	0.7	...	0.6	1.5	0.1	0.4
Forestry products	...	...	...	...	...	...	...	...	0.6	1.4	...	0.2
Fish and other marine products	...	...	...	...	...	...	...	...	...	...	...	...
Metallic ores and concentrates	...	...	...	...	...	...	...	...	...	...	...	...
Bituminous coal and lignite	...	...	...	...	...	...	...	...	...	...	...	...
Crude petroleum and natural gas	...	...	...	...	...	...	...	...	...	...	...	...
Nonmetallic materials	...	...	...	0.1	0.1	0.2	0.4	...	...	...	...	0.2
Scrap and waste	...	...	...	...	...	...	0.3	...	...	...	...	...
Used merchandise	...	...	...	...	...	...	...	...	...	...	...	...
Goods imported and returned unchanged	...	...	...	...	...	...	...	...	...	...	...	...
Special classification provisions	...	...	...	...	...	...	...	...	...	...	...	...

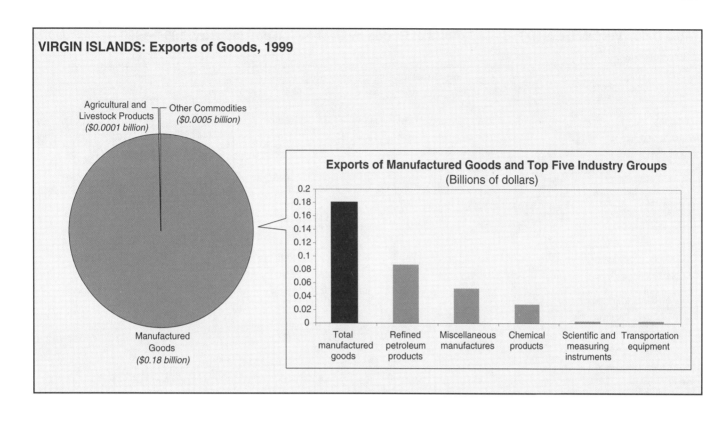

VIRGIN ISLANDS: Exports of Goods, 1999

Agricultural and Livestock Products ($0.0001 billion)

Other Commodities ($0.0005 billion)

Manufactured Goods ($0.18 billion)

Exports of Manufactured Goods and Top Five Industry Groups (Billions of dollars)

Table D-50. VIRGIN ISLANDS: State Exports of Goods by Destination and Industry, 1994–1999

(Millions of dollars.)

Industry	All destinations						Canada					
	1994	1995	1996	1997	1998	1999	1994	1995	1996	1997	1998	1999
ALL GOODS	158.0	228.6	192.4	242.7	114.5	180.9	7.5	12.4	7.4	4.3	2.8	2.9
Manufactured Goods	157.6	226.9	191.1	240.8	112.9	180.3	7.3	11.9	7.1	3.2	2.7	2.6
Food products	5.6	4.2	2.0	2.4	0.4	0.7	0.5	0.3	0.3	0.3	0.2	0.3
Tobacco products	0.4	0.6	...	...	...	...	...	...	...	...	...	...
Textile mill products	0.1	0.1	...	...	0.2	...	...	...	...	...	...	...
Apparel	3.5	2.3	1.3	0.3	...	0.2	...	...	...	...	...	0.1
Lumber and wood products	...	0.2	0.2	0.1	0.1	0.1	...	...	...	...	...	...
Furniture and fixtures	...	0.1	0.1	0.1	...	...	...	...	...	0.1	...	...
Paper products	0.1	0.6	0.4	0.3	0.1	0.3	...	0.1	0.1	0.1	...	0.1
Printing and publishing	3.8	6.4	11.7	1.6	0.4	...	2.4	0.1	...	0.2	...	...
Chemical products	55.0	49.9	20.3	52.8	19.0	28.1	2.1	4.6	3.7	0.7	1.3	0.6
Refined petroleum products	63.9	137.1	136.5	168.1	53.3	87.3	...	...	0.2	...	...	...
Rubber and plastic products	0.3	0.2	0.5	0.4	0.2	0.8	0.2	0.1	0.2	0.2	...	0.1
Leather products	0.4	0.1	0.1	0.1	0.1	1.1	...	...	...	...	...	...
Stone, clay and glass products	1.3	1.1	1.0	0.8	0.6	1.1	0.1	0.1	0.1	0.1	...	0.5
Primary metals	1.5	1.3	0.4	0.6	0.5	0.3	...	0.3	...	...	0.5	0.1
Fabricated metal products	0.3	0.4	2.0	0.1	1.0	0.1	...	...	...	...	...	...
Industrial machinery and computers	6.5	8.0	2.5	1.9	1.1	1.2	0.8	5.3	0.6	0.5	0.1	0.3
Electric and electronic equipment	2.1	1.8	3.6	0.9	0.7	0.4	0.7	0.8	0.7	...	...	...
Transportation equipment	2.0	1.1	0.7	0.9	2.7	2.9	0.3	0.1	...	0.1	...	...
Scientific and measuring instruments	6.5	5.2	3.5	4.1	7.7	3.2	0.1	...	...	0.1	0.2	0.4
Miscellaneous manufactures	3.8	5.8	3.9	5.1	24.4	51.8	...	...	1.0	0.9	...	...
Unidentified manufactures	0.4	0.3	0.2	0.3	0.5	0.7	...	...	0.1	...	...	...
Agricultural And Livestock Products	...	...	...	0.2	...	0.1	...	...	...	...	...	0.1
Agricultural products	...	...	...	...	...	0.1	...	...	...	...	...	0.1
Livestock and livestock products	...	...	...	0.2	...	...	...	...	...	...	...	...
Other Commodities	0.4	1.7	1.3	1.7	1.5	0.5	0.1	0.5	0.3	1.1	0.1	0.3
Forestry products	...	...	...	...	...	0.2	...	...	...	...	...	...
Fish and other marine products	...	0.1	...	0.1	...	...	...	...	...	...	...	...
Metallic ores and concentrates	...	...	...	...	...	...	...	...	...	...	...	...
Bituminous coal and lignite	...	...	...	...	...	...	...	...	...	...	...	...
Crude petroleum and natural gas	...	...	...	...	...	0.2	...	...	...	...	...	...
Nonmetallic minerals	0.1	1.1	1.0	0.3	0.8	0.2	0.1	0.3	0.1	...	...	0.1
Scrap and waste	...	0.1	...	...	...	...	...	...	...	...	...	...
Used merchandise	0.2	0.2	0.1	0.1	0.3	...	...	...	...	...	...	...
Goods imported and returned unchanged	0.1	0.2	0.2	1.0	0.1	...	0.1	0.2	0.2	1.0	0.1	...
Special classification provisions	...	...	...	0.1	...	0.1	...	...	...	...	...	0.1

Table D-50. VIRGIN ISLANDS: State Exports of Goods by Destination and Industry, 1994–1999—*Continued*

(Millions of dollars.)

Industry	South and Central America and Caribbean						Mexico					
	1994	1995	1996	1997	1998	1999	1994	1995	1996	1997	1998	1999
ALL GOODS	71.6	134.6	123.7	114.8	73.7	92.2	3.8	5.6	11.7	3.9	0.7	1.9
Manufactured Goods	71.4	133.5	122.7	114.4	72.7	92.0	3.8	5.6	11.6	3.9	0.7	1.9
Food products	4.7	3.1	1.7	2.0	0.1	...	...	...	...	...	...	...
Tobacco products	0.4	0.6	...	...	...	...	...	...	...	...	...	...
Textile mill products	0.1	...	...	...	...	...	...	...	...	...	...	...
Apparel	3.4	2.2	1.2	0.3	...	0.1	...	...	...	...	...	...
Lumber and wood products	...	0.1	0.1	0.1	0.1	0.1	...	...	...	...	...	...
Furniture and fixtures	...	...	...	...	...	...	...	...	...	...	...	...
Paper products	0.1	0.5	0.1	...	...	0.2	...	...	...	...	...	...
Printing and publishing	0.9	0.9	0.6	0.7	0.3	...	0.4	5.3	11.0	0.6	...	...
Chemical products	2.7	2.3	1.0	1.9	1.2	5.3	3.2	0.1	...	2.5	0.2	1.8
Refined petroleum products	46.0	112.7	110.0	100.6	37.9	28.4	...	...	...	...	...	...
Rubber and plastic products	...	...	0.2	...	0.1	0.2	...	...	...	...	...	...
Leather products	0.4	0.1	0.1	...	...	...	...	...	...	...	...	...
Stone, clay and glass products	1.2	0.9	0.8	0.7	0.6	0.6	...	...	...	...	...	...
Primary metals	1.1	0.6	0.3	0.2	...	0.2	...	0.1	...	...	...	...
Fabricated metal products	0.1	0.2	0.2	...	0.9	0.1	...	...	...	...	...	...
Industrial machinery and computers	2.0	1.3	1.2	0.4	0.3	0.6	0.1	...	...	...	0.4	...
Electric and electronic equipment	0.6	0.1	1.0	0.2	0.2	...	...	0.1	0.4	0.4	...	...
Transportation equipment	1.4	1.1	0.6	0.7	2.4	1.9	0.1	...	...	...	...	...
Scientific and measuring instruments	3.4	2.9	2.0	2.8	4.8	2.6	...	...	0.1	0.3	...	...
Miscellaneous manufactures	2.4	3.6	1.4	3.5	23.3	51.2	...	...	...	...	...	...
Unidentified manufactures	0.4	0.2	0.1	0.2	0.5	0.6	...	...	...	...	...	...
Agricultural And Livestock Products	...	...	...	...	...	...	...	...	...	...	...	...
Agricultural products	...	...	...	...	...	...	...	...	...	...	...	...
Livestock and livestock products	...	...	...	...	...	...	...	...	...	...	...	...
Other Commodities	0.3	1.1	0.9	0.5	0.9	0.2	...	...	...	0.1	...	...
Forestry products	...	...	...	...	0.1	...	...	...	...	...	...	...
Fish and other marine products	...	...	...	...	...	...	...	...	...	...	...	...
Metallic ores and concentrates	...	...	...	...	...	...	...	...	...	...	...	...
Bituminous coal and lignite	...	...	...	...	...	...	...	...	...	...	...	...
Crude petroleum and natural gas	...	...	...	...	...	...	...	...	...	...	...	...
Nonmetallic minerals	...	0.8	0.8	0.2	0.5	0.2	...	...	0.1	...	...	...
Scrap and waste	...	0.1	...	...	...	...	...	...	...	...	...	...
Used merchandise	0.2	0.2	0.1	0.1	0.3	...	...	...	...	...	...	...
Goods imported and returned unchanged	...	...	...	...	...	...	...	...	...	...	...	...
Special classification provisions	...	...	...	0.1	...	...	...	...	...	...	...	...

Industry	European Union						United Kingdom					
	1994	1995	1996	1997	1998	1999	1994	1995	1996	1997	1998	1999
ALL GOODS	32.4	14.3	24.4	83.2	20.4	43.6	1.0	0.7	1.0	0.4	0.9	1.4
Manufactured Goods	32.4	14.3	24.4	82.9	20.3	43.6	1.0	0.7	1.0	0.2	0.9	1.4
Food products	...	...	...	...	...	...	...	...	...	...	...	...
Tobacco products	...	...	...	...	...	...	...	...	...	...	...	...
Textile mill products	...	...	...	...	...	...	...	...	...	...	...	...
Apparel	...	0.1	0.1	...	...	...	...	...	...	...	...	...
Lumber and wood products	...	...	...	...	...	...	...	...	...	...	...	...
Furniture and fixtures	...	...	...	...	...	...	...	...	...	...	...	...
Paper products	...	...	...	0.1	...	...	...	...	...	...	...	...
Printing and publishing	...	0.1	...	...	...	...	...	...	...	...	...	...
Chemical products	19.3	9.3	5.7	26.2	14.1	12.8	0.2	...	...	...	...	0.1
Refined petroleum products	9.3	2.6	17.0	55.3	3.1	28.1	...	...	...	...	0.1	...
Rubber and plastic products	...	0.1	...	...	...	...	...	0.1	...	...	...	...
Leather products	...	...	...	...	...	1.1	...	...	...	...	...	...
Stone, clay and glass products	...	...	...	...	...	...	...	...	...	...	...	...
Primary metals	0.3	...	...	...	...	...	...	...	...	...	...	...
Fabricated metal products	0.1	0.1	0.1	...	...	...	...	...	...	...	...	...
Industrial machinery and computers	1.7	0.8	0.3	0.9	0.2	0.2	0.2	0.2	...	...	0.2	0.1
Electric and electronic equipment	0.3	0.5	0.2	0.1	0.3	...	0.2	...	...	...	0.3	...
Transportation equipment	...	...	...	...	0.2	1.1	...	...	...	...	...	1.1
Scientific and measuring instruments	1.0	0.4	0.3	0.1	2.1	0.1	0.3	0.3	0.2	...	0.3	...
Miscellaneous manufactures	0.2	0.1	0.7	0.1	0.2	...	0.1	0.1	0.7	0.1	...	...
Unidentified manufactures	...	0.1	...	...	...	...	...	...	...	...	...	...
Agricultural And Livestock Products	...	...	...	0.2	...	...	...	...	...	0.2	...	...
Agricultural products	...	...	...	...	...	...	...	...	...	...	...	...
Livestock and livestock products	...	...	...	0.2	...	...	...	...	...	0.2	...	...
Other Commodities	...	...	...	0.1	0.1	...	...	...	...	...	...	...
Forestry products	...	...	...	...	...	...	...	...	...	...	...	...
Fish and other marine products	...	...	...	0.1	...	...	...	...	...	...	...	...
Metallic ores and concentrates	...	...	...	...	...	...	...	...	...	...	...	...
Bituminous coal and lignite	...	...	...	...	...	...	...	...	...	...	...	...
Crude petroleum and natural gas	...	...	...	...	0.1	...	...	...	...	...	...	...
Nonmetallic minerals	...	...	...	...	...	...	...	...	...	...	...	...
Scrap and waste	...	...	...	...	...	...	...	...	...	...	...	...
Used merchandise	...	...	...	...	...	...	...	...	...	...	...	...
Goods imported and returned unchanged	...	...	...	...	...	...	...	...	...	...	...	...
Special classification provisions	...	...	...	...	...	...	...	...	...	...	...	...

Table D-50. VIRGIN ISLANDS: State Exports of Goods by Destination and Industry, 1994–1999—*Continued*

(Millions of dollars.)

Industry	Germany						France					
	1994	1995	1996	1997	1998	1999	1994	1995	1996	1997	1998	1999
ALL GOODS	0.3	0.6	0.1	5.8	1.8	0.3	0.3	0.1	0.1	1.8	0.1	0.7
Manufactured Goods	0.3	0.6	0.1	5.8	1.7	0.3	0.3	0.1	0.1	1.7	0.1	0.7
Food products	...	...	...	...	...	...	...	...	...	...	...	...
Tobacco products	...	...	...	...	...	...	...	...	...	...	...	...
Textile mill products	...	...	...	...	...	...	...	...	...	...	...	...
Apparel	...	...	...	...	...	...	...	...	...	...	...	...
Lumber and wood products	...	...	...	...	...	...	...	...	...	...	...	...
Furniture and fixtures	...	...	...	...	...	...	...	...	...	...	...	...
Paper products	...	...	...	0.1	...	...	...	...	...	...	...	...
Printing and publishing	...	...	...	...	...	...	...	...	...	...	...	...
Chemical products	...	...	...	0.6	...	...	...	...	...	1.6	0.1	...
Refined petroleum products	...	...	...	5.0	...	...	...	...	...	...	...	...
Rubber and plastic products	...	...	...	...	...	...	...	...	...	...	...	...
Leather products	...	...	...	...	...	0.2	...	...	...	...	...	0.7
Stone, clay and glass products	...	...	...	...	...	...	...	...	...	...	...	...
Primary metals	...	...	...	...	...	...	...	...	...	...	...	...
Fabricated metal products	...	...	...	...	...	...	...	...	...	...	...	...
Industrial machinery and computers	...	...	...	...	...	...	...	...	...	...	...	...
Electric and electronic equipment	...	0.4	...	...	...	...	0.1	...	0.1	0.1	...	...
Transportation equipment	...	...	...	...	...	...	...	...	...	...	...	...
Scientific and measuring instruments	0.3	0.1	0.1	...	1.7	0.1	0.2	...	...	...	...	...
Miscellaneous manufactures	...	...	...	...	...	...	...	...	...	...	...	...
Unidentified manufactures	...	...	...	...	...	...	...	...	...	...	...	...
Agricultural And Livestock Products	...	...	...	...	...	...	...	...	...	...	...	...
Agricultural products	...	...	...	...	...	...	...	...	...	...	...	...
Livestock and livestock products	...	...	...	...	...	...	...	...	...	...	...	...
Other Commodities	...	...	...	...	0.1	...	...	...	...	0.1	...	...
Forestry products	...	...	...	...	...	...	...	...	...	...	...	...
Fish and other marine products	...	...	...	...	...	...	...	...	...	0.1	...	...
Metallic ores and concentrates	...	...	...	...	...	...	...	...	...	...	...	...
Bituminous coal and lignite	...	...	...	...	...	...	...	...	...	...	...	...
Crude petroleum and natural gas	...	...	...	...	0.1	...	...	...	...	...	...	...
Nonmetallic minerals	...	...	...	...	...	...	...	...	...	...	...	...
Scrap and waste	...	...	...	...	...	...	...	...	...	...	...	...
Used merchandise	...	...	...	...	...	...	...	...	...	...	...	...
Goods imported and returned unchanged	...	...	...	...	...	...	...	...	...	...	...	...
Special classification provisions	...	...	...	...	...	...	...	...	...	...	...	...

Industry	The Netherlands						Asian 10					
	1994	1995	1996	1997	1998	1999	1994	1995	1996	1997	1998	1999
ALL GOODS	16.4	2.5	8.4	57.5	0.7	10.9	38.4	45.6	14.7	19.2	1.9	10.7
Manufactured Goods	16.4	2.5	8.4	57.5	0.7	10.9	38.4	45.6	14.7	19.2	1.7	10.7
Food products	...	...	...	...	...	...	0.2	...	...	...	...	0.1
Tobacco products	...	...	...	...	...	...	...	...	...	...	...	...
Textile mill products	...	...	...	...	...	...	...	...	...	...	...	...
Apparel	...	...	...	...	...	...	...	...	...	...	...	...
Lumber and wood products	...	...	...	...	...	...	...	0.1	0.1	...	...	...
Furniture and fixtures	...	...	...	...	...	...	...	...	...	...	...	...
Paper products	...	...	...	...	...	...	...	...	0.1	...	...	...
Printing and publishing	...	...	...	...	...	...	...	...	...	...	...	...
Chemical products	6.7	2.3	0.5	15.9	0.5	10.9	27.6	28.4	8.8	18.5	1.3	6.5
Refined petroleum products	9.3	...	7.9	41.5	...	...	8.1	15.4	2.3	...	...	3.9
Rubber and plastic products	...	...	...	...	...	...	...	...	...	0.1	...	...
Leather products	...	...	...	...	...	...	...	...	...	...	...	...
Stone, clay and glass products	...	...	...	...	...	...	...	...	...	0.1	...	...
Primary metals	...	...	...	...	...	...	0.1	...	...	0.3	...	...
Fabricated metal products	...	...	...	...	...	...	...	...	1.7	...	...	0.1
Industrial machinery and computers	0.4	...	...	...	...	...	1.1	0.5	0.2	0.1	...	...
Electric and electronic equipment	...	...	...	...	...	...	0.2	0.2	1.2	0.1	0.1	0.1
Transportation equipment	...	...	...	...	...	...	0.2	...	...	...	...	...
Scientific and measuring instruments	...	...	...	...	0.1	...	0.2	0.1	0.1	0.1	...	...
Miscellaneous manufactures	...	...	...	...	...	...	0.8	0.9	...	...	0.2	...
Unidentified manufactures	...	...	...	...	...	...	...	...	...	...	...	...
Agricultural And Livestock Products	...	...	...	...	...	...	...	...	...	...	...	...
Agricultural products	...	...	...	...	...	...	...	...	...	...	...	...
Livestock and livestock products	...	...	...	...	...	...	...	...	...	...	...	...
Other Commodities	...	...	...	...	...	...	...	0.1	...	...	0.2	...
Forestry products	...	...	...	...	...	...	...	...	...	...	...	...
Fish and other marine products	...	...	...	...	...	...	...	0.1	...	...	...	...
Metallic ores and concentrates	...	...	...	...	...	...	...	...	...	...	...	...
Bituminous coal and lignite	...	...	...	...	...	...	...	...	...	...	...	...
Crude petroleum and natural gas	...	...	...	...	...	...	...	...	...	...	...	...
Nonmetallic minerals	...	...	...	...	...	...	...	...	...	...	0.2	...
Scrap and waste	...	...	...	...	...	...	...	...	...	...	...	...
Used merchandise	...	...	...	...	...	...	...	...	...	...	...	...
Goods imported and returned unchanged	...	...	...	...	...	...	...	...	...	...	...	...
Special classification provisions	...	...	...	...	...	...	...	...	...	...	...	...

Table D-50. VIRGIN ISLANDS: State Exports of Goods by Destination and Industry, 1994–1999—*Continued*

(Millions of dollars.)

Industry	Japan						South Korea					
	1994	1995	1996	1997	1998	1999	1994	1995	1996	1997	1998	1999
ALL GOODS	1.9	16.1	6.4	0.1	1.1	0.8	18.3	17.3	6.3	18.4	...	5.8
Manufactured Goods	1.9	16.1	6.4	0.1	1.1	0.8	18.3	17.3	6.3	18.4	...	5.8
Food products	0.1	...	...	...	...	0.1	...	...	...	...	...	...
Tobacco products	...	...	...	...	...	...	...	...	...	...	...	...
Textile mill products	...	...	...	...	...	...	...	...	...	...	...	...
Apparel	...	...	...	...	...	...	...	...	...	...	...	...
Lumber and wood products	...	...	0.1	...	...	...	...	...	...	...	...	...
Furniture and fixtures	...	...	...	...	...	...	...	...	...	...	...	...
Paper products	...	...	0.1	...	...	...	...	...	...	...	...	...
Printing and publishing	...	...	...	...	...	...	...	...	...	...	...	...
Chemical products	0.2	...	3.6	...	1.1	0.7	18.0	17.2	5.2	18.3	...	5.8
Refined petroleum products	...	15.4	2.3	...	...	...	...	...	...	...	...	...
Rubber and plastic products	...	...	...	...	...	...	...	...	...	...	...	...
Leather products	...	...	...	...	...	...	...	...	...	...	...	...
Stone, clay and glass products	...	...	...	...	...	...	...	...	...	0.1	...	...
Primary metals	...	...	...	...	...	...	...	...	...	...	...	...
Fabricated metal products	...	...	...	...	...	...	...	...	...	...	...	...
Industrial machinery and computers	0.5	0.3	0.1	...	...	...	0.2	...	...	...	...	...
Electric and electronic equipment	0.2	...	...	...	...	...	...	...	1.1	0.1	...	...
Transportation equipment	0.1	...	...	...	...	...	...	...	...	...	...	...
Scientific and measuring instruments	0.1	0.1	...	...	...	...	0.1	...	...	...	...	...
Miscellaneous manufactures	0.6	0.3	...	...	...	...	...	...	...	...	...	...
Unidentified manufactures	...	...	...	...	...	...	...	...	...	...	...	...
Agricultural And Livestock Products	...	...	...	...	...	...	...	...	...	...	...	...
Agricultural products	...	...	...	...	...	...	...	...	...	...	...	...
Livestock and livestock products	...	...	...	...	...	...	...	...	...	...	...	...
Other Commodities	...	...	...	...	...	...	...	0.1	...	...	...	...
Forestry products	...	...	...	...	...	...	...	...	...	...	...	...
Fish and other marine products	...	...	...	...	...	...	...	0.1	...	...	...	...
Metallic ores and concentrates	...	...	...	...	...	...	...	...	...	...	...	...
Bituminous coal and lignite	...	...	...	...	...	...	...	...	...	...	...	...
Crude petroleum and natural gas	...	...	...	...	...	...	...	...	...	...	...	...
Nonmetallic minerals	...	...	...	...	...	...	...	...	...	...	...	...
Scrap and waste	...	...	...	...	...	...	...	...	...	...	...	...
Used merchandise	...	...	...	...	...	...	...	...	...	...	...	...
Goods imported and returned unchanged	...	...	...	...	...	...	...	...	...	...	...	...
Special classification provisions	...	...	...	...	...	...	...	...	...	...	...	...

Industry	Taiwan						Singapore					
	1994	1995	1996	1997	1998	1999	1994	1995	1996	1997	1998	1999
ALL GOODS	6.0	7.4	0.1	0.1	0.1	...	8.5	0.8	0.1	0.1	...	3.9
Manufactured Goods	6.0	7.4	0.1	0.1	0.1	...	8.5	0.8	0.1	0.1	...	3.9
Food products	0.1	...	...	...	...	...	...	...	...	...	...	...
Tobacco products	...	...	...	...	...	...	...	...	...	...	...	...
Textile mill products	...	...	...	...	...	...	...	...	...	...	...	...
Apparel	...	...	...	...	...	...	...	...	...	...	...	...
Lumber and wood products	...	...	...	...	...	...	...	...	...	...	...	...
Furniture and fixtures	...	...	...	...	...	...	...	...	...	...	...	...
Paper products	...	...	...	...	...	...	...	...	...	...	...	...
Printing and publishing	...	...	...	...	...	...	...	...	...	...	...	...
Chemical products	5.8	7.4	...	0.1	...	...	...	0.7	...	...	...	...
Refined petroleum products	...	...	...	...	...	...	8.1	...	...	...	...	3.9
Rubber and plastic products	...	...	...	...	...	...	...	...	...	...	...	...
Leather products	...	...	...	...	...	...	...	...	...	...	...	...
Stone, clay and glass products	...	...	...	...	...	...	...	...	...	...	...	...
Primary metals	...	...	...	...	...	...	...	...	...	...	...	...
Fabricated metal products	...	...	...	...	...	...	...	...	...	...	...	...
Industrial machinery and computers	...	0.1	...	...	...	...	0.3	...	...	...	...	...
Electric and electronic equipment	...	...	...	...	...	...	...	0.1	...	...	...	...
Transportation equipment	...	...	...	...	...	...	...	...	...	...	...	...
Scientific and measuring instruments	...	...	0.1	...	...	...	0.1	...	...	...	...	...
Miscellaneous manufactures	...	...	...	...	...	...	...	...	...	...	...	...
Unidentified manufactures	...	...	...	...	...	...	...	...	...	...	...	...
Agricultural And Livestock Products	...	...	...	...	...	...	...	...	...	...	...	...
Agricultural products	...	...	...	...	...	...	...	...	...	...	...	...
Livestock and livestock products	...	...	...	...	...	...	...	...	...	...	...	...
Other Commodities	...	...	...	...	...	...	...	...	...	...	...	...
Forestry products	...	...	...	...	...	...	...	...	...	...	...	...
Fish and other marine products	...	...	...	...	...	...	...	...	...	...	...	...
Metallic ores and concentrates	...	...	...	...	...	...	...	...	...	...	...	...
Bituminous coal and lignite	...	...	...	...	...	...	...	...	...	...	...	...
Crude petroleum and natural gas	...	...	...	...	...	...	...	...	...	...	...	...
Nonmetallic minerals	...	...	...	...	...	...	...	...	...	...	...	...
Scrap and waste	...	...	...	...	...	...	...	...	...	...	...	...
Used merchandise	...	...	...	...	...	...	...	...	...	...	...	...
Goods imported and returned unchanged	...	...	...	...	...	...	...	...	...	...	...	...
Special classification provisions	...	...	...	...	...	...	...	...	...	...	...	...

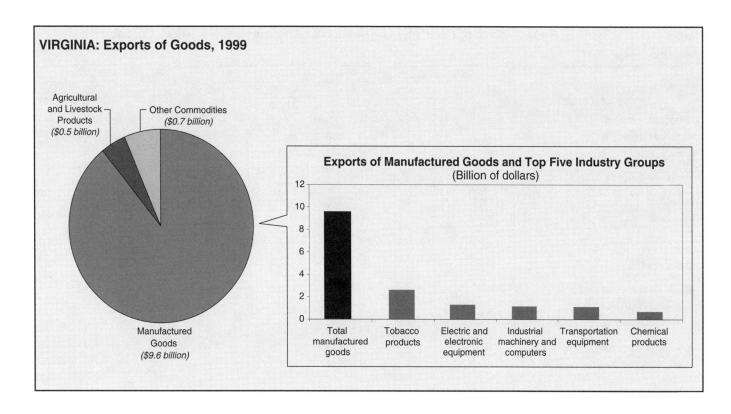

VIRGINIA: Exports of Goods, 1999

Agricultural and Livestock Products ($0.5 billion)

Other Commodities ($0.7 billion)

Manufactured Goods ($9.6 billion)

Exports of Manufactured Goods and Top Five Industry Groups
(Billion of dollars)

Total manufactured goods | Tobacco products | Electric and electronic equipment | Industrial machinery and computers | Transportation equipment | Chemical products

Table D-51. VIRGINIA: State Exports of Goods by Destination and Industry, 1994–1999

(Millions of dollars.)

Industry	All destinations						Canada					
	1994	1995	1996	1997	1998	1999	1994	1995	1996	1997	1998	1999
ALL GOODS	9 947.3	10 425.2	10 926.0	11 512.4	11 459.9	10 722.4	1 220.5	1 465.8	1 356.7	1 535.8	1 835.9	2 138.0
Manufactured Goods	8 793.6	9 294.1	9 699.0	10 158.5	10 092.2	9 559.0	1 154.9	1 366.3	1 246.6	1 413.2	1 661.3	1 971.0
Food products	201.0	175.0	234.4	235.7	206.5	139.9	16.0	16.3	21.8	31.9	23.5	27.1
Tobacco products	3 506.1	3 185.5	3 646.8	3 530.3	3 424.9	2 619.6	0.1	0.1	0.1	0.1	. . .	0.3
Textile mill products	79.1	99.6	94.4	118.5	113.2	124.8	41.1	49.2	48.1	59.6	56.6	62.7
Apparel	100.2	88.4	116.6	134.6	148.1	108.1	17.8	17.7	15.3	24.5	24.7	25.8
Lumber and wood products	119.4	110.7	108.5	118.7	102.9	121.3	21.8	21.0	22.4	21.2	20.0	29.3
Furniture and fixtures	49.6	42.4	49.5	50.6	43.6	45.1	24.4	20.7	23.4	25.0	25.2	25.4
Paper products	140.3	181.8	157.7	142.7	157.5	175.0	54.5	61.4	68.3	74.7	92.1	110.5
Printing and publishing	26.8	35.3	41.8	39.5	46.7	49.6	14.5	12.9	19.9	17.6	30.3	30.8
Chemical products	702.0	902.7	735.2	745.8	777.0	690.5	205.8	317.2	214.2	187.6	175.4	178.6
Refined petroleum products	130.1	124.5	109.2	92.1	88.0	127.1	18.4	22.5	26.8	27.1	25.1	38.7
Rubber and plastic products	192.7	233.5	228.6	266.7	265.5	295.1	51.7	63.9	74.7	90.9	102.7	99.5
Leather products	2.6	4.0	3.0	3.1	2.6	3.3	0.8	1.0	0.6	0.8	0.7	0.7
Stone, clay and glass products	64.8	76.0	89.5	82.3	75.2	86.9	27.7	27.0	23.9	30.8	33.3	41.0
Primary metals	206.7	296.6	258.2	291.5	187.4	139.4	69.6	87.5	44.9	46.1	34.7	26.9
Fabricated metal products	233.8	313.6	435.3	376.8	542.8	553.4	44.9	57.4	82.1	115.6	133.7	171.2
Industrial machinery and computers	853.1	1 008.0	1 044.0	1 112.9	1 085.0	1 165.9	149.8	157.4	151.2	172.5	204.5	266.7
Electric and electronic equipment	566.4	652.1	726.7	1 013.8	1 105.3	1 298.7	179.5	181.1	192.9	233.4	281.6	228.2
Transportation equipment	980.5	988.6	868.5	821.0	966.0	1 122.2	157.4	195.2	165.2	191.0	338.7	547.1
Scientific and measuring instruments	226.7	311.2	241.0	392.6	373.4	324.9	39.0	42.8	35.7	49.7	43.5	43.3
Miscellaneous manufactures	150.0	163.6	131.6	187.1	115.3	84.2	14.8	8.8	9.6	7.8	8.2	9.9
Unidentified manufactures	261.9	301.1	378.5	402.3	265.2	284.0	5.0	5.1	5.6	5.4	6.7	7.3
Agricultural And Livestock Products	630.5	486.2	408.8	391.3	382.3	466.5	16.4	13.0	14.4	12.9	18.8	13.2
Agricultural products	617.3	475.6	401.0	384.6	371.2	459.7	9.1	12.5	13.8	12.5	18.2	12.5
Livestock and livestock products	13.2	10.6	7.9	6.7	11.2	6.8	7.3	0.5	0.6	0.4	0.6	0.7
Other Commodities	523.2	644.9	818.1	962.6	985.5	696.8	49.2	86.5	95.7	109.7	155.8	153.8
Forestry products	3.5	3.3	3.9	4.2	1.7	2.0	3.3	3.2	3.8	3.6	1.4	1.8
Fish and other marine products	15.3	16.9	19.5	27.1	31.9	23.0	4.5	4.9	5.9	10.9	12.3	10.5
Metallic ores and concentrates	1.4	1.5	1.4	0.6	0.5	7.1	1.3	1.4	0.3	0.6	0.2	. . .
Bituminous coal and lignite	403.9	499.8	673.6	821.0	863.2	560.1	8.4	35.6	39.4	37.8	92.6	86.6
Crude petroleum and natural gas	. . .	. . .	0.5	2.7	. . .	2.1	. . .	. . .	. . .	. . .	. . .	2.1
Nonmetallic minerals	7.4	7.9	10.2	8.6	7.5	8.4	1.4	1.6	1.4	1.3	1.4	1.5
Scrap and waste	43.7	74.7	48.7	43.7	27.4	16.6	7.7	14.7	10.7	19.4	14.4	4.2
Used merchandise	10.2	7.5	13.1	10.1	13.3	11.3	0.8	0.6	0.9	1.4	2.3	1.1
Goods imported and returned unchanged	19.6	21.9	30.8	32.9	29.1	36.7	19.6	21.9	30.8	32.9	29.1	36.7
Special classification provisions	18.1	11.4	16.4	11.7	10.7	29.6	2.2	2.6	2.3	1.7	2.0	9.3

Table D-51. VIRGINIA: State Exports of Goods by Destination and Industry, 1994–1999—Continued

(Millions of dollars.)

Industry	South and Central American and Caribbean						Mexico					
	1994	1995	1996	1997	1998	1999	1994	1995	1996	1997	1998	1999
ALL GOODS	619.5	694.4	750.1	903.6	833.0	608.6	365.8	320.8	342.1	430.2	547.2	644.6
Manufactured Goods	519.2	632.1	687.1	795.6	709.1	528.7	363.3	318.4	339.2	426.1	542.3	641.0
Food products	24.3	22.5	25.5	20.7	14.5	12.8	16.2	4.3	2.9	7.1	5.3	5.2
Tobacco products	109.1	94.6	113.8	100.8	76.9	31.1	0.1	0.3	0.3	0.6	0.2	...
Textile mill products	3.3	5.2	5.1	10.5	8.4	7.8	5.2	5.2	5.7	8.5	16.1	19.1
Apparel	59.2	45.2	53.7	45.5	39.6	27.6	8.9	9.7	25.7	43.2	69.1	41.7
Lumber and wood products	2.9	0.9	1.7	4.5	2.6	2.4	0.8	0.1	0.1	0.2	1.2	0.7
Furniture and fixtures	2.3	1.6	1.7	5.0	2.1	1.4	3.1	0.9	0.4	1.2	1.8	2.0
Paper products	7.0	15.3	13.0	14.7	14.6	7.2	13.3	12.3	23.9	18.1	23.3	28.4
Printing and publishing	0.7	1.5	0.9	0.9	0.9	0.9	1.4	1.4	2.2	1.6	1.8	2.1
Chemical products	59.8	57.4	61.6	59.0	72.8	62.0	31.0	39.9	49.7	60.7	59.1	52.8
Refined petroleum products	19.5	24.4	11.6	11.4	8.2	23.0	22.9	24.7	12.2	1.3	...	9.3
Rubber and plastic products	8.9	14.7	16.9	28.6	27.2	26.4	36.9	38.2	22.9	29.8	30.6	42.5
Leather products	0.3	0.2	1.1	0.9	0.3	0.3	0.1	...	...	...	...	0.1
Stone, clay and glass products	2.5	1.6	6.8	9.3	4.9	4.0	10.0	7.1	3.1	3.5	4.7	7.4
Primary metals	45.7	86.0	93.9	145.6	68.0	29.5	9.7	18.5	14.8	15.9	17.3	20.9
Fabricated metal products	47.6	59.4	53.3	18.2	31.0	23.4	23.2	30.7	60.6	56.9	87.1	109.3
Industrial machinery and computers	62.4	97.2	84.6	86.0	74.9	66.0	35.1	24.8	20.7	32.9	42.6	60.2
Electric and electronic equipment	37.2	62.0	101.3	135.0	173.7	100.8	75.3	90.5	80.5	126.0	152.6	204.5
Transportation equipment	13.1	21.9	20.8	21.2	20.7	22.0	57.0	3.8	6.7	7.2	6.5	5.1
Scientific and measuring instruments	7.6	9.0	10.0	62.3	51.1	33.0	10.6	5.0	4.9	7.1	11.1	21.2
Miscellaneous manufactures	1.6	2.5	2.9	3.7	3.9	5.4	1.2	0.4	0.5	2.6	7.8	4.4
Unidentified manufactures	4.1	8.9	6.8	11.9	12.7	41.6	1.3	0.6	1.1	1.8	4.1	3.9
Agricultural And Livestock Products	49.3	15.8	10.8	5.0	4.3	7.0	1.1	0.9	1.5	2.3	3.1	0.9
Agricultural products	49.3	15.7	10.7	4.3	4.3	6.9	0.9	0.8	1.5	2.0	3.1	0.7
Livestock and livestock products	0.1	0.1	0.1	0.7	0.1	0.1	0.3	0.1	...	0.2	...	0.2
Other Commodities	51.0	46.5	52.2	103.0	119.5	72.9	1.5	1.5	1.4	1.9	1.8	2.7
Forestry products	...	...	...	0.1	0.1	0.1	...	...	...	0.1	...	...
Fish and other marine products	...	0.1	...	0.6	0.6	0.5	...	0.8	...	0.1	...	...
Metallic ores and concentrates	...	...	...	...	...	...	...	...	...	...	...	...
Bituminous coal and lignite	45.8	41.0	48.5	97.4	116.8	68.9	...	...	...	...	...	...
Crude petroleum and natural gas	...	...	0.5	2.7	...	...	...	...	...	...	...	...
Nonmetallic materials	0.4	0.3	0.9	0.4	0.2	0.3	0.8	0.7	1.3	1.3	1.2	1.3
Scrap and waste	4.2	4.0	0.1	0.3	0.3	0.9	0.1	...	...	0.4	0.5	0.2
Used merchandise	0.3	0.6	0.7	1.2	0.7	0.5	0.4	...	...	...	...	0.1
Goods imported and returned unchanged	...	...	...	...	...	...	...	...	...	...	...	...
Special classification provisions	0.1	0.4	1.6	0.3	0.9	1.7	0.2	...	0.1	0.1	0.1	1.1

Industry	European Union						United Kingdom					
	1994	1995	1996	1997	1998	1999	1994	1995	1996	1997	1998	1999
ALL GOODS	3 077.9	3 244.3	3 414.4	3 326.2	3 389.8	2 670.1	286.0	315.7	338.2	323.3	346.2	338.1
Manufactured Goods	2 613.4	2 749.8	2 811.5	2 668.9	2 707.4	2 094.5	254.4	284.0	300.7	275.5	300.4	302.2
Food products	28.1	16.8	25.7	18.9	34.0	6.5	5.0	6.2	4.8	5.7	8.0	0.4
Tobacco products	1 421.0	1 343.8	1 282.5	1 141.2	1 086.9	505.1	5.7	1.7	...	0.1	...	...
Textile mill products	12.0	21.8	15.9	17.0	11.7	13.8	1.6	4.4	4.2	5.7	3.0	2.8
Apparel	3.8	3.2	4.3	4.9	3.7	2.2	0.6	0.6	1.5	0.7	0.8	1.1
Lumber and wood products	47.5	52.5	49.3	50.2	50.5	53.5	4.1	5.7	6.4	7.2	6.6	6.7
Furniture and fixtures	4.0	6.1	9.0	6.8	6.5	5.3	0.4	0.6	5.5	2.3	2.9	2.7
Paper products	50.2	72.3	26.8	9.4	6.0	10.3	23.7	31.7	10.7	2.6	1.9	1.9
Printing and publishing	7.8	13.5	15.1	11.4	9.6	9.7	3.1	6.4	8.2	6.9	5.9	7.0
Chemical products	169.1	222.6	169.5	185.8	213.3	140.8	15.7	19.5	16.6	18.4	19.5	30.0
Refined petroleum products	4.4	12.2	4.0	11.1	5.9	9.0	0.1	0.1	...	0.1	0.4	0.1
Rubber and plastic products	28.7	38.1	29.7	34.3	44.1	56.5	8.3	9.9	6.3	9.9	14.6	15.2
Leather products	0.5	1.7	0.5	0.5	0.6	1.2	0.1	0.4	...	0.1	0.4	0.6
Stone, clay and glass products	7.4	11.8	16.5	12.9	10.5	12.4	0.5	3.2	2.1	5.0	4.0	2.7
Primary metals	26.3	34.1	41.2	33.3	31.3	35.7	12.3	9.4	17.0	18.5	14.0	21.9
Fabricated metal products	51.9	101.6	162.3	84.6	109.4	54.3	11.5	15.4	16.2	10.2	18.5	15.9
Industrial machinery and computers	175.4	244.5	289.6	291.5	336.4	317.8	50.5	64.6	72.6	65.2	69.6	74.0
Electric and electronic equipment	120.3	124.9	140.9	170.5	227.7	414.5	34.8	36.8	32.2	39.0	46.5	30.2
Transportation equipment	210.8	210.9	223.2	184.6	210.3	165.2	44.7	33.8	72.7	51.0	49.4	45.1
Scientific and measuring instruments	74.1	83.8	73.1	86.1	91.6	101.5	20.2	20.6	16.7	16.8	21.6	31.5
Miscellaneous manufactures	28.7	22.2	22.3	27.4	34.9	30.3	10.5	8.4	5.3	8.8	11.4	11.1
Unidentified manufactures	141.4	111.3	210.1	286.6	182.3	149.2	1.1	4.5	1.6	1.4	1.5	1.3
Agricultural And Livestock Products	151.0	146.8	161.6	160.7	160.5	234.3	17.9	21.7	16.1	18.4	12.1	14.1
Agricultural products	148.3	143.8	159.4	158.4	157.8	231.6	17.2	21.4	15.7	18.0	11.4	13.6
Livestock and livestock products	2.7	3.0	2.2	2.3	2.7	2.7	0.8	0.3	0.3	0.4	0.7	0.5
Other Commodities	313.5	347.8	441.3	496.5	522.0	341.2	13.7	10.0	21.4	29.4	33.7	21.9
Forestry products	0.1	0.1	...	0.1	0.1	...	...	...	...	...	...	...
Fish and other marine products	4.7	5.0	4.3	6.4	10.9	6.2	0.2	0.1	0.1	0.1	0.4	0.2
Metallic ores and concentrates	...	...	1.1	...	0.3	7.1	...	...	1.1	...	...	...
Bituminous coal and lignite	289.9	328.9	417.8	475.7	494.6	312.5	9.0	5.8	14.1	25.9	30.0	17.9
Crude petroleum and natural gas	...	...	...	...	...	...	...	...	...	...	...	...
Nonmetallic materials	2.3	2.9	3.1	3.3	2.8	2.9	0.6	0.7	0.9	0.7	0.7	0.9
Scrap and waste	1.1	0.4	0.4	0.4	1.2	0.1	0.3	0.1	0.1	...	...	...
Used merchandise	6.2	4.7	7.3	3.9	7.2	3.3	3.4	2.0	3.6	1.8	1.3	1.0
Goods imported and returned unchanged	...	...	...	...	...	...	...	...	...	...	...	...
Special classification provisions	9.1	5.8	7.2	6.7	4.8	9.2	0.1	1.3	1.6	0.9	1.2	1.8

Table D-51. VIRGINIA: State Exports of Goods by Destination and Industry, 1994–1999—*Continued*

(Millions of dollars.)

Industry	Germany						France					
	1994	1995	1996	1997	1998	1999	1994	1995	1996	1997	1998	1999
ALL GOODS	480.4	531.0	672.5	670.7	620.4	679.0	153.8	154.0	194.7	210.5	249.0	204.6
Manufactured Goods	407.8	480.7	585.8	588.8	521.7	580.7	105.4	111.5	132.4	144.8	166.1	141.2
Food products	0.5	0.6	8.5	1.3	0.4	1.1	0.9	0.5	0.1	0.5	0.9	0.2
Tobacco products	22.4	18.3	18.3	14.7	12.0	17.2	. . .	0.2	. . .	. . .	. . .	. . .
Textile mill products	0.9	2.4	1.6	0.9	0.6	3.9	0.8	1.0	0.9	0.4	0.5	0.3
Apparel	1.1	0.5	0.8	0.6	0.8	0.1	0.4	0.1	0.1	0.1	. . .	0.1
Lumber and wood products	15.6	16.2	16.0	12.0	9.6	7.4	0.5	0.2	0.1	0.1	0.1	0.1
Furniture and fixtures	1.3	3.1	2.2	2.8	1.3	0.9	1.2	0.8	0.1	0.3	1.4	0.3
Paper products	9.2	16.8	5.3	1.1	0.6	6.4	1.1	0.2	0.8	0.3	1.1	0.4
Printing and publishing	2.2	2.2	1.5	1.5	1.1	1.2	0.4	1.4	0.7	0.7	0.4	0.2
Chemical products	12.4	19.7	18.5	39.1	29.2	21.7	16.3	21.1	26.2	22.8	20.9	19.2
Refined petroleum products	0.2	0.7	0.1	. . .	0.1	1.3	0.1	1.3	1.9	2.7	4.4	5.7
Rubber and plastic products	10.2	8.1	7.6	6.0	11.7	21.6	4.0	8.1	2.8	1.9	1.2	2.7
Leather products	0.1	0.4	0.2	0.1	. . .	. . .	. . .	0.3	. . .	0.1	. . .	0.2
Stone, clay and glass products	5.4	7.5	8.1	5.9	4.2	5.8	0.2	0.1	2.6	0.4	0.4	2.0
Primary metals	0.8	11.9	4.3	5.9	1.2	2.2	1.0	0.8	2.9	1.0	3.1	3.6
Fabricated metal products	26.1	69.0	109.3	38.6	26.5	19.3	1.9	5.5	20.4	23.5	27.5	8.7
Industrial machinery and computers	51.5	70.8	80.5	90.2	97.8	79.6	23.4	32.7	39.8	34.9	36.5	39.7
Electric and electronic equipment	23.5	25.6	25.5	22.8	36.8	149.0	12.0	11.8	13.4	34.5	36.4	39.2
Transportation equipment	89.5	84.1	59.1	43.9	101.6	79.0	31.1	15.1	9.6	2.5	3.8	5.0
Scientific and measuring instruments	10.5	16.3	12.7	14.1	8.4	17.2	6.0	7.2	7.2	13.8	22.1	9.5
Miscellaneous manufactures	5.5	2.6	7.4	7.8	5.1	6.5	2.4	2.3	1.5	3.0	4.5	3.2
Unidentified manufactures	118.9	103.9	198.4	279.4	172.6	139.2	1.7	0.8	1.1	1.3	1.0	0.7
Agricultural And Livestock Products	59.0	45.3	68.2	72.1	78.1	91.3	3.6	4.7	1.6	3.1	2.3	4.1
Agricultural products	58.9	44.6	68.1	72.0	78.1	91.2	2.5	3.5	0.8	1.9	1.0	3.3
Livestock and livestock products	0.1	0.6	0.1	0.1	. . .	0.1	1.1	1.2	0.8	1.2	1.3	0.8
Other Commodities	13.6	5.0	18.4	9.9	20.6	6.9	44.8	37.7	60.6	62.6	80.6	59.2
Forestry products	. . .	. . .	. . .	. . .	. . .	. . .	. . .	. . .	. . .	. . .	. . .	. . .
Fish and other marine products	0.9	1.0	1.0	0.6	0.7	0.6	1.4	2.5	1.3	3.9	7.7	4.4
Metallic ores and concentrates	. . .	. . .	. . .	. . .	. . .	. . .	. . .	. . .	. . .	. . .	. . .	0.1
Bituminous coal and lignite	3.6	. . .	13.0	3.3	16.7	2.0	42.9	34.6	58.3	58.0	70.5	54.3
Crude petroleum and natural gas	. . .	. . .	. . .	. . .	. . .	. . .	. . .	. . .	. . .	. . .	. . .	. . .
Nonmetallic materials	0.3	0.4	0.3	0.4	0.6	0.3	0.3	0.3	0.3	. . .	. . .	0.1
Scrap and waste	. . .	. . .	. . .	0.4	. . .	. . .	. . .	. . .	. . .	. . .	. . .	. . .
Used merchandise	0.7	0.8	0.7	0.8	0.2	1.2	. . .	0.2	0.2	0.6	2.2	. . .
Goods imported and returned unchanged	. . .	. . .	. . .	. . .	. . .	. . .	. . .	. . .	. . .	. . .	. . .	. . .
Special classification provisions	8.1	2.9	3.5	4.5	2.4	2.8	0.2	0.2	0.6	0.1	0.1	0.3

Industry	The Netherlands						Asian 10					
	1994	1995	1996	1997	1998	1999	1994	1995	1996	1997	1998	1999
ALL GOODS	185.2	262.0	202.6	211.0	331.4	285.7	2 907.6	3 008.5	2 899.7	3 094.5	2 813.2	2 861.7
Manufactured Goods	129.0	186.1	142.6	140.2	235.9	174.6	2 603.0	2 698.7	2 565.5	2 746.9	2 539.7	2 635.8
Food products	0.8	0.6	4.4	6.3	0.6	3.3	24.5	47.4	46.4	46.7	48.9	49.6
Tobacco products	67.2	101.2	39.3	54.9	104.8	57.1	1 274.6	1 135.8	1 217.0	1 253.0	1 189.1	. . .
Textile mill products	0.2	0.6	0.3	0.3	0.4	0.4	11.9	12.2	13.4	13.3	12.3	15.2
Apparel	0.4	0.6	0.4	0.2	0.5	0.2	8.8	10.1	16.0	14.0	7.2	6.9
Lumber and wood products	2.1	2.1	3.1	0.6	0.3	0.9	25.5	30.7	29.9	36.9	23.1	28.5
Furniture and fixtures	0.3	0.4	0.3	0.3	0.4	0.4	3.9	5.3	4.4	3.7	2.2	2.7
Paper products	10.8	15.3	6.9	0.4	0.1	0.3	10.2	12.7	17.2	18.2	12.2	12.0
Printing and publishing	0.5	0.9	2.1	0.8	1.0	0.2	0.9	2.0	1.6	2.9	1.7	2.7
Chemical products	9.9	17.7	18.4	13.4	23.0	19.8	154.2	173.9	144.6	176.5	174.3	178.7
Refined petroleum products	0.5	1.3	0.1	0.1	0.3	0.5	36.3	17.7	9.0	6.5	4.3	4.6
Rubber and plastic products	3.0	5.9	8.1	6.7	6.4	9.6	54.2	64.8	64.4	61.8	43.7	52.3
Leather products	. . .	0.2	0.2	0.1	0.1	0.1	0.4	0.7	0.7	0.7	0.6	0.4
Stone, clay and glass products	0.5	0.1	0.2	0.2	0.3	0.2	13.0	22.8	33.0	18.2	16.2	15.3
Primary metals	0.5	0.9	2.8	1.9	0.8	1.0	40.3	30.9	39.1	30.3	17.5	12.4
Fabricated metal products	1.9	3.9	3.1	1.8	2.5	2.9	28.1	43.1	45.4	60.9	142.0	161.5
Industrial machinery and computers	16.2	13.0	17.8	27.0	53.7	36.2	168.8	223.7	245.9	247.8	184.6	177.5
Electric and electronic equipment	3.1	5.9	11.7	9.5	6.7	15.2	86.9	106.9	113.8	165.4	144.1	223.5
Transportation equipment	1.5	2.9	2.1	2.9	0.9	0.5	499.3	510.2	357.8	354.7	341.8	305.4
Scientific and measuring instruments	7.6	9.0	11.3	9.0	19.5	21.1	55.1	120.7	69.9	95.6	103.5	68.9
Miscellaneous manufactures	1.9	3.2	2.7	1.6	9.8	4.1	97.5	122.6	89.4	134.4	48.4	23.8
Unidentified manufactures	0.3	0.5	7.4	2.2	3.7	0.5	8.9	4.5	6.4	5.4	22.2	27.0
Agricultural And Livestock Products	4.7	4.3	2.5	1.5	4.6	45.0	227.8	168.2	152.0	168.0	140.7	139.4
Agricultural products	4.3	3.7	1.8	1.2	4.4	44.8	226.2	166.6	150.7	167.1	139.8	138.2
Livestock and livestock products	0.4	0.6	0.7	0.3	0.3	0.2	1.6	1.6	1.3	0.9	0.9	1.1
Other Commodities	51.4	71.6	57.6	69.3	90.8	66.1	76.8	141.6	182.2	179.6	132.8	86.5
Forestry products	. . .	. . .	. . .	. . .	. . .	. . .	0.1	. . .	. . .	0.3	. . .	. . .
Fish and other marine products	1.5	1.2	1.6	1.3	1.1	0.1	5.6	5.3	8.8	7.7	7.2	. . .
Metallic ores and concentrates	. . .	. . .	. . .	. . .	. . .	. . .	0.1	. . .	. . .	. . .	. . .	. . .
Bituminous coal and lignite	47.5	68.9	55.0	67.1	86.7	62.0	44.3	82.3	134.7	149.2	111.8	. . .
Crude petroleum and natural gas	. . .	. . .	. . .	. . .	. . .	. . .	. . .	. . .	. . .	. . .	. . .	. . .
Nonmetallic materials	0.4	0.1	0.1	0.3	0.2	0.2	0.6	0.5	1.2	0.9	1.6	2.3
Scrap and waste	0.7	0.3	. . .	. . .	. . .	. . .	25.3	53.2	34.0	20.5	10.0	10.1
Used merchandise	1.3	1.0	0.8	0.1	2.7	. . .	0.5	0.2	0.4	0.3	0.3	2.3
Goods imported and returned unchanged	. . .	. . .	. . .	. . .	. . .	. . .	. . .	. . .	. . .	. . .	. . .	. . .
Special classification provisions	. . .	0.2	0.1	0.4	. . .	. . .	0.4	0.2	3.0	0.8	1.8	4.4

Table D-51. VIRGINIA: State Exports of Goods by Destination and Industry, 1994–1999—*Continued*

(Millions of dollars.)

Industry	Japan						South Korea					
	1994	1995	1996	1997	1998	1999	1994	1995	1996	1997	1998	1999
ALL GOODS	1 401.9	1 256.2	1 385.5	1 434.2	1 458.0	1 476.2	856.4	971.6	737.6	751.7	605.1	645.6
Manufactured Goods	1 194.2	1 095.5	1 190.7	1 235.0	1 297.8	1 347.8	803.6	898.8	669.7	681.9	548.0	591.1
Food products	7.9	6.2	9.3	7.7	10.1	9.5	5.2	6.2	7.8	11.9	2.5	11.6
Tobacco products	976.5	844.9	934.6	964.4	1 027.0	1 094.9	86.6	107.7	107.8	129.5	8.6	44.7
Textile mill products	2.4	3.1	0.9	1.1	0.8	0.5	0.4	0.4	0.9	0.9	0.9	0.9
Apparel	8.1	9.2	15.2	13.2	6.7	6.4	0.1	0.1	0.1	0.1	. . .	0.3
Lumber and wood products	17.5	20.7	19.3	22.3	10.6	7.3	1.8	1.9	1.6	2.8	0.7	1.6
Furniture and fixtures	2.4	3.2	3.0	2.7	1.6	1.4	0.6	1.2	0.8	0.2	. . .	0.3
Paper products	1.2	1.3	1.4	1.6	1.7	2.2	1.9	1.2	1.1	1.1	0.5	2.3
Printing and publishing	0.4	1.0	0.4	1.5	0.6	0.5	0.1	0.1	. . .	0.2	0.1	0.5
Chemical products	54.7	61.5	48.1	58.9	73.9	56.8	25.7	25.3	24.6	34.4	27.8	30.4
Refined petroleum products	2.2	0.8	2.1	0.9	0.6	0.6	2.3	2.8	1.9	0.3	0.3	1.0
Rubber and plastic products	32.5	29.4	24.4	24.6	20.0	20.2	8.9	14.9	16.9	9.8	3.9	5.4
Leather products	0.1	0.3	0.4	0.3	0.1	0.2	. . .	. . .	. . .	. . .	0.3	0.1
Stone, clay and glass products	8.2	16.0	22.1	10.5	6.7	6.8	3.1	4.9	6.8	3.7	3.7	3.1
Primary metals	2.3	4.9	7.2	4.5	3.7	1.3	16.1	3.3	4.6	3.7	1.4	0.7
Fabricated metal products	4.0	3.1	6.3	8.6	11.6	7.1	15.8	29.2	12.6	21.5	107.6	141.1
Industrial machinery and computers	22.7	29.6	42.5	42.4	38.9	51.3	54.6	65.1	62.2	56.1	27.1	19.7
Electric and electronic equipment	16.1	21.7	22.6	23.8	18.3	34.0	21.4	13.6	13.0	13.2	12.5	15.3
Transportation equipment	4.1	3.0	4.2	6.6	15.4	8.5	474.1	484.6	342.6	331.2	312.0	287.3
Scientific and measuring instruments	21.9	20.0	14.6	22.0	32.4	22.2	14.9	78.0	27.7	32.0	36.2	21.2
Miscellaneous manufactures	8.5	14.9	11.6	17.1	14.3	6.4	68.8	57.7	35.9	28.7	1.4	2.1
Unidentified manufactures	0.5	0.8	0.5	0.6	2.7	9.6	1.4	0.6	0.6	0.7	0.6	1.6
Agricultural And Livestock Products	191.1	122.3	111.9	107.1	97.9	85.8	4.2	7.2	11.7	19.8	9.1	22.9
Agricultural products	190.0	121.3	110.8	106.3	97.3	84.9	4.2	6.7	11.5	19.8	9.1	22.9
Livestock and livestock products	1.1	1.0	1.0	0.8	0.6	0.9	. . .	0.6	0.2	. . .	. . .	. . .
Other Commodities	16.6	38.4	82.9	92.2	62.3	42.6	48.6	65.5	56.2	50.0	48.0	31.6
Forestry products	. . .	. . .	. . .	. . .	. . .	. . .	. . .	. . .	. . .	. . .	. . .	. . .
Fish and other marine products	3.1	2.1	1.8	1.9	1.5	1.7	0.7	. . .	0.1	0.1	. . .	0.1
Metallic ores and concentrates	0.1	. . .	. . .	. . .	. . .	. . .	. . .	. . .	. . .	. . .	. . .	. . .
Bituminous coal and lignite	12.8	34.4	78.8	89.4	59.4	35.3	24.6	37.2	45.7	46.6	40.8	22.6
Crude petroleum and natural gas	. . .	. . .	. . .	. . .	. . .	. . .	. . .	. . .	. . .	. . .	. . .	. . .
Nonmetallic materials	0.1	0.1	0.8	0.1	0.1	0.1	0.2	0.3	0.2	0.4	0.4	0.8
Scrap and waste	0.1	1.5	0.6	0.4	0.5	0.7	23.1	27.9	10.0	2.5	6.0	7.3
Used merchandise	0.4	0.2	0.3	0.1	0.1	2.2	. . .	. . .	. . .	0.1	. . .	. . .
Goods imported and returned unchanged	. . .	. . .	. . .	. . .	. . .	. . .	. . .	. . .	. . .	. . .	. . .	. . .
Special classification provisions	0.1	0.1	0.6	0.2	0.7	2.8	. . .	. . .	0.1	0.3	0.8	0.7

Industry	Taiwan						Singapore					
	1994	1995	1996	1997	1998	1999	1994	1995	1996	1997	1998	1999
ALL GOODS	202.2	181.5	156.1	152.8	135.6	112.6	96.3	126.3	107.7	133.4	118.7	159.1
Manufactured Goods	186.9	161.9	136.8	126.5	118.9	104.4	95.4	124.8	107.0	132.7	117.0	157.3
Food products	0.1	0.8	3.5	1.6	3.9	3.8	1.9	2.4	2.5	3.3	2.0	3.3
Tobacco products	60.9	26.2	39.1	42.5	42.9	35.5	30.6	29.2	30.8	38.5	48.2	. . .
Textile mill products	2.0	1.3	1.3	0.5	1.2	1.1	0.2	0.1	0.1	0.2	0.1	0.2
Apparel	0.1	0.1	. . .	0.2	. . .	. . .	. . .	. . .	0.1	0.1	. . .	. . .
Lumber and wood products	4.0	4.1	4.8	4.7	2.6	3.0	0.1	0.2	0.1	0.1	0.1	0.6
Furniture and fixtures	0.4	0.3	0.2	0.3	0.1	. . .	0.2	0.2	0.2	0.3	0.1	0.4
Paper products	2.0	1.7	2.6	2.8	2.0	1.3	0.1	0.3	0.3	0.3	0.8	0.1
Printing and publishing	. . .	. . .	0.1	0.2	0.2	0.4	0.5	0.2	0.1	0.3	0.1	0.1	0.2
Chemical products	14.8	16.5	12.9	14.1	11.0	12.0	18.0	30.6	20.9	19.8	12.1	17.8
Refined petroleum products	18.7	1.0	2.1	1.4	1.0	1.1	10.6	10.3	0.1	0.2	0.1	. . .
Rubber and plastic products	1.5	1.2	1.0	1.2	0.8	2.4	3.9	4.1	4.3	3.0	1.1	2.6
Leather products	. . .	. . .	0.2	. . .	0.1	0.1	. . .	. . .	. . .	. . .	. . .	. . .
Stone, clay and glass products	0.6	0.3	1.4	1.0	0.9	2.5	0.2	0.1	0.1	0.2	0.2	0.1
Primary metals	15.4	11.4	8.7	7.9	1.4	2.3	1.3	2.1	1.0	1.1	1.2	1.5
Fabricated metal products	1.8	2.5	7.7	3.2	4.5	0.8	2.2	2.0	0.3	2.8	2.9	0.7
Industrial machinery and computers	8.1	10.4	10.7	10.8	10.9	9.2	9.8	15.5	16.3	13.0	9.8	9.3
Electric and electronic equipment	17.1	35.0	26.4	20.7	23.7	21.4	10.7	14.3	23.6	35.6	22.9	75.6
Transportation equipment	12.7	10.4	7.2	4.3	1.3	1.2	0.8	8.4	1.2	8.3	9.7	2.7
Scientific and measuring instruments	5.7	4.0	3.9	6.8	7.7	4.8	3.7	4.2	3.4	3.9	5.0	4.3
Miscellaneous manufactures	16.4	33.9	2.6	2.1	1.4	0.9	0.7	0.6	1.2	1.4	0.6	0.6
Unidentified manufactures	4.7	0.4	0.3	0.3	1.3	0.3	0.2	0.1	0.1	0.4	0.3	0.2
Agricultural And Livestock Products	7.7	5.3	2.3	5.3	4.5	1.8	0.7	1.3	0.4	0.4	1.2	1.4
Agricultural products	7.1	5.3	2.3	5.3	4.4	1.7	0.7	1.3	0.4	0.4	1.2	1.4
Livestock and livestock products	0.5	. . .	. . .	. . .	0.1	0.1	. . .	. . .	. . .	. . .	. . .	. . .
Other Commodities	7.6	14.3	17.0	21.0	12.2	6.4	0.2	0.2	0.2	0.2	0.4	0.4
Forestry products	. . .	. . .	. . .	. . .	. . .	. . .	. . .	. . .	. . .	. . .	. . .	. . .
Fish and other marine products	0.3	. . .	0.3	. . .	0.1	0.1	. . .	0.2	0.1	. . .	. . .	. . .
Metallic ores and concentrates	. . .	. . .	. . .	. . .	. . .	. . .	. . .	. . .	. . .	. . .	. . .	. . .
Bituminous coal and lignite	6.9	10.7	10.2	13.2	11.6	4.8	. . .	. . .	. . .	. . .	. . .	. . .
Crude petroleum and natural gas	. . .	. . .	. . .	. . .	. . .	. . .	. . .	. . .	. . .	. . .	. . .	. . .
Nonmetallic materials	0.2	0.1	0.2	0.1	0.2	0.2	. . .	. . .	. . .	0.1	0.3	0.1
Scrap and waste	. . .	3.5	6.3	7.6	0.1	1.1	0.2	. . .	. . .	. . .	. . .	. . .
Used merchandise	. . .	. . .	. . .	. . .	. . .	. . .	. . .	. . .	. . .	0.1	. . .	. . .
Goods imported and returned unchanged	. . .	. . .	. . .	. . .	. . .	. . .	. . .	. . .	. . .	. . .	. . .	. . .
Special classification provisions	0.2	. . .	. . .	0.1	0.2	0.2	. . .	. . .	0.2	0.1	0.1	0.3

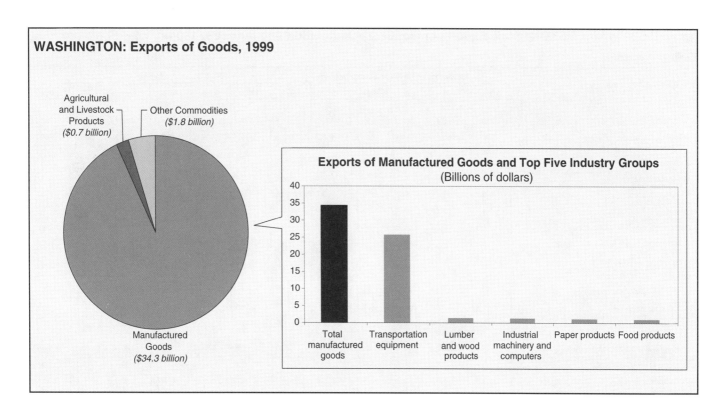

WASHINGTON: Exports of Goods, 1999

Agricultural and Livestock Products ($0.7 billion)

Other Commodities ($1.8 billion)

Manufactured Goods ($34.3 billion)

Exports of Manufactured Goods and Top Five Industry Groups
(Billions of dollars)

Total manufactured goods / Transportation equipment / Lumber and wood products / Industrial machinery and computers / Paper products / Food products

Table D-52. WASHINGTON: State Exports of Goods by Destination and Industry, 1994–1999

(Millions of dollars.)

Industry	All destinations						Canada					
	1994	1995	1996	1997	1998	1999	1994	1995	1996	1997	1998	1999
ALL GOODS	25 062.3	22 032.0	25 498.0	31 745.6	37 960.4	36 825.9	1 856.4	2 288.6	2 437.4	2 457.5	2 360.0	2 507.7
Manufactured Goods	22 356.4	18 945.6	22 741.3	29 184.9	35 936.8	34 301.4	1 546.7	1 959.2	2 074.7	2 085.4	1 999.8	2 099.5
Food products	828.9	967.1	915.8	919.5	865.9	1 026.7	157.9	175.3	164.3	167.3	180.3	207.5
Tobacco products	0.1	0.1	0.1	0.3	0.6	1.4	0.1	. . .	. . .	0.1	0.2	0.2
Textile mill products	24.8	33.4	33.7	31.5	34.2	32.8	4.7	6.3	7.8	9.4	12.2	15.5
Apparel	49.3	53.0	55.5	57.9	52.1	42.8	26.8	23.7	24.2	28.6	27.5	20.4
Lumber and wood products	2 643.0	2 870.2	2 893.3	2 286.8	1 469.2	1 400.3	127.6	173.4	161.8	204.5	149.8	154.4
Furniture and fixtures	20.7	24.4	27.5	31.4	28.1	33.5	11.1	11.2	11.0	11.4	9.6	8.8
Paper products	1 018.9	1 600.0	1 285.2	1 240.6	1 121.6	1 175.8	90.9	131.6	121.8	126.8	127.9	115.9
Printing and publishing	76.3	75.3	75.6	85.5	86.2	72.5	40.5	48.3	45.9	31.9	27.5	38.5
Chemical products	372.4	276.0	371.7	601.0	425.5	649.4	69.0	80.6	98.6	95.4	82.9	87.5
Refined petroleum products	72.9	94.4	177.4	147.1	73.3	68.1	59.6	81.1	131.3	138.2	58.1	58.9
Rubber and plastic products	75.2	94.7	97.5	113.5	116.8	131.8	44.0	45.2	48.4	61.0	66.1	66.5
Leather products	9.7	13.2	16.9	20.8	18.1	23.6	2.6	3.5	7.1	9.9	8.6	6.7
Stone, clay and glass products	46.5	51.2	53.4	62.4	52.5	54.1	20.2	19.8	21.0	21.0	20.6	21.3
Primary metals	226.1	301.9	327.7	399.1	354.0	393.7	74.9	96.7	108.8	125.6	136.8	158.5
Fabricated metal products	129.6	142.4	126.2	195.0	185.9	154.7	55.8	80.1	67.2	95.8	71.5	77.6
Industrial machinery and computers	822.4	1 055.1	1 060.3	1 275.8	1 313.7	1 331.3	180.7	213.7	237.4	311.6	339.9	319.4
Electric and electronic equipment	795.5	947.4	881.0	990.9	907.4	792.8	272.7	301.9	269.8	230.0	215.5	132.4
Transportation equipment	14 450.4	9 581.7	13 402.7	19 711.3	27 817.5	25 777.2	174.3	340.2	377.9	237.4	249.8	367.3
Scientific and measuring instruments	532.1	583.9	672.3	785.5	740.7	821.3	68.1	67.9	74.8	90.4	85.6	100.6
Miscellaneous manufactures	137.5	153.5	239.3	199.6	233.0	270.5	56.1	48.8	85.6	77.2	117.9	129.5
Unidentified manufactures	24.0	26.6	28.1	29.5	40.3	47.2	9.1	9.8	10.1	12.1	11.7	12.1
Agricultural And Livestock Products	748.5	993.5	902.2	907.1	700.4	746.9	132.2	133.6	132.4	138.4	133.2	121.0
Agricultural products	664.6	917.6	800.2	825.3	631.7	672.0	113.6	119.1	121.6	125.7	121.0	107.3
Livestock and livestock products	83.8	75.9	102.0	81.8	68.6	75.0	18.7	14.5	10.9	12.7	12.2	13.6
Other Commodities	1 957.5	2 092.9	1 854.6	1 653.6	1 323.2	1 777.5	177.5	195.8	230.2	233.7	226.9	287.2
Forestry products	19.7	21.7	22.4	27.0	31.2	32.1	1.9	2.2	2.3	2.4	2.5	2.6
Fish and other marine products	1 691.3	1 755.2	1 511.8	1 298.3	1 020.2	1 301.7	90.9	102.1	109.5	98.3	108.8	129.2
Metallic ores and concentrates	8.3	8.4	8.0	10.1	11.9	13.6	2.2	0.4	0.2	1.3	1.8	0.4
Bituminous coal and lignite	2.9	2.2	0.7	0.7	. . .	0.3	. . .	. . .	. . .	0.5	. . .	0.3
Crude petroleum and natural gas	4.5	5.6	5.3	3.9	4.3	5.3	4.3	5.2	5.1	3.8	4.3	5.1
Nonmetallic minerals	9.4	10.6	16.7	19.4	12.2	11.9	8.0	8.8	9.6	9.1	9.1	7.9
Scrap and waste	104.4	168.1	107.2	102.5	87.9	87.3	10.0	10.2	4.2	5.8	5.6	4.4
Used merchandise	17.7	17.3	23.3	26.6	21.0	17.0	5.3	4.6	5.9	6.6	6.6	5.5
Goods imported and returned unchanged	51.6	56.8	86.8	102.8	84.1	77.5	51.6	56.8	86.8	102.8	84.1	77.5
Special classification provisions	47.7	47.1	72.4	62.3	50.5	230.8	3.3	5.4	6.6	3.1	4.2	54.3

Table D-52. WASHINGTON: State Exports of Goods by Destination and Industry, 1994–1999—*Continued*

(Millions of dollars.)

Industry	South and Central American and Caribbean						Mexico					
	1994	1995	1996	1997	1998	1999	1994	1995	1996	1997	1998	1999
ALL GOODS	410.4	482.4	651.0	952.2	1 193.6	979.5	411.2	188.1	254.9	272.4	582.9	385.2
Manufactured Goods	382.3	450.1	614.3	917.3	1 150.3	912.6	391.0	167.0	233.1	239.3	535.9	306.2
Food products	8.9	16.1	14.5	20.7	14.5	17.8	3.0	3.7	4.2	4.9	16.3	19.0
Tobacco products	...	...	...	...	...	...	...	...	...	...	...	...
Textile mill products	0.5	2.9	3.3	1.7	2.2	2.1	2.5	2.4	2.7	2.3	3.8	3.7
Apparel	1.6	0.6	3.7	1.6	1.1	0.8	0.9	1.5	0.4	0.7	1.0	4.3
Lumber and wood products	0.5	0.6	1.9	2.0	1.5	2.2	0.4	16.0	1.3	1.1	1.2	1.0
Furniture and fixtures	0.5	0.9	0.8	0.7	0.7	0.6	0.4	0.1	0.3	0.5	0.4	1.3
Paper products	18.9	33.2	27.6	36.9	26.2	27.9	39.8	31.8	31.4	35.3	37.4	46.5
Printing and publishing	4.5	3.7	1.3	4.9	6.0	1.3	4.0	1.3	0.9	1.8	1.6	2.1
Chemical products	3.0	4.7	4.6	7.8	11.6	40.1	7.9	6.5	19.1	14.9	13.2	13.8
Refined petroleum products	1.1	0.9	0.9	0.9	0.2	0.8	0.3	0.6	0.6	0.9	0.1	0.1
Rubber and plastic products	1.0	7.1	4.4	3.4	4.5	3.8	2.0	1.5	1.7	2.6	3.7	4.2
Leather products	0.3	0.5	0.1	1.4	2.6	2.2	0.7	...	0.1	0.1	0.1	0.3
Stone, clay and glass products	1.5	3.3	0.5	1.0	3.1	0.6	0.5	0.9	0.5	0.5	0.5	0.6
Primary metals	0.7	1.1	1.3	3.8	2.3	1.8	2.2	2.5	6.6	26.2	17.3	9.4
Fabricated metal products	3.1	5.4	5.4	7.1	12.3	6.6	3.2	4.6	1.8	2.7	5.2	5.2
Industrial machinery and computers	28.1	42.9	42.5	81.7	65.7	43.6	67.3	64.8	106.0	76.7	62.2	56.9
Electric and electronic equipment	66.8	69.1	66.0	126.6	104.7	22.4	16.9	15.3	27.1	42.4	40.4	41.5
Transportation equipment	217.8	227.5	395.0	573.9	837.2	683.5	223.3	1.5	1.3	2.1	287.7	49.6
Scientific and measuring instruments	19.3	21.5	34.5	37.7	48.8	50.2	12.3	9.9	21.0	16.2	35.9	30.7
Miscellaneous manufactures	3.2	7.3	4.7	2.9	2.8	2.9	3.2	1.8	5.4	5.8	3.8	8.4
Unidentified manufactures	1.1	0.8	1.5	0.7	2.3	1.4	0.3	0.3	0.8	1.5	4.0	7.8
Agricultural And Livestock Products	25.5	30.7	33.9	31.7	38.0	28.8	15.6	11.8	16.2	26.3	40.4	61.0
Agricultural products	25.2	30.3	33.6	31.7	37.8	28.8	15.5	11.8	16.2	26.2	40.4	60.7
Livestock and livestock products	0.3	0.4	0.3	0.1	0.2	...	0.1	...	0.1	0.1	0.1	0.3
Other Commodities	2.5	1.6	2.8	3.1	5.4	38.2	4.7	9.2	5.5	6.8	6.6	18.0
Forestry products	0.1	0.1	0.2	...	...	...	1.1	1.8	1.5	1.6	0.7	0.9
Fish and other marine products	0.1	0.1	0.6	0.2	2.4	1.0	0.8	1.4	0.5	0.5	0.4	1.7
Metallic ores and concentrates	...	...	...	...	...	...	...	...	...	...	...	...
Bituminous coal and lignite	...	...	0.1	...	...	...	...	...	...	...	...	...
Crude petroleum and natural gas	...	...	...	...	...	0.1	...	...	...	...	...	...
Nonmetallic minerals	...	...	0.1	...	...	0.2	0.1	0.3	0.4	0.4	0.4	0.6
Scrap and waste	0.1	0.1	0.1	...	0.2	0.3	2.2	5.6	2.8	3.5	5.0	6.5
Used merchandise	1.7	1.0	1.5	1.8	1.5	1.2	0.4	0.1	0.1	...	0.1	0.5
Goods imported and returned unchanged	...	...	...	...	...	...	...	...	...	...	...	...
Special classification provisions	0.4	0.2	0.2	1.1	1.3	35.2	0.1	0.1	0.3	0.7	...	7.8

Industry	European Union						United Kingdom					
	1994	1995	1996	1997	1998	1999	1994	1995	1996	1997	1998	1999
ALL GOODS	5 114.5	4 469.0	4 869.4	8 889.1	10 281.5	13 815.8	2 297.4	1 272.3	1 688.5	4 488.1	4 455.9	4 431.9
Manufactured Goods	4 984.2	4 339.2	4 730.9	8 730.1	10 066.5	13 580.7	2 273.7	1 247.2	1 662.8	4 454.5	4 418.6	4 388.2
Food products	118.2	142.3	111.8	93.3	99.7	134.6	81.7	99.7	83.0	67.7	66.1	89.7
Tobacco products	...	...	...	...	...	...	...	...	...	...	...	...
Textile mill products	2.1	2.0	2.2	3.8	4.2	2.4	0.1	0.4	0.4	1.1	1.5	0.5
Apparel	2.4	2.7	3.3	9.2	11.4	6.1	0.5	1.4	1.6	6.7	6.9	2.9
Lumber and wood products	52.9	78.6	107.7	136.6	91.2	77.5	5.2	5.3	4.3	7.1	3.6	2.6
Furniture and fixtures	1.6	1.8	3.0	6.6	5.8	11.0	1.0	0.6	1.6	2.3	3.5	9.4
Paper products	220.1	406.1	253.4	264.6	257.3	250.1	36.6	68.8	39.7	28.1	21.7	17.6
Printing and publishing	5.6	6.9	13.3	12.2	20.0	10.1	1.3	2.2	5.1	2.8	7.6	3.4
Chemical products	152.0	75.4	100.1	171.1	75.6	173.7	5.4	6.4	43.3	10.6	8.6	16.1
Refined petroleum products	0.1	...	0.1	...	0.1	0.1	...	...	...	...	0.1	0.1
Rubber and plastic products	3.4	5.4	6.4	7.2	7.6	8.5	0.6	1.3	1.4	2.0	2.1	3.5
Leather products	0.9	1.3	1.7	2.2	2.5	2.3	0.1	0.5	0.4	0.8	1.1	1.1
Stone, clay and glass products	3.6	3.7	2.7	4.0	5.0	7.6	0.5	0.7	0.6	0.7	0.8	2.9
Primary metals	10.8	18.4	25.6	46.4	47.5	35.0	2.7	5.6	8.3	14.3	24.2	15.1
Fabricated metal products	11.9	11.8	15.5	22.7	24.6	25.5	5.2	4.6	7.4	12.6	10.7	12.5
Industrial machinery and computers	304.4	358.8	292.1	401.8	470.6	539.1	70.2	61.1	80.5	126.2	154.4	172.4
Electric and electronic equipment	174.1	197.6	168.0	257.6	287.2	282.9	53.3	62.1	54.1	74.7	78.4	86.1
Transportation equipment	3 674.6	2 758.2	3 323.9	6 932.8	8 295.7	11 585.5	1 958.9	867.7	1 274.8	4 024.4	3 951.7	3 860.3
Scientific and measuring instruments	207.1	231.4	254.6	313.5	311.3	375.0	38.9	50.1	43.2	60.2	59.9	75.5
Miscellaneous manufactures	34.8	32.0	40.0	41.4	43.0	46.9	10.4	7.3	11.0	11.6	13.8	14.1
Unidentified manufactures	3.4	4.8	5.5	3.1	6.4	6.9	1.1	1.3	2.1	0.7	1.9	2.4
Agricultural And Livestock Products	39.9	36.5	46.6	55.2	77.5	55.6	13.8	13.3	15.2	17.3	20.6	13.2
Agricultural products	34.0	33.6	41.1	43.2	57.6	49.0	13.0	12.6	14.5	14.8	18.6	13.0
Livestock and livestock products	5.9	2.9	5.4	12.0	19.9	6.5	0.8	0.6	0.7	2.5	2.0	0.2
Other Commodities	90.5	93.3	91.9	103.8	137.5	179.6	9.9	11.9	10.4	16.3	16.7	30.5
Forestry products	15.4	16.8	17.7	21.9	27.2	27.7	...	0.1	0.1	0.3	0.2	0.2
Fish and other marine products	62.3	53.3	45.6	47.4	75.1	72.5	5.7	7.3	5.3	4.6	4.9	6.7
Metallic ores and concentrates	...	...	...	...	...	...	...	...	...	...	...	...
Bituminous coal and lignite	...	...	...	...	...	...	...	...	...	...	...	...
Crude petroleum and natural gas	0.1	0.2	0.1	0.1	...	...	...	...	...	...	...	...
Nonmetallic minerals	0.2	0.4	4.8	5.8	0.6	0.1	0.2	...	...	0.1	...	...
Scrap and waste	3.3	10.0	4.7	2.1	0.9	0.7	...	0.2	0.1	0.2	...	0.1
Used merchandise	3.3	5.2	4.9	8.9	5.4	2.7	0.8	1.8	1.2	4.9	2.4	0.8
Goods imported and returned unchanged	...	...	...	...	...	...	...	...	...	...	...	...
Special classification provisions	5.9	7.3	13.9	17.6	28.3	75.7	3.3	2.4	3.6	6.2	9.2	22.7

Table D-52. WASHINGTON: State Exports of Goods by Destination and Industry, 1994–1999—Continued

(Millions of dollars.)

Industry	Germany						France					
	1994	1995	1996	1997	1998	1999	1994	1995	1996	1997	1998	1999
ALL GOODS	829.1	896.6	923.4	1 518.4	2 401.9	2 249.2	415.7	297.5	218.9	342.5	971.3	1 500.9
Manufactured Goods	803.7	878.1	893.4	1 489.7	2 350.9	2 212.4	392.6	273.9	200.5	322.5	944.8	1 468.6
Food products	5.3	7.0	5.3	5.2	6.1	7.4	1.2	1.4	3.0	2.3	5.4	7.7
Tobacco products	...	...	...	...	...	...	...	...	...	...	...	...
Textile mill products	0.1	0.1	0.2	0.2	0.1	0.2	0.2	0.1	0.2	0.1	0.1	...
Apparel	0.4	0.7	0.3	0.4	0.6	0.5	0.5	0.1	0.1	0.2	0.2	0.1
Lumber and wood products	22.0	41.1	51.7	68.4	46.9	31.8	0.5	1.2	1.7	3.0	3.1	3.4
Furniture and fixtures	0.2	0.3	0.2	0.4	0.4	0.3	0.1	0.1	0.1	1.3	0.4	0.4
Paper products	62.0	116.7	79.8	80.2	88.9	101.2	37.8	65.4	40.9	30.2	32.2	31.7
Printing and publishing	0.7	0.4	0.9	0.7	0.7	0.6	0.3	1.7	4.2	5.8	1.3	0.4
Chemical products	132.4	43.8	6.8	113.6	49.0	35.2	5.9	10.4	7.3	5.7	6.5	7.0
Refined petroleum products	0.1	...	...	...	...	...	...	...	...	...	...	...
Rubber and plastic products	0.6	1.0	1.1	2.2	1.6	1.1	0.7	0.6	0.4	1.0	1.2	0.4
Leather products	0.1	0.2	0.2	0.1	0.2	0.2	...	...	0.1	0.2	0.2	0.3
Stone, clay and glass products	2.0	1.6	1.3	1.8	3.1	3.5	0.1	0.1	0.1	0.1	0.1	0.1
Primary metals	2.2	5.2	2.2	5.6	4.8	3.1	0.9	1.4	5.3	16.4	9.9	6.4
Fabricated metal products	2.7	2.5	1.6	2.5	3.7	3.1	0.6	0.4	0.8	1.0	1.5	2.3
Industrial machinery and computers	62.6	88.1	60.7	52.9	55.9	87.1	68.8	92.2	33.3	53.5	62.2	86.3
Electric and electronic equipment	28.1	30.8	28.7	43.9	68.8	47.2	32.9	41.4	34.0	72.6	66.0	93.6
Transportation equipment	425.5	497.5	583.1	1 030.3	1 941.3	1 780.9	216.6	35.0	47.7	104.1	726.7	1 188.4
Scientific and measuring instruments	47.4	30.0	55.6	69.8	66.4	89.8	23.6	19.6	19.5	21.9	23.2	36.6
Miscellaneous manufactures	8.5	9.8	12.9	11.2	11.5	18.5	1.5	2.4	1.3	2.5	4.0	2.9
Unidentified manufactures	0.7	1.2	0.8	0.5	0.9	0.8	0.4	0.4	0.8	0.5	0.6	0.6
Agricultural And Livestock Products	7.7	8.7	13.5	10.0	18.5	9.0	1.5	0.7	0.7	1.4	2.2	1.7
Agricultural products	4.3	7.7	11.9	6.4	7.0	4.6	1.4	0.6	0.7	1.2	1.3	1.5
Livestock and livestock products	3.4	1.0	1.5	3.6	11.5	4.4	0.1	...	...	0.2	0.9	0.3
Other Commodities	17.7	9.8	16.5	18.6	32.5	27.8	21.6	22.9	17.7	18.6	24.3	30.5
Forestry products	5.3	2.8	3.0	4.2	6.3	3.4	...	0.1	...	0.2	...	0.1
Fish and other marine products	10.8	3.7	5.0	4.6	19.0	9.3	18.9	19.9	13.0	14.8	19.2	20.1
Metallic ores and concentrates	...	...	...	...	...	...	...	...	...	...	...	...
Bituminous coal and lignite	...	...	...	...	...	...	...	...	...	...	...	...
Crude petroleum and natural gas	0.1	0.2	...	...	...	...	...	...	...	...	...	...
Nonmetallic minerals	...	0.4	4.5	5.8	0.6	0.1	...	...	...	...	...	...
Scrap and waste	0.7	1.3	...	...	...	...	...	...	...	...	...	...
Used merchandise	0.2	0.3	0.3	0.1	0.1	0.8	1.9	2.0	1.3	0.7	1.2	0.5
Goods imported and returned unchanged	...	...	...	...	...	...	...	...	...	...	...	...
Special classification provisions	0.7	1.2	3.7	4.0	6.6	14.2	0.8	0.9	3.4	3.0	3.9	9.8

Industry	The Netherlands						Asian 10					
	1994	1995	1996	1997	1998	1999	1994	1995	1996	1997	1998	1999
ALL GOODS	448.4	713.7	904.2	877.1	479.3	961.3	14 039.7	13 043.6	13 920.2	14 870.6	16 362.0	12 860.7
Manufactured Goods	426.7	692.4	881.0	846.3	445.7	919.5	11 880.4	10 539.4	11 797.6	12 999.7	15 106.8	11 234.1
Food products	21.1	22.7	13.1	10.6	16.0	16.5	487.8	541.1	522.1	509.4	443.4	578.3
Tobacco products	...	...	...	...	...	...	...	...	...	0.2	0.3	1.1
Textile mill products	0.7	0.8	0.5	0.8	1.5	0.3	10.3	14.8	13.3	9.7	7.4	4.7
Apparel	0.1	0.1	0.1	0.4	0.7	1.3	15.2	21.8	21.5	15.4	8.8	9.5
Lumber and wood products	1.8	2.2	2.9	5.5	3.0	1.9	2 451.9	2 589.9	2 607.3	1 929.2	1 216.8	1 158.5
Furniture and fixtures	...	0.4	0.5	0.1	0.5	0.3	4.5	8.4	10.0	9.1	7.5	7.0
Paper products	4.1	17.4	2.9	8.0	8.2	3.8	589.5	914.8	796.8	727.1	619.5	684.5
Printing and publishing	0.4	0.3	0.8	1.0	2.9	4.4	8.3	7.7	8.9	9.9	18.2	15.4
Chemical products	1.9	1.9	1.6	4.5	3.4	3.5	128.5	94.9	131.3	293.5	218.9	297.4
Refined petroleum products	...	...	...	...	...	...	10.9	10.7	43.0	4.5	1.8	6.4
Rubber and plastic products	0.5	1.3	0.8	0.5	0.6	0.9	19.9	31.1	31.1	27.4	24.9	37.1
Leather products	0.4	0.4	0.6	0.5	0.5	0.3	3.8	6.8	6.9	6.4	3.6	10.1
Stone, clay and glass products	0.2	0.1	...	...	...	0.1	19.6	22.3	26.4	33.1	20.8	21.3
Primary metals	0.5	1.0	0.3	0.5	1.7	1.1	129.9	176.1	177.9	188.0	143.1	181.5
Fabricated metal products	1.0	1.1	1.1	2.0	1.9	1.5	18.7	31.2	24.9	50.3	60.0	28.3
Industrial machinery and computers	16.3	35.5	39.7	51.7	104.6	98.2	146.2	270.4	226.3	277.0	230.6	242.8
Electric and electronic equipment	11.8	13.4	12.9	14.2	24.2	25.4	140.8	231.2	218.8	248.6	197.4	257.4
Transportation equipment	313.5	525.9	727.3	666.6	197.2	669.4	7 503.2	5 341.9	6 646.3	8 382.2	11 660.1	7 442.5
Scientific and measuring instruments	44.7	62.1	70.4	74.6	75.6	87.0	156.8	167.9	190.3	216.0	163.5	171.0
Miscellaneous manufactures	7.4	5.3	5.0	4.8	2.7	3.1	29.1	48.8	88.1	55.7	49.8	64.1
Unidentified manufactures	0.3	0.3	0.3	0.3	0.5	0.6	5.5	7.5	6.5	6.9	10.5	14.8
Agricultural And Livestock Products	5.5	4.8	5.9	10.6	8.5	10.4	492.5	731.3	622.4	594.1	353.4	426.5
Agricultural products	5.2	4.8	5.9	10.6	8.5	10.4	435.2	674.8	538.6	539.2	318.3	372.4
Livestock and livestock products	0.3	...	...	...	...	...	57.3	56.4	83.9	55.0	35.1	54.1
Other Commodities	16.2	16.5	17.3	20.2	25.1	31.3	1 666.7	1 772.9	1 500.2	1 276.8	901.8	1 200.1
Forestry products	9.1	9.5	13.3	15.6	17.0	20.6	0.9	0.5	0.5	0.7	0.5	0.6
Fish and other marine products	5.4	2.7	1.6	2.2	6.4	4.5	1 534.2	1 586.6	1 345.9	1 137.7	808.5	1 078.8
Metallic ores and concentrates	...	...	...	...	...	...	6.1	8.0	7.8	8.9	10.0	13.1
Bituminous coal and lignite	...	...	...	...	...	...	2.9	2.2	0.6	0.1	...	...
Crude petroleum and natural gas	...	...	...	...	...	...	0.1	0.1	...	0.1	...	...
Nonmetallic minerals	...	...	0.1	...	...	...	0.9	1.0	1.6	3.7	1.8	3.0
Scrap and waste	1.3	2.7	1.0	1.0	0.6	0.2	88.2	141.0	88.3	87.0	67.8	65.7
Used merchandise	0.1	0.5	0.1	0.1	0.4	0.2	4.6	4.6	7.9	5.7	3.8	3.9
Goods imported and returned unchanged	...	...	...	...	...	...	...	...	...	...	...	...
Special classification provisions	0.3	1.1	1.2	1.2	0.7	5.8	28.9	28.9	47.6	32.9	9.4	35.1

Table D-52. WASHINGTON: State Exports of Goods by Destination and Industry, 1994–1999—*Continued*

(Millions of dollars.)

Industry	Japan						South Korea					
	1994	1995	1996	1997	1998	1999	1994	1995	1996	1997	1998	1999
ALL GOODS	6 372.5	6 703.0	6 316.4	6 561.6	6 287.0	6 056.1	1 408.3	1 851.6	2 023.9	1 889.2	965.3	1 398.8
Manufactured Goods	4 747.3	4 968.9	4 899.3	5 311.1	5 434.0	4 948.3	1 226.8	1 528.1	1 766.8	1 690.0	854.4	1 196.8
Food products	345.8	365.5	330.5	323.4	306.6	386.9	28.2	32.7	33.9	25.8	21.1	43.1
Tobacco products	...	...	...	0.2	0.1	1.1	...	...	...	...	...	...
Textile mill products	4.9	6.2	5.9	5.0	3.2	1.1	2.7	5.1	4.7	1.6	1.4	1.5
Apparel	13.4	16.4	17.9	10.3	5.9	6.9	0.4	3.6	1.4	1.8	0.8	1.0
Lumber and wood products	2 247.1	2 379.1	2 407.3	1 721.7	1 140.6	1 046.7	133.7	156.8	147.7	150.2	38.2	69.5
Furniture and fixtures	2.9	6.1	5.0	4.6	3.7	5.1	0.5	0.9	2.8	1.5	0.5	0.4
Paper products	385.4	571.6	480.1	426.9	380.8	415.3	76.9	137.6	105.2	93.5	48.3	71.4
Printing and publishing	2.7	4.0	5.0	5.3	12.2	10.7	0.7	1.0	1.1	1.3	0.6	0.7
Chemical products	26.3	59.6	83.6	168.5	135.1	177.6	5.4	11.1	12.5	15.3	10.1	30.9
Refined petroleum products	1.0	7.1	1.7	1.6	1.0	1.1	2.0	2.1	21.7	1.7	0.3	1.7
Rubber and plastic products	10.1	21.1	20.2	15.9	17.6	23.6	2.0	5.7	4.6	5.9	1.0	5.8
Leather products	1.5	4.6	5.5	4.7	0.8	1.7	0.4	0.5	0.7	1.2	0.1	0.2
Stone, clay and glass products	2.9	3.8	7.3	15.7	8.5	10.1	1.3	2.0	4.1	4.3	0.4	0.8
Primary metals	36.6	49.3	57.4	82.2	93.8	95.9	33.4	44.0	33.4	31.2	10.0	20.1
Fabricated metal products	7.2	14.1	10.4	8.7	10.6	16.5	0.8	4.5	2.2	3.0	1.3	4.2
Industrial machinery and computers	39.3	77.0	80.2	94.1	66.9	105.3	23.9	28.9	29.2	38.3	19.2	17.5
Electric and electronic equipment	44.5	65.2	87.0	112.7	77.3	60.6	16.8	23.0	17.5	14.5	8.9	24.8
Transportation equipment	1 476.6	1 198.2	1 149.0	2 183.8	3 071.1	2 461.4	876.5	1 036.6	1 300.6	1 254.7	668.8	872.1
Scientific and measuring instruments	74.1	78.6	78.2	86.5	67.0	72.1	18.2	25.7	33.5	36.4	16.7	23.0
Miscellaneous manufactures	22.2	37.1	64.2	36.7	27.2	42.7	2.2	5.4	9.3	7.0	5.4	6.3
Unidentified manufactures	2.8	4.1	3.1	2.6	4.3	6.0	1.0	0.8	0.6	0.8	1.4	1.9
Agricultural And Livestock Products	198.6	239.5	193.1	251.0	157.0	196.9	52.6	192.6	127.1	73.4	11.9	33.0
Agricultural products	191.8	234.3	189.0	246.4	154.3	194.2	16.4	155.9	77.0	41.4	7.0	11.5
Livestock and livestock products	6.8	5.3	4.1	4.6	2.7	2.7	36.2	36.7	50.1	32.0	4.9	21.4
Other Commodities	1 426.6	1 494.6	1 224.0	999.5	696.1	911.0	128.9	130.9	130.0	125.8	99.0	169.1
Forestry products	0.5	0.3	0.3	0.3	0.2	0.2	...	...	...	...	...	...
Fish and other marine products	1 401.9	1 461.3	1 202.6	971.9	673.6	871.8	76.9	56.4	79.8	77.8	62.0	125.0
Metallic ores and concentrates	6.1	8.0	7.8	8.9	10.0	13.0	...	...	...	...	...	0.1
Bituminous coal and lignite	...	...	...	0.1	...	...	2.9	2.2	0.6	0.1	...	...
Crude petroleum and natural gas	...	0.1	...	...	...	...	...	...	...	...	...	...
Nonmetallic minerals	0.2	0.3	0.1	0.4	0.2	0.5	...	0.1	0.1	...	0.2	0.9
Scrap and waste	14.1	21.4	7.9	7.6	7.3	6.0	47.6	69.8	48.1	46.6	36.5	40.6
Used merchandise	3.4	2.7	4.5	2.4	1.6	2.4	...	0.1	0.2	...	...	...
Goods imported and returned unchanged	...	...	...	...	...	...	...	...	...	...	...	...
Special classification provisions	0.4	0.4	0.8	7.9	3.2	17.1	1.4	2.5	1.2	1.3	0.3	2.5

Industry	Taiwan						Singapore					
	1994	1995	1996	1997	1998	1999	1994	1995	1996	1997	1998	1999
ALL GOODS	993.8	933.0	893.6	797.0	1 541.6	550.9	1 295.0	1 037.4	966.3	1 276.1	1 403.4	1 218.9
Manufactured Goods	801.9	715.9	687.0	636.4	1 446.9	459.2	1 289.2	1 029.2	958.0	1 265.5	1 393.8	1 209.8
Food products	42.7	40.3	39.3	49.3	28.0	37.2	7.7	8.9	9.5	12.3	11.9	12.6
Tobacco products	...	...	...	...	...	...	...	...	...	...	...	...
Textile mill products	0.8	1.0	0.2	0.5	0.5	0.5	0.1	0.2	0.2	1.0	0.8	0.2
Apparel	...	...	0.6	1.0	0.7	0.8	0.5	0.5	0.6	0.5	0.6	0.2
Lumber and wood products	11.5	28.1	22.6	24.2	10.6	16.8	0.2	0.3	0.6	1.1	0.3	0.7
Furniture and fixtures	0.4	0.4	0.8	0.7	1.4	0.4	0.2	0.2	0.3	1.2	0.8	0.2
Paper products	32.5	56.7	45.8	54.2	50.7	53.0	15.3	25.3	23.4	18.1	11.3	12.6
Printing and publishing	0.9	0.6	0.5	0.6	0.5	0.4	0.9	0.5	0.5	0.6	0.8	1.9
Chemical products	85.4	5.9	7.1	85.9	50.7	23.1	2.0	2.0	4.5	2.1	1.6	12.7
Refined petroleum products	0.7	0.4	0.3	0.2	0.1	0.2	0.5	...	1.9	...	...	0.1
Rubber and plastic products	0.7	0.2	0.6	0.7	1.0	1.3	0.8	1.0	1.0	1.6	0.7	1.2
Leather products	0.4	0.3	0.1	0.1	0.1	0.3	0.1	0.1	...	...	...	...
Stone, clay and glass products	6.3	5.9	5.9	3.6	2.6	3.3	1.5	1.3	2.0	0.6	0.2	0.3
Primary metals	15.1	20.0	20.4	16.0	10.3	15.3	6.6	7.5	10.3	9.2	8.0	11.8
Fabricated metal products	3.2	0.7	2.7	2.3	1.9	1.2	2.0	0.9	2.0	2.5	4.3	0.7
Industrial machinery and computers	15.4	22.8	21.2	16.9	23.1	30.8	22.4	49.7	24.4	36.4	28.3	20.1
Electric and electronic equipment	12.6	16.1	18.9	15.3	17.8	65.3	25.4	67.5	46.5	56.1	29.8	46.9
Transportation equipment	559.5	504.3	483.6	343.6	1 228.4	190.3	1 189.1	851.0	816.0	1 105.2	1 284.5	1 070.7
Scientific and measuring instruments	12.6	10.7	13.2	18.7	15.3	15.7	13.0	11.1	12.3	14.5	8.1	14.2
Miscellaneous manufactures	0.8	0.9	2.5	1.7	1.3	1.2	0.6	1.0	1.6	2.0	1.4	1.2
Unidentified manufactures	0.3	0.3	0.7	1.0	1.6	1.9	0.3	0.4	0.3	0.4	0.4	1.3
Agricultural And Livestock Products	172.0	191.6	185.9	138.6	75.0	71.2	5.1	6.8	6.0	6.3	5.4	4.3
Agricultural products	171.8	191.5	185.5	137.9	74.9	71.2	5.1	6.8	6.0	6.3	5.4	4.3
Livestock and livestock products	0.2	...	0.4	0.8	0.1	...	...	...	...	...	...	...
Other Commodities	20.0	25.6	20.8	22.0	19.7	20.5	0.7	1.4	2.3	4.3	4.3	4.8
Forestry products	...	...	...	0.1	0.1	0.1	...	...	...	...	...	...
Fish and other marine products	10.2	11.1	13.8	10.1	10.3	9.8	0.1	0.4	1.6	1.9	3.5	0.9
Metallic ores and concentrates	...	...	...	...	...	...	...	...	...	...	...	...
Bituminous coal and lignite	...	...	...	...	...	...	...	...	...	...	...	...
Crude petroleum and natural gas	...	...	...	...	...	...	...	...	...	...	...	...
Nonmetallic minerals	0.4	0.1	0.2	0.3	0.4	0.4	...	...	...	...	...	...
Scrap and waste	8.2	13.9	6.3	10.9	8.1	6.8	0.1	...	...	1.1	...	0.1
Used merchandise	0.5	...	...	0.1	...	0.6	0.2	0.5	0.4	0.1	...	0.1
Goods imported and returned unchanged	...	...	...	...	...	...	...	...	...	...	...	...
Special classification provisions	0.6	0.5	0.5	0.5	0.9	2.8	0.3	0.5	0.3	1.2	0.6	3.5

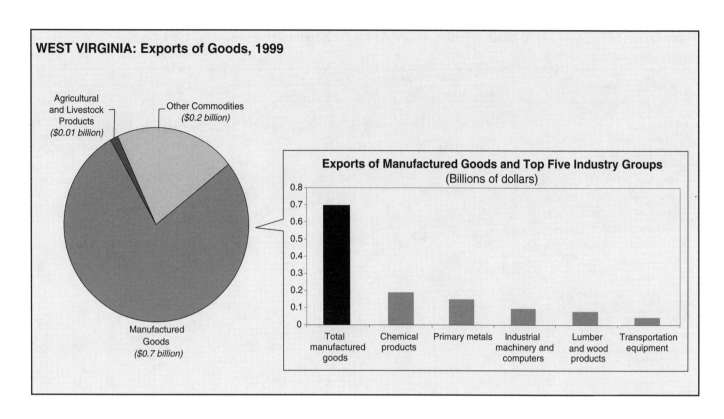

WEST VIRGINIA: Exports of Goods, 1999

Agricultural and Livestock Products ($0.01 billion)

Other Commodities ($0.2 billion)

Manufactured Goods ($0.7 billion)

Exports of Manufactured Goods and Top Five Industry Groups
(Billions of dollars)

Total manufactured goods | Chemical products | Primary metals | Industrial machinery and computers | Lumber and wood products | Transportation equipment

Table D-53. WEST VIRGINIA: State Exports of Goods by Destination and Industry, 1994–1999

(Millions of dollars.)

Industry	All destinations						Canada					
	1994	1995	1996	1997	1998	1999	1994	1995	1996	1997	1998	1999
ALL GOODS	940.6	1 097.9	1 217.9	1 298.8	1 178.2	897.1	334.6	334.2	377.5	478.5	503.4	373.0
Manufactured Goods	637.3	708.4	820.2	867.7	827.4	694.6	245.3	255.2	292.0	313.9	337.4	348.3
Food products	2.9	14.1	5.9	5.2	5.7	4.8	2.3	2.6	2.3	2.2	4.0	2.0
Tobacco products	...	4.0	...	0.2	0.1	0.4	...	...	...	...	...	0.4
Textile mill products	3.7	3.7	4.9	7.1	6.6	7.8	1.2	1.3	1.8	2.6	1.7	2.7
Apparel	0.9	1.4	1.3	4.7	2.2	1.8	0.1	0.3	0.4	0.4	0.6	0.3
Lumber and wood products	38.2	37.6	45.6	61.1	57.8	78.5	14.1	15.5	23.4	27.8	26.9	38.3
Furniture and fixtures	1.4	2.5	2.1	2.8	6.4	2.2	0.8	0.8	0.4	0.3	4.9	1.2
Paper products	3.9	5.4	6.2	7.1	11.1	5.4	3.4	4.5	4.9	4.6	5.3	4.3
Printing and publishing	2.1	3.2	1.0	0.7	2.3	1.0	0.5	1.2	0.9	0.3	0.9	0.4
Chemical products	280.5	232.3	289.2	249.6	262.9	189.8	98.2	80.1	85.0	83.0	99.0	96.1
Refined petroleum products	7.0	3.3	8.8	9.3	11.9	9.0	7.0	1.4	1.4	5.1	6.4	5.7
Rubber and plastic products	11.3	10.8	11.6	9.1	10.9	11.1	4.5	4.9	5.0	5.1	5.7	6.5
Leather products	0.3	0.2	3.3	1.5	0.6	3.0	0.3	0.1	0.1	...	0.1	2.8
Stone, clay and glass products	15.9	30.1	31.7	28.9	26.3	21.5	3.3	4.5	6.5	7.1	6.9	6.4
Primary metals	127.9	161.6	212.6	289.8	200.1	150.2	66.0	71.6	98.8	118.3	99.1	94.7
Fabricated metal products	13.3	18.2	18.3	16.6	23.5	24.3	8.6	11.0	12.0	10.2	16.1	16.5
Industrial machinery and computers	49.9	57.0	75.5	79.6	112.6	95.0	15.5	20.0	24.5	21.3	37.5	39.2
Electric and electronic equipment	8.7	15.7	19.5	30.5	19.8	19.0	4.1	5.9	5.6	5.3	5.5	9.3
Transportation equipment	45.0	81.1	58.2	38.4	41.7	44.0	11.9	24.5	15.8	15.9	12.8	16.8
Scientific and measuring instruments	21.9	22.6	21.5	22.3	19.8	15.3	2.7	3.9	2.4	3.6	2.7	3.6
Miscellaneous manufactures	1.2	2.1	1.8	2.2	2.8	2.7	0.4	0.6	0.5	0.5	0.8	0.8
Unidentified manufactures	1.3	1.4	1.1	1.2	2.4	7.8	0.5	0.6	0.5	0.3	0.4	0.5
Agricultural And Livestock Products	6.1	12.3	5.9	8.0	7.0	13.2	5.8	6.3	3.7	4.3	4.6	8.2
Agricultural products	3.8	7.4	1.5	1.7	1.7	6.3	3.7	3.1	1.2	1.4	1.2	5.6
Livestock and livestock products	2.3	4.9	4.5	6.3	5.4	6.8	2.1	3.2	2.5	2.9	3.3	2.6
Other Commodities	297.2	377.3	391.8	423.1	343.8	189.4	83.5	72.7	81.8	160.3	161.4	16.5
Forestry products	3.5	3.6	2.6	1.4	1.0	1.7	0.1	0.6	0.1	...	...	0.2
Fish and other marine products	0.3	0.3	0.2	1.6	0.6	0.7	0.2	0.3	0.1	...	0.6	0.7
Metallic ores and concentrates	...	1.3	0.1	0.1	0.5	0.3	...	...	0.1	0.1	0.2	0.2
Bituminous coal and lignite	277.3	360.4	367.2	394.2	327.5	173.1	67.7	61.7	61.2	136.5	149.0	4.1
Crude petroleum and natural gas	0.2	...	...	5.1	...	...	0.2	...	...	5.1	...	...
Nonmetallic minerals	0.9	0.7	1.4	2.1	1.6	0.9	0.7	0.6	1.0	1.6	0.3	0.3
Scrap and waste	2.7	4.0	2.9	3.0	3.7	3.0	2.6	3.1	2.1	2.2	2.7	2.7
Used merchandise	0.5	0.8	0.8	2.0	0.8	0.6	0.2	0.3	0.6	1.3	0.7	0.5
Goods imported and returned unchanged	11.6	5.9	16.3	13.3	7.5	7.4	11.6	5.9	16.3	13.3	7.5	7.4
Special classification provisions	0.3	0.3	0.4	0.3	0.5	1.7	0.3	0.2	0.3	0.3	0.4	0.4

Table D-53. WEST VIRGINIA: State Exports of Goods by Destination and Industry, 1994–1999—Continued

(Millions of dollars.)

Industry	South and Central American and Caribbean						Mexico					
	1994	1995	1996	1997	1998	1999	1994	1995	1996	1997	1998	1999
ALL GOODS	66.2	91.1	101.7	65.5	62.6	70.0	16.7	16.4	19.3	34.4	55.8	29.6
Manufactured Goods	46.6	56.4	62.4	38.8	37.0	22.9	16.6	16.4	19.0	33.5	55.4	29.2
Food products	...	1.5	2.0	0.5	0.1	0.4	0.2	...	...	0.2	0.6	2.1
Tobacco products	...	...	...	...	...	...	...	...	...	...	...	...
Textile mill products	0.2	0.4	0.2	0.3	0.2	0.1	0.2	0.1	0.4	0.9	0.4	0.7
Apparel	0.3	0.4	0.3	...	...	0.1	...	0.1	0.2	3.7	0.4	0.8
Lumber and wood products	1.4	...	...	0.5	...	1.9	...	...	0.1	...	1.3	0.5
Furniture and fixtures	...	...	...	...	0.4	...	0.1	...	...	...	0.1	0.1
Paper products	...	...	0.1	0.2	0.1	0.4	0.3	...	...	1.5	0.7	0.2
Printing and publishing	...	...	...	...	...	0.1	...	...	...	0.1	...	...
Chemical products	15.0	12.2	15.3	17.7	17.2	6.8	7.4	6.4	6.4	7.7	3.9	4.5
Refined petroleum products	...	...	...	...	...	0.4	...	...	0.2	1.0	0.7	0.5
Rubber and plastic products	0.3	0.2	0.2	0.2	0.3	0.2	0.3	0.2	1.4	0.6	0.4	0.5
Leather products	...	...	...	...	...	...	...	...	...	...	...	...
Stone, clay and glass products	0.8	0.6	1.4	0.7	0.4	0.5	0.2	1.0	1.5	0.8	0.4	1.7
Primary metals	0.5	0.1	0.6	6.1	2.6	0.1	0.6	1.9	2.7	2.7	12.3	3.8
Fabricated metal products	0.3	0.6	1.4	0.4	0.8	0.7	0.3	2.0	0.8	1.7	0.6	0.7
Industrial machinery and computers	4.1	5.6	15.3	7.6	8.9	5.4	2.7	2.3	3.6	6.0	24.0	8.2
Electric and electronic equipment	0.1	1.1	1.0	0.7	1.5	0.4	0.9	0.7	0.3	2.0	3.6	1.7
Transportation equipment	22.7	32.6	22.6	2.4	2.3	4.0	0.5	0.8	0.7	3.6	4.6	2.5
Scientific and measuring instruments	0.6	0.9	1.8	1.3	1.9	1.2	2.9	0.5	0.4	0.8	0.6	0.3
Miscellaneous manufactures	0.2	...	0.1	0.2	0.1	0.1	...	0.1	0.2	0.3	0.2	0.1
Unidentified manufactures	0.2	0.1	0.1	0.1	0.1	0.3	...	0.1	0.1	0.1	0.4	0.4
Agricultural And Livestock Products	...	0.2	0.3	0.1	0.2	0.8	...	...	0.1	...	0.2	0.1
Agricultural products	...	0.2	0.1	0.1	0.2	0.3	...	...	...	...	0.2	0.1
Livestock and livestock products	...	...	0.2	0.1	...	0.5	...	...	...	...	...	...
Other Commodities	19.6	34.5	39.0	26.7	25.4	46.3	...	...	0.2	0.8	0.3	0.2
Forestry products	...	...	...	...	...	...	...	...	...	...	...	...
Fish and other marine products	...	...	...	1.6	...	...	...	...	...	...	...	...
Metallic ores and concentrates	...	...	...	...	...	...	...	...	...	...	...	...
Bituminous coal and lignite	19.3	33.8	39.0	25.0	25.3	46.1	...	...	...	...	...	...
Crude petroleum and natural gas	...	...	...	...	...	...	...	...	...	...	...	...
Nonmetallic minerals	0.1	...	...	...	...	...	...	...	0.2	0.5	0.2	0.1
Scrap and waste	...	0.3	...	...	...	...	...	...	...	...	...	0.1
Used merchandise	0.1	0.3	...	...	0.1	...	...	...	...	0.3	...	...
Goods imported and returned unchanged	...	...	...	...	...	...	...	...	...	...	...	...
Special classification provisions	...	...	...	...	...	0.1	...	...	...	...	...	...

Industry	European Union						United Kingdom					
	1994	1995	1996	1997	1998	1999	1994	1995	1996	1997	1998	1999
ALL GOODS	291.5	412.9	419.6	403.3	305.9	259.0	57.7	100.6	100.0	127.2	116.4	76.8
Manufactured Goods	126.5	191.9	217.4	230.8	209.3	166.6	42.3	70.6	71.5	91.6	74.4	43.1
Food products	...	2.5	0.1	0.7	0.5	0.1	...	1.1	...	0.6	0.4	0.1
Tobacco products	...	4.0	...	...	...	...	...	...	...	...	...	...
Textile mill products	1.3	1.1	1.3	1.7	2.1	0.7	0.3	0.3	0.4	0.5	1.1	0.6
Apparel	...	0.2	0.1	0.2	0.6	0.1	...	0.1	...	0.1	0.5	0.1
Lumber and wood products	20.4	19.1	17.8	24.0	22.3	26.2	0.5	1.0	1.1	1.9	2.7	5.0
Furniture and fixtures	0.3	0.2	0.5	0.5	0.4	0.4	...	...	0.4	...	...	...
Paper products	...	0.2	...	0.1	4.7	...	...	0.1	...	...	...	...
Printing and publishing	1.3	1.9	0.1	0.1	1.2	0.3	1.2	0.2	0.1	0.1	0.1	0.1
Chemical products	30.2	42.6	75.5	62.0	64.3	41.3	0.8	2.6	3.0	1.1	2.1	4.5
Refined petroleum products	...	1.9	7.2	2.8	...	...	...	...	...	...	...	...
Rubber and plastic products	2.2	3.2	1.1	1.2	3.3	2.8	0.4	0.8	0.6	0.2	0.4	0.2
Leather products	...	0.1	...	...	...	...	...	...	...	...	...	...
Stone, clay and glass products	4.9	15.6	12.0	11.7	12.1	6.9	0.7	0.7	1.0	2.1	2.5	1.1
Primary metals	36.0	56.2	68.2	84.9	57.1	38.4	24.5	42.6	51.9	72.1	46.7	20.0
Fabricated metal products	1.2	1.9	2.0	1.5	3.1	3.3	0.7	1.1	0.9	0.9	1.6	2.2
Industrial machinery and computers	13.7	15.7	12.4	12.2	17.2	20.2	8.1	6.2	5.5	3.6	5.9	3.1
Electric and electronic equipment	1.1	2.0	6.3	13.0	1.6	3.7	0.4	0.6	1.4	2.1	0.7	0.9
Transportation equipment	5.4	14.1	4.7	6.1	11.3	10.1	2.8	9.5	2.4	2.5	6.6	3.8
Scientific and measuring instruments	8.2	8.4	7.7	7.2	6.4	5.7	1.9	3.1	2.6	3.5	2.8	1.1
Miscellaneous manufactures	0.1	0.9	0.3	0.8	0.4	0.4	...	0.5	0.1	...	...	...
Unidentified manufactures	0.2	0.3	0.2	0.3	0.7	5.8	0.1	0.1	0.1	0.1	0.3	0.2
Agricultural And Livestock Products	0.2	5.5	1.7	2.4	1.7	2.0	...	0.1	...	...	...	...
Agricultural products	...	3.9	0.1	0.2	0.1	0.1	...	0.1	...	...	...	...
Livestock and livestock products	0.2	1.6	1.6	2.2	1.6	2.0	...	...	...	...	...	...
Other Commodities	164.7	215.5	200.5	170.1	94.9	90.4	15.3	29.9	28.5	35.6	42.0	33.8
Forestry products	0.1	0.1	0.1	...	...	...	...	...	...	...	...	...
Fish and other marine products	...	...	...	...	...	...	...	...	...	...	...	...
Metallic ores and concentrates	...	1.3	...	...	0.3	...	...	...	...	...	...	...
Bituminous coal and lignite	164.5	213.8	199.9	169.0	93.1	89.1	15.2	29.8	28.4	35.6	41.5	33.7
Crude petroleum and natural gas	...	...	...	...	...	...	...	...	...	...	...	...
Nonmetallic minerals	0.1	0.1	0.1	0.1	0.7	...	0.1	...	...	...	...	...
Scrap and waste	...	0.1	0.3	0.6	0.8	0.2	...	0.1	0.1	...	0.4	...
Used merchandise	...	...	0.1	0.4	...	...	...	...	...	...	...	...
Goods imported and returned unchanged	...	...	...	...	...	...	...	...	...	...	...	...
Special classification provisions	...	0.1	0.1	...	...	1.0	...	...	...	...	...	...

Table D-53. WEST VIRGINIA: State Exports of Goods by Destination and Industry, 1994–1999—*Continued*

(Millions of dollars.)

Industry	Germany 1994	1995	1996	1997	1998	1999	France 1994	1995	1996	1997	1998	1999
ALL GOODS	24.1	29.3	19.4	28.0	22.1	24.8	20.9	23.3	24.0	34.0	19.0	37.4
Manufactured Goods	15.7	25.5	18.7	24.2	19.6	23.3	12.8	17.5	16.3	17.6	14.5	16.8
Food products	...	0.6	...	0.1	...	...	...	0.1	...	...	...	...
Tobacco products	...	...	...	...	...	...	...	...	...	...	...	...
Textile mill products	0.7	0.6	0.8	1.0	0.6	0.1	...	...	...	...	...	...
Apparel	...	...	...	...	...	...	...	...	...	...	...	...
Lumber and wood products	6.4	5.7	4.5	7.4	4.6	4.3	1.5	0.7	0.2	0.3	0.4	1.1
Furniture and fixtures	...	0.1	...	0.1	0.1	...	...	...	...	...	...	...
Paper products	...	0.1	...	...	...	...	...	...	...	...	...	...
Printing and publishing	...	0.2	...	...	0.7	...	...	1.1	...	...	...	...
Chemical products	1.0	1.3	2.0	1.0	0.5	0.5	2.0	2.7	0.6	2.7	1.2	0.8
Refined petroleum products	...	...	...	...	...	...	...	...	...	...	...	...
Rubber and plastic products	1.4	0.4	0.2	0.1	0.2	0.3	...	0.5	0.1	0.1	...	0.4
Leather products	...	...	...	...	...	...	...	...	...	...	...	...
Stone, clay and glass products	0.2	5.2	2.1	1.0	2.0	0.9	1.0	3.4	3.8	5.1	5.5	2.2
Primary metals	2.0	5.2	4.8	4.3	5.8	6.6	4.5	4.0	5.8	2.9	1.6	3.3
Fabricated metal products	0.2	0.1	0.7	0.1	0.8	0.5	0.1	0.2	...	0.2	0.3	0.2
Industrial machinery and computers	1.1	1.4	0.8	1.5	1.7	1.8	1.5	3.4	1.4	2.4	2.4	5.5
Electric and electronic equipment	0.2	0.8	2.0	5.0	0.4	0.5	0.2	0.3	1.1	2.1	0.1	0.3
Transportation equipment	1.2	2.7	0.5	1.8	1.9	2.0	0.4	0.4	1.4	0.8	2.3	1.7
Scientific and measuring instruments	1.3	1.0	0.2	0.2	0.3	0.5	1.7	0.8	1.8	0.9	0.5	0.9
Miscellaneous manufactures	0.1	...	...	0.6	...	0.1	...	...	0.1	0.1	...	...
Unidentified manufactures	...	0.1	...	...	0.1	5.1	...	...	...	...	0.1	0.1
Agricultural And Livestock Products	0.1	3.7	0.7	1.6	1.6	1.4	...	...	...	0.1	...	0.6
Agricultural products	...	3.6	...	...	...	...	...	...	...	0.1	...	...
Livestock and livestock products	0.1	0.1	0.7	1.5	1.6	1.4	...	...	...	0.1	...	0.6
Other Commodities	8.2	0.1	0.1	2.3	0.9	0.1	8.0	5.8	7.7	16.4	4.5	20.0
Forestry products	0.1	0.1	...	...	...	...	...	...	...	...	...	...
Fish and other marine products	...	...	...	...	...	...	...	...	...	...	...	...
Metallic ores and concentrates	...	...	...	...	0.3	...	...	...	...	...	...	...
Bituminous coal and lignite	8.2	...	...	2.2	...	...	8.0	5.8	7.7	16.2	4.5	19.9
Crude petroleum and natural gas	...	...	...	...	...	...	...	...	...	...	...	...
Nonmetallic minerals	...	...	...	...	0.6	...	...	...	...	...	...	...
Scrap and waste	...	...	...	...	...	...	...	...	...	...	...	...
Used merchandise	...	...	...	...	...	...	...	...	...	0.1	...	0.1
Goods imported and returned unchanged	...	...	...	...	...	...	...	...	...	...	...	...
Special classification provisions	...	...	...	...	...	...	...	...	...	...	...	...

Industry	The Netherlands 1994	1995	1996	1997	1998	1999	Asian 10 1994	1995	1996	1997	1998	1999
ALL GOODS	71.3	73.0	57.2	64.4	26.9	32.6	200.1	193.4	231.1	218.3	188.9	124.2
Manufactured Goods	26.4	21.5	19.1	20.9	22.5	29.9	170.8	145.2	172.1	159.0	128.6	88.0
Food products	...	0.4	0.1	...	...	...	0.3	1.6	1.5	1.4	0.3	0.3
Tobacco products	...	...	...	...	...	...	...	...	...	...	...	...
Textile mill products	...	...	...	...	...	...	0.6	0.6	1.0	1.6	1.6	2.9
Apparel	...	...	...	...	...	...	0.5	0.3	0.2	0.1	0.1	0.1
Lumber and wood products	2.8	0.1	0.3	0.3	0.1	0.1	2.3	2.7	4.1	8.0	6.8	9.9
Furniture and fixtures	0.1	0.1	0.1	0.3	0.3	0.3	...	...	0.7	1.1	0.1	0.1
Paper products	...	0.1	...	...	1.6	...	0.1	0.5	1.0	0.7	0.3	0.4
Printing and publishing	0.1	0.3	...	...	...	...	0.1	0.1	...	0.1	0.2	0.1
Chemical products	20.6	14.0	14.1	16.8	15.7	21.8	125.1	82.2	95.8	69.1	66.4	34.5
Refined petroleum products	...	...	...	...	...	...	...	...	...	...	...	...
Rubber and plastic products	0.2	1.1	...	0.4	0.9	1.3	3.5	1.4	3.2	1.3	0.7	0.8
Leather products	...	...	...	...	...	...	...	...	3.2	1.5	0.4	0.1
Stone, clay and glass products	...	0.1	0.1	0.1	1.0	0.1	2.6	6.1	7.8	7.4	5.0	5.2
Primary metals	0.8	0.5	0.3	...	0.2	3.1	15.9	24.5	23.9	37.3	17.7	7.8
Fabricated metal products	...	0.1	...	...	...	...	2.4	1.8	1.7	1.4	1.2	0.7
Industrial machinery and computers	0.7	1.6	2.1	1.1	1.8	1.7	8.7	7.5	9.5	7.7	6.9	9.9
Electric and electronic equipment	0.1	...	0.2	0.6	0.1	...	1.5	4.2	3.6	6.1	6.2	3.5
Transportation equipment	0.1	0.9	0.1	0.1	...	0.5	1.6	4.2	8.3	6.4	7.4	7.7
Scientific and measuring instruments	1.0	1.9	1.5	1.0	0.5	0.7	5.2	6.8	6.0	7.3	5.9	3.2
Miscellaneous manufactures	...	0.3	0.1	...	0.2	0.1	0.3	0.3	0.6	0.2	0.9	0.4
Unidentified manufactures	...	...	...	...	...	...	0.3	0.3	0.1	0.3	0.5	0.5
Agricultural And Livestock Products	0.1	1.5	0.8	0.1	...	...	...	...	...	...	...	0.2
Agricultural products	...	...	...	0.1	...	...	...	...	...	...	...	0.2
Livestock and livestock products	0.1	1.5	0.7	...	...	...	...	...	...	...	...	...
Other Commodities	44.8	50.0	37.3	43.4	4.4	2.6	29.2	48.2	58.9	59.3	60.3	36.0
Forestry products	...	...	...	...	...	...	3.3	2.9	2.4	1.4	1.0	1.5
Fish and other marine products	...	...	...	...	...	...	...	...	...	...	...	...
Metallic ores and concentrates	...	1.3	...	...	...	...	...	...	0.1	...	...	...
Bituminous coal and lignite	44.8	48.7	37.1	43.0	4.1	2.5	25.8	45.2	56.3	57.7	58.7	33.9
Crude petroleum and natural gas	...	...	...	...	...	...	...	...	...	...	...	...
Nonmetallic minerals	...	...	...	...	...	...	...	...	...	...	0.5	0.4
Scrap and waste	...	...	0.2	0.3	0.3	0.1	...	...	...	0.1	0.1	...
Used merchandise	...	...	...	...	...	...	...	...	0.1	0.2	0.1	...
Goods imported and returned unchanged	...	...	...	...	...	...	...	...	...	...	...	...
Special classification provisions	...	...	...	...	...	0.1	...	...	...	...	0.1	0.2

Table D-53. WEST VIRGINIA: State Exports of Goods by Destination and Industry, 1994–1999—*Continued*

(Millions of dollars.)

Industry	Japan						South Korea					
	1994	1995	1996	1997	1998	1999	1994	1995	1996	1997	1998	1999
ALL GOODS	58.7	94.7	112.0	105.5	115.2	70.6	16.7	21.2	24.5	29.8	11.6	14.0
Manufactured Goods	32.8	49.4	55.6	47.8	56.4	36.7	16.7	21.1	24.4	29.8	11.1	13.6
Food products	0.1	1.1	0.7	0.6	0.3	0.2	...	...	0.4	0.1	...	...
Tobacco products	...	...	...	...	...	...	...	...	...	...	...	...
Textile mill products	...	0.1	0.2	0.1	0.2	0.1	0.1	...	0.1	...	...	...
Apparel	0.1	0.2	0.1	...	0.1	...	...	...	...	0.1	...	...
Lumber and wood products	1.0	0.5	0.3	1.0	1.0	2.3	0.5	0.7	0.6	1.0	0.3	1.7
Furniture and fixtures	...	...	...	0.1	0.1	...	...	...	0.5	1.0	...	...
Paper products	...	...	...	...	...	0.1	...	0.4	0.6	0.4	...	0.2
Printing and publishing	...	...	...	...	...	...	...	...	0.1	0.1	0.1	...
Chemical products	14.5	16.6	24.9	16.2	24.5	13.1	11.5	13.3	15.4	14.3	7.5	7.5
Refined petroleum products	...	...	...	...	...	...	...	...	...	...	...	...
Rubber and plastic products	1.6	0.9	0.8	0.6	0.4	0.3	0.4	0.2	0.3	0.1	0.1	0.1
Leather products	...	...	...	...	...	...	...	...	...	...	...	...
Stone, clay and glass products	1.5	4.6	1.5	4.2	4.1	3.7	0.7	0.3	0.3	0.4	0.2	0.3
Primary metals	8.1	18.2	16.2	16.0	13.5	7.1	0.8	1.8	1.3	7.2	1.1	0.1
Fabricated metal products	0.9	1.2	0.4	0.3	0.4	0.1	0.1	...	0.4	0.1	0.2	0.1
Industrial machinery and computers	0.8	1.0	2.2	1.5	1.6	1.9	1.4	3.0	3.9	1.9	0.5	2.0
Electric and electronic equipment	0.6	2.1	1.9	3.0	4.4	1.6	0.4	0.3	0.1	0.3	0.3	1.0
Transportation equipment	1.0	1.5	4.6	3.1	4.3	4.7	...	...	0.1	...	...	0.1
Scientific and measuring instruments	2.3	1.3	1.5	1.0	1.3	0.9	0.8	1.0	0.6	2.6	0.6	0.3
Miscellaneous manufactures	0.1	...	0.4	...	0.1	0.3	...	...	...	0.1	0.1	0.1
Unidentified manufactures	0.1	0.1	...	0.1	0.1	0.1	...	...	...	0.1	0.1	0.1
Agricultural And Livestock Products	...	...	...	...	...	...	...	...	...	...	...	...
Agricultural products	...	...	...	...	...	...	...	...	...	...	...	...
Livestock and livestock products	...	...	...	...	...	...	...	...	...	...	...	...
Other Commodities	25.8	45.3	56.4	57.7	58.8	33.9	...	...	...	...	0.5	0.4
Forestry products	...	...	...	...	...	...	...	...	...	...	...	...
Fish and other marine products	...	...	0.1	...	...	...	...	...	...	...	...	...
Metallic ores and concentrates	...	...	...	...	...	...	...	...	...	...	...	...
Bituminous coal and lignite	25.8	45.2	56.3	57.7	58.7	33.9	...	...	...	...	...	...
Crude petroleum and natural gas	...	...	...	...	...	...	...	...	...	...	...	...
Nonmetallic minerals	...	...	...	...	...	...	...	...	...	...	0.5	0.4
Scrap and waste	...	...	...	...	...	...	...	...	...	...	...	...
Used merchandise	...	...	...	...	...	...	...	...	...	...	...	...
Goods imported and returned unchanged	...	...	...	...	...	...	...	...	...	...	...	...
Special classification provisions	...	...	...	...	...	...	...	...	...	...	...	...

Industry	Taiwan						Singapore					
	1994	1995	1996	1997	1998	1999	1994	1995	1996	1997	1998	1999
ALL GOODS	15.2	10.1	17.1	13.2	7.5	6.1	30.5	18.9	28.0	21.0	21.0	7.2
Manufactured Goods	15.2	10.1	17.1	13.2	7.5	6.1	30.5	18.9	28.0	21.0	21.0	7.2
Food products	...	...	...	...	...	...	...	0.2	0.2	0.1	...	...
Tobacco products	...	...	...	...	...	...	...	...	...	...	...	...
Textile mill products	0.1	0.1	...	...	...	...	...	...	0.1	...	...	...
Apparel	...	...	...	...	...	...	...	...	0.1	...	...	...
Lumber and wood products	0.3	0.4	1.3	1.3	1.8	2.3	...	...	0.2	0.1	...	0.1
Furniture and fixtures	...	...	...	...	...	...	...	...	...	...	...	0.1
Paper products	...	...	...	...	...	...	...	...	...	...	...	...
Printing and publishing	0.1	...	...	...	...	0.1	...	...	...	...	...	...
Chemical products	10.4	7.1	7.3	6.8	3.9	2.3	25.7	10.6	18.3	13.3	11.0	2.1
Refined petroleum products	...	...	...	...	...	...	...	...	...	...	...	...
Rubber and plastic products	...	0.1	...	0.1	...	...	0.3	0.2	0.2	0.1	0.1	0.1
Leather products	...	...	...	...	...	...	...	...	...	...	...	...
Stone, clay and glass products	0.1	0.1	4.7	1.4	0.3	0.6	...	...	0.3	0.2	0.1	0.1
Primary metals	2.4	0.9	1.0	2.1	0.3	...	1.7	2.3	2.3	2.1	1.5	0.1
Fabricated metal products	0.8	...	0.4	0.4	0.3	0.2	0.4	0.4	...	0.1	...	...
Industrial machinery and computers	0.2	0.3	0.2	0.1	0.2	0.1	0.5	0.5	1.7	0.6	2.2	0.5
Electric and electronic equipment	0.1	0.7	1.3	0.8	0.1	0.1	0.2	0.8	...	0.2	...	...
Transportation equipment	...	...	...	...	...	...	0.4	2.2	3.1	2.7	2.8	2.5
Scientific and measuring instruments	0.5	0.3	0.8	0.1	0.4	0.2	1.2	1.6	1.5	1.5	3.2	1.4
Miscellaneous manufactures	0.2	0.1	0.1	...	...	...	...	...	...	...	0.1	0.1
Unidentified manufactures	...	...	...	...	...	...	...	...	...	...	...	...
Agricultural And Livestock Products	...	...	...	...	...	...	...	...	...	...	...	...
Agricultural products	...	...	...	...	...	...	...	...	...	...	...	...
Livestock and livestock products	...	...	...	...	...	...	...	...	...	...	...	...
Other Commodities	...	...	...	...	...	...	...	...	...	...	...	...
Forestry products	...	...	...	...	...	...	...	...	...	...	...	...
Fish and other marine products	...	...	...	...	...	...	...	...	...	...	...	...
Metallic ores and concentrates	...	...	...	...	...	...	...	...	...	...	...	...
Bituminous coal and lignite	...	...	...	...	...	...	...	...	...	...	...	...
Crude petroleum and natural gas	...	...	...	...	...	...	...	...	...	...	...	...
Nonmetallic minerals	...	...	...	...	...	...	...	...	...	...	...	...
Scrap and waste	...	...	...	...	...	...	...	...	...	...	...	...
Used merchandise	...	...	...	...	...	...	...	...	...	...	...	...
Goods imported and returned unchanged	...	...	...	...	...	...	...	...	...	...	...	...
Special classification provisions	...	...	...	...	...	...	...	...	...	...	...	...

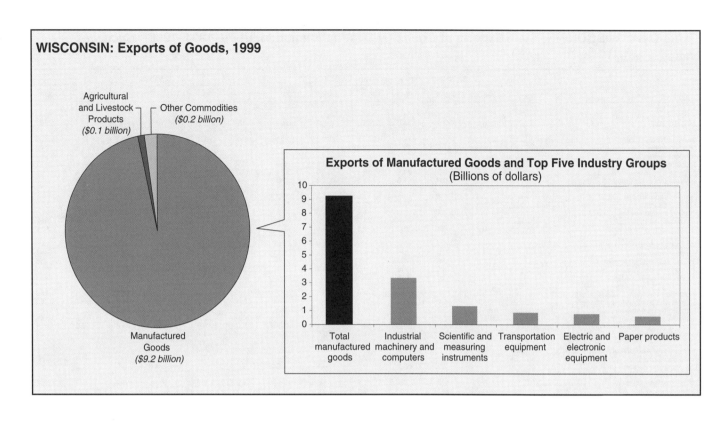

WISCONSIN: Exports of Goods, 1999

Agricultural and Livestock Products ($0.1 billion)

Other Commodities ($0.2 billion)

Manufactured Goods ($9.2 billion)

Exports of Manufactured Goods and Top Five Industry Groups
(Billions of dollars)

Total manufactured goods | Industrial machinery and computers | Scientific and measuring instruments | Transportation equipment | Electric and electronic equipment | Paper products

Table D-54. WISCONSIN: State Exports of Goods by Destination and Industry, 1994–1999

(Millions of dollars.)

Industry	All destinations						Canada					
	1994	1995	1996	1997	1998	1999	1994	1995	1996	1997	1998	1999
ALL GOODS	6 927.9	8 004.5	8 409.7	9 791.5	9 221.4	9 546.3	2 438.4	2 808.6	2 685.6	3 096.3	3 457.3	3 716.2
Manufactured Goods	6 636.7	7 643.3	8 095.1	9 455.1	9 032.3	9 227.8	2 254.6	2 549.0	2 503.3	2 870.6	3 360.6	3 520.6
Food products	280.3	389.4	395.8	423.3	433.6	417.3	104.6	114.7	135.6	147.1	148.9	145.4
Tobacco products	. . .	1.0	. . .	. . .	. . .	. . .	. . .	. . .	. . .	. . .	. . .	. . .
Textile mill products	31.1	42.6	48.8	51.5	54.0	51.3	14.6	22.7	23.6	23.2	25.8	25.1
Apparel	37.5	58.3	82.4	66.5	70.6	65.1	5.5	6.7	10.9	15.5	16.5	5.3
Lumber and wood products	59.9	66.9	70.5	82.7	79.3	75.7	27.1	32.0	37.4	42.8	45.2	46.6
Furniture and fixtures	56.6	42.6	47.9	48.7	56.4	44.4	32.1	26.4	25.2	27.6	33.8	22.8
Paper products	323.7	364.6	369.6	390.0	456.2	614.8	232.2	286.6	255.8	244.6	249.8	341.7
Printing and publishing	40.1	45.0	51.2	59.8	62.0	95.7	22.7	29.3	30.1	33.3	30.0	47.7
Chemical products	300.5	346.9	367.6	441.6	435.5	499.1	123.7	143.8	158.0	165.2	161.3	173.2
Refined petroleum products	21.9	21.4	22.5	19.6	17.9	20.0	18.8	15.6	16.3	11.5	9.5	9.1
Rubber and plastic products	173.5	194.9	180.6	213.5	220.8	243.1	91.8	96.7	95.3	116.0	123.9	118.9
Leather products	83.8	66.8	69.2	68.1	71.0	57.5	17.4	14.2	13.1	13.9	13.1	12.8
Stone, clay and glass products	52.9	59.1	68.9	62.3	50.2	56.6	13.6	13.6	15.8	19.2	20.0	22.2
Primary metals	52.8	81.7	101.5	115.3	106.3	103.3	25.6	33.3	35.9	47.8	49.6	45.4
Fabricated metal products	314.4	337.5	358.6	381.0	379.9	382.8	118.3	128.4	129.9	147.3	163.8	171.9
Industrial machinery and computers	2 719.6	3 029.8	3 167.4	4 178.5	3 522.4	3 339.5	845.4	961.8	908.1	1 058.6	1 251.5	1 197.8
Electric and electronic equipment	590.5	725.7	769.6	859.9	967.9	780.3	155.5	187.4	187.8	226.0	291.6	218.8
Transportation equipment	450.5	502.7	479.7	603.4	729.8	863.2	243.1	250.2	201.8	286.4	451.2	614.0
Scientific and measuring instruments	855.0	1 051.5	1 216.2	1 145.7	1 100.0	1 326.8	87.7	109.5	144.2	166.0	198.7	236.8
Miscellaneous manufactures	164.8	185.9	200.8	218.9	184.1	153.2	65.8	64.6	64.9	67.2	67.4	55.4
Unidentified manufactures	27.4	29.0	26.4	24.8	34.5	38.2	9.1	11.8	13.6	11.3	9.1	9.6
Agricultural And Livestock Products	66.8	78.0	92.9	75.0	70.8	99.1	16.6	21.0	33.8	23.6	20.2	36.9
Agricultural products	31.6	45.1	57.6	37.5	37.9	51.2	8.7	13.8	23.2	12.1	11.6	9.7
Livestock and livestock products	35.3	32.9	35.3	37.5	32.8	47.8	7.9	7.2	10.6	11.5	8.5	27.2
Other Commodities	224.4	283.2	221.7	261.4	118.4	219.5	167.2	238.7	148.5	202.1	76.5	158.6
Forestry products	29.3	24.4	27.7	20.7	16.9	8.7	1.8	1.8	1.6	2.2	2.1	1.3
Fish and other marine products	1.1	1.1	1.2	1.1	1.2	1.0	0.9	0.5	0.5	0.4	1.0	0.8
Metallic ores and concentrates	111.5	130.3	82.0	62.1	. . .	. . .	111.5	130.2	81.9	62.0	. . .	. . .
Bituminous coal and lignite	0.3	2.3	2.3	3.1	16.1	81.3	0.3	. . .	2.2	3.1	16.1	81.3
Crude petroleum and natural gas	0.2	0.1	2.3	1.8	1.5	0.7	0.2	0.1	2.0	1.8	1.5	0.5
Nonmetallic minerals	6.5	7.3	7.6	8.3	5.6	6.4	1.6	2.3	2.6	1.8	2.1	3.7
Scrap and waste	30.5	35.8	50.6	46.4	25.5	23.8	26.2	32.5	24.6	24.1	20.8	20.2
Used merchandise	9.4	8.0	9.9	15.0	10.0	9.2	1.3	1.3	1.5	9.6	1.6	1.1
Goods imported and returned unchanged	18.5	63.5	25.8	94.0	27.1	27.5	18.5	63.5	25.8	94.0	27.1	27.5
Special classification provisions	17.0	10.3	12.3	8.8	14.6	60.9	5.0	6.5	5.6	3.1	4.3	22.1

Table D-54. WISCONSIN: State Exports of Goods by Destination and Industry, 1994–1999—Continued

(Millions of dollars.)

Industry	South and Central American and Caribbean						Mexico					
	1994	1995	1996	1997	1998	1999	1994	1995	1996	1997	1998	1999
ALL GOODS	464.1	577.6	664.0	785.1	736.3	604.1	411.9	311.0	350.5	427.3	512.1	596.1
Manufactured Goods	453.2	567.5	645.9	770.6	722.8	595.8	385.7	288.0	327.8	419.2	502.0	589.2
Food products	24.8	42.9	40.9	32.3	26.0	25.9	21.2	15.5	18.9	26.0	41.9	46.3
Tobacco products	. . .	. . .	. . .	. . .	. . .	. . .	. . .	. . .	. . .	. . .	. . .	. . .
Textile mill products	2.6	3.7	5.8	8.3	6.1	5.0	0.9	1.4	1.8	2.4	4.8	4.1
Apparel	15.5	20.2	20.9	16.2	17.6	30.4	2.3	1.4	3.0	2.7	1.4	1.6
Lumber and wood products	0.5	0.9	1.8	1.6	2.3	0.9	1.8	2.1	2.5	1.7	3.2	4.4
Furniture and fixtures	1.6	1.8	3.5	3.3	5.2	6.2	3.1	0.6	0.7	1.2	3.1	1.7
Paper products	5.4	8.5	8.9	12.6	31.7	49.8	16.8	11.9	16.9	24.5	27.5	32.7
Printing and publishing	0.7	1.1	0.9	1.2	1.6	1.8	2.2	1.0	1.0	2.5	6.9	14.4
Chemical products	13.4	20.3	19.4	28.3	29.9	30.8	17.7	16.7	26.9	27.4	33.1	37.1
Refined petroleum products	0.3	0.4	0.8	1.2	0.9	1.4	0.1	0.1	0.2	0.2	0.2	0.6
Rubber and plastic products	5.5	10.2	10.5	14.7	14.3	11.5	25.9	19.5	15.0	15.0	26.2	34.2
Leather products	5.7	3.9	1.5	3.9	4.9	2.9	0.8	0.7	1.3	0.9	1.4	2.1
Stone, clay and glass products	4.6	2.0	1.1	2.7	1.8	1.9	1.4	1.4	1.2	1.1	1.3	2.5
Primary metals	1.2	1.6	2.9	4.9	2.1	3.1	5.0	5.4	9.9	8.1	8.5	11.4
Fabricated metal products	15 0	22.2	20.0	27.1	19.1	10.0	48.6	16.1	21.3	23.8	31.6	38.2
Industrial machinery and computers	165.2	221.6	283.5	373.8	310.6	209.2	111.7	87.0	89.7	114.1	122.8	159.9
Electric and electronic equipment	34.6	45.2	48.7	63.7	65.3	44.1	66.4	62.6	69.7	91.9	96.7	108.3
Transportation equipment	17.0	13.6	20.8	24.7	25.3	20.3	9.1	4.9	9.7	19.2	26.2	23.3
Scientific and measuring instruments	121.8	121.7	126.0	112.3	129.9	113.5	34.9	29.0	30.8	48.9	51.8	54.4
Miscellaneous manufactures	16.7	24.1	26.9	36.1	25.1	22.2	15.0	9.2	5.8	5.4	6.6	5.9
Unidentified manufactures	1.2	1.6	1.1	1.7	3.0	4.9	1.0	1.4	1.6	2.1	6.9	6.0
Agricultural And Livestock Products	5.1	7.3	13.7	12.7	10.8	4.8	22.1	18.4	19.3	3.9	4.8	3.5
Agricultural products	0.1	0.2	9.0	7.6	5.7	0.2	16.0	17.1	16.5	0.4	0.3	0.3
Livestock and livestock products	5.0	7.2	4.7	5.0	5.1	4.6	6.1	1.3	2.8	3.5	4.5	3.2
Other Commodities	5.7	2.8	4.4	1.8	2.6	3.5	4.2	4.6	3.3	4.2	5.3	3.4
Forestry products	0.2	0.1	. . .	0.1	0.1	0.1	0.1	. . .	. . .	. . .	0.1	. . .
Fish and other marine products	. . .	. . .	. . .	. . .	. . .	. . .	. . .	. . .	0.2	0.2	. . .	. . .
Metallic ores and concentrates	. . .	. . .	. . .	. . .	. . .	. . .	. . .	. . .	. . .	. . .	. . .	. . .
Bituminous coal and lignite	. . .	. . .	. . .	. . .	. . .	. . .	. . .	. . .	. . .	. . .	. . .	. . .
Crude petroleum and natural gas	. . .	. . .	. . .	. . .	. . .	0.1	. . .	. . .	. . .	. . .	. . .	0.1
Nonmetallic minerals	1.1	0.6	0.7	0.9	0.5	0.1	3.3	3.7	3.0	3.7	1.0	1.5
Scrap and waste	0.4	0.8	0.6	0.3	0.6	0.8	0.4	. . .	. . .	. . .	. . .	0.6
Used merchandise	0.3	1.0	2.6	0.1	0.7	0.8	0.2	0.9	. . .	0.1	4.0	0.3
Goods imported and returned unchanged	. . .	. . .	. . .	. . .	. . .	. . .	. . .	. . .	. . .	. . .	. . .	. . .
Special classification provisions	3.8	0.3	0.3	0.4	0.6	1.6	0.1	. . .	0.1	0.2	0.1	1.0

Industry	European Union						United Kingdom					
	1994	1995	1996	1997	1998	1999	1994	1995	1996	1997	1998	1999
ALL GOODS	1 725.6	1 915.6	2 097.3	2 493.0	2 203.9	2 299.0	447.2	400.3	441.9	612.6	513.1	583.4
Manufactured Goods	1 698.0	1 892.9	2 069.1	2 472.0	2 186.1	2 259.2	441.3	397.8	438.7	609.7	510.6	574.2
Food products	53.0	71.3	66.1	74.3	86.4	69.5	12.4	15.5	13.7	20.9	14.4	16.1
Tobacco products	. . .	. . .	. . .	. . .	. . .	. . .	. . .	. . .	. . .	. . .	. . .	. . .
Textile mill products	6.0	6.0	6.8	8.5	8.5	8.7	0.4	0.3	0.6	0.7	1.4	2.4
Apparel	6.9	13.6	25.9	18.7	23.8	14.3	2.0	6.6	19.7	16.0	20.9	12.5
Lumber and wood products	18.1	14.3	7.8	10.8	12.4	13.6	5.8	6.5	2.2	4.8	4.3	6.6
Furniture and fixtures	6.9	5.8	6.8	9.2	7.1	6.3	1.9	1.6	2.4	2.2	2.6	2.6
Paper products	37.3	24.1	39.5	51.0	68.5	73.4	19.2	9.1	11.7	14.7	12.8	16.2
Printing and publishing	10.5	8.4	13.0	15.2	14.9	20.5	4.6	4.3	6.6	7.7	6.0	8.6
Chemical products	78.2	79.4	88.9	124.1	125.0	165.7	18.3	17.3	16.5	29.3	23.8	40.2
Refined petroleum products	0.8	1.3	2.1	2.1	3.3	3.3	0.1	. . .	0.1	0.1	0.1	0.1
Rubber and plastic products	28.4	26.7	33.0	27.3	30.5	36.3	5.5	6.0	8.1	6.9	7.1	8.4
Leather products	11.9	10.2	12.3	14.1	16.3	13.4	3.4	1.3	3.2	3.5	2.0	1.0
Stone, clay and glass products	11.8	20.3	32.3	20.3	8.0	12.1	0.8	1.1	1.4	2.0	1.0	2.2
Primary metals	11.8	27.8	38.6	36.8	32.1	28.7	1.4	2.8	4.4	6.8	8.1	9.6
Fabricated metal products	54.4	65.4	75.2	81.6	84.8	80.4	23.6	25.8	32.6	27.3	33.6	31.9
Industrial machinery and computers	790.3	778.9	861.5	1 226.4	965.4	931.1	207.4	140.5	154.8	284.9	179.4	225.9
Electric and electronic equipment	141.6	185.8	210.9	200.5	215.7	187.2	55.6	67.0	62.8	70.0	80.7	82.0
Transportation equipment	104.2	137.3	147.8	148.3	119.9	115.8	17.6	16.8	27.2	39.4	38.4	35.3
Scientific and measuring instruments	294.9	379.0	356.4	359.2	317.2	437.7	52.0	64.8	57.1	56.0	55.5	55.9
Miscellaneous manufactures	24.8	30.2	39.3	39.5	38.1	31.9	7.5	8.4	12.2	15.0	14.7	12.5
Unidentified manufactures	6.1	6.9	4.7	4.1	8.0	9.3	1.8	2.3	1.6	1.7	3.7	4.2
Agricultural And Livestock Products	12.8	14.4	12.3	11.3	10.1	11.0	1.6	1.4	1.6	1.7	1.4	1.7
Agricultural products	4.0	5.6	3.4	2.6	3.4	3.8	. . .	0.2	0.3	0.3	0.5	0.9
Livestock and livestock products	8.8	8.8	8.8	8.6	6.7	7.2	1.5	1.1	1.3	1.4	0.9	0.8
Other Commodities	14.8	8.4	15.9	9.7	7.8	28.8	4.3	1.1	1.5	1.1	1.0	7.5
Forestry products	0.3	0.5	0.6	0.4	0.5	0.3	. . .	. . .	. . .	. . .	. . .	. . .
Fish and other marine products	0.1	0.6	0.2	0.1	0.1	0.1	. . .	. . .	. . .	0.1	0.1	. . .
Metallic ores and concentrates	. . .	0.1	. . .	. . .	. . .	. . .	. . .	. . .	. . .	. . .	. . .	. . .
Bituminous coal and lignite	. . .	2.3	0.1	. . .	. . .	. . .	. . .	. . .	. . .	. . .	. . .	. . .
Crude petroleum and natural gas	. . .	. . .	0.2	. . .	. . .	. . .	. . .	. . .	. . .	. . .	. . .	. . .
Nonmetallic minerals	0.3	0.5	0.4	0.9	1.4	0.7	. . .	. . .	0.1	0.1	0.1	0.1
Scrap and waste	2.1	0.8	9.2	3.3	1.5	0.3	0.8	0.1	. . .	0.2	. . .	. . .
Used merchandise	5.4	1.5	1.3	1.9	1.6	4.4	0.1	0.2	0.1	0.2	0.3	0.1
Goods imported and returned unchanged	. . .	. . .	. . .	. . .	. . .	. . .	. . .	. . .	. . .	. . .	. . .	. . .
Special classification provisions	6.6	2.1	3.8	3.0	2.6	22.9	3.4	0.8	1.3	0.5	0.5	7.2

Table D-54. WISCONSIN: State Exports of Goods by Destination and Industry, 1994–1999—*Continued*

(Millions of dollars.)

Industry	Germany						France					
	1994	1995	1996	1997	1998	1999	1994	1995	1996	1997	1998	1999
ALL GOODS	325.0	387.1	441.4	462.2	445.6	382.5	317.4	358.2	319.4	454.0	327.7	412.5
Manufactured Goods	318.7	382.1	438.5	459.6	443.4	368.5	314.2	355.8	315.6	450.6	324.8	406.9
Food products	3.1	9.7	10.1	10.5	13.6	5.7	1.7	2.0	3.5	2.6	1.6	1.1
Tobacco products	. . .	. . .	. . .	. . .	. . .	. . .	. . .	. . .	. . .	. . .	. . .	. . .
Textile mill products	0.5	2.5	1.8	2.2	2.3	2.2	1.3	1.4	1.8	2.8	1.7	2.4
Apparel	2.6	1.6	1.5	0.5	0.3	0.2	0.1	0.2	0.4	0.1	0.2	0.3
Lumber and wood products	7.7	3.4	2.6	2.7	2.1	0.8	1.3	0.9	0.6	0.9	1.5	1.6
Furniture and fixtures	1.1	0.6	0.8	1.2	1.4	1.0	0.3	0.4	0.4	0.7	0.8	0.6
Paper products	4.7	2.3	4.5	9.4	14.4	9.3	2.0	0.5	1.6	1.9	10.5	12.8
Printing and publishing	2.7	1.8	2.4	3.0	3.4	5.7	1.5	0.5	0.8	1.4	0.6	2.1
Chemical products	13.0	11.6	14.5	24.5	15.0	19.4	6.5	8.1	10.6	15.5	17.3	37.1
Refined petroleum products	. . .	. . .	0.1	0.1	. . .	. . .	0.1	0.1	0.1	0.1	0.2	0.2
Rubber and plastic products	4.0	4.4	7.7	5.6	5.0	4.9	3.3	3.0	1.7	1.9	2.9	5.3
Leather products	0.8	1.3	1.4	2.1	0.7	0.5	0.3	0.2	. . .	0.1	0.1	0.1
Stone, clay and glass products	3.4	4.6	5.3	4.7	1.8	4.9	3.1	2.7	3.9	4.3	2.8	3.4
Primary metals	2.5	6.0	9.5	7.3	4.5	6.4	0.5	0.9	1.5	3.3	1.3	0.4
Fabricated metal products	12.1	16.5	18.2	20.1	21.1	19.8	6.1	6.4	4.7	8.0	8.2	6.9
Industrial machinery and computers	155.1	178.4	195.6	222.8	214.1	135.0	145.9	143.8	142.1	255.9	152.6	150.1
Electric and electronic equipment	19.8	34.9	39.2	34.0	38.7	31.3	10.0	12.5	12.9	13.5	15.2	7.1
Transportation equipment	23.7	32.2	41.2	30.1	21.6	16.6	18.4	17.9	15.4	11.0	8.7	7.7
Scientific and measuring instruments	54.4	64.7	75.4	71.0	75.7	100.9	107.1	149.3	106.9	119.6	90.9	160.5
Miscellaneous manufactures	6.0	3.8	5.8	7.0	6.3	2.8	3.9	4.0	6.2	6.7	7.1	6.5
Unidentified manufactures	1.5	1.6	1.1	0.7	1.3	1.1	0.8	0.9	0.6	0.4	0.6	0.8
Agricultural And Livestock Products	1.9	3.2	1.3	1.0	0.7	3.7	2.9	1.6	2.2	1.9	2.2	2.2
Agricultural products	0.3	1.9	. . .	. . .	0.2	0.4	1.8	0.9	1.1	0.4	0.9	1.6
Livestock and livestock products	1.6	1.3	1.3	1.0	0.6	3.3	1.1	0.8	1.1	1.5	1.3	0.6
Other Commodities	4.5	1.8	1.6	1.7	1.4	10.3	0.3	0.8	1.6	1.5	0.7	3.4
Forestry products	0.2	0.3	0.3	0.2	0.3	0.1	. . .	. . .	0.1	. . .	0.1	. . .
Fish and other marine products	. . .	. . .	. . .	. . .	. . .	. . .	. . .	. . .	. . .	. . .	0.1	. . .
Metallic ores and concentrates	. . .	. . .	. . .	. . .	. . .	. . .	. . .	. . .	. . .	. . .	. . .	. . .
Bituminous coal and lignite	. . .	. . .	. . .	. . .	. . .	. . .	. . .	. . .	. . .	. . .	. . .	. . .
Crude petroleum and natural gas	. . .	. . .	. . .	. . .	. . .	. . .	. . .	. . .	. . .	. . .	. . .	. . .
Nonmetallic minerals	. . .	0.1	. . .	0.2	0.3	. . .	. . .	. . .	0.1	0.1	0.2	0.2
Scrap and waste	0.1	0.5	0.5	. . .	. . .	. . .	. . .	0.2	0.6	0.4	0.1	0.2
Used merchandise	3.4	0.3	. . .	0.6	0.4	4.2	. . .	0.4	0.4	0.1	0.1	. . .
Goods imported and returned unchanged	. . .	. . .	. . .	. . .	. . .	. . .	. . .	. . .	. . .	. . .	. . .	. . .
Special classification provisions	0.8	0.5	0.7	0.7	0.4	5.9	0.3	0.3	0.6	0.8	0.2	3.0

Industry	The Netherlands						Asian 10					
	1994	1995	1996	1997	1998	1999	1994	1995	1996	1997	1998	1999
ALL GOODS	179.4	238.9	254.8	238.9	261.2	268.3	1 172.6	1 557.6	1 696.5	1 830.6	1 470.2	1 547.7
Manufactured Goods	175.2	236.0	252.5	235.6	258.7	264.9	1 139.3	1 529.2	1 645.6	1 775.4	1 432.9	1 497.0
Food products	15.7	22.8	16.7	17.7	26.2	25.5	65.5	115.0	99.0	107.5	101.5	113.9
Tobacco products	. . .	. . .	. . .	. . .	. . .	. . .	. . .	0.9	. . .	. . .	. . .	. . .
Textile mill products	2.5	0.7	1.2	1.3	2.1	0.5	3.8	5.9	7.3	6.6	5.9	5.0
Apparel	0.8	3.4	1.8	1.6	1.6	0.7	5.0	14.5	19.3	10.6	9.1	11.7
Lumber and wood products	1.2	1.1	0.8	0.5	1.1	1.0	10.1	13.9	16.5	21.7	12.2	8.2
Furniture and fixtures	0.9	0.8	1.1	0.3	0.2	0.2	2.8	3.0	3.4	3.7	2.6	4.8
Paper products	3.9	5.3	8.6	9.8	7.7	12.2	21.7	22.7	35.9	42.6	60.2	91.0
Printing and publishing	0.7	0.5	1.0	1.2	1.6	1.3	2.4	3.2	4.1	4.9	4.4	6.2
Chemical products	10.5	14.2	14.1	18.3	21.6	30.5	43.5	54.8	54.0	64.3	64.2	66.1
Refined petroleum products	0.1	0.1	. . .	. . .	0.3	. . .	1.2	3.3	2.3	3.3	2.6	4.3
Rubber and plastic products	1.2	3.3	4.4	1.4	3.4	3.5	15.1	32.6	19.5	30.0	18.4	29.3
Leather products	1.8	3.0	3.7	2.3	4.5	4.1	45.6	36.1	36.9	32.4	33.9	23.7
Stone, clay and glass products	2.3	2.7	3.5	3.1	0.5	0.2	16.6	18.0	15.8	16.1	14.6	13.9
Primary metals	4.4	6.6	5.7	5.9	11.0	5.9	6.6	9.6	8.7	12.8	8.5	6.8
Fabricated metal products	4.8	5.5	7.9	6.2	6.1	5.5	56.7	74.7	81.4	68.3	51.2	52.3
Industrial machinery and computers	69.5	85.7	96.9	112.9	120.0	116.6	440.0	598.8	563.4	730.6	468.3	498.9
Electric and electronic equipment	31.7	26.3	34.6	18.5	19.5	12.8	120.8	130.9	152.3	171.6	215.9	153.7
Transportation equipment	14.6	36.1	29.4	16.4	12.2	23.6	22.4	30.7	41.7	40.7	27.6	23.9
Scientific and measuring instruments	6.5	9.7	13.0	15.9	15.9	17.8	225.1	315.2	432.8	354.5	295.3	351.3
Miscellaneous manufactures	1.7	7.8	7.9	2.1	2.6	1.7	29.4	41.8	48.2	50.2	32.2	26.4
Unidentified manufactures	0.4	0.4	0.2	0.4	0.9	1.4	4.9	3.5	3.0	3.0	4.4	5.5
Agricultural And Livestock Products	2.3	2.2	1.7	1.9	1.5	1.4	3.2	3.1	5.4	16.1	18.0	35.3
Agricultural products	0.3	0.6	0.6	0.5	0.4	0.2	0.8	0.8	1.5	12.7	16.0	32.6
Livestock and livestock products	2.0	1.6	1.1	1.5	1.1	1.3	2.4	2.4	3.9	3.4	2.0	2.7
Other Commodities	1.9	0.6	0.7	1.4	1.0	1.9	30.1	25.2	45.4	39.2	19.3	15.4
Forestry products	. . .	. . .	. . .	. . .	. . .	. . .	26.9	22.0	25.4	17.9	14.0	6.9
Fish and other marine products	. . .	. . .	. . .	. . .	. . .	. . .	0.1	. . .	0.1	. . .	. . .	. . .
Metallic ores and concentrates	. . .	. . .	. . .	. . .	. . .	. . .	. . .	. . .	. . .	. . .	. . .	. . .
Bituminous coal and lignite	. . .	. . .	. . .	. . .	. . .	. . .	. . .	. . .	. . .	. . .	. . .	. . .
Crude petroleum and natural gas	. . .	. . .	. . .	. . .	. . .	. . .	. . .	. . .	. . .	. . .	. . .	. . .
Nonmetallic minerals	. . .	. . .	. . .	0.1	. . .	. . .	0.1	0.1	0.7	0.7	0.2	0.3
Scrap and waste	1.0	. . .	. . .	. . .	. . .	. . .	1.4	1.6	15.8	18.7	2.4	1.8
Used merchandise	. . .	0.6	0.6	0.9	0.7	0.1	1.0	0.8	2.3	0.5	0.4	0.9
Goods imported and returned unchanged	. . .	. . .	. . .	. . .	. . .	. . .	. . .	. . .	. . .	. . .	. . .	. . .
Special classification provisions	0.8	. . .	0.1	0.3	0.4	1.8	0.6	0.6	1.1	1.3	2.2	5.4

Table D-54. WISCONSIN: State Exports of Goods by Destination and Industry, 1994–1999—*Continued*

(Millions of dollars.)

Industry	Japan						South Korea					
	1994	1995	1996	1997	1998	1999	1994	1995	1996	1997	1998	1999
ALL GOODS	463.9	581.6	677.9	693.7	639.6	680.6	123.4	167.4	172.1	187.9	79.7	119.7
Manufactured Goods	461.2	578.2	658.0	671.3	634.0	672.3	121.4	165.8	170.1	186.9	78.7	118.6
Food products	34.3	52.7	51.3	49.9	41.2	46.3	11.4	14.2	12.2	12.8	17.8	26.6
Tobacco products	...	...	...	...	...	...	...	...	...	...	...	...
Textile mill products	0.4	0.6	0.8	2.1	2.0	1.8	0.7	0.5	0.3	0.6	0.6	1.0
Apparel	2.8	10.0	16.5	6.8	7.6	11.0	0.4	0.5	0.4	1.0	...	0.1
Lumber and wood products	7.3	10.1	10.8	11.1	7.3	4.4	1.9	2.5	1.8	5.9	2.3	1.4
Furniture and fixtures	0.9	1.0	1.0	0.6	0.7	0.9	0.4	0.6	0.4	0.5	0.1	1.2
Paper products	6.3	2.7	4.9	6.0	34.3	52.8	5.6	6.2	11.1	9.1	5.1	7.8
Printing and publishing	1.2	1.3	1.8	2.1	1.9	1.4	0.1	0.2	0.3	0.3	0.1	1.5
Chemical products	18.4	21.6	19.1	26.8	25.9	27.7	7.2	9.0	10.1	11.7	8.6	10.0
Refined petroleum products	0.1	0.4	0.1	0.3	...	...	0.3	0.3	0.4	0.6	0.2	0.3
Rubber and plastic products	5.4	18.9	4.4	6.7	3.8	8.3	1.5	1.4	1.4	1.6	1.0	0.9
Leather products	1.6	1.5	1.6	0.6	1.1	0.4	2.2	1.3	0.6	0.7	...	...
Stone, clay and glass products	2.8	3.6	3.9	7.0	5.3	3.0	1.5	2.5	2.1	2.4	0.7	1.8
Primary metals	0.8	1.4	3.0	3.0	3.0	1.7	0.3	0.8	1.3	1.2	0.8	0.8
Fabricated metal products	14.2	17.1	24.6	24.5	21.6	27.7	7.4	7.7	7.8	4.8	1.9	3.5
Industrial machinery and computers	197.7	174.4	141.8	228.6	221.3	209.3	34.4	64.1	65.9	84.4	20.1	20.5
Electric and electronic equipment	17.9	22.2	37.5	28.9	25.5	28.2	11.3	18.7	14.3	13.6	5.6	8.2
Transportation equipment	5.6	9.1	8.6	10.2	6.8	8.1	3.3	2.2	3.3	5.4	3.7	1.6
Scientific and measuring instruments	135.1	216.8	313.6	244.4	212.4	228.7	28.1	27.4	31.7	23.5	8.3	29.7
Miscellaneous manufactures	7.4	11.3	11.8	10.8	11.0	9.0	2.8	5.3	4.4	6.3	1.4	1.0
Unidentified manufactures	1.0	1.5	1.1	1.1	1.2	1.5	0.4	0.5	0.5	0.5	0.4	0.8
Agricultural And Livestock Products	1.7	2.2	3.1	3.1	2.4	4.4	0.7	0.5	0.5	0.3	0.1	0.3
Agricultural products	0.3	0.5	0.5	0.7	0.8	2.2	...	...	0.1	0.1	...	0.1
Livestock and livestock products	1.4	1.7	2.6	2.4	1.6	2.2	0.7	0.5	0.4	0.2	...	0.1
Other Commodities	1.1	1.3	16.8	19.3	3.2	3.9	1.3	1.1	1.5	0.7	0.9	0.9
Forestry products	...	...	...	...	...	0.2	...	...	...	0.3	0.4	...
Fish and other marine products	...	...	...	...	...	...	...	...	0.1	...	...	...
Metallic ores and concentrates	...	...	...	...	...	...	...	...	...	...	...	...
Bituminous coal and lignite	...	...	...	...	...	...	...	...	...	...	...	...
Crude petroleum and natural gas	...	...	...	...	...	...	...	...	...	...	...	...
Nonmetallic minerals	...	0.1	0.4	0.3	0.2	0.1	...	...	...	0.1	...	...
Scrap and waste	...	0.3	14.0	18.0	1.6	0.1	1.1	1.0	1.2	0.2	0.1	0.2
Used merchandise	0.8	0.5	1.8	0.3	0.2	0.7	...	...	0.1	...	...	...
Goods imported and returned unchanged	...	...	...	...	...	...	...	...	...	...	...	...
Special classification provisions	0.2	0.4	0.6	0.5	1.1	2.8	0.2	0.1	0.1	0.2	0.4	0.6

Industry	Taiwan						Singapore					
	1994	1995	1996	1997	1998	1999	1994	1995	1996	1997	1998	1999
ALL GOODS	119.1	214.2	164.6	160.3	147.7	151.6	112.8	124.5	137.3	149.3	87.5	123.8
Manufactured Goods	117.3	213.1	164.1	158.9	146.9	149.8	112.2	123.9	136.8	148.9	86.3	123.1
Food products	15.0	24.3	22.2	31.9	28.3	21.4	1.2	1.3	0.8	1.5	0.6	0.4
Tobacco products	...	...	...	...	...	...	...	...	...	...	...	...
Textile mill products	0.7	2.2	2.5	0.5	0.8	0.3	...	0.3	0.2	0.2	0.1	0.1
Apparel	0.1	0.1	0.1	0.1	0.1	...	1.1	1.7	0.9	1.0	0.2	0.3
Lumber and wood products	0.4	0.5	0.7	1.9	0.9	0.4	...	0.2	0.1	0.3	...	0.1
Furniture and fixtures	0.1	0.2	0.1	0.2	0.1	0.1	0.1	0.1	0.1	0.1	0.3	0.1
Paper products	0.6	1.6	4.4	4.9	4.6	5.2	1.7	3.0	3.3	4.2	3.4	4.3
Printing and publishing	0.1	0.4	0.4	0.1	0.3	0.3	0.2	0.3	0.2	0.3	0.1	0.3
Chemical products	5.3	9.2	6.5	6.5	7.9	8.5	2.6	3.1	6.0	3.0	2.4	3.3
Refined petroleum products	0.2	1.6	0.7	1.2	1.4	2.7	0.1	0.1	0.3	...	...	...
Rubber and plastic products	2.6	2.8	2.0	3.2	1.4	3.0	1.6	2.3	3.7	5.2	3.8	4.7
Leather products	3.2	0.5	0.3	0.6	0.2	0.3	0.3	0.2	0.1	0.4	0.5	0.2
Stone, clay and glass products	0.8	1.4	0.8	0.7	1.5	2.5	1.2	1.5	1.4	0.5	1.0	0.6
Primary metals	0.8	1.5	0.4	0.7	1.2	1.5	2.1	2.2	1.5	2.4	1.1	1.0
Fabricated metal products	9.2	6.6	3.6	4.4	4.1	4.3	5.8	7.1	5.3	4.1	3.3	2.7
Industrial machinery and computers	35.8	117.4	85.7	63.6	62.0	58.2	49.2	59.0	59.2	68.5	31.9	65.5
Electric and electronic equipment	24.8	28.3	15.2	14.9	13.1	12.7	24.0	16.2	24.4	28.2	15.6	18.1
Transportation equipment	1.1	1.7	1.1	4.9	2.0	3.2	1.8	3.3	4.5	4.4	3.9	5.4
Scientific and measuring instruments	12.5	11.3	15.5	15.4	13.9	20.9	10.3	11.5	14.1	12.5	12.0	12.0
Miscellaneous manufactures	1.3	1.2	1.9	3.0	2.8	3.3	8.6	10.3	10.4	11.8	5.4	3.5
Unidentified manufactures	2.6	0.3	0.3	0.2	0.5	0.5	0.3	0.3	0.3	0.3	0.8	0.7
Agricultural And Livestock Products	0.3	0.1	0.1	0.2	0.1	0.5	0.4	...	0.1	...	0.4	...
Agricultural products	...	...	...	...	...	0.4	0.4	...	0.1	...	0.4	...
Livestock and livestock products	0.3	0.1	0.1	0.1	0.1	0.1	...	...	...	...	...	...
Other Commodities	1.5	1.0	0.3	1.2	0.8	1.3	0.2	0.6	0.4	0.4	0.8	0.6
Forestry products	1.5	1.0	0.3	0.8	0.4	0.2	0.2	0.3	0.2	...	0.3	0.1
Fish and other marine products	...	...	...	...	...	...	...	...	...	...	...	...
Metallic ores and concentrates	...	...	...	...	...	...	...	...	...	...	...	...
Bituminous coal and lignite	...	...	...	...	...	...	...	...	...	...	...	...
Crude petroleum and natural gas	...	...	...	...	...	...	...	...	...	...	...	...
Nonmetallic minerals	...	...	...	0.1	...	0.1	...	...	0.1	0.1	...	...
Scrap and waste	...	...	...	0.2	0.4	0.7	...	0.1	...	...	...	...
Used merchandise	...	...	...	0.1	...	...	...	0.2	0.1	...	0.1	...
Goods imported and returned unchanged	...	...	...	...	...	0.3	...	...	...	...	...	...
Special classification provisions	...	...	...	...	...	0.3	...	...	...	0.1	0.4	0.4

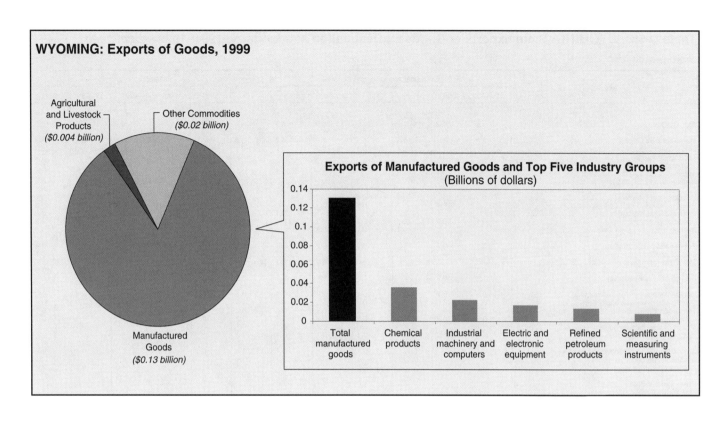

WYOMING: Exports of Goods, 1999

Agricultural and Livestock Products ($0.004 billion)

Other Commodities ($0.02 billion)

Manufactured Goods ($0.13 billion)

Exports of Manufactured Goods and Top Five Industry Groups
(Billions of dollars)

Total manufactured goods / Chemical products / Industrial machinery and computers / Electric and electronic equipment / Refined petroleum products / Scientific and measuring instruments

Table D-55. WYOMING: State Exports of Goods by Destination and Industry, 1994–1999

(Millions of dollars.)

Industry	All destinations						Canada					
	1994	1995	1996	1997	1998	1999	1994	1995	1996	1997	1998	1999
ALL GOODS	95.4	101.2	123.7	175.9	158.4	155.8	48.6	50.7	69.4	88.3	75.9	89.1
Manufactured Goods	80.4	83.0	100.8	122.4	120.2	130.2	39.6	39.8	55.1	69.9	66.6	77.1
Food products	3.4	8.7	14.8	5.2	3.2	3.0	1.8	0.9	1.0	2.0	1.8	1.5
Tobacco products	. . .	. . .	. . .	. . .	. . .	. . .			. . .	. . .	. . .	. . .
Textile mill products	0.2	0.1	0.5	0.8	0.3	0.9	0.1	0.1	0.2	0.2	0.1	0.2
Apparel	1.1	0.7	0.4	0.5	0.4	0.6	0.1	0.1	0.1	0.2	. . .	0.1
Lumber and wood products	0.9	1.6	2.3	4.1	3.1	2.3	0.8	1.3	1.5	0.9	0.6	0.7
Furniture and fixtures	0.3	0.1	0.3	0.4	0.7	0.7	0.2	0.1	0.1	0.2	0.2	0.1
Paper products	0.2	0.3	0.4	3.0	0.8	0.7	. . .	0.1	0.1	0.3	0.1	0.3
Printing and publishing	0.5	1.3	0.5	0.4	0.4	1.2	0.2	0.2	0.1	0.3	0.1	. . .
Chemical products	18.4	18.5	24.6	42.0	41.2	35.9	12.1	15.4	22.3	37.1	33.6	32.6
Refined petroleum products	. . .	. . .	1.1	0.2	0.1	13.7	. . .	. . .	0.9	. . .	. . .	7.8
Rubber and plastic products	0.8	1.0	1.0	1.0	1.6	2.4	0.3	0.6	0.5	0.4	0.8	0.8
Leather products	0.2	. . .	0.1	0.1	0.3	0.3	0.1					0.1
Stone, clay and glass products	0.4	0.6	0.4	0.5	1.0	0.5	0.1	0.1	0.2	0.3	0.5	0.3
Primary metals	2.7	2.0	3.1	2.8	1.7	2.3	2.3	1.2	0.7	1.7	1.1	1.3
Fabricated metal products	5.6	6.6	3.0	5.1	5.9	7.5	2.9	3.2	1.9	3.6	3.4	2.9
Industrial machinery and computers	27.2	19.9	24.5	34.2	30.2	22.5	15.8	10.2	12.4	13.7	13.4	11.0
Electric and electronic equipment	9.1	10.3	4.7	8.1	9.1	17.2	1.1	1.5	1.7	3.0	4.0	8.5
Transportation equipment	3.8	4.1	10.1	6.8	4.8	5.0	0.6	2.0	5.3	2.5	2.2	2.0
Scientific and measuring instruments	3.2	5.2	7.5	5.8	8.7	8.3	0.8	2.4	5.5	3.1	4.2	3.9
Miscellaneous manufactures	1.7	1.3	1.3	0.8	6.1	4.5	0.2	0.1	0.1	0.2	0.1	2.7
Unidentified manufactures	0.6	0.7	0.5	0.5	0.7	0.9	0.2	0.4	0.3	0.3	0.2	0.3
Agricultural And Livestock Products	1.6	1.6	2.5	5.2	2.9	3.5	1.1	1.5	1.9	3.3	1.4	2.0
Agricultural products	0.7	0.7	1.5	2.0	0.8	1.7	0.6	0.6	1.1	1.4	0.4	1.3
Livestock and livestock products	0.9	0.9	1.0	3.2	2.1	1.8	0.5	0.8	0.8	1.9	1.0	0.7
Other Commodities	13.4	16.6	20.3	48.3	35.3	22.0	7.9	9.5	12.3	15.1	7.9	9.9
Forestry products	0.2	0.1	. . .	. . .	0.1	. . .	0.1	. . .	. . .	. . .	. . .	. . .
Fish and other marine products	0.1	0.3	0.6	10.3	8.8	10.1	. . .	0.1	0.2	. . .	0.1	0.1
Metallic ores and concentrates	. . .	. . .	. . .	17.0	16.7	1.1	. . .	. . .	. . .	. . .	. . .	. . .
Bituminous coal and lignite	2.3	2.7	6.0	4.3	. . .	. . .	. . .	. . .	0.1	. . .	. . .	. . .
Crude petroleum and natural gas	0.1	. . .	. . .	0.8	. . .	. . .	0.1	. . .	. . .	0.8	. . .	. . .
Nonmetallic minerals	0.9	1.4	1.0	1.1	3.5	5.6	0.7	0.8	0.7	0.8	2.9	5.4
Scrap and waste	1.1	1.5	1.6	0.5	0.7	0.4	1.0	1.5	1.5	0.2	0.1	0.1
Used merchandise	3.1	4.2	1.5	1.5	0.8	0.4	0.6	0.8	0.4	0.7	0.3	0.1
Goods imported and returned unchanged	5.3	6.3	9.4	12.6	4.5	3.8	5.3	6.3	9.4	12.6	4.5	3.8
Special classification provisions	0.3	0.1	0.2	0.2	0.1	0.6	0.1	0.1	0.1	. . .	. . .	0.4

Table D-55. WYOMING: State Exports of Goods by Destination and Industry, 1994–1999—*Continued*

(Millions of dollars.)

Industry	South and Central American and Caribbean						Mexico					
	1994	1995	1996	1997	1998	1999	1994	1995	1996	1997	1998	1999
ALL GOODS	3.5	4.2	4.2	11.7	8.9	6.4	4.1	4.1	3.5	4.9	5.9	12.6
Manufactured Goods	3.4	4.1	4.1	10.5	7.8	4.7	3.7	4.0	3.1	3.8	5.2	11.8
Food products	0.1	1.3	0.1	0.1	0.2	0.2	0.2	0.1	0.5	0.4	0.3	0.2
Tobacco products	...	...	...	...	...	...	...	...	...	...	...	...
Textile mill products	0.1	...	0.2	0.3	...	0.3	...	...	...	...	...	0.1
Apparel	...	0.1	...	...	0.1	0.1	...	...	...	0.1	...	...
Lumber and wood products	...	...	...	0.3	...	...	...	...	...	...	0.3	0.5
Furniture and fixtures	0.1	...	0.1	0.1	...	...	...	...	...	...	...	...
Paper products	...	0.1	...	0.5	0.1	...	0.1	0.1	0.1	0.1	0.3	0.2
Printing and publishing	...	...	...	...	...	0.1	...	0.2	...	...	...	0.9
Chemical products	0.1	0.2	0.4	0.5	0.3	0.4	0.2	1.5	0.6	1.3	1.2	1.6
Refined petroleum products	...	...	0.1	0.1	0.1	...	...	...	...	...	...	5.9
Rubber and plastic products	0.1	0.1	...	0.2	0.2	0.3	0.1	0.1	0.1	0.2	0.3	0.4
Leather products	...	...	...	...	...	...	...	...	...	...	...	0.1
Stone, clay and glass products	...	...	...	...	0.4	0.1	...	...	...	0.1	...	...
Primary metals	0.1	0.1	0.1	0.2	...	...	0.1	0.1	0.1	0.1	0.4	0.3
Fabricated metal products	1.3	0.3	...	0.7	1.1	0.8	0.2	0.2	0.1	0.1	...	0.1
Industrial machinery and computers	0.5	0.7	2.3	5.4	2.6	1.4	0.5	0.5	0.7	0.7	1.1	0.6
Electric and electronic equipment	0.2	0.6	0.2	0.7	1.5	0.5	1.5	0.8	0.5	0.5	1.0	0.5
Transportation equipment	0.5	0.4	0.3	1.2	0.5	0.4	0.2	0.2	0.2	...	0.1	0.1
Scientific and measuring instruments	0.3	0.3	0.2	0.2	0.2	0.1	0.2	0.2	0.1	0.2	0.1	0.1
Miscellaneous manufactures	...	...	...	0.2	0.2	0.1	0.1	...	...	...	0.1	...
Unidentified manufactures	...	...	...	0.1	0.1	0.1	0.1	...	...	...	0.1	0.2
Agricultural And Livestock Products	0.1	...	...	0.2	...	0.1	0.4	0.1	0.3	1.1	0.7	0.7
Agricultural products	...	...	...	...	...	0.1	0.1	...	0.2	0.1	...	...
Livestock and livestock products	0.1	...	...	0.2	...	...	0.3	...	0.2	1.0	0.7	0.7
Other Commodities	...	...	0.1	1.0	1.1	1.6	...	...	...	...	...	...
Forestry products	...	...	...	...	...	...	...	...	...	...	...	...
Fish and other marine products	...	...	...	0.9	0.9	1.4	...	...	...	...	...	...
Metallic ores and concentrates	...	...	...	...	...	...	...	...	...	...	...	...
Bituminous coal and lignite	...	...	...	...	...	...	...	...	...	...	...	...
Crude petroleum and natural gas	...	...	...	...	...	...	...	...	...	...	...	...
Nonmetallic minerals	...	...	...	...	...	...	...	...	...	...	...	...
Scrap and waste	...	...	...	...	0.1	...	...	...	...	...	...	...
Used merchandise	...	...	...	...	0.1	...	...	...	...	...	...	...
Goods imported and returned unchanged	...	...	...	...	...	...	...	...	...	...	...	...
Special classification provisions	...	...	0.1	...	...	0.1	...	...	...	...	...	...

Industry	European Union						United Kingdom					
	1994	1995	1996	1997	1998	1999	1994	1995	1996	1997	1998	1999
ALL GOODS	16.5	17.4	17.8	39.5	46.4	21.2	8.6	7.6	6.8	6.9	10.2	9.9
Manufactured Goods	14.4	11.8	13.3	18.6	25.4	17.3	8.1	6.4	6.5	6.8	10.1	9.6
Food products	...	0.1	0.1	0.2	0.2	0.1	...	...	0.1	...	0.1	0.1
Tobacco products	...	...	...	...	...	...	...	...	...	...	...	...
Textile mill products	...	...	...	0.1	...	...	...	...	...	0.1	...	...
Apparel	0.1	...	0.1	0.1	0.1	0.2	...	...	...	...	...	0.2
Lumber and wood products	...	0.1	0.5	2.7	2.2	1.1	...	...	0.3	2.3	1.3	0.4
Furniture and fixtures	0.1	...	...	...	...	...	...	...	...	...	...	...
Paper products	...	...	...	0.1	0.2	0.1	...	...	...	...	...	0.1
Printing and publishing	0.1	0.6	0.2	0.1	0.3	0.1	0.1	0.1	...	...	0.1	...
Chemical products	5.5	0.9	1.0	1.0	5.6	0.7	5.3	0.7	0.8	0.7	5.1	0.3
Refined petroleum products	...	...	...	...	...	...	...	...	...	...	...	...
Rubber and plastic products	0.1	0.1	...	0.1	0.1	0.3	...	0.1	...	...	0.1	0.3
Leather products	...	...	...	...	...	...	...	...	...	...	...	...
Stone, clay and glass products	0.1	0.1	0.1	...	...	...	0.1	...	0.1	...	...	...
Primary metals	0.1	0.2	0.1	0.2	0.1	...	...	0.2	...	...	...	...
Fabricated metal products	0.1	0.5	0.1	0.1	0.1	0.4	...	...	...	...	...	0.1
Industrial machinery and computers	3.0	3.4	5.6	9.9	8.2	4.7	1.4	1.7	1.9	1.9	1.1	1.8
Electric and electronic equipment	2.1	4.0	0.9	1.1	1.0	4.6	0.7	3.1	0.6	0.2	0.4	4.2
Transportation equipment	1.2	0.7	3.4	2.2	1.3	1.8	0.2	0.1	2.6	1.4	0.1	1.0
Scientific and measuring instruments	0.8	0.6	0.6	0.7	1.8	2.1	0.1	...	0.1	0.1	0.7	0.3
Miscellaneous manufactures	0.9	0.4	0.4	0.1	4.2	1.0	...	0.4	...	...	1.0	0.9
Unidentified manufactures	0.1	0.1	...	...	0.1	0.1	0.1	0.1	...	...	...	...
Agricultural And Livestock Products	...	...	0.2	...	0.2	...	...	...	...	...	...	...
Agricultural products	...	...	0.2	...	...	...	...	...	...	...	...	...
Livestock and livestock products	...	...	...	...	0.2	...	...	...	...	...	...	...
Other Commodities	2.1	5.6	4.4	20.9	20.8	3.9	0.5	1.2	0.3	0.2	0.2	0.2
Forestry products	...	...	...	...	0.1	...	...	...	...	...	...	...
Fish and other marine products	0.1	...	0.2	3.0	2.9	2.3	...	...	...	...	...	0.1
Metallic ores and concentrates	...	...	...	16.9	16.7	1.1	...	...	...	...	...	...
Bituminous coal and lignite	0.2	2.7	3.0	...	...	...	...	...	...	...	...	...
Crude petroleum and natural gas	...	...	...	...	...	...	...	...	...	...	...	...
Nonmetallic minerals	0.2	0.6	0.3	0.3	0.6	0.2	...	...	...	0.1	...	...
Scrap and waste	...	...	...	...	...	...	...	...	...	...	...	...
Used merchandise	1.6	2.3	0.9	0.6	0.3	0.2	0.5	1.2	0.3	0.1	0.1	0.1
Goods imported and returned unchanged	...	...	...	...	...	...	...	...	...	...	...	...
Special classification provisions	0.1	...	...	0.1	...	...	...	...	...	...	...	...

Table D-55. WYOMING: State Exports of Goods by Destination and Industry, 1994–1999—*Continued*

(Millions of dollars.)

Industry	Germany						France					
	1994	1995	1996	1997	1998	1999	1994	1995	1996	1997	1998	1999
ALL GOODS	4.0	2.7	1.9	1.7	3.4	0.5	1.2	1.5	0.6	1.3	1.9	0.9
Manufactured Goods	3.4	2.3	1.3	1.6	3.3	0.4	0.9	1.3	0.4	1.0	1.6	0.9
Food products	...	...	...	...	...	...	...	...	...	...	...	...
Tobacco products	...	...	...	...	...	...	...	...	...	...	...	...
Textile mill products	...	...	...	...	...	...	...	...	...	...	...	...
Apparel	...	...	...	...	0.1	...	...	...	...	...	...	...
Lumber and wood products	...	...	...	...	...	...	...	0.1	...	...	...	...
Furniture and fixtures	...	...	...	...	...	...	0.1	...	...	...	...	...
Paper products	...	...	...	...	...	...	...	...	...	...	...	...
Printing and publishing	...	...	...	...	0.1	...	...	0.5	...	...	...	...
Chemical products	...	...	0.2	0.2	0.1	...	...	0.1	...	...	0.1	0.1
Refined petroleum products	...	...	...	...	...	...	...	...	...	...	...	...
Rubber and plastic products	...	...	...	...	...	...	...	...	...	...	...	...
Leather products	...	...	...	...	...	...	...	...	...	...	...	...
Stone, clay and glass products	0.1	...	...	...	...	...	...	...	...	...	...	...
Primary metals	...	...	...	...	...	...	...	...	...	...	...	...
Fabricated metal products	0.1	0.5	...	0.1	...	...	...	...	...	...	...	...
Industrial machinery and computers	0.9	0.8	0.3	0.2	0.1	0.2	0.1	0.3	0.3	0.5	0.1	0.1
Electric and electronic equipment	1.0	0.5	0.1	0.1	...	...	0.2	0.1	...	...	0.1	0.1
Transportation equipment	0.3	0.4	0.2	0.7	0.5	0.1	0.4	...	...	0.1	0.5	0.6
Scientific and measuring instruments	0.3	0.1	...	0.2	0.1	...	...	0.2	...	0.2	0.1	...
Miscellaneous manufactures	0.6	...	0.3	...	2.4	...	...	...	...	0.1	0.6	...
Unidentified manufactures	...	0.1	...	...	...	...	...	...	...	...	...	...
Agricultural And Livestock Products	...	...	...	...	...	...	...	...	0.1	...	0.2	...
Agricultural products	...	...	...	...	...	...	...	...	0.1	...	...	...
Livestock and livestock products	...	...	...	...	...	...	...	...	...	...	0.2	...
Other Commodities	0.6	0.4	0.5	0.1	...	...	0.3	0.2	0.1	0.2	0.1	...
Forestry products	...	...	...	...	...	...	...	...	...	...	...	...
Fish and other marine products	...	...	...	...	...	...	...	...	...	...	...	...
Metallic ores and concentrates	...	...	...	...	...	...	...	...	...	...	...	...
Bituminous coal and lignite	...	...	...	...	...	...	...	...	...	...	...	...
Crude petroleum and natural gas	...	...	...	...	...	...	...	...	...	...	...	...
Nonmetallic minerals	...	0.1	0.2	...	...	...	...	...	...	...	...	...
Scrap and waste	...	...	...	...	...	...	...	...	...	...	...	...
Used merchandise	0.6	0.3	0.3	0.1	...	...	0.3	0.2	0.1	0.2	0.1	...
Goods imported and returned unchanged	...	...	...	...	...	...	...	...	...	...	...	...
Special classification provisions	...	...	...	...	...	...	...	...	...	...	...	...

Industry	The Netherlands						Asian 10					
	1994	1995	1996	1997	1998	1999	1994	1995	1996	1997	1998	1999
ALL GOODS	0.5	1.1	0.9	15.0	18.2	3.6	13.3	17.2	24.0	22.8	15.1	18.8
Manufactured Goods	0.4	0.5	0.7	0.5	0.9	2.2	10.5	16.3	20.6	12.4	10.1	13.0
Food products	...	...	...	...	...	...	1.2	5.4	13.0	2.5	0.6	0.7
Tobacco products	...	...	...	...	...	...	...	...	...	...	...	...
Textile mill products	...	...	...	...	...	...	...	...	...	...	0.1	0.2
Apparel	...	...	...	...	...	...	0.8	0.4	0.1	0.1	0.1	0.2
Lumber and wood products	...	...	...	...	...	...	0.1	0.1	0.2	0.2	...	...
Furniture and fixtures	...	...	...	...	...	...	...	...	...	0.1	0.4	0.5
Paper products	...	...	...	0.1	...	...	...	...	0.1	1.9	0.1	...
Printing and publishing	...	...	0.1	...	0.2	0.1	0.1	...	...	...	...	...
Chemical products	...	...	...	...	0.1	...	0.4	0.3	0.2	1.1	0.4	0.4
Refined petroleum products	...	...	...	...	...	...	...	...	...	...	...	...
Rubber and plastic products	...	...	...	...	...	...	0.1	0.1	0.1	0.1	0.1	0.2
Leather products	...	...	...	...	...	...	...	...	...	0.1	0.1	...
Stone, clay and glass products	...	...	...	...	...	...	0.1	0.4	...	0.1	0.2	0.1
Primary metals	...	...	0.1	...	...	...	0.2	...	2.0	0.4	0.1	0.6
Fabricated metal products	...	...	...	...	...	...	0.9	2.1	0.7	0.4	0.8	2.5
Industrial machinery and computers	0.1	0.2	0.1	0.4	0.2	1.3	2.1	2.2	1.5	1.6	3.8	4.0
Electric and electronic equipment	...	0.1	0.1	...	0.2	0.1	3.1	2.6	0.8	1.8	0.8	1.8
Transportation equipment	0.1	0.1	...	...	0.1	...	0.3	0.6	0.5	0.6	0.3	0.6
Scientific and measuring instruments	0.1	...	0.2	...	...	0.7	0.8	1.3	0.6	1.0	1.7	0.6
Miscellaneous manufactures	...	...	...	...	0.1	...	0.3	0.7	0.6	0.2	0.3	0.6
Unidentified manufactures	...	...	...	...	...	...	0.1	0.1	...	0.1	0.1	0.1
Agricultural And Livestock Products	...	...	0.1	...	...	...	...	...	...	0.4	0.3	0.3
Agricultural products	...	...	0.1	...	...	...	...	...	...	0.4	0.3	0.2
Livestock and livestock products	...	...	...	...	...	...	...	...	...	...	...	0.1
Other Commodities	...	0.6	0.1	14.5	17.3	1.4	2.8	0.9	3.4	10.0	4.7	5.6
Forestry products	...	...	...	...	0.1	...	0.1	0.1	...	...	...	...
Fish and other marine products	...	...	...	0.1	0.1	0.1	...	0.3	0.2	5.2	4.2	5.2
Metallic ores and concentrates	...	...	...	14.1	16.7	1.1	...	...	...	0.1	...	...
Bituminous coal and lignite	...	...	...	...	...	...	2.2	...	3.0	4.3	...	...
Crude petroleum and natural gas	...	...	...	...	...	...	...	...	...	...	...	...
Nonmetallic minerals	...	0.5	0.1	0.2	0.4	0.2	...	...	...	...	...	...
Scrap and waste	...	...	...	...	...	...	0.1	...	0.1	0.3	0.5	0.3
Used merchandise	...	0.1	0.1	0.1	...	...	0.3	0.5	0.1	0.1	0.1	0.1
Goods imported and returned unchanged	...	...	...	...	...	...	0.1	...	...	...	...	...
Special classification provisions	...	...	...	...	...	...	...	...	...	...	...	...

Table D-55. WYOMING: State Exports of Goods by Destination and Industry, 1994–1999—*Continued*

(Millions of dollars.)

Industry	Japan						South Korea					
	1994	1995	1996	1997	1998	1999	1994	1995	1996	1997	1998	1999
ALL GOODS	6.9	9.6	18.4	11.1	3.6	4.7	1.1	0.9	1.2	3.3	3.8	5.3
Manufactured Goods	4.6	9.4	15.3	5.4	2.9	4.0	1.1	0.9	1.2	1.5	1.0	0.8
Food products	0.9	5.1	12.7	2.4	0.3	0.2	...	...	0.2	0.1	0.1	0.3
Tobacco products	...	...	...	...	...	...	...	...	...	...	...	...
Textile mill products	...	...	...	...	0.1	...	...	...	...	...	...	...
Apparel	0.8	0.4	0.1	0.1	0.1	0.2	...	...	...	...	...	...
Lumber and wood products	0.1	0.1	0.2	0.2	...	...	...	...	0.1	...	...	...
Furniture and fixtures	...	...	...	...	0.3	0.5	...	...	...	...	...	...
Paper products	...	...	...	0.3	0.1	...	...	...	...	...	...	...
Printing and publishing	...	...	...	...	...	...	...	...	...	...	...	...
Chemical products	...	0.3	0.1	0.3	0.1	0.1	0.1	...	0.1	0.3	0.1	0.1
Refined petroleum products	...	...	...	...	...	...	...	...	...	...	...	...
Rubber and plastic products	...	...	0.1	...	...	0.1	...	...	...	...	...	...
Leather products	...	...	...	...	...	...	...	...	...	...	...	...
Stone, clay and glass products	0.1	0.2	...	0.1	...	...	...	...	...	...	...	...
Primary metals	...	...	0.1	0.3	0.3	0.4	...	...	0.2	...	...	...
Fabricated metal products	0.9	0.9	0.4	0.1	0.7	0.8	...	...	...	0.3	...	0.1
Industrial machinery and computers	0.1	0.1	0.2	0.2	0.4	0.2	0.6	0.3	0.2	0.1	0.1	0.3
Electric and electronic equipment	0.7	0.9	0.3	0.4	...	0.4	0.2	0.2	0.1	0.3	0.4	...
Transportation equipment	0.1	0.1	0.3	0.1	0.1	0.3	...	...	...	0.1	0.1	0.1
Scientific and measuring instruments	0.5	0.7	0.3	0.6	0.3	0.4	0.2	...	0.2	0.2	0.2	...
Miscellaneous manufactures	0.2	0.3	0.5	0.2	0.3	0.4	...	...	...	...	...	...
Unidentified manufactures	0.1	...	...	...	...	...	...	...	...	...	...	...
Agricultural And Livestock Products	...	...	...	...	...	0.2	...	...	...	0.3	...	...
Agricultural products	...	...	...	...	...	0.2	...	...	...	0.3	...	...
Livestock and livestock products	...	...	...	...	...	...	...	...	...	...	...	...
Other Commodities	2.4	0.2	3.1	5.7	0.7	0.5	...	...	...	1.5	2.8	4.5
Forestry products	0.1	0.1	...	...	...	...	...	...	...	...	...	...
Fish and other marine products	...	...	0.1	1.0	0.5	0.3	...	...	...	1.5	2.8	4.5
Metallic ores and concentrates	...	...	...	0.1	...	...	...	...	...	...	...	...
Bituminous coal and lignite	2.2	...	3.0	4.3	...	...	...	...	...	...	...	...
Crude petroleum and natural gas	...	...	...	...	...	...	...	...	...	...	...	...
Nonmetallic minerals	...	...	...	...	...	...	...	...	...	...	...	...
Scrap and waste	...	...	0.1	0.2	0.2	0.2	...	...	...	...	...	...
Used merchandise	...	...	...	...	...	...	...	...	...	...	...	...
Goods imported and returned unchanged	...	...	...	...	...	...	...	...	...	...	...	...
Special classification provisions	...	...	...	...	...	...	...	...	...	...	...	...

Industry	Taiwan						Singapore					
	1994	1995	1996	1997	1998	1999	1994	1995	1996	1997	1998	1999
ALL GOODS	2.0	1.8	0.7	1.1	1.9	2.1	1.0	1.1	0.6	1.3	1.8	1.7
Manufactured Goods	1.9	1.8	0.6	1.1	1.9	2.0	0.9	1.0	0.6	1.3	1.8	1.7
Food products	...	0.2	0.1	...	0.1	0.1	0.1	...	...	...	...	...
Tobacco products	...	...	...	...	...	...	...	...	...	...	...	...
Textile mill products	...	...	...	...	...	0.2	...	...	...	...	...	...
Apparel	...	...	...	...	...	...	...	...	...	...	...	...
Lumber and wood products	...	...	...	...	...	...	...	...	...	...	...	...
Furniture and fixtures	...	...	...	0.1	0.1	...	...	...	...	...	...	...
Paper products	...	...	...	...	...	...	...	...	...	...	...	...
Printing and publishing	...	...	...	...	...	...	...	...	...	...	...	...
Chemical products	...	...	...	0.2	0.1	0.1	0.1	...	...	...	0.1	0.1
Refined petroleum products	...	...	...	...	...	...	...	...	...	...	...	...
Rubber and plastic products	...	...	...	0.1	0.1	...	...	...	...	...	...	...
Leather products	...	...	...	...	...	...	...	...	...	...	...	...
Stone, clay and glass products	...	...	...	...	0.1	...	...	...	...	...	...	...
Primary metals	0.1	...	...	...	...	...	...	...	...	0.1	...	0.1
Fabricated metal products	...	1.0	0.2	...	...	...	...	0.1	...	...	0.1	0.1
Industrial machinery and computers	0.9	0.1	0.1	0.1	0.7	0.8	0.2	0.3	0.4	0.9	1.4	0.9
Electric and electronic equipment	0.7	0.2	0.1	0.4	0.1	0.6	0.3	0.2	...	0.1	0.1	0.3
Transportation equipment	...	0.2	0.1	0.2	...	...	0.1	...	0.1	...	0.1	...
Scientific and measuring instruments	...	0.1	0.1	...	0.6	...	0.1	0.1	...	0.1	...	...
Miscellaneous manufactures	...	...	...	...	...	0.1	...	0.2	...	...	...	0.1
Unidentified manufactures	...	...	...	...	...	...	...	...	...	...	...	...
Agricultural And Livestock Products	...	...	...	...	...	...	...	...	...	...	...	...
Agricultural products	...	...	...	...	...	...	...	...	...	...	...	...
Livestock and livestock products	...	...	...	...	...	...	...	...	...	...	...	...
Other Commodities	0.1	...	...	0.1	...	0.1	...	0.1	...	...	...	...
Forestry products	...	...	...	...	...	...	...	...	...	...	...	...
Fish and other marine products	...	...	...	...	...	...	...	...	...	...	...	...
Metallic ores and concentrates	...	...	...	...	...	...	...	...	...	...	...	...
Bituminous coal and lignite	...	...	...	...	...	...	...	...	...	...	...	...
Crude petroleum and natural gas	...	...	...	...	...	...	...	...	...	...	...	...
Nonmetallic minerals	...	...	...	...	...	...	...	...	...	...	...	...
Scrap and waste	...	...	...	0.1	...	0.1	...	...	...	...	...	...
Used merchandise	...	...	...	...	...	...	...	0.1	...	...	...	...
Goods imported and returned unchanged	...	...	...	...	...	...	...	...	...	...	...	...
Special classification provisions	...	...	...	...	...	...	...	...	...	...	...	...

PART E. METROPOLITAN AREA EXPORTS OF GOODS

Leading Exporting Metropolitan Areas, 1999
(Billions of dollars)

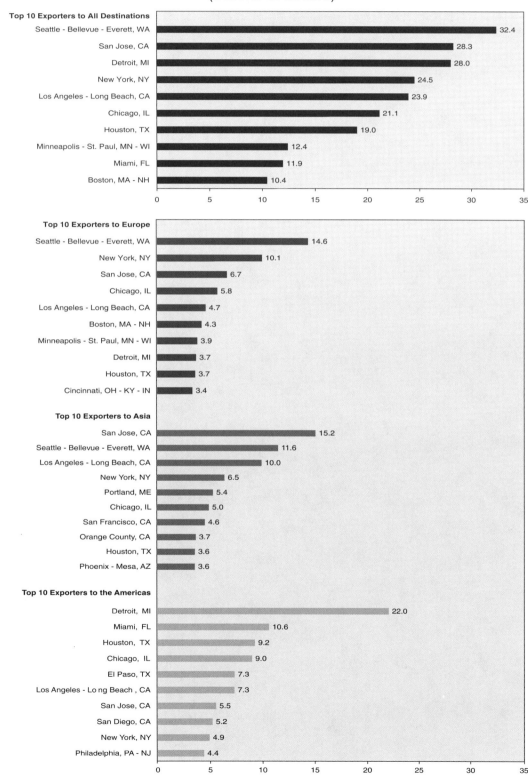

Top 10 Exporters to All Destinations

Seattle - Bellevue - Everett, WA	32.4
San Jose, CA	28.3
Detroit, MI	28.0
New York, NY	24.5
Los Angeles - Long Beach, CA	23.9
Chicago, IL	21.1
Houston, TX	19.0
Minneapolis - St. Paul, MN - WI	12.4
Miami, FL	11.9
Boston, MA - NH	10.4

Top 10 Exporters to Europe

Seattle - Bellevue - Everett, WA	14.6
New York, NY	10.1
San Jose, CA	6.7
Chicago, IL	5.8
Los Angeles - Long Beach, CA	4.7
Boston, MA - NH	4.3
Minneapolis - St. Paul, MN - WI	3.9
Detroit, MI	3.7
Houston, TX	3.7
Cincinnati, OH - KY - IN	3.4

Top 10 Exporters to Asia

San Jose, CA	15.2
Seattle - Bellevue - Everett, WA	11.6
Los Angeles - Long Beach, CA	10.0
New York, NY	6.5
Portland, ME	5.4
Chicago, IL	5.0
San Francisco, CA	4.6
Orange County, CA	3.7
Houston, TX	3.6
Phoenix - Mesa, AZ	3.6

Top 10 Exporters to the Americas

Detroit, MI	22.0
Miami, FL	10.6
Houston, TX	9.2
Chicago, IL	9.0
El Paso, TX	7.3
Los Angeles - Long Beach, CA	7.3
San Jose, CA	5.5
San Diego, CA	5.2
New York, NY	4.9
Philadelphia, PA - NJ	4.4

PART E. METROPOLITAN AREA EXPORTS OF GOODS

NOTES AND DEFINITIONS

Metropolitan Area Exporter Location (EL) Data

Source: Bureau of the Census; compiled by Office of Trade and Economic Analysis (OTEA), International Trade Administration.

DATA NOTES

All of the metropolitan area data shown have been compiled from the Census Bureau's Exporter Location series by the Office of Trade and Economic Analysis, International Trade Administration, U.S. Department of Commerce. All of the metropolitan area export data are based on f.a.s. (free alongside ship) value. All metropolitan area data exclude timing adjustments and Canada adjustment. Timing adjustment is adjustment to a previous period's data because the data were not reported in a timely manner; the Canada adjustment is for inland freight that is sometimes included in Canadian exports. All figures are based on initial, unrevised data.

The EL series show export sales by exporters of record located in the metropolitan area listed. Typically, the EL data reflect the point of sale, that is, the marketing origin of the exports. This is not necessarily the location where the goods are produced. *Thus, the EL series provide an approximation, rather than a precise record, of the production origin of U.S. exports.* The data are best viewed as a measure of international sales activity. They should be interpreted with caution as a measure of export-related production or jobs.

About three-fourths of manufacturing exports are generated by manufacturers who do their own exporting. For these shipments the production origin and the sales origin are generally, but not always, the same. For the remaining one-fourth of manufactured exports and most non-manufactured exports, the seller (the exporter of record) is not the producer. The production may or may not have occurred in the same metropolitan area. In some cases, the exporter of record may be a headquarters or central office that may or may not engage in international marketing activity. Overall, Census Bureau research suggests that, for manufacturing establishments, the zip code location of the exporter of record is the same as the physical location of production for about 88 percent of the value of exports.

The data measure final sales of goods leaving the country. Even where the final product was produced in the same location as the sale, it may contain raw materials and intermediate products produced elsewhere.

There are significant differences between the EL series and the alternative Origin of Movement (OM) state export series, also prepared by the Bureau of the Census. Data from these two series cannot be compared to each other. The OM series measures the transportation origin of exports, which inflates the exports of states with major shipping ports. Also, the OM series is only available for states, while the EL series can show both states and metropolitan areas.

The export figures shown in these tables for states and metropolitan areas can be used together. That is, it is possible to use the data for a metropolitan area to estimate its share of the state's export sales.

When calculating these data, the Census Bureau was unable to allocate about 7.5 percent of exports to any local jurisdiction, because of faulty reporting of zip codes by exporters. Thus, it can be inferred that export totals for at least some of the metropolitan areas are understated. Further, improvements in reporting may cause one-time statistical 'gains' in exports, simply because the data become available. As an example, Detroit, MI, showed a 10.7 billion dollar, or 65 percent, gain in 1994. Upon closer inspection, it was found that as much as 6 billion of this may have been due to better reporting on export declarations.

Commodity categories shown in metropolitan tables are based on the Standard Industrial Classification (SIC) product codes. (See the general notes for Section C for an explanation of SIC and other classifications.) Manufactured goods that cannot be classified by type, for example those with incomplete data, are labeled "unidentified manufactures".

Metropolitan areas. In general, a metropolitan statistical area (MSA) is a geographic area consisting of a large population nucleus together with adjacent communities that have a high degree of economic and social integration with that nucleus. MSAs consist of groups of adjacent counties. Metropolitan complexes with populations of one million or more may be divided into two or more primary metropolitan statistical areas (PMSAs). When PMSAs are defined, the larger metropolitan area of which they are components is designated a consolidated metropolitan statistical area (CMSA), for example, Dallas-Forth Worth. The metropolitan area data tables cover both MSAs and PMSAs, (for example, Dallas and Fort Worth are shown separately), but CMSAs are not shown.

The metropolitan area export data were tabulated based on the five-digit zip codes entered by businesses on the export declarations. Zip codes that cross from a metropolitan area into an adjacent rural area were assigned to the metro area. Where two adjacent metropolitan areas share the same zip code, the zip code was assigned to a catch-all "crossover" category. The crossover category accounted for 2.9 percent of total goods exports in 1997.

DATA AVAILABILITY

All data are available on the OTEA web site.

Table E-1. Metropolitan Area Exports of Goods, 1993–1999

DATA NOTES

Out of a total of 335 metropolitan areas, this table shows the 256 for which export data are available. Data are not available for the other metropolitan areas for one of two reasons. One is that there is no export business reported from that area. The other is that the federal government restricts disclosure of confidential business data of individual companies. If an individual company could be identified by the data, then the data are suppressed. This prevents publication of data for some relatively large metropolitan areas.

Table E-2. Metropolitan Area Exports of Goods by Industry, 1994–1999

DATA NOTES

This table includes 43 of the 50 largest exporters. Some metropolitan area tables may show two or more classifications combined. This is done to prevent disclosure of data on individual firms, while still providing a sense of the exports from these classifications. Other metropolitan areas could not be shown due to the disclosure restrictions.

Table E-3. Metropolitan Area Exports of Goods by Destination, 1994–1999

DATA NOTES

This table shows 181 metropolitan areas. As in the previous tables, some metropolitan areas could not be shown due to the disclosure restrictions.

North America includes Canada and Mexico.

Caribbean countries include the Bahamas, Barbados, Belize, Cayman Islands, Dominican Republic, Guyana, Haiti, Jamaica, Leeward and Windward Islands (i.e., Antigua, British Virgin Islands, Dominica, Grenada, Montserrat, St. Christopher-Nevis and Anguilla, St. Lucia, and St. Vincent), Netherlands Antilles and Aruba, Suriname, Trinidad and Tobago, and Turks and Caicos Islands.

Central American countries consist of Costa Rica, El Salvador, Guatemala, Honduras, Nicaragua, and Panama.

South America includes Argentina, Bolivia, Brazil, Chile, Colombia, Ecuador, Paraguay, Peru, Uruguay, and Venezuela.

Europe consists of Western Europe and Eastern Europe.

Western Europe includes the European Union (EU) and non-EU Western Europe.

The European Union includes Austria, Belgium/Luxembourg, Denmark, Finland, France, Germany (both East and West), Greece, Ireland, Italy, Netherlands, Portugal (including Azores and the Madeira Islands), Spain (including Spanish Africa and the Canary Islands), Sweden, and the United Kingdom.

Western Europe, except European Union include Cyprus, Gibraltar, Iceland, Malta, Norway, Switzerland, Turkey, Yugoslavia (former), and, after 1987, other non-EU Western Europe (Andorra, Faroe Islands, Liechtenstein, Monaco, San Marino, Svalbard and Jan Mayen Island, and Vatican City).

Eastern Europe and Former Soviet Republics includes Albania, Bulgaria, Czech Republic and Slovakia (former Czechoslovakia), Hungary, Poland, Romania and the Former Soviet Republics.

Former Soviet Republics consist of Armenia, Azerbaijan, Belarus, Estonia, Georgia, Kazakhstan, Kyrgyzstan, Latvia, Lithuania, Russia, Tajikistan, Turkmenistan, Ukraine and Uzbekistan.

Asia, including Middle East includes Afghanistan, Bangladesh, Bhutan, Brunei, Burma, Cambodia, China, Hong Kong, India, Indonesia, Japan, Laos, Macao, Malaysia, Maldive Islands, Mongolia, Nepal, North Korea, Pakistan, Philippines, Singapore, South Korea, Sri Lanka, Taiwan, Thailand, Vietnam and the Middle East

The Middle East includes Bahrain, Iran, Iraq, Israel (including the Gaza Strip and the West Bank), Jordan, Kuwait, Lebanon, the Neutral Zone, Oman, Qatar, Saudi Arabia, Syria, United Arab Emirates and the Yemen Arab Republic.

Africa consists of all the countries on the continent.

Table E-1. Metropolitan Area Exports of Goods, 1993–1999

(Millions of dollars.)

Metropolitan area	1993	1994	1995	1996	1997	1998	1999
Akron, OH	1 434.9	1 606.3	1 931.7	2 260.3	2 353.3	2 266.1	2 207.6
Albany - Schenectady - Troy, NY	676.2	831.4	1 061.2	1 101.0	1 666.2	1 613.0	1 302.5
Albany, GA	26.4	31.8	31.5	52.5	57.3	36.9	23.6
Albuquerque, NM	256.7	335.5	270.1	740.3	1 564.6	1 694.4	2 714.9
Alexandria, LA	15.8	16.9	18.7	21.6	17.9	23.5	14.4
Allentown - Bethlehem - Easton, PA	1 273.9	1 371.1	1 492.8	1 477.2	1 808.9	1 535.0	1 203.4
Altoona, PA	42.6	46.4	74.2	80.2	85.9	80.6	81.9
Anchorage, AK	128.8	198.2	150.4	109.0	213.1	146.0	197.7
Ann Arbor, MI	2 218.1	2 075.8	1 157.9	1 311.1	1 520.9	1 594.9	1 745.6
Appleton - Oshkosh - Neenah, WI	529.5	507.7	593.7	608.5	647.9	658.0	768.0
Asheville, NC	232.3	228.6	185.2	236.7	294.2	233.0	268.6
Atlanta, GA	3 870.6	4 739.1	5 811.4	5 891.5	6 604.6	7 904.6	7 574.5
Augusta - Aiken, GA - SC	227.4	326.3	405.2	443.9	433.8	519.6	569.0
Austin - San Marcos, TX	1 721.5	2 128.8	2 929.2	2 743.1	3 354.8	3 802.4	4 931.4
Bakersfield, CA	480.7	780.4	730.5	721.3	835.6	695.3	419.4
Baltimore, MD	1 783.4	1 869.0	2 209.2	2 110.4	2 171.3	2 331.0	2 328.1
Baton Rouge, LA	564.6	458.0	569.6	552.9	577.1	509.9	525.1
Beaumont - Port Arthur, TX	87.7	97.0	118.9	115.4	133.4	127.2	108.5
Bellingham, WA	206.8	210.7	253.5	275.4	316.7	256.4	328.7
Benton Harbor, MI	338.7	368.8	369.3	317.2	260.6	275.9	286.8
Bergen - Passaic, NJ	3 924.9	4 387.0	4 784.0	4 499.9	4 789.8	4 228.6	4 181.5
Biloxi - Gulfport - Pascagoula, MS	108.1	281.6	281.0	119.9	76.9	117.9	195.9
Binghamton, NY	316.2	474.9	558.1	443.3	513.3	440.2	524.5
Birmingham, AL	533.9	453.8	550.5	625.8	941.4	533.8	448.5
Bloomington, IN	113.6	115.7	127.6	198.8	166.8	75.3	85.2
Boise City, ID	1 022.7	1 289.8	1 635.0	1 338.5	1 407.3	1 114.4	1 734.7
Boston, MA - NH	6 472.5	7 095.3	7 902.7	8 715.8	9 570.6	9 556.3	10 427.0
Bremerton, WA	45.0	54.6	109.8	79.9	102.4	76.2	66.8
Bridgeport, CT	1 125.9	918.8	952.9	788.6	981.4	895.0	795.3
Brockton, MA	107.0	113.1	144.0	159.7	268.7	342.3	492.9
Brownsville - Harlingen - San Benito, TX	1 904.4	2 113.4	2 245.9	2 612.6	2 697.1	2 421.3	2 571.4
Buffalo - Niagara Falls, NY	1 135.2	1 569.7	2 295.8	2 262.2	2 667.3	2 222.7	2 225.4
Canton - Massillon, OH	250.2	315.9	377.2	406.0	421.6	359.5	339.3
Cedar Rapids, IA	342.4	363.8	402.2	391.1	429.8	537.6	535.2
Champaign - Urbana, IL	87.8	89.3	103.4	214.4	423.6	394.0	336.7
Charleston - North Charleston, SC	597.3	388.5	501.6	595.1	827.6	837.9	985.7
Charleston, WV	178.9	277.6	394.4	412.2	393.4	396.7	287.2
Charlotte - Gastonia - Rock Hill, NC--SC	1 563.7	1 782.8	2 088.0	2 291.3	2 588.8	2 628.9	2 751.0
Charlottesville, VA	113.8	123.0	157.4	140.2	195.4	191.4	196.5
Chattanooga, TN - GA	218.3	237.3	301.0	273.5	331.4	337.1	372.0
Chicago, IL	14 446.6	17 333.6	21 083.4	22 030.1	23 209.9	22 929.4	21 144.1
Chico - Paradise, CA	71.0	77.2	70.1	78.1	58.1	59.7	56.9
Cincinnati, OH - K - IN	3 898.2	4 056.5	4 256.7	4 784.1	5 674.1	6 682.5	6 783.1
Cleveland - Lorain - Elyria, OH	3 582.8	4 093.3	4 707.0	5 075.2	5 511.0	5 347.0	5 894.2
Colorado Springs, CO	664.3	900.7	954.7	857.0	1 006.0	1 103.2	1 174.2
Columbia, MO	42.9	50.2	51.1	57.9	74.9	131.5	197.0
Columbia, SC	212.9	300.4	343.3	310.8	328.5	346.6	360.7
Columbus, GA - AL	183.8	172.8	245.4	253.2	282.3	276.5	233.4
Columbus, OH	1 167.0	1 295.5	1 358.2	1 497.2	1 660.7	1 753.2	1 966.6
Corpus Christi, TX	186.8	153.6	162.4	241.8	387.2	308.7	309.4
Cumberland, MD - WV	54.9	64.3	53.8	45.9	48.3	42.6	38.2
Dallas, TX	4 817.6	5 679.7	6 870.4	7 096.9	8 645.9	8 449.6	8 188.4
Danbury, CT	316.7	393.0	421.6	531.9	482.9	425.9	530.6
Danville, VA	173.0	202.7	155.7	89.1	104.4	74.9	141.7
Davenport - Moline - Rock Island, IA - IL	1 102.6	1 098.9	1 291.0	1 576.1	1 933.9	1 745.8	1 381.2
Dayton - Springfield, OH	2 479.9	2 671.3	2 404.8	2 201.5	2 271.5	2 253.0	2 198.7
Daytona Beach, FL	140.5	110.3	85.9	111.7	137.5	142.8	119.7
Decatur, AL	42.3	54.5	65.6	91.6	109.5	124.5	84.7
Denver, CO	931.0	1 089.8	1 385.3	1 502.9	1 738.1	1 806.3	1 558.5
Des Moines, IA	337.2	348.9	378.5	426.0	450.5	476.1	362.4
Detroit, MI	16 780.9	27 469.7	27 314.7	27 531.2	25 967.4	27 004.7	28 008.3
Dubuque, IA	93.1	177.6	180.7	183.5	181.2	162.6	101.0
Eau Claire, WI	289.7	465.7	399.9	320.6	507.3	583.4	456.6
El Paso, TX	2 967.0	3 561.3	4 120.8	5 212.7	5 833.9	6 544.6	7 793.2
Elkhart - Goshen, IN	419.9	460.4	501.5	367.5	414.7	411.4	400.9

Table E-1. Metropolitan Area Exports of Goods, 1993–1999—*Continued*

(Millions of dollars.)

Metropolitan area	1993	1994	1995	1996	1997	1998	1999
Elmira, NY	70.2	116.8	139.5	196.9	241.8	205.5	281.4
Erie, PA	311.6	285.4	490.8	321.9	598.2	621.2	536.3
Eugene - Springfield, OR	157.9	173.1	190.3	168.9	190.5	373.9	693.4
Evansville - Henderson, IN--KY	448.5	487.4	525.1	545.1	588.0	595.4	323.3
Fargo - Moorhead, ND - MN	111.8	137.3	155.0	181.9	208.5	158.1	136.7
Fayetteville - Springdale - Rogers, AR	250.4	433.8	669.3	801.2	732.8	597.7	477.8
Fayetteville, NC	54.3	57.9	66.6	65.4	105.3	96.4	70.0
Flint, MI	958.9	1 032.1	1 451.7	1 318.8	1 475.3	1 417.8	1 165.2
Florence, AL	29.8	25.7	29.5	25.2	35.9	37.0	80.4
Florence, SC	66.3	117.2	249.0	121.6	75.8	71.4	133.4
Fort Collins - Loveland, CO	284.3	354.5	373.9	468.1	433.3	340.7	699.0
Fort Lauderdale, FL	1 321.4	1 506.7	1 774.7	1 864.5	2 143.0	2 086.6	2 393.2
Fort Pierce - Port St. Lucie, FL	73.5	92.3	114.2	107.6	118.5	108.7	99.0
Fort Wayne, IN	640.6	770.9	1 029.4	991.4	1 078.2	1 192.8	1 236.9
Fort Worth - Arlington, TX	1 600.2	2 052.0	1 915.0	2 372.7	3 045.9	3 455.9	3 971.0
Fresno, CA	673.1	763.4	714.4	691.8	739.8	822.7	712.4
Gainesville, FL	62.6	65.7	91.6	88.3	79.6	70.2	62.3
Gary, IN	225.3	267.5	310.6	303.2	336.9	356.0	362.5
Grand Rapids - Muskegon - Holland, MI	1 705.0	1 993.5	2 304.1	2 656.5	2 933.1	3 063.5	3 255.5
Greeley, CO	276.0	501.8	582.9	558.8	693.9	631.8	755.6
Green Bay, WI	134.1	187.3	212.7	189.0	281.9	224.6	220.1
Greensboro - Winston - Salem - High Point, NC	2 453.1	2 773.3	3 356.3	3 495.6	4 050.8	4 037.2	4 313.1
Greenville - Spartanburg - Anderson, SC	1 462.1	1 745.0	2 305.3	2 720.4	3 076.9	3 124.2	3 357.0
Hamilton - Middletown, OH	49.3	66.3	78.3	90.1	98.2	83.2	107.3
Harrisburg - Lebanon - Carlisle, PA	339.2	535.0	601.0	775.5	964.4	952.9	938.7
Hartford, CT	1 926.1	1 967.1	2 167.6	2 416.0	3 219.8	3 758.1	3 875.5
Hickory - Morganton, NC	335.2	397.9	476.1	464.3	501.2	529.9	572.1
Honolulu, HI	187.8	215.5	228.2	265.7	269.5	172.2	204.2
Houma, LA	58.3	53.8	60.0	58.0	86.4	128.6	83.4
Houston, TX	12 284.6	13 388.2	16 247.9	16 541.5	18 595.9	19 119.0	18 967.6
Huntington - Ashland, WV - KY - OH	136.6	162.4	237.2	193.9	218.7	138.9	84.4
Huntsville, AL	573.6	672.1	829.0	899.1	1 071.8	1 055.3	1 095.7
Indianapolis, IN	2 626.6	3 003.8	3 555.9	4 012.8	4 301.8	4 771.3	5 187.1
Jackson, MI	95.5	96.3	98.5	128.1	135.0	159.1	159.7
Jackson, MS	141.2	154.3	203.0	231.4	318.1	219.6	159.7
Jackson, TN	108.0	132.5	175.3	155.2	167.8	241.8	245.5
Jacksonville, FL	404.9	500.4	604.1	677.0	721.3	777.2	796.9
Jamestown, NY	156.9	209.4	256.6	241.2	283.5	285.9	293.7
Janesville - Beloit, WI	76.6	76.3	80.2	107.1	128.5	125.2	103.8
Jersey City, NJ	986.2	1 351.2	1 159.9	1 140.8	1 319.4	1 402.8	1 247.1
Johnson City - Kingsport - Bristol, TN - VA	1 356.7	1 580.8	1 677.5	1 566.5	1 698.6	1 587.4	1 596.3
Joplin, MO	52.1	44.6	50.3	71.4	73.5	68.2	90.3
Kalamazoo - Battle Creek, MI	650.3	869.0	897.3	836.1	919.5	929.7	1 051.8
Kankakee, IL	79.1	86.0	137.8	113.7	118.7	108.3	92.2
Kansas City, MO - KS	2 225.9	2 578.6	3 350.2	3 985.1	3 817.6	3 631.7	3 306.2
Kenosha, WI	126.9	117.7	133.9	154.3	232.1	564.8	683.9
Knoxville, TN	580.4	689.2	633.2	764.1	884.2	858.3	881.4
Kokomo, IN	1 727.5	1 858.4	1 648.9	2 056.4	2 213.1	2 180.7	2 312.2
La Crosse, WI - MN	90.6	93.1	276.2	273.2	297.8	230.0	292.1
Lafayette, IN	75.2	74.9	116.2	133.2	172.7	289.1	366.2
Lafayette, LA	93.6	148.7	192.7	164.8	202.2	190.4	156.0
Lake Charles, LA	56.1	55.9	64.6	48.2	77.9	74.3	110.6
Lakeland - Winter Haven, FL	187.0	199.2	237.7	241.5	243.6	233.3	249.6
Lancaster, PA	406.1	469.3	581.5	626.2	620.3	591.0	539.2
Lansing - East Lansing, MI	185.7	208.6	224.0	202.2	217.5	186.0	243.8
Laredo, TX	4 061.8	4 157.4	2 897.8	3 440.7	3 959.1	3 633.6	2 681.7
Lawrence, KS	5.2	6.2	4.1	5.7	6.5	10.0	56.8
Lawrence, MA - NH	822.6	806.4	841.7	1 033.6	1 810.2	1 544.9	1 749.5
Lexington, KY	624.2	1 078.6	1 235.0	1 499.9	1 886.8	1 838.1	1 837.6
Lima, OH	294.1	166.2	226.0	207.3	242.0	264.1	262.4
Lincoln, NE	188.5	207.2	208.8	225.3	264.6	261.7	275.6
Little Rock - North Little Rock, AR	200.1	219.0	193.6	210.4	349.4	262.3	311.9
Longview - Marshall, TX	85.0	97.3	121.2	144.2	183.6	226.5	148.3
Los Angeles - Long Beach, CA	20 013.6	22 224.8	24 731.0	24 437.9	25 816.4	25 554.7	23 904.7
Louisville, KY - IN	1 673.8	1 798.8	2 199.8	2 327.1	2 449.1	2 290.4	2 392.7

Table E-1. Metropolitan Area Exports of Goods, 1993–1999—*Continued*

(Millions of dollars.)

Metropolitan area	1993	1994	1995	1996	1997	1998	1999
Lowell, MA - NH	867.5	890.1	1 079.9	1 119.9	1 396.5	1 449.8	1 237.6
Lubbock, TX	98.6	165.1	258.7	189.0	262.2	225.1	132.3
Lynchburg, VA	143.2	152.5	192.1	258.8	439.2	442.8	451.6
Macon, GA	160.5	173.3	197.6	220.1	241.3	253.3	302.1
Madison, WI	357.7	417.1	497.5	522.4	603.0	587.8	657.9
Manchester, NH	107.0	115.3	146.3	198.3	237.8	219.7	237.3
Mansfield, OH	367.6	349.9	394.9	413.0	444.0	430.7	462.8
McAllen - Edinburg - Mission, TX	1 510.2	1 826.4	1 617.1	1 579.7	1 872.9	1 791.8	1 991.5
Melbourne - Titusville - Palm Bay, FL	315.2	315.9	310.1	635.0	408.8	538.5	635.8
Memphis, TN - AR - MS	2 055.1	2 729.5	4 163.8	3 786.1	3 636.9	3 615.5	3 135.2
Miami, FL	8 264.3	9 266.7	10 200.8	10 681.2	12 692.3	12 943.4	11 942.1
Middlesex - Somerset - Hunterdon, NJ	2 840.6	3 035.9	3 448.1	3 628.1	4 385.4	4 879.7	4 857.8
Milwaukee - Waukesha, WI	2 337.3	2 913.5	3 506.9	3 717.2	3 837.6	3 570.3	3 720.2
Minneapolis - St. Paul, MN - WI	9 003.8	8 863.5	11 071.8	12 384.0	12 006.7	11 652.4	12 401.3
Mobile, AL	356.7	395.3	415.8	459.9	498.7	426.1	570.8
Modesto, CA	201.1	236.7	279.2	359.6	387.5	378.4	373.6
Monmouth - Ocean, NJ	373.4	410.2	471.8	478.2	504.8	508.8	493.4
Monroe, LA	77.1	107.1	167.8	134.0	101.9	69.3	63.2
Montgomery, AL	157.8	231.0	244.1	192.9	185.5	135.3	141.1
Muncie, IN	64.3	107.4	158.3	137.6	157.6	105.3	121.4
Naples, FL	55.6	56.0	75.0	76.0	35.0	20.5	16.8
Nashua, NH	290.2	235.4	282.2	291.3	339.8	364.5	391.9
Nashville, TN	1 104.1	1 310.5	1 412.3	1 445.5	1 767.1	1 868.7	1 836.6
Nassau - Suffolk, NY	2 803.2	2 866.3	3 558.6	3 680.2	4 208.5	4 438.6	4 686.5
New Bedford, MA	141.6	154.5	186.8	165.8	153.4	161.9	180.8
New Haven - Meriden, CT	1 035.6	1 075.5	1 106.3	1 012.4	1 179.8	1 200.4	1 112.4
New London - Norwich, CT - RI	136.5	141.5	178.2	157.5	192.1	191.4	171.8
New Orleans, LA	2 034.2	2 326.2	3 037.8	3 316.8	2 770.8	2 776.2	2 409.0
New York, NY	28 192.8	23 543.7	27 131.1	27 970.5	29 082.6	26 578.4	24 484.7
Newark, NJ	4 287.4	5 205.5	5 640.0	5 044.2	5 201.8	4 866.1	5 397.5
Newburgh, NY - PA	382.3	152.8	148.9	153.3	222.1	419.3	337.6
Norfolk - Virginia Beach - Newport News, VA - NC	677.2	807.7	1 005.5	1 256.9	1 396.9	1 587.3	1 390.0
Oakland, CA	4 181.5	5 113.2	6 372.5	7 309.2	6 920.4	6 263.9	6 709.5
Odessa - Midland, TX	50.0	68.3	118.2	92.1	99.7	96.5	104.0
Oklahoma City, OK	478.9	488.6	485.8	483.9	520.0	552.5	525.9
Omaha, NE - IA	299.8	393.3	425.9	608.3	691.4	753.7	949.5
Orange County, CA	5 653.4	6 716.0	8 041.1	8 309.3	8 798.3	8 198.9	9 323.7
Orlando, FL	930.4	848.5	968.8	1 219.0	1 662.8	1 477.3	1 500.0
Panama City, FL	90.9	121.2	216.5	174.8	221.1	246.7	167.5
Parkersburg - Marietta, WV - OH	298.8	313.6	186.6	211.9	262.3	246.6	234.2
Pensacola, FL	38.8	34.0	32.2	36.8	59.8	47.9	52.3
Philadelphia, PA--NJ	5 869.1	6 545.8	7 896.9	7 727.9	8 027.8	8 397.2	9 267.1
Phoenix - Mesa, AZ	4 498.9	5 561.1	6 780.4	7 912.1	11 108.4	8 102.8	7 531.7
Pine Bluff, AR	125.3	152.5	153.7	152.8	139.2	129.7	152.3
Pittsburgh, PA	2 989.7	3 150.6	3 982.2	3 933.7	4 352.2	4 079.2	3 940.3
Pittsfield, MA	77.2	112.2	151.9	175.5	219.3	203.6	219.6
Portland - Vancouver, OR - WA	5 698.5	6 448.8	8 931.3	9 234.3	8 926.5	8 283.3	9 366.6
Portland, ME	355.2	319.5	373.1	339.2	617.4	755.6	757.1
Portsmouth - Rochester, NH - ME	465.0	470.2	553.6	574.8	486.0	555.2	588.4
Providence - Fall River - Warwick, RI - MA	1 141.7	1 246.0	1 241.0	1 296.2	1 601.8	1 670.6	1 554.4
Provo - Orem, UT	170.4	200.2	201.6	301.9	360.5	320.4	284.1
Racine, WI	365.1	403.2	335.1	493.2	992.0	482.5	240.7
Raleigh - Durham - Chapel Hill, NC	1 620.9	1 758.7	2 093.2	2 609.8	2 713.1	2 665.6	2 981.3
Reading, PA	300.6	271.6	293.4	326.2	429.5	454.2	481.0
Redding, CA	32.3	28.6	41.0	53.0	39.3	31.8	36.5
Reno, NV	184.1	213.7	368.2	314.6	399.7	384.4	588.2
Richland - Kennewick - Pasco, WA	220.3	271.6	146.6	228.1	457.9	309.2	342.5
Richmond - Petersburg, VA	4 012.2	5 260.6	5 389.3	5 609.4	5 571.7	5 396.0	4 587.2
Riverside - San Bernardino, CA	1 093.8	1 458.9	1 856.5	1 982.1	2 067.9	1 861.2	2 076.9
Roanoke, VA	164.0	195.9	231.3	238.3	285.2	436.7	293.5
Rochester, MN	53.0	72.7	93.9	92.9	131.8	172.0	169.8
Rochester, NY	3 091.5	3 143.7	3 860.5	4 307.7	4 694.5	4 489.8	4 370.2
Rockford, IL	521.6	616.1	641.4	721.9	758.7	926.5	857.2
Sacramento, CA	1 075.6	1 087.9	1 448.3	1 908.6	1 669.5	1 731.9	2 337.6
Saginaw - Bay City - Midland, MI	855.4	776.8	1 035.6	1 254.5	1 654.4	1 557.9	1 831.0

Table E-1. Metropolitan Area Exports of Goods, 1993–1999—*Continued*

(Millions of dollars.)

Metropolitan area	1993	1994	1995	1996	1997	1998	1999
Salem, OR	66.3	72.9	112.0	123.0	160.6	138.8	180.6
Salinas, CA	294.5	322.0	359.9	337.6	393.2	350.5	313.0
Salt Lake City - Ogden, UT	1 660.9	1 808.7	1 838.2	2 111.5	2 593.6	2 494.8	2 260.0
San Antonio, TX	563.9	656.3	771.1	1 050.0	1 342.8	1 640.8	2 003.7
San Diego, CA	4 357.7	4 867.3	5 860.9	6 719.4	7 810.0	8 591.6	8 963.8
San Francisco, CA	9 264.9	9 303.8	8 133.7	8 560.4	9 978.5	9 123.2	9 035.0
San Jose, CA	16 171.6	19 942.7	26 822.8	29 331.3	29 057.2	26 111.9	28 255.7
Santa Barbara - Santa Maria - Lompoc, CA	424.0	420.2	565.2	648.0	623.3	501.3	581.4
Santa Cruz - Watsonville, CA	664.3	857.4	1 408.2	1 943.1	2 298.5	1 800.8	2 366.4
Santa Rosa, CA	409.1	485.2	572.9	681.8	856.3	862.7	865.5
Sarasota - Bradenton, FL	186.9	187.4	182.8	180.2	184.8	208.5	202.5
Savannah, GA	442.5	423.3	567.5	459.4	633.4	665.7	624.6
Scranton - Wilkes -Barre - Hazleton, PA	266.6	328.2	431.9	392.0	442.4	438.2	565.5
Seattle - Bellevue - Everett, WA	23 815.6	21 753.0	17 815.4	21 391.1	27 005.8	34 003.3	32 356.1
Sharon, PA	44.1	40.4	60.7	56.9	83.9	81.1	82.0
Sheboygan, WI	207.1	244.3	258.7	283.3	320.9	316.4	306.4
Sherman - Denison, TX	34.7	36.1	90.7	147.5	172.4	116.9	99.6
Shreveport - Bossier City, LA	108.4	134.6	169.1	172.6	180.8	143.3	141.3
South Bend, IN	179.7	160.3	389.5	494.8	522.1	586.9	493.8
Spokane, WA	254.4	269.4	310.9	347.9	445.7	392.7	447.1
Springfield, IL	23.9	29.8	35.1	35.5	44.4	38.6	30.9
Springfield, MA	389.8	434.8	512.1	530.3	568.0	442.1	432.9
Springfield, MO	81.1	103.8	120.2	120.3	141.4	174.4	200.5
St. Joseph, MO	36.9	39.2	49.6	94.4	116.4	138.3	78.8
St. Louis, MO - IL	3 400.0	3 673.3	3 997.7	4 497.4	4 711.5	4 315.5	4 879.2
Stamford - Norwalk, CT	3 366.6	3 452.7	4 937.6	4 424.3	3 387.6	2 778.9	2 573.0
Stockton - Lodi, CA	287.5	320.3	355.7	357.8	341.6	339.9	311.6
Syracuse, NY	1 374.1	1 600.9	1 894.3	1 665.5	1 846.7	1 514.8	1 553.7
Tacoma, WA	1 115.3	774.9	1 098.9	1 179.7	1 403.8	1 254.3	1 224.9
Tallahassee, FL	16.1	18.7	24.2	27.2	32.7	47.6	38.0
Tampa - St. Petersburg - Clearwater, FL	1 295.7	1 835.8	2 116.1	1 921.8	2 273.8	2 471.5	2 403.8
Terre Haute, IN	67.3	88.8	163.6	253.7	264.7	559.3	446.4
Texarkana, TX - Texarkana, AR	26.7	24.6	52.2	64.1	31.4	55.1	59.4
Toledo, OH	836.1	986.9	1 177.7	1 207.5	1 261.1	1 056.6	867.6
Topeka, KS	121.1	125.2	133.0	130.2	140.7	160.3	154.1
Trenton, NJ	223.8	237.5	392.5	267.8	343.4	276.9	330.6
Tucson, AZ	487.1	638.1	671.7	800.1	1 060.5	1 253.4	1 064.6
Tulsa, OK	1 273.0	1 241.0	1 485.1	1 549.6	1 626.4	1 558.1	1 423.8
Utica - Rome, NY	188.3	269.3	238.0	278.0	238.8	240.3	248.2
Vallejo - Fairfield - Napa, CA	171.7	264.0	238.1	278.0	384.9	398.8	284.0
Ventura, CA	640.3	698.7	953.4	967.3	1 128.9	1 192.5	1 577.5
Visalia - Tulare - Porterville, CA	119.6	107.7	120.6	143.7	160.5	178.1	160.6
Washington, DC - MD - VA - WV	7 250.6	7 969.3	8 350.4	8 083.5	7 980.7	7 347.8	7 213.3
Waterbury, CT	187.5	179.6	207.6	221.6	252.0	258.8	235.9
Waterloo - Cedar Falls, IA	102.7	149.7	194.6	200.9	282.8	200.8	86.4
Wausau, WI	122.5	113.6	117.3	148.9	184.8	158.9	177.7
West Palm Beach - Boca Raton, FL	764.8	834.3	898.0	955.8	1 156.0	959.0	948.4
Wheeling, WV - OH	7.4	10.8	9.0	15.1	77.1	99.7	8.3
Wichita Falls, TX	49.6	65.1	80.7	77.0	91.2	105.3	98.4
Wichita, KS	1 444.0	1 540.6	1 727.7	1 916.8	2 273.4	1 689.2	2 286.1
Williamsport, PA	105.2	123.3	150.4	151.0	182.5	171.2	172.9
Wilmington - Newark, DE--MD	3 423.8	3 720.4	4 361.1	4 551.1	5 140.6	5 027.4	4 903.2
Wilmington, NC	147.1	180.7	211.7	301.7	422.9	478.7	483.7
Worcester, MA - CT	1 017.9	603.8	757.6	685.7	772.1	745.5	655.8
Yakima, WA	135.8	147.6	168.9	176.0	213.1	256.7	264.1
York, PA	751.8	952.0	973.9	945.1	1 015.4	1 089.1	1 012.6
Youngstown - Warren, OH	189.3	185.3	225.9	223.1	323.0	296.6	239.8
Yuba City, CA	62.8	61.5	70.5	74.0	78.5	86.4	90.1
Other Metropolitan Areas	19 963.5	24 124.6	30 744.9	30 793.3	33 363.5	30 397.5	29 657.4
Non - Metropolitan Areas	25 932.9	29 367.1	34 188.8	36 892.0	41 567.4	40 376.9	44 196.7
Crossovers	10 146.1	11 085.6	13 376.1	16 339.3	19 942.0	21 602.7	23 952.4
Unknown	38 889.6	35 565.6	37 062.3	44 315.9	51 718.5	51 716.5	53 195.3

Table E-2. Metropolitan Area Exports of Goods by Industry, 1994–1999

(Millions of dollars.)

Industry	Atlanta, GA					
	1994	1995	1996	1997	1998	1999
ALL GOODS	4 739.1	5 811.4	5 891.5	6 604.6	7 904.6	7 574.5
Manufactured Products	4 406.7	5 475.2	5 561.0	6 239.0	7 537.7	7 183.0
Food products	418.0	616.4	767.3	556.8	502.9	444.2
Tobacco products	2.7	3.9	3.5	5.4	10.9	7.7
Textile mill products	144.4	106.2	134.0	111.6	102.0	114.4
Apparel	138.8	173.0	227.5	295.8	344.0	207.0
Lumber and wood products	210.4	197.8	157.8	202.1	122.8	97.1
Furniture and fixtures	28.4	26.9	33.5	46.7	40.6	28.8
Paper products	444.8	687.6	673.2	641.5	533.8	473.4
Printing and publishing	39.8	50.0	45.5	42.2	48.2	37.4
Chemical and petroleum products	344.8	407.4	455.8	722.6	1 241.2	638.3
Refined Petroleum Products	59.0	77.1	76.9	80.9	52.5	44.5
Rubber and plastic products	170.9	166.9	151.4	162.4	175.3	144.5
Leather products	3.4	3.9	5.0	4.9	4.5	8.2
Stone, clay, and glass products	27.1	17.4	20.8	30.5	45.4	46.8
Primary metals	138.6	177.7	229.3	246.8	514.3	516.8
Fabricated metal products	90.4	105.6	119.1	118.6	134.1	163.8
Industrial machinery and computers	707.1	851.8	867.2	1 016.3	972.4	920.5
Electric and electronic equipment	656.7	674.7	725.7	910.1	1 123.0	1 289.4
Transportation equipment	378.7	651.3	387.8	457.1	1 000.9	1 400.0
Scientific and measuring instruments	345.9	420.3	417.8	511.2	478.6	487.4
Miscellaneous manufactures	39.3	40.5	44.3	54.9	55.8	71.4
Unidentified manufactures	17.6	18.9	17.9	20.6	34.6	41.4
Nonmanufactured Commodities	332.4	336.2	330.4	365.6	366.9	391.6

Exports of Goods, Manufactures, and Top Five Industry Groups, 1999
(Billions of dollars)

Industry	Austin - San Marcos, TX					
	1994	1995	1996	1997	1998	1999
ALL GOODS	2 128.8	2 929.2	2 743.1	3 354.8	3 802.4	4 931.4
Manufactured Products	2 120.4	2 922.0	2 735.0	3 335.3	3 781.0	4 885.6
Food products	2.0	2.9	10.0	4.0	10.1	7.1
Tobacco products	. . .	. . .	. . .	. . .	. . .	. . .
Textile mill products	0.5	1.4	4.7	5.4	6.2	2.2
Apparel	0.7	0.6	3.5	1.1	1.2	1.7
Lumber and wood products	1.1	0.8	0.6	2.4	11.6	7.1
Furniture and fixtures	1.6	0.5	1.0	1.9	1.6	1.7
Paper products	0.6	1.7	1.2	1.1	6.2	5.8
Printing and publishing	4.3	9.1	12.4	16.8	14.6	8.7
Chemical and petroleum products	11.4	18.0	24.0	31.3	38.6	40.6
Rubber and plastic products	3.4	3.7	3.9	5.9	5.6	9.2
Leather products	0.2	0.5	0.4	0.5	0.2	0.8
Stone, clay, and glass products	1.6	3.2	7.5	5.2	10.9	7.6
Primary metals	2.2	3.4	4.6	4.0	6.0	8.1
Fabricated metal products	5.8	13.8	15.5	12.9	10.9	13.6
Industrial machinery and computers	435.6	600.4	574.8	819.8	1 120.2	1 463.5
Electric and electronic equipment	1 515.0	2 079.2	1 830.7	2 182.3	2 267.0	3 038.4
Transportation equipment	23.6	33.8	36.0	39.6	43.2	35.5
Scientific and measuring instruments	102.2	138.2	172.3	188.1	206.3	208.8
Miscellaneous manufactures	4.2	5.7	26.8	6.5	9.6	14.2
Unidentified manufactures	4.2	5.1	5.1	6.4	11.1	11.1
Nonmanufactured Commodities	8.3	7.2	8.1	19.5	21.4	45.9

Exports of Goods, Manufactures, and Top Five Industry Groups, 1999
(Billions of dollars)

Table E-2.   Metropolitan Area Exports of Goods by Industry, 1994–1999 —*Continued*

(Millions of dollars.)

Industry	Bergen - Passaic, NJ					
	1994	1995	1996	1997	1998	1999
ALL GOODS	4 387.0	4 784.0	4 499.9	4 789.8	4 228.6	4 181.5
Manufactured Products	4 286.1	4 643.5	4 398.7	4 673.9	4 104.7	4 040.8
Food products	293.1	339.5	297.5	306.0	246.0	227.6
Textile mill products	57.0	65.5	70.4	79.8	80.5	73.2
Apparel	58.8	76.6	119.8	114.6	91.5	74.6
Lumber and wood products	8.9	7.4	15.8	13.6	10.8	13.6
Furniture and fixtures	10.2	9.4	12.6	10.1	10.7	10.4
Paper and tobacco products	322.0	548.3	370.9	276.8	201.0	100.8
Printing and publishing	69.9	87.8	112.1	116.2	131.0	134.9
Chemical products	939.0	1 055.9	1 045.4	1 015.7	803.3	820.1
Refined petroleum products	13.1	9.7	7.6	9.1	9.4	9.5
Rubber and plastic products	101.7	97.6	89.1	105.9	101.1	111.6
Leather products	26.9	31.6	I7.6	21.2	25.6	19.7
Stone, clay, and glass products	42.0	45.6	51.1	51.0	47.7	46.8
Primary metals	66.6	107.4	88.6	78.1	53.0	66.6
Fabricated metal products	93.8	99.9	104.9	112.0	93.4	103.1
Industrial machinery and computers	584.8	675.4	548.7	663.6	517.0	423.7
Electric and electronic equipment	712.1	490.1	479.7	602.0	678.7	632.4
Transportation equipment	344.2	395.4	396.9	487.5	426.0	459.0
Scientific and measuring instruments	474.0	424.7	495.9	536.1	492.2	521.5
Miscellaneous manufactures	48.4	57.1	57.6	57.3	55.5	90.0
Unidentified manufactures	19.7	18.5	16.5	17.4	30.6	101.6
Nonmanufactured Commodities	100.9	140.5	101.2	115.8	124.0	140.7

Industry	Boston, MA - NH					
	1994	1995	1996	1997	1998	1999
ALL GOODS	7 095.3	7 902.7	8 715.8	9 570.6	9 556.3	10 427.0
Manufactured Products	6 802.5	7 606.3	8 395.6	9 280.8	9 267.1	9 996.0
Food products	118.6	146.8	217.5	215.2	200.7	170.0
Tobacco products	0.1	. . .	. . .	. . .	. . .	. . .
Textile mill products	60.1	61.1	60.9	77.0	78.4	73.6
Apparel	30.4	30.8	48.4	43.6	26.7	40.5
Lumber and wood products	72.7	80.5	89.1	113.4	108.5	115.0
Furniture and fixtures	12.3	11.1	11.5	13.6	21.5	28.9
Paper products	110.2	166.4	194.4	219.6	151.9	155.5
Printing and publishing	90.4	92.1	111.0	111.2	124.1	101.3
Chemical and petroleum products	436.2	531.1	642.1	799.8	871.7	1 033.5
Rubber and plastic products	368.0	338.6	271.1	297.9	282.5	310.9
Leather products	82.9	80.1	77.8	75.5	61.0	54.7
Stone, clay, and glass products	22.6	24.0	26.0	35.1	28.1	70.7
Primary metals	62.0	78.1	80.4	110.5	104.8	92.4
Fabricated metal products	266.3	291.2	325.2	321.0	374.7	409.3
Industrial machinery and computers	1 911.5	2 037.2	2 315.2	2 400.4	2 251.0	2 302.2
Electric and electronic equipment	1 495.4	1 763.3	1 927.9	2 225.1	2 316.6	2 472.8
Transportation equipment	91.5	109.0	121.8	101.9	111.0	128.4
Scientific and measuring instruments	1 449.1	1 632.9	1 738.0	1 965.8	1 987.2	2 278.7
Miscellaneous manufactures	81.0	93.7	104.9	122.6	116.1	110.2
Unidentified manufactures	41.4	38.5	32.4	31.6	50.6	47.4
Nonmanufactured Commodities	292.8	296.4	320.2	289.8	289.2	431.0

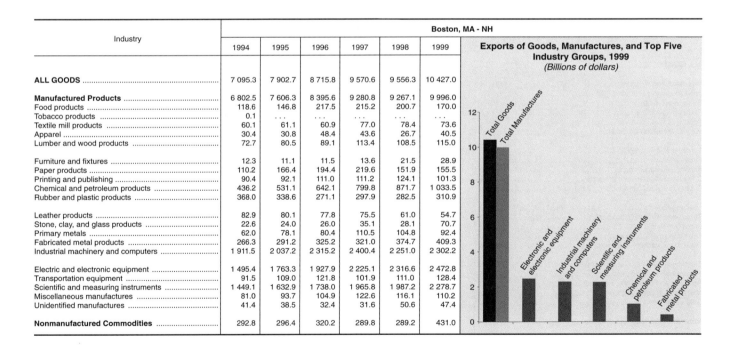

Table E-2. Metropolitan Area Exports of Goods by Industry, 1994–1999 —*Continued*

(Millions of dollars.)

Industry	Brownsville - Harlingen - San Benito, TX					
	1994	1995	1996	1997	1998	1999
ALL GOODS	2 113.4	2 245.9	2 612.6	2 697.1	2 421.3	2 571.4
Manufactured Products	1 855.1	1 999.8	2 358.1	2 459.9	2 207.1	2 337.3
Food and tobacco products	100.1	59.2	73.7	80.1	58.6	59.4
Textiles and apparel	81.1	126.7	193.8	130.4	105.2	141.8
Lumber and wood products	9.6	10.7	4.1	3.6	4.3	7.2
Furniture and fixtures	7.8	6.1	8.6	5.0	3.4	2.3
Paper products	63.4	59.4	52.2	41.2	42.3	43.6
Printing and publishing	6.1	6.3	6.6	5.5	4.8	5.0
Chemical products	277.5	260.0	349.8	339.6	348.5	337.2
Refined petroleum products	115.5	70.2	171.0	165.0	164.9	184.7
Rubber and plastic products	73.3	58.6	62.3	74.9	84.4	88.6
Leather products	2.5	0.3	3.8	8.1	5.6	1.6
Stone, clay, and glass products	18.1	22.6	20.4	18.5	19.1	22.4
Primary metals	60.8	79.4	106.5	135.8	113.7	95.0
Fabricated metal products	90.7	107.4	121.1	106.2	94.9	134.2
Industrial machinery and computers	187.9	133.1	129.3	127.6	138.4	159.5
Electric and electronic equipment	443.2	716.6	762.6	825.9	604.7	731.7
Transportation equipment	220.1	150.9	189.5	279.3	313.7	250.3
Scientific and measuring instruments	68.1	109.8	86.7	94.8	81.5	56.8
Miscellaneous manufactures	22.4	14.6	11.5	12.8	11.2	8.6
Unidentified manufactures	6.9	8.0	4.5	5.6	7.7	7.2
Nonmanufactured Commodities	258.2	246.1	254.5	237.3	214.2	234.2

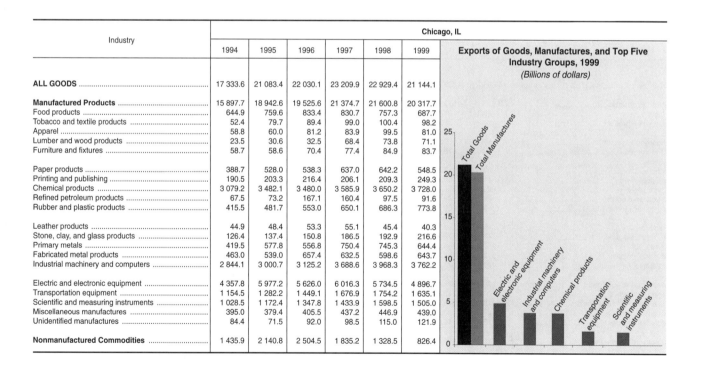

Industry	Chicago, IL					
	1994	1995	1996	1997	1998	1999
ALL GOODS	17 333.6	21 083.4	22 030.1	23 209.9	22 929.4	21 144.1
Manufactured Products	15 897.7	18 942.6	19 525.6	21 374.7	21 600.8	20 317.7
Food products	644.9	759.6	833.4	830.7	757.3	687.7
Tobacco and textile products	52.4	79.7	89.4	99.0	100.4	98.2
Apparel	58.8	60.0	81.2	83.9	99.5	81.0
Lumber and wood products	23.5	30.6	32.5	68.4	73.8	71.1
Furniture and fixtures	58.7	58.6	70.4	77.4	84.9	83.7
Paper products	388.7	528.0	538.3	637.0	642.2	548.5
Printing and publishing	190.5	203.3	216.4	206.1	209.3	249.3
Chemical products	3 079.2	3 482.1	3 480.0	3 585.9	3 650.2	3 728.0
Refined petroleum products	67.5	73.2	167.1	160.4	97.5	91.6
Rubber and plastic products	415.5	481.7	553.0	650.1	686.3	773.8
Leather products	44.9	48.4	53.3	55.1	45.4	40.3
Stone, clay, and glass products	126.4	137.4	150.8	186.5	192.9	216.6
Primary metals	419.5	577.8	556.8	750.4	745.3	644.4
Fabricated metal products	463.0	539.0	657.4	632.5	598.6	643.7
Industrial machinery and computers	2 844.1	3 000.7	3 125.2	3 688.6	3 968.3	3 762.2
Electric and electronic equipment	4 357.8	5 977.2	5 626.0	6 016.3	5 734.5	4 896.7
Transportation equipment	1 154.5	1 282.2	1 449.1	1 676.9	1 754.2	1 635.1
Scientific and measuring instruments	1 028.5	1 172.4	1 347.8	1 433.9	1 598.5	1 505.0
Miscellaneous manufactures	395.0	379.4	405.5	437.2	446.9	439.0
Unidentified manufactures	84.4	71.5	92.0	98.5	115.0	121.9
Nonmanufactured Commodities	1 435.9	2 140.8	2 504.5	1 835.2	1 328.5	826.4

Table E-2. Metropolitan Area Exports of Goods by Industry, 1994–1999 —*Continued*

(Millions of dollars.)

Industry	Cincinnati, OH - KY - IN						
	1994	1995	1996	1997	1998	1999	Exports of Goods, Manufactures, and Top Five Industry Groups, 1999 (Billions of dollars)
ALL GOODS	4 056.5	4 256.7	4 784.1	5 674.1	6 682.5	6 783.1	
Manufactured Products	3 883.9	4 000.7	4 565.2	5 441.4	6 509.4	6 540.2	
Food products	170.6	209.9	204.4	154.3	211.3	230.5	
Tobacco products	. . .	. . .	. . .	. . .	. . .	. . .	
Textile mill products	8.9	7.6	19.8	35.7	22.9	32.3	
Apparel	9.5	9.7	31.7	112.1	726.0	78.9	
Lumber and wood products	15.5	15.8	15.6	23.1	15.0	18.2	
Furniture and fixtures	5.0	5.7	5.0	5.2	9.2	8.0	
Paper products	88.1	194.9	239.4	120.4	114.0	96.2	
Printing and publishing	45.1	60.2	67.7	65.5	67.8	73.0	
Chemical products	585.2	681.1	667.8	637.8	552.5	663.4	
Refined petroleum products	4.4	5.4	5.1	5.1	2.8	13.5	
Rubber and plastic products	52.6	52.8	57.8	71.3	89.9	100.5	
Leather products	21.5	21.5	42.5	38.8	29.1	62.5	
Stone, clay, and glass products	33.2	31.4	36.8	34.3	38.5	62.6	
Primary metals	89.7	59.0	62.9	91.7	86.3	55.3	
Fabricated metal products	62.0	75.9	121.3	121.4	116.6	124.2	
Industrial machinery, computers, and transportation equipment	2 440.3	2 228.7	2 580.5	3 455.0	3 858.6	4 246.6	
Electric and electronic equipment	140.3	180.0	197.6	245.4	318.3	333.6	
Scientific and measuring instruments	91.6	132.3	178.1	204.0	224.3	302.5	
Miscellaneous manufactures	14.0	22.0	26.1	14.5	17.4	28.8	
Unidentified manufactures	6.4	6.7	5.1	5.9	9.1	9.6	
Nonmanufactured Commodities	172.6	256.0	219.0	232.8	173.0	242.9	

Industry	Cleveland - Lorain - Elyria, OH						
	1994	1995	1996	1997	1998	1999	Exports of Goods, Manufactures, and Top Five Industry Groups, 1999 (Billions of dollars)
ALL GOODS	4 093.3	4 707.0	5 075.2	5 511.0	5 347.0	5 894.2	
Manufactured Products	3 882.1	4 512.8	4 535.6	4 898.7	4 946.1	5 156.6	
Food products	25.3	25.4	18.8	22.5	24.3	32.6	
Tobacco and textile products	4.3	5.9	5.2	7.5	6.9	13.6	
Apparel	3.5	3.7	5.4	7.6	7.1	12.4	
Lumber and wood products	31.1	32.0	30.3	36.2	30.2	37.7	
Furniture and fixtures	14.6	19.0	18.7	17.7	17.4	8.7	
Paper products	53.0	62.3	69.7	99.2	102.7	105.9	
Printing and publishing	14.3	24.1	17.9	22.0	16.2	21.0	
Chemical products	1 064.4	1 226.0	1 157.8	1 221.3	964.5	1 028.0	
Refined petroleum products	63.3	39.5	80.7	46.6	50.9	36.3	
Rubber and plastic products	96.3	100.5	96.5	98.4	107.4	136.4	
Leather products	0.8	1.7	1.5	1.3	1.3	1.6	
Stone, clay, and glass products	46.1	72.2	83.7	115.7	102.7	104.2	
Primary metals	291.2	358.4	369.1	468.3	531.0	496.0	
Fabricated metal products	313.6	392.3	374.1	294.5	438.1	597.6	
Industrial machinery and computers	772.9	927.3	995.4	1 114.8	1 188.9	1 174.3	
Electric and electronic equipment	529.2	524.8	488.7	519.0	541.7	517.7	
Transportation equipment	207.4	318.2	343.6	364.9	275.8	369.4	
Scientific and measuring instruments	315.3	343.4	342.2	398.2	479.2	403.6	
Miscellaneous manufactures	22.5	23.3	25.0	31.9	43.3	42.3	
Unidentified manufactures	13.2	12.9	11.4	10.9	16.5	17.4	
Nonmanufactured Commodities	211.2	194.2	539.6	612.3	400.9	737.6	

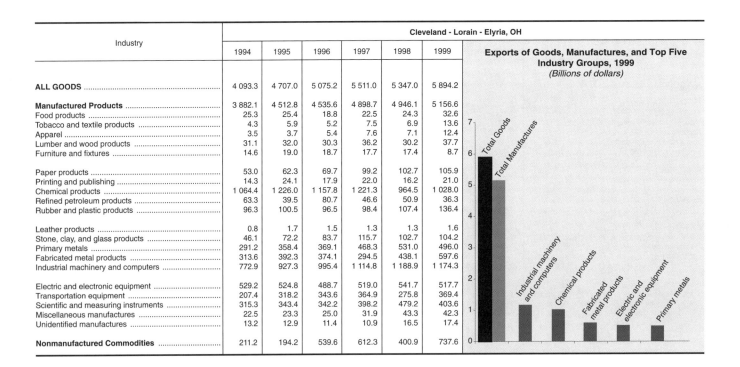

Table E-2. Metropolitan Area Exports of Goods by Industry, 1994–1999 —*Continued*

(Millions of dollars.)

Industry	Dallas, TX					
	1994	1995	1996	1997	1998	1999
ALL GOODS	5 679.7	6 870.4	7 096.9	8 645.9	8 449.6	8 188.4
Manufactured Products	5 308.8	6 343.8	6 757.2	8 285.9	8 055.0	7 930.3
Food products	158.1	155.0	167.1	199.1	202.1	186.2
Tobacco products	. . .	. . .	. . .	. . .	. . .	. . .
Textile mill products	11.9	20.6	24.6	20.8	23.6	23.9
Apparel	123.4	96.2	76.8	82.1	89.8	75.8
Lumber, wood, furniture, and fixtures	67.6	69.4	73.0	75.9	68.7	51.0
Paper products	33.1	34.8	40.0	53.5	54.9	69.8
Printing and publishing	26.0	27.2	33.2	29.7	26.5	23.5
Chemical products	860.5	1 242.5	1 096.9	1 108.3	962.9	953.4
Refined petroleum products	22.4	28.2	26.7	274.9	305.5	229.2
Rubber and plastic products	38.5	45.2	57.8	56.1	48.3	79.4
Leather products	4.6	8.6	7.5	6.4	6.2	7.4
Stone, clay, and glass products	17.9	16.4	18.9	19.9	23.4	23.9
Primary metals	82.6	115.0	123.4	184.0	126.0	168.3
Fabricated metal products	107.8	112.2	93.5	141.6	156.3	146.0
Industrial machinery and computers	808.0	928.7	1 069.4	1 256.0	1 214.9	967.5
Electric and electronic equipment	1 963.8	2 413.3	2 716.8	3 468.4	3 267.3	3 496.0
Transportation equipment	545.0	501.0	554.7	676.2	814.3	734.4
Scientific and measuring instruments	375.7	471.9	509.4	553.3	568.7	588.8
Miscellaneous manufactures	41.8	42.7	52.6	62.1	65.9	66.2
Unidentified manufactures	19.8	15.0	15.0	17.7	29.4	39.5
Nonmanufactured Commodities	370.9	526.6	339.6	360.0	394.6	258.1

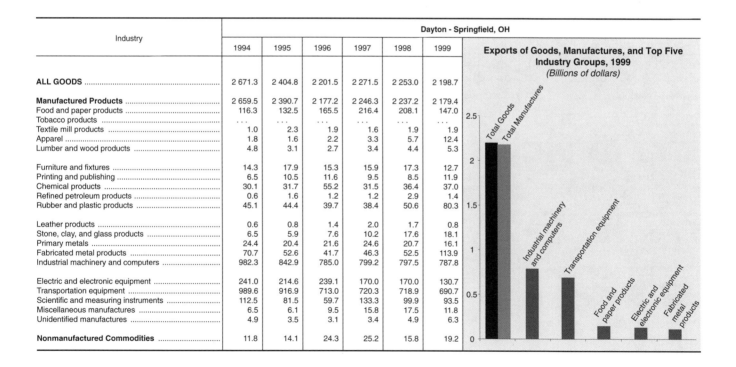

Exports of Goods, Manufactures, and Top Five Industry Groups, 1999
(Billions of dollars)

Industry	Dayton - Springfield, OH					
	1994	1995	1996	1997	1998	1999
ALL GOODS	2 671.3	2 404.8	2 201.5	2 271.5	2 253.0	2 198.7
Manufactured Products	2 659.5	2 390.7	2 177.2	2 246.3	2 237.2	2 179.4
Food and paper products	116.3	132.5	165.5	216.4	208.1	147.0
Tobacco products	. . .	. . .	. . .	. . .	. . .	. . .
Textile mill products	1.0	2.3	1.9	1.6	1.9	1.9
Apparel	1.8	1.6	2.2	3.3	5.7	12.4
Lumber and wood products	4.8	3.1	2.7	3.4	4.4	5.3
Furniture and fixtures	14.3	17.9	15.3	15.9	17.3	12.7
Printing and publishing	6.5	10.5	11.6	9.5	8.5	11.9
Chemical products	30.1	31.7	55.2	31.5	36.4	37.0
Refined petroleum products	0.6	1.6	1.2	1.2	2.9	1.4
Rubber and plastic products	45.1	44.4	39.7	38.4	50.6	80.3
Leather products	0.6	0.8	1.4	2.0	1.7	0.8
Stone, clay, and glass products	6.5	5.9	7.6	10.2	17.6	18.1
Primary metals	24.4	20.4	21.6	24.6	20.7	16.1
Fabricated metal products	70.7	52.6	41.7	46.3	52.5	113.9
Industrial machinery and computers	982.3	842.9	785.0	799.2	797.5	787.8
Electric and electronic equipment	241.0	214.6	239.1	170.0	170.0	130.7
Transportation equipment	989.6	916.9	713.0	720.3	718.9	690.7
Scientific and measuring instruments	112.5	81.5	59.7	133.3	99.9	93.5
Miscellaneous manufactures	6.5	6.1	9.5	15.8	17.5	11.8
Unidentified manufactures	4.9	3.5	3.1	3.4	4.9	6.3
Nonmanufactured Commodities	11.8	14.1	24.3	25.2	15.8	19.2

Exports of Goods, Manufactures, and Top Five Industry Groups, 1999
(Billions of dollars)

Table E-2. Metropolitan Area Exports of Goods by Industry, 1994–1999—*Continued*

(Millions of dollars.)

Industry	Detroit, MI						Exports of Goods, Manufactures, and Top Five Industry Groups, 1999 (Billions of dollars)
	1994	1995	1996	1997	1998	1999	
ALL GOODS	27 469.7	27 314.7	27 531.2	25 967.4	27 004.7	28 008.3	
Manufactured Products	27 122.0	26 982.6	27 219.9	25 627.0	26 689.2	27 598.2	
Food products	99.0	127.2	114.0	126.4	126.3	79.5	
Tobacco and textile products	70.7	70.8	35.1	35.8	29.0	33.5	
Apparel	83.1	118.6	152.0	133.7	120.0	82.8	
Lumber and wood products	19.4	24.7	14.1	11.4	15.8	21.6	
Furniture and fixtures	324.2	380.4	260.7	264.2	292.6	26.8	
Paper products	58.7	66.7	67.5	68.7	60.1	65.4	
Printing and publishing	50.0	54.2	43.6	43.1	39.2	40.2	
Chemical products	252.2	233.3	272.5	316.8	357.2	310.2	
Refined petroleum products	44.5	44.5	52.2	48.2	34.9	51.8	
Rubber, plastic, and leather products	451.4	437.8	419.3	428.6	422.2	527.4	
Stone, clay, and glass products	246.9	250.8	293.4	284.7	287.3	309.4	
Primary metals	601.1	621.9	494.9	518.8	563.1	498.7	
Fabricated metal products	1 031.8	764.5	835.1	783.5	1 127.8	1 513.9	
Industrial machinery and computers	2 169.5	2 256.1	2 387.9	3 173.9	2 571.9	2 987.0	
Electric and electronic equipment	1 161.2	965.8	967.2	1 223.4	1 243.1	1 337.8	
Transportation equipment	19 985.6	20 113.9	20 387.4	17 622.4	18 771.8	19 082.9	
Scientific and measuring instruments	393.0	374.9	368.2	465.6	548.7	562.4	
Miscellaneous manufactures	47.3	45.1	33.9	55.4	50.8	35.1	
Unidentified manufactures	32.3	31.4	21.0	22.3	27.5	31.9	
Nonmanufactured Commodities	347.6	332.1	311.3	340.4	315.5	410.0	

Industry	El Paso, TX						Exports of Goods, Manufactures, and Top Five Industry Groups, 1999 (Billions of dollars)
	1994	1995	1996	1997	1998	1999	
ALL GOODS	3 561.3	4 120.8	5 212.7	5 833.9	6 544.6	7 793.2	
Manufactured Products	3 452.0	3 983.7	5 032.6	5 697.4	6 417.8	7 609.0	
Food products	108.4	75.3	113.5	131.0	159.9	141.4	
Tobacco products	14.5	10.3	6.8	1.8	1.0	0.2	
Textile mill products	173.1	207.5	232.3	259.3	406.3	569.3	
Apparel	372.0	347.9	432.8	410.2	460.8	417.1	
Lumber and wood products	22.6	7.8	9.7	9.4	8.9	12.6	
Furniture and fixtures	130.2	114.0	222.7	298.5	252.4	9.7	
Paper products	174.7	193.9	216.3	195.0	256.0	255.9	
Printing and publishing	5.7	7.4	9.3	12.0	19.0	28.7	
Chemical products	53.3	67.0	73.2	74.4	90.3	156.3	
Refined petroleum products	1.9	2.2	3.1	2.6	4.1	3.2	
Rubber and plastic products	155.1	166.3	379.9	509.1	637.9	806.2	
Leather products	6.8	5.7	5.5	7.2	7.9	155.6	
Stone, clay, and glass products	36.1	31.3	18.8	16.5	27.8	44.4	
Primary metals	170.6	270.5	359.0	388.1	437.4	539.8	
Fabricated metal products	115.6	115.5	191.0	234.9	341.2	409.5	
Industrial machinery and computers	191.3	160.9	199.6	256.2	390.6	808.5	
Electric and electronic equipment	1 518.0	1 959.9	2 245.4	2 505.2	2 513.7	2 641.7	
Transportation equipment	68.4	64.3	49.5	135.4	112.6	262.0	
Scientific and measuring instruments	93.0	137.5	229.8	218.2	242.0	268.9	
Miscellaneous manufactures	30.8	25.5	24.2	21.4	23.4	38.3	
Unidentified manufactures	9.6	13.0	10.0	10.8	24.9	39.9	
Nonmanufactured Commodities	109.3	137.0	180.1	136.6	126.8	184.2	

Table E-2. Metropolitan Area Exports of Goods by Industry, 1994–1999—*Continued*

(Millions of dollars.)

Industry	Fort Worth - Arlington, TX						Exports of Goods, Manufactures, and Top Five Industry Groups, 1999 *(Billions of dollars)*
	1994	1995	1996	1997	1998	1999	
ALL GOODS	2 052.0	1 915.0	2 372.7	3 045.9	3 455.9	3 971.0	
Manufactured Products	2 018.3	1 881.8	2 330.7	2 995.0	3 404.6	3 910.6	
Food products	47.3	53.2	45.4	37.4	32.1	33.9	
Tobacco products	. . .	. . .	. . .	. . .	. . .	. . .	
Textile mill products	3.5	4.3	9.1	16.4	20.3	17.7	
Apparel	69.3	69.0	62.8	80.3	77.5	83.9	
Lumber and wood products	1.7	4.6	3.0	1.9	2.6	3.5	
Furniture and fixtures	1.9	3.3	4.2	5.8	5.5	4.1	
Paper products	7.0	5.8	6.7	6.2	30.5	70.8	
Printing and publishing	5.2	4.2	6.5	8.6	8.6	14.1	
Chemical products	52.2	67.2	73.7	98.8	115.8	135.0	
Refined petroleum products	4.6	3.6	5.6	4.3	3.5	5.2	
Rubber and plastic products	20.4	22.3	31.1	53.1	82.0	112.5	
Leather products	9.0	9.8	7.4	10.6	8.8	4.6	
Stone, clay, and glass products	6.7	7.0	7.3	6.8	11.3	38.5	
Primary metals	27.6	33.4	37.3	35.3	41.4	29.7	
Fabricated metal products	36.9	51.7	79.5	65.8	46.9	36.5	
Industrial machinery and computers	415.0	340.7	565.6	419.2	357.8	298.9	
Electric and electronic equipment	394.0	547.7	718.0	1 358.1	1 703.8	2 002.5	
Transportation equipment	695.9	495.9	516.0	611.7	674.7	861.0	
Scientific and measuring instruments	195.1	132.3	124.0	145.6	146.2	117.5	
Miscellaneous manufactures	18.6	18.7	20.9	19.9	21.2	20.8	
Unidentified manufactures	6.3	6.8	6.7	9.2	14.1	19.8	
Nonmanufactured Commodities	33.7	33.2	42.0	50.9	51.3	60.4	

Exports of Goods, Manufactures, and Top Five Industry Groups, 1999 (Billions of dollars). Bars: Total Goods, Total Manufactures, Electric and electronic equipment, Transportation equipment, Industrial machinery and computers, Chemical products, Scientific and measuring instruments.

Industry	Greensboro - Winston - Salem - High Point, NC						Exports of Goods, Manufactures, and Top Five Industry Groups, 1999 *(Billions of dollars)*
	1994	1995	1996	1997	1998	1999	
ALL GOODS	2 773.3	3 356.3	3 495.6	4 050.8	4 037.2	4 313.1	
Manufactured Products	2 699.8	3 276.2	3 439.8	3 962.2	3 939.8	4 225.3	
Food products	27.3	28.8	29.9	33.4	23.1	18.7	
Tobacco and textile products	1 112.3	1 152.6	1 029.4	869.8	924.9	841.7	
Apparel	479.9	821.2	951.7	1 159.1	1 036.1	1 227.0	
Lumber and wood products	31.8	31.3	29.7	38.5	42.2	51.5	
Furniture and fixtures	66.3	84.0	97.4	101.3	78.2	85.7	
Paper products	14.7	26.0	32.0	51.5	40.7	46.0	
Printing and publishing	3.6	5.1	6.2	9.3	9.9	18.6	
Chemical products	279.6	372.3	396.0	551.5	476.9	475.8	
Refined petroleum products	0.4	0.2	0.5	1.7	0.4	1.1	
Rubber and plastic products	19.4	25.5	32.9	38.5	38.6	51.8	
Leather products	4.7	5.4	6.5	9.1	5.3	8.4	
Stone, clay, and glass products	8.3	11.9	10.5	33.5	11.5	20.9	
Primary metals	19.0	17.8	20.5	22.9	34.1	41.2	
Fabricated metal products	70.6	57.9	47.1	64.0	75.5	91.0	
Electric and electronic equipment	107.5	144.1	202.7	350.2	438.7	563.7	
Transportation equipment	56.6	51.8	59.2	55.0	76.0	145.6	
Scientific and measuring instruments	127.8	160.9	177.8	215.1	245.6	214.2	
Assorted manufactures	266.5	275.7	305.9	352.6	371.1	307.0	
Unidentified manufactures	3.6	3.4	3.8	5.3	11.2	15.5	
Nonmanufactured Commodities	73.5	80.1	55.9	88.6	97.3	87.8	

Exports of Goods, Manufactures, and Top Five Industry Groups, 1999 (Billions of dollars). Bars: Total Goods, Total Manufactures, Apparel, Tobacco and textile products, Electric and electronic equipment, Chemical products, Assorted manufactures.

Table E-2. Metropolitan Area Exports of Goods by Industry, 1994–1999 —*Continued*

(Millions of dollars.)

Industry	\multicolumn{6}{c}{Houston, TX}					
	1994	1995	1996	1997	1998	1999
ALL GOODS	13 388.2	16 247.9	16 541.5	18 595.9	19 119.0	18 967.6
Manufactured Products	12 957.7	15 666.2	15 954.6	17 951.4	18 542.5	18 233.8
Food products	438.7	464.2	465.4	378.5	460.0	423.3
Textile mill products	12.0	14.8	13.1	14.8	15.9	18.1
Apparel	13.0	15.6	21.9	19.1	22.2	13.5
Lumber and wood products	56.9	62.6	69.3	78.8	47.8	44.9
Furniture and fixtures	16.8	12.3	14.8	20.6	22.7	13.7
Paper products	31.7	37.3	29.7	43.1	46.2	69.2
Printing and publishing	13.9	15.4	15.0	14.9	14.5	16.9
Chemical products	3 626.8	4 810.9	4 107.8	4 436.8	4 221.9	5 644.6
Refined petroleum products	1 460.6	1 843.3	2 045.6	2 103.1	1 687.2	1 647.7
Rubber and plastic products	143.9	155.0	161.1	167.6	174.3	155.0
Leather products	5.0	5.3	5.2	8.1	6.4	2.7
Stone, clay, and glass products	64.7	79.8	104.9	125.0	159.1	160.4
Primary metals	287.9	475.0	536.0	601.8	595.9	401.1
Fabricated metal products	371.7	380.4	494.3	642.4	700.4	619.6
Industrial machinery and computers	4 973.2	5 787.3	6 264.4	7 224.3	7 923.2	6 488.1
Electric and electronic equipment	549.1	641.7	563.7	762.1	792.0	792.4
Transportation equipment	402.3	334.2	444.2	556.5	739.7	952.1
Scientific and measuring instruments	408.3	453.0	526.8	685.3	809.3	659.4
Miscellaneous manufactures	58.3	48.5	49.4	45.8	50.8	50.0
Unidentified manufactures	22.9	29.7	22.0	22.8	53.0	61.1
Nonmanufactured Commodities	430.5	581.7	586.8	644.5	576.5	733.8

Exports of Goods, Manufactures, and Top Five Industry Groups, 1999
(Billions of dollars)

Industry	\multicolumn{6}{c}{Indianapolis, IN}					
	1994	1995	1996	1997	1998	1999
ALL GOODS	3 003.8	3 555.9	4 012.8	4 301.8	4 771.3	5 187.1
Manufactured Products	2 968.8	3 523.9	3 970.7	4 263.2	4 744.2	5 078.5
Food products	38.3	40.7	42.8	63.6	60.0	30.3
Tobacco products	...	...	...	...	...	...
Textile mill products	1.0	3.9	2.6	3.4	3.5	3.8
Apparel	7.1	7.3	6.5	7.7	7.8	11.1
Lumber and wood products	83.8	69.0	74.9	83.2	80.2	62.2
Furniture and fixtures	36.9	6.9	9.6	10.6	39.3	16.9
Paper products	22.1	60.3	56.8	53.6	56.2	55.1
Printing and publishing	35.5	48.7	55.6	78.1	90.1	81.3
Chemical products	733.8	873.7	1 034.7	1 168.3	1 233.1	1 259.1
Refined petroleum products	4.3	3.4	5.2	2.3	3.0	2.1
Rubber and plastic products	82.8	94.3	129.4	130.4	110.5	98.5
Leather products	1.7	2.3	2.2	3.3	3.0	1.9
Stone, clay, and glass products	24.7	54.3	35.4	46.9	41.6	20.8
Primary metals	44.1	65.5	76.7	61.5	82.6	70.6
Fabricated metal products	144.3	116.3	135.4	128.9	230.2	282.5
Industrial machinery and computers	300.5	332.7	410.1	470.0	445.2	389.1
Electric and electronic equipment	911.5	1 029.5	1 096.3	1 043.8	1 395.6	1 555.5
Transportation equipment	369.4	585.9	626.3	765.7	719.0	877.9
Scientific and measuring instruments	110.5	112.2	151.5	118.0	121.9	237.8
Miscellaneous manufactures	10.1	8.2	9.7	14.8	11.3	12.9
Unidentified manufactures	6.5	8.9	9.1	8.9	10.0	9.1
Nonmanufactured Commodities	35.0	32.0	42.0	38.6	27.1	108.6

Exports of Goods, Manufactures, and Top Five Industry Groups, 1999
(Billions of dollars)

Table E-2. Metropolitan Area Exports of Goods by Industry, 1994–1999—*Continued*

(Millions of dollars.)

Industry	Kansas City, MO - KS						
	1994	1995	1996	1997	1998	1999	Exports of Goods, Manufactures, and Top Five Industry Groups, 1999 *(Billions of dollars)*
ALL GOODS	2 578.6	3 350.2	3 985.1	3 817.6	3 631.7	3 306.2	
Manufactured Products	1 347.7	1 425.3	1 503.5	1 910.9	1 862.6	1 623.8	
Food products	266.0	272.6	263.0	322.2	325.9	290.0	
Tobacco products	. . .	. . .	. . .	. . .	. . .	. . .	
Textiles and apparel	38.5	55.4	79.7	111.8	23.9	14.2	
Lumber and wood products	14.7	14.7	13.5	14.3	15.2	14.2	
Furniture and fixtures	4.1	3.8	4.5	6.7	3.8	3.0	
Paper products	15.0	21.9	19.2	23.4	22.4	20.2	
Printing and publishing	38.9	36.6	44.4	48.5	39.5	51.4	
Chemical products	160.0	175.1	206.0	263.6	290.4	336.0	
Refined petroleum products	2.6	2.8	2.7	3.2	2.3	3.6	
Rubber and plastic products	26.3	30.1	25.1	31.5	53.7	48.0	
Leather products	1.4	0.9	0.8	1.3	1.5	1.3	
Stone, clay, and glass products	28.5	22.9	22.0	14.7	17.3	23.3	
Primary metals	18.2	12.4	15.7	52.6	63.3	18.6	
Fabricated metal products	102.3	129.5	129.7	175.4	143.9	91.5	
Industrial machinery and computers	216.5	243.5	288.2	361.2	349.3	232.5	
Electric and electronic equipment	175.0	128.5	111.5	157.6	145.1	130.0	
Transportation equipment	98.8	122.0	102.3	122.4	151.5	142.4	
Scientific and measuring instruments	116.0	129.1	146.0	168.4	179.9	174.2	
Miscellaneous manufactures	10.2	12.4	11.9	18.6	21.5	15.7	
Unidentified manufactures	14.7	10.8	17.3	13.6	12.4	13.7	
Nonmanufactured Commodities	1 230.8	1 924.9	2 481.6	1 906.8	1 769.1	1 682.4	

Industry	Laredo, TX						
	1994	1995	1996	1997	1998	1999	Exports of Goods, Manufactures, and Top Five Industry Groups, 1999 *(Billions of dollars)*
ALL GOODS	4 157.4	2 897.8	3 440.7	3 959.1	3 633.6	2 681.7	
Manufactured Products	3 969.1	2 722.0	3 298.4	3 816.4	3 468.4	2 554.2	
Food products	392.7	273.8	275.6	311.6	274.2	215.0	
Tobacco products	17.8	7.5	19.4	13.2	1.7	0.1	
Textile mill products	54.7	36.3	46.4	43.7	59.1	76.7	
Apparel	46.5	23.9	29.2	41.5	58.2	24.5	
Lumber and wood products	24.1	9.5	7.3	8.6	8.0	6.9	
Furniture and fixtures	45.0	21.2	5.6	11.2	8.5	6.5	
Paper products	240.4	245.2	185.9	254.8	207.9	191.3	
Printing and publishing	27.9	12.9	12.8	15.7	14.2	12.3	
Chemical products	269.9	244.7	226.3	282.6	288.9	176.0	
Refined petroleum products	5.9	4.8	15.6	23.7	15.3	15.0	
Rubber and plastic products	202.9	150.3	144.2	228.8	223.4	191.7	
Leather products	31.3	29.0	30.4	48.1	51.2	48.0	
Stone, clay, and glass products	51.0	32.6	36.6	43.0	46.2	40.1	
Primary metals	193.4	200.4	204.6	196.6	230.7	112.6	
Fabricated metal products	244.5	186.4	359.6	89.3	109.2	88.6	
Industrial machinery and computers	704.2	327.6	333.1	486.6	542.1	458.3	
Electric and electronic equipment	549.0	577.5	589.2	745.6	542.5	506.5	
Transportation equipment	702.8	254.8	671.0	805.8	582.4	229.6	
Scientific and measuring instruments	102.6	49.6	56.5	113.7	116.8	78.4	
Miscellaneous manufactures	52.2	24.8	42.1	37.9	51.1	27.8	
Unidentified manufactures	10.1	9.1	7.1	14.3	36.8	48.5	
Nonmanufactured Commodities	188.2	175.8	142.3	142.8	165.2	127.5	

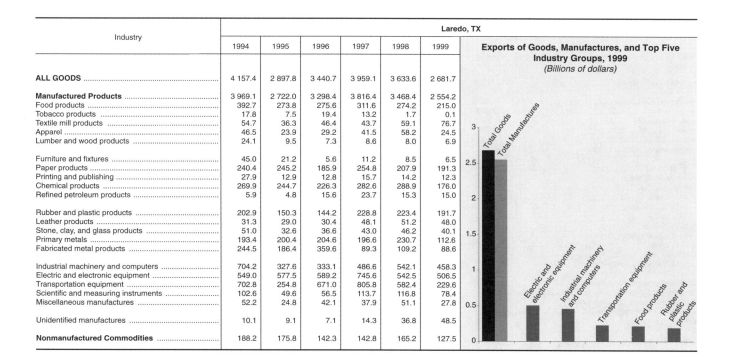

Table E-2. Metropolitan Area Exports of Goods by Industry, 1994–1999 —*Continued*

(Millions of dollars.)

Industry	Los Angeles - Long Beach, CA						Exports of Goods, Manufactures, and Top Five Industry Groups, 1999 (Billions of dollars)
	1994	1995	1996	1997	1998	1999	
ALL GOODS	22 224.8	24 731.0	24 437.9	25 816.4	25 554.7	23 904.7	
Manufactured Products	20 526.0	22 603.3	22 602.4	23 987.6	23 740.6	21 989.4	
Food products	1 311.1	1 536.1	1 526.8	1 490.5	1 185.8	1 198.4	
Tobacco and textile products	135.2	149.0	165.8	205.7	201.6	286.6	
Apparel	619.4	775.6	871.9	838.3	778.7	740.9	
Lumber and wood products	93.5	115.7	118.4	114.9	101.1	95.9	
Furniture and fixtures	118.3	116.0	129.9	149.3	187.4	111.3	
Paper products	149.3	172.2	220.7	218.2	176.5	189.3	
Printing and publishing	167.9	143.5	149.8	176.6	192.1	151.7	
Chemical products	930.2	1 106.4	1 066.6	1 277.5	1 240.5	1 169.9	
Refined petroleum products	559.6	467.0	560.5	491.5	363.1	467.8	
Rubber and plastic products	278.8	298.1	350.8	367.7	333.6	341.0	
Leather products	126.7	133.0	122.6	109.2	88.6	134.3	
Stone, clay, and glass products	94.2	126.3	118.3	136.0	130.5	129.3	
Primary metals	302.5	442.5	485.4	448.2	428.2	427.8	
Fabricated metal products	433.3	528.5	593.0	628.9	654.0	820.7	
Industrial machinery and computers	2 553.8	2 836.9	3 382.3	3 350.2	2 980.2	2 910.2	
Electric and electronic equipment	2 467.8	2 617.9	2 548.7	2 836.7	2 903.8	2 640.6	
Transportation equipment	8 331.8	8 885.9	7 732.1	8 363.4	9 208.6	7 381.8	
Scientific and measuring instruments	1 125.8	1 243.5	1 526.3	1 718.3	1 589.8	1 619.8	
Miscellaneous manufactures	596.8	779.6	823.4	903.7	802.7	873.8	
Unidentified manufactures	130.2	129.6	109.1	162.8	193.7	298.1	
Nonmanufactured Commodities	1 698.8	2 127.6	1 835.6	1 828.8	1 814.1	1 915.3	

Industry	Memphis, TN - AR - MS						Exports of Goods, Manufactures, and Top Five Industry Groups, 1999 (Billions of dollars)
	1994	1995	1996	1997	1998	1999	
ALL GOODS	2 729.5	4 163.8	3 786.1	3 636.9	3 615.5	3 135.2	
Manufactured Products	1 525.3	1 856.0	1 949.9	2 335.0	2 475.9	2 522.5	
Food and tobacco products	71.8	86.8	130.1	93.4	82.8	96.9	
Textile mill products	2.9	3.1	7.7	6.8	8.2	...	
Apparel	10.8	4.8	4.3	5.2	4.0	9.3	
Lumber and wood products	35.2	35.2	26.3	15.1	11.8	12.7	
Furniture and fixtures	7.3	5.2	4.7	7.1	5.9	3.1	
Paper products	624.9	814.4	698.5	726.5	716.5	724.1	
Printing and publishing	12.9	13.7	9.8	11.1	10.2	12.0	
Chemical products	95.9	129.6	132.2	147.8	181.1	169.7	
Refined petroleum products	1.3	2.2	1.1	2.7	3.2	2.5	
Rubber and plastic products	29.5	39.8	41.8	59.0	58.6	72.6	
Leather products	2.0	2.4	2.9	3.2	5.1	5.6	
Stone, clay, and glass products	3.6	3.2	3.1	4.6	7.4	14.5	
Primary metals	10.6	12.7	13.0	32.6	35.6	33.1	
Fabricated metal products	13.5	19.7	41.9	46.3	40.2	42.5	
Industrial machinery and computers	215.0	247.3	270.4	439.1	416.2	436.0	
Electric and electronic equipment	80.2	91.7	105.8	129.1	156.7	232.7	
Transportation equipment	178.1	184.1	262.5	311.7	382.8	340.8	
Scientific and measuring instruments	107.0	138.9	168.4	258.6	310.6	268.8	
Miscellaneous manufactures	18.4	16.2	20.6	28.5	28.9	22.5	
Unidentified manufactures	4.3	4.9	4.7	6.4	10.1	13.4	
Nonmanufactured Commodities	1 204.2	2 307.8	1 836.2	1 302.0	1 139.6	612.6	

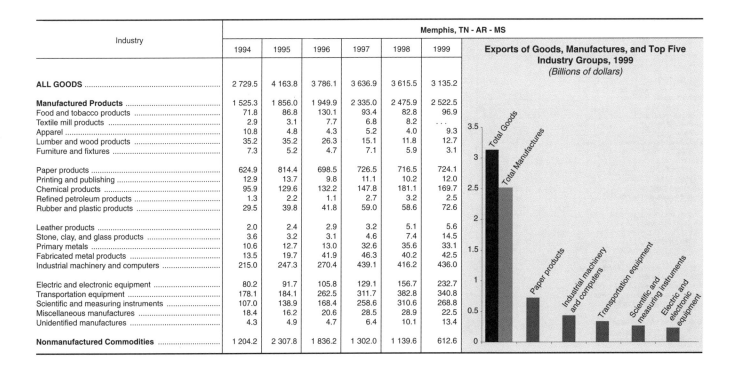

Table E-2. Metropolitan Area Exports of Goods by Industry, 1994–1999 —*Continued*

(Millions of dollars.)

Industry	Miami, FL						Exports of Goods, Manufactures, and Top Five Industry Groups, 1999 (Billions of dollars)
	1994	1995	1996	1997	1998	1999	
ALL GOODS	9 266.7	10 200.8	10 681.2	12 692.3	12 943.4	11 942.1	
Manufactured Products	8 572.2	9 773.2	10 266.6	12 250.5	12 463.5	11 491.7	
Food products	380.1	392.9	390.9	430.8	446.4	434.5	
Tobacco products	5.6	12.9	18.6	18.5	7.0	9.6	
Textile mill products	123.1	146.2	203.5	315.5	358.2	301.2	
Apparel	387.1	377.1	408.9	524.6	488.8	463.5	
Lumber and wood products	93.7	110.7	106.3	137.7	156.7	155.9	
Furniture and fixtures	76.9	80.5	92.8	115.6	123.8	83.4	
Paper products	252.7	355.4	350.1	363.9	354.9	413.4	
Printing and publishing	66.7	71.5	59.3	73.3	107.8	87.2	
Chemical products	456.1	552.3	641.2	780.2	740.5	644.5	
Refined petroleum products	69.2	61.1	36.2	53.1	53.9	43.8	
Rubber and plastic products	221.4	294.8	275.1	322.1	292.0	274.8	
Leather products	44.2	44.8	47.2	58.1	60.4	54.5	
Stone, clay, and glass products	80.3	86.5	85.3	88.6	85.8	88.9	
Primary metals	358.6	421.2	284.7	354.6	411.5	354.3	
Fabricated metal products	203.1	245.4	234.3	312.2	298.2	249.5	
Industrial machinery and computers	2 098.2	2 679.8	3 167.4	3 744.5	3 623.2	2 969.0	
Electric and electronic equipment	1 461.5	1 690.5	1 764.5	2 263.4	2 424.2	2 347.8	
Transportation equipment	1 271.4	1 229.2	1 123.6	1 204.5	1 333.1	1 320.2	
Scientific and measuring instruments	659.3	627.8	709.5	767.9	711.0	730.8	
Miscellaneous manufactures	192.5	228.8	208.9	245.9	255.3	321.5	
Unidentified manufactures	70.5	63.9	58.5	75.4	130.8	143.6	
Nonmanufactured Commodities	694.5	427.7	414.6	441.7	479.8	450.4	

Industry	Middlesex - Somerset - Hunterdon, NJ						Exports of Goods, Manufactures, and Top Five Industry Groups, 1999 (Billions of dollars)
	1994	1995	1996	1997	1998	1999	
ALL GOODS	3 035.9	3 448.1	3 628.1	4 385.4	4 879.7	4 857.8	
Manufactured Products	2 653.8	3 099.2	3 299.6	4 039.7	4 546.8	4 540.2	
Food and tobacco products	77.5	105.1	110.6	130.7	168.8	134.0	
Textile mill products	7.7	7.4	10.9	18.4	18.4	. . .	
Apparel	35.4	27.4	18.1	22.0	31.2	22.0	
Lumber and wood products	4.1	2.9	11.8	6.9	4.4	7.6	
Furniture and fixtures	3.8	3.9	4.1	6.3	7.6	6.7	
Paper products	44.9	44.9	38.2	54.0	70.4	72.2	
Printing and publishing	52.7	58.8	54.7	57.6	56.3	58.9	
Chemical products	934.4	1 077.9	1 254.4	1 855.4	1 877.2	1 988.1	
Refined petroleum products	21.5	18.8	13.1	12.2	20.0	28.5	
Rubber and plastic products	46.8	45.7	48.7	70.6	62.7	82.5	
Leather products	8.1	7.6	8.2	12.8	7.9	9.5	
Stone, clay, and glass products	21.8	20.5	23.4	30.2	32.7	39.2	
Primary metals	341.4	321.7	268.9	417.0	727.3	650.3	
Fabricated metal products	59.6	203.0	185.0	109.3	197.0	227.3	
Industrial machinery and computers	311.5	284.4	326.4	343.2	314.5	385.3	
Electric and electronic equipment	216.4	281.9	260.1	246.1	282.6	246.3	
Transportation equipment	122.5	181.2	235.2	241.0	198.9	140.9	
Scientific and measuring instruments	318.7	371.7	366.1	340.5	394.2	361.9	
Miscellaneous manufactures	16.8	18.9	21.8	34.3	32.8	32.5	
Unidentified manufactures	8.0	15.3	40.0	31.0	42.0	30.6	
Nonmanufactured Commodities	382.1	348.9	328.5	345.7	332.9	317.6	

Table E-2. Metropolitan Area Exports of Goods by Industry, 1994–1999 —*Continued*

(Millions of dollars.)

Industry	\multicolumn{6}{c}{Milwaukee - Waukesha, WI}	
	1994	1995	1996	1997	1998	1999	
ALL GOODS	2 913.5	3 506.9	3 717.2	3 837.6	3 570.3	3 720.2	
Manufactured Products	2 857.8	3 449.3	3 618.1	3 769.3	3 523.9	3 645.5	
Food and tobacco products	120.9	173.7	180.8	157.5	108.4	79.0	
Textile mill products	2.8	4.5	4.9	3.9	4.0	5.0	
Apparel	8.7	13.5	12.2	7.8	7.1	5.1	
Lumber and wood products	4.5	7.1	8.5	13.3	13.5	12.9	
Furniture and fixtures	7.2	7.2	9.5	9.2	11.6	5.0	
Paper products	17.9	24.0	29.6	31.7	62.4	70.7	
Printing and publishing	18.0	17.6	22.2	26.9	29.7	52.7	
Chemical products	147.4	164.8	184.3	206.6	210.6	232.0	
Refined petroleum products	17.4	16.7	17.6	8.4	6.3	6.6	
Rubber and plastic products	41.0	44.4	44.5	48.1	44.7	50.4	
Leather products	76.4	59.9	61.6	58.9	54.8	42.8	
Stone, clay, and glass products	5.8	6.0	7.2	10.7	7.1	7.7	
Primary metals	25.2	35.0	39.9	48.3	57.0	52.1	
Fabricated metal products	147.6	154.0	146.1	141.7	140.0	137.9	
Industrial machinery and computers	1 025.1	1 261.2	1 230.0	1 360.4	1 166.1	1 212.3	
Electric and electronic equipment	311.9	400.5	421.9	469.9	446.8	359.5	
Transportation equipment	184.0	199.7	206.6	253.4	257.4	230.7	
Scientific and measuring instruments	648.1	810.5	950.1	870.1	852.9	1 041.2	
Miscellaneous manufactures	38.3	38.1	31.1	33.5	30.3	28.2	
Unidentified manufactures	9.5	10.8	9.4	9.1	13.1	13.4	
Nonmanufactured Commodities	55.7	57.6	99.1	68.3	46.3	74.7	

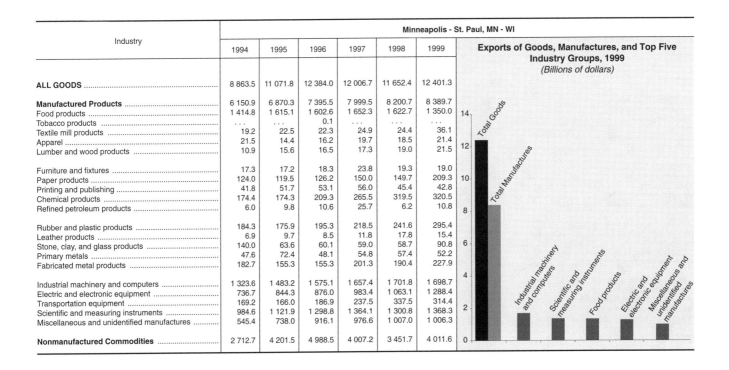

Exports of Goods, Manufactures, and Top Five Industry Groups, 1999
(Billions of dollars)

Industry	\multicolumn{6}{c}{Minneapolis - St. Paul, MN - WI}	
	1994	1995	1996	1997	1998	1999	
ALL GOODS	8 863.5	11 071.8	12 384.0	12 006.7	11 652.4	12 401.3	
Manufactured Products	6 150.9	6 870.3	7 395.5	7 999.5	8 200.7	8 389.7	
Food products	1 414.8	1 615.1	1 602.6	1 652.3	1 622.7	1 350.0	
Tobacco products	. . .	. . .	0.1	. . .	. . .	. . .	
Textile mill products	19.2	22.5	22.3	24.9	24.4	36.1	
Apparel	21.5	14.4	16.2	19.7	18.5	21.4	
Lumber and wood products	10.9	15.6	16.5	17.3	19.0	21.5	
Furniture and fixtures	17.3	17.2	18.3	23.8	19.3	19.0	
Paper products	124.0	119.5	126.2	150.0	149.7	209.3	
Printing and publishing	41.8	51.7	53.1	56.0	45.4	42.8	
Chemical products	174.4	174.3	209.3	265.5	319.5	320.5	
Refined petroleum products	6.0	9.8	10.6	25.7	6.2	10.8	
Rubber and plastic products	184.3	175.9	195.3	218.5	241.6	295.4	
Leather products	6.9	9.7	8.5	11.8	17.8	15.4	
Stone, clay, and glass products	140.0	63.6	60.1	59.0	58.7	90.8	
Primary metals	47.6	72.4	48.1	54.8	57.4	52.2	
Fabricated metal products	182.7	155.3	155.3	201.3	190.4	227.9	
Industrial machinery and computers	1 323.6	1 483.2	1 575.1	1 657.4	1 701.8	1 698.7	
Electric and electronic equipment	736.7	844.3	876.0	983.4	1 063.1	1 288.4	
Transportation equipment	169.2	166.0	186.9	237.5	337.5	314.4	
Scientific and measuring instruments	984.6	1 121.9	1 298.8	1 364.1	1 300.8	1 368.3	
Miscellaneous and unidentified manufactures	545.4	738.0	916.1	976.6	1 007.0	1 006.3	
Nonmanufactured Commodities	2 712.7	4 201.5	4 988.5	4 007.2	3 451.7	4 011.6	

Exports of Goods, Manufactures, and Top Five Industry Groups, 1999
(Billions of dollars)

Table E-2. Metropolitan Area Exports of Goods by Industry, 1994–1999 —*Continued*

(Millions of dollars.)

Industry	Nassau - Suffolk, NY						
	1994	1995	1996	1997	1998	1999	
ALL GOODS	2 866.3	3 558.6	3 680.2	4 208.5	4 438.6	4 686.5	
Manufactured Products	2 730.4	3 407.8	3 484.8	4 035.6	4 268.3	4 467.0	
Food products	52.6	47.5	56.0	71.5	71.5	98.5	
Tobacco products	0.2	0.3	1.3	2.3	1.6	0.2	
Textile mill products	42.6	45.8	42.6	41.4	35.4	31.2	
Apparel	47.2	26.7	26.5	34.0	31.4	56.9	
Lumber and wood products	8.2	8.2	16.7	14.9	9.5	14.7	
Furniture and fixtures	11.6	10.5	8.4	12.8	14.6	10.1	
Paper products	73.6	102.2	96.1	82.4	105.6	83.2	
Printing and publishing	57.7	54.5	53.2	64.6	73.1	66.3	
Chemical products	181.3	226.6	279.7	366.1	438.8	518.7	
Refined petroleum products	6.3	5.4	12.9	5.8	7.1	4.9	
Rubber and plastic products	53.2	57.8	70.2	96.6	89.1	84.3	
Leather products	23.8	27.5	28.1	32.8	27.3	16.4	
Stone, clay, and glass products	13.5	13.7	15.8	17.7	17.5	18.4	
Primary metals	66.1	164.8	79.2	104.6	89.4	60.3	
Fabricated metal products	68.9	73.1	83.8	111.7	95.1	87.2	
Industrial machinery and computers	521.3	629.0	696.2	822.7	832.7	877.5	
Electric and electronic equipment	802.6	917.4	998.8	1 149.0	1 256.2	1 386.8	
Transportation equipment	247.5	542.6	296.5	227.0	251.3	273.8	
Scientific and measuring instruments	265.7	305.2	487.2	656.0	695.3	638.1	
Miscellaneous manufactures	120.0	121.8	112.0	91.1	89.6	100.1	
Unidentified manufactures	66.7	27.1	23.8	30.8	36.0	39.3	
Nonmanufactured Commodities	135.8	150.8	195.3	172.9	170.4	219.5	

Exports of Goods, Manufactures, and Top Five Industry Groups, 1999
(Billions of dollars)

Industry	Newark, NJ						
	1994	1995	1996	1997	1998	1999	
ALL GOODS	5 205.5	5 640.0	5 044.2	5 201.8	4 866.1	5 397.5	
Manufactured Products	4 959.0	5 320.1	4 778.3	4 965.7	4 688.9	5 250.0	
Food and tobacco products	565.9	422.0	462.8	433.0	382.7	317.3	
Textile mill products	31.4	26.4	24.6	34.6	30.7	26.8	
Apparel	36.1	27.6	25.8	35.1	20.7	18.7	
Lumber and wood products	5.3	9.1	15.1	19.0	6.9	7.9	
Furniture and fixtures	36.6	30.3	24.5	26.3	32.2	11.6	
Paper products	85.7	155.8	154.5	132.1	91.8	108.0	
Printing and publishing	31.6	45.2	46.3	83.1	60.8	48.8	
Chemical products	1 493.5	1 708.6	1 678.7	2 169.5	1 981.9	2 271.3	
Refined petroleum products	44.0	66.6	23.0	21.2	11.4	22.3	
Rubber and plastic products	77.9	92.6	101.7	115.1	100.6	101.4	
Leather products	6.2	7.5	8.3	7.4	11.6	17.4	
Stone, clay, and glass products	22.7	20.4	27.3	29.3	22.5	37.8	
Primary metals	173.1	183.1	153.4	127.1	132.8	127.0	
Fabricated metal products	115.5	126.2	145.1	167.7	140.4	177.9	
Industrial machinery and computers	412.8	440.2	398.6	489.2	475.9	451.6	
Electric and electronic equipment	1 354.1	1 356.8	728.9	416.9	421.0	712.3	
Transportation equipment	188.3	307.8	421.0	264.4	289.9	281.7	
Scientific and measuring instruments	205.8	216.7	263.5	312.5	383.5	372.4	
Miscellaneous manufactures	41.2	50.4	46.4	53.4	59.8	86.9	
Unidentified manufactures	31.2	26.8	28.7	29.0	32.0	50.9	
Nonmanufactured Commodities	246.5	319.9	265.9	236.2	177.2	147.4	

Exports of Goods, Manufactures, and Top Five Industry Groups, 1999
(Billions of dollars)

Table E-2. Metropolitan Area Exports of Goods by Industry, 1994–1999 —*Continued*

(Millions of dollars.)

Industry	New Orleans, LA						Exports of Goods, Manufactures, and Top Five Industry Groups, 1999 (Billions of dollars)
	1994	1995	1996	1997	1998	1999	
ALL GOODS	2 326.2	3 037.8	3 316.8	2 770.8	2 776.2	2 409.0	
Manufactured Products	1 255.5	1 476.1	1 250.3	1 201.1	1 417.4	1 180.5	
Food and tobacco products	377.6	464.3	226.4	237.5	321.2	229.9	
Textile mill products	14.6	12.4	14.7	17.2	18.4	16.9	
Apparel	3.0	3.7	6.8	4.8	18.4	26.3	
Lumber and wood products	19.2	28.1	31.3	19.0	16.0	14.6	
Furniture and fixtures	8.5	3.2	2.8	3.7	3.8	3.1	
Paper products	27.3	34.9	13.1	11.7	13.8	11.6	
Printing and publishing	0.8	1.8	1.0	0.9	0.9	1.0	
Chemical products	191.0	272.1	278.3	276.0	265.3	303.2	
Refined petroleum products	51.6	83.6	133.8	108.5	56.2	140.0	
Rubber and plastic products	34.6	26.5	26.4	25.2	28.1	31.7	
Leather products	3.2	1.2	0.9	4.3	6.7	5.5	
Stone, clay, and glass products	4.0	6.2	11.5	6.6	5.4	5.6	
Primary metals	53.6	121.1	66.9	55.1	53.9	43.2	
Fabricated metal products	37.2	28.3	39.9	36.0	29.7	22.2	
Industrial machinery and computers	224.3	189.2	180.5	183.1	164.8	128.8	
Electric and electronic equipment	79.6	65.3	72.7	87.7	62.1	53.4	
Transportation equipment	46.4	46.3	58.1	34.5	262.8	63.4	
Scientific and measuring instruments	73.6	80.9	80.3	84.5	82.1	70.5	
Miscellaneous manufactures	2.0	2.6	2.4	1.9	2.4	4.4	
Unidentified manufactures	3.5	4.5	2.6	3.0	5.5	5.3	
Nonmanufactured Commodities	1 070.7	1 561.7	2 066.4	1 569.7	1 358.8	1 228.5	

Industry	New York, NY						Exports of Goods, Manufactures, and Top Five Industry Groups, 1999 (Billions of dollars)
	1994	1995	1996	1997	1998	1999	
ALL GOODS	23 543.7	27 131.1	27 970.5	29 082.6	26 578.4	24 484.7	
Manufactured Products	19 038.3	21 769.5	22 508.1	23 831.0	21 637.9	20 504.3	
Food and tobacco products	1 947.4	2 123.9	2 025.4	2 384.3	1 937.6	1 152.3	
Textile mill products	605.7	631.7	625.3	651.7	541.6	436.9	
Apparel	523.5	529.8	493.6	543.3	463.8	384.4	
Lumber and wood products	102.1	76.7	62.3	67.9	72.4	144.4	
Furniture and fixtures	57.0	52.9	51.1	60.7	50.3	38.2	
Paper products	935.1	1 368.7	1 107.5	1 125.5	1 101.5	1 013.5	
Printing and publishing	579.5	552.8	506.0	534.5	587.8	610.2	
Chemical products	2 324.3	2 396.1	2 241.2	2 086.9	1 837.6	1 863.5	
Refined petroleum products	266.2	294.8	320.8	357.8	236.6	127.0	
Rubber and plastic products	157.0	186.7	190.4	306.2	237.6	208.9	
Leather products	94.1	87.3	94.0	80.0	76.8	86.4	
Stone, clay, and glass products	105.8	116.9	125.2	142.1	113.7	88.3	
Primary metals	2 314.0	3 563.0	5 081.2	4 368.8	3 742.3	3 803.8	
Fabricated metal products	239.3	311.8	309.6	321.2	459.4	292.1	
Industrial machinery and computers	2 647.1	3 041.9	2 619.3	3 377.2	2 537.2	2 240.0	
Electric and electronic equipment	1 026.3	1 059.3	974.3	1 189.4	1 027.3	929.0	
Transportation equipment	2 017.2	2 032.4	2 180.5	2 559.5	2 870.1	2 805.7	
Scientific and measuring instruments	635.3	673.6	596.3	542.8	510.1	514.1	
Miscellaneous manufactures	2 306.8	2 584.6	2 821.0	3 018.3	3 061.2	3 607.1	
Unidentified manufactures	154.3	84.6	83.0	113.1	172.9	158.5	
Nonmanufactured Commodities	4 505.5	5 361.6	5 462.4	5 251.6	4 940.6	3 980.4	

Table E-2. Metropolitan Area Exports of Goods by Industry, 1994–1999—*Continued*

(Millions of dollars.)

Industry	Oakland, CA						
	1994	1995	1996	1997	1998	1999	Exports of Goods, Manufactures, and Top Five Industry Groups, 1999 (Billions of dollars)
ALL GOODS	5 113.2	6 372.5	7 309.2	6 920.4	6 263.9	6 709.5	
Manufactured Products	4 802.6	5 995.1	6 917.8	6 532.3	5 977.7	6 157.5	
Food and tobacco products	373.7	512.3	551.7	544.4	491.4	425.6	
Textile mill products	6.7	9.7	9.8	8.8	9.9	9.0	
Apparel	6.6	8.3	12.5	16.9	10.4	10.5	
Lumber and wood products	25.5	21.9	21.7	22.1	16.7	13.2	
Furniture and fixtures	6.4	11.5	8.7	12.2	13.3	5.4	
Paper products	114.5	162.1	167.6	154.2	161.8	112.8	
Printing and publishing	17.9	23.4	29.0	31.8	30.3	36.6	
Chemical and petroleum products	429.9	455.2	531.4	534.1	478.5	503.1	
Rubber and plastic products	50.3	52.8	49.1	51.0	42.1	67.0	
Leather products	2.4	2.3	3.1	4.4	2.9	2.7	
Stone, clay, and glass products	15.5	17.1	23.4	22.4	22.5	23.3	
Primary metals	73.5	152.6	246.4	266.0	144.6	112.1	
Fabricated metal products	245.3	253.6	254.5	121.9	120.2	108.6	
Industrial machinery and computers	1 021.5	1 326.4	1 758.8	1 804.5	1 631.9	1 967.3	
Electric and electronic equipment	1 764.7	2 306.6	2 419.1	2 114.5	2 045.5	1 960.5	
Transportation equipment	169.4	168.5	162.5	215.5	163.3	217.6	
Scientific and measuring instruments	408.2	457.1	572.6	536.4	509.2	491.8	
Miscellaneous manufactures	52.3	36.5	36.3	36.1	35.3	43.8	
Unidentified manufactures	18.3	17.3	59.6	35.0	47.8	46.7	
Nonmanufactured Commodities	310.6	377.3	391.4	388.1	286.2	552.0	

Exports of Goods, Manufactures, and Top Five Industry Groups, 1999 (Billions of dollars) — Oakland, CA: Total Goods, Total Manufactures, Industrial machinery and computers, Electric and electronic equipment, Chemical and petroleum products, Scientific and measuring instruments, Food and tobacco products

Industry	Orange County, CA						
	1994	1995	1996	1997	1998	1999	Exports of Goods, Manufactures, and Top Five Industry Groups, 1999 (Billions of dollars)
ALL GOODS	6 716.0	8 041.1	8 309.3	8 798.3	8 198.9	9 323.7	
Manufactured Products	6 407.5	7 597.6	7 852.2	8 403.3	7 984.2	9 019.4	
Food products	131.8	182.1	198.4	180.1	168.9	173.4	
Tobacco products	. . .	. . .	. . .	. . .	0.3	0.4	
Textile mill products	17.4	34.6	39.2	37.4	38.7	51.9	
Apparel	98.0	91.3	105.4	139.7	138.0	178.1	
Lumber and wood products	18.7	16.6	25.2	31.4	31.7	26.4	
Furniture and fixtures	21.3	20.6	20.2	32.6	30.4	21.7	
Paper products	44.1	56.4	66.5	67.1	63.7	63.0	
Printing and publishing	23.5	29.9	42.7	35.3	30.5	34.6	
Chemical products	343.5	420.8	473.6	491.2	458.5	463.0	
Refined petroleum products	69.0	12.8	66.1	67.0	43.1	26.1	
Rubber and plastic products	112.7	126.9	135.8	169.0	154.3	158.1	
Leather products	14.0	17.8	29.4	35.3	15.4	23.8	
Stone, clay, and glass products	18.9	32.0	42.8	39.5	46.9	43.6	
Primary metals	450.4	346.8	73.6	83.8	98.1	101.8	
Fabricated metal products	128.3	152.6	171.6	198.5	195.8	222.2	
Industrial machinery and computers	1 833.7	2 325.1	2 255.7	2 245.0	2 052.2	2 300.0	
Electric and electronic equipment	1 728.5	2 193.1	2 516.1	2 888.4	2 948.8	3 570.1	
Transportation equipment	518.4	619.8	648.8	574.5	469.5	497.7	
Scientific and measuring instruments	589.6	676.5	720.8	861.2	820.7	853.3	
Miscellaneous manufactures	201.3	196.2	186.2	192.2	127.6	153.0	
Unidentified manufactures	44.2	45.5	34.2	34.3	51.2	57.3	
Nonmanufactured Commodities	308.5	443.5	457.1	395.0	214.7	304.3	

Exports of Goods, Manufactures, and Top Five Industry Groups, 1999 (Billions of dollars) — Orange County, CA: Total Goods, Total Manufactures, Electric and electronic equipment, Industrial machinery and computers, Scientific and measuring instruments, Transportation equipment, Chemical products

Table E-2. Metropolitan Area Exports of Goods by Industry, 1994–1999 —*Continued*

(Millions of dollars.)

Industry	Philadelphia, PA - NJ						Exports of Goods, Manufactures, and Top Five Industry Groups, 1999 (Billions of dollars)
	1994	1995	1996	1997	1998	1999	
ALL GOODS	6 545.8	7 896.9	7 727.9	8 027.8	8 397.2	9 267.1	
Manufactured Products	5 843.3	7 112.1	6 970.6	7 286.8	7 622.4	8 353.5	
Food and tobacco products	343.8	315.8	363.7	379.4	328.9	314.3	
Textile mill products	72.9	95.6	113.2	84.7	53.9	67.1	
Apparel	57.1	89.5	112.3	87.9	75.8	58.8	
Lumber and wood products	16.9	13.8	17.1	14.1	22.1	15.1	
Furniture and fixtures	18.4	20.7	26.7	23.9	24.9	15.4	
Paper products	107.6	166.1	153.9	166.8	159.2	158.3	
Printing and publishing	254.0	264.7	292.3	290.1	278.3	281.9	
Chemical products	1 815.0	2 467.8	2 172.3	2 224.3	2 608.8	2 650.1	
Refined petroleum products	71.1	69.4	95.5	108.0	128.4	87.6	
Rubber and plastic products	263.0	306.2	337.4	358.0	400.5	411.4	
Leather products	11.0	8.1	11.7	13.6	14.2	10.6	
Stone, clay, and glass products	50.5	52.9	62.2	76.2	79.3	77.5	
Primary metals	232.1	363.1	324.2	300.4	321.2	271.1	
Fabricated metal products	180.1	191.1	181.1	212.9	247.1	266.5	
Industrial machinery and computers	881.4	1 216.5	1 132.7	1 213.6	1 095.9	1 258.9	
Electric and electronic equipment	706.1	732.6	723.6	815.5	628.2	1 262.0	
Transportation equipment	196.0	219.8	293.4	298.7	534.4	434.8	
Scientific and measuring instruments	437.3	375.7	396.8	430.3	413.0	494.3	
Miscellaneous manufactures	105.5	122.1	141.7	162.4	178.6	187.7	
Unidentified manufactures	23.4	20.7	18.8	25.9	29.9	30.3	
Nonmanufactured Commodities	702.5	784.8	757.4	741.0	774.8	913.6	

Industry	Phoenix - Mesa, AZ						Exports of Goods, Manufactures, and Top Five Industry Groups, 1999 (Billions of dollars)
	1994	1995	1996	1997	1998	1999	
ALL GOODS	5 561.1	6 780.4	7 912.1	11 108.4	8 102.8	7 531.7	
Manufactured Products	5 316.8	6 380.7	7 649.8	10 836.4	7 927.1	7 330.7	
Food products	57.6	37.5	37.5	70.4	53.0	44.1	
Tobacco products	...	...	...	...	...	...	
Textile mill products	2.3	2.9	2.3	4.3	3.0	5.0	
Apparel	7.6	9.4	9.4	11.5	19.7	7.6	
Lumber and wood products	1.4	1.6	2.9	2.5	3.3	4.7	
Furniture and fixtures	6.0	5.4	8.7	11.3	12.5	8.2	
Paper products	11.5	11.0	12.0	12.8	14.5	13.6	
Printing and publishing	8.5	7.4	8.6	6.5	7.7	10.6	
Chemical products	90.9	162.0	133.5	107.6	112.8	146.9	
Refined petroleum products	1.0	0.9	0.7	62.7	49.6	107.8	
Rubber and plastic products	44.3	43.1	47.2	60.7	74.8	67.1	
Leather products	4.2	4.2	3.3	4.0	5.5	7.0	
Stone, clay, and glass products	7.0	5.2	10.1	11.3	8.0	10.1	
Primary metals	213.0	324.3	313.9	134.0	97.1	62.5	
Fabricated metal products	54.0	40.7	73.5	89.9	120.6	171.7	
Industrial machinery and computers	550.3	608.0	719.9	2 770.8	1 574.2	837.9	
Electric and electronic equipment	3 262.8	3 963.6	4 877.3	5 860.3	3 872.3	3 975.9	
Transportation equipment	592.9	667.3	860.3	1 093.2	1 406.0	1 306.6	
Scientific and measuring instruments	341.4	417.6	456.6	460.4	419.7	467.9	
Miscellaneous manufactures	46.4	54.7	59.4	46.7	45.5	57.0	
Unidentified manufactures	13.6	13.9	12.5	15.5	27.1	18.5	
Nonmanufactured Commodities	244.3	399.7	262.3	272.0	175.7	201.0	

Table E-2. Metropolitan Area Exports of Goods by Industry, 1994–1999 —*Continued*

(Millions of dollars.)

Industry	Pittsburgh, PA						Exports of Goods, Manufactures, and Top Five Industry Groups, 1999 *(Billions of dollars)*
	1994	1995	1996	1997	1998	1999	
ALL GOODS	3 150.6	3 982.2	3 933.7	4 352.2	4 079.2	3 940.3	
Manufactured Products	2 800.1	3 529.7	3 491.2	3 902.9	3 560.1	3 593.5	
Food products	26.5	27.5	32.5	30.9	34.6	42.1	
Tobacco and textile products	5.9	8.9	15.6	13.7	6.3	6.4	
Apparel	8.7	11.0	13.7	11.2	15.1	20.7	
Lumber and wood products	32.4	41.0	35.4	39.1	46.5	58.0	
Furniture and fixtures	7.9	2.8	3.4	6.2	7.3	3.9	
Paper products	10.6	11.6	16.4	25.1	16.8	29.5	
Printing and publishing	4.8	5.6	6.3	6.6	5.7	5.0	
Chemical products	567.9	734.5	777.5	965.8	982.9	1 102.9	
Refined petroleum products	20.3	25.1	27.5	21.3	24.0	31.1	
Rubber and plastic products	28.8	27.2	25.7	31.7	35.7	36.0	
Leather products	0.6	0.7	1.2	1.0	1.1	2.6	
Stone, clay, and glass products	238.8	285.8	299.2	338.0	289.7	240.6	
Primary metals	456.6	1 036.0	744.8	731.9	477.0	472.0	
Fabricated metal products	87.5	104.2	102.6	124.6	151.0	141.4	
Industrial machinery and computers	658.6	572.4	704.1	803.3	698.2	617.5	
Electric and electronic equipment	361.6	321.0	298.4	334.1	339.4	334.0	
Transportation equipment	72.6	93.0	105.1	136.5	101.6	105.1	
Scientific and measuring instruments	164.4	174.8	221.1	234.4	264.7	285.1	
Miscellaneous manufactures	33.0	38.2	51.8	39.1	40.1	31.1	
Unidentified manufactures	12.7	8.4	9.0	8.4	22.5	28.6	
Nonmanufactured Commodities	350.5	452.4	442.5	449.3	519.1	346.9	

Industry	Portland - Vancouver, OR - WA						Exports of Goods, Manufactures, and Top Five Industry Groups, 1999 *(Billions of dollars)*
	1994	1995	1996	1997	1998	1999	
ALL GOODS	6 448.8	8 931.3	9 234.3	8 926.5	8 283.3	9 366.6	
Manufactured Products	4 095.2	5 540.9	5 800.9	6 037.4	6 376.9	7 673.2	
Food and tobacco products	151.9	160.3	182.8	198.7	196.5	173.2	
Textile mill products	17.1	20.4	20.5	17.5	22.8	14.4	
Apparel	22.1	31.5	37.5	66.8	49.3	36.1	
Lumber and wood products	632.6	580.2	573.5	526.1	321.1	317.1	
Furniture and fixtures	6.8	6.4	7.4	9.2	11.3	14.6	
Paper products	211.4	313.2	348.8	338.8	265.5	318.8	
Printing and publishing	27.1	22.0	24.4	25.0	23.3	20.7	
Chemical products	41.6	55.4	68.8	87.1	186.8	509.2	
Refined petroleum products	21.2	22.4	22.3	18.4	20.5	28.4	
Rubber, plastic, and leather products	89.7	121.2	192.8	165.4	149.9	208.8	
Stone, clay, and glass products	20.1	21.9	32.3	41.2	34.9	71.5	
Primary metals	152.6	193.8	161.3	181.0	210.7	154.6	
Fabricated metal products	70.4	88.8	98.1	118.1	125.1	138.6	
Industrial machinery and computers	1 100.2	1 703.2	1 432.6	1 694.0	1 631.2	1 502.2	
Electric and electronic equipment	700.3	1 270.3	1 685.5	1 565.2	1 977.7	2 572.8	
Transportation equipment	366.0	389.2	317.8	407.1	686.8	1 067.2	
Scientific and measuring instruments	405.8	481.6	535.3	522.4	407.7	459.2	
Miscellaneous manufactures	45.0	47.6	39.7	33.1	27.5	31.6	
Unidentified manufactures	13.3	11.7	19.6	22.2	28.5	34.2	
Nonmanufactured Commodities	2 353.7	3 390.4	3 433.4	2 889.0	1 906.3	1 693.4	

Table E-2. Metropolitan Area Exports of Goods by Industry, 1994–1999 —*Continued*

(Millions of dollars.)

Industry	Rochester, NY						Exports of Goods, Manufactures, and Top Five Industry Groups, 1999 (Billions of dollars)
	1994	1995	1996	1997	1998	1999	
ALL GOODS	3 143.7	3 860.5	4 307.7	4 694.5	4 489.8	4 370.2	
Manufactured Products	3 078.9	3 789.0	4 243.0	4 635.1	4 424.8	4 272.3	
Food products	21.4	30.1	33.6	61.8	62.4	73.2	
Tobacco products	...	...	...	...	...	...	
Textile mill products	7.3	7.1	5.0	6.0	4.7	6.2	
Apparel	1.9	1.2	2.7	3.8	3.2	2.2	
Furniture and fixtures	3.7	2.4	2.9	4.2	6.3	4.0	
Paper and chemical products	227.2	281.0	308.3	299.8	328.8	333.3	
Printing, publishing, and lumber	14.2	64.9	57.8	16.1	29.7	41.3	
Refined petroleum products	0.4	1.1	0.5	0.8	0.7	0.7	
Rubber, plastic, and leather products	215.1	278.8	243.6	229.4	198.8	199.9	
Stone, clay, and glass products	30.7	25.7	25.4	25.5	32.9	34.0	
Primary metals	28.6	25.7	37.8	38.0	40.2	49.1	
Fabricated metal products	30.9	27.5	41.5	46.4	60.1	53.7	
Industrial machinery and computers	361.0	496.8	487.1	636.9	675.5	600.9	
Electric and electronic equipment, and scientific instruments	2 062.1	2 404.9	2 869.0	3 106.7	2 870.5	2 769.3	
Transportation equipment	57.7	118.2	100.5	126.0	77.8	70.6	
Miscellaneous manufactures	11.0	17.6	22.6	29.6	27.2	27.4	
Unidentified manufactures	5.7	5.8	4.6	4.2	5.9	6.4	
Nonmanufactured Commodities	64.7	71.5	64.7	59.4	64.9	97.9	

Industry	San Diego, CA						Exports of Goods, Manufactures, and Top Five Industry Groups, 1999 (Billions of dollars)
	1994	1995	1996	1997	1998	1999	
ALL GOODS	4 867.3	5 860.9	6 719.4	7 810.0	8 591.6	8 963.8	
Manufactured Products	4 754.0	5 752.9	6 583.0	7 649.4	8 444.4	8 712.4	
Food and tobacco products	209.0	185.6	137.1	172.1	183.9	224.4	
Textile mill products	22.4	21.0	29.8	36.3	41.8	49.9	
Apparel	98.6	111.2	128.4	115.7	97.1	115.7	
Lumber and wood products	134.9	64.5	76.9	83.8	103.3	116.3	
Furniture and fixtures	34.0	26.5	37.3	39.8	39.4	49.6	
Paper products	117.3	149.1	170.8	204.5	222.8	198.2	
Printing and publishing	65.9	57.5	55.2	65.6	93.1	59.5	
Chemical products	209.4	255.9	302.6	349.6	376.4	395.8	
Refined petroleum products	10.5	10.2	11.1	18.3	20.5	22.1	
Rubber and plastic products	208.5	257.6	316.4	324.6	267.5	323.5	
Leather products	18.5	23.3	29.2	22.0	21.5	19.9	
Stone, clay, and glass products	29.9	33.0	31.9	41.7	48.5	47.0	
Primary metals	134.4	170.9	188.5	216.1	206.7	217.2	
Fabricated metal products	141.9	167.7	222.1	187.1	229.1	222.4	
Industrial machinery and computers	989.8	1 066.9	1 237.6	1 295.9	1 539.5	1 584.5	
Electric and electronic equipment	1 432.0	2 122.6	2 489.7	3 078.5	3 318.8	3 480.0	
Transportation equipment	182.2	236.8	211.9	299.5	505.7	508.5	
Scientific and measuring instruments	470.1	490.8	552.9	618.0	654.5	606.0	
Miscellaneous manufactures	211.4	270.9	323.4	441.5	428.4	420.9	
Unidentified manufactures	33.3	30.8	30.2	38.8	46.2	51.0	
Nonmanufactured Commodities	113.3	108.0	136.4	160.6	147.3	251.4	

Table E-2. Metropolitan Area Exports of Goods by Industry, 1994–1999 —*Continued*

(Millions of dollars.)

Industry	San Francisco, CA						Exports of Goods, Manufactures, and Top Five Industry Groups, 1999 (Billions of dollars)
	1994	1995	1996	1997	1998	1999	
ALL GOODS	9 303.8	8 133.7	8 560.4	9 978.5	9 123.2	9 035.0	
Manufactured Products	8 781.5	7 532.3	8 066.6	9 508.3	8 676.6	8 349.8	
Food and tobacco products	1 032.4	957.5	896.9	836.5	771.8	710.6	
Textiles, tobacco, and furniture	153.0	134.5	152.6	134.6	136.2	154.6	
Apparel	266.8	279.7	298.1	345.3	287.3	247.7	
Lumber and wood products	29.0	39.9	39.8	36.5	39.2	42.5	
Paper products	175.5	184.8	150.8	157.9	149.2	147.9	
Printing and publishing	34.0	31.1	33.1	35.1	44.3	38.6	
Chemical and petroleum products	859.5	654.0	704.5	789.5	687.2	633.3	
Rubber and plastic products	95.6	49.0	63.1	79.3	75.6	112.0	
Leather products	16.6	14.9	15.1	10.8	5.8	6.8	
Stone, clay, and glass products	59.0	39.7	42.0	52.6	49.7	50.3	
Primary metals	171.5	179.3	223.7	283.6	147.8	139.9	
Fabricated metal products	168.3	129.9	153.5	150.3	166.8	129.8	
Industrial machinery and computers	1 652.0	882.8	1 309.0	1 727.0	2 016.4	2 148.3	
Electric and electronic equipment	1 393.3	1 491.0	1 620.5	2 170.1	2 040.8	1 916.6	
Transportation equipment	2 086.1	1 824.9	1 555.2	1 725.1	1 246.8	1 219.5	
Scientific and measuring instruments	384.1	420.8	609.6	787.0	665.1	543.7	
Miscellaneous manufactures	178.2	198.8	180.5	167.4	121.0	77.2	
Unidentified manufactures	26.8	19.8	18.6	19.5	25.5	30.4	
Nonmanufactured Commodities	522.3	601.3	493.8	470.3	446.6	685.2	

Industry	San Jose, CA						Exports of Goods, Manufactures, and Top Five Industry Groups, 1999 (Billions of dollars)
	1994	1995	1996	1997	1998	1999	
ALL GOODS	19 942.7	26 822.8	29 331.3	29 057.2	26 111.9	28 255.7	
Manufactured Products	19 709.1	26 597.6	29 047.9	28 791.1	25 868.0	27 612.8	
Food products	114.0	122.2	136.7	138.1	130.7	109.7	
Tobacco products	. . .	. . .	. . .	. . .	. . .	0.1	
Textile mill products	4.4	5.7	4.8	4.1	3.4	2.9	
Apparel	4.8	5.5	6.3	6.6	6.5	6.2	
Lumber and wood products	3.9	6.6	6.8	7.8	7.7	5.2	
Furniture and fixtures	11.6	15.5	13.5	15.6	22.0	8.2	
Paper products	15.2	29.6	37.4	47.2	52.0	32.5	
Printing and publishing	86.1	90.0	87.5	105.0	125.2	114.1	
Chemical products	206.0	209.2	231.5	252.2	228.0	233.3	
Refined petroleum products	4.1	1.3	0.7	1.6	1.1	0.5	
Rubber and plastic products	62.6	83.0	101.9	99.2	74.9	71.7	
Leather products	1.5	2.1	3.6	3.3	3.0	6.8	
Stone, clay, and glass products	16.9	20.6	28.2	35.0	24.8	43.4	
Primary metals	107.8	117.9	102.8	120.6	100.2	92.7	
Fabricated metal products	57.1	80.7	93.0	68.5	43.6	75.6	
Industrial machinery and computers	7 659.5	10 279.7	12 395.2	13 044.5	10 994.6	12 003.1	
Electric and electronic equipment	9 445.3	13 254.6	13 210.2	11 855.1	10 879.3	11 461.2	
Transportation equipment	123.6	160.1	149.5	211.7	172.9	122.5	
Scientific and measuring instruments	1 657.7	2 001.6	2 325.1	2 671.7	2 860.7	3 084.7	
Miscellaneous manufactures	71.9	62.9	65.3	51.7	59.7	50.7	
Unidentified manufactures	55.3	48.5	48.1	51.5	77.8	87.6	
Nonmanufactured Commodities	233.6	225.3	283.4	266.1	243.9	642.9	

Table E-2. Metropolitan Area Exports of Goods by Industry, 1994–1999 —*Continued*

(Millions of dollars.)

Industry	Seattle - Bellevue - Everett, WA						Exports of Goods, Manufactures, and Top Five Industry Groups, 1999 (Billions of dollars)
	1994	1995	1996	1997	1998	1999	
ALL GOODS	21 753.0	17 815.4	21 391.1	27 005.8	34 003.3	32 356.1	
Manufactured Products	19 703.6	15 661.9	19 430.0	25 266.1	32 644.9	30 566.0	
Food products	558.3	631.4	607.6	591.9	527.3	601.4	
Tobacco products	. . .	0.1	0.1	0.3	0.5	0.2	
Textile mill products	10.6	12.6	13.4	15.4	16.4	16.0	
Apparel	33.3	38.2	44.4	51.8	47.7	36.4	
Lumber and wood products	2 126.8	2 306.6	2 313.7	1 726.0	1 097.0	1 050.6	
Furniture and fixtures	14.9	18.8	18.1	22.7	20.9	28.3	
Paper, printing, and publishing	667.0	958.1	714.1	405.7	272.3	262.4	
Chemical products	71.0	84.2	82.7	109.4	103.2	113.8	
Refined petroleum products	22.9	38.5	94.5	63.4	46.9	36.3	
Rubber and plastic products	49.7	67.6	67.3	74.9	82.9	96.4	
Leather products	9.3	11.9	14.2	17.0	16.4	21.7	
Stone, clay, and glass products	36.2	39.0	37.5	39.8	31.3	31.7	
Primary metals	61.8	91.0	90.8	106.8	118.6	104.6	
Fabricated metal products	87.0	73.9	76.0	117.0	139.7	93.5	
Industrial machinery and computers	385.3	474.3	548.7	775.6	876.7	973.0	
Electric and electronic equipment	655.9	724.7	609.2	692.3	693.4	524.1	
Transportation equipment	14 352.9	9 472.9	13 289.2	19 574.7	27 679.1	25 632.6	
Scientific and measuring instruments	424.0	468.8	579.3	683.8	635.7	672.5	
Miscellaneous manufactures	120.5	131.0	211.6	177.5	211.2	240.8	
Unidentified manufactures	16.3	18.3	17.8	20.3	27.9	29.8	
Nonmanufactured Commodities	2 049.4	2 153.5	1 961.1	1 739.8	1 358.4	1 790.0	

Exports of Goods, Manufactures, and Top Five Industry Groups, 1999 (Billions of dollars) — Seattle - Bellevue - Everett, WA

Industry	St. Louis, MO - IL						Exports of Goods, Manufactures, and Top Five Industry Groups, 1999 (Billions of dollars)
	1994	1995	1996	1997	1998	1999	
ALL GOODS	3 673.3	3 997.7	4 497.4	4 711.5	4 315.5	4 879.2	
Manufactured Products	3 251.5	3 598.3	3 871.3	4 109.2	3 866.7	4 387.0	
Food products	147.7	207.5	239.4	342.4	464.3	482.4	
Tobacco products	. . .	. . .	. . .	. . .	. . .	. . .	
Textile mill products	5.6	9.6	9.6	8.1	9.5	10.5	
Apparel	35.3	41.8	43.3	40.6	31.2	26.5	
Lumber and wood products	12.3	13.0	11.5	8.9	13.5	11.4	
Furniture and fixtures	19.7	17.6	19.6	17.2	22.3	15.9	
Paper products	15.5	26.0	32.4	27.4	25.1	27.1	
Printing and publishing	31.6	46.3	43.4	61.4	71.1	70.7	
Chemical products	1 245.9	1 368.8	1 404.5	1 287.8	930.0	1 481.2	
Refined petroleum products	72.1	68.5	108.2	147.1	81.5	146.5	
Rubber and plastic products	102.9	113.8	116.4	174.3	162.1	162.2	
Leather products	5.5	6.7	9.2	16.3	15.3	10.2	
Stone, clay, and glass products	18.0	15.6	14.4	15.2	15.7	18.1	
Primary metals	101.6	141.0	152.1	179.5	156.3	135.7	
Fabricated metal products	171.9	133.9	117.1	156.3	164.2	163.6	
Industrial machinery and computers	377.8	445.2	497.0	573.7	601.9	648.6	
Electric and electronic equipment	337.1	355.6	403.3	416.8	393.8	404.1	
Transportation equipment	340.0	366.7	407.5	393.9	469.7	303.8	
Scientific and measuring instruments	183.9	197.3	219.5	217.7	205.2	239.5	
Miscellaneous manufactures	17.9	12.5	13.4	15.5	20.5	15.5	
Unidentified manufactures	9.4	10.9	9.6	9.0	13.8	13.3	
Nonmanufactured Commodities	421.8	399.4	626.2	602.3	448.8	492.2	

Exports of Goods, Manufactures, and Top Five Industry Groups, 1999 (Billions of dollars) — St. Louis, MO - IL

Table E-2. Metropolitan Area Exports of Goods by Industry, 1994–1999—*Continued*

(Millions of dollars.)

Industry	Stamford - Norwalk, CT						
	1994	1995	1996	1997	1998	1999	Exports of Goods, Manufactures, and Top Five Industry Groups, 1999 (Billions of dollars)
ALL GOODS	3 452.7	4 937.6	4 424.3	3 387.6	2 778.9	2 573.0	
Manufactured Products	2 403.4	3 576.4	3 095.1	2 727.2	2 325.6	2 251.8	
Food products	178.6	214.9	116.2	115.7	180.3	201.3	
Tobacco products	0.2	0.3	0.8	1.6	0.7	2.9	
Textile mill products	1.9	2.7	2.2	2.4	2.1	2.1	
Apparel	2.1	1.7	2.5	4.2	2.9	1.3	
Lumber and wood products	1.9	5.5	1.7	2.2	4.1	8.2	
Furniture and fixtures	2.0	2.1	2.1	4.9	6.2	3.9	
Paper, printing, and publishing	457.6	634.6	619.5	568.6	499.5	198.3	
Chemical products	826.9	1 188.2	1 233.9	1 121.8	832.9	842.5	
Refined petroleum products	435.2	551.4	490.3	435.3	375.3	391.3	
Rubber and plastic products	12.5	12.6	10.9	13.3	10.8	17.0	
Leather products	4.3	3.0	1.8	3.1	2.6	2.9	
Stone, clay, and glass products	3.9	4.1	5.1	2.9	2.1	5.4	
Primary metals	172.0	297.1	168.6	65.2	74.1	78.6	
Fabricated metal products	13.0	11.9	13.2	19.0	22.2	30.8	
Industrial machinery and computers	102.7	133.5	119.6	135.2	107.0	156.5	
Electric and electronic equipment	94.9	116.7	83.9	70.0	65.2	67.0	
Transportation equipment	35.6	262.2	152.9	70.1	31.6	19.2	
Scientific and measuring instruments	43.5	118.3	55.0	75.5	85.4	204.6	
Miscellaneous manufactures	8.9	6.1	6.6	7.2	7.7	6.8	
Unidentified manufactures	5.7	9.3	8.4	9.0	12.9	11.1	
Nonmanufactured Commodities	1 049.3	1 361.1	1 329.2	660.4	453.3	321.2	

Exports of Goods, Manufactures, and Top Five Industry Groups, 1999 (Billions of dollars) — Total Goods, Total Manufactures, Chemical products, Refined petroleum products, Scientific and measuring instruments, Food products, Paper printing and publishing

Industry	Washington, DC - MD - VA - WV						
	1994	1995	1996	1997	1998	1999	Exports of Goods, Manufactures, and Top Five Industry Groups, 1999 (Billions of dollars)
ALL GOODS	7 969.3	8 350.4	8 083.5	7 980.7	7 347.8	7 213.3	
Manufactured Products	7 558.8	7 968.9	7 784.0	7 791.5	7 140.2	6 927.4	
Food products	186.2	119.6	154.6	143.5	151.2	128.5	
Tobacco products	. . .	0.7	0.5	0.1	2.1	1.0	
Textile mill products	6.5	9.3	11.1	8.3	9.5	9.8	
Apparel	17.1	18.9	23.6	24.6	30.1	17.6	
Lumber and wood products	32.7	15.8	12.8	14.9	15.8	17.4	
Furniture and fixtures	18.5	13.7	17.8	20.5	13.2	14.0	
Paper products	15.1	16.0	13.2	12.5	22.3	23.1	
Printing and publishing	30.7	35.9	35.3	38.3	46.6	59.5	
Chemical and petroleum products	409.2	540.0	429.1	306.8	293.7	352.7	
Rubber and plastic products	44.2	57.4	100.6	105.8	131.2	56.1	
Leather products	1.6	2.4	1.2	1.1	2.0	1.5	
Stone, clay, and glass products	18.0	20.5	15.9	14.0	12.5	14.9	
Primary metals	29.6	40.6	32.2	66.6	182.0	280.8	
Fabricated metal products	781.7	1 024.5	534.0	550.6	823.7	597.6	
Industrial machinery and computers	633.8	675.9	637.2	781.9	674.1	696.3	
Electric and electronic equipment	619.6	843.5	733.1	983.6	1 182.6	1 214.0	
Transportation equipment	3 620.3	3 359.6	4 010.9	3 265.9	2 540.9	2 448.7	
Scientific and measuring instruments	371.9	422.4	280.0	726.5	464.1	464.1	
Miscellaneous manufactures	17.8	40.9	40.6	44.0	29.6	35.5	
Unidentified manufactures	704.3	711.3	700.3	681.9	513.1	494.4	
Nonmanufactured Commodities	410.5	381.6	299.5	189.3	207.6	286.0	

Exports of Goods, Manufactures, and Top Five Industry Groups, 1999 (Billions of dollars) — Total Goods, Total Manufactures, Transportation equipment, Electric and electronic equipment, Industrial machinery and computers, Fabricated metal products, Unidentified manufactures

Table E-2. Metropolitan Area Exports of Goods by Industry, 1994–1999 —*Continued*

(Millions of dollars.)

Industry	Wilmington - Newark, DE - MD						Exports of Goods, Manufactures, and Top Five Industry Groups, 1999 (Billions of dollars)
	1994	1995	1996	1997	1998	1999	
ALL GOODS	3 720.4	4 361.1	4 551.1	5 140.6	5 027.4	4 903.2	
Manufactured Products	3 631.3	4 248.6	4 442.1	5 043.6	4 945.4	4 820.0	
Food products	11.1	11.0	8.4	19.9	43.1	44.6	
Textile and paper products	189.5	159.0	165.1	254.1	210.7	199.2	
Apparel	2.5	1.8	2.8	3.6	3.9	1.7	
Lumber and wood products	7.9	10.7	8.4	4.0	3.3	3.3	
Furniture and fixtures	0.5	0.5	1.2	2.0	1.0	1.4	
Paper and chemical products	2 572.1	3 120.1	3 257.5	3 675.3	3 512.3	3 440.4	
Printing and publishing	2.1	1.9	2.3	2.3	3.5	11.0	
Refined petroleum products	1.7	1.2	2.2	1.7	3.0	9.4	
Rubber, plastics, stone, clay, and glass	308.2	419.6	438.4	528.7	457.5	406.5	
Leather products	0.6	0.3	0.2	0.5	0.3	0.3	
Fabricated metal products	34.6	31.0	24.8	13.6	10.5	12.6	
Industrial machinery and computers	69.8	77.6	82.9	113.9	146.3	169.3	
Electric and electronic equipment, and scientific instruments	299.9	324.5	305.7	286.7	374.8	385.2	
Transportation equipment	56.4	42.3	80.3	87.9	130.7	84.9	
Assorted manufactures	71.7	45.5	59.3	47.8	40.9	47.7	
Unidentified manufactures	2.8	1.6	2.7	1.6	3.5	2.6	
Nonmanufactured Commodities	89.1	112.5	109.0	97.0	82.0	83.2	

Table E-3. Metropolitan Area Exports of Goods by Destination, 1994–1999

(Millions of dollars.)

Destination	Akron, OH						Albany - Schenectady - Troy, NY					
	1994	1995	1996	1997	1998	1999	1994	1995	1996	1997	1998	1999
ALL DESTINATIONS	1 606.3	1 931.7	2 260.3	2 353.3	2 266.1	2 207.6	831.4	1 061.2	1 101.0	1 666.2	1 613.0	1 302.5
North America	885.2	1 006.7	1 184.8	1 270.9	1 345.7	1 371.1	489.2	704.6	715.0	1 140.6	1 120.4	887.3
Canada	778.9	895.9	1 067.6	1 134.3	1 193.9	1 200.8	483.9	696.9	704.3	1 123.9	1 104.7	853.8
Mexico	106.3	110.7	117.2	136.6	151.7	170.3	5.3	7.7	10.6	16.8	15.7	33.5
Caribbean And Central America	16.6	22.5	23.1	22.5	28.5	24.7	7.9	6.2	3.9	3.9	6.2	4.3
South America	96.2	156.1	193.5	212.6	174.8	125.4	21.9	27.7	27.4	27.6	30.5	32.1
Argentina	14.0	13.5	15.3	22.3	19.1	11.7	3.3	4.3	3.2	4.6	5.2	5.0
Brazil	37.1	57.0	96.9	92.0	77.3	55.4	11.6	10.5	16.0	14.4	15.8	17.3
Other South America	45.2	85.7	81.3	98.4	78.3	58.3	7.0	13.0	8.3	8.6	9.5	9.7
Europe	305.6	400.5	458.2	435.6	385.8	373.7	171.6	124.1	124.2	166.1	200.7	221.6
Belgium	41.7	65.4	116.5	107.1	85.8	37.0	2.1	2.1	2.2	2.5	6.4	10.5
France	35.2	44.6	48.1	48.9	40.7	43.6	14.3	20.9	11.9	10.5	15.6	15.2
Germany	63.8	79.8	74.5	63.7	57.8	76.6	9.5	8.5	11.1	9.6	12.6	15.7
Netherlands	23.2	24.4	15.4	10.1	6.4	17.0	98.6	30.8	34.5	45.1	37.8	81.7
United Kingdom	81.1	98.6	110.8	115.9	93.3	84.6	18.7	21.0	18.2	25.5	36.2	25.9
Turkey	1.9	2.9	5.6	8.6	9.4	13.3	0.6	0.2	0.5	1.4	0.4	0.6
Former Soviet Republics	1.9	3.7	2.2	1.8	1.2	1.3	2.2	6.0	8.8	12.3	10.9	8.3
Poland	0.8	0.5	1.5	3.3	1.9	1.3	0.3	0.1	0.2	0.2	0.4	0.1
Other Eastern Europe	1.5	1.4	3.3	1.8	6.2	4.0	0.2	0.2	0.5	0.8	0.4	1.4
Other Europe	54.5	79.3	80.2	74.4	83.1	94.9	25.1	34.3	36.1	58.3	79.9	62.1
Asia	217.0	256.7	304.3	322.0	246.2	243.5	109.4	170.2	202.0	265.1	219.7	140.7
Japan	102.2	108.3	109.4	113.5	101.7	81.4	28.5	33.1	44.2	33.0	32.7	17.6
China	10.5	6.3	17.2	28.0	14.8	17.4	4.5	9.2	14.0	12.3	16.1	18.2
Hong Kong	12.2	13.6	19.7	29.4	25.3	30.9	12.6	31.0	41.1	41.7	44.4	29.8
Taiwan	26.6	22.0	18.9	25.6	21.4	21.8	17.1	23.2	31.8	45.5	50.7	27.8
Singapore	7.6	10.7	16.9	12.4	10.5	9.9	8.4	12.1	13.7	19.7	18.7	7.0
South Korea	22.2	41.3	44.8	35.1	19.6	25.5	19.0	36.6	29.9	30.3	31.6	23.4
Indonesia	10.2	12.3	14.0	14.3	7.2	9.0	3.4	5.2	6.1	59.9	2.4	1.1
India	3.0	9.6	13.1	10.8	6.0	6.3	3.5	1.7	3.5	3.5	9.2	3.4
Other Asia	22.4	32.6	50.3	52.8	39.6	41.4	12.4	18.1	17.6	19.3	13.9	12.5
Africa	32.8	11.6	14.8	19.8	17.5	15.9	3.8	6.5	3.6	2.9	2.6	2.3
North Africa	21.3	3.3	3.3	4.8	5.7	5.1	0.6	3.1	0.8	1.4	1.1	1.0
Republic of South Africa	6.4	5.5	8.4	11.0	9.0	8.1	1.9	2.7	1.6	0.7	0.8	0.7
Other Subsaharan Africa	5.0	2.8	3.1	4.0	2.8	2.8	1.3	0.7	1.1	0.7	0.7	0.6
Middle East	34.6	48.8	40.9	40.4	36.9	32.5	11.8	8.2	10.0	44.2	17.5	5.9
Australia	18.2	28.8	40.8	29.4	30.8	20.7	15.8	13.7	15.0	15.8	15.4	8.4
Rest Of World	...	...	...	...	...	0.1	...	...	...	...	...	...

Destination	Albuquerque, NM						Allentown - Bethlehem - Easton, PA					
	1994	1995	1996	1997	1998	1999	1994	1995	1996	1997	1998	1999
ALL DESTINATIONS	335.5	270.1	740.3	1 564.6	1 694.4	2 714.9	1 371.1	1 492.8	1 477.2	1 808.9	1 535.0	1 203.4
North America	44.9	25.5	22.0	29.6	32.1	34.3	373.8	419.5	421.4	497.0	520.6	468.6
Canada	19.7	17.2	17.8	22.5	26.8	25.6	342.4	380.4	376.3	436.6	423.9	382.9
Mexico	25.2	8.3	4.2	7.1	5.3	8.6	31.4	39.2	45.1	60.3	96.6	85.7
Caribbean And Central America	1.5	3.4	1.5	6.8	11.7	40.5	15.5	18.4	30.5	27.2	27.4	31.6
South America	1.3	4.4	2.1	2.7	7.6	9.3	50.1	101.9	115.1	134.7	91.3	37.9
Argentina	0.3	0.9	0.3	0.6	0.9	1.1	4.6	3.6	5.3	10.4	9.9	5.3
Brazil	0.2	0.5	0.3	0.6	0.6	1.8	16.3	21.5	33.5	24.4	20.0	10.8
Other South America	0.8	3.0	1.4	1.5	6.1	6.4	29.3	76.8	76.3	99.9	61.4	21.7
Europe	105.8	80.2	85.4	121.3	92.9	156.2	328.7	358.6	303.8	381.1	348.1	251.6
Belgium	0.6	1.0	5.1	21.4	8.4	2.0	29.4	40.3	27.5	36.3	43.0	17.6
France	6.6	14.6	26.5	31.7	28.9	39.3	16.9	25.3	46.0	61.1	23.1	12.2
Germany	28.7	13.1	13.6	12.9	7.8	17.1	76.4	77.8	27.4	48.4	52.1	55.0
Netherlands	3.1	14.9	4.0	5.3	4.8	16.6	132.3	130.3	97.5	119.1	89.4	8.4
United Kingdom	44.7	23.7	7.8	10.4	11.2	15.2	27.3	27.6	38.2	52.6	62.9	90.4
Turkey	...	...	...	0.3	0.2	0.4	0.6	1.1	2.3	1.6	3.0	3.2
Former Soviet Republics	14.5	0.6	0.7	1.6	1.9	2.0	2.0	1.4	9.6	4.0	0.2	0.2
Poland	...	...	...	0.1	...	...	3.6	8.8	12.1	11.3	7.7	1.4
Other Eastern Europe	0.2	0.1	0.4	...	0.2	0.2	2.9	0.9	3.5	0.9	1.0	1.0
Other Europe	7.4	12.1	27.3	37.7	29.5	63.4	37.1	45.0	39.7	37.4	66.2	62.3
Asia	175.1	150.6	619.5	1 390.9	1 538.9	2 427.3	542.5	496.9	528.1	678.2	461.4	364.7
Japan	36.5	14.8	40.2	52.3	19.5	22.1	58.4	74.2	55.2	83.3	59.3	39.5
China	1.6	8.0	9.7	28.3	146.8	204.8	8.9	18.4	18.9	23.6	15.4	10.5
Hong Kong	19.1	13.3	9.7	7.7	6.5	11.5	14.8	24.9	18.0	17.2	21.9	26.1
Taiwan	6.4	13.1	53.1	103.0	49.7	66.0	16.4	24.3	28.7	38.0	16.2	15.1
Singapore	1.9	5.4	2.7	1.6	1.2	5.7	174.4	143.3	212.9	206.0	102.4	110.7
South Korea	67.4	56.7	183.5	195.9	374.2	778.9	45.3	50.3	34.7	40.9	12.4	16.1
Indonesia	...	...	...	0.1	...	0.3	2.5	27.4	31.7	61.7	7.6	1.7
India	0.4	0.2	0.6	1.6	0.3	0.2	7.0	3.7	6.6	5.6	12.8	1.7
Other Asia	41.8	39.0	320.0	1 000.5	940.7	1 337.8	214.9	130.4	121.2	201.9	213.5	143.3
Africa	1.5	0.3	0.7	0.9	4.0	1.6	18.0	14.2	12.4	17.2	17.6	11.4
North Africa	0.7	0.1	...	0.2	0.3	0.9	3.0	3.2	3.0	6.4	9.8	6.5
Republic of South Africa	0.2	0.1	0.3	0.6	3.4	0.5	5.5	5.7	6.0	6.8	5.4	3.3
Other Subsaharan Africa	0.6	0.1	0.4	0.1	0.3	0.3	9.5	5.3	3.5	4.0	2.5	1.6
Middle East	3.4	3.3	5.8	3.4	5.4	32.3	19.2	36.6	25.8	28.9	33.8	17.1
Australia	1.9	2.4	3.3	9.1	1.8	13.3	23.3	46.8	40.0	44.5	34.8	20.4
Rest Of World	...	...	0.1	...	...	...	...	...	0.2	...	...	...

Table E-3. Metropolitan Area Exports of Goods by Destination, 1994–1999—*Continued*

(Millions of dollars.)

Destination	Anchorage, AK						Appleton - Oshkosh - Neenah, WI					
	1994	1995	1996	1997	1998	1999	1994	1995	1996	1997	1998	1999
ALL DESTINATIONS	198.2	150.4	109.0	213.1	146.0	197.7	507.7	593.7	608.5	647.9	658.0	768.0
North America	15.9	32.4	19.8	141.2	89.4	109.3	357.7	402.8	363.1	374.8	354.8	421.8
Canada	15.8	32.4	19.7	141.1	89.3	107.0	320.2	367.5	339.9	343.0	314.2	379.9
Mexico	0.1	0.1	0.1	...	...	2.3	37.5	35.3	23.2	31.8	40.6	42.0
Caribbean And Central America	0.1	0.3	...	0.1	...	...	10.9	9.2	17.0	13.4	15.3	20.7
South America	0.6	0.5	0.3	0.4	0.4	0.3	19.3	23.8	29.4	42.9	45.8	62.3
Argentina	...	...	...	...	0.2	...	5.1	6.2	6.9	10.6	15.5	21.2
Brazil	...	...	...	0.1	...	0.1	3.9	3.2	4.8	5.1	7.4	10.2
Other South America	0.6	0.4	0.2	0.2	0.2	0.2	10.3	14.4	17.7	27.2	23.0	30.9
Europe	75.6	20.9	15.1	14.7	12.7	14.8	53.5	73.5	76.8	96.2	105.5	116.4
Belgium	...	...	0.1	...	...	0.1	1.2	2.8	1.9	4.0	2.5	3.5
France	4.1	...	0.1	0.4	0.4	0.1	4.5	3.6	3.8	6.2	11.7	10.6
Germany	0.4	0.2	0.2	0.6	0.4	2.1	7.9	14.8	15.1	13.7	19.7	11.6
Netherlands	0.1	0.2	0.2	0.2	0.4	0.3	6.9	6.6	8.4	14.8	16.7	21.9
United Kingdom	2.4	0.6	1.3	4.0	5.1	4.9	14.2	12.2	17.5	16.9	16.4	26.3
Turkey	...	...	...	...	...	0.3		0.7	0.8	3.2	1.4	1.2
Former Soviet Republics	37.4	16.3	12.3	7.6	5.4	3.4	0.2	0.6	0.3	0.3	0.2	0.1
Poland	...	...	...	...	...	...	...	0.3	0.1	0.1	2.1	4.2
Other Eastern Europe	0.7	0.1	...	...	...	...	0.2	1.5	1.1	0.5	0.8	2.1
Other Europe	30.4	3.5	0.9	1.9	0.9	3.6	18.4	30.3	27.8	36.4	34.0	34.9
Asia	102.8	96.2	73.6	56.1	43.4	71.9	40.7	39.6	79.0	72.6	73.1	87.4
Japan	54.7	38.2	21.8	11.3	11.6	30.1	3.4	3.8	7.6	7.1	24.6	32.7
China	7.9	0.2	4.2	0.3	0.2	0.2	6.3	4.1	6.1	7.1	7.5	9.1
Hong Kong	1.4	0.9	0.5	1.5	1.1	1.1	4.3	5.5	5.4	8.2	8.3	10.9
Taiwan	0.8	12.6	0.3	1.9	5.6	8.0	2.7	1.0	17.0	4.6	3.6	4.1
Singapore	0.4	0.3	0.3	0.8	1.9	1.7	5.3	5.5	15.7	14.9	4.5	8.7
South Korea	37.2	39.9	45.0	39.6	22.7	30.3	10.0	6.4	10.2	5.9	5.2	8.1
Indonesia	...	...	...	0.1	...	...	1.7	1.3	1.7	4.3	0.9	0.8
India	...	...	...	...	...	...	0.1	0.3	0.4	1.3	2.4	0.4
Other Asia	0.3	4.1	1.4	0.8	0.4	0.5	6.9	11.7	14.9	19.3	16.2	12.6
Africa	0.2	...	0.1	0.2	...	...	3.2	7.6	8.9	14.8	17.2	8.7
North Africa	...	...	0.1	...	...	...	0.4	1.5	1.7	7.4	9.4	3.3
Republic of South Africa	0.1	...	...	0.1	...	...	2.6	5.6	6.8	6.9	6.7	3.9
Other Subsaharan Africa	...	...	...	...	...	0.8	0.2	0.5	0.5	0.5	1.1	1.5
Middle East	2.9	...	...	0.4	...	0.5	9.0	19.4	19.7	14.4	32.7	34.1
Australia	0.1	0.1	...	0.1	...	...	13.4	17.8	14.5	18.9	13.6	16.5
Rest Of World	...	...	...	...	...	...	...	...	...	...	...	...

Destination	Asheville, NC						Atlanta, GA					
	1994	1995	1996	1997	1998	1999	1994	1995	1996	1997	1998	1999
ALL DESTINATIONS	228.6	185.2	236.7	294.2	233.0	268.6	4 739.1	5 811.4	5 891.5	6 604.6	7 904.6	7 574.5
North America	171.8	130.7	168.2	202.2	140.7	199.0	1 260.3	1 300.5	1 373.6	1 578.5	2 029.1	2 216.8
Canada	160.5	116.5	152.3	177.2	123.5	179.1	903.3	1 004.5	1 010.2	1 024.2	1 081.2	1 148.9
Mexico	11.3	14.2	15.9	25.0	17.2	19.9	357.0	296.0	363.4	554.3	947.9	1 067.9
Caribbean And Central America	0.8	0.9	0.6	2.6	2.0	2.2	325.0	399.5	380.6	431.4	494.5	424.4
South America	5.7	7.8	5.2	7.6	10.0	7.4	534.1	708.5	650.0	748.0	968.0	614.0
Argentina	0.5	0.1	0.2	1.0	0.7	0.6	182.3	134.7	105.1	126.2	168.1	98.1
Brazil	3.1	4.8	2.3	4.1	7.3	4.9	113.3	287.3	248.8	304.8	434.1	247.4
Other South America	2.1	2.9	2.7	2.4	2.0	1.9	238.5	286.5	296.0	317.0	365.8	268.4
Europe	28.9	28.3	41.7	51.5	56.6	40.8	1 346.0	1 549.9	1 678.2	1 914.3	2 540.0	2 223.3
Belgium	0.7	1.4	2.6	2.8	4.3	2.1	100.1	83.7	78.8	202.0	430.7	237.5
France	1.0	2.8	1.9	2.5	2.4	3.6	98.4	116.6	158.1	198.7	191.4	162.0
Germany	6.6	3.7	5.2	6.3	5.9	9.5	183.3	204.4	207.0	192.2	182.3	215.2
Netherlands	7.2	5.5	9.5	8.8	8.6	2.6	192.5	217.2	212.8	262.6	302.4	382.4
United Kingdom	6.4	8.9	14.3	16.7	19.7	11.7	284.1	347.0	305.3	358.2	879.9	772.8
Turkey	0.3	0.2	0.2	0.6	0.1	0.1	15.3	30.9	30.0	33.9	17.3	20.3
Former Soviet Republics	0.2	0.6	0.2	0.6	1.6	0.1	113.3	120.0	284.2	148.1	83.7	30.2
Poland	...	0.2	0.2	0.1	0.2	0.1	19.4	9.9	10.3	15.0	12.9	8.8
Other Eastern Europe	...	0.3	1.9	0.4	0.5	0.7	19.7	20.5	19.7	21.7	20.4	12.8
Other Europe	6.4	4.7	5.8	12.7	13.0	10.4	319.7	399.7	372.0	481.8	419.0	381.3
Asia	18.8	15.9	17.6	23.8	17.6	14.5	993.4	1 546.1	1 467.7	1 553.5	1 411.4	1 388.2
Japan	2.1	2.7	4.3	5.8	3.7	2.6	278.8	394.7	419.8	420.0	455.0	466.9
China	6.7	0.2	0.7	5.0	3.1	1.0	49.3	88.5	117.4	106.5	112.0	106.6
Hong Kong	2.1	2.9	1.1	1.6	1.9	1.7	137.0	200.5	220.3	242.1	183.1	178.3
Taiwan	0.7	0.9	0.8	1.4	1.5	1.6	114.8	119.6	99.2	109.9	116.6	90.4
Singapore	0.5	1.0	0.7	0.7	1.4	1.0	63.6	81.4	126.0	172.9	108.5	144.0
South Korea	4.5	4.8	4.5	3.9	2.9	2.8	121.2	377.0	154.3	125.9	92.9	87.2
Indonesia	0.8	0.5	1.8	0.1	0.2	0.5	56.6	29.7	64.9	69.4	38.4	42.0
India	0.1	0.3	1.0	1.3	1.1	0.9	59.6	84.6	78.3	89.6	92.5	82.4
Other Asia	1.3	2.7	2.6	4.0	1.7	2.5	112.5	170.1	187.7	217.1	212.4	190.5
Africa	0.4	0.4	1.4	1.1	0.8	0.5	90.9	104.8	115.5	118.2	123.7	91.9
North Africa	0.1	0.1	0.4	0.3	0.2	0.2	38.5	37.4	27.2	24.0	33.6	30.6
Republic of South Africa	0.3	0.3	0.9	0.3	0.2	0.2	35.3	57.1	64.2	61.6	52.0	28.5
Other Subsaharan Africa	...	...	0.1	0.5	0.4	...	17.1	10.2	24.1	32.6	38.1	32.8
Middle East	0.7	0.5	1.1	4.4	2.5	1.8	120.6	102.8	102.4	113.8	160.9	183.2
Australia	1.5	0.6	0.9	0.8	2.6	2.4	68.9	99.2	123.5	146.8	177.1	432.7
Rest Of World	...	...	...	...	...	...	...	...	...	...	...	...

Table E-3. Metropolitan Area Exports of Goods by Destination, 1994–1999—*Continued*

(Millions of dollars.)

Destination	Augusta - Aiken, GA - SC						Austin - San Marcos, TX					
	1994	1995	1996	1997	1998	1999	1994	1995	1996	1997	1998	1999
ALL DESTINATIONS	326.3	405.2	443.9	433.8	519.6	569.0	2 128.8	2 929.2	2 743.1	3 354.8	3 802.4	4 931.4
North America	124.5	158.0	207.4	219.8	232.8	227.9	327.7	369.9	472.8	719.7	875.3	1 138.4
Canada	105.4	142.2	188.0	199.9	208.8	188.4	281.3	334.6	417.2	607.7	720.5	853.0
Mexico	19.1	15.9	19.4	19.9	24.0	39.5	46.4	35.4	55.6	112.0	154.8	285.3
Caribbean And Central America	21.6	19.0	11.1	5.0	4.7	6.1	10.9	13.8	12.9	17.2	27.1	24.8
South America	11.3	34.6	19.8	13.2	36.6	18.5	21.8	31.3	30.2	34.8	61.7	43.7
Argentina	1.2	3.4	1.6	2.1	3.8	1.3	4.5	4.4	3.1	4.8	6.9	4.3
Brazil	7.8	19.4	11.8	4.2	9.1	4.8	6.3	10.0	6.8	10.1	17.3	20.8
Other South America	2.4	11.8	6.4	6.9	23.8	12.4	11.1	17.0	20.3	19.9	37.4	18.6
Europe	111.5	129.0	146.7	141.8	187.4	246.4	495.3	642.5	541.3	599.4	818.2	718.0
Belgium	8.9	20.4	14.9	6.9	16.3	43.0	14.5	29.5	10.2	8.1	11.6	12.5
France	36.2	40.2	26.8	28.5	48.2	71.2	30.8	51.6	31.9	50.6	100.1	72.6
Germany	14.2	12.1	18.6	23.5	13.4	24.4	51.4	111.9	112.5	154.3	181.1	143.7
Netherlands	6.1	6.2	5.9	11.5	9.8	6.5	18.2	19.2	24.6	28.5	27.6	34.7
United Kingdom	15.7	17.9	35.7	22.4	25.5	26.6	291.5	315.2	261.7	256.5	293.3	199.1
Turkey	1.1	0.3	1.1	0.7	0.4	0.4	0.5	1.0	1.6	3.2	2.0	3.1
Former Soviet Republics	. . .	0.3	0.7	0.5	1.2	1.2	1.5	0.8	1.0	1.4	1.6	1.7
Poland	0.2	0.7	1.8	1.7	3.4	6.3	1.3	0.9	0.8	0.3	0.8	1.3
Other Eastern Europe	0.5	0.4	1.2	1.5	3.0	5.7	2.5	1.9	3.9	2.4	3.6	2.8
Other Europe	28.5	30.5	39.9	44.7	66.3	61.2	82.9	110.6	93.2	94.1	196.4	246.5
Asia	41.7	37.2	35.9	33.4	36.1	42.1	1 204.9	1 781.0	1 604.3	1 909.8	1 936.5	2 949.2
Japan	12.2	16.2	14.7	9.7	12.5	18.3	150.2	303.8	343.8	372.8	287.1	242.0
China	1.6	1.8	0.6	1.1	1.1	6.2	7.0	20.8	48.7	69.9	59.8	112.4
Hong Kong	3.0	3.3	2.5	4.1	1.4	0.9	223.7	346.2	298.2	370.0	262.7	219.9
Taiwan	9.4	2.4	3.1	3.4	8.7	4.6	66.5	86.4	124.0	174.1	232.3	361.3
Singapore	0.6	2.0	2.8	5.5	4.5	3.4	166.4	188.7	146.9	202.7	258.8	292.3
South Korea	5.7	1.5	1.5	2.2	2.8	2.2	50.1	118.9	118.5	182.9	293.3	890.2
Indonesia	0.2	0.5	1.0	0.5	. . .	0.1	2.7	8.3	7.0	18.1	15.4	26.5
India	0.4	0.6	1.8	0.5	0.6	1.0	7.5	21.0	7.8	5.6	3.0	5.0
Other Asia	8.6	8.7	8.1	6.5	4.5	5.3	530.7	686.9	509.5	513.9	524.0	799.6
Africa	1.6	3.8	3.9	4.0	5.3	4.9	7.2	12.4	13.1	6.7	7.4	6.8
North Africa	0.2	1.0	0.9	0.5	0.7	0.5	3.4	9.3	2.2	2.2	1.5	2.7
Republic of South Africa	1.2	2.3	2.7	3.3	4.4	3.7	2.7	2.5	2.6	3.2	4.5	2.8
Other Subsaharan Africa	0.2	0.5	0.4	0.3	0.2	0.7	1.0	0.6	8.3	1.3	1.4	1.3
Middle East	3.4	9.2	4.6	8.3	7.2	4.6	46.3	62.2	50.5	41.1	56.9	24.5
Australia	10.7	14.4	14.4	8.3	9.4	18.6	14.7	16.1	18.1	26.2	19.4	26.0
Rest Of World	. . .	. . .	. . .	. . .	. . .	. . .	. . .	. . .	. . .	. . .	. . .	0.1

Destination	Bakersfield, CA						Baltimore, MD					
	1994	1995	1996	1997	1998	1999	1994	1995	1996	1997	1998	1999
ALL DESTINATIONS	780.4	730.5	721.3	835.6	695.3	419.4	1 869.0	2 209.2	2 110.4	2 171.3	2 331.0	2 328.1
North America	68.7	77.0	82.6	98.2	105.4	105.2	492.4	430.0	453.6	478.6	535.7	682.6
Canada	62.0	71.1	75.8	90.4	95.2	94.9	429.2	376.9	378.6	429.9	456.9	596.0
Mexico	6.7	6.0	6.8	7.7	10.2	10.4	63.2	53.1	75.0	48.7	78.8	86.6
Caribbean And Central America	1.5	2.2	2.4	2.7	4.8	3.7	52.8	38.1	38.8	34.1	57.7	40.3
South America	6.3	4.5	9.8	68.5	77.1	29.5	100.4	154.3	128.7	130.0	113.6	68.1
Argentina	3.9	1.0	2.1	0.4	0.2	0.1	13.9	17.6	14.4	14.9	9.8	8.8
Brazil	. . .	0.3	0.6	1.5	11.0	0.9	19.0	54.6	34.4	26.8	28.6	22.7
Other South America	2.3	3.1	7.2	66.6	65.8	28.5	67.4	82.1	79.9	88.4	75.2	36.6
Europe	88.7	113.3	137.7	119.0	133.3	95.0	667.1	894.7	788.7	752.4	890.7	937.0
Belgium	5.4	8.0	10.4	10.3	8.8	4.0	136.1	108.0	96.6	92.0	143.2	182.9
France	4.3	5.7	2.9	3.9	7.9	6.5	64.3	58.1	53.1	72.4	83.8	57.4
Germany	20.0	31.9	40.1	33.9	35.1	26.0	41.2	62.6	68.3	89.3	74.2	105.4
Netherlands	4.3	8.0	11.6	9.5	8.8	5.1	156.8	206.9	182.9	107.6	143.3	171.6
United Kingdom	15.7	12.1	17.8	10.5	11.8	5.2	128.1	218.1	192.9	184.8	209.1	160.2
Turkey	. . .	. . .	0.4	17.4	25.1	15.9	14.9	17.8	12.3	21.7	15.6	11.1
Former Soviet Republics	0.4	. . .	0.2	2.4	0.4	1.1	14.6	6.6	14.5	10.3	9.6	11.9
Poland	0.1	3.3	4.0	. . .	. . .	. . .	3.3	6.7	1.8	7.3	7.6	14.9
Other Eastern Europe	6.1	3.1	1.5	0.9	0.9	0.7	15.5	34.9	31.2	41.3	15.3	15.2
Other Europe	32.5	41.3	48.7	30.2	34.4	30.4	92.3	174.9	135.1	125.7	189.1	206.4
Asia	587.8	432.7	453.6	526.7	344.6	169.3	262.4	308.0	355.0	370.7	345.6	312.4
Japan	162.3	164.6	141.7	125.5	79.1	45.6	66.3	83.2	78.4	80.4	107.9	95.0
China	181.4	15.2	99.8	150.5	26.3	14.9	10.8	22.5	36.4	16.9	14.8	14.7
Hong Kong	13.8	13.8	15.6	14.0	32.4	8.3	22.8	23.4	26.6	27.6	35.9	27.3
Taiwan	37.7	25.3	21.2	25.1	31.0	16.0	45.1	36.5	42.0	39.8	34.7	36.1
Singapore	3.8	4.4	2.8	3.5	2.6	1.7	20.8	46.6	53.6	31.0	24.7	16.2
South Korea	70.6	73.7	71.5	79.5	80.0	28.9	30.0	33.6	43.0	48.6	31.6	48.7
Indonesia	71.4	80.7	68.2	76.8	35.7	23.9	7.3	4.8	15.7	15.2	8.2	4.6
India	1.0	12.9	0.3	4.4	7.4	4.7	6.6	10.2	11.8	8.0	8.3	9.9
Other Asia	45.6	42.0	32.6	47.4	50.2	25.3	52.8	47.1	47.5	103.3	79.4	60.0
Africa	20.7	92.5	25.1	6.7	5.7	3.9	115.1	137.3	207.2	206.1	159.8	106.1
North Africa	20.0	91.6	24.9	5.8	5.3	3.4	63.1	82.7	127.0	131.6	67.7	35.8
Republic of South Africa	0.5	0.6	0.2	0.3	0.3	0.3	40.6	42.8	67.9	58.3	73.6	27.9
Other Subsaharan Africa	0.2	0.3	0.1	0.7	0.1	0.1	11.4	11.8	12.3	16.3	18.5	42.4
Middle East	3.4	4.5	5.1	8.7	8.7	5.7	150.8	198.8	95.9	152.1	167.2	143.4
Australia	3.4	3.8	4.9	5.2	15.6	7.1	27.8	48.0	42.5	47.2	60.6	38.2
Rest Of World	. . .	. . .	. . .	. . .	. . .	. . .	. . .	. . .	. . .	. . .	0.1	. . .

Table E-3. Metropolitan Area Exports of Goods by Destination, 1994–1999—*Continued*

(Millions of dollars.)

Destination	Bellingham, WA						Benton Harbor, MI					
	1994	1995	1996	1997	1998	1999	1994	1995	1996	1997	1998	1999
ALL DESTINATIONS	210.7	253.5	275.4	316.7	256.4	328.7	368.8	369.3	317.2	260.6	275.9	286.8
North America	120.8	159.3	184.1	212.5	169.1	235.8	126.8	88.3	108.9	88.9	127.4	138.2
Canada	117.6	155.8	179.7	210.4	166.7	232.8	66.9	79.2	80.8	79.3	119.3	123.2
Mexico	3.2	3.4	4.5	2.1	2.3	3.0	59.9	9.1	28.1	9.5	8.0	15.0
Caribbean And Central America	0.9	0.2	0.7	0.6	1.9	1.3	1.8	3.8	0.8	0.2	1.0	0.4
South America	1.9	10.6	5.9	7.0	6.9	3.1	9.5	9.8	6.1	6.6	6.2	9.1
Argentina	0.9	0.8	0.8	2.1	2.7	0.8	3.5	1.5	0.5	0.6	0.2	0.6
Brazil	0.2	4.0	2.3	1.3	1.9	0.2	4.8	6.7	4.7	3.5	2.7	6.0
Other South America	0.7	5.8	2.8	3.6	2.3	2.2	1.3	1.6	0.9	2.5	3.2	2.5
Europe	23.9	18.1	14.8	25.3	19.0	20.3	123.6	129.0	70.8	64.7	63.7	65.6
Belgium	4.0	3.7	3.0	3.7	1.3	1.3	1.4	1.9	0.7	3.4	3.8	3.2
France	1.6	1.6	0.8	1.4	0.8	1.4	59.8	54.4	18.6	10.5	12.3	12.0
Germany	1.7	2.6	2.7	2.9	1.6	2.2	22.0	22.0	10.2	8.6	8.1	5.5
Netherlands	0.3	0.8	0.3	2.6	1.7	3.6	6.4	11.0	14.5	12.9	12.1	16.9
United Kingdom	1.8	2.3	2.3	5.1	7.8	8.1	13.8	21.3	10.8	15.5	12.1	18.0
Turkey	...	...	...	...	...	...	0.1	0.5	0.5	0.9	1.8	0.4
Former Soviet Republics	3.3	1.0	0.6	...	...	...	0.8	0.2	0.2	0.1	...	0.1
Poland	...	...	0.1	0.1	...	0.1	0.4	0.4	0.8	0.3	0.8	0.2
Other Eastern Europe	0.1	0.1	0.1	...	...	0.1	5.4	0.5	0.7	0.8	0.5	0.6
Other Europe	11.0	5.9	4.9	9.4	5.8	3.4	13.5	16.6	13.8	11.8	12.1	8.6
Asia	57.3	51.0	57.8	63.4	46.2	55.0	72.4	102.4	85.7	65.9	39.1	42.6
Japan	40.3	40.8	37.2	37.8	31.5	32.8	25.0	21.4	18.1	10.0	10.5	9.6
China	0.5	1.7	7.9	8.7	3.6	3.0	3.2	2.1	1.2	0.7	3.3	1.4
Hong Kong	1.5	1.7	2.6	2.3	1.4	2.7	5.5	18.6	7.0	2.8	1.5	2.8
Taiwan	1.4	1.2	1.3	2.6	3.8	4.6	17.6	26.9	22.0	16.1	8.1	8.4
Singapore	0.7	0.8	2.4	1.4	1.3	1.5	1.7	2.6	4.7	1.9	1.6	3.1
South Korea	3.9	1.0	2.6	2.0	1.9	5.3	16.0	18.0	24.4	24.2	8.4	10.2
Indonesia	0.5	0.4	0.1	0.9	...	0.2	0.3	1.0	0.8	0.7	0.0	0.2
India	0.5	1.1	...	...	0.1	0.1	0.5	2.4	2.1	1.6	0.7	1.9
Other Asia	8.0	2.2	3.8	7.5	2.7	5.0	2.7	9.4	5.4	8.0	5.0	5.0
Africa	0.1	0.2	0.2	0.4	0.5	0.3	6.7	6.5	7.8	5.5	6.7	4.4
North Africa	...	0.1	...	...	0.4	0.2	0.6	0.6	0.5	0.4	0.4	0.7
Republic of South Africa	0.1	...	0.1	0.2	0.1	0.1	5.7	5.3	7.1	5.0	6.3	3.6
Other Subsaharan Africa	...	0.1	...	0.2	...	...	0.4	0.6	0.3	0.1	0.1	0.1
Middle East	0.9	0.9	1.0	1.0	1.2	1.5	13.8	13.0	17.3	13.2	13.7	9.6
Australia	4.8	13.3	10.9	6.5	11.7	11.5	14.1	16.5	19.6	15.6	18.1	17.0
Rest Of World	...	...	...	...	...	...	...	...	0.1	...	...	...

Destination	Bergen - Passaic, NJ						Binghamton, NY					
	1994	1995	1996	1997	1998	1999	1994	1995	1996	1997	1998	1999
ALL DESTINATIONS	4 387.0	4 784.0	4 499.9	4 789.8	4 228.6	4 181.5	474.9	558.1	443.3	513.3	440.2	524.5
North America	960.6	779.6	818.5	992.0	1 063.8	929.1	207.8	259.7	233.0	243.9	208.8	258.1
Canada	588.7	662.4	678.8	779.3	830.6	711.0	196.8	251.1	224.8	231.4	197.9	249.3
Mexico	371.9	117.2	139.8	212.7	233.1	218.0	11.0	8.6	8.2	12.6	10.9	8.8
Caribbean And Central America	120.2	184.4	153.6	122.1	125.7	119.6	2.3	2.0	1.4	1.9	1.4	1.0
South America	262.4	308.3	316.1	360.1	269.0	211.1	18.7	15.5	16.4	17.7	10.2	9.2
Argentina	60.7	35.0	42.8	47.5	39.4	31.5	3.3	2.6	2.4	3.0	3.1	2.5
Brazil	82.7	121.1	131.3	139.8	108.6	75.6	11.6	10.4	12.3	11.0	4.1	4.7
Other South America	119.0	152.1	142.0	172.7	121.0	104.1	3.8	2.5	1.7	3.7	3.0	2.1
Europe	1 343.9	1 552.5	1 336.2	1 347.4	1 297.0	1 287.5	106.6	129.2	96.8	126.6	121.7	117.4
Belgium	165.8	193.3	163.3	161.0	178.3	191.3	1.0	1.3	5.7	10.5	8.6	1.9
France	142.9	194.9	177.5	210.7	233.2	300.4	24.4	22.5	18.1	16.0	20.4	12.0
Germany	143.4	218.2	148.4	124.2	175.4	172.7	16.2	22.5	18.0	23.2	23.8	20.4
Netherlands	200.0	161.4	146.6	157.4	141.0	74.7	4.0	4.8	3.4	1.7	3.0	2.6
United Kingdom	301.3	308.7	276.0	248.2	268.3	296.4	11.2	37.0	28.9	48.7	38.2	39.1
Turkey	10.5	17.6	11.3	16.4	11.7	11.1	8.5	13.9	0.3	0.1	0.5	0.1
Former Soviet Republics	26.1	32.3	28.5	37.9	21.1	14.6	0.8	0.3	0.3	0.9	1.0	0.7
Poland	3.0	8.3	7.1	3.6	5.6	4.3	0.5	0.2	1.3	...	0.1	3.2
Other Eastern Europe	9.7	13.2	24.1	25.5	13.1	17.4	0.3	1.3	1.4	0.9	...	7.2
Other Europe	341.2	404.5	353.4	362.5	249.4	204.5	39.8	25.4	19.4	24.7	25.9	30.2
Asia	1 442.2	1 688.5	1 628.8	1 714.2	1 242.6	1 406.0	127.1	141.5	83.3	115.6	88.9	134.2
Japan	343.5	375.5	401.4	486.2	410.0	525.2	25.3	12.4	11.0	7.3	11.3	24.5
China	57.3	88.2	94.0	96.4	110.3	68.6	14.7	23.2	17.5	47.1	23.4	36.8
Hong Kong	66.9	92.8	81.4	96.7	92.7	89.7	5.3	10.4	9.0	16.0	14.8	8.3
Taiwan	139.8	143.4	100.3	95.7	84.7	84.9	9.8	24.3	11.9	11.9	10.6	25.2
Singapore	105.3	95.7	80.0	96.3	62.3	80.3	14.3	19.8	14.9	9.4	9.2	14.9
South Korea	627.3	745.3	713.4	718.9	378.3	403.4	29.9	16.6	5.5	5.4	1.4	3.6
Indonesia	15.4	22.1	28.0	20.1	12.1	15.8	1.8	2.8	3.1	1.9	2.9	0.1
India	21.6	30.7	25.9	16.2	15.0	18.7	3.3	3.8	0.4	3.9	0.3	1.4
Other Asia	65.0	94.7	104.4	87.7	77.2	119.5	22.8	28.2	10.1	12.7	15.1	19.2
Africa	39.1	47.9	45.8	50.6	36.6	33.1	3.4	4.1	3.5	1.9	2.4	1.0
North Africa	11.8	11.2	11.5	17.9	13.5	11.8	2.3	1.9	1.6	0.9	2.1	0.2
Republic of South Africa	15.6	21.5	22.4	20.3	14.6	12.3	0.9	1.5	1.8	0.9	0.3	0.7
Other Subsaharan Africa	11.7	15.2	11.8	12.3	8.5	9.0	0.2	0.7	...	...	...	...
Middle East	167.9	161.9	144.3	151.1	143.9	135.0	2.6	2.7	4.8	3.3	2.7	1.6
Australia	50.7	60.9	56.4	52.3	50.1	60.1	6.4	3.4	4.1	2.4	4.0	2.1
Rest Of World	...	...	0.1	...	...	...	...	...	...	...	...	...

Table E-3. Metropolitan Area Exports of Goods by Destination, 1994–1999—*Continued*

(Millions of dollars.)

Destination	Bloomington, IN						Boston, MA - NH					
	1994	1995	1996	1997	1998	1999	1994	1995	1996	1997	1998	1999
ALL DESTINATIONS	115.7	127.6	198.8	166.8	75.3	85.2	7 095.3	7 902.7	8 715.8	9 570.6	9 556.3	10 427.0
North America	46.0	30.9	36.9	34.3	23.7	32.0	1 523.5	1 488.8	1 640.5	1 605.9	1 711.7	1 930.4
Canada	43.3	29.4	34.8	32.8	21.7	31.3	1 189.5	1 355.7	1 465.4	1 408.3	1 488.8	1 540.9
Mexico	2.6	1.5	2.1	1.5	2.0	0.6	334.1	133.1	175.1	197.6	222.9	389.5
Caribbean And Central America	0.2	0.4	0.4	0.3	1.1	0.9	86.7	94.1	101.2	98.2	101.4	96.8
South America	3.0	1.7	4.0	3.2	1.0	1.6	253.2	293.9	301.2	341.6	320.5	327.3
Argentina	. . .	. . .	0.3	. . .	. . .	. . .	53.1	42.5	36.9	43.9	39.3	57.1
Brazil	2.4	1.4	2.1	2.0	0.8	1.4	95.2	123.7	158.5	165.0	142.8	163.1
Other South America	0.6	0.2	1.5	1.3	0.3	0.2	104.8	127.8	105.8	132.6	138.4	107.1
Europe	9.8	16.2	28.1	26.2	18.0	18.4	3 102.3	3 492.1	3 728.5	3 862.4	4 124.9	4 275.2
Belgium	0.2	0.6	0.5	0.5	0.1	. . .	133.6	196.6	349.6	298.6	208.6	177.6
France	0.4	1.9	1.1	1.4	1.4	1.1	331.0	339.5	415.7	399.3	413.7	535.8
Germany	0.8	0.8	0.3	0.4	1.4	1.1	497.6	601.7	693.3	588.7	631.1	615.6
Netherlands	1.1	2.0	0.1	0.9	1.3	1.0	486.0	481.3	418.9	663.4	704.8	779.4
United Kingdom	0.6	1.6	0.4	0.5	1.4	1.1	698.0	808.3	863.9	893.8	1 058.5	1 075.2
Turkey	0.1	. . .	. . .	. . .	0.5	. . .	11.2	15.8	28.1	34.0	27.0	33.5
Former Soviet Republics	. . .	. . .	. . .	. . .	. . .	. . .	42.8	38.9	32.2	43.5	30.7	13.3
Poland	. . .	. . .	. . .	0.3	2.0	. . .	12.7	19.3	21.2	20.3	21.4	21.1
Other Eastern Europe	. . .	. . .	. . .	. . .	. . .	. . .	23.1	25.7	23.6	23.0	21.7	30.6
Other Europe	6.6	9.3	25.6	22.1	9.9	14.0	866.3	964.9	882.0	897.9	1 007.3	993.2
Asia	48.7	68.0	125.9	94.6	24.6	21.1	1 764.5	2 117.1	2 453.3	3 171.7	2 834.6	3 302.9
Japan	11.4	10.9	15.2	9.2	11.8	9.0	718.5	806.9	907.5	1 139.2	1 144.6	1 193.3
China	11.2	33.3	88.2	54.1	1.7	3.3	73.3	80.0	95.9	90.2	111.2	144.9
Hong Kong	11.2	6.9	11.8	17.0	2.7	2.5	182.7	233.4	234.9	341.4	281.4	261.6
Taiwan	0.1	0.6	0.9	1.1	0.7	1.0	222.2	242.9	277.6	382.6	388.7	539.8
Singapore	6.5	2.2	3.3	2.4	1.3	1.7	208.2	206.7	292.0	394.0	330.1	378.1
South Korea	0.9	2.9	2.4	2.2	3.2	2.1	182.5	239.6	305.5	386.5	231.0	318.1
Indonesia	. . .	0.1	. . .	0.4	. . .	. . .	22.1	22.5	31.9	27.6	13.0	14.9
India	. . .	0.1	. . .	0.1	0.1	. . .	36.8	39.9	33.6	42.0	44.4	34.3
Other Asia	7.4	11.0	4.0	8.0	3.1	1.5	118.2	245.2	274.4	368.2	290.1	417.9
Africa	0.2	1.4	0.2	0.4	0.1	0.4	53.9	65.9	81.1	87.4	83.6	87.1
North Africa	0.2	0.9	0.2	. . .	. . .	. . .	15.9	15.8	11.2	15.6	22.9	19.8
Republic of South Africa	. . .	. . .	. . .	. . .	. . .	0.2	32.2	41.5	47.2	56.6	45.3	60.3
Other Subsaharan Africa	. . .	0.5	. . .	0.3	0.1	0.2	5.8	8.6	22.7	15.1	15.5	6.9
Middle East	3.8	5.3	0.9	2.6	1.4	5.7	121.6	143.1	187.0	215.0	208.6	224.6
Australia	4.1	3.6	2.4	5.2	5.5	5.0	189.6	207.6	223.1	188.5	170.6	182.7
Rest Of World	. . .	. . .	. . .	. . .	. . .	. . .	0.1	. . .	. . .	. . .	0.3	. . .

Destination	Bridgeport, CT						Brownsville - Harlingen - San Benito, TX					
	1994	1995	1996	1997	1998	1999	1994	1995	1996	1997	1998	1999
ALL DESTINATIONS	918.8	952.9	788.6	981.4	895.0	795.3	2 113.4	2 245.9	2 612.6	2 697.1	2 421.3	2 571.4
North America	188.3	170.4	194.5	237.3	212.8	181.9	2 060.9	2 178.1	2 560.9	2 634.0	2 301.2	2 448.6
Canada	115.2	133.9	148.3	170.9	161.9	151.4	133.9	453.1	372.9	467.8	361.8	397.7
Mexico	73.1	36.5	46.2	66.4	50.9	30.6	1 927.0	1 725.0	2 188.0	2 166.3	1 939.4	2 050.9
Caribbean And Central America	48.7	70.8	78.3	186.5	131.8	101.0	19.0	21.6	13.6	14.3	18.2	39.7
South America	49.9	40.6	20.4	22.1	32.0	17.8	2.0	3.0	1.5	6.6	4.4	4.5
Argentina	19.1	3.4	2.1	1.1	2.0	1.1	0.1	0.2	0.2	0.4	1.0	1.2
Brazil	11.4	12.8	10.2	13.1	10.4	9.4	0.5	0.5	0.3	1.7	1.1	1.5
Other South America	19.3	24.4	8.1	7.9	19.6	7.4	1.4	2.3	1.0	4.5	2.3	1.8
Europe	364.2	409.0	281.3	278.5	235.9	341.8	18.3	24.9	20.5	24.0	70.4	53.7
Belgium	16.9	6.4	4.2	4.6	4.3	5.5	. . .	0.2	0.8	0.7	0.6	0.4
France	9.0	13.5	15.0	9.2	11.2	14.1	1.2	3.8	1.0	1.3	9.1	8.2
Germany	47.6	51.0	25.7	37.2	42.6	36.2	2.8	3.2	5.7	7.6	13.1	12.1
Netherlands	16.4	16.2	13.2	24.5	15.8	16.8	0.7	2.2	1.9	2.4	7.4	2.0
United Kingdom	82.3	82.9	118.6	125.8	46.1	41.2	7.8	8.6	6.4	7.1	12.6	13.5
Turkey	74.4	15.4	16.4	9.1	10.3	178.0	. . .	. . .	0.1	0.1	0.2	. . .
Former Soviet Republics	1.3	2.2	2.0	1.2	1.2	0.8	. . .	. . .	. . .	. . .	. . .	. . .
Poland	0.4	0.7	4.4	0.4	0.5	0.7	0.4	. . .	. . .	0.1	0.1	. . .
Other Eastern Europe	0.8	0.6	0.5	3.0	8.6	2.9	. . .	0.5	0.1	0.1	0.2	. . .
Other Europe	115.2	220.1	81.3	63.6	95.4	45.6	5.2	6.3	4.5	4.6	27.3	17.4
Asia	214.3	216.6	169.3	229.8	247.1	125.4	10.3	15.8	13.1	14.3	23.0	22.0
Japan	27.9	23.6	29.1	18.0	17.1	15.2	0.6	2.2	3.1	2.4	4.0	4.4
China	8.1	8.3	5.4	6.2	21.2	8.9	1.5	1.1	0.1	0.2	1.0	1.0
Hong Kong	16.0	26.7	20.6	15.0	10.0	9.9	0.4	1.0	0.9	2.3	6.3	5.9
Taiwan	15.3	16.9	9.3	6.8	77.0	10.7	1.0	1.8	0.4	1.0	0.9	1.5
Singapore	11.9	8.9	6.4	7.5	2.9	4.9	0.6	1.8	4.1	5.4	7.5	1.1
South Korea	107.2	104.9	80.1	108.5	78.1	47.3	4.1	3.9	2.4	2.1	0.9	3.7
Indonesia	2.6	2.0	1.2	1.5	1.0	0.2	. . .	. . .	0.4	. . .	. . .	. . .
India	2.9	3.1	1.7	1.6	1.9	1.4	. . .	0.6	0.5	0.1	0.3	0.1
Other Asia	22.4	22.3	15.5	64.7	37.8	26.9	2.0	3.4	1.1	0.8	2.0	4.3
Africa	8.6	3.6	4.3	3.2	9.2	6.7	0.2	0.7	1.0	2.5	2.2	1.8
North Africa	6.6	2.3	3.1	0.7	7.5	2.2	. . .	. . .	. . .	0.3	0.5	0.2
Republic of South Africa	1.8	1.2	0.9	2.4	1.4	1.5	0.1	. . .	. . .	0.3	0.1	. . .
Other Subsaharan Africa	0.2	0.1	0.3	0.1	0.2	3.1	0.1	0.7	1.0	2.0	1.6	1.5
Middle East	10.5	15.9	16.4	10.7	13.4	9.2	1.4	0.9	1.1	0.7	0.9	0.3
Australia	34.3	26.0	24.1	13.3	12.9	11.4	1.1	1.1	0.9	0.7	1.0	0.8
Rest Of World	. . .	. . .	. . .	. . .	. . .	. . .	. . .	. . .	. . .	. . .	. . .	. . .

Table E-3. Metropolitan Area Exports of Goods by Destination, 1994–1999—*Continued*

(Millions of dollars.)

Destination	Buffalo - Niagara Falls, NY						Canton - Massillon, OH					
	1994	1995	1996	1997	1998	1999	1994	1995	1996	1997	1998	1999
ALL DESTINATIONS	1 569.7	2 295.8	2 262.2	2 667.3	2 222.7	2 225.4	315.9	377.2	406.0	421.6	359.5	339.3
North America	1 051.0	1 702.5	1 638.7	1 943.7	1 588.4	1 563.5	156.5	178.6	193.6	203.8	192.8	194.8
Canada	997.7	1 660.3	1 599.5	1 881.1	1 466.8	1 438.4	128.2	170.5	174.3	195.6	184.1	185.6
Mexico	53.3	42.2	39.1	62.7	121.6	125.0	28.3	8.1	19.3	8.2	8.8	9.2
Caribbean And Central America	5.5	7.6	6.0	8.7	8.4	7.9	3.0	3.2	2.2	2.6	5.4	3.5
South America	32.5	80.0	63.3	77.1	56.5	48.3	32.0	22.4	33.2	41.2	42.9	22.8
Argentina	4.8	6.4	7.1	15.8	12.1	14.8	2.7	1.3	7.3	8.5	8.4	0.4
Brazil	9.9	23.1	25.9	32.7	25.2	17.3	20.6	11.7	13.7	24.3	30.2	21.1
Other South America	17.8	50.4	30.3	28.7	19.2	16.2	8.7	9.4	12.2	8.4	4.4	1.3
Europe	202.9	200.0	238.8	278.1	284.5	287.9	52.5	72.6	79.0	63.3	56.7	62.8
Belgium	12.8	18.6	27.5	19.0	14.3	12.0	0.8	1.7	1.6	1.1	0.3	0.4
France	18.7	19.2	20.4	28.1	34.2	39.2	11.8	12.8	9.8	9.3	9.4	6.4
Germany	29.5	33.3	41.7	59.6	57.2	59.5	8.0	19.4	34.7	20.2	18.3	18.0
Netherlands	7.9	9.9	8.4	7.7	8.7	12.5	7.6	9.7	7.0	5.6	5.1	8.4
United Kingdom	38.6	38.8	54.1	65.2	73.3	62.1	13.0	16.8	14.4	14.9	10.9	10.6
Turkey	3.2	3.3	8.4	5.0	4.8	3.2	0.2	0.9	0.6	0.3	0.1	5.0
Former Soviet Republics	11.2	5.2	0.6	1.8	2.7	3.0	0.5	. . .	0.1	0.2	1.3	0.6
Poland	0.3	0.8	5.5	2.9	2.7	2.1	. . .	. . .	. . .	. . .	1.4	1.2
Other Eastern Europe	2.1	2.6	4.7	2.8	4.3	4.3	0.8	0.1	0.1	0.1	1.1	2.8
Other Europe	78.6	68.2	67.6	86.2	82.4	90.1	9.8	11.0	10.7	11.5	8.9	9.5
Asia	228.3	267.1	267.3	308.9	235.5	256.5	43.0	71.0	70.1	81.4	34.0	33.3
Japan	77.0	93.0	86.8	95.0	82.1	97.9	2.0	2.4	4.7	3.3	5.7	1.7
China	14.6	19.2	12.5	32.5	18.1	13.1	6.2	9.9	6.0	20.6	10.6	6.5
Hong Kong	18.8	21.0	22.2	28.0	28.0	24.8	1.7	8.4	6.4	14.1	1.3	6.8
Taiwan	30.6	22.9	24.1	23.1	20.0	30.4	2.0	3.7	2.4	0.8	1.0	1.9
Singapore	21.6	19.3	18.3	18.7	18.0	12.7	0.8	1.2	1.4	0.6	0.8	2.3
South Korea	32.0	47.9	60.4	54.7	18.2	26.0	6.4	13.3	6.3	3.4	3.2	3.7
Indonesia	6.5	9.4	6.4	4.0	2.9	4.0	3.4	11.1	13.2	12.6	0.7	0.6
India	4.7	4.6	5.8	14.1	13.5	6.7	0.9	2.9	5.8	5.1	3.2	1.6
Other Asia	22.6	29.8	30.9	38.9	34.7	41.0	19.7	18.2	24.0	21.1	7.6	8.2
Africa	14.5	10.4	13.1	14.6	10.2	10.1	10.3	10.0	10.9	13.6	11.6	10.9
North Africa	1.8	1.5	1.7	1.5	2.3	2.3	0.2	0.3	0.2	0.5	1.6	0.7
Republic of South Africa	11.3	8.2	10.0	11.7	7.3	6.9	9.5	9.0	10.0	12.4	9.4	9.3
Other Subsaharan Africa	1.3	0.6	1.4	1.4	0.6	0.9	0.7	0.7	0.7	0.8	0.6	1.0
Middle East	19.9	15.4	20.9	21.7	23.8	25.6	3.6	2.0	2.1	2.2	4.4	3.7
Australia	15.1	12.9	14.1	14.3	15.3	25.5	15.1	17.5	15.0	13.4	11.8	7.5
Rest Of World	. . .	. . .	. . .	. . .	. . .	. . .	. . .	. . .	. . .	. . .	. . .	. . .

Destination	Charleston - North Charleston, SC						Charlotte - Gastonia - Rock Hill, NC - SC					
	1994	1995	1996	1997	1998	1999	1994	1995	1996	1997	1998	1999
ALL DESTINATIONS	388.5	501.6	595.1	827.6	837.9	985.7	1 782.8	2 088.0	2 291.3	2 588.8	2 628.9	2 751.0
North America	106.6	140.3	122.9	197.4	255.2	250.8	714.0	806.2	838.0	997.1	1 051.4	1 120.7
Canada	71.9	96.9	99.0	169.6	162.5	157.9	559.5	682.0	683.3	819.6	767.6	818.1
Mexico	34.7	43.4	24.0	27.8	92.7	92.9	154.5	124.3	154.7	177.5	283.9	302.6
Caribbean And Central America	4.5	12.7	6.2	15.2	19.6	19.9	26.9	50.2	55.3	71.0	97.3	98.4
South America	12.0	33.7	32.5	85.0	91.4	102.2	116.2	157.5	168.6	193.9	187.9	145.2
Argentina	1.8	2.0	5.2	15.9	15.8	3.9	14.6	11.2	28.6	20.5	18.0	15.5
Brazil	1.7	14.6	9.6	40.4	46.4	75.5	43.0	65.2	65.5	90.9	74.9	56.3
Other South America	8.5	17.2	17.7	28.7	29.1	22.8	58.6	81.1	74.5	82.4	94.9	73.4
Europe	148.9	150.1	190.8	251.6	271.8	292.3	453.6	495.4	579.1	686.8	718.5	790.3
Belgium	8.7	12.4	18.7	27.5	36.8	47.4	91.7	103.3	117.1	101.1	109.4	118.4
France	4.5	9.6	18.0	20.9	19.5	10.4	33.7	39.4	53.7	83.8	70.4	72.1
Germany	47.8	46.9	58.3	91.6	101.4	92.6	89.1	108.1	96.7	134.1	168.8	133.9
Netherlands	34.8	27.1	27.3	35.5	24.4	42.5	25.4	32.3	43.0	43.7	67.8	113.9
United Kingdom	35.5	29.6	30.9	43.2	38.5	38.8	82.7	90.1	101.2	155.9	137.7	189.5
Turkey	0.6	3.0	3.2	1.8	6.4	5.3	5.9	4.5	9.0	12.0	10.5	17.8
Former Soviet Republics	0.1	0.2	0.3	3.2	1.8	1.9	1.1	2.4	1.1	5.8	2.0	3.7
Poland	0.1	0.1	. . .	0.8	5.3	0.6	0.8	0.5	2.0	4.5	3.5	3.0
Other Eastern Europe	0.2	0.3	0.9	0.9	0.7	1.1	2.1	3.3	5.1	16.3	10.3	12.2
Other Europe	16.7	20.9	33.1	26.2	37.2	51.6	121.1	111.5	150.2	129.7	138.2	125.8
Asia	89.3	119.4	185.9	238.3	147.6	258.5	362.6	471.6	543.0	510.5	448.9	479.0
Japan	11.8	16.7	21.2	29.4	18.7	16.2	90.6	110.4	147.2	114.3	114.7	101.5
China	13.7	21.4	18.3	15.1	12.3	14.5	86.1	111.2	114.5	106.6	121.9	119.2
Hong Kong	6.6	12.9	14.7	13.2	11.2	8.0	27.3	32.8	39.3	49.6	34.6	35.6
Taiwan	8.6	10.3	82.3	112.1	54.5	69.6	23.6	21.6	25.1	38.0	31.6	21.5
Singapore	8.9	5.9	3.0	1.7	3.7	4.5	21.6	27.7	33.4	33.0	17.8	46.4
South Korea	27.2	28.8	18.7	20.6	16.8	118.4	36.6	57.1	80.6	62.3	41.4	55.2
Indonesia	2.9	5.1	3.0	22.5	5.7	4.6	31.4	48.2	29.8	21.5	28.2	33.4
India	3.9	4.9	5.6	4.1	2.6	2.2	6.2	8.5	11.9	13.1	9.2	18.8
Other Asia	5.7	13.4	19.0	19.6	22.1	20.6	39.4	54.2	61.2	72.1	49.5	47.4
Africa	6.3	6.5	17.9	10.3	18.0	8.2	26.1	18.1	17.5	31.9	30.7	34.4
North Africa	1.5	2.3	11.9	5.3	5.0	4.6	4.2	4.7	7.0	16.1	16.5	20.5
Republic of South Africa	3.3	4.0	5.1	4.5	12.3	2.9	8.1	9.1	7.5	9.2	11.2	10.7
Other Subsaharan Africa	1.5	0.1	0.9	0.5	0.7	0.6	13.8	4.4	3.0	6.6	3.1	3.2
Middle East	10.7	15.8	25.4	21.4	19.3	19.3	47.6	53.9	55.8	57.0	61.6	45.9
Australia	10.1	23.1	13.5	8.4	15.0	34.5	35.8	35.0	33.9	40.6	32.7	36.9
Rest Of World	. . .	. . .	. . .	. . .	. . .	. . .	. . .	. . .	. . .	. . .	. . .	. . .

Table E-3. Metropolitan Area Exports of Goods by Destination, 1994–1999—*Continued*

(Millions of dollars.)

Destination	Chattanooga, TN - GA						Chicago, IL					
	1994	1995	1996	1997	1998	1999	1994	1995	1996	1997	1998	1999
ALL DESTINATIONS	237.3	301.0	273.5	331.4	337.1	372.0	17 333.6	21 083.4	22 030.1	23 209.9	22 929.4	21 144.1
North America	107.5	122.6	124.7	146.7	162.2	180.9	4 830.9	5 137.8	5 701.9	6 733.8	6 849.5	7 116.5
Canada	97.6	116.6	114.9	127.8	123.3	128.7	3 582.1	4 180.2	4 412.7	5 203.0	4 922.9	5 012.9
Mexico	9.9	6.0	9.9	18.9	38.8	52.2	1 248.8	957.6	1 289.2	1 530.7	1 926.6	2 103.6
Caribbean And Central America	6.8	19.7	25.4	39.8	38.4	18.3	262.4	305.5	301.8	321.2	423.0	368.6
South America	8.0	11.7	9.6	15.4	18.0	19.7	1 091.4	1 118.0	1 294.8	1 825.2	1 767.4	1 467.9
Argentina	0.2	1.4	1.3	2.3	6.1	7.5	172.8	187.9	186.9	322.3	252.9	268.0
Brazil	0.5	2.0	2.8	5.5	4.5	6.1	432.7	440.7	541.5	722.2	810.2	719.7
Other South America	7.2	8.3	5.6	7.7	7.4	6.0	485.9	489.4	566.3	780.7	704.4	480.2
Europe	44.5	60.1	44.1	56.9	57.5	70.7	4 317.5	5 214.7	5 659.3	6 006.0	6 309.4	5 803.8
Belgium	8.2	9.7	5.1	5.0	12.4	11.8	481.7	500.2	561.8	665.7	751.3	666.2
France	2.7	5.0	3.2	4.4	4.7	7.8	386.7	413.9	468.4	563.9	486.9	471.2
Germany	7.8	15.3	8.6	14.4	5.8	13.6	903.6	1 040.2	1 112.7	1 140.4	1 206.4	1 106.5
Netherlands	5.7	9.0	5.9	6.8	7.0	4.8	352.3	463.5	594.9	703.1	579.1	587.8
United Kingdom	12.1	11.6	12.1	9.9	9.7	10.3	1 009.5	1 227.3	1 218.2	1 305.1	1 360.8	1 154.0
Turkey	0.3	0.7	0.3	2.2	2.4	2.4	25.7	55.0	86.3	106.9	78.7	51.1
Former Soviet Republics	0.2	0.2	0.2	0.4	2.6	...	90.0	84.5	73.8	104.1	206.0	108.6
Poland	0.1	0.7	0.3	0.3	0.1	3.2	55.9	71.3	106.4	123.8	106.3	103.8
Other Eastern Europe	0.1	0.4	0.5	0.9	0.3	0.1	51.6	61.0	62.7	58.6	61.2	33.8
Other Europe	7.2	7.4	8.0	12.5	12.4	16.6	960.5	1 297.9	1 374.1	1 234.4	1 472.9	1 520.7
Asia	53.3	69.4	50.2	53.6	37.2	65.6	5 508.9	7 459.8	7 291.7	6 653.7	5 905.9	4 965.9
Japan	11.9	14.0	16.3	9.9	10.6	8.9	1 777.8	2 343.4	2 453.5	1 962.0	2 506.0	1 882.8
China	0.9	14.2	2.3	2.8	4.9	4.8	915.0	938.8	894.6	816.4	609.5	578.2
Hong Kong	3.9	6.0	4.1	5.5	4.9	5.5	338.3	663.1	553.8	810.9	425.8	321.1
Taiwan	10.6	8.0	5.8	15.0	5.8	31.8	575.5	491.8	411.5	396.2	445.4	347.4
Singapore	12.1	9.8	8.0	8.0	3.8	2.8	295.3	356.9	427.5	492.2	357.9	382.6
South Korea	2.0	1.8	3.3	2.2	0.9	2.8	652.2	1 099.4	1 136.7	781.6	572.2	610.2
Indonesia	0.6	0.4	0.2	0.5	0.3	1.3	111.0	169.3	238.4	253.3	72.8	40.3
India	0.7	0.8	0.2	0.9	0.2	0.1	138.5	188.1	124.1	169.7	243.5	307.4
Other Asia	10.5	14.4	9.9	8.9	5.7	7.6	705.3	1 209.0	1 051.6	971.3	672.8	496.0
Africa	3.0	1.9	4.9	2.9	4.0	4.6	340.5	579.0	558.1	459.5	381.6	231.4
North Africa	0.9	1.2	0.6	0.3	1.5	2.0	192.6	369.7	305.2	207.5	118.2	83.1
Republic of South Africa	0.9	0.6	3.2	2.5	2.1	2.5	104.9	163.2	183.6	176.9	200.1	110.5
Other Subsaharan Africa	1.2	0.1	1.1	0.1	0.4	0.1	42.9	46.1	69.3	75.1	63.3	37.9
Middle East	6.4	8.1	7.2	5.7	13.1	6.5	483.0	661.1	662.0	639.0	650.6	577.7
Australia	7.7	7.6	7.2	10.3	6.8	5.7	492.1	515.2	478.1	561.8	606.6	612.2
Rest Of World	...	...	...	...	...	...	7.0	92.3	82.5	9.9	35.2	...

Destination	Cincinnati, OH - KY - IN						Cleveland - Lorain - Elyria, OH					
	1994	1995	1996	1997	1998	1999	1994	1995	1996	1997	1998	1999
ALL DESTINATIONS	4 056.5	4 256.7	4 784.1	5 674.1	6 682.5	6 783.1	4 093.3	4 707.0	5 075.2	5 511.0	5 347.0	5 894.2
North America	904.8	1 040.9	1 194.8	1 153.3	1 212.1	1 244.4	1 633.7	1 822.1	1 988.4	2 148.3	2 339.7	2 616.5
Canada	686.3	885.1	1 010.4	914.4	934.2	905.2	1 294.3	1 445.9	1 610.7	1 717.9	1 876.5	2 023.3
Mexico	218.4	155.8	184.4	239.0	277.9	339.2	339.4	376.1	377.6	430.4	463.2	593.2
Caribbean And Central America	109.1	146.6	130.8	137.6	649.2	138.8	39.9	37.7	33.1	43.1	46.5	40.8
South America	98.2	192.9	171.9	348.6	350.1	399.4	281.8	322.2	322.3	387.4	437.5	303.1
Argentina	10.6	16.7	19.4	20.7	17.1	21.6	58.5	54.2	79.7	65.1	59.4	58.4
Brazil	14.8	63.8	45.8	190.6	236.4	266.9	85.9	117.7	111.2	163.8	211.7	159.6
Other South America	72.8	112.3	106.7	137.3	96.6	110.8	137.5	150.3	131.5	158.4	166.5	85.1
Europe	2 193.1	1 972.2	2 157.3	2 656.4	3 083.7	3 371.0	959.5	1 095.0	1 067.0	1 109.2	1 127.8	1 188.3
Belgium	94.3	99.1	91.0	85.5	133.5	162.8	66.2	57.8	58.8	55.0	61.5	61.4
France	1 467.5	963.8	984.3	1 390.2	1 553.8	1 574.5	165.0	188.0	145.4	156.4	197.8	233.7
Germany	120.6	150.9	186.2	230.1	243.6	306.7	163.8	198.9	211.5	212.3	203.0	225.4
Netherlands	54.2	55.7	60.1	75.1	89.0	114.8	55.4	62.4	75.0	113.8	106.1	124.6
United Kingdom	181.9	313.4	436.2	446.2	647.2	786.3	181.0	194.4	207.9	223.6	198.8	228.8
Turkey	82.0	147.6	111.1	97.8	45.0	33.5	23.6	50.1	40.3	64.6	29.3	12.4
Former Soviet Republics	1.3	2.4	1.5	3.0	4.5	5.1	6.1	16.2	9.9	12.4	12.8	6.2
Poland	6.4	6.5	6.7	8.5	3.7	6.5	2.1	3.3	7.5	4.9	4.6	3.1
Other Eastern Europe	2.1	3.2	11.3	12.7	13.9	9.5	8.6	6.0	18.3	23.5	25.1	29.3
Other Europe	182.8	229.8	268.8	307.4	349.7	371.2	287.5	317.9	292.4	242.7	288.8	263.4
Asia	652.5	787.3	968.5	1 195.8	1 184.2	1 431.5	871.2	1 132.7	1 410.5	1 523.2	1 122.7	1 459.0
Japan	281.1	313.6	415.1	595.0	579.6	647.6	276.7	327.2	365.4	324.1	248.5	457.5
China	51.3	34.6	55.7	69.4	53.3	70.6	65.2	74.4	74.7	185.4	150.0	184.7
Hong Kong	31.3	39.4	52.5	40.9	50.0	89.0	69.2	69.4	87.5	121.3	77.1	68.5
Taiwan	52.5	93.3	43.7	50.4	47.5	54.5	84.2	118.5	178.7	133.2	131.3	111.8
Singapore	111.4	132.0	182.7	219.0	240.5	308.4	133.3	175.9	158.7	172.8	116.2	130.3
South Korea	47.8	45.6	73.6	55.6	36.6	52.4	123.4	195.8	391.2	444.2	255.7	403.1
Indonesia	13.6	17.7	10.1	12.9	3.0	10.0	6.5	22.7	22.4	18.0	11.4	12.9
India	4.8	7.3	14.4	21.9	27.7	34.3	38.4	49.4	27.2	32.4	24.9	25.0
Other Asia	58.7	103.8	120.7	130.7	146.0	164.8	74.4	99.5	104.7	91.8	107.4	65.2
Africa	16.7	27.6	55.4	38.3	22.4	18.3	87.6	95.3	71.5	73.5	74.7	52.6
North Africa	5.6	17.2	30.9	21.1	7.9	4.6	15.1	13.0	11.9	12.6	17.7	11.4
Republic of South Africa	10.4	8.3	23.1	14.4	13.3	11.2	68.4	78.2	56.3	55.1	49.8	37.2
Other Subsaharan Africa	0.7	2.1	1.4	2.8	1.3	2.5	4.2	4.1	3.4	5.9	7.2	4.0
Middle East	49.4	44.1	43.4	66.6	96.1	65.4	89.3	85.4	80.1	117.1	96.2	91.0
Australia	32.7	45.2	62.0	77.5	84.7	114.2	130.3	116.6	101.6	109.1	101.9	142.6
Rest Of World	...	...	...	...	...	...	...	...	0.6	...	...	0.1

Table E-3. Metropolitan Area Exports of Goods by Destination, 1994–1999—Continued

(Millions of dollars.)

Destination	Colorado Springs, CO						Columbia, SC					
	1994	1995	1996	1997	1998	1999	1994	1995	1996	1997	1998	1999
ALL DESTINATIONS	900.7	954.7	857.0	1 006.0	1 103.2	1 174.2	300.4	343.3	310.8	328.5	346.6	360.7
North America	84.6	113.2	70.5	115.8	90.0	90.2	86.6	94.4	97.7	106.6	107.9	133.6
Canada	77.0	110.5	63.6	60.6	71.3	68.4	80.6	91.7	92.1	100.2	98.9	97.3
Mexico	7.6	2.8	6.9	55.2	18.8	21.9	6.0	2.7	5.5	6.3	9.0	36.4
Caribbean And Central America	0.7	1.7	1.2	1.4	1.5	3.8	4.9	9.4	11.7	8.7	3.9	10.6
South America	3.2	5.1	7.2	6.7	7.0	13.3	8.9	12.4	11.8	17.4	16.6	10.3
Argentina	0.6	0.9	0.4	0.3	0.1	1.0	1.7	4.0	1.2	1.9	3.0	1.0
Brazil	1.4	1.3	2.3	3.8	4.6	10.4	2.9	5.4	7.4	9.8	5.4	6.6
Other South America	1.2	2.8	4.6	2.6	2.3	1.9	4.2	3.0	3.2	5.7	8.1	2.6
Europe	376.8	416.5	336.6	380.1	462.4	482.0	138.8	140.9	106.6	126.4	113.3	146.3
Belgium	2.3	3.5	4.2	2.4	2.2	2.2	15.9	16.7	12.7	9.5	3.4	4.5
France	21.6	20.5	17.7	22.0	25.5	38.2	14.5	22.7	20.2	27.3	14.0	39.1
Germany	39.0	56.4	57.3	58.6	75.9	75.7	42.4	17.7	14.7	22.1	22.6	22.9
Netherlands	115.3	100.6	76.9	41.2	61.0	70.8	8.9	10.6	11.3	7.5	4.4	5.3
United Kingdom	121.8	138.1	70.9	75.3	98.3	85.8	10.6	23.9	14.5	13.1	14.2	14.6
Turkey	. . .	0.4	0.3	0.5	0.7	0.6	0.3	0.8	0.2	0.4	0.5	0.1
Former Soviet Republics	0.1	0.6	0.2	0.5	0.1	0.1	0.2	0.4	2.6	0.2	0.7	0.2
Poland	0.2	0.3	1.2	0.5	0.2	0.8	0.1	0.3	0.1	0.1	0.1	0.1
Other Eastern Europe	1.3	1.6	1.1	1.3	0.2	0.2	0.9	0.3	0.5	2.6	4.7	1.1
Other Europe	75.2	94.7	106.8	177.8	198.4	207.6	45.0	47.5	29.9	43.6	49.0	58.5
Asia	422.3	404.4	426.4	482.6	516.2	562.5	51.8	71.5	66.5	57.7	88.7	51.7
Japan	153.8	178.1	185.7	157.2	128.4	139.5	11.1	16.3	26.2	20.6	19.5	12.3
China	0.7	1.5	6.3	13.7	41.5	51.8	0.9	9.2	0.4	0.6	1.2	1.7
Hong Kong	89.7	59.9	47.9	75.4	82.5	71.8	9.9	7.1	3.7	10.2	7.7	6.6
Taiwan	26.7	23.8	36.2	43.9	38.7	32.3	2.5	6.8	16.6	6.9	47.7	10.6
Singapore	61.8	50.7	36.1	34.7	54.2	82.7	0.4	0.8	1.4	1.3	0.5	1.2
South Korea	33.6	38.9	51.2	75.2	74.8	38.8	24.2	25.2	14.0	15.2	6.1	13.7
Indonesia	0.1	11.6	0.3	0.2	0.1	0.6	0.3	0.1	0.1	0.1	. . .	. . .
India	0.2	1.0	0.9	0.4	2.4	4.2	0.7	3.6	2.1	1.2	1.6	0.6
Other Asia	55.7	39.0	61.9	81.9	93.7	140.8	1.8	2.4	2.1	1.7	4.5	4.9
Africa	2.8	1.8	1.4	1.7	3.5	1.9	0.9	1.2	2.2	1.7	1.2	0.8
North Africa	0.1	0.1	0.2	0.5	0.7	0.4	0.1	. . .	. . .	0.4	0.1	0.3
Republic of South Africa	2.3	0.5	0.7	0.8	2.6	1.3	0.7	0.6	2.1	1.0	0.5	0.2
Other Subsaharan Africa	0.4	1.2	0.5	0.4	0.2	0.2	0.1	0.6	0.1	0.3	0.6	0.3
Middle East	1.6	2.9	5.4	6.3	8.0	10.3	6.1	9.9	10.2	6.6	12.6	4.7
Australia	8.8	9.1	8.4	11.5	14.7	10.2	2.3	3.5	4.3	3.6	2.5	2.8
Rest Of World	. . .	. . .	. . .	. . .	. . .	. . .	. . .	. . .	. . .	. . .	. . .	. . .

Destination	Columbus, OH						Corpus Christi, TX					
	1994	1995	1996	1997	1998	1999	1994	1995	1996	1997	1998	1999
ALL DESTINATIONS	1 295.5	1 358.2	1 497.2	1 660.7	1 753.2	1 966.6	153.6	162.4	241.8	387.2	308.7	309.4
North America	635.1	699.9	766.0	838.1	863.8	1 148.3	113.0	93.1	180.0	291.3	242.2	254.6
Canada	570.2	629.0	692.1	757.3	743.4	1 003.7	88.6	68.7	139.6	201.6	203.6	210.7
Mexico	64.9	71.0	74.0	80.8	120.3	144.6	24.4	24.4	40.4	89.7	38.5	43.9
Caribbean And Central America	14.4	13.8	13.9	16.5	21.2	23.7	0.9	0.8	0.7	1.0	1.3	4.2
South America	48.2	47.2	38.3	57.6	83.8	55.1	5.2	5.4	7.1	5.3	10.4	7.4
Argentina	5.1	4.8	5.5	6.3	7.8	6.1	3.8	0.5	1.1	0.2	1.6	0.4
Brazil	20.8	24.3	13.8	22.9	28.4	28.9	. . .	0.2	0.2	0.2	0.6	0.2
Other South America	22.2	18.1	19.0	28.4	47.7	20.1	1.5	4.6	5.8	4.9	8.3	6.8
Europe	305.0	313.1	300.7	357.3	440.8	411.1	11.8	37.1	21.9	39.4	31.7	22.6
Belgium	12.4	12.4	19.8	32.0	32.5	13.7	1.3	0.5	0.1	. . .	0.1	0.1
France	12.9	15.0	14.0	18.4	26.3	22.4	1.0	1.0	1.5	0.7	0.4	1.0
Germany	84.0	77.5	63.8	44.6	48.9	58.2	1.8	2.4	1.1	3.0	3.9	2.3
Netherlands	11.1	16.8	36.9	37.4	48.3	30.6	0.1	0.1	. . .	1.0	0.3	0.3
United Kingdom	52.1	67.7	61.0	70.6	92.7	99.9	3.2	3.1	2.8	3.5	5.7	11.3
Turkey	0.5	1.2	1.4	2.2	1.9	2.7	. . .	. . .	. . .	. . .	0.1	. . .
Former Soviet Republics	1.0	2.3	1.4	1.7	4.8	5.9	4.1	29.2	14.6	20.8	17.8	0.2
Poland	0.4	1.7	0.4	1.8	2.0	3.8	. . .	. . .	. . .	. . .	. . .	. . .
Other Eastern Europe	4.2	2.5	2.4	2.4	2.9	3.2	. . .	0.2	1.2	. . .	. . .	0.1
Other Europe	126.6	116.1	99.8	146.3	180.4	170.7	0.5	0.5	0.5	10.2	3.2	7.2
Asia	244.4	233.6	315.7	328.3	289.9	275.8	10.0	21.9	29.1	42.0	20.3	18.2
Japan	89.3	70.9	116.3	113.2	93.6	61.8	1.9	3.7	2.8	10.1	3.7	2.5
China	9.4	18.0	10.6	10.8	20.3	15.4	3.7	0.3	1.0	14.5	0.1	2.3
Hong Kong	11.7	18.2	21.9	21.9	26.9	24.9	0.3	2.3	1.1	0.4	0.4	0.8
Taiwan	37.6	40.9	61.0	82.2	49.7	43.3	0.7	4.8	7.2	2.7	6.8	1.3
Singapore	9.5	11.6	22.8	18.1	19.2	18.1	1.7	5.8	4.6	3.7	2.3	6.3
South Korea	47.7	43.4	51.7	45.2	49.2	87.1	0.1	0.2	0.5	0.5	0.4	0.3
Indonesia	7.1	0.3	1.2	3.2	0.5	1.9	. . .	0.1	1.3	0.7	0.5	0.5
India	8.8	10.0	7.4	7.2	5.6	6.8	0.1	0.9	0.1	. . .	0.1	0.5
Other Asia	23.3	20.2	22.7	26.4	24.9	16.6	1.5	3.8	10.5	9.4	6.1	3.7
Africa	8.1	6.6	10.7	9.0	12.3	8.6	0.2	0.4	0.3	2.1	0.4	0.8
North Africa	2.5	1.3	4.1	2.3	2.5	2.0	0.1	0.1	. . .	0.3	0.2	0.6
Republic of South Africa	2.9	3.7	5.7	4.4	6.5	4.8	0.1	0.2	0.2	0.1	0.1	0.1
Other Subsaharan Africa	2.7	1.6	0.9	2.3	3.3	1.9	. . .	0.1	. . .	1.7	0.1	0.1
Middle East	25.6	29.4	24.6	25.2	18.6	19.0	11.6	3.4	1.6	2.4	1.6	1.2
Australia	14.7	14.4	27.2	28.6	22.7	24.9	0.8	0.3	1.1	3.7	0.7	0.5
Rest Of World	. . .	. . .	. . .	. . .	. . .	. . .	. . .	. . .	. . .	. . .	. . .	. . .

Table E-3. Metropolitan Area Exports of Goods by Destination, 1994–1999—*Continued*

(Millions of dollars.)

Destination	Dallas, TX						Danbury, CT					
	1994	1995	1996	1997	1998	1999	1994	1995	1996	1997	1998	1999
ALL DESTINATIONS	5 679.7	6 870.4	7 096.9	8 645.9	8 449.6	8 188.4	393.0	421.6	531.9	482.9	425.9	530.6
North America	1 485.9	1 559.7	1 692.1	2 282.9	2 567.6	2 528.4	93.6	98.6	97.2	107.6	139.4	130.9
Canada	773.0	847.9	996.6	1 309.6	1 400.7	1 301.1	85.5	94.6	94.0	102.9	126.2	123.8
Mexico	713.0	711.7	695.5	973.3	1 166.8	1 227.3	8.1	4.0	3.3	4.7	13.2	7.1
Caribbean And Central America	150.2	147.0	139.3	293.0	299.8	129.5	3.4	3.7	5.1	5.8	6.4	5.7
South America	377.4	447.0	418.8	471.4	479.0	341.0	36.8	38.4	46.1	60.5	51.7	58.8
Argentina	49.7	71.0	76.6	68.9	60.4	45.8	11.1	11.2	11.5	13.8	16.6	20.0
Brazil	69.1	117.0	130.9	142.1	115.8	122.3	5.6	10.5	11.5	18.2	14.5	17.1
Other South America	258.6	258.9	211.3	260.4	302.8	173.0	20.2	16.7	23.1	28.6	20.6	21.7
Europe	1 062.0	1 227.9	1 368.5	1 611.3	1 613.1	1 459.2	82.2	85.1	137.1	91.6	110.7	143.3
Belgium	37.6	39.8	52.3	83.2	102.0	93.0	7.5	11.4	7.4	6.6	19.6	18.4
France	114.3	105.2	114.5	137.0	138.1	142.3	6.2	6.1	13.7	7.5	8.0	10.1
Germany	209.5	257.7	257.9	283.2	275.0	274.3	11.0	17.2	23.3	17.9	15.6	31.5
Netherlands	163.8	227.1	219.7	234.1	215.3	177.5	5.1	8.6	17.5	10.5	13.8	14.4
United Kingdom	231.8	245.1	287.2	324.7	410.1	285.2	14.3	18.7	35.8	24.4	26.6	23.0
Turkey	52.0	59.3	69.5	103.8	63.7	60.7	0.1	0.5	1.2	1.2	2.1	0.8
Former Soviet Republics	11.8	12.3	29.5	29.6	21.8	8.9	0.2	1.9	3.5	2.6	2.3	0.4
Poland	2.6	6.4	8.5	7.5	6.5	10.9	1.5	1.3	1.9	1.4	1.9	0.6
Other Eastern Europe	9.5	13.0	14.3	21.4	11.1	10.7	0.2	0.2	0.9	0.7	0.6	0.8
Other Europe	229.2	262.0	315.2	386.8	369.5	395.8	36.0	19.2	31.9	18.8	20.1	43.3
Asia	2 290.7	3 066.6	3 019.6	3 530.5	3 055.1	3 310.6	139.4	164.1	185.7	186.9	88.6	141.8
Japan	496.7	715.4	677.5	901.5	746.7	806.8	61.0	76.4	79.1	40.1	33.5	42.9
China	109.4	163.6	123.4	100.7	92.2	86.9	3.3	4.9	3.0	12.5	4.6	3.7
Hong Kong	100.2	145.7	179.7	159.3	116.7	146.7	36.5	30.7	33.3	40.8	16.9	45.1
Taiwan	396.6	478.0	422.5	469.5	451.2	603.1	4.4	11.6	10.7	10.2	7.1	14.1
Singapore	246.1	381.8	309.9	437.5	328.2	264.1	13.0	12.6	10.0	7.2	7.4	8.4
South Korea	225.5	283.8	279.6	271.7	210.0	198.5	7.0	8.8	24.0	58.8	11.7	16.8
Indonesia	59.6	85.6	85.3	65.6	29.0	14.8	5.7	7.7	8.0	5.4	0.3	1.3
India	50.7	46.1	49.9	51.0	43.1	53.4	1.3	2.0	5.3	2.7	1.9	2.8
Other Asia	605.9	766.5	891.8	1 073.8	1 038.0	1 136.4	7.0	9.4	12.3	9.2	5.3	6.6
Africa	77.1	101.7	107.0	152.5	157.8	144.9	9.3	4.1	6.8	4.8	8.3	5.9
North Africa	26.3	36.6	43.0	41.8	42.0	45.9	2.5	0.9	0.9	0.5	1.4	0.8
Republic of South Africa	34.4	44.6	39.4	49.8	49.0	47.1	0.6	0.8	2.4	1.4	2.0	1.3
Other Subsaharan Africa	16.4	20.6	24.6	61.0	66.9	51.9	6.1	2.4	3.5	2.9	4.9	3.8
Middle East	149.7	161.3	206.4	192.7	154.6	150.5	11.9	11.7	40.8	9.4	10.0	36.0
Australia	86.6	159.2	145.1	111.4	122.7	124.2	16.5	15.8	13.0	16.3	10.8	8.0
Rest Of World	. . .	. . .	. . .	0.1	. . .	. . .	. . .	. . .	. . .	. . .	. . .	. . .

Destination	Davenport - Moline - Rock Island, IA-IL						Dayton - Springfield, OH					
	1994	1995	1996	1997	1998	1999	1994	1995	1996	1997	1998	1999
ALL DESTINATIONS	1 098.9	1 291.0	1 576.1	1 933.9	1 745.8	1 381.2	2 671.3	2 404.8	2 201.5	2 271.5	2 253.0	2 198.7
North America	332.9	328.3	455.4	609.9	597.0	510.5	2 019.7	1 594.5	1 403.1	1 437.6	1 507.0	1 568.7
Canada	270.6	299.9	393.4	511.7	504.5	448.8	1 845.3	1 473.8	1 272.7	1 310.6	1 354.1	1 454.4
Mexico	62.3	28.4	62.0	98.2	92.5	61.7	174.4	120.7	130.4	127.0	152.9	114.2
Caribbean And Central America	23.2	23.8	24.8	27.5	26.9	22.8	7.3	7.6	6.0	10.5	18.0	8.8
South America	102.3	98.4	141.2	203.4	164.2	63.3	30.6	37.5	33.6	41.3	39.2	28.4
Argentina	46.0	40.7	62.3	74.7	67.9	22.4	3.9	4.3	6.4	6.9	7.5	5.6
Brazil	12.1	15.3	15.1	46.8	32.0	22.6	9.5	20.5	12.4	18.4	20.8	15.0
Other South America	44.1	42.5	63.9	81.9	64.4	18.2	17.2	12.8	14.9	16.0	10.9	7.8
Europe	397.2	523.0	598.5	663.9	651.8	547.0	368.6	452.5	456.9	479.8	421.6	345.5
Belgium	9.1	12.9	11.9	8.9	10.2	12.5	11.6	17.8	19.8	19.5	15.4	16.5
France	69.6	99.5	92.5	95.1	93.0	74.2	43.7	47.6	46.4	58.3	53.9	44.5
Germany	166.5	218.6	234.2	230.8	239.7	210.7	77.5	86.3	84.5	89.5	67.7	54.2
Netherlands	19.5	27.0	22.7	29.0	40.5	64.8	26.9	31.5	26.0	26.9	22.2	26.6
United Kingdom	34.6	55.3	48.9	54.5	57.1	68.7	86.1	102.3	105.0	111.0	95.1	90.2
Turkey	0.1	0.2	. . .	1.0	0.5	0.2	9.4	5.7	5.3	10.1	5.3	7.2
Former Soviet Republics	26.7	0.9	43.8	93.1	67.8	2.0	0.7	2.2	1.1	2.6	2.5	0.9
Poland	0.4	. . .	0.8	3.2	2.6	3.2	0.4	0.8	1.0	2.5	1.1	1.1
Other Eastern Europe	12.2	25.5	30.8	34.8	29.8	23.5	2.0	1.8	1.6	2.3	3.5	2.6
Other Europe	58.6	83.1	112.9	113.6	110.6	87.1	110.5	156.5	166.2	157.0	154.8	101.8
Asia	118.1	176.3	158.6	162.0	97.8	107.0	163.7	218.4	228.7	229.6	192.9	178.9
Japan	51.4	73.6	61.8	62.3	51.1	44.4	65.2	87.2	110.2	99.3	107.0	92.6
China	3.8	4.0	3.8	5.1	8.0	16.0	8.7	15.5	13.7	19.3	8.4	15.0
Hong Kong	6.5	5.9	6.7	7.9	5.0	3.4	12.7	16.5	14.2	13.2	13.9	10.6
Taiwan	6.7	10.5	8.7	9.3	6.9	4.5	22.5	20.0	12.4	16.2	14.3	14.4
Singapore	7.9	8.6	7.4	9.9	3.4	2.9	14.2	16.1	15.0	10.4	6.6	9.8
South Korea	15.0	34.7	27.1	27.3	5.4	13.6	18.4	26.5	25.8	24.0	11.0	11.4
Indonesia	3.8	3.9	3.5	5.0	0.6	2.5	1.0	2.1	4.0	2.6	0.5	0.5
India	0.6	1.7	0.8	0.7	1.7	0.7	2.3	6.9	3.9	5.4	4.3	2.8
Other Asia	22.4	33.5	38.8	34.7	15.7	19.0	18.7	27.7	29.5	39.2	27.0	21.8
Africa	32.4	32.9	38.9	49.5	33.5	19.1	19.1	20.2	24.5	15.6	19.8	17.2
North Africa	2.1	2.7	4.0	2.8	1.3	0.4	7.0	7.8	9.0	4.6	4.6	8.6
Republic of South Africa	29.4	29.8	34.2	46.2	31.8	18.7	10.9	10.6	13.2	9.7	14.7	8.0
Other Subsaharan Africa	0.9	0.3	0.7	0.5	0.5	. . .	1.2	1.9	2.2	1.3	0.5	0.6
Middle East	7.6	11.8	14.0	14.5	10.6	4.3	21.0	31.5	26.8	27.4	30.5	23.4
Australia	85.1	96.4	144.7	203.2	163.9	107.2	41.3	42.5	21.9	29.7	24.0	27.9
Rest Of World	. . .	. . .	. . .	. . .	. . .	. . .	. . .	. . .	. . .	. . .	. . .	. . .

Table E-3. Metropolitan Area Exports of Goods by Destination, 1994–1999—*Continued*

(Millions of dollars.)

Destination	Daytona Beach, FL						Denver, CO					
	1994	1995	1996	1997	1998	1999	1994	1995	1996	1997	1998	1999
ALL DESTINATIONS	110.3	85.9	111.7	137.5	142.8	119.7	1 089.8	1 385.3	1 502.9	1 738.1	1 806.3	1 558.5
North America	26.1	17.3	24.5	36.7	46.0	39.1	231.0	261.5	329.9	337.6	404.2	410.7
Canada	15.4	15.5	23.7	33.9	43.5	36.2	166.2	190.8	254.5	268.7	332.7	354.1
Mexico	10.7	1.8	0.8	2.9	2.4	3.0	64.8	70.7	75.3	68.9	71.5	56.6
Caribbean And Central America	6.5	6.3	7.5	10.3	9.5	8.0	13.7	14.7	12.3	12.9	14.4	14.3
South America	3.4	6.9	4.8	4.9	6.5	2.0	61.6	67.4	65.6	89.9	70.3	53.9
Argentina	0.8	1.4	0.4	2.1	1.9	0.2	11.3	8.7	9.4	9.6	5.9	5.4
Brazil	0.7	2.3	2.1	0.7	1.7	0.4	14.1	21.9	16.0	37.6	17.2	18.4
Other South America	1.9	3.3	2.3	2.1	2.8	1.4	36.3	36.8	40.2	42.6	47.3	30.0
Europe	47.8	34.1	43.1	46.3	43.6	43.3	362.3	448.0	474.3	639.3	741.1	600.4
Belgium	1.1	1.3	3.5	2.1	0.4	0.6	92.4	60.9	68.2	68.8	62.1	57.4
France	2.6	2.2	1.3	5.3	2.5	2.9	23.1	33.1	32.2	67.2	64.5	61.9
Germany	9.2	9.5	10.2	10.1	11.3	6.7	38.2	71.1	68.6	64.3	112.1	113.9
Netherlands	9.3	8.3	10.0	9.2	9.4	12.2	28.0	58.0	57.7	96.7	123.6	106.6
United Kingdom	5.1	3.9	9.2	10.4	9.6	13.3	60.8	78.6	73.7	73.7	81.4	74.6
Turkey	. . .	0.1	. . .	. . .	0.4	0.1	1.9	3.2	3.1	3.6	5.8	4.1
Former Soviet Republics	0.1	0.4	0.5	0.1	. . .	. . .	26.9	25.1	44.2	85.5	36.1	12.2
Poland	. . .	. . .	. . .	0.1	0.1	. . .	3.6	2.7	3.0	2.8	2.2	3.0
Other Eastern Europe	0.3	0.2	0.2	0.1	0.1	0.2	7.3	13.9	7.2	4.7	3.5	2.5
Other Europe	20.1	8.3	8.0	8.9	9.8	7.3	80.2	101.4	116.5	172.1	249.7	164.1
Asia	18.9	14.3	21.7	30.4	16.4	22.8	329.8	483.3	505.5	572.3	482.9	406.5
Japan	4.7	3.2	3.2	4.7	2.8	9.1	136.0	240.2	266.2	304.0	264.7	201.2
China	0.4	. . .	0.6	0.2	1.8	0.6	14.5	12.6	25.5	11.0	16.0	16.8
Hong Kong	0.9	0.8	1.1	2.1	1.0	1.0	24.2	58.7	37.0	45.9	31.9	25.4
Taiwan	2.5	3.7	5.6	6.6	4.9	2.3	32.3	22.3	17.1	22.8	20.2	31.3
Singapore	1.7	0.6	1.0	1.7	0.3	0.8	30.1	32.5	48.6	58.9	53.8	42.9
South Korea	1.8	2.1	4.2	5.9	1.4	4.8	32.4	40.9	39.9	58.7	18.3	22.1
Indonesia	0.4	0.3	0.5	3.7	0.2	0.1	2.3	4.4	1.7	10.8	8.9	12.7
India	1.4	2.0	2.1	1.8	1.8	1.5	3.7	6.7	12.8	12.0	10.2	9.0
Other Asia	5.1	1.8	3.3	3.7	2.2	2.6	54.3	65.0	56.9	48.3	58.8	45.1
Africa	1.2	0.4	0.5	0.6	1.3	0.7	22.9	28.2	33.9	21.8	22.6	9.9
North Africa	0.9	. . .	0.1	. . .	0.6	0.4	10.6	14.4	25.6	7.3	4.5	1.3
Republic of South Africa	0.3	0.3	0.3	0.3	0.5	0.1	7.8	8.0	5.9	9.8	16.7	7.5
Other Subsaharan Africa	. . .	0.1	0.1	0.2	0.2	0.2	4.4	5.8	2.4	4.6	1.4	1.1
Middle East	5.1	5.4	8.4	6.9	18.1	2.5	30.4	34.7	39.4	22.3	26.2	20.3
Australia	1.3	0.9	1.2	1.4	1.6	1.2	37.8	47.5	41.9	42.0	44.7	42.6
Rest Of World	. . .	. . .	. . .	. . .	. . .	. . .	0.2	. . .	. . .	. . .	. . .	. . .

Destination	Detroit, MI						Elkhart - Goshen, IN					
	1994	1995	1996	1997	1998	1999	1994	1995	1996	1997	1998	1999
ALL DESTINATIONS	27 469.7	27 314.7	27 531.2	25 967.4	27 004.7	28 008.3	460.4	501.5	367.5	414.7	411.4	400.9
North America	21 734.2	20 821.2	19 963.9	18 434.6	19 216.0	21 295.7	239.2	234.6	225.8	269.1	293.5	292.3
Canada	15 214.8	16 351.4	15 995.5	12 907.4	12 498.7	13 933.7	231.0	230.6	218.3	254.5	262.4	265.8
Mexico	6 519.5	4 469.8	3 968.4	5 527.2	6 717.3	7 362.0	8.2	4.0	7.5	14.6	31.1	26.5
Caribbean And Central America	63.1	87.7	83.0	85.0	247.1	113.9	2.5	3.3	3.4	4.9	2.9	3.2
South America	449.0	633.1	763.6	1 120.7	979.0	614.5	13.6	13.2	13.3	17.3	13.0	7.5
Argentina	26.7	24.1	67.1	97.3	156.9	46.1	4.1	3.3	4.0	4.2	2.1	1.4
Brazil	218.8	330.9	317.0	394.1	430.6	297.0	1.3	3.1	3.6	6.7	4.3	3.8
Other South America	203.5	278.1	379.5	629.3	391.4	271.3	8.3	6.8	5.7	6.4	6.6	2.4
Europe	2 691.7	3 244.7	3 229.9	3 634.7	3 842.9	3 726.0	120.6	170.4	49.8	57.8	63.6	55.1
Belgium	413.0	438.6	431.3	893.5	771.9	648.8	3.3	19.3	0.5	0.6	0.4	0.3
France	147.3	168.7	158.3	171.5	169.3	129.5	9.0	5.1	4.7	4.6	3.3	2.4
Germany	690.6	819.8	756.4	748.5	742.2	654.9	17.1	24.4	12.6	12.1	9.0	6.5
Netherlands	85.8	96.5	103.2	112.2	99.7	90.2	4.3	8.4	3.8	6.0	6.0	5.2
United Kingdom	436.9	282.3	331.3	365.2	478.6	898.0	59.4	92.9	12.4	12.9	11.9	9.7
Turkey	46.0	16.0	20.9	24.4	15.4	41.2	0.6	0.7	1.7	2.4	2.2	0.6
Former Soviet Republics	57.8	66.3	62.7	86.0	55.7	6.6	0.1	0.4	0.3	0.5	0.7	1.0
Poland	3.8	19.7	14.8	3.4	8.0	9.3	0.7	2.6	2.4	1.8	2.6	2.0
Other Eastern Europe	21.5	30.7	53.2	75.4	73.3	96.2	0.7	1.0	1.7	2.1	1.6	1.0
Other Europe	789.0	1 306.2	1 297.7	1 154.5	1 428.8	1 151.3	25.4	15.6	9.7	14.8	25.9	26.4
Asia	1 220.2	1 309.8	1 635.3	1 397.4	1 214.1	1 107.3	61.0	59.0	58.3	47.6	24.0	28.7
Japan	661.4	750.6	1 031.7	599.0	621.2	503.4	31.9	23.2	19.8	15.4	10.1	13.4
China	96.2	74.4	92.2	289.1	180.0	147.6	1.6	2.7	1.2	2.0	0.8	0.2
Hong Kong	45.9	37.2	51.7	44.2	81.2	61.2	4.7	6.9	9.6	7.0	4.2	4.2
Taiwan	132.5	110.3	67.8	78.7	61.8	46.3	5.1	3.4	2.7	2.4	1.2	1.7
Singapore	35.6	59.1	45.4	51.4	48.9	56.1	4.7	4.2	4.8	2.9	1.6	2.7
South Korea	104.6	135.4	145.9	133.1	50.8	66.6	6.0	7.7	9.7	7.0	2.9	2.8
Indonesia	17.8	15.1	22.7	21.4	13.4	16.7	0.5	0.4	0.7	0.7	. . .	. . .
India	10.3	30.7	29.4	25.5	17.6	9.9	1.5	3.6	1.0	1.2	0.9	0.3
Other Asia	116.0	97.0	148.5	155.0	139.2	199.5	4.9	6.8	8.8	9.0	2.4	3.4
Africa	33.5	38.4	67.2	55.8	67.3	33.9	1.5	2.5	4.5	2.5	2.4	2.9
North Africa	14.1	16.8	36.3	33.2	30.2	17.2	0.4	0.7	1.4	1.0	1.0	1.2
Republic of South Africa	15.2	16.6	18.4	13.5	11.6	7.1	1.0	1.5	1.7	1.1	1.2	1.3
Other Subsaharan Africa	4.2	4.9	12.5	9.0	25.4	9.6	. . .	0.3	1.4	0.4	0.2	0.4
Middle East	1 124.9	950.4	1 421.1	909.4	1 073.0	751.2	8.4	8.4	5.8	7.6	4.7	5.3
Australia	152.9	224.4	367.2	329.9	365.3	365.8	13.7	10.1	6.7	7.9	7.3	5.8
Rest Of World	0.1	5.1	. . .	. . .	. . .	. . .	. . .	. . .	. . .	. . .	. . .	. . .

Table E-3. Metropolitan Area Exports of Goods by Destination, 1994–1999—*Continued*

(Millions of dollars.)

Destination	Elmira, NY						El Paso, TX					
	1994	1995	1996	1997	1998	1999	1994	1995	1996	1997	1998	1999
ALL DESTINATIONS	116.8	139.5	196.9	241.8	205.5	281.4	3 561.3	4 120.8	5 212.7	5 833.9	6 544.6	7 793.2
North America	32.8	38.0	39.6	34.3	32.4	36.6	3 307.8	3 732.6	4 882.1	5 435.8	6 129.9	7 223.3
Canada	27.5	37.6	38.7	32.8	30.8	34.6	396.7	558.1	509.8	663.8	624.9	920.1
Mexico	5.4	0.4	0.9	1.5	1.6	2.0	2 911.1	3 174.5	4 372.2	4 772.0	5 504.9	6 303.2
Caribbean And Central America	1.1	1.0	0.8	2.7	1.1	0.8	25.1	24.7	24.7	17.8	15.5	16.0
South America	6.2	4.9	4.2	8.9	12.6	26.4	7.1	19.5	17.6	79.3	23.4	36.1
Argentina	1.5	0.7	0.5	1.4	2.8	1.4	2.4	2.8	5.8	5.1	1.8	7.1
Brazil	3.0	2.8	2.2	4.3	5.0	24.2	1.6	4.8	4.5	4.9	11.7	19.7
Other South America	1.6	1.3	1.5	3.2	4.8	0.7	3.2	11.8	7.3	69.4	9.9	9.3
Europe	33.2	39.5	49.7	57.4	45.5	83.8	106.8	131.1	131.5	157.0	184.2	275.8
Belgium	...	1.0	1.9	4.6	7.2	17.0	5.9	7.0	4.5	6.9	11.8	13.2
France	2.6	7.4	11.5	7.9	9.3	10.4	9.3	13.3	18.1	17.2	23.8
Germany	4.1	4.5	5.9	9.9	11.6	19.6	22.0	16.1	20.6	18.5	29.5	48.4
Netherlands	1.2	2.1	3.4	3.6	2.8	9.4	13.5	27.8	26.7	30.5	37.9	40.1
United Kingdom	9.9	11.7	9.4	19.8	6.4	14.1	36.6	39.0	24.9	37.8	43.0	78.5
Turkey	0.1	2.6	1.0	0.3	0.4	1.0	1.4	0.8	1.7	1.8	0.2	1.1
Former Soviet Republics	0.1	...	0.4	0.2	0.2	...	0.1	0.2	0.1	...	0.2	0.7
Poland	0.7	0.1	0.3	0.1	...	0.5	0.1	...	...	0.1	1.1	0.5
Other Eastern Europe	0.7	0.3	1.2	0.8	1.4	0.8	0.5	1.2	1.0	1.0	1.5	1.4
Other Europe	13.9	9.9	14.8	10.3	6.2	11.1	17.5	25.7	36.0	42.4	41.8	68.0
Asia	37.8	48.4	92.4	125.1	98.9	117.8	103.5	202.3	148.9	131.0	176.2	227.9
Japan	12.7	26.6	52.7	67.1	48.1	32.3	17.4	29.8	24.2	27.2	38.1	27.3
China	5.6	7.9	8.2	5.4	8.0	7.8	6.1	19.3	18.2	14.4	12.2	42.5
Hong Kong	0.4	0.4	0.2	1.9	2.0	1.8	9.4	10.3	5.5	9.0	21.7	35.3
Taiwan	0.6	1.0	1.9	4.8	1.6	4.2	7.0	9.1	63.1	11.8	26.1	27.0
Singapore	0.3	0.7	1.3	5.6	1.9	1.4	17.4	81.6	11.7	28.5	38.0	41.7
South Korea	2.8	4.1	20.4	26.6	20.1	46.5	6.6	9.7	2.3	3.5	1.4	6.3
Indonesia	0.4	0.1	0.1	2.4	5.6	9.9	0.9	1.5	3.4	3.4	2.8	4.7
India	4.5	3.0	4.0	3.8	3.6	2.8	0.1	10.8	0.1	0.2	0.8	0.6
Other Asia	10.5	4.6	3.7	7.4	7.9	11.1	38.5	30.2	20.4	32.9	35.1	42.5
Africa	2.1	2.5	2.3	4.5	3.5	6.4	0.5	2.0	0.8	1.1	1.1	0.8
North Africa	0.2	0.2	0.5	2.0	0.1	0.7	...	0.6	...	0.1	...	0.2
Republic of South Africa	1.9	2.0	1.7	2.3	2.7	5.6	0.5	1.4	0.5	0.6	0.5	0.6
Other Subsaharan Africa	...	0.2	0.1	0.1	0.8	...	0.1	...	0.3	0.5	0.6	...
Middle East	0.5	0.9	0.9	2.3	3.7	2.7	1.8	2.0	2.5	4.7	4.8	4.4
Australia	3.0	4.4	7.1	6.7	7.9	6.9	8.6	6.6	4.5	7.3	9.5	8.8
Rest Of World	...	...	...	...	...	...	...	...	...	...	...	...

Destination	Erie, PA						Eugene - Springfield, OR					
	1994	1995	1996	1997	1998	1999	1994	1995	1996	1997	1998	1999
ALL DESTINATIONS	285.4	490.8	321.9	598.2	621.2	536.3	173.1	190.3	168.9	190.5	373.9	693.4
North America	174.4	304.5	175.0	386.4	452.4	275.9	76.9	85.2	69.3	79.1	97.5	80.3
Canada	166.3	298.4	161.9	380.7	428.0	203.8	71.1	73.0	66.9	75.8	91.1	74.0
Mexico	8.1	6.1	13.1	5.6	24.4	72.1	5.8	12.2	2.5	3.3	6.5	6.3
Caribbean And Central America	2.6	2.7	1.8	2.4	2.7	1.8	0.8	0.5	0.6	1.1	2.0	1.2
South America	9.0	11.1	11.4	20.4	18.7	114.5	4.1	5.6	8.2	11.3	5.6	8.5
Argentina	0.7	1.5	1.6	2.8	3.8	1.3	0.4	1.2	1.9	1.9	0.6	0.3
Brazil	4.5	5.3	4.2	12.1	10.0	108.6	1.4	2.1	3.4	5.2	2.4	5.5
Other South America	3.7	4.2	5.6	5.5	4.9	4.6	2.3	2.4	3.0	4.1	2.6	2.7
Europe	38.7	72.7	62.4	59.8	54.0	54.5	41.1	43.0	43.0	52.5	61.0	72.9
Belgium	2.6	8.0	2.8	5.4	2.1	0.8	1.6	2.2	2.2	2.0	1.4	1.9
France	2.2	5.9	5.1	6.2	6.6	5.4	9.6	8.2	10.4	12.4	14.9	20.9
Germany	6.3	8.2	10.6	13.9	14.0	13.6	10.1	8.5	8.8	11.1	13.8	17.9
Netherlands	1.1	4.3	4.7	1.3	2.7	3.4	2.9	3.8	4.2	7.8	10.6	7.2
United Kingdom	6.3	15.6	14.0	9.3	8.0	10.0	7.6	7.1	7.6	6.5	5.0	6.9
Turkey	0.5	1.9	2.9	1.8	1.0	0.9	0.1	0.1	...	...	0.1	0.1
Former Soviet Republics	0.1	0.9	3.5	1.5	1.2	0.1	2.8	3.6	0.4	0.7	0.2	0.2
Poland	0.1	0.4	0.6	0.6	0.2	0.8	...	...	0.2	0.3	1.4	1.0
Other Eastern Europe	1.0	0.5	0.3	0.5	0.6	0.1	0.2	0.3	0.6	0.7	2.4	1.8
Other Europe	18.5	27.1	18.0	19.3	17.7	19.3	6.2	9.2	8.5	11.0	11.2	15.0
Asia	42.2	48.3	49.0	83.4	61.4	58.1	42.7	47.4	39.1	39.4	200.3	522.5
Japan	6.6	6.5	6.8	9.8	9.7	10.5	24.0	27.4	19.9	17.5	20.4	19.4
China	2.7	3.4	1.7	4.3	7.3	4.7	0.1	0.3	1.6	1.1	1.2	1.7
Hong Kong	2.8	3.0	4.1	6.2	4.1	6.3	2.8	2.9	3.3	3.4	3.9	3.9
Taiwan	6.8	5.9	4.1	7.7	7.9	8.8	2.5	3.0	1.1	3.0	1.5	1.6
Singapore	1.7	2.7	3.4	2.4	1.8	5.0	1.7	3.2	3.3	3.3	1.7	2.6
South Korea	12.2	11.4	10.6	15.3	5.8	6.3	7.6	5.7	3.9	4.7	167.8	485.5
Indonesia	0.6	1.4	2.5	7.0	4.2	5.5	0.6	0.1	0.3	0.8	0.1	1.5
India	1.8	2.5	2.7	2.0	2.6	1.6	...	0.1	...	0.1	0.2	0.1
Other Asia	7.2	11.5	13.0	28.7	17.9	9.3	3.3	4.7	5.7	5.6	3.7	6.1
Africa	5.2	27.7	6.3	25.7	12.2	9.8	0.4	0.5	0.6	1.4	0.9	1.5
North Africa	0.5	1.3	1.7	15.5	2.2	4.0	...	...	...	...	...	...
Republic of South Africa	4.4	4.5	4.2	5.6	3.9	3.0	0.4	0.4	0.5	1.3	0.9	1.5
Other Subsaharan Africa	0.3	21.8	0.4	4.6	6.1	2.7	...	0.1	...	...	...	...
Middle East	8.4	18.7	10.2	9.7	9.5	8.5	1.1	2.2	1.0	0.4	1.3	1.2
Australia	4.8	5.0	5.7	10.4	10.2	13.3	6.0	5.8	7.1	5.3	5.1	5.4
Rest Of World	...	...	...	...	...	...	...	...	...	...	...	...

Table E-3. Metropolitan Area Exports of Goods by Destination, 1994–1999—*Continued*

(Millions of dollars.)

Destination	Fargo - Moorhead, ND - MN						Flint, MI					
	1994	1995	1996	1997	1998	1999	1994	1995	1996	1997	1998	1999
ALL DESTINATIONS	137.3	155.0	181.9	208.5	158.1	136.7	1 032.1	1 451.7	1 318.8	1 475.3	1 417.8	1 165.2
North America	103.5	117.7	121.3	152.9	110.6	74.4	730.5	1 095.9	974.9	1 057.9	1 021.3	996.7
Canada	103.0	107.2	113.6	145.0	105.7	67.3	639.1	990.6	884.1	1 036.2	1 013.0	982.9
Mexico	0.5	10.6	7.8	7.9	5.0	7.1	91.4	105.4	90.7	21.7	8.3	13.8
Caribbean And Central America	0.2	0.1	0.4	0.1	0.1	0.5	2.1	2.9	3.1	4.0	2.8	1.9
South America	1.4	1.1	0.4	0.8	1.0	1.6	47.7	64.9	67.2	129.4	162.2	13.4
Argentina	1.1	0.5	0.2	0.3	0.4	1.5	23.8	24.0	13.2	66.9	96.3	3.1
Brazil	. . .	0.2	. . .	0.1	0.1	. . .	18.6	27.2	47.9	54.5	59.5	7.5
Other South America	0.3	0.4	0.2	0.5	0.4	0.1	5.3	13.6	6.1	8.1	6.5	2.8
Europe	24.3	31.8	50.1	45.6	37.8	49.7	28.0	30.3	34.8	48.4	41.7	46.5
Belgium	1.2	1.7	1.3	1.1	0.5	1.9	0.2	0.1	3.3	2.1	1.6	0.4
France	0.3	0.7	2.1	2.9	1.5	1.3	1.4	0.6	0.6	1.3	2.6	1.7
Germany	9.8	12.7	15.6	17.6	14.2	15.9	1.4	6.1	6.9	21.5	6.1	4.0
Netherlands	1.1	2.1	10.3	3.9	2.4	2.9	10.4	8.6	7.4	8.4	6.9	4.6
United Kingdom	1.4	2.0	4.2	6.8	7.1	9.5	4.7	4.3	5.1	6.3	7.4	4.8
Turkey	0.2	1.2	1.1	0.8	0.5	1.7	0.9	2.3	1.2	0.3	. . .	. . .
Former Soviet Republics	0.9	1.2	2.4	1.4	1.3	1.0	2.9	0.5	0.1	0.1	0.1	. . .
Poland	0.1	0.2	0.2	0.3	0.1	0.2	. . .	. . .	. . .	. . .	. . .	0.2
Other Eastern Europe	. . .	0.1	. . .	0.2	0.2	0.2	. . .	. . .	. . .	. . .	. . .	. . .
Other Europe	9.2	9.9	12.8	10.7	9.9	15.2	6.0	7.8	10.1	8.4	16.9	30.8
Asia	7.3	3.1	7.5	7.0	6.9	7.7	67.9	72.6	38.4	48.3	39.5	34.2
Japan	1.9	2.1	2.5	4.8	2.7	3.0	11.2	32.8	19.4	30.9	25.7	17.0
China	. . .	. . .	. . .	0.5	1.0	1.3	1.7	1.6	0.2	0.2	1.2	4.6
Hong Kong	0.1	. . .	1.5	0.1	0.3	0.4	11.5	5.8	5.1	6.1	5.3	4.0
Taiwan	4.1	0.2	0.1	0.4	1.2	0.7	16.4	15.5	8.7	7.7	5.5	3.9
Singapore	0.1	. . .	0.3	0.2	. . .	0.2	6.1	3.1	0.7	0.2	0.2	0.7
South Korea	0.6	0.2	2.4	0.4	0.7	1.3	0.3	1.1	0.6	0.8	0.5	3.4
Indonesia	. . .	0.1	. . .	. . .	. . .	. . .	. . .	0.1	0.7	0.6	0.2	0.1
India	. . .	. . .	. . .	. . .	. . .	0.1	1.6	3.7	1.3	0.3	0.1	0.1
Other Asia	0.6	0.3	0.7	0.5	0.9	0.7	19.1	9.1	1.7	1.7	0.7	0.4
Africa	0.2	0.3	0.3	0.2	0.5	0.2	3.2	3.9	3.2	0.9	0.6	0.3
North Africa	. . .	. . .	. . .	. . .	. . .	. . .	0.5	0.3	0.3	0.6	0.3	0.2
Republic of South Africa	0.2	0.3	0.3	0.1	0.3	0.2	2.7	3.4	2.5	0.2	0.1	. . .
Other Subsaharan Africa	. . .	. . .	. . .	0.1	0.1	0.1	. . .	0.2	0.3	0.1	0.3	0.1
Middle East	0.2	0.5	0.7	0.7	0.6	2.0	85.1	115.0	125.0	129.0	94.5	68.1
Australia	0.3	0.4	1.1	1.2	0.6	0.5	67.5	66.2	72.3	57.3	55.1	4.1
Rest Of World	. . .	. . .	. . .	. . .	0.1	. . .	. . .	. . .	. . .	. . .	. . .	. . .

Destination	Florence, SC						Fort Lauderdale, FL					
	1994	1995	1996	1997	1998	1999	1994	1995	1996	1997	1998	1999
ALL DESTINATIONS	117.2	249.0	121.6	75.8	71.4	133.4	1 506.7	1 774.7	1 864.5	2 143.0	2 086.6	2 393.2
North America	17.7	28.7	35.5	41.1	40.8	35.2	202.7	181.5	199.6	332.8	353.0	338.6
Canada	16.3	27.0	32.1	36.3	34.9	33.1	122.4	139.6	127.7	164.3	162.4	161.5
Mexico	1.4	1.7	3.4	4.9	5.9	2.1	80.3	41.9	71.9	168.5	190.6	177.1
Caribbean And Central America	0.5	0.4	2.0	1.8	0.9	1.3	294.5	354.2	364.7	485.9	515.2	613.6
South America	2.3	15.2	4.3	4.1	2.2	1.1	430.1	544.9	590.1	632.7	567.0	521.1
Argentina	0.2	2.5	0.2	1.0	0.1	0.2	77.4	62.6	89.4	94.2	86.5	88.3
Brazil	0.5	9.0	2.6	1.7	1.0	0.4	80.8	130.9	145.0	133.3	140.5	136.7
Other South America	1.6	3.7	1.5	1.4	1.0	0.5	271.9	351.4	355.6	405.1	340.0	296.2
Europe	24.5	30.8	31.6	20.6	20.8	85.0	309.3	388.4	360.0	372.2	371.0	494.0
Belgium	1.5	2.5	0.8	0.1	. . .	0.1	10.1	15.6	18.4	16.7	19.9	17.0
France	1.9	2.1	1.5	1.4	1.7	0.8	42.1	45.7	47.1	41.4	36.1	41.3
Germany	2.0	3.9	3.9	1.6	1.9	1.6	42.6	67.0	64.2	56.5	56.3	88.7
Netherlands	4.9	6.6	5.0	4.1	5.4	8.1	14.9	24.7	23.5	20.1	21.5	23.3
United Kingdom	4.0	5.4	11.8	7.3	4.9	3.7	99.0	81.7	70.9	80.7	73.5	122.3
Turkey	2.7	0.4	. . .	0.1	0.2	. . .	3.2	4.9	7.3	11.3	7.5	7.2
Former Soviet Republics	. . .	. . .	. . .	. . .	. . .	. . .	7.2	10.5	7.1	10.5	5.8	4.1
Poland	. . .	. . .	. . .	. . .	. . .	. . .	1.2	1.2	0.8	1.7	2.8	1.9
Other Eastern Europe	. . .	. . .	. . .	. . .	. . .	. . .	5.4	13.2	13.6	10.0	8.0	6.2
Other Europe	7.5	9.9	8.6	6.1	6.8	70.6	83.5	123.8	107.3	123.3	139.7	182.1
Asia	61.8	157.5	40.4	5.4	4.3	8.1	139.9	175.1	186.9	177.3	149.8	264.4
Japan	3.4	5.4	4.0	1.2	2.6	3.5	31.9	41.3	50.2	39.2	26.6	27.5
China	7.3	6.8	3.4	0.4	0.5	2.2	10.4	12.9	9.4	6.8	11.0	52.2
Hong Kong	15.9	47.5	0.7	0.3	. . .	. . .	12.1	21.7	18.2	21.9	19.6	30.3
Taiwan	18.9	81.5	27.4	0.7	0.3	0.4	7.3	12.1	11.3	9.3	8.1	10.9
Singapore	0.4	0.5	1.0	0.6	0.5	0.5	32.1	38.0	40.4	39.3	25.3	33.4
South Korea	1.8	6.1	0.8	0.8	0.2	1.1	16.6	16.6	18.5	15.9	12.8	27.3
Indonesia	3.5	2.3	0.8	0.1	. . .	. . .	3.4	4.6	5.6	2.7	0.7	3.9
India	3.8	1.2	0.1	0.6	0.1	0.1	2.6	2.9	3.5	2.4	3.1	9.0
Other Asia	6.8	6.2	2.3	0.7	0.1	0.2	23.6	24.9	29.8	39.9	42.7	69.8
Africa	7.7	13.4	4.0	0.8	1.2	0.9	43.2	34.6	36.2	46.0	34.1	35.5
North Africa	6.9	13.1	3.7	0.5	0.8	0.5	3.4	13.2	17.8	15.4	11.4	17.0
Republic of South Africa	0.8	0.3	0.3	0.3	0.3	0.5	11.5	12.1	13.8	15.4	12.7	9.4
Other Subsaharan Africa	0.1	. . .	. . .	. . .	0.1	. . .	28.4	9.3	4.7	15.1	10.0	9.0
Middle East	2.3	2.5	3.0	1.3	1.0	0.9	62.2	73.7	104.2	62.0	74.5	95.6
Australia	0.4	0.5	0.8	0.6	0.3	0.9	24.8	22.3	22.8	34.1	22.0	30.3
Rest Of World	. . .	. . .	. . .	. . .	. . .	. . .	. . .	. . .	. . .	. . .	. . .	. . .

Table E-3. Metropolitan Area Exports of Goods by Destination, 1994–1999—*Continued*

(Millions of dollars.)

Destination	Fort Wayne, IN						Fort Worth - Arlington, TX					
	1994	1995	1996	1997	1998	1999	1994	1995	1996	1997	1998	1999
ALL DESTINATIONS	770.9	1 029.4	991.4	1 078.2	1 192.8	1 236.9	2 052.0	1 915.0	2 372.7	3 045.9	3 455.9	3 971.0
North America	517.8	707.4	691.9	773.2	872.7	982.3	451.0	413.6	697.3	844.3	1 159.2	1 608.5
Canada	421.9	544.3	496.9	591.0	634.2	756.0	288.0	293.8	542.9	578.2	731.0	850.8
Mexico	95.9	163.1	195.0	182.1	238.5	226.3	163.1	119.7	154.4	266.1	428.2	757.6
Caribbean And Central America	5.9	3.7	3.2	6.3	4.6	7.4	54.2	57.8	61.0	81.8	86.9	155.4
South America	22.7	35.6	25.0	30.0	23.7	16.0	127.4	148.6	193.8	355.7	475.3	552.2
Argentina	3.5	7.8	3.6	4.1	3.7	4.0	24.5	19.2	31.2	48.5	32.1	53.0
Brazil	3.7	4.7	5.9	7.9	6.2	4.5	22.5	54.1	55.6	117.9	139.5	257.6
Other South America	15.5	23.0	15.5	18.0	13.8	7.4	80.4	75.3	107.1	189.4	303.8	241.6
Europe	133.5	167.1	157.1	137.6	171.7	126.4	764.6	477.2	437.2	424.7	574.7	583.9
Belgium	4.1	12.3	5.2	8.5	11.0	9.2	23.6	20.7	22.8	36.3	74.5	16.5
France	11.2	14.3	18.4	22.0	31.9	30.3	51.2	47.3	26.8	30.3	51.2	27.9
Germany	30.5	31.7	27.2	21.8	19.3	17.3	36.8	34.2	28.9	40.1	33.0	38.6
Netherlands	12.8	9.1	11.5	4.9	7.1	6.7	88.0	81.5	105.9	72.5	107.3	115.1
United Kingdom	21.7	29.4	29.9	23.5	27.9	27.5	65.5	55.4	85.6	110.0	150.6	198.0
Turkey	1.9	9.7	0.9	0.9	2.3	2.5	347.3	104.3	53.0	25.6	5.6	18.1
Former Soviet Republics	0.1	1.6	0.3	1.6	0.8	0.3	1.4	5.1	8.6	15.4	4.4	9.9
Poland	1.5	2.7	2.2	2.5	1.5	0.6	3.2	1.6	4.6	2.8	2.2	2.7
Other Eastern Europe	2.1	2.4	1.3	2.3	1.6	1.1	13.5	5.9	2.0	4.5	2.4	6.4
Other Europe	47.5	53.9	60.3	49.6	68.4	31.0	134.0	121.4	99.0	87.3	143.5	150.7
Asia	60.0	75.0	83.5	95.7	87.7	82.9	493.0	615.1	730.8	1 071.3	935.1	891.5
Japan	12.8	12.1	11.8	14.5	14.3	14.3	40.7	54.7	29.7	35.1	43.2	255.1
China	1.0	2.3	3.8	2.7	10.0	12.8	19.7	45.5	51.2	66.5	49.1	16.5
Hong Kong	2.0	1.6	2.6	2.5	4.1	4.3	70.5	104.5	92.4	125.8	130.7	93.5
Taiwan	7.8	8.7	7.1	9.3	8.7	9.5	22.3	33.2	23.1	49.0	46.1	23.3
Singapore	9.1	11.3	13.4	12.9	6.8	8.8	166.4	180.8	219.0	388.2	333.2	164.2
South Korea	5.5	9.7	9.3	13.3	8.7	8.6	62.8	85.1	189.5	217.6	132.1	73.9
Indonesia	1.9	1.5	0.9	0.9	1.2	0.5	13.8	10.7	21.6	16.4	21.9	9.9
India	0.8	1.9	3.0	5.6	2.7	2.6	8.9	19.9	11.1	16.1	38.2	7.2
Other Asia	18.9	26.0	31.6	34.1	31.3	21.3	88.0	80.7	93.3	156.5	140.7	247.7
Africa	8.1	9.6	6.6	10.2	8.2	6.8	58.9	36.1	39.8	48.0	42.0	28.6
North Africa	1.7	3.1	1.2	3.0	2.5	4.0	28.4	10.6	15.8	22.6	13.8	8.4
Republic of South Africa	5.3	4.6	4.2	4.0	3.7	2.2	19.3	9.9	4.1	4.2	2.6	3.8
Other Subsaharan Africa	1.1	1.9	1.2	3.2	2.1	0.6	11.2	15.7	20.0	21.2	25.6	16.5
Middle East	11.0	20.1	11.8	13.8	13.5	8.0	64.0	110.0	160.0	167.9	139.7	125.2
Australia	11.9	11.0	12.3	11.5	10.5	7.1	38.8	56.6	52.8	52.2	43.1	25.7
Rest Of World	...	...	...	...	...	...	...	...	...	...	...	...

Destination	Fresno, CA						Gary, IN					
	1994	1995	1996	1997	1998	1999	1994	1995	1996	1997	1998	1999
ALL DESTINATIONS	763.4	714.4	691.8	739.8	822.7	712.4	267.5	310.6	303.2	336.9	356.0	362.5
North America	177.7	176.4	185.1	198.9	210.2	224.3	134.2	153.9	145.7	164.9	185.5	214.0
Canada	152.2	164.0	173.6	182.2	191.5	202.6	128.0	147.5	138.2	146.1	165.2	195.0
Mexico	25.5	12.4	11.5	16.7	18.7	21.8	6.2	6.5	7.5	18.8	20.4	19.0
Caribbean And Central America	5.7	3.0	2.8	2.5	10.9	5.2	2.3	2.4	1.2	3.6	3.1	2.7
South America	20.3	21.9	27.2	26.3	29.0	20.6	11.3	14.5	11.7	18.2	17.2	9.6
Argentina	1.8	1.5	1.3	3.0	3.5	2.8	2.7	3.2	3.4	4.7	3.6	3.2
Brazil	6.8	9.8	13.0	8.4	9.5	4.2	3.6	3.6	1.8	3.1	3.7	1.9
Other South America	11.6	10.5	12.9	14.9	16.0	13.5	5.0	7.7	6.5	10.4	9.9	4.4
Europe	141.4	136.3	132.3	162.2	216.0	212.1	53.2	57.1	56.6	57.4	73.7	68.6
Belgium	11.0	10.5	7.3	11.3	19.1	11.1	2.5	2.1	2.0	1.4	2.2	1.0
France	6.1	5.6	8.6	7.7	9.2	8.4	14.2	14.6	12.7	10.4	12.5	14.2
Germany	28.9	32.2	22.3	24.9	38.2	33.1	9.6	10.3	10.8	10.2	9.4	9.4
Netherlands	12.8	10.6	11.9	17.6	24.7	42.0	4.1	4.7	6.1	6.1	8.7	6.7
United Kingdom	34.7	33.3	35.3	40.9	58.1	52.8	13.8	12.5	13.8	16.2	23.0	21.8
Turkey	0.1	0.6	0.4	1.0	0.8	0.7	0.1	0.3	0.4	0.8	0.8	0.3
Former Soviet Republics	2.4	2.6	0.7	0.5	1.2	0.2	0.1	...	...	...	0.3	...
Poland	0.3	1.0	1.1	2.5	4.1	2.8	0.7	0.9	0.7	0.2	1.1	0.9
Other Eastern Europe	0.2	0.3	0.7	0.8	0.6	0.7	0.3	0.7	0.2	0.4	2.1	0.7
Other Europe	44.9	39.7	44.0	55.1	60.0	60.2	7.9	10.9	9.9	11.9	13.5	13.4
Asia	381.8	346.2	301.4	311.2	324.2	220.1	57.0	71.7	75.7	76.6	64.6	56.6
Japan	115.5	135.4	105.6	82.6	97.2	98.5	9.6	14.7	12.2	13.4	10.6	11.8
China	63.1	27.2	13.5	35.9	26.6	12.7	3.2	7.5	6.8	5.9	6.0	8.2
Hong Kong	15.5	13.5	17.2	19.6	14.1	14.6	2.3	2.8	1.8	2.4	2.6	1.4
Taiwan	25.5	18.5	18.9	28.3	20.5	17.3	5.6	7.1	6.1	9.3	10.4	5.4
Singapore	7.5	7.0	4.3	10.0	5.5	16.1	19.1	19.2	23.9	27.4	24.7	19.5
South Korea	102.6	83.1	70.8	59.6	94.9	13.4	7.2	9.5	9.8	7.2	4.6	4.5
Indonesia	24.6	22.8	33.6	30.8	25.0	17.6	1.0	2.5	1.5	2.3	0.3	0.6
India	0.3	2.6	0.8	1.4	1.6	1.7	0.8	0.8	1.5	0.5	0.3	0.6
Other Asia	27.2	36.2	36.8	43.0	38.8	28.1	8.2	7.6	12.1	8.1	5.1	4.6
Africa	5.9	5.3	5.2	6.5	7.6	6.5	1.3	3.7	2.4	3.6	3.7	2.2
North Africa	1.4	2.4	1.0	2.0	2.1	1.7	0.2	0.6	0.2	0.2	1.5	0.5
Republic of South Africa	1.8	2.6	4.0	1.8	1.7	2.2	0.8	1.7	2.0	3.1	2.2	1.5
Other Subsaharan Africa	2.7	0.4	0.1	2.6	3.8	2.7	0.2	1.4	0.2	0.3	...	0.3
Middle East	19.9	15.6	24.1	17.2	13.4	11.7	2.0	1.5	2.8	3.7	3.7	4.1
Australia	10.7	9.6	13.7	15.0	11.4	11.8	6.2	5.8	7.2	8.8	4.5	4.7
Rest Of World	...	...	...	...	...	...	...	...	...	...	...	...

Table E-3. Metropolitan Area Exports of Goods by Destination, 1994–1999—*Continued*

(Millions of dollars.)

Destination	Grand Rapids - Muskegon - Holland, MI						Green Bay, WI					
	1994	1995	1996	1997	1998	1999	1994	1995	1996	1997	1998	1999
ALL DESTINATIONS	1 993.5	2 304.1	2 656.5	2 933.1	3 063.5	3 255.5	187.3	212.7	189.0	281.9	224.6	220.1
North America	906.5	1 037.1	1 179.9	1 429.2	1 745.1	1 963.2	110.8	116.0	108.6	177.3	126.7	125.7
Canada	779.1	907.6	1 016.8	1 192.5	1 510.5	1 732.8	96.3	100.3	98.8	167.8	110.8	111.1
Mexico	127.4	129.5	163.1	236.6	234.6	230.4	14.6	15.7	9.7	9.5	15.9	14.6
Caribbean And Central America	26.2	22.1	23.9	18.8	18.5	21.2	2.7	2.5	1.4	2.3	2.2	1.8
South America	40.9	55.8	53.6	64.3	69.7	53.9	3.2	6.1	4.0	5.6	11.0	8.4
Argentina	6.3	8.3	7.7	16.0	9.4	5.5	0.2	1.2	0.8	0.1	0.5	0.4
Brazil	20.5	24.9	16.8	17.8	22.9	20.0	0.9	1.7	1.3	2.8	6.5	1.7
Other South America	14.1	22.6	29.2	30.6	37.4	28.5	2.2	3.2	1.9	2.7	4.1	6.3
Europe	289.3	351.9	394.0	462.4	522.4	540.6	34.4	42.2	30.7	46.2	44.6	41.0
Belgium	7.6	11.1	10.3	10.0	11.9	12.1	3.5	3.4	2.4	4.4	3.8	4.9
France	18.4	27.0	24.1	38.6	45.7	66.2	2.8	3.8	1.2	8.5	2.3	2.8
Germany	60.1	73.7	99.3	132.8	151.2	122.1	3.7	2.5	4.0	6.3	4.0	3.6
Netherlands	24.6	24.8	40.7	55.2	59.3	79.5	10.7	17.1	5.8	4.5	5.3	1.6
United Kingdom	75.4	92.4	96.0	105.0	120.7	110.2	6.6	9.1	7.7	9.7	10.1	12.4
Turkey	2.0	2.8	3.9	6.1	3.0	5.4	0.1	1.0	...	0.4	0.4	0.1
Former Soviet Republics	1.4	1.8	1.4	1.8	1.2	1.8	...	...	0.1	...	0.2	0.1
Poland	7.3	11.9	15.2	9.3	5.1	4.4	...	...	0.2	...	...	0.2
Other Eastern Europe	7.2	6.0	7.8	8.4	8.6	3.7	0.1	...	0.9	...	...	...
Other Europe	85.3	100.4	95.4	95.2	115.7	135.3	6.8	5.2	8.4	12.5	18.5	15.4
Asia	636.1	763.9	928.4	864.7	564.4	601.9	29.9	37.1	35.3	42.3	31.9	33.3
Japan	292.9	343.4	417.1	433.8	330.8	284.6	17.2	17.7	15.1	18.6	14.1	14.9
China	12.6	39.0	78.6	54.1	17.8	28.1	0.6	0.1	0.1	0.7	4.2	2.1
Hong Kong	37.9	55.7	57.3	72.5	54.6	60.7	0.6	1.1	1.1	1.0	1.5	1.5
Taiwan	134.3	97.0	58.9	52.8	43.3	39.9	0.5	1.4	3.9	5.0	6.7	6.0
Singapore	19.2	22.1	24.1	19.0	11.3	19.7	0.5	0.9	0.4	1.3	0.1	0.5
South Korea	55.8	112.6	159.7	101.3	28.1	72.2	6.3	5.9	4.3	11.5	1.6	5.5
Indonesia	8.1	7.9	8.3	7.2	7.7	6.1	...	0.2	0.5	1.0	1.3	0.1
India	2.1	5.5	6.2	4.6	4.6	6.3	0.6	1.6	0.2	0.1	0.1	1.1
Other Asia	73.2	80.8	118.1	119.4	66.3	84.3	3.6	8.1	9.5	3.1	2.2	1.7
Africa	5.3	9.3	9.0	13.5	26.2	12.3	1.6	1.1	3.3	2.1	0.7	0.8
North Africa	1.3	3.2	1.3	4.3	10.3	1.7	0.7	0.4	...	0.5	...	...
Republic of South Africa	3.5	5.6	7.1	8.4	14.1	8.8	0.7	0.6	3.2	1.5	0.6	0.7
Other Subsaharan Africa	0.4	0.5	0.6	0.8	1.8	1.8	0.2	0.1	...	...	...	...
Middle East	48.8	27.2	32.2	31.8	80.4	26.7	1.5	5.3	2.2	1.0	2.1	1.3
Australia	40.4	36.8	35.4	48.4	36.8	35.7	3.2	2.4	3.4	5.1	5.3	7.7
Rest Of World	...	...	...	...	...	...	...	...	...	...	...	...

Destination	Greensboro - Winston-Salem - High Point, NC						Greenville - Spartanburg - Anderson, SC					
	1994	1995	1996	1997	1998	1999	1994	1995	1996	1997	1998	1999
ALL DESTINATIONS	2 773.3	3 356.3	3 495.6	4 050.8	4 037.2	4 313.1	1 745.0	2 305.3	2 720.4	3 076.9	3 124.2	3 357.0
North America	684.0	935.2	1 148.0	1 588.7	1 667.3	1 827.5	952.0	1 307.1	1 247.5	1 433.5	1 519.8	1 964.0
Canada	497.8	537.2	541.3	669.8	677.6	640.4	658.8	853.8	808.4	832.7	891.1	1 117.4
Mexico	186.2	398.0	606.6	919.0	989.7	1 187.1	293.2	453.3	439.0	600.7	628.6	846.5
Caribbean And Central America	425.1	604.3	665.6	711.0	614.0	729.6	55.4	69.7	59.5	84.4	116.8	95.3
South America	164.4	223.9	208.2	239.5	212.6	207.2	67.0	58.9	73.8	84.9	71.8	55.7
Argentina	28.6	34.6	35.2	50.3	38.4	34.3	5.1	7.7	10.7	13.3	15.8	10.1
Brazil	47.4	82.8	79.9	89.5	64.8	86.3	13.9	22.6	22.7	21.0	19.6	20.1
Other South America	88.4	106.5	93.1	99.7	109.3	86.6	47.9	28.6	40.4	50.5	36.4	25.4
Europe	877.5	945.9	864.2	867.1	935.3	849.4	320.3	449.5	936.8	1 016.9	1 038.3	903.0
Belgium	257.9	258.7	159.0	118.4	131.8	80.7	26.2	45.6	46.9	47.1	57.9	46.7
France	32.1	36.4	35.7	45.4	54.3	44.0	26.0	35.0	36.7	35.4	33.4	25.3
Germany	149.3	131.6	110.8	94.6	109.7	123.0	82.6	129.6	620.0	699.7	576.0	501.3
Netherlands	36.8	49.9	62.3	83.4	72.3	43.3	27.6	41.0	37.4	22.0	31.7	49.1
United Kingdom	85.1	104.1	107.8	110.3	111.6	132.1	83.7	111.0	97.9	93.0	222.7	181.3
Turkey	16.0	6.1	8.9	30.6	61.0	59.3	2.6	3.9	3.8	5.1	2.7	1.9
Former Soviet Republics	2.2	12.0	18.1	12.1	9.4	22.5	1.5	0.2	0.4	0.6	0.8	0.3
Poland	4.1	5.4	10.7	12.9	17.3	8.4	0.1	0.4	0.8	0.6	0.2	0.9
Other Eastern Europe	2.6	3.6	11.2	9.3	16.1	16.7	0.9	0.5	1.3	1.0	1.0	1.3
Other Europe	291.3	338.2	339.8	350.0	351.8	319.4	69.2	82.4	91.6	112.4	112.0	94.8
Asia	361.4	411.1	429.7	455.7	419.7	513.0	296.4	351.7	315.0	363.5	301.2	252.7
Japan	158.0	182.9	199.3	183.4	160.7	140.4	136.7	107.6	87.2	131.0	124.9	121.4
China	6.8	13.3	9.1	15.2	8.9	21.3	4.4	8.1	19.1	17.8	11.6	18.2
Hong Kong	58.9	60.1	45.3	51.8	56.7	90.5	54.9	67.5	60.3	58.5	62.4	29.2
Taiwan	26.7	32.8	23.7	34.3	27.5	22.0	25.4	45.4	30.1	29.7	21.3	14.0
Singapore	17.2	10.7	13.9	22.9	38.7	67.4	15.0	29.3	34.4	36.5	23.4	13.7
South Korea	36.9	34.4	22.4	35.2	50.0	77.3	34.3	35.7	25.7	20.8	15.4	21.3
Indonesia	14.3	16.1	16.0	28.4	8.9	12.0	2.3	3.6	4.8	9.9	2.5	1.5
India	1.7	3.1	7.0	6.9	8.8	11.5	2.3	20.7	11.6	15.0	8.1	11.6
Other Asia	40.9	57.5	92.9	77.6	59.5	70.6	21.1	33.7	41.9	44.3	31.7	21.8
Africa	54.9	61.4	47.1	58.7	58.2	52.9	9.8	13.6	15.2	12.6	12.6	16.7
North Africa	25.3	31.1	10.7	10.6	13.5	21.5	1.3	2.9	2.4	2.8	3.8	7.4
Republic of South Africa	20.2	26.0	31.8	35.4	41.3	27.5	4.2	7.1	9.9	6.4	5.0	5.8
Other Subsaharan Africa	9.4	4.3	4.6	12.8	3.4	3.9	4.4	3.6	2.9	3.3	3.8	3.6
Middle East	164.4	135.2	82.3	77.1	78.7	81.0	25.0	37.1	50.1	28.9	32.7	34.9
Australia	41.6	39.1	50.4	52.6	51.3	52.4	19.1	17.8	22.5	52.2	30.8	34.5
Rest Of World	...	0.2	0.2	0.3	0.1	0.2	...	...	...	...	0.2	0.2

Table E-3. Metropolitan Area Exports of Goods by Destination, 1994–1999—*Continued*

(Millions of dollars.)

Destination	Harrisburg - Lebanon - Carlisle, PA						Hartford, CT					
	1994	1995	1996	1997	1998	1999	1994	1995	1996	1997	1998	1999
ALL DESTINATIONS	535.0	601.0	775.5	964.4	952.9	938.7	1 967.1	2 167.6	2 416.0	3 219.8	3 758.1	3 875.5
North America	264.8	274.6	387.6	445.9	474.4	542.6	414.3	406.6	452.4	567.5	589.6	659.4
Canada	164.9	164.2	229.8	269.6	292.8	311.2	333.1	349.7	392.3	477.9	499.7	519.9
Mexico	99.9	110.4	157.7	176.3	181.6	231.4	81.1	56.9	60.1	89.6	89.8	139.5
Caribbean And Central America	6.5	4.8	4.6	8.7	6.6	7.7	54.5	66.5	55.6	99.4	102.0	120.6
South America	19.3	33.7	32.8	39.7	22.3	14.9	47.7	57.3	83.6	63.1	81.4	103.4
Argentina	1.9	3.1	4.5	4.4	2.5	1.1	12.0	9.7	6.7	7.4	19.2	8.6
Brazil	7.9	12.1	8.7	11.4	10.2	7.3	11.0	15.3	18.0	22.1	21.4	72.9
Other South America	9.5	18.5	19.6	23.9	9.6	6.5	24.8	32.2	58.9	33.5	40.8	22.0
Europe	98.4	118.3	143.7	203.1	207.1	176.5	687.7	810.9	919.6	1 222.9	1 800.4	1 796.7
Belgium	3.3	4.1	3.1	5.1	5.3	6.6	17.5	31.2	42.0	50.3	82.6	71.9
France	17.0	17.1	18.4	25.9	19.7	18.4	79.1	39.6	40.4	96.4	563.8	708.3
Germany	3.0	3.7	6.6	11.1	31.9	36.6	150.1	171.9	201.2	244.9	291.5	236.8
Netherlands	0.7	1.1	1.4	21.3	29.1	16.0	19.2	44.8	30.4	72.0	64.0	41.2
United Kingdom	62.9	73.7	82.9	98.5	68.8	42.3	160.9	190.3	194.5	277.6	332.0	255.5
Turkey	. . .	0.1	0.5	0.5	0.5	1.2	3.5	6.8	5.5	6.5	3.5	4.2
Former Soviet Republics	2.6	4.0	2.2	5.6	2.0	2.4	8.5	10.3	7.4	13.0	7.4	2.9
Poland	0.3	0.1	0.1	0.4	0.4	0.3	4.8	4.4	6.2	3.0	1.9	0.9
Other Eastern Europe	0.4	0.4	1.3	2.1	1.4	1.8	3.7	4.3	3.4	7.1	14.7	8.1
Other Europe	8.2	13.9	27.2	32.5	48.1	50.9	240.3	307.4	388.7	452.1	439.1	466.9
Asia	139.2	162.6	197.6	255.5	226.1	178.7	652.8	711.5	726.8	1 145.1	983.5	1 015.8
Japan	41.9	54.1	63.1	71.0	44.2	35.3	177.6	221.5	196.9	317.5	278.5	310.2
China	0.2	1.1	4.3	4.9	21.9	22.3	50.0	33.9	22.0	27.4	34.5	46.3
Hong Kong	40.2	44.0	57.0	64.3	47.3	27.8	17.9	26.8	30.0	34.0	36.7	61.9
Taiwan	4.3	4.9	5.3	8.8	16.3	17.1	65.0	42.9	55.2	73.5	92.5	80.5
Singapore	32.5	39.6	43.7	62.4	53.3	21.1	218.4	192.7	146.5	157.1	182.0	127.6
South Korea	7.2	9.1	10.7	12.9	8.2	9.9	51.3	110.1	167.5	206.8	186.5	280.9
Indonesia	. . .	. . .	0.1	0.3	. . .	0.1	5.6	9.3	21.2	108.9	29.1	3.6
India	0.4	1.4	2.0	5.7	9.0	2.7	5.1	8.7	9.3	109.3	14.1	17.2
Other Asia	12.5	8.3	11.3	25.2	25.9	42.4	61.8	65.6	78.2	110.6	129.5	87.6
Africa	1.2	0.9	1.9	1.1	1.4	1.7	37.2	60.6	138.1	68.1	143.8	110.4
North Africa	0.4	0.1	0.2	0.1	0.3	0.1	10.3	11.0	98.1	2.9	75.0	87.4
Republic of South Africa	0.6	0.7	1.5	0.6	0.9	0.9	22.1	36.3	33.6	49.3	51.4	19.8
Other Subsaharan Africa	0.2	0.1	0.2	0.4	0.3	0.7	4.8	13.2	6.3	15.9	17.4	3.2
Middle East	4.1	3.5	5.4	5.3	8.2	8.9	53.0	36.8	21.8	33.1	38.9	50.8
Australia	1.5	2.6	1.9	5.1	6.8	7.6	19.9	17.4	17.6	20.5	18.5	18.2
Rest Of World	. . .	. . .	. . .	. . .	. . .	. . .	. . .	. . .	0.4	. . .	. . .	. . .

Destination	Hickory - Morganton, NC						Honolulu, HI					
	1994	1995	1996	1997	1998	1999	1994	1995	1996	1997	1998	1999
ALL DESTINATIONS	397.9	476.1	464.3	501.2	529.9	572.1	215.5	228.2	265.7	269.5	172.2	204.2
North America	172.8	168.2	125.3	165.2	228.8	263.6	14.5	48.4	63.9	26.5	11.2	12.3
Canada	121.2	125.9	106.7	123.4	151.5	193.1	8.6	48.1	63.7	25.8	9.4	11.7
Mexico	51.6	42.3	18.6	41.8	77.2	70.5	5.9	0.2	0.3	0.7	1.9	0.6
Caribbean And Central America	16.6	22.4	22.2	19.0	14.6	11.9	0.6	0.6	0.5	0.9	1.8	0.4
South America	40.8	35.6	42.1	45.4	20.0	19.2	0.1	0.1	0.2	0.3	0.1	0.4
Argentina	21.3	10.2	5.6	9.1	4.0	5.3	. . .	. . .	. . .	. . .	. . .	. . .
Brazil	5.8	6.8	20.8	23.1	7.8	7.6	. . .	. . .	. . .	0.1	. . .	0.2
Other South America	13.6	18.7	15.7	13.2	8.2	6.3	0.1	. . .	0.2	0.1	0.1	0.1
Europe	75.2	90.1	97.0	104.0	93.3	99.3	5.8	6.8	7.9	7.4	12.9	11.0
Belgium	2.6	1.9	1.2	4.3	9.8	3.8	. . .	. . .	. . .	. . .	. . .	0.3
France	4.9	4.1	2.6	2.1	6.2	6.7	1.4	1.2	0.7	1.0	0.9	1.2
Germany	11.3	18.8	20.5	36.9	22.0	20.1	1.9	2.0	2.0	1.1	2.6	2.6
Netherlands	9.6	8.0	9.7	9.5	7.2	8.0	0.3	0.4	0.7	0.2	0.2	0.6
United Kingdom	28.9	39.3	35.2	23.2	21.9	29.1	0.7	1.0	2.6	1.7	1.9	3.3
Turkey	0.1	0.4	2.0	1.3	0.9	0.8	. . .	. . .	. . .	. . .	. . .	. . .
Former Soviet Republics	0.1	. . .	0.4	1.8	1.7	1.6	. . .	. . .	. . .	0.2	0.3	0.9
Poland	. . .	0.1	0.1	1.0	0.8	0.6	. . .	. . .	. . .	. . .	. . .	. . .
Other Eastern Europe	3.2	2.9	7.0	2.3	1.8	3.1	. . .	. . .	0.1	0.1	0.5	. . .
Other Europe	14.5	14.5	18.4	21.6	21.1	25.6	1.5	2.2	1.7	3.0	6.4	2.0
Asia	71.8	123.5	140.9	134.3	152.7	156.9	168.0	167.3	188.0	228.6	142.0	173.1
Japan	43.4	71.6	91.0	90.2	113.9	114.0	96.0	108.6	143.4	153.7	101.8	113.5
China	2.4	0.2	3.1	3.3	2.6	1.6	4.0	0.3	0.7	6.1	1.1	1.3
Hong Kong	8.6	7.1	4.3	6.4	6.1	5.5	12.4	4.1	4.3	7.6	6.0	4.3
Taiwan	1.7	7.5	5.7	3.7	14.2	14.0	9.5	5.3	4.1	1.8	3.1	1.2
Singapore	1.6	2.0	4.5	3.9	5.1	4.8	2.1	5.6	5.0	11.7	6.5	7.4
South Korea	1.6	19.3	11.3	7.8	1.0	3.4	26.1	24.8	9.0	9.2	5.4	10.7
Indonesia	0.9	0.9	0.5	2.0	0.3	0.8	0.5	0.4	0.6	3.7	0.5	0.8
India	1.6	4.3	3.1	3.5	3.7	6.0	. . .	. . .	. . .	0.1	. . .	. . .
Other Asia	10.0	10.6	17.4	13.5	5.9	6.8	17.4	18.3	20.8	34.6	17.6	33.8
Africa	1.4	1.9	1.5	1.4	4.1	4.6	12.4	0.1	0.1	0.2	0.4	0.4
North Africa	. . .	0.2	0.2	0.3	1.9	4.0	11.8	. . .	. . .	. . .	. . .	. . .
Republic of South Africa	1.2	0.9	1.2	1.0	2.1	0.4	0.5	. . .	. . .	. . .	0.4	0.1
Other Subsaharan Africa	0.1	0.9	. . .	0.2	. . .	0.3	0.1	. . .	0.1	0.1	0.1	0.3
Middle East	15.0	7.9	7.7	20.1	10.4	8.8	0.2	0.3	0.2	3.1	1.1	1.0
Australia	4.4	26.4	27.6	11.8	6.0	7.8	13.8	4.7	4.9	2.7	2.6	5.6
Rest Of World	. . .	. . .	. . .	. . .	. . .	. . .	. . .	. . .	. . .	. . .	. . .	. . .

Table E-3. Metropolitan Area Exports of Goods by Destination, 1994–1999—*Continued*

(Millions of dollars.)

Destination	Houston, TX						Huntsville, AL					
	1994	1995	1996	1997	1998	1999	1994	1995	1996	1997	1998	1999
ALL DESTINATIONS	13 388.2	16 247.9	16 541.5	18 595.9	19 119.0	18 967.6	672.1	829.0	899.1	1 071.8	1 055.3	1 095.7
North America	2 839.7	3 166.6	3 525.5	4 728.3	5 113.8	5 339.8	350.2	427.4	531.2	678.3	651.5	695.3
Canada	1 513.6	1 726.8	1 965.2	2 548.4	2 699.0	2 746.8	293.5	382.7	470.5	492.8	499.3	565.4
Mexico	1 326.0	1 439.8	1 560.3	2 179.9	2 414.8	2 593.1	56.6	44.7	60.7	185.4	152.2	129.9
Caribbean And Central America	726.1	858.7	828.4	1 071.6	954.2	850.3	1.2	9.9	1.9	2.6	2.6	1.8
South America	1 908.0	2 724.9	2 870.0	3 320.3	3 083.7	3 034.9	11.6	14.1	12.3	18.1	13.8	10.7
Argentina	236.4	371.8	278.1	288.8	319.2	324.3	2.9	1.1	1.4	2.7	1.3	0.9
Brazil	294.3	601.3	704.3	790.3	719.3	699.6	6.0	10.0	6.3	11.4	8.2	5.7
Other South America	1 377.3	1 751.8	1 887.6	2 241.1	2 045.1	2 011.0	2.8	3.0	4.6	4.0	4.3	4.2
Europe	2 610.7	3 023.7	2 984.7	3 187.9	3 747.3	3 652.4	190.4	242.8	225.3	233.0	258.9	257.3
Belgium	206.8	233.1	183.3	180.8	265.1	427.9	2.6	1.6	1.0	1.9	2.0	2.7
France	268.8	250.7	301.7	272.5	312.9	358.8	22.7	25.2	9.6	14.9	28.3	25.4
Germany	126.8	151.1	171.4	220.0	233.0	279.7	59.1	55.4	33.6	37.0	55.7	42.4
Netherlands	430.9	480.0	552.2	553.6	732.2	556.7	40.6	62.9	82.9	64.9	62.1	51.1
United Kingdom	839.3	1 024.3	872.5	985.8	1 095.1	666.4	24.2	56.4	69.7	84.3	83.2	87.7
Turkey	68.7	128.1	97.4	124.8	174.4	161.8	0.6	0.9	2.7	0.6	0.5	0.3
Former Soviet Republics	182.2	189.5	252.1	224.9	186.5	321.4	2.6	2.9	1.5	4.7	2.8	0.8
Poland	9.3	20.1	11.6	10.2	7.5	3.6	1.1	0.9	0.5	0.6	1.2	1.0
Other Eastern Europe	24.7	38.3	39.0	25.1	44.8	61.1	3.6	1.8	0.6	1.6	1.1	1.6
Other Europe	453.3	508.5	503.4	590.3	695.8	815.0	33.4	34.7	23.2	22.5	22.1	44.3
Asia	3 532.6	4 412.6	3 717.9	3 442.8	3 159.8	3 614.2	92.2	101.4	107.5	118.3	104.1	108.7
Japan	617.4	765.9	623.2	552.3	491.2	538.7	30.5	31.5	33.0	30.1	38.7	38.2
China	270.4	403.1	281.0	261.7	312.8	491.1	4.2	6.4	5.3	6.1	4.3	4.9
Hong Kong	182.6	394.6	242.4	223.1	178.2	158.6	10.7	18.2	14.6	18.1	8.3	9.4
Taiwan	601.7	633.1	398.9	452.8	323.3	428.8	7.1	5.6	3.9	7.6	4.9	4.4
Singapore	830.8	775.4	677.5	799.1	848.6	785.5	9.4	8.8	16.2	13.2	7.3	7.3
South Korea	405.5	768.5	585.8	473.6	355.1	552.7	24.2	17.0	14.0	21.0	11.8	13.6
Indonesia	152.2	158.0	250.6	202.1	145.9	156.6	0.2	0.2	0.9	1.2	0.3	0.1
India	76.1	146.5	158.2	140.5	193.5	112.7	1.2	4.1	6.0	3.6	5.2	10.0
Other Asia	395.8	367.4	500.4	337.5	311.1	389.5	4.8	9.6	13.6	17.5	23.3	20.8
Africa	721.9	928.5	1 101.7	1 223.0	1 263.5	977.8	2.4	3.3	2.5	4.5	7.3	11.0
North Africa	364.3	326.1	274.7	360.2	404.0	225.9	1.0	0.9	0.1	0.6	0.1	0.2
Republic of South Africa	88.3	105.9	147.4	148.4	116.1	119.8	1.3	2.3	2.3	3.8	7.1	10.8
Other Subsaharan Africa	269.3	496.5	679.5	714.4	743.4	632.1	0.1	0.1	0.1	0.1	0.1	0.1
Middle East	845.0	906.9	1 176.4	1 342.8	1 531.8	1 202.0	14.4	15.6	8.4	8.6	11.4	4.3
Australia	204.2	226.0	336.9	279.2	264.7	296.0	9.7	14.4	10.0	8.5	5.6	6.6
Rest Of World	. . .	. . .	. . .	. . .	0.2	. . .	. . .	. . .	. . .	. . .	. . .	. . .

Destination	Indianapolis, IN						Jackson, MS					
	1994	1995	1996	1997	1998	1999	1994	1995	1996	1997	1998	1999
ALL DESTINATIONS	3 003.8	3 555.9	4 012.8	4 301.8	4 771.3	5 187.1	154.3	203.0	231.4	318.1	219.6	159.7
North America	1 728.4	1 974.6	2 139.7	2 069.3	2 498.8	2 848.8	45.8	48.3	50.8	65.3	88.1	89.5
Canada	1 088.6	1 079.1	1 099.2	1 302.4	1 309.1	1 487.7	37.3	44.6	42.9	53.9	70.8	66.3
Mexico	639.8	895.5	1 040.5	766.9	1 189.7	1 361.1	8.4	3.7	7.9	11.4	17.3	23.2
Caribbean And Central America	32.4	37.0	36.4	34.6	33.8	37.8	9.0	11.8	11.4	6.2	8.0	8.4
South America	102.9	223.2	273.4	384.4	513.9	567.8	13.6	16.6	11.4	12.2	12.5	8.2
Argentina	21.5	26.1	40.5	62.5	40.1	48.1	3.6	0.5	2.4	0.8	0.4	0.3
Brazil	38.1	103.1	142.1	243.5	384.3	469.1	1.6	1.3	1.5	2.9	4.9	5.3
Other South America	43.3	94.0	90.9	78.5	89.5	50.6	8.4	14.7	7.5	8.5	7.1	2.6
Europe	654.6	720.0	886.8	1 071.3	1 047.4	1 089.5	47.6	69.1	123.4	197.4	87.0	33.0
Belgium	32.7	31.1	37.7	46.5	49.5	36.7	0.3	1.4	4.7	1.6	1.1	1.1
France	88.7	105.4	201.3	280.6	263.4	306.2	4.3	3.2	4.8	4.3	3.9	3.3
Germany	87.7	77.2	100.0	142.0	165.1	186.5	6.0	6.3	7.5	6.9	8.1	9.0
Netherlands	66.4	99.2	129.2	149.1	72.3	58.1	2.8	6.1	2.5	6.0	4.6	3.3
United Kingdom	165.8	155.9	215.6	219.8	257.6	252.6	3.9	5.7	8.4	8.1	10.8	7.9
Turkey	10.0	33.5	17.8	25.4	20.8	23.0	1.1	0.7	0.7	0.5	0.5	0.3
Former Soviet Republics	4.2	2.1	5.4	2.5	2.8	2.6	21.9	37.7	82.4	147.3	41.8	0.5
Poland	2.8	2.1	0.9	1.7	2.3	7.0	1.2	1.7	2.1	3.5	2.2	1.0
Other Eastern Europe	3.3	10.8	14.1	17.5	13.3	9.3	1.4	1.6	3.1	1.5	1.0	0.5
Other Europe	193.0	202.6	165.0	186.3	200.2	207.5	4.7	4.8	7.3	17.9	12.8	6.2
Asia	413.1	505.3	565.9	633.7	573.2	516.1	26.4	46.2	25.4	27.2	16.3	12.5
Japan	265.8	312.8	326.5	282.5	282.9	279.8	7.9	8.1	9.0	12.4	9.3	4.4
China	7.9	6.1	9.3	19.9	21.7	25.9	0.5	4.4	1.4	0.9	0.8	1.3
Hong Kong	23.9	29.4	33.7	57.3	47.6	37.0	7.3	15.7	4.8	1.9	1.3	0.9
Taiwan	31.2	28.2	31.7	34.6	38.9	24.0	4.2	5.6	1.7	3.5	1.3	1.5
Singapore	15.6	28.5	30.2	35.0	23.2	19.5	0.4	0.7	1.8	1.4	0.9	1.7
South Korea	29.0	38.3	48.8	40.6	34.7	39.5	4.8	10.1	4.8	2.7	0.9	1.0
Indonesia	3.4	6.6	7.9	9.2	5.4	6.7	0.1	0.1	0.5	0.3	. . .	0.1
India	2.9	10.4	14.4	23.8	15.4	12.1	0.1	0.1	0.1	2.8	0.3	0.6
Other Asia	33.5	45.1	63.5	130.8	103.4	71.5	1.0	1.5	1.3	1.4	1.4	0.9
Africa	14.3	18.4	20.4	26.4	22.6	22.9	4.9	2.5	2.7	2.1	2.7	2.5
North Africa	5.4	5.9	6.2	7.2	7.3	7.0	2.9	0.5	0.5	0.2	0.3	0.8
Republic of South Africa	8.4	10.2	12.7	17.6	13.4	14.9	1.3	1.7	1.9	1.7	0.8	1.2
Other Subsaharan Africa	0.5	2.3	1.4	1.7	1.8	1.1	0.7	0.3	0.4	0.2	1.6	0.5
Middle East	29.9	40.0	42.4	38.5	38.2	57.4	5.4	7.1	4.3	5.4	3.6	4.7
Australia	26.8	36.7	47.7	43.5	43.4	46.7	1.7	1.5	1.9	2.3	1.5	0.9
Rest Of World	1.3	0.7	. . .	. . .	. . .	. . .	. . .	. . .	. . .	. . .	. . .	. . .

Table E-3. Metropolitan Area Exports of Goods by Destination, 1994–1999—*Continued*

(Millions of dollars.)

Destination	Jackson, TN						Jacksonville, FL					
	1994	1995	1996	1997	1998	1999	1994	1995	1996	1997	1998	1999
ALL DESTINATIONS	132.5	175.3	155.2	167.8	241.8	245.5	500.4	604.1	677.0	721.3	777.2	796.9
North America	68.4	86.7	83.9	119.0	155.6	164.7	116.4	106.5	123.0	160.7	176.1	186.5
Canada	66.3	83.1	79.6	108.0	140.7	150.3	85.7	87.5	98.3	131.5	150.0	151.2
Mexico	2.1	3.5	4.3	11.0	14.9	14.3	30.7	19.0	24.7	29.2	26.1	35.3
Caribbean And Central America	1.0	1.8	1.1	2.1	1.4	0.9	78.9	97.2	108.1	116.0	131.1	140.7
South America	2.3	4.9	5.0	2.7	13.5	14.0	64.9	69.7	43.0	32.7	42.3	36.2
Argentina	2.1	3.2	1.8	0.5	3.4	4.4	2.3	2.8	3.6	4.4	8.3	8.7
Brazil	...	1.3	2.2	1.2	8.4	3.0	6.0	8.0	7.7	11.7	12.7	13.2
Other South America	0.3	0.4	0.9	1.0	1.7	6.6	56.6	59.0	31.6	16.5	21.2	14.4
Europe	51.6	70.8	57.2	34.2	60.3	45.7	136.1	166.5	183.6	204.2	184.6	211.6
Belgium	4.2	33.8	34.3	9.7	7.4	3.3	5.6	5.9	5.6	7.6	8.1	10.0
France	20.8	13.5	5.8	0.6	1.6	0.6	15.3	16.7	24.4	23.7	23.3	16.2
Germany	11.6	7.3	4.4	3.5	3.6	5.1	19.0	25.4	20.4	15.6	14.8	10.0
Netherlands	5.9	5.7	4.8	3.8	2.7	2.1	11.3	12.9	12.7	12.5	14.0	16.0
United Kingdom	2.4	4.7	2.4	8.3	16.3	27.5	42.2	51.0	48.8	62.4	39.4	74.1
Turkey	...	...	...	...	...	0.1	0.5	0.8	0.5	2.1	2.4	1.6
Former Soviet Republics	...	...	...	...	17.1	0.1	0.9	0.6	1.0	0.6	1.2	0.6
Poland	...	0.1	...	...	3.7	0.1	1.6	0.5	0.5	0.8	1.4	1.5
Other Eastern Europe	1.4	1.5	0.7	...	0.1	2.0	0.3	0.4	0.8	1.6	2.0	2.4
Other Europe	5.2	4.2	4.7	8.3	7.8	4.7	39.4	52.2	68.8	77.4	78.1	79.1
Asia	3.9	8.6	4.3	6.9	4.3	13.7	86.2	143.4	190.5	176.7	206.8	187.6
Japan	1.7	5.5	2.0	3.7	1.9	3.3	44.8	79.6	108.9	105.6	141.4	119.1
China	...	...	0.1	0.5	0.9	8.3	1.2	1.6	4.3	7.0	11.3	8.6
Hong Kong	0.1	...	0.1	0.3	...	0.4	4.9	7.5	8.9	11.3	9.8	11.8
Taiwan	0.1	0.2	0.3	0.3	0.5	0.1	8.7	12.2	16.2	19.9	18.0	17.7
Singapore	0.6	1.2	0.5	0.1	0.1	0.4	2.8	5.5	8.9	7.4	6.8	6.8
South Korea	0.4	0.8	0.2	0.6	0.4	0.6	11.5	14.3	18.8	10.0	9.2	12.0
Indonesia	0.1	...	...	...	...	...	2.2	13.1	12.2	2.8	1.8	2.3
India	...	...	...	0.2	0.1	0.1	2.9	3.7	3.7	3.3	1.5	1.6
Other Asia	0.8	0.8	1.1	1.2	0.3	0.5	7.3	6.0	8.6	9.3	6.9	7.8
Africa	0.1	0.2	0.3	0.3	1.1	0.1	5.1	6.2	7.1	7.6	9.2	8.4
North Africa	...	...	...	0.1	0.5	...	0.4	1.2	1.3	1.5	0.9	0.9
Republic of South Africa	0.1	0.2	0.2	0.2	0.2	...	3.3	4.1	4.6	3.9	7.8	5.9
Other Subsaharan Africa	...	...	...	...	0.4	...	1.4	0.9	1.2	2.2	0.5	1.5
Middle East	0.3	0.5	0.5	0.2	3.5	5.4	6.7	7.9	12.8	10.6	17.3	12.8
Australia	4.9	1.9	2.9	2.5	2.1	1.2	6.1	6.6	9.0	13.0	9.7	13.2
Rest Of World	...	...	...	...	...	...	...	...	...	...	...	...

Destination	Jamestown, NY						Jersey City, NJ					
	1994	1995	1996	1997	1998	1999	1994	1995	1996	1997	1998	1999
ALL DESTINATIONS	209.4	256.6	241.2	283.5	285.9	293.7	1 351.2	1 159.9	1 140.8	1 319.4	1 402.8	1 247.1
North America	168.6	178.3	162.6	195.4	206.7	192.6	135.3	152.1	197.1	206.4	193.8	176.3
Canada	159.9	175.6	154.2	177.1	194.9	184.4	92.3	111.8	153.4	153.9	132.5	115.2
Mexico	8.7	2.8	8.4	18.4	11.8	8.2	42.9	40.3	43.8	52.5	61.4	61.1
Caribbean And Central America	0.8	0.9	1.2	1.4	1.9	2.0	39.6	47.0	39.5	48.9	39.4	30.8
South America	3.8	5.4	4.7	3.6	2.4	6.5	29.9	36.1	30.7	38.7	33.5	39.3
Argentina	0.2	0.1	...	1.1	0.3	3.0	3.6	2.2	3.6	2.2	2.6	6.0
Brazil	1.8	3.6	1.6	1.5	1.2	3.0	7.5	14.6	9.5	6.9	8.7	9.6
Other South America	1.9	1.7	3.1	0.9	1.0	0.5	18.8	19.3	17.6	29.6	22.2	23.8
Europe	20.7	49.5	56.4	62.0	57.8	70.8	410.9	173.7	96.5	121.0	130.2	113.6
Belgium	0.6	0.3	0.5	0.8	1.4	2.3	3.5	3.6	5.8	2.5	1.6	2.3
France	3.4	3.5	1.4	3.3	4.4	3.4	7.1	6.2	7.1	12.3	10.6	6.7
Germany	0.9	1.4	0.7	1.9	0.4	4.6	46.3	24.9	16.5	21.5	20.0	16.6
Netherlands	...	1.5	1.3	0.1	0.3	0.3	5.4	6.1	4.8	8.5	12.4	10.3
United Kingdom	13.1	37.5	46.6	51.5	47.9	57.3	23.4	23.4	15.2	14.0	14.8	15.3
Turkey	...	0.8	0.1	...	...	0.1	267.9	59.1	7.9	2.3	1.7	1.7
Former Soviet Republics	0.6	0.4	0.5	0.5	1.1	...	12.1	5.5	4.5	3.6	5.3	5.3
Poland	0.4	...	...	...	...	...	17.9	13.7	1.1	1.7	3.5	5.3
Other Eastern Europe	0.2	0.3	...	...	...	0.5	2.7	2.3	1.7	2.4	1.4	0.5
Other Europe	1.6	3.8	5.4	3.8	2.1	2.1	24.5	28.9	31.8	52.2	58.8	49.6
Asia	13.3	19.9	12.4	16.0	13.9	17.8	150.8	147.3	129.3	129.9	104.0	108.3
Japan	7.9	9.7	7.8	8.6	8.5	11.5	42.4	38.0	38.7	34.6	35.9	31.3
China	0.1	0.4	...	1.1	0.4	0.9	23.3	26.3	26.3	22.9	13.5	11.1
Hong Kong	2.5	1.9	1.9	2.1	2.3	2.1	20.9	29.2	20.2	18.2	17.0	13.8
Taiwan	0.2	0.6	0.2	0.1	0.2	0.6	3.9	3.1	2.0	2.3	4.4	4.5
Singapore	0.3	0.1	1.0	1.7	1.3	1.0	17.9	6.5	6.2	8.1	7.3	12.8
South Korea	1.1	3.3	0.8	0.4	...	0.3	17.8	15.1	12.8	23.9	8.8	17.0
Indonesia	...	2.5	...	0.1	...	...	2.1	1.0	2.1	1.8	0.6	1.3
India	0.2	0.8	...	0.6	0.1	0.5	9.8	11.0	6.2	1.9	3.8	8.3
Other Asia	1.0	0.6	0.6	1.4	1.1	1.0	12.7	17.0	14.8	16.2	12.7	8.1
Africa	0.9	1.5	1.9	0.5	0.3	0.7	13.4	13.8	6.1	20.9	13.9	9.3
North Africa	...	...	0.1	...	...	0.1	1.6	2.7	1.9	11.7	4.6	2.2
Republic of South Africa	0.9	1.5	1.8	0.5	0.3	0.2	10.0	7.9	2.2	5.1	4.5	2.9
Other Subsaharan Africa	...	...	...	...	...	0.3	1.8	3.3	2.0	4.1	4.8	4.2
Middle East	0.8	0.5	0.5	0.5	0.3	0.5	564.6	583.9	636.8	747.9	882.9	767.2
Australia	0.5	0.4	1.5	4.1	2.6	2.9	6.7	5.9	4.7	5.8	5.1	2.5
Rest Of World	...	...	...	...	...	...	...	...	...	...	...	...

Table E-3. Metropolitan Area Exports of Goods by Destination, 1994–1999—*Continued*

(Millions of dollars.)

Destination	Kalamazoo - Battle Creek, MI						Kansas City, MO - KS					
	1994	1995	1996	1997	1998	1999	1994	1995	1996	1997	1998	1999
ALL DESTINATIONS	869.0	897.3	836.1	919.5	929.7	1 051.8	2 578.6	3 350.2	3 985.1	3 817.6	3 631.7	3 306.2
North America	361.8	386.6	358.6	420.5	477.4	618.2	847.5	876.5	1 357.2	1 189.8	1 277.7	1 194.4
Canada	305.4	347.3	312.4	350.5	390.2	564.9	339.1	367.1	367.9	428.5	429.2	408.2
Mexico	56.4	39.2	46.1	70.0	87.1	53.3	508.4	509.4	989.3	761.3	848.5	786.2
Caribbean And Central America	10.8	13.6	14.1	16.6	14.2	10.5	103.4	145.6	199.9	201.3	114.9	114.5
South America	32.4	33.8	34.2	27.3	29.0	25.6	210.1	347.1	430.4	465.8	337.2	289.5
Argentina	6.4	4.1	8.6	5.7	4.4	4.1	14.9	25.2	27.0	58.3	25.3	15.3
Brazil	12.5	15.3	10.8	10.3	12.4	13.0	20.4	35.2	53.9	32.0	35.2	35.1
Other South America	13.5	14.4	14.8	11.3	12.2	8.5	174.8	286.7	349.5	375.5	276.8	239.1
Europe	271.6	257.3	233.4	250.0	233.0	221.1	362.0	437.1	468.4	553.0	536.8	525.2
Belgium	65.3	94.4	66.7	65.4	82.8	64.8	51.1	56.6	46.8	18.2	52.8	52.2
France	103.8	44.0	31.8	28.4	31.5	18.3	21.1	33.4	21.2	43.7	64.7	56.1
Germany	13.0	12.9	11.2	12.5	13.5	16.5	55.7	63.6	57.3	92.0	113.3	110.0
Netherlands	10.0	11.8	9.9	9.2	6.2	5.7	26.2	31.5	50.8	34.6	32.0	20.1
United Kingdom	36.7	53.9	47.1	78.8	55.2	67.7	61.0	51.6	76.2	83.5	121.6	90.5
Turkey	1.8	1.9	1.6	2.4	1.3	0.9	1.6	4.2	19.0	78.9	29.3	22.9
Former Soviet Republics	0.9	1.9	2.2	0.4	0.3	0.1	38.2	51.5	53.6	37.8	12.4	14.6
Poland	0.1	0.3	0.6	0.6	0.7	0.3	1.5	2.3	10.8	8.9	6.6	5.3
Other Eastern Europe	0.2	0.3	0.2	1.8	0.4	1.3	26.3	11.5	21.3	19.6	18.2	9.5
Other Europe	39.8	36.0	62.1	50.6	41.2	45.6	79.2	130.9	111.4	135.9	85.9	144.0
Asia	149.3	164.3	152.9	153.0	137.7	153.0	639.1	1 150.3	1 120.3	997.3	918.4	856.6
Japan	62.1	72.5	59.9	63.1	64.2	74.9	253.7	537.5	641.3	506.3	478.8	429.3
China	5.5	5.5	2.8	3.2	7.2	5.8	43.3	53.8	61.3	94.9	65.6	25.1
Hong Kong	28.7	15.9	13.4	13.4	10.9	8.2	12.0	20.1	14.2	14.1	17.0	15.0
Taiwan	12.8	11.4	9.0	6.8	10.4	11.7	96.3	147.6	131.1	134.8	73.8	160.2
Singapore	3.7	3.3	5.1	13.2	23.1	28.1	21.8	21.6	26.8	27.5	25.0	26.0
South Korea	22.3	35.8	31.4	28.4	7.9	9.9	60.7	225.7	142.7	88.4	57.5	58.1
Indonesia	1.2	2.7	2.0	2.1	1.0	1.4	5.5	17.6	24.3	48.5	62.2	42.2
India	4.5	6.2	9.9	12.1	7.2	5.6	6.9	4.1	5.9	11.7	19.6	8.6
Other Asia	8.6	11.1	19.3	10.8	5.7	7.5	138.9	122.3	72.7	71.0	118.9	92.2
Africa	4.9	6.1	6.0	6.2	3.0	4.4	154.5	151.0	146.6	138.9	155.9	134.8
North Africa	1.3	1.8	3.1	1.3	0.7	0.7	106.9	67.7	57.8	77.4	85.1	39.7
Republic of South Africa	3.3	2.6	2.7	4.8	2.2	3.7	16.5	40.1	17.3	11.6	12.8	14.7
Other Subsaharan Africa	0.3	1.7	0.2	0.1	0.1	0.1	31.1	43.3	71.6	49.9	58.0	80.5
Middle East	10.3	12.7	12.2	10.4	6.8	5.5	167.8	163.5	167.7	209.3	189.8	130.1
Australia	27.9	22.9	24.7	35.4	28.6	13.6	41.7	34.7	63.0	41.4	53.9	53.5
Rest Of World	...	...	...	...	...	...	52.4	44.3	31.5	20.8	47.1	7.6

Destination	Kenosha, WI						Knoxville, TN					
	1994	1995	1996	1997	1998	1999	1994	1995	1996	1997	1998	1999
ALL DESTINATIONS	117.7	133.9	154.3	232.1	564.8	683.9	689.2	633.2	764.1	884.2	858.3	881.4
North America	45.7	47.0	57.1	93.5	430.3	520.7	273.0	195.2	263.0	265.8	280.4	321.9
Canada	40.8	44.1	54.6	86.9	420.1	507.1	259.1	169.8	215.5	187.0	199.6	220.2
Mexico	4.9	2.8	2.4	6.5	10.3	13.6	13.9	25.4	47.5	78.8	80.8	101.8
Caribbean And Central America	14.3	18.6	18.1	16.9	18.9	34.1	13.7	17.3	22.3	40.4	54.0	38.9
South America	2.3	3.9	2.9	4.5	5.4	4.2	31.5	35.8	41.8	51.2	51.4	57.8
Argentina	0.3	0.2	0.2	0.6	0.6	0.3	13.5	10.8	19.6	15.9	7.8	26.0
Brazil	0.2	1.8	0.5	0.9	2.4	1.9	1.7	2.1	3.6	8.2	13.6	5.3
Other South America	1.8	1.9	2.3	2.9	2.4	2.1	16.3	22.9	18.7	27.1	30.1	26.5
Europe	26.0	31.0	43.5	51.6	58.5	55.8	163.0	194.3	230.4	291.2	264.5	263.8
Belgium	0.6	0.6	0.4	1.9	3.2	2.8	1.8	2.3	2.9	3.1	4.1	16.8
France	0.5	1.0	1.1	2.1	3.2	4.8	12.8	14.8	22.4	35.5	19.5	14.4
Germany	2.5	2.6	3.8	3.3	3.0	2.5	35.5	42.2	31.5	26.5	39.0	31.3
Netherlands	1.8	3.9	4.1	5.8	7.2	4.9	12.7	12.6	13.5	22.9	24.4	30.0
United Kingdom	14.3	15.7	24.4	19.1	25.9	27.4	75.4	71.4	97.9	157.0	115.8	104.1
Turkey	0.1	0.1	0.2	0.2	0.1	...	0.6	1.3	2.4	3.5	1.8	2.6
Former Soviet Republics	...	0.1	...	0.3	0.2	0.3	1.1	1.0	1.6	1.2	4.7	0.7
Poland	0.1	...	0.1	0.1	0.1	...	0.5	1.1	1.2	0.4	0.2	0.2
Other Eastern Europe	0.3	0.4	1.1	0.6	0.3	0.4	0.7	3.8	4.0	5.6	6.8	6.8
Other Europe	5.8	6.7	8.2	18.2	15.4	12.8	21.8	43.8	53.1	35.5	48.4	57.0
Asia	23.1	23.9	26.2	57.1	44.5	59.6	180.4	156.0	168.1	183.7	154.1	162.4
Japan	13.3	15.3	17.5	39.8	32.0	47.8	112.0	53.4	60.8	67.2	75.2	80.8
China	1.3	0.8	0.5	1.8	2.5	2.8	5.5	5.0	2.9	2.4	6.6	5.7
Hong Kong	2.5	1.4	0.9	2.4	1.9	2.0	3.9	7.4	12.1	19.2	19.7	12.3
Taiwan	1.5	1.0	2.1	3.1	3.0	3.4	7.4	7.5	11.8	12.1	10.5	14.4
Singapore	1.0	1.0	1.1	1.9	1.3	0.8	6.6	4.1	5.3	7.7	7.3	3.8
South Korea	2.2	2.2	0.8	5.5	0.9	0.5	31.1	55.8	40.1	44.0	15.2	18.9
Indonesia	0.2	0.5	0.7	0.7	0.1	0.1	0.8	0.1	4.9	0.4	0.1	0.5
India	0.2	0.1	0.1	0.2	1.4	0.7	0.4	1.5	3.2	4.5	1.5	2.2
Other Asia	0.9	1.6	2.5	1.7	1.3	1.4	12.9	21.2	26.9	26.3	18.0	23.8
Africa	1.0	2.4	1.9	2.1	2.3	1.8	5.4	6.1	7.6	6.6	17.7	6.1
North Africa	0.2	0.3	0.4	0.2	0.5	0.2	1.8	1.4	2.2	1.8	13.2	1.8
Republic of South Africa	0.7	1.1	1.5	1.7	1.8	1.6	3.5	4.6	4.9	4.3	3.7	3.7
Other Subsaharan Africa	0.1	1.0	0.1	0.2	...	...	0.1	0.1	0.5	0.5	0.8	0.6
Middle East	2.3	1.3	1.0	1.5	1.7	1.2	12.8	13.7	10.8	13.1	9.7	5.1
Australia	2.9	5.8	3.5	4.9	3.1	6.5	9.3	14.8	20.0	32.2	26.6	25.3
Rest Of World	...	...	...	...	...	...	...	...	...	...	...	...

Table E-3. Metropolitan Area Exports of Goods by Destination, 1994–1999—*Continued*

(Millions of dollars.)

Destination	Lafayette, LA						Lakeland - Winter Haven, FL					
	1994	1995	1996	1997	1998	1999	1994	1995	1996	1997	1998	1999
ALL DESTINATIONS	148.7	192.7	164.8	202.2	190.4	156.0	199.2	237.7	241.5	243.6	233.3	249.6
North America	32.7	43.4	45.2	71.2	79.1	73.6	54.0	64.6	40.6	43.5	49.5	64.0
Canada	26.4	36.4	34.9	63.6	66.9	66.1	49.4	56.8	38.7	41.8	45.1	37.6
Mexico	6.2	7.0	10.3	7.6	12.2	7.5	4.6	7.8	1.9	1.7	4.4	26.4
Caribbean And Central America	12.1	11.9	8.2	8.7	9.6	11.1	26.0	25.7	23.8	31.0	30.4	34.9
South America	46.8	35.1	45.2	54.4	42.1	22.5	6.6	8.3	10.8	11.9	19.7	11.5
Argentina	5.3	1.1	2.4	1.2	1.2	2.4	1.0	0.5	1.8	1.5	2.7	2.7
Brazil	3.4	5.0	2.2	3.1	2.8	3.6	1.6	2.0	2.3	1.9	0.9	1.1
Other South America	38.0	29.0	40.7	50.2	38.1	16.5	4.0	5.7	6.7	8.4	16.2	7.6
Europe	21.7	69.9	34.9	31.3	26.0	21.7	72.0	109.9	117.2	109.4	92.3	85.6
Belgium	0.1	11.9	0.3	0.6	0.2	0.2	6.7	9.1	2.3	2.4	8.6	2.5
France	3.8	4.7	1.2	1.2	1.3	2.0	7.9	9.2	23.3	24.4	5.4	7.5
Germany	0.7	1.9	0.4	0.7	0.7	0.7	4.3	6.0	5.3	4.9	4.9	5.7
Netherlands	1.0	22.7	12.3	3.6	5.2	1.7	12.6	33.8	26.9	37.3	37.8	41.6
United Kingdom	3.6	13.4	8.2	13.6	10.4	8.8	22.1	8.7	6.3	5.0	5.6	6.2
Turkey	0.2	0.2	0.1	0.2	0.4	0.2	...	2.6	7.8	0.4	1.4	0.2
Former Soviet Republics	1.5	5.2	5.4	...	...	...	0.4	0.5	0.2	0.2	1.9	0.2
Poland	...	0.1	...	0.1	0.6	...	...	1.2	3.1	1.7	1.4	0.8
Other Eastern Europe	0.1	0.2	0.2	0.5	...	0.1	0.2	1.7	0.4	0.2	0.5	0.6
Other Europe	10.8	9.4	6.8	10.8	7.2	7.9	17.7	37.0	41.5	32.8	24.8	20.2
Asia	12.9	9.8	16.2	9.8	9.9	12.3	35.0	22.2	37.1	39.1	29.0	44.1
Japan	2.3	1.3	0.8	1.4	1.0	1.2	27.7	14.7	28.0	22.6	20.3	28.0
China	0.3	0.2	1.0	1.3	0.2	0.1	3.9	1.0	2.0	2.0	0.6	1.0
Hong Kong	2.9	2.2	0.7	0.8	0.7	0.3	0.4	0.5	1.1	0.5	1.4	2.6
Taiwan	0.5	0.1	0.1	0.3	...	0.2	1.0	0.4	0.9	1.9	0.6	1.3
Singapore	3.0	2.0	1.3	1.5	3.2	4.0	0.7	0.6	1.3	0.5	0.8	0.7
South Korea	...	0.5	0.9	0.5	0.2	0.1	0.6	2.1	1.5	4.3	4.6	8.9
Indonesia	0.4	0.7	0.5	0.2	1.3	0.1	...	1.3	0.1	2.0	0.1	...
India	0.1	0.2	0.9	1.0	1.3	0.2	...	0.1	0.1	0.1	0.1	0.1
Other Asia	3.4	2.8	10.1	2.8	2.0	6.2	0.7	1.6	2.0	5.1	0.5	1.5
Africa	19.7	11.4	11.3	13.8	14.1	6.2	3.6	2.4	3.8	3.3	5.7	1.6
North Africa	0.7	1.0	0.3	4.8	0.9	0.3	...	1.1	2.5	1.5	1.7	0.4
Republic of South Africa	1.0	2.5	...	...	0.1	0.2	2.8	1.0	0.9	1.8	1.4	0.6
Other Subsaharan Africa	18.1	7.9	10.9	9.0	13.1	5.8	0.8	0.4	0.4	0.1	2.7	0.6
Middle East	2.1	9.8	2.1	9.7	7.6	6.7	1.0	3.7	4.4	3.4	5.7	7.1
Australia	0.7	1.5	1.8	3.2	2.0	1.7	1.0	0.9	3.8	2.0	0.9	0.8
Rest Of World	...	...	...	...	...	...	...	...	...	...	...	...

Destination	Lancaster, PA						Lansing - East Lansing, MI					
	1994	1995	1996	1997	1998	1999	1994	1995	1996	1997	1998	1999
ALL DESTINATIONS	469.3	581.5	626.2	620.3	591.0	539.2	208.6	224.0	202.2	217.5	186.0	243.8
North America	219.7	197.4	218.0	215.2	256.5	267.5	157.4	165.6	146.6	168.4	134.8	201.8
Canada	163.3	171.3	181.0	186.7	211.0	223.3	155.2	162.1	138.1	161.4	121.8	178.9
Mexico	56.4	26.1	37.0	28.4	45.5	44.2	2.3	3.5	8.5	7.0	13.0	22.9
Caribbean And Central America	19.9	23.0	34.0	40.1	49.6	59.2	2.7	1.2	1.5	1.5	1.0	1.1
South America	35.3	53.1	77.4	75.7	49.3	28.3	2.0	1.7	5.0	3.8	2.9	5.4
Argentina	5.7	7.5	6.5	15.2	13.9	4.0	0.3	0.4	0.6	1.3	0.8	0.8
Brazil	21.9	37.6	63.2	52.6	29.1	20.8	0.9	0.8	2.0	1.0	1.2	3.5
Other South America	7.7	7.9	7.7	7.9	6.3	3.5	0.8	0.5	2.5	1.5	0.9	1.1
Europe	113.1	159.4	132.3	129.5	147.4	116.8	19.7	20.9	22.8	24.5	28.2	18.7
Belgium	23.7	19.6	13.3	9.9	11.8	0.5	0.4	0.6	0.1	0.6	0.1	2.2
France	13.3	18.4	21.8	17.0	19.9	9.3	0.6	0.3	1.2	2.1	1.3	1.0
Germany	9.3	11.5	11.1	13.4	15.8	10.2	5.1	8.7	8.0	8.2	5.8	4.1
Netherlands	2.7	13.7	7.9	20.2	35.9	41.7	1.6	0.4	0.9	0.9	0.5	0.4
United Kingdom	41.9	39.4	34.8	22.4	35.6	24.2	5.2	6.7	5.9	9.9	16.1	5.5
Turkey	0.7	1.1	0.5	0.8	0.4	0.1	1.0	...	0.1	0.1	0.1	0.1
Former Soviet Republics	0.9	4.7	1.7	12.4	1.0	0.3	...	0.3	...	0.3	...	0.1
Poland	0.8	0.9	0.9	0.3	1.0	0.4	...	...	0.3	...	...	0.1
Other Eastern Europe	1.1	1.0	1.9	1.2	1.4	2.5	0.1	...	3.3	0.2	...	1.4
Other Europe	18.8	49.1	38.4	31.9	24.7	27.6	5.8	3.7	3.0	2.2	4.1	3.9
Asia	48.1	97.6	120.9	132.6	63.6	52.3	19.7	21.3	16.5	9.0	8.5	8.8
Japan	11.8	25.0	24.8	22.3	16.7	16.7	13.8	11.9	8.8	3.8	2.9	1.9
China	8.2	2.2	3.9	2.5	3.1	2.3	0.8	1.1	0.4	...	1.7	0.5
Hong Kong	4.2	17.4	14.3	16.8	8.7	11.0	1.3	1.9	1.3	1.1	0.5	1.2
Taiwan	5.9	8.9	16.0	11.9	14.4	7.9	0.4	0.4	0.4	0.1	0.2	0.7
Singapore	4.1	3.6	5.2	7.8	5.3	6.0	0.8	1.1	1.0	0.7	0.1	0.6
South Korea	6.4	18.7	39.0	54.2	8.9	3.1	1.8	2.2	2.4	1.2	0.6	1.9
Indonesia	0.2	0.2	...	...	...	...	...	...	...	...	...	...
India	1.1	2.4	1.0	1.2	2.0	0.6	...	0.2	0.7	0.4	0.6	1.4
Other Asia	6.3	19.2	16.8	15.9	4.4	4.8	0.8	2.6	1.6	1.5	1.9	0.6
Africa	3.3	7.3	5.5	2.8	2.0	0.9	0.8	4.0	0.6	0.5	0.3	0.3
North Africa	0.7	0.9	0.1	0.3	0.4	0.1	0.2	3.5	0.5	0.3	0.1	0.1
Republic of South Africa	2.0	5.2	4.8	0.9	1.0	0.7	0.5	0.4	0.1	0.1	0.1	0.1
Other Subsaharan Africa	0.5	1.2	0.6	1.6	0.6	0.2	0.1	0.1	...	0.1	...	0.2
Middle East	4.2	14.9	7.9	6.6	6.0	3.4	5.8	7.9	7.9	7.8	8.0	5.5
Australia	25.8	28.8	30.3	17.8	16.7	10.7	0.4	1.3	1.3	2.0	2.3	2.3
Rest Of World	...	...	...	...	...	...	...	...	...	...	...	...

Table E-3. Metropolitan Area Exports of Goods by Destination, 1994–1999—Continued

(Millions of dollars.)

Destination	Laredo, TX						Lawrence, MA - NH					
	1994	1995	1996	1997	1998	1999	1994	1995	1996	1997	1998	1999
ALL DESTINATIONS	4 157.4	2 897.8	3 440.7	3 959.1	3 633.6	2 681.7	806.4	841.7	1 033.6	1 810.2	1 544.9	1 749.5
North America	4 135.7	2 880.4	3 420.5	3 927.6	3 597.6	2 660.1	153.6	185.3	188.7	240.1	252.8	291.8
Canada	87.1	295.1	242.3	268.2	162.8	55.1	142.7	179.1	178.5	226.7	235.9	265.5
Mexico	4 048.6	2 585.2	3 178.2	3 659.5	3 434.8	2 605.0	10.9	6.3	10.2	13.4	16.9	26.3
Caribbean And Central America	4.9	3.4	2.1	1.1	4.4	1.4	3.5	3.6	5.7	6.7	12.8	7.6
South America	1.6	6.1	3.3	3.8	3.2	3.1	10.2	15.5	15.2	33.3	42.5	38.1
Argentina	0.3	0.1	0.5	0.1	0.1	. . .	1.2	2.5	2.5	5.8	6.1	6.4
Brazil	0.3	0.3	0.1	. . .	0.1	2.0	3.9	6.3	6.4	18.1	18.3	19.6
Other South America	1.1	5.7	2.7	3.7	3.0	1.1	5.0	6.7	6.3	9.4	18.1	12.1
Europe	12.1	4.0	8.0	6.9	7.7	8.5	378.3	375.9	354.1	728.0	701.1	733.1
Belgium	0.3	0.6	2.2	0.7	0.7	1.6	6.2	6.8	7.8	7.9	6.9	7.6
France	1.0	0.7	1.0	0.7	0.8	0.4	79.6	43.6	30.8	49.5	72.1	63.1
Germany	0.3	0.4	0.8	0.1	0.3	0.4	119.0	118.4	133.4	139.8	130.3	140.0
Netherlands	7.4	0.8	. . .	0.6	2.0	0.7	15.2	29.9	22.2	54.4	41.3	58.5
United Kingdom	1.8	0.6	1.8	1.2	1.8	1.7	66.0	61.3	62.0	349.1	284.1	317.0
Turkey	. . .	0.1	. . .	. . .	. . .	. . .	0.3	0.2	0.5	0.8	0.4	1.8
Former Soviet Republics	. . .	. . .	. . .	. . .	. . .	. . .	4.3	2.1	4.6	10.1	3.4	4.9
Poland	0.1	. . .	. . .	. . .	. . .	. . .	1.1	3.4	0.9	3.6	1.3	7.1
Other Eastern Europe	. . .	. . .	. . .	. . .	. . .	. . .	2.0	2.8	2.4	1.8	2.1	4.2
Other Europe	1.3	0.7	2.2	3.6	2.1	3.7	84.6	107.3	89.5	111.1	159.2	128.8
Asia	2.6	3.1	5.3	18.1	18.3	6.6	216.8	219.1	433.9	735.1	460.9	571.0
Japan	0.8	1.4	0.6	4.7	3.5	1.0	112.9	111.0	192.8	325.0	256.3	259.1
China	. . .	0.1	0.1	5.2	4.8	1.2	10.1	11.4	16.4	24.3	36.8	43.8
Hong Kong	0.7	0.3	0.2	2.3	5.3	2.2	17.9	20.8	23.2	38.7	42.1	38.6
Taiwan	0.4	0.6	0.6	0.1	0.2	0.2	17.6	23.6	147.6	251.0	63.7	45.4
Singapore	0.4	0.3	2.3	3.0	2.0	0.9	18.8	16.9	12.3	22.0	17.1	103.9
South Korea	0.3	0.3	1.3	1.5	0.7	0.2	22.0	20.2	22.2	39.3	18.2	46.9
Indonesia	. . .	. . .	. . .	. . .	0.2	. . .	0.4	0.7	0.8	1.2	1.0	1.1
India	0.1	. . .	. . .	0.4	0.5	0.8	4.0	3.1	2.8	4.4	5.3	9.3
Other Asia	. . .	0.1	0.2	0.9	1.2	0.2	13.0	11.5	15.9	29.2	20.3	23.0
Africa	. . .	. . .	. . .	. . .	. . .	0.2	7.4	8.4	5.3	7.4	7.9	9.6
North Africa	. . .	. . .	. . .	. . .	. . .	. . .	1.3	1.1	0.6	1.0	0.7	2.3
Republic of South Africa	. . .	. . .	. . .	. . .	. . .	. . .	6.0	7.0	4.7	6.3	6.5	5.1
Other Subsaharan Africa	. . .	. . .	. . .	. . .	. . .	0.2	0.1	0.3	. . .	0.1	0.6	2.2
Middle East	0.4	0.3	0.9	0.2	0.5	0.8	18.3	16.6	11.6	29.9	41.0	62.6
Australia	0.1	0.5	0.5	1.4	1.8	1.0	18.4	17.4	19.1	29.7	26.0	35.8
Rest Of World	. . .	. . .	. . .	. . .	. . .	. . .	. . .	. . .	. . .	. . .	. . .	. . .

Destination	Lexington, KY						Lima, OH					
	1994	1995	1996	1997	1998	1999	1994	1995	1996	1997	1998	1999
ALL DESTINATIONS	1 078.6	1 235.0	1 499.9	1 886.8	1 838.1	1 837.6	166.2	226.0	207.3	242.0	264.1	262.4
North America	535.9	629.6	690.9	897.5	810.6	957.8	96.8	142.7	112.5	146.3	154.3	176.7
Canada	493.8	589.5	619.5	793.6	681.7	771.8	91.6	140.2	109.3	140.3	145.8	170.1
Mexico	42.2	40.0	71.4	103.9	129.0	186.0	5.3	2.6	3.2	6.1	8.5	6.6
Caribbean And Central America	2.8	4.8	7.4	5.2	7.3	7.8	0.3	0.8	0.4	1.3	3.2	1.2
South America	29.1	36.0	45.8	64.3	78.1	70.0	6.3	6.3	12.1	13.0	9.8	7.5
Argentina	12.9	9.1	13.5	16.6	23.6	21.8	1.0	1.4	2.4	3.8	1.7	0.7
Brazil	2.7	11.8	14.0	24.0	28.2	22.6	1.6	1.3	4.4	3.4	2.9	3.1
Other South America	13.5	15.1	18.3	23.7	26.2	25.6	3.7	3.5	5.3	5.8	5.2	3.7
Europe	226.5	236.6	410.4	467.7	490.4	496.4	24.5	24.7	20.3	16.1	29.2	26.7
Belgium	8.2	2.6	4.6	4.3	2.6	1.8	3.6	2.7	2.7	2.1	4.3	5.0
France	123.3	108.4	195.7	279.8	241.2	166.3	0.9	3.3	2.7	1.1	2.5	0.7
Germany	5.7	20.5	25.1	19.1	17.2	18.7	3.2	4.5	3.4	3.0	4.0	3.8
Netherlands	32.4	27.1	47.7	56.5	46.6	45.1	0.6	0.5	1.0	0.3	0.5	1.5
United Kingdom	31.9	61.8	113.7	64.1	94.7	141.6	10.0	6.8	2.7	4.0	6.3	6.7
Turkey	7.3	0.4	10.0	21.2	18.3	11.5	0.2	. . .	0.1	0.2	1.0	0.1
Former Soviet Republics	0.1	0.3	0.1	0.5	0.5	0.2	. . .	0.1	0.1	0.4	. . .	. . .
Poland	0.1	. . .	0.2	0.2	0.1	0.2	0.2	. . .	0.1	0.1	0.1	0.1
Other Eastern Europe	0.2	0.1	0.1	4.9	41.5	78.8	0.1	. . .	1.6	. . .	0.2	. . .
Other Europe	17.5	15.4	13.1	17.1	27.6	32.3	5.8	6.8	5.9	4.7	10.2	8.9
Asia	248.1	287.8	291.7	377.6	380.7	249.0	23.2	25.0	28.8	38.8	34.6	15.3
Japan	206.7	229.9	208.1	300.2	332.5	164.1	5.7	8.2	6.4	17.6	21.2	5.1
China	1.8	2.2	5.5	2.9	3.6	10.6	4.4	5.4	3.8	5.8	4.1	1.1
Hong Kong	5.1	7.1	6.7	10.2	8.9	9.9	0.4	0.7	0.7	0.7	0.4	0.2
Taiwan	2.3	5.9	11.3	8.6	7.6	10.6	3.2	1.0	1.7	0.2	0.6	0.2
Singapore	8.5	8.8	9.5	13.0	9.7	8.6	1.4	2.8	4.1	4.5	1.5	1.8
South Korea	14.6	23.3	35.0	26.0	6.5	13.9	3.6	1.3	3.1	3.8	0.9	1.0
Indonesia	0.5	1.3	1.2	7.0	2.2	1.0	0.4	1.2	0.8	0.4	. . .	0.2
India	0.9	1.6	1.6	1.4	1.7	1.1	. . .	. . .	. . .	. . .	0.1	0.1
Other Asia	7.7	7.7	12.6	8.3	8.1	29.3	4.1	4.5	8.1	5.8	5.8	5.6
Africa	1.6	5.5	6.7	9.1	5.5	4.2	0.6	1.8	1.6	1.4	2.0	0.7
North Africa	0.3	0.8	2.9	4.7	2.9	0.6	. . .	0.1	. . .	0.3	0.2	0.2
Republic of South Africa	0.6	3.9	3.3	3.7	2.2	3.4	0.6	1.6	1.4	0.8	1.5	0.5
Other Subsaharan Africa	0.6	0.8	0.5	0.6	0.3	0.3	. . .	0.1	0.1	0.2	0.4	. . .
Middle East	6.3	5.4	3.7	4.0	5.2	6.3	0.7	0.5	0.9	2.0	2.7	1.1
Australia	28.2	29.5	43.4	61.5	60.2	46.0	13.7	24.2	30.7	23.0	28.3	33.2
Rest Of World	. . .	. . .	. . .	. . .	. . .	. . .	. . .	. . .	. . .	. . .	. . .	. . .

Table E-3. Metropolitan Area Exports of Goods by Destination, 1994–1999—*Continued*

(Millions of dollars.)

Destination	Lincoln, NE						Little Rock - North Little Rock, AR					
	1994	1995	1996	1997	1998	1999	1994	1995	1996	1997	1998	1999
ALL DESTINATIONS	207.2	208.8	225.3	264.6	261.7	275.6	219.0	193.6	210.4	349.4	262.3	311.9
North America	51.4	58.6	68.3	94.9	90.3	94.5	107.9	85.6	93.4	194.9	116.0	177.7
Canada	42.4	53.7	64.2	89.8	84.1	78.1	76.9	77.8	82.3	162.5	90.0	99.6
Mexico	9.0	4.9	4.1	5.1	6.2	16.4	31.0	7.8	11.1	32.5	26.0	78.2
Caribbean And Central America	1.3	0.6	0.4	1.2	2.1	1.8	3.9	3.1	4.2	5.0	5.4	4.2
South America	3.3	4.6	6.3	9.0	12.3	10.8	4.3	5.7	6.8	12.5	20.0	5.7
Argentina	1.2	0.9	0.7	1.0	1.4	1.1	1.1	1.0	0.8	2.4	4.6	0.7
Brazil	0.7	1.5	3.1	3.9	5.4	6.2	0.6	1.2	2.6	4.3	7.8	1.4
Other South America	1.4	2.3	2.5	4.1	5.5	3.5	2.7	3.5	3.4	5.9	7.6	3.6
Europe	70.9	57.0	55.5	79.9	88.4	83.4	40.2	41.0	46.8	57.7	53.6	56.2
Belgium	1.3	1.5	5.6	9.5	17.0	16.2	0.3	0.6	0.9	0.8	1.0	4.0
France	7.4	2.5	1.9	3.6	7.3	6.5	5.6	7.7	17.3	7.9	5.3	8.4
Germany	13.4	8.6	12.7	17.7	21.4	16.7	1.6	2.6	1.8	1.8	1.9	3.1
Netherlands	19.3	12.8	8.5	10.6	11.2	9.8	2.4	2.2	2.8	7.9	8.7	17.1
United Kingdom	13.5	14.0	12.9	20.1	13.5	13.3	13.5	11.4	10.8	11.1	14.9	11.5
Turkey	...	0.2	0.2	0.2	0.8	0.4	...	...	0.1	0.1	0.2	0.1
Former Soviet Republics	0.3	0.2	0.2	1.0	0.1	0.3	9.2	6.7	4.5	12.6	6.6	1.2
Poland	0.4	0.7	0.1	0.3	0.2	0.4	...	...	...	1.7	0.6	0.3
Other Eastern Europe	1.3	1.0	0.4	0.5	0.2	0.5	0.1	0.1	0.2	2.1	1.3	1.3
Other Europe	13.9	15.5	12.9	16.6	16.5	19.5	7.4	9.7	8.6	11.8	13.2	9.3
Asia	61.6	73.1	72.9	63.5	50.5	63.2	43.2	42.0	45.4	59.2	51.4	54.7
Japan	45.4	50.9	46.2	35.4	28.8	39.8	3.4	5.5	6.7	5.7	5.9	7.8
China	0.2	0.6	2.7	4.7	5.7	4.0	0.9	1.2	2.1	1.0	1.3	1.5
Hong Kong	1.8	1.2	0.7	1.4	2.5	1.6	0.7	2.7	5.9	5.8	3.3	1.7
Taiwan	2.0	1.7	3.8	2.7	2.3	3.0	4.0	5.3	3.2	4.0	4.8	3.3
Singapore	0.7	0.8	1.4	1.4	1.1	1.3	2.7	3.8	3.5	5.2	5.3	3.8
South Korea	3.3	7.8	4.1	3.7	1.7	6.2	2.6	5.1	3.7	4.4	1.5	5.2
Indonesia	0.1	0.2	0.4	2.5	0.1	...	0.7	0.9	1.1	0.9	...	0.2
India	0.6	0.4	0.2	0.4	0.9	0.5	0.2	0.3	0.4	0.6	0.9	0.2
Other Asia	7.5	9.6	13.3	11.2	7.3	6.9	28.1	17.1	18.7	31.6	28.2	30.3
Africa	2.1	2.8	2.4	4.5	2.8	2.5	1.6	1.7	2.2	2.0	1.8	1.4
North Africa	0.8	1.1	0.4	1.4	0.6	0.5	0.2	0.1	0.6	0.6	0.8	1.0
Republic of South Africa	1.0	1.5	1.7	2.4	1.9	1.6	1.0	1.3	1.4	1.0	0.6	0.2
Other Subsaharan Africa	0.2	0.2	0.4	0.7	0.3	0.4	0.3	0.2	0.1	0.4	0.4	0.2
Middle East	2.7	1.3	2.3	2.3	1.8	2.5	12.2	8.6	7.6	9.0	6.5	4.6
Australia	13.7	10.7	17.2	9.3	13.6	16.9	5.8	5.8	4.0	8.9	7.6	7.4
Rest Of World	...	...	...	...	...	...	...	...	...	...	...	...

Destination	Los Angeles - Long Beach, CA						Louisville, KY - IN					
	1994	1995	1996	1997	1998	1999	1994	1995	1996	1997	1998	1999
ALL DESTINATIONS	22 224.8	24 731.0	24 437.9	25 816.4	25 554.7	23 904.7	1 798.8	2 199.8	2 327.1	2 449.1	2 290.4	2 392.7
North America	3 232.6	3 558.2	4 044.4	4 949.8	5 666.0	6 217.6	372.1	381.2	445.7	574.6	611.4	767.7
Canada	1 894.6	2 378.7	2 457.5	2 831.3	3 204.0	3 325.3	279.9	357.6	411.5	534.8	553.1	692.3
Mexico	1 337.9	1 179.5	1 586.8	2 118.5	2 461.9	2 892.3	92.2	23.6	34.2	39.8	58.4	75.4
Caribbean And Central America	173.2	175.1	206.6	225.4	405.2	279.6	28.6	26.0	24.8	27.2	29.7	37.8
South America	885.5	1 155.0	992.6	1 030.4	1 176.6	775.0	54.1	78.1	55.9	91.9	51.2	45.5
Argentina	122.6	112.3	122.7	142.5	144.9	121.6	8.3	16.9	5.9	30.9	6.5	4.1
Brazil	361.2	445.2	478.2	363.8	416.6	279.7	8.5	19.3	15.9	20.6	18.8	17.6
Other South America	401.7	597.5	391.6	524.1	615.1	373.7	37.3	41.9	34.2	40.3	25.9	23.8
Europe	4 987.5	4 875.6	4 337.3	4 681.8	5 489.7	4 662.6	432.1	471.3	591.0	699.6	672.3	597.4
Belgium	167.4	180.1	298.5	192.6	319.0	181.3	94.8	28.6	24.1	30.7	31.4	32.6
France	583.3	401.3	479.5	474.3	408.9	498.0	24.9	26.5	45.1	57.2	47.1	44.5
Germany	548.2	536.1	545.7	508.0	1 077.4	1 027.8	124.7	174.6	154.9	172.6	165.9	134.2
Netherlands	1 178.6	1 353.9	473.9	613.7	660.1	531.9	8.5	16.3	30.3	39.4	33.7	27.7
United Kingdom	718.5	824.8	911.4	824.2	1 094.3	1 029.3	40.7	47.1	84.7	109.9	100.6	95.4
Turkey	23.2	27.3	38.0	321.3	138.6	64.4	3.7	9.1	33.4	60.1	10.5	3.1
Former Soviet Republics	89.4	124.9	167.7	120.1	151.0	52.2	3.3	7.5	10.0	26.1	82.4	30.2
Poland	15.1	14.3	14.6	15.0	14.2	11.0	0.1	0.8	0.7	1.6	0.4	0.7
Other Eastern Europe	34.6	39.0	42.8	50.0	45.3	31.7	1.4	3.0	4.2	7.2	17.9	7.4
Other Europe	1 629.0	1 374.0	1 365.1	1 562.6	1 581.1	1 234.9	130.1	157.8	203.5	194.8	182.3	221.6
Asia	11 960.7	13 759.0	13 562.6	13 209.1	10 327.5	10 031.4	713.2	1 020.6	1 017.3	875.9	772.8	837.6
Japan	5 806.9	7 060.5	6 719.4	5 907.4	4 904.6	4 464.4	453.8	712.9	709.3	601.8	611.8	691.9
China	522.7	482.3	751.1	857.1	798.6	922.1	1.4	10.4	13.6	22.9	13.6	11.6
Hong Kong	763.0	1 010.1	893.7	952.3	811.1	703.8	53.9	40.7	30.8	17.9	13.9	14.6
Taiwan	2 140.1	1 977.4	1 325.7	1 532.7	1 285.0	1 046.9	24.0	37.9	47.5	43.6	22.3	24.3
Singapore	464.8	481.8	524.6	576.5	411.2	433.3	76.8	70.4	87.2	65.9	47.2	29.8
South Korea	1 395.3	1 698.1	2 086.3	1 835.0	1 026.0	1 537.6	42.8	73.8	67.6	59.8	31.8	42.4
Indonesia	113.7	167.6	334.9	361.7	70.8	91.6	2.3	6.1	6.6	3.4	1.4	1.0
India	35.8	66.2	70.0	61.9	53.3	53.8	0.7	2.7	7.4	6.2	2.5	3.4
Other Asia	718.5	815.0	856.9	1 124.3	967.0	777.9	57.5	65.8	47.3	54.5	28.3	18.6
Africa	105.1	110.2	144.9	153.4	120.7	158.9	6.8	10.4	11.9	12.7	11.8	8.4
North Africa	30.1	29.5	70.0	79.5	36.6	99.6	3.1	5.6	6.4	5.8	3.8	2.8
Republic of South Africa	38.3	38.6	50.1	42.5	54.9	35.6	1.5	2.6	4.1	5.5	6.5	4.5
Other Subsaharan Africa	36.6	42.1	24.8	31.3	29.2	23.7	2.2	2.3	1.4	1.4	1.5	1.1
Middle East	283.4	404.9	464.1	849.5	1 574.3	1 018.6	157.6	170.3	135.9	128.4	112.3	70.5
Australia	596.8	692.9	685.5	717.0	794.7	761.1	34.3	41.6	44.5	38.9	28.9	27.8
Rest Of World	...	...	...	0.1	...	...	...	0.2	...	...	...	...

Table E-3. Metropolitan Area Exports of Goods by Destination, 1994–1999—*Continued*

(Millions of dollars.)

Destination	Lowell, MA - NH						Lubbock, TX					
	1994	1995	1996	1997	1998	1999	1994	1995	1996	1997	1998	1999
ALL DESTINATIONS	890.1	1 079.9	1 119.9	1 396.5	1 449.8	1 237.6	165.1	258.7	189.0	262.2	225.1	132.3
North America	122.2	144.9	161.8	175.2	224.6	236.0	62.6	70.1	65.7	79.8	83.4	56.5
Canada	103.8	131.0	146.2	152.3	191.6	202.5	11.9	17.9	12.2	9.4	15.1	17.8
Mexico	18.4	13.9	15.6	22.9	33.1	33.5	50.7	52.3	53.5	70.4	68.3	38.7
Caribbean And Central America	4.1	3.2	3.8	7.7	8.4	11.2	1.0	0.4	0.9	1.2	1.4	2.1
South America	28.1	26.4	19.1	49.8	34.1	31.5	16.9	29.3	29.5	34.3	13.5	7.6
Argentina	3.7	3.1	3.8	6.8	4.5	2.3	0.1	0.2	8.3	0.8	0.3	0.1
Brazil	10.5	17.0	8.0	28.5	16.4	18.3	1.7	1.7	0.1	11.2	1.4	0.3
Other South America	13.9	6.3	7.3	14.4	13.2	10.9	15.2	27.4	21.1	22.4	11.7	7.2
Europe	442.5	501.8	482.9	623.4	674.1	567.8	13.7	20.9	14.2	33.2	51.5	24.5
Belgium	30.4	31.7	31.4	11.6	19.6	22.6	0.1	0.1	0.3	0.8	0.8	2.0
France	68.0	69.9	41.8	95.0	75.5	64.3	0.1	0.9	0.9	0.6	0.8	0.8
Germany	63.1	86.5	75.2	117.7	224.5	98.5	1.7	1.1	1.0	1.0	1.2	1.0
Netherlands	62.1	74.3	84.3	81.9	48.9	65.5	2.1	1.4	1.3	0.2	1.1	2.0
United Kingdom	95.2	105.0	90.8	116.4	108.7	119.7	2.4	1.0	1.0	3.1	2.4	1.2
Turkey	1.1	1.4	1.2	1.3	2.4	1.6	...	1.2	0.8	19.7	38.4	12.8
Former Soviet Republics	0.7	10.8	2.0	7.1	7.0	2.5	...	...	...	...	...	0.1
Poland	1.1	0.7	0.5	1.0	1.9	2.2	...	...	...	0.5	0.4	0.1
Other Eastern Europe	2.1	4.0	7.1	7.8	5.9	7.7	0.3	1.4	1.1	0.6	...	0.1
Other Europe	118.9	117.5	148.8	183.5	179.6	183.2	7.1	13.8	8.0	6.7	6.5	4.6
Asia	222.6	343.0	391.4	464.8	441.3	325.0	62.6	130.2	62.3	106.0	67.6	38.0
Japan	108.4	160.7	217.2	238.5	233.4	116.2	1.1	2.2	0.8	1.0	0.6	0.4
China	5.7	10.6	16.5	8.0	41.0	17.0	16.5	15.0	15.0	28.5	1.3	0.2
Hong Kong	27.2	43.6	27.6	26.6	27.6	28.7	2.3	7.5	1.9	2.1	2.3	4.9
Taiwan	14.3	27.4	17.1	35.3	28.6	29.0	3.7	13.8	9.3	22.5	13.8	4.3
Singapore	22.4	29.1	23.8	37.4	40.1	45.9	0.5	0.5	0.5	0.4	0.7	0.1
South Korea	26.8	46.9	60.0	73.2	29.0	38.6	4.7	4.2	2.2	1.1	3.8	6.2
Indonesia	1.2	1.8	5.8	6.9	1.7	2.6	7.9	12.8	3.1	5.9	8.3	0.6
India	2.7	4.6	3.8	4.1	4.5	8.5	...	15.1	1.2	0.3	0.8	0.7
Other Asia	13.9	18.2	19.7	34.9	35.5	38.5	25.9	59.1	28.3	44.1	36.0	20.5
Africa	14.2	9.7	8.1	9.4	12.1	19.9	4.7	2.4	10.8	3.9	1.3	0.5
North Africa	1.5	0.7	0.5	1.1	1.0	10.9	4.6	2.4	10.7	1.1	0.2	0.1
Republic of South Africa	10.9	7.6	6.7	6.6	10.0	6.9	...	...	...	...	...	0.1
Other Subsaharan Africa	1.8	1.5	0.9	1.7	1.1	2.0	0.1	...	0.1	2.7	1.1	0.3
Middle East	30.2	15.9	14.2	22.6	17.6	21.7	2.9	2.3	2.9	2.9	2.7	2.1
Australia	26.2	35.0	38.5	43.6	37.4	24.5	0.7	3.1	2.7	0.8	3.8	1.0
Rest Of World	...	...	...	...	...	...	...	...	...	...	...	...

Destination	Lynchburg, VA						Madison, WI					
	1994	1995	1996	1997	1998	1999	1994	1995	1996	1997	1998	1999
ALL DESTINATIONS	152.5	192.1	258.8	439.2	442.8	451.6	417.1	497.5	522.4	603.0	587.8	657.9
North America	75.6	73.6	86.3	144.1	161.7	229.6	120.5	127.2	140.1	183.6	216.0	237.1
Canada	62.0	63.0	74.2	110.7	122.8	105.3	105.0	118.4	132.4	165.7	192.6	218.9
Mexico	13.6	10.6	12.1	33.4	38.9	124.4	15.6	8.8	7.7	18.0	23.5	18.2
Caribbean And Central America	1.1	1.9	2.3	3.5	7.0	12.4	3.7	3.5	3.6	2.8	3.8	6.9
South America	15.2	36.1	66.5	79.2	117.2	60.2	18.3	29.3	27.1	31.5	24.3	17.0
Argentina	2.6	8.2	5.5	25.3	9.3	3.4	3.3	3.7	2.6	3.4	4.2	3.1
Brazil	7.1	15.9	34.2	24.8	25.0	16.3	7.0	16.3	13.6	12.4	12.6	7.5
Other South America	5.4	12.0	26.8	29.1	82.9	40.5	7.9	9.4	11.0	15.7	7.5	6.4
Europe	33.9	42.3	50.9	70.9	80.6	84.2	156.7	178.8	197.4	220.3	215.5	251.6
Belgium	1.3	1.2	0.4	0.5	0.8	1.2	1.3	2.4	4.0	3.3	3.0	4.7
France	5.4	1.6	2.8	3.5	4.5	4.3	20.9	20.9	20.2	36.2	33.5	53.8
Germany	5.9	8.2	12.8	9.3	7.1	6.1	34.8	40.4	51.2	47.8	31.6	46.4
Netherlands	0.7	1.0	2.1	3.3	6.6	15.3	13.3	15.2	19.7	21.0	18.6	21.2
United Kingdom	8.2	10.0	9.7	11.6	12.6	12.5	36.8	43.4	44.3	52.8	60.6	62.5
Turkey	0.2	0.7	0.1	0.1	...	...	1.4	0.5	0.9	2.0	3.8	1.6
Former Soviet Republics	1.7	0.8	0.3	18.0	12.5	3.0	4.6	4.1	1.6	1.7	4.2	1.3
Poland	1.9	1.3	0.9	2.0	2.6	1.0	1.0	0.8	2.7	1.3	2.2	2.2
Other Eastern Europe	0.2	0.6	0.2	1.0	1.7	0.5	3.5	3.5	5.5	4.7	4.2	2.7
Other Europe	8.5	17.0	21.6	21.5	32.2	40.2	39.1	47.7	47.2	49.6	53.9	55.1
Asia	19.3	28.8	37.9	75.5	54.9	39.2	82.6	105.2	107.9	115.1	87.1	109.2
Japan	5.6	8.1	9.3	10.9	9.1	5.4	34.7	50.2	50.2	50.4	40.7	48.7
China	2.4	3.7	3.1	3.1	2.0	1.3	5.2	5.9	5.1	6.1	7.6	9.4
Hong Kong	1.9	2.6	6.0	34.5	25.8	13.4	8.5	5.2	6.7	7.8	9.2	13.9
Taiwan	3.2	3.4	3.3	7.7	4.0	4.1	7.6	8.2	9.1	10.4	7.6	9.9
Singapore	1.3	3.0	3.2	3.1	0.9	1.8	8.8	8.3	7.9	10.5	5.0	4.4
South Korea	2.0	2.1	5.7	5.0	3.0	2.2	8.9	14.9	12.5	13.4	5.5	9.7
Indonesia	0.3	0.6	1.2	1.4	0.2	1.1	0.2	0.6	0.3	1.2	0.4	0.1
India	0.1	...	0.1	1.3	0.2	0.2	3.1	3.1	2.9	3.1	3.8	3.2
Other Asia	2.5	5.5	6.1	8.4	9.6	9.7	5.6	8.8	13.1	12.2	7.2	9.9
Africa	1.8	2.7	4.7	3.8	1.2	1.8	7.2	18.2	12.2	14.1	5.7	6.3
North Africa	...	...	1.6	2.5	0.7	1.0	3.1	13.3	5.9	6.8	1.4	1.6
Republic of South Africa	1.7	2.7	3.1	0.5	0.4	0.6	3.1	4.3	5.8	6.4	3.8	4.1
Other Subsaharan Africa	0.1	...	...	0.7	...	0.2	1.1	0.6	0.4	0.9	0.5	0.7
Middle East	2.8	5.4	7.5	55.2	15.5	20.2	16.9	22.5	21.1	20.3	23.7	19.8
Australia	2.9	1.3	2.7	7.1	4.7	4.1	11.1	12.7	13.0	15.1	11.6	10.0
Rest Of World	...	...	...	...	...	...	...	...	...	...	...	...

Table E-3. Metropolitan Area Exports of Goods by Destination, 1994–1999—*Continued*

(Millions of dollars.)

Destination	Manchester, NH						Mansfield, OH					
	1994	1995	1996	1997	1998	1999	1994	1995	1996	1997	1998	1999
ALL DESTINATIONS	115.3	146.3	198.3	237.8	219.7	237.3	349.9	394.9	413.0	444.0	430.7	462.8
North America	67.8	72.4	115.1	134.0	111.6	104.5	219.1	251.7	279.2	313.6	301.9	358.8
Canada	51.0	57.9	96.9	114.9	91.8	88.5	194.7	235.2	259.4	269.3	267.3	316.2
Mexico	16.8	14.6	18.2	19.1	19.7	16.0	24.4	16.5	19.7	44.3	34.6	42.5
Caribbean And Central America	4.6	6.1	5.9	7.7	10.3	13.5	2.0	2.6	2.8	2.5	2.8	3.1
South America	1.9	4.1	5.7	3.1	6.1	6.5	13.2	10.8	8.0	7.8	6.3	5.1
Argentina	0.4	0.1	0.1	0.3	1.1	1.1	1.2	1.7	0.6	1.8	0.8	0.8
Brazil	0.3	2.0	1.3	1.4	2.8	1.7	3.7	2.8	1.3	0.8	2.0	2.1
Other South America	1.2	1.9	4.3	1.4	2.2	3.8	8.2	6.4	6.1	5.2	3.5	2.2
Europe	24.9	39.3	44.7	53.4	58.1	60.7	51.0	73.7	70.5	71.8	79.0	54.3
Belgium	4.8	0.3	1.4	3.2	2.6	3.6	1.0	1.0	1.4	0.7	0.3	0.5
France	3.4	2.5	2.4	3.3	3.8	3.0	6.0	9.7	12.6	8.2	8.3	4.3
Germany	3.1	5.1	6.2	7.8	11.7	15.0	15.1	18.7	13.7	20.2	25.8	15.3
Netherlands	2.3	9.0	15.9	12.1	10.7	12.6	2.8	5.1	2.3	2.1	2.4	3.1
United Kingdom	5.7	13.1	9.7	11.8	15.6	12.4	10.2	22.9	22.9	19.7	22.7	20.2
Turkey	0.2	0.2	0.1	0.1	0.2	0.8	0.4	0.6	0.3	0.4	0.2	0.5
Former Soviet Republics	0.4	0.7	0.9	0.8	0.1	0.1	...	...	0.1	0.3	0.4	0.1
Poland	0.1	0.1	...	0.1	0.7	0.6	...	...	0.2	0.2	0.2	0.3
Other Eastern Europe	...	1.4	0.8	0.3	0.2	1.7	...	...	...	0.3	0.8	0.2
Other Europe	5.0	6.9	7.3	13.9	12.6	11.0	15.6	15.7	16.9	19.9	17.9	9.7
Asia	11.9	18.5	23.3	28.7	21.9	34.5	37.4	31.3	26.4	29.2	22.6	20.2
Japan	2.8	2.7	4.0	5.8	4.4	4.4	15.0	6.2	5.4	6.9	6.9	3.4
China	0.6	1.6	0.5	2.0	1.3	1.2	3.4	0.9	1.2	2.1	1.3	1.8
Hong Kong	1.3	5.1	6.8	5.3	4.7	6.3	0.3	0.6	1.3	1.9	3.7	2.7
Taiwan	1.7	1.9	3.4	4.6	4.7	1.8	2.1	2.3	2.2	3.0	1.7	1.8
Singapore	2.0	1.4	2.1	2.5	1.5	3.9	1.3	1.5	1.0	1.7	1.0	0.7
South Korea	1.6	3.1	2.6	3.6	1.9	10.1	2.9	5.7	5.5	3.0	3.7	5.1
Indonesia	...	0.4	0.2	0.2	...	0.1	...	...	0.3	0.4	...	0.1
India	0.3	0.4	0.2	0.2	0.7	0.3	6.0	10.6	6.0	4.6	1.8	2.6
Other Asia	1.7	2.0	3.5	4.4	2.7	6.4	6.3	3.6	3.5	5.7	2.4	2.0
Africa	0.7	0.9	0.6	1.5	1.5	1.1	7.3	6.3	9.4	3.7	4.2	3.7
North Africa	0.4	0.6	0.6	0.9	0.9	0.2	0.8	0.6	2.2	1.0	1.1	1.0
Republic of South Africa	0.2	0.2	0.1	0.5	0.5	0.9	6.0	5.6	6.8	2.4	3.2	2.7
Other Subsaharan Africa	0.1	0.1	...	...	...	...	0.4	0.1	0.3	0.2	...	...
Middle East	0.7	1.1	1.0	5.0	2.3	6.8	4.0	2.0	2.2	2.9	1.8	1.8
Australia	2.7	3.9	1.9	4.5	8.0	9.8	15.9	16.5	14.6	12.4	12.0	15.7
Rest Of World	...	...	...	...	...	...	...	...	...	...	...	0.1

Destination	McAllen - Edinburg - Mission, TX						Melbourne - Titusville - Palm Bay, FL					
	1994	1995	1996	1997	1998	1999	1994	1995	1996	1997	1998	1999
ALL DESTINATIONS	1 826.4	1 617.1	1 579.7	1 872.9	1 791.8	1 991.5	315.9	310.1	635.0	408.8	538.5	635.8
North America	1 798.3	1 576.4	1 533.8	1 786.0	1 682.9	1 891.8	62.5	79.6	137.4	144.4	143.4	164.0
Canada	78.3	121.8	126.8	173.8	178.5	231.4	53.7	76.2	127.4	123.5	120.5	129.4
Mexico	1 720.0	1 454.6	1 407.0	1 612.2	1 504.4	1 660.4	8.8	3.4	10.0	20.8	22.9	34.6
Caribbean And Central America	5.8	4.9	5.7	2.1	6.4	17.5	16.1	5.5	6.0	8.2	22.6	32.2
South America	0.7	5.9	2.3	4.1	3.3	4.2	11.9	10.4	12.7	32.7	31.7	35.0
Argentina	0.4	0.4	0.6	0.4	0.2	0.2	5.3	0.9	1.3	1.0	3.0	4.3
Brazil	0.1	4.9	1.2	1.1	1.2	1.9	2.0	3.2	4.9	9.7	7.9	6.2
Other South America	0.2	0.5	0.5	2.6	2.0	2.1	4.6	6.3	6.5	22.0	20.9	24.4
Europe	14.7	21.4	27.2	60.4	80.3	55.2	81.1	75.4	334.1	99.4	132.2	195.0
Belgium	...	0.2	0.2	0.2	0.3	0.2	3.5	2.0	3.3	5.4	3.5	2.5
France	1.7	1.6	1.5	1.5	1.6	1.7	12.2	13.3	129.4	11.4	25.0	88.3
Germany	1.6	2.5	5.3	15.1	38.0	29.1	11.6	14.2	20.9	13.2	19.5	19.1
Netherlands	1.2	2.7	1.4	2.6	3.1	2.4	3.8	2.8	5.8	4.8	13.4	3.5
United Kingdom	6.5	9.4	13.4	31.7	27.5	10.8	33.8	22.5	30.5	35.6	46.6	34.5
Turkey	...	0.2	0.1	0.1	0.1	...	0.7	...	1.5	1.9	0.3	0.2
Former Soviet Republics	...	...	...	...	...	0.1	0.7	1.9	1.0	4.0	3.5	7.8
Poland	...	...	0.1	...	...	...	...	0.2	0.1	0.3	0.3	0.3
Other Eastern Europe	0.1	...	...	0.1	...	0.1	1.5	1.8	1.6	0.6	0.9	1.9
Other Europe	3.5	4.7	5.2	9.1	9.8	10.8	13.1	16.6	139.9	22.2	19.2	36.8
Asia	5.4	6.1	7.8	18.4	16.8	20.3	112.4	116.3	119.2	100.1	111.6	178.0
Japan	0.9	1.3	0.9	10.5	4.0	7.4	12.0	7.7	4.1	6.3	5.6	7.0
China	1.4	...	...	0.2	0.1	1.6	22.0	2.7	1.6	2.3	1.8	3.3
Hong Kong	0.4	2.0	1.7	0.7	2.1	3.9	11.5	7.2	6.2	6.0	4.5	7.7
Taiwan	0.3	0.3	0.5	0.4	2.1	0.2	2.6	1.8	1.9	4.1	2.0	62.5
Singapore	0.4	0.8	1.0	3.9	6.9	3.9	17.2	62.5	77.9	12.4	2.0	1.7
South Korea	0.1	0.3	0.4	0.4	0.2	0.5	4.2	11.5	4.8	15.2	10.4	15.2
Indonesia	...	...	...	0.1	...	...	1.6	2.6	1.5	0.3	0.6	0.2
India	0.1	0.1	0.2	...	0.1	...	1.2	1.5	2.7	1.1	1.1	1.1
Other Asia	1.8	1.3	3.0	2.2	1.1	2.7	40.1	18.8	18.6	52.2	83.1	79.5
Africa	0.1	0.6	1.0	0.4	0.4	0.5	3.8	13.0	7.7	7.1	3.1	5.3
North Africa	...	...	...	...	...	...	1.4	9.3	5.7	4.5	0.6	2.0
Republic of South Africa	...	0.2	0.1	0.1	0.1	0.2	1.1	0.8	0.8	0.5	1.2	0.6
Other Subsaharan Africa	0.1	0.4	1.0	0.3	0.3	0.3	1.2	2.8	1.2	2.1	1.4	2.8
Middle East	0.5	0.8	1.1	0.9	0.7	0.9	7.3	5.6	9.6	14.2	14.9	15.4
Australia	1.0	1.0	0.8	0.6	1.0	1.0	18.8	4.2	6.7	2.8	2.5	11.0
Rest Of World	...	...	...	...	...	...	1.9	...	1.7	...	76.4	...

Table E-3. Metropolitan Area Exports of Goods by Destination, 1994–1999—*Continued*

(Millions of dollars.)

Destination	Memphis, TN - AR - MS						Miami, FL					
	1994	1995	1996	1997	1998	1999	1994	1995	1996	1997	1998	1999
ALL DESTINATIONS	2 729.5	4 163.8	3 786.1	3 636.9	3 615.5	3 135.2	9 266.7	10 200.8	10 681.2	12 692.3	12 943.4	11 942.1
North America	598.6	623.7	665.6	790.8	985.1	794.6	976.7	659.2	725.6	1 066.8	1 170.6	1 237.3
Canada	359.7	433.3	468.4	522.9	594.6	577.3	314.5	366.2	322.2	379.2	450.2	418.9
Mexico	238.8	190.5	197.2	267.9	390.5	217.3	662.2	293.1	403.4	687.6	720.4	818.4
Caribbean And Central America	58.1	88.2	82.0	82.4	118.5	69.7	2 608.2	2 808.0	2 907.5	3 449.3	3 731.3	3 814.5
South America	152.2	253.7	287.8	263.9	273.0	241.8	4 620.1	5 241.5	5 718.9	6 855.4	6 764.3	5 522.0
Argentina	9.4	12.5	18.3	18.9	21.6	24.0	723.8	536.5	626.4	705.9	724.8	562.4
Brazil	84.3	137.4	171.2	130.7	96.3	82.3	868.8	1 336.5	1 696.5	2 128.8	1 934.0	1 793.6
Other South America	58.6	103.8	98.4	114.2	155.2	135.5	3 027.4	3 368.4	3 396.0	4 020.7	4 105.5	3 166.0
Europe	590.0	732.0	755.6	1 013.9	1 039.3	936.8	629.7	847.5	836.7	829.8	854.1	933.5
Belgium	43.9	54.6	64.7	110.2	96.2	108.3	35.8	25.3	23.3	47.1	43.4	26.2
France	99.6	90.4	111.9	151.6	179.5	134.4	103.2	145.2	138.1	146.7	125.3	186.6
Germany	66.4	73.7	118.9	111.7	101.5	94.2	70.7	75.5	48.6	52.6	84.1	108.4
Netherlands	75.2	100.7	69.4	97.5	137.3	139.1	82.9	95.7	106.8	111.8	119.4	141.1
United Kingdom	69.3	99.2	101.5	110.3	138.4	125.1	93.1	131.9	150.0	159.9	172.6	147.0
Turkey	25.6	76.4	54.6	124.6	105.2	53.2	2.7	3.0	5.0	8.9	8.8	12.0
Former Soviet Republics	13.9	8.7	20.8	121.5	25.1	11.7	11.0	12.2	13.9	12.1	9.2	7.8
Poland	0.3	0.1	0.7	0.7	1.0	7.1	2.4	2.0	1.6	1.3	1.7	4.0
Other Eastern Europe	23.2	12.3	20.7	8.8	11.0	21.2	9.1	8.8	8.9	5.1	3.0	7.2
Other Europe	172.6	216.0	192.4	177.0	244.1	242.5	218.8	347.8	340.4	284.4	286.6	293.3
Asia	1 133.7	2 137.5	1 654.5	1 169.1	863.0	741.6	302.9	478.3	327.5	319.2	249.9	270.1
Japan	224.7	324.1	250.8	263.5	255.1	239.3	120.9	114.1	81.7	102.6	89.4	78.7
China	350.1	1 023.8	806.5	362.2	90.8	30.8	10.1	38.9	11.4	12.5	15.0	21.2
Hong Kong	116.5	113.0	49.6	58.8	67.6	39.2	72.8	99.6	64.9	64.9	48.9	38.6
Taiwan	72.1	81.4	65.3	102.9	88.9	90.7	23.4	68.5	28.5	20.3	13.6	15.9
Singapore	12.9	15.3	23.6	62.1	77.5	98.0	24.0	29.7	27.1	27.7	26.7	29.5
South Korea	112.2	137.2	196.2	113.9	97.3	71.9	18.0	62.7	29.8	16.9	7.0	31.0
Indonesia	59.9	131.9	93.9	45.6	35.6	29.0	4.4	7.7	7.6	5.0	4.0	5.0
India	12.1	30.0	8.2	10.1	13.9	21.3	5.7	5.9	7.3	7.6	8.5	3.7
Other Asia	173.1	280.7	160.6	149.9	136.4	121.4	23.6	51.2	69.2	61.7	36.8	46.6
Africa	112.2	183.6	215.1	161.7	163.4	183.1	54.0	67.4	62.7	65.5	83.5	51.4
North Africa	69.2	136.4	166.8	89.6	67.1	117.2	8.6	13.2	16.9	13.3	16.3	8.6
Republic of South Africa	41.5	44.2	44.3	32.7	37.1	21.8	12.8	15.2	16.8	22.8	26.2	16.0
Other Subsaharan Africa	1.4	3.0	4.0	39.4	59.2	44.2	32.6	39.0	29.0	29.4	41.0	26.8
Middle East	49.4	94.5	72.6	74.1	79.9	66.2	50.9	69.1	73.1	74.4	68.7	87.5
Australia	35.4	49.8	52.8	79.8	93.3	101.3	24.4	29.8	29.3	31.7	20.3	25.6
Rest Of World	. . .	0.7	. . .	1.2	. . .	. . .	. . .	. . .	. . .	0.2	0.7	. . .

Destination	Middlesex - Somerset - Hunterdon, NJ						Milwaukee - Waukesha, WI					
	1994	1995	1996	1997	1998	1999	1994	1995	1996	1997	1998	1999
ALL DESTINATIONS	3 035.9	3 448.1	3 628.1	4 385.4	4 879.7	4 857.8	2 913.5	3 506.9	3 717.2	3 837.6	3 570.3	3 720.2
North America	710.3	747.2	807.9	875.7	861.7	917.0	961.3	1 088.7	1 082.0	1 242.9	1 345.1	1 422.3
Canada	624.1	679.3	714.3	742.3	696.7	813.6	764.7	946.1	918.6	1 045.0	1 126.2	1 189.3
Mexico	86.2	68.0	93.7	133.4	165.0	103.4	196.6	142.6	163.5	197.9	218.9	233.0
Caribbean And Central America	63.4	55.9	46.7	65.6	112.4	104.5	45.6	55.8	50.9	52.3	52.5	51.9
South America	139.6	149.4	177.2	241.4	246.0	181.9	222.1	275.2	333.1	309.1	307.7	238.7
Argentina	29.4	24.9	22.4	39.2	48.5	29.4	44.2	28.7	32.0	37.8	38.8	42.0
Brazil	58.0	73.9	90.4	123.9	122.6	53.6	70.8	105.2	130.8	118.4	121.1	94.5
Other South America	52.1	50.6	64.3	78.3	74.8	98.9	107.0	141.3	170.3	152.9	147.9	102.2
Europe	1 273.2	1 389.4	1 565.3	2 051.6	2 399.1	1 984.0	848.7	1 014.9	1 085.0	1 131.6	1 008.2	1 094.5
Belgium	82.8	109.5	73.6	89.3	108.8	120.6	98.5	106.9	128.8	135.2	82.5	47.6
France	141.3	113.2	67.7	122.3	142.4	133.2	164.1	211.4	161.3	178.0	151.0	216.0
Germany	248.8	247.9	288.3	320.2	294.2	280.4	126.8	158.5	170.5	188.6	178.7	178.9
Netherlands	120.9	162.1	296.1	593.9	622.0	548.9	59.6	89.9	105.1	96.5	96.5	112.3
United Kingdom	272.0	169.6	176.1	199.8	281.6	268.7	140.8	170.2	174.0	197.0	176.9	196.3
Turkey	3.5	145.5	284.4	222.9	219.8	86.6	10.0	6.0	16.9	8.1	7.9	10.3
Former Soviet Republics	17.5	33.0	16.1	14.0	57.9	17.7	3.6	3.6	13.0	19.3	7.3	5.2
Poland	3.6	5.5	4.2	8.0	8.6	7.0	1.7	2.9	3.8	7.3	4.3	4.2
Other Eastern Europe	4.3	7.0	5.8	5.7	9.6	7.1	11.4	7.8	12.1	10.3	11.3	10.9
Other Europe	378.7	396.2	353.1	475.5	654.1	513.8	232.2	257.8	299.5	291.4	291.7	312.8
Asia	639.2	907.5	805.3	884.3	967.9	1 322.4	591.3	821.0	904.0	829.4	647.0	688.1
Japan	321.9	388.1	391.6	438.6	441.2	607.7	196.6	279.7	386.6	316.9	275.1	296.3
China	30.8	145.8	81.9	43.1	116.6	199.0	49.7	44.3	43.6	54.8	60.2	71.7
Hong Kong	47.7	57.3	45.6	68.5	83.6	100.3	74.8	83.0	87.2	82.5	71.9	54.4
Taiwan	61.4	67.9	53.8	64.0	93.9	123.2	64.7	131.5	62.3	65.0	43.0	46.8
Singapore	33.5	36.1	41.5	36.8	29.9	38.2	53.3	46.7	48.5	43.7	37.7	43.9
South Korea	87.8	109.2	91.7	107.0	91.0	141.6	59.7	75.4	81.3	75.4	41.7	57.4
Indonesia	4.2	9.9	13.8	19.7	16.1	18.0	5.6	13.2	25.0	19.7	12.1	3.8
India	15.1	25.4	20.4	24.3	23.1	25.6	10.5	26.2	22.5	22.5	23.9	30.2
Other Asia	36.7	67.7	65.0	82.4	72.4	68.7	76.3	120.9	147.0	148.9	81.6	83.5
Africa	54.2	50.6	47.9	58.6	92.8	117.4	63.1	59.6	70.7	70.3	49.0	44.0
North Africa	24.1	12.8	9.6	13.4	15.0	21.9	27.0	18.9	16.0	26.5	19.3	17.4
Republic of South Africa	25.2	35.8	35.3	41.6	74.2	90.4	32.2	38.1	50.7	39.2	24.5	19.8
Other Subsaharan Africa	4.9	1.9	3.0	3.6	3.5	5.1	3.9	2.6	4.1	4.6	5.2	6.8
Middle East	66.0	53.0	61.7	78.3	94.8	103.9	62.1	62.5	67.1	67.4	55.9	44.6
Australia	89.9	95.2	116.1	129.8	104.9	126.7	119.3	129.2	124.3	134.8	104.8	136.0
Rest Of World	. . .	. . .	. . .	. . .	0.1	0.1	. . .	. . .	. . .	. . .	. . .	. . .

Table E-3. Metropolitan Area Exports of Goods by Destination, 1994–1999—*Continued*

(Millions of dollars.)

Destination	Minneapolis - St. Paul, MN - WI						Mobile, AL					
	1994	1995	1996	1997	1998	1999	1994	1995	1996	1997	1998	1999
ALL DESTINATIONS	8 863.5	11 071.8	12 384.0	12 006.7	11 652.4	12 401.3	395.3	415.8	459.9	498.7	426.1	570.8
North America	1 805.4	2 213.2	2 854.7	3 014.3	3 149.4	3 233.1	85.5	78.8	105.1	111.3	106.6	94.3
Canada	1 492.4	1 719.2	2 025.2	2 208.7	2 307.2	2 293.2	73.5	66.4	89.2	92.6	90.0	78.2
Mexico	313.1	494.0	829.5	805.6	842.2	940.0	11.9	12.4	15.9	18.6	16.7	16.1
Caribbean And Central America	180.1	246.5	270.7	276.8	298.3	247.2	13.0	19.1	31.1	29.7	28.9	34.6
South America	244.1	408.8	458.5	474.2	464.8	410.1	21.0	19.7	18.7	25.4	28.9	16.7
Argentina	42.2	30.1	36.4	83.9	51.4	36.8	1.2	1.1	1.8	3.7	2.9	0.8
Brazil	85.5	73.7	135.3	110.2	136.0	80.4	3.5	7.8	6.5	10.1	16.9	9.8
Other South America	116.4	305.0	286.8	280.0	277.4	292.9	16.3	10.8	10.5	11.6	9.1	6.1
Europe	3 479.4	4 101.6	4 293.2	4 111.3	3 878.5	3 860.2	186.3	177.8	167.3	146.3	105.1	137.6
Belgium	159.0	238.9	235.1	166.5	215.0	172.3	5.3	4.9	5.7	3.2	9.5	4.3
France	226.2	253.4	270.3	350.5	412.2	387.1	19.2	14.1	22.6	16.6	14.8	21.7
Germany	444.3	477.7	612.7	545.1	546.8	516.1	16.5	19.8	12.6	14.1	13.0	22.1
Netherlands	888.4	996.9	941.6	821.6	740.2	610.2	33.0	24.8	13.4	12.9	16.2	21.5
United Kingdom	403.5	487.9	556.8	653.3	598.6	656.3	19.3	38.1	39.1	62.9	16.2	25.6
Turkey	53.5	118.9	167.7	173.9	131.2	143.2	1.3	0.2	0.2	0.2	0.1	0.5
Former Soviet Republics	95.0	31.1	120.0	43.1	35.7	28.1	. . .	0.6	0.5	0.6	0.4	. . .
Poland	12.2	13.7	54.1	14.5	12.5	11.9	0.2	0.6	0.2	. . .	0.1	0.1
Other Eastern Europe	25.0	26.8	39.1	35.6	25.4	28.6	0.8	0.1	1.0	0.3	0.2	0.9
Other Europe	1 172.3	1 456.3	1 295.9	1 307.2	1 161.0	1 306.5	90.7	74.6	72.1	35.5	34.5	40.9
Asia	2 141.9	2 798.4	2 950.3	2 771.4	2 713.0	3 259.4	68.4	103.6	115.6	163.9	135.4	263.0
Japan	709.6	817.2	993.5	1 016.5	755.7	772.2	55.8	73.2	67.4	43.4	48.3	32.5
China	89.2	393.6	160.0	208.6	253.5	277.3	0.7	3.1	1.4	6.0	6.1	2.6
Hong Kong	133.7	207.1	193.8	164.4	211.1	188.0	0.2	1.7	2.7	4.4	1.7	1.6
Taiwan	250.6	242.0	436.0	249.6	267.4	354.6	1.0	3.3	11.9	4.0	2.5	3.1
Singapore	177.1	213.0	230.8	213.9	272.4	259.5	0.6	3.7	5.2	3.2	2.4	3.0
South Korea	245.1	403.8	466.6	244.6	293.4	561.8	4.0	13.7	19.6	95.8	70.6	217.9
Indonesia	69.3	64.0	87.3	143.5	49.2	123.2	1.7	0.8	1.7	0.9	0.1	. . .
India	16.2	39.5	32.2	28.3	27.8	29.0	0.4	0.3	. . .	0.3	0.3	0.2
Other Asia	451.1	418.2	350.0	502.0	582.4	693.9	3.9	3.8	5.7	5.9	3.5	2.2
Africa	454.6	511.1	810.2	747.1	610.4	705.4	7.7	3.9	7.2	5.9	6.3	14.0
North Africa	347.1	354.9	657.3	619.3	502.6	579.2	5.3	1.1	3.0	2.6	0.2	3.3
Republic of South Africa	55.9	69.5	58.6	65.0	51.4	71.4	1.8	1.3	1.6	3.0	3.3	1.5
Other Subsaharan Africa	51.7	86.7	94.3	62.8	56.4	54.8	0.7	1.5	2.5	0.3	2.8	9.3
Middle East	373.9	427.5	381.4	332.4	254.1	395.7	8.5	8.6	9.1	9.2	9.8	6.3
Australia	145.2	162.2	172.4	179.4	174.4	166.3	5.0	4.2	5.7	7.0	5.1	4.2
Rest Of World	38.8	202.5	192.5	99.8	109.6	123.9	. . .	. . .	. . .	. . .	. . .	. . .

Destination	Modesto, CA						Monmouth - Ocean, NJ					
	1994	1995	1996	1997	1998	1999	1994	1995	1996	1997	1998	1999
ALL DESTINATIONS	236.7	279.2	359.6	387.5	378.4	373.6	410.2	471.8	478.2	504.8	508.8	493.4
North America	54.3	56.1	63.0	68.9	70.8	74.2	119.7	123.7	138.7	145.1	150.2	182.1
Canada	47.2	49.7	56.0	61.0	61.4	61.7	77.5	79.2	91.7	98.6	98.1	107.3
Mexico	7.1	6.4	7.1	7.9	9.4	12.5	42.3	44.5	47.0	46.5	52.1	74.8
Caribbean And Central America	7.5	7.7	8.0	10.0	11.6	10.7	6.1	7.3	8.4	11.9	13.8	11.4
South America	7.6	9.7	11.3	15.1	13.4	11.4	47.9	44.8	52.8	43.6	40.8	31.0
Argentina	1.6	1.2	2.3	2.9	2.2	2.3	7.9	4.3	8.4	7.2	6.0	6.3
Brazil	1.4	3.3	3.8	5.5	4.6	3.8	10.9	14.9	14.8	13.8	13.9	13.3
Other South America	4.6	5.2	5.1	6.6	6.6	5.3	29.1	25.6	29.6	22.6	20.9	11.4
Europe	119.3	139.8	202.3	207.9	194.0	193.5	112.8	143.5	139.6	151.6	179.4	150.0
Belgium	4.3	5.9	7.2	6.8	3.9	3.5	2.3	2.5	2.2	4.3	7.6	4.5
France	11.9	7.4	6.4	12.7	8.5	6.4	15.6	14.9	14.1	16.0	13.7	10.1
Germany	40.3	46.7	69.1	61.9	30.5	19.0	13.9	14.8	16.1	12.6	14.1	14.8
Netherlands	10.4	11.4	11.0	16.3	37.3	65.2	19.3	23.9	21.8	20.8	23.6	21.5
United Kingdom	28.7	38.2	59.3	67.9	72.7	60.4	20.4	24.6	27.4	32.0	37.1	43.8
Turkey	0.2	0.3	0.7	0.3	0.7	0.1	1.3	1.3	1.8	1.8	2.9	2.3
Former Soviet Republics	0.8	2.6	0.9	0.7	0.3	0.4	6.9	8.8	4.7	2.9	5.5	3.6
Poland	0.4	0.4	0.6	0.5	0.7	0.6	0.6	1.4	1.6	3.0	1.3	1.2
Other Eastern Europe	0.2	0.3	0.3	0.8	1.1	0.5	3.1	3.9	1.9	5.3	1.3	1.1
Other Europe	22.1	26.9	46.9	40.2	38.4	37.4	29.4	47.4	48.0	52.9	72.4	47.0
Asia	31.4	48.0	52.7	65.9	69.2	63.3	89.4	115.2	105.9	118.9	84.2	88.3
Japan	12.6	23.6	20.3	22.5	47.4	40.5	23.3	26.7	18.9	21.1	21.9	19.1
China	0.7	0.4	0.4	1.4	1.5	0.4	6.5	5.4	14.7	13.8	15.0	13.4
Hong Kong	5.3	5.2	5.6	9.5	4.8	3.9	19.7	24.1	19.6	15.4	10.9	11.1
Taiwan	4.2	5.9	5.2	10.4	4.5	4.2	4.4	3.8	4.7	22.4	10.1	8.4
Singapore	1.8	2.8	2.1	2.3	1.3	3.2	5.2	6.8	6.1	6.3	5.1	6.3
South Korea	2.5	4.2	5.8	5.6	3.1	2.8	14.3	10.3	16.3	14.5	7.6	10.8
Indonesia	0.5	0.3	0.7	0.8	0.4	0.9	5.4	5.1	5.3	6.9	3.7	4.7
India	0.2	0.3	3.8	5.9	1.1	1.0	1.2	3.3	2.2	5.1	2.1	1.6
Other Asia	3.6	5.4	8.6	7.5	5.0	6.4	9.6	29.6	18.0	13.3	7.7	13.0
Africa	1.7	2.4	1.9	1.4	2.9	2.5	4.8	10.6	6.8	5.5	6.6	4.0
North Africa	1.1	1.5	0.5	0.6	1.9	1.5	1.4	6.3	3.1	2.8	3.0	2.3
Republic of South Africa	0.5	0.8	1.1	0.6	0.8	0.7	2.7	3.9	3.0	2.3	3.0	1.5
Other Subsaharan Africa	0.1	0.1	0.3	0.2	0.3	0.3	0.8	0.4	0.8	0.4	0.6	0.3
Middle East	8.4	6.5	8.9	12.2	11.2	13.0	21.3	14.7	17.3	22.4	26.1	19.9
Australia	6.7	9.0	11.5	6.1	5.2	5.0	8.1	12.0	8.6	5.7	7.8	6.7
Rest Of World	. . .	. . .	. . .	. . .	. . .	. . .	. . .	. . .	. . .	. . .	. . .	. . .

Table E-3. Metropolitan Area Exports of Goods by Destination, 1994–1999—Continued

(Millions of dollars.)

Destination	Monroe, LA						Muncie, IN					
	1994	1995	1996	1997	1998	1999	1994	1995	1996	1997	1998	1999
ALL DESTINATIONS	107.1	167.8	134.0	101.9	69.3	63.2	107.4	158.3	137.6	157.6	105.3	121.4
North America	26.8	39.0	31.5	39.2	35.0	43.9	54.9	98.4	84.0	101.7	77.3	79.9
Canada	24.2	36.7	28.5	33.4	26.0	29.8	51.9	95.9	82.7	95.6	72.3	77.7
Mexico	2.5	2.3	3.0	5.8	9.0	14.1	2.9	2.4	1.3	6.1	5.0	2.2
Caribbean And Central America	0.7	1.9	0.9	0.8	1.7	0.7	0.3	0.3	0.5	0.1	0.1	0.2
South America	6.0	14.6	6.8	4.8	1.5	0.5	1.1	1.4	0.9	2.3	1.2	0.4
Argentina	0.2	0.3	0.1	0.1	0.1	...	0.2	0.1	...	0.1	0.1	0.1
Brazil	4.4	9.8	5.1	3.1	0.5	0.2	0.7	0.8	0.6	1.7	0.6	0.1
Other South America	1.5	4.5	1.6	1.6	1.0	0.3	0.2	0.5	0.3	0.5	0.5	0.2
Europe	42.0	68.1	58.6	35.6	27.3	15.0	9.9	11.8	11.4	7.3	5.4	9.1
Belgium	3.7	0.4	0.8	1.9	1.5	0.4	1.0	1.1	1.0	1.2	1.4	1.9
France	1.8	1.9	2.1	0.9	0.2	0.1	0.2	0.3	0.3	...	...	...
Germany	4.8	7.2	8.4	12.1	13.2	8.1	0.3	0.3	0.5	0.2	0.2	0.1
Netherlands	8.2	27.8	18.9	5.8	2.5	1.3	0.2	0.1	0.2	...	0.1	0.1
United Kingdom	16.1	20.6	18.4	8.9	8.6	4.3	7.7	8.8	8.4	4.2	2.2	5.5
Turkey	0.1	0.1	0.2	0.1	...	...	...	...	...	...	...	...
Former Soviet Republics	0.3	0.2	0.2	0.1	...	...	...	...	...	...	...	...
Poland	...	...	...	...	...	...	...	...	...	...	...	...
Other Eastern Europe	0.1	0.1	0.1	...	0.1	...	...	...	...	...	...	...
Other Europe	6.7	9.6	9.5	5.9	1.2	0.7	0.6	1.2	0.9	1.6	1.5	1.5
Asia	14.2	27.7	24.1	16.0	2.3	2.8	37.4	44.2	38.5	44.5	20.6	31.3
Japan	4.3	7.9	6.4	6.3	0.1	0.2	0.2	0.2	0.6	1.2	1.6	1.1
China	1.2	1.7	0.9	0.7	...	1.2	3.3	2.6	0.5	1.0	0.7	0.4
Hong Kong	0.4	3.8	7.2	2.7	0.2	0.1	0.4	10.8	9.4	4.8	0.2	0.1
Taiwan	0.1	0.1	0.1	0.2	...	0.1	0.4	0.2	0.1	0.1	0.2	0.1
Singapore	0.5	0.4	0.7	1.5	0.2	0.4	1.0	0.2	0.4	0.2	0.1	0.2
South Korea	...	...	0.3	0.1	...	0.2	31.7	29.5	25.5	36.4	15.2	27.6
Indonesia	0.5	2.0	1.9	0.6	...	...	...	...	1.1	...	0.1	0.1
India	0.1	0.1	...	...	0.6	...	0.1	0.5	0.4	0.4	0.8	1.4
Other Asia	7.1	11.6	6.7	3.9	1.1	0.4	0.3	0.1	0.5	0.4	1.7	0.3
Africa	1.3	0.7	0.6	0.1	0.4	...	0.2	0.4	0.1	0.1	0.1	0.1
North Africa	...	0.1	0.1	...	...	...	...	...	...	...	...	...
Republic of South Africa	0.6	0.7	0.5	0.1	0.4	...	0.2	0.4	0.1	0.1	0.1	0.1
Other Subsaharan Africa	0.7	...	...	...	...	...	...	...	...	...	...	...
Middle East	2.0	1.5	1.2	1.0	0.7	0.1	...	...	0.2	0.1	0.3	0.1
Australia	14.2	14.3	10.3	4.4	0.4	0.3	3.7	1.9	2.0	1.5	0.5	0.4
Rest Of World	...	...	...	...	...	...	...	...	...	...	...	...

Destination	Nashua, NH						Nashville, TN					
	1994	1995	1996	1997	1998	1999	1994	1995	1996	1997	1998	1999
ALL DESTINATIONS	235.4	282.2	291.3	339.8	364.5	391.9	1 310.5	1 412.3	1 445.5	1 767.1	1 868.7	1 836.6
North America	70.6	79.2	79.2	95.2	113.2	122.2	596.3	694.0	617.5	777.7	869.0	985.6
Canada	64.2	63.4	63.8	76.2	94.7	102.6	348.6	404.2	416.9	465.2	516.4	598.5
Mexico	6.4	15.8	15.4	18.9	18.5	19.6	247.7	289.8	200.7	312.5	352.7	387.1
Caribbean And Central America	1.2	1.1	4.4	11.0	11.2	12.3	38.5	39.2	28.9	53.4	65.2	65.3
South America	8.2	5.2	4.6	6.8	6.9	9.3	21.7	28.1	38.9	84.1	103.1	85.7
Argentina	3.1	1.4	0.4	1.7	2.3	2.9	4.4	5.1	5.6	13.3	22.3	15.7
Brazil	3.3	2.0	3.3	3.7	3.0	3.7	7.9	13.0	13.2	20.7	17.3	31.4
Other South America	1.8	1.9	0.9	1.3	1.6	2.8	9.3	10.1	20.1	50.2	63.5	38.7
Europe	73.9	96.5	101.4	108.0	127.1	120.4	352.0	323.4	331.4	398.0	461.9	433.5
Belgium	2.6	3.8	2.0	3.9	13.7	3.7	9.2	9.7	7.5	20.3	7.4	5.3
France	3.5	5.6	7.2	4.9	6.8	6.6	39.3	33.7	32.3	36.3	45.5	37.1
Germany	16.4	23.6	20.0	16.1	21.4	18.8	61.7	51.6	61.8	79.1	69.1	79.1
Netherlands	11.3	11.4	12.6	11.7	15.2	14.4	27.4	29.8	24.3	25.9	20.2	26.5
United Kingdom	11.8	14.9	14.1	25.0	22.7	24.2	138.1	130.3	126.2	144.3	226.7	206.1
Turkey	0.2	0.7	...	0.3	0.5	0.8	0.6	2.2	3.0	4.6	7.2	6.0
Former Soviet Republics	0.2	0.2	7.7	1.5	0.7	1.1	0.3	2.9	1.2	1.9	2.2	1.1
Poland	0.2	0.1	...	...	0.5	1.2	4.1	6.1	9.2	8.8	4.8	1.4
Other Eastern Europe	2.4	1.8	0.7	1.4	0.8	1.0	2.3	2.6	3.1	1.2	5.1	2.0
Other Europe	25.4	34.5	37.0	43.2	44.9	48.5	69.0	54.5	62.7	75.6	73.8	68.8
Asia	68.0	88.7	85.6	95.0	74.6	95.4	257.0	264.2	368.4	357.6	286.7	215.5
Japan	16.7	12.1	14.0	37.1	15.0	13.8	110.3	137.9	262.5	224.3	172.1	120.7
China	2.7	1.3	1.8	3.0	1.0	3.6	1.5	2.3	3.3	6.4	6.1	7.9
Hong Kong	2.0	4.4	6.3	8.3	6.6	4.5	4.7	6.2	5.9	14.0	13.3	11.1
Taiwan	13.3	8.4	13.0	4.4	4.4	4.9	119.8	81.7	55.5	55.6	59.0	40.6
Singapore	21.2	35.0	16.6	24.9	36.9	61.0	4.4	9.5	9.8	11.2	6.9	11.0
South Korea	9.4	20.5	8.3	4.0	2.3	2.3	9.3	14.0	13.8	23.2	9.2	7.7
Indonesia	0.1	0.3	...	0.3	0.8	0.3	0.4	1.6	0.9	2.6	0.4	1.2
India	0.2	0.5	0.8	0.7	0.8	0.4	1.0	1.2	1.9	2.5	6.7	3.8
Other Asia	2.4	6.1	24.8	12.3	6.8	4.6	5.7	9.8	14.8	17.7	13.0	11.5
Africa	5.6	3.3	3.1	10.0	9.8	6.7	4.7	7.4	6.9	10.3	14.3	13.4
North Africa	3.3	0.2	0.9	8.1	8.0	5.8	2.0	1.3	2.3	2.4	4.0	2.9
Republic of South Africa	2.1	2.7	2.0	1.9	1.8	0.6	2.3	3.1	3.3	5.2	7.1	6.5
Other Subsaharan Africa	0.2	0.4	0.3	0.1	...	0.3	0.4	3.0	1.3	2.7	3.2	3.9
Middle East	5.5	5.4	10.1	10.3	15.9	22.3	24.9	33.6	32.1	62.2	44.5	15.8
Australia	2.3	2.9	2.9	3.6	5.7	3.2	15.2	22.4	21.3	23.8	24.0	21.8
Rest Of World	...	...	...	...	...	...	...	...	...	...	...	...

Table E-3. Metropolitan Area Exports of Goods by Destination, 1994–1999—*Continued*

(Millions of dollars.)

Destination	Nassau - Suffolk, NY						Newark, NJ					
	1994	1995	1996	1997	1998	1999	1994	1995	1996	1997	1998	1999
ALL DESTINATIONS	2 866.3	3 558.6	3 680.2	4 208.5	4 438.6	4 686.5	5 205.5	5 640.0	5 044.2	5 201.8	4 866.1	5 397.5
North America	640.4	692.9	787.2	889.5	921.9	1 029.9	1 244.7	1 061.0	1 052.3	1 291.1	1 333.7	1 436.7
Canada	505.7	569.6	607.4	657.0	639.1	722.2	828.8	819.3	855.0	1 020.9	1 023.1	1 008.1
Mexico	134.7	123.3	179.8	232.4	282.8	307.7	415.9	241.7	197.3	270.2	310.6	428.6
Caribbean And Central America	100.2	74.0	74.7	91.1	102.6	132.0	118.9	157.3	168.3	187.7	194.0	167.3
South America	163.5	163.3	165.0	223.1	345.5	307.9	324.7	427.0	436.4	513.4	464.6	515.0
Argentina	22.1	19.9	20.8	28.0	27.0	46.2	46.4	46.6	48.6	76.0	60.3	61.0
Brazil	49.9	60.7	56.1	95.8	232.2	192.2	95.0	166.3	188.3	266.3	241.7	276.2
Other South America	91.5	82.7	88.1	99.3	86.3	69.5	183.3	214.1	199.4	171.2	162.6	177.8
Europe	969.1	1 107.0	1 346.2	1 644.4	1 825.2	1 897.9	1 508.9	1 754.1	1 587.0	1 659.6	1 676.9	1 818.1
Belgium	23.1	29.0	57.1	87.1	90.6	78.4	108.4	129.1	89.5	124.4	167.2	234.4
France	97.9	112.3	190.1	267.8	351.2	309.2	138.3	128.0	145.6	129.4	105.0	157.1
Germany	184.0	208.0	278.0	316.9	267.5	351.0	265.0	323.2	289.5	287.1	240.0	221.3
Netherlands	73.1	72.9	82.0	102.9	102.5	104.6	168.0	225.5	157.0	117.7	134.1	134.9
United Kingdom	258.7	278.1	278.9	372.1	477.4	532.0	184.5	224.5	207.7	235.8	250.3	231.2
Turkey	12.7	19.7	20.9	26.9	28.0	27.8	42.8	52.3	35.0	30.9	21.1	17.7
Former Soviet Republics	19.4	16.3	17.7	24.6	18.3	25.6	82.7	62.1	83.1	94.3	27.8	24.1
Poland	5.2	5.8	10.3	14.8	11.9	6.9	20.5	15.7	20.6	18.1	13.8	12.6
Other Eastern Europe	27.8	32.8	42.4	25.0	28.8	23.4	5.9	11.4	8.3	8.6	14.8	25.4
Other Europe	267.3	332.1	368.8	406.4	448.9	439.1	492.9	582.3	550.8	613.3	702.7	759.5
Asia	648.9	1 131.3	931.4	954.5	832.8	933.4	1 729.5	1 826.4	1 490.5	1 184.0	876.5	1 165.1
Japan	123.1	158.6	200.3	227.4	264.5	299.4	525.7	530.1	482.8	361.8	280.6	462.1
China	45.4	38.1	56.1	60.0	40.4	41.9	139.1	171.1	100.0	59.0	89.9	64.6
Hong Kong	96.5	126.5	101.4	126.1	103.8	115.4	132.8	164.6	184.5	135.4	105.5	125.8
Taiwan	128.0	454.9	171.8	135.9	171.2	152.0	209.4	235.3	203.1	167.0	128.5	119.2
Singapore	47.1	49.4	72.0	93.5	59.7	73.8	67.2	71.9	64.0	97.5	70.1	121.4
South Korea	73.8	117.1	138.9	126.3	72.8	79.5	361.5	287.3	157.8	132.7	80.0	119.4
Indonesia	8.9	11.9	18.4	14.2	5.0	7.2	29.1	72.7	40.4	56.5	6.6	7.8
India	31.4	50.0	53.9	34.6	43.3	66.7	30.9	40.8	62.3	27.2	19.7	28.9
Other Asia	94.6	124.8	118.6	136.3	72.2	97.5	233.8	252.5	195.6	147.0	95.6	115.9
Africa	42.4	64.6	55.8	62.0	73.9	67.5	63.1	83.2	77.5	77.8	66.5	64.2
North Africa	10.0	9.5	10.8	15.7	16.4	11.0	25.2	21.9	25.3	24.2	24.7	28.6
Republic of South Africa	22.7	29.7	26.8	29.2	34.1	29.8	15.5	21.0	24.9	23.5	19.4	17.4
Other Subsaharan Africa	9.6	25.4	18.2	17.2	23.4	26.7	22.4	40.4	27.3	30.1	22.3	18.1
Middle East	248.0	259.8	260.3	255.3	243.3	209.2	135.9	228.1	154.8	196.5	168.0	152.7
Australia	53.8	65.7	59.6	88.6	93.5	108.0	78.8	102.6	76.9	91.4	86.0	78.3
Rest Of World	. . .	. . .	. . .	. . .	. . .	. . .	1.1	0.3	0.6	0.4	. . .	. . .

Destination	New Bedford, MA						Newburgh, NY - PA					
	1994	1995	1996	1997	1998	1999	1994	1995	1996	1997	1998	1999
ALL DESTINATIONS	154.5	186.8	165.8	153.4	161.9	180.8	152.8	148.9	153.3	222.1	419.3	337.6
North America	57.6	85.7	65.3	54.7	62.9	65.3	90.2	77.2	75.5	145.3	273.9	246.2
Canada	42.5	57.8	41.0	31.4	33.4	36.5	77.5	61.4	61.8	137.9	270.4	241.8
Mexico	15.0	27.8	24.3	23.3	29.4	28.9	12.7	15.8	13.7	7.4	3.4	4.4
Caribbean And Central America	3.8	4.3	3.0	1.2	1.4	1.9	2.4	2.7	1.5	2.0	2.7	2.2
South America	0.7	1.2	2.8	3.0	1.9	1.4	5.0	6.0	6.7	9.5	6.1	6.4
Argentina	0.1	. . .	0.3	0.5	0.2	0.4	0.4	0.3	1.9	2.6	1.2	1.3
Brazil	0.2	0.9	1.7	2.0	1.2	0.8	2.7	2.9	2.6	4.5	2.4	3.0
Other South America	0.5	0.3	0.9	0.4	0.5	0.2	1.9	2.8	2.2	2.4	2.5	2.2
Europe	58.7	63.6	65.4	55.3	60.1	63.7	30.3	36.4	35.4	38.1	35.0	35.2
Belgium	2.8	2.4	6.0	3.5	0.8	1.2	1.6	2.2	4.2	2.5	4.0	1.5
France	17.9	20.6	23.9	22.3	14.8	5.6	2.5	4.4	2.2	7.4	2.6	2.5
Germany	10.2	16.4	14.4	6.9	14.5	16.5	4.5	8.6	9.2	8.1	9.1	7.3
Netherlands	1.8	1.7	0.9	1.3	2.3	2.9	3.7	2.4	2.3	3.1	1.7	2.6
United Kingdom	19.2	14.8	14.3	14.4	18.8	27.2	10.7	9.1	9.8	8.2	9.9	11.3
Turkey	0.1	0.3	0.2	0.5	0.6	0.4	0.2	0.1	. . .	0.3	0.1	0.4
Former Soviet Republics	. . .	0.1	. . .	. . .	. . .	0.2	1.0	0.8	0.3	0.1	0.1	0.2
Poland	. . .	. . .	. . .	. . .	. . .	0.1	0.2	0.2	0.1	0.1	0.3	0.5
Other Eastern Europe	0.2	. . .	0.1	0.1	. . .	0.3	0.1	0.3	0.2	0.3	0.2	0.3
Other Europe	6.5	7.3	5.5	6.3	8.1	9.4	5.7	8.3	7.0	8.0	6.9	8.5
Asia	29.6	27.6	25.7	35.8	29.2	44.8	21.2	23.7	31.3	24.3	22.4	27.2
Japan	16.9	9.1	10.7	16.0	10.6	18.2	3.7	5.2	5.7	5.8	10.0	10.3
China	0.1	1.0	0.9	1.3	0.2	2.9	3.6	1.4	8.2	4.2	0.6	4.6
Hong Kong	2.2	1.8	2.4	4.6	1.5	2.2	3.1	4.1	5.4	3.3	2.5	3.7
Taiwan	2.8	3.8	1.8	2.3	5.1	6.3	1.2	1.6	1.5	1.3	2.2	2.0
Singapore	1.3	3.3	1.6	2.2	1.9	3.8	2.7	1.9	1.6	1.7	0.8	1.4
South Korea	4.2	7.0	6.6	6.9	5.5	8.1	2.6	3.1	2.4	1.6	1.0	2.0
Indonesia	0.5	0.1	0.1	0.1	0.4	0.4	0.1	0.2	0.3	0.4	. . .	0.1
India	. . .	0.2	0.5	0.2	0.9	0.3	0.2	0.8	0.3	0.6	0.4	0.5
Other Asia	1.5	1.3	1.0	2.1	3.2	2.5	4.0	5.5	5.8	5.5	4.9	2.6
Africa	0.4	0.6	1.3	0.3	1.1	0.4	0.6	0.4	0.4	0.7	0.6	0.5
North Africa	. . .	0.4	1.1	. . .	. . .	0.2	0.2	0.1	0.1	0.3	0.1	0.1
Republic of South Africa	0.2	0.1	0.1	. . .	0.2	1.0	0.3	0.2	0.2	0.2	0.4	0.3
Other Subsaharan Africa	0.1	0.1	. . .	. . .	. . .	0.1	0.1	0.1	0.1	0.2	0.1	0.1
Middle East	1.6	0.4	1.0	0.5	1.1	1.7	1.2	1.3	0.8	0.7	1.1	1.4
Australia	2.2	3.3	1.3	2.6	4.4	1.5	1.9	1.2	1.6	1.5	77.6	18.5
Rest Of World	. . .	. . .	. . .	. . .	. . .	. . .	. . .	. . .	. . .	. . .	. . .	. . .

Table E-3. Metropolitan Area Exports of Goods by Destination, 1994–1999—*Continued*

(Millions of dollars.)

Destination	New Haven - Meriden, CT						New London - Norwich, CT - RI					
	1994	1995	1996	1997	1998	1999	1994	1995	1996	1997	1998	1999
ALL DESTINATIONS	1 075.5	1 106.3	1 012.4	1 179.8	1 200.4	1 112.4	141.5	178.2	157.5	192.1	191.4	171.8
North America	332.6	399.7	316.7	362.1	381.1	414.7	67.0	78.9	76.4	98.0	102.4	93.2
Canada	298.9	378.0	291.1	335.9	339.8	343.3	64.3	77.9	73.7	95.0	95.2	87.3
Mexico	33.7	21.7	25.7	26.2	41.2	71.4	2.6	0.9	2.7	3.0	7.2	5.9
Caribbean And Central America	15.6	20.7	25.5	30.3	32.3	29.6	0.9	1.2	1.4	2.1	1.9	1.9
South America	43.4	45.5	49.7	52.2	50.4	39.6	2.7	9.0	10.4	11.7	9.4	3.7
Argentina	9.2	6.2	6.1	11.1	9.2	7.3	0.4	0.6	0.9	0.2	1.8	0.3
Brazil	18.8	15.1	19.5	19.3	14.5	12.4	1.3	6.3	4.8	6.6	3.1	1.5
Other South America	15.4	24.2	24.2	21.8	26.7	20.0	1.0	2.2	4.7	4.8	4.5	1.8
Europe	407.7	346.3	317.5	399.5	410.4	329.1	43.4	61.9	48.6	52.5	63.0	53.5
Belgium	6.4	5.9	7.1	10.1	20.0	30.9	2.6	2.9	3.2	3.0	11.0	4.9
France	70.6	48.6	12.6	18.2	14.2	14.2	10.1	10.2	9.9	7.2	5.9	8.2
Germany	116.2	115.5	155.6	193.9	183.9	84.4	9.1	24.6	16.1	14.1	10.0	5.5
Netherlands	12.7	9.5	9.7	18.2	16.0	20.2	1.7	2.3	1.2	0.9	1.3	0.8
United Kingdom	47.6	52.5	52.4	55.4	61.3	67.3	8.6	7.1	8.1	9.2	11.1	13.4
Turkey	2.9	5.3	5.9	8.3	9.1	6.1	0.3	0.8	0.7	0.5	0.5	0.5
Former Soviet Republics	21.9	3.9	2.0	5.0	5.4	2.8	. . .	0.9	0.3	1.2	0.2	0.1
Poland	4.7	5.8	1.1	1.8	3.8	0.8	0.6	0.7	0.5	2.3	1.5	0.8
Other Eastern Europe	7.7	2.4	2.1	3.5	8.6	13.2	0.1	0.6	0.5	0.1	0.5	0.2
Other Europe	117.0	96.9	68.9	85.1	88.3	89.2	10.5	11.8	8.2	14.0	21.1	19.2
Asia	226.1	236.8	251.7	287.7	268.9	232.3	23.6	19.2	15.7	24.3	10.7	15.5
Japan	126.6	134.1	153.7	153.4	151.6	86.9	1.5	2.1	1.6	2.6	2.6	2.8
China	10.5	15.6	13.0	16.2	14.1	10.2	10.4	1.9	1.8	3.3	1.9	1.9
Hong Kong	14.6	15.5	12.7	15.8	19.3	14.0	3.0	1.4	2.8	6.9	2.5	2.8
Taiwan	17.5	16.1	15.9	20.4	30.3	46.9	1.5	4.4	4.6	0.8	0.2	1.2
Singapore	18.4	23.2	29.2	14.1	18.9	23.0	1.4	2.3	0.9	1.4	1.6	1.5
South Korea	13.6	12.7	9.3	28.2	11.4	24.9	1.7	1.2	1.2	1.4	0.7	0.8
Indonesia	2.2	2.4	2.7	2.8	0.9	2.6	0.1	1.3	0.6	0.9	. . .	0.1
India	2.1	1.8	1.2	3.1	3.0	3.0	0.4	1.3	0.5	2.2	0.3	1.3
Other Asia	20.6	15.5	13.9	33.7	19.5	20.7	3.6	3.3	1.7	4.8	0.9	3.2
Africa	8.4	8.7	9.1	6.9	10.6	9.0	1.4	3.5	2.3	1.0	1.3	1.5
North Africa	4.4	3.2	4.1	2.0	3.8	2.5	0.1	2.4	1.9	0.4	0.4	0.7
Republic of South Africa	3.4	4.5	4.3	3.8	5.5	5.9	1.0	0.5	0.4	0.6	0.9	0.4
Other Subsaharan Africa	0.6	0.9	0.8	1.1	1.3	0.6	0.3	0.6	. . .	. . .	. . .	0.4
Middle East	22.9	31.7	26.5	28.8	33.9	40.5	1.3	2.6	1.7	1.2	0.6	1.3
Australia	18.7	16.7	15.6	12.3	12.7	17.4	1.2	1.8	0.9	1.4	2.2	1.3
Rest Of World	. . .	0.2	0.1	. . .	0.1	0.2	. . .	. . .	. . .	. . .	. . .	. . .

Destination	New Orleans, LA						New York, NY					
	1994	1995	1996	1997	1998	1999	1994	1995	1996	1997	1998	1999
ALL DESTINATIONS	2 326.2	3 037.8	3 316.8	2 770.8	2 776.2	2 409.0	23 543.7	27 131.1	27 970.5	29 082.6	26 578.4	24 484.7
North America	203.3	202.6	235.8	259.4	263.5	304.7	2 493.4	2 371.9	2 722.6	3 412.0	3 337.8	3 013.7
Canada	139.3	157.0	158.9	204.8	208.1	227.6	1 851.1	1 916.8	2 099.0	2 458.9	2 416.8	2 156.2
Mexico	64.0	45.7	76.9	54.6	55.5	77.1	642.3	455.1	623.6	953.1	921.0	857.5
Caribbean And Central America	121.1	156.9	149.6	159.1	370.9	172.1	868.6	837.4	961.3	1 092.5	1 004.5	711.8
South America	117.5	192.3	209.9	181.5	194.7	151.6	1 349.2	1 601.1	1 584.6	1 850.4	1 724.1	1 152.4
Argentina	11.7	7.0	6.5	17.6	27.7	19.2	214.6	170.8	192.7	250.5	323.6	168.7
Brazil	13.6	24.7	24.9	39.9	25.9	27.8	465.0	485.4	425.1	579.3	453.8	414.8
Other South America	92.2	160.7	178.6	124.0	141.0	104.7	669.6	944.9	966.9	1 020.5	946.7	568.9
Europe	554.5	700.5	713.4	535.3	460.1	359.6	7 484.5	9 175.4	10 145.3	9 791.1	10 187.9	10 112.1
Belgium	102.1	123.8	154.0	103.4	42.6	12.8	777.1	861.6	742.4	753.1	801.4	823.5
France	61.9	81.5	34.6	34.9	29.1	15.4	412.8	421.6	440.1	455.6	483.9	527.2
Germany	42.6	27.3	84.9	45.2	36.5	34.3	706.6	940.0	772.7	859.3	994.4	990.4
Netherlands	111.4	168.8	153.5	119.2	89.4	65.7	507.0	798.8	588.8	515.1	561.0	629.7
United Kingdom	26.4	40.2	35.5	40.8	40.0	37.5	1 912.9	1 800.8	2 613.9	1 943.4	2 573.9	2 042.9
Turkey	18.6	28.7	14.1	12.6	20.4	33.7	276.0	239.4	237.9	231.3	204.0	104.4
Former Soviet Republics	29.7	13.0	6.5	4.1	11.7	4.5	432.0	407.2	310.2	269.6	315.6	334.1
Poland	3.1	0.2	0.2	0.6	2.8	0.3	36.8	42.7	39.4	47.9	35.7	22.3
Other Eastern Europe	2.5	0.3	7.9	4.2	0.6	7.4	164.8	190.7	157.5	118.7	81.1	103.1
Other Europe	156.1	216.7	222.3	170.3	186.9	147.9	2 258.4	3 472.6	4 242.6	4 597.0	4 136.9	4 534.5
Asia	1 080.9	1 504.0	1 782.4	1 389.8	1 235.1	1 127.4	8 772.7	10 355.6	9 645.3	9 500.4	7 035.0	6 459.9
Japan	734.4	805.7	1 053.3	916.9	732.2	673.3	3 832.3	4 538.1	4 355.6	4 289.3	3 590.6	3 181.1
China	44.7	226.0	120.8	71.1	164.1	63.8	461.3	456.7	625.2	512.8	484.6	417.3
Hong Kong	11.5	16.7	11.7	13.9	17.6	10.0	1 280.2	1 312.5	1 070.1	1 211.4	802.8	834.5
Taiwan	26.2	214.0	294.2	150.3	142.9	153.7	771.4	806.2	626.3	600.8	428.0	294.1
Singapore	24.1	14.8	20.7	24.5	14.8	17.9	249.0	272.9	238.6	242.2	143.0	169.9
South Korea	22.1	59.1	109.2	86.2	102.7	123.9	964.1	1 457.0	1 271.5	959.7	472.9	564.9
Indonesia	201.0	75.3	58.5	33.0	14.8	20.1	173.9	284.7	146.5	119.3	66.5	94.7
India	5.7	20.0	15.4	4.0	1.3	5.6	345.2	443.5	401.4	443.2	269.5	354.8
Other Asia	11.3	72.5	98.7	89.9	44.6	59.1	695.5	784.2	910.2	1 121.7	777.1	548.7
Africa	47.6	62.0	62.5	74.5	80.1	121.2	746.2	835.7	793.6	888.7	681.0	447.1
North Africa	23.6	18.2	13.8	22.8	34.8	71.3	383.9	336.1	289.2	353.8	264.7	123.5
Republic of South Africa	5.7	9.0	9.0	9.7	12.8	26.4	130.4	168.0	136.9	150.4	153.0	113.3
Other Subsaharan Africa	18.3	34.9	39.7	42.0	32.5	23.5	232.0	331.6	367.5	384.5	263.3	210.4
Middle East	175.1	197.5	131.1	129.6	149.4	140.2	1 605.7	1 736.0	1 862.8	2 331.4	2 442.5	2 415.7
Australia	26.2	22.0	31.9	41.6	22.5	32.2	221.1	217.9	254.9	215.3	164.9	172.0
Rest Of World	. . .	. . .	. . .	. . .	. . .	. . .	2.3	. . .	0.1	0.8	0.8	. . .

Table E-3. Metropolitan Area Exports of Goods by Destination, 1994–1999—*Continued*

(Millions of dollars.)

Destination	Norfolk - Virginia Beach - Newport News, VA - NC						Oakland, CA					
	1994	1995	1996	1997	1998	1999	1994	1995	1996	1997	1998	1999
ALL DESTINATIONS	807.7	1 005.5	1 256.9	1 396.9	1 587.3	1 390.0	5 113.2	6 372.5	7 309.2	6 920.4	6 263.9	6 709.5
North America	181.5	249.5	287.0	317.1	383.7	411.1	763.7	713.7	878.9	1 022.5	1 124.5	1 210.6
Canada	157.0	219.2	205.6	230.1	265.8	280.1	586.0	598.2	747.2	855.1	943.6	989.1
Mexico	24.5	30.3	81.4	87.1	117.9	131.1	177.7	115.5	131.7	167.4	180.9	221.5
Caribbean And Central America	5.2	6.6	16.3	20.2	16.3	17.8	19.4	45.8	58.5	72.1	60.0	35.4
South America	54.6	78.7	90.2	98.0	119.4	104.3	76.5	67.5	120.0	161.9	95.0	97.8
Argentina	6.5	9.3	6.6	10.6	13.3	9.5	18.1	14.3	10.0	23.8	9.8	13.8
Brazil	37.1	47.1	53.8	59.7	85.7	73.5	13.4	23.2	86.2	92.4	36.9	34.6
Other South America	11.0	22.3	29.8	27.7	20.4	21.3	45.0	30.1	23.8	45.8	48.2	49.5
Europe	402.0	455.6	574.8	610.9	736.6	507.6	1 022.0	1 440.5	1 382.5	1 371.8	1 539.1	1 809.0
Belgium	36.3	52.0	56.5	66.9	36.2	18.9	48.0	53.3	39.7	29.5	47.7	32.4
France	55.3	66.5	95.8	101.4	116.7	85.2	103.0	122.7	132.7	131.0	152.0	131.0
Germany	68.4	83.3	110.1	118.8	126.1	79.1	250.5	353.9	339.5	315.1	380.7	432.7
Netherlands	31.4	58.1	49.2	46.5	96.9	63.1	117.9	169.8	150.2	143.0	151.1	358.5
United Kingdom	23.4	28.5	37.5	43.1	68.6	77.1	209.1	341.6	346.0	370.7	377.5	377.8
Turkey	20.9	7.9	3.3	7.2	14.3	12.2	1.5	1.3	4.7	5.3	6.7	30.1
Former Soviet Republics	5.4	6.3	5.0	5.2	8.9	2.6	28.5	20.7	22.4	29.5	24.3	19.8
Poland	0.2	0.6	1.0	1.3	2.2	2.7	2.9	3.8	4.9	5.2	7.7	5.6
Other Eastern Europe	0.4	2.5	7.0	7.3	5.0	4.5	8.8	24.6	21.8	16.0	25.7	22.3
Other Europe	160.4	149.8	209.4	213.2	261.7	162.1	251.8	348.7	320.6	326.6	365.7	398.8
Asia	118.5	167.6	207.5	253.3	222.7	206.5	2 976.8	3 903.0	4 649.5	4 029.3	3 212.5	3 338.9
Japan	31.4	33.0	49.2	56.8	47.9	59.7	1 043.0	1 343.1	1 647.0	1 262.8	1 109.0	1 100.4
China	4.8	24.2	15.4	21.5	28.5	21.1	70.6	94.5	133.9	168.5	152.6	153.7
Hong Kong	10.1	13.0	18.5	29.4	24.4	20.2	305.2	336.9	278.8	342.5	295.1	292.3
Taiwan	9.7	14.6	22.3	23.1	18.2	12.0	460.1	610.0	746.5	699.7	558.4	620.9
Singapore	4.2	5.0	7.9	11.9	12.3	9.1	367.3	535.3	833.5	651.4	466.7	381.3
South Korea	45.4	61.4	39.4	29.1	33.2	45.3	351.4	491.6	492.8	410.3	236.1	289.3
Indonesia	0.7	1.5	15.9	26.7	6.4	4.4	28.6	40.3	74.1	59.7	27.3	36.0
India	4.6	0.4	3.5	2.4	2.5	3.3	21.3	58.8	44.0	16.1	23.9	21.2
Other Asia	7.7	14.5	35.5	52.3	49.3	31.4	329.3	392.5	399.0	418.3	343.3	443.7
Africa	23.2	25.3	17.9	29.9	33.1	50.9	85.5	25.6	38.8	42.8	29.5	43.8
North Africa	18.0	20.2	11.3	21.2	28.2	42.2	8.3	3.8	7.2	14.5	12.0	17.7
Republic of South Africa	4.0	4.0	5.2	7.9	3.6	6.3	11.5	12.9	22.8	15.7	12.6	14.2
Other Subsaharan Africa	1.3	1.0	1.3	0.8	1.3	2.4	65.7	8.9	8.8	12.5	4.9	11.9
Middle East	14.6	11.0	37.8	45.2	57.0	31.9	54.8	52.5	61.4	72.6	69.8	67.9
Australia	8.0	11.3	24.9	22.3	18.5	59.7	114.6	123.8	119.7	147.4	133.6	106.1
Rest Of World	. . .	. . .	0.5	. . .	. . .	0.3	. . .	. . .	. . .	. . .	. . .	. . .

Destination	Omaha, NE - IA						Orange County, CA					
	1994	1995	1996	1997	1998	1999	1994	1995	1996	1997	1998	1999
ALL DESTINATIONS	393.3	425.9	608.3	691.4	753.7	949.5	6 716.0	8 041.1	8 309.3	8 798.3	8 198.9	9 323.7
North America	137.9	150.6	257.0	231.9	218.9	261.9	1 585.3	1 962.5	2 208.3	2 442.2	2 413.9	2 930.9
Canada	94.7	103.5	127.3	153.3	153.0	168.5	833.0	1 004.0	1 033.3	1 024.0	1 047.3	1 203.7
Mexico	43.3	47.2	129.7	78.6	65.9	93.4	752.3	958.5	1 175.1	1 418.2	1 366.7	1 727.2
Caribbean And Central America	11.2	7.4	7.4	4.5	3.3	39.0	37.8	32.5	38.9	62.5	77.7	101.7
South America	46.5	50.0	81.0	120.6	79.4	65.8	132.1	192.8	208.9	242.8	266.3	213.6
Argentina	0.4	0.2	0.6	1.3	2.1	2.4	29.8	47.1	33.5	42.0	38.5	31.8
Brazil	0.6	0.5	3.1	6.9	9.5	14.9	50.8	90.0	120.0	131.6	152.4	122.9
Other South America	45.5	49.3	77.4	112.3	67.8	48.5	51.6	55.7	55.4	69.2	75.4	59.0
Europe	91.1	94.3	122.5	149.2	238.7	233.8	2 016.9	2 293.4	1 918.2	2 012.6	2 005.4	2 073.3
Belgium	16.2	10.2	22.7	32.3	63.4	35.6	38.9	56.9	55.6	58.1	50.7	73.7
France	2.7	2.8	4.8	9.1	6.6	8.3	640.4	657.2	461.1	423.5	244.5	260.5
Germany	4.3	4.0	6.8	7.2	11.3	14.0	322.8	363.3	286.9	302.3	289.4	284.7
Netherlands	38.8	48.2	46.9	43.6	55.7	39.4	141.6	176.5	219.1	221.0	272.1	263.4
United Kingdom	11.8	6.9	13.1	16.5	38.4	32.3	400.2	443.4	359.0	454.6	596.7	593.5
Turkey	0.2	0.2	0.4	0.1	. . .	14.6	4.6	7.9	9.2	11.9	10.5	8.9
Former Soviet Republics	0.5	1.2	12.6	0.7	0.4	0.4	16.0	14.5	24.7	24.8	17.2	10.3
Poland	. . .	0.9	0.6	0.1	0.9	0.1	2.6	6.4	8.6	8.2	7.1	8.8
Other Eastern Europe	1.1	4.1	1.4	0.8	5.9	4.6	17.0	17.3	20.7	24.1	24.8	22.0
Other Europe	15.5	15.9	13.3	38.8	56.1	84.4	432.7	550.0	473.3	484.1	492.5	547.5
Asia	58.6	78.9	91.9	122.8	164.2	240.8	2 651.7	3 243.9	3 623.9	3 706.9	3 106.1	3 701.0
Japan	14.7	20.1	29.2	26.2	28.6	31.7	1 160.7	1 380.1	1 531.8	1 393.1	1 144.0	1 164.9
China	2.3	3.2	5.6	1.5	14.9	3.6	65.7	147.3	133.0	87.6	121.7	149.7
Hong Kong	12.6	10.6	2.6	2.9	3.6	6.3	226.8	257.9	243.4	313.8	289.7	366.4
Taiwan	1.9	1.9	3.1	7.4	7.7	14.6	330.4	376.5	425.4	512.7	610.7	716.0
Singapore	10.5	16.5	15.7	26.3	22.1	29.6	297.5	325.4	358.4	299.6	291.9	366.9
South Korea	6.5	4.6	7.3	6.7	3.6	40.3	315.0	458.4	537.9	686.8	340.6	518.9
Indonesia	1.3	3.3	2.5	9.0	0.7	3.6	12.6	10.9	56.2	50.5	9.9	19.2
India	0.4	1.6	0.5	1.2	0.7	0.6	15.7	26.6	33.7	27.7	27.4	28.8
Other Asia	8.5	17.1	25.5	41.6	82.4	110.5	227.3	260.8	304.1	335.2	270.2	370.2
Africa	16.3	10.8	15.0	17.6	9.1	27.7	40.6	50.7	43.2	48.9	45.4	44.5
North Africa	9.6	6.3	11.3	9.5	4.5	13.9	11.6	21.4	10.2	13.9	12.8	7.0
Republic of South Africa	2.3	2.9	3.2	2.3	2.2	5.3	25.1	26.2	27.8	26.9	26.3	29.0
Other Subsaharan Africa	4.4	1.6	0.5	5.8	2.4	8.4	3.9	3.1	5.2	8.1	6.3	8.5
Middle East	24.4	23.4	14.1	12.1	8.7	42.4	88.0	97.9	101.0	125.5	143.5	124.0
Australia	7.1	10.5	19.4	32.7	31.4	27.5	163.6	167.4	166.8	156.8	140.2	134.6
Rest Of World	. . .	. . .	. . .	. . .	. . .	10.6	. . .	0.1	. . .	. . .	0.2	. . .

Table E-3. Metropolitan Area Exports of Goods by Destination, 1994–1999—*Continued*

(Millions of dollars.)

Destination	Orlando, FL						Parkersburg - Marietta, WV - OH					
	1994	1995	1996	1997	1998	1999	1994	1995	1996	1997	1998	1999
ALL DESTINATIONS	848.5	968.8	1 219.0	1 662.8	1 477.3	1 500.0	313.6	186.6	211.9	262.3	246.6	234.2
North America	222.0	176.1	177.6	237.4	188.1	303.2	98.0	80.6	97.4	113.8	113.7	103.4
Canada	146.9	131.6	151.9	201.1	145.0	258.7	89.9	74.8	90.7	106.7	109.0	96.7
Mexico	75.1	44.5	25.7	36.3	43.1	44.5	8.1	5.8	6.8	7.1	4.6	6.6
Caribbean And Central America	45.5	39.8	63.6	74.0	90.7	92.4	3.1	1.2	1.5	2.9	0.5	0.7
South America	122.0	114.6	100.5	134.1	84.5	70.9	9.7	3.3	4.8	5.6	6.5	3.1
Argentina	6.8	20.8	8.2	13.0	9.3	6.3	2.2	1.4	1.4	1.4	1.1	1.3
Brazil	24.9	50.2	40.8	35.2	26.5	32.7	2.3	1.2	2.1	2.7	4.0	1.1
Other South America	90.3	43.6	51.6	85.9	48.7	31.8	5.2	0.8	1.4	1.5	1.4	0.7
Europe	186.1	250.4	348.0	297.1	352.5	366.6	55.7	39.0	44.9	72.5	70.2	68.3
Belgium	8.6	19.1	16.3	13.1	16.3	10.8	19.0	17.6	17.9	30.6	34.2	37.2
France	20.9	22.1	23.7	22.9	25.5	30.0	1.9	2.1	2.5	6.6	5.0	2.6
Germany	32.2	42.8	46.4	54.4	70.7	53.5	2.7	1.6	1.8	3.5	5.9	3.0
Netherlands	16.9	25.9	39.4	25.7	39.4	36.0	21.4	4.4	4.2	7.8	7.0	5.6
United Kingdom	32.5	47.6	61.8	83.4	95.3	136.9	5.6	8.9	13.2	15.6	9.6	12.8
Turkey	2.8	2.5	3.7	4.7	13.2	5.2	...	0.4	0.3	0.2	0.1	0.1
Former Soviet Republics	4.9	3.1	3.6	3.0	3.1	3.1	0.1	...	...	...	...	...
Poland	0.6	11.3	49.9	10.2	12.4	2.9	...	...	...	...	0.1	...
Other Eastern Europe	1.7	1.8	8.7	5.1	5.7	3.6	0.3	0.1	0.1	0.1	...	0.3
Other Europe	65.1	74.2	94.5	74.6	70.8	84.6	4.5	3.9	4.9	8.1	8.3	6.4
Asia	179.5	295.6	433.9	741.5	627.6	568.3	139.7	57.1	55.9	58.0	46.1	54.0
Japan	23.3	29.4	49.1	45.6	30.6	22.6	20.8	13.5	8.2	23.7	22.9	32.0
China	14.8	28.0	80.4	282.6	88.8	27.3	16.6	14.8	12.2	1.1	4.1	2.5
Hong Kong	9.8	10.8	7.5	13.4	20.1	26.6	28.1	5.2	5.5	4.0	3.3	2.8
Taiwan	7.2	9.1	10.0	13.8	6.6	4.9	11.2	1.9	1.3	1.4	1.2	1.2
Singapore	14.5	28.3	35.0	173.0	342.8	338.6	30.4	12.2	18.1	16.5	10.5	10.0
South Korea	74.5	162.0	191.1	179.8	88.3	71.3	13.1	5.6	5.6	4.3	2.3	2.8
Indonesia	1.2	3.4	2.7	3.5	1.0	0.2	0.6	0.5	0.3	0.6	...	0.2
India	1.4	2.9	5.6	3.7	3.4	5.5	0.7	0.6	0.7	0.7	0.5	0.6
Other Asia	32.9	21.5	52.4	26.2	46.0	71.4	18.2	2.9	3.8	5.9	1.4	1.9
Africa	20.0	24.2	16.4	14.8	16.4	11.3	0.2	0.3	0.3	1.8	1.1	1.1
North Africa	12.8	10.1	6.5	2.7	3.9	3.2	0.2	0.2	0.1	1.5	0.5	0.4
Republic of South Africa	3.7	5.1	7.2	7.5	4.9	3.6	...	...	0.2	0.2	0.6	0.5
Other Subsaharan Africa	3.6	9.0	2.8	4.7	7.6	4.5	0.1	...	...	0.1	0.1	0.2
Middle East	66.9	60.1	65.7	151.8	105.9	76.2	2.6	0.9	1.7	2.1	1.2	1.6
Australia	6.4	8.0	13.3	12.1	11.7	11.2	4.7	4.1	5.4	5.5	7.2	2.0
Rest Of World	...	...	...	...	...	...	...	...	...	...	...	...

Destination	Philadelphia, PA - NJ						Phoenix - Mesa, AZ					
	1994	1995	1996	1997	1998	1999	1994	1995	1996	1997	1998	1999
ALL DESTINATIONS	6 545.8	7 896.9	7 727.9	8 027.8	8 397.2	9 267.1	5 561.1	6 780.4	7 912.1	11 108.4	8 102.8	7 531.7
North America	1 771.5	1 942.3	1 994.3	2 171.5	2 473.3	3 436.9	772.6	916.9	1 045.0	1 253.0	1 173.7	1 404.7
Canada	1 426.5	1 641.4	1 690.9	1 845.7	1 999.3	2 225.5	455.6	630.7	690.2	794.8	771.1	848.7
Mexico	345.0	300.9	303.4	325.7	474.0	1 211.5	317.0	286.2	354.8	458.2	402.5	556.0
Caribbean And Central America	240.4	307.3	409.2	369.2	360.9	359.1	8.4	8.3	10.5	17.4	42.7	119.0
South America	696.1	870.1	682.7	778.3	651.5	560.0	69.1	87.9	125.0	147.7	182.0	176.3
Argentina	124.4	106.4	75.3	81.8	86.2	85.5	12.5	9.6	10.7	13.1	10.4	10.1
Brazil	325.8	450.1	344.9	410.3	279.5	247.0	28.4	43.7	65.9	98.2	122.7	127.8
Other South America	245.9	313.6	262.5	286.2	285.8	227.5	28.2	34.7	48.3	36.5	49.0	38.4
Europe	1 761.2	2 280.4	2 386.1	2 313.4	2 534.8	2 492.7	1 766.6	2 295.3	2 291.4	3 744.6	2 598.3	1 977.5
Belgium	137.3	199.1	168.0	168.8	303.8	159.3	55.7	68.6	73.2	78.6	88.7	73.1
France	129.7	180.7	186.0	168.6	211.1	239.5	182.4	246.8	284.5	335.1	396.5	335.7
Germany	232.0	262.3	264.9	299.7	282.5	318.5	288.3	337.7	316.3	336.2	445.9	356.9
Netherlands	217.4	363.7	313.3	262.6	355.2	340.9	125.0	281.5	550.6	1 421.7	386.5	91.5
United Kingdom	464.0	691.8	800.5	793.7	807.7	788.9	877.1	1 046.9	781.9	1 010.6	647.1	695.5
Turkey	21.0	17.7	29.9	28.8	39.4	25.4	18.0	7.8	11.1	18.2	32.8	13.0
Former Soviet Republics	30.2	40.6	86.6	53.8	42.5	9.6	7.0	8.2	6.7	165.7	89.2	7.5
Poland	6.8	9.2	16.4	20.7	9.6	9.3	1.2	0.9	1.5	0.8	3.8	4.4
Other Eastern Europe	14.4	19.3	12.4	26.8	11.9	24.8	3.9	3.4	4.6	10.0	21.3	17.6
Other Europe	508.3	496.0	508.0	489.8	471.2	576.5	208.1	293.5	261.1	367.9	486.6	382.2
Asia	1 732.1	2 041.9	1 833.2	1 954.3	1 921.6	2 023.4	2 784.2	3 319.4	4 292.4	5 767.2	3 881.3	3 610.5
Japan	411.4	423.5	492.8	479.0	467.8	483.8	753.7	1 049.3	1 275.3	1 716.0	514.0	697.7
China	92.9	123.8	111.6	119.5	125.6	131.6	61.2	90.6	119.9	120.1	238.7	160.7
Hong Kong	140.6	167.3	186.9	183.0	170.9	177.3	269.6	375.5	381.3	477.2	309.6	346.4
Taiwan	408.1	469.0	219.1	303.2	350.3	437.3	585.3	618.7	855.1	1 013.2	581.3	443.1
Singapore	125.3	163.2	128.4	154.6	163.4	209.2	347.5	297.2	345.9	452.6	279.2	295.5
South Korea	270.3	306.4	259.4	273.5	320.9	206.9	202.3	227.5	279.1	289.0	348.0	331.1
Indonesia	45.2	72.3	56.7	78.0	40.6	52.8	13.0	15.7	13.7	18.9	24.7	26.2
India	43.9	60.2	67.1	82.9	74.7	60.7	19.9	25.1	14.3	33.9	18.5	12.8
Other Asia	194.5	256.2	311.2	280.6	207.4	263.8	531.8	619.8	1 007.8	1 646.4	1 567.2	1 296.8
Africa	85.1	86.0	75.8	80.3	93.3	95.5	18.6	24.6	21.3	28.4	34.5	36.3
North Africa	34.3	28.4	19.9	30.7	28.6	27.4	10.6	6.8	6.2	8.3	9.3	18.3
Republic of South Africa	36.2	44.4	42.5	37.7	51.1	44.9	4.5	12.1	11.8	15.0	21.5	13.6
Other Subsaharan Africa	14.5	13.1	13.5	12.0	13.6	23.3	3.5	5.6	3.2	5.1	3.8	4.4
Middle East	119.8	145.0	153.7	170.9	171.8	143.3	46.9	57.7	65.4	77.8	90.7	111.0
Australia	139.5	224.1	192.9	189.8	190.0	156.2	94.6	70.4	61.0	72.3	99.5	96.4
Rest Of World	0.1	...	...	...	...	0.1	...	...	...	...	...	...

Table E-3. Metropolitan Area Exports of Goods by Destination, 1994–1999—*Continued*

(Millions of dollars.)

Destination	Pittsburgh, PA						Pittsfield, MA					
	1994	1995	1996	1997	1998	1999	1994	1995	1996	1997	1998	1999
ALL DESTINATIONS	3 150.6	3 982.2	3 933.7	4 352.2	4 079.2	3 940.3	112.2	151.9	175.5	219.3	203.6	219.6
North America	955.1	1 010.3	1 170.4	1 564.1	1 717.1	1 808.0	51.0	58.5	75.8	95.7	108.0	112.1
Canada	731.0	823.6	948.5	1 222.5	1 356.2	1 410.5	33.1	36.1	52.7	55.6	61.9	93.7
Mexico	224.1	186.7	221.9	341.6	360.9	397.5	17.9	22.4	23.1	40.1	46.1	18.4
Caribbean And Central America	56.2	68.6	72.0	66.8	79.7	74.8	0.3	0.5	9.6	10.0	9.8	4.7
South America	288.5	281.6	266.3	374.5	252.4	156.7	3.6	3.5	13.8	14.2	12.9	5.2
Argentina	62.3	30.7	29.2	36.9	24.6	15.1	1.0	0.4	1.7	0.8	0.3	0.4
Brazil	89.5	118.3	121.6	213.9	122.3	80.6	0.3	1.5	2.3	5.6	5.3	1.6
Other South America	136.7	132.6	115.5	123.7	105.5	61.0	2.4	1.7	9.7	7.8	7.4	3.2
Europe	728.6	1 103.0	1 077.3	1 099.3	1 078.7	977.9	31.3	49.1	33.1	34.7	45.2	57.1
Belgium	55.5	141.0	143.1	149.9	97.3	86.8	0.5	2.3	0.3	0.2	0.1	0.1
France	45.7	76.5	72.7	81.5	94.0	78.1	0.5	1.5	2.2	2.1	2.9	1.9
Germany	110.2	143.3	161.3	149.9	147.1	183.4	5.8	5.5	4.6	5.2	4.3	8.1
Netherlands	74.1	116.2	139.8	120.4	118.5	132.7	14.5	23.1	19.1	18.2	31.8	31.7
United Kingdom	166.5	184.7	190.4	230.0	222.3	177.7	2.3	6.8	3.6	4.4	2.2	1.1
Turkey	8.3	35.4	15.0	26.0	54.2	13.9	. . .	. . .	. . .	. . .	0.1	0.3
Former Soviet Republics	11.8	22.3	23.8	21.3	21.5	13.3	0.1	2.6	. . .	0.1	. . .	10.3
Poland	6.4	6.7	5.5	7.2	5.2	3.6	0.8	. . .	. . .	0.1	. . .	0.5
Other Eastern Europe	16.4	19.3	26.3	47.8	66.3	35.1	0.6	. . .	. . .	. . .	. . .	. . .
Other Europe	233.7	357.6	299.2	265.3	252.3	253.4	6.3	7.2	3.3	4.4	3.8	3.1
Asia	807.7	1 156.8	964.8	944.1	668.6	710.4	23.8	33.3	40.0	61.1	25.4	35.9
Japan	205.9	350.8	309.6	295.6	199.7	153.8	6.6	8.5	10.8	8.4	9.4	9.6
China	115.1	125.5	72.7	63.3	63.6	88.5	8.2	1.4	3.3	3.9	6.0	5.6
Hong Kong	27.9	49.6	39.5	53.9	49.4	91.2	3.3	3.4	9.0	9.7	4.0	2.5
Taiwan	63.7	158.1	116.2	97.1	75.3	106.1	3.1	3.5	3.5	2.4	1.7	4.4
Singapore	51.5	91.3	109.4	107.5	82.6	60.0	0.4	1.1	1.8	20.8	1.3	1.2
South Korea	176.6	187.2	149.6	111.5	66.3	101.3	1.1	1.9	2.7	7.1	1.0	0.7
Indonesia	11.2	18.7	27.9	16.1	10.4	9.1	0.1	11.6	6.4	4.6	0.3	7.7
India	33.2	41.1	37.9	48.9	49.0	20.0	. . .	0.2	0.8	0.2	0.1	0.1
Other Asia	122.5	134.6	102.0	150.3	72.3	80.6	1.0	1.7	1.6	4.0	1.5	4.0
Africa	75.7	75.5	107.7	93.5	97.0	58.3	0.2	0.5	0.3	0.2	0.7	1.2
North Africa	22.4	13.1	42.6	36.1	28.4	14.7	. . .	. . .	. . .	0.1	0.1	. . .
Republic of South Africa	48.2	56.5	58.4	49.6	59.9	37.5	0.2	0.5	0.1	0.1	0.6	1.2
Other Subsaharan Africa	5.1	6.0	6.7	7.9	8.8	6.1	. . .	. . .	0.1	. . .	. . .	. . .
Middle East	178.9	206.7	192.4	127.7	131.7	104.8	1.5	1.9	0.3	2.0	0.5	0.1
Australia	59.9	79.7	82.8	82.0	54.0	49.4	0.4	4.4	2.8	1.4	1.1	3.4
Rest Of World	. . .	. . .	. . .	. . .	. . .	. . .	. . .	. . .	. . .	. . .	. . .	. . .

Destination	Portland, ME						Portland - Vancouver, OR - WA					
	1994	1995	1996	1997	1998	1999	1994	1995	1996	1997	1998	1999
ALL DESTINATIONS	319.5	373.1	339.2	617.4	755.6	757.1	6 448.8	8 931.3	9 234.3	8 926.5	8 283.3	9 366.6
North America	61.2	61.7	61.5	69.3	72.1	90.8	919.4	927.9	960.1	1 099.8	1 679.8	2 325.5
Canada	59.0	60.6	58.3	67.0	69.8	84.9	759.7	843.9	839.1	994.1	1 206.6	1 366.0
Mexico	2.3	1.2	3.2	2.3	2.3	5.9	159.7	84.0	121.1	105.8	473.2	959.5
Caribbean And Central America	11.5	8.1	14.4	13.2	15.0	21.0	16.7	23.5	25.9	34.8	34.1	31.4
South America	3.6	4.2	6.8	8.8	7.6	7.3	91.8	157.2	106.0	182.1	177.2	114.2
Argentina	0.3	0.5	0.6	0.7	0.5	0.6	7.6	6.9	7.4	15.9	11.7	10.5
Brazil	0.9	1.6	2.5	2.9	1.9	3.5	15.7	24.8	23.6	41.8	49.6	44.4
Other South America	2.4	2.0	3.8	5.2	5.2	3.1	68.4	125.5	75.0	124.3	115.9	59.3
Europe	82.9	74.3	77.7	78.4	53.4	52.8	1 133.0	1 497.0	1 248.4	1 297.3	1 189.9	1 239.4
Belgium	24.6	2.3	2.3	3.1	1.7	2.3	43.4	69.5	43.7	49.2	50.4	145.2
France	24.3	34.1	37.9	18.7	13.8	10.4	117.3	142.5	93.7	100.3	87.6	80.3
Germany	3.9	4.3	5.6	5.1	5.5	3.4	208.1	264.1	240.1	194.5	163.3	187.2
Netherlands	1.6	2.5	3.7	2.4	4.8	10.6	96.9	169.2	185.7	280.8	238.8	191.2
United Kingdom	6.8	8.7	6.5	7.3	8.0	8.0	295.9	328.7	299.4	332.0	342.0	290.8
Turkey	0.7	0.5	1.5	0.8	0.7	1.1	3.3	13.7	30.7	3.2	8.4	6.4
Former Soviet Republics	0.9	0.1	0.7	0.2	0.1	0.2	40.3	30.6	13.9	22.7	32.7	28.0
Poland	. . .	. . .	. . .	. . .	. . .	. . .	1.4	2.9	2.5	4.2	4.5	3.8
Other Eastern Europe	0.2	0.2	0.4	0.8	1.9	2.4	10.3	10.3	7.9	5.5	6.1	17.4
Other Europe	19.8	21.5	19.2	39.9	16.8	14.5	316.1	465.5	330.8	304.8	256.0	289.1
Asia	149.2	213.5	167.3	437.5	602.7	580.4	3 780.5	5 800.7	6 284.5	5 884.7	4 847.1	5 363.4
Japan	29.8	25.6	26.4	25.0	23.6	26.0	1 359.7	1 677.9	1 804.3	1 558.0	1 379.1	1 475.6
China	0.2	1.2	1.9	2.4	0.7	0.2	37.2	71.1	109.0	120.2	117.9	203.3
Hong Kong	5.1	1.7	2.0	1.9	3.6	2.4	139.0	260.2	521.9	291.6	240.0	187.8
Taiwan	1.7	2.3	2.5	1.7	2.0	1.1	688.3	1 051.1	1 078.9	1 121.5	653.3	630.1
Singapore	12.2	17.9	31.0	155.4	281.5	377.4	123.3	311.0	331.5	221.0	137.4	140.0
South Korea	0.9	1.5	3.0	7.2	1.9	2.2	527.3	911.4	977.0	1 099.3	1 195.1	1 426.0
Indonesia	0.1	. . .	1.3	0.9	. . .	0.1	41.3	141.0	146.7	96.7	59.6	77.5
India	0.1	0.1	0.4	0.2	0.2	0.4	1.7	9.2	16.5	18.6	14.8	17.2	18.9
Other Asia	99.1	163.1	98.8	242.9	289.1	169.4	855.0	1 360.4	1 296.6	1 361.6	1 047.5	1 204.2
Africa	1.5	1.9	3.3	3.7	2.1	1.6	234.8	112.0	125.7	97.8	139.1	94.4
North Africa	0.7	0.5	1.0	0.5	. . .	0.2	183.2	68.0	80.5	26.9	79.8	46.5
Republic of South Africa	0.6	1.2	1.7	2.6	1.1	1.0	16.7	23.8	34.8	63.9	46.6	41.7
Other Subsaharan Africa	0.2	0.2	0.7	0.5	0.9	0.4	34.9	20.2	10.4	7.0	12.7	6.2
Middle East	7.8	6.2	4.2	4.7	1.7	2.2	81.1	133.4	206.8	135.1	86.9	76.7
Australia	1.8	3.2	3.8	2.0	1.0	1.2	191.7	279.7	276.9	194.8	125.3	121.0
Rest Of World	. . .	. . .	. . .	. . .	. . .	. . .	. . .	. . .	. . .	0.2	3.8	0.6

Table E-3. Metropolitan Area Exports of Goods by Destination, 1994–1999—Continued

(Millions of dollars.)

Destination	Portsmouth - Rochester, NH - ME						Providence - Fall River - Warwick, RI - MA					
	1994	1995	1996	1997	1998	1999	1994	1995	1996	1997	1998	1999
ALL DESTINATIONS	470.2	553.6	574.8	486.0	555.2	588.4	1 246.0	1 241.0	1 296.2	1 601.8	1 670.6	1 554.4
North America	157.6	173.6	234.7	192.2	221.6	250.0	365.1	383.0	445.2	528.5	570.5	598.1
Canada	131.5	159.8	224.8	179.0	195.3	226.4	312.4	345.7	385.2	408.4	445.2	433.0
Mexico	26.1	13.8	9.9	13.2	26.3	23.6	52.7	37.3	60.0	120.1	125.3	165.1
Caribbean And Central America	18.0	32.2	28.0	33.9	37.3	25.4	15.9	12.7	11.9	14.0	12.0	15.2
South America	18.7	33.0	23.5	21.1	11.7	10.0	43.9	37.3	24.8	59.4	47.5	44.4
Argentina	1.3	1.5	1.7	1.6	1.4	1.3	10.9	4.2	2.7	6.0	5.0	5.0
Brazil	11.9	27.1	15.8	13.2	4.1	4.4	11.7	13.4	11.1	37.0	19.4	15.6
Other South America	5.4	4.5	6.0	6.3	6.2	4.4	21.3	19.7	11.0	16.4	23.1	23.8
Europe	173.5	203.3	175.3	156.2	191.3	229.9	520.6	452.8	437.3	542.2	576.9	433.7
Belgium	2.3	7.8	3.0	4.9	7.4	6.7	53.2	29.2	33.6	48.6	36.9	28.5
France	19.5	19.2	25.1	25.0	17.9	15.0	23.7	23.9	21.2	25.4	37.9	28.9
Germany	20.1	24.8	19.9	20.4	14.8	17.8	39.9	45.8	56.1	67.5	58.5	48.6
Netherlands	11.8	10.9	9.4	17.1	15.0	22.6	55.0	38.2	30.0	33.3	22.5	38.0
United Kingdom	47.0	35.0	27.2	20.1	29.5	32.2	161.3	118.5	94.8	134.6	202.1	96.8
Turkey	1.4	0.6	0.6	1.5	1.1	0.5	0.6	2.4	5.4	9.8	4.8	2.7
Former Soviet Republics	. . .	0.8	0.1	0.3	0.2	1.3	3.0	2.8	3.3	4.4	1.8	1.3
Poland	0.6	. . .	. . .	0.1	0.2	0.4	8.4	4.0	4.1	4.3	2.7	2.4
Other Eastern Europe	4.2	1.0	0.6	0.5	1.1	0.8	6.0	3.2	3.8	2.8	5.2	5.5
Other Europe	66.5	103.2	89.4	66.3	104.0	132.6	169.5	184.7	185.1	211.7	204.6	180.9
Asia	88.8	98.1	101.7	67.1	81.8	66.9	262.0	312.5	330.7	418.4	421.6	397.7
Japan	19.2	16.9	27.6	22.7	30.2	20.8	61.1	85.1	86.0	126.3	166.5	105.3
China	2.6	7.6	2.4	1.8	2.4	5.7	17.3	7.1	10.0	6.3	10.8	12.3
Hong Kong	18.7	22.5	11.4	8.5	6.4	6.0	46.5	47.7	55.7	52.2	57.0	61.4
Taiwan	17.8	15.6	20.3	7.4	16.8	10.6	23.1	30.1	33.0	42.1	38.1	42.6
Singapore	7.7	11.2	13.2	13.3	12.6	11.7	26.0	28.0	25.2	34.1	27.7	40.6
South Korea	8.4	4.5	9.7	5.5	2.4	3.0	27.6	32.7	30.9	37.3	14.4	28.2
Indonesia	3.8	3.5	3.5	1.6	1.3	0.6	1.6	0.9	2.0	1.2	0.9	1.7
India	3.1	5.9	3.4	2.6	0.9	1.2	5.3	5.7	3.6	5.0	3.3	5.3
Other Asia	7.6	10.3	10.3	3.7	8.7	7.3	53.6	75.3	84.5	114.1	102.9	100.3
Africa	1.1	1.0	0.6	1.6	1.5	0.7	5.1	6.2	5.5	6.5	6.4	38.0
North Africa	0.1	0.1	0.1	1.0	0.1	0.1	0.6	2.0	0.9	1.0	1.7	3.3
Republic of South Africa	0.4	0.8	0.5	0.5	0.3	0.5	3.6	2.9	3.8	4.2	3.0	29.1
Other Subsaharan Africa	0.6	. . .	0.1	. . .	1.1	0.1	0.8	1.3	0.8	1.3	1.7	5.6
Middle East	3.5	3.6	3.5	3.5	5.4	2.4	19.7	18.8	21.5	16.0	14.2	12.6
Australia	8.9	8.7	7.4	10.5	4.6	3.1	13.7	17.7	19.3	16.7	21.5	14.5
Rest Of World	. . .	. . .	. . .	. . .	. . .	. . .	. . .	. . .	. . .	. . .	. . .	0.2

Destination	Provo - Orem, UT						Racine, WI					
	1994	1995	1996	1997	1998	1999	1994	1995	1996	1997	1998	1999
ALL DESTINATIONS	200.2	201.6	301.9	360.5	320.4	284.1	403.2	335.1	493.2	992.0	482.5	240.7
North America	67.5	63.1	45.6	55.3	61.0	61.1	207.3	213.8	162.5	190.5	221.6	171.0
Canada	59.9	58.5	40.9	51.5	55.6	53.7	202.9	211.5	157.0	177.9	206.0	161.1
Mexico	7.6	4.6	4.7	3.9	5.4	7.4	4.4	2.3	5.5	12.6	15.6	9.9
Caribbean And Central America	0.3	1.0	1.3	1.0	2.1	3.0	1.7	2.7	5.1	12.5	14.6	6.4
South America	4.2	5.7	7.2	8.0	11.6	13.8	7.0	8.7	41.6	122.7	50.2	8.6
Argentina	0.1	0.1	0.1	0.8	0.4	1.1	0.3	1.7	17.6	22.5	9.1	3.7
Brazil	1.5	2.4	4.1	3.6	5.3	3.1	3.8	3.5	7.0	66.8	29.5	1.1
Other South America	2.7	3.2	2.9	3.7	5.9	9.7	2.9	3.5	16.9	33.3	11.6	3.8
Europe	22.4	31.7	66.3	56.4	51.4	45.5	98.2	68.4	143.3	438.9	119.2	31.2
Belgium	1.4	1.7	4.0	4.3	5.3	1.9	2.2	0.5	3.3	3.2	1.3	0.9
France	1.4	2.3	7.8	5.8	3.3	1.9	26.1	11.7	29.1	82.9	31.0	4.1
Germany	2.7	4.3	9.7	4.5	4.4	5.8	24.6	12.7	27.4	56.6	17.7	6.2
Netherlands	4.4	6.6	10.1	8.4	7.7	5.7	8.9	23.4	21.2	3.0	2.2	0.9
United Kingdom	4.4	5.0	11.0	10.4	11.9	13.1	17.3	5.8	15.7	60.2	14.8	5.6
Turkey	0.1	0.1	0.1	0.1	0.3	0.3	0.1	1.1	2.4	4.4	1.5	0.4
Former Soviet Republics	0.6	2.6	0.9	2.8	2.9	0.5	2.5	0.3	4.7	135.6	23.6	0.6
Poland	0.1	0.1	0.1	. . .	0.2	. . .	0.6	0.1	2.9	13.3	0.2	0.3
Other Eastern Europe	0.2	0.1	0.2	0.3	0.5	0.4	2.9	0.1	8.2	9.6	0.7	0.1
Other Europe	7.3	9.0	22.3	19.8	14.9	15.9	12.9	12.7	28.4	70.1	26.1	12.1
Asia	96.3	91.3	170.4	224.9	180.4	145.7	19.1	19.7	33.9	51.9	17.1	13.1
Japan	47.1	41.7	75.7	134.4	119.4	77.3	8.7	5.4	7.6	10.6	5.9	3.8
China	1.5	0.8	1.7	1.2	4.9	1.6	0.7	0.4	2.1	1.3	1.0	0.8
Hong Kong	4.5	4.2	4.4	8.2	6.5	12.8	0.7	1.6	1.7	2.5	1.4	0.7
Taiwan	35.7	29.0	36.0	34.5	23.6	17.3	0.6	2.3	2.8	4.1	1.2	0.9
Singapore	1.8	2.7	3.0	3.6	3.5	4.0	0.8	1.2	1.1	2.5	1.4	1.6
South Korea	1.4	3.3	38.8	19.8	2.3	5.4	1.5	1.3	1.0	1.5	0.2	0.4
Indonesia	. . .	0.1	0.1	0.1	0.3	0.1	0.2	0.4	1.0	2.4	0.3	. . .
India	0.1	0.2	0.9	1.5	4.0	2.7	1.8	2.8	1.2	1.0	0.8	3.1
Other Asia	4.4	9.3	9.4	21.6	15.9	24.5	4.1	4.3	15.5	26.0	4.9	1.9
Africa	1.2	1.3	0.9	1.4	2.2	2.8	3.3	2.7	19.7	24.4	6.7	2.9
North Africa	0.6	0.7	0.3	0.5	0.1	1.3	0.5	0.2	2.7	3.1	0.7	0.8
Republic of South Africa	0.5	0.5	0.4	0.8	1.0	0.3	2.4	2.2	15.1	19.4	4.9	1.9
Other Subsaharan Africa	0.2	0.1	0.3	0.2	1.0	1.1	0.4	0.3	1.8	1.9	1.1	0.2
Middle East	2.2	1.4	3.4	3.4	2.9	3.0	5.5	4.5	7.4	10.3	6.1	2.8
Australia	5.9	6.1	6.8	10.0	8.9	9.1	61.2	14.5	79.8	140.7	47.0	4.7
Rest Of World	. . .	. . .	. . .	. . .	. . .	. . .	. . .	. . .	. . .	. . .	. . .	. . .

Table E-3. Metropolitan Area Exports of Goods by Destination, 1994–1999—*Continued*

(Millions of dollars.)

Destination	Raleigh - Durham - Chapel Hill, NC						Reading, PA					
	1994	1995	1996	1997	1998	1999	1994	1995	1996	1997	1998	1999
ALL DESTINATIONS	1 758.7	2 093.2	2 609.8	2 713.1	2 665.6	2 981.3	271.6	293.4	326.2	429.5	454.2	481.0
North America	857.5	1 055.9	1 363.3	1 117.0	1 123.4	1 146.2	187.1	170.8	205.3	241.3	222.1	221.7
Canada	810.0	1 005.2	1 282.9	1 050.4	1 041.0	1 043.6	173.4	152.6	181.5	213.1	167.6	150.0
Mexico	47.5	50.8	80.4	66.6	82.4	102.6	13.7	18.2	23.8	28.2	54.5	71.7
Caribbean And Central America	29.6	35.3	58.3	66.1	57.6	59.5	2.0	2.0	2.3	2.8	2.8	2.5
South America	81.2	111.0	138.4	182.5	167.6	184.1	5.2	6.2	7.8	7.6	8.8	7.9
Argentina	14.6	15.5	23.2	31.6	21.8	19.6	0.3	0.6	0.7	0.8	1.6	1.3
Brazil	34.0	51.0	54.4	88.7	76.3	73.6	1.0	2.5	3.3	1.7	1.4	1.8
Other South America	32.7	44.6	60.8	62.2	69.5	90.9	3.9	3.0	3.8	5.0	5.8	4.8
Europe	378.0	475.7	586.4	816.4	731.4	943.9	34.1	47.6	42.8	50.8	69.0	81.0
Belgium	15.1	31.8	45.3	51.5	31.7	48.6	1.6	1.7	1.9	1.6	6.9	19.7
France	37.2	46.6	66.1	101.9	136.1	138.9	1.9	2.9	2.7	6.8	6.5	5.8
Germany	49.1	101.3	104.3	131.1	79.6	212.6	5.2	7.2	6.2	9.1	6.0	11.4
Netherlands	107.7	94.1	91.1	110.4	97.3	98.7	1.0	3.0	4.1	7.8	14.0	7.4
United Kingdom	81.4	62.3	105.6	220.0	234.0	252.6	17.3	17.5	14.7	14.0	17.7	18.3
Turkey	0.7	4.1	13.9	21.8	10.9	19.8	. . .	0.4	2.2	0.4	1.5	0.4
Former Soviet Republics	2.9	9.6	19.2	17.5	14.5	13.6	0.2	1.7	0.3	. . .	0.2	0.1
Poland	1.3	2.9	2.5	1.4	2.9	1.5	. . .	0.1	0.1	0.1	0.2	0.5
Other Eastern Europe	3.5	4.5	1.9	2.5	3.7	7.2	. . .	0.5	1.7	0.7	0.4	3.1
Other Europe	78.9	118.5	136.4	158.4	120.7	150.4	6.9	12.6	8.9	10.3	15.6	14.3
Asia	321.1	313.3	359.5	449.8	469.3	514.4	31.6	47.1	50.9	112.4	135.4	153.3
Japan	180.9	122.0	159.1	178.9	191.3	212.4	15.6	19.5	17.8	18.4	27.0	25.6
China	6.2	10.7	14.4	19.1	38.5	51.6	0.8	0.7	1.7	1.0	2.0	2.0
Hong Kong	33.3	52.0	51.0	88.4	61.5	56.9	1.5	2.8	6.2	4.0	4.0	7.0
Taiwan	18.6	19.0	19.4	47.4	60.0	43.2	1.7	4.0	4.0	3.4	3.2	8.8
Singapore	11.9	17.8	26.3	27.0	27.3	29.5	5.1	3.7	3.1	15.8	14.8	16.6
South Korea	21.1	17.8	21.8	28.5	16.2	19.6	2.6	4.6	5.8	10.4	3.5	6.2
Indonesia	6.5	7.1	5.6	7.4	6.6	10.8	0.1	0.4	0.2	0.3	0.2	0.2
India	7.4	5.5	7.4	6.9	8.4	8.0	0.9	1.3	1.7	1.9	1.6	3.2
Other Asia	35.2	61.3	54.4	46.2	59.6	82.4	3.4	10.1	10.5	57.1	79.2	83.6
Africa	31.7	26.1	21.1	19.8	37.1	32.6	2.7	6.7	5.0	2.0	3.2	4.2
North Africa	22.6	12.7	5.2	7.8	7.9	9.3	0.1	0.4	1.1	0.2	0.1	0.4
Republic of South Africa	7.0	10.4	10.5	8.8	20.7	14.9	2.0	5.9	3.4	1.6	3.0	3.1
Other Subsaharan Africa	2.2	3.0	5.4	3.2	8.5	8.3	0.5	0.3	0.4	0.1	0.1	0.7
Middle East	22.1	26.8	35.2	24.6	26.1	40.6	3.8	7.6	7.6	7.5	7.3	6.5
Australia	37.5	49.0	47.6	36.8	53.1	59.9	5.2	5.5	4.5	5.2	5.6	4.0
Rest Of World	. . .	. . .	. . .	. . .	0.1	. . .	. . .	. . .	. . .	. . .	. . .	. . .

Destination	Reno, NV						Richmond - Petersburg, VA					
	1994	1995	1996	1997	1998	1999	1994	1995	1996	1997	1998	1999
ALL DESTINATIONS	213.7	368.2	314.6	399.7	384.4	588.2	5 260.6	5 389.3	5 609.4	5 571.7	5 396.0	4 587.2
North America	76.8	100.0	157.5	198.8	199.2	398.1	537.6	697.2	543.4	514.8	551.8	590.7
Canada	73.5	98.0	155.0	148.7	190.7	353.6	390.7	521.5	417.6	374.8	388.4	434.4
Mexico	3.3	2.0	2.5	50.2	8.4	44.6	146.9	175.7	125.7	140.0	163.4	156.2
Caribbean And Central America	1.7	3.4	5.3	2.2	4.7	5.0	81.3	60.3	73.9	57.2	27.5	25.0
South America	4.0	16.0	18.5	16.6	11.6	11.7	223.9	301.5	279.7	321.0	245.0	132.2
Argentina	0.3	4.3	2.9	2.8	1.6	3.3	19.7	34.8	19.3	30.1	15.1	13.2
Brazil	1.5	2.7	2.7	3.9	2.1	3.4	103.0	158.9	143.4	180.7	110.8	58.9
Other South America	2.3	9.1	12.9	9.9	7.9	5.0	101.2	107.8	117.0	110.2	119.1	60.1
Europe	51.2	58.4	62.1	80.9	88.9	77.1	2 140.6	2 128.3	2 370.3	2 185.4	2 204.4	1 437.2
Belgium	0.8	1.5	1.5	8.7	6.1	3.5	1 320.0	1 268.8	1 207.5	1 053.3	974.5	386.7
France	8.9	8.1	12.4	11.9	10.6	12.0	21.0	28.7	24.7	31.4	39.1	32.6
Germany	4.5	6.8	6.2	6.4	6.6	7.3	108.8	103.8	118.0	111.4	130.1	196.9
Netherlands	7.0	4.7	9.0	9.1	8.9	8.5	92.1	136.3	63.1	99.8	182.3	153.4
United Kingdom	7.5	9.7	9.5	20.0	24.5	20.5	75.4	91.1	69.5	68.5	63.9	61.4
Turkey	13.2	0.4	2.2	0.5	0.3	0.4	71.3	105.7	108.5	103.8	125.2	72.0
Former Soviet Republics	1.2	0.4	1.7	0.6	1.3	0.2	177.6	65.0	406.8	316.8	244.5	25.3
Poland	. . .	0.1	0.1	0.1	0.4	0.2	11.6	11.8	25.3	42.8	44.2	41.9
Other Eastern Europe	0.2	0.3	1.7	0.3	1.8	0.7	1.9	28.2	23.8	30.5	67.9	55.3
Other Europe	7.9	26.5	17.9	23.3	28.5	23.8	260.9	289.1	323.3	327.2	332.8	411.6
Asia	62.9	168.9	54.1	83.0	39.5	74.5	1 755.0	1 683.2	1 732.4	1 844.8	1 643.4	1 704.0
Japan	14.0	16.3	21.3	22.1	12.9	21.3	1 193.1	1 066.5	1 179.1	1 216.6	1 263.8	1 262.1
China	3.8	1.0	1.2	0.8	2.2	3.1	32.5	45.0	41.5	66.4	33.4	24.4
Hong Kong	1.7	3.5	2.6	3.0	3.9	6.9	102.0	111.5	118.5	131.9	93.8	73.8
Taiwan	1.8	2.0	3.3	2.4	3.2	4.4	96.5	78.3	58.9	64.9	63.2	48.9
Singapore	2.6	1.4	1.7	3.2	4.0	3.1	46.6	57.4	57.0	75.2	70.4	112.6
South Korea	5.3	4.4	4.1	4.4	4.6	17.9	193.2	221.4	177.8	202.2	51.9	77.6
Indonesia	0.3	0.5	0.5	0.5	0.3	0.4	18.4	22.5	10.2	11.9	4.9	9.8
India	0.2	1.2	1.3	0.5	0.4	1.0	9.3	7.3	12.2	10.3	7.1	11.3
Other Asia	33.3	138.7	18.1	46.0	8.0	16.4	63.3	73.3	77.7	65.3	54.9	83.6
Africa	3.7	6.2	4.8	5.1	19.2	11.9	70.6	94.3	110.1	120.7	161.6	193.6
North Africa	0.4	0.3	0.2	0.4	0.7	0.6	57.1	66.6	82.5	96.8	127.1	152.1
Republic of South Africa	2.1	5.3	3.6	4.1	15.2	8.6	4.9	9.3	4.1	3.7	8.9	14.7
Other Subsaharan Africa	1.3	0.5	1.0	0.6	3.4	2.8	8.6	18.3	23.5	20.2	25.5	26.8
Middle East	6.9	5.6	4.0	3.2	10.1	2.3	417.1	398.0	466.7	502.5	527.3	472.1
Australia	6.2	9.7	8.3	9.9	11.2	7.6	34.6	26.6	32.9	25.4	35.0	32.5
Rest Of World	. . .	. . .	. . .	. . .	. . .	. . .	. . .	. . .	. . .	. . .	. . .	. . .

Table E-3. Metropolitan Area Exports of Goods by Destination, 1994–1999—Continued

(Millions of dollars.)

Destination	Riverside - San Bernardino, CA						Roanoke, VA					
	1994	1995	1996	1997	1998	1999	1994	1995	1996	1997	1998	1999
ALL DESTINATIONS	1 458.9	1 856.5	1 982.1	2 067.9	1 861.2	2 076.9	195.9	231.3	238.3	285.2	436.7	293.5
North America	344.5	352.3	379.4	496.3	511.5	585.8	46.8	53.7	55.5	95.8	234.5	103.2
Canada	176.8	213.6	219.3	260.9	311.9	352.2	42.4	49.5	51.1	63.8	194.7	75.2
Mexico	167.6	138.7	160.1	235.4	199.6	233.6	4.4	4.3	4.4	32.0	39.8	28.1
Caribbean And Central America	9.3	10.5	8.3	13.9	20.9	12.8	8.7	10.0	7.6	10.5	7.7	8.5
South America	28.4	34.0	40.7	68.9	61.5	56.8	9.0	10.5	11.6	21.7	19.3	9.5
Argentina	5.9	5.6	8.9	22.8	8.5	12.8	1.2	0.5	0.7	0.7	3.5	0.8
Brazil	9.2	14.9	14.0	15.1	10.7	10.1	1.4	3.1	4.9	7.8	7.5	1.5
Other South America	13.2	13.6	17.9	31.0	42.3	33.9	6.3	6.8	6.0	13.2	8.4	7.1
Europe	251.8	490.7	505.5	407.0	406.9	488.3	39.5	51.2	73.4	84.7	93.2	77.8
Belgium	4.6	8.6	8.8	12.1	15.7	30.1	1.0	0.5	1.7	1.8	0.5	1.5
France	23.0	67.2	176.8	24.7	42.9	44.9	14.5	17.7	25.1	32.1	36.6	31.0
Germany	54.2	66.7	77.3	78.8	63.4	73.8	4.6	12.9	7.1	6.8	7.2	6.1
Netherlands	15.7	30.3	18.9	29.8	45.8	51.2	5.3	4.0	6.7	2.3	10.1	4.2
United Kingdom	83.8	224.8	124.8	115.1	118.6	117.1	8.0	7.1	7.9	15.2	15.3	14.6
Turkey	2.8	3.1	3.9	4.1	4.0	6.7	0.2	1.0	3.5	5.9	4.6	0.4
Former Soviet Republics	3.2	2.0	5.3	46.4	10.6	1.8	. . .	0.2	0.2	4.0	2.4	1.9
Poland	0.4	0.9	0.9	1.4	1.6	1.2	0.1	0.1	0.2	0.1	0.1	. . .
Other Eastern Europe	2.4	3.3	4.4	4.9	5.6	5.9	0.2	0.3	5.4	0.3	0.4	0.5
Other Europe	61.6	83.7	84.3	89.6	98.8	155.6	5.8	7.4	15.8	15.4	15.9	17.5
Asia	725.3	861.2	932.5	956.3	744.1	815.4	71.8	73.5	52.9	57.1	50.6	58.6
Japan	247.9	307.4	339.7	294.5	290.2	300.0	6.5	8.3	7.6	8.7	10.2	9.3
China	50.5	41.0	45.7	60.8	58.2	67.6	4.1	5.9	2.2	1.7	1.2	4.7
Hong Kong	58.4	83.2	101.8	138.0	93.8	100.8	8.1	6.5	5.0	4.5	3.2	5.3
Taiwan	94.0	97.5	92.8	104.8	98.7	102.2	10.7	19.4	8.1	7.8	10.4	9.7
Singapore	58.2	72.5	82.5	73.3	56.0	56.0	10.1	10.5	6.9	10.2	7.5	7.2
South Korea	87.9	112.8	125.0	124.6	45.7	62.8	21.0	12.4	12.5	13.2	9.8	15.6
Indonesia	8.2	18.9	13.2	13.0	5.7	4.9	0.1	0.6	0.3	0.3	0.2	0.2
India	15.8	10.8	11.1	10.4	9.2	13.9	3.3	0.6	2.1	1.0	2.3	1.3
Other Asia	104.3	117.0	120.6	137.0	86.4	107.2	7.7	9.3	8.2	9.7	5.7	5.4
Africa	11.2	9.2	11.3	15.0	14.5	14.1	8.8	1.6	3.7	2.4	4.1	1.6
North Africa	4.2	2.4	4.7	3.0	3.9	2.4	8.1	0.4	0.7	0.5	0.8	0.3
Republic of South Africa	4.3	4.5	5.3	10.0	7.9	8.5	0.7	0.8	1.0	1.2	2.6	0.8
Other Subsaharan Africa	2.8	2.4	1.3	2.0	2.7	3.2	. . .	0.4	2.0	0.6	0.7	0.5
Middle East	23.3	32.5	21.5	30.4	29.8	24.9	2.5	21.4	23.2	3.2	8.0	3.7
Australia	65.0	66.1	83.0	80.1	72.0	78.8	8.7	9.4	10.5	9.8	19.4	30.6
Rest Of World	. . .	. . .	. . .	. . .	. . .	. . .	. . .	. . .	. . .	. . .	. . .	. . .

Destination	Rochester, NY						Rockford, IL					
	1994	1995	1996	1997	1998	1999	1994	1995	1996	1997	1998	1999
ALL DESTINATIONS	3 143.7	3 860.5	4 307.7	4 694.5	4 489.8	4 370.2	616.1	641.4	721.9	758.7	926.5	857.2
North America	1 198.0	1 306.7	1 437.9	1 612.7	1 576.4	1 746.9	321.7	341.2	363.2	372.8	445.0	370.6
Canada	862.9	1 036.1	1 123.6	1 224.0	1 131.1	1 263.3	306.1	332.6	340.2	339.2	409.8	347.7
Mexico	335.1	270.6	314.3	388.7	445.3	483.6	15.5	8.6	23.0	33.5	35.1	22.8
Caribbean And Central America	17.8	19.0	17.4	23.8	22.0	26.8	3.1	2.9	2.3	3.0	3.5	2.6
South America	218.7	299.2	306.1	305.0	376.8	281.6	11.5	8.9	12.0	14.3	20.6	16.5
Argentina	11.3	9.9	7.4	17.0	23.2	26.8	1.3	1.1	1.9	3.5	4.4	3.0
Brazil	149.7	237.9	260.6	244.3	286.0	215.3	2.5	2.9	3.7	4.8	6.2	5.5
Other South America	57.8	51.4	38.0	43.7	67.6	39.5	7.7	5.0	6.4	6.0	10.1	8.0
Europe	846.7	1 190.0	1 361.6	1 491.2	1 486.5	1 242.3	166.0	188.5	206.4	233.2	294.8	321.0
Belgium	34.1	75.6	39.8	22.2	41.6	59.9	5.6	2.9	4.9	3.4	8.3	14.4
France	168.4	222.3	291.1	379.5	320.1	249.6	25.0	30.8	44.2	59.1	65.1	68.9
Germany	144.1	239.0	277.3	289.9	257.7	215.6	33.8	37.4	41.9	57.6	55.6	50.4
Netherlands	115.2	121.1	146.7	158.0	259.7	159.4	16.5	15.5	7.8	6.1	6.1	7.4
United Kingdom	262.5	343.5	364.8	369.8	427.6	380.1	43.2	50.3	53.4	60.4	103.0	114.0
Turkey	7.2	2.5	1.4	2.7	5.5	1.8	0.7	3.6	2.9	2.4	2.0	2.2
Former Soviet Republics	2.0	5.1	8.8	3.4	5.8	5.0	0.1	0.1	0.4	1.0	1.0	0.7
Poland	0.4	0.5	1.2	1.2	2.7	0.9	0.2	1.3	0.9	1.0	1.4	1.5
Other Eastern Europe	3.5	2.3	1.8	3.1	3.5	13.0	2.1	0.6	1.6	1.0	2.1	2.7
Other Europe	109.2	178.2	228.6	261.3	162.4	157.1	38.9	45.9	48.5	41.2	50.2	58.7
Asia	685.9	810.3	892.3	920.7	754.0	838.2	90.9	79.8	114.4	103.8	128.2	107.8
Japan	394.5	472.5	494.5	464.9	360.9	412.0	13.7	15.7	17.6	23.4	27.9	27.9
China	9.9	13.8	8.4	16.2	28.0	65.0	19.7	10.6	18.5	14.6	43.5	16.5
Hong Kong	36.3	47.2	116.1	142.4	112.3	110.8	7.9	3.9	7.9	5.2	6.0	10.0
Taiwan	21.9	24.6	40.5	38.3	46.5	24.5	16.9	18.1	13.9	9.4	7.9	5.5
Singapore	172.7	180.4	125.9	123.8	105.8	104.6	12.4	9.7	16.1	19.8	16.6	17.8
South Korea	27.6	43.1	61.7	72.4	40.7	81.8	10.6	9.1	17.6	9.6	4.8	14.6
Indonesia	7.0	3.5	4.8	3.0	7.0	1.2	3.1	3.8	1.4	4.9	3.2	0.6
India	4.7	4.8	15.2	26.9	33.1	16.8	0.6	0.5	0.6	1.8	6.0	1.3
Other Asia	11.4	20.5	25.2	32.9	19.7	21.6	6.1	8.4	20.8	15.2	12.2	12.0
Africa	7.1	14.9	9.7	9.9	10.3	15.3	3.7	3.0	3.6	6.2	5.2	6.6
North Africa	1.3	9.2	3.7	3.7	3.7	9.6	0.6	0.2	0.6	2.7	1.8	2.7
Republic of South Africa	4.6	3.3	4.1	5.0	3.4	2.8	2.0	2.6	2.5	2.7	3.0	3.4
Other Subsaharan Africa	1.2	2.5	1.9	1.3	3.2	2.9	1.1	0.2	0.5	0.8	0.4	0.5
Middle East	24.2	33.0	23.9	31.2	32.0	24.4	8.3	6.9	8.8	9.0	8.9	11.4
Australia	145.2	187.4	258.8	300.0	231.8	194.7	11.1	10.3	11.1	16.4	20.3	20.8
Rest Of World	. . .	. . .	. . .	. . .	. . .	. . .	. . .	. . .	. . .	. . .	. . .	. . .

Table E-3. Metropolitan Area Exports of Goods by Destination, 1994–1999—*Continued*

(Millions of dollars.)

Destination	Sacramento, CA						Salinas, CA					
	1994	1995	1996	1997	1998	1999	1994	1995	1996	1997	1998	1999
ALL DESTINATIONS	1 087.9	1 448.3	1 908.6	1 669.5	1 731.9	2 337.6	322.0	359.9	337.6	393.2	350.5	313.0
North America	134.7	148.2	180.2	239.4	345.0	451.8	152.4	182.6	159.5	180.4	174.1	164.0
Canada	81.5	101.3	114.7	169.5	283.3	324.9	143.9	176.8	156.6	171.4	168.0	154.2
Mexico	53.1	46.8	65.5	69.9	61.7	126.9	8.5	5.8	3.0	8.9	6.2	9.8
Caribbean And Central America	4.1	4.4	19.8	11.2	18.4	30.8	0.5	0.4	0.2	0.6	0.7	0.5
South America	23.2	45.7	52.1	81.2	72.1	79.5	1.3	1.2	1.4	3.1	4.4	2.2
Argentina	5.9	9.7	11.2	14.6	14.0	20.3	0.3	0.5	0.3	0.1	0.8	0.6
Brazil	12.9	18.3	27.5	44.0	35.7	38.9	0.2	0.1	0.1	0.6	1.9	0.3
Other South America	4.3	17.7	13.4	22.6	22.4	20.3	0.9	0.6	1.0	2.4	1.7	1.4
Europe	412.1	494.1	637.0	530.7	662.3	745.7	37.7	22.5	25.9	46.8	26.3	27.2
Belgium	19.7	10.8	14.9	8.5	7.4	7.4	2.7	1.2	0.6	1.4	1.6	1.9
France	105.7	129.9	193.8	138.9	168.1	166.8	2.1	1.5	1.9	3.4	2.4	2.1
Germany	127.7	131.4	189.8	180.7	276.4	359.4	1.6	1.7	3.2	3.1	3.8	1.6
Netherlands	51.4	98.2	56.8	45.5	39.8	63.7	4.1	1.3	2.6	8.2	1.8	2.9
United Kingdom	24.8	31.1	47.3	48.7	56.9	82.8	9.8	5.3	7.1	12.3	10.3	7.7
Turkey	0.3	0.3	0.5	0.8	1.6	1.6	0.1	0.3	0.3	0.4	0.2	. . .
Former Soviet Republics	3.2	3.4	2.8	4.3	7.4	1.2	0.1	0.6	0.2	0.8	0.3	0.1
Poland	3.7	0.2	0.6	0.5	0.4	0.3	. . .	0.1	0.1	0.1	0.1	. . .
Other Eastern Europe	0.7	1.5	3.1	3.6	3.2	4.5	0.4	0.2	0.3	0.3	0.7	0.6
Other Europe	75.0	87.1	127.3	99.2	101.1	57.9	16.7	10.3	9.8	16.7	5.3	10.1
Asia	435.5	656.0	909.6	712.2	554.1	898.8	126.1	148.6	146.0	154.9	138.6	110.5
Japan	204.9	310.6	470.2	360.6	263.6	230.4	74.9	80.4	66.3	66.7	61.6	54.3
China	6.6	6.6	14.5	11.7	32.7	186.3	1.3	5.8	8.4	7.9	3.8	5.5
Hong Kong	37.2	59.8	47.3	28.6	26.4	40.9	20.9	26.8	36.1	46.2	49.0	25.6
Taiwan	19.6	34.1	45.7	35.6	72.9	109.5	12.1	10.7	12.9	14.1	9.5	9.5
Singapore	84.6	90.8	140.3	79.7	61.6	106.8	6.2	8.1	6.9	6.0	5.7	3.4
South Korea	39.8	82.6	111.2	106.8	25.3	115.6	5.3	5.1	3.5	2.8	1.7	2.4
Indonesia	2.3	4.4	7.6	13.3	6.1	6.2	0.5	1.6	3.1	4.1	1.0	0.7
India	9.8	16.3	14.2	16.0	21.0	26.3	0.5	2.1	0.1	0.1	0.5	1.8
Other Asia	30.7	50.8	58.6	59.9	44.6	76.7	4.6	7.9	8.8	6.9	5.9	7.1
Africa	6.7	6.5	10.9	8.3	19.5	18.5	1.0	1.1	0.8	0.8	0.8	0.5
North Africa	2.8	3.4	6.8	3.2	4.4	6.2	0.3	0.2	0.2	0.1	0.1	. . .
Republic of South Africa	3.5	2.8	3.0	4.7	14.5	11.3	0.4	0.7	0.2	0.5	0.5	0.3
Other Subsaharan Africa	0.5	0.3	1.0	0.4	0.6	1.1	0.3	0.2	0.3	0.3	0.3	0.1
Middle East	17.6	15.4	22.5	21.3	28.7	31.4	2.3	2.3	1.7	3.8	3.1	3.5
Australia	54.1	78.0	76.5	65.2	31.7	81.2	0.6	1.2	2.0	2.8	2.3	4.7
Rest Of World	. . .	. . .	. . .	. . .	. . .	. . .	. . .	. . .	. . .	. . .	. . .	. . .

Destination	Salt Lake City - Ogden, UT						San Antonio, TX					
	1994	1995	1996	1997	1998	1999	1994	1995	1996	1997	1998	1999
ALL DESTINATIONS	1 808.7	1 838.2	2 111.5	2 593.6	2 494.8	2 260.0	656.3	771.1	1 050.0	1 342.8	1 640.8	2 003.7
North America	323.6	369.7	424.1	474.6	474.8	546.9	384.5	408.7	663.0	886.0	1 229.2	1 484.7
Canada	251.4	310.0	355.7	411.7	403.5	454.6	100.1	204.5	110.2	113.7	131.9	214.3
Mexico	72.2	59.8	68.4	62.9	71.3	92.3	284.4	204.2	552.7	772.3	1 097.3	1 270.4
Caribbean And Central America	5.5	10.9	16.6	8.9	8.8	11.2	15.9	7.4	7.0	15.5	11.0	26.2
South America	35.8	62.7	62.9	76.7	69.3	68.3	13.7	23.5	30.0	35.3	70.9	88.2
Argentina	3.0	3.1	3.2	3.8	2.9	4.5	4.6	7.4	12.7	8.5	10.1	4.7
Brazil	6.1	3.8	14.3	21.8	30.6	40.0	2.7	6.4	4.3	6.0	19.1	47.4
Other South America	26.7	55.8	45.3	51.1	35.8	23.8	6.4	9.7	13.0	20.8	41.7	36.1
Europe	485.0	497.5	750.2	1 122.0	1 012.0	1 048.5	114.9	129.0	122.0	120.0	105.3	171.9
Belgium	81.1	125.2	57.5	74.1	38.0	38.7	5.8	3.3	4.1	5.3	14.2	7.2
France	12.6	22.8	32.6	33.8	32.1	44.6	11.5	10.1	9.0	6.3	7.4	6.6
Germany	166.3	141.6	155.4	97.0	71.6	100.6	21.2	22.2	16.3	21.4	11.7	56.9
Netherlands	42.8	40.8	73.3	71.0	57.9	91.2	4.4	2.9	2.6	5.5	4.4	8.5
United Kingdom	52.5	96.2	346.4	712.4	676.4	597.4	31.8	34.3	24.5	25.6	25.3	50.7
Turkey	2.3	1.8	1.7	4.0	7.6	18.5	6.9	7.8	3.0	0.6	0.2	0.4
Former Soviet Republics	2.8	8.9	4.3	4.2	7.3	5.5	0.5	9.3	9.6	16.0	12.8	0.4
Poland	0.3	0.8	1.1	2.2	1.6	1.0	0.2	0.4	0.8	1.9	1.4	0.7
Other Eastern Europe	1.6	1.8	3.4	3.3	2.3	3.1	1.4	2.9	1.5	0.5	0.3	0.4
Other Europe	122.8	57.5	74.4	120.0	117.3	147.9	31.3	35.7	50.7	36.9	27.5	40.1
Asia	925.6	849.3	775.7	858.9	604.6	521.9	93.4	161.5	189.8	250.8	195.4	210.1
Japan	191.9	322.9	275.1	296.1	192.0	161.1	23.9	60.3	71.5	74.4	53.6	53.8
China	11.8	12.6	20.3	9.9	11.7	21.5	9.4	5.1	12.8	22.4	11.3	11.6
Hong Kong	378.8	50.9	23.1	29.0	24.5	28.5	4.1	4.4	7.2	8.7	8.2	7.3
Taiwan	129.1	90.2	69.8	55.9	25.0	32.7	4.5	6.7	12.4	33.2	31.6	45.5
Singapore	20.1	77.3	127.3	57.0	35.4	39.3	3.0	3.8	4.5	4.5	3.9	3.7
South Korea	84.8	150.1	94.4	70.7	41.8	82.8	18.9	14.1	23.8	36.5	35.2	55.0
Indonesia	7.5	7.1	11.3	7.9	2.8	3.6	0.1	3.2	1.8	0.7	0.5	0.3
India	1.5	3.9	2.5	2.7	3.7	3.1	2.0	0.8	0.6	2.0	0.9	1.2
Other Asia	100.1	134.4	151.9	329.8	267.6	149.3	27.5	63.1	55.2	68.5	50.1	31.6
Africa	3.8	6.6	15.6	9.2	8.0	9.3	3.0	2.6	11.0	8.3	3.4	3.6
North Africa	0.5	1.5	5.0	2.2	1.4	1.0	0.7	0.6	8.7	5.8	1.1	1.3
Republic of South Africa	2.5	3.8	6.6	4.7	4.2	3.0	1.1	1.5	1.4	1.0	1.6	1.3
Other Subsaharan Africa	0.8	1.3	3.9	2.3	2.4	5.3	1.3	0.5	0.8	1.5	0.6	1.0
Middle East	9.2	15.9	42.9	19.5	20.7	25.1	10.1	9.6	10.9	13.9	16.7	11.7
Australia	20.1	25.3	23.6	23.8	296.6	29.0	20.8	28.8	16.3	13.0	8.9	7.4
Rest Of World	. . .	0.2	. . .	. . .	. . .	. . .	. . .	. . .	. . .	. . .	. . .	. . .

Table E-3. Metropolitan Area Exports of Goods by Destination, 1994–1999—*Continued*

(Millions of dollars.)

Destination	San Diego, CA						San Francisco, CA					
	1994	1995	1996	1997	1998	1999	1994	1995	1996	1997	1998	1999
ALL DESTINATIONS	4 867.3	5 860.9	6 719.4	7 810.0	8 591.6	8 963.8	9 303.8	8 133.7	8 560.4	9 978.5	9 123.2	9 035.0
North America	2 473.5	2 981.5	3 587.2	4 155.7	4 819.7	4 771.8	788.9	740.5	697.2	826.8	898.4	872.4
Canada	441.3	496.8	613.2	793.2	1 025.5	914.3	392.0	438.5	422.4	479.6	516.9	446.3
Mexico	2 032.2	2 484.7	2 973.9	3 362.6	3 794.2	3 857.5	396.9	302.0	274.9	347.2	381.6	426.1
Caribbean And Central America	51.0	71.9	57.1	81.9	75.7	138.6	237.8	203.9	212.0	271.5	293.8	259.3
South America	149.3	195.1	197.3	281.6	311.8	259.2	486.8	429.7	307.2	452.5	479.0	402.7
Argentina	54.6	19.8	15.5	55.6	55.0	22.4	75.0	34.9	56.1	92.7	58.4	53.9
Brazil	53.1	93.6	94.1	127.5	134.1	131.6	182.3	85.4	140.2	208.7	201.7	148.1
Other South America	41.6	81.7	87.8	98.5	122.8	105.2	229.5	309.4	111.0	151.0	218.9	200.7
Europe	898.0	1 035.3	1 152.5	1 387.0	1 701.6	1 770.2	2 457.1	2 085.1	2 411.6	2 929.4	3 028.1	2 470.4
Belgium	32.7	37.2	44.2	53.4	91.2	99.9	383.5	398.8	374.3	415.7	393.6	325.9
France	88.7	108.7	107.9	144.5	220.9	260.0	172.6	174.9	124.0	138.2	166.7	173.2
Germany	227.7	245.4	275.1	266.8	245.3	212.9	482.0	267.9	323.5	388.2	410.2	406.0
Netherlands	92.3	117.1	136.4	202.5	266.3	311.6	239.5	159.4	220.1	279.9	467.2	392.3
United Kingdom	179.3	230.7	277.5	329.0	390.9	449.3	487.4	442.0	568.1	653.9	563.5	407.9
Turkey	6.2	9.2	6.1	6.2	11.3	12.8	26.2	17.3	56.7	132.5	73.4	12.2
Former Soviet Republics	11.0	13.4	24.7	47.4	63.0	10.6	57.8	73.5	72.1	74.5	38.8	20.2
Poland	2.7	2.1	2.9	4.3	5.5	7.4	4.7	1.7	7.1	9.3	6.6	4.5
Other Eastern Europe	9.5	12.9	13.4	20.0	18.9	16.2	11.0	9.7	9.9	10.9	22.0	15.7
Other Europe	247.9	258.7	264.3	312.9	385.2	389.5	592.4	539.8	655.8	826.4	886.1	712.4
Asia	1 049.5	1 311.6	1 526.4	1 620.9	1 384.5	1 710.7	4 516.6	4 267.4	4 485.3	5 031.9	4 035.9	4 581.2
Japan	360.2	506.2	517.5	580.4	474.9	512.9	1 818.0	1 926.6	2 049.5	2 123.5	1 910.5	1 870.8
China	21.1	37.0	57.9	82.8	79.9	103.6	241.4	181.8	172.1	269.3	279.8	291.5
Hong Kong	166.5	141.4	165.8	142.0	131.2	156.0	563.8	488.7	491.4	498.9	340.6	449.7
Taiwan	97.4	123.2	154.8	151.9	130.6	144.7	506.3	513.8	355.7	366.8	255.2	318.8
Singapore	126.2	137.2	156.2	155.0	112.1	203.5	631.0	433.2	419.6	406.9	378.2	417.3
South Korea	85.6	111.3	181.5	164.1	154.2	328.3	223.8	234.2	295.2	288.0	163.9	392.1
Indonesia	17.2	22.9	37.8	44.2	59.1	3.0	65.1	42.2	43.3	55.2	26.8	47.3
India	10.1	15.6	19.9	15.8	25.7	16.2	34.8	27.6	17.7	25.1	30.4	49.5
Other Asia	165.2	216.7	235.0	284.7	216.9	242.5	432.5	419.4	640.8	1 001.8	650.5	744.1
Africa	106.2	123.9	57.5	77.2	85.4	62.2	134.5	60.5	66.1	72.9	88.8	67.4
North Africa	85.7	90.4	34.0	31.7	52.1	14.8	95.5	45.7	32.8	26.9	16.3	17.6
Republic of South Africa	16.7	21.6	19.4	26.0	25.2	23.5	25.8	8.7	26.6	33.9	63.1	44.0
Other Subsaharan Africa	3.9	11.9	4.1	19.5	8.1	23.9	13.2	6.1	6.7	12.1	9.3	5.8
Middle East	62.0	68.4	52.1	95.8	95.5	96.8	273.0	191.5	210.3	228.7	136.0	158.9
Australia	77.7	73.2	89.3	109.9	117.2	154.2	409.2	155.0	170.7	164.8	163.2	222.2
Rest Of World	...	...	...	...	0.2	...	...	...	...	...	...	0.4

Destination	San Jose, CA						Santa Barbara - Santa Maria - Lompoc, CA					
	1994	1995	1996	1997	1998	1999	1994	1995	1996	1997	1998	1999
ALL DESTINATIONS	19 942.7	26 822.8	29 331.3	29 057.2	26 111.9	28 255.7	420.2	565.2	648.0	623.3	501.3	581.4
North America	2 796.5	3 273.3	3 990.4	4 201.4	4 230.3	4 680.2	51.2	39.0	58.0	71.8	75.4	96.0
Canada	2 395.9	2 918.4	3 532.4	3 434.7	3 581.3	3 972.3	42.9	36.0	51.9	61.3	64.6	85.7
Mexico	400.6	354.9	457.9	766.7	648.9	707.9	8.3	3.0	6.1	10.5	10.8	10.3
Caribbean And Central America	15.8	18.2	29.8	55.1	103.0	112.4	1.5	2.0	6.5	5.5	3.7	5.1
South America	270.8	388.0	511.6	708.0	799.2	714.7	16.9	13.0	21.8	35.0	41.2	13.7
Argentina	42.6	63.2	98.7	170.1	233.7	127.1	0.6	1.0	1.1	0.7	1.0	0.6
Brazil	138.6	201.9	233.1	309.9	329.5	333.7	0.7	1.3	1.0	4.5	2.8	4.3
Other South America	89.6	123.0	179.8	227.9	236.0	253.9	15.5	10.7	19.7	29.8	37.5	8.9
Europe	5 136.4	6 097.1	6 232.6	6 818.0	6 342.3	6 726.9	123.3	147.5	154.6	163.1	175.0	189.4
Belgium	142.7	115.5	143.5	148.1	116.2	116.0	2.6	1.3	1.1	2.4	2.5	5.0
France	541.8	633.0	703.2	740.0	566.0	570.7	9.5	9.1	8.9	11.7	16.8	17.1
Germany	1 017.0	1 387.2	1 298.6	1 265.2	1 171.1	994.3	52.7	55.8	61.0	50.0	65.3	69.8
Netherlands	628.0	624.2	679.3	1 302.0	1 278.2	1 276.3	8.0	9.3	10.5	11.5	12.4	18.4
United Kingdom	1 381.0	1 553.2	1 632.0	1 696.2	1 540.6	1 477.2	17.7	33.4	27.8	26.4	25.7	23.9
Turkey	28.7	14.9	16.1	25.7	19.5	35.8	4.3	1.6	1.5	1.9	1.8	2.9
Former Soviet Republics	46.1	46.5	44.1	61.6	154.9	368.1	0.7	2.2	1.6	1.4	0.9	0.6
Poland	22.7	20.6	20.5	28.4	33.4	63.5	0.4	0.2	0.2	0.8	0.6	1.1
Other Eastern Europe	55.6	67.8	69.2	68.3	68.7	81.9	0.4	0.8	0.9	1.4	1.4	0.9
Other Europe	1 272.8	1 634.1	1 625.9	1 482.5	1 393.8	1 743.2	27.0	33.8	41.1	55.7	47.6	49.7
Asia	11 089.3	16 341.0	17 899.6	16 504.3	13 947.3	15 213.2	203.7	260.7	307.0	318.3	182.9	250.7
Japan	2 843.4	4 158.4	5 122.9	4 789.6	3 643.8	3 744.5	45.5	88.2	66.0	57.1	50.3	49.2
China	228.3	253.0	338.6	415.7	760.7	636.2	2.3	3.4	3.2	3.2	5.0	3.6
Hong Kong	709.6	930.3	965.6	1 137.2	1 079.6	1 091.1	4.1	6.1	7.5	5.5	7.3	8.4
Taiwan	1 074.0	1 539.1	1 983.3	2 474.4	2 230.5	3 066.9	4.5	7.6	12.6	11.4	12.6	12.1
Singapore	1 468.7	1 974.0	2 333.2	2 223.9	1 862.5	1 721.8	5.4	5.3	11.5	10.6	8.1	89.2
South Korea	1 688.0	2 792.1	3 132.3	2 464.8	1 706.8	2 413.9	24.5	27.6	26.2	32.0	20.7	12.5
Indonesia	39.1	73.5	85.3	74.8	38.9	21.7	3.2	1.9	0.7	1.6	0.6	0.8
India	76.7	117.7	150.3	162.9	147.9	133.2	4.0	6.2	5.0	5.8	3.9	3.3
Other Asia	2 961.5	4 502.8	3 788.2	2 761.0	2 476.7	2 383.9	110.1	114.4	174.4	191.1	74.4	71.5
Africa	111.9	103.5	108.9	105.6	108.0	90.8	3.5	3.2	3.4	3.6	5.5	4.9
North Africa	30.7	17.3	19.2	24.7	18.8	20.7	0.6	0.6	0.4	1.0	0.7	2.6
Republic of South Africa	68.7	79.0	84.1	73.0	82.1	60.3	1.9	1.8	2.8	2.3	3.9	1.9
Other Subsaharan Africa	12.5	7.2	5.6	7.9	7.1	9.8	1.0	0.8	0.2	0.4	0.8	0.5
Middle East	165.1	216.1	212.0	241.9	244.7	348.6	12.3	90.6	86.9	14.3	4.9	10.0
Australia	356.7	385.7	346.3	422.1	337.1	368.9	7.8	9.0	9.8	11.8	12.7	11.7
Rest Of World	0.1	...	0.1	0.8	0.1	...	...	...	0.1	...	...	...

Table E-3. Metropolitan Area Exports of Goods by Destination, 1994–1999—*Continued*

(Millions of dollars.)

Destination	Santa Cruz - Watsonville, CA						Santa Rosa, CA					
	1994	1995	1996	1997	1998	1999	1994	1995	1996	1997	1998	1999
ALL DESTINATIONS	857.4	1 408.2	1 943.1	2 298.5	1 800.8	2 366.4	485.2	572.9	681.8	856.3	862.7	865.5
North America	95.5	78.9	108.5	178.4	152.6	349.7	78.0	86.4	101.3	148.3	196.5	178.7
Canada	49.8	44.5	45.9	54.3	55.6	46.4	61.9	69.8	76.7	111.3	166.6	146.9
Mexico	45.7	34.5	62.6	124.1	97.0	303.3	16.2	16.5	24.6	37.1	29.9	31.8
Caribbean And Central America	0.8	0.8	2.1	0.6	2.1	1.8	2.5	2.7	3.1	4.1	5.6	6.7
South America	17.1	8.7	7.9	12.2	11.9	17.5	7.0	8.9	13.2	19.5	20.9	16.8
Argentina	2.8	0.4	0.4	0.7	0.5	0.6	2.7	1.6	1.2	2.0	2.0	1.3
Brazil	7.9	4.4	5.0	8.8	9.4	16.3	2.8	5.5	9.7	14.5	10.7	5.6
Other South America	6.3	4.0	2.5	2.7	2.0	0.7	1.5	1.9	2.2	3.1	8.2	9.9
Europe	107.5	185.6	215.6	263.8	308.6	792.3	180.7	216.8	223.3	297.8	306.4	354.0
Belgium	0.9	0.5	0.9	0.3	0.7	0.4	1.8	3.0	4.2	4.5	6.7	5.9
France	7.0	8.0	13.9	13.7	8.2	4.6	20.1	18.5	22.7	27.6	32.7	29.5
Germany	14.0	14.0	21.7	10.5	16.8	11.7	29.0	32.6	34.4	54.6	51.3	39.0
Netherlands	34.0	69.2	53.6	87.1	170.9	625.1	5.6	6.8	8.9	20.7	20.3	17.8
United Kingdom	30.4	39.4	80.5	112.4	80.6	91.9	54.5	66.0	68.1	84.2	81.2	99.4
Turkey	0.1	0.3	0.1	0.1	0.4	0.8	0.1	0.4	0.3	1.4	1.4	2.4
Former Soviet Republics	0.5	0.8	1.3	1.0	0.7	0.2	2.2	0.8	0.3	0.2	0.4	0.2
Poland	0.2	0.2	0.2	0.1	0.8	3.3	0.1	0.4	0.4	0.3	0.5	0.4
Other Eastern Europe	0.3	0.3	0.7	0.6	1.4	5.4	0.1	0.5	0.7	1.0	1.1	1.2
Other Europe	20.1	53.0	42.8	38.0	28.3	48.8	67.1	87.9	83.3	103.2	110.8	158.3
Asia	626.1	1 120.6	1 591.2	1 824.6	1 301.3	1 144.6	196.0	238.0	323.7	361.9	311.4	281.8
Japan	28.8	42.3	67.7	60.4	59.7	66.2	122.3	147.0	188.9	208.1	184.4	163.1
China	3.9	2.5	92.8	32.5	37.3	25.4	9.9	5.7	10.8	4.8	15.4	4.3
Hong Kong	6.4	8.3	47.4	46.5	36.0	18.9	8.6	14.4	29.4	32.2	17.2	10.5
Taiwan	22.0	33.1	40.7	39.6	69.1	141.2	13.6	17.2	23.2	18.8	15.8	13.3
Singapore	354.1	458.9	560.8	706.1	607.0	563.0	9.8	13.6	15.5	23.1	20.5	14.4
South Korea	19.3	35.9	55.4	30.9	10.2	17.1	18.0	23.1	21.6	35.8	19.6	15.7
Indonesia	0.5	0.1	1.8	0.3	...	0.2	0.6	0.5	0.2	0.5	0.3	0.7
India	0.7	0.6	2.5	0.7	1.0	1.3	0.6	1.8	3.5	3.3	4.0	4.3
Other Asia	190.5	538.8	722.2	907.6	480.9	311.2	12.7	14.6	30.6	35.2	34.2	55.6
Africa	2.1	4.1	0.8	0.9	2.2	2.0	1.3	1.5	1.3	1.5	2.4	4.9
North Africa	...	0.1	0.1	0.1	0.3	0.5	0.3	0.3	0.2	0.1	0.2	0.4
Republic of South Africa	2.1	3.9	0.6	0.8	1.9	1.4	0.7	0.9	1.1	1.3	2.0	4.5
Other Subsaharan Africa	...	0.1	...	0.1	0.1	0.1	0.2	0.3	...	0.1	0.2	0.1
Middle East	1.5	2.0	2.9	4.4	3.4	5.7	3.6	3.6	3.5	6.4	4.6	8.5
Australia	6.8	7.5	14.2	13.6	18.6	52.9	16.0	15.2	12.3	16.9	14.7	14.0
Rest Of World	...	...	...	...	...	...	...	...	...	...	...	...

Destination	Savannah, GA						Scranton -Wilkes - Barre - Hazleton, PA					
	1994	1995	1996	1997	1998	1999	1994	1995	1996	1997	1998	1999
ALL DESTINATIONS	423.3	567.5	459.4	633.4	665.7	624.6	328.2	431.9	392.0	442.4	438.2	565.5
North America	91.8	69.7	80.0	75.7	66.5	105.3	171.4	222.0	195.4	204.3	217.3	288.6
Canada	71.3	53.4	55.4	57.0	50.3	50.6	163.0	215.9	189.4	193.6	207.0	258.2
Mexico	20.5	16.3	24.6	18.7	16.2	54.7	8.4	6.0	6.0	10.6	10.3	30.4
Caribbean And Central America	51.8	36.6	29.4	24.4	59.3	93.0	13.1	15.3	6.5	8.0	13.0	5.0
South America	26.6	29.7	33.1	37.3	49.5	30.3	17.3	13.7	11.7	19.1	10.2	7.5
Argentina	1.0	3.1	6.7	4.2	2.3	2.2	1.5	0.8	0.5	2.0	2.2	0.8
Brazil	4.1	4.2	2.9	11.1	6.8	2.2	12.0	8.5	7.2	10.6	2.9	3.0
Other South America	21.5	22.3	23.5	21.9	40.3	25.9	3.8	4.4	4.0	6.5	5.1	3.6
Europe	66.1	215.6	127.8	211.8	222.9	179.4	41.0	52.1	61.4	64.8	48.9	65.3
Belgium	3.6	16.8	8.0	6.4	5.5	1.4	1.4	2.2	3.7	1.6	1.6	2.0
France	5.0	25.6	15.4	12.3	12.1	8.1	5.9	6.6	9.3	12.7	8.0	6.3
Germany	4.7	14.5	23.6	29.8	38.6	22.8	6.5	10.4	11.7	10.5	8.4	12.3
Netherlands	15.3	28.2	13.2	32.2	26.7	11.0	8.4	13.3	16.0	13.1	8.4	5.8
United Kingdom	17.9	28.1	28.3	25.5	21.8	27.0	4.2	6.4	8.3	12.5	8.9	15.1
Turkey	2.1	7.5	5.0	8.3	4.4	1.8	0.3	0.2	0.2	0.4	1.3	0.8
Former Soviet Republics	0.9	3.2	2.1	1.6	0.7	1.1	0.3	1.3	0.8	0.6	0.2	0.2
Poland	...	0.2	0.3	0.1	...	...	0.4	0.1	0.1	0.1	0.1	0.1
Other Eastern Europe	...	0.1	0.4	...	0.1	0.2	0.7	0.4	0.4	0.4	0.1	0.6
Other Europe	16.5	91.3	31.5	95.5	113.0	105.9	13.0	11.4	10.8	12.8	11.8	22.0
Asia	150.3	165.7	127.4	197.0	171.7	137.0	75.8	116.5	101.0	138.3	141.0	189.7
Japan	16.5	53.6	22.8	15.4	10.8	47.1	7.8	9.6	10.9	10.8	11.5	13.1
China	49.4	31.5	6.7	49.0	18.3	14.5	1.6	2.1	3.2	5.0	4.8	4.4
Hong Kong	0.4	1.3	3.0	4.5	1.3	2.1	5.1	6.6	5.4	5.6	4.5	4.2
Taiwan	1.0	2.1	2.4	6.0	10.8	47.2	5.6	2.1	2.9	4.6	2.8	3.5
Singapore	1.6	20.2	3.1	4.5	1.8	5.5	43.3	85.7	69.8	102.2	100.9	2.6
South Korea	27.2	17.3	53.5	95.2	117.9	6.1	3.6	2.9	2.9	2.6	2.0	6.2
Indonesia	9.4	1.4	6.7	1.5	0.9	1.4	0.1	0.2	0.5	1.3	0.4	0.7
India	1.6	2.1	1.8	7.6	1.7	3.2	0.5	1.5	1.3	1.3	1.6	0.6
Other Asia	43.2	36.2	27.5	13.3	8.4	9.9	8.2	5.9	4.1	4.8	12.5	154.3
Africa	24.7	17.0	30.1	33.0	23.2	34.4	0.9	0.9	0.9	1.3	2.0	1.4
North Africa	6.0	4.7	2.5	4.9	5.2	4.3	0.4	0.2	0.4	0.7	0.4	0.5
Republic of South Africa	4.8	5.0	9.4	10.8	8.2	4.3	0.3	0.3	0.4	0.5	0.9	0.3
Other Subsaharan Africa	13.8	7.3	18.2	17.3	9.8	25.4	0.2	0.4	0.2	0.1	0.8	0.6
Middle East	10.3	30.4	13.1	16.6	16.3	42.1	3.0	3.4	9.6	3.6	2.7	4.5
Australia	1.6	2.9	18.4	37.6	56.3	3.2	5.6	8.0	5.4	3.0	3.1	3.4
Rest Of World	...	...	...	...	...	...	...	...	...	...	...	...

Table E-3. Metropolitan Area Exports of Goods by Destination, 1994–1999—*Continued*

(Millions of dollars.)

Destination	Seattle - Bellevue - Everett, WA						Sheboygan, WI					
	1994	1995	1996	1997	1998	1999	1994	1995	1996	1997	1998	1999
ALL DESTINATIONS	21 753.0	17 815.4	21 391.1	27 005.8	34 003.3	32 356.1	244.3	258.7	283.3	320.9	316.4	306.4
North America	1 344.7	1 417.0	1 503.0	1 400.6	1 729.3	1 633.4	92.8	94.5	118.1	138.1	159.9	162.2
Canada	1 064.0	1 351.8	1 450.3	1 341.9	1 358.7	1 460.8	62.5	70.6	95.4	116.1	134.2	138.5
Mexico	280.8	65.2	52.7	58.7	370.6	172.6	30.3	23.9	22.7	22.1	25.7	23.8
Caribbean And Central America	102.1	21.5	19.8	26.1	145.2	187.1	8.3	7.3	4.8	5.1	6.9	4.4
South America	245.7	369.8	535.4	796.5	953.7	657.9	15.9	16.4	8.5	15.3	21.0	13.9
Argentina	30.9	85.2	24.9	34.1	101.5	248.0	3.3	4.7	0.9	2.3	2.3	5.3
Brazil	76.5	68.5	80.0	379.6	347.5	142.5	1.0	3.8	0.9	1.4	6.8	1.2
Other South America	138.4	216.1	430.5	382.8	504.6	267.4	11.6	7.8	6.7	11.7	11.9	7.4
Europe	5 568.0	4 187.6	4 972.9	8 956.0	11 689.4	14 564.7	57.1	61.5	60.7	63.9	59.6	54.8
Belgium	151.2	114.0	159.8	233.8	309.4	91.5	2.7	3.0	1.5	1.0	0.5	0.9
France	322.7	146.4	134.4	252.1	895.2	1 437.7	4.6	3.2	2.6	6.2	5.0	6.1
Germany	569.3	634.6	720.2	1 204.7	2 181.0	2 012.8	19.6	17.3	11.0	13.2	12.2	11.1
Netherlands	404.4	650.8	857.2	822.5	422.9	900.1	7.9	2.4	1.4	1.9	1.1	2.3
United Kingdom	2 182.4	1 118.3	1 503.0	4 345.2	4 322.5	4 276.9	11.5	14.8	13.9	13.8	15.3	15.5
Turkey	320.7	129.1	13.1	20.4	487.8	604.5	0.1	4.3	4.5	4.8	5.2	2.5
Former Soviet Republics	431.8	266.4	547.4	263.3	976.6	479.8	0.1	0.4	0.1	0.1	3.5	0.4
Poland	78.5	88.9	49.8	272.0	11.5	12.4	0.3	0.5	1.0	1.6	2.1	1.5
Other Eastern Europe	151.7	17.6	19.4	182.1	164.2	127.6	0.2	1.4	0.2	0.7	0.8	0.6
Other Europe	955.3	1 021.4	968.5	1 359.8	1 918.3	4 621.4	10.0	14.2	24.4	20.6	13.9	13.9
Asia	13 089.3	11 166.6	12 940.5	13 076.8	15 406.5	11 612.2	52.6	57.2	72.5	74.7	45.7	48.9
Japan	5 568.6	5 730.0	5 317.1	5 221.4	5 127.6	4 835.4	4.3	4.2	6.3	10.7	8.1	6.2
China	1 852.8	1 026.3	1 391.3	1 730.1	3 090.9	1 990.0	2.1	4.1	8.5	10.8	5.5	5.4
Hong Kong	398.2	449.0	733.0	214.7	501.9	321.3	16.6	14.4	8.7	10.0	13.4	10.2
Taiwan	748.7	708.7	693.3	560.3	1 404.3	388.4	11.2	9.9	9.2	7.2	4.4	6.1
Singapore	1 246.9	921.1	890.3	1 176.4	1 342.7	1 138.6	8.7	8.0	10.8	10.7	6.9	6.5
South Korea	1 203.0	1 436.0	1 746.5	1 624.0	846.0	1 175.2	4.1	8.4	7.1	13.6	1.5	4.3
Indonesia	376.3	42.4	48.9	226.5	257.8	26.2	. . .	0.8	4.3	3.6	0.9	1.1
India	163.7	31.0	405.0	197.5	384.8	340.1	. . .	0.2	3.7	0.9	0.1	0.7
Other Asia	1 531.1	822.1	1 715.0	2 125.9	2 450.6	1 396.9	5.6	7.3	13.9	7.2	4.9	8.4
Africa	244.2	215.0	276.2	681.2	743.5	722.0	2.8	3.7	5.5	7.8	9.7	7.4
North Africa	155.1	120.5	18.5	487.9	113.1	376.2	0.6	0.8	0.1	1.5	6.4	4.2
Republic of South Africa	43.3	73.4	79.5	49.5	563.8	17.2	0.3	1.5	1.1	1.4	1.5	0.7
Other Subsaharan Africa	45.8	21.1	178.2	143.9	66.6	328.5	1.8	1.4	4.2	4.9	1.9	2.5
Middle East	727.8	249.4	605.0	1 644.2	2 877.5	2 453.0	10.7	13.1	6.1	9.3	9.6	9.5
Australia	430.8	188.3	538.2	424.0	458.3	525.8	4.3	5.1	7.2	6.6	3.9	5.2
Rest Of World	0.3	0.2	0.2	0.5	. . .	. . .	. . .	. . .	. . .	. . .	. . .	. . .

Destination	Shreveport - Bossier City, LA						South Bend, IN					
	1994	1995	1996	1997	1998	1999	1994	1995	1996	1997	1998	1999
ALL DESTINATIONS	134.6	169.1	172.6	180.8	143.3	141.3	160.3	389.5	494.8	522.1	586.9	493.8
North America	52.7	63.0	64.4	60.9	65.4	82.9	88.1	173.7	209.1	180.5	205.7	210.2
Canada	51.0	61.8	58.9	55.8	55.6	70.2	64.9	110.6	122.9	126.7	156.8	170.9
Mexico	1.7	1.2	5.5	5.1	9.9	12.7	23.2	63.1	86.1	53.8	48.8	39.3
Caribbean And Central America	2.8	2.8	2.6	1.6	0.8	0.7	1.6	2.8	1.5	2.2	2.0	3.0
South America	3.5	4.2	3.8	5.1	6.6	4.6	11.9	11.3	8.7	10.5	10.2	12.4
Argentina	1.8	0.9	1.5	1.8	1.1	1.6	1.4	1.7	3.1	4.3	4.3	7.6
Brazil	0.2	0.2	0.3	1.2	4.2	0.6	7.5	5.9	2.2	1.6	3.1	2.6
Other South America	1.6	3.1	2.0	2.0	1.3	2.4	3.1	3.6	3.4	4.7	2.8	2.2
Europe	56.5	73.5	79.7	91.9	52.4	26.9	20.8	91.0	164.9	242.8	291.9	214.5
Belgium	0.6	0.8	0.3	0.8	0.9	1.2	0.5	7.3	2.6	1.0	0.6	0.6
France	5.5	10.0	9.0	9.0	5.8	2.7	3.1	4.9	7.7	7.0	10.4	5.7
Germany	14.0	16.1	20.0	21.0	6.6	5.5	4.9	13.4	23.2	19.6	32.2	6.7
Netherlands	1.3	2.3	2.8	4.9	2.2	4.7	0.8	1.4	29.0	87.8	103.1	91.6
United Kingdom	6.1	10.6	6.5	7.8	7.0	3.8	6.8	45.0	68.5	110.8	108.7	72.7
Turkey	0.6	0.2	. . .	0.1	. . .	0.3	0.1	1.4	0.8	1.8	1.6	2.0
Former Soviet Republics	1.7	9.8	14.8	18.1	9.3	3.3	0.5	0.9	1.9	1.4	1.2	0.3
Poland	0.8	0.9	2.6	3.1	2.0	0.7	. . .	. . .	. . .	. . .	0.2	0.1
Other Eastern Europe	2.6	1.3	0.9	0.9	1.3	0.3	1.4	0.6	1.1	0.5	1.2	1.6
Other Europe	23.4	21.6	22.8	26.2	17.3	4.3	2.7	16.1	30.2	13.0	32.7	33.1
Asia	10.3	14.8	12.2	10.3	10.1	19.9	20.8	34.8	51.1	56.4	47.1	26.2
Japan	2.2	4.5	2.0	1.6	1.5	4.0	4.9	16.7	21.1	33.2	24.3	9.9
China	. . .	0.7	0.1	0.2	1.3	1.4	0.5	0.2	1.5	0.6	0.6	0.7
Hong Kong	0.6	0.2	0.5	2.0	1.3	2.4	3.1	3.3	3.0	4.9	3.8	3.7
Taiwan	2.9	4.5	3.7	0.9	0.5	1.5	1.4	2.2	11.4	3.4	6.5	2.9
Singapore	1.3	0.6	0.9	2.6	3.9	7.1	2.5	2.8	4.0	3.8	4.3	1.3
South Korea	1.6	2.1	2.3	1.7	0.2	1.4	5.2	4.7	4.1	4.0	2.6	3.7
Indonesia	. . .	0.1	. . .	0.1	. . .	. . .	0.2	0.3	0.2	0.3	. . .	0.1
India	. . .	. . .	0.3	0.1	0.5	0.7	. . .	1.1	1.5	1.5	2.2	1.8
Other Asia	1.7	2.1	2.5	1.2	1.0	1.3	3.0	3.4	4.4	4.5	2.7	2.1
Africa	0.7	0.1	0.2	1.0	1.2	1.4	3.2	44.9	8.6	5.2	5.2	5.2
North Africa	0.3	. . .	. . .	0.4	0.4	0.1	0.5	37.5	2.0	1.6	1.5	1.0
Republic of South Africa	0.2	. . .	0.2	0.1	0.6	0.5	0.6	0.7	2.6	2.1	2.3	2.5
Other Subsaharan Africa	0.2	0.1	. . .	0.4	0.2	0.8	2.2	6.7	4.1	1.6	1.3	1.7
Middle East	5.0	3.6	2.0	3.0	3.8	0.9	13.1	28.3	39.3	14.2	12.3	12.6
Australia	3.1	7.1	7.6	7.0	3.0	4.1	0.8	2.8	11.8	10.2	12.6	9.8
Rest Of World	. . .	. . .	. . .	. . .	. . .	. . .	0.1	. . .	. . .	. . .	. . .	. . .

Table E-3. Metropolitan Area Exports of Goods by Destination, 1994–1999—*Continued*

(Millions of dollars.)

Destination	Spokane, WA						Springfield, MA					
	1994	1995	1996	1997	1998	1999	1994	1995	1996	1997	1998	1999
ALL DESTINATIONS	269.4	310.9	347.9	445.7	392.7	447.1	434.8	512.1	530.3	568.0	442.1	432.9
North America	76.8	97.9	111.0	161.3	150.5	184.9	156.9	204.6	238.5	289.5	220.1	189.9
Canada	54.3	64.4	64.8	73.6	78.5	121.1	142.0	194.2	221.2	272.3	199.2	171.3
Mexico	22.5	33.6	46.2	87.6	72.0	63.8	14.9	10.4	17.3	17.2	20.9	18.6
Caribbean And Central America	1.2	1.3	0.7	0.9	5.6	7.3	3.2	2.6	2.1	2.8	3.5	3.1
South America	6.3	8.9	18.8	24.1	15.2	19.3	15.2	15.2	13.8	12.8	11.0	10.8
Argentina	1.2	4.8	3.2	2.0	2.1	1.0	3.5	2.1	1.8	2.2	1.7	3.3
Brazil	1.7	1.8	3.6	4.2	5.6	13.7	4.7	5.0	5.2	3.9	3.8	2.8
Other South America	3.4	2.2	11.9	18.0	7.6	4.6	7.0	8.2	6.8	6.7	5.5	4.7
Europe	74.2	90.3	90.8	123.4	90.9	96.1	109.4	121.0	133.1	151.6	136.5	149.1
Belgium	0.4	0.1	0.4	0.3	0.2	1.0	12.4	9.0	6.8	13.9	12.5	13.9
France	5.1	5.1	6.8	18.1	16.4	6.5	7.2	8.4	11.9	9.4	6.5	10.6
Germany	17.4	20.3	32.6	39.1	11.1	6.0	17.5	20.8	22.3	12.8	11.9	20.4
Netherlands	3.7	3.8	1.8	2.2	3.9	8.6	6.9	11.4	15.3	22.5	18.3	21.1
United Kingdom	28.5	34.6	26.6	30.6	27.6	42.9	25.8	32.7	34.0	33.6	29.7	27.8
Turkey	0.6	0.1	0.6	0.5	0.7	0.8	1.9	2.3	6.9	8.7	2.2	0.8
Former Soviet Republics	1.0	0.6	0.4	0.2	0.8	0.2	0.6	0.4	0.2	1.3	0.1	0.2
Poland	0.1	0.1	0.1	...	0.8	1.5	17.6	18.2	15.4	14.6	12.0	13.1
Other Eastern Europe	0.2	0.4	0.6	0.9	1.1	2.9	0.2	1.0	0.7	0.6	0.7	0.8
Other Europe	17.2	25.3	20.8	31.4	28.4	25.7	19.4	16.9	19.7	34.4	42.5	40.5
Asia	87.1	91.7	104.2	117.3	115.4	112.6	108.4	126.4	108.6	90.2	57.2	59.5
Japan	41.1	41.5	50.1	45.2	49.2	47.9	31.0	35.8	30.1	21.6	15.6	23.4
China	0.3	0.7	1.2	2.6	6.5	6.9	2.2	2.9	3.1	3.3	5.4	2.2
Hong Kong	9.1	7.2	3.5	4.8	14.6	6.9	13.6	10.9	11.6	14.4	15.5	12.2
Taiwan	3.7	11.5	9.3	14.1	11.4	18.8	10.7	3.8	4.5	5.5	3.7	3.0
Singapore	11.8	9.6	13.5	13.7	9.6	9.4	12.4	14.1	17.6	14.6	6.6	8.1
South Korea	5.0	8.3	12.1	21.0	10.1	12.8	16.1	21.8	14.7	12.7	3.3	5.8
Indonesia	0.3	0.3	1.4	0.3	0.1	0.1	2.3	0.4	0.5	0.2	0.2	0.4
India	2.3	1.4	1.4	1.8	1.1	0.5	1.0	0.9	0.3	0.4	0.9	0.4
Other Asia	13.5	11.3	11.6	13.7	12.8	9.4	19.1	35.9	26.1	17.3	5.9	4.0
Africa	9.2	1.7	3.1	2.7	3.7	4.6	12.9	12.7	8.6	2.5	2.3	4.8
North Africa	6.9	0.6	2.1	1.9	0.7	0.4	0.5	0.6	0.8	0.6	1.1	3.2
Republic of South Africa	1.9	0.8	1.0	0.5	2.9	3.9	8.7	9.9	6.4	1.6	1.1	1.4
Other Subsaharan Africa	0.4	0.3	0.1	0.3	0.1	0.3	3.7	2.2	1.4	0.4	0.1	0.2
Middle East	8.1	5.2	8.2	5.5	3.5	9.5	16.4	16.1	14.0	12.4	4.9	4.6
Australia	6.5	13.9	11.1	10.6	7.9	12.8	12.4	13.3	11.5	6.3	6.7	11.1
Rest Of World	...	...	...	...	...	...	...	...	...	...	...	...

Destination	Springfield, MO						Stamford - Norwalk, CT					
	1994	1995	1996	1997	1998	1999	1994	1995	1996	1997	1998	1999
ALL DESTINATIONS	103.8	120.2	120.3	141.4	174.4	200.5	3 452.7	4 937.6	4 424.3	3 387.6	2 778.9	2 573.0
North America	56.9	60.2	63.7	75.7	72.9	74.8	464.1	478.2	533.6	553.2	555.7	669.7
Canada	47.3	54.0	56.5	70.6	63.0	62.7	316.8	342.5	306.6	327.0	317.1	353.0
Mexico	9.7	6.2	7.2	5.1	9.9	12.1	147.3	135.7	227.0	226.2	238.7	316.7
Caribbean And Central America	3.3	2.7	3.6	6.2	46.2	49.0	161.2	252.9	217.6	230.3	206.3	188.2
South America	4.6	8.8	6.6	7.5	7.7	11.2	457.2	570.5	519.0	382.8	368.9	279.9
Argentina	1.9	0.9	0.7	0.8	0.8	0.6	29.9	35.4	30.8	42.8	33.4	23.4
Brazil	1.0	1.8	1.3	2.1	1.8	2.8	150.0	260.5	224.7	132.0	120.3	103.4
Other South America	1.7	6.1	4.5	4.6	5.1	7.7	277.3	274.6	263.5	208.0	215.1	153.1
Europe	22.9	30.8	30.8	30.8	21.6	42.7	857.4	1 401.1	1 321.3	861.8	648.2	529.7
Belgium	5.5	10.4	0.4	0.5	1.2	3.1	82.8	78.6	119.0	77.0	25.3	32.3
France	1.7	2.1	5.5	2.9	4.1	3.8	58.5	129.8	157.9	81.5	36.3	20.9
Germany	0.7	2.8	1.2	0.9	0.4	1.0	93.1	121.9	138.1	106.7	87.3	54.8
Netherlands	0.7	0.6	0.4	0.4	0.3	0.9	166.1	234.6	228.7	120.8	105.1	152.4
United Kingdom	1.0	2.1	3.6	3.5	3.1	2.9	114.1	186.5	201.9	215.7	203.3	145.6
Turkey	...	...	...	0.2	0.5	0.1	79.4	109.7	128.7	70.5	18.0	20.7
Former Soviet Republics	...	...	0.3	0.9	0.4	0.5	18.6	15.3	18.9	9.0	10.0	3.2
Poland	...	...	...	...	...	...	1.7	0.3	3.9	1.2	1.3	1.6
Other Eastern Europe	...	...	0.1	...	0.1	0.3	4.7	19.4	39.9	27.3	13.8	2.1
Other Europe	13.2	12.7	19.3	21.6	11.3	30.1	238.2	505.0	284.3	152.0	147.9	96.2
Asia	13.0	14.8	13.6	17.9	21.3	20.3	1 166.3	1 793.5	1 392.6	1 073.8	802.2	721.5
Japan	4.6	3.5	4.6	4.5	8.0	3.5	441.2	484.8	309.8	265.8	213.7	206.7
China	0.5	0.3	0.7	0.5	0.7	2.2	67.0	150.2	131.0	96.4	85.7	31.8
Hong Kong	1.2	0.7	0.7	1.4	2.3	2.3	51.3	87.6	81.2	45.0	38.1	38.9
Taiwan	0.9	3.3	0.7	1.5	2.6	1.5	99.7	207.5	120.1	98.5	78.8	56.2
Singapore	1.0	1.3	1.4	1.6	1.5	2.0	44.6	68.7	54.7	32.1	23.4	46.7
South Korea	2.1	1.6	1.7	2.7	1.0	1.7	271.8	368.9	359.3	285.3	196.0	185.4
Indonesia	0.8	0.9	0.7	0.3	0.2	0.1	58.9	83.6	91.0	83.4	54.3	38.0
India	...	0.1	0.2	...	0.1	0.3	45.4	119.4	43.1	48.1	31.6	36.8
Other Asia	1.9	3.1	3.0	5.4	5.1	6.6	86.5	222.8	202.4	119.0	80.6	81.0
Africa	0.5	0.5	0.3	1.0	1.9	0.5	274.0	310.0	298.1	167.5	133.0	97.7
North Africa	0.1	0.1	...	0.4	0.6	0.1	238.5	232.6	180.0	73.9	62.0	60.6
Republic of South Africa	0.1	0.2	0.1	0.4	0.8	0.1	23.8	36.5	65.4	21.4	19.6	15.1
Other Subsaharan Africa	0.4	0.3	0.2	0.2	0.5	0.3	11.7	40.9	52.8	72.2	51.4	21.9
Middle East	1.0	0.7	0.8	0.6	1.2	0.6	37.8	88.7	96.7	84.3	43.1	65.7
Australia	1.6	1.6	1.0	1.6	1.6	1.5	34.7	42.7	45.5	32.0	21.5	20.7
Rest Of World	...	...	...	...	...	...	...	...	...	1.9	...	...

Table E-3. Metropolitan Area Exports of Goods by Destination, 1994–1999—*Continued*

(Millions of dollars.)

Destination	St. Louis, MO - IL						Stockton - Lodi, CA					
	1994	1995	1996	1997	1998	1999	1994	1995	1996	1997	1998	1999
ALL DESTINATIONS	3 673.3	3 997.7	4 497.4	4 711.5	4 315.5	4 879.2	320.3	355.7	357.8	341.6	339.9	311.6
North America	1 272.7	1 194.2	1 265.6	1 314.9	1 488.0	1 464.5	107.7	107.1	109.3	92.4	99.7	92.5
Canada	837.3	783.9	724.8	789.5	893.4	864.8	98.2	99.7	96.4	80.9	72.2	81.9
Mexico	435.5	410.3	540.8	525.3	594.6	599.6	9.5	7.4	13.0	11.5	27.5	10.6
Caribbean And Central America	133.0	143.8	187.1	229.1	183.1	227.9	1.2	1.1	2.0	2.2	11.5	11.0
South America	319.2	398.0	487.3	458.3	387.4	509.9	6.6	11.2	8.0	22.0	16.1	6.5
Argentina	62.7	64.1	100.1	94.3	72.7	163.4	0.4	0.4	0.4	0.6	0.8	0.7
Brazil	98.7	133.3	153.0	173.3	108.4	159.1	0.4	0.6	0.4	11.9	2.8	1.4
Other South America	157.8	200.6	234.2	190.6	206.2	187.5	5.8	10.2	7.2	9.6	12.5	4.4
Europe	1 010.4	1 219.9	1 347.4	1 529.5	1 267.5	1 379.7	103.8	124.4	129.6	112.2	111.5	99.7
Belgium	251.9	328.8	342.6	376.0	184.6	349.0	2.8	5.4	1.9	2.0	1.7	2.7
France	65.7	84.1	68.0	69.5	100.3	71.1	7.8	11.8	9.3	7.2	3.7	5.5
Germany	71.0	99.0	81.8	100.5	121.5	131.2	26.3	24.5	18.0	20.9	25.6	20.4
Netherlands	137.3	120.7	131.1	129.5	64.8	101.0	6.3	9.0	11.7	9.9	7.2	10.7
United Kingdom	222.5	155.6	148.9	187.7	206.3	285.1	10.9	15.4	13.7	18.2	19.9	17.6
Turkey	0.7	9.1	3.9	25.5	5.1	38.7	0.4	1.5	1.2	0.7	5.6	0.4
Former Soviet Republics	9.9	7.2	6.I	32.7	20.3	19.5	2.4	0.1	2.0	1.3	2.2	0.5
Poland	3.2	5.0	10.0	13.6	19.0	5.4	. . .	0.3	0.1	. . .	. . .	. . .
Other Eastern Europe	5.3	13.5	18.9	8.6	7.1	16.4	1.0	0.6	2.1	0.5	0.5	0.3
Other Europe	242.9	396.9	536.1	585.8	538.6	362.5	45.8	55.9	69.7	51.5	45.1	41.5
Asia	730.1	806.6	927.0	947.4	705.6	954.8	78.4	92.5	88.6	86.4	73.3	77.9
Japan	193.1	201.8	196.8	220.0	188.5	192.3	42.5	44.5	45.8	32.4	33.1	41.1
China	39.6	48.7	106.1	108.4	92.9	124.7	0.3	0.8	0.6	8.8	1.3	1.8
Hong Kong	60.8	94.4	72.7	56.0	69.7	42.9	10.3	12.0	12.8	10.8	18.5	13.7
Taiwan	111.1	93.4	145.3	141.6	87.1	106.4	3.8	7.8	5.1	6.1	6.5	6.5
Singapore	71.5	90.6	90.5	89.2	74.7	97.5	5.6	9.7	4.9	7.6	2.9	1.1
South Korea	85.6	103.0	124.9	121.5	58.1	107.1	5.0	6.0	7.2	6.8	2.3	3.0
Indonesia	21.2	23.4	45.5	46.5	8.7	36.1	0.2	0.3	0.1	0.1	0.1	0.4
India	18.6	17.3	21.0	19.2	31.8	27.8	2.9	1.4	1.6	6.9	3.9	3.6
Other Asia	128.5	133.9	124.2	145.0	94.2	220.0	7.7	10.0	10.5	6.9	4.7	6.7
Africa	37.1	57.6	79.2	48.0	102.8	104.2	2.5	2.0	1.9	2.7	8.5	2.9
North Africa	27.1	43.8	59.0	17.1	63.0	68.9	1.8	1.7	1.4	1.7	6.8	1.4
Republic of South Africa	8.4	10.4	13.3	21.0	32.1	28.1	0.4	0.2	0.1	0.4	0.3	0.3
Other Subsaharan Africa	1.6	3.4	6.9	9.9	7.7	7.2	0.2	0.1	0.3	0.6	1.4	1.2
Middle East	74.6	67.2	68.6	61.6	70.7	119.4	15.8	12.7	12.8	17.9	14.1	14.8
Australia	89.5	107.3	135.2	122.7	110.5	118.8	4.5	4.5	5.6	5.7	5.4	6.4
Rest Of World	6.7	3.1	. . .	. . .	. . .	. . .	. . .	. . .	. . .	. . .	. . .	. . .

Destination	Syracuse, NY						Tacoma, WA					
	1994	1995	1996	1997	1998	1999	1994	1995	1996	1997	1998	1999
ALL DESTINATIONS	1 600.9	1 894.3	1 665.5	1 846.7	1 514.8	1 553.7	774.9	1 098.9	1 179.7	1 403.8	1 254.3	1 224.9
North America	781.9	943.8	859.1	908.3	582.2	759.6	128.5	142.2	172.3	202.3	223.4	172.6
Canada	711.8	912.6	822.1	866.6	544.7	708.7	114.4	125.3	149.7	176.8	188.9	137.8
Mexico	70.1	31.2	37.1	41.7	37.5	50.9	14.0	16.9	22.6	25.5	34.5	34.8
Caribbean And Central America	7.1	9.6	8.7	8.3	10.9	14.0	2.0	3.6	5.7	2.1	2.7	4.2
South America	38.0	34.5	39.4	60.2	43.1	43.5	4.5	7.7	12.8	27.4	16.0	21.0
Argentina	13.5	6.1	6.2	11.9	9.2	10.9	1.1	3.4	7.4	9.4	6.5	6.3
Brazil	10.2	17.3	21.3	34.4	17.0	21.0	0.3	1.0	1.9	10.5	4.6	5.5
Other South America	14.3	11.2	11.9	13.8	16.9	11.6	3.1	3.3	3.5	7.5	4.9	9.2
Europe	352.7	384.4	257.1	345.4	503.5	366.0	127.2	303.4	304.5	316.6	320.2	315.9
Belgium	5.1	6.8	5.5	7.7	6.3	8.9	5.6	17.4	15.6	25.9	33.0	28.2
France	30.9	23.8	19.4	26.6	38.8	56.5	24.1	54.8	46.3	39.0	40.8	43.5
Germany	64.7	58.9	36.9	44.6	67.4	43.1	26.2	77.2	88.2	86.6	97.3	106.4
Netherlands	17.8	29.3	20.7	17.6	18.1	17.8	3.4	14.8	8.0	12.3	10.5	7.0
United Kingdom	46.1	69.6	59.3	78.1	76.5	54.7	24.7	50.7	48.5	40.0	29.8	25.5
Turkey	25.7	3.6	2.9	6.3	3.2	4.5	2.4	6.7	6.4	10.1	11.3	14.6
Former Soviet Republics	1.1	4.8	1.8	0.8	1.6	1.2	0.8	1.4	2.2	4.9	9.7	1.1
Poland	0.9	1.9	1.0	2.6	2.6	1.6	. . .	0.5	4.0	6.7	9.3	6.5
Other Eastern Europe	1.0	2.2	1.7	1.6	49.7	16.2	0.2	0.3	0.5	1.2	1.6	1.0
Other Europe	159.4	183.5	107.7	159.5	239.4	161.7	39.7	79.5	84.8	89.9	76.9	81.9
Asia	353.8	396.8	377.1	392.5	300.3	309.2	489.1	615.2	662.7	828.9	671.0	695.5
Japan	49.3	40.6	47.0	84.3	58.6	54.0	294.6	320.6	375.5	526.5	450.0	441.1
China	19.3	32.8	29.1	47.6	36.3	55.3	17.7	40.7	47.4	47.6	52.5	37.4
Hong Kong	25.8	51.2	67.6	47.8	32.9	24.7	10.1	22.8	27.9	20.0	17.1	20.4
Taiwan	15.7	13.8	6.8	16.4	17.0	16.5	20.3	36.1	33.8	35.9	27.2	28.4
Singapore	77.8	47.8	52.4	63.9	48.3	54.8	5.7	7.1	8.8	23.6	14.6	11.1
South Korea	134.6	154.9	122.5	86.6	59.0	78.8	117.2	151.0	106.7	123.5	73.5	106.9
Indonesia	3.9	7.3	2.0	2.4	0.1	0.2	2.9	6.9	11.9	14.2	5.2	14.7
India	2.5	4.6	7.3	2.4	4.1	6.9	0.8	1.3	5.1	3.8	1.8	1.3
Other Asia	24.8	43.6	42.5	41.1	44.0	18.0	19.8	28.8	45.6	33.8	29.2	34.4
Africa	5.7	10.3	6.7	12.3	12.4	22.3	6.8	6.5	5.9	4.6	5.1	5.7
North Africa	1.6	1.8	1.0	6.6	7.6	16.2	0.2	0.2	0.6	0.2	0.6	1.7
Republic of South Africa	3.2	6.8	4.4	4.7	3.8	5.1	4.9	5.0	4.2	3.4	3.1	3.0
Other Subsaharan Africa	0.9	1.6	1.3	1.0	1.0	1.0	1.6	1.3	1.1	1.0	1.4	1.0
Middle East	40.3	19.1	50.0	53.1	43.8	25.5	13.6	17.1	13.0	12.6	9.8	6.5
Australia	21.5	95.7	67.2	66.6	18.5	13.6	3.3	3.3	2.9	9.4	6.1	3.6
Rest Of World	. . .	. . .	. . .	. . .	0.1	. . .	. . .	. . .	. . .	. . .	. . .	. . .

Table E-3. Metropolitan Area Exports of Goods by Destination, 1994–1999—*Continued*

(Millions of dollars.)

Destination	Tampa - St. Petersburg - Clearwater, FL						Toledo, OH					
	1994	1995	1996	1997	1998	1999	1994	1995	1996	1997	1998	1999
ALL DESTINATIONS	1 835.8	2 116.1	1 921.8	2 273.8	2 471.5	2 403.8	986.9	1 177.7	1 207.5	1 261.1	1 056.6	867.6
North America	345.1	344.9	391.0	452.4	431.6	429.9	586.8	785.8	729.8	891.0	700.8	549.9
Canada	284.0	271.9	279.3	325.8	349.9	339.0	536.1	742.6	693.6	803.4	606.5	488.6
Mexico	61.1	73.0	111.8	126.7	81.7	90.9	50.7	43.1	36.2	87.7	94.3	61.3
Caribbean And Central America	164.4	164.8	194.4	213.6	244.9	182.0	10.7	12.7	13.1	11.8	14.8	11.8
South America	160.6	176.7	187.3	215.4	191.4	159.6	53.6	63.2	67.3	61.8	47.2	42.6
Argentina	19.2	41.4	40.7	44.7	38.4	38.8	8.7	5.2	7.0	4.2	5.2	3.2
Brazil	73.0	54.7	67.5	79.0	74.3	48.6	9.8	12.7	14.3	20.4	11.4	18.6
Other South America	68.4	80.5	79.1	91.7	78.7	72.2	35.0	45.3	46.1	37.2	30.6	20.9
Europe	279.7	343.3	328.5	471.7	476.0	414.5	128.6	151.5	183.6	133.4	165.1	126.5
Belgium	5.7	14.8	7.3	17.7	14.5	15.4	37.3	41.1	58.8	51.3	48.9	14.6
France	42.4	42.7	33.7	38.1	38.9	39.2	8.3	6.8	8.3	6.8	12.7	5.1
Germany	51.3	65.9	74.5	67.5	90.1	72.1	10.9	16.1	11.0	10.2	12.9	14.5
Netherlands	30.8	35.8	63.1	105.1	76.4	45.6	6.2	11.3	10.4	8.8	9.3	19.8
United Kingdom	61.5	65.2	59.6	86.6	107.4	115.5	29.3	44.6	42.8	28.2	26.7	38.4
Turkey	3.5	14.4	6.7	23.8	14.7	4.9	0.8	1.1	3.0	3.3	8.9	2.0
Former Soviet Republics	5.9	4.0	5.1	28.7	7.0	2.3	0.2	0.5	1.5	0.8	0.7	. . .
Poland	0.6	0.8	0.7	2.1	9.9	3.7	5.4	6.6	3.9	4.3	6.3	2.2
Other Eastern Europe	4.2	3.5	3.4	7.8	14.7	7.7	0.4	1.1	1.4	0.6	0.7	7.3
Other Europe	73.8	96.2	74.4	94.1	102.5	108.1	29.8	22.2	42.6	19.0	37.9	22.6
Asia	708.1	826.5	537.2	700.1	814.1	996.5	105.7	115.6	142.7	108.6	74.8	97.0
Japan	33.7	108.2	62.2	66.8	95.4	124.3	40.2	27.8	28.4	30.8	23.6	39.2
China	447.9	466.2	226.2	304.6	347.9	368.5	9.2	18.2	21.1	6.8	7.0	9.2
Hong Kong	21.3	20.9	25.2	26.4	26.0	40.8	6.1	9.1	13.4	7.1	5.1	6.0
Taiwan	63.6	15.3	17.7	22.2	16.9	32.5	9.5	8.3	7.3	9.2	11.4	8.5
Singapore	9.7	10.2	15.1	21.9	11.8	41.9	6.6	5.9	7.7	7.0	6.6	12.0
South Korea	6.1	13.6	13.4	21.3	29.1	20.9	22.8	22.7	36.5	22.7	8.3	5.9
Indonesia	9.4	1.3	16.9	2.7	0.9	0.9	1.3	9.1	9.2	0.9	0.5	0.6
India	36.5	119.6	36.9	135.8	156.1	247.1	1.0	3.1	7.4	13.5	7.6	5.4
Other Asia	79.9	71.4	123.4	98.3	129.9	119.8	8.9	11.4	11.7	10.6	4.8	10.1
Africa	20.0	77.3	50.4	36.6	37.4	32.4	12.3	7.7	13.5	6.6	10.0	4.2
North Africa	12.0	62.3	36.6	23.7	20.1	16.5	7.0	1.0	0.7	0.5	0.7	0.6
Republic of South Africa	5.5	8.7	6.6	11.1	11.9	7.1	4.6	6.1	10.6	5.7	7.3	3.4
Other Subsaharan Africa	2.5	6.3	7.3	1.9	5.4	8.9	0.7	0.5	2.2	0.3	2.1	0.2
Middle East	38.1	49.4	25.9	29.2	73.6	35.5	12.7	16.0	33.5	23.4	20.6	11.2
Australia	119.8	133.2	207.1	154.8	202.4	153.3	. 25.5	12.2	16.1	18.3	21.2	24.4
Rest Of World	. . .	. . .	. . .	. . .	. . .	. . .	51.1	13.1	7.8	6.2	2.1	. . .

Destination	Topeka, KS						Trenton, NJ					
	1994	1995	1996	1997	1998	1999	1994	1995	1996	1997	1998	1999
ALL DESTINATIONS	125.2	133.0	130.2	140.7	160.3	154.1	237.5	392.5	267.8	343.4	276.9	330.6
North America	19.5	14.1	21.9	33.5	54.4	68.5	104.3	104.2	122.2	197.9	125.2	127.1
Canada	18.5	13.1	20.4	32.1	42.7	66.0	85.6	92.4	107.9	178.7	96.0	87.4
Mexico	1.0	1.0	1.5	1.4	11.7	2.5	18.7	11.8	14.3	19.2	29.2	39.7
Caribbean And Central America	0.7	0.4	0.6	0.8	1.2	1.5	3.9	3.0	1.4	1.9	4.9	14.0
South America	0.7	3.1	3.1	4.4	6.5	5.3	14.5	16.8	25.0	11.4	11.3	27.8
Argentina	0.4	0.7	1.3	0.5	2.4	2.5	2.9	1.1	0.6	0.7	1.0	4.4
Brazil	. . .	0.7	0.1	0.8	0.6	1.6	7.6	11.5	13.5	5.9	6.0	16.5
Other South America	0.3	1.8	1.7	3.1	3.5	1.2	4.0	4.2	10.9	4.8	4.3	6.9
Europe	53.6	51.0	56.4	26.5	22.7	18.8	49.6	70.6	65.5	81.3	79.6	93.6
Belgium	0.1	2.3	13.6	13.7	12.0	8.9	1.4	0.9	1.4	2.3	1.3	1.6
France	8.5	8.7	6.4	0.3	0.2	0.2	5.4	7.1	11.2	14.7	11.4	8.2
Germany	4.5	5.8	5.8	0.6	0.3	0.1	12.7	13.2	13.9	10.8	11.0	13.0
Netherlands	5.3	3.9	1.3	0.8	0.1	0.1	2.3	15.4	16.4	22.9	5.1	3.0
United Kingdom	18.1	14.2	14.7	5.0	4.8	3.7	11.0	11.8	9.1	13.5	18.9	15.0
Turkey	. . .	0.1	0.3	0.2	. . .	. . .	0.1	0.3	0.6	0.7	1.3	0.6
Former Soviet Republics	0.3	0.1	. . .	. . .	. . .	. . .	0.2	0.6	0.6	0.3	0.7	19.4
Poland	. . .	0.1	0.1	. . .	. . .	. . .	0.2	0.7	0.5	0.5	0.6	1.6
Other Eastern Europe	0.3	0.4	0.1	. . .	. . .	. . .	0.7	1.7	1.1	1.9	1.9	2.1
Other Europe	16.5	15.4	14.3	5.9	5.2	5.8	15.5	19.0	10.9	13.7	27.5	29.1
Asia	48.5	60.9	43.8	69.2	67.7	52.9	57.2	191.2	44.0	43.1	44.7	45.1
Japan	43.7	53.0	35.4	59.8	57.3	43.4	9.3	12.5	11.6	11.2	14.5	13.9
China	. . .	. . .	0.4	0.4	0.7	0.2	8.8	137.4	2.7	6.1	7.7	4.7
Hong Kong	1.0	1.4	1.1	1.9	1.6	3.9	5.8	5.3	2.4	2.6	3.1	2.1
Taiwan	1.1	2.2	2.5	2.1	1.8	1.1	14.6	5.0	2.8	3.2	3.3	5.9
Singapore	0.3	0.4	0.7	0.7	0.6	0.6	2.1	3.5	1.4	1.8	2.2	1.3
South Korea	0.3	0.3	0.5	0.6	0.7	0.7	4.0	5.9	4.1	3.8	2.0	2.3
Indonesia	0.4	0.1	. . .	0.1	. . .	0.1	2.8	3.7	4.3	1.7	1.2	1.1
India	. . .	. . .	0.1	0.3	2.1	0.2	3.3	7.8	4.0	1.7	2.7	2.6
Other Asia	1.6	3.4	3.2	3.3	2.9	2.8	6.4	10.1	10.8	11.1	8.0	11.2
Africa	0.2	0.4	1.5	2.7	3.7	3.7	3.7	2.1	2.7	2.0	3.7	12.6
North Africa	. . .	. . .	0.1	0.2	. . .	. . .	1.2	0.3	0.9	0.8	1.6	1.8
Republic of South Africa	0.2	0.4	1.3	2.5	3.7	3.6	1.4	1.0	0.6	0.6	0.7	10.0
Other Subsaharan Africa	. . .	. . .	. . .	0.1	. . .	. . .	1.2	0.8	1.2	0.7	1.4	0.8
Middle East	0.1	0.6	1.0	0.8	0.5	0.7	3.0	2.8	3.2	3.8	5.5	8.3
Australia	2.0	2.3	1.9	2.6	3.5	2.8	1.3	1.7	3.9	2.0	2.1	2.0
Rest Of World	. . .	. . .	. . .	. . .	. . .	. . .	. . .	. . .	. . .	. . .	. . .	. . .

Table E-3. Metropolitan Area Exports of Goods by Destination, 1994–1999—*Continued*

(Millions of dollars.)

Destination	Tucson, AZ						Utica - Rome, NY					
	1994	1995	1996	1997	1998	1999	1994	1995	1996	1997	1998	1999
ALL DESTINATIONS	638.1	671.7	800.1	1 060.5	1 253.4	1 064.6	269.3	238.0	278.0	238.8	240.3	248.2
North America	385.1	387.4	470.5	621.2	649.6	587.8	69.0	68.8	120.9	106.4	142.3	155.4
Canada	89.5	83.6	134.1	129.8	147.1	155.9	65.2	65.9	116.8	103.6	137.5	147.0
Mexico	295.6	303.8	336.4	491.4	502.5	431.8	3.7	2.9	4.2	2.8	4.8	8.5
Caribbean And Central America	4.4	1.9	1.3	1.6	3.0	1.6	0.6	1.5	1.4	1.5	1.1	1.7
South America	9.9	8.4	14.2	46.3	62.8	56.1	1.9	1.6	3.4	2.5	2.4	1.4
Argentina	1.0	0.9	1.0	5.6	12.2	0.6	0.4	0.1	0.3	0.7	. . .	0.2
Brazil	0.9	1.7	2.0	25.3	11.3	13.2	0.5	0.4	2.5	0.7	0.4	0.5
Other South America	8.0	5.8	11.1	15.4	39.3	42.3	1.0	1.1	0.6	1.0	1.9	0.7
Europe	133.4	149.4	161.9	194.1	292.7	221.6	114.1	89.1	93.1	85.7	58.3	59.9
Belgium	0.8	3.0	2.4	1.7	2.3	5.6	1.5	2.1	14.1	2.4	1.1	2.6
France	16.3	30.3	23.7	27.5	22.9	28.2	9.5	25.3	11.6	14.6	16.0	21.4
Germany	46.4	50.4	57.0	48.6	74.2	81.7	5.4	7.1	5.8	5.6	5.7	5.5
Netherlands	6.9	6.9	5.5	26.1	16.1	5.6	5.5	2.1	1.6	1.4	2.1	1.9
United Kingdom	22.9	25.7	32.8	37.3	61.4	41.8	77.7	38.9	46.9	47.6	20.5	12.0
Turkey	0.6	0.5	0.2	0.3	38.5	0.7	0.1	0.2	0.7	0.7	0.4	0.3
Former Soviet Republics	0.9	0.6	0.6	0.4	0.4	0.3	. . .	0.9	0.4	0.1	0.1	0.3
Poland	0.1	0.6	1.1	0.5	0.7	1.0	0.1	0.3	0.3	0.7	0.2	0.1
Other Eastern Europe	0.2	0.2	0.7	1.2	1.1	2.3	0.4	0.4	0.9	0.3	0.2	1.2
Other Europe	38.3	31.0	38.0	50.6	75.1	54.5	14.0	11.9	10.9	12.3	11.9	14.8
Asia	86.6	109.8	126.8	156.8	213.2	165.7	76.5	64.5	46.4	34.4	23.3	22.6
Japan	46.8	59.1	53.4	64.0	134.2	61.7	6.0	10.1	11.2	10.2	8.4	7.4
China	1.7	0.9	1.0	2.2	4.0	5.9	1.4	0.9	2.8	2.1	2.3	0.9
Hong Kong	4.7	4.4	4.9	9.5	9.8	13.6	1.5	1.2	1.0	1.6	1.2	0.7
Taiwan	18.7	28.3	35.8	40.8	34.9	44.0	61.1	39.2	16.6	3.1	1.9	2.6
Singapore	2.9	3.1	9.9	7.3	7.3	5.5	1.7	4.2	6.3	6.3	4.8	5.5
South Korea	2.5	2.3	6.8	5.4	2.7	2.8	3.1	4.8	3.9	5.9	1.1	2.1
Indonesia	0.5	1.2	1.2	0.8	0.5	0.3	. . .	0.1	0.5	0.2	0.1	0.7
India	1.8	1.1	1.3	0.7	0.8	1.1	0.2	1.0	0.8	1.2	0.8	0.3
Other Asia	6.9	9.4	12.6	26.0	19.1	30.7	1.5	3.0	3.2	3.7	2.7	2.3
Africa	2.7	3.8	1.8	16.8	7.9	9.5	0.9	1.4	1.8	0.9	1.7	0.8
North Africa	0.3	0.2	0.1	0.5	0.9	0.2	0.1	0.2	0.5	0.5	0.3	0.3
Republic of South Africa	1.9	2.4	1.5	10.0	3.4	9.0	0.7	1.2	1.3	0.4	1.4	0.4
Other Subsaharan Africa	0.6	1.3	0.2	6.4	3.6	0.3	. . .	. . .	. . .	. . .	. . .	. . .
Middle East	5.7	3.7	4.8	4.8	5.7	7.2	3.4	8.9	9.2	5.4	8.9	4.2
Australia	10.4	7.3	18.9	18.7	18.6	15.1	2.9	2.2	1.7	2.1	2.4	2.1
Rest Of World	. . .	. . .	. . .	. . .	. . .	. . .	. . .	. . .	. . .	. . .	. . .	. . .

Destination	Vallejo - Fairfield - Napa, CA						Ventura, CA					
	1994	1995	1996	1997	1998	1999	1994	1995	1996	1997	1998	1999
ALL DESTINATIONS	264.0	238.1	278.0	384.9	398.8	284.0	698.7	953.4	967.3	1 128.9	1 192.5	1 577.5
North America	46.1	46.5	56.1	115.4	140.5	68.9	153.1	160.9	168.7	211.0	222.4	243.3
Canada	43.7	45.3	55.0	106.0	134.0	60.6	110.8	118.7	133.2	171.7	179.6	191.4
Mexico	2.4	1.2	1.1	9.4	6.5	8.3	42.3	42.1	35.5	39.3	42.8	51.9
Caribbean And Central America	1.6	1.0	1.6	1.6	2.5	1.3	8.3	11.0	15.0	18.0	18.0	39.3
South America	2.3	5.8	7.3	36.3	9.6	4.2	31.0	39.6	38.0	54.5	47.5	39.9
Argentina	0.6	1.1	0.3	18.0	0.9	1.3	7.4	8.9	5.8	7.4	8.5	7.2
Brazil	0.7	2.6	3.3	4.0	4.7	0.8	11.0	16.0	14.3	27.1	19.1	18.3
Other South America	1.0	2.1	3.7	14.4	4.0	2.1	12.7	14.7	17.9	20.0	20.0	14.4
Europe	46.9	83.4	89.0	106.5	138.3	124.9	187.7	246.7	262.3	320.5	342.8	327.6
Belgium	2.2	15.1	4.1	4.4	20.6	24.9	4.3	33.3	20.5	19.8	10.3	10.2
France	4.7	6.9	4.3	6.6	8.1	6.5	19.5	24.3	42.4	46.9	54.6	52.2
Germany	6.7	10.4	10.9	11.8	13.6	13.0	47.4	43.8	54.0	58.6	48.2	72.9
Netherlands	4.3	7.7	10.2	12.3	21.6	13.8	13.0	15.0	16.3	15.6	23.6	22.6
United Kingdom	10.5	14.9	26.3	26.1	30.5	25.9	49.1	53.3	53.6	75.8	85.3	87.1
Turkey	0.5	0.3	0.5	0.3	0.4	0.4	1.3	2.2	3.0	5.9	4.0	12.6
Former Soviet Republics	2.2	0.1	0.2	0.2	0.3	0.2	7.9	14.3	4.8	3.2	0.5	0.4
Poland	0.4	0.3	0.5	1.1	1.6	2.0	0.3	0.3	0.3	0.4	0.3	0.3
Other Eastern Europe	1.0	2.5	0.9	2.1	1.2	0.4	1.1	1.9	2.7	2.1	2.6	2.5
Other Europe	14.4	25.2	30.9	41.8	40.4	37.9	43.8	58.3	64.8	92.3	113.2	66.8
Asia	136.8	89.0	101.0	106.8	77.5	66.5	271.4	421.8	411.2	450.1	480.9	841.8
Japan	17.6	44.0	46.4	43.9	34.5	26.3	75.2	111.3	131.6	142.5	130.0	253.1
China	2.0	8.2	4.9	9.4	0.8	1.6	5.7	7.1	8.2	11.9	11.6	16.9
Hong Kong	1.7	2.9	5.0	7.0	3.9	6.8	21.8	34.7	36.8	56.9	147.4	297.9
Taiwan	3.1	9.9	14.4	23.1	15.2	11.5	18.1	28.3	43.6	51.8	59.3	79.5
Singapore	11.6	3.8	6.9	5.0	3.1	6.2	50.6	42.2	38.7	46.4	32.6	43.6
South Korea	5.3	11.9	9.8	7.7	3.0	6.3	28.2	57.2	48.7	37.7	12.6	35.2
Indonesia	2.8	1.2	1.9	2.1	6.8	0.3	5.6	3.2	2.4	4.2	1.7	1.3
India	0.9	1.0	2.0	0.9	0.2	0.3	12.8	14.9	11.1	16.0	11.4	12.3
Other Asia	91.9	6.1	9.8	7.7	10.0	7.1	53.6	122.9	90.0	82.8	74.3	102.1
Africa	25.2	1.5	2.4	2.4	2.7	1.4	7.7	12.0	10.0	13.1	19.4	9.6
North Africa	23.6	0.2	0.4	0.6	0.6	0.2	2.8	4.5	3.1	5.6	6.8	5.4
Republic of South Africa	1.6	1.1	1.8	1.4	1.6	0.6	3.8	5.5	5.7	6.1	10.6	2.5
Other Subsaharan Africa	0.1	0.2	0.2	0.4	0.5	0.6	1.0	1.9	1.3	1.4	1.9	1.7
Middle East	1.7	3.7	12.7	3.1	16.6	6.9	15.5	24.5	17.1	18.8	26.8	41.2
Australia	3.3	7.2	7.9	12.8	11.2	9.9	24.0	36.8	45.0	42.8	34.8	34.8
Rest Of World	. . .	. . .	. . .	. . .	. . .	. . .	. . .	0.1	. . .	. . .	. . .	. . .

Table E-3. Metropolitan Area Exports of Goods by Destination, 1994–1999—*Continued*

(Millions of dollars.)

Destination	Visalia - Tulare - Porterville, CA						Washington, DC - MD - VA - WV					
	1994	1995	1996	1997	1998	1999	1994	1995	1996	1997	1998	1999
ALL DESTINATIONS	107.7	120.6	143.7	160.5	178.1	160.6	7 969.3	8 350.4	8 083.5	7 980.7	7 347.8	7 213.3
North America	63.6	63.5	74.0	81.8	79.4	91.1	517.6	416.2	442.3	582.4	817.8	741.5
Canada	62.1	61.4	69.5	75.2	73.7	73.5	364.5	336.8	325.3	412.9	536.5	458.3
Mexico	1.4	2.1	4.5	6.5	5.7	17.6	153.1	79.4	117.0	169.5	281.3	283.1
Caribbean And Central America	0.4	1.1	2.6	2.0	4.9	6.1	81.3	60.6	56.9	61.0	72.0	127.2
South America	1.6	2.0	3.8	6.8	5.9	6.5	333.5	203.4	240.0	361.3	310.4	243.3
Argentina	1.1	. . .	0.2	0.1	0.1	. . .	42.5	26.0	13.2	28.8	35.4	28.3
Brazil	. . .	0.8	1.5	1.0	0.2	0.2	70.9	86.3	136.7	201.1	148.7	121.4
Other South America	0.5	1.1	2.1	5.7	5.6	6.2	220.1	91.1	90.0	131.4	126.3	93.6
Europe	6.5	11.6	12.1	15.5	32.7	23.9	2 037.5	2 617.4	2 770.7	2 798.3	2 365.6	2 537.4
Belgium	1.2	1.9	1.1	1.2	1.6	1.3	86.9	87.3	85.2	122.1	103.5	113.5
France	0.3	0.9	1.0	1.6	2.6	2.9	107.5	145.5	98.9	103.3	165.6	346.7
Germany	0.8	1.6	1.5	1.7	4.4	5.5	406.0	400.0	504.0	590.4	407.4	413.4
Netherlands	0.1	0.7	0.6	0.6	1.4	1.5	37.9	53.8	64.2	47.4	63.6	69.1
United Kingdom	1.2	1.9	2.4	2.6	7.7	4.0	652.1	565.9	769.5	661.0	736.7	745.0
Turkey	0.1	0.4	0.1	0.7	1.7	0.1	24.0	27.0	23.9	28.5	29.6	45.2
Former Soviet Republics	. . .	. . .	. . .	0.1	. . .	0.3	231.2	334.6	339.6	326.8	220.5	157.2
Poland	. . .	. . .	. . .	0.1	0.1	0.3	9.9	11.9	15.0	16.6	17.1	15.0
Other Eastern Europe	0.1	0.2	0.2	0.1	0.5	0.7	28.1	39.7	52.8	32.9	35.3	55.8
Other Europe	2.7	4.1	5.3	6.9	12.7	7.2	454.0	951.6	817.7	869.5	586.3	576.4
Asia	30.9	39.1	45.4	48.0	41.1	22.1	2 040.8	2 385.1	1 981.7	2 237.5	1 826.8	2 012.8
Japan	11.2	21.9	27.7	24.6	18.9	12.1	196.7	288.5	178.3	186.6	370.7	554.4
China	0.6	0.3	0.3	0.4	0.1	0.2	40.6	54.8	71.8	62.5	50.9	92.5
Hong Kong	9.2	8.4	7.5	7.9	6.4	2.7	27.3	49.5	50.7	44.1	36.1	32.5
Taiwan	2.9	2.5	2.8	1.9	1.8	2.2	750.9	724.8	547.8	643.9	488.5	560.0
Singapore	0.7	1.4	1.9	2.2	1.9	1.6	56.8	77.7	55.3	63.7	60.1	69.9
South Korea	3.3	1.1	1.6	2.5	7.9	1.4	584.2	655.4	495.1	484.0	487.3	498.1
Indonesia	. . .	. . .	0.2	0.7	0.2	. . .	14.2	75.2	80.7	92.2	19.5	16.4
India	0.2	0.3	0.2	1.2	0.2	. . .	94.4	142.5	111.9	133.7	95.1	61.5
Other Asia	2.7	3.3	3.2	6.7	3.8	1.8	275.6	316.7	390.2	526.9	218.6	127.5
Africa	2.1	0.8	0.5	1.3	3.0	4.4	1 151.4	667.5	608.6	637.4	698.3	558.8
North Africa	1.9	0.4	0.1	0.9	1.0	0.5	930.8	493.0	429.8	538.9	574.5	434.3
Republic of South Africa	0.1	0.3	0.4	0.3	1.9	3.8	20.9	66.2	93.0	24.2	37.2	24.9
Other Subsaharan Africa	0.1	0.1	. . .	0.1	0.1	0.1	199.7	108.3	85.9	74.3	86.7	99.6
Middle East	0.6	0.5	1.0	0.6	3.5	2.7	1 563.5	1 720.1	1 764.1	1 014.9	784.7	476.6
Australia	2.0	2.1	4.6	4.7	7.5	3.8	243.6	280.1	219.1	287.9	472.2	515.6
Rest Of World	. . .	. . .	. . .	. . .	. . .	. . .	. . .	. . .	. . .	. . .	. . .	. . .

Destination	Waterbury, CT						Waterloo - Cedar Falls, IA					
	1994	1995	1996	1997	1998	1999	1994	1995	1996	1997	1998	1999
ALL DESTINATIONS	179.6	207.6	221.6	252.0	258.8	235.9	149.7	194.6	200.9	282.8	200.8	86.4
North America	84.3	76.3	90.4	112.3	105.6	108.1	127.4	166.7	172.2	248.5	177.4	62.7
Canada	64.3	59.0	69.5	85.4	81.0	86.2	126.1	165.9	171.1	246.3	172.2	55.3
Mexico	20.0	17.2	20.9	26.9	24.6	21.9	1.3	0.8	1.1	2.2	5.2	7.5
Caribbean And Central America	0.6	1.8	3.6	4.5	7.9	5.0	0.1	0.5	0.4	0.2	0.2	0.4
South America	8.7	12.5	12.6	14.4	8.3	5.0	1.5	3.1	2.0	4.6	2.8	1.9
Argentina	3.4	5.3	3.9	4.6	3.1	1.0	0.4	0.3	0.3	2.9	0.6	0.5
Brazil	2.0	3.7	4.3	6.0	2.8	0.7	0.3	2.2	0.8	0.5	1.2	0.5
Other South America	3.4	3.6	4.3	3.8	2.4	3.3	0.8	0.6	0.9	1.1	1.0	0.9
Europe	42.1	65.0	64.1	63.6	57.5	64.4	10.9	10.6	11.4	8.4	7.5	9.1
Belgium	1.3	8.6	9.5	12.7	5.0	5.4	0.6	1.6	1.2	2.0	0.6	0.6
France	5.3	8.7	5.9	4.7	5.5	7.2	1.3	0.3	1.1	0.2	0.3	0.1
Germany	6.3	9.8	9.2	9.5	9.9	11.3	0.7	0.9	0.1	0.2	0.1	0.2
Netherlands	2.5	3.3	3.1	8.3	11.6	7.8	2.1	2.7	2.3	2.6	1.8	2.0
United Kingdom	16.7	17.9	18.8	16.0	13.6	20.1	2.6	1.5	2.8	0.7	1.2	3.4
Turkey	. . .	0.2	0.1	0.1	0.2	0.2	0.1	. . .	. . .	. . .	. . .	. . .
Former Soviet Republics	0.5	1.7	0.4	0.7	1.1	0.2	. . .	. . .	. . .	. . .	. . .	. . .
Poland	0.2	0.8	0.3	0.2	0.3	0.1	. . .	0.1	. . .	. . .	0.1	. . .
Other Eastern Europe	0.5	0.8	1.1	0.6	0.8	0.8	. . .	0.1	. . .	. . .	. . .	. . .
Other Europe	8.9	13.3	15.8	10.9	9.5	11.1	3.5	3.5	3.8	2.7	3.3	2.7
Asia	37.0	46.0	46.1	51.7	73.6	48.9	8.3	12.2	12.3	17.9	10.2	10.8
Japan	6.4	7.1	6.7	8.5	9.1	9.7	4.5	6.5	5.6	6.7	6.7	7.1
China	0.2	1.0	1.3	2.3	1.0	2.8	. . .	0.2	1.0	0.3	0.3	0.2
Hong Kong	3.3	6.4	5.7	11.2	14.1	6.0	0.1	0.2	0.3	0.2	0.1	0.3
Taiwan	2.3	5.5	5.6	7.3	31.0	7.8	0.6	0.8	0.7	2.5	1.1	0.3
Singapore	13.1	6.6	4.4	5.3	5.2	4.5	0.6	1.1	0.7	0.9	0.7	0.7
South Korea	2.7	3.3	3.8	3.1	2.3	2.5	1.3	1.6	1.5	1.3	0.5	0.4
Indonesia	0.2	0.5	0.4	0.4	0.6	0.2	0.1	0.1	0.1	0.1	. . .	. . .
India	0.4	2.2	1.6	0.8	1.5	1.9	0.1	0.2	0.1	0.1	0.2	0.2
Other Asia	8.4	13.4	16.5	12.8	8.8	13.5	0.9	1.6	2.3	5.7	0.5	1.5
Africa	3.9	0.7	0.4	0.4	0.9	0.4	0.6	0.6	0.8	0.5	0.9	0.5
North Africa	0.9	0.1	0.2	0.3	0.3	0.2	0.1	0.1	. . .	0.1	0.5	0.2
Republic of South Africa	3.0	0.4	0.2	0.1	0.5	0.1	0.5	0.5	0.5	0.4	0.5	0.2
Other Subsaharan Africa	. . .	0.1	. . .	. . .	0.1	0.1	. . .	. . .	0.3	. . .	. . .	. . .
Middle East	1.4	1.7	2.0	2.0	2.0	1.5	0.2	0.3	0.6	1.3	0.8	0.3
Australia	1.5	3.6	2.4	3.0	2.9	2.7	0.7	0.7	1.2	1.5	1.0	0.7
Rest Of World	. . .	. . .	. . .	. . .	. . .	. . .	. . .	. . .	. . .	. . .	. . .	. . .

Table E-3. Metropolitan Area Exports of Goods by Destination, 1994–1999—*Continued*

(Millions of dollars.)

Destination	Wausau, WI						West Palm Beach - Boca Raton, FL					
	1994	1995	1996	1997	1998	1999	1994	1995	1996	1997	1998	1999
ALL DESTINATIONS	113.6	117.3	148.9	184.8	158.9	177.7	834.3	898.0	955.8	1 156.0	959.0	948.4
North America	59.4	59.3	65.2	79.7	80.2	84.0	193.7	169.0	225.0	282.7	304.8	267.7
Canada	50.1	52.1	56.1	67.4	69.0	71.6	168.3	149.7	187.5	192.9	186.1	176.2
Mexico	9.3	7.2	9.1	12.3	11.2	12.5	25.4	19.3	37.5	89.7	118.6	91.6
Caribbean And Central America	0.8	0.2	0.6	1.0	0.5	0.4	109.8	108.3	112.0	128.6	134.1	135.7
South America	2.0	1.4	1.9	3.4	4.3	4.3	136.9	152.7	179.9	222.9	96.0	88.9
Argentina	0.5	0.4	0.6	1.5	2.0	1.8	18.0	14.1	10.9	13.6	15.4	12.6
Brazil	1.3	0.3	0.1	0.1	0.1	0.1	37.6	65.2	103.3	125.3	38.0	28.2
Other South America	0.1	0.7	1.2	1.7	2.2	2.4	81.4	73.3	65.7	84.0	42.6	48.1
Europe	7.1	10.8	14.8	19.5	13.6	15.6	180.9	250.6	251.5	258.1	260.6	300.9
Belgium	...	...	...	...	0.6	...	6.4	9.3	7.6	13.7	23.2	29.6
France	0.5	0.5	0.9	1.1	1.8	0.9	22.5	24.6	17.0	22.8	21.9	21.0
Germany	1.2	2.0	2.0	2.1	2.5	1.5	26.0	35.6	53.1	47.9	40.9	72.2
Netherlands	0.3	0.5	2.5	0.8	1.2	0.5	8.0	19.2	23.2	14.5	22.1	31.4
United Kingdom	2.3	3.8	5.3	4.6	3.9	6.6	43.6	57.6	54.9	66.3	64.5	73.9
Turkey	...	0.1	2.7	2.9	0.9	0.4	1.1	2.0	3.5	7.9	3.7	1.7
Former Soviet Republics	0.2	...	...	...	...	...	2.7	24.1	2.0	4.3	2.0	1.7
Poland	...	...	...	0.1	...	...	4.3	1.7	2.2	2.6	1.2	0.9
Other Eastern Europe	...	...	...	1.2	...	0.1	1.8	2.0	3.1	3.2	2.2	0.4
Other Europe	2.5	3.8	1.4	6.6	2.8	5.5	64.5	74.5	84.8	74.8	78.8	68.1
Asia	42.0	42.9	63.9	77.7	57.4	70.0	174.4	164.7	148.8	194.4	113.2	116.2
Japan	5.6	9.0	9.9	10.9	8.3	4.3	78.0	55.5	49.9	74.1	37.3	38.2
China	0.8	1.4	4.1	4.2	1.6	2.0	18.0	7.2	9.1	10.0	7.4	9.3
Hong Kong	24.5	20.4	24.5	26.9	26.1	35.8	10.8	23.1	22.2	23.2	10.7	11.0
Taiwan	2.5	3.8	5.3	8.2	9.7	8.9	8.2	9.2	5.1	9.3	7.1	6.9
Singapore	4.6	1.3	5.9	10.0	4.9	5.6	21.5	26.3	10.2	16.0	19.2	10.8
South Korea	2.9	5.0	9.0	9.0	2.3	8.0	14.8	17.7	32.1	32.6	13.6	13.0
Indonesia	...	0.2	0.7	0.4	0.5	0.5	0.8	0.4	2.3	0.9	1.3	1.6
India	0.1	0.4	0.5	0.4	0.3	0.2	2.8	9.1	3.2	3.2	4.1	3.0
Other Asia	1.0	1.3	4.0	7.7	3.7	4.6	19.4	16.1	14.8	25.2	12.6	22.5
Africa	0.3	0.8	0.4	0.6	0.6	0.3	14.1	28.8	19.1	25.5	24.1	11.4
North Africa	0.3	...	0.3	0.2	0.3	0.1	6.2	21.0	10.9	11.1	12.2	1.1
Republic of South Africa	...	0.8	0.1	0.4	0.3	0.1	4.7	3.6	5.1	7.2	8.7	9.5
Other Subsaharan Africa	...	...	...	...	...	...	3.2	4.2	3.2	7.2	3.2	0.8
Middle East	1.7	1.4	1.6	2.2	1.3	2.7	13.7	14.1	14.0	24.2	15.5	15.7
Australia	0.2	0.5	0.6	0.8	0.9	0.5	10.9	9.6	5.5	19.6	10.7	11.9
Rest Of World	...	...	...	...	...	...	...	0.2	...	...	...	...

Destination	Williamsport, PA						Wilmington, NC					
	1994	1995	1996	1997	1998	1999	1994	1995	1996	1997	1998	1999
ALL DESTINATIONS	123.3	150.4	151.0	182.5	171.2	172.9	180.7	211.7	301.7	422.9	478.7	483.7
North America	69.7	79.6	71.5	92.9	79.8	80.3	86.8	93.9	141.8	124.9	186.9	291.8
Canada	65.9	76.5	68.7	90.7	77.5	77.4	86.3	93.5	139.1	119.9	182.7	278.9
Mexico	3.8	3.1	2.8	2.1	2.3	2.9	0.5	0.4	2.8	5.0	4.2	12.9
Caribbean And Central America	0.6	1.5	4.6	12.3	23.5	21.1	1.4	5.8	14.0	29.3	48.8	44.4
South America	3.4	4.6	2.2	7.6	4.7	3.0	0.7	1.9	7.1	32.3	10.8	1.5
Argentina	0.2	0.5	0.2	0.1	0.3	0.1	...	0.1	0.1	0.6	0.8	0.1
Brazil	2.0	2.8	1.1	3.0	2.7	1.6	0.4	1.2	6.8	28.7	5.8	0.9
Other South America	1.2	1.3	0.8	4.5	1.7	1.3	0.3	0.6	0.3	3.0	4.2	0.4
Europe	32.7	42.5	50.1	43.4	46.6	45.9	17.8	20.2	45.1	86.0	94.2	53.5
Belgium	5.0	5.4	8.2	6.8	5.5	4.2	0.1	0.5	0.3	0.3	1.3	0.2
France	5.9	7.1	5.1	7.8	7.6	8.7	0.5	0.6	0.8	12.9	3.8	1.2
Germany	9.6	12.2	13.2	9.2	10.3	10.3	1.1	4.5	19.5	20.5	26.5	4.5
Netherlands	1.1	1.1	1.3	0.8	0.6	0.7	1.4	1.7	1.5	3.6	3.4	1.9
United Kingdom	5.4	7.6	11.5	7.8	7.8	8.3	1.2	3.4	4.2	3.0	3.4	3.9
Turkey	0.2	0.2	0.3	...	0.1	0.2	...	0.3	0.4	0.5	1.1	1.5
Former Soviet Republics	0.2	...	0.2	...	...	0.1	0.1	0.1	...	1.0	3.1	9.4
Poland	...	...	...	0.2	0.4	0.1	...	...	...	...	0.3	...
Other Eastern Europe	0.6	0.3	0.6	0.2	0.4	0.7	0.1	0.5	0.1	0.1	1.0	...
Other Europe	4.6	8.7	9.7	10.5	14.0	12.6	13.4	8.7	18.3	44.0	50.3	30.9
Asia	10.3	15.1	14.2	19.2	9.7	14.3	40.6	52.3	62.1	124.4	102.5	63.4
Japan	1.0	1.4	1.4	1.2	1.0	1.3	8.9	6.4	13.3	15.5	8.8	9.0
China	0.8	0.9	0.5	1.3	1.2	1.7	20.1	24.2	37.2	69.9	25.0	3.9
Hong Kong	0.9	1.0	1.0	2.9	2.3	1.9	4.3	13.6	5.0	26.3	58.7	42.4
Taiwan	2.2	3.3	2.5	2.7	2.5	2.6	0.2	3.4	2.9	6.4	3.8	4.1
Singapore	1.1	4.8	4.4	0.6	0.9	1.0	1.2	1.0	1.1	1.3	3.1	2.8
South Korea	1.1	1.0	1.3	8.0	0.2	2.5	5.7	2.9	1.6	2.4	0.2	0.3
Indonesia	...	0.1	...	0.1	0.1	0.1	...	0.1	...	...	...	...
India	1.2	0.7	0.3	...	0.3	0.3	0.1	0.2	0.6	1.3	0.5	0.2
Other Asia	2.0	2.0	2.9	2.4	1.2	3.0	0.1	0.5	0.5	1.2	2.4	0.6
Africa	0.6	1.3	1.5	0.9	1.8	1.1	17.6	27.5	22.7	21.5	26.1	22.2
North Africa	...	0.4	0.3	0.1	0.3	0.3	0.5	12.1	...	1.5	3.5	1.3
Republic of South Africa	0.4	0.7	1.1	0.8	1.3	0.8	...	...	0.1	...	0.2	0.2
Other Subsaharan Africa	0.2	0.1	0.1	0.1	0.2	...	17.1	15.4	22.6	20.0	22.4	20.7
Middle East	1.5	1.7	2.0	1.7	2.6	2.4	15.5	9.7	8.7	4.4	8.0	6.8
Australia	4.5	4.2	4.9	4.4	2.5	4.8	0.2	0.3	0.2	0.1	1.2	0.2
Rest Of World	...	...	...	...	...	...	...	...	...	...	...	...

Table E-3. Metropolitan Area Exports of Goods by Destination, 1994–1999—*Continued*

(Millions of dollars.)

Destination	Wilmington - Newark, DE - MD						Worcester, MA - CT					
	1994	1995	1996	1997	1998	1999	1994	1995	1996	1997	1998	1999
ALL DESTINATIONS	3 720.4	4 361.1	4 551.1	5 140.6	5 027.4	4 903.2	603.8	757.6	685.7	772.1	745.5	655.8
North America	851.3	854.4	989.0	1 065.6	1 193.0	1 181.5	252.7	249.6	247.8	331.7	360.7	268.5
Canada	646.8	675.7	706.6	765.3	921.2	943.5	181.9	189.5	173.2	237.6	243.0	201.0
Mexico	204.5	178.6	282.4	300.3	271.8	238.0	70.8	60.1	74.6	94.1	117.7	67.5
Caribbean And Central America	59.9	42.9	27.8	33.1	38.2	28.0	1.7	2.5	2.6	2.4	10.4	5.2
South America	353.3	456.3	484.1	574.3	455.5	401.4	9.4	15.8	12.4	16.4	19.3	14.8
Argentina	59.7	83.3	102.5	119.5	90.8	74.9	2.0	1.3	1.2	2.0	1.4	2.3
Brazil	165.9	213.5	228.8	276.0	236.5	218.3	2.8	6.5	4.9	7.9	10.5	8.6
Other South America	127.7	159.5	152.9	178.8	128.2	108.2	4.6	8.1	6.3	6.6	7.4	3.8
Europe	1 215.7	1 538.1	1 520.7	1 616.0	1 786.5	1 686.0	162.7	225.1	193.8	205.1	188.9	205.0
Belgium	488.8	701.6	663.6	657.5	739.6	678.9	3.0	8.3	3.1	3.1	1.7	1.3
France	100.6	114.1	90.2	99.7	107.4	122.0	17.8	17.8	14.9	20.7	23.8	29.6
Germany	171.4	163.0	190.9	191.2	239.0	205.8	48.6	76.5	62.9	56.4	54.0	52.2
Netherlands	157.7	190.2	192.7	256.0	260.7	240.2	16.6	23.5	21.9	23.7	23.4	17.4
United Kingdom	147.5	171.3	181.0	213.0	244.0	210.7	40.2	52.5	39.9	48.3	41.2	55.9
Turkey	19.3	35.6	28.8	23.6	7.6	17.4	0.3	0.6	0.7	0.9	0.6	0.7
Former Soviet Republics	14.8	11.1	6.0	9.4	3.4	7.9	0.8	0.7	1.2	0.8	0.6	0.8
Poland	0.2	0.3	0.4	1.6	0.6	0.8	0.3	0.5	0.6	0.3	0.3	0.2
Other Eastern Europe	1.7	2.2	1.0	3.1	5.3	12.2	0.6	0.7	1.0	0.7	0.7	0.8
Other Europe	113.6	148.7	166.1	160.9	179.0	190.1	34.6	43.9	47.8	50.2	42.6	45.9
Asia	1 060.0	1 255.8	1 344.6	1 649.4	1 341.6	1 428.7	150.2	228.6	201.4	192.0	140.8	135.2
Japan	374.4	439.1	447.6	572.0	550.9	465.3	29.9	37.3	38.3	40.0	32.5	28.6
China	54.8	64.7	68.5	75.7	71.7	105.3	12.1	17.3	4.9	7.2	5.7	5.8
Hong Kong	60.7	75.6	94.9	104.2	104.1	126.7	9.7	18.2	35.4	29.1	15.8	13.0
Taiwan	149.1	170.5	167.9	208.4	170.0	202.7	13.9	18.8	16.4	19.8	12.9	9.7
Singapore	77.3	94.3	112.3	157.1	142.5	173.4	11.2	22.6	36.7	19.1	9.4	10.7
South Korea	156.3	172.6	209.2	195.3	117.3	179.9	17.1	29.1	27.2	21.4	9.0	8.6
Indonesia	50.0	67.5	68.2	80.3	42.9	43.2	1.9	2.0	2.6	6.9	1.8	1.2
India	25.2	41.8	39.7	45.6	42.3	42.8	3.3	7.5	5.2	5.9	4.8	2.2
Other Asia	112.2	129.6	136.3	210.9	99.8	89.2	51.1	75.7	34.7	42.6	49.0	55.3
Africa	40.0	54.2	52.0	61.9	60.8	46.3	3.5	13.6	5.9	3.6	6.0	4.8
North Africa	6.5	8.8	4.7	9.8	7.3	11.9	0.7	2.3	1.6	0.3	1.0	1.2
Republic of South Africa	24.8	30.9	23.0	25.5	25.7	18.4	2.4	10.6	3.9	2.6	2.9	3.4
Other Subsaharan Africa	8.7	14.5	24.3	26.7	27.8	16.0	0.4	0.7	0.4	0.7	2.1	0.3
Middle East	41.4	59.4	49.8	56.8	57.4	49.9	8.5	7.8	9.1	8.7	7.7	13.4
Australia	98.8	100.1	83.1	83.6	94.4	81.5	15.1	14.5	12.7	12.2	11.7	8.9
Rest Of World	. . .	. . .	. . .	. . .	. . .	. . .	. . .	. . .	. . .	. . .	. . .	. . .

Destination	Yakima, WA						York, PA					
	1994	1995	1996	1997	1998	1999	1994	1995	1996	1997	1998	1999
ALL DESTINATIONS	147.6	168.9	176.0	213.1	256.7	264.1	952.0	973.9	945.1	1 015.4	1 089.1	1 012.6
North America	87.2	84.2	94.9	109.1	133.1	135.1	216.6	226.0	238.5	298.3	316.9	306.5
Canada	79.4	78.3	84.9	92.7	100.3	87.7	172.2	194.2	211.0	225.4	236.4	247.7
Mexico	7.9	5.8	10.0	16.4	32.8	47.5	44.4	31.8	27.5	72.9	80.5	58.8
Caribbean And Central America	2.7	3.7	3.7	4.3	6.7	6.6	9.3	16.7	14.0	9.7	6.1	8.6
South America	14.8	15.7	17.4	17.4	12.9	9.9	16.0	33.2	31.6	33.1	30.5	23.5
Argentina	0.9	0.4	3.3	1.4	0.2	1.0	4.2	7.5	6.2	3.3	9.4	3.3
Brazil	7.7	11.4	8.6	9.4	7.5	5.2	3.2	6.2	4.9	11.9	7.4	7.6
Other South America	6.2	3.9	5.5	6.6	5.2	3.7	8.5	19.5	20.4	17.9	13.7	12.7
Europe	23.0	29.7	31.4	41.0	30.8	37.8	229.8	276.6	293.0	316.8	342.5	341.5
Belgium	1.4	0.8	0.7	0.5	2.6	3.7	4.0	3.0	4.3	5.3	2.2	2.5
France	1.7	1.1	2.3	4.1	1.7	1.4	9.6	12.3	18.2	33.6	31.9	30.2
Germany	7.7	10.6	9.5	11.1	9.6	12.8	77.8	88.0	77.8	68.8	72.8	71.9
Netherlands	0.9	0.8	1.1	2.3	3.2	1.8	38.4	50.2	50.4	57.0	63.2	59.8
United Kingdom	6.9	12.2	13.0	9.5	9.2	9.2	44.1	52.8	61.6	63.6	68.5	64.5
Turkey	. . .	. . .	. . .	0.9	. . .	0.1	1.0	1.1	1.7	2.6	6.6	1.9
Former Soviet Republics	0.7	0.7	0.6	1.0	0.1	0.4	0.2	0.1	0.3	2.0	4.9	0.8
Poland	. . .	. . .	0.1	0.1	0.1	0.3	1.0	0.4	0.2	0.3	0.8	. . .
Other Eastern Europe	0.3	0.1	0.4	0.1	. . .	0.2	0.3	1.0	0.6	0.6	0.4	0.6
Other Europe	3.3	3.5	3.7	11.5	4.4	8.0	53.4	67.8	77.9	83.1	91.1	109.3
Asia	17.2	30.0	23.2	35.3	68.0	70.3	301.3	317.6	266.9	248.3	290.2	250.1
Japan	6.2	15.0	8.5	22.6	53.8	51.4	38.9	53.6	60.9	76.8	92.7	99.9
China	0.5	1.5	1.8	0.3	0.3	0.3	23.9	32.5	16.3	20.3	40.7	34.9
Hong Kong	2.1	1.9	2.3	1.5	3.4	1.6	23.1	20.0	15.2	16.1	7.9	8.3
Taiwan	1.7	4.2	3.3	2.3	2.8	2.9	40.7	24.0	19.7	37.5	91.3	36.0
Singapore	0.6	0.4	0.7	0.3	0.8	1.4	40.0	42.6	29.4	18.3	19.3	28.9
South Korea	1.8	1.6	2.7	3.6	1.7	4.4	100.3	113.6	78.6	44.9	14.6	23.1
Indonesia	0.9	2.0	0.8	0.5	0.1	0.4	1.1	2.5	1.2	1.6	0.6	0.4
India	. . .	. . .	0.2	0.1	0.1	. . .	7.4	7.1	2.8	2.2	2.6	2.5
Other Asia	3.5	3.4	3.0	4.2	4.9	8.0	26.1	21.7	42.8	30.6	20.4	16.1
Africa	0.6	0.4	1.2	1.3	1.0	0.8	95.8	17.3	11.1	15.7	19.9	11.3
North Africa	0.3	. . .	1.0	0.1	. . .	0.4	83.8	13.3	4.8	11.0	15.7	5.2
Republic of South Africa	0.3	0.4	0.2	0.9	1.0	0.3	11.5	3.9	6.0	4.0	3.6	5.6
Other Subsaharan Africa	. . .	. . .	. . .	0.2	. . .	0.1	0.5	0.1	0.3	0.7	0.5	0.5
Middle East	0.1	1.0	0.9	1.1	1.7	1.1	43.3	36.3	40.8	45.9	32.9	35.2
Australia	1.9	4.3	3.2	3.6	2.5	2.5	39.9	50.3	49.3	47.6	50.0	35.9
Rest Of World	. . .	. . .	. . .	. . .	. . .	. . .	. . .	. . .	. . .	. . .	. . .	. . .

Table E-3. Metropolitan Area Exports of Goods by Destination, 1994–1999—*Continued*

(Millions of dollars.)

Destination	Youngstown - Warren, OH					
	1994	1995	1996	1997	1998	1999
ALL DESTINATIONS	185.3	225.9	223.1	323.0	296.6	239.8
North America	105.9	136.1	128.8	188.9	150.6	168.4
Canada	98.3	115.0	120.9	174.4	134.3	158.4
Mexico	7.5	21.1	7.9	14.5	16.3	10.0
Caribbean And Central America	3.2	4.3	2.7	5.6	1.0	0.7
South America	12.4	13.3	10.8	10.7	12.7	3.1
Argentina	7.3	4.2	3.2	3.8	2.0	0.9
Brazil	1.1	3.3	1.7	0.9	6.7	0.7
Other South America	4.0	5.8	5.9	5.9	4.0	1.5
Europe	38.9	38.4	39.5	58.5	52.5	46.2
Belgium	0.4	0.6	0.5	5.2	0.4	5.1
France	7.5	4.8	7.4	13.1	16.0	9.8
Germany	5.5	8.5	7.2	8.7	7.3	5.0
Netherlands	4.7	3.9	3.0	2.6	2.8	2.4
United Kingdom	7.6	l0.6	12.1	21.6	20.4	17.3
Turkey	3.2	2.2	0.5	0.1	0.1	2.3
Former Soviet Republics	. . .	. . .	. . .	. . .	0.3	. . .
Poland	. . .	. . .	0.1	0.3	. . .	0.1
Other Eastern Europe	0.2	0.1	0.1	0.1	0.3	0.6
Other Europe	9.9	7.7	8.6	6.7	4.8	3.6
Asia	17.3	25.8	30.3	45.6	65.7	15.6
Japan	2.0	2.2	7.4	6.6	6.0	2.1
China	5.9	5.4	2.1	2.6	0.9	1.7
Hong Kong	0.5	0.6	0.6	0.8	0.8	0.9
Taiwan	2.8	1.9	3.1	2.5	48.6	5.3
Singapore	0.4	2.6	6.0	2.6	0.2	0.5
South Korea	3.9	9.3	2.2	13.1	5.0	2.2
Indonesia	. . .	0.3	2.4	0.7	0.2	0.1
India	1.0	1.4	1.6	1.7	1.8	1.8
Other Asia	0.7	2.2	4.8	15.1	2.2	1.1
Africa	1.1	2.9	1.5	2.1	2.3	1.4
North Africa	0.3	0.3	0.4	0.7	0.3	0.3
Republic of South Africa	0.5	2.6	1.0	1.1	1.8	1.0
Other Subsaharan Africa	0.3	. . .	0.1	0.3	0.2	. . .
Middle East	3.0	1.5	7.8	7.7	8.5	1.2
Australia	3.5	3.7	1.7	3.7	3.1	3.2
Rest Of World	. . .	. . .	. . .	. . .	. . .	. . .

INDEX